THE OXFORD HANDBOOK OF
CASTE

THE OXFORD HANDBOOK OF
CASTE

Edited by
SURINDER S. JODHKA
JULES NAUDET

Great Clarendon Street, Oxford, OX2 6DP,
United Kingdom

Oxford University Press is a department of the University of Oxford.
It furthers the University's objective of excellence in research, scholarship,
and education by publishing worldwide. Oxford is a registered trade mark of
Oxford University Press in the UK and in certain other countries

© Oxford University Press 2023

The moral rights of the authors have been asserted

First Edition published in 2023

All rights reserved. No part of this publication may be reproduced, stored in
a retrieval system, or transmitted, in any form or by any means, without the
prior permission in writing of Oxford University Press, or as expressly permitted
by law, by licence or under terms agreed with the appropriate reprographics
rights organization. Enquiries concerning reproduction outside the scope of the
above should be sent to the Rights Department, Oxford University Press, at the
address above

You must not circulate this work in any other form
and you must impose this same condition on any acquirer

Published in the United States of America by Oxford University Press
198 Madison Avenue, New York, NY 10016, United States of America

British Library Cataloguing in Publication Data

Data available

Library of Congress Control Number: 2023937656

ISBN 978–0–19–889671–5

DOI: 10.1093/oxfordhb/9780198896715.001.0001

Links to third party websites are provided by Oxford in good faith and
for information only. Oxford disclaims any responsibility for the materials
contained in any third party website referenced in this work.

Contents

Acknowledgements — xi
Notes on Editors and Contributors — xiii

Introduction—Studying Caste: Conceptual Currents and Emergent Perspectives — 1
SURINDER S. JODHKA AND JULES NAUDET

SECTION I. CONCEPTUAL FRAMES

Editors' Introduction — 25

1. The Idea of Caste through the Ages: Concept, Words, and Things — 31
   ROLAND LARDINOIS

2. Hierarchy — 48
   MARTIN FUCHS

3. The Jajmani System — 60
   PETER MAYER

4. Caste and Capital — 76
   CAROL UPADHYA

5. Caste and Class — 91
   JULES NAUDET

6. Caste and Kinship — 104
   JANAKI ABRAHAM

SECTION II: HISTORY, STATE, AND THE SHAPING OF CASTE

Editors' Introduction — 121

7. Caste and Kingship — 127
   HARALD TAMBS-LYCHE

8. Transformations of Caste in Colonial India — 139
   DILIP M. MENON

9. Census, Caste Enumeration and the British Legacy — 154
   LEIGH DENAULT

10. Caste Disputes in Colonial India: Conflicts and the Legal Shaping of Caste — 176
    JULIE MARQUET

11. Caste and the Law — 188
    GAUTAM BHATIA

12. Reservations and Affirmative Action — 199
    ASHWINI DESHPANDE

13. 'Backwardness': Reviewing the Emergence of a Concept — 213
    S. ANANDHI AND KALPANA KANNABIRAN

SECTION III: CASTE AND THE RELIGIOUS REALM

Editors' Introduction — 231

14. Hinduism and Caste System — 235
    MATHIEU CLAVEYROLAS

15. Hindu Sects and Caste — 247
    RAPHAËL VOIX

16. Sanskritization: The Inheritance of an Ideational Category — 266
    GEORGE KUNNATH

17. Caste and Hindutva — 279
    JOEL LEE

18. Caste among Muslims in North India and Pakistan   290
JULIEN LEVESQUE

SECTION IV: LOCAL POWER AND THE POLITICAL PROCESS

Editors' Introduction   305

19. The Dominant Caste   309
NICOLAS MARTIN

20. Caste Associations and the Post-Mandal Politics of Caste   320
RAJESHWARI DESHPANDE

21. Do Indians Vote Their Caste—or Their *Jati*, or Their Class, or ...?   331
CHRISTOPHE JAFFRELOT

22. Caste, Patronage and Criminalization of Politics   345
LUCIA MICHELUTTI

SECTION V. COMMUNITY PROFILES AND REGIONAL TRAJECTORIES

Editors' Introduction   357

23. How to Write New Histories of Caste: A Dalit History of Chamars   361
RAMNARAYAN S. RAWAT

24. The Brahmins of Urban India   375
HARIPRIYA NARASIMHAN

25. Agarwal Banias of Delhi   388
UJITHRA PONNIAH

26. Caste Logos: A View from Tamil Nadu   399
ZOE E. HEADLEY

27. The Invisibility of Caste in Bengal   413
SARBANI BANDYOPADHYAY

28. Caste in Punjab   428
SURINDER S. JODHKA

29. Caste, Ethnicity, and the State in Nepal 443
DAVID N. GELLNER

SECTION VI. DALIT LIVES AND PREDICAMENTS OF CHANGE

Editors' Introduction 459

30. Ambedkar's Legacy 463
ANAND TELTUMBDE

31. Changing Dynamics of Untouchability 478
SURYAKANT WAGHMORE

32. Dalit Movements in India 488
HUGO GORRINGE AND KARTHIKEYAN DAMODARAN

33. The Mahars and Dalit Movement of Maharashtra 502
HARISH WANKHEDE

34. Dalit Activism and Transnational Mobilization 514
EVA-MARIA HARDTMANN

35. Caste, Race and Ethnicity 527
DEEPA S. REDDY

36. Caste and Tribe 539
JAI PRASAD

37. Denotified Communities 554
KALPANA KANNABIRAN

SECTION VII: EMERGING ENTANGLEMENTS OF CASTE

Editors' Introduction 569

38. The Economics of Caste 573
GUILHEM CASSAN

39. Caste and Merit 586
AJANTHA SUBRAMANIAN

40. Caste and Mobility 595
    Divya Vaid

41. Caste and Gender 609
    Pushpesh Kumar

42. Caste and the Diaspora 623
    Radha Modi

Name Index 637
Subject Index 643

Acknowledgements

As editors of this volume, we wish to acknowledge the help and support we have received from colleagues, friends, and family, without which it would not have been possible for us to complete the Handbook.

We are grateful to the institutions where we are employed for providing us with a conducive environment and continuous support for our academic work. Surinder S. Jodhka greatly benefitted from the support of his colleagues and students at the Centre for the Study of Social Systems (CSSS) at Jawaharlal Nehru University, New Delhi. Jules Naudet is grateful to the CNRS as well as to the Centre d'Etudes de l'Inde et de l'Asie du Sud (CEIAS, EHESS, Paris). He is particularly indebted to its directors Michel Boivin, Vanessa Caru, Rémy Delage, and Zoe Headley who spared no efforts to support him while he was learning to live with his new disability. Jules Naudet also thanks the staff of the Centre for Advanced Studies in Behavioural Sciences (CASBS) at Stanford University, where he completed the final bit of work on the Handbook while being offered the best mix of material conditions and intellectual atmosphere that he has ever experienced. The Centre for Social Sciences and Humanities (CSH) in New Delhi deserves a special mention as this was where we began collaborating and discussing about the possibility of working on such a project.

We also wish to thank Vanessa Caru, Bruno Cousin, Sébastien Chauvin, Mathieu Ferry, David Gellner, Lise Guilhamon, Sneha S. Komath, and Ujithra Ponniah for their valuable feedback on the drafts of our Introduction. Their critical comments helped us sharpen the framework that we have tried to propose as an alternative to existing 'theories' of caste.

We express our gratitude to the editors and staff at the Oxford University Press. Barun Sarkar and Moutushi Mukherjee showed exceptional flexibility with regard to the timeline. We thank Thomas Perridge for taking this project toward completion with a great deal of enthusiasm despite the interruptions imposed by the Covid-19 pandemic.

Most of all, we heartfully thank the contributors who, despite the trying times, readily agreed to share their in-depth and empirically rich understanding of the subject that have been put together in this volume. We particularly appreciate their patience and grace as we were painstakingly compiling this monumental collection of chapters.

Surinder S. Jodhka
Jules Naudet

Notes on Editors and Contributors

EDITORS:

Surinder S. Jodhka is a Professor of Sociology at the Jawaharlal Nehru University, New Delhi. He researches on social inequalities, caste, and its articulation in contemporary India, rural/agrarian change, and the political sociology of community identities. His recent publications include *India's Villages in the 21st Century: Revisits and Revisions* (co-edited with Edward Simpson, OUP, 2019); *Mapping the Elite: Power, Privilege, and Inequality* (co-edited with Jules Naudet, OUP, 2019); *A Handbook of Rural India* (Orient Blackswan, 2018); *Contested Hierarchies, Persisting Influence: Caste and Power in Twenty-First Century India* (co-edited with James Manor, Orient Blackswan, 2018); *Inequality in Capitalist Societies* (co-authored with Boike Rehbien and Jesse Souza, Routledge, 2018); *The Indian Middle-Class* (co-authored with Aseem Prakash, OUP, 2016); *Caste in Contemporary India* (Routledge, 2015/2018); *Caste: Oxford India Short Introductions* (OUP, 2012). He is among the first recipients of the ICSSR-Amartya Sen Award for Distinguished Social Scientists, for the year 2012.

Jules Naudet is a CNRS Associate Research Professor at the Centre for South-Asian and Himalayan Studies (CESAH) at EHESS, Paris, an Associate Researcher at the Centre de Sciences Humaines, New Delhi, and a 2021–2022 CASBS Fellow at Stanford University. His earlier work looked at upward social mobility in India, the US, and France and he is the author of *Stepping into the Elite* (OUP, 2018), a book that revisits the classical question of the experience of moving from one class to another. He also co-edited *Justifier l'ordre social* with Christophe Jaffrelot (University Press of France, 2013) and is the co-author, with Serge Paugam, Bruno Cousin, and Camila Giorgetti, of *Ce que les riches pensent des pauvres* (Le Seuil, 2017), a comparative analysis of the representations of the poor by the inhabitants of upper-class neighbourhoods in Paris, Delhi, and São Paulo. Naudet holds several editorial positions. He is a member of the editorial board of *SAMAJ (South Asia Multidisciplinary Academic Journal)* as well as the co-editor-in-chief of *La Vie des Idées/ Books & Ideas*, an online journal hosted by the Collège de France. Along with Surinder Jodhka, he co-edits the book series *Exploring India's Elite*. He also co-organizes the research seminar 'Sociology of Inequalities in India' at the EHESS, in Paris (along with Joël Cabalion, Mathieu Ferry, Odile Henry, Clémence Jullien, and Olivier Roueff). Naudet currently devotes his research to the study of the Indian and French economic elites.

CONTRIBUTORS

Janaki Abraham is an Associate Professor of Sociology in the Department of Sociology, Delhi School of Economics, Delhi University. Her research interests include the study of kinship, gender and caste, visual anthropology, sexual harassment, and gender and space, particularly the study of towns. She is the co-editor, with Sanjay Srivastava and Yasmeen Arif, of *Critical Themes in Indian Sociology* (SAGE, 2019) and the author of several articles in journals and edited books. From 2012 to 2016, she was co-editor of the Book Reviews section of the journal *Contributions to Indian Sociology*.

S. Anandhi is a Professor at the Madras Institute of Development Studies, Chennai, India. She is a historian with research interests in political movements and social processes in colonial and postcolonial Tamil Nadu, India. She has contributed several articles on caste, gender, and sexual politics in the Dravidian movement and on Dalit Women's Struggles. Her recent publications include *Rethinking Social Justice* (co-edited, Orient Blackswan, 2020); and *Dalit Women: Vanguard of an Alternative Politics* (co-edited, Routledge, London and New York, South Asia edition in India, 2017).

Sarbani Bandyopadhyay teaches sociology in St. Xavier's College (autonomous) Kolkata. She has a PhD from the Department of Humanities and Social Sciences, IIT Bombay. Her PhD thesis is titled 'The Lives of Caste among the Bengali Middle Class: A Study of the Contemporary'. She has published a couple of papers from her thesis and presented at several international conferences. Currently she is working on the intersections of the caste and the Muslim questions in post-Partition West Bengal.

Gautam Bhatia graduated from the National Law School of India University. He has BCL and MPhil degrees from the University of Oxford and an LLM from Yale Law School. His essays have appeared in the *Oxford Handbook for the Indian Constitution*, *Max Planck Encyclopedia of Comparative Constitutional Law*, and in journals such as *Constellations* and *Global Constitutionalism*. He has published three books—*Offend, Shock, or Disturb: Freedom of Speech under the Indian Constitution*, *The Transformative Constitution: A Radical Biography in Nine Acts*, and a novel, *The Wall*. As a lawyer, he has been part of legal teams involved in contemporary constitutional cases such as the challenge to criminal defamation, the nine-judge bench right to privacy case, the Section 377 challenge, and the Aadhaar challenge. His work has been cited thrice by the Indian Supreme Court, and once by the High Court of Kerala. He founded and writes the Indian Constitutional Law and Philosophy Blog (http://indconlawphil.wordpress.com).

Guilhem Cassan is a Professor of Economics at the University of Namur and Fellow of the CEPR. His work revolves around the study of the role of identity—caste and gender—in economics behaviour as well as the study of the political economy of inequality, both in history and in contemporary times. His research has notably been published in *American Economic Journal: Applied Economics*, *American Economic Journal: Economic Policy* and the *Journal of Development Economics*.

Mathieu Claveyrolas is an Anthropologist at the CNRS, Paris and Member of the Center for South-Asian Studies (EHESS/CNRS). He specializes in Hinduism through ethnographic methods focusing on temples, actors, and practices. He first studied Indian Hinduism (in Varanasi) before turning to Mauritian, Creole, Hinduism, and, more recently, Guyanese Hinduism in New York City. Among his main publications are *Quand le temple prend vie. Atmosphère et dévotion à Bénarès* (2003), *Quand l'hindouisme est* *créole. Plantation et indianité à l'île Maurice* (2017), *Les territoires du religieux dans les mondes indiens* (edited, 2016), and *Les Hindous, les Autres et l'Ailleurs* (edited, 2021).

Karthikeyan Damodaran is a Post-Doctoral Researcher at the Centre for Modern Indian Studies, University of Goettingen. He has previously held posts at Goettingen and Jain (deemed-to-be) University, Bangalore. His research interests include Dalit politics, caste, commemorations, Urban Cultures, and Tamil Cinema. He is the author of numerous articles on Dalit politics and Tamil cinema.

Leigh Denault is a Fellow and Director of Studies in History at Churchill College, Cambridge University. Her first monograph focused on the social, cultural, and legal history of the family in colonial North India at the University of Cambridge (*Publicising Family in Colonial North India, c. 1780–1930*, Faculty of History, University of Cambridge, 2009). Her current research focuses on conceptions of social welfare in 20th-century India. She is also working on a digital history project mapping newspaper networks and debates about press freedom across mid-19th-century India.

Ashwini Deshpande is a Professor of Economics, and Founding Director of Centre for Economic Data and Analysis at Ashoka University, India. Her PhD and early publications have been on the international debt crisis of the 1980s. Subsequently, she has been working on the economics of discrimination and affirmative action, with a focus on caste and gender in India. She has published extensively in leading scholarly journals. She is the author of *Grammar of Caste: Economic Discrimination in Contemporary India* (OUP, hardcover 2011 and paperback 2017); and *Affirmative Action in India* (OUP, Oxford India Short Introductions series, 2013). She received the EXIM Bank award for outstanding dissertation (now called the IERA Award) in 1994, and the VKRV Rao Award for Indian economists under 45 in 2007.

Rajeshwari Deshpande is a Professor of Politics at the Savitribai Phule Pune University. She was the ICCR Visiting Professor (Rajiv Gandhi Chair in Contemporary Indian Studies) at the University of Technology, Sydney, and UKIERI Visiting Fellow at King's India Institute, London. Her research interests are in areas such as intellectual traditions of Maharashtra, politics of the urban poor, urban caste-class realities, women's politics, and politics and policies related to social welfare. Her recent publications include *Last Fortress of Congress Dominance: Maharashtra since the 1990s* (with Suhas Palshikar, SAGE, 2021), *Gandhinchya Shodhat Javdekar* (Marathi-Javdekar in search of Gandhi, Samkaleen Prakashan, 2019), *Politics of Welfare: Comparisons across Indian States* (edited, with Louise Tillin and KK Kailash, OUP, 2015).

Martin Fuchs is trained in Sociology and Anthropology. He is Professor of Indian Religious History at the Max Weber Centre for Advanced Cultural and Social Studies, University of Erfurt, Germany. He is also a member and temporarily Director of the M.S. Merian—R. Tagore International Centre of Advanced Studies in the Humanities and Social Sciences 'Metamorphoses of the Political' (ICAS:MP) in Delhi, India. He has published books and articles on Max Weber, Louis Dumont, B. R. Ambedkar, Indian social movements, religious individualization (*bhakti*), Indian modernity, urban poor

(Mumbai), reflexive anthropology, ethnographic representation, intercultural translation, and comparison.

David N. Gellner is a Professor of Social Anthropology and a Fellow of All Souls College, University of Oxford. He has worked on religion, ethnicity, class, politics, activism, and borderlands in Nepal, and occasionally over the border in eastern UP, since the 1980s. Among his many publications are *Rebuilding Buddhism: The Theravada Movement in Twentieth-Century Nepal* (Harvard University Press, 2005), *Global Nepalis: Religion, Culture, and Community in a New and Old Diaspora* (OUP, 2018), 'Masters of Hybridity: How Activists Reshaped Nepali Society' in the *Journal of the Royal Anthropological Institute* (2019), and 'Nepali Dalits in Transition' in a special issue of *Contributions to Nepalese Studies* (2019).

Hugo Gorringe is a Senior Lecturer in Sociology and the Co-Director of the Centre for South Asian Studies at the University of Edinburgh. His research focuses on the interplay between caste, politics, and Dalit movements in Tamil Nadu. He is author of *Untouchable Citizens* (SAGE, 2005) and *Panthers in Parliament: Dalits, Caste and Political Power in South India* (OUP, 2017), as well as numerous articles and chapters on identity, violence, space, caste, and politics.

Eva-Maria Hardtmann is an Associate Professor in the Department of Social Anthropology at Stockholm University. Her research areas include social movements, citizenship, transnationalism, gender, and power relations. She specializes in South Asia and her fieldwork has been carried out mainly in northern India, but also among immigrated Dalit activists in Great Britain, in relation to the U.N. and among Dalit activists in the Global Justice Movement. Her writings include the ethnographies *Dalit Movement in India: Local Practices, Global Connections* (OUP, 2009) and *South Asian Activists in the Global Justice Movement* (OUP, 2017).

Zoe E. Headley is a CNRS Associate Research Professor and Director of the Centre for South Asian Studies at EHESS, Paris.

Christophe Jaffrelot is Director of Research at CERI-Sciences Po/CNRS in Paris, Professor of Indian Politics and Sociology at King's College London, and a nonresident scholar at the Carnegie Endowment for International Peace. He was elected President of the French Association of Political Science in July 2020. He is the author of numerous books, including *Modi's India: Hindu Nationalism and the Rise of Ethnic Democracy* (2021), *Hindu Nationalism: A Reader* (2007), and *India's Silent Revolution: The Rise of the Lower Castes in North India* (2003).

Kalpana Kannabiran is a Distinguished Professor at the Council for Social Development. Her work focuses on the intersections of sociology, law, gender studies, and social movements. She is a co-founder of Asmita Resource Centre for Women, Secunderabad. She has taught in NALSAR University of Law, Hyderabad and was the Director of the Council for Social Development, Hyderabad. She is the author of *Tools of Justice: Non-Discrimination and the Indian Constitution* (2012), co-author of *Gender*

Regimes and the Politics of Privacy: A Feminist Re-Reading of Puttaswamy v. Union of India (2021), and author of *Law, Justice and Human Rights in India: Short Reflections* (2021). She was a recipient of the VKRV Rao Prize for Social Science Research in 2003, and has also received the Amartya Sen Award for Distinguished Social Scientists in 2012, for her work in the field of law.

Pushpesh Kumar teaches sociology at the University of Hyderabad. He has written extensively on gender and sexuality issues. He has recently published an edited volume entitled *Sexuality, Abjection and Queer Existence in Contemporary India* (Routledge, 2022). He also serves on the international advisory committee of the *Community Development Journal* (OUP).

George Kunnath is a Research Fellow at the International Inequalities Institute, LSE. Kunnath received his PhD in Social Anthropology from SOAS, University of London. His work focuses on caste and class relations; relationality of inequality, conflict, and development, and research ethics. Kunnath has published his research in *Current Anthropology, Journal of Peasant Studies,* and *Dialectical Anthropology,* among others. His book *Rebels from the Mud Houses: Dalits and the Making of the Maoist Revolution in Bihar* (Social Science Press, 2012; Routledge, 2017) discusses Dalit agency and the Maoist movement in the eastern Indian state of Bihar.

Roland Lardinois sociologist is a Senior and a Research Fellow emeritus at the French National Center for Scientific Research, Paris. His field of research deals, on the one hand, with modern and contemporary India, in particular the sociology of engineers and, on the other hand, on the history of Indian studies in France. He has published *Scholars and Prophets: Sociology of India in France in the 19th–20th centuries*, translated from the French by Renuka George (Social Science Press, 2013), and edited, in collaboration with Charles Gadéa, *Les mondes de l'ingénieur en Inde XIXe–XXIe siècle*, Paris, Classiques Garnier (Classiques Garnier, 2022).

Joel Lee is the author of *Deceptive Majority: Dalits, Hinduism, and Underground Religion* (Cambridge University Press, 2021). He teaches anthropology at Williams College in Massachusetts.

Julien Levesque is currently a Senior Teaching and Research Assistant in Indian Studies and a Postdoctoral Fellow at the Department of Indian Studies, Asien-Orient Institut, University of Zürich. He has previously worked at Ashoka University and the Centre de Sciences Humaines in New Delhi. He is also affiliated with the Centre for South Asian Studies (CEIAS), EHESS, Paris. He holds a PhD (2016) in Political Science from the School of Advanced Studies in Social Sciences (EHESS), Paris. His first monograph, published in 2022, investigates nationalism and identity construction in Sindh after Pakistan's independence. His ongoing work examines the politics of the Muslim caste in North India and Pakistan.

Julie Marquet is an Assistant Professor at the Université du Littoral Côte d'Opale in France. She works on caste disputes in the French settlements of India in the 18th and 19th centuries and on citizenship under colonial rule.

Nicolas Martin is an Assistant Professor in Indian/South Asian studies at the Institute of Oriental and Asian Studies of the University of Zurich. He was trained as a social anthropologist at the London School of Economics where he produced a dissertation and a subsequent book about landed power in the rural Pakistani Punjab. Since 2012 he has shifted his attention to the Indian rural Punjab where he has been researching democracy, elections, violence and criminality, clientelism, caste, and local government.

Peter Mayer is an Associate Professor of Politics and Visiting Research Fellow at the University of Adelaide. He has written on many aspects of Indian politics, international relations, economics, history, anthropology, and sociology—especially the sociology of suicide. His recent publications have examined issues including a zone of weak governance in the Indus-Ganges plains, India's engagement with economic reforms, long-term trends in the real wages of agricultural labourers in the Kaveri Delta, the foreign relations of Australia and India, why elections in India appear to defy Duverger's Law of party competition, and the declining rate of massacres of India's Dalits.

Dilip M. Menon is the Mellon Chair in Indian Studies in Africa and the Director of the Centre for Indian Studies in Africa at the University of Witwatersrand. He works on South Asian history, oceanic history, and the idea of knowledge from the global south. His recent publications are a co-edited volume *Capitalisms: Towards a Global History* (OUP, 2020) and the forthcoming *Changing Theory: Concepts from the Global South* (Routledge, 2022).

Lucia Michelutti is a Professor of Anthropology at the University College London. She writes on issues of democracy, politics, leadership, violence, and crime in South Asia, specifically Uttar Pradesh and in Latin America in Venezuela. She is the author of *The Vernacularization of Democracy* (Routledge), co-editor of *The Wild East* (with Barbara Harriss-White, UCL Press) and co-author of *Mafia Raj* (with Hoque, Martin, Picherit, Rollier, Ruud, and Still, Stanford University Press).

Radha Modi is an Associate Teaching Professor at Florida State University. She specializes in research on race relations, immigrant incorporation, and economic inequality. Her research and publications investigate the role of skin colour in the racialization of second-generation South Asians in the US with a publication in *Ethnic and Racial Studies*. She also has publications on wealth inequality during the Great Recession of 2008. In collaboration with South Asian Americans Leading Together, a national nonpartisan organization working on civil rights, she authored a report entitled *Communities on Fire: Confronting Hate Violence and Xenophobic Political Rhetoric*, documenting the hate violence experienced by South Asian, Middle Eastern, and Arab communities following the 2016 election. In addition to research, she works with national organizations such as South Asian American Digital Archive.

Haripriya Narasimhan is an Anthropologist and a Faculty in the Department of Liberal Arts at IIT Hyderabad. Her research interests are in the areas of media, health, and globalisation. She has previously worked on caste, and with C.J. Fuller

(Prof Emeritus, LSE), published *Tamil Brahmans: A Middle Class Caste* (University of Chicago Press, 2014).

Ujithra Ponniah is a Wealth Inequality and Elite Studies Fellow in the Southern Centre for Inequality Studies at the University of Witwatersrand, Johannesburg. Previously she taught at the School of Gender Studies at Tata Institute of Social Sciences, Hyderabad, India. She has a doctorate in Sociology from Jawaharlal Nehru University, New Delhi (2018) and a master's in Development Studies from Tata Institute of Social Sciences, Mumbai. She works on inequality with a focus on elites and ascriptive hierarchies. She is in the process of converting her doctoral thesis into a book manuscript.

Jai Prasad is a Doctoral candidate and Research Fellow in the Department of Politics, South Asia Institute, Centre for Asian and Transcultural Studies, Universität Heidelberg, Germany. Prior to this, he was a publishing editor with a renowned academic press in New Delhi. He is currently researching the ideational roots of institutional change in forest governance in India, with particular focus on the landmark Forest Rights Act (FRA), 2006. His broader research interests include policy and politics of redistributive welfare, and political sociology of indigeneity and sustainable natural resource use.

Ramnarayan S. Rawat is an Associate Professor of History at the University of Delaware. He co-edited the *Dalit Studies* (2016) with K. Satyanarayana. He is currently co-editing the second *Dalit Studies* volume. His second book, *The Language of Liberalism: The Dalit Public Sphere in Late Colonial India*, is in the advanced stages of completion. His first book, *Reconsidering Untouchability: Chamars and Dalit History in North India*, received Joseph W. Elder Book Prize (2009) awarded by the American Institute of Indian Studies and a honorable mention in the Bernard S. Cohn Book Prize (2013) awarded by the Association of Asian studies.

Deepa S. Reddy received her BA in Anthropology and English Literature from the University of Toronto, and her PhD in Anthropology from Rice University. She teaches anthropology and cross-cultural studies at the University of Houston-Clear Lake. Her research foci have ranged from religious nationalism and identitarian politics, the internationalization/globalization of 'caste', bioethics and biopolitics, to air quality and environmental governance in India. She blogs on paticheri.com

Ajantha Subramanian is a Professor of Anthropology and South Asian Studies at Harvard University. Her first book, *Shorelines: Space and Rights in South India* (Stanford University Press, 2009; Yoda Press, 2013), chronicles the struggles for resource rights by Catholic fishers on India's southwestern coast, with a focus on how they have used spatial imaginaries and practices to constitute themselves as political subjects. Her second book, *The Caste of Merit: Engineering Education in India* (Harvard University Press, 2019), analyses meritocracy as a terrain of caste struggle in India and its implications for democratic transformation.

Harald Tambs-Lyche is a social anthropologist. He received his PhD from the University of Bergen in 1972, becoming a Professor at the University of Picardie in 1996. He has written four monographs: *London Patidars* (1980); *Power, Profit and Poetry: Traditional Society in Kathiawar, Western India* (1997); *The Good Country: Individual, Situation and Society in Saurashtra* (2004); and *Business Brahmins: The Gauda Saraswat Brahmins of South Kanara* (2011), edited several books and written a large number of articles.

Anand Teltumbde was a Senior Professor and Chair of Big Data Analytics at the Goa Institute of Management. He is a leading Indian intellectual and the author of several books on Ambedkar and the Dalits in India, including *Khairlanji: A Strange and Bitter Crop* (Navayana, 2008).

Carol Upadhya is a social anthropologist and a Professor in the School of Social Sciences at the National Institute of Advanced Studies, Bangalore, India, where she leads the Urban and Mobility Studies Programme. Her research interests include Indian software capital and labour, the reconstitution of the Indian middle class, transnational migration and regional diasporas in India, and real estate development and the urbanization of rural landscapes. She is the author of *Reengineering India: Work, Capital, and Class in an Offshore Economy* (2016) and co-editor of *Provincial Globalization in India: Transregional Mobilities and Development Politics* (2018).

Divya Vaid teaches sociology at Jawaharlal Nehru University, New Delhi. She has an MSc and DPhil from Oxford. Her research interests include the study of social mobility and inequalities, social stratification and educational attainment, and the application of quantitative methods. Her work has appeared in the *Annual Review of Sociology*, *Contemporary South Asia*, *Asian Survey* and the *Economic and Political Weekly* among others. She is the author of *Uneven Odds: Social Mobility in Contemporary India* (OUP, 2018).

Raphaël Voix is a social anthropologist, Research Fellow at the National Centre for Scientific Research, member of the French Institute of Pondicherry (MEAE/CNRS), and associate member of the Centre for Indian and South Asian Studies, Paris. His research focuses on sectarian Hinduism through fieldwork done mainly in Bengali communities. He has published extensively in journals and edited books on the themes such as asceticism and violence, Hindu utopia and millennial movements, contemporary uses of Vedic texts, Hinduism and the courts, politics and contemporary yoga.

Suryakant Waghmore is a Professor of Sociology in the Department of Humanities and Social Sciences at the IIT Bombay. He is the author of *Civility against Caste* (2013) and co-editor of *Civility in Crisis* (2020).

Harish Wankhede is an Assistant Professor at the Centre for Political Sciences, JNU. He is recipient of the prestigious Raman Fellowship for conducting Post-Doctoral Research at Stanford University as Visiting Scholar. His research interests are political theory, public institutions, secularism and social justice, and Hindi cinema. He has published widely in peer-reviewed journals and edited books, and regularly contributes opinion pieces to national newspapers and magazines.

INTRODUCTION

STUDYING CASTE
Conceptual Currents and Emergent Perspectives

SURINDER S. JODHKA AND JULES NAUDET

'Caste' often invokes tradition, as if a remnant of the ancient past. According to this popular view, caste was a closed system of hierarchy, unique to South Asia, which presumably tied everyone to the social collective that they were born into, with no individual choice of occupation, mobility, or marriage. Privileges and statuses were all pre-given, with no one ever questioning the social order. This notion of caste also claimed that the source of its origin and legitimacy lay in the religious cosmos of the Hindus, who practised it as a matter of *dharma* or faith. The traditional order thus persisted without any change and reproduced itself for ages in the spatial universe of its innumerable village communities.

A corollary to this textbook formulation of India's past tradition would go on to suggest that it was only during the British colonial rule that Indians were first introduced to modernity. This march of India becoming 'modern' was significantly accelerated after Independence from colonial rule when the post-colonial state initiated the process of development with much enthusiasm. With India moving ahead on the path of development and modernization, caste ought to have become a thing of the past. The lingering traces of survival in modern times could only be a product of social, mental, and political anomalies, often attributed to the crooked world of electoral politics and the quota system born out of it. These lingering traces of it are also sometimes perceived as an evidence of the inability of the Indians/Hindus to move forward on the path of modernity and progress. Fixing these anomalies would, in this narrative, lead to the disappearance of caste, at least from the urban and modern landscapes of India's national life.

This is an outdated and, dare we say, deceptive or misleading view of India's past as well as of the experiences of caste on the ground in contemporary times. However, such a view persists across sections of the world community, in textbooks of social sciences, in popular writings and media representations and even amongst large sections of Indian middle classes as well as the elite. This is despite the fact that, academic or social science writings on the subject have come a long way and their understandings of the lived realities of caste have undergone profound transformations.

Where do such views come from and why do they persist? As historians have pointed out, such notions of India's past tradition were largely drawn from the early conceptualizations of South Asian societies by the Orientalist scholarship and the colonial administrators (Bayly, 2001; Cohn, 1996; Dirks, 2001). They drew their conceptions almost entirely from select classical texts, which indeed represented 'the caste system' as an aspect of 'native' religious tradition, an ideology that shaped minds and behaviour patterns of the Hindus in the Indian subcontinent, and had remained unchanged over centuries. Such a representation of the 'orient' was to also contrast it with the West, which was presented as a land of progress, science, and reason. However, this view completely ignored the easily observable empirics of ascription-based hierarchies (Jodhka, 2016). On the ground, caste had been very diverse across regions, often fluid, occasionally contested, and ever changing. Nevertheless, this view was accepted quite uncritically even by western-educated Indians, which included a large section of the nationalist leadership, who also later on came to be the first generation of native rulers and elite in independent India. Such an understanding of caste was also accepted by the elite in other countries of the region where caste exists in some form and impacts social structures: Sri Lanka (Lecamwasam and Peiris, 2020), Nepal (see David Gellner's chapter on *Caste in Nepal*), Bangladesh, and Pakistan (see Julien Levesque's chapter on *Caste among Muslims in North India and Pakistan* also see Jodhka and Shah, 2010).

Such a conceptual trajectory of caste has had lasting impact. According to this evolving common-sense view of caste among India's emerging middle-class elite during the late colonial period and soon after Independence, the introduction of western-style liberal democracy as a system of political organization (along with economic growth) was to dismantle caste on its own. The working assumption was that with equal rights to participate, without any weight of status and class, electoral democracy would undermine, and eventually erase caste-based divisions and hierarchies. The founding leaders of India's constitutional democracy explicitly expressed such a view in their writings. The first Prime Minister of independent India, Jawaharlal Nehru, put it quite sharply:

> In the context of society today, the caste system and much that goes with it are wholly incompatible, reactionary, restrictive, and barriers to progress. There can be no equality in status and opportunity within its framework, nor can there be political democracy ... Between these two conceptions conflict is inherent and only one of them can survive. (Nehru, 1946, p. 257)

Another important architect of the Indian democracy, chairman of the Drafting Committee of the Indian Constitution, B. R. Ambedkar, put it even more emphatically:

> You cannot build anything on the foundations of caste. You cannot build up a nation; you cannot build up a morality. Anything you will build on the foundations of caste will crack and will never be a whole. (Ambedkar, 2002, p. 102)

With the exception of B. R. Ambedkar and a few others, this early generation of India's elite that inherited power from the colonial rulers thus saw caste primarily from a culturalist perspective, informed by the apolitical ideas of tradition and modernization. A direct implication of this was that caste was not seen as a relevant variable shaping and structuring deprivations and the economic well-being of different sections of India's populace. Even when it was included in the policy, it was not seen as a reality that structured poverties and privileges. As David Mosse puts it:

> The manner in which caste has entered social policy largely overlooks caste as a continuing structural cause of inequality and poverty in present-day market-led development, and instead treats it as an archaic Indian cultural and ritual phenomenon erased by such development, or as a social disability subject to (in principle, temporary) 'special measures'. (Mosse, 2018, p. 423)

Despite many changes over time, such a view persists within the Indian state system. For example, when a section of civil society activists mobilized for recognition of the caste system as a form of racism at the Durban conference in 2011, the Indian government actively lobbied against it (see Deepa Reddy's chapter on *Caste, Race, and Ethnicity* and Eva-Maria Hardtmann's chapter on *Dalit Transnational Mobilization*). It obviously feared that such recognition would create ground for the close monitoring of caste-related violence and other forms of discrimination by UN treaty bodies. Upper-caste Indian diaspora groups in the UK lobbied against caste being included under 'race' as a 'protected characteristic' under the new Equality Act (see Dhanda et al., 2014).

However, given its centrality in India's social and political life, caste did enter the institutional process and state policy-making right from the days of colonial rule. It was in the british colonial period, during the 1920s and 1930s that a system of classification that identified communities suffering from caste-induced disabilities began to be developed. Under pressure from some of the non-Brahmin castes, the colonial state initiated affirmative action to provide representation for them in the emerging political system. Such a policy perspective also found space in the Constitution of independent India (see Gautam Bhatia's chapter on *Caste and Law*). Those who framed the Indian Constitution mostly agreed on working towards making India a society free of caste-based inequality and discrimination.

Not only does the Indian Constitution affirm its commitment to the value of equality among all, it also assigns the task of defending such values to the Indian State. It goes on to recognize social, economic, and political disabilities that caste has historically inflicted on a section of the Indian population. It even lays down provisions for a range of pro-active legal interventions and affirmative action policies that would expand the domain of citizenship and help create a level playing field (see Ashwini Deshpande's chapter on *Reservations and Affirmative Action*). Over the years, India has indeed expanded its policies of affirmative action that have produced positive outcomes. However, despite these forces at play, the deepening of democracy or India's economic growth and its increasing globalization, caste shows no sign of fading away. In some ways, the salience of caste seems to have grown in Indian public life since the early 1990s.

It is this paradox of contemporary Indian society and its economic and political processes that shapes the contributions to this volume. The essays presented in the volume help us make sense of this puzzle and contribute to the understanding of the forces behind the continued reproduction of caste, with many of its features intact—hierarchy, patriarchy, humiliation, deprivations, exclusions, and economic disparities—even while changes on the ground are surely not insignificant.

In our attempt to engage with this paradox, we argue for a new narrative of caste, going beyond the Orientalist formulations of Indian culture or the modernization theories of change. As is evident from the wide range of essays written by a diverse galaxy of authors from various academic disciplines, such a narrative is clearly emerging. This innovative literature draws from grounded and empirical studies of the different aspects of caste that have flourished since Independence. The perspective we present in this Introduction and those presented in the chapters also reflect emerging diverse voices from the margins, articulated through social movements, autobiographies, and scholarship.

Conceptual Currents: Caste, like other social phenomena, is not simply a thing out there, a *sui generis* social fact, as Emile Durkheim would have put it. It is also a construct, a conceptual framing of the 'thing out there'. Concepts in the social sciences have a life of their own. They are not simply words that denote a certain reality or process. While some are indeed used as technical terms with a limited descriptive or explanatory value, some others have capacious, and complicated careers. Their origins are important but their meanings and significations change over time, moulded, and twisted by the world in which they travel and the contexts in which they get deployed. Some of them even have the potential to shape, or at least influence, the very process, and realities they describe. As sources of meanings and meaningful/interpretative systems, they carry within them political possibilities and potentials for a wide range of imaginations and actions.

Caste is one such category. Even though it has been widely regarded as the most popular and lasting signifier of Indian social life and its ancient tradition, the term—not the reality that it has come to signify—has its origin in the western European linguistic cosmos. Native words such as *jati* and *varna* did not easily translate into its European counterpart. Over the years, it has also evolved into a category that did not simply describe a system of inequality or hierarchy that marked social and economic life almost everywhere in the subcontinent but a unique cultural universe that was fundamentally different from that of the Western world. In the evolving Orientalist scholarship of 18th- and 19th-century Europe, the Portuguese word *casta* was no longer a generic category. It came to be associated with Hindu religion, and its ritual life, as the Europeans had imagined it, their 'other'. Coupled with this was also the claim that everything Indian was determined by or reducible to the Hindu religious worldview, which, they underlined, had also remained stable and static for centuries, bereft of any history, contestation, and agency.

However, the Orientalist and colonial narratives simplified it as a pan-Indian 'system' (see Roland Lardinois's chapter on *The Idea of Caste through the Ages: Concept, Words, and Things*) and caste came to be imagined as being devoid of any materiality, constructed simply as a feature of the Hindu mind, shaped and structured by the dialectics of 'purity' and 'pollution', with which it has presumably been forever obsessed. As Louis Dumont translates this classical orientalist view in his much-celebrated book *Homo Hierarchicus*, the hierarchy that the Hindu mind produced was purely ideological, of status, and not of power or the material world (see Martin Fuchs's chapter on *Hierarchy* and Mathieu Claveyrolas chapter on *Hinduism and Caste System*). While such an autonomy or separation of status from power was unthinkable in the western world, this was not the case in India, Dumont had argued. Thus, by implication, in this culture-centric orientalist view of caste, the inequality that caste produced was not to be seen through questions of distribution and discrimination or through the deprivations and exclusionary patterns of life and residence that it produced. Even untouchability was a matter of cultural consensus and not of violence and humiliation, which it most obviously is and would always have been (see Suryakant Waghmore's chapter on *Dynamics of Untouchability*). Caste, as we see it, was never simply an ideological system, prescribing a social order of hierarchy based on cultural consensus. It always carried with it a system of domination and power, which produced deprivations and material inequalities.

As historians have rightly pointed out, the popular orientalist view of caste and India also ignored the significant regional diversities of the social arrangements on ground, as they would have evolved over time, intersecting with local economies, political histories and ecological possibilities (see Harald Tambs-Lyche's chapter on *Caste and Kingship*). Even when caste was ideologically embedded in the religious and ideational frameworks of the South Asian region, it was not simply a mental construct. Moreover, like some other religious philosophies, Hinduism too had its fluidities and varieties that were evolving and changing over time and space (see Raphaël Voix's chapter on *Hindu Sects and Caste*). The religious universe of South Asia has always been marked by diversities and contestations from within and from without (Raheja, 1988a; Thapar, 1989; Frykenberg, 1989; Lorenzen, 1999; Fuller, 1992). A case in point is the Nepal experience, where in absence of colonial encounter, caste, and its narratives evolved very differently (see David Gellner's chapter on *Caste, Ethnicity and the State in Nepal*).

Most importantly, the Orientalist framing of Hinduism and the ascription-based hierarchies in the region produced a hegemonic narrative of caste as a static and closed system, which the British colonial rulers strategically deployed to legitimize India's colonization. The colonial rulers used this formulation with their own people to make a case for India's colonization and show to them how their presence in the region was an act of benevolence (Cohn, 1987; Metcalf, 1997). They, thus, implicitly professed that the colonizers were there to help India get out of its inherent inertia and enable it to move forward on the path of progress, which the western civilization had already accomplished and charted out for others. The classical orientalist writings by scholars such as Hegel had already produced an account of the Indians and Hindus as being people with no agency (see Inden, 1986) and who hence could not move on the path of 'progress' on their own. Even radical scholars like Karl Marx accepted the Orientalist and colonial view of India and saw British rule as being positive for India, in the sense that it would help the country to extricate itself from its 'asiatic mode of production' (see Thorner, 1966).

Thus, caste conceptualised as a Hindu religious value, along with its presumed spatial locale, the 'village communities', came to be deployed as a foundational category of classification in the colonial administrative system. As has been widely documented by historians of colonial India, the use of such a framework in the Colonial Census, initiated during the latter half of the 19th century, had far-reaching implications for the realities of caste on ground. The process of enumeration with a *varna* model as an operative framework across regions of the subcontinent set in motion a process of mobilizations and self-identification across significantly diverse cultures and communities through identities that best fitted the *varna* model of caste. Many also wanted to be placed in a higher varna than what they had been granted by the enumerators (see Leigh Denault's chapter on *Census, Caste Enumeration, and the British Legacy*). The colonial categorization involved a very tedious and thorough process of engagements with the ground realities of caste. The data collected by colonial ethnographers continues to be a valuable source of information for scholars, though the though the publications they addressed to their European counterparts interpreted facts drawing upon a biased imperial lens, which perpetuated stereotypes of making caste appear as a part of the Hindus' religious practices.

As we have mentioned above, the Orientalist and colonial framing of caste had been so hegemonic that it came to be accepted uncritically by nearly everyone, including those fighting for India's independence from colonial rule. Even when they actively campaigned for reforms within their communities or in the broader relational frames of caste, they tended to work with the Orientalist/colonial view of caste. Thus, the Hindu religion-centric view of caste emerged as a hegemonic frame in yet another way. Conflation of caste with Hinduism also implied that all other religious communities of India, who too had caste or caste like divisions, implicitly shared a Hindu worldview based on the opposition between the pure and the impure. On this view, the Jains, the Buddhists, the Sikhs (Jodhka, 2004) or even the Muslims (see Julien Levesque's chapter on *Caste among Muslims in North India and Pakistan*), and Christians (Mosse, 2012) of the region had either converted out of Hinduism (such as the Indian Muslims or the Indian Christians) or their faith systems were branches and varieties of the broader Hindu family (such as the Buddhists and the Jains, or even the Sikhs) (see Gellner and Quigley, 1997).

Such a view of India and its pasts also found interesting synergies with the emerging social science theories and thinking of the time in the Western world. The Eurocentric social science frameworks on social and economic change that developed in the mainstream of Western academy tended to view caste as a classic case of 'tradition' stuck in time, not having reached yet the realm of reason and rationality. The classical functionalist and evolutionary thinking dominant within the disciplines of sociology and social anthropology found the colonial/orientalist view of caste as a form of traditional social order fitting very well in the theories of modernization and development that emerged in the western hemisphere during the middle of the 20th century.

Caste also acquired a special spatial identity, as an institution originating from India that came to be seen as being synonym of extreme social closure and anti-meritocratic in spirit. Caste was thus invoked to describe processes of social closure present in Western societies while at the same time 'othering' them by pointing to their oriental and Indian origin. For example, it often came to be invoked to describe enclosed elite formations or political establishments through expressions such as 'the Boston Brahmins' or 'the political pundits'. The term had also been popular with scholars of race studies as a metaphor to describe impermeable boundaries and ascription-based status hierarchies across racial groupings, presumably found among the Hindus of India (Cox, 1945; Myrdal, 2017; Ogbu, 1979; Berreman, 1960). 'Caste' thus came to be inscribed in the textbooks of sociology as a form of social stratification that was closed and rigid with no possibility of mobility across strata, that was to be found in its purest form among the Hindus of India and its South-Asian neighbourhood.

Such an understanding of caste and its invocation as an example of 'a type of society' could also be witnessed in the sociological theories of social change; whereby all societies move from one kind of order to another. As these functionalist theories of change suggested, the social structure of pre-modern societies was characterized by 'status' and 'communities', which are ultimately bound to transform into associational collectives of individuals marked by distinctions of class. While the former and traditional social order was invariably a closed system of hierarchy based on the logic of ascription, the latter was an open system of stratification, which reflected differential individual achievements. Even the Marxian theory of capitalist transformation underlined the radical nature of change in social relations that capitalism had been able to bring about, dissolving all the pre-capitalist structures of belonging and distinction.

Interestingly, the functionalist thinking on a subject like caste, or its counterpart, the orientalist view of Indian tradition, or even the nationalist common-sense did not view caste as a 'problem' that produced deprivations and marginalities. They did not see the need for an active political engagement with such exclusionary realities on ground that produced poverty, conflict, and violence. As indicated above, in the eyes of the modernizers and of the developmental state, caste was primarily a cultural hangover that needed to be dealt with ideologically, like a deceptive myth. Caste, had thus to be overcome mentally. Its eventual disappearance, as a natural consequence of the forward march of history, was taken for granted. It is this **imperative of disappearance** that has informed much of the common-sense view of caste, and pervasively continues to do so even today.

Social Science Engagements with Caste: The early social science research and writing in India was also informed largely by a similar understanding of the caste system. This naturally made it a subject of lesser significance. In the given context where the 'new nation' was preoccupied with questions of development and change, thinking of caste appeared to be a regressive move. The economists, who were in the driving seat along with the political elite during the initial decades after Independence, designed India's path of development while hardly recognizing caste as a variable of any critical significance even when studying subjects such as poverty (Mosse, 2018). Surprisingly, the early historians too did not take caste seriously. They tended to work with categories such as class, community, religion, and region to make sense of India's pasts. Even their accounts of rural life focused mostly on the land revenue system and the changing relationships between the peasantry and the state(s).

However, there were also counter-currents that this Handbook draws upon in order to lay the foundations of a re-framing of caste. The size of social science academy and institutional funding for field-based research expanded quite significantly after India's Independence from colonial rule. India's development planning was accompanied by the introduction of new systems of data collection. The process of evaluating the impacts of development planning and programmes also required qualitative empirical studies. India's development planning and its choice of political democracy thus generated a great deal of interest in the 'new' nation-state among the academics of the western world. A wide range of scholars from the United States and Western Europe began to engage with the empirics of the Indian social, economic, and political life. This process has continued over time, including a growing number of collaborations with local scholars. Many of the Indian scholars who initiated surveys and qualitative empirical studies were also trained in Western universities.

With growing engagements of the social science scholarship, the Orientalist reading of caste drawn mostly from select classical texts and loaded with a Eurocentric bias began to be revised. One of the most popular subjects of enquiry that emerged during the 1950s was the empirical study of India's rural life, mainly pursued by social anthropologists, many of whom later began to identify themselves as sociologists. Unlike their counterpart economists and political scientists of the time who were mostly preoccupied with questions of change, sociologists and social anthropologists were far more comfortable with exploring what existed on the ground. Given the popular view of India as a land of villages, the Indian village emerged as an obvious methodological entry point for the study of its social structure. For a social anthropologist approaching rural life from a cultural perspective, caste was its obvious core—the life blood of rural communities. Post-independence social scientists were thus sharing a common assumption with their colonial predecessors. Though this common interest in caste in its rural setting helped bridge the production of knowledge on caste from one epistemic moment to the other, the tireless fieldwork of social scientists from the post-colonial period led them to gradually emancipate themselves from the assumption that religion is the cornerstone of caste.

Over the years, caste thus came to be described as the stock-in-trade of the social anthropologists and sociologists working in/on India. Even when many of them shared the mainstream middle-class elite view of caste being a cultural hangover of the past, and that with India moving on the path of modernization it would die out on its own, they could rarely ignore its all-pervasive presence while constructing their ethnographic 'field-views' of village life, the presumed signifier of its authentic native self. They extensively explored the nature of jajmani relations, the inter-dependence among caste groups, the nature of hierarchy, and structures of domination through which it reproduced itself (for a review of village studies, see Jodhka, 1998; Madan, 2002; Thakur, 2013; Cabalion and Thivet, 2019).

The early generation of sociologists and social anthropologists worked with the received notions of caste, inherited from the colonial and orientalist constructs of 'Indian tradition'. However, they soon started to question the stated and unstated assumptions about the so-called unity of caste as an ideological construct and its 'continuity' with virtually no internal changes over the centuries. The early social anthropological monographs on individual villages pointed to the fluidities and diversities of rural social structures. They also pointed to aspects of power and dominance as being inherent to caste relations and the possibilities of mobility even within the so-called tradition-governed hierarchies (see Nicolas Martin's chapter on *The Dominant Caste*, and George Kunnath's chapter on *Sanskritization*). They underlined the need to move away from the simple 'book-view' of caste to a 'field-view' to unearth its varied manifestations and internal dynamics of change and adaptability. They argued that the complexities of caste in the real world were often not easily captured in neatly worked-out theories and conceptions of the 'system' as present in some of the Western writings on the subject. Through empirical studies of village life and caste communities, they showed how caste changed with time and revealed possibilities of movement within this so-called 'closed' system of stratification (see Jules Naudet's chapter on *Caste and Class*, and Divya Vaid's chapter on *Caste and Mobility*). In particular, these studies documented caste's capacity to adapt and change, which underpinned its remarkable endurance.

As studies on the subject progressed, some of them also looked at broader processes that were being shaped by caste. They underlined the need for taking it seriously as a lived reality that structured social life even beyond its rural settlements. Some of them also looked at caste-based community networks and the ways in which they were mobilized to achieve social and economic mobility (Hardgrave, 1969; Béteille, 2012). Still others looked at the emerging regional networks of caste communities, the 'horizontal consolidations' of the *jatis* (Srinivas, 1959).

Parallel to the shifts brought about by the field-view on caste, another epistemic change began to unfold itself during the 1980s and 1990s with a growing participation of Dalits, Adivasis, and OBCs in academic debates. Following the path opened by Ambedkar and drawing upon new upward mobility pathways created by the implementation of reservations, they gradually entered the well-guarded upper-caste bastion of academia. Their voice and their scholarship slowly gained influence in intellectual debates. They brought to these debates their experiences of exclusion and humiliation and insisted on recognizing its persistence, even beyond the space of village and tradition, in labour markets, urban settlements, and the rapidly globalizing India. The popular view of caste was thus provincialized as the brahminical view on caste.

This growing influence partly drew upon the consolidation and radicalization of the Dalit movement, epitomized by the invigorating emergence of the Dalit Panther movement (see Hugo Gorringe and Karthikeyan Damodaran's chapter on *Dalit Movements* and Harish Wankhede's chapter on *The Mahars and Dalit Movements of*

Maharashtra). Dalit perspectives on caste made their way into the intellectual debate from multiple entry-points, some of which were not necessarily academic. The emergence of a Dalit literature (Satyanarayana, 2019), the publication of the radical weekly magazine 'Dalit Voice' in 1981 and the mushrooming of Dalit civil society organizations following the Durban World Conference against Racism of 2001 were among the most visible emanations of these multiple assertions. From then on, no scholarship on caste could ignore this new reality anymore.

Sociological and anthropological scholarship on caste has continued to diversify during the following decades. While questions such as kinship networks and their ideological effects remain important (see Janaki Abraham's chapter on *Caste, and Kinship*), sociologists are also beginning to explore its continued significance in shaping democratic politics (see Christophe Jaffrelot's chapter on *Do Indians Vote their Caste, or Their jati, or Their Class, or...?* Lucia Michelutti's chapter on *Caste, Patronage, and Criminalization of Politics*; and David Gellner's chapter on *Caste, Ethnicity, and The State in Nepal*); opportunity structures in labour markets of the neo-liberal economy (Vaid, 2018; also see Carol Upadhya's chapter on *Caste and Capital*; and Divya Vaid's chapter on *Caste and Mobility*); or everyday urban life and its exclusionary character. Sociologists today continue to explore the multiple modes and manifestations of caste, trying to figure out the mechanisms that account for its incredible resilience.

Political scientists were drawn to the subject of caste when they began to explore the empirical dynamics of the modern western-style democracy that independent India had ushered in individual-centric universal adult franchise in a society marked by group-based hierarchies. The early generation of political scientists observing the intersection of caste with the newly introduced democratic politics found caste to be a potentially active and adaptive institution (see Frankel and Rao, 1989; Rudolph and Rudolph, 1967). They examined the ways in which the 'traditional' institution of caste could rather quickly adapt to the 'modern' systems of democratic political processes. Even though it had to undergo a process of internal change as it entered and interacted with electoral politics, it also adapted the western representative system to the local organization of caste-communities and hierarchical cultures (Michelutti, 2008).

Political scientists discovered that politicians found it convenient to organize their efforts to reach out to collectives around caste-based identities. In response, caste acquired new salience and substance, as leaders of organized interests stressed caste (the category that politicians used) in their efforts to seek benefits from elected governments and state bureaucracy. Democracy did not erode caste. Nor did caste always find democracy inimical. Beginning with the writings of scholars like Lloyd Rudolph and Susanne Rudolph, studies on electoral processes showed how caste communities mobilized themselves to effectively participate in the democratic political process (Rudolph and Rudolph, 1967). While caste entered the democratic political process, it also underwent some significant changes and had to adapt to some of the normative demands of democratic politics in forming 'caste associations' (see Kothari, 1976). Interestingly, sociologists too had observed this process of caste adapting to the changing realities of social and political life. While G. S. Ghurye had described this as 'caste patriotism', Srinivas had famously seen it as a process of 'horizontal consolidation of caste' (see Jodhka, 2010). Many other concepts such as the 'ethnicization' or the 'substantialization' of caste emerged during this period, as if the nature of caste itself had changed, making it amenable to democratic politics.

As caste came to occupy a greater and more visible place in India's democratic politics, the engagement of political scientists with the subject has also persistently grown, particularly among those working on the empirics of the dynamics of Indian politics. Their focus has also shifted from an earlier preoccupation with its compatibility with democracy to more critical questions, such as its implications on building citizenship or on identifying backwardness (see S. Anandhi and Kalpana Kannabiran's chapter on *Backwardness*), its exclusionary effects and the rise of identity politics (Frankel and Rao, 1989; Jayal and Mehta, 2010; Guru and Sarukkai, 2019). One of the most influential pieces of work in the emerging political sociology in more recent time has been Christophe Jaffrelot's book *India's Silent Revolution: The Rise of the Lower Castes* (2003) that comprehensively examined the growing political participation of those lower down in the local hierarchies in north India. The book also shows how over the years they came to even occupy positions of leadership at different levels in the Indian democratic political system. This academic and popular interest in the complex relationship between caste and democratic politics in India has continued to grow with time and is currently one of the most dynamic and fertile areas of research for social scientists (see Jodhka and Manor, 2017).

Beginning with the early 1990s, the **historical** scholarship on the subject also began to grow and greatly influence scholars working in other disciplines as well. As is evident from the discussion, the historical scholarship has over the years made a substantial contribution to the contemporary understanding of caste. Historians explored the past of the 'caste system'—or rather *systems*—and have provided rich empirical details of the wide varieties and modes through which the local systems of hierarchy were integrated with the regional economic and political regimes and manners in which they were reproduced (see Julie Marquet's chapter on *Caste Disputes in Colonial India: Conflicts and the Legal Shaping of Caste*). Their work has also had very significant theoretical implications. Caste was not simply a subject for making sense of the 'peculiar' social organization of Indian society, in the past or in the present. It was also a construct, which acquired a particular shape with growing influence of what Bernard Cohn described as the 'colonial forms of knowledge' of India (Cohn, 1996).

As we have argued above, and as it has also been elaborated in several chapters of this volume (see Dilip Menon's chapter on *Transformations of Caste in Colonial India* and Leigh Denault's chapter on *Census, Caste Enumeration, and the British Legacy*), the making of such theories about India's 'exceptionalism' was not simply an academic fallacy. It was primarily driven by an attempt at producing an ideological and political legitimization of the 'foreign' rule. The colonial reading of caste gradually became the unquestioned common-sense view of Indian society. For the nationalists, it helped craft a coherent idea of India as a nation cemented around the Hindu religion's capacity to weave together a complex social fabric. On their side, social scientists endorsed this idea of caste having been a stable and coherent system for centuries and, from there, they speculated on the ways in which it could adjust/change to the forces of modernization.

Historical research proved decisive in questioning and challenging such assumptions. Rosalind O'Hanlon's work, for example, points to the deep historical roots of the 'fissiparous' dimension of caste that most anthropologists and sociologists saw as a resolutely modern process unfolding in forms such as its substantialization or ethnicization. It has been underway even in the pre-colonial times (O'Hanlon, 2017; O'Hanlon, Hidass, and Kiss, 2015). Sadly though, such researches have still not become common knowledge and find no mention in the textbooks. The same is the case with popular political narratives. They tend to stay content with the simplistic view framed around categories of *varna* and *jati*.

Economists have been the last to come on board in the social science of caste (see Guilhem Cassan's chapter on *The Economics of Caste*). Even though some economists had documented aspects of the rural economy during the 1950s and even earlier and pointed to the relationship of caste with landlessness and its significance in the rural economic life (Jodhka and Simpson, 2019), it was around the turn of the century that, along with a section of those involved with state policy, they began to look at the economic dimensions of caste while exploring patterns of exclusion and group identity. They advocated the value of recognizing caste and other such group identities as critical variables in mapping and understanding persistent poverty and deprivation in countries like India.

Though work on the social organization of labour markets in India is just beginning, the new language of community-centric social exclusion is being increasingly used and recognized in the policy discourses, not only by planners and policymakers in the Government of India but also by global development agencies such as the World Bank and the UNDP that are concerned with questions of poverty and human well-being in countries of the South. Economists have also mobilized their conceptual tools to highlight how caste networks remain important sources of security and stability across social groups, ranging from the most deprived to the most endowed (Munshi, 2016). Indeed, in the absence of a strong welfare state and of universalistic solidarities, caste is often seen as a protection from uncertainties (Munshi and Rosenzweig, 2009). Hoping for privileged access to certain rare resources, actors are thus often ready to sacrifice a part of their individual freedom and yield to the subjugation and social control of their caste peers. The economists' transactional way of looking at caste could prove crucial to our understanding of the mechanisms of its reproduction and help extend inter-disciplinary dialogue on the subject.

This emerging social science scholarship has also quite fundamentally transformed the conception of caste. Through the essays presented in this handbook, written by scholars from a wide range of disciplines, we hope to showcase the evolving inter-disciplinary understanding of caste, which contests and complicates the simplistic notions of it merely being a rigid system of ascription-based hierarchy. It also demonstrates the diversities of themes and thinking on the subject as it becomes increasingly popular with practitioners of a wide range of scholars within the social sciences and humanities.

Changing Dynamics of Caste: Over the last century or so the institution of caste has undergone striking changes. A great deal of occupational differentiation has occurred that has substantially eroded the old *jajmani* system (see Peter Mayer's chapter on *The Jajmani System*), which provided caste hierarchies with their material underpinnings. Not only has the caste-based framework of the organization of rural societies been declining, but local level political processes have also become more inclusive. To put it differently, while caste-based politics is still blossoming, its custodians now tend to resort to alternative ways of exerting caste domination (see Lucia Michelutti's chapter on *Caste, Patronage, and Criminalization of Politics*). More importantly the so-called low-caste groupings have become serious and effective contenders in the political and electoral games of the Indian democracy. We now hear little about polling booths being captured by the armies of dominant landlords in the hinterlands of India. Caste violence has to contend with the 'silent revolution' impulse of the lower castes and their growing resistance to traditional upper-caste modes of domination.

Despite all changes, the institution survives and thrives in many different ways. The most obvious evidence of its persistence is its continued overlap with the prevailing patterns of inequality. Available analyses of official data on poverty and productive assets clearly show significant variations across caste lines (see Jules Naudet's chapter on *Caste and Class* and Divya Vaid's chapter on *Caste and Mobility*). Those located at the lower end of the traditional caste hierarchy tend to be significantly over-represented among the poor and the marginal. The positive correlation at the other end is equally strong. Those at the upper end of the caste hierarchy are far less likely to be present among the economically most depressed categories (also see Vaid, 2018). In other words, even if we're at a point in history when caste has weakened ideologically, the process has so far not produced any kind of levelling in Indian society. Even when Dalits and others located lower in the hierarchical structures do not subscribe to any of the popular theories that provide justification for their subjugation, hierarchies persist. Not only do traditional inequalities continue to be reproduced in the economic domain, the emerging opportunity structures at different levels of the labour market, and urban economy also tend to be skewed against the traditionally underprivileged and socially marginalized (see Carol Upadhya's chapter on *Caste and Capital*; Kalpana Kannabiran's chapter on *De-Notified Communities*; and Jai Prasad's chapter on *Caste and Tribe*). This only restates the point we have made above that caste does not merely exist in people's minds. It has *materiality*, in that it shapes and structures the nature of opportunities available to different strata of the erstwhile hierarchies.

While it is important to highlight the material side of caste, its persistence, albeit in a different form, in everyday culture is also not to be ignored or undermined. Even when it is hard to find an unapologetic advocate of the traditional system of caste hierarchy, and those at the lower down in the hierarchy no longer accept their position as a consequence of their past *karma* (if they ever did), status hierarchies continue to be cherished and legitimized (see Rajeshwari Deshpande's chapter on *Caste Associations and The Post-Mandal Politics of Caste*). This is also reflected in marriage and kinship patterns. Even when boundaries of endogamous jati groups expand, the logic of caste remains very strong (see Janaki Abraham's chapter on *Caste and Kinship*). Statistically speaking, inter-caste marriages are still an exception (Ahuja and Ostermann, 2016; Ray, Chaudhuri, and Sahay, 2017). The caste question is thus also closely intertwined with the gender question (see Pushpesh Kumar's chapter on *Caste and Gender*).

The neo-liberal turn and the so-called opening of markets appear to have had the opposite effect on caste and kinship bonding. The myth of modernity and individual achievement, unfettered by ascription, has been responsible for the invisibilization of caste, and other such realities (Deshpande, 2013). The burden of inequality is then transferred on the individual, who had presumably failed to achieve despite having been given equal opportunity. Such narratives tend to provide legitimacy to differentially endowed cultural and social capital, acquired mostly through caste, and family-based habitus (see Ajantha Subramanian's chapter on *Caste and Merit*). Growth of capitalism or the so-called process of modernization does not always erase the pre-existing structures of hierarchy and difference. Capitalism re-shapes them, and often uses them, ideologically and structurally (see Jodhka, Rehbein, and Souza, 2017). Emerging research on urban spatial formations too suggests that these have been increasingly becoming exclusionary and caste-like (Bharati, Malghan, and Rahman, 2018; Srivastava, 2014). The frequent reports of caste-based violence and never-ending news of atrocities on the Dalits who dare to assert themselves for their basic rights as citizens of a democratic country further provide proof of its endurance (Narula, 2008).

The emerging literature on caste does not deny the profound changes that have come about in almost every aspect of caste in India over the past century, but it explores the different ways in which it continues to matter even when it undergoes profound change(s) and simultaneously extends its influence beyond the boundaries of South Asia (see Radha Modi's chapter on *Caste and the Diaspora*). It might not be wrong to say that the public salience of caste is far greater today than it has ever been in the past when institutionally the old hierarchies were much stronger and the ideologies sustaining it much less contested. Anti-caste movements are far noisier now than ever before (see Hugo Gorringe and Karthikeyan Damodaran's chapter on *Dalit Movements*). They have also been able to draw upon social media and international networks to spread their ideas across all segments of society, nationally and globally (see Eva-Maria Hardtmann's chapter on *Dalit Transnational Mobilizations*). Politicians of all hues today applaud the legacy of Ambedkar (see Anand Teltumbde's chapter on *Ambedkar's Legacy*). Even the Hindu right-wing organizations that mobilize their cadre around the idea of the greatness of India's past 'tradition' publically profess their commitment to making the country and Hinduism a casteless religious collective (see Joel Lee's chapter on *Caste and Hindutva*).

This compilation of essays thus aspires to provide a comprehensive account of the available social science research on this crucial subject. We also hope that this volume would help orient future research on caste and related subjects. Study of caste is no longer a monopoly of sociologists and social anthropologists. We believe that the growing multidisciplinary approach as being presented in this book will enrich our understanding of caste and help reframe our approach to the study of it, transcending Indian exceptionalism, within which it has remained trapped for long.

Moving Forward: In this final section, we propose a way forward to the study of caste and possible modes of approaching it empirically and conceptually. The essays presented in this volume provide a useful resource for doing so. They reflect conceptual shifts emanating from emerging research on the subject as well as from the political dynamics unfolding on the ground as India has been witnessing a surge of subaltern movements centred on caste identities since the early 1990s. They question, directly or implicitly, the classical orientalist views on the subject, the presumed exceptionalism of India's social and cultural life woven around caste. It was also around this time that caste came to be recognized as a relevant 'variable' in development and policy narratives (see Jodhka, 2018).

As is evident from empirical and historical research, caste is not simply a fossilized tradition embedded in a pre-modern religiosity, waiting to dissolve, and disappear with the onset of modernity. Its survival in the present time is not simply a result of India's 'progress deficit', nor is it a problem of mental evolution or a cultural and religious hangover. It is a living reality that structures social, economic, and political life, ever changing but still persisting. It is capable of resilience, agility, and flexibility. Caste in fact was, and is, a profoundly diverse and dynamic institution. Thus, what emerges from the essays presented in the volume is not a singular view, which is reducible to one definite principle, a timeless character, of the so-called Indian culture, as Louis Dumont had once attempted (Lardinois, 2013 [2007]). Such a view also tends to essentialize, overgeneralize, and explain everything about the subject, making the need for any further research unnecessary. The dynamics of social institutions are always fluid, with multiple dimensions, and varied possibilities of articulation with other structures and processes of social life.

The social science scholarship and its conceptual tools should be such that they help us explore and understand its dynamic without suggesting a teleological path of its dissolution into a known phenomenon: from caste to class or tradition to modernity. Such attempts simplify complex processes of change and mislead political action. As an alternative to such simplistic views, we approach caste both as a complex social reality and also a conceptual tool, a kind of heuristic device, that enables us to look at ascription-based structures **of hierarchy and inequality** (see Jodhka, 2016, 2018). It could help us explore and understand how ascription-based hierarchies persist in contemporary times—in capitalist social and economic order—and intersect with other aspects of social, economic and political life. Agreeing with Max Weber, we see caste as a form of **status group**, a kind of ethnic formation, with vertically drawn boundaries. As he argued,

> The 'caste' is, indeed, the normal form in which ethnic communities usually live side by side in a 'societalized' manner. These ethnic communities believe in blood relationship and exclude exogamous marriage and social intercourse. Such a caste situation is part of the phenomenon of 'pariah' peoples and is found all over the world. These people form communities, acquire specific occupational traditions... (Weber, 1946, pp. 188–189)

We further follow B. R. Ambedkar when he argues that what shapes the specificity of caste *vis-à-vis* other forms of ethnic groupings is the very high number of such endogamous groups among South Asian societies. The principle regulating the relations between such an innumerable myriad of endogamous groups is, according to him, the idea of 'graded inequality'. In his own words, this refers to the fact that:

> There is no such class as a completely underprivileged class except the one which is at the base of the social pyramid. The privileges of the rest are graded. Even the low is a privileged class as compared with the lower. Each class being privileged, every class is interested in maintaining the social system. (Ambedkar, 1979, vol. 5, p. 102)

For Ambedkar, 'graded inequality' is the key explanation to the stability of India's unequal social order. Ascription-based relational structures and status groupings are nonetheless not unique to India or Hinduism. They exist in all societies. What we learn from the study of caste is not the uniqueness or exceptionalism of India but its being a useful conceptual tool for the comparative understanding of inequalities.

Thus, a non-teleological approach to caste must not only recognize its pervasive character, but also its multi-dimensionality, its ability to manifest itself in a wide variety of forms and practices. It being an aspect of the Brahmanical Hindu religious philosophy does not exhaust the reality of caste. Caste has also shaped agrarian land relation even in absence of Brahmanical Hinduism (see Surinder S. Jodhka's chapter on *Caste in Punjab*). It could similarly play a critical role in shaping aspects of secular and modern institutions, ranging from elected bodies of local governance to elite urban housing societies and top-end corporate offices (see Jodhka, 2018; Naudet, 2018).

We propose a polythetic definition of caste, that is, a definition that invokes a number of different criteria, not all of which will necessarily be present in every case and no one of which is all-determining or ever-present. Caste, we argue, is a status group based on an ideal of endogamy that is the result of several heterogeneous dimensions being twisted together, just like 'the strength of the thread does not reside in the fact that someone fibre runs through its whole length, but in the overlapping of many fibres' (Wittgenstein, *Philosophical Investigations*, I, sec. 67). We suggest that there are five different dimensions structuring caste. This implies that caste hierarchies are necessarily multidimensionales and cannot be reduced to one single criterion (purity, dominance, etc.). While these dimensions are all related, none of them totally prevails. When some of these dimensions weaken, others may not, and could even become stronger. The intensity of these dimensions also varies in time and in space and their effects may manifest themselves in a variety of different forms and practices, leading to a perpetual re-shaping of the contours of caste as an endogamous group.

First, caste has a religious dimension within Brahmanical Hinduism where ideas of purity and pollution play a critical structuring role in shaping cultural values and everyday social practices. However, Hinduism, as we know it today, is an internally diverse religious system and there are sects and sections within Hinduism which question the sanctity of such ideas and practices. Further, there are religions in India, such as

Christianity, Buddhism, Sikhism, and Islam, whose religious ideologies do not advocate caste but many of whose adherents practice it in their everyday social life.

As we have argued above, a religion-centric view of caste has its roots in the Orientalist writings on India and Louis Dumont later developed it into an elaborate theory of caste and Hindu society. While we do not deny its presence and influence, the reality of caste is much more than simply an ideological system of a specific religion. Further, unlike Dumont, we see such a structure of hierarchical relations embedded by 'power' and shaped by as well as shaping materialities, thereby constricting the possibility of building a democratic culture grounded on the values of common humanity and equal citizenship (Naudet, 2015).

Second, 'power' is also an independent dimension of caste, which is not always reducible or even related to religious ideology. Caste has, for example, widely come to be seen as an important aspect of India's democratic politics. It functions as a site or platform of mobilization or networks of influence and/or coercion at different levels of the Indian political system: local, regional, and national. Beyond the electoral politics, caste is also by itself political, structuring power relations, institutionally, and in everyday life. It interacts and intersects with gender and shapes interpersonal relations, within and across caste communities. The distribution of power, in all its different forms, is intimately tied to caste and caste often also functions as a power resource.

A related, third dimension of caste is its relationship with the state system. Beyond the classical debate around the question of the relationship between the 'king' and the 'priest' (see Raheja, 1988b, for a summary), hierarchies of caste are often sustained, shaped, and transformed by the state system. In the process of its institutional regulation, the state may become source for its legitimacy. It could also make it illegitimate through its legislative systems. It often superimposes a classificatory order through enumerative strategies and/or the policies of affirmative action. Categories such as Scheduled Castes (SCs) and Other Backward Classes (OBCs), introduced by the state for administering its policies of affirmative action tend to acquire a life of their own and begin to shape ideas of the 'self' and the 'other'.

Fourth, the 'economic' dimension of caste has always been important and widely recognized. It remains so even today, in urban India and the modern sectors of the economy. As Ambedkar famously argued, it facilitates the division of labour by dividing the labourers on caste lines. Such an ethnic segmentation of labour markets has increasingly become a feature of modern-day capitalist economy in different parts of the world. Such hierarchies produce exclusionary outcomes, often in correspondence with the pre-existing social differences of caste. It does so because of the widespread cultures and practices of discrimination, co-optation and 'opportunity-hoarding' that perpetuate around pre-existing social identities.

Finally, caste thrives because it continues to be an important aspect of living culture. We argue that its religious or institutional dimension does not encompass its entire cultural dimension, as we understand it. As is evident from several chapters presented in this volume, cultures of caste present themselves around notions of collective histories of communitarian pride, which inspires them to mobilize and form collective institutions such as caste associations, caste-community specific temples, restricted urban neighbourhoods, and sometimes even political parties (see Ujithra Ponniah's chapters on *Agarwal Banias of Delhi*; Zoe Headley's chapter on *Caste Logoes: A View from Tamil Nadu*; Haripriya Narasimhan's chapter on *The Brahmins of Urban India*; and Ramnarayan Rawat's chapter on *A Dalit History of Chamars in Uttar Pradesh*). They collectively promote specific values and belief systems, which in some cases could even be 'secular' in nature (e.g. the Bengali Bhadralok, see Sarbani Bandyopadhyay chapter on *The Invisibility of Caste in Bengal*).

This dimension also includes the promotion and propagation of communitarian myths, common dress codes, culinary traditions (Baviskar, 2018), cultivation of tastes. Caste also continues to promote negative impulses, such as commonly shared senses of repulsion towards certain groups and things. Distinctive caste cultures further imply specific matrices of socialization, which end up producing a range of discrete caste habitus, in the sense in which Bourdieu defines it, that is, a set of learned dispositions organizing how we see the world and act in our everyday lives. They help create and reinforce 'symbolic boundaries' across groups and communities that are not simply about cultural difference. They produce and promote a sense of judgment and hierarchy across symbolically marked groupings (Lamont and Molnar, 2002; Pachuki, Pendergrass, and Lamont, 2007).

Our purpose in identifying these different dimensions is to propose a new relational framework of approaching caste that better accommodates the contributions made by most recent researches on the subject. Social science researches coming from a range of disciplines over the past three decades enables us to see and study caste better. We hope that the proposed framework will help raise relevant questions for empirical research, without proposing a telos for its future. It is through the interactions and intersection of these dimensions at a given time and context that the relational structures of caste, such as the jajmani system, marriage and kinship, community identities, segmented labour markets or patterns of social networks, are produced and practised. Even when the five dimensions of caste proposed above overlap and closely intersect with each other, they tend to also function with a degree of autonomy. The weight and value of each dimension changes depending upon the given historical, spatial, and political context. It is possible that in a given context, a specific dimension may prevail over the others while in another context some other dimension may acquire greater salience.

The nature and degree of change in any one or more dimensions of caste indeed change relations on the ground, but such changes tend to only reconfigure the reality of caste, and do not necessarily weaken it. For example, in an emerging democratic polity, the Brahmins or Banias may align with Dalits to form a viable alliance to counter the influence of dominant OBC caste groupings but that is unlikely to promote inter-marriage across the two sets of caste groups. It may not even make any difference to pervasive caste prejudice that the former may have for the latter and which may compel them to continue to treat them as 'impure' and 'untouchable'. However, such a process indeed weakens the religious and ideological underpinnings of the so-called upper-caste groups by allowing so-called lower caste groups to rise up and acquire and consolidate new sources of secular power. Their access to institutional power enables them—though not always successfully—to convert the newly acquired political resource into economic capital, thus further reconfiguring caste hierarchies.

Such a reshuffling of the rules of the competition between caste groups could also lead to a redrawing of group boundaries. For instance, Lucia Michelutti (2008) shows how in order to increase their political weight in Uttar Pradesh, Ahirs, and Yadavs dissolved their distinctions and came together to form a new caste collective. They even induced a change in endogamy practices by encouraging fusion of the numerous sub-jatis into one single kinship unit, the *Krishnavanshi Yadav*. This was critical for the emergence of a resurgent Yadav culture and viable political formations, which in turn impacted other dimensions of the system. Over a period of time the caste hierarchies in the region were significantly reconfigured and the morphology of caste groups altered. A similar kind of process was also witnessed in the Punjab region though in a completely different historical context and through a very different set of re-configurations. Similarly, the chapters in this volume on the regional contexts of Bengal, Tamil Nadu, and Nepal as well as the chapter on *Caste and Kinship* could be read through such an angle.

Approaching caste purely from the aspects likely to bring about its disappearance tends only to impede the framing of relevant research questions. The need is to explore and understand the different ways in which caste perpetually reconfigures itself across these dimensions and the implications of their outcomes for a democratic political life.

Such a perspective on the subject could also help understand caste in a comparative frame, its similarities and differences from ascription-based hierarchies and classifications in other parts of the world. If caste is an institution that becomes a locus around which social hierarchies are produced and contested, it compares well with categories and constructs like gender, ethnicity, race, or in some contexts even class. As ideological systems, they all enable the production of a common sense that provides *justification to why certain groups ought to be privileged while others be deprived of those privileges and instead be subjugated to 'lower' positions*. The sum total of this is the production of a multifaceted justification for persistent structures of inequality that acts as the backdrop for the unequal *distribution of positions and resources*. Seen from a comparative perspective, caste could easily be viewed as a form of 'categorical distinction' producing 'durable inequality', a concept proposed by Charles Tilly (1998). It quite closely resembles other forms of categorical distinctions—race, ethnicity, religion, gender, sexuality—that tend to produce durable inequalities.

While such an approach indeed helps us to escape the trap of Indian exceptionalism, we do not propose that all forms of durable inequalities are similar in nature (Brubaker and Fernandez, 2019). Caste is both comparable and different from race or ethnicity. Not because the content of caste is substantially different from that of race or ethnicity, but because it is relationally different, in the sense that caste is part of a social topography that organizes the relationships between nature, biology, nation, and religion differently.

However, caste, race, and ethnicity tend to produce similar kinds of relational dynamics: endogamy, commensality, segregated settlements, communal solidarity, opportunity hoarding, business networks, or even music cultures, literature, and art. They tend to similarly instil a negative attitude and orientation towards the 'other': distance, prejudice and avoidance. Following Andreas Wimmer's theory of ethnic boundary-making, we argue that it is important to think of caste the way he thinks of ethnicity, that is, as 'the outcome of the classificatory struggles and negotiations between actors situated in a social field' (Wimmer, 2008, p. 970).

Such a relational framing could thus help in bringing caste back to the centre stage of the dynamics of reproduction of inequality and help identify the numerous commonalities that it shares with other forms of difference producing durable inequalities. In so doing, it further helps us take the research on caste beyond the traps of methodological nationalism. Patterns of change taking place in India—its economy, society, and culture—are not fundamentally different from what is happening elsewhere in the world. This is not to undermine the historical trajectories and cultural specificities of India but to broaden the research and perspective on caste and place it in a wider comparative perspective. Such a comparative perspective on caste could also help us approach it in relation to the global dynamics of capital, making it possible to approach it as a part of mainstream discussions of politics and policy dealing with inequality.

To conclude, we thus call for a re-framing of caste by setting down the following goals: (i) it is necessary to abandon the Orientalist worldview and its ideas about caste being a fixed, never-changing, and closed system of ascription; (ii) we must also reject its later avatars, the essentialist view of caste as being a *sui generis* institution, uniquely present among the Hindus of India, as was proposed by Dumont; (iii) it is important to shift to the available empirically grounded research and historical scholarship on caste, and broadly on India, for us to think of caste as a fluid ever-changing reality with multiple dimensions and varied manifestations; (iv) a better understanding of caste would be possible by looking at its different dimensions and recognizing that they could all function autonomously, not only independently of each other, but sometimes also in contradiction to each other, shaping its forms and identities depending upon the context; and finally, (v) caste as a structure shaping inequalities, opportunities, and power could be best understood through a sociology or social science that compares it with other forms of similar realities.

The essays presented in this Handbook provide numerous examples of how caste perpetually reconfigures itself as the balance between these different dimensions evolve. We hope that these essays and the framework we have proposed above will help in framing further questions for empirical research on the subject.

References

Ahuja, Amit, and Susan L. Ostermann. 2016. 'Crossing Caste Boundaries in the Modern Indian Marriage Market'. *Studies in Comparative International Development,* 51(3): 365–387.

Ambedkar, Bhimrao Ramji (edited by Valerian Rodrigues). 2002. *The Essential Writings of BR Ambedkar*. New Delhi: Oxford University Press.

Baviskar, Amita. 2016. 'New Cultures of Food Studies'. In S. Srivastava Y. Arif, and J. Abraham (Eds.), *Critical Themes in Indian Sociology* (pp.361–374). SAGE Publications Pvt Ltd, https://www.doi.org/10.4135/9789353287801.n25

Bayly, Susan. 2001. *Caste, Society and Politics in India from the Eighteenth Century to the Modern Age*. Vol. 3. Cambridge University Press.

Berreman, Gerald D. 1960. 'Caste in India and the United States'. *American Journal of Sociology*, 66(2): 120–127.

Béteille, Andre. 2012. *Caste, Class and Power: Changing Patterns of Stratification in a Tanjore Village*. New Delhi: Oxford University Press.

Bharathi, Naveen, Deepak V. Malghan, and Andaleeb Rahman. 2018, 14 June. Isolated by Caste: Neighbourhood-Scale Residential Segregation in Indian Metros. IIM Bangalore Research Paper No. 572. DOI: 10.2139/ssrn.3195672.

Brubaker, Rogers, and Matías Fernández. 2019. 'Cross-Domain Comparison and the Politics of Difference'. *The British Journal of Sociology*, 70(4): 1135–1158.

Cabalion, Joël, and Delphine Thivet. 2019. 'Who Speaks for the Village? Representing and Practicing the "Rural" in India from the Colonial to the Post-Colonial'. *South Asia Multidisciplinary Academic Journal*, 21. http://journals.openedition.org/samaj/5384; DOI: https://doi.org/10.4000/samaj.5384

Cohn, Bernard S. 1987. *An Anthropologist Among the Historians and Other Essays*. New Delhi: Oxford University Press (pp. 173–187).

Cohn, Bernard S. 1996. *Colonialism and Its Forms of Knowledge: The British in India*. Princeton: Princeton University Press.

Cox, Oliver C. 1945. 'Race and Caste: A Distinction'. *American Journal of Sociology*, 50(5): 360–368.

Deshpande, Satish. 2013. 'Caste and Castelessness: Towards a Biography of the "General Category"'. *Economic and Political Weekly*, 48(15): 32–39.

Meena Dhanda, Annapurna Waughray, David Keane, David Mosse, Roger Green and Stephen Whittle. 2014. *Caste in Britain: Socio-Legal Review*. Equality and Human Rights Commission Research Report No. 91. Manchester: Equality and Human Rights Commission.

Dirks, Nicholas B. 2001. *Castes of Mind: Colonialism and the Making of Modern India*. Princeton: Princeton University Press.

Frankel, Francine R., and Madhugiri Shamarao Ananthapadmanabha Rao. 1989. *Dominance and State Power in Modern India: Decline of a Social Order* (Vol. 2). New Delhi: Oxford University Press.

Frykenberg, Robert E. 1989. 'The Emergence of Modern 'Hinduism'as a Concept and as an Institution: A Reappraisal with Special Reference to South India'. In *Hinduism Reconsidered*, pp. 29–49. New Delhi: Manohar.

Fuller, Christoph. J. 1992. 'The Camphor Flame: Popular Hinduism and Society in India'. Princeton: Princeton University Press.

Gellner, David N., and Declan Quigley (Eds.) 1997. *Contested Hierarchies: A Collaborative of Caste among the Newars of the Kathmandu Valley, Nepal*. Oxford: Clarendon.

Guru, Gopal, and Sundar Sarukkai. 2019. *Experience, Caste and the Everyday Social*. New Delhi: Oxford University Press.

Hardgrave, Robert L. 1969. *The Nadars of Tamilnad*. Berkeley and Los Angeles: University of California Press.

Inden, Ronald. 1986. 'Orientalist Constructions of India'. *Modern Asian Studies*, 20(3): 401–446.

Jaffrelot, Christophe. 2003. *India's Silent Revolution: The Rise of the Lower Castes in North India*. Bangalore: Orient Blackswan, 2003.

Jayal, Niraja Gopal, and Pratap Bhanu Mehta. 2010. *The Oxford Companion to Politics in India*. New Delhi: Oxford University Press.

Jodhka, Surinder S. 1998. 'From "Book View" to "Field View": Social Anthropological Constructions of the Indian Village'. *Oxford Development Studies*, 26(3): 311–331.

Jodhka, Surinder S. 2004. 'Sikhism and the Caste Question: Dalits and Their Politics in Contemporary Punjab'. *Contributions to Indian Sociology*, 38(1–2): 165–192.

Jodhka, Surinder S. 2010. *Caste and Politics*. New Delhi: Oxford University Press.

Jodhka, Surinder S. 2016. 'Ascriptive Hierarchies: Caste and Its Reproduction in Contemporary India'. *Current Sociology* (Monograph), 64(2): 228–243.

Jodhka, Surinder S. 2018. *Caste in Contemporary India* (2nd edition). London, New Delhi: Routledge.

Jodhka, Surinder S., and Edward Simpson (Eds.) 2019. *India's Villages in the 21st Century: Revisits and Revisions*. Delhi: Oxford University Press.

Jodhka, Surinder S., and Ghanshyam Shah. 2010. 'Comparative Contexts of Discrimination: Caste and Untouchability in South Asia'. *Economic and Political Weekly*, 45(48): 99–106.

Jodhka, Surinder S., and James Manor (Eds.) 2017. *Contested Hierarchies, Persisting Influence: Caste and Power in Twenty-First Century India*. Hyderabad: Orient Black Swan.

Jodhka, Surinder S., Boike Rehbein, and Jessé Souza. 2017. *Inequality in Capitalist Societies*. Oxfordshire [England], New York: Routledge.

Kothari, Rajni. 1976. *Democratic Polity and Social Change in India: Crisis and Opportunities*. Bombay: Allied Publishers.

Lamont, Michèle, and Virág Molnár. 2002. 'The Study of Boundaries in the Social Sciences'. *Annual Review of Sociology*, 28(1): 167–195.

Lardinois, Roland (tr. by Renuka George). 2013 [2007]. *Scholars and Prophets. Sociology of India from France in the 19th–20th Centuries*. Delhi: Social Science Press.

Lorenzen, David N. 'Who Invented Hinduism?' *Comparative Studies in Society and History*, 41(4): 630–659.

Madan, Vandana. 2002. *The Village in India/Edited by Vandana Madan*. New Delhi: Oxford University Press.

Metcalf, Thomas R. 1997. *Ideologies of the Raj* (Vol. 4). Cambridge: Cambridge University Press.

Michelutti, Lucia. 2008. *The Vernacularisation of Democracy: Politics, Caste and Religion in India*. India: Routledge.

Mosse, David. 2012. *The Saint in the Banyan Tree: Christianity and Caste Society in India* (Vol. 14). Berkeley and Los Angeles: University of California Press.

Mosse, David. 2018. 'Caste and Development: Contemporary Perspectives on a Structure of Discrimination and Advantage'. *World Development*, 110: 422–436.

Munshi, Kaivan. 2016. 'Caste Networks in the Modern Indian Economy'. In S. Mahendra Dev and P.G. Babu (Eds.) *Development in India*, pp. 13–37. New Delhi: Springer.

Munshi, Kaivan, and Mark Rosenzweig. 2009. *Why is Mobility in India So Low? Social Insurance, Inequality, and Growth*. No. w14850. National Bureau of Economic Research.

Myrdal, Gunnar. 2017 [1944]. *An American Dilemma: The Negro Problem and Modern Democracy* (Vol. 1). New York: Routledge.

Narula, Smita. 2008. 'Equal by Law, Unequal by Caste: The Untouchable Condition in Critical Race Perspective'. *Wisconsin International Law Journal*. 26: 255.

Naudet, Jules. 2015, August. '"Equality as Relationship", Special Issue on "Exclusion, Discrimination, Disparity: Emerging Patterns of Social Inequality in India'. *Seminar*, number 672: 16–20.

Naudet, Jules. 2018. *Stepping into the Elite: Trajectories of Social Achievement in India, France and the United States*. New Delhi: Oxford University Press.

Nehru, Jawaharlal. 1946. *The Discovery of India*. New York: The John Day Company.

Ogbu, John U. 1979. 'Minority Education and Caste: The American System in Cross-Cultural Perspective'. *Crisis*, 86(1): 17–21.

O'Hanlon, Rosalind. 2017. 'Caste and Its Histories in Colonial India: A Reappraisal'. *Modern Asian Studies*, 51(2): 432–461.

O'Hanlon, Rosalind, Gergely Hidas, and Csaba Kiss. 2015. 'Discourses of Caste Over the Longue durée: Gopīnātha and Social Classification in India, ca. 1400–1900'. *South Asian History and Culture*, 6(1): 102–129.

Pachucki, Mark A., Sabrina Pendergrass, and Michèle Lamont. 2007 'Boundary Processes: Recent Theoretical Developments and New Contributions'. *Poetics*, 35(6): 331–351.

Peiris, Pradeep and Hasini Lecamwasam. 2020. 'Caste-based Differentiation in Sinhalese Society Role of Buddhism and Democracy'. *EPW Economic & Political Weekly*, 55(32&33): 64–71.

Raheja, Gloria Goodwin. 1988a. *The Poison in the Gift: Ritual, Prestation, and the Dominant Caste in a North Indian Village*. Chicago: University of Chicago Press.

Raheja, Gloria Goodwin. 1988b. 'India: Caste, Kingship, and Dominance Reconsidered'. *Annual Review of Anthropology*, 17(1): 497–522.

Ray, Tridip, A. Chaudhuri, and Komal Sahai. 2017. *Whose Education Matters? An Analysis of Intercaste Marriage in India*. Technical report, Indian Statistical Institute, Delhi Economics and Planning Unit.

Rudolph, Lloyd I., and Susanne Hoeber Rudolph. 1967. *The Modernity of Tradition: Political Development in India*. Chicago: University of Chicago Press.

Satyanarayana, K. 2019. 'The Political and Aesthetic Significance of Contemporary Dalit Literature'. *The Journal of Commonwealth Literature*, 54(1): 9–24.

Srinivas, Mysore Narasimhachar. 1959. 'The Dominant Caste in Rampura'. *American Anthropologist*, 61(1): 1–16.

Srivastava, Sanjay. 2014. *Entangled Urbanism: Slum, Gated Community and Shopping Mall in Delhi and Gurgaon*. New Delhi: Oxford University Press.

Thakur, Manish K. 2013. 'Of "Village Studies" and the "Village": A Disputed Legacy'. *Sociological Bulletin*, 62(1): 138–151.

Thapar, Romila. 1989. 'Imagined Religious Communities? Ancient History and the Modern Search for a Hindu Identity'. *Modern Asian Studies*, 23(2): 209–231.

Thorner, Daniel. 1966. 'Marx on India and the Asiatic Mode of Production'. *Contributions to Indian Sociology*, 9(1): 3–66.

Tilly, Charles. 1998. *Durable Inequality*. Berkeley & Los Angeles: University of California Press.

Vaid, Divya. 2018. *Uneven Odds: Social Mobility in Contemporary India*. Oxford University Press.

Weber, Max, Hans Gerth, and C. Wright Mills. 1946. *From Max Weber: Essays in sociology*. New York: Oxford University Press.

Wimmer, Andreas. 2008. 'The Making and Unmaking of Ethnic Boundaries: A Multilevel Process Theory'. *American Journal of Sociology*, 113(4): 970–1022.

SECTION I

CONCEPTUAL FRAMES

Editors' Introduction

The opening section of the Handbook has six chapters that, in significantly different ways, map the diverse modes through which the subject of caste has been framed in modern times. These framings have functioned like paradigms for research and debates on the subject, in popular imaginations, in public politics, and in the social sciences. These essays also directly extend some of the points discussed in the Introduction. As is evident from their titles, they do not necessarily gel together around a single theme of discussion or research; they rather reflect how the different perspectives on the subject have evolved over time; and the different ways in which caste has come to be comprehended. Thus, they foreground the diversity of perspectives that the volume proposes to exhibit.

Unlike some other terms or concepts used in the social sciences, 'caste' did not emerge from the writings of a distinguished scholar or from an ethnographic monograph of an anthropologist. The category has had a rather peculiar trajectory. Even though it has come to be seen as the encompassing matrix of social life in the South Asian region, the term arrived in the subcontinent with the Europeans. Over the years, it has come to acquire a life of its own and has widely come to be accepted as English translation of the pre-existing hierarchies of *varna* and *jati*.

In Castilian and Portuguese, this term initially referred to the lineage and the purity of animal and vegetal species, before being extended to human ancestries as well. It perhaps found currency in the South Asian region because it closely resembled the local realities. With changing political dynamics, social, and economic churnings and scholarly engagements, the categories through which caste is described and represented have also been changing. Roland Lardinois discusses these trajectories at considerable length in his chapter and provides a broad and rich overview of the conceptual history of the term, from the Buddhist criticism of the Brahmanic conception of *chaturvarna* frame of social organization in the 5th century BCE to the statist classifications of caste communities used for identifying and enumerating them for caste-based quotas (Reservations).

Besides the category of caste, the idea of *hierarchy* too has been a key-word, a kind of short-hand term, in the western scholarly discussions on the Indian society that is invoked to describe the distinctive nature of its social structure. Interestingly, quite like the word caste, hierarchy also originated in the western European context, sometime in the 6th century CE within the Christian religious domain 'to designate the "celestial" and, by extension, the clerical hierarchies and the order given to the world with its estates, or classes, by God'. In his chapter, Martin Fuchs provides an exhaustive and critical overview of the history of the term, its uses and its extensive criticisms. As Fuchs shows, despite its origin in the European context, over the years the idea of hierarchy came to signify the Indian caste system, in a rather pejorative sense. Perhaps the credit for this goes to Louis Dumont, who initially invoked it as a Weberian 'ideal type'. Dumont conveniently shifted to representing caste as a category that was best understood by contrasting what he assumed as the all-encompassing ideology of inequality prevailing in India with the presumed value of equality dominating in the West. Such a totalizing framing of caste and India conveyed a hegemonic agenda, implicitly suggesting the superiority of the West's agential subjects over the tradition-bound social structure of India characterized by its virtual incapacity for internal change or agency. The idea of hierarchy, as popularized by Dumont, thus became a restatement of the orientalist constructs of India and its caste system. He goes on to argue how much before Dumont, B. R. Ambedkar had provided a significantly richer and critical conceptualization of such a reality highlighting 'both the value and the power basis of caste hierarchy'. Such a system thus produced a divided and segregated social life marked by 'an ascending scale of hatred and descending scale of contempt'.

Another influential and popular framework through which caste has been imagined empirically is that of the *Jajmani* system. Advocates of this framework contend that, on ground, caste functions as a structure or system of relationships organizing the social division of labour. In his chapter on the *jajmani* system, Peter Mayer provides a broad overview of the anthropological and historical writings on the subject. 'The *jajmani* system, refers to hereditary patron-client ties between members of land-owning castes with other caste groups in a village setting who provide them with services throughout the year. The textbook view of *jajmani* system tends to claim that this was a pan-Indian system, which existed almost everywhere, though known differently in different linguistic regions of the subcontinent.

However, as Mayer shows, even while the mid-20th century scholarship on the subject largely agreed on its presence across regions of India, they considerably differed on its substantive character and relational features. Some anthropologists presented it as a harmonious system of interdependence across caste groups sustained by an underlying logic of reciprocity, others argued that it ought to be seen within the framework of hierarchy. There were also many who cited evidence of persistent conflict across caste groups and an inherently unequal and exploitative nature of the system, underlining the centrality, and domination of the dominant castes. Further, there were those who contested its pan-India presence. Through their historical research, they showed that *jajmani* type relations existed only in some regions of the subcontinent and that the system had not been around since the ancient times. They showed that, in fact, such a social division of labor came into being only during the 19th century, in response to changing state policies of the colonial rulers. However, they all seem to agree on the fact that it has now largely disintegrated and that this process began sometime during the 1960s, or earlier.

The demise of *jajmani* system did not end caste. As indicated in the Introduction, caste survives even when its structural frames undergo changes, defeating the Eurocentric theories of change and their predictions. In her chapter on *caste and capitalism*, Carol Upadhya shows how the so-called classical thinking in sociology and economic history remained trapped in Eurocentric imaginations of the 'Eastern World'. Scholars like Max Weber and Karl Marx saw caste as a source of India's economic stagnation and an active impediment to the growth of capital. Even the later day scholarship that showed how 'industrialization in England was built on the destruction of flourishing "proto-industrial" economies' of India and other colonies' did not give much credence to caste as a structuring economic institution. Indian sociologists too worked with 'straightjacketed binaries that separated culture from the domain of the economy and equated caste with "traditional culture", which in turn was counterpoised to liberal capitalism', which is presumably grounded in modern values of reason and individual choice.

This has been changing over the past decades. As she shows through an extensive review of the emerging literature, scholars no longer work with the 'economy-culture binary' and argue that besides being many other things, caste is also '*constitutive of capital or class*'. She identifies three sets of writings that have shifted the paradigm of approaching caste and capital. First are the early writings on 'the organization and activities of India's "traditional" business communities'; the second are the writings that 'view caste more broadly as a form of "social capital" or "structure of accumulation", which works in different ways to facilitate the generation and preservation of capital by some groups while disadvantaging others'; the third are those who 'attempt to locate capital within caste in a more fundamental way'. She concludes her chapter by arguing that: 'Rather than asking how caste ... facilitates or hinders accumulation or economic action, we might explore the various ways caste and capital ... are co-constituted and embedded in one another.'

The following chapter extends this discussion by looking at 'caste' in relation to 'class'. At the level of its empirical explorations, caste has often been invoked as an axis of inequality, comparable or contrastable to class. The obvious reason for this is the persisting influence of the notion of *Jajmani* system on the way caste is approached, leading to the popular idea that there is an inextricable association between caste and occupation. 'Class' thus came to be imagined as a western reality, representing an open and mobile system of stratification, while caste, presumably unique to India, was understood as a traditional and closed system of hierarchy. Such a binary framing of systems of inequality implicitly relies upon a theory of change, embedded in the Marxist theory of history as well as in the functionalist view of modernization. Jules Naudet takes us through the conceptual journey of this relationship and shows how scholarship on the subject has progressively moved away from either seeing caste as class or counterposing caste with class, whereby 'caste' ought to evolve into 'class' with India progressing from a pre-capitalist to a capitalist mode of production; or from traditional order to a modern society. Scholarship has increasingly shown that the dynamics of caste are quite distinct from those of 'class' and that the two persist side by side, often intersecting with each other in multiple ways. Actors, for example, may deploy 'caste' as a resource for class competition, even when they inhabit the modern-day corporate world.

While the intersections of caste with class or their conceptual overlap and distinctiveness speaks of caste in the 'outer' world, in relation to economy, politics, and spatiality, it is through kinship and marriage that caste reproduces itself 'internally'. One of the defining features of caste groupings is their constant ability to mark boundaries, both of the 'collective self' as well as of the 'other'. And this is ensured by strictly regulated norms of kinship and marriage. Caste groupings prescribe whom one can marry and whom one cannot. The governing norms do allow for transgression of boundaries but only for some and under certain circumstances.

The idea of kinship also helps us question some of the popular notions that draw from a textual view of caste, and construct it as a singular pan-Indian system, represented through the notion of a timeless varna hierarchy. This has very little resemblance to the ground realities or the real life of caste. Caste communities in the past reproduced themselves locally, within a specific kinship and cultural or linguistic region, rarely going beyond an extended group of villages. It is only during the past century that this began to change, with India moving on the path of economic growth and development and mobility becoming the norm. With change accelerating, individuals and families began to routinely migrate, not only out of their villages but also away from their kinship and cultural regions, to different parts of the nation-state and sometimes even across national boundaries.

In her chapter, Janaki Abraham provides an account of caste and kinship dynamics. She offers an extensive overview of the emerging trends as sociologists and social anthropologists are documenting them. Caste and kinship have always been 'enmeshed and *mutually* constituted', she argues. The changing dynamics of caste also changed marriage practices. However, this shift is not a radical one, which would imply a disintegration of caste or a moving away from caste as an endogamous group. On the contrary, caste is alive and kicking, though its boundaries are being re-imagined with the generational shifts, particularly among the mobile middle classes. Her historical perspective on the evolution of kinship boundaries thus suggests that castes were never rigid and static. When needed, they could turn flexible and adapt to the requirements of economic change and political opportunities.

As is evident from the chapters of this opening section, far from disappearing with India's modernization, caste persists even while it changes. They also reveal how scholarship on the subject has been progressing, and growing substantially, in complexity and richness.

CHAPTER 1

THE IDEA OF CASTE THROUGH THE AGES
Concept, Words, and Things

ROLAND LARDINOIS

THE INDO-PORTUGUESE MOMENT: 15TH-16TH CENTURY

The word caste is derived from the Portuguese *casta* which is imported into India by Europeans arriving in the wake of Vasco da Gama (1498). The chronology of its dissemination is well established by historians (Subrahmanyam, 2017; Xavier, 2016; Xavier and Zupanov, 2015). The word first appears in *Duarte Barbosa's Livro* (circa 1515), but on rare occasions. Duarte Barbosa uses more often the terms *lei* (law), *costume* (custom), but also *linhagem* (lineage) or *fidalguia* (nobility). Rare before 1550 in the writings of Portuguese soldiers, merchants, or bureaucrats, the word *casta* became more frequent in the second half of the 16th century. After 1600, it became widespread as churchmen, Jesuits, Catholic, and Protestant missionaries learned Sanskrit, like the Italian Jesuit Roberto de Nobili (1577–1656), often from Brahmins, especially in southern India, and wrote essays and travelogues about India. As early as 1590, the division of the Hindu society in four *varna* (*Brahmin, Kshatriya, Vaishya, Shudra*), which are still called nations (*nações*), is established.

To understand the spread of the word *casta* in India, we must look back at its uses in the Iberian Christian world of the 15th–16th centuries when the Christians nobles were confronted with Jews and Moors who had been forcibly converted following the massacres of which they were victims in the 14th century (Xavier, 2011; Guha, 2016). In order to stop the mixing of the Iberian populations, the Nobility of 'old Christians' fearing of being stained by a macule of Jewish or Muslim blood of 'new Christians' and

Marranos ('crypto Jews and former Moors'), church, and bureaucracy established the statutes of 'purity of blood' (spanish *'limpieza de sangre'*) first in Toledo (1449–1547). The Inquisition courts were opened in Spain (1480) and Portugal (1536), and finally these policies led to the expulsion of Jews from Spain (1492) and Portugal (1496), just before Vasco da Gama opened the road to India.

It is in this context that the use of the word *casta* developed in the Iberian world. Dictionaries (Castilian and Portuguese) attest to the existence of the word *casta* since the end of the 15th century to designate, first, animal (bull) or vegetable species and then, by extension, humans, in the sense of '*casta buen linage*' ('of good lineage'). The use of the word became widespread to denote Jews and Muslims in inquisition's investigations. But *casta* is also associated with the notion of purity, as in the expression '*casta sangue*' (of 'pure blood').

These usages circulated very quickly in India as evidenced by Duarte Barbosa's statement: 'The Nayres ... say that their blood [*sangue*] may not be tainted [*macularem*] (by the contact with a vile man [*vilões*])' (Machado, 1946, p. 144). Two factors are related to the spread of the word *casta* in the subcontinent. First, following their expulsion from the Iberian Peninsula, many Jews moved to India where they met and traded with Jews formerly settled on the Malabar Coast (Fischel, 1962). Second, the Portuguese imported to India the policies of blood purity in order to regulate the relations between the Portuguese who considered themselves as 'old Christians' and the new social groups which emerged from the mixing of Indian and Portuguese, or from Indian converts, but also to track Jews and 'crypto-Jews' who settled in India. In 1560, the inquisition was established at Goa (Révah, 2001). The word *casta* was then part of the mental tools of Europeans who came to India from the Iberian Peninsula at the end of the 15th century.

The morphology of the word *casta* and its semantic field attest to its filiation with Indo-European languages (Benveniste, 1973). Castilian dictionaries associate *casta* with the Greek *genos* and Latin *gens*, people, strain, race. According to linguist Émile Benveniste, Sanskrit *jati-* (root *JAN*—'to be born') belongs to the same lexical family of Latin *gens to* whom it is morphologically related. In their usages, *jati* and *genti* refer both to birth as a social fact. Finally, the dictionaries bring etymologically *casta* closer to the Latin *castus*, chaste, hence purity (*contra* Dumont, 1966), whose meaning is also attested in the Spanish literature.

The word *casta*, whose semantic field originally applied to both humans and non-humans, was therefore used in India from the early 16th century to designate a type of social morphology that was not foreign to Europeans. Coming from the Iberian world where birth, blood purity and rank were questioned, the latter found in India people and groups of different *varna*, of different *jati*, who were separated along the rules of commensality, endogamy, purity, and rank, according to the first European testimonies.

Buddhist Criticism of the Naturalization of Caste

In order to break away from a European point of view focused on the concept of caste and its criticism, we must turn to ancient India. Indeed, from the 6th–5th century

BCE, Buddhism challenged the Brahmanic world in its soteriological, social, and political dimensions. The Brahmanic definition of caste is at the heart of controversies in which, during the first millennium CE, two opposing gnoseological points of view struggled (Eltschinger, 2012). The first point of view is that of Brahmanism, according to which the representation of the social world is structured by the combination of two collective entities, *varna* and *jati*. The term *varna* (skt. 'color') refers to the four classes of the Brahmanic society *Brahmin, Kshatriya, Vaishya, Shudra* (Aktor, 2018), who are ordered according to their social function and their relationship to Vedic sacrifice. Indeed, this one is reserved for the men of the first three *varna* that the initiation rite distinguishes as twice-born (*dvija*), thus separating *Shudra* who are excluded from this rite. The notion of *jati* ('class', 'specie'), whose semantic field is much broader than *varna*, applies to grammar, logic, non-humans (plants, animals), and humans to designate the birth group. In this respect, the Brahmins defend a caste theory based on a naturalistic philosophy of knowledge. According to this conception, each *jati* is defined by an innate character acquired by birth, this character engaging a specific being, an essence of the *jati* that determines the reality of this class in the world: for example, a 'Brahman being' or '*Brahmatva*' defines the class (*jati*) 'Brahmin'. The idea of blood purity is central to this conception of the *jati*, to which is added an anthropogonic dimension, because Brahmins were born from the mouth, the organ of the body considered as the purest, of the primordial *Purusha* (*Rg Veda* X, 90).

In contrast to this naturalism, the Buddhist criticism of the Brahmanic concept of caste exposed in Sanskrit by the logician Dharmakirti (7th century CE) is grounded on a nominalist philosophy of knowledge. This criticism addresses questions of filiation and the notion of species (*jati*), at the crossroads of genealogy and biology. First, with regard to filiation, Buddhists highlight the contradictions and inconsistencies of Brahmanic arguments to support the idea of blood purity over several generations. For Buddhists, the designations of the *jati* are only language conventions superimposed on reality, but they do not divide distinct species classes in the world (nominalism). Then, Dharmakirti criticizes the Brahmanic theory of classes considered as a continuous analogical chain from non-humans to humans. He distinguishes between humans and non-humans and, above all, he affirms the ontological unity of the human species, which he believes constitutes a single undifferentiated class, *ekavarna*. Thus, in the middle of the first millennium of our CE, Dharmakirti invalidated the division of Brahmanic society into *varna*, understood as functional classes, and he delegitimized the naturalization of *jati* as different species.

However, Buddhists are not abolitionists of caste. They criticize the Brahmanic definition of it, which is incompatible with the new ways of salvation they bring, but they continue to think of the world in the very categories of Indian society, in terms of *varna* and *jati*, which they redefine.[1]

---

[1] For the Buddhist conception of caste, which is not our purpose in this article, see Bailey (2014).

Bhakti and Anti-Caste Movements in Medieval India

The memory of this Buddhist criticism of caste informs the different Hindu devotional currents of bhakti that developed in medieval India. Bhakti designs sectarian theist movements (*sampradaya*) that favour a personal relationship between the devotee (*bhakta*) and his or her chosen divinity, in contrast to the Vedic ritualism of the Brahmanic circles. The point that retains us here is the following. Even though these popular sectarian currents are crossed by hostility towards the institution of caste and the Brahmins, who are considered at its proponents (Lele, 1980), bhakti does not propose any radical criticism of the concept of caste, as Buddhists had developed it.

We examine three points of view presented by historians of religions. First, in Maharashtra, the poet Jnandev (1275–1296), a Brahmin educated in Sanskrit, uses the emerging popular language, Marathi, to spread among the masses, that is, 'women, low castes and others' (skt. *strishudradika*), the message of the *Bhagavad Gita* (Novetzke, 2016). According to Jnandev, salvation can be universalized to all and no longer only to the religious virtuosos of high castes. Everything happens as if the demands for equality and social justice, carried by the mass of the population, were reduced to the cosmic level where all the social distinctions of castes of the daily world are resolved, but without calling into question the Hindu social order.

Secondly, David Lorenzen defends the existence of a casteless Hinduism represented by the current initiated by Kabir (c. 1440–1518), the Kabir Panth, established particularly in North India (Lorenzen, 1987). However, it is a sect whose abolition of caste distinctions applies to ascetics but not to devotees who continue to live in the secular world governed by caste rules. It should also be noted that the history of the Kabir Panth follows the segmental logic of the division of the *jati*.

Finally, with regard to high castes, considered as twice-born (*dvija*), several treaties of *Dharmashastra*, used in the Deccan, in the 15th–18th centuries, attest that these groups were obsessed with the mixing of *varna* (*samkara*), which might put in danger the proper nature (*svabhava*) of the groups concerned (O'Hanlon, Hidas, and Kiss, 2015). In a context of economic, social, and political upheavals, these treaties were used in pamphlets and petitions, particularly by the castes of scribes and Brahmins involved in 'identity wars' to legitimize their access to new employment opportunities in the Deccan bureaucracies. In order to resolve these statutory struggles recourse to State power was frequent, whether that of Shivaji (c. 1627/1630–1680) in Pune or the Portuguese in Goa.

Indo-Persian View of Caste: From Al Biruni to Abu'l Fazl

At the beginning of the year 1000, Al-Biruni, a scholar trained in Persian, wrote in Arabic a history of India, a country where he had lived for many years near actual Punjab (Marlow, 1995). Ten centuries before the subject divides Western anthropologists (Gaborieau, 1993), Al-Biruni, who had learned Sanskrit, contrasted the principle of equality in Islam with that of hierarchy in Hinduism. 'We Muslims (...) stand entirely on the other side of the question, considering all men as equal, except in piety; and this is the greatest obstacle which prevents any approach or understanding between Hindus and Muslims. The Hindus call their caste [*tabaqah*, i.e. generation] *varna*, i.e. colours [*alwan*], and from a genealogical point of view they call them *jataka*, that is births. These castes [*tabaqat*] are from the very beginning four' (trad. Sachau, 1910: 100). Al-Biruni then presents the four *varna* of the Brahmanic society and their common Vedic myth of origin (which he does not name). To these classes, he adds two groups that are not recognized as castes in the sense of *varna*, he says: the first, which he names the *antyaja* (skt. last, the lowest), and the second in which he includes the *candalas* whose service activities are even more vile than those attached to the first. We note that the notions of *varna* and *jati* seem to merge in Al-Biruni's presentation.

This book has had little posterity in the Indo-Muslim world (Ernst, 2003). This is not the case, six centuries later, of the *A'in-i Akbari* (*Akbar's Institutes*), composed in Persian by Shaikh Abu'l Fazal in the 1590s. In its Book IV, 'Account of India', *A'in-I Akbari* contains the most complete and coherent account of the philosophical and religious systems of the Hindus—that is the populations who inhabit Hindustan but do not belong to the Islamic faith community—written by a foreign author at this time. Abu'l Fazl, who used translation of texts into Sanskrit, a language he did not know, describes the composition of Hindu society in three superior *varna* whose members carry the 'sacred cord', to which he adds the *varna* of the *Shudra*, that is those who serve the three superior *varna*. The author adds: 'Other than these are termed *mleccha* [skt. non-aryen, barbarian]; those of the fifth class[2] are reckoned as beyond the pale of religion like infidels, Jews and the like' (trad. Jarret, 1894: 221). Alongside this division of the Indian society, the *Ain-i-Akbari de facto* recognizes the existence of social groups that make up the military-administrative elites of North India's Mughal power, for example: Afghans, Ahirs, Brahmans, Chauhans, Jats, Kayasths, or Rajputs. But the two types of social groups are not integrated into a totalizing representation of the Indian social world.

---

[2] According to the authors of the *dharmashastra*, there is no fifth (*pañcama*) *varna*.

The Co-Production of Otherness: Islam Versus Hinduism

At the end of the 16th century, Abu'l Fazl's work attests that the Mughal elites had acquired a good knowledge of Sanskrit treaties, particularly those that set out the theory of *varna* and the position of the 'out-caste'. Meanwhile, literary sources in North India since the end of the 14th–early 15th century reveal that Hindu theist sects (*sampradaya*) share a common consciousness of evolving within a *dharma* distinct from that of Muslims. The term 'Hindu', according to Lorenzen, has both an ethno-geographical and religious qualification: it refers to the former inhabitants of the 'Hindustan' who are neither Muslims, nor Jews, nor Christians, as also noted by European travellers. But this does not mean in any way that there is the consciousness of a unified vision of this *dharma* under the term Hinduism, a Western designation that only appeared in the 19th century (Lorenzen, 1999).

Making Up Caste: The State and the Statistician

A history of the concept of caste, such as this notion developed in the mass of colonial bureaucratic publications, in particular the censuses reports (Bayly, 1999; Cohn, 1987; Kalpagam, 2014), is impeded by the notion of orientalism or, more precisely, by criticism of orientalism. Many scholars who expose this criticism reduce any process of knowledge to an external purpose of domination; they then consider caste, unilaterally, as a 'colonial invention' (Dirks 2001), confusing the concept of caste with the reality that this concept designates. At this point, three remarks are necessary.

First, pre-colonial states, for tax reasons, practised partial enumeration of population per caste and house (*khanasumari*), modelled on the *Ain-i Akbari*, as in Marwar State in Rajasthan in the second half of the 17th century (Peabody, 2001). However, this State taxation was not oriented towards the public needs of a modern State. It was defined by an economy of gift and redistribution (land, food) that was part of the religious or soteriological order. Second, to consider caste as a type of unqualified group, culturally speaking, one should be located oneself in a naturalist ontological regime that empowers spheres of action leading to the separation of the religious properties of caste from its strictly social component, even for the purpose of conversion. Last, modern censuses derive their characteristics, first of all, from their own statistical methods, such as counting and classifying, independently of any colonial situation (Desrosières, 1998).

Modern censuses, which take the person as the unit of counting and no longer the house, construct classifications that involve three ways of thinking that are relevant with regard to the concept of caste. The first way of thinking is statistical: it is a matter of making groups as homogeneous as possible according to criteria to be defined. Yet, sociologists raise two criticisms of census classifications. One criticism addresses the formation of groups that bring together different castes or caste segments and thus make these groups artifacts (Sundar, 2000). The other criticism insists on the reification of the constituted groups, but it ignores the need for statistical stabilization of the classifications so that they can be subject to quantitative analysis. The second way of thinking is political in that censuses produce a total quantitative representation of a population referred to a hierarchical and delimited administrative and political territory, which takes the form of a nation. Finally, the third mode, of a cognitive nature, is linked to the fact that censuses operate a double task: on the one hand, they differentiate groups according to various socio-demographic, religious, cultural, and linguistic criteria and, on the other hand, they bring these same groups together by developing links between them that must give meaning to the total representation of a social space that is then called Indian society.

From this point of view, colonial censuses have oscillated, depending on year and province, between two main modes of classifying people, which are not independent. On the one hand, census classified persons according to their occupation or work, based on the state of the division of labour in India and, on the other hand, they classified them according to caste whose debates over definition feed the colonial anthropological reports (Fuller, 2017; Pant, 1987; Samarendra, 2003). In addition, the definition of caste is itself difficult to separate from the definition of religion, tribe, and race, according to colonial categories (Gottschalk, 2013).

Over nearly two centuries of British colonial history, it is the classification of individuals according to their caste, of castes according to their social precedence and, finally, the interlocking of the latter according to the encompassing classification scheme of the four *varna* of Hindu society which was the most efficient way to give meaning to the representation of Indian society produced by the censuses. These rankings have given rise to unprecedented struggles between castes to ensure that the rank they claimed prevails, thus illustrating the way in which classifications act on classified persons. In any case, we should consider these classifications as a 'colonial census idea of caste'.

Historians and anthropologists, alike who criticize the orientalist construction of caste through the colonial censuses, describe these modes of classification as Brahmanical, and they attribute it to the determining position of the high castes in the colonial bureaucracy. However, we must ask why, in the *longue durée* of the history of India, no other modes of ranking individuals and groups has ever emerged as a way of making society.

From Caste to Caste System in Indian Sociology

The knowledge accumulated by colonial administrators, from the mid-19th century onwards, shifted the focus from the notion of caste to that of a caste system[3] considered as a pan-Indian structure. This notion, which was not elaborated from the outset from a sociological point of view, was nevertheless taken up by all the authors who published on this subject from the end of the 19th century onwards, in India and Europe. These are as much administrators (Hocart, 1938; Hutton, 1946; Malley, 1932; Risley, 1908), Sanskrit scholars (Senart, 1896), sociologists (Ambedkar, 1917; Bouglé, 1908; Ghurye, 1932; Weber, 1916–17), or missionaries (Wiser, 1936). But in all these studies, 'the system is taken as a mere collection of "blocks" and their arrangement is neglected' writes Louis Dumont in *Homo hierarchicus* (Dumont, 1980: 32).

In this book, Dumont presents the most coherent model of the caste system to date, but also the most disputed (Lardinois, 2013 [2007]). According to Dumont, caste, that is *jati*, is a segmental social unit defined according to three criteria: endogamy, professional specialization, and ritual hierarchy oriented by the polarity of the values of the pure (Brahmin) and the impure (Untouchable). *Jati* as interdependent groups are included in the four functional classes of the *varna*, which constitute a structure 'underlying and completing the *jati* ideology' (Dumont, 1971: 73): *jati* and *varna* are organized in relation to the rite of sacrifice that gives the caste system its overall coherence (Hocart, 1950). In this system, status (Brahmin) and power (king) are separated, ritual status having supremacy over politics. Finally, the figure of the renouncer offers a way of abandoning caste while remaining in Hinduism.

Numerous criticisms have been addressed to the caste system model proposed by Dumont. Some Sanskrit scholars criticize the definition of the ideology encompassing the pure and the impure and its modes of operation (Olivelle, 1998), which has led some anthropologists to substitute this opposition by the ideology of gift and the idea of auspiciousness (Raheja, 1988). Other anthropologists dispute the centrality of the Brahmin (Dirks, 1987; Quigley, 1993), or even the specificity of a hierarchical model (Appadurai, 1996). Still others see the caste system as an example of social stratification and exploitation that would be similar to the forms of racial segregation observed in the United States (Berreman, 1972). Finally, it is both the very idea of the caste system and its pan-Indian dimension that are rejected in favour of an understanding of its local dimension (Das, 2015).

The anthropologist M. N. Srinivas describes Louis Dumont's model as a 'book view' to which he contrasts the empirical 'field view', but on which Dumont's work is

---

[3] To speak of a 'caste system' would imply examining the concept of 'system' in the social sciences, a point that is out of the purpose of this article.

also grounded. Nevertheless, Srinivas uses *varna* theory to define the structure of the caste system and study its social transformation. According to Srinivas, the lower castes (*Shudra*) adopt the values and practices of the higher castes twice-born (*dvija*), thus testifying to what Srinivas calls a process of Sanskritization of the lower castes.

However, a question of method remains with regard to the model developed by Dumont in *Homo hierarchicus*. The aim of this book can be considered as being to identify an ideal-type, in the logical sense, of the caste system, that is, to use Max Weber's language, an abstract, revisable 'thought picture' with which partial field studies can be compared, making it possible to identify the gap between the empirical and the ideal-type. But when Dumont makes the caste system an organic whole regulated by consensus and social harmony, is there not confusion between, on the one hand, the ideal-type of the caste system that the scholar must build and, on the other hand, the evaluative judgment that he makes on what he thinks is the ideal (in the normative sense and no longer logical) of the Hindu caste system[4]?

The debates on the values that are at the core of the caste system are concerned with the political dimension of the Hindu social order that social agents, including scholars, seek to preserve or transform. This is the case of struggles that took place in the Indian National Congress in the first half of the 20th century. In this respect, the work of B. R. Ambedkar, which neither Louis Dumont nor M. N. Srinivas considered, makes it possible to discuss this blind spot in the sociology of India.

'Graded Inequality', Caste, and Hinduism

B. R. Ambedkar elaborated a critical sociology of the caste system and Hinduism, which is driven by a political goal: the emancipation of the Untouchables from their position as dominated group within the caste structure, with a broader focus, 'the annihilation of caste' (Ambedkar, 2014 [1936]; Herrenschmidt, 1987). Ambedkar asserted, as early as 1916, the cultural unity of the Hindu world and the existence of a pan-Indian caste system (Ambedkar, 1979). This system articulates the two social institutions that are the *varna* and the *jati*. The caste system operates a 'division of laborers' which is based on a hierarchical order of ritual precedence that Ambedkar describes as 'graded inequality'. In this system, 'there is no such class as completely underprivileged class (. . .). Each class being privileged, every class is interested in maintaining the social system' (Ambedkar, 1989: 102, quoted by Herrenschmidt). The Vedic hymn of the *Purusha* (*Rg Veda* X, 90), which gives birth to the *Shudra* from the feet of cosmic man, expresses this principle of 'graduated inequality'. This hymn is a Brahmanic cosmogony, argues Ambedkar, that is

---

[4] On the distinction between ideal-type (logic) and normative practical-idea, see Max Weber's remarks about historians' works on medieval Christianity (Weber, 2012).

a religious discourse of human origin, which is the object of a collective belief. Breaking the caste order means breaking with beliefs in the sanctity of Hindu texts. However, this movement faces a particular difficulty: since each group competes with the next higher and lower groups, the unity of the lower castes is practically impossible, each caste closing in on itself: 'caste is a state of mind' (Ambedkar, 1979: 28).

This sociological criticism of the caste system that Ambedkar aimed to annihilate was in opposition to the point of view defended by Gandhi, who condemned untouchability but adhered to the representation of Hindu society grounded on the *varna* system that he simply intended to reform (Zelliot, 1972). In this respect, Gandhi's viewpoint remained close to the positions defended by the reformist movement of Arya Samaj, whose writings value the *varna* system to the detriment of the *jati*, according to the old idea that caste (assimilated to *varna*) is a matter of merit and not of birth. This is the reason why Arya Samaj differed from Brahmo Samaj, which tried to respond to requests for social reforms aimed in particular at the caste system (female infanticide, child marriage, intercaste marriage, widow remarriage). In both cases, however, the notion of caste and caste system, held by the 'spirit of the system', to use Max Weber's expression, remains. Ambedkar had declared in 1935 that he would not die a Hindu. In 1956, a few months before his death, he converted to Buddhism, engaging with him mass conversions of Untouchable Mahars.

However, Ambedkar's conversion cannot be interpreted as a break with the Hindu cultural world because Ambedkar draws from it a repertoire of cognitive patterns guiding his action. This is evidenced by the collective work of defining Hindu identity carried out during the debates on the codification of Hindu Code Bill (HCB) conducted under the responsibility of Ambedkar in the early 1950s (Clémentin-Ojha, 2019; Herrenschmidt, 2009). While the HCB was finally abandoned, clause 2, which defines the groups to which the concept of Hindu law applies, was included in the family law passed in 1955–1956. This clause, defended by Ambedkar, provides an inclusive definition of the term 'Hindu' which, on the one hand, includes Jains, Sikhs but also Buddhists and, on the other hand, excludes Muslims, Christians, and Parsis. Two arguments were used in these debates. The first argument is of a historical-genealogical nature. Jains, Buddhists, and Sikhs are legally Hindus, says Ambedkar, because while their beliefs (creed) differ from those of Hindus, they do share the same right (law). Indeed, their respective founders, all Indians, having aimed for salvation and not for the transformation of society, did not give them any other legal right. The second argument is territorial. Members of religions from outside India, such as Islam, Christianism, and Judaism, are *de facto* excluded from the application of Hindu law.

In fact, Ambedkar conceives the relationship of the Jain, Buddhist, and Sikh religions to Hindu society in the same way as the relationship of *sampradaya* to it. Membership in any of these religions, in terms of creed, nor did membership in a Hindu sect, affects membership in the Hindu cultural world. From then on, by converting to Buddhism and rejecting the caste system, Ambedkar was not breaking away but moving from one creed to another creed within Hinduism, which was now conceived as an inclusive national religion.

From the Varna Structure to the State Classes

Ambedkar's sociological criticism of the caste system and his work on redefining Hinduism are related to the constitution of the Untouchables as a political group that was unified, under State control (Indian Act 1935), in the category known as Scheduled Castes (SC), followed by the elaboration of the Scheduled Tribes (ST) category (Charsley, 1996). The policy of positive discrimination was extended, in the aftermath of Independence, to new groups of beneficiaries, that of intermediate castes grouped in the category of Other Backward Classes (OBC), first at the level of the regional States, in the years 1950–1960 (Galanter, 1984), then at the level of the Indian Union in the years 1990.

The OBC includes the castes belonging to the *Shudra varna*. This intermediate position in the structure of the *varna* system is explicitly deduced from the place of the OBCs between the lower class of Scheduled Castes (ex-Untouchables) and the upper class of the General Category (GC), which is negatively defined as all the groups that remain once the SC, ST, and OBC have been removed from the Hindu population. Caste classified in the GC belongs to the three higher *varna*, *Brahmin*, *Kshatriya*, and *Vaishya*, have a high ritual status (*dvija*), and are considered historically favoured, particularly in terms of education and culture; this is why members of these groups have been excluded from the benefits of compensatory discrimination policies.

The making of these four categories, which are State classes—SC, ST, OBC, and GC—highlights anew, as noted in the case of Ambedkar, the process by which collective thought structures inform the institutionalization of an inseparable political and religious representation of Indian society, regardless of the will of the actors. The definition of the groups benefiting from the compensatory policies implemented by the State is based on the division of Hindu society into *varna*, but on condition that the *sa-varna*, that is persons who share the common characteristic of belonging to one of the four *varna*, are joined by those who are *a-varna*, that is socially without *varna* (Figure 1.1). In total, all persons (of Hindu religion) are classified into castes (*jati*) which, in their contemporary forms, are the result of past and present census classifications, and these castes are in turn included in defined and ordered State classes, at the end of a historical construction process, according to the *varna* model.

The two structures considered of *varna* and State classes are each composed of four elements that seem to correspond. However, they differ in their internal composition. On the one hand, the structure in four *varna* can be analysed, following the Sanskrit scholar Charles Malamoud, in mode 4 = 3 + 1, the first three *varna* being considered as twice-born (*dvija*) unlike the *Shudra* (Malamoud, 1981), with however an additional group, sociologically, that of the *a-varna*, composed of the Untouchables and Tribes. On the other hand, the structure of the four State classes (which is not the subject of Malamoud's study) may be analysed in the opposite way 4 = 1 + 3, the GC, which is outside the reservation policy, opposing the three quota beneficiary classes. To these

Ancient India sa-varna, a-varna, jatis		**Contemporary India** State, legal categories, jatis	
sa-varna	dvija Brahmans Kshatriyas Vaishyas	General Category (GC)	Muslims, Buddhists, Christians, Others
		Eco. Weaker Section	
	Sat-Shudras	Creamy layer	
	Shudras	Other Backward Classes (OBC)	
a-varna	Candalas, Pariahs, Untouchables, Outcastes, Exterior Castes, Depressed Classes, Harijans	Creamy layer	
		Scheduled Castes (SC) Dalits	
	Excluded areas Tribes	Creamy layer	
		Scheduled Tribes (ST)	

FIGURE 1.1 Representation of Indian Society through Indian Categories

elements, however, a residual category must be added, that of persons belonging to a religion other than Hinduism, who are excluded, at least in principle, from compensatory policies.

However, the Constitution (103rd Amendment) Act of January 2019 introduces a new 10 per cent reservation class for a legal category of citizens called the 'Economically Weaker Section' (EWS) defined according to strictly economic criteria. This amendment excludes SC, ST, and OBC groups and targets economically disadvantaged members of the GC, a class that has been excluded from compensatory policies until now. The spirit of the reservation system has been changed in two ways. First, the EWS is defined according to an economic principle, while the reservation classes are defined according to a sociological principle. Second, the economic principle is attached to the person when the sociological principle characterizes a collective. In one case, the beneficiary of the reservation policy is an unqualified (sociologically) citizen, in the other case it is a citizen assigned to a reservation class constituted with reference to the caste system. More fundamentally, it is the internal structure of the reservation system that is affected.

This tends to take the form of a stacking of classes in mode 4= 1 + 1 + 1 + 1 opening each class to compensatory benefits, even if in a differentiated way varying with the groups.

This socio-political representation of Indian society thus takes the external form of a social stratification composed of four State classes subdivided into castes, products of the census categories, these classes being hierarchized according to a historically reified principle of statutory economic, social, and cultural inequality. These four State classes form a system, at the national level, because they are united by the struggles for equal access to the benefits of these compensatory policies, each change that affects one class or one of its elements causing chain reactions of other groups. That the structure of the *varna* social order informs this new stratified representation of Indian society attests that the *varna* system, as a shared and active collective representation of the (Hindu) social world, is part of the objective reality of the caste system.

Equality of Citizens and Spheres of Justice

The categorization of Indian society into caste and State classes benefiting from compensatory policies is an example of the co-construction of categories that involves, before and after the Independence, colonial administrators, bureaucrats, politicians, caste associations, and social science scholars. This work is part of a long-term process at the end of which the concepts of caste and caste system are redefined legally, in the political and social field, according to new principles of citizenship and justice enshrined in the 1947 Constitution, which Ambedkar chaired.

Breaking with the old social order based on the graduated hierarchy of castes, the Constitution abolishes Untouchability, prohibits all 'discrimination on grounds of religion, race, caste, sex or place of birth' (CoI art. 15.1), and thus makes each person a citizen to whom an 'equality of status and opportunity' is recognized.

The State's responsibility is to ensure social, economic, and political justice 'not only amongst individuals but also amongst [. . .] any socially and educationally backward classes of citizens or for the Scheduled Castes and the Scheduled Tribes' (CoI art. 15.4, 38.2). In other words, the principles of justice are pluralistic in their forms according to the types of goods and spheres of justice concerned (Walzer, 1983), but also according to the recipients who are persons who belong, as citizens, to one of the collectives, castes, and classes, legalized by the State which makes them the beneficiaries of compensatory policies.

This arrangement must be seen as an effect of modernity that marks the advent of a divided citizenship in which people are equal in dignity, but unequal in differentiated access to goods and services according to the ascriptive status of the old social order, formally abolished, but which is legally redefined and enshrined in the Constitution. This division has consequences on the political and social field in contemporary India.

On the one hand, the persons referred to the GC have as their political identity, from the State viewpoint, only their status as citizens that they can universalize, this category having been legally emptied of caste qualification; but these same persons retain in the social imaginary, and also in the reality of the world, the mark of the privileges attached to the twice-born (*dvija*). On the other hand, people belonging to the groups benefiting from compensatory policies, who are also citizens, remain assigned to the old status of their caste and class, which is still stigmatized and transformed into State categories, but from which they now derive social and political benefits (Deshpande, 2013). However, for everyone, 'equality may be a fiction, but nonetheless one must accept it as the governing principle' (Ambedkar, 2014, p. 261).

References

Aktor, Mikael. 2018. 'Social Classes Varna'. In P. Olivelle and D. R. Davis Jr. (Eds.), *Hindu Law. A New History of Dharmaśāstra* (pp. 60–77). The Oxford History of Hinduism. Oxford: Oxford University Press.

Ambedkar, Bhimrao R. 1979 [1917]. 'Caste in India. Their Mechanism, Genesis and Development'. In Vasant Moon *Dr. Babasaheb Ambedkar. Writings and Speeches* (Vol. 1, pp. 3–22). Bombay: Educational Department, Government of Maharashtra.

Ambedkar, Bhimrao R. 1989 [1979]. 'The Untouchables or the Children of India's Ghetto'. In Vasant Moon (Eds.), *Dr. Babasaheb Ambedkar. Writings and Speeches* (Vol. 5, pp. 1–124). Bombay: Education Department, Government of Maharashtra.

Ambedkar, Bhimrao R. 2014 [1936]. *The Annihilation of Caste*. The Annotated Critical Edition edited and annotated by S. Anand. Introduced with the Essay *The Doctor and the Saint* by Arundhati Roy. London: Verso.

Appadurai, Arjun. 1996. 'Is Homo Hierarchicus?' *American Ethnologist*, 13(4): 745–761.

Bailey, Greg. 2014. 'Buddhism and Caste'. *Oxford Bibliographies*. DOI: 10.1093/obo/9780195393521-0191.

Bayly, Susan. 1999. *Caste, Society and Politics in India from the Eighteenth Century to the Modern Age*. The New Cambridge History of India IV. 3. Cambridge: Cambridge University Press.

Benveniste, Émile (tr. from French by Elizabeth Palmer). 1973 [1969]. *Indo-European Language and Society*. London: Faber.

Berreman, Gerald D. 1972. 'Race, Caste, and Other Invidious Distinctions in Social Stratification'. *Race and Class*, 13(4): 385–414.

Bouglé, Célestin (tr. by David F. Pocock). 1971 [1908]. *Essays on the Caste System*. Cambridge: Cambridge University Press.

Charsley, Simon. 1996. '"Untouchable" What Is in a Name?' *The Journal of the Royal Anthropological Institute*, 2(1): 1–23.

Clémentin-Ojha, Catherine. 2019. 'La question de la définition de l'identité hindoue. La contribution de B. R. Ambedkar à son règlement politique (1951)'. *Archives des sciences sociales des religions*, 186(avril–juin): 163–182.

Cohn, Bernard. S. 1990 [1987]. 'The Census, Social Structure and Objectication in South Asia'. In Cohn S. Bernard (Ed.), *An Anthropologist among Historians and Other Essays* (pp. 224–252). Delhi: Oxford University Press.

Das, Veena. 2015. 'Caste'. In James Wright (Ed.), *International Encyclopedia of the Social & Behavioral Sciences* (2nd ed., Vol. 3, pp. 223–227). Amsterdam: Elsevier. DOI: 10.1016/B978-0-08-097086-8.12030-6.

Deshpande, Satish. 2013. 'Caste and Castelessness. Towards a Biography of the "General Category"'. *Economic and Political Weekly*, 48(15): 32–39.

Desrosières, Alain (tr. by Camille Naish). 1998 [1993]. *The Politics of Large Numbers. A History of Statistical Reasoning.* Cambridge, MA: Harvard University Press.

Dirks, Nicholas B. 1987. *The Hollow Crown: Ethnohistory of an Indian Kingdom.* Cambridge: Cambridge University Press.

Dirks, Nicholas B. 2001. *Caste of Mind: Colonialism and the Making of Modern India.* Princeton: Princeton University Press.

Dumont, Louis (tr. by Mark Sainsbury, Louis Dumont, and Basia Gulati). 1980 [1966]. *Homo Hierarchicus. The Caste System and It Implications.* Chicago: University of Chicago Press.

Dumont, Louis. 1971. 'On Putative Hierarchy and Some Allergies to It'. *Contributions to Indian Sociology (n.s.)*, 5: 58–81.

Eltschinger, Vincent (tr. from French by Raynald Prévèreau in Collaboration with the Author). 2012 [2000]. *Caste and Buddhist Philosophy: Continuity of Some Buddhist Arguments against the Realist Interpretation of Social Denominations.* Delhi: Motilal Banarsidass.

Ernst, Carl W. 2003. 'Muslim Studies of Hinduism? A Reconsideration of Arabic and Persian Translations from Indian Languages'. *Iranian Studies*, 36(2): 173–195.

Fischel, Walter J. 1962. 'Cochin in Jewish History: Prolegomena to a History of the Jews in India'. *Proceedings of the American Academy for Jewish Research*, 30: 37–59.

Fuller, C. J. 2017. 'Ethnographic Inquiry in Colonial India: Herbert Risley, William Crooke, and the Study of Tribes and Castes'. *Journal of the Royal Anthropological Institute (n.s.)*, 23: 603–662.

Gaborieau, Marc. 1993. *Ni brahmanes ni ancêtres. Colporteurs musulmans du Népal.* Nanterre: Société d'ethnologie.

Galanter, Marc. 1984. *Competing Equalities. Law and the Backward Classes in India.* Delhi: Oxford University Press.

Gottschalck, Peter. 2013. *Religion, Science and Empire. Classifying Hinduism and Islam in British India.* New York: Oxford University Press.

Guha, Sumit. 2016 [2013]. *Beyond Caste. Identity and Power in South Asia. Past and Present.* Ranikhet: Permanent Black.

Gurhye, G. S. 1932. *Caste and Race in India.* London: Routledge and Kegan Paul.

Herrenschmidt, Olivier. 1987. ''L'inégalité graduée' ou la pire des inégalités. L' analyse de la société hindoue par Ambedkar'. *Archives Européennes de Sociologie*, 37(1): 3–22.

Herrenschmidt, Olivier. 2009. 'The Indians' Impossible Civil Code'. *Archives Européennes de Sociologie*, 50(2): 309–347.

Hocart, Arthur M. (tr. from French edition). 1950 [1938]. *Caste. A Comparative Study.* New York: Russell and Russell.

Hutton, John H. 1946. *Caste in India, Its Nature, Function and Origins.* Cambridge: Cambridge University Press.

Jarret, Colonel H. S. (tr. from the Original Persian). 1894. *The Ain i Akbari by Abul Fazl 'Allami.* Calcutta: The Baptist Mission Press.

Kalpagam, U. 2014. *Rule by Numbers. Governmentality in Colonial India.* Lanham: Lexington Books.

Lardinois, Roland (tr. by Renuka George). 2013 [2007]. *Scholars and Prophets. Sociology of India from France in the 19th–20th Centuries*. Delhi: Social Science Press.

Lele, Jayant. 1980. 'The Bhakti Movement in India: A Critical Introduction'. *Journal of Asian and African Studies*, 15(1–2): 1–15.

Lorenzen, David. 1987. 'Traditions of Non-Caste Hinduism: The Kabir Panth'. *Contributions to Indian Sociology (n.s.)*, 21(2): 263–283.

Lorenzen, David. 1999. 'Who Invented Hinduism?' *Comparative Studies in Society and History*, 41(4): 630–659.

Machado, A. R. (Ed.). 1946. *Livro. Em que da relação do que viu et ouviu no Oriente Duarte Barbosa*. Lisboa: Divisão de Publicacões e Biblioteca Agencia General das Colonias.

Marlow, Louise. 1995. 'Some Classical Muslim Views of the Caste System'. *The Muslim World*, 85(1–2): 1–22.

Malamoud, Charles. 1981. 'On the Rhetoric and Semantics of Puruṣārtha'. *Contributions to Indian Sociology (n.s.)*, 15(1–2): 33–54.

Novetzke, Christian Lee. 2016. *The Quotidian Revolution. Vernacularization, Religion, and the Premodern Public Sphere in India*. New York: Columbia University Press.

O'Hanlon, Rosalind, Gergely Hidas, and Csaba Kiss. 2015. 'Discourses of Caste over the Longue Durée: Gopīnātha and Social Classification in India, ca.1400–1900'. *South Asian History and Culture*, 6(1): 102–129. DOI: 10.1080/19472498.2014.969013.

Olivelle, Patrick. 1998. 'Caste and Purity: A Study in the Language of Dharma Literature'. *Contributions to Indian Sociology (n.s.)*, 32(2): 189–216.

O'Malley, Lewis S. S. 1932. *Indian Caste Customs*. Cambridge: Cambridge University Press.

Pant, Rashmi. 1987. 'The Cognitive Status of Caste in Colonial Ethnography: A Review of Some Literature on the Northwest Provinces and Oudh'. *The Indian Economic and Social History Review*, 24(2): 145–162.

Peabody, Norbert. 2001. 'Cents, Sense, Census: Human Inventories in Late Precolonial and Early Colonial India'. *Comparative Studies in Society and History*, 43(4): 819–850.

Quigley, Declan. 1993. *The Interpretation of Caste*. Oxford: Clarendon Press.

Raheja, Gloria Goodwin. 1988. *The Poison in the Gift. Ritual, Prestation, and the Dominant Caste in a North Indian Village*. Chicago: University of Chicago Press.

Révah, I.-S. 2001. 'Pour une histoire religieuse de l'Asie portugaise: l'activité du tribunal inquisitorial de Goa'. In Henry Méchoulan and Gérard Nahon (Eds.), *Mémorial I.-S. Révah: études sur le marranisme, l'hétérodoxie juive et Spinoza* (pp. 545–560). Paris: Louvain.

Risley, Herbert (Revised Edition by W. Crooke). 1915 [1908]. *The People of India*. London: W. Thacker.

Sachau, Edward C. (tr.). 1910. *Alberuni's India: An Account of the Religion, Philosophy, Literature, Geography, Chronology, Astronomy, Customs, Laws and Astrology of India about A.D. 1030* (2 vol.). London: Trubner.

Samarendra, Padmanabh. 2003. 'Classifying Caste: Census Surveys in India in the Late Nineteenth and Early Twentieth Centuries'. *South Asia: Journal of South Asia Studies*, 26(2): 141–164.

Senart, Émile (tr. by E. Denison Ross). 1930 [1896]. *Caste in India. The Facts and the System*. London: Methuen and Company.

Srinivas, M. N. 1996. *Caste. Its Twentieth Century Avatar*. Delhi: Viking, Penguin.

Subrahmanyam, Sanjay. 2017. *Europe's India. Words, People, Empires, 1500–1800*. Cambridge: Harvard University Press.

Sundar, Nandini. 2000. 'Caste as Census Category: Implications for Sociology'. *Current Sociology*, 48(3): 111–126.

Walzer, Michael. 1983. *Spheres of Justice. A Defense of Pluralism and Equality*. Oxford: Martin Robertson.

Weber, Max (tr. by Hans H. Gerth and D. Martindale). 1958 [1916–1917]. *The Religion of India. The Sociology of Hinduism and Buddhism*. Glencoe III: The Free Press.

Weber, Max. 2012. 'The "Objectivity" of Knowledge in Social Science and Social Policy: Critical Studies in the Logic of Cultural Sciences'. In Hans Henrik Bruun and Sam Whimster (Eds.), *Collected Methodological Writings*. London, New York: Routledge.

Wiser, William H. 1936. *The Hindu Jajmani System. A Socio-Economic System Interrelating Members of a Hindu Village Community in Services*. Lucknow: Lucknow Publishing House.

Xavier, Angela Barreto. 2011. '*Conversos* and *Novamente Convertidos*: Law, Religion, and Identity in the Portuguese Kingdom and Empire'. *Journal of Early Modern History*, 15: 255–287.

Xavier, Angela Barreto. 2016. 'Languages of Difference in the Portuguese Empire. The Spread of "Caste" in the Indian World'. *Anuario Colombiano de Historia Social y de la Cultura*, 43(2): 89–119.

Xavier, Angela Barreto, and Ines G. Županov. 2015. *Catholic Orientalism, Portuguese Empire, Indian Knowledge (16th–18th Centuries)*. Delhi: Oxford University Press.

Zelliot, Eleanor. 1972. 'Gandhi and Ambedkar. A Study in Leadership'. In Michael Mahar (Ed.), *The Untouchable in Contemporary India* (pp. 69–95). Tucson: University of Arizona Press.

CHAPTER 2

HIERARCHY

MARTIN FUCHS

CONSIDERED as ensemble, if not as system, caste seems to signify the prototype of social hierarchy. On the other hand, hierarchy grasps only one dimension, even be it a central one, of caste.

Hierarchy refers to a ranked order, of people or values. In an institutional and political sense, hierarchy has been applied to relations of dominion, rule, or authority, and at the other end, subordination. With respect to social order reference is to status differences or, more generally, to classifications of whole categories of people. Being an originally Western term, derived from ancient Greek, hierarchy has its origin in sacred and church contexts. First introduced at the end of the 6th century, hierarchy became prominent in the Christian context as a term designating the 'celestial' as well as clerical hierarchies and by extension the order given to the world with its estates, or classes, by God (Rausch, 1982, p. 103ff.). Hierarchy thus originally referred to 'the yearning of man for something outside and above him' (Kolnai, 1971, p. 210).[1] Hierarchy gained a pejorative sense after the Reformation (Rausch, 1982, p. 110). Its use as socio-philosophical term seems to have started after the French Revolution. The term can be found in texts of authors like Henri de Saint Simon, Auguste Comte, and Georg Wilhelm Friedrich Hegel (Rausch, 1982, pp. 118–120). Hegel seems to have been one of the first to contrast the hierarchy of the socio-political order with a social condition based on autonomous human activity (*Selbstbetätigung*).

There is no general agreement regarding what hierarchy is to be opposed with. Not being divided into different levels of importance or status can be understood as referring to either 'collegial' and 'anti-authoritarian' (Merriam-Webster) or 'egalitarian' (Oxford Online Dictionary) modes of relationship.

---

[1] The word hierarchy derives from Greek hierarkhiā, 'rule of a high priest', and hierarkhēs, 'leader of sacred rites', and made its appearance in Late Middle English via medieval Latin and Old French. The earliest meaning in English was 'system of orders of angels and heavenly beings'; the other significations date from the 17th century (OED).

Within debates on caste one can observe two ways of approaching hierarchy. Approaches focusing on ground realities attempt to set out the various contextual forms and registers of super- and subordination. Approaches that start from the idea of a social model or a guiding social ideal tend to look for structuring principles configuring or underlying the hierarchical order. Social actors may, explicitly or implicitly, refer to images of an ideal order, as a condition advocated or contested, in either dichotomous form—like *savarna-avarna*, Brahminical-non-Brahminical, polluting or non-polluting—or by employing the *chaturvarna* model originally laid out in the Rigveda and afterwards the *dharmashastra*-s that comprises a series of dichotomizing strides (Dumont, 1980a, p. 67). Taking an analytical perspective, hierarchy in the strict sense appears as a socio-historical 'ideal-type', as Max Weber suggested the term, against which one measures the structures of relationships found historically as either close to, or 'deviating' from, the ideal-type (Weber, 2004). Louis Dumont in his discourse-setting book on hierarchical India, *Homo Hierarchicus* (published in French in 1966; first English edition 1970), makes use of Weber's 'ideal-type' with respect to both the (hierarchical) disjunction of power and (ritual) status, and the hierarchy of pure and impure (1980b, p. 260). Be it as an image of an ideal order, or understood as an ideal-type, a conceptual model can be clearly laid out, but, by definition, can never be regarded as translatable into social reality in an unadulterated form.

In the Indian case, it is of course Louis Dumont whose thinking provides the prototype of hierarchical analysis. His approach has dominated debates on caste in India since the 1970s. Dumont combines a sociological ideal-typical model of caste hierarchy with an image of an ideal social or even cosmic order shared at least by certain elite sections. While himself not fully clear about the historical beginnings of full-fledged caste hierarchies he then treats hierarchy as a single and ahistorical system of order, with variations regarded as just contextualized articulations, which experienced stronger modal changes (like that of a 'substantialization' of caste; 1980a, p. 222) only with colonialism and in the context of the processes of what has been called modernization. Putting his approach into the centre allows discussing the logic and the limits of his approach and bring alternative views into sharper relief. Whereas Dumont subscribes to hierarchy, other views are often informed by more critical perspectives.

Louis Dumont

Louis Dumont[2] designs hierarchy, and the Indian caste system as its clearest instantiation, as an essentially 'rational system', a logical order, and tries to use deductive arguments to the extent possible (1980a, pp. xlix, 35). Dumont takes off from earlier,

---

[2] For a systematic exposition, defense and application of Dumont's concept of hierarchy (hierarchical opposition) see Robert Parkin (2003).

primarily Western attempts at theorizing caste (Émile Senart, Célestin Bouglé, Arthur Maurice Hocart) and builds on a Maussian-Durkheimian and partially Hegelian legacy of holistic conceptualizations of social relations, enshrined in a structuralist language adapted to his purpose ('hierarchical structuralism'). Empirical findings are fitted into, or are made to accommodate to, the structural model of order, and when they do not fit, are treated as exceptions or imperfections. At certain points the intervention of other social registers, especially, but not only, politics and power, is being acknowledged.

For Dumont, hierarchy has to be approached from the extremes, the in-between and less clear-cut layers being considered by him of secondary importance (1980a, p. 76). On the one hand taken as a ranking along one dimension, the underlying structure is being conceived on the other hand as a relationship between two contrasting terms that presuppose each other. Hierarchy, as Dumont sees it, is based on a dichotomy, the opposition of extremes. Seen from either perspective, both hierarchy and the underlying dichotomy in Dumont's sense stand for a closed system.[3] Hierarchy for Dumont entails holism, the submission of each group and each individual to the whole (1980a, pp. 40f., 76, 131, 1977a, p. 4), a prerequisite if there is to be society in the proper sense (1980a, p. 9f.).

In the Dumontian concept, it is decisive to have the ideas in view with which he compares both of the terms, hierarchy and holism. For Dumont it is the oppositions—of hierarchy to equality, and holism to individualism—that are central. The idea of hierarchy lives from the contrast with equality, as does holism from the contrast with individuality. Again, equivalent to the holism-hierarchy relationship, the ideas of individuality and equality are seen by Dumont as entailing each other (1977a, p. 4).[4] Dumont's overriding concern is with the notions of individualism and equality as they, assumedly, are ruling the modern Western world, to which he opposes holism and hierarchy as represented by India. India is meant to hold up the mirror to the modern West: 'the ideal of equality' has to be realized as being 'artificial', a deliberate denial of hierarchy, which is meant constituting a 'universal phenomenon' (Dumont, 1980a, p. 20, 1977a and b, 1986, cf. Fuchs, 1988, pp. 587–627).[5] Dumont moreover sees the West giving priority to economics and politics against the Indian emphasis on the religious. It is the contrast of the Indian value system with the values of the modern West that is the ultimate driving force behind Dumont's deliberations on India. Each of the two regions (civilizations) stands for one principle or value. As in other Orientalist schemes (starting with Hegel),

---

[3] On the difference between closed and open systems of hierarchy see Gupta (2000, p. 23ff.).

[4] In this respect, Bouglé can also be seen as a precursor. Not only did he write a treatise on caste that Dumont built on, as he distanced himself from it, Bouglé also, like Dumont, but in his case predating his work on caste, wrote a treatise on the development of the idea of equality, *Les idée égalitaires* (1899), and already linked equality with individualism (1899, pp. 25–28). Dumont's book titled *From Mandeville to Marx* in English had the title *Homo Aequalis* in French (both books 1977) to emphasize its complementarity to *Homo Hierarchicus*.

[5] '... the main comparative task is to account for ... the modern case in traditional terms' (Dumont, 1975b, p. 169).

India is given a place in a grid, meant to feed a general argument in a largely Western debate, employed as tool of the critique of individualism and equality.

The primary focus of Dumont's argument concerns the dominant social values, or what he calls the 'system of ideas and values', which he subjects to a logical analysis. Dumont sees these general 'ideas and values' (or 'basic ideology'; Dumont, 1980a, p. 343) as prime factor or force determining society, the social order. In the Indian case it is the religious notion of (ritual) purity that represents the lead value, allowing for rankings according to grades of purity. Looking from a structural angle the value hierarchy is viewed as couched in the opposition between 'purity' and 'impurity'. This opposition historically pre-dates as it logically underlies hierarchy (1980a, pp. 43, 47). Empirically, 'purity' is not a straightforward value category though. The term stands for 'a welter of heterogeneous notions' in 'the Indian vocabulary' (Dumont, 1971, p. 75). Impurity on the other hand, even if required as foundational opposite of purity to sustain the system, is itself not a value, but derivative of purity, the negative of the prime value, designating conditions where what is considered polluted and polluting is concentrated (Dumont, 1980a, p. 54f.). Permanent impurity has its source in temporary impurity in relation to the 'organic' aspects of life by way of relieving people of high status from polluting tasks and offloading these onto categories of people to whom then permanent impurity is being attributed (1980a, p. 47).[6] Having to shield the sphere in which purity is to rule, the connection of the pole of impurity with its opposite has to be regarded, the way Dumont depicts it, as one of essential, but unequal complementarity: 'The whole is founded on the necessary and hierarchical coexistence of the two opposites' (1980a, p. 43; sentence emphasized by author). In an attempt to resolve the tension between (the notions of) opposition, negation, and (logical, physical, as well as social) inequality Dumont introduces the concept of hierarchical 'encompassment' to characterize the relationship of the two poles (1980a, pp. 60f., 76). This concept he took from one of his students, Raymond Apthorpe, who himself relates back to Susan Stebbing and Leonhard Euler (Dumont, 1966, p. 19f., 1980a, pp. xvii, 241; Apthorpe, 1984). That the opposite of the supreme value, the assemblage point of impurities discarded or disposed of, is not just considered as negation of, but as also being encompassed, and that means included by, the prime value on the level of logical argument, seems sociologically problematic. Encompassment is a condition that on top of everything denies agency to those who are already hierarchically subordinate.[7]

Conceived by Dumont as closed order, no one considered a member of society, including those who are encompassed as depositories of impurity, can be outside the reach of the hierarchical value structure (1980a, p. 215). Dumont equates society with

---

[6] Dumont does not consider the fact that pollution does not exhaust states of being non-pure (Das and Uberoi, 1971, pp. 35, 41f.; Gupta, 2000, p. 67f.).

[7] While this formula reminds one of what today is being termed by the itself paradoxically sounding phrase of 'inclusion by exclusion', it is, in the second case, not the top position that 'includes' those who otherwise are excluded, but the overall social order that gives an ambivalent place to the marginalized.

one value system. Instead of looking for the different value orders upheld, followed, or forwarded by different members of society, other value orders are dismissed from the very start. But Dumont takes one further step. Not satisfied with seeing in the Indian case one value system reigning nearly unopposed by other values, he furthermore equates the prime value with the position of one social group, the Brahmins, who by definition and in toto stand for, or even inhabit, purity and thus represent the apex of the social order (1980a, pp. 47, 70),[8] while the 'Untouchables', who have to 'absorb pollution' (Kolenda, 1976, p. 584), are equally sweepingly equated with impurity and pollution. It is this what led to the critique that Dumont identifies with an idealized Brahmanical view of the social order.

For status hierarchy to function in principle independently, and thus to firmly ground his conception of social hierarchy, Dumont had to make two further moves—disentangle religion from its social context and relegate individuality. Dumont sees the establishment of ritual hierarchy grounded in a dissociation that again is claimed to predate logically as well as historically the instalment of the purity value hierarchy (so that a purely religiously instituted hierarchy becomes possible) and that anchors the social value order at an even higher point:[9] the categorial as well as categorical separation between priesthood and royalty, *brahman* and *kshatra*, (hierarchical) status and (secularized) power (or even force), the 'spiritual' and the 'temporal', or the 'religious'— that is the ritualistic-religious explicitly taken by Dumont as 'group religion' (1980e, pp. 278, 285f.)[10]—and the 'politico-economic'. All these binaries are being deployed by Dumont as practical synonyms (1980a, pp. 37, 71–79, 165, 215, 1980c, pp. 291, 293, 301, 303f., 1980d, p. 317, 1975a, p. 58; cf. Fuchs, 1988, pp. 454–469).[11] Assuming that a social order is based on values, Dumont takes religion as the highest value field with the political sphere taking a secondary place. He here again applies the concept of 'encompassment', the politico-economic being hierarchically 'encompassed' by religion as its contradictory-complementary, which thus establishes the societal whole: a duplication of hierarchy.

While Dumont himself, on the level of values, finds no (significant) traces of hierarchy's direct opposite, equality, in India, he does so with respect to holism's other. The contrast to the holistically closed social structure, individualism, against all odds actually finds space in Dumont's model and, in addition, receives a prominent place. For Dumont, the locus of this anti-, or non-hierarchical value lies outside society proper, its representatives being people, largely men, who 'leave' society, live 'outside the world',

---

[8] For Dumont Brahmins on the one hand are 'in principle priests', no matter what their actual practice is. On the other hand, he acknowledges Brahmins who do not serve others or serve as priests to be of higher rank (1980, pp. 47, 70). Several scholars have pointed out that priests are not occupying the top rank (Heesterman, 1985; Fuller, 1979).

[9] The distinction he claims goes back to around 800 years BCE (Dumont, 1980a, p. 37).

[10] 'The religion of gods is secondary; the religion of caste is fundamental' (Dumont, 1959, p. 34).

[11] Before Dumont, Max Weber (1978, p. 139) had already underlined this dissociation, which however was not acknowledged by Dumont, who otherwise had read Weber's study on Hinduism and Buddhism closely (Fuchs, 1988, p. 45, fn. 1).

act as individuals and represent religions of salvation: the renouncers or *samnayasin*-s (1980e, 1980a, pp. 184–187). Again, Dumont clubs together various individual as well as collective forms of asceticism and *samnyas* (Gupta, 2000, pp. 30–32, with reference to Thapar, 1978, p. 64) and identifies a whole field of action—the search for religious iberation—with one institution and one social category. From the angle of caste society, the institution of (social or world) renunciation—individualizing religion—acts like a safety valve that allows for individualistic articulations (Dumont, 1980a, p. 186).

Dumont thus effectively ends up applying two different concepts of society, that of society in the shape of a closed caste order, and that of society in a wider (and sociologically more conventional) sense, which comprises opposite values and opposing institutions (Fuchs, 1988, p. 417ff.). Paradoxically then, and combining both concepts of society,[12] Dumont finally makes the individual, who renounces society, the apex of society (in the larger sense) and top hierarchy: '... hierarchy in actual fact culminated in its contrary, the renouncer' (1980a, p. 194). Moreover, in Dumont's analysis renouncers also turned out as having been the main creative agents in Indian history (1965, p. 91, 1975a, p. 55, 1975b, p. 163), and he even suggested seeing them as having played a major role in world history.[13]

ALTERNATIVES AND CRITIQUES

A largely intellectualist exercise, the strict rigidity of Dumont's outline of caste hierarchy, which he tried stubbornly to uphold, cannot be sustained. He had to make concessions, which others would see as undermining his approach. The first thing he had to acknowledge was the fact that power intervenes in status ranking. However, he tried to budge as little as possible. Hierarchy 'must give a place to power without saying so' (1980a, p. 77). 'Surreptitiously', Dumont states, power makes itself felt as a factor that influences ranking and 'makes itself the equal of status at the interstitial level' (1980a, p. 153, also pp. 167, 212), sometimes even 'victoriously offsetting' purity (1980a, p. 89). However, Dumont lets power hold sway in the 'median zone' only. Kshatriyas for example, who do not follow major purity rules, often rank higher than others who do (1980a, p. 77). Since this would have undermined his whole model, Dumont denies power the position of an equal principle of order. Instead, he wants to see power and status, like the first two *varna*-s, as being in alliance under real life conditions (1980a, pp. 77, 88). His concession

---

[12] Individualism opposes the holistic social order, characterized by hierarchy, 'from the outside', and thus becomes the opposite not just of holism, but indirectly also of hierarchy, but without any egalitarian implication.

[13] Dumont (1975b, p. 168f.) suggests that Indian renouncers, the individuals 'outside' society, influenced developments in the West during antiquity through contacts with the Greek world, and formulates the hypothesis that the idea of the otherworldly individual, as precursor of the inner-worldly individual, might have been invented only once in world history, and, even if this seems ironic, the place where this happened was India.

to acknowledge the ways in which power intervenes in the scales of hierarchy, is not extended by him to the lowest position affecting people exposed to permanent impurity, nor to the other extreme, the top-positioned Brahmins. What Dumont does not concede is that ascription of pollution is itself a question of power, a condition forced on people. The placement at the bottom of the value order is not based on value decisions the people concerned themselves have taken—some may even follow the so-called purity rules meticulously—it is imposed on them (Gupta, 2000, p. 182). Dumont's defence of hierarchy makes him show no concern for, nor extend recognition to, those who are the victims of hierarchization.

A little different is the way in which Dumont deals with the other element he had cut off from (caste) society, the occurrence and the very possibility of social forms of individualization. Again, Dumont has to concede that individuality exists within the realm of caste and feels forced to acknowledge that *bhakti*, which provides ideas of salvation without renunciation, shows the option of individualization within society. With *bhakti* 'one can leave the world from within', 'everybody can become free individuals' (1980e, p. 282f.). Dumont even acknowledges that his dichotomous model of religion is thus getting undermined and that the two kinds of religion, the two 'ideal types' that he had set out to distinguish, in actual fact 'mingle', 'and some men who in spirit are sanyasis live in the world' (1980e, p. 285). However, having made these concessions, Dumont, like Max Weber in a different way before him, hereafter puts *bhakti* to the side and makes no attempt whatsoever to integrate *bhakti* into his overall model of Indian society. He, like Weber, locked away his own insights, as these did not fit his basic analytical agenda (Fuchs, 2018, p. 128f.; Fuchs, 1988, pp. 469–486). *Bhakti* would also have provided him an occasion to pinpoint the mutual entailment of individualization and egalitarian ideas in the Indian case (Fuchs, 2019b).[14]

Bhakti shows that other value systems and possibilities of value critique did exist in Indian society, even if in most cases in a secondary, marginalized position. Others underlined other moments of equality, reciprocity, and mutuality in Indian society with respect to the lower and medium rungs of the caste system, including the removal of impurities, or regard centrality and mutuality together with hierarchy as the principles that make up the elementary structure of local caste systems (Das and Uberoi, 1971, pp. 39–41; Raheja, 1989).

Most debate was triggered by Dumont's notion of caste ranking and revolved around suggestions of alternatives. No scholar denies the social significance of hierarchy in the Indian context, but many scholars point out that caste hierarchies can be diverse or multiple; can be based on other principles, especially that of power; that there exists hierarchy beyond caste; and also that there are forces, principles and values in India that cannot be submerged in hierarchy.

---

[14] On *bhakti* as a site of endeavours of individualization see also Banerjee-Dube (2019), Feldhaus (2019).

Dumont intentionally overruled the fact that it was different local or regional social orders in which Indians lived throughout their history ('concrete wholes' or small political units, as he called these) and insisted that the principles and the 'basic ideology' were the same throughout (1980a, pp. 33, 35, 46). It is, however, the very fact of this diversity that many critics hold against him. Even if one would accept the wide presence of purity as symbolic and hierarchizing code, application of this code does not result in the same kind of hierarchical order in each context. More generally, there is wide agreement that caste ranking, even when reference is to the purity-impurity code, has to be seen as being underwritten by political as well as economic power: 'the rule of caste is only obeyed when it is accompanied by the rule of power' (Gupta, 2000, pp. 67, 68).[15] Some, like Pauline Kolenda (1976, p. 595), regard 'close-to-absolute politico-economic power' as a second value system (ideology) or principle, balanced with purity-pollution in caste-ranking.

In particular it has been pointed out that Brahmins were not always in the top position, that this position was often claimed by *kshatriya*-s and even *baniya*-s, that both *kshatriya*-s and *baniya*-s can be the reference point for members of other groups or serve as model of emulation, and that historically the caste system was generally ordered in relation to the king, or even the *kshatriya*-s more generally (Dirks, 1987; Quigley, 1993; Gupta, 2000, pp. 9, 35, 124ff.; Jodhka, 2012, pp. 42–51; Tambs-Lyche, 2017). In several cases, different hierarchical models coexist(ed) or compete (Gupta, 2000, p. 142). Taking 18th and early- 19th centuries Nepal as example, Richard Burghart (1978) showed the coexistence of three conflicting hierarchical models, the Brahmin claiming supremacy based on purity (according to the hierarchy of the sacrificial body of Brahma), the ascetic claiming supremacy based on the assumption that he is released from rebirth, and the king claiming supremacy as Lord of the Land (*bhupati*), and, as Protector of the Earth (*bhupalan*) identifying with Vishnu. Moreover, individual castes, even while sharing some common principles, often articulate very different ideologies and very different notions 'of who they are and what positions they should occupy', many of these distinctly different from Brahmanical versions, and sometimes even hostile to Brahmins (Gupta, 2000, pp. 64, 69ff., 135). Dipankar Gupta here specifically includes what subaltern castes think of their position and of the caste order as a whole, views which Dumont completely ignores. Such differences can often lead to disagreements and conflicts regarding the actual positioning of *jati*-s (Gupta, 2000, pp. 9, 35).

At the same time, attempts are made to strengthen a side of hierarchy that Dumont took all effort to downplay, namely that of the segregation between castes. Dumont had tried to downgrade segregation to a secondary phenomenon derivative of hierarchy and was occupied with minimizing, against Célestin Bouglé, the effect of segregation and repulsion that the earlier scholar had emphasized. Dumont undertook every

---

[15] Gupta (2000, p. 143f.) strengthens this argument further by claiming that the institution of untouchability and the notion of purity and pollution are a 'historical accretion', a 'later addition in the history of the Indian caste system' and 'not its essence'.

effort to make segregation look a derivative of hierarchy—again not completely distinct from hierarchy, but 'implied by and encompassed in' hierarchy (1980a, pp. 130f., 109, 197). Even then he had to concede that separation and repulsion might 'somewhere' be present as an 'independent factor' (1980, pp. 308, fn. 55b).[16] While also not following Bouglé, Dipankar Gupta points out that castes are not to be seen as aligned on one scale, on which they, or rather individual members, could move up and down—this mode represents what Gupta calls an open system—but are each considered, and consider themselves, as unique and bearers of differences, characterized by pride in their own community and its customs and traditions, and as hierarchized not necessarily with respect to purity-pollution but 'on the basis of supposed natural substances' (2000, pp. 42, 80, 84). Analytically for Gupta caste groups exist as discrete categories first; he regards hierarchies as a later introduction. Only this can for him explain the multiplicity of hierarchies, of models of emulation, as well as the tensions in the ways power and ritual status are being weighted (2000, p. 147).

A very different perspective is gained when one looks at hierarchy from the bottom up, and this is usually combined with a particularly harsh social critique. Dumont has been widely criticized for what looks like a defence of the practice of untouchability, namely to assume that Untouchables have no voice of their own and accept the value system and their social position. Dalit scholars—taking up the social critique of activists and scholars like Jyotiba Phule, Iyothee Thass, or Bhimrao Ambedkar—as well as some non-Dalit scholars, articulate strong normative critique of what for Dumont and others represent the core elements of hierarchy and social integration through hierarchy, the predetermination of one's social belonging and status; the legitimation of the pre-eminence of Brahmins; the purity-pollution system of ideas and values, which they regard as ideology in the sense of critical theory; and the practices of segregation and exclusion of the lower castes. Specifically targeted are systematic practices of stigmatization and humiliation entailed by this exclusion (Guru, 2009).

Before Dumont, and not acknowledged by Dumont, Ambedkar had already tried to find a scholarly informed understanding of caste (Fuchs, 2019a). Trained as a social science scholar he had in an early essay laid his finger less on hierarchy but rather on the self-enclosed 'fissiparous' character of caste, emphasized endogamy, for which Brahmins set the example, and the control of women, and did not see in the 'idea of pollution' a structuring factor (1998b). Later he advanced the concept of 'graded inequality' to pinpoint a system that assigned people to separate, hierarchically ordered categories (Ambedkar, 1992, pp. 87–91, 301; cf. Herrenschmidt, 2004, pp. 42–47; Fuchs, 2019a, p. 378f.). That people are assigned to their position in advance and permanently, made Ambedkar describe this as a 'division of labourers' instead of just a division of

---

[16] Repulsion, even 'magical distance' and 'deadly enmity' between castes are also the main characteristics of caste society in the eyes of Max Weber (1978, pp. 36, 40), who read at least summaries of Bouglé's work. It is interesting that Dumont did not refer to Weber in this regard, whose writings on India he otherwise appreciated.

labour (Ambedkar, 1989a, p. 47, 1987, p. 67). Taking, like Dumont, a unitary perspective, Ambedkar addressed both the value and the power basis of caste hierarchy, but foregrounded (using John Dewey's approach) the habitual dimension, the inscription of hierarchizing and denigrating attitudes into the dispositions and the conduct of social actors (Ambedkar, 1989a, pp. 59, 68, 78, 1992, pp. 218, 284f.). Ambedkar attacked not only the maltreatment caste hierarchy involved but also its consequences. As he put it, the hierarchical organization 'produces an ascending scale of hatred and descending scale of contempt' (Ambedkar, 1987, p. 48) and excludes members of subaltern castes from access to life-chances and the possibility 'to develop the capacity of an individual' (Ambedkar, 1989a, pp. 47f., 57). Ambedkar too emphasized the aspect of segregation and particularly criticized the effects segregation has on society at large—the 'spirit of rivalry' among castes that it produces; the division and fragmentation of society; the focus by each group on the 'interests of its own'; the dearth of 'social efficiency' of caste society, which harms and weakens Indian society; and the fact that members of the lower castes cannot contribute to the flourishing of society (Ambedkar, 1989a, pp. 38, 47f., 51f., 55; Ambedkar, 1987, pp. 48, 67f.). Dispositionally, this peaks in an attitude of 'indifferentism' that both lies at the origin as it is the consequence of the social division: the absence of 'fellow-feeling' and the lack of a social or 'public' spirit and of concern for those not belonging to one's immediate group (Ambedkar, 1989a, pp. 55–57).

References

Ambedkar, Bhimrao Ramji. 1987. 'The Philosophy of Hinduism (ms.)'. In Vasant Moon (Ed.), *Dr. Babasaheb Ambedkar Writings and Speeches* (Vol. 3, pp. 1–92). Bombay: Education Department, Government of Maharashtra.
Ambedkar, Bhimrao Ramji. 1989a [1936/1944]. 'Annihilation of Caste—with a Reply to Mahatma Gandhi'. In Vasant Moon (Ed.), *Dr. Babasaheb Ambedkar, Writings and Speeches* (Vol. 1, pp. 23–96). Bombay: Education Department, Government of Maharashtra.
Ambedkar, Bhimrao Ramji. 1989b [1917]. 'Castes in India. Their Mechanism, Genesis and Development'. In Vasant Moon (Ed.), *Dr. Babasaheb Ambedkar, Writings and Speeches* (Vol. 1, pp. 3–22). Bombay: Education Department, Government of Maharashtra.
Ambedkar, Bhimrao Ramji. 1992 [1957]. 'The Buddha and His Dhamma'. In Vasant Moon (Ed.), *Dr. Babasaheb Ambedkar, Writings and Speeches* (Vol. 11). Bombay: Education Department, Government of Maharashtra.
Apthorpe, Raymond. 1984. 'Hierarchy and Other Social Relations: Some Categorical Logic'. In Jean-Claude Galey (Ed.), *Différences, valeurs, hiérarchie: Textes offertes à Louis Dumont* (pp. 285–298). Paris: Éditions de l'École des Hautes Études en Sciences Sociales.
Banerjee-Dube, Ishita. 2019. 'Religious Individualisation and Collective Bhakti: Sarala Dasa and Bhima Bhoi'. In Martin Fuchs, Antje Linkenbach, Martin Mulsow, Bernd-Christian Otto, Rahul Parson, and Jörg Rüpke (Eds.), *Religious Individualisation: Historical Dimensions and Comparative Perspectives* (pp. 841–858). Berlin: de Gruyter.
Bouglé, Célestin. 1899. *Les idées égalitaires. Étude sociologique*. Paris: Alcan.
Bouglé, Célestin. 1971 [1908]. *Essays on the Caste System*. Cambridge: Cambridge University Press.

Burghart, Richard. 1978. 'Hierarchical Models of the Hindu Social System'. *Man (n.s.)*, 13(4): 519–536.

Das, Veena, and Jit Singh Uberoi. 1971. 'The Elementary Structure of Caste (A Review Symposium on Louis Dumont's *Homo Hierarchicus*)'. *Contributions to Indian Sociology (n.s.)*, 5: 33–43.

Dirks, Nicholas B. 1987. *The Hollow Crown. Ethnohistory of an Indian Kingdom*. Cambridge: Cambridge University Press.

Dumont, Louis. 1959. 'Pure and Impure'. *Contributions to Indian Sociology*, 3: 9–39.

Dumont, Louis. 1965. 'The Functional Equivalents of the Individual in Caste Society'. *Contributions to Indian Sociology*, 8: 13–61.

Dumont, Louis. 1966. 'A Fundamental Problem in the Sociology of Caste'. *Contributions to Indian Sociology*, 9: 17–32.

Dumont, Louis. 1971. 'On Putative Hierarchy and Some Allergies to It (A Review Symposium on Louis Dumont's Homo Hierarchicus)'. *Contributions to Indian Sociology (n.s.)*, 5: 58–78.

Dumont, Louis. 1975a. *La civilisation indienne et nous*. Paris: Armand Colin.

Dumont, Louis. 1975b. 'On the Comparative Understanding of Non-Modern Civilizations'. *Daedalus*, 104: 153–172.

Dumont, Louis. 1977a. *From Mandeville to Marx*. Chicago: University of Chicago Press.

Dumont, Louis. 1977b. *Homo Aequalis. Genèse et épanouissement de l'idéologie économique*. Paris: Gallimard.

Dumont, Louis. 1980a. *Homo Hierarchicus. The Caste System and Its Implications. Complete Revised English Edition*. Chicago: University of Chicago Press.

Dumont, Louis. 1980b. 'Caste, Racism and "Stratification". Reflections of a Social Anthropologist'. In Louis Dumont, (Ed.), *Homo Hierarchicus* (pp. 247–266, and 421–425). Chicago: University of Chicago Press.

Dumont, Louis. 1980c. 'The Conception of Kingship in Ancient India'. In Louis Dumont, (Ed.), *Homo Hierarchicus* (pp. 287–313 and 439–443). Chicago: University of Chicago Press.

Dumont, Louis. 1980d. 'Nationalism and Communalism'. In Louis Dumont, (Ed.), *Homo Hierarchicus* (pp. 314–334 and 443–447). Chicago: University of Chicago Press.

Dumont, Louis. 1980e. 'World Renunciation in Indian Religions'. In Louis Dumont, (Ed.), *Homo Hierarchicus. The Caste System and Its Implications. Complete Revised English Edition* (pp. 267–286 and 425–439). Chicago University of Chicago Press.

Dumont, Louis. 1986. *Essays on Individualism. Modern Ideology in Anthropological Perspective*. Chicago: University of Chicago Press.

Feldhaus, Anne. 2019. 'Individualisation, Deindividualisation, and Institutionalisation among the Early Mahānubhāvs'. In Martin Fuchs, Antje Linkenbach, Martin Mulsow, Bernd-Christian Otto, Rahul Parson, and Jörg Rüpke (Eds.), *Religious Individualisation: Historical Dimensions and Comparative Perspectives* (pp. 823–840). Berlin: de Gruyter.

Fuchs, Martin. 1988. *Theorie und Verfremdung. Max Weber, Louis Dumont und die Analyse der indischen Gesellschaft*. Frankfurt/Main: Peter Lang.

Fuchs, Martin. 2018. 'Indian Imbroglios: Bhakti Neglected, or: The Missed Opportunities for a New Approach to a Comparative Analysis of Civilizational Diversity'. In Johann Arnason and Chris Hann (Eds.), *Anthropology and Civilizational Analysis. Eurasian Explorations* (pp. 121–154). Albany, NY: SUNY Press.

Fuchs, Martin. 2019a. 'Dhamma and the Common Good: Religion as Problem and Answer—Ambedkar's Critical Theory of Social Relationality'. In Martin Fuchs and Vasudha

Dalmia (Eds.), *Religious Interactions in Modern India* (pp. 364–413). New Delhi: Oxford University Press.

Fuchs, Martin. 2019b. 'Self-Affirmation, Self-Transcendence and the Relationality of Selves: The Social Embedment of Individualisation in *Bhakti*'. In Martin Fuchs, Antje Linkenbach, Martin Mulsow, Bernd-Christian Otto, Rahul Parson, and Jörg Rüpke (Eds.), *Religious Individualisation: Historical Dimensions and Comparative Perspectives* (pp. 255–286). Berlin: de Gruyter.

Fuller, Chris J. 1979. 'Gods, Priests and Purity: On the Relation between Hinduism and the Caste System'. *Man (n.s.)*, 14(3): 459–476.

Fuller, Chris J. 1992. *The Camphor Flame. Popular Hinduism and Society in India*. New Delhi: Viking.

Gupta, Dipankar. 2000. *Interrogating Caste. Understanding Hierarchy and Difference in Indian Society*. New Delhi: Penguin.

Guru, Gopal (Ed.). 2009. *Humiliation. Claims and Context*. New Delhi: Oxford University Press.

Heesterman, J. C. 1985. 'Brahmin, Ritual, and Renouncer'. In J. C. Heesterman (Ed.), *The Inner Conflict of Tradition. Essays in Indian Ritual, Kingship, and Society* (pp. 26–44). Chicago: University of Chicago Press.

Herrenschmidt, Olivier. 2004. 'Ambedkar and the Hindu Social Order'. In Surendra Jondhale and Johannes Beltz (Eds.), *Reconstructing the World: B.R. Ambedkar and Buddhism in India* (pp. 37–48). New Delhi: Oxford University Press.

Jodhka, Surinder S. 2012. *Caste*. New Delhi: Oxford University Press.

Kolenda, Pauline. 1976. 'Seven Kinds of Hierarchy in *Homo Hierarchicus*'. *Journal of Asian Studies*, 35 (4): 581–596.

Kolnai, Aurel. 1971. 'The Concept of Hierarchy'. *Philosophy*, 46 (177): 201–221.

Parkin, Robert. 2003. *Louis Dumont and Hierarchical Opposition*. New York: Berghahn.

Quigley, Declan. 1993. *The Interpretation of Caste*. Oxford: Clarendon.

Rausch, Heinz. 1982. 'Hierarchie'. In Otto Brunner, Werner Conze, and Reinhart Koselleck (Eds.), *Geschichtliche Grundbegriffe. Historisches Lexikon zur politisch-sozialen Sprache in Deutschland, Band 3* (pp. 103–129). Stuttgart: Klett-Cotta.

Raheja, Gloria Goodwin. 1989. 'Centrality, Mutuality and Hierarchy. Shifting Aspects of Inter-Caste Relationships in North India'. *Contributions to Indian Sociology (n.s.)*, 23(1): 79–101.

Tambs-Lyche, Harald. 2017. *Transaction and Hierarchy. Elements for a Theory of Caste*. New Delhi: Manohar.

Thapar, Romila. 1978. *Ancient Indian Social History. Some Interpretations*. New Delhi: Orient Longman.

Weber, Max. 1978 [1921]. *Gesammelte Aufsätze zur Religionssoziologie, Bd. 2: Hinduismus und Buddhismus*. Tübingen: Mohr.

Weber, Max. 2004. 'The "Objectivity" of Knowledge in Social Science and Social Policy'. In Sam Whimster (Ed.), *The Essential Weber. A Reader* (pp. 359–404). London: Routledge.

CHAPTER 3

THE JAJMANI SYSTEM

PETER MAYER

INTRODUCTION

Definition

The *jajmani* system refers to hereditary patron-client ties between members of land-owning castes and members of other castes who provide them with services throughout the year. Prakash Tandon in his autobiography *Punjabi Century* provided a clear, untechnical description of what those relations entailed:

> We had a family barber, whose father before him had been our family's barber, and so the barber's family and ours were indissolubly bound. Good or bad we could not get rid of him, nor could he refuse to serve us, unless we went to live in another place and adopted a local barber family. But whenever we returned to our home town the old barber was there, and there was no changing him. (Tandon, 1968, p. 79)

William Wiser, who gave what is usually regarded as the first formal description of the *jajmani* system in 1936, offered this account of the obligations of a village carpenter:

> The carpenter during the sowing season must remove and sharpen the plough point once or twice a week. During the harvest he must keep sickles sharp and renew handles as often as demanded. He must be ready to repair a cart whenever called upon by a customer, or to make minor repairs on the customer's house. In exchange he receives at each harvest, twenty-eight pounds of grain, for every plough owned by his client. (Wiser, 1958 [1936], pp. xvii–xviii)

Peter Mayer, by contrast, placed emphasis not on the obligations but on the value as property for a client such as Tandon's barber:

the irreducible essence of the jajmani relationship is the exclusive property right possessed by a member of an artisan or servant caste to serve a specific patron family. (Mayer, 1993, p. 360)

Pauline Kolenda offered a more formal description of the jajmani system:

[T]he *jajmani* system is a system of distribution in Indian villages whereby high-caste landowning families called *jajmans* are provided services and products by various lower castes such as carpenters, potters, blacksmiths, watercarriers, sweepers, and laundrymen. Purely ritual services may be provided by Brahman priests and various sectarian castes, and almost all serving castes have ceremonial and ritual duties at their jajman's births, marriages, funerals, and at some of the religious festivals....

The landowning jajmans pay the serving castes in kind, with grain, clothing, sugar, fodder, and animal products like butter and milk. Payment may amount to a little of everything produced on the land, in the pastures and in the kitchen. Sometimes land is granted to servants, especially as charity to Brahman priests. In this system, the middle and lower castes either subscribe to each other's services in return for compensations and payments, or exchange services with one another. (Kolenda, 1963, pp. 11–12)

This reciprocity was particularly stressed by Wiser:

Each [caste] serves the others. Each in turn is master. Each in turn is servant. Each has his own clientele comprising members of different castes which is his 'jajmani' or 'birt'. This system of interrelatedness in service within the Hindu community is called the Hindu 'Jajmani system'. (Wiser, 1958 [1936], p. xxi)

In the terminology found in Karimpur, the village studied by Wiser, the patron of a specialist was called a *jajman*, the specialist was a *kam-wala*, a *kam karne-wala* or elsewhere a *kamin* (all mean 'worker'). The word *jajman* is derived from the Sanskrit *yajman*, the person who employs a Brahman to perform religious ceremonies (Wilson, 1968 [1855], p. 226). The Brahman who performed the ceremony was referred to as the *jackak* or sacrificer (Nesfield, 1885, p. 71). In many villages, the term *jajman* referred only to the patron of a Brahman. In other villages, such as that studied by Wiser, the term *jajman* was extended to any patron in a similar patron-client relationship.

Explorations of the *jajmani* system in Indian villages, especially in the 1950s to 1970s, gave important insight into the nature of the economic relationships between castes. A common feature of many studies was the enumeration of the different castes in a village and a detailed accounting of the payments made to different caste specialists at harvest time from the grain heap (e.g. Mann, 1917; Wiser, 1958 [1936]; Lewis, 1958; Gould, 1964; Caldwell, 1991).

In Wiser's seminal account of Karimpur[1] in the early 1930s, the *jajmani* system had several distinctive elements: the system was of great antiquity, perhaps over 2000 years old; it was a 'system'; relationships within the system were essentially harmonious;

---

[1] Karimpur was later re-studied by the Wisers (Wiser and Wiser, 1963) and later still by Susan Wadley (Wadley, 1994).

because all served all, they were reciprocal and essentially the same; and, finally, with minor variations, the *jajmani* system could be found in all parts of India. In an influential article, Simon Commander identified five assumptions made by Wiser and others (Commander, 1983, pp. 286–288). In addition to its great antiquity and a harmony embedded in the very nature of the caste system, Commander noted that there is an assumption that *jajmani* operates in largely self-sufficient villages; that village property is relatively equally distributed amongst a small-holding peasantry; that the economic rationality of *jajmani* is 'wholly disconnected from that of a market nature' (Commander, 1983, p. 297); that status and hierarchy, rather than contract, govern the distribution of rewards; and that labour is largely immobile.

As village studies emerged in the 1960s and 1970s, all of the features identified by Wiser came to be questioned by different scholars and Commander himself questioned each of the assumptions he identified.

Major Debates

Complementary Interdependence?

One of the most fundamental disagreements among students of the *jajmani* system concerns its involvement with the very structure of caste itself. Wiser, as we have seen, reported that *jajmani* relations included all castes in his village. David Pocock disagreed, arguing that the essence of 'true specialization' in *jajmani* relations arises 'from the basic opposition of purity and impurity and only by extension of this idea can other castes be said to be "specialized"' (Pocock, 1962, p. 82). Thus the relation between a Brahman and a client is part of *jajmani*, but relations with artisans or unskilled labourers are not.[2]

Louis Dumont greatly expanded this line of analysis to the entire village economy:

> It has become common practice to apply the term 'the *jajmani* system' to the prestations [payments in money or services] and counter-prestations by which the castes as a whole are bound together in the village, and which is more or less universal in India. To a large extent it is a question of natural as opposed to monetary economy. It is also a question of the closed economy of the Indian village in which essential goods and especially services are found, or used to be found, either on the spot or in the immediate vicinity... (Dumont, 1972, pp. 138–139)

> [The essence of *jajmani* is] interdependence. While directly religious prestations and 'economic' prestations are mingled together, this takes place within the prescribed

---

[2] Mayer argued that the evidence from Bengal suggested that it was service roles which first took on the individual patron-client relationship typical of *jajmani*. Those relationships were only subsequently applied to religious specialists (Mayer, 1993, p. 380).

order, the religious order. The needs of each are conceived to be different, depending on caste, on hierarchy, but this fact should not disguise the entire system's *orientation towards the whole* [emphasis in original]. Thus ... distribution on the threshing floor is essentially different from a market in that it takes place in virtue of the fact that everyone is interdependent. (Dumont, 1972, p. 147)

[T]he jajmani system ... eludes what we call economics because it is founded on an implicit reference to the whole, which, in its nature, is religious or, if one prefers, a matter of ultimate values. (Dumont, 1972, p. 148)

There are several important issues and assertions in Dumont's argument which will be discussed below; for the moment, the most important point to note is his assertion that *jajmani* relations emerge directly from the very encompassing or totalizing nature of the caste system itself (Dumont, 1972, p. 148). Chris Fuller observes:

It is in Dumont's analysis, more than anyone else's, that the contrast between holistic interdependence, said to characterise jajmani, and individualist exclusive rights, characteristic of capitalist market systems, is most subtly developed into a comparison of opposed value systems. (Fuller, 1989, p. 55)

A 'System'?

Wiser described *jajmani* as a 'system', and Dumont enlarged it from a system of economic relationships to a manifestation of the caste system as a whole. Miller, too, on the basis of fieldwork with potters in Malwa argued that there is a system along the lines suggested by Dumont and that, making appropriate adjustments for local differences, that it is an India-wide system (Miller, 1986). We have seen that Pocock challenged this, seeking to restrict usage to a narrower conception of what constitute religious services. Commander, reviewing historical evidence from the 19th century, concluded that, apart from the Brahman-*jajman* relationship, there was no persuasive evidence that that was a 'system' 'flowing from the Hindu theory of the social order' (Commander, 1983, p. 310) or evident even at the micro-level (Commander, 1983, fn. 105). This point was made even more emphatically by Chris Fuller in an influential review article:

In my opinion, it is now time that the notion of a jajmani system, with its distinctive functionalist overtones, was abandoned once and for all .... these relationships and payments cannot all be subsumed within a single analytical category and they do not, even when taken together, define or constitute an integrated system. (Fuller, 1989, p. 41)

Sumit Guha made a particularly compelling argument against the existence of a system which emerges directly from the opposition of purity and impurity underlying the caste system in Dumont's influential analysis. Evidence from *The Committee on the Customary Rights to Scavenging* in 1966 found relations indistinguishable from *jajmani* which existed between households and the Untouchable [= Scheduled Caste, = Dalit] families which cleaned their dry latrines-one of the most-polluting activities (Guha, 2004, p. 89). Yet, these relations only existed in the western and central parts of Uttar Pradesh and other locations in central western India.

> The status of human faeces in the purity-pollution schema must be obvious. If jajmani was an institution designed to cope with this (and other) polluting substances, it should have been present almost everywhere. But contrary to Dumont's belief that jajmani was 'more or less universal' in India, the Committee found the 'old form' (or what anthropological literature described as jajmani) did not extend even to eastern Uttar Pradesh. (Guha, 2004, p. 89)

Essentially Religious or Economic? Harmonious or Exploitative?

In the accounts of Wiser and Dumont, there is an essential village harmony in *jajmani* relations because they are subsumed by the totality of the caste system and offer basic subsistence to all castes. Both, as we have seen, argued that because *jajmani* relations were traditional, payments were largely fixed in amounts of grain and involved reciprocity, they should be understood as being outside of individualistic market relationships. Orenstein, who studied a village in Maharashtra, also argued that the *baluta* system he found in operation there 'prevent[s] power from dominating interpersonal relations and thus to increase the feasibility of village solidarity' (Orenstein, 1962, p. 311).

By contrast, Sumit Guha cites 18th-century evidence from Maharashtra to show that well before British rule, conflicts over wages were common. '[C]onflict was always present, and recurred as individuals felt that they could exploit some fresh advantage' (Guha, 2004, p. 94).

Other scholars have questioned whether there is integrated harmony in *jajmani* relations. Susan Wadley, summing up her re-study of Karimpur, the village first studied by Wiser, observed: 'At the outset, we must recognize that the network of mutual obligations and dependencies related to *jajmani* and large landlords was based on exploitation of those who did not have primary tenancy rights' (Wadley, 1994, p. 251). Biedelman drew attention to the very unequal power relationships between landowning *jajmans* and their dependent *kamins* (Beidelman, 1959, pp. 31–50). The former wielded potential and actual coercive control over the latter.

> A *jajman* may coerce other castes as tenants or laborers; he may coerce them by his control of farm implements and oxen, carts, seed, food, pasture, forage, and sometimes even housesites and wells. (Beidelman, 1959, p. 74)

The near-total control which patrons exerted over their clients is well-illustrated by Ram Manohar Vikas et al. who studied a village in Bihar.

> [*Kamins*] had to get approvals from landlords before entering into economic transactions with others. The Jajmani system was so dominant that low castes had to either run away from the village or lose their lives if they violated this principle. Even the low caste artisans had to sell their produce through patron landlords, who acted as middlemen between producers and traders. (Vikas, Varman, and Belk, 2015, p. 478)

Nor were *jajmans* always constrained by existing religious restrictions on some activities. Biedelman cites examples in which services which were once deemed to be the religious monopolies of certain castes were taken over by their *jajmans* following disputes. When barbers protesting a reduction in traditional payments in one village refused to shave their *jajmans*, the latter bought safety razors and began to shave themselves. In a similar dispute, *jajmans* began to perform their own carpentry and blacksmithing. Yet others undertook night watchman duties, performed services such as drumming at ceremonies when Untouchable castes refused, and so forth (Beidelman, 1959, p. 67).

Henry Orenstein rejected the view that *jajmani* relations were exploitative. He studied *baluta* villages near Poona in Maharashtra and concluded that most payments allowed the service providers to make a profit when compared to market rates. Only the barber incurred a loss and might thus be considered to have been exploited by his patrons (Orenstein, 1962, p. 310). 'The nature of the *baluta* payment gives reason to view the system as contributing to village cohesion, and it provides some insight into the social asymmetry contained by the village' (Orenstein, 1962, p. 313). Orenstein himself notes that *balutedars* did not consider themselves to have a one-to-one relationship with individual landholders but rather 'to the village as a whole' (Orenstein, 1962, p. 314). On that basis, there are grounds for questioning whether *jajmani* relations were involved.

The significance of *jajmani* payments in kind from the grain-heap has also been contested. While there is recognition that payment in kind offered security, especially in hard times, there is ample evidence of *jajmans* seeking to reduce payments when market conditions would make it advantageous to put the share of their clients onto the market. Commander in particular argues that it is immaterial whether a wage is paid in kind or in cash; in either case there is a labour market which is uncompetitive and where wages are set by the relative strengths of *jajmans* and *kamins* (Commander, 1983, p. 305).

Geographic Distribution

Wiser believed that *jajmani* or its near equivalent existed in all parts of India (Wiser, 1958 [1936], p. ix) as did Dumont (Dumont, 1972, p. 144). Others, taking as their point of departure Hiroshi Fukazawa's detailed description of village servants in 18th-century

Maharashtra, questioned whether the one-to-one relationship between *jajman* and *kamin* was indeed found all over India (e.g. Commander, 1983; Fuller, 1989; Guha, 2004). In the *baluta* system, as described by Fukazawa, service castes were servants of the entire village and were compensated by the whole, often by grants of village land.

> Of the records I have consulted there is none which indicates that the *baluta*-servants in the Maharashtrian villages were employed by specific families in the village. Rather all of them show that they were servants of the village as a whole. (Fukazawa, 1972, p. 25)

Those who looked at economic relations in south Indian villages usually reported that *jajmani* relations did not exist. In a village in Andhra Pradesh, Dirk Bronger reported that patrons in the village were regularly re-distributed by clients every 5–8 years to ensure a more equal distribution of income (Bronger, 1975, p. 29).[3] Edward Harper described what he termed the 'Malnad system' which he found in Karnataka. In that system, most labourers were employed on short-term contracts for cash payments: 'the employer-employee relationship is characterized by intense bargaining and by instability of ties' (Harper, 1959, p. 767, also see Benson, 1976). There were, however, also some attached workers, tied to landlords by debt bondage (Harper, 1959, pp. 767–768, cf. attached labourers in the Kaveri Delta Mayer, 2006). Another to survey south Indian agricultural relations was Mayer who found that in pre-colonial Tamil Nadu cultivation was undertaken 'by hereditary classes of untouchable slaves and by hereditary share-croppers' (Mayer, 1993, p. 362). Like Fukazawa, Mayer found that village servants were precisely that: servants of entire villages, not individual patrons (Mayer, 1993, pp. 363–364).

Origin, Age of Jajmani

Wiser believed that the origins of the *jajmani* system which he studied in the early 1930s could be traced far back in pre-history:

> [it is] a system which is very similar to or identical with the religio-socio-economic plan of occupations outlined two thousand years ago by Hindu philosophers and lawmakers [such as Manu]. (Wiser, 1958 [1936], pp. 1–2)

Dumont, as we have seen, considered *jajmani* to be inseparable from the essential hierarchical principle on which the caste system was founded, perhaps 2,800 years ago (Dumont, 1972, p. 74).

---

[3] This is similar to the periodic re-distribution of landholdings found in villages in the Kaveri delta in Tamil Nadu (see Mayer, 1980).

Other authors have questioned whether we have evidence that the system is of such antiquity. Kathleen Gough argued that British colonialism had forcibly introduced a 'generalised capitalist market system' which wrought a 'profound and revolutionary change' in the existing society.

> [T]he jajmani system as a legal system was abolished whenever and wherever the British introduced the capitalist form of land ownership, even though some of its customary features persisted in areas of subsistence cultivation right up to the period of Independence. (Gough, 1960, p. 88)

Fuller argued that the historical evidence shows that the British rule did not introduce a major change in economic relations, because the pre-colonial Indian economy was not static.

> Market exchange was in fact an important feature and, most crucial in this context, there were significant internal developments, notably the changeover to cash revenue systems and the emergence of proprietary rights. (Fuller, 1989, p. 54)

Mayer concluded from a survey of historical documents and sources that there were no references to the *jajmani* system as described by Wiser before the middle of the 19th century. Prior to that, the evidence is that instead of an individual patron-client relationship, village artisans were considered 'village servants' and were employed by villages as wholes.

> what emerges consistently and clearly from these accounts of the relations between village cultivators and artisans is that the system which prevailed widely in north India, at least until the second half of the 19th century, was one in which the artisans and others like Chamars had general obligations of service to the entire class of village land-holders and were compensated for those services by all cultivators, either directly by payment at harvest time, or indirectly through grants of village land. (Mayer, 1993, p. 373, see also Neale, 1971, p. 224)

Mayer argued that, in all likelihood, the *jajmani* system became widespread only in the final quarter of the 19th century following population growth, legal changes in land ownership, and the emergence of alternative opportunities for employment of artisans in public works introduced by the British.

> There were ... two forces of change from whose convergence jajmani emerged. The first of these was the growing partition of zamindari and bhaiyachara [brotherhood] villages into individual holdings. The second was the mounting pressure on landholders to offer significant incentives to village artisans in order to retain their services. (Mayer, 1993, p. 385)

Mayer suggests, paradoxically, that *jajmani* relations may actually have had their origins in towns and cities and then spread out to villages (Mayer, 1993, p. 378).

Sumit Guha, while accepting Mayer's general thesis about the relatively recent origins of the *jajmani* system, argues that 'village servants' were themselves a relatively recent development in the areas under Maratha rule. In the 18th century the *baluta* form of village service was strongest in the relatively well-off regions of western Maharashtra, but almost unknown in poorer parts of contemporary Chhattisgarh. Where elements of *balutadari* were creeping in, the impetus was the possibility of securing 'rents' such as fines from the possession of hereditary office (Guha, 2004, pp. 98–101).

Only One Kind of Relationship, or Many?

In Wiser's initial account where each in turn might be master or servant, there appeared to be essentially a single form of the relationship. Pocock argued we should distinguish between two types of services specialists. The term *jajmani* should be restricted to services which deal with the impurities which arise in daily life. The others are those who provide a commodity (Pocock, 1962, p. 85). Gerald Berreman in his study of a Himalayan village reported that villagers distinguished four types of service relationships: *jajman* was restricted to the patron of a Brahman'; *gaikh* was used to describe a patron who purchases the services of another; a third form, for which no name was given, is reciprocal exchanges among artisans; finally, many services in his village were paid for either in cash or kind, on a piece-work or a daily wage rate (Berreman, 1962, pp. 388–389). Harold Gould reported that in his Uttar Pradesh village there were five distinct forms of payment to traditional specialists. The first was the payment by a patron to a Brahman; next were regular half-yearly grain payments to permanently engaged specialists; third were payments in kind or cash to permanently engaged specialists on a piecework basis; fourth were reciprocal payments between specialists; and last were payments in kind or cash on a piecework basis 'to any specialist who happens to be handy and is willing to provide a particular service' (Gould, 1964, p. 16). Gould notes that '... what has been conceived of as the ideal traditional economic relationship between a Hindu household and caste specialists is limited ... to a very small proportion of the entire spectrum of specialists' (Gould, 1964, p. 17).

Only in Kind, or Cash?

Another disputed topic is the significance, if any, of payments made in grain and those made in cash. For Wiser, payments of grain in customary amounts had a dual significance. Their relatively settled quantities, paid on a regular basis which did not correspond to the work performed, were evidence of a village-wide system ensuring the subsistence of all. The fact that they were fixed by custom and thus not the subject of negotiation was evidence that the village economy lay outside the world of the marketplace.

[F]ixed cash and kind payments [are] made in the village. They cannot be compared with payments made for similar kinds of work outside of the jajmani system ... The Jajman when he makes a cash payment thinks not in terms of value for value received, but that the payments together with certain concessions will give the 'kam karne-wala' his livelihood. (Wiser, 1958 [1936], p. 42)

For Dumont, too, regular payments to clients from the harvested grain heap were clear evidence that the encompassing whole of the caste system distinguished it utterly from the individualism of the capitalist market.

[D]istribution on the threshing floor is essentially different from a market in that it takes place in virtue of the fact that everyone is interdependent. If we look closely and see the farmer part with a significant portion of his crop for the benefit of a whole series of different people, we shall feel in the end that we are not in the world of the modern economic individual, but in a sort of cooperative where the main aim is to ensure the subsistence of everyone in accordance with his social function, almost to the extent of sharing out the produce of each piece of land. In the one case, the reference is to the *individual* pursuing his own gain, in the other to the *hierarchical collectivity*. (Dumont, 1972, p. 147)

The view of *jajmani* payments as being of a different world than those of the market was sharply contested by Simon Commander who reviewed a wide range of historical documents and contemporary village studies and concluded:

Enough evidence has been presented to demonstrate the wide variations in the rates of remuneration. Moreover, it is clear that such rates were closely determined by very local factors, the conditions of settlement, the distribution of power and, above all, the land/labour ratio and the state of labour supply. Recognizing this necessarily means that we should modify the original conception of customary grain payment. Rather than a time-honoured set of rates tending to equality, they appear on closer examination to be closely related to the type of labour, the quantity of labour power expended and the relative availability of labour. The fact that there is no formal adjustment vis-a-vis price does not really subvert the fact that what we are speaking about is a wage-in-kind, where the wage rate is determined, in the context of an improperly integrated market, by relative bargaining powers. (Commander, 1983, p. 304)

Other scholars also argued that individual economic rationality underpinned the *jajmani* system. Harold Gould, while noting that traditional economic relations continued in his U.P. village because they reinforced established relations of social status, nevertheless reported that

Relative to total grain and pea production ... the amount involved in traditional economic interaction is remarkably small-only 1.5 per cent of the gross harvest. (Gould, 1964, pp. 30–31)

Oscar Lewis, while arguing that *jajmani* was not a market-oriented system, did see that there were clear elements of economic rationality on the part of both patrons and clients. Clients preferred payment in kind because grain prices had risen greatly in the decade before he conducted his study of a Haryana village near New Delhi. For *jajmans* a 'major function of the *jajmani* system is to assure a stable labor supply for the dominant agricultural caste ... by limiting the mobility of the lower castes, especially those who assist in agricultural work' (Lewis, 1958, p. 57).

Bruce Caldwell noted that Lingayats in his Karnataka village did not believe that Hindu ideas of purity and impurity applied to them. They nevertheless had a small number of *jajmani*-like relations. Caldwell concluded that the most convincing reason they did so was 'the lack of cash and the easy availability of grain means that payment in kind is preferred, and the permanent tie ensures the provision of needed services' (Caldwell, 1991, p. 96).

Peter Mayer argued the market nature of jajmani relations was incontestable.

> what is striking about the new jajmani relations is that they so clearly took the form of property... in 1911 jajmani rights could be not only inherited but also transferred to another in lieu of dowry. By 1930 the United Provinces Provincial Banking Enquiry Committee found in Meerut that 'no less than 84 mortgages of jajmanis had been registered, most of which belonged to Bhangis, ... some belonged to Mahabrahmans..., whilst one was the purohiti of a Brahman'. (Mayer, 1993, p. 285)

Perspectives

Dissolution of Jajmani Relations

Even in his initial description of the *jajmani* system, Wiser recognized that the system was undergoing significant changes. Every subsequent village study has made similar findings. Wiser felt that centuries of rule by Muslim kings followed by British colonization, which introduced private land ownership and free public schools, had made the system which he had studied 'a corruption of the ancient system' of communal ownership (Wiser, 1958 [1936], pp. 110–112). Various castes were taking up aspects of agriculture which were once the specializations of specific castes. Castes such as merchants and goldsmiths were outside of *jajmani* relations. Above all, villagers were obtaining services and manufactured goods from nearby towns for which, of course, they paid in cash (Wiser, 1958 [1936], pp. 114–116). The 'system' which should provide livelihoods for all was failing to do so for most client families who of necessity worked in other jobs and outside the village (Wiser, 1958 [1936], pp. 117–121).

Wiser gives details of a telling incident in which a jajman in his village sought to profit from high international prices for grain by selling all in his granary. When his clients learned of this, they stopped his carts and distributed the traditional amount to each client, keeping a careful record of their actions. The furious *jajman* had his clients arrested, but a sympathetic Superintendent of Police let them off with a warning. 'If many jajmans treated their 'kam karnewalas' in this way the Hindu Jajmani System would soon break down' (Wiser, 1958 [1936], p. 116).

In a study of a village near Kanchipuram in Tamilnadu, Joan Mencher found 'considerable change as many traditional roles have acquired a more temporary contractual nature' (Mencher, 1970, p. 208). Brahman landowners were leaving the village to pursue urban employment. Other villagers were increasingly obtaining goods, including wooden plows, from nearby towns. 'Traditional economic roles for service castes are changing as modern technology ... including modern transportation, makes it feasible for both poor and middle-class people to resort to more impersonal services' (Mencher, 1970, p. 209).

Joseph Elder found in his study of a U.P. village that many service castes were greatly affected by economic change. Potters had given up their traditional trade in the face of competition from mass-produced metal vessels. Chamar leather-workers had given up skinning cattle and tanning hides because of its stigma and competition from factory-made shoes. In addition, the availability of galvanized steel buckets had replaced those of leather in field irrigation. There was less work for Carpenters, too; one family had turned its *jajmans* over to other families and set up a carpenter shop outside the village. 'It was better that one family leave the jajmani system and take its chances on the open market than for all the Barhais to starve slowly' (Elder, 1970, p. 13). The village Blacksmith family faced falling demand for their services in the face of competition from machine shops in the neighbouring town. The last Lohar informed his *jajmans* that he could no longer afford to perform their ironwork. Barbers were now performing shaves and haircuts for cash payments. The demand for the products of Oil Pressers had also largely been extinguished by petroleum lubricants and commercially available cooking oils. There were no Washermen in Elder's village, so residents made arrangements with Dhobis from other villages, paying either in kind or cash.[4]

Most striking of all, cheap hand pumps had devastated the income of Water Carriers. 'Once the price of a hand pump came within the range of the Jat families, its convenience spelled the end of the harvest grain payments to the Dimars, and with it the end of their core jajmani relationship' (Elder, 1970, p. 121).

The only relationship which did not seem threatened by technological competition was the service of the Brahman.

> So long as people view rituals and ceremonies as an important part of their lives, and so long as Brahmans are the only ones trained to perform these rituals and ceremonies, their services will be needed. (Elder, 1970, p. 121)

---

[4] Berreman found similar changes in his Himalayan village (Berreman, 1962, p. 390).

Elder concluded: 'as a rule, where core jajmani relationships have ended in the face of competitive technology, the terminating initiative has come from the jajman [patrons] rather than the kam karnewala workers' (Elder, 1970, pp. 122–123).

S. G. Sapre and colleagues at the Gokhale Institute of Politics and Economics resurveyed a Nasik District village in 1960–1961 which had previously been studied in 1939–1940. They found that the introduction of irrigation had led to an increase in the production of commercial crops such as onions, sugarcane, and groundnuts (peanuts) and a decline in the production of cereal crops such as wheat and bajri (Sapre, 1962, p. 243). This change in cropping pattern had severe consequences for artisans who received traditional *baluta* payments as shares of the cereal crop: 'the share of the baluta in the total produce has nearly halved during the intervening period' (Sapre, 1962, p. 243). While payments for a few artisans such as the rope-maker and the potter had not changed greatly, payments to washermen, barbers, and others had shrunk considerably (Sapre, 1962, p. 246). In the case of the barbers, an emerging preference for more sophisticated, urban styles of haircutting were a cause of patrons ceasing to use their services. In addition, the state government in Maharashtra had abolished *vatan* land grants which once supported village servants. Sapre concluded that urbanization and the growth of mechanization in agriculture would in time result in the elimination of the baluta system (Sapre, 1962, p. 246).

That, indeed, is what M. P. Kaushal found in a study of a village in Patiala, Punjab. Mechanized farmers displayed attitudes of

> Prodigality, profit motivation, lack of interest in family and community traditions and a preference for kinship rather than for caste or community ... Agriculture for them carries an economic value and is a source of livelihood rather than a communal undertaking or a source of community participation .... [They] now have a greater dependence upon the urban centres for their implements, their repairs and maintenance and many other occupational requirements. (Kaushal, 1972, p. 56)

The consequence of these changes in technology and attitude were predictable: former service castes 'agreed that the indifferent attitudes of the mechanized farmers and their commercial outlook on life had affected the community's solidarity and its other aspects of social life' (Kaushal, 1972, p. 56). The loss of traditional payments and entitlements produced an interesting reaction among the lower-ranked castes: they were 'more united and willing to participate and bargain with other castes not as individuals but through their leaders' (Kaushal, 1972, p. 59). Overall, *jajmani* relations, where they persisted, had shrunk to minimal obligations on both sides; patrons made no informal concessions to clients and clients gave no informal help to patrons 'in any sphere except those covered by contract' (Kaushal, 1972, p. 61).

Tom Kessinger, in his study of Vilyatpur in the Punjab between 1848 and 1968, traces changes in the village's *sepidar* system over the course of a century. Artisans rose from 10 per cent of men of working age in 1848 to 14 per cent in 1922. Wages for many artisans also increased in that period.

Since the nineteen twenties, however, the *sepidar* system (for agricultural labor) has slowly disintegrated ... [permanent employment] has been replaced by annual agreements on the amount of work expected and the rate of compensation received ... By 1947 the last vestiges of the system had disappeared for agricultural labor, the yearly contracts giving way to daily arrangements at cash rates for certain jobs and piece-work rates for others. (Kessinger, 1974, pp. 123–124, 156ff.)

Vikas recounts sweeping changes in his Bihar village. Most service castes have freed themselves from the domination of their former *jajmans* by setting up small businesses and migration. At the state level, lower caste political parties have captured political power, challenging the dominance of once all-powerful upper castes. With their newfound wealth and independence, they have begun to set standards for conspicuous consumption in the village. A village Brahman now prefers to serve these lower castes because they pay more and don't expect him to provide services for free the way his old *jajmans* do (Vikas, Varman, and Belk, 2015, p. 488). Some Bhumihar landlords who have remained in the village are now economically worse off and no longer able to either dominate or set social standards (Vikas et al., 2015, pp. 479–490).

Susan Wadley too, in her re-study of Karimpur, the village first studied by Wiser, found that the *jajmani* system had largely lapsed by 1984. She emphasized the importance of government programs of education and reservation for former Untouchables. She quotes the observations on social changes made by Mohan, an elderly Brahman landowner:

These people don't work that much any more. Moreover, in former times these people were poor and weak. So they were happy with what we gave to them. They were satisfied. But now the government has moved these people ahead and we have been pulled back. Now these people have reached where we were and we have reached where they were. Now they have no need for us. Just suppose-earlier, if a Midwife man or Shepherd came to my door in the evening, and the poor fellow was hungry and I was cutting fodder for the animals, I would say,"-All right, sit down, cut the fodder."- I would go inside and bring out some vegetables, lentils and four breads to give him. He would cut my fodder and throw it to the animals. But nowadays, those who used to come to us for two breads don't need to. They don't need the breads. This is because their seats [in schools and government jobs] have been reserved [set aside for the scheduled castes]. Because of Jagjivan Ram [a leader of the Untouchables], they got their seats reserved. We are small in numbers, so we get only one seat while these people get ten of fifteen seats. So these people have become big men now, and they know that they are big. They get money; they help in reading and writing. So why would they cut our fodder for our two breads? This is the situation. (Wadley, 1994, p. 220)

In these accounts of the dissolution of the *jajmani* system in post-Independence India we can see that in many cases village patrons were responding to changes wrought by technology and growing access to markets. In a few cases, *jajmani* relations were retained because they were perceived to be integral to the functioning of caste *as a system*. It is possible, as Pocock suggested, that the original relationship between Brahman and *jajman* was also the last to succumb to the forces of change. In some villages, that too, was subject to change: in Karimpur, Wadley reported that a man of the Cultivator caste was now performing marriages, once a Brahman monopoly (Wadley, 1994, p. 247).

Mayer, in summing up his argument that the *jajmani* system itself was of late 19th century origins, concluded that '[l]ike many transitional systems of labour relationships, the jajmani system was in dissolution almost from its coming into being' (Mayer, 1993, p. 386). By the third decade of the 21st century, that dissolution is virtually complete.

References

Beidelman, T. O. 1959. 'A Comparative Analysis of the *Jajmani* System'. In *Monographs of the Association of Asian Studies*. Locust Valley, NY: J.J. Augustin Inc. for the Association for Asian Studies.

Benson, Janet. 1976. 'A South Indian Jajmani System'. *Ethnology*, 15(3): 239–250. DOI: 10.2307/3773133.

Berreman, G. D. 1962. 'Caste and Economy in the Himalayas'. *Economic Development and Cultural Change*, 10(4): 386–394.

Bronger, Dirk. 1975. 'Jajmani System in Southern India'. *Journal of the Indian Anthropological Society*, 10: 1–38.

Caldwell, Bruce. 1991. 'The Jajmani System: An Investigation'. In M. N. Srinivas (Ed.), *Studies in Sociology and Social Anthropology*. Delhi: Hindustan Publishing Corporation.

Commander, Simon. 1983. 'The Jajmani System in North India: An Examination of Its Logic and Status across Two Centuries'. *Modern Asian Studies*, 17(2): 283–311. DOI: 10.1017/s0026749x0001564x.

Dumont, Louis. 1972. *Homo Hierarchicus: The Caste System and Its Implications*. London: Paladin.

Elder, Joseph W. 1970. 'Rajpur: Change in the Jajmani System of an Uttar Pradesh Village'. In K. Ishwaran (Ed.), *Change and Continuity in India's Villages*. New York: Columbia University Press.

Fukazawa, Hiroshi. 1972. 'Rural Servants in the 18th Century Maharashtrian Village—Demiurgic or Jajmani System?' *Hitotsubashi Journal of Economics*, 12(2): 14–40.

Fuller, C. J. 1989. 'Misconceiving the Grain Heap: A Critique of the Concept of the Indian Jajmani System'. In J. Parry and M. Bloch (Eds.), *Money and the Morality of Exchange*. Cambridge: Cambridge University Press.

Gough, Kathleen. 1960. 'The Hindu Jajmani System'. *Economic Development and Cultural Change*, IX(1, Part 1): 83–91.

Gould, H. A. 1964. 'A Jajmani System of North India: Its Structure, Magnitude, and Meaning'. *Ethnology*, 3(1): 12–41. DOI: 10.2307/4617554.

Guha, Sumit. 2004. 'Civilisations, Markets and Services: Village Servants in India from the Seventeenth to the Twentieth Centuries'. *Indian Economic Social History Review*, 41(1): 79–101.

Harper, Edward B. 1959. 'Two Systems of Economic Exchange in Village India'. *American Anthropologist*, 61: 760–778.

Kaushal, M. P. 1972. 'The Mechanisation of Agriculture and Its Effect on the Jajmani System in the Punjab'. *Pacific Viewpoint*, 13(1): 49–61.

Kessinger, Tom G. 1974. *Vilyatpur 1848–1968: Social and Economic Change in a North Indian Village*. Berkeley: University of California Press.

Kolenda, Pauline Mahar. 1963. 'Toward a Model of the Hindu Jajmani System'. *Human Organization*, 22(1): 11–31. DOI: 10.17730/humo.22.1.x011620468995q1j.

Lewis, Oscar. 1958. *Village Life in North India*. Urbana: University of Illinois Press.

Mann, Harold H. 1917. *Land and Labour in a Deccan Village*. London and Bombay: Oxford University Press.

Mayer, Peter. 1980. 'The Penetration of Capitalism in a South Indian District: The First 60 Years of Colonial Rule in Tiruchirapalli'. *South Asia*, III(2): 1–24. DOI: 10.1080/00856408008723003.

Mayer, Peter. 1993. 'Inventing Village Tradition—The Late-19th-Century Origins of the North Indian "Jajmani System"'. *Modern Asian Studies*, 27: 357–395. DOI: 10.1017/s0026749x00011537.

Mayer, Peter. 2006. 'Trends of Real Income in Tiruchirapalli and the Upper Kaveri Delta, 1819–1980: A Footnote in Honour of Dharma Kumar'. *Indian Economic and Social History Review*, 43(3): 349–364.

Mencher, Joan P. 1970. 'A Tamil Village: Changing Socioeconomic Structure in Madras State'. In K. Ishwaran (Ed.), *Change and Continuity in India's Villages* (pp. 197–218). New York and London: Columbia University Press.

Miller, Daniel. 1986. 'Exchange and Alienation in the Jajmani System'. *Journal of Anthropological Research*, 42(4): 535–556. DOI: 10.1086/jar.42.4.3630107.

Neale, Walter C. 1971. 'Reciprocity and Redistribution in the Indian Village: Sequel to Some Notable Discussions'. In Karl Polanyi, Conrad M. Arensberg, and Harry W. Pearson (Eds.), *Trade & Market in the Early Empires*. Chicago: Chicago: Henry Regnery Company.

Nesfield, John C. 1885. *Brief View of the Caste System of the North-Western Provinces and Oudh*. Allahabad: North-Western Provinces and Oudh Government Press.

Orenstein, Henry. 1962. 'Exploitation or Function in the Interpretation of Jajmani'. *Southwestern Journal of Anthropology*, 18(4): 302–316. DOI: 10.1086/soutjanth.18.4.3628985.

Pocock, David F. 1962. 'Notes on Jajmani Relationships'. *Contributions to Indian Sociology*, 6: 78–95.

Sapre, S. G. 1962. 'A Study of Changes in the Baluta-Payments Over the Last Two Decades in an Irrigated Village in the Nasik District'. *Artha Vijnana*, 4(3): 242–252.

Tandon, Prakash. 1968. *Punjabi Century, 1857–1947*. Berkeley: University of California Press.

Vikas, Ram Manohar, Rohit Varman, and Russell W. Belk. 2015. 'Status, Caste, and Market in a Changing Indian Village'. *Journal of Consumer Research*, 42: 427–497. DOI: 10.1093/jcr/ucv038.

Wadley, Susan S. 1994. *Struggling with Destiny in Karimpur, 1925–1984*. Berkeley: University of California Press.

Wilson, H. H. 1968 [1855]. *A Glossary of Judicial and Revenue Terms and of Useful Words Occurring in Official Documents Relating to the Administration of the Government of British India*. Delhi: Munshiram Manoharlal.

Wiser, William Henricks. 1958 [1936]. *The Hindu Jajmani System*. Lucknow, UP: Lucknow Publishing House.

Wiser, William H., and Charlotte Viall Wiser. 1963. *Behind Mud Walls, 1930–1960*. Berkeley: University of California Press.

CHAPTER 4

CASTE AND CAPITAL

CAROL UPADHYA

MAX Weber, writing in the late- 19th century, was perhaps the first major scholar to consider the question of caste and capital. In *Religion of India* (1958; originally published in 1916), Weber identified the caste system as the major impediment to the emergence of industrial capitalism in India. Although he recognized that traditional mercantile communities (or castes) had long been engaged in sophisticated trading and financial transactions in the sub-continent and across Asia, he argued that India's vibrant precolonial economy failed to develop into modern capitalism in part because of the rigid occupational structure and ritualism of the caste system. While Weber's analysis of capitalism highlighted its cultural and ethical foundations in the Protestantism of particular European countries, Marx (1969) too presumed that the strict social hierarchies of India's ancient civilization would disintegrate under the onslaught of colonial capitalism.

Modern scholarship has moved far beyond these Eurocentric theories of capitalist development, for instance by showing that industrialization in England was built on the destruction of flourishing 'proto-industrial' economies of the 'East'. However, revisionist economic histories of India have largely ignored caste, even as they have documented the sophisticated commercial activities of precolonial merchant groups and their displacement or solidification under colonial rule. Tirthankar Roy (2010), for instance, draws on institutional economics to describe the corporate structuring of the Indian economy without specifically invoking a theory of caste. Christopher Bayly (1975), in his work on the early colonial period, highlights several key elements of merchant culture, including the importance of the family in marshalling, and preserving financial resources and the role of social networks in the establishment of trust and credit relations (Kudsaiya, 2016, p. 264). Yet Bayly (1983) and other prominent historians such as Sanjay Subrahmanyam (1990) argue that caste played little role in the operations of the 'portfolio capitalists' who were key players in the early colonial economy (Subrahmanyam and Bayly, 1988).

In contrast, sociologists have been more interested in the role of caste in economic organization and development, yet much of the sociological literature has been straightjacketed by the foundational binaries that opposed 'economy' to 'culture'—class/status group, modernity/tradition, achievement/ascription, and so on. In academic scholarship as well as in political and legal institutions, caste was largely relegated to sphere of culture or religion and emptied of its material content, in what Natrajan (2012) terms the 'culturalization of caste'. Ritu Birla (2009) traces this discursive split to colonial writings and governance systems, which separated culture from the domain of the economy and equated 'culture' with 'tradition', which in turn was counterposed to liberal capitalism based on British laws of contract (cf. Viswanath, 2014). This conceptual scaffolding deeply shaped academic research on Indian society and economy from the 1950s until recently, and was elaborated particularly in the work of Louis Dumont (1981) who theorized the 'caste system' as a distinctive form of social structure rooted in religious ideology and radically different from the class-based social hierarchies of the West. Within this framework, the main question became—how are these different dimensions of stratification interconnected or inflect one another (see chapter on *Caste and Class*, this volume)—rather than asking how caste might be *constitutive of* capital or class. Consequently, mainstream scholarly literature on the Indian economy as well as policy debates have tended to ignore the question of caste, despite its clearly central role in the organization of economic activities (Jodhka, 2012, 2016; Mosse, 2018). As Mosse (2020, p. 1262) argues:

> ... the neo-liberal framing of social transformation separates out caste as a matter of religion/culture or special-interest politics, making it harder to acknowledge caste as a social structure of the modern market economy itself that works to help some get ahead and sorely burdens others, as indeed does the way of talking or *not* talking about caste.

More recently, scholars have attempted to destabilize the economy-culture binary by pointing to the numerous ways in which caste is implicated in processes of capital accumulation and class formation, yet the view of caste as somehow premodern and antithetical to capitalist development still casts a long shadow over academic scholarship. In this essay I elaborate this argument by summarizing several bodies of literature that have explored the multifarious entanglements of caste and capital in South Asia. The next section discusses the early stream of studies on the organization and activities of India's 'traditional' business communities. In this literature, caste is largely understood as a social formation that facilitates economic transactions and accumulation within relatively closed spheres, enabling particular groups to monopolize specific economic domains. In the third section, I review work that views caste more broadly as a form of 'social capital' or 'structure of accumulation' that works in different ways to facilitate the generation and preservation of capital by some groups while disadvantaging others. While these rich bodies of work illustrate the varied ways in which caste and the market are entangled, in the final section I turn to scholarship that challenges received categories of thought and attempts to locate capital within caste in a more fundamental way.

Caste and Commerce

Many observers have noted that business activities in India are concentrated in the hands of a few mercantile communities, and that most of the major industrial houses have emerged from the family businesses of 'traditional' mercantile communities. The tendency for production and trade to be organized through social ties of community and kinship, and the historical monopolization of economic niches by particular groups, is often traced to the *varna* system that designates a separate category of merchants (Vaisya) within the four-fold scaffolding of 'Hindu' society. The fact that the Vaisya is given third rank, below the Brahmin and the Kshatriya, is often cited as evidence that commerce is devalued in Hindu ideology relative to religious and political authority—reinforcing the Orientalist argument about India's fundamental difference from the West (Chakrabarty, 2000; Dumont, 1981).

Studies of South Asian mercantile communities carried out in the 1960s and 1970s (many inspired by Weber's Protestant Ethic thesis) explored their histories, social organization and business practices, providing us with in-depth accounts of the role of caste in the economy. These scholars documented the tight-knit social fabric that structured commercial operations; the institutions that facilitated financial and trade transactions, often across long distances; and the role of endogamy and strategic marriage alliances in the consolidation of business relations (Fox, 1967; Hazlehurst, 1966; Mahadevan, 1978). Timberg's (1978) classic study of the Marwaris traced the history of their migration out of Rajasthan and their establishment as a major mercantile and banking ('moneylending') community across India, showing how they captured certain domains of trade and finance. Other studies explored how caste networks enabled business transactions and capital accumulation by easing access to credit, markets, labour, and capital (Tripathi, 1984). More recent studies have similarly highlighted the role of kinship and caste relations in the management of risk and in helping new entrepreneurs set up businesses, as well as the organizational advantages of the 'joint family system' (Cadene and Vidal, 1997; Kudaisya, 2016; Tripathi and Jumani, 2013).

Under the sway of modernization theory, these early scholars were especially interested in tracing the emergence of industrial entrepreneurship within the mercantile castes (Lamb, 1955; Nafziger, 1975; Singer, 1973; Tripathi, 1971). They also investigated the hypothesis that the significance of 'traditional' social institutions in economic life would wither away with the advance of modern capitalism, which is supposedly structured by impersonal contractual ties and markets based on individual self-interest. For instance, in his work on merchant castes in Chennai, Mattison Mines argued that 'impersonal contractual relationships, law and governmental bureaucracy' were replacing personal ties (Mines, 1994, p. 79, cited in Harriss, 2003, p. 758). This formulation reflects the popular notion that Indian business culture is characterized by 'selective trust' (rather than generalized trust in institutions and law) due to the predominance of family control, which in turn stems from the 'cellularity' of Indian society (Saberwal, 1996, p. 39, cited in Harriss, 2003, p. 759). Against such culturalist arguments, Harriss suggests that the language of 'trust' often conceals relationships of power—both within and between firms (Harriss, 2003, p. 769)—as in the antagonistic relations between 'untouchable' Jatav producers and high caste dealers in the leather footwear cluster of Agra (Knorringa, 1996). However, Harriss also concludes from his study of entrepreneurs in Ahmedabad and Chennai that 'selective trust' is being eroded by the professionalization of business practices under the influence of globalization.

In contrast to the dominant framing of caste as somehow extraneous to economic activity, David Rudner (1995) argues explicitly that capitalism in India is (and has long been) embedded in caste. In his historical anthropology of the Nattukottai Chettiars of Tamil Nadu, he shows how caste served as an institution of banking and trade, and conversely how 'a specific financial institution functioned as a caste' (1995, p. 7). Rudner details how structures of caste and kinship as well as marriage alliances and temple donations facilitated long-distance trade and financial activities, allowing the Nakarattars to dominate segments of the maturing colonial economy. Contrary to the mainstream view of caste as the fundamental structure of Indian society through which economic activities may or may not be organized, he suggests that the social organization and practices of the Nakarattar community were deeply shaped by their commercial activities. Thus, far from being incompatible with modern capitalism, Rudner presents the Chettiar example as a 'corporate' form of capitalism, in the sense that they act as a group in the accumulation and distribution of capital.

It is important to note here that it was not only mercantile (Hindu) *castes* that flourished under colonial rule—other kinds of (religious/regional) communities also emerged as key players in particular sectors, such as the Gujarati and Marwari Jains, the Parsis, the Muslim Bohras, and the Sindhi diaspora (Markovits, 2000, 2008)—all wealthy trading and industrial communities of western India—which suggests that the significance of community in Indian business extends beyond caste *per se*. The example of the Parsis is particularly noteworthy—a religious and ethnic minority, they became successful merchants through their links with the colonial state, and later established themselves as major industrialists and business entrepreneurs of postcolonial India (Desai, 1968; Luhrmann, 1996). These studies suggest that strong social networks, binding moral norms, and a common social identity are important in building mutual trust and coordinating commercial transactions, which in turn helps to sequester and multiply wealth within the community.

However, a strong community identity, shared values, and relations of trust are not simply by-products of caste organization—they are crucial ingredients of business relations that are actively created and sustained through various social strategies. The

Marwaris provide a key example. Popularly imagined as a long-standing and solidary 'caste' or community with strong social boundaries, the Marwaris had no social existence prior to the early 20th century. It was only after moving out their home region to different parts of India that members of disparate merchant *jatis* of Rajasthan began to create the social and political associations that united them as a 'community' under this label. Hardgrove (2004) traces the adoption of the term 'Marwari' (which was used by local elites a negative way to refer to these migrant merchants) by community leaders in colonial Calcutta to construct a powerful business class out of disparate social components. Birla's (2009) later study of the Marwaris further illustrates how they engaged with the colonial state and law to carve out a key place for themselves within the modernizing economy.

The ideological and social strategies that were employed to create 'the Marwaris' as the most prominent indigenous trading and mercantile community of India find echoes in the present, as Ponniah (2017) demonstrates in her ethnography of the Aggarwals of Delhi. She documents the role of Aggarwal women in producing and maintaining caste and family relations and sustaining a common cultural identity—elements that are crucial to the success of Aggarwal family businesses.

The colonial period also saw the refashioning of non-mercantile castes into new 'business communities'. A notable example are the Patels (or Patidars) of central and western Gujarat, an agricultural and landowning caste which began to consolidate and reinvent itself as a higher caste merchant community by emulating the cultural and business practices of Gujarati *banias*. Through outward migration, Patels became significant actors in the trade across the Indian Ocean (Guha, 2013, p. 191). This trend continued after Independence as Patels spread out from Gujarat to the UK, North America, and Africa and established themselves as small traders and businessmen, creating strong cross-border networks which in turn facilitated additional migration and entrepreneurial activity within the community (Lyon and West, 1995; Oonk, 2013; Poros, 2011; Rutten, 2008). The gradual monopolization of particular domains of business in the US by Patels—such as motels and newspaper kiosks—shows how 'caste' continues to structure Indian business beyond the sub-continent (Dhingra, 2012). Similarly, 'Kathiawari' Kanbi Patels from Saurashtra shifted from their business specialization in cutting and polishing diamonds in Surat to enter international trade, displacing the Palanpur Jains who had earlier become key players in the diamond trade between Surat, Mumbai, and Antwerp (Engelshoven, 1999; Munshi, 2007; Tumbe, 2017). Transnational caste networks allowed these groups to gain control over a notoriously secretive, high-value business that depends heavily on personal relations and trust. The spatial expansion and reconfiguration of caste as it becomes a vehicle of commerce and business organization, in the past (Chettiars) as well as the present (Gujarati Jains and Patels), points to its malleability and multi-functionality as a social structure of accumulation.

Planned economic development in the postcolonial period expanded the range of non-Vaisya groups entering business and industry in India, often building on pre-existing forms of capital (especially land), as well as on expertise gained through hereditary occupations such as toddy-tapping (Hardgrave, 1970) and weaving (Haynes, 2012; Mines, 1984). Harish Damodaran, in *India's New Capitalists: Caste, Business, and Industry in a Modern Nation* (2008), provides a comprehensive account of the formation of new business communities from castes whose traditional occupation was not commerce. He shows how the monopoly of some mercantile groups in several arenas of business was slowly eroded by the entry of landowning agrarian castes such as the Kammas and Reddys of Andhra Pradesh, the Patidars and Marathas in western India, and Naidus and Gounders in Kongunad (Tamil Nadu); upper caste groups such as the Khatris; 'lower' caste groups such as the Nadars of Tamil Nadu; as well as various Muslim groups and the Syrian Christians of Kerala. While his survey demonstrates that the social base of capital accumulation widened after independence, it also suggests a loosening of the connections between caste and business. Damodaran uses the term 'business community' to describe these groups, but it is important to note that within new entrepreneurial groups such as the Gounders and Kammas, only a minority are business owners, in contrast to mercantile castes for whom 'business' (large or small) is usually the main occupation of most members.

Caste networks have been important for the operations of these 'new capitalists' as well (Chari, 2004a; Rutten, 1995; Rutten and Upadhya, 1997; Upadhya, 1988, 1997a), but caste and modes of accumulation may differ from what has been described for 'traditional' mercantile castes. Thus, rather than understanding caste as a pre-existing social structure that may support or hinder processes of capital accumulation in specific ways, it may be more usefully regarded as a flexible and adaptable form of sociality and identity (or social and cultural capital) that is variously deployed, reconstituted, or reconfigured for different purposes (Upadhya, 1997b).

Caste as Social Network

Although it is well known that capital and other resources are unequally distributed along the lines of caste (yet not entirely in synch with the ritual caste hierarchy), the question of caste and the economy is often regarded as merely a distributional one—a problem of 'discrimination' (most notably, Deshpande, 2011)—rather than a structural one. To explain its distributional effects, caste is usually conceptualized as a kind of social network that creates economic effects or differential outcomes. For instance, economists have noted that spatially dispersed caste networks may serve as a source of insurance (Munshi and Rosenzweig, 2009), suggesting that these networks compensate for market imperfections (Witsoe, 2017, p. 42). Several popular commentators have even lauded the role of caste as valuable 'social capital' that promotes entrepreneurship and business success—for instance, by facilitating trust and credit relations.

However, the operation of caste networks in the economy also creates exclusionary effects. Alha's (2018) study of entrepreneurs in a Rajasthan industrial estate maps the ways in which caste membership allows some groups to monopolize business opportunities, reinforcing structural inequalities. Similarly, strong caste-based networks enabled Gounders to succeed in the Tiruppur knitwear industry (Chari, 2004a) while also creating barriers to entry for entrepreneurs from other castes—especially Dalits (Vijaybaskar and Kalaiyarasan, 2014). According to Mosse:

> ... modern caste persists in the age of the market because of its advantages – its discriminations are opportunities for others, although rarely examined as such ... Caste is a resource, perhaps best conceived as a network, in part of actual or potential kin; a network of enormous durability and spatial reach ... offering protection (social insurance), access (to jobs, business, the state), mediation (of disputes) and control (over resources), beyond state regulation (Mosse, 2018, p. 430).

Bandyopadhyay and Samaddar (2017) suggest that organizational analysis would be useful here, by focusing on how caste operates in key elements of capital accumulation such as managing capital-labour relations and sourcing finance. Revisiting the case of Mahisya entrepreneurs in Howrah's engineering industry first documented by Owens and Nandy (1977), they trace the role of caste in supply chains, business networks, property transfers, and other factors that create durable market positions.

One might have expected the growth of the private sector after the economic reforms of the 1990s to have weakened the role of caste in the economy, but empirical studies suggest otherwise (Deshpande, 2011; Iyer, Khanna, and Varshney, 2013). Caste networks and family control over business continue to be central to the generation and multiplication of wealth and economic power even in the 'formal economy', especially by maintaining control over markets and capital (Munshi, 2016). Members of mercantile castes still predominate in the ownership and control of large corporate organizations (Naudet and Dubost, 2016; Naudet et al., 2018). A study of 1000 companies found that 92.6 per cent of board members of Indian corporate houses are from upper castes, while OBCs constituted 3.8 per cent and members of SC and ST communities 3.5 per cent (Ajit et al., 2012, p. 41).

In these discussions, the intimate connection between caste and kinship is often elided—the relations that are labelled as 'caste' might be better understood as kinship ties. Jodhka and Manor (2017) point to the crucial role of kinship networks in urban business and in the reproduction of inequalities, as caste- and kinship-based communities try to preserve their monopolies in particular sectors of the economy: 'Kinship networks matter as social capital, as resources that help in mobilizing other forms of capital, such as bank loans and access to networks required for a successful urban business' (2017, p. 7). In the higher echelons of the corporate sector, for instance, we find the children of owners of major business houses marrying across caste or regional lines—suggesting that in forming business alliances, at some level class and capital may trump caste.

Nonetheless, the unequal distribution of capital and resources along the lines of caste creates unequal possibilities for business enterprise and economic mobility—in particular, for Dalits and other marginalized groups who are relatively excluded from participating in valuable productive or commercial activities. As Prakash argues, 'caste identity can confer an unfair advantage or disadvantage (depending on one's caste location) vis-à-vis one's competitors in the market. Therefore, caste in its contemporary form is often deployed to manage competition in the market in a manner which is mostly detrimental to the economic interests of Dalits' (2018, pp. 58–59). Across economic sectors, capital and wealth (such as land and financial resources) remain largely in the hands of the 'upper' castes, while the '"lowest" castes participate in the economy primarily as wage laborers' (Mosse, 2018, p. 423).

These effects of caste are reinforced by the fact that most economic activity in India remains in the informal sector, which is regulated through social structures of gender, religion, and caste (Harriss-White, 2003, p. 241; Mosse, 2018, p. 430). Barbara Harriss-White (2003) has elaborated the concept of 'social structures of accumulation' to integrate the social dimensions of caste and gender into her analysis of the informal economy (also see Basile and Harriss-White, 2001). She argues that caste

> ... has a perplexing capacity to dissolve, as ascriptive characteristics give way to acquired ones (such as skills, compliance and trust, experience and creative competence), and as capital becomes mobile. But at the same time it persists and transforms itself as a regulative structure of the economy—sometimes in the same site (Harriss-White and Vidyarthee, 2010, p. 318).

Harriss-White highlights the operations of caste in the organization of production and distribution, which creates structures of disadvantage as well as accumulation (2003, p. 239).

An emerging body of literature on Dalit entrepreneurship has documented the strong barriers faced by Dalits, such as restricted access to business networks, capital, finance, infrastructure, and supply chains, and markets controlled by other castes (Harriss-White et al., 2014). Mosse points out that Dalit businesses are mostly 'survival-oriented rather than entrepreneurial businesses, owner-operated or reliant on family labor, without formal credit, and mostly rural and male' (2018, p. 429). Prakash's (2015) study of Dalit entrepreneurs illustrates the mechanisms and consequences of exclusion from crucial networks. While the share of enterprises owned by Dalits has risen since 2005, and there has been some diversification in rural areas, 'prejudice still enclaves Dalit businesses in towns and cities' (Mosse, 2018, p. 429). Caste inequalities in ownership of private enterprises are evident in NSSO and other official data sources as well (Thorat, Kundu, and Sadana, 2010). These observations call into question the hopes placed on 'Dalit capitalism' by actors such as the Dalit Indian Chamber of Commerce and the state (Mosse, 2018, p. 429; Prakash, 2018). For critics, this expectation (voiced mainly by Dalit elites) that participation in the formal economy would be liberating fails to recognize the situation of most Dalits (Vidyarthee, 2016, cited in Mosse, 2018, p. 431). Gopal Guru (2012) calls the celebration of the rise of Dalit millionaires a 'low intensity spectacle' that arises from corporate patronage and operates as an ideological justification for neoliberalism.

Summarizing this literature, Mosse (2018, p. 429) identifies three major 'caste effects' on business: (1) network effects, (2) the ranking of markets, and (3) caste exclusion and barriers. Caste networks are particularly important where risks are high, such as in the diamond industry in Mumbai and Antwerp (Munshi, 2011, cited in Mosse, 2018, p. 429), and in 'shunned markets' dominated by Dalits such as leather, sanitary ware, and cleaning services (Jodhka, 2010, cited in Mosse, 2018, p. 429). However, mapping the effects of caste networks is not a straightforward process—recent quantitative and formal analyses of social networks highlight the variability and complexity of networks, for instance in the ownership and control of Indian businesses (Mani and Moody, 2014; Naudet and Dubost, 2016; Naudet et al., 2018). Clearly, caste does not structure markets in a uniform way, but has variable effects and modalities across different domains such as the corporate sector, land and real estate markets, trade, agriculture, and so on.

More broadly, networks may maintain caste dominance and exclusion of others not only through control over material resources but also the use of violence. Gupta (1998) points to the shift from patronage-based caste dominance based on land ownership to 'brokerage' based on control over development resources in independent India, which created a nexus between local landowning elites, politicians, bureaucrats, and contractors—networks that were often based on caste connections (Witsoe, 2017, p. 43). Witsoe's (2017) work on Bihar shows how dominant caste networks work to capture and control particular economic activities and resources, especially through connections with the state: 'Caste networks connect regional business activities with politics, provide members with influence over government institutions and access to "muscle", shaping the regional political economy' (Witsoe, 2017, p. 39). His case studies of caste networks in the 'sand mafia' and 'cooperative mafia' underline the 'materiality of caste' (2017, p. 56).

According to Mosse (2018), although caste is well-recognized as a source of social exclusion and everyday humiliation, its role in governing access to economic opportunities has been relatively neglected in social policy as well as anti-caste struggles. This is because caste, 'reworked as private connections and capital, is not so easily perceived as such, even by those affected' (Mosse, 2018, p. 427). But Mosse also points to the limitations of conceptualizing caste mainly as a social network, an understanding that ignores the effects of circulating cultural and political discourses as well as the ways in which power operates through such networks (2018, p. 432). He argues that caste should instead be understood as a key social structure of the modern market economy.

Rethinking Caste Through Capital

Moving beyond questions about how caste enables or limits capital accumulation, several scholars have attempted to rethink the categories of caste and capital more fundamentally, 'putting caste back' into our understanding of capitalism in India and trying to unsettle the conceptual straitjacket discussed at the beginning of this essay. Rather than asking how caste (as a social/cultural phenomenon) facilitates or hinders market participation, we might explore the various ways caste and capital (as structure and practice) are co-constituted and embedded in one another.

Chari's (2004a, 2004b) study of the transition of Gounder cultivators into a class of industrial capitalists in the Tiruppur knitwear industry of Tamil Nadu represents one such reformulation. By foregrounding cultural politics within an analysis of changing class relations, he shows how caste identity, ideology, and *habitus* may be reconstituted in the service of accumulation. Chari uses the term 'fraternal capital' to describe how Gounder industrialists from modest rural backgrounds rework meanings derived from the region's agrarian past to represent themselves as hard-working, self-made men. Chari's work suggests that caste may be productively understood as a set of practices and orientations which, although rooted in particular histories and geographies, may be altered over time as they become imbricated in processes of accumulation.

Similarly, Vinay Gidwani, in his work on agrarian capitalism in central Gujarat, conceptualizes capitalism as a 'complex whole' in which profit-oriented production 'interdigitates with other value-creating practices' (2008, p. 198)—including of caste. Like Chari, he examines the self-fashioning of agrarian capitalists (the Patels) and explores the intersections between caste mobility, the politics of labour, and processes of capital accumulation in the context of colonial and postcolonial projects of development. These examples point to ways in which we might begin to liberate caste from the sociological stranglehold of culture, and capital from the universalizing grip of political economy (Chakrabarty, 2000).

In another attempt to 'provincialize' Indian capitalism, Birla (2009) traces the emergence of an Indian capitalist class from a merchant community (the Marwaris) as they negotiated with new forms of market governance and law. She shows how colonial discourses and legal codes placed the Marwaris and their commercial practices in the domain of 'tradition' or 'culture', viewed as the opposite of modern, rational economic practices. The relegation of Indian business practices to the realm of 'tradition' is echoed in the contemporary circulation of self-orientalizing popular business discourses that essentialize and romanticize an 'Indian' (i.e., Hindu) way of doing business (Inamdar, 2014; Jodhka and Naudet, 2017). The invocation of high-caste Hindu notions of duty, tradition, and devotion in these writings is yet another example of the ideological reverberations of caste within contemporary Indian capitalism.

While the colonial state attempted to dismantle indigenous capitalism and institutionalize 'modern' norms of capitalism through changes in law and governance, Birla shows that these steps also encompassed existing practices—for instance, through the institutionalization of the 'Hindu Undivided Family' (HUF). The HUF legal structure continues to provide substantial tax and fiscal benefits to business communities that organize their business activities through the presumptively 'traditional' joint family system (Das Gupta and Gupta, 2017). Similarly, Viswanath's history of caste in colonial Madras Presidency shows how the question of caste (and especially of the 'Untouchable' communities) was neatly delinked from that of land and control over labour and framed as one of 'culture' or religion through colonial texts and policies.

By privileging the landed castes within the village power structure, a highly unequal caste-based economy was inscribed in the land administration system, even as caste (now located in the domain of 'custom') was placed beyond the reach of legal reform by the state.

This short and necessarily incomplete overview of a vast and variegated literature suggests that much intellectual work remains to be done to develop a deeper theoretical understanding of the materialities of caste; its imbrication within 'modern' institutions of the economy and state; the ways in which caste relations and ideologies permeate business practices and their implications for accumulation; and more broadly, the role of caste in the widening of inequalities in contemporary India.

Acknowledgements

Many thanks to Jules Naudet for his perceptive comments and suggestions on an earlier draft of this essay. All errors and omissions are my own.

References

Ajit, D., Han Donker, and Ravi Saxena. 2012. 'Corporate Boards in India: Blocked by Caste?' *Economic & Political Weekly*, 11(31): 39–43.

Alha, Akhil. 2018. 'The Other Side of Caste as Social Capital'. *Social Change*, 48(4): 575–588.

Bandyopadhyay, Ritajyoti, and Ranabir Samaddar. 2017. 'Caste and the Frontiers of Post-Colonial Capital Accumulation'. In Iman Kumar Mitra, Ranabir Samaddar, and Samita Sen (Eds.), *Accumulation in Post-Colonial Capitalism* (pp. 189–214). Singapore: Springer.

Basile, Elisabetta, and Barbara Harriss-White. 2001. 'Corporative Capitalism: Civil Society and the Politics of Accumulation in Small Town India'. QEH Working Paper Series 38.

Bayly, Christopher A. 1975. *The Local Roots of Indian Politics: Allahabad, 1880–1920*. Oxford: Clarendon Press.

Bayly, Christopher A. 1983. *Rulers, Townsmen and Bazaars; North Indian Society in the Age of British Expansion, 1770–1870*. Delhi: Oxford University Press.

Birla, Ritu. 2009. *Stages of Capital: Law, Culture, and Market Governance in Late Colonial India*. Durham: Duke University Press.

Cadene, Philippe, and Denis Vidal (Eds.) 1997. *Webs of Trade: Dynamics of Business Communities in Western India*. Delhi: Manohar.

Chakrabarty, Dipesh. 2000. *Provincializing Europe: Postcolonial Thought and Historical Difference*. Princeton: Princeton University Press.

Chari, Sharad. 2004a. *Fraternal Capital: Peasant-Workers, Self-Made Men and Globalization in Provincial India*. Delhi: Permanent Black.

Chari, Sharad. 2004b. 'Provincializing Capital: The Work of an Agrarian Past in South Indian Industry'. *Comparative Studies in Society and History*, 46(4): 760–785.

Damodaran, Harish. 2008. *India's New Capitalists: Caste, Business and Industry in a Modern Nation*. New Delhi: Palgrave Macmillan.

Das Gupta, Chirashree, and Mohit Gupta. 2017. 'The *Hindu Undivided Family* in Independent India's Corporate Governance and Tax Regime'. *South Asia Multidisciplinary Academic Journal* [Online], 15. http://journals.openedition.org/samaj/4300.

Desai, Ashok V. 1968. 'The Origins of Parsi Enterprise'. *Indian Economic & Social History Review*, 5(4): 307–317.

Deshpande, Ashwini. 2011. *The Grammar of Caste: Economic Discrimination in Contemporary India*. New Delhi: Oxford University Press.

Dhingra, Pawan. 2012. *Life behind the Lobby: Indian American Motel Owners and the American Dream*. Stanford: Stanford University Press.

Dumont, Louis. 1981. *Homo Hierarchicus: The Caste System and Its Implications* (2nd ed.). Chicago: University of Chicago Press.

Engelshoven, Miranda. 1999. 'Diamonds and Patels: A Report on the Diamond Industry of Surat'. *Contributions to Indian Sociology (N.S.)*, 33: 353–377.

Fox, Richard G. 1967. 'Family, Caste, and Commerce in a North Indian Market Town'. *Economic Development and Cultural Change*, 15(3): 297–314.

Gidwani, Vinay. 2008. *Capital, Interrupted; Agrarian Development and the Politics of Work in India*. Ranikhet: Permanent Black.

Guha, Sumit. 2013. *Beyond Caste: Identity and Power in South Asia, Past and Present*. Leiden: Brill.

Gupta, Akhil. 1998. *Postcolonial Developments: Agriculture in the Making of Modern India*. Durham: Duke University Press.

Guru, Gopal. 2012. 'Rise of the "Dalit Millionaire": A Low Intensity Spectacle'. *Economic & Political Weekly*, 47(50): 41–49.

Hardgrave, Robert. 1970. *The Nadars of Tamilnad*. Berkeley and Los Angeles: University of California Press.

Hardgrove, Anne. 2004. *Community and Public Culture: The Marwaris in Calcutta*. New Delhi: Oxford University Press.

Harriss, John. 2003. '"Widening the Radius of Trust": Ethnographic Explorations of Trust and Indian Business'. *Journal of the Royal Anthropological Institute*, 9(4): 755–773.

Harriss-White, Barbara. 2003. *India Working: Essays on Society and Economy*. Cambridge: Cambridge University Press.

Harriss-White, Barbara, et al. 2014. *Dalits and Adivasis in India's Business Economy: Three Essays and an Atlas*. Gurgaon, India: Three Essays Collective.

Harriss-White, Barbara, and Kaushal Vidyarthee. 2010. 'Stigma and Regions of Accumulation: Mapping Dalit and Adivasi Capital in the 1990s'. In Barbara Harriss-White and Judith Heyer (Eds.), *The Comparative Political Economy of Development: Africa and South Asia* (pp. 317–349). Abingdon & New York: Routledge.

Haynes, Douglas. 2012. *Small Town Capitalism in Western India: Artisans, Merchants and the Making of the Informal Economy, 1870–1960*. Cambridge: Cambridge University Press.

Hazlehurst, Leighton W. 1966. *Entrepreneurship and the Merchant Castes in a Punjabi City*. Durham, NC: Duke University Program in Comparative Studies on Southern Asia, Monograph and Occasional Papers Series, Number 1.

Inamdar, Nikhil. 2014. *Rokda: How Baniyas Do Business*. Delhi: Random House.

Iyer, Lakshmi, Tarun Khanna, and Ashutosh Varshney. 2013. 'Caste and Entrepreneurship in India'. *Economic & Political Weekly*, 48(6): 52–60.

Jodhka, Surinder S. 2010. 'Dalits in Business: Self-Employed Scheduled Castes in Northwest India'. *Economic & Political Weekly*, 45(11): 41–48.

Jodhka, Surinder S. 2012. 'The Problem'. *Seminar* No. 633.

Jodhka, Surinder S. 2016. 'Ascriptive Hierarchies: Caste and Its Reproduction in Contemporary India'. *Current Sociology*, 64(2): 228–243.

Jodhka, Surinder S. and James Manor. 2017. 'Introduction'. In Surinder S. Jodhka and James Manor (Eds.), *Contested Hierarchies, Persisting Influence: Caste and Power in Twenty-first Century India* (pp. 1–38). Hyderabad: Orient BlackSwan.

Jodhka, Surinder S. and Jules Naudet. 2017. 'Introduction. Towards a Sociology of India's Economic Elite: Beyond the Neo-Orientalist and Managerialist Perspectives'. *South Asia Multidisciplinary Academic Journal*. http://journals.openedition.org/samaj/4316.

Knorringa, Peter. 1996. *Economics of Collaboration: Indian Shoemakers between Market and Hierarchy*. Delhi: SAGE.

Kudaisya, Medha. 2016. 'Mercantile Communities, Business and State in Twentieth-Century India: State of the Field'. *South Asia: Journal of South Asian Studies*, 39(1): 262–270.

Lamb, Helen. 1955. 'The Indian Business Communities and the Evolution of an Industrialist Class'. *Pacific Affairs*, 28: 101–116.

Luhrmann, Tanya M. 1996. *The Good Parsi: The Fate of a Colonial Elite in a Postcolonial Society*. Cambridge: Harvard University Press.

Lyon, Michael H., and Bernice J. M. West. 1995. 'London Patels: Caste and Commerce'. *Journal of Ethnic and Migration Studies*, 21(3): 399–419.

Mahadevan, Raman. 1978. 'Immigrant Entrepreneurs in Colonial Burma: An Exploratory Study of the Role of Nattukottai Chettiars of Tamil Nadu, 1880–1930'. *Indian Economic & Social History Review*, 15(3): 329–358.

Mani, Dalhia, and James Moody. 2014. 'Moving beyond Stylized Economic Network Models: The Hybrid World of the Indian Firm Ownership Network'. *American Journal of Sociology*, 119(6): 1629–1669.

Markovits, Claude. 2000. *The Global World of Indian Merchants, 1750–1947. Traders of Sind from Bukhara to Panama*. Cambridge: Cambridge University Press.

Markovits, Claude. 2008. *Merchants, Traders, Entrepreneurs: Indian Business in the Colonial Era*. Ranikhet: Permanent Black.

Marx, Karl. 1969. 'The Future Results of British Rule in India'. In Shlomo Avineri (Ed.), *Karl Marx on Colonialism and Modernization* (pp. 132–139). New York: Anchor Books.

Mines, Mattison. 1984. *The Warrior Merchants: Textiles, Trade and Territory in South India*. Cambridge: Cambridge University Press.

Mines, Mattison. 1994. *Public Faces, Private Voices: Community and Individuality in South India*. Cambridge: Cambridge University Press.

Mosse, David. 2018. 'Caste and Development: Contemporary Perspectives on a Structure of Discrimination and Advantage'. *World Development*, 110: 422–436.

Mosse, David. 2020. 'The Modernity of Caste and the Market Economy'. *Modern Asian Studies*, 54(4): 1225–1271.

Munshi, Kaivan. 2007. 'From Farming to International Business: The Social Auspices of Entrepreneurship in a Growing Economy'. NBER Working Paper 13065. Cambridge, MA: National Bureau of Economic Research. https://www.nber.org/papers/w13065.pdf.

Munshi, Kaivan. 2011. 'Strength in Numbers: Networks as a Solution to Occupational Traps'. *Review of Economic Studies*, 78(3): 1069–1101.

Munshi, Kaivan. 2016. 'Caste Networks in the Modern Indian Economy'. In S. Mahindra Dev and P. G. Babu (Eds.), *Development in India: Micro and Macro Perspectives* (pp. 13–37). New Delhi: Springer India.

Munshi, Kaivan, and Mark Rosenzweig. 2009. 'Why Is Mobility in India so Low? Social Insurance, Inequality and Growth'. National Bureau of Economic Growth, Working Paper 14850. Cambridge, MA. https://ideas.repec.org/p/nbr/nberwo/14850.html.

Nafziger, E. Wayne. 1975. 'Class, Caste and Community of South Indian Industrialists: An Examination of the Horatio Alger Model'. *Journal of Development Studies*, 11: 131–148.

Natrajan, Balmurli. 2012. *The Culturalization of Caste in India: Identity and Inequality in a Multicultural Age*. Oxon: Routledge.

Naudet, Jules, Adrien Allorant, and Mathieu Ferry. 2018. 'Heirs, Corporate Aristocrats and "Meritocrats": The Social Space of Top CEOs and Chairmen in India'. *Socio-Economic Review*, 16(2): 307–339.

Naudet, Jules, and Claire-Lise Dubost. 2016. 'The Indian Exception: The Densification of the Network of Corporate Interlocks and the Specificities of the Indian Business System (2000–2012)'. *Socio-Economic Review*, 15(2): 405–434.

Oonk, Gijsbert. 2013. *Settled Strangers: Asian Business Elites in East Africa, 1800–2000*. New Delhi: SAGE.

Owens, Raymond, and Ashish Nandy. 1977. *The New Vaishyas*. Bombay: Allied Publishers.

Ponniah, Ujithra. 2017. 'Reproducing Elite Lives: Women in Aggarwal Family Businesses'. *South Asia Multidisciplinary Academic Journal* [Online], 15. http://journals.openedition.org/samaj/4280.

Poros, Maritsa V. 2011. *Modern Migrations; Gujarati Indian Networks in New York and London*. Stanford: Stanford University Press.

Prakash, Aseem. 2015. *Dalit Capital: State, Markets and Civil Society in Urban India*. New Delhi: Routledge India.

Prakash, Aseem. 2018. 'Dalit Capital and Markets: A Case of Unfavourable Inclusion'. *Journal of Social Inclusion Studies*, 4(1): 51–61.

Roy, Tirthankar. 2010. *Company of Kinsmen: Enterprise and Community in South Asian History 1700–1940*. New Delhi: Oxford University Press.

Rudner, David. 1995. *Caste and Capitalism in Colonial India: The Nattukottai Chettiars*. Berkeley: University of California Press.

Rutten, Mario. 1995. *Farms and Factories; Social Profile of Large Farmers and Rural Industrialists in Central Gujarat, India*. New Delhi: Oxford University Press.

Rutten, Mario. 2008. 'Caste and Religion in a Transnational Context: The Patidars of Central Gujarat'. In S. Mahendra Dev and K. S. Babu (Eds.), *India's Development: Social and Economic Disparities* (pp. 347–364). Delhi: Manohar/IDPAD.

Rutten, Mario, and Carol Upadhya (Eds.). 1997. *Small Business Entrepreneurs in Asia and Europe: Towards a Comparative Perspective*. New Delhi: SAGE.

Saberwal, Satish. 1996. *The Roots of Crisis: Interpreting Contemporary Indian Society*. Delhi: Oxford University Press.

Singer, Milton (Ed.). 1973. *Entrepreneurship and Modernization of Occupational Cultures in South Asia*. Durham: Duke University Press.

Subrahmanyam, Sanjay. 1990. *The Political Economy of Commerce*. Cambridge: Cambridge University Press.

Subrahmanyam, Sanjay and Christopher A. Bayly. 1988. 'Portfolio Capitalists and Political Economy in Early Modern India'. *Indian Economic and Social History Review*, 25(4): 401–424.

Timberg, Thomas A. 1978. *The Marwaris: From Traders to Industrialists*. New Delhi: Vikas Publishing House.

Thorat, Sukhdeo, Debolina Kundu, and Nidhi Sadana. 2010. 'Caste and Ownership of Private Enterprises'. In Sukhdeo Thorat and Katherine Newman (Eds.), *Blocked by Caste: Economic Discrimination in Modern India* (pp. 311–327). New Delhi: Oxford University Press.

Tripathi, Dwijendra. 1971. 'Indian Entrepreneurship in Historical Perspective: A Re-interpretation'. *Economic and Political Weekly*, 6(22): M59–M66.

Tripathi, Dwijendra (Ed.). 1984. *Business Communities in India: A Historical Perspective*. Delhi: Manohar.

Tripathi, Dwijendra and Jyoti Jumani (Eds.). 2013. *The Oxford History of Contemporary Indian Business*. New Delhi: Oxford University Press.

Tumbe, Chinmay. 2017. 'Transnational Indian Business in the Twentieth Century'. *Business History Review*, 91: 651–679.

Upadhya, Carol. 1988. 'The Farmer Capitalists of Coastal Andhra Pradesh'. *Economic & Political Weekly*, 23(27&28): 1376–1382, 1433–1442.

Upadhya, Carol. 1997a. 'Culture, Class and Entrepreneurship: A Case Study of Coastal Andhra Pradesh, India'. In Mario Rutten and Carol Upadhya (Eds.), *Small Business Entrepreneurs in Asia and Europe: Towards a Comparative Perspective* (pp. 47–80). New Delhi: SAGE.

Upadhya, Carol. 1997b. 'Social and Cultural Strategies of Class Formation in Coastal Andhra Pradesh'. *Contributions to Indian Sociology (n.s.)*, 31(2): 169–193.

Vidyarthee, Kaushal K. 2016. 'The Incorporation of Dalits into India's Business Economy and Its Implications for Social and Economic Policies'. DPhil dissertation, University of Oxford.

Vijayabaskar, M. and A. Kalaiyarasan. 2014. 'Caste as Social Capital'. *Economic & Political Weekly*, 49(10): 34–38.

Viswanath, Rupa. 2014. *The Pariah Problem: Caste, Religion, and the Social in Modern India*. New York: Columbia University Press.

Weber, Max. 1958. *The Religion of India: The Sociology of Hinduism and Buddhism* (translated by Hans H. Gerth and Don Martindale). New York: The Free Press.

Witsoe, Jeffrey. 2017. 'Caste Networks and Regional Political Economy'. In Surinder S. Jodhka and James Manor (Eds.), *Contested Hierarchies, Persisting Influence: Caste and Power in Twenty-first Century India* (pp. 39–59). Hyderabad: Orient BlackSwan.

CHAPTER 5

CASTE AND CLASS

JULES NAUDET

This chapter[1] intends to offer an analytical perspective on one of the most debated issues among sociologists of the Indian society: the nature of the relation between caste and class. A brief look at the literature immediately reveals how scholars hold very contrasted positions on this issue. Scholarship has progressively moved from a debate constructed around the idea of a necessity to choose between either caste or class and marked by the imperative of an analytical move from caste to class with India's modernization and capitalist development, to a situation in which most scholars reckon that class dynamics and caste dynamics are distinct though they intersect in multiple ways. This chapter acknowledges that the alternative between caste or class is outdated and argues that the most heuristic position consists in acknowledging the co-existence of caste and class processes and in investigating the various modalities through which they interact.

THE VAGARIES OF THE CASTE 'OR' CLASS DEBATE

A lot of scholars have engaged in the 'caste or class debate' (Gupta, 1981; Ilaiah, 2004). The simple fact that it is often referred to as a 'debate' is quite revealing. The stake was indeed to know whether class is a consequence of caste or caste a consequence of class, whether class is embedded in caste or caste embedded in class. The alternative was thus framed in terms of a precedence of one over the other, the ultimate challenge being to identify the matrix of social hierarchies. Whatever the position held, this reveals a predominantly unidimensional approach to social stratifications: there is either a caste system or a class structure.

---

[1] I warmly thank Joël Cabalion, Mathieu Ferry, Odile Henry, Surinder Jodhka, and Olivier Roueff for their remarks on the first draft of this text.

The necessity to decide between caste or class can be linked to the domination of three paradigms in social sciences in the period following independence in India till the late 80s. The first one consists in a 'neo-orientalist' vision of Indian society inherited from colonialism (Deshpande, 2001) that places castes at the centre of every social fact and whose most visible proponent is probably Louis Dumont (in the sense that he pushed the theorization of caste as a system of values encompassing all aspects of social life to its furthest point). The second one consists in an orthodox approach to Marxism that takes the exact opposite stand: it regards caste as a specific avatar of class or, at least, sees caste as embedded in class. The third one consists in a structuring opposition between 'modern' and 'traditional' societies. Such an opposition was generally considered mutually exclusive, drawing upon the exaggeratedly optimist postulate that modernization and industrialization would inescapably lead to the erosion of caste. In order to assess the 'modern' (class) or 'traditional' (caste) nature of a society, sociologists would then consider social mobility as the most decisive criterion. Following a simplistic reading of Sorokin's work, they would indeed often consider that societies would either be 'open' or 'closed' (Sorokin, 1927; Naudet, 2018). According to this logic, caste societies would necessarily be societies where statuses are ascribed and where only collective mobility is possible while class societies would be characterized by a social structure allowing for individual mobility. Here again, the ultimate challenge lies in getting to know whether India is still constructed around a caste system or if it has finally become a class society.

Class as the Matrix of All Oppressions

With an intensity that decreases as Marxist ideology loses grip in academia, it has often been argued that Indian society is, first and foremost, a class society. In this perspective, most conflicts in Indian society would actually be buttressed by class, even though they sometimes take forms that are difficult to identify as class conflicts. Caste would mainly be an aggravating factor of class struggles. Or, alternatively, caste would be seen as a crystallization of class or, in a more teleological vision, as a kind of remnant of a feudal past.

Such conceptions of caste rely upon an historical assumption regarding the formation of caste and postulate that caste is above all the reflection (or the product) of class oppositions. As Dipankar Gupta puts it, the orthodox Marxist approach 'seeks to unearth the material and historical roots of the caste system and in particular searches for those peculiar features of India's material history which were responsible for the genesis of the caste system and which contributed to its development' (Gupta, 1981, p. 2093).

This approach draws upon the idea, expressed by Marx himself, that, 'legislation may perpetuate land ownership in certain families, or allocate labour as a hereditary privilege, thus consolidating it into a caste system' (Marx, 1859, p. 201). This resorts to negating the distinction between caste and class and to argue that what is called caste is actually a specific and reified incarnation of class. Marxism, 'in its reduction of all oppressions to class', argues Aditya Nigam, led to 'the absolute prioritization of "class" and made caste oppression unspeakable' (Nigam, 2006, p. 195).

If scholars like Maurice Godelier and Gail Omvedt developed a nuanced—and somehow heterodox—Marxist understanding of caste as (understanding of caste as built into) is built into the relations of production (Godelier, 1977, pp. IX, 96–97, 275–276; Omvedt, 1978), such positions remain exceptions and most Marxists would keep locating caste at the superstructure level rather than at the infrastructure level. These readings remain in line with Marx's own idea that 'Modern industry, resulting from the railway system, will dissolve the hereditary divisions of labor, upon which rest the Indian castes, those decisive impediments to Indian progress and Indian power' (Marx, 1853, p. 497).

These interrogations have somehow been taken up by scholars who extensively discussed whether the Indian social structure can be characterized as feudal, semi-feudal, or as capitalist (Thorner, 1982). If class is the main engine of social change, then the central preoccupation is indeed to figure out at what stage of historical development India is located. These debates have recently been further developed by Jens Lerche, Alpa Shah, and Barbara Hariss-White (2013) in their discussion of the role of agrarian economy in India.

Such a teleological vision of historical development finds its alter-ego in its non-Marxist avatar known as the 'modernization' theory that is the proposition that modernity will ultimately crush caste distinctions and replace them with pure class distinctions, that caste is bound to be wiped away by economic modernization. In this perspective *homo œconomicus* is bound to replace *homo hierarchicus*.

CLASS EMBEDDED IN CASTE

It is interesting to note that the proponents of the alternative position, that is those who argue that caste prevails over class, also struggled to make sense of the massive social changes at work in independent India. Coming from a neo-orientalist scholarship that sees caste as the main vehicle of social cohesion, they consider that class positions are embedded in an all-encompassing caste structure. But in a context where the *jajmani* system loses its grip and where the religious dimension of caste (Dumont, 1980) is being partly eroded by the secularization of the country's institutions, they need to make sense of these transformations.

M. N. Srinivas has brilliantly retraced the evolution across time of the various ways in which class was built into caste, with opportunities, and paths of class mobility evolving along with the changes in the way caste operates (Srinivas, 1968). M. N. Srinivas notably distinguishes between the medieval period, the British period, and the postcolonial one, each being associated with specific forms of class mobility.

In such a perspective, class mobility is not autonomous from caste dynamics. This is notably illustrated by the fact that it often entails a process of sanskritization. The importance of such strategies would be dictated by the fact that the ideological—and religious—foundations of caste have not disappeared and that ritual purity still matters. This amounts to the idea that caste structures the position one occupies in society and is the main mould of all other kinds of social hierarchies. Such a perspective generally stresses the fact that India is a 'closed social stratification' system (Bailey, 1963): class dynamics would be too anecdotal to matter in the way stratification operates and would thus be overweighed by caste.

The persistence of the centrality of caste in spite of the erosion of its most traditional structures is thus explained through various theories of caste transformation. Srinivas writes an obituary of 'caste as a system' and focuses on its 'twentieth century avatar'. His diagnostic is clear: 'while caste as a system is dead, individual castes are flourishing' (Srinivas, 2003, p. 459). On his side, F. G. Bailey writes that 'Castes still exist: but they are used as building blocks in a different kind of system' (Bailey, 1963, p. 123). As Dumont is concerned, the transformation of caste should be understood through a process of 'substantialization of caste' in which caste no longer operates as a system. Caste entities would now function as 'impenetrable blocks, self-sufficient, essentially identical and in competition with one another' (Dumont, 1980, p. 222).

Decoupling Caste from Class to Escape Conceptual Confusion

The transformation of the social structure in post-independent India poses a tremendous dilemma to anthropologists and sociologists who struggle with theories of tradition, modernity, and development to make sense of what André Béteille diagnoses as a 'dissociation of class relations from the caste structure' caused by the modernization of the occupational structure (Béteille, 2011, p. 191). In 1987, M. N. Srinivas thus humbly admits his difficulty to make sense of what's happening and describes the academic debates as a sort of theoretical mess: 'All the three systems, jajmani (including jajmani in decline), castes in acute conflict with each other, and networks involving individuals from different castes, coexist in the country today, and are likely to coexist in the immediate future. But jajmani system will continue to decline, inter-caste conflict will increase in the future, and the character of networks is likely to change. Class and life-style may assume increasing importance in social relations, especially in urban areas. All this sounds conceptually very messy and far from clear but that is how the immediate future appears to be' (Srinivas, 2002, p. 250). His humbling confession of his hardships at making sense of the various ways in which caste and class intersect can actually be read as a plea for a non-monolithic approach of the Indian social structure.

In many ways, Srinivas' statement was visionary of what scholarship on caste and class was to become. If the opposition between caste 'or' class has long been structuring of debates on the Indian stratification system, they now seem to have been relegated to the past. Trying to move beyond an overwhelmingly ideological alternative between caste *or* class, sociologists now increasingly argue that the Indian social structure is constructed around both caste *and* class. Rather than deciding which has precedence over the other, the challenge mainly consists in identifying how caste dynamics co-exist along class dynamics, how they intersect and interact.

Such an approach first necessitates to define caste and class in a way that does not necessarily imply that one is subjugated to the other and that rather reckons that each is prompted by partly autonomous ways of functioning. Weber, who has often been misread, is certainly the author who first offered the most comprehensive distinction allowing for a heuristic decoupling of caste from class. As he reminds in *The Sociology of Hinduism and Buddhism*, caste is a specific case of *Stand* (status group). Unlike the frequent cases where social honour is directly linked to class status, caste modifies the relationship between social status and class (understood as the possession or non-possession of material goods or professional qualifications of a certain type).[2] According to Weber, caste is a closed *Stand* to the extent that it imposes highly restrictive professional, religious, and social obligations.

While there has always been a high congruence between caste and class, this congruence was never perfect. The post-independence challenges of the modernization of the Indian economy, combined with the implementation of reservation quotas, have accelerated the disassociation of caste and class.[3] In addition, the country's secularization has accelerated the erosion of the ideological and religious foundations of caste. This contributed to widen the breach in the principles that maintained the Indian social order. The Indian theodicy, which Weber described as 'the most consistent theodicy ever produced by history' (Weber, 1967, p. 39), thus found itself in competition with an ideology of merit, according to which an individual's value no longer depends on his birth, but on his professional success.

Nonetheless, such a process has not completely wiped away the ideological foundations of caste. The devaluation of religious justifications of caste went along with a concomitant transformation of the principles of meritocracy that found themselves increasingly infused by the notion of caste. This indeed led to the emergence of a new 'language of caste' in which caste discrimination is now increasingly justified by attempts at maintaining meritocracy (Jodhka and Newman, 2010).

---

[2] It should be noted here that Weber's definition of class differs from Marx's. If Marx insists on the property of means of production in his definition of class, Weber rather lays the emphasis on the volume of economic resources at one's disposal. Weber is thus concerned by the differences in life chances that result from class differences while Marx is more concerned with dynamics of appropriation and exploitation. This difference in conceptions of class probably explains why Marxist scholars have mainly focused on the relationship between caste and division of labour and were consequently led to mainly focus on caste as a system of birth-ascribed hierarchy.

[3] One of the main effects of the introduction of the reservation policy was 'classification struggles' between the different caste groups who sought to monopolize the benefits of these quota policies. According to Christophe Jaffrelot (2003), the main impact of these policies has been a 'silent revolution' which has led to a decline in the political domination by the upper castes, who are slowly being replaced by SC, ST, and *Other Backward Classes* elites.

This points to two things. First, it reveals that the ideological foundations of caste have changed and are becoming increasingly complex, characterized by an instable mix of ideologies pertaining to the realm of the religious, and others pertaining to the realm of power. Second, in so far as meritocracy is one of the most powerful repertoires of justification of class inequalities, it also reveals that caste ideologies tend to be intimately tied with class ideologies.

These developments have also led to a blurring of the principles defining status. While caste remains a closed *Stand* in the Weberian sense, status in India is not only defined by belonging to a specific caste. Status is also a function of the prestige of the profession one exercises. Hence, one's social status and life chances are concomitantly defined by one's caste as well as by one's profession. This basically means that caste and class cannot be examined separately. A good way of arguing in favour of the inextricable tie between caste and class consists in asking if there can be such a thing as an autonomous 'class habitus' that would act independently from caste (Bourdieu, 1998). This is very unlikely as dispositions of Indian actors are constructed by their caste ethos as well as by their class ethos. A poor agricultural labourer from a Patel background will not have the same social dispositions as a Patel who is an executive corporate in a multinational company. And, similarly, the strong cultural autonomy of caste groups (Natrajan, 2012) is such that, to take one example, a Dalit IAS officer and a Marwari IAS officer generally have a very different set of dispositions.

All the difficulty thus lies in how to apprehend the way caste and class mutually produce an unequal and hierarchical social order. In the face of such a confused and confusing situation, David Mosse's diagnostic is particularly enlightening. He indeed argues that though 'the intersecting nature of identities (caste, class, gender, religion) that give poverty in India its distinctive social face means that ultimately caste cannot be independently examined (Shah et al., 2018)', it is nonetheless still possible to 'identify the "grammar" of caste (Deshpande, 2011) at work behind persisting socioeconomic and human capital disparities in India' (Mosse, 2018, p. 423). The intersectionality of social identities does not necessarily prevent from analytically distinguishing between the various logics at work. The last three sections of this chapter thus give a few examples of the various ways in which sociologists can empirically interrogate the modalities in which caste and class are built one into another.

The Issue of the Congruence of Caste and Class

Weber's distinction between honour and class thus leads to posit the debate in terms of the congruence between caste and class. This approach supposes a certain distance from the issue of knowing whether caste or class prevails and is mainly motivated by the will to empirically assess the extent to which both dimensions overlap.

Disregarding the issue of knowing whether caste religious and ideological foundations are still alive, such an approach indeed looks at the objectivity of facts, thus bringing a precious contribution to the debate. The most robust assessment of this congruence has certainly been conducted by Divya Vaid in her book *UnEven Odds* (Vaid, 2018). Her conclusions suffer no ambiguity. If, she notices that 'high castes dominate in the more "clean" white collar classes and a strong manual-non-manual barrier seems to exist where the high-castes seem to be avoiding "unclean" manual work' (Vaid, 2018, p. 200), she nonetheless remarks that 'the association between caste and class origins is seen to weaken marginally over time' (Vaid, 2018, p. 200). Moreover, her data reveals that 'the effect of class origins is [. . .] much stronger than the effect of community or caste' (Vaid, 2018, p. 201). In sum, she argues that if the relationship between class and caste is still relatively strong and that there is still 'a pervasive effect of caste', 'class origins, rather than caste, have long been the major factor influencing one's class destinations' (Vaid, 2018, p. 202).

If Vaid's work mainly focuses on the issue of the role of caste and class in the chances of being socially mobile, she is less attentive to the weight of caste on the microstratifications within each social class. Other empirical studies indeed suggest that within each class, there exist caste hierarchies that mainly align with the traditional varna hierarchy. Studying in detail the local hierarchies of the non-farm economy of a village in the Madhubani district of Bihar, Surinder Jodhka and Adarsh Kumar show that the 'low'-status caste groups 'are often located at the lower end of the occupational hierarchy' while 'Upper and trading castes are over-represented in activities that generate higher income and carry superior status' (Jodhka and Kumar, 2017, p. 23). In their macro-sociological study of the Indian social space, Ferry, Naudet, and Roueff (2018) have noticed that 'among the populations that possess no economic or cultural capital, the caste one belongs to [. . .] make[s] an enormous difference in terms of creating a minimum distance from the weight of need, much more so than social class or education'. This points to the specific resources caste offers and that alter the class competition even if, as Divya Vaid's work reminds us, one's class position can help counterbalance the effects of caste assignation. It thus appears that more research looking at the way caste structures hierarchies within a given social class is needed in order to gain more clarity on these issues.

To account for the persistence of the congruence between caste and class, the most basic explanation is that though the *jajmani* system has almost entirely disappeared and has been replaced by a global market economy, it has nonetheless left its mark on the contemporary Indian social structure. Rippling across time, it would hence still be shaping the life chances of individuals because the privileges (or the disadvantages) accumulated under the *jajmani* have been passed over generations through caste. This would be one of the mechanisms accounting for why all the most exploited and dominated individuals belong to Adivasi or Dalit communities while almost all the richest and most powerful individuals belong to higher castes. Such an argument is nonetheless insufficient to account for the strength of the caste and class congruence.

Caste as a Resource in Class Struggles: Converting Caste Capital into Class Capital

One way of exploring this inextricable knot consists in being attentive to the way caste constitutes a resource in the struggle for attaining the best class positions. Conceptualizing caste as a resource suggests that caste privileges cannot solely be thought of as ascribed at birth and produced by an encompassing and unchallenged ideology but are also, to a great extent, the product of intense efforts at reproducing them.

Many of these mechanisms actually deal with what Surinder Jodhka has termed 'caste as power' (Jodhka, 2012) and highlight how caste positively or negatively influence the capacity to access education (Paik, 2009; Jeffrey et al., 2005), to access business opportunities, to access political power, to access law and order (Narula, 2007), to access basic public infrastructure (Shah et al., 2006), etc. The relative ease or difficulty with which these resources are accessed is actually decisive of an individual's life chances and capacity to reproduce his or her privileges or even of his or her capacity to move up the class structure. Being able to file a complaint at the police station, being allowed to sit in the classroom rather than outside of it, not being afraid to be beaten-up if you publicly contradict somebody, being able to leverage capital to start business, being able to access reliable business information, being confident you can trust your business partners because they belong to the same community as you, being offered good water or electricity access because your neighbourhood is the electoral stronghold of the local M.L.A., etc.: these are all basic facts that shape one's confidence, one's life chances, and ultimately one's class position. And all these facts are directly aligned on caste identity.

If they are so, this is generally because resourceful people engage in activities that explicitly aim at either excluding people from certain networks or that aim at ensuring the impermeability of caste networks in order to preserve their homogeneity. Such activities can either be linked to caste-based associations that actively develop the cohesion of their caste group, its endogamy, its privileges, and its influence or to the fact that caste and traditional customs are embedded in local governance (Ananth Pur, 2007) and tend to lead to the development of patron-client politics. The extreme intensity with which caste functions as a group of interest thus leads to the development of a caste-based 'Mafia Raj' in certain areas of the country (Michelutti et al., 2018). In order to objectify such mechanisms from a quantitative perspective, Jaffrelot reminds us that 'one needs to disaggregate the meta categories that are "Upper Castes", "OBCs" and "Scheduled Castes", in order to look at the *jatis* and, similarly, one needs to shift from a pan-Indian level to the State level' (Jaffrelot, 2019, p. 155).

CLASS HIERARCHIES WITHIN CASTE GROUPS AND ACROSS CASTE GROUPS

Conceptualizing caste as a group of interest working at converting caste into class (or into power) is nonetheless reductive and should not obliterate that caste groups generally encompass very disparate class positions. This aspect of the interaction between caste and class has led to less research than the other aspects mentioned above but it reminds us that caste unity often acts as a silencer of class inequalities within a given caste group.

Jaffrelot notably points at this fact in the case of Patels in Gujarat: *'There is a popular view evident in the saying, 'P for P', that a Patel would always support a Patel, making the community a close-knit one. But there is a clear differentiation of the caste along class lines—in addition to sub-caste lines, even though they sometimes overlap: Leuva Patels and Kadva Patels, respectively in Saurashtra as well as central Gujarat and Northern Gujarat represent the dominant jatis (whereas the Satpanthis of Kutch and the Chaudhary Patel of North Gujarat are not as affluent, the latter are even part of the OBCs), but there are inequalities within the jatis'* (Jaffrelot, 2016). A recent World-Bank study has similarly shown the importance of these intra-jati inequalities in the case of Bihar (Joshi, Kocchar, and Rao, 2018). On their side, Jaffrelot and Kalaiyarasan have systematically explored intra-group inequality among caste groups in Haryana and point to the fact that 'Jats have seen the sharpest internal differentiation along class lines' (Jaffrelot and Kalaiyarasan, 2019, p. 36).

The fact people occupy different class positions within a same caste hints at the fact that class is mediated by caste. Naudet thus stresses that caste deeply affects the way one's group of reference (to borrow Merton's concept) is defined and perceived. He particularly shows that Dalits and upwardly mobile upper-caste people tend to have a differing subjective appreciation of their trajectories (Naudet, 2018, p. 64). Consequently, upper-caste people often experience their upward mobility as simply catching-up with their caste peers while most Dalits have to deal with the ordeal of keeping ties with a caste-group that is dissonant with their class of arrival.

These remarks on the variations in the way class is differently experienced across different castes as well as within a given caste points to fruitful paths of research for the future. An increasing number of researchers have indeed recently highlighted the mechanisms through which caste identity is produced in spite of class disparities within the caste group. Ujithra Ponniah, for example, has shown how Agarwal women actively forge fictive kinship ties across caste strata and thus play a major role in the reproduction of Agarwal privileges (see her chapter *Aggarwal Banias of Delhi* in this volume). Lucia Michelutti had already pointed at the role of fictive kinship in creating a Yadav identity transcending all the jatis of this group (Michelutti, 2008).

On her side, Zoe Headley offers illuminating insights on how the Pramalai Kallar's sense of identity and collective memory draws upon a substantial corpus of narratives that constitutes a 'potential pool of reference, or resource, constantly accessible to all, and it is as such that it is "collective" because at any given moment any PK can appropriate its content in his or her definition or counterdefinition of his belonging to this subcaste' (Headley, 2011, p. 103). Sanam Roohi is also attentive to the way caste identity crystallizes around common narratives and she more specially analyses how, in the case of Kammas, the production of a sense of caste pride centred around a strong valorization of cosmopolitanism leads to a consolidation of a specifically Kamma caste habitus (Roohi, 2019).

Towards a Renewal of the Scholarship on Caste and Class

All the elements presented in this chapter indicate how crucial is the need to better understand the mechanisms through which caste identity manages to silence intra-caste inequalities. But they simultaneously point at the necessity to better understand the consequences of the situations, particularly under-researched, in which differing class-positions bring dissonance to caste-based identities. Finally, as noted in the section on caste and class congruence, we also lack precise data on the way hierarchies within a given social class align along caste lines. These are probably the three lines of enquiry that should be the most urgently pursued in order to better understand the social mechanisms through which caste is articulated with class.

On a larger note, as the caste segmentation of class and the class segmentation of caste suggest 'a cultural logic embedded within and perpetuated through economic activity' (Mosse, 2019), understanding the complexity of the relation between caste and class implies moving beyond monolithic approaches of stratification and developing innovative multidimensional approaches of the Indian society. Though it requires to be adapted to the Indian context, Bourdieu's approach in terms of a multidimensional social space probably offers the most operative conceptual toolkit to seize these processes (Ferry, Naudet, and Roueff, 2018). It offers one of the most convincing models to accomplish both empirically and theoretically Shah and Lerche's wish when they argue that, more than looking at whether categories 'may or may not "interact" or "intersect" or "correlate" in a particular circumstance', it is important to keep in mind that 'class relations, caste, tribe, gender and region are inextricably linked' as 'identity-based social oppression is constitutive of and shapes people's relationships to the means of their production and reproduction' (Shah et al., 2018, p. 13).

References

Ananth Pur, Kripa. 2007. 'Rivalry or Synergy? Formal and Informal Local Governance in Rural India'. *Development and Change*, 38(3): 401–421.

Bailey, F. G. 1963. 'Closed Social Stratification in India'. *European Journal of Sociology*, 4(1): 107–124.

Béteille, André. 2011. *Caste, Class and Power: Changing Patterns of Stratification in a Tanjore Village*. New Delhi: Oxford University Press.

Bourdieu, Pierre. 1998. *Practical Reason: On the Theory of Action*. Stanford: Stanford University Press.

Deshpande, Ashwini. 2011. *The Grammar of Caste: Economic Discrimination in Contemporary India*. New Delhi: Oxford University Press.

Deshpande, Satish. 2001. 'Disciplinary Predicaments: Sociology and Anthropology in Postcolonial India'. *Inter-Asia Cultural Studies*, 2(2): 247–260.

Dumont, Louis. 1980. *Homo Hierarchicus: The Caste System and Its Implications*. Chicago: University of Chicago Press.

Ferry, Mathieu, Jules Naudet, and Olivier Roueff. 2018. 'Seeking the Indian Social Space'. *South Asia Multidisciplinary Academic Journal* [Online]. http://journals.openedition.org/samaj/4462.

Godelier, Maurice. 1977. *Perspectives in Marxist Anthropology*. Cambridge: Cambridge University Press.

Gupta, Dipankar. 1981. 'Caste, Infrastructure and Superstructure: A Critique'. *Economic and Political Weekly*, 16(51): 2093–2104.

Headley, Zoe. 2011. Caste Belonging and Collective Memory: Locating the Past and Negotiating the Present among a South Indian subcaste. In Clark-Deces, I. (Ed.), *A Companion to the Anthropology of India* (pp. 98–113).. Blackwell Publishing, Oxford.

Ilaiah, Kancha. 2004. 'Caste or Class or Caste-Class: A Study in Dalit-Bahujan Consciousness and Struggles in Andhra Pradesh in 1980s'. In Mohanty Manoranjan (Ed.), *Class, Caste, Gender* (227– 254). New Delhi: SAGE.

Jaffrelot, Christophe. 2003. *India's Silent Revolution, The Rise of the Lower Castes in North India*. London: Hurst.

Jaffrelot, Christophe. 2016. Quota for Patels? The Neo-Middle-Class Syndrome and the (Partial) Return of Caste Politics in Gujarat. *Studies in Indian Politics*, 4(2): 218–232.

Jaffrelot, Christophe. 2019. 'Class and Caste in the 2019 Indian Election—Why Have So Many Poor Started Voting for Modi?' *Studies in Indian Politics*, 7(2): 149–160.

Jaffrelot, Christophe, and A. Kalaiyarasan. 2019. 'The Political Economy of the Jat Agitation for Other Backward Class Status'. *Economic and Political Weekly*, 54(7): 29–37.

Jeffrey, Craig, Patricia Jeffery, and Roger Jeffery. 2005. 'When Schooling Fails: Young Men, Education and Low–Caste Politics in Rural North India'. *Contributions to Indian Sociology*, 39(1): 1–38.

Jodhka, Surinder S. 2012. *Caste. Oxford India Short Introductions*. Delhi: Oxford University Press.

Jodhka, Surinder S., and Adarsh Kumar. 2017. 'Non-Farm Economy in Madhubani, Bihar Social Dynamics and Exclusionary Rural Transformations'. *Economic and Political Weekly*, lII(25 and 26): 14–24.

Jodhka, Surinder S., and Katherine S. Newman. 2010. 'In the Name of Globalization: Meritocracy, Productivity, and the Hidden Language of Caste'. In Sukhadeo Thorat and Katherine S. Newman (Eds.), *Economic Discrimination in Modern India* (pp. 52–87). New Delhi, Oxford University Press.

Jodhka, Surinder S. and Adarsh Kumar. 2017. 'Non-farm Economy in Madhubani, Bihar Social Dynamics and Exclusionary Rural Transformations'. *Economic and Political Weekly*, lII (25 and 26): 14–24.

Joshi, Shareen and Kochhar, Nishtha and Rao, Vijayendra, Jati Inequality in Rural Bihar (July 10, 2018). World Bank Policy Research Working Paper No. 8512, Available at SSRN: https://ssrn.com/abstract=3238352.

Lerche, Jens, Alpa Shah, and Barbara Harriss-White. 2013, July. 'Introduction: Agrarian Questions and Left Politics in India'. *Journal of Agrarian Change*, 13(3): 337–350.

Marx, Karl. 1973 [1853]. 'The Future Results of British Rule in India'. In Marx and Engels (Eds.), *Selected Works* (Vol. 1, pp. 494–499). Moscow: Progress Publishers.

Marx, Karl. 1973 [1859]. *A Contribution to the Critique of Political Economy*. Moscow: Progress Publishers.

Michelutti, Lucia. 2008. *The Vernacularisation of Democracy: Politics, Caste and Religion in India*. New Delhi: Routledge.

Michelutti, Lucia, Ashraf Hoque, Nicolas Martin, David Picherit, Paul Rollier, Arild Engelsen Ruud, and Clarinda Still. 2019. *Mafia Raj: The Rule of Bosses in South Asia*. Stanford, California : Stanford University Press.

Mosse, David. 2018. 'Caste and Development: Contemporary Perspectives on a Structure of Discrimination and Advantage'. *World Development*, 110: 422–436.

Mosse, David. 2019. 'The Modernity of Caste and the Market Economy'. *Modern Asian Studies*, 54(4): 1225–71.

Narula, Smita. 2007. 'Equal by Law, Unequal by Caste: The "Untouchable" Condition in Critical Race Perspective'. *Wisconsin International Law Journal*, 26(2): 255–344.

Natrajan, Balmurli. 2012. *The Culturalization of Caste in India: Identity and Inequality in Multicultural Age*. London: Routledge.

Naudet, Jules. 2018. *Stepping into the Elite: Trajectories of Social Achievement in India, France, and the United States*. New Delhi: Oxford University Press.

Nigam, Aditya. 2006. *The Insurrection of Little Selves: The Crisis of Secular-Nationalism in India*. USA: Oxford University Press.

Omvedt, Gail. 1978. 'Class Struggle or Caste War'. *Frontier*, 11: 30–40.

Paik, Shailaja. 2009. 'Chhadi Lage Chham, Vidya Yeyi Gham (The Harder the Stick Beats, the Faster the Flow of Knowledge): Dalit Women's Struggle for Education'. *Indian Journal of Gender Studies*, 16: 95.

Roohi, Sanam. 2019. Kula Gauravam, Transnational Migration, and Class Mobility: Reconfiguring the Dominant Caste Status in Coastal Andhra. In Surinder S. Jodhka and Jules Naudet (Eds.), *Mapping the Elite: Power, Privilege, and Inequality*. Delhi: Oxford University Press. Oxford Scholarship Online. doi: 10.1093/oso/9780199491070.003.0006.

Shah, Alpa et al. 2018. *Ground Down by Growth. Tribe, Caste, Class, and Inequality in Twenty-First Century India*. London: Pluto Press.

Shah, Ganshyam et al. 2006. *Untouchability in Rural India, New Delhi*. Thousand Oaks, CA: SAGE, 2006.

Sorokin, Pitirim. 1927. *Social Mobility*. New York: Harper and Brothers.

Srinivas, M. N. 1968. 'Mobility in the Caste System'. In Milton B. Singer and Bernard S. Cohn (Eds.), *Structure and Change in Indian Society* (p. 194). Chicago: Aldine Publishing Company.

Srinivas, M. N. 2002f/1987. 'The Caste System and Its Future'. In M. N. Srinivas (Ed.), *Collected Essays* (pp. 236–250). New Delhi: Oxford University Press.

Srinivas, M. N. 2003. An Obituary on Caste as a System. *Economic and Political Weekly*, 38(5): 455–459, http://www.jstor.org/stable/4413162.

Thorner, Alice. 1982. 'Semi-Feudalism or Capitalism? Contemporary Debate on Classes and Modes of Production in India'. *Economic and Political Weekly*, 17(50): 1961–1968.

Vaid, Divya. 2018. *Uneven Odds: Social Mobility in Contemporary India*. New Delhi: Oxford University Press.

Weber, Max. 1967. *The Sociology of Hinduism and Buddhism* [trans. H. H. Gerth and D. Martindale]. Glencoe, IL: Free Press.

CHAPTER 6

CASTE AND KINSHIP

JANAKI ABRAHAM[*]

The ways in which caste and kinship[1] have been understood as entangled has changed over time, especially as a result of the theoretical and methodological changes in the study of each. Writing in the 1960s, Adrian Mayer conceptualized caste as effectively the unit of the sub-caste comprising two concentric circles—'the kindred of cooperation' and 'the kindred of recognition' (1960) in which the later was the circle with in which marriage alliances would be sought. Mayer and others[2] could count the number of villages that included intermarrying descent groups that constituted a *jati* (the effective unit of caste or a sub-caste).[3]

Caste as an institution has altered dramatically and today, even if many towns and villages have caste based residential clusters or caste-based panchayats, the idea of the marriage circle or the circles that constitute the *jati* are far wider and may include families and groups who have migrated to far flung regions of the country or world or those linked though caste associations, matrimonial sites, or social media. Thus, while the local carries salience in understanding the meaning and practice of caste, castes can no longer be imagined as embedded in a narrowly defined local. Further, what has also been contested is the idea that kinship is encompassed by caste (*al la* Dumont 1957; 1966[4]). Lambert (2000) for example argues that the 'treatment of caste and kinship has been coloured by the systematic male bias' (pp. 118–19) particularly the neglect of kinship that cuts across castes.

---

[*] I am grateful to Surinder Jodhka and Jules Naudet for asking me to write this, and to Rajni Palriwala for comments.

[1] In this paper I use a broad definition of kinship which includes forms of relatedness through descent (restricted to a biological relatedness), intimate relationships, and marriage, family formations, living arrangements, and friendship.

[2] See also for example Madan (1989 [1965]).

[3] Although, this understanding was not shared by everyone (see, e.g. Parry, 1979).

[4] Lambert reminds us of Dumont and Pocock's words that kinship 'does not exist in the face of caste' (Dumont and Pocock 1970 quoted in Lambert 1996: 93).

Before proceeding it will be useful to briefly lay out changes in our understanding of caste. Colonial descriptions embodied in the ethnographies, District Gazetteers, and in census reports presented caste as a substance—discrete and describable through an intricate network of customs and rituals, and unambiguously classifiable in the varna scheme.[5] Caste emerged in these descriptions as static and timeless.[6] M. N. Srinivas' work on caste mobility which described strategies of not only marriage alliance, but changes in rituals and customs, described as 'sanskritization', was important in challenging the static view of caste created in colonial descriptions and in conceptualizing caste as one system (see, e.g. Srinivas, 1995 [1966]). These changes in rituals and customs[7] are critically linked to ideas of relatedness and in this have contributed to our understanding of the intersection of caste and kinship.

Further, in contrast to the conceptualization of caste as a multitude of localized groups within a given territory with distinct customs and rituals (as described by colonial ethnographers and several anthropologists), Louis Dumont (1972) argued that caste had to be understood as a pan Indian ideology that structured all relationships. Caste was then more than just a shell within which kinship was played out, it was the principle on which kinship was structured. And marriage alliance was the critical structuring feature that linked caste and kinship (Dumont, 1957). While this has been useful in furthering our understanding of the enmeshed nature of caste and kinship, Dumont's view of caste drew heavily from a Brahmanical textual tradition and was conceptualized through the lens of consensus across the caste system.[8] In doing this it failed to consider 'the political nature of caste hierarchy' (Quigley, 1993, p. 111), most notably exploitation, subordination, and violence that are critical to the institution of caste and its perpetuation (see e.g. Ambedkar (1916; 2004 [1936]).

An understanding of caste as a system of stratification in which power ran through every capillary of the system, was strengthened by the comparative scholarship on race for example, and critically by both anti-caste movements and dalit literature from across the country. Critical to this was the 'discovery' of B. R. Ambedkar's writings which mainstream scholarship had overlooked for decades (Rege 2013). Starting from the second decade of the 20th century, Ambedkar had described the way kinship practices around marriage such as widow remarriage, sati and child marriage were structured by the institution of caste and were fundamentally gendered (Ambedkar, 1916, 2004 [1936]; Rege, 2013).

---

[5] For a flavour of this see for example Thurston and Rangachari (1909); Ibbetson (1916).

[6] These descriptions have perpetuated into the present in a variety of forms. The People of India volumes brought out by the Anthropological Society of India and edited by K. S. Singh (1993) is one such example of a view of castes as describable through their distinct birth and death rituals and customs, kinship, and religious practices. This was also true of several ethnographies of different castes.

[7] The changes need to be understood not so much as imitation but as a form of resistance in the appropriation of what was forbidden (see Abraham forthcoming).

[8] For critiques on multiple counts see for example Ambedkar's writing (1916; 2004 [1936]); and for more direct critiques see Khare (2006); Madan (1971); Quigley (1993).

More recently feminist scholarship has contributed significantly to our understanding of the gendered nature of caste and in this has explored the intersection of gender, caste, and kinship. This literature is vast and looks at a range of issues from the control of women's sexuality, negotiations around marriage; caste and gendered violence; caste, kinship and labour and so on (see, e.g. Chakravarti, 1993, 2003; Chowdhry, 2007a; Dube, 1996; Fruzzetti, 1991, 2013; Ganesh, 1993; Grover, 2011; Kapadia 1996; Nitya Rao, 2014, 2015; and the articles in Anupama Rao, 2003, 2018). Dalit women's autobiographies have substantially deepened our understanding of caste, kinship, family, and marriage while highlighting the implications of poverty, discrimination, and violence on the everyday lives of dalit women (see, e.g. Pawar, 2008; Rege 2006; Viramma, Racine, and Racine, 2005).

If our conceptualization of caste has changed dramatically, so has our understanding of kinship. Kinship for too long was seen by anthropologists to be based in a biological relationship and hence the several titles of books 'Kinship and marriage among the …'. Kinship then expanded to include both relationships of blood and of marriage, or consanguinity and affinity. This happened in the 1980s, around the time that David Schneider argued in his *Critique of Kinship* (1984) that anthropologists had imposed Eurocentric categories of kinship onto other cultures. In particular, he argued that sexual procreation and biological relatedness had been assumed to be central to definitions of kinship. It was following this 'bomb' that the study of kinship moved out of its narrow confines to be far more encompassing of different forms of relatedness not limited by marriage and descent. This included non-heterosexual relationships, friendships, and other kinship relationships that were made rather than assumed as a result of genealogical relationships or marriage. In this conception of kinship, the focus was simultaneously on the processes and practices by which kin relatedness was established (see, e.g. Carstens, 2000) and the idea of kinship expanded to embrace 'family' and 'marriage' and intimate relationships of different kinds, kinship-like relationships that were earlier termed 'fictive kinship', and friends who were like family.

In this chapter, then I consider the expanded understandings of caste and kinship in looking at how they are entangled and mutually constituted over time. Socio-economic and political changes, including changes in state policy, have altered in multiple ways the mutual constitution of caste and kinship. Rather than try to summarize what is an extremely vast literature on caste and kinship, in what follows I focus on a few areas in which caste and kinship are mutually constituted and try to draw out these multiple influences and shifts over time. I will start by looking at kinship among castes through theories of origin—a focus that is not generally seen in discussions of kinship and caste. I will then look at kin-like relationships across caste that were termed 'fictive kinship'. The second section, titled 'Caste, hierarchy and marriage', looks at hypergamy and endogamy as central to the reproduction of caste and outlines these through a discussion of changing rural and urban landscapes and aspirations. The last section titled 'Caste, Kinship and Power' focuses on the shifts over time in what is considered a 'contentious' marriage or relationship and argues that power and control over resources is at the heart of the assertion of endogamy. This chapter then simultaneously highlights the importance of looking at temporal shifts in the entangled nature of kinship and caste.

THE KINSHIP OF CASTES

The scaffolding for the institution of caste was a robust ideology built through several texts written at different periods of time. Central to this ideology were theories of the origin of castes that harped on their differential origin in order to justify the fate of different castes and their members. Thus, for example, *Purushashukta* in the *Rg Veda* described the birth of different castes where the Brahmin was born from the head, the Kshatriya from the shoulders, the Vaishya from the thighs, and the Shudra from the feet.[9] The Laws of Manu described the birth of 'low castes' as resulting from sexual unions that were prohibited and abhorred and were clearly a mechanism to deter the violation of rules.

Theories of the origin of different castes were an important part of the descriptions of caste by colonial administrators and early anthropologists (see, e.g. Ibbetson, 1916; Risley, 1915; Thurston and Rangachari, 1909). These theories can be read as a way in which kinship across castes was imagined.[10] Colonial texts often drew from Brahmanical texts or from 'upper caste' versions of history and origins, and became a site of robust contestation.

Several contestations about the origin of a caste challenged their ranking in the putative caste hierarchy,[11] that is, their relationship or kinship with other castes. For example, the Nadars with a traditional occupation of coconut climbing and a history of working in agriculture, argued that they were Kshatriya (Hardgrave, 1969), or the Bedias of North India who also claimed Kshatriya status, drawing from the identities of the patrons of the women in the community who worked as sex workers (Agarwal, 2004). What is clear in many alternate theories of origin is that while caste groups tended to reconceptualize the structural relationship with other castes, and claimed a new kinship for themselves, they often did not challenge the institution of caste per se (Deliége, 1999). Many other theories contested the racial classification of the caste (see, e.g. Ambedkar, 2004 [1936]). Some theories including the one presented by Ambedkar in his book '*Who Are the Sudras*' (1949) strongly critiqued the way upper castes asserted caste power and privilege and subordinated and marginalized others. By pointing to

---

[9] There is no mention of those who ranked below the Shudras!

[10] The colonial texts often reproduced theories in upper caste texts or presented theories that were from the perspective of the ethnographer's upper castes respondents.

[11] This rewriting of history often ran in parallel with the process that M. N. Srinivas (1995) called 'sanskritization'.

a system of oppression in which castes were not innately different, but instead were subordinated and marginalized by virtue of the power some yield, these theories did in fact critique caste as a system. Below, I draw from my research of the Thiyyas in North Kerala to argue that these contestations over caste relatedness or kinship in the past were critical to the formation of social identities in the present (cf. Ali, 1999).

Thiyyas in North Kerala, who suffered caste based discrimination and are classified as an Other Backward Class, contested the theory given in Brahmanical texts *Keralolpatti* and *Keralamahatmyan* (written in Malayalam and Sanskrit, respectively) and reproduced in colonial texts such as William Logan's two volume *Malabar Manual* and the District Gazetteers. The theory stated that the Thiyyas were descendants of people who migrated to India from Ceylon around the 5th century AD bringing with them the coconut tree, which they cultivated and climbed—and hence their traditional occupation of toddy tapping. This theory was contested by several writers.

What is significant is the shift in the nature of the different arguments made over time. One theory presented by two authors somewhat differently, sought to prove that the Thiyyas were native to Kerala. While one did this by arguing that there is reference to the Thiyyas in the *Ramayana*, the other author argued that they were Aryans who came to India well before the 5th century. In contrast, two theories written and published in the first decade of the 21st century, move out to claim the world, pointing to a place of origin in ancient Crete or Africa via Kyrgyzstan. The former was presented in a self-published book by a professional who lived in Delhi, while the other, done on the basis of the DNA of the author based in the US, argued that Thiyyas migrated from Africa 30,000 years ago to Kyrgyzstan in central Asia and then moved to Kerala from there. The details of these theories are less significant here, than the idea embodied in them that the Thiyyas are an autonomous community outside the narrow confines of stratified caste society. It was apparent that while the question of origins had been asked through the 20th century, the motivation to ask this question and the answers sought emerged from a present. For the Thiyyas this was a present characterized by a mismatch: on the one hand a history of caste discrimination, and on the other professional success in different spheres over the last century. It was this perceived mismatch that prompted people to probe into the past and enquire about the origins of the caste. Thus, what emerges from these alternative theories of kinship with other castes is a critique of the knowledge produced by those with caste privilege, and unlike theories that sought a positional change in caste ranking, here we see an aspiration for the future via 'stepping out' of the narrow confines of caste society. While this discussion has briefly dealt with changing ideas about a kinship between castes (or the lack of one), below I turn to looking at practices by which a kinship may or may not be forged across castes.

Given the description of caste groups as bounded endogamous groups with innumerable rules restricting marriage and a sociality between castes, especially pertaining to food and space sharing, in the 1960s anthropologists asked if kin-like relationships or 'fictive kinship' was established across caste. This was particularly important because so much of the writing on kinship focused only on intra-caste consanguineal and affinal relationships (Lambert, 2000). Across India, it is common for people to communicate a strong relationship through the language of kinship so that a brother can mean someone you share parents with; a cousin; someone from your village or even state; or from the same caste. Writing in the 1960s, Mandelbaum (1967) argued that 'fictive kinship' relationships were indeed established between castes but cautioned that they were largely restricted to the two people concerned, and unlike other kinship relationships did not extend to the wider groups on both sides. Stanley Freed (1963) argued that fictive kinship terms are linked to the caste identities of the person concerned (p. 102) such that kinship with a person considered superior in caste is expressed with a term showing age hierarchy.[12] More recently Geert de Neve (2008) shows in his discussion of an industry in Tamil Nadu that 'fictive kinship' is strategically employed in this setting, even if it has its limits. Employers then use the language of kinship (including for those they do not share a caste identity with) for recruitment, retaining and disciplining labour, but as de Neve argues, while this helped in mobalizing workers' co-operation and silencing them on the shop floor, the kinship morality did not prevent workers from leaving when they did not like the labour conditions.

Helen Lambert's (1996, 2000) rich ethnography from a village in Rajasthan on the other hand indicates that not only are there kinship relationships in the local that go beyond relationships based on descent and alliance, but these kinship relationships[13] cut across caste. For example, she describes the way given a woman's subordinate position in her husband's village (her *sasural*), she may enter into two kinds of relationships: *jholi* or *dharm*. *Jholi* relationships with a family which is often from another caste are chosen by in-laws so that the daughter-in-law has a house where she is like a daughter (she does not veil and her interactions are more open and free). This family then can stand in for her family in order to fulfil obligations at death, marriage, etc. *Dharm* relations are also adoptive relations but are contracted by a woman herself. Although a *jholi* relationship is generally only established with a caste from whom water can be accepted, this is not necessarily true of *dharm* relationships. Thus a *dharm bhai/behen* (brother/sister), or *dharam ma* (mother) may be established with someone from a caste with which there are no commensal relations but commensality will be practised by those concerned. Contrary to Mandelbaum's argument (1967), Lambert (2000) argues that this kinship extends to others in the family and often continues for at least another generation, if not more. These adoptive relationships that are locality based are considered consanguineous ties and are in fact considered purer than ones based on shared blood (Lambert, 2000). These kinship ties across castes are then, she argues, made through processes by which kinship is made: shared locality or feeding/eating or the fulfilment of obligations. The varied examples above express both the possibility of kinship across castes, while also pointing to the possible limits of such a kinship in the absence of contexts in which affective ties are created over time through certain processes. A concern for changes in

---

[12] For example a man will be referred to as an uncle rather than a brother if he belongs to a superior caste Freed (1963).

[13] She uses the term 'kinship' rather than 'fictive kinship' in accordance with the shift to a broader idea of kinship.

the kinship between castes continues in the rest of the chapter through a focus on the rules of marriage and their violation.

Caste, Hierarchy, and Marriage

Endogamy and hypergamy are central structuring principles that ensure the reproduction of caste and caste status (Ghurye 2000 [1932]; Srinivas, 1995 [1966]). Writing in 1916, Ambedkar not only stressed the centrality of endogamy in both the making of caste and its perpetuation, but argued that sati, the enforcement of widowhood, and child marriage were central to this. Endogamy could thus only be upheld through the control of women's sexuality.[14] Nur Yalman (1963) stressed that it was ritual purity, women, and land that castes sought to protect in the maintenance of caste hierarchy and caste power.

Although endogamy (and hypergamy) is considered ideal across the caste hierarchy, some women did not have the 'luxury' of practising it, since their bodies were seen to be 'available' to men of 'superior' castes and economic status. Thus, not all castes have policed their caste boundaries in the same way, either because they did not have the privilege to do this or because they did not feel the need to. B. R. Ambedkar (1916) articulated this well through the idea that caste was a system of graded inequalities, and entailed graded violence against women. At the same time, given that the sharp and violent response to non-endogamous relationships is far from restricted to what are considered 'upper' or *savarna* (twice-born) castes, it is important to recognize that hypogamous relationships are prohibited (and feared) across all caste communities. The prohibition of hypogamous relationships and the endorsement of hypergamous relationships indicates the way patriarchy is entangled with the logic of caste such that caste power and privilege and gender power overlap in the case of hypergamous relationships or do not contradict each other, unlike in hypogamous ones where the woman is of higher caste status to the man (see Abraham, 2014).

Hypergamy or the practice of a woman marrying a man of higher status is consistent with the idea of *kanyadaan* or the ritual gift of the bride which is believed to bring religious merit (*punya*) in Hindu marriages. It is also consistent with the status differential between 'wife-givers' and 'wife takers' such that gifts have to flow from 'givers' of a bride to 'takers' throughout her life and even after (Madan, 1989 [1965]; Vatuk, 1975). This is particularly so in north India where affinal relationships are ordered by caste and hypergamy, and there is a prohibition of exchange[15] marriages. This is in sharp contrast to south India where there was a preference for consanguineal marriages (cousin marriages or uncle-niece marriages) and no prohibition of exchange marriages (see, e.g. Dumont, 1957, 1961, 1964, 1966; Kapadia, 1996). This difference between north India and

---

[14] See also Sharmila Rege (2013). For an elaboration of this see for example Uma Chakravarti (1993; 2003).

[15] Where a sister and brother pair are married to a brother and sister pair.

south India is seen to have strong implications for women's experience of marriage in the two regions (see Palriwala, 1994; Uberoi, 1993).

Hypergamy, Pocock (1972) argued, was the structuring principle within the caste and a central mechanism by which castes were internally organized, i.e. differentiated. His study of the Patidars in Gujarat described hypergamous marriage strategies in which a woman married into a family of higher status. In 19th-century Bengal, Kulin Brahmin men entered into polygynous marriages with women who ranked below them. In turn rich families whose link to a Kulin Brahmin was distant, sought an alliance for a daughter in order to enhance their status. In fact several different kinds of marital arrangements were followed (Béteille, 1996).[16] As in the case of many other hypergamous marriages, large dowries accompanied the marriage[17] and men thus gained a lot materially from their several marriages.

Also writing about Gujarat, A. M. Shah points out that hypergamous relationships led to a surfeit of unmarried women among the high status groups in the castes, addressed through polygyny and even female infanticide; and a number of bachelor men among the lower status groups in the caste[18] or marriage with women of a lower caste (2014, p. 412). Shah writes that among the Khedawal Brahmins in Radhvanaj, among four of the five fraternal units 'the eldest brother is a bachelor, and genealogies since 1825 show that in almost every generation the line of descent was continued by the youngest son, while the others remained unmarried' (2014, p. 412). Given their caste orthodoxy it was not very common for a man to marry a woman of a 'lower' caste, nor was widow remarriage allowed. This was in contrast to the Patidars in Gujarat among whom widow remarriage was practised until the 1950s (Pocock, 1972).[19]

The consolidation and protection of material resources, particularly land, through rules of marriage and inheritance was a strategy to consolidate caste power. The Nambudiris of Kerala, for example, sought to keep property intact through a kinship rule called primogeniture in which only the eldest son could marry a Nambuduri woman and other sons were forced to enter into *sambandham*[20] relations with Nayar women. While the Nambudiris were strongly patrilineal, Nayars were matrilineal and the children born of these *sambandham* ties belonged to their mother's matrilineal joint

---

[16] In some cases where the girl was from a poor family, she may have remained in her parental house after getting married and her husband would visit her there (Béteille 1996).

[17] See for example Parry (1979) for a discussion of the escalation of dowries in the practice of hypergamy among the Rajputs in Kangra, North West India.

[18] This is one of the examples Shah (2014: 63) uses to point to the way the composition of households is affected by the customs and institutions of particular castes. For a discussion on caste and changes in the family and household composition see Patel (2005).

[19] In a fascinating article Tilche and Simpson (2018) discuss changes in the marriage market among Patidars in Gujarat. The adverse sex ratio, which is a fall out of practices of hypergamy, has led to a large number of bachelors in the 21st century as well. This has been exacerbated by the desire for men who migrate abroad and for those engaged in non-agriculture jobs.

[20] Literally 'a connection'. There was considerable debate among anthropologists on whether *sambandham* could be considered marriage or not.

family tharavad and had no rights in their father's house or his wealth. For the Nayar tharavads, a *sambandham* with a Nambudiri man brought prestige and status. However, scores of Nambudiri women remained unmarried or were married to much older men leading to many child widows who were forced to follow stringent rules of widowhood. In the 20th century these and other forms of hypergamy and polygyny were critiqued and were the focus of social reform.[21]

Writing about the Newars in Kathmandu, Quigley (1993) says that isogamy was the response to an outside politically dominant force usurping their power and denying them the opportunity of marriage alliances with the new elite. 'Hypergamy and isogamy' he argues 'are two sides of the same hierarchical coin' by which groups attempted to maximize their 'status given the political constraints of a society where power ultimately derive[d] from control over land' (pp. 112–113). The changing response to kinship arrangements over time indicates the importance of not only looking at kinship rules and practices as being dynamic over time, but also of understanding the social context of these changes. Below, I will further elaborate on changes in marriage circles over time.

In her discussion of shifts in marriage practices of Kayasths in Hyderabad, Karen Leonard (1978) argues that over a period of time there was a relaxation in the restricted circle of endogamy such that marriages that were once prohibited between say the Mathurs and Srivastavs or Saxenas became normative. She documents the way marriage strategies sought to maximize economic and political opportunities to the extent that there was a sharp increase in the number of marriages with non-Kayasths and even a preference for marrying a Hyderabadi rather than a non-Hyderabadi. This included a questioning of intra-subcaste rules of prohibited degrees of relationships, which came to be seen as 'unnecessary, old fashioned barriers to desirable marriages' (Leonard, 1978, p. 276). Leonard (1978) thus argues that there was an 'adaptability' in Kayasth marriage networks in order to maximize economic, political, and social status. This adaptability and negotiation is important to understand in other contexts as well.

Béteille points out, for example, that among Tamil Brahmans, 'the horizons of endogamy were being extended from sub-sub caste to sub caste, and then to caste' (1996, p. 164).[22] This expansion of circles of endogamy was a result of the importance given to education, occupation, and income. At the end of the 20th century however, unlike the case of the Kayasths in which the local came to take precedence over caste, Béteille (1996) writes that a parent would prefer that their child marry a Brahman from another region rather than a non-Brahmin.[23] This redefinition of caste endogamy in the face of dramatic geographical mobility can be read as a need to reproduce Brahmanism, and

---

[21] For a discussion of this and an excellent contemporary study of the Nambudiris see Gallo (2017).

[22] Béteille (1996) thus cautions us to the use of the word inter-caste, as this label may be used for alliances that are now part of the new circle of endogamy.

[23] For example in arranged marriages or strategically maneuvered self-arranged marriages, a Haryana Brahman father may agree to a proposal from a Brahman from Bihar who has a good job because of the anxiety that they may not be able to find a groom from within their caste who is as qualified as their daughter.

was clearly not unrelated to the strong non-Brahmin movement in Tamil Nadu. Writing about young middle class IT sector employees in Tamil Nadu in the first decade of the 21st century, Fuller and Narasimhan (2008) argue that although interpersonal compatibility is now considered a priority, this choice is exercised within the circle of caste endogamy.

While the authority of parents to arrange a marriage contrary to the will of the young person has reduced substantially and been bolstered by the law, 'consent' is constrained by the pressure to marry and marry with parental approval. Based on her study of middle class, upper caste young people in Delhi, Parul Bhandari (2017) argues that familial approval remains for young people an important priority along with 'love' and hence caste and class remain considerations even in self-arranged marriages. Thus, while among the people she interviewed there were some inter-caste marriages, these were between the upper castes, and Bhandari 'did not encounter a single "serious" relationship between a member of an upper caste and one of a so-called lower caste' (2017).[24] Thus, choice and desire in even pre-marital relationships among young people are structured by caste, class, and ethnicity.

Through a moving case study of a dalit women in Andhra Pradesh, Clarinda Still (2011) points to the sense of shame at the elopement of a woman who is then brought back by her parents, beaten and married off to someone quickly. The dominant narrative she argues was of how education for girls was risky. This idea of education being 'risky' can be seen to be enacted in the stringent regimes of gender segregation in colleges, inscribed in the architectural design of buildings that have separate staircases, canteens, and corridors (Hebbar, 2018), uniforms for all students and tight curfew hours in hostels.

As several scholars have pointed out this focus on parental approval and the continued respectability of 'arranged marriages' then leads people to describe their self-chosen marriage as 'love and arranged marriage' or 'arranged love marriage' (see de Neve, 2016; Grover, 2011; Mody, 2008).[25] Sometimes approval for a self-chosen non-endogamous relationship is negotiated by following a traditional form in which a marriage proposal is formally brought by the groom's family.

On the other hand, choice marriages without the approval of parents, even if within the caste, may result in the couple or one of them being distanced from the family, disinherited, excommunicated from the caste or village, shamed by being paraded through the village, or in some cases even murdered (see Chowdhury, 2007a; Kannabiran and Kannabiran, 2003; Chakravarti, 2005). In some cases, the family may file a case of kidnapping, abduction and rape against the man (see Baxi, 2015). In other cases however, inter-caste or inter-religious marriages may be accepted by parents and even by a wider community. It is productive then to ask why certain marriages

---

[24] This is precisely why scholars prefer the term 'self-arranged' rather than 'love' marriage to indicate the way 'love', and 'choice' are also structured.

[25] The various ways in which a marriage may be categorized as 'love and arranged' or even as an 'arranged marriage' and the shifting circles of permissible marriage which complicate the term 'inter-caste', means that statistics on inter-caste marriages are not reliable.

are contentious and provoke a violent reaction at a certain point in time and others are accepted even if after a lapse of time. This forces us to ask what is at stake in choice marriages that cut across boundaries of permissible marriage. In the section titled Caste, Kinship and Power below I turn to this by first drawing from my research on the Thiyyas in North Kerala.

Caste, Kinship, and Power

During colonial rule some Thiyya women in north Kerala (north Malabar to be precise) had liaisons with British men. Thiyyas, who were seen to rank below the Nayars in the caste hierarchy, suffered caste-based discrimination and violence including the denial of temple entry and practices of untouchability. Early colonial texts suggest that women were not ex-communicated from the caste as a result of the liaisons.[26] However, it was in the late 19th century, early 20th century that the liaisons with British men began to be seen as being 'dishonourable', and 'degrading to the community' and women who had liaisons and their children born of these relationships were ex-communicated from the caste, or a matrilineal joint family *tharavad* ex-communicated the woman and her children. It is no coincidence that this break in kinship took place at the height of the social reform movement in the late 19th century and the early 20th century when caste associations were being formed.[27] Thus, 'social reform' was addressed in a context of castes competing for social legitimacy and political and economic power, and was equally a time when castes were challenging processes that were *not* seen as status enhancing (Abraham, 2014). The 'honour' and status of the community was thus sought to be restored by policing the boundaries of the Thiyya caste and especially through the control of women's sexuality.

Thus, while the principle of endogamy may have be critical to the reproduction of caste, the contexts and manner in which it has been enforced has varied. One critical distinction was between primary and secondary marriages (Dumont 1964) in which primary marriages were more strictly regulated, and secondary marriages may have crossed caste lines (Parry 2001). In addition, Parry (2001, p.787) points to the correlation between marital instability and intercaste marriage. On the basis of his research in an industrial town in India, he argues that under modern conditions this was strengthened. Not only then does the assertion of endogamy vary between different castes in the caste hierarchy but among a working-class marital practices have been 'progressively polarized' (Parry 2001, p. 788). Parry writes, 'For those with informal sector industrial jobs, divorce remains as frequent as formerly and remarriage more commonly crosses caste boundaries. For

---

[26] For details, see Abraham (2006).
[27] The Sri Narayana Dharma Paripalana Yogam was formed in 1903; the Nayar Service Society in 1908, the Yogakshema Sabha which built a movement for social reform among the Nambudiris started much later in 1930.

those with public sector employment, a new companionate ideology of marriage and stress on intimacy is accompanied by a decline in divorce (hence a lesser likelihood of intercaste marriage)...' (ibid.). Added then to this shift in relation to the practice of endogamy is the understanding that the response to the breach of endogamy shifts across time as I have tried to show in the discussion on liaisons above (Abraham, 2014). Thus, while Yalman (1963) argued that caste blood was bilateral and hence women's sexuality was to be controlled, the extent to which this was done was not uniform through time hence indicating Yalman's neglect of 'the historicity of facts and practices' (Palriwala, 1994, p. 24). In addition, as I will discuss below, a consideration of the web of power and status in the local is critical to understanding the very varied responses to non-endogamous intimate relationships and marriages.[28]

A study of the responses to non-endogamous marriages indicates a distinct pattern. During field work in North Kerala, for example I was struck by how marriages with even someone from another country would be accepted and collectively celebrated, while a marriage with someone from a caste earlier considered stigmatized in the local was resisted, condemned, or minimally whispered about. The issue at stake then was less about the ideal of endogamy or the 'purity of blood' but rather was linked to the anxiety about *changing relationships of power* in the local.

Reports of women and men killed because they loved across caste or community in both north and south India has entered into the media with frightening frequency in the last decade or so. This extreme reaction is not only to inter-caste or inter-community relationships but also to those that are seen as violating rules of marriage of one kind or another—for example, village exogamy or gotra (clan) exogamy. These killings, inappropriately termed 'honour killings', are so varied that it is hard to succinctly capture all their complexities. However, I would like to consider a few cases to highlight the web of issues at play.

Hypogamous relationships have been seen as far more of a threat than hypergamous ones. Thus, when the man has belonged to a caste considered 'inferior' to that of the woman, the response has often been sharper. For example, in a case in Haryana in which a Jat woman (Jats are a dominant landowning intermediate caste in north India) and a Jatav man (a scheduled caste) ran away to get married, the village reacted sharply. Jats saw this as a sign of Jatavs becoming too powerful, and were expressing this by laying claim to a woman of the dominant caste (Chowdhry, 2009). Enforcing endogamy, then, is one way in which communities seek to reassert their caste/community power. In some cases, the whole dalit hamlet was burnt down in an attempt to reiterate caste/community power.

However, even hypergamous relationships between a man and woman who are from castes very differently ranked have met with violence, though not necessarily with death.

---

[28] It is important to point out here that all non-endogamous marriages are not 'love marriages' or self-chosen marriages. Especially in urban India, inter-caste family arranged marriages among a middle class are not uncommon and have received insufficient attention. Equally, as Donner (2002) points out, the most common form of love marriage in a neighbourhood in Kolkata was within the caste group.

Prem Chowdhry (2007a) describes a case in which in a Jat dominated village, a Jat man and a Balmiki (scheduled caste) woman were hauled up by an all-caste panchayat for their 'love affair'. Their faces were blackened, their hair was cut and they were paraded on donkeys in the village.

Here too it is important to look at the shifts in the assertion of endogamy. Prem Chowdhry describes how during colonial rule some Jat men married women from castes considered 'lower' such as Churhi or Chamar castes, and the children of such marriages were called Jats even if they may have been 'ridiculed as *Churhike* or *Chamaranke*' (1994, p. 127); see also Chowdhry, 2007b). This openness was captured by a local belief, 'The Jat is like an ocean and whichever river falls into this ocean loses its identity and become the ocean itself' (1994, p. 127). However, this tolerance changed as members of the caste acquired more property and sought upward mobility.

In several instances the relative caste positioning of the couple was not the issue, as much as the way the authority of the family and the community were seen as undermined in the self-chosen relationship. At the same time, this perceived threat to the masculinity of the men in the group needs to be understood in relation to its material basis (Chowdhry 1998). One fear is that a woman's agency in the choice of spouse will lead to her claiming her share of property (Chowdhry, 1998), while another is linked to a perception that Dalits are usurping the jobs of the dominant caste (Chowdhry, 2009).

The nature of these responses becomes clearer when we look at what would appear to be an 'endogamy paradox' (Abraham 2014). Men, and mainly Jat men, in Haryana have been going to far flung places like Kerala and Assam to find brides because of the skewed sex ratio in the state (877 women per 1000 men, according to the 2011 Census). During a visit to Payyanur, in north Kerala, from where several women have migrated to Haryana for marriage, I interviewed marriage brokers and family members of women who had married men from Haryana. Both groups spoke about how Haryanvi men had no idea about what the local caste terms meant but they asked for girls of 'good' castes (see also Kaur, 2004). In many cases, the mothers of these men were told that the women did not eat meat. This and the relatively lighter skin of the women were read as markers of a 'good' caste.[29]

What marked these marriages out from those which were self-arranged was that here the Haryanvi men were choosing brides with the consent of their families when they could not find a bride at home. When marriages are contracted far from the local, they avoid setting up a marriage alliance with another family, and thus do not establish a web of relationships. In such a context, a woman can be incorporated completely into the family without upsetting local hierarchies. Thus the assertion of endogamy is less about maintaining the 'purity of blood' than about the fear of changing power equations, whether in the family, caste group, village, or beyond.

---

[29] These are marriages in which no dowry is transacted; in fact, the groom pays for all the marriage expenses.

Conclusion

In this chapter, I have looked at the question of kinship between castes, and at marriage, which critically structures the relationship between caste and kinship. Here I have tried to show that transformations in particular castes may result in contesting histories and presenting alternative ones of how they relate to other castes in the region. Thus, although theories of origin were part of a strategy by which a caste sought to, or seeks to change its position, the nature of the theories change with changes in the caste.

Further, through a discussion of endogamy and hypergamy, and the enforcement of rules of marriage I have tried to argue that kinship practices, especially marriage, have been critically tied to the ways in which the boundaries of a caste have been imagined and asserted. Further, endogamy is reproduced less as a value in itself and more as an ideal that is critically tied to material and symbolic power and forms of social status. What the contingencies in the enforcement of endogamy tell us is that ideas of purity and pollution are another of the ideological cloaks that shroud something else—an attempt to maintain power and the status quo whether in terms of prestige, caste superiority, jobs, or property.

What we learn about caste by looking at the entangled nature of caste and kinship is that caste is agile—it shifts and transforms itself according to context. The complicated ways in which it works on the ground bring together both past memory of stigma and discrimination, relationships of power and domination in the present, and aspirations for the future. It will then do us good to recognize the flexibility and agility of caste[30] and kinship and understand that this entangled relationship is dynamic and critically linked to power, whether caste power, familial power, or patriarchal power.

References

Abraham, J. 2006. 'The Stain of White: Liaisons, Memories, and White Men as Relatives'. *Men and Masculinities*, 9(2): 131–151.

Abraham, J. 2014. 'Contingent Caste Endogamy and Patriarchy: Lessons for Our Understanding of Caste'. *Economic and Political Weekly*, 49(2): 56–65.

Abraham, Janaki. 'Sanskritisation' as appropriation of what was denied: A view from the Sree Narayana Guru Movement in Kerala. *Sociological Bulletin*. Forthcoming.

Agarwal, Anuja. 2004. '"The Bedias Are Rajputs": Caste Consciousness of a Marginal Community'. *Contributions to Indian Sociology*, 38(1&2): 221–246.

Ambedkar, B. R. 1916. 'Castes in India: Their Mechanism, Genesis and Development'. *Online*. http://www.columbia.edu/itc/mealac/pritchett/00ambedkar/txt_ambedkar_castes.html. accessed 12 September 2019.

Ambedkar, B. R. 1949. *Who Were the Shudras?* Bombay: Thackers.

---

[30] See for example Sharma (1999) who argues that caste must be seen as a contingent category with ever changing content.

Ambedkar, B. R. 2004 (1936). 'The Annihilation of Caste'. In Valerian Rodrigues (Ed.), *Essential Writings of B. R. Ambedkar*. New Delhi: Oxford University Press.

Ali, Daud. (Ed.). 1999. *Invoking the Past: The Uses of History in South Asia*. New Delhi: Oxford University Press.

Baxi, Pratiksha. 2015. '"Pyar Kiya to Darna Kya": On Criminalising Love'. In Daniela Berti and Devika Bordia (Eds.), *Regimes of Legality: Ethnography of Criminal Cases in South Asia* (pp. 52–90). Oxford: Oxford University Press.

Béteille, André. 1990. 'Race, Caste and Gender'. *Man*, 25(3): 489–504.

Béteille, André. 1996. 'Caste in Contemporary India'. In C. J. Fuller (Ed.), *Caste Today* (pp. 150–179). Delhi: Oxford University Press.

Bhandari, Parul. 2017. 'Pre-Marital Relationships and the Family in Modern India'. *South Asia Multidisciplinary Academic Journal* [Online], 16. http://samaj.revues.org/4379.

Carsten, J. (Ed.). 2000. *Cultures of Relatedness: New Approaches to the Study of Kinship*. Cambridge: Cambridge University Press.

Chakravarti, Uma. 1993. 'Conceptualising Brahmanical Patriarchy in Early India: Gender, Caste, Class and State'. *Economic and Political Weekly*, 28(14): 579–585.

Chakravarti, Uma. 2003. *Gendering Caste: Through a Feminist Lens*. Calcutta: Stree.

Chakravarti, Uma. 2005. 'From Fathers to Husbands: Of Love, Death and Marriage in North India'. In Lynn Welchman and Sara Hossain (Eds.), *Honour: Crimes, Paradigms and Violence against Women* (pp. 308–331). New Delhi: Zubaan.

Chowdhry, Prem. 1994. *The Veiled Women: Shifting Gender Equations in Rural Haryana 1880–1990*. Delhi: Oxford University Press.

Chowdhry, Prem. 1998. 'Enforcing Cultural Codes: Gender and Violence in Northern India'. In Mary E. John and Janaki Nair (Eds.), *A Question of Silence? The Sexual Economies of Modern India* (pp. 332–367). New Delhi: Kali for Women.

Chowdhry, Prem. 2007a. *Contentious Marriages, Eloping Couples: Gender, Caste and Patriarchy in North India*. New Delhi: Oxford University Press.

Chowdhry, Prem. 2007b. 'Fluctuating Fortunes of Wives: Creeping Rigidity in Inter-Caste Marriages in the Colonial Period'. *Indian Historical Review*, 34(1): 210–243.

Chowdhry, Prem. 2009. '"First Our Jobs Then Our Girls": The Dominant Caste Perceptions on the "Rising" Dalits'. *Modern Asian Studies*, 43(2): 437–479.

de Neve, Geert. 2008. '"We Are All *Sondukarar* (Relatives)!": Kinship and Its Morality in an Urban Industry of Tamil Nadu, South India'. *Modern Asian Studies*, 42(1): 211–246.

de Neve, Geert. 2016. 'The Economies of Love: Love Marriage, Kin Support, and Aspiration in a South Indian Garment City'. *Modern Asian Studies*, 50(4): 1220–1249.

Deliége, Robert. 1999. *Untouchables of India* [tr. Nora Scott]. New York: Berg.

Donner, H. 2002. '"One's Own Marriage": Love Marriages in a Calcutta Neighbourhood'. *South Asia Research*, 22(1): 79–94.

Dube, Leela. 1996. 'Caste and Women'. In M. N. Srinivas (Ed.), *Caste: Its Twentieth Century Avatar* (pp. 1–27). New Delhi: Viking Penguin India.

Dumont, Louis. 1957. *Hierarchy and Marriage Alliance in South Indian Kinship*. Occasional Papers of the Royal Anthropological Institute. London: Royal Anthropological Institute.

Dumont, Louis. 1961. 'Marriage in India: The Present State of the Question'. *Contributions to Indian Sociology*, 5: 75–95.

Dumont, Louis. 1964. 'Marriage in India: The Present State of the Question: Postscript to Part I–II. Nayar and Newar'. *Contributions to Indian Sociology*, 7: 77–98.

Dumont, Louis. 1966. 'Marriage in India: The Present State of the Question: North India in Relation to South India. Part-III'. *Contributions to Indian Sociology*, 9: 90–114.

Dumont, Louis. 1972. *Homo Hierarchicus: The Caste System and Its Implications*. London: Paladin.
Freed, Stanley. 1963. 'Fictive Kinship in a North Indian Village'. *Ethnology*, 1(1): 86–103.
Fuller, C. J. (Ed.). 1996. *Caste Today*. Delhi: Oxford University Press.
Fuller, C. J., and Haripriya Narasimhan. 2008. 'Companionate Marriage in India: The Changing Marriage System in a Middle-Class Brahman Subcaste'. *The Journal of the Royal Anthropological Institute*, 14(4): 736–754.
Fruzzetti, Lina M. 1991. *The Gift of a Virgin: Women, Marriage, and Ritual in a Bengali Society*. New Delhi: Oxford University Press.
Fruzzetti, Lina M. 2013. *When Marriages Go Astray: Choices Made, Choices Challenged*. New Delhi: Orient BlackSwan.
Gallo, Ester. 2017. *The Fall of Gods: Memory, Kinship, and Middle Classes in South India*. New Delhi: Oxford University Press.
Ganesh, Kamala. 1993. *Boundary Walls: Caste and Women in a Tamil Community*. Delhi: Hindustan Publishing Corporation.
Grover, Shalini. 2011. *Marriage, Love, Caste and Kinship Support: Lived Experiences of the Urban Poor in India*. New Delhi: Social Science Press.
Ghurye, G. S. 2000 [1932]. *Caste and Race in India*. Bombay: Popular Prakashan.
Hebbar, Nandini N. 2018. 'Subjectivities of Suitability: "Intimate Aspirations" in an Engineering College'. *South Asia Multidisciplinary Academic Journal* [Online], 19. http://journals.openedition.org/samaj/4578.
Hardgrave, Robert L. Jr. 1969. *The Nadars of TamilNad: The Political Culture of a Community in Change*. Berkeley and Los Angeles: University of California Press.
Ibbetson, D. C. J. 1916. *Punjab Castes*. Lahore: Government Press.
Kannabiran, Vasanth, and Kalpana Kannabiran. 2003. 'Caste and Gender: Understanding Dynamics of Power and Violence'. In Anupama Rao (Ed.), *Gender & Caste* (pp. 249–260). Delhi: Kali for Women.
Kapadia, Karin. 1996. *Siva and Her Sisters: Gender, Caste, and Class in Rural South India*. Delhi: Oxford University Press.
Kaur, Ravinder. 2004. 'Across-Region Marriages: Poverty, Female Migration and the Sex Ratio'. *Economic and Political Weekly*, 39(25): 2595–2603.
Khare, R. S. 2006. *Caste, Hierarchy, and Individualism: Indian Critiques of Louis Dumont's Contributions*. New Delhi and New York: Oxford University Press.
Lambert, Helen. 1996. 'Caste, Gender and Locality in Rural Rajasthan'. In C. J. Fuller (Ed.), *Caste Today*. Delhi: Oxford University Press.
Lambert, Helen. 2000. 'Sentiment and Substance in North Indian Forms of Relatedness'. In Janet Carsten (Ed.), *Cultures of Relatedness: New Approaches to the Study of Kinship* (pp. 73–89). Cambridge: Cambridge University Press.
Leonard, Karen Isaksen. 1978. *Social History of an Indian Caste: The Kayasths of Hyderabad*. Berkeley: University of California Press.
Madan, T. N. 1989 [1965]. *Family and Kinship: A Study of the Pandits of Rural Kashmir*. Delhi: Oxford University Press.
Madan, T. N. 1971. 'On the Nature of Caste in India: A Review Symposium on Louis Dumont's Homo Hierarchicus'. *Contributions to Indian Sociology*, 5(1): 1–13.
Mandelbaum, David G. 1967. 'Some Meanings of Kinship in Village India'. *Economic and Political Weekly*, 2(3/5): 237+239–40.
Mayer, Adrian C. 1960. *Caste and Kinship in Central India: A Village and Its Region*. London: Routledge & Kegan Paul.

Mody, Parveez. 2008. *The Intimate State: Love-Marriage and the Law in Delhi*. New Delhi: Routledge.
Palriwala, Rajni. 1994. *Changing Kinship, Family, and Gender Relations in South Asia: Processes, Trends, and Issues*. Leiden: Women and Autonomy Centre (VENA), Leiden University.
Parry, J. 1979. *Caste and Kinship in Kangra*. London: Routledge and Kegan Paul.
Parry, J. 2001. 'Ankalu's Errant Wife: Sex, Marriage and Industry in Contemporary Chhattisgarh'. *Modern Asian Studies*, 35(4): 783–820.
Patel, Tulsi (Ed.). 2005. *The Family in India: Structure and Practice*. California and London: SAGE.
Pawar, Urmila. 2008. *The Weave of My Life: A Dalit Woman's Memoir*. Kolkata: Stree.
Pocock, David. 1972. *Kanbi and Patidar. A Study of the Patidar Community of Gujarat*. Oxford: Clarendon Press.
Quigley, Declan. 1993. *The Interpretation of Caste*. Oxford: Clarendon Press.
Rao, Anupama (Ed.). 2003. *Gender and Caste*. New Delhi: Kali for Women.
Rao, Anupama. 2018. *Gender, Caste and the Imagination of Equality*. New Delhi: Women unlimited.
Rao, Nitya. 2014. 'Caste, Kinship, and Life Course: Rethinking Women's Work and Agency in Rural South India'. *Feminist Economics*, 20(3): 78–102.
Rao, Nitya. 2015. 'Marriage, Violence and Choice: Understanding Dalit Women's Agency in Rural Tamil Nadu'. *Gender and Society*, 29(3): 410–433.
Rege, Sharmila. 2006. *Writing Caste Writing Gender: Narrating Dalit Women's Testimonios*. New Delhi: Zubaan.
Rege, Sharmila. 2013. Against the *Madness of Manu: B.R. Ambedkar's Writings on Brahmanical Patriarchy*. New Delhi: Navayana.
Risley, H. H. 1915. *People of India*. Calcutta and Simla: Thaker, Spink & Co.
Shah, A. M. 2014. *The Writings of A M Shah: The Household and Family in India*. Hyderabad: Orient Blackswan.
Sharma, U. 1999. *Caste*. Buckingham: Open University Press.
Srinivas, M. N. 1995 [1966]. *Social Change in Modern India*. New Delhi: Orient Blackswan.
Still, Clarinda. 2011. 'Spoiled Brides and the Fear of Education: Honour and Social Mobility among Dalits in South India'. *Modern Asian Studies*, 45(5): 1119–1146.
Thurston, E., and K. Rangachari. 1909. *Castes and Tribes in Southern India*. Madras: Government Press.
Tilche, Alice, and Edward Simpson. 2018. 'Marriage and the Crisis of Peasant Society in Gujarat, India'. *The Journal of Peasant Studies*. DOI: 10.1080/03066150.2018.1477759.
Uberoi, Patricia, (Ed.). 1993. 'Introduction' in *Family, Kinship and Marriage in India* (pp. 1–44). Delhi: Oxford University Press.
Vatuk, Sylvia. 1975. 'Gifts and Affines in North India'. *Contributions to Indian Sociology*. 9(1):155–96.
Viramma, Josiane Racine, and Jean-Luc Racine. 2005. *Viramma: Life of a Dalit*. New Delhi: Social Science Press.
Yalman, N. 1963. 'On the Purity of Women in the Castes of Ceylon and Malabar'. *The Journal of the Royal Anthropological Institute of Great Britain and Ireland*, 93(1): 25–58.
Yalman, N. 1967. *Under the Bo Tree: Studies in Caste, Kinship and Marriage in the Interior of Ceylon*. Berkeley: University of California Press.

SECTION II

HISTORY, STATE, AND THE SHAPING OF CASTE

Editors' Introduction

THE most commonly spoken feature of the Indian caste system is its timeless continuity, since its origin in the ancient past, sometime at the beginning of the Vedic civilization. References to the idea of *Varna* and its cosmic origin could indeed be traced back to the Rig Veda. The text that spelt out the four-fold varna order, the *Manusmriti*, is believed to have been composed sometime around the 1st century of the Common Era. However, much of the social science writing on the subject has been on its modern and contemporary dynamics. Many of them have specifically underlined the role played by the orientalist imaginary and the colonial state practices in giving caste its contemporary shape. Beginning with works of Bernard Cohn, some historians and anthropologists have critically explored aspects of the colonial knowledge production and the state administrative processes as influencing and shaping local identities, including those of caste. The colonial shaping of caste continued to be a governing framework for the Indian state even after Independence. Classification of caste groups into pan-Indian aggregate categories for the affirmative action policy (such as the

Scheduled Castes) is a good example of this key influence of the colonial governance system on the imaginings of caste in the post-colonial times.

While the influence of colonial state on the shaping of caste has come to be widely recognized, its pre-colonial life is still largely attributed to the sphere of 'culture'. In the opening chapter of this section Harald Tambs-Lyche explores the diverse modes in which the state-power or 'kingship' interacted and intersected with the local orders of caste. His chapter questions the view popularized by the orientalist writings on the Indian social life, but also widely accepted uncritically by the sociologists and social anthropologists. The underlying assumption of this textbook view is the autonomy and superiority of the so-called religious domain of caste over the secular order of politics and state power during the pre-colonial times. As he argues, scholars like Louis Dumont 'postulated a hierarchical relation between king and Brahmin where the Brahmin dealt with the relation to the entire cosmos, including the supernatural, while the king's sphere was restricted to the exercise of power in this world'. However, such an overgeneralized claim relies upon very fragile and weak empirical evidence. It was a mythical construct derived conveniently from some select Brahmanic texts. The relationship between the two domains was not singularly and uniformly structured everywhere. It changed across regions of India, as well as over time, very similar to what was happening in the medieval Europe where different forms of arrangement between royalty and the church existed. Distinctive path dependencies developed across South-Asia, and Brahmin status in a given region and time depended largely on material factors, such as political patronage and their control over land.

The following chapter by Dilip Menon focusses on the range of changes introduced by the British colonial rule, some of which have had far reaching implications for the order of caste and its conceptions. As the British extended their rule over large parts of the Subcontinent, they also introduced a singular perspective of administration, which had profound implications for social life, including the Indian caste system. The new legal and administrative framework along with the colonial Census, encouraged groups with common status to come together and form associations. Similarly, 'secular' education and the new administrative system opened-up spaces for formal education to the Dalits, but it also crafted new experiences of untouchability and humiliation. However, he underlines that though caste was profoundly transformed during the colonial period, its ideological and ontological tenets, the ideas of hierarchy as well as practices of exclusion and humiliation, preceded and transcended its colonial tweaking.

The Colonial Census and its far-reaching implications for the processes of caste-identity formation has indeed been among the most commented upon topic, particularly in historical writings on the subject. In the next chapter of this section, Leigh Denault provides an introduction to the rich literature on the subject and debates among historians on the intents and expands of the changes that came about in the conceptions of caste through 'imperial information-gathering' projects. As she argues, 'the colonial state indeed did not invent caste'. However, its policies, particularly 'the census did much to promote the popular idea of a singular caste "system" as a universal governing principle underlying Indian society'. Quoting Susan Bayly, she also qualifies that 'while caste, like Hinduism itself, had become prominent as an ordering factor in Indian lives by the end of the 19th century, it still wasn't a 'single "system" regulating all aspects of life – regional diversity and social mobility persisted'.

Historical research on caste has also helped us revise some of the popular formulations about its working, those developed by anthropologists borrowing from orientalist readings of India's past. For example, in popular textbooks on Indian society, caste is often presented as a 'harmonious system', integrated vertically and rarely contested from within. Even processes like Sanskritization are believed to have been slow and smooth instances of status mobility within the hierarchical logic of the system. Inter-caste conflict, which presupposes substantialized identities of individual caste communities mobilizing themselves to push their interests, was virtually unthinkable in the presumed harmonious and smooth social order of caste. Julie Marquet's chapter contests such an understanding with rich evidence and provides a counter-view to the orientalist mythology of the Indian caste system. Drawing her evidence from southern India, she shows how even in the 17th century there were cases of individual caste groups confronting each other over questions of status/honor and claims over material resources, frequency of which increased with time, particularly during the 19th century. Even Sanskritization, which involved claims over higher status following the economic mobility of a given group, was often violently resisted by the already privileged sections. This, she rightly argues, goes on to show 'that Indian society was not static, fixed in a traditional system'. Indians were 'actively shaping identities and boundaries of caste'.

As she argues, caste identities appeared 'to be instrumental in many cases' and that

> this ... demonstrates the agency of individuals or social groups: they were not locked into a system that went beyond them but participated in shaping that system. In particular, they used the language of the "community" and the rights of the caste as a social entity because that language was acceptable to the authorities and it had a mobilizing effect on the members of the caste-group.

Interaction of caste with the political process continued even after India's independence from the colonial rule in 1947. As Gautam Bhatia argues in his chapter, once the Indian state chose to be a liberal and constitutional democracy, its governing values stood directly opposed to those of the caste, often viewed as the most evident example of the modernity-tradition conflict. It thus became inevitable for the new legal system to intervene and confront caste-based hierarchies. The new law enabled an agency that was supposed to transform the interpersonal relations across sections of the citizenry. However, in order to do so, the Indian Constitution had little choice but to deploying 'caste *as* a marker of identification'. Thus, 'the very act of doing so ...

becomes constitutive of changes in the concept of caste itself, under pressure from the force of law'. Law and caste, as he argues, are in constant tension with one another, and their relationship remains a fluid and dynamic one. His chapter dwells upon four different aspects of the Indian law in relation to caste: the manner in which caste appears in the Indian Constitution; engagements of the Indian Supreme Court with caste in relation to reservations; an examination of the legal actors and their mores of establishing jurisprudential link between caste, territory, and religion; and finally, the different legislative attempts at preventing and redressal of caste-based atrocities and violence.

The following chapter by Ashwini Deshpande extends this discussion by focusing on the Indian systems of affirmative action, the reservations, which until 2019 were based on caste and community identities alone. In January 2019, the Government of India introduced a new quota of 10 per cent seats in the government jobs and in admissions to state-run educational institutions for the Economically Weaker Sections. The origin of the caste-based affirmative action policy lay in the colonial period. As the British introduced a western-style legal framework, caste-based disparities and disabilities began to be viewed from the angle of justice and equality. The colonial Census too aided to the process by enhancing awareness of caste-based deprivations, eventually leading to the identification of untouchable castes as a category needing special attention. The independent Indian state worked with similar approach and promulgated a Scheduled Castes Order in 1950 to list communities needing special attention, 'which was a restatement of the 1936 list'. A similar list was prepared of the so-called Scheduled Tribes (also see Jai Prasad's chapter in this volume). These groups were given quotas in admissions to state-run educational institutions, in government jobs and in elections to representative bodies. Over the year, the quotas have expanded, the most important addition being the inclusion of the Other Backward Classes (OBCs). Quite like the colonial policies, these classificatory strategies too are shaping caste identities and the nature of their political self-imaginations.

The roots of Indian affirmative action lie in the framing of caste as being a source of backwardness. The following chapter by S. Anandhi and Kalpana Kannabiran provides an exhaustive account of the evolution of the idea of 'backwardness' and how its relationship with caste came to be imagined and contested by a range of actors. It was during the 19th century that this relationship was first put forward by a section of the Christian missionaries working in India. Their writings also influenced the colonial rulers and their modes of approaching the Indian social order. The idea of 'caste' underlining India's social and economic backwardness was soon picked-up by the 'native' reformers, particularly by those from the 'lowest' segments of caste hierarchy or those speaking on their behalf. These reformers were quite successful in politicizing the idea of the caste-linked backwardness of a section of the Indian society. It was in this context that the issue came to be discussed in the Constituent Assembly, which decided on introducing various systems of quotas that would help create a level playing field for all sections of Indians. The idea of 'backwardness' continues to be invoked by different sections of Indian population, such as women and religious minorities, to make case for their demands from the Indian state, which often also involves pronouncements from the Indian courts.

These chapters together provide a broad overview of the evolving nature of caste, historically, and in the present time. They also show how its popular articulation has been shaped by the active relationship caste has with the state and the political process, not merely during the colonial period, but also before and after.

CHAPTER 7

CASTE AND KINGSHIP

HARALD TAMBS-LYCHE

Introduction: The Communitarian Base of Kingship in India

The relation between caste and kingship in India is complex. Mythical accounts speak of how kings 'ordered' the caste system, but it is unlikely that early kings had the power to do so. There are close links between the political system and the order of castes from an early date, but kings in different parts of India and at different periods had various power bases and different degrees of sacredness, and then we do not really know when caste emerged as an integral social order in India. Before the Common Era there is little evidence of caste as we understand the term today. During the early middle age we come across a number of communities still found as castes today; others were about to take form. By the early modern era—the 15th to 16th century—a caste order clearly existed, though it has changed continuously since. Thus there can be no fixed relationship between kingship and caste.

Dumont (1962; 1966) postulated a hierarchical relation between king and Brahmin where the Brahmin dealt with the relation to the entire cosmos, including the supernatural, while the king's sphere was restricted to the exercise of power in this world. In modern terms, he was a secular ruler. But Dumont's proposition suffers from overgeneralization: he never studied any Indian kingdom empirically. Conversely, Hocart (1950) and Quigley (1993) proposed that the caste system is centred on the king. From his interviews with an ex-ruler in Madhya Pradesh, Mayer (1981) stressed the paternal role of the king in relation to his subjects, and his relations to the local communities. This is the lead I shall follow here.

We know that, in many kingdoms, the king was taking counsel with leaders of identifiable groups: heads of merchant guilds, head priests of important temples, leaders of sects, chiefs of tribes, heads of clans from dominant castes, or caste representatives. Quigley proposed that the king rules with the aid of clan leaders (1994), but there were many other influential groups in the kingdoms, depending on the type of state and the historic period we are dealing with. Still, Guha (2013) shows that, from the beginning of the early modern period, castes played an important part in governance and government.

This contrasts with conventional wisdom about the same period in Europe, where early modernity is associated with a rise in royal power and attempts to dissolve communities that had been important earlier: orders, estates, and guilds. In India, the communitarian political structure remained fundamental, and continues even today, as Jaffrelot (2005) and others have argued. Why the two regions developed differently, we do not yet know.

This communitarian structure is fundamental to the relationship between kingship and caste. I shall now look more closely at historical and regional differences between selected Indian kingdoms and relate each type to the communitarian structure.

Moral Kingship: Buddhist and Jain Rulers

We know little of kingship in the Indus Valley civilization, or in the long period until the rise of the Mauryas, the first Indian rulers we have real information about. Kosambi (1975) held that their rule was based on a monopoly on iron extraction and produce. Its maintenance is the main theme of the Arthashastra (ca. 300 BC), in which the minister Kautilya describes a powerful, centralized state. His assertions may represent the statesman's utopia, but most scholars feel that Kautilya is realistic in his descriptions, which show merchants and artisans as servants of the state, a form Polanyi (1944; 1957) proposed for early empires in general. These groups lived in separate villages.

But the Mauryan empire changed under Ashoka (ca. 273–237 BC), a generation later. The territory expanded to Saurashtra in the west, Orissa in the east, and northwards into Afghanistan. The control implied by the Arthashastra became impracticable, villages grew autonomous, and craftsmen and merchants dispersed to serve the population directly (Kosambi, 1975, pp. 240–242). The Jatakas describe villages formed from numerous communities, though they probably did not form a 'caste system' yet.

Now power had to be supported by other sources of authority, and as Ashoka converted to Buddhism and propagated its principles, the amoral Arthashastra state changed into a 'moral' kingdom, as defined by Stein (1978) for South India. The Mauryan Empire was based on commerce, and many merchants were Buddhist. Political control mainly concerned the safety of trade routes; agricultural revenue played a secondary part. Ashoka erected his pillars at the crossroads of trade. His kingdom must have been like a grid, with the interstices filled by 'tribals', bound by treaty or tribute arrangements so they did not harm the commerce.

A similar type of state founded by the viceroys of the Guptas, last of the 'classical' Indian empires, survived as the Vallabhi or Maitraka kingdom in Saurashtra till 784 CE. As with the Guptas, guilds and trade were important here (Tambs-Lyche, 2017, pp. 208–210), and the state fits the pattern of 'moral kingship'. The secondary importance of land revenue avoided exploitation of peasants, enabling the king to pose as a 'mediator' or 'umpire' between the various groups.

'Moral kingship' was current in the Tamil heartland from the 3rd to the 8th century CE, a period when Jain influence in South India was strong. Here, the conception of the righteous king as upholder of *dharma* is central, and society is seen as consisting of various interest groups, *sreni*, capable of self-management and self-rule, needing the king only as a referee, and a 'model of moral standing' (Stein, 1978, p. 150). This corresponds to Buddhist and Jain ideals of kingship (Arai, 1978), but Buddhism was much less important than Jainism in South India (Stein, 1978, p. 122). Both religions have been identified with merchant communities, and *Sreni* is commonly translated as 'guild'. Guilds were central to this society, where trade, crafts, and towns were important. Jain kingship was ephemeral in Tamil Nadu, but it remained important in Karnataka much later.

In coastal Karnataka we still find the families of Jain kings (Tambs-Lyche, *forthcoming*). Established from around the 13th century, these kingdoms were based on the export of spices from plantations on the foothills of the Western Ghats. These states formed a grid: people living along the routes were 'vassals' who desisted from attacking the trade routes and served to defend the kingdom. The vassals later became the Bunt chiefdoms described below. The Jain ex-rulers still claim to follow the moral ideals of the Jain king, acting as an umpire between conflicting interests (Tambs-Lyche, 2017, pp. 218–219).

In extreme cases of 'moral kingship' the ruler was seen to incarnate the deity, or, in the case of the Buddhist kings, the Bodhisattvas. Here, sacredness is inherent in the king's status. Sometimes, the sacred king was kept apart from politics, while other powerful figures did the dirty political work for him. The king's role as 'umpire' implied that communities and castes were left to develop without state inference, except when the king was mediating conflicts between them.

Buddhist rulers disappeared from India in the 11th century, but they furnished the model for the monarchies of South East Asia. In India, however, a similar model of kingship persisted in the *Vishnudharmottarapurana* (ca. 700–1200 AD) (Inden, 1978). This model, where the king is 'a microcosm of the Cosmic Man', characterized some Hindu kingdoms, like Puri, whose king was the overlord of medieval Orissa. Seen as incarnating Vishnu, through his avatar Jagannath, royalty was closely integrated with Jagannath's temples and the king participated in divine authority. In this form of kingship, divine authority compensated inadequate resources (Kulke, 1978, pp. 147–150). Most of Puri's vassal states were based on a tribe-king alliance (below). The nexus, in Puri, was the king—Brahman alliance, and many villages near Puri were donated to temples, with Brahmins as the landlords *(brahmadeya)* (Pfeffer, 1976).

We may see a parallel in Bengal, where the Hindu Sena dynasty succeeded to the Buddhist Palas. They invited Brahmins and Kayasthas from Northern India, and it is likely that they were at the origin of the privileged Kulani groups among these castes (Inden, 1976). How far these kings were able to 'order' the caste system in Bengal is questionable, since central power was weak, and Sena rule depended on the consent of regional authorities.

THE KALI AGE AND THE DEVELOPMENT OF FEUDALISM

The period between the end of the Maurya Empire (185 BC) and the beginning of Gupta rule has been treated variously by historians; statements on continuity vie with those stressing disruption. The Kushanas, conquering Northern India in the 1st century CE, were the first to call themselves 'devaputra' (sons of gods) (Kulke and Rothermund, 1990, pp. 77–79). The Buddhists saw them as Buddhist, which is debatable (Kulke and Rothermund, 1990, pp. 80–81), but they started the deification of the king typical of later Buddhist rulers. Despite considerable political unrest, trade, merchants, and guilds prospered in the centuries following the fall of the Mauryas (Kulke and Rothermund, 1990, p. 90).

Yet it was now that the idea of a 'Kali age' was born, in the early Puranas. R. S. Sharma sees it as a time of political instability and crisis. The puranas talk about the mixing of the varnas, of hostility between Shudras and Brahmans, refusal of Vaishyas to sacrifice, and so on (Sharma, 2002, p. 63). The Brahmin authors describe themselves as suffering from unjust rulers, exploitation by traders and lack of respect from Shudras, all blatantly in conflict with the laws of Manu, which were written about this time. Sharma sees the coercive measures of the Manusmruti as a reaction to the crisis (2002, p. 66).

It is indeed as if Brahmins were casting a charter for society and simultaneously complaining that things were evolving quite differently. These texts point to a society that was gradually, through conflict, coming to resemble a 'caste system'. From this period Indian discourse on society takes caste for granted—as a system, and not just a conglomeration of communities. By this it is meant that each member of society is member of a caste, and that there exists some idea of an ordered hierarchy of these communities.

Sharma stresses how servants of the state, at this time, began to receive land grants, and places the beginning of feudalization at the late 3rd and 4th centuries (2002, pp. 73–74).[1] The ruler-merchant nexus that characterized the moral kingdoms was replaced by that of the ruler and his military vassals.

---

[1] Yadava places this transformation later, in the centuries following the fall of the Gupta Empire (2002).

Indeed, at the time of the fall of Vallabhi in 784 CE, immigration swelled the 'tribal' population between the trade routes, and the centre of gravity shifted to the countryside. There, kingdoms arose that were based on an alliance between a king, come from afar, and a tribe which retained control of the land. There are several examples of such kingdoms in early medieval Saurashtra and Rajasthan. The Junagadh rulers were known as kings of the Ahirs, the Jethwas of Porbandar built their power on the Mer 'tribe', and the Mewar kingdom, in Rajasthan, began as an alliance between Bhils and foreign rulers (Tambs-Lyche, 2017, pp. 210–212). In Junagadh villages the Ahirs were dominant till the Muslim conquest in 1470, when *zamindars* (Muslims but also Nagar Brahmins) were given control of villages. In Porbandar, Mers are still dominant in the villages. In Mewar the Rajputs, often kin of the rulers, became dominant: *jagirdars* were allotted many villages. But many local Rajputs may have Bhil origins.

The king-tribe alliance reappeared, at different times, in the North Indian peripheries: in the Western Himalayan foothills and in Nepal before the rise of the Malla dynasty (Galey, 1989; 1991–1992; Lecomte-Tilouine, 2009, pp. 195–197), in Bundelkhand (Jain, 2002) and in inland Orissa. Princely adventurers carved out chiefdoms in 'tribal' areas, but even tribes that refused them were conversant with the idea. Thus the Santals—who never had a king—conceive of the king as a foreign prince (Carrin-Bouez, 1991).

In Saurashtra and Rajasthan, this alliance developed into the Rajput state. It began, typically, with raids of armed bands, who may not have been kin at first but gradually became a 'clan'. Subjugating the population, the leaders of these bands founded kingdoms. A process of segmentation characterized these states. Junior clansmen—the king's *bhayats*—were allotted territory in fief from the king, so that royal kin were implanted all over the kingdom. In Saurashtra the Jhalas, who received their fief from the Chalukya ruler of Gujarat, were the first to follow this policy (Tambs-Lyche, 2017, p. 211). Rajput domains were secondary kingdoms (Fried, 1967), located in the periphery, as seen in their relations to the Mogul empire.

Junior descendants of the founder became the 'Rajputs' of the land, nobles that controlled the periphery on behalf of the chief: the Rajput caste and political system developed together. Agricultural revenue flowed from the peasant through the vassals to the chief. Central power was weak, and each chief depended on his strength to defend or extend his 'rights'.

This system had no place for sacred kings, and divinity rested with the chiefs' goddess, seen as arbitrator of political fortunes as well as guardian of the *dharma*—moral order— that the chiefs should uphold. The chiefs' halo came from the warlike exploits of their forefathers, sung by the Charan bards—far more important at this stage than the Brahmins were. But the vassals, like their chiefs, always had to deal with the various subject communities in their domain, among which the merchants remained a distinct and important interest group.

Beginnings of Centralization and the Early Modern State

A very different configuration arose in Central Gujarat during the same period. From the 10th to 11th century, the Chaulukya kingdom engaged heavily in agricultural development through the construction of stepwells, often financed by the king, the queen, or a minister. Clearly state revenues now came from agriculture, implying a new relation between villagers and the state, and changes in village structure. Traders (*vaniks*), however, rather than a landed aristocracy, channelled revenue from the farmer to the state (Hardiman, 1996, pp. 18–20), and merchants were often ministers of the state. Farming castes probably remained dominant in the villages, which must have become more complex with the intensification of agriculture, with more specialist and labouring castes.

Parallel developments took place on the North Indian plain, where the Persian wheel was introduced at about the same time. Concurrently, Muslim conquest led to introduction of zamindari tenure, where notables from the court were granted the revenue of villages. In a zamindari village, there can be no dominant caste, and the formerly dominant become simple peasants. In theory, zamindars served the state: in practice they often kept small armies to keep the locals in check, and sometimes used them to gain autonomy when central power was weak. In villages held by a Rajput jagirdar, such as Ranawaton-ki-Sadri (Chauhan, 1967), he similarly kept the village under his control, and no local caste was dominant. Often, as in Praj, Saurashtra (Tambs-Lyche, 2017, pp. 161–168), which may once have been a chiefdom, Rajputs, aided by their allied castes (Mayer, 1958) were dominant. In this, Praj resembles Ramkheri in Malwa (Mayer, 1960). This pattern was typical of the Rajput domains.

The Muslim conquests probably contributed to the transition towards the modern state. Sheikh (2008) has shown how the Gujarat sultanate replaced the earlier alliance-based politics of vassalage and strategic marriages in the second half of the 15th century, with a polity centred on the figure of the sultan. Similarly, while Stein thoroughly discusses Krishnadevaraja's efforts at centralization of the Vijayanagara Empire in the 16th century, he also stresses that the Deccan sultanates which eventually vanquished the empire, represented a more centralized political order (Stein, 1989). These and other Muslim states were using slaves as elite personnel to diminish the decentralizing force of the nobility, and several Hindu rulers also adopted this strategy later. Generally, the centralizing changes in the Muslim states predated similar concentration of power in the Hindu kingdoms.

Some areas, like those controlled by the Jats, escaped zamindari. Controlled by a council and chief from the dominant caste, these were the villages that gave rise to the idea of the Indian village as a 'little republic'. Here, as in villages led by a zamindar or a jagirdar, specialist and labouring castes led to complex, multi-caste villages.

In Saurashtra, the Rajput states began to change when the ruler of the northwestern corner of the peninsula founded the port of Navanagar (Jamnagar) in 1540. Control of trade brought revenues independent of the vassals' tribute, so he, and rulers that followed his example, could raise mercenary armies and acquire artillery, gaining military strength no vassal could match (Tambs-Lyche, 2017, pp. 214–215). Thus the segmentary nature of the Rajput state gave way to centralization, vassals lost their autonomy, and small chiefdoms were annexed by large ones. The early modern state had arrived, but modernity did not reduce the importance of caste (Guha, 2013). Rather, the ruler now developed relations to all important groups in his domain, bypassing the vassal intermediaries, and the king's role became that of listening to, and wielding paternalistic power over, all caste groups.

This centralization was accompanied by religious change. A new cult, of Rama the god-king, was established, and Rama temples, founded and funded by the king, were built all over Saurashtra, as rulers identified themselves with the *dharmic* prince of the Ramayana. Unlike the goddess cults, which had sustained the position of the Charan bards—the goddesses were deified Charan women—the Rama temples were served by Brahmins (Tambs-Lyche, 2017, p. 215), who thus became far more important to the state, while the king's role changed. Yet Rajput kings did not follow the model of the *Vishnudharmottarapurana*: they wanted to be *like* Rama, not his incarnations, and they certainly did not want to cede their sovereignty to god or man.

Development of Kingship Specific to South India

For South India, Stein (1978) distinguishes three types of kingship. 'Tamil heroic kingship' the first, centred on warriors and their martial valour. This type is firmly based in the kinship group, with commemoration of ancestors through memorial stones. Stein relates it to a 'tribal' polity, and it was gradually superseded in the central plains of the Tamil Nadu by 'moral kingship' during the early centuries of the common era. When, later, the plains empires declined, the tribal chiefs from the dry highland regions of Tamil Nadu established 'little kingdoms' there. Puddukottai (Dirks, 1987), ruled by chiefs from the Kallar caste, belongs to a whole family of 'poligar' states ruled by Maravars or Kallars. There is a parallel to early Rajput kingship, in that these states were secondary developments, but the network of junior kinsmen as vassals, typical of the Rajput state, never developed to the same extent in South India.

Like post-16th century Rajput rulers, the later poligars projected a double image: the warrior hero, inherited from the past, and the moral king, adapted from his former superiors. Gifts to Brahmins were central to this second image, and Brahmins were heavily patronized (Dirks, 1987, p. 10). But they were not at the centre of the social order: rather, 'caste was embedded in a political context of kingship' (1987, p. 7).

Another variant of 'heroic kingship' is found in South Kanara. The ancestors of the Bunt chiefs controlled the interstices between trade routes controlled by Jain kingdoms, of whom they were the vassals. They headed matrilineal lineages, having what Stein calls a 'tribal' base. In the 15th and 16th centuries, the river valleys here were drained and prepared for rice cultivation (Vasantha Madhava, 1991). Bunts became the chiefs of the new villages, while the tenants and labourers were Billavas. When the Ikkeri Nayaks extended their authority to South Kanara in the 17th century, the Bunt chiefdoms prospered while the power of the Jain kings declined, and some of them became more powerful than their Jain 'superiors'.

Each Bunt chief is seen as holding his land in fief from a 'royal' bhuta, a deity who manifests in oracles through low-caste mediums (Carrin and Tambs-Lyche, 2003). The bhuta is seen as inspecting his domain, overseeing the chief's role as protector of *dharma,* and dispensing divine justice—recalling, rather, the justice dispensed by the Jain kings, as if the 'tribal' chiefdoms were invested with the moral dimension from Jain kingship (Tambs-Lyche, 2017, p. 217).

Stein's third type is 'ritual kingship', identified with the great Tamil kingdoms: the Pallavas, the Cholas, and the Pandyas. This form is notable for its large, central temples, whose presiding deities are made to stand in the same relation to lesser gods as the king does to the regional authorities. Centralization of the realm is thus expressed symbolically and ritually. Crucial here is the role of Brahmins. The Pallava king Nandivarman, who ruled from Kanchi in the 8th century, invited great numbers of Brahmins from the North. He is credited with starting the practice of *brahmadeya* grants of villages to Brahmins, and effectively established the new type of kingship (Stein, 1978).

Brahmadeya grants at once founded a temple and the settlement *(agrahara)* of Brahmins to serve it: the latter controlled the temple lands, which other castes worked for them. Ritual kingship thus corresponds to a village model that was to become typical of Tamil Nadu, as the system spread to the Cholas and the Pandyas. It provided for a neat and fixed rank order, where all other castes were defined in relation to the Brahmins (Gough, 1962; Béteille, 1965; Mines, 2002). With the temple as the reference point for social positions, this type of village also instituted 'village ritual' in which 'all' local castes participated, expressing and confirming the hierarchical order. Such villages became the model for Dumont's view of the caste system, which fits these villages better than any others.

In the ritual type of kingdom, the king rules in the name of a sovereign among the Gods—Shiva or Vishnu—and through the Brahmins, over an integrated caste order which expresses the *dharma* for which the king is responsible. Identified with the god, though not incarnating him, the ruler is lord of the *gana* (Stein, 1978)—the regional or local assemblies that united all castes—and thus of the 'people' as a whole: he no longer represents his *kula* (lineage), nor is he the impartial umpire mediating between interest groups. The ritual kingdom as defined by Stein is found only in Tamil Nadu and has no counterpart in North India.

Nepal: A Special Case

Nepal, historically the last Hindu kingdom, which some scholars have seen as a model for Hindu kingship, is a special case. Its kings claimed Rajput descent, and in the early days their kingdom resembled the king-tribe alliance (Lecomte-Tillouine, 2009). By the 18th century, however, Nepal entered a process of centralization unique in South Asia, where the king acquired a degree of sacredness setting him apart from the Rajput rulers. At the same time, Nepal got a constitution where each caste or tribe had its social position formally defined in writing. Nepal, then, stands out as a singular development of the Hindu state, in which elements from various earlier forms converge.

A Tentative Typology of Kingship in India

This overview of kingship in the subcontinent suggests a tentative typology. First, we have 'tribal' chiefs, based in kin groups, who lead their 'tribe' as *primus inter pares*. This form, close to Stein's 'heroic kingship', is still present among indigenous populations all over India. Here, the majority of the population belong to a single community. Then, under the king-tribe alliance this remains true, though we may get a 'foreign' elite clustering around the king, as well as an increase in specialist, minority populations. We may get an aristocratic 'caste' as well as specialist communities, but we do not really get a 'caste system'.

This type evolved, in Western India, into a third, the Rajput state with its segmentation of the clan, where junior lines become the vassals of the chief. As this form of state became generalized, the rulers and their vassals became one aristocratic caste—the Rajputs. The king is separated from the population as part of the conquering 'nobility' but is still in many ways a *primus inter pares* among his clansmen. With a separate aristocratic caste at the top goes a segregation of low castes from the cultivators, who, along with some specialist castes, become 'allies' of the aristocracy (Mayer, 1960; Tambs-Lyche, 2017, p. 161). The larger number of castes among the villagers sets the Rajput state apart from the tribe-caste alliance type. Then, as the Rajput state developed into early modernity, the vassals lost much of their power, and the king dealt more directly with the various castes that made up the population of his domain.

These were 'secondary' states formed on the peripheries of states with more complex populations. The first type of such central states was based on 'moral kingship' and on control of trade. Such control implied a merchant community, but beyond the elite there was no need for the king to interfere in the order of the communities over which he ruled. The key here is the relative independence of cultivators from state interference, so that villages could retain their old form, 'tribal' or otherwise. Thus there was not yet a caste system under the Mauryas, and even in the latest avatars of this form, the Jain kingdoms of South Kanara, the king did not meddle with the caste order which, by then, had become an established feature of society.

When the Pandyas in Tamil Nadu and, later, the Senas of Bengal and the kings of Puri invited Brahmins from outside and offered them privileges, however, we get a second type of central state, where kings engaged directly with the caste order, actively supporting Brahmin claims to superiority. In the variant of this type found in Tamil Nadu and in Kerala, this king-Brahmin nexus resulted in a systematic ranking of all other communities as castes.

In fertile areas such as central Tamil Nadu or the Gangetic plain, villages may well have acquired a multi-community form at an early date. If so, the dominant must have been able to maintain themselves locally without relying on higher authority. This points to villages run by a farming community—Vellalars in Tamil Nadu—under their chief, or, as the Tamil sources indicate, a council. This would seem to be the essence of the relatively autonomous village assemblies we find at the early stage of the great Tamil kingdoms. In the north, their closest parallel is in the areas controlled by councils of a dominant caste, as in the Jat areas.

In the 'ritual kingship' that characterizes this variant of the second type of central kingdoms, initiated by the Pallavas in Tamil Nadu, the role of temples and Brahmins is central: indeed, this is the first time we see Brahmins forming an essential link in the State structure. This gave Brahmins local power corresponding with their status in the texts, removing the ambiguity of being prestigious but not powerful. The land grants to Brahmins reduced the status and power of those who held the land earlier: Brahmins reduced Vellalars to peasant status, but their dominance depended on central authority. No wonder that the main political force in Tamil Nadu since the kings disappeared has been the anti-Brahmin movements. We may add medieval Kerala here, where indeed the *brahmadeya* settlements were constituent of the state formation (Veluthat, 2000).

In the densely settled plains of Northern India, a second sub-type emerged, where the caste order was not controlled by the king in the same way: rather, the king's power relied on caste relationships as they existed in the region. Here, two types of village emerged, producing a secondary distinction: where there was no *zamindar*, strong council-organized dominant castes like the Jats controlled the others; but they were reduced to peasant status under *zamindari*. In both cases, the advanced division of labour in agriculture implied a large number of castes per village. Typical of the North Indian plains was the large community of agricultural labourers, forming the 'untouchable' Chamar caste. Kings ruled through their influence over zamindars and dominant caste councils.

Central Gujarat differed, on the same secondary level, in that merchant moneylenders occupied the position between the peasants and the state, while the caste order otherwise resembled that of Northern India. Merchant castes were therefore more important to the rulers than elsewhere. The territories of the Maratha confederacy from the 18th century onwards formed an interesting variation of this pattern, since the merchant moneylenders were Brahmins.

Conclusion

In all regions of India, kings ruled through their links to representatives of the various communities or castes, so the caste order of villages was closely related to the larger political system and to the various forms of kingship. This pattern, which may have had its parallel in medieval Europe, has persisted throughout the modern period in India, while it seems to have disappeared in the West. Indian villages have of course changed, in recent times, with new forms of government, such as Panchayati Raj, and with economic change. But the old patterns are still visible, and they remain a major factor behind regional variations in the caste order.

References

Arai, T. 1978. 'Jaina Kingship as Viewed in the Prabandhacintamani'. In J. F. Richards (Ed.), *Kingship and Authority in South Asia* (pp. 74–114). Madison: University of Wisconsin.

Béteille, A. 1965. *Caste, Class and Power: Changing Patterns of Stratification in a Tanjore Village.* Berkeley: University of California Press.

Carrin, M., and H. Tambs-Lyche. 2003. 'You Don't Joke with These Fellows: Power and Ritual in South Canara, India'. *Social Anthropology,* 11(1): 23–42.

Carrin-Bouez, M. 1991. 'Un roi venu d'ailleurs … ou la conception santal du roi dans les contes'. *Cahiers de Littérature Orale,* 29: 89–124.

Chauhan, B. R. 1967. *A Rajasthan Village.* Delhi: Vir Publishing House.

Dirks, N. 1987. *The Hollow Crown: Ethnohistory of an Indian Kingdom.* Cambridge: Cambridge University Press.

Dumont, L. 1962. 'The Conception of Kingship in Ancient India'. *Contributions to Indian Sociology,* I: 48–77.

Dumont, L. 1966. *Homo Hierarchicus.* Paris: Gallimard (English translation, same title, University of Chicago Press, 1970).

Fried, M. H. 1967. *The Evolution of Political Society.* New York: Random House.

Galey, J-C. 1989. 'Reconsidering Kingship in India; An Ethnological Perspective'. In J-C. Galey (Ed.), *Kingship and the Kings, History and Anthropology* (Vol. 4, pp. 123–187). London: Harwood Academic Publishers.

Gough, K. 1962. 'Caste in a Tanjore Village'. In E. R. Leach (Ed.), *Aspects of Caste in South India, Ceylon and North West Pakistan* (pp. 11–60). Cambridge: Cambridge University Press.

Guha, Sumit. 2013. *Beyond Caste: Identity and Power in South Asia, Past and Present.* Leiden: Brill.

Hardiman, D. 1996. *Feeding the Bania: Peasants and Usurers in Western India.* Delhi: Oxford University Press.

Hocart, A. M. 1950. *Caste.* London: Methuen. (First edition, in French, 1938.)

Inden, R. B. 1976. *Marriage and Rank in Bengali Culture.* Delhi: Vikas. (Published simultaneously by University of California Press.)

Inden, R. B. 1978. 'Ritual, Authority and Cyclic Time in Hindu Kingship'. In J. F. Richards (Ed.), *Kingship and Authority in South Asia* (pp. 28–73). Madison: University of Wisconsin.

Jaffrelot, C. 2005. *Inde: la démocratie par la caste*. Paris: Fayard.

Jain, R. K. 2002. *Between History and Legend: Status and Power in Bundelkhand*. Hyderabad: Orient Longmans.

Kosambi, D. D. 1975. *An Introduction to Indian History*. Bombay: Popular Prakashan (1st edition 1956).

Kulke, H. 1978. 'Early Royal Patronage of the Jagannatha Cult'. In A.-M. Eschmann, H. Kulke, and G. C. Tripathi (Eds.), *The Cult of Jagannath and the Regional Traditions of Orissa* (pp. 139–155). Delhi: Manohar.

Kulke, H., and D. Rothermund. 1990. *A History of India*. London and New York: Routledge.

Lecomte-Tilouine, M. 2009. *Hindu Kingship, Ethnic Revival, and Maoist Rebellions in Nepal*. Delhi: Oxford University Press.

Mayer, A. C. 1958. 'The Dominant Caste in a Region of Northern India'. *Southwestern Journal of Anthropology*, 14: 407–427.

Mayer, A. C. 1960. *Caste and Kinship in Central India*. London: Routledge and Kegan Paul.

Mayer, A. C. 1981. 'Perceptions of Princely Rule: Perspectives from a Biography'. *Contributions to Indian Sociology (n.s.)*, 15: 127–154.

Mines, D. P. 2002. 'Hindu Nationalism, Untouchable Reform, and the Ritual Production of a South Indian Village'. *American Ethnologist*, 29(1): 58–85.

Pfeffer, G. 1976. *Puris Sasandörfer: Basis einer regionalen Elite*. Doctoral Thesis. Berlin: Freie Universität.

Polanyi, K. 1944. *The Great Transformation*. New York: Rinehart.

Quigley, D. 1993. *The Interpretation of Caste*. Oxford: Clarendon.

Quigley, D. 1994. 'Is a Theory of Caste Still Possible?' In M. Searle-Chatterjee and U. Sharma (Eds.), *Contextualising Caste* (pp. 25–48). Oxford: Blackwell.

Sharma, R. S. 2002. 'The Kali Age: A Period of Social Crisis'. In D. N. Jha (Ed.), *The Feudal Order: State, Society and Ideology in Early Medieval India* (pp. 61–77). Delhi: Manohar.

Sheikh, S. 2008. 'Alliance, Genealogy and Political Power: The Cudasamas of Junagadh and the Sultans of Gujarat'. *The Medieval History Journal*, 11(1): 29–61.

Stein, B. 1978. 'All the King's Mana: Perspectives on Kingship in Medieval South India'. In J. F. Richards (Ed.), *Kingship and Authority in South Asia* (pp. 115–167). Madison: University of Wisconsin.

Stein, B. 1989. *Vijayanagara*. The Cambridge History of India I-2. Cambridge: Cambridge University Press.

Tambs-Lyche, H. 2017. *Transaction and Hierarchy: Elements for a Theory of Caste*. Delhi: Manohar.

Vasantha Madhava, K. G. 1991. *Western Karnataka: Its Agrarian Relations, A.D. 1500–1800*. Delhi: Navrang.

Veluthat, K. 2010. *The Early Medieval in South India*. Delhi: Oxford University Press.

Yadava, B. N. S. 2002. 'The Accounts of the Kali Age and the Social Transition from Antiquity to the Middle Ages'. In D. N. Jha (Ed.), *The Feudal Order: State, Society and Ideology in Early Medieval India* (pp. 79–120). Delhi: Manohar.

CHAPTER 8

TRANSFORMATIONS OF CASTE IN COLONIAL INDIA

DILIP M. MENON

Introduction

Caste hierarchy is fundamental to social and political life in India. There has been much debate over whether a statement such as this falls prey to an essentialist portrayal of a society believed to be mired in 'tradition'. The word caste is itself of Portuguese origin (*casta*) and moreover, it covers too much terrain, taking in both the idea of *varna* (a conceptual category) and *jati* (the sociological variations). What does it mean to ask a question regarding changes in caste under a temporal regime—the time of colonialism? Are the ideologies and practices of caste malleable, flexible, and responsive to conjunctural pressures: whether from state initiatives or movements for social reform from within communities? Caste has been studied by some as a timeless essence of Hindu society, while recent arguments state that caste was substantially reinvented under colonial rule. The latter position rests on two very different ideas. The first is that of a fundamental misrecognition, by an alien power, of social reality. A reliance on textual traditions and their guardians, whether out of administrative convenience or epistemic misrecognition, seemingly entailed that multiple practices, and social variations were given short shrift in the attempt to create a uniform and universal model for India. The second sees colonialism as opening up fissures within society substantially altering conceptions of ineffable social hierarchy. Processes of education, and political and social reform meant a re-evaluation of the very idea of the value of human being. However, the central question is of the nature of change in society, and how in the middle of transformation, certain elements like patriarchy, racism, and casteism are perpetuated or continued through other means. The central argument of this chapter is that while colonialism, and subsequently, the nation-state, created a legal apparatus of equality under the law, caste discrimination persisted in the impossibility of generating equality of relationships between humans. This question can be posed more bluntly: does the dalit have a right to dignity, and indeed, life in India?

THINKING WITH CASTE

Untouchability may not have vanished, nor a belief in the indefinable worth of the brahman, but alternative values of equality and fraternity were theorized, circulated, and took root. BR Ambedkar wrote in 1930 that an ascending scale of reverence and a descending scale of contempt characterized caste (Ambedkar, 1931). Such attitudes exist in the present, but they operate within a space where theoretically all Indians are equal under a secular law. There are still restrictions on who one eats with, who one marries, and spaces that one can inhabit, but arguably the flawed projects of colonialism and nationalism opened up spaces of contradiction within a seemingly hermetic ideology. While, as Aniket Jaaware puts it, as a Hindu, one's caste precedes one's birth and survives one's death, the space of action, and thought while one lives, can be conceived of, for the most part, as one where mobility and sociability can be aspired to (Jaaware, 2019). If one moves away from the sociological and anthropological focus on endogamy, purity, and pollution and structures of kinship, there still remains the experiential questions of humiliation and violence for those at the bottom of an extremely segmented society. And, as Jaaware has powerfully argued recently, caste is premised, at a primary level, on whom one can touch, and who can touch one (Jaaware, 2019). Society is still constituted by the passable and impassable spaces between people. The dilemma remains; modern governmentality can legislate equality and liberty, both values enshrined in the Constitution of India, but fraternity cannot be legislated into existence. Much may have changed in the colonial period, and new spaces of conviviality, aspiration, and anonymity created, but caste persisted at the ontological, interpersonal, and phenomenological levels.

There are multiple ways to read caste as a phenomenon as much as a way of thinking in India. Within classical Indian thought, there has been a structural tendency to create taxonomies of phenomena, qualities, persons, and states and these habits of thinking may have spilled over into social classifications, hardening over time with the flux of social and political relations (Smith, 1994). The fourfold classification of *varna* (with the constitutive outside of the untouchable) has been seen to have parallels with historical Indo-European three-fold classifications of sovereignty, military, and productivity, which signals longer histories of a hierarchical conception (Dumezil, 1958). The debate, however, has hinged on whether one is to take the centrality of the brahman (an ineffable category) or that of the king (a secular category) as central to the constitution of the idea of caste. The first position is seen as being too idealist, deriving from a classical textual understanding of Hindu society, and at the same time arising from the self-serving projections of the Brahmins themselves (Inden, 1990). The second, while it is able to account for a material politics of conjunctural power and is premised on social transactions of some texture, has again been criticized as ahistorical as crowns were rendered hollow under colonialism (Hocart, 1936, 1970; Dirks, 1987).

The royal model has found more takers of late, with studies looking at the organization of village society around the idea of the dominant caste *jajman* (replicating the kingly sacrificer) as central to transactions of an economic, political as much as of a ritual nature. The idea of a *jajmani* 'system', as first articulated, with services rendered by dependent castes in return for a share of the harvest, has been undermined, and it has been argued that colonial agrarian settlements reconstituted village society substantially (Wiser, 1936; Quigley, 1993, 2005; Commander, 1983; Fuller, 1989; Fukuzawa, 1972). The fact that patronage and dependence continue and are central to the practices of contemporary village life has allowed for arguments such as the role of the *jajman* in regulating 'auspiciousness' and 'inauspiciousness' in the reproduction of social life (Raheja, 1988). Academic wisdom has always resisted seeing caste as a 'system' and attempted to detail its protean, local, and contextual nature. One must consider the fact that caste is also an ideological phenomenon and places a value on hierarchy at the same time as there is a social regulation of transgressions relating to everyday practices as much as kinship arrangements. Louis Dumont's work attempted to understand this hierarchical principle in a magisterial comparative trilogy, and much of the criticism of his work proceeds surprisingly from a reading of the work on India alone (Dumont, 1966, 1980, 1977, 1986). He urged a moving away from the conceits of modernity—a trajectory arcing to individualism and egalitarianism—towards more hybrid forms of thinking and understanding the presence of equality and hierarchy in some manner in all societies. Dumont's lapidary formulation on the value of hierarchy that underlies caste is worth reflecting on: 'It is clear that the impurity of the Untouchable is conceptually inseparable from the purity of the Brahman ... untouchability will not truly disappear until the purity of the Brahman is itself radically devalued ...' (Dumont, 1980, p. 54).

COLONIAL INVENTION OF CASTE?

Caste relations and identities underwent transformation from the 18th century onwards along particular fault lines: within the crucible of war; state formation in the shadow of the demise of indigenous empires; and the transition of the East India Company (EIC) from commercial organization to state post-1757 (Bayly, 1987, 1999; Alavi, 2007). By 1830, the EIC had consolidated its finances as a military-fiscal state through a variety of land settlements that invested control over land and the powers of revenue collection in landlords (Bengal and Malabar); peasant proprietors (Madras Presidency); and peasant communities believed to be constituted through kinship relations (Northwest India) (Ludden, 1994; Prakash, 1992; Bose, 1994). This consolidation of land under the sovereignty of the EIC state meant that the spaces for negotiation and movement of lower caste labour diminished, and agrestic servitude was entrenched. The 'golden age of the pariah' was over and increasingly the process of sedentarization meant that cultivators as much as pastoralists were drawn into vertical relations of dependence (Washbrook, 1993). Indigenous state formation in the 18th century also tended to draw upon classic notions of royalty involving consolidation of hierarchies around temples, Brahmins, and courts (Bayly, 1989).

However, it was the EIC's attempts to create an all-India paradigm for governance that drew in textual prescriptions—both Hindu and Muslim—and the *pandit* and *maulavi* into creating an Anglo-Indian law. Derrett has spoken of the generation of 'responsive texts' as native intellectuals were drawn into the enterprise of power in attempting to find a new relevance for themselves (Derrett, 1968). While Islamic law and its strictures were increasingly jettisoned, leading to piquant results like the proscription on the cutting of limbs and an encouragement of hanging for offences (Fisch, 1983), Hindu texts found a new lease of life. Translations produced by Orientalist scholars like William Jones, Nathaniel Halhed, and Henry Thomas Colebrooke began to undergird the new judicial system that emerged, and, over time, the idea of a uniform all-India, Anglo-Hindu law administered by the courts came into existence unmoored from local circumstances and history. If in an earlier period, kings and chieftains had arbitrated in caste disputes at the local level, and there had been a relative fluidity of interpretation, case-law, and precedent in the courts created a more intransigent regime (McCormack, 1966). Brahmins, possessing historical traditions of literacy as also service to government, began to populate the legal and administrative structure further orienting the understanding of society towards the texts of a high tradition. In one sense, EIC and British rule created the sense of a caste system through incorporating both Sanskrit texts and Brahmin administrators within the colonial order thus helping to promote a fault line of Brahmin and non-brahmin within Indian society. Jotirao Phule's *The Cultivators Whip Cord* in the later 19th century was one of the first texts to bring together a set of arguments against Brahmins as purveyors of useless rituals as much as monopolists of education and employment under British rule (Phule, 1883, 2002).

The emergence of the Brahmin-nonbrahmin divide was the catalyst for the emergence of caste associations as much as non-brahmin movements in southern India in the late 19th century. Trautmann has pointed to the Madras School of Orientalism and the work of FW Ellis in the early 19th century who argued for the separate origin of Dravidian languages (Trautmann, 2006, 2009). Bishop Caldwell further expanded this idea in the mid-19th century and argued linguistically and philologically for a separate Dravidian identity in south India as against the foreign Brahmin (Irschick, 1969; Ramaswamy, 1997). However, there were also deep-seated local histories. The states of the Deccan Sultanate had inherited from the medieval Yadava kingdoms a layer of Brahmin administrators, who generated 'vernacular sociologies' of caste. Gopinatha wrote his *Jativiveka* (Discernment of jati) sometime between 1350 and 1400 CE, based on the *Manusmriti*, arguing for Brahmins as being of pure birth and the other castes as characterized by miscegenation. This text was to have its own life in the 18th and 19th centuries as Brahmins as much as colonial administrators drew upon it to serve their own political purposes (O'Hanlon, 2017). This is mentioned here as a caution against arguments regarding the 'colonial invention of caste' which, through a misreading of

Nicholas Dirks' original formulation, make it appear as if colonialism was able to conjure up categories *ex nihilo* which were then appropriated and inhabited by an indigenous population (Dirks, 1987).

If caste was at all invented, it was invented time and again within particular conjunctures and for specific agendas over a long historical period. We have spoken earlier of the role of law courts in administering Hindu 'custom' as it were and creating all India paradigms. The effects of this were to become evident in the late 19th century in diverse instances. The transformation of matrilineal systems in Kerala was the result initially of the weight of Victorian patriarchal norms and then of the weight of Brahmin patriliny (Arunima, 2003). There were failed attempts to impose upper caste norms of marriage on lower caste communities as in the *cause celebre* of Rakhmabai, of the carpenter caste, who refused to return to her husband to whom she had been married off to as a child. The case went up to the Privy Council and Queen herself before it was resolved (Chandra, 1998). The most discussed instance of colonial transformation was the introduction of the Census in 1881 with its hard delineation of caste, religious, and community categories, and ascribing particular practices of belonging to each within a putative hierarchy of castes (Cohn, 1987, 1996; Barrier, 1981).

The Census generated a slew of caste associations that compelled category alignment among the population and sought to create new consolidated constituencies to engage with colonial governmentality. It is important to remember that Princely states like Marwar in Rajasthan had been conducting censuses since the 18th century, and in these, the hierarchy reflected the dominant mercantile vision of the world rather than a brahminical one (Peabody, 2001). It has been argued that the idea of 'numbers' reflecting the strength of a caste or community became significant as the public sphere opened up, albeit in limited ways, to native participation in politics and institutions (Appadurai, 1993). While Census classifications may not have replaced lived social criteria with regard to rankings, a political discourse of diminishing numbers of Hindus (through conversion), and the 'dying' Hindu community became prevalent from the early 20th century (Datta, 1993). This was to have significant consequences in the emergence of a Hindu right-wing discourse that saw movements for caste mobility as much as Muslim politics as the primary enemies of the nation in the making.

Education and Empowerment

A major transformation that occurred under colonialism was the access that untouchables and lower castes gained to education, as government funding for aided schools became conditional on schools being open for all castes. This was resisted by many conservatives but the presence of missionary schools; the setting up of schools by lower caste reformers like Phule; and progressive measures in princely states like Travancore and Mysore created a space for engagement with knowledge and ideas of mobility (O'Hanlon, 1985; Kawashima, 1998; Bhagavan, 2003). This was not an easy transition and many untouchables still had to sit like modern Ekalavyas on the school veranda apart from their school mates (Constable, 2000). It is not without significance that education became the watchword for the challenge to the caste order in a society where knowledge was traditionally presented as the preserve of the Brahmin. Many of these caste movements were also spurred by an engagement with the cash crop economy as opposed to agrarian servitude on wetlands: Phule came from the gardener caste; the Nadars and Ezhavas were associated with the coconut economy in Madras Presidency. Whether it was the Sri Narayana Dharma Paripalana Yogam (SNDP) movement of the Ezhava, Narayana Guru in Travancore; the Ad Dharm movement founded by Acchutanand in Punjab; the movement among the Nadar caste in Tamil Nadu; or the Namasudra movement in Bengal, education and the opportunities offered by the colonial opening up of schools created a vision of social mobility (Jeffrey, 1974; Juergensmeyer, 1982; Templeman, 1996; Bandyopadhyay, 1997). B. R. Ambedkar's meteoric rise to education in prestigious institutions like Columbia University and the London School of Economics and his motto: 'Educate, Agitate, Organize' summarized this impulse of knowledge and freedom.

Education also created a space for the emergence of a new idiom in the vernacular, escaping the hegemony of a sanskritized high register; new forms of engagement in the public sphere ranging from pamphlets, chapbooks, and novels as also more ephemeral forms like oratory; and a new audience forged within the crucible of discussions on equality and liberty (Bate, 2009). One of the earliest vernacular novels by a lower caste was *Saraswativijayam* (The Victory of Learning), written in Malayalam by the Tiyya pleader, Potheri Kunhambu in 1893. It told the story of an untouchable, attacked, and left for dead for the crime of singing in the presence of a Brahmin, who survives, converts to Christianity, gains an education, and in the denouément of the novel, sits in judgement on the very Brahmin believed to have caused his death (Kunhambu, 1893, 2002). One of the intellectual consequences of the British project of translation and the rise of a new audience invested in counter-histories was the recuperation of histories of Buddhism in southern India (Kemper, 2015). The idea that a materialist religion invested in equality had been defeated in the ancient past and submerged by an orthodox Hinduism became the spur to a rethinking of Buddhism as a religion for modern times. A remarkable figure in this neo-Buddhist revival was Iyothee Thass, whose assiduous recovery of the histories of equality and its suppression in southern India was central to discussions in the southern public sphere (Aloysius, 1998; Surendran, 2013). B. R. Ambedkar turned to Buddhism in 1956, when after a life-long fight against caste prejudice and authoring a Constitution for India that had equality written on every page, he found the persistence of an unchanging and implacable caste hierarchy. His conversion along with half a million of his followers, reflected the failure of the modernist, nationalist vision of creating equality through the notion of citizenship.

One of the concepts that has dogged interpretations of 'social change' in modern India has been the idea of 'sanskritization'. This view sees social mobility as slowly incremental without affecting structures of caste or the ideology of hierarchy, through lower castes adopting vegetarianism, temperance, and rituals akin to higher Hindu practices

(Srinivas, 1952, 1966). The idea was rooted in a reaction to the modernization theory of the 1960s and the idea of 'westernization' as the form of the modern in former colonized societies. It reflected the reaction of an upper caste nationalist elite who argued that Indians changed in Indian ways. Lucy Carroll's extensive work questioning the sentimentality, flabbiness, and conservatism of this notion has surprisingly received little traction within Indian academe (Carroll, 1975, 1977, 1978). Arguably, it is the belief in change and mobility without social conflict that has been extremely appealing to a version of social sciences, which has been non-cognizant of the ontological humiliation of caste and its being rooted in a dialectic of violence and struggle. Arguably, the experience of Partition in 1947, and of civil war between Hindus and Muslims in northern India, has meant that 'communalism', or religious violence, has come to be seen as the central faultline in Indian society (Menon, 2007).

Caste, Religion, Migration

That caste hierarchies are kept in place through everyday violence, reflected in a slew of continuing killings of dalits from Kilvenmani (1968) to Karamchedu (1985), Tsunduru (1991), Khairlanji (2006), and Bhima Koregaon (2018) reflects that little has changed (Teltumbde, 2008; Omvedt, 2009; *Human Rights Watch*, 1999). Even the adoption of the ritual and lifestyle practices of upper castes is met less with approbation than condign punishment. However, throughout the colonial period and beyond, there has been an intimate dialectic between lower caste mobility and attempts to consolidate a 'Hindu' identity for which numbers within its putative constituency were crucial. Periods of lower caste mobility, whether through associational politics or secular economic processes, accompanied by resentment, and agitation against a hierarchical order have resulted in conjunctures of the assertion of a Hindu identity as against Muslims, seen as the internal enemy. This displacement of the inner violence characteristic of caste onto an external object reflects an intimate relation between caste and communal violence that has not been taken seriously enough (Menon, 2007). A study of the transformation of caste, whether in colonial or postcolonial India, must take in a field larger than a set of relations within a putative Hindu society alone.

Even as we argue for caste bleeding into other forms of politics in India, it is important to remember that with the abolition of slavery in the 19th century, we have the phenomenon of indentured labour and the creation of an Indian diaspora from the Caribbean to South Africa. Most of the indentured labourers came from the exhausted agrarian economies of the Gangetic plain and the dry areas of the Madras Presidency in the Tamil and Telugu speaking regions. Many were from the lower ends of the caste and class hierarchy and carried with them beliefs, ideologies, and attitudes from India to form a set of similar, yet altered practices, of Hinduism and Islam in their new spaces (Gillion, 1962; Carter, 1996; Kale, 1998; Desai, 2010; Allen, 2017; Bahadur, 2013). Much of the debate has centred on whether caste 'survives' in these spaces and the question of whether people thrown pell-mell into the discipline of hard labour and regimes of punishment across an ocean continue to be invested in maintaining ineffable differences. At the level of ideology, it has been asked whether caste as a phenomenon can survive outside of spaces not determined by caste ideology and differences of purity and impurity (Younger, 2009). The history of indenture must be seen alongside the voluntary migration, of labour and capital, across the oceans to Southeast Asia, and the opening up of the land frontier in Burma and Malaya (Baker, 1985; Adas, 2011). Mercantile groups as much as labouring classes were to influence hugely the development of the public sphere in southern India, funding educational organizations as much as new social movements like the Dravidian movements of the early 20th century (Bate, 2009).

A similar movement of labour from eastern and northwest India to the USA and Canada was also to inflect the developing politics of nationalism and the internal fissures of caste and other hierarchies within India (Mawani, 2018; Shah, 2011; Bald, 2013). The Punjabi dalit, Mangoo Ram, who founded the first untouchable movement in north India, the Ad Dharm movement, travelled through Southeast Asia to California to work as an agricultural labour. He came back imbued with ideas of equality as much as a belief in the power of education and labour to create a powerful constituency in Punjab (Juergensmeyer, 1982). Again, one must not forget the experience of Indian soldiers, recruited to fight in the cause of empire in Europe, Africa, and the Middle East during the First and Second World Wars who then returned to an uncomfortable location within local society. Returning soldiers were to be catalysts and constituents of social and political movements in the United Provinces and Punjab, from where the most recruitment had taken place (Singha, 2021). While Gandhi's role of making haste slowly regarding caste and social transformation needs to be the subject of another essay, a forgotten vignette needs to be stated here. When Gandhi returned from South Africa to India, his initial campaigns in Champaran and Kheda tended to work along the lines of petitions and the networks of colonial officials that Gandhi knew. Meanwhile, in the United Provinces, a returned indentured labourer from Fiji, calling himself Baba Ramachandra, forged a powerful peasant movement in the 1920s melding together religiosity, anti-caste sentiments, and a radical peasant politics. Arguably, this movement, which was hijacked by the Indian National Congress, represented the radicalizing of nationalism by a labour diaspora towards addressing issues of caste and class which has received little recognition in the literature (Pandey, 1978; K. Kumar, 1978; A. Kumar, forthcoming; Siddiqui, 1978).

Gandhi, Ambedkar, and Caste

In the early years of nationalism, after the formation of the Indian National Congress in 1885, annual sessions had always co-hosted conferences regarding social reform. The late 19th century had seen agitations for the abolition of *sati* and child marriage and the promotion of widow remarriage, though the question of caste inequality was not yet raised. This has been studied generally as social reform and an engagement with the 'women's question', notwithstanding the fact that these were issues that concerned only the reform of the upper caste family as B. R. Ambedkar pointed out in a graduate essay in 1916 (Heimsath, 1964; Jones, 1990; Ambedkar, 1916). The relation of organized nationalism to caste had always been ambivalent reflecting the social composition of the leadership. Gandhi brought a new radicalism to nationalist understanding characterizing caste as an 'excrescence on Hinduism' at the Nagpur session of the Congress in 1920 and put the issue of untouchability on the national agenda. However, his emphasis that transformation would come through a change of heart among upper castes and his ambivalence regarding *varnasrama* and the respective roles of castes within a system meant a de-politicization of the issue of inequality and hierarchy.

Ambedkar was insistent that there had to be a political solution to caste, and this was to lead to a stand-off with Gandhi over the issue of separate electorates for untouchables in 1932. Gandhi insisted that he would fast unto death if the issue of separate electorates was granted, and Ambedkar backed down, and a compromise was reached in the Poona Pact. This conjuncture has led to a linking of Gandhi and Ambedkar as a dyad and attempts to think through Ambedkar's work only in the shadow of Gandhian politics. However, from 1916 to 1956, Ambedkar produced a corpus of work that in lapidary formulations defined caste as a 'graded system of sovereignties' and a 'division of labourers rather than a division of labour' and attempted to understand the peculiarities of caste as a social phenomenon that could not be reduced to relations of class or indeed to Hindu mystifications. He mined classical texts to forge a history of the emergence of the *sudra* and the 'broken people' and was convinced that the palliatives that nationalism and democracy offered would be nothing more than a thin crust on a society that was ineffably hierarchical and had little place for fraternity between humans. While Ambedkar is seen sentimentally in the popular imagination as the 'father of the Indian constitution', it is forgotten that he had little faith in parliamentary democracy as offering a solution to the denial of dignity to the untouchable. In 1946, in his sharply titled *What Congress and Gandhi Have Done to the Untouchables*, an adept analysis of Congress funds and election results, he showed the influence of caste, money, and factions in determining popular elections. It is significant that even as the Constituent Assembly was being set up in 1946, and Ambedkar was preparing to take over as Chairman, he was already sceptical of the outcome of parliamentary democracy in relation to social equality.

What Ambedkar's unstinting research in history, politics, and sociology did was to put caste in a transnational frame while at the same time recognizing the quiddity of caste as an Indian phenomenon. His uncovering of a genealogy and the suggestion of a therapeutic for caste points to a larger and ignored history of the traditions of intellection and reflection of caste in colonial India (Kumar, 2015). Modern Indian intellectual history has worked with the thought of elites—Gandhi, Nehru, Ambedkar, Bankimchandra—pointing out both possibilities and aporias. Lower castes have been largely studied in their actions, whether in peasant and tribal revolts or in the formation of associations towards political and institutional action. Arguably, the writings of Phule, Iyothee Thass, and Ambedkar have served to broaden our vision of democracy and inclusion and provide intellectual frameworks for the working out of the as yet unfulfilled project of equality and fraternity in our country (Rao, 2009; Aloysius, 1997). Orientalists like William Jones and others through the translation of classical texts made legible what had been largely an opaque and inaccessible tradition. The exposure, as it were, of the textual underpinnings of a brahminical hierarchy produced the classical texts of Hinduism as the villains of a historical drama of inequality, and the Manusmriti was to gain an indexical status with public burnings of it in 1927, by Ambedkar at Mahad and MC Rajah in Madras.

Untouchability and Freedom

An intellectual history of the idea of freedom as expounded by dalit and lower caste intellectuals awaits its author (Rao, 2009). While reflections on self, dignity, and newer forms of relating to the ineffable have been written about for the medieval and early modern period, through the histories of *bhakti* saints, the colonial and modern period have been dominated by studies on nationalism and political activity directed towards the state. Ravindra Khare's magisterial *The Untouchable as Himself*, an intellectual biography of the Chamar thinker, Jigyasu who wrote in the United Provinces in the 1930s is a unique exception. Jigyasu plumbs the Hindu philosophical tradition within its vernacular renditions to mine a relation to self and others that is premised on oneness. He renders the sophisticated idea of *advaita* or monism to establish that individual souls and the transcendent soul are one, negating the very possibility of inequality, and difference in the world (Khare, 1984). The cities of the United Provinces like Kanpur and Agra had under colonialism attracted large numbers of untouchables and lower castes from the rural areas towards service within the cantonments and colonial establishments. Communities dealing with carcases, hitherto scorned, now found that they had a monopoly on the leather industry. There was a new constituency emerging that experienced wealth, education, and mobility, but the story needs to be supplemented with the emergence of newer forms of thinking which were not parochial but reflected on the human condition (Gooptu, 2001; Jodhka, 2010; Harriss-White, 2014).

If we are to truly think about caste, not from the sterile standpoint of understanding it as a system and studying its putative rules, we need to address what the experience of the lowest in society entails. There have been significant new writings particularly by Gopal Guru, Sundar Sarukkai, and Aniket Jaaware which try and address the question of caste as experience: an ontology and phenomenology of caste as it were (Guru, 2009; Sarukkai and Guru, 2012; Jaaware, 2019). This literature addresses the ethical question of rendering the lives of others and theorizing from the experience of the subaltern. One could possibly argue that the experience of being an untouchable or a dalit has not substantially changed from colonial to postcolonial times. While arguably, programmes of affirmative action have promoted access to education and state employment, the fact remains that the life of the dalit is a parlous one, despite the existence of legal protections and remedies. This is most evident not only in the violence that disciplines attempts at social mobility and aspirations to equality, but also in a simple fact. Manual scavenging continues to be done by dalit castes in contemporary India, and the cleaning of noxious manholes and the carrying of excreta through a metonymic transference condemns these castes to a life tainted by opprobrium and disgust. The everyday violence on the dalit body, epistemic, and physical is matched by the violence of the law; in its inability, perhaps refusal, to recognize the worth of all human life. V. Geetha has characterized this fundamental feature of Indian democracy as the pervasiveness of impunity (Geetha, 2016). If the illusion of the colonial period was the rule of law, so far as the dalit is concerned, this continues to be true for independent India.

Towards a Conclusion

Caste and its forms—rigid endogamy, untouchability—may be unique to India but it shares a lot with forms of discrimination like racism in the USA epistemologically and ontologically. As the black sociologist WEB du Bois argued being black was about the experience of being black: 'the black man is a person who must ride Jim Crow in Georgia' i.e. at the back of the bus (du Bois, 1940, p. 77). To be a dalit in India or to be an African–American the USA is to experience indignity—the lack of fraternity, and violence—the force of the law enacted through the state or social ostracism. It is not without significance that when Jotiba Phule wrote the first systematic attack on caste in Marathi titled *Gulamgiri* (Slavery) in 1873, he dedicated it to the freed slaves of the America, in the hope that Indian untouchables too would see the day of freedom. And when Oliver Cox, the Chicago sociologist, wrote his *Caste, Class, and Race* in 1959, he too was reaching across the ocean to understand the experience of blackness in the USA which neither the rhetoric of democracy or equality had ameliorated (Visweswaran, 2010). Finally, the lightning bolt of dalit writing by Namdeo Dhasal, Raja Dhale, and others that struck Marathi literature was aligned with the dalit Panther manifesto of 1973, which drew upon the conjuncture of the formation of the Black Panther liberation party in the USA (Dangle, 2010, 1992). The generation of affinities across a landscape of inequality and humiliation suggests that while caste, race, ethnicity, and so on may sociologically be explained only within particular landscapes, the spirit of political fraternity has a wider geography.

References

Adas, Michael. 2011. *The Burma Delta: Economic Development and Social Change on an Asian Rice Frontier, 1852–1941*. Madison: University of Wisconsin Press.
Alavi, Seema. 2007. *The Eighteenth Century in India*. Delhi: Oxford University Press.
Allen, R. B. 2017. 'Asian Indentured Labour in the 19th and Early 20th Century Colonial Plantation World'. In *Oxford Research Encyclopaedia of Asian History*.

Aloysius, G. 1997. *Nationalism without a Nation in India*. Delhi: Oxford University Press.

Aloysius, G. R. 1998. *Religion as Emancipatory Ideology: A Buddhist Movement among the Tamils under Colonialism*. Chennai: New Age International.

Ambedkar, B. R. 1916. 'Castes in India: Their Mechanism, Genesis and Development'. In *Dr Babasaheb Ambedkar: Writings and Speeches* (Vol. 1, pp. 3–22). Bombay: Education Department, Govt. of Maharashtra.

Ambedkar, B. R. 1931. *Indian Round Table Conference*. 12 November 1930–19 January 1931 Proceedings. Government of India, Central Publications Branch, Calcutta.

Appadurai, Arjun. 1993. 'Number in the Colonial Imagination'. In Carol Breckenridge and Peter van der Veer (Eds.), *Orientalism and the Postcolonial Predicament: Perspectives on South Asia*. Philadelphia: University of Pennsylvania Press.

Arunima, G. 2003. *'There Comes Papa': Colonialism and the Transformation of Matriliny in Kerala, Malabar c. 1850–1940*. Hyderabad: Orient Blackswan.

Bahadur, G. 2013. *Coolie Woman: The Odyssey of Indenture*. Chicago: University of Chicago Press.

Baker, C. J. 1985. *An Indian Rural Economy, 1880–1955*. Oxford: Oxford University Press.

Bald, Vivek. 2013. *Bengali Harlem and the Lost Histories of South Asian America*. Cambridge, MA: Harvard University Press.

Bandyopadhyay, Sekhar. 1997. *Caste, Protest and Identity in Colonial India: The Namasudras of Bengal, 1872–1947*. Delhi: Oxford University Press.

Barrier, N. G. 1981. *The Census in British India*. Delhi: Manohar Publications.

Bate, Bernard. 2009. *Tamil Oratory and the Dravidian Aesthetic: Democratic Practice in South India*. New York: Columbia University Press.

Bayly, C. A. 1987. *Indian Society and the Making of the British Empire*. Cambridge: Cambridge University Press.

Bayly, Susan. 1989. *Saints, Goddesses and Kings: Muslims and Christians in South Indian Society*. Cambridge: Cambridge University Press.

Bayly, Susan. 1999. *Caste, Society and Politics in India from the Early 18th Century to the Modern Age*. Cambridge: Cambridge University Press.

Bhagavan, Manu. 2003. *Sovereign Spheres: Princes, Education, and Empire in Colonial India*. Delhi: Oxford University Press.

Bose, Sugata. 1994. *Credit, Markets and the Agrarian Economy of Colonial India*. Delhi: Oxford University Press.

Carroll, L. M. 1975. 'Caste, Social Change and the Social Scientist: A Note on the Ahistorical Approach to Indian Social History'. *Journal of Asian Studies*, XXXV(1): 63–84.

Carroll, L. M. 1977. '"Sanskritization", "Westernization", and "Social Mobility": A Reappraisal of the Relevance of Anthropological Concepts to the Social Historian of Modern India'. *Journal of Anthropological Research*, 33(4): 355–371.

Carroll, L. M. 1978. 'Colonial Perception of Indian Society and the Emergence of Caste(s) Associations'. *Journal of Asian Studies*, XXXVII(2): 233–250.

Carter, M. 1996. *Voices from Indenture: Experiences of Indian Migrants in the British Empire*. Leicester: Leicester University Press.

Chandra, Sudhir. 1998. *Enslaved Daughters: Colonialism, Law and Womens Rights*. Delhi: Oxford University Press.

Cohn, Bernard. 1987. *An Anthropologist among the Historians and Other Essays*. Delhi: Oxford University Press.

Cohn, Bernard. 1996. *Colonialism and Its Forms of Knowledge*. Delhi: Oxford University Press.

Commander, Simon. 1983. 'The Jajmani System in North India; An Examination of Its Logic and Status across Two Centuries'. *Modern Asian Studies*, 17(2): 283–311.

Constable, Philip. 2000. 'Sitting on the School Verandah: The Ideology and Practice of "Untouchable" Educational Protest in Late Nineteenth Century Western India'. *Indian Economic and Social History Review*, 37(4): 383–422.

Dangle, Arjun. 2010 (1992). *Poisoned Bread: Translations from Marathi Dalit Literature*. Hyderabad: Orient Blackswan.

Datta, P. K. 1993. '"Dying Hindus": Production of Communal Commonsense in Early 20th Century Bengal'. *Economic and Political Weekly*, 28(25): 1305–1319.

Derrett, J. D. M. 1968. *Religion, Law and the State in India*. London: Faber and Faber.

Desai, Ashvin, and G. Vahed. 2010. *Inside Indian Indenture: A South African Story, 1860–1914*. Pretoria: HSRC Press.

Dirks, Nicholas. 1987. *The Hollow Crown: Ethnohistory of an Indian Kingdom*. Cambridge: Cambridge University Press.

Dumezil, Georges. 1958. *L'ideologie Tripartite Des Indo-Europeens* (Vol. 31). Brussels: Collection Latomus.

Du Bois, W. E. B. 1940. *Dusk of Dawn*. Oxford: Oxford University Press.

Dumont, Louis. 1966. *1980 Homo Hierarchicus: The Caste System and Its Implications*. Chicago: Chicago University Press.

Dumont, Louis. 1977. *From Mandeville to Marx: The Genesis and Triumph of Economic Ideology*. Chicago: Chicago University Press.

Dumont, Louis. 1986. *Essays on Individualism: Modern Ideology in Anthropological Perspective*. Chicago: Chicago University Press.

Fisch, Jorg. 1983. *Cheap Lives and Dear Limbs: The British Transformation of the Bengal Criminal Law, 1769–1817*. Wiesbaden: F Steiner.

Fukuzawa, H. 1972. 'Rural Servants in the 18thc Maharashtrian Village-Demiurgic or Jajmani System'. *Hitotsubashi Journal of Economics*, XII(2): 14–40.

Fuller, C. J. 1989. 'Misconceiving the Grain Heap: A Critique of the Indian Jajmani System'. In Jonathan Parry and Maurice Bloch (Eds.), *Money and the Morality of Exchange*., Cambridge: Cambridge University Press.

Geetha, V. 2016. *Undoing Impunity: Speech after Sexual Violence*. New Delhi: Zubaan.

Gillion, K. L. 1962. *Fiji's Indian Migrants: A History to the End of Indenture in 1920*. Melbourne: Oxford University Press.

Gooptu, Nandini. 2001. *The Politics of the Urban Poor in Early Twentieth Century India*. Cambridge: Cambridge University Press.

Guru, Gopal. 2009. *Humiliation: Claims and Contexts*. New Delhi: Oxford University Press.

Guru, Gopal, and S. Sarukkai. 2012. *The Cracked Mirror: An Indian Debate on Experience and Theory*. New Delhi: Oxford University Press.

Harriss-White, B. et al. 2014. *Dalits and Adivasis in India's Business Economy: Three Essays and an Atlas*. Gurgaon: Three Essays Collective.

Heimsath, Charles. 1964. *Indian Nationalism and Hindu Social Reform*. New Jersey: Princeton University Press.

Hocart, A. M. 1936 (1970). *Kings and Councillors: An Essay in the Comparative Anatomy of Human Society*. Chicago: Chicago University Press.

Human Rights Watch. 1999. *Broken People: Caste Violence against India's Untouchables*. New York.

Inden, Ronald. 1990. *Imagining India*. London: Hurst and Company.

Irschick, Eugene. 1969. *Politics and Social Conflict in South India*. Berkeley: University of California Press.

Jaaware, Aniket. 2019. *Practicing Caste: On Touching and Not Touching*. New York: Fordham University Press.

Jeffrey, Robin. 1974. 'The Social Origins of a Caste Association, 1875–1905: The Founding of the SNDP Yogam'. *South Asia: Journal of South Asian Studies*, 4(1): 39–59.

Jodhka, Surinder. 2010. 'Dalits in Business: Self Employed Scheduled Castes in North-West India'. *Economic and Political Weekly*, 45(11): 41–48.

Jones, Kenneth. 1990. *The New Cambridge History of Modern India: Socio-Religious Reform Movements in British India*. Cambridge: Cambridge University Press.

Juergensmeyer, Mark. 1982. *Religion as Social Vision: The Movement against Untouchability in 20th Century Punjab*. Berkeley: University of California Press.

Kale, M. 1998. *Fragments of Empire: Capital, Slavery and Indian Indentured Labour in the British Caribbean*. Philadelphia: University of Pennsylvania Press.

Kawashima, Koji. 1998. *Missionaries and a Hindu State: Travancore 1858–1936*. Delhi: Oxford University Press.

Kemper, Steven. 2015. *Rescued from the Nation: Anagarika Dharmapala and the Buddhist World*. Chicago: Chicago University Press.

Khare, Ravindra. 1984. *The Untouchable as Himself: Ideology, Identity and Pragmatism among the Lucknow Chamars*. Cambridge: Cambridge University Press.

Kumar, Aishwary. 2015. *Radical Equality: Ambedkar, Gandhi and the Risk of Democracy*. Stanford: Stanford University Press.

Kumar, Ashutosh. n.d. *Baba Ramchandra: Fiji Girmitiya*. Forthcoming.

Kumar, Kapil. 1978. 'Baba Ramchandra and the Peasant Upsurge in Oudh: 1920–21'. *Social Scientist*, 6(11): 35–56.

Kunhambu, Potheri. 1893(2002). *Saraswativijayam* (trans. Dilip Menon). Delhi: Book Review Literary Trust.

Ludden, David. 1994. *Agricultural Production and Indian History*. Delhi: Oxford University Press.

Mawani, Renisa. 2018. *Across Oceans of Law: The Komagata Maru and Jurisdiction in the Time of Empire*. Durham: Duke University Press.

McCormack, William. 1966. 'Caste and the British Administration of Hindu Law'. *Journal of Asian Studies*, 1(1): 27–34.

Menon, Dilip. 2007. 'An Inner Violence: why Communalism in India Is About Caste'. In T. N. Srinivasan (Ed.), *The Future of Secularism*. New Delhi: Oxford University Press.

O'Hanlon, Rosalind. 1985. *Caste Conflict and Ideology: Mahatma Jotirao Phule and Low Caste Protest in Nineteenth Century Western India*. Cambridge: Cambridge University Press.

O'Hanlon, Rosalind. 2017. 'Caste and Its Histories in Colonial India: A Reappraisal'. *Modern Asian Studies*, 51(2): 432–461.

Omvedt, Gail. 2009. *Seeking Begumpura: The Social Vision of Anti-Caste Intellectuals*. Delhi: Navayana.

Pandey, Gyanendra. 1978. *The Ascendancy of the Congress in Uttar Pradesh 1926–34: A Study in Imperfect Mobilization*. Delhi: Oxford University Press.

Peabody, Norbert. 2001. 'Cents, Sense, Census: Human Inventories in Later Precolonial and Early Colonial India'. *Comparative Studies in Society and History*, 43(4): 819–850.

Phule, Jotirao. 1883 (2002). Cultivators Whipcord (trans. Aniket Jaaware). In G. P. Deshpande (Ed.), *Selected Writings of Jotirao Phule*. Delhi: Leftword Books.

Prakash, Gyan. 1992. *World of the Rural Labourer in Colonial India*. Delhi: Oxford University Press.

Quigley, Declan. 1993. *The Interpretation of Caste*. Oxford: Oxford University Press.

Quigley, Declan. 2005. *The Character of Kingship*. London: Bloomsbury.

Raheja, G. G. 1988. *The Poison in the Gift; Ritual, Prestation and the Dominant Caste in a North Indian Village*. Chicago: Chicago University Press.

Ramaswamy, Sumathi. 1997. *Passions of the Tongue: Language Devotion in Tamil India, 1891–1970*. Berkeley: University of California Press.

Rao, Anupama. 2009. *The Caste Question: Dalits and the Politics of Modern India*. Berkeley: University of California Press.

Shah, Nayan. 2011. *Stranger Intimacy: Contesting Race, Sexuality and the Law in the North American West*. Berkeley: University of California Press.

Siddiqui, Majid. 1978. *Agrarian Unrest in North India: The United Provinces, 1918–22*. Delhi: Vikas Publishing House.

Singha, Radhika. 2021. *The Coolies' Great War: Indian Labour in a Global Conflict, 1914–1921*. London: C. Hurst and Publishers.

Smith, Brian K. 1994. *Classifying the Universe: The Ancient Indian varna System and the Origins of Caste*. New York: Oxford University Press.

Srinivas, M. N. 1952. *Religion and Society among the Coorgs of South India*. Oxford: Clarendon Press.

Srinivas, M. N. 1966. *Social Change in Modern India*. Berkeley: University of California Press.

Surendran, G. 2013. ' "The Indian Discovery of Buddhism": Buddhist Revival in India c. 1890–1956'. Unpublished PhD Dissertation, Harvard University.

Teltumbde, Anand. 2008. *Khairlanji: A Strange and Bitter Crop*. Delhi: Navayana.

Templeman, Dennis. 1996. *The Northern Nadars of Tamil Nadu: An Indian Caste in the Process of Change*. Delhi: Oxford University Press.

Trautmann, Thomas. 2006. *Languages and Nations: The Dravidian Proof in Colonial Madras*. Berkeley: University of California Press.

Trautmann, Thomas. 2009. *The Madras School of Orientalism: Producing Knowledge in Colonial South India*. Delhi: Oxford University Press.

Visweswaran, Kamala. 2010. *Un/Common Cultures: Racism and the Re-Articulation of Cultural Difference*. Durham, NC: Duke University Press.

Washbrook, David. 1993. 'Land and Labour in Late Eighteenth-Century South India: The Golden Age of the Pariah'. In P. G. Robb (Ed.), *Dalit Movements and the Meanings of Labour in India*. Delhi: Oxford University Press.

Wiser, W. H. 1936. *The Hindu Jajmani System*. Lucknow: Lucknow Publishing House.

Younger, Paul. 2009. *New Homelands: Hindu Communities in Mauritius, Guyana, Trinidad, South Africa, Fiji and East Africa*. New York: Oxford University Press.

CHAPTER 9

CENSUS, CASTE ENUMERATION AND THE BRITISH LEGACY

LEIGH DENAULT

INTRODUCTION

Rich debates on colonial knowledge and state power in colonial India have focused on the nature of imperial information-gathering projects and agendas, and their impact on South Asian subjects. What processes transformed people into 'legible bodies'[1] that could be classified, counted (and controlled) by the state? How were plural South Asian socio-political identities fit into 'universal' categories by the end of the 19th century? Historians from the 1980s focused on how the politics of community and belonging were entangled with classification and codification in colonial India, and on how volatile and often violent eruptions of communalism could be tied directly to the ways in which colonial representation and enumeration deconstructed and reconstructed Indian identities.[2]

Work on the decennial censuses has revealed both the operation of the colonial state, and the vocal South Asian publics whom they consulted and categorized. Drawing on Karin Barber's use of Mikhail Bakhtin's concept of 'addressivity',[3] we might anthropologize the census itself. The census of India purported to uncover the nature of Indian personhood, and to establish 'social facts' about South Asia. But the

---

[1] Anderson, *Legible Bodies: Race, Criminality, and Colonialism in South Asia*.
[2] See Thapar, 'Imagined Religious Communities?' and also the work of A. M. Rajni Kothari, Shah, Gyanendra Pandey, and Bernard Cohn, 'Barrier's Edited Volume Brought Together Many Early Studies'; Barrier, *The Census in British India: New Perspectives*.
[3] Barber, 'The Anthropology of Texts, Persons and Publics by Karin Barber'.

massive collation of data produced by and for the census, and its highly public and publicized reports, resulted in a document more as 'hypertext' than text: censuses referenced rumours and petitions from phantom 'Indian publics' as well as orientalist and ethnographic scholars, while commissioners reflexively reflected on omissions and mischaracterizations, yet ultimately papered over these fissures, quite literally, with hundreds of pages of statistical tables that told their own essentializing story.

This chapter will first explore how scholarly debates on caste, colonial knowledge, and power, stemming from the pathbreaking work of Cohn and others, focused on the census as a crucial site for the creation of discourse. It will then consider how the operation of the decennial censuses in India intersected with social and political movements, suggesting that while the census inflected both South Asian and imperial understandings of caste, South Asians also challenged the new 'demographic thinking' of the colonial state, or absorbed new conceptualizations into pre-existing social movements. Finally, it will examine how late colonial censuses, and more recent thinking on a 'caste census', evolved from, and in some cases perpetuated, colonialism's statistical view of Indian society.

THE CENSUS IN HISTORY AND ANTHROPOLOGY

Bernard Cohn and Talal Asad[4] were among the first to identify colonial epistemology, and, for Cohn, the census in particular, as a crucial tool in conquest. Cohn argued that colonialism was not solely a process of military and economic domination, but a 'conquest of knowledge',[5] producing what Nicholas Dirks termed 'cultural technologies of rule'.[6] For both Cohn and Dirks, the census was the critical operation through which colonial administrators, who believed that 'caste and religion were the sociological keys to understanding the Indian people',[7] attempted to systematize, and thereby objectify and essentialize, Indian subjects. This argument is sometimes summarized as a 'postcolonial' or 'discursive' understanding of the relationship between colonial power and colonial knowledge. While both Cohn and Dirks emphasized the fragmentary and contradictory ways in which census ethnography operated, their arguments about the impact of colonial knowledge were criticized as overstating the extent to which this colonial 'dream of order' was ever achieved. C. A. Bayly suggested that 'orientalism' was instead a project marked by incoherence, and that the colonial stereotyping of Indian

---

[4] Asad, *Anthropology & the Colonial Encounter*.
[5] Cohn, *Colonialism and Its Forms of Knowledge: The British in India*, p. 16
[6] Their early work predated the publication of Edward Said's *Orientalism* in 1978, but presaged a wider interest in intersections between colonial knowledge and conquest. See Dirks, Introduction, in Cohn (1996), p. ix.
[7] Cohn, *An Anthropologist among the Historians and Other Essays*, p. 242.

society was the result of 'the weakness and blindness of the state at the fringes of its knowledge, rather than a set of governing assumptions at its core'.[8] Bayly argued that the colonial state was most effective, epistemologically, when it was able to successfully 'graft' European knowledge onto 'indigenous stock'. This 'grafting' was itself a process of subordination which required stressing 'sameness', rather than 'otherness'. While Indians were, he suggests, 'temporarily' subordinated to new colonial discourses and cultural technologies, they were almost immediately able to deploy these 'forms of social power' in ways that subverted colonial intentions, drawing on their ability to operate effectively as publicists in both the domain of colonial officialdom, and within burgeoning Indian public spheres.[9] Drawing on the arguments of Eugene Irschick, Bayly argued that the colonial state was instead engaged in a 'dialogic' project, which, while continually asserting European knowledge as 'superior', was forced to borrow legitimacy from South Asian concepts, institutions, and individuals.

While the colonial state did unquestionably attempt to impose essentialized group identities, historians have asked to what extent the colonial state was able to realize its vision of order, and how far its enumeration projects diverged from precolonial statecraft. Brian Pennington also cautions against overplaying the power and agency of colonial rulers, as historians could mis-read both resistance, and creative uses of precolonial tradition. The argument that a state has the capacity to 'invent' identities suggests that such identities are somehow 'false'. As Conlon put it, however, even if castes were 'reinvented', both from above and below, during the colonial period, are invented identities necessarily less 'real' than organic ones?[10]

Caste was not simply constructed by British rulers, as Dirks himself makes clear, and Susan Bayly and Rosalind O'Hanlon elaborate, but it did acquire a new significance in the colonial period. Norbert Peabody, Sumit Guha, and Philip Wagoner have argued that British projects of enumeration drew heavily on precolonial precursors as templates. They note that the caste categories which so preoccupied British census administrators were present in precolonial enumerations, and suggest that their adoption by the British was seen as a 'necessary evil'. Peabody suggests that colonial discourses of identity and personhood were palimpsest, 'built upon indigenous ones in ways that inflected local politics about which the British initially were only dimly aware and indirectly concerned, but which later had a major impact on the constitution of colonial rule'.[11]

However, as Peter Gottschalk argues, it was the 'differing quality' of the categories which British administrators adopted, and 'the divergent contexts' of British 'knowledge projects', which constructed a 'singular information order with multiple facets, each expected to reinforce one another's conclusions within a context of top-down

---

[8] Bayly, *Empire and Information: Intelligence Gathering and Social Communication in India, c. 1780–1870*, p. 370.

[9] Ibid., 373–374.

[10] Conlon, 'Speaking of Caste? Colonial and Indigenous Interpretations of Caste and Community in Nineteenth Century Bombay', p. 293.

[11] Peabody, 'Cents, Sense, Census'.

standardization'.[12] Gottschalk's focus on the extent to which an ostensibly secular, 'progressive' colonial scientific vision reproduced medieval Christian categories[13] in colonial information orders adds another dimension to Bernard Cohn's earlier work on the census as a part of a Victorian 'quest for total knowledge'.[14] By insisting that the census could be, and should be, universal, and that every colonial subject could be counted and categorized according to a uniform system which identified personhood through monolithic religious and caste categories, and, crucially, by making the results of the census both official and highly public, and publicized, the colonial government simultaneously destroyed the last remnants of a plural Mughal information order and forced countless individuals to rethink their identity in relation to a new state-produced rubric.

In identifying the origins of what Cohn would call the enumerative 'modality' of colonialism, Richard Smith has argued that around 1850, coinciding with the conquest and settlement of Punjab, censuses and surveys, intended to administer an agrarian economy and focussing on the household and village as primary units of measurement, ceased to function primarily as determinants of taxation. Instead, the census was transformed from 'an instrument of taxes to an instrument of knowledge'.[15] Immediately after the 1853 censuses of Punjab, as revenue officials handed off to colonial administrators, caste became the key container for identification. The expansion of formal empire disrupted individuals and groups whose lives, both settled and peripatetic, had relied on precolonial institutions and systems. Appadurai notes that this 'unyoking' of social groups took place in two significant periods of dislocation: first, prior to 1870, during the period of major colonial revisions to land settlement and taxation regimes; and second, the late 19th and early 20th centuries, during which the work of cataloguing India's people became a primary occupation.[16]

The rebellion of 1857 motivated further shifts in colonial understanding of Indian society. Dirks notes that 'after 1857, anthropology supplanted history as the principal colonial modality of knowledge and rule'.[17] The census became a measurement of fealty, and a tool for understanding subjecthood. Karuna Mantena further suggests that the colonial state after 1858 moved away from a model in which India's progress was regarded as desirable or even possible, instead citing Indian racial otherness and incapacity for change as a core justification for continued rule. New legal and surveillance systems which privileged ethnography as a source of knowledge focused on managing Indian *difference*, rather than promoting Indian 'progress'.[18] Mantena and Gottschalk challenge lingering notions of a 'modern' and 'scientific' colonial regime confronting a 'traditional' people. Rather than harbingers of 'secular' Western science, the colonial census

---

[12] Gottschalk, *Religion, Science, and Empire*, p. 184.
[13] Ibid., p. 187.
[14] Cohn, *Colonialism and Its Forms of Knowledge: The British in India*, p. 8.
[15] Smith, *Rule by Records*. See also his article on the census: 'Between Local Tax and Global Statistic: The Census as Local Record'.
[16] Appadurai, 'Number in the Colonial Imagination', p. 327.
[17] Dirks, *Castes of Mind: Colonialism and the Making of Modern India*, p. 43.
[18] Mantena, *Alibis of Empire: Henry Maine and the Ends of Liberal Imperialism*.

reports, and the broader project of enumeration, were steeped in both religious and racial/civilizational prejudices. The insistence on classifying Indian subjects according to caste and religion, while Western subjects were more usually grouped by their country of origin, reinforced South Asian people as 'other'.

The decennial censuses from 1871 to 1941 have been singled out as representing the nexus of a colonial 'information matrix', relying on earlier orientalist archives as well as the wealth of 'cadastral' knowledge[19] contained in the records and surveys generated by British imperial expansion across South Asia. India's decennial censuses, Gottschalk notes, while clearly based in some respects on prior British censuses, diverged wildly in their focus on religion and caste. Nowhere else in the empire was religious identity given such primacy: British census respondents would not be asked to provide their religious affiliation until 2001.[20] By the 1881 Indian census, the colonial government aimed to list the names 'of every person in India' and to compile information about age, sex, occupation, caste, religion, literacy, place of birth, and current residence.[21] The census reports did not merely describe statistical data, but included long treatises on the nature of caste, Indian religion, and Indian households, and local economies. While this information purported to be purely descriptive,[22] it was linked with ethnographic projects to distinguish 'authentic' Hindus, and upper-caste Hindus, from people who had attained a higher caste identity through service in the Mughal administration or military, or who had claimed an upper caste identity through literacy.[23]

In other words, censuses produce, rather than merely collect or collate, data.[24] Bruce Curtis, writing on the 1861 Canadian census, has noted that those responsible for contact with each household, and the translators and compilers of census data, all left their mark on the production of categories.[25] Enumerators often 'corrected' questionnaires based on their own understanding, and census officials, overworked and overwhelmed, misreported or underreported information. In their turn, commissioners, in abstracting the data provided to them, could also fundamentally alter the context and categories provided by local sub-divisions. The colonial government relied on the census as a process which relayed information about territories and peoples to support and validate administration, but the information itself was, as all data is, a construct, rather than an unfiltered reflection of reality. Curtis suggests that we see census data as 'made, not taken, fabricated through processes that select, and do not simply reflect dimensions of social organization'.[26]

---

[19] Appadurai, 'Number in the Colonial Imagination', 321.
[20] Gottschalk, *Religion, Science, and Empire*, 199.
[21] Cohn, *Colonialism and Its Forms of Knowledge: The British in India*, p. 8.
[22] Lelyveld, *Aligarh's First Generation*.
[23] Bandyopadhyay, 'Construction of Social Categories: The Role of the Colonial Census'. See also O'Hanlon and Minkowski, 'What Makes People Who They Are?'
[24] For more on the idea that there is 'no such thing as raw data,' see: Owens, 'Defining Data for Humanists'.
[25] See Curtis, 'On the Local Construction of Statistical Knowledge'.
[26] Ibid.

Counting Castes, Casting Doubt

In order to understand how the information that the census produced affected the lived experience of colonized subjects, we must therefore think about how census categories were generated. Gottschalk identifies four stages of census work.[27] First, enumerators numbered each house in their area, and administered a questionnaire to the identified 'head' of the household. Enumerators were often blamed for substituting what they felt were more accurate answers to their questions, and were constantly reminded to record only the householder's response. In the second phase, census officials construed categories from the enumerator's data, deploying, from 1901,[28] pigeonholes and coloured slips of paper to ensure each enumeration slip went into a single category. The third and fourth stages involved the transmission of data from sub-divisions to the provincial government's census operation, and finally, the production of an interpretive essay to contextualize the data provided. The physical ordering of data into a set number of boxes precluded plural identities: with a matter of days or weeks to organize millions of enumerator's slips, any identity which did not tally with the pre-agreed categories either had to be made to fit an existing one, or put into a box marked 'other'.

There were, however, two additional 'stages': first, publicity, and last, publication. Publicizing the census was critical to the success of the entire enterprise, not least because the newly reconstituted Government of India was concerned about provoking further unrest following 1857. But publicity also made the census, and its wider mission and implications, a topic of discussion and debate across British India. The publication of the census and its reports meant that it entered the multilingual and multivocal public spheres spanning the subcontinent. The way that the census represented India, and Indians, therefore became synonymous with a 'state's-eye view' of Indian society, but it was also a public property, open to manipulation, petitions, and dissent. There was tension within the colonial state regarding its information policy: as C. A. Bayly argued, the events of 1857–1858 had revealed the inadequacy of the vast reams of data collected by Company officials at all levels of administration, creating an 'information panic'.[29] Far from an omniscient and omnipotent 'panopticon' state, the rebellion had demonstrated that the government had not been collecting, organizing, and prioritizing information to produce actionable intelligence. Officials were simultaneously anxious to construct better surveillance networks, and concerned that large-scale enquiries would be seen as threatening in recently re-conquered territories.

---

[27] Gottschalk, *Religion, Science, and Empire*, p. 198.
[28] *Report on the 1901 Census of India*, p. xviii.
[29] Bayly, *Empire and Information: Intelligence Gathering and Social Communication in India, c. 1780–1870*, Chapter 4.

The government went so far as to disallow the 1863 Bombay Census Bill, produced by a number of provincial governors who had been petitioning the central administration to undertake a national census.[30] Despite this reluctance, census operations had been gradually extending across the provinces of British India, and Company directors had themselves previously proposed a census of the entire country for 1861. The rebellion brought a new urgency to these demands. The Home Office now saw a national census for India as 'most desirable' and 'absolutely necessary'.[31] Provinces and towns pressed ahead with local enumerations intended to provide vital demographic data, and these projects became test-cases for a national decennial census in 1871, when the central government, somewhat unwillingly, agreed to act, receiving Crown permission in November of 1870.

The 1871–1872 census was not carried out in several of the provinces most severely affected by the violence of 1857. The ostensible reason was that there had been enumerations within the previous decade in those areas which made the 'expense' 'undesirable', however, Henry M. Waterfield noted in the first census report that there had also been concerns about 'disturb[ing] the people' of Awadh and Berar.[32] Public mistrust in government had been one of the key issues raised by earlier regional and local censuses. In Calcutta's 1866 census, 'the general impression which prevailed amongst the lower classes of Natives that the object of the Census was the imposition of some new tax', led the chair of the census committee to argue that a public relations campaign would be critical in determining the success of any future census. Legislative Council of India members Maulvi Abdul Latif and Babu Ramanath Tagore had provided a paper laying out the advantages of the census to provide talking points for 'Native Justices', who were to act as intermediaries in dispelling rumours. The 'advantages' aligned closely with caste association welfare and reform programs, and were intended to win over new 'public men' in the towns and cities of British India to the census project.[33]

The creation of uniform, comparable data about India's population was the chief goal from the outset, but this proved much more difficult than colonial officials had imagined. The pursuit of categories which would encompass India's diversity, rendering it susceptible to administration and analysis, would lead officials both to experiment with new, 'scientific' forms of classification and to the revival of Brahminical models. They also reveal the extent to which multivocal and noisy Indian public spheres refused to be 'pigeonholed'. Comparing the tone and content of the chapters on 'Caste, Tribe, and Race' in the eight colonial census reports from 1871 to 1941 reveals both the diversity

---

[30] Maheshwari, *The Census Administration under the Raj and After*, p. 27.
[31] 'That a census of the whole people is most desirable, or rather we may say is absolutely necessary, as a sound basis of almost every economical reform, has long since been admitted as a simple truism … thus the census should proceed with a view to secure uniformity and thus facilitate comparison.' Cited in Natarajan, *A Century of Social Reform in India*, pp. 3–4.
[32] Waterfield, *Memorandum on the Census of British India of 1871–72*.
[33] Ibid.

of colonial ethnographic and administrative 'facts' about caste, and shifting attitudes toward Indian reception.

The most 'remarkable' quality of the census of 1871–1872 was its 'uniform absence of uniformity'.[34] Waterfield's own *Memorandum* on the census noted that 1871 marked a 'first approach' rather than a successful attempt.[35] The census did, however, reveal how diverse practices and understandings of 'caste' were across British India. The unclassifiable mass of data on caste was generally believed to be the result of open-ended questions, poorly trained enumerators, and poorly instructed administrators. There is another interpretation: that the data generated did in fact reflect a genuine uncertainty about 'caste' within both local and pan-regional communities, and among imperial officialdom. What individuals and meant by 'caste' could be at times nebulous, at times rigid, depending on one's position within nested hierarchies.

The 1871–1872 census assumed 'Hindu' and 'Muslim' to be monolithic categories, although Waterfield somewhat undermined this point by noting that not all of those enumerated as 'Hindu' might be generally acknowledged as such.[36] Untouchables were sometimes included among 'Other' (non-Hindu) populations, alongside 'Hill Tribes', sometimes as 'Hindu'. Ramnarayan Rawat has noted that the census produced 'caste-based occupational stereotypes', linking 'Chamar' with 'leatherworker' and 'untouchable' or 'unclean' caste by connecting Sanskrit etymology to a 'traditionally impure' occupation. This identification persisted despite extensive evidence that Chamars were engaged in a myriad of occupations, most notably agrarian labour. The census powerfully reinforced anti-Chamar prejudice, exposing individuals to accusations of cattle poisoning and slaughter.[37] The census would continue to make racialized distinctions, despite qualifications about internal diversity and high levels of syncretism, following earlier Orientalist categorizations of India's population into Hindu and Muslim 'races'.[38] Moreover, by focusing on the geographical distribution of religious groups, and areas of relative concentration, the census created a highly public demographic geography of different communities across the subcontinent. This mapping extended to caste groups, and, although the 1871 and 1881 censuses did not separate castes into 'inferior' and 'superior' groupings, Waterfield's *Memorandum* makes clear where populations of 'untouchables' or 'Brahmins' were more densely situated, making it possible for the first time to begin to visualize, however erroneously, the distribution of India's caste 'communities'.[39]

---

[34] Ibbetson, *Report on the Census of the Panjáb Taken on the 17th of February 1881*. Vol. 1, p. 2. The census was not conducted simultaneously, nor was it 'All-India' in scope, and there was considerable local variation in questionnaires and responses.

[35] Waterfield, *Memorandum on the Census of British India of 1871–72*, p. 5.

[36] Ibid., 17. Waterfield includes a note on the 'doubtful castes' of Kumaon, 'of which it is difficult to say where they should be classed'.

[37] See Rawat, *Reconsidering Untouchability*.

[38] Rocher, 'British Orientalism in the Eighteenth Century'.

[39] For dalit groups and other marginalized people, this mapping could be both empowering and dangerous: see Rawat, *Reconsidering Untouchability*.

Waterfield opened the section on 'Nationality, language, and caste' in the first census memorandum by suggesting that it was the *race* of those who practised Hinduism, rather than doctrinal and cultural variation across time and space, which provided an explanation for divergences from an assumed 'pure' form of Hinduism. Bengalis were described in the report as 'nourished on a watery rice diet, looking weak and puny, but able to bear much exposure, timid and slothful, but sharp-witted, industrious, and fond of sedentary employment'.[40] Oriyas, in turn, were seen as 'more timid, conservative, bigoted, and priest-ridden', while the people of Assam were seen to be 'proud and indolent ... and addicted to opium' due to their 'large mixture of Indo-Chinese blood'.[41] The Hindus of the North-Western Provinces were depicted as simple cultivators, with Urdu culture and language dominant among more cultured elites in the towns and cities.[42] These caricatures, published in a high-profile official government report, gave authority to long-standing official and popular stereotypes, and would prompt outraged responses from Indian publics. They also set a precedent, aptly summarized by Appadurai: the project of enumeration, alongside these new classification schemes, cemented 'the link between the orientalizing thrust of the British state, which saw India as a museum or zoo of difference and of differences, and the project of reform, which involved cleaning up the sleazy, flabby, frail, feminine, obsequious bodies of natives into clean, virile, muscular, moral, and loyal bodies that could be moved into the subjectivities proper to colonialism'.[43]

As far as caste itself was concerned, census administrators confessed that the result was unsatisfactory. Waterfield suggested that the lack of a 'uniform plan of classification' had led to each enumerator and writer 'adopting that which seemed to him best suited for the purpose'. This had produced, Waterfield noted, a 'mass of detailed information' which was impossible to clearly categorize or tabulate.[44] The 1871 commissioners settled on slotting the dense local information generated by the census into varna categories.[45]

The 1881 census would use measures of demographic 'significance' to sort out the confusing concatenation of Orientalist racial theory and Mughlai-era hyper-local societal detail which the 1871 census had revealed. Commissioner W. C. Plowden, who once had argued against using caste at all in the census,[46] instead ordered provincial census officials to consider only caste communities numbering over 100,000. Although he had initially intended to classify 'major' castes according to their social standing, Plowden abandoned this scheme after his office was inundated by petitions from caste

---

[40] Waterfield, *Memorandum on the Census of British India of 1871–72*, p. 19.
[41] Ibid.
[42] Ibid.
[43] Appadurai, 'Number in the Colonial Imagination', 134.
[44] Waterfield, *Memorandum on the Census of British India of 187–72*, p. 20.
[45] 'Varna' refers to a four-fold caste division, and in the 19th century this was increasingly in reference the social order described in the *Manusmriti*. Vedic texts used a corporeal metaphor for society, in which Brahmins, priests, were the mouth or head of the *purusha*, kshatriya (warriors) were his arms, vaishya his thighs, and shudra his feet.
[46] Dirks, *Castes of Mind: Colonialism and the Making of Modern India*, pp. 207–208.

associations 'complaining of the position assigned to castes to which the petitioners belong'.[47] These petitions represented the extent to which the census had entered into public life and public debate in colonial India. Efforts to publicize the census operations had centred on convincing the population that its goal was not to institute a new poll tax, mass conscription for forced labour projects or to fight Russian imperial expansion.[48] As Dirks notes, however, the census data was of course intended to further aims of imperial control and administration, which did correspond to the recruitment and retention of military personnel and labour, particularly in the context of the recent uprising, increasing plantation-style agriculture across British India, and renewed competition among imperial powers.[49]

The use of varna as a 'primary principle of classification',[50] according to Dirks, was the moment at which the census, as an 'empirical project', was 'wedded to the most general of Orientalist categories for the classification of the social order, with built-in assumptions about hierarchy and precedence'.[51] Census officials, starting with Waterfield, were able to argue for the usefulness of varna as a general system of classification while heavily qualifying it,[52] as it was apparent that there were substantial numbers engaged in occupations far from those designated by their ostensible varna rank. Varna had been introduced as the answer to the need for a 'uniform' and universalizing system of categorization, and Waterfield urged regional reports to make use of it, but was seen from the start even by colonial census officials to be inadequate for the purpose.

A racialized understanding of varna would later be taken up by H. H. Risley, commissioner of the 1901 census and a devotee of the new biological and sociological sciences. However, the racialization of religious and caste differences is apparent from the very start of colonial attempts to understand the population of India, stemming from discourses of civilizational 'progress' and 'stagnation' at a much earlier phase of encounter. In Madras in 1881, W. R. Cornish, after complaining of the intricacies and abstruse nature of the caste system, upon which 'no two divisions, or sub-divisions, of the people themselves are agreed, and upon which European authorities who have paid any attention to it differ hopelessly', expounded on how race might explain such variance, suggesting that caste had been a means to 'prevent the admixture of the white and dark races'.[53] It was the blending of these discourses with information given by a population used to Mughlai censuses which produced colonial definitions of caste. But the publicity which census operations generated, and the public spheres of debate which they created, also helped to construct new popular, and official understandings of caste.

---

[47] Ibid., see also Plowden, *Report on the Census of British India, Taken on the 17th February 1881*. Vol. 1, p. 277.
[48] Beverley, *Report of the Census of Bengal 1872*, p. 58.
[49] Dirks, *Castes of Mind: Colonialism and the Making of Modern India*, p. 201.
[50] Ibid., p. 202.
[51] Ibid.
[52] Waterfield, *Memorandum on the Census of British India of 1871–72*, p. 21.
[53] Dirks, *Castes of Mind: Colonialism and the Making of Modern India*, pp. 205–207.

In his general report on the 1891–1892 census, J. A. Baines stated that caste was 'the most important of the ethnographic elements included in the census scheme'.[54] Following the work of M. Barth, which Baines quoted extensively throughout the report, caste was deemed 'the stronghold' of Hinduism. Yet Baines also argued that the sections on language and religion should provide a wider context for caste, which he saw as 'a development of the special tendency to which the social atmosphere of India is abnormally favourable', rather than a product of Brahminical Hinduism. To support the argument that caste was endemic to South Asia's people, and not an attribute of a singular religious culture, Baines pointed out how many 'tribes' or 'castes', that is Jats and Rajputs, contained Hindu, Sikh, and Muslim adherents, and the extent to which caste persisted among Christian converts in South India. Baines also exhibited a broader tendency to correlate caste, race, skin colour, and civilizational attainment, accepting as historical fact an invasion of Aryans 'white in colour, and more hardy and advanced in the arts of war and husbandry than his antagonists, but not so far removed in race as to prevent successful interbreeding'.[55] Baines briefly mapped out 'the evolution of caste from the comparatively simple basis of race and function into its present complicated shape', noting forces which would later be summarized as 'Sanskritization'.[56] He also took note of historical non-Brahmin movements, some of which gave rise to new castes, such as the Lingayat sect. He saw this process however in terms of caste rules and doctrinal differences, including no discussion of the rise and spread of Bhakti, an omission which would continue to shape official understandings of socio-religious change in South Asia.

By 1901, H. H. Risley and E. A. Gait's *Report* would open with a section on the 'Ethnic isolation of India'.[57] Risley, in his posthumously published *People of India* series,[58] would argue for an absolute equation of caste and race.[59] C. J. Fuller has challenged the extent to which Risley's particular vision was accepted, or acted upon, by the Government of India,[60] and William Crooke's introduction certainly suggests that Risley's theories were no longer accepted by the Indian ethnographic community: '. . . like all pioneer work, some of his conclusions are open to criticism in the light of later researches'.[61] The bulk of Crooke's introduction was a careful refutation of 'caste as race'. Risley, Crookes argued, 'greatly exaggerated' the extent to which caste had maintained endogamous, and therefore inappropriately applied new biological theory about racial divisions which could be

---

[54] Baines, *Census of India, 1891*, p. 182.
[55] Ibid., p. 183.
[56] Ibid., p. 185: 'The gradual acquisition of a higher caste by the lower ...' See also: Srinivas, 'A Note on Sanskritization and Westernization'. Baines however explained most divergences from the Vedic period as 'degradation rather than usurpation', stemming from excommunications.
[57] Gait, *Census of India, 1901*.
[58] Risley and Crooke, *The People of India*.
[59] Discussion of anthropometry?
[60] Fuller, 'Colonial Anthropology and the Decline of the Raj: Caste, Religion and Political Change in India in the Early Twentieth Century'.
[61] Risley and Crooke, *The People of India*. Introduction, p. xvi.

measured scientifically using anthropometry. Crookes stated that 'caste, in its modern, rigid form, is of comparatively recent origin'.[62] In the next census report for 1911, census commissioner O'Malley would write that 'anthropometry as a test of race has begun to fall out of favour'.[63] *People of India*, however, became a hugely popular reference book, and thus formed a part of the climate in which new civil servants, as well as the general public, understood caste, becoming a landmark work in the global history of anthropology.[64] Further, the census reports and ethnographic monographs produced by census commissioners would provide source material for an array of publications, from popular histories such as James Hewitt's *The Ruling Races of Prehistoric Times* to the caste 'biographies' published by burgeoning caste associations.

The 19th-century census reports heavily qualified their use of caste and religious categories, and even the 1901 and 1911 census reports tended to hedge their arguments about the nature of personhood (although their tabulated data had no compunction in privileging these categories). The 1921 census report, on the other hand, is extraordinarily perfunctory in its discussion of caste. While Risley and Gait had spent paragraphs explaining that caste was highly relational, and that people tended to answer questions about caste based on the identity and mission of the questioner, rather than recourse to a 'universal' catalogue of caste identities, the 1921 census commissioner, J. T. Marten, took a different view. He wrote that in 'the more advanced countries', intermarriage and 'national sentiment' had done away with 'racial distinctions', and therefore, their censuses had no need of taking account of such categories.[65] In the Americas, Eastern Europe, and India, however, he saw the population as 'divided on fundamental lines of race or colour which correspond to differences in cultural or economic progress', and he claimed that it was common to use such categories in compiling census statistics for these regions. Bizarrely, given that the rise of mass nationalism, the Lucknow Pact, and the Khilafat Movement were all roughly contemporaneous with his report, Marten continued:

> In India the sense of a common political nationality has never in the history of the people achieved sufficient intensity to override the factors of cleavage which are inherent in the social system. In a population divided into innumerable groups, each having its own character and traditions, the enquiry 'what caste are you?' or more simply 'who are you?', is recognized as referring to the racial, tribal or social group and is a question which has to be asked wherever clear identification is required, whether it be in the courts of law or in every day life. The question is always understood by the individual to whom it is put and the answer immediately gives his recognized place in the social structure.[66]

---

[62] Ibid., p. xvii.
[63] Ibid., p. xviii.
[64] I am grateful to my conversations with Harry Stockwell, MPhil student in World History at Cambridge in 2016–2017, for bringing new insight to Risley's work during this period.
[65] Marten, *Census Of India 1921 Vol.1 India Pt.1 (Report)*, p. 221.
[66] Ibid.

Baines, in his essay on the 1921 census operation for the Royal Statistical Society,[67] commended Marten for having 'restricted himself to the ethnographic details of the present day which are essential to the adequate interpretation of his demographic statistics', noting that this information was necessary 'in the case of a population like India, which is permeated from top to bottom by differentiation of class and custom maintained by the sanction of religion from time immemorial'.[68] Marten's report documented the rise of what would be called 'communalism', arguing that modernity had strengthened, rather than weakened, what he called 'caste patriotism' and 'caste jealousy'. In his chapter on 'Caste, Tribe, Race and Nationality', Marten defended even more vehemently the continued inclusion of a question on caste, in the face of demands, in 1920, from the Legislative Council, that it be removed as it was 'undesirable to recognize and perpetuate, by official action, the system of caste differentiation'.[69] Caste, Marten insisted, was still the 'foundation of the Indian social fabric'. Chastising caste sabhas for providing misleading information, Marten noted that 'there is probably no part of the census which interests the general public so much as the entry on caste'.[70] The 1921 census administrators would discount what they saw as 'false' claims for upper-caste status by removing the varna categories to which these groups aspired, simply listing castes in alphabetical order.

By 1931, widespread protests against the use of caste in the census, including Gandhi's demands for non-cooperation with the census enumeration, resulted in significant numbers of people insisting that they be recorded as having 'no caste'. Hutton's 1931 report paradoxically asserted, following Marten, that the term 'caste' 'needs no definition in India',[71] while simultaneously addressing criticisms regarding the use of caste as a census category: 'it has been alleged that the mere act of labelling persons as belonging to a caste tends to perpetuate the system, and on this excuse a campaign against any record of caste was attempted in 1931'.[72] Hutton further noted the rise of lower-caste movements to consolidate groupings of jatis around new caste identities (singling out Yadavs for comment) without acknowledging that these movements were longstanding. Significantly, the 1931 census abandoned varna, stating that 'practically every Hindu who claims to be a Hindu at all would claim to be either Brahmin or Kshatriya'.[73] The census reverted to religion as a means of 'sorting' India's population, claiming, in a victory for the nascent Hindu nationalists, that 'rigid caste distinctions appear to be broken down'.[74]

---

[67] Baines, 'The Census of India, 1921'.
[68] Ibid.
[69] Marten, *Census of India 1921 Vol.1 India Pt.1 (Report)*, p. 222. The Legislative Council further noted that the returns were in any event inaccurate, given the widespread practice of lower-caste groups claiming higher-caste status.
[70] Ibid., p. 223.
[71] Hutton, *Census of India 1931 Vol.1 (Report)*, p. 425.
[72] Ibid., 430.
[73] Ibid., 432. Note that the commissioner makes an unconscious distinction here, between 'Hindus' and those who 'claim to be' Hindus, suggesting that only an external, Western observer is qualified to explain 'what makes people who they are'.
[74] Ibid.

What Appadurai has called 'self-consciously enumerated communities' had taken over the census operations, most strikingly in terms of the efforts of the Hindu Mahasabha to include Buddhists, Sikhs, Jains, and Adivasis as 'Hindu'.[75]

Yet caste would continue to haunt the final colonial census, even as census officials themselves were almost, but not quite, ready to dispense with caste altogether. In his opening note, census commissioner M. W. M. Yeatts called the censuses 'the silent ambassadors of India all over the world'. The 1941 census took place despite the war, suggesting the continued importance of the census to both domestic and international imperial policy, despite its prohibitive cost during a turbulent and uncertain period.[76] It was however a divergence from what had come before. Census officials were subject to intense questioning by elected members of the legislative assemblies. Groups that felt themselves marginalized by nationalist and imperial politics campaigned for inclusion, and encouraged their members to, quite literally, be counted, in ever greater number.[77] Instead of the sweeping narrative 'report' which had characterized the published censuses from 1881, Yeatts simply provided an 'introduction', almost an apologia, to the tabulated data. He argued that the 'old style of omnibus report was out of date'.[78] Yeatts further insisted that the primary function of the census had never been anthropological, and that its 'excessive association with anthropology' had acted 'to obscure the basic importance of the country-wide determinations which so far the census was the only means of securing; and the tendency to dismiss it as something concerned with the peculiar activities of castes and tribes'[79] had both contributed to a dismissal of the census as a unique scientific operation and resulted in an underfunding of anthropological field work.[80]

Although the stated reason for excluding all-India caste tables in 1941 was the expense of tabulation, in fact, they were unfeasible because large numbers of self-identified Hindus had refused to answer questions on their caste.[81] Yeatts had planned for a single essay and map of India's natural resources to replace the wide-ranging and anthropologically minded census report with a different kind of visualization, one that Yeatts said could be summarized as a meditation on 'the unity of the land against the variety of its divisions and the need for the synoptic view if that unity was to receive its full consideration'. Prophetically, given that this was a document whose maps and data would be used to draw the Radcliffe line, the essay project was abandoned and even

---

[75] Gottschalk, *Religion, Science, and Empire*, 217–218.
[76] Yeatts, *Census of India 1941 India Part I Tables*, p. 11. The census of 1941 was not even formally approved and authorized by the Government of India until 1940.
[77] Arya Samaj examples, 1901–1931; and Hindu Mahasabha, 1941.
[78] Yeatts, *Census of India 1941 India Part I Tables*, p. 2.
[79] Ibid.
[80] Ibid., 2. While caste information was collected at the local level, the national tabulation for 1941 did not cover caste, as no all-India caste table was prepared. (Censuses from 1911 to 1931 had relied on the 1901 tables, in modified form, which were produced by the Ethnographic Survey of India.)
[81] Ibid., 14. This trend was, as in 1931, especially prominent in Bengal.

the map, purporting to demonstrate India's unity, was left unprinted due to wartime pressures on the Survey of India.[82]

Across the eight decennial censuses and within the administration and ethnographic community, there was never a singular 'take' on caste, nor was the colonial government fully in control of what happened to the morass of facts packed into their censuses once they left the stationer's office. This does not, however, undermine the fundamental arguments of Cohn and Dirks, that the 'reality effect', or what Peabody calls the 'generative' effect of the government's collective 'vision' of India's population, exerted a powerful force on the imaginations of Indians. But as Dirks himself would argue, this power was not ever exerted in a straightforward way:

> ... the assumption that the colonial state could manipulate and invent Indian tradition at will ... is clearly inadequate and largely wrong ... The power of colonial discourse was not that it created whole new fields of meaning instantaneously, but that it shifted old meanings slowly, sometimes imperceptibly, through the colonial control of a range of new institutions ... Transformation occurred because of the ways colonial discourse inscribed its peculiar, often masterful, combination of old and new meanings in institutional theatres ...[83]

Just as colonial officials struggled to repurpose the Mughlai data generated by census operations across the 19th century, South Asian writers, activists, and thinkers would assess, absorb, and reject the ways in which enumerative projects sought to define and describe them, in the 'theatres' of print and public debate.

The Census as a Public Property

The problems revealed in the classificatory systems deployed by early decennial census administrators led to numerous ethnographic surveys, all attempting to repair the 'chaos' of categories which had been identified by commissioners. The census was not initially conceived, as Padmanabh Samarendra points out, as an ethnographic exercise. After the divergence in classification tactics in 1871 and 1881 rendered the decennial censuses non-comparable, and therefore useless for their stated purpose, however, 'it was being recognized that to count, it was first necessary to know'.[84] As with caste, census commissioners recognized that religious categorization was a crude measure of identity in the diverse landscape of South Asia: many officials commented, in publications as well as in official communication, that it was not even usually possible to easily distinguish

---

[82] Ibid., 2
[83] Dirks, 'The Invention of Caste', 50–51.
[84] Samarendra, 'Between Number and Knowledge: Career of Caste in Colonial Census', 50.

between Hindus and Muslims in north India.[85] Nonetheless, census commissioners had repeatedly accepted racialized religious, and therefore, caste, divisions as central categories for the statistical comparison of India's population.

All-India decennial censuses began at the same time that Indian-language print became ubiquitous across rural and urban South Asia. As a result, the census-taking operations, and the consultations, committees, and policy decisions which preceded them, addressed an 'All-India' public sphere of debate, discussion, and dissent. Editors of Indian newspapers not only reproduced government directives, but engaged with them in editorials, and conducted investigations and analyses of their own. On the eve of the 1891 census, the *Times of India* 'called attention' to the publication of detailed census operation guidelines, and then noted with satisfaction that the experience of the 1881 census had resulted in a 'simpler' form for enumerators.[86] When J. A. Baines, Census Commissioner, passed through Allahabad, it was considered a newsworthy event.[87] By 1881, in anticipation of the second decennial census, Indian newspapers reported extensively on 'census meetings' being held in every town, leading the *Vrat* to declare them 'the fashion of the day'.[88]

In this noisy public arena, caste associations disputed not just with census commissioners, but among themselves.[89] From the outset of the census project, very few Indians felt that the varna system, as the decennial census commissioners understood it, held any historical or contemporary legitimacy. Historians should, however, be careful in assuming that caste association leaders were exclusively motivated by the census in arguing for their own social position, or that they were motivated solely by concerns about their status before the state.[90] This argument was first deployed, in print, by Kumar Cheda Singh Varma, in his 1904 book, *Kshatriyas and Would-be Kshatriyas*.[91] Singh Varma focused on Khatri, Kayastha, Jat, and Kurmi caste associations, attacking their arguments with both South Asian and colonial legal and ethnographic authority, and blaming the practice of lower-caste claims to 'kshatriya' status on Risley's 1901 schema.

Singh Varma's interpretation became commonplace in assessments of caste uplift movements. Marten would write in his 1921 report that 'the opportunity of the census was therefore seized by all but the highest caste to press for recognition of social claims and to secure, if possible, a step upwards in the social ladder'.[92] Lucy Carroll's work on

---

[85] See Gottschalk, 182; see also Denault, 'Partition and the Politics of the Joint Family,' IESHR 2009, on the legal difficulties presented in defining a family as Hindu or Muslim in the courts, for the purposes of applying personal law to inheritance.
[86] *Times of India*, 22 July 1890, p. 4.
[87] Ibid., 7 January 1891, p. 3.
[88] 'The Native Papers,' *Times of India*, 18 February 1881, p. 3.
[89] Carroll, 'Colonial Perceptions of Indian Society and the Emergence of Caste(s) Associations'.
[90] Pinch, *Peasants and Monks in British India*, pp. 115–117.
[91] Singh Varma, *Kshatriyas and Would-Be Kshatriyas: A Consideration of the Claims of Certain Hindu Castes to Rank with the Rajputs, the Descendants of the Ancient Kshatriyas*.
[92] Marten, *Census of India 1921 Vol.1 India Pt.1 (Report)*, p. 223.

caste associations also ascribes the rise of caste associations to the publicity that census operations and court decisions brought to the classification of castes according to 'superior' or 'inferior' varnas. Singh Varma's argument, however, emanated from groups attempting to police longer-standing social hierarchies, and ignores the groundswell of socio-cultural changes which led to the formation and proliferation of active caste associations across the social spectrum in the late 19th and early 20th centuries. While there is no doubt that lower-caste and middle-caste activists and publicists paid a great deal of attention to official publications during this period, the census, rather than a primary raison d'etre for these groups, may simply have provided an additional platform. Pinch suggests that while 'the thoughts, words, and deeds of peasants and monks in the colonial era confirm that caste was a subject of great interest to all', this was because 'the ideology of inequality and status (and, by implication, equality, and identity) implicit to caste enabled individuals, communities, and the state to facilitate, moderate, or obliterate social change'.

The Khattri Hitkari Association, for example, held a large conference in Bareilly in June of 1901 to discuss the ramifications of the census report. The Khattris were members of a 'middle' caste who, like the Kayasthas, could, broadly, already claim 'middle class' status. They had risen to higher status as clerks and administrators within the Mughal bureaucracy, and their literacy had left them better-positioned under the colonial government than many other groups. The Standing Committee appointed to draft a resolution to government following the conference in 1901 included wealthy landowners, advocates and barristers, a school headmaster, inspector of schools, and a professor. But the assembled Khattri groups adopted a resolution formally objecting entirely to any hierarchization of caste within the census.[93]

Kurmi and Goala peasants, whom Buchanan called 'other pretenders' to the rank of Kshatriya, also objected to colonial caste hierarchy. While many historians of the census have singled out the caste-uplift projects of the Arya Samaj, which encouraged lower castes to self-designate as 'Aryans' from the late 19th century, Pinch and Rawat have both called attention to the extent to which marginalized groups of peasants and untouchables, some organized around emerging Vaishnava and Bhakti centres of worship, some around committees and associations, contested their 'inferior' status as assigned by government only *because* they had already forged new socio-political communities.[94] Nor were these trends confined to those labelled, or claiming to be, 'Hindus:' Muslim peasants in Bihar, for example, laid claim to the status of *Shekh*. Disputes over the census gave rise not only to groups adhering to new, more rigid and exclusivist definitions of caste, but to social and political movements among groups who saw opportunities to argue for their rights via this exercise in self-identification. New religious movements gave these groups a language in which to challenge the colonial classifications, a language which was

---

[93] Seth, *A Brief Ethnological Survey of the Khattris*.
[94] Rawat, *Reconsidering Untouchability*.

still outside the Brahmin-driven logics of caste which the colonial census projects continued to deploy.

Conclusion

B. R. Ambedkar, when asked his opinion on the census in 1947, responded:

> The Census of India has over a number of decades ceased to be an operation in demography. It has become a Political affair. Every community seems to be attempting to artificially argument its numbers at the cost of some other community for the sake of capturing greater and greater degree of political power in its own hands. The Scheduled Castes seem to have been made a common victim for the satisfaction of the combined greed of the other communities who through their propagandists or enumerators are able to control the operations and the results of the Census.[95]

Ambedkar analysed the census in several works, in particular in his article on 'A Need for Checks and Balances', on arguments for and against linguistic states. His assessment damned decades of census ethnography at a stroke: 'Unfortunately no student has devoted himself to a demographic survey of the population of India. We only know from our census reports how many are Hindus, how many are Muslims, how many Jews, how many Christians and how many untouchables. Except for the knowledge we get as to how many religions there are this information is of no value.'[96]

C. J. Fuller has argued that an increasing divergence between a colonial ethnographic 'vision', as enshrined in the census operations, and conditions on the ground rendered 'official anthropology ... increasingly irrelevant to policy making', such that it 'could no longer strengthen the colonial state'.[97] However, Fuller's own case studies of the later careers of census officials, and in particular involvement of Blunt in the Montagu-Chelmsford reforms, go some way to contradict this argument.[98] The census may have ceased to be a tool which usefully authorized empire, but that did not make the decisions drawn from its data, or the officials trained by its operations, any less central to both imperial and domestic politics in India. After the 1921 report's insistence on the universality of experiences of caste, subsequent commissioners were more tentative in their assertions. Yet throughout its history, despite official awareness of the limitations of its data, the census of India was used extensively by colonial governors to visualize South Asian society for the purposes of administration. The census became more, rather than less, of a 'political tool' of colonial administration as time went on.

---

[95] Ambedkar, *Dr. Babasaheb Ambedkar: Writings and Speeches*, Vol. 17, p. 1.
[96] Ambedkar, Vol. 1, p. 134.
[97] Fuller, 'Colonial Anthropology and the Decline of the Raj: Caste, Religion and Political Change in India in the Early Twentieth Century', 463.
[98] Ibid., 479–485.

Much has been written about the connection between the census and what Jinnah called 'minoritarian' thinking on the politics of representation, or what Gyanendra Pandey terms the 'construction of communalism', but the politicization of demography was not due solely to its uses by nationalist groups and Indian social movements. Colonial officials increasingly applied census knowledge to political problems. H. H. Risley, whose blending of racial theory with the varna typology would enshrine 'caste/religion as race' in the popular imagination, was Home Secretary during the first partition of Bengal, and was instrumental in encouraging partition as a political solution. The phrase 'scheduled castes' is taken directly from the census reports. Cyril Radcliffe relied on the 1941 census data, even though it was known to be incomplete, as the basis for the 1947 Radcliffe line that 'cracked' India into two separate countries.

The census, and debates about the census, reflect a piecemeal and halting knowledge project, but one which had enormous power. While it would be going too far to say that it forced colonized subjects to entirely 'rethink themselves', the enterprise of explaining oneself, and of seeing 'all-India' as part of a unified and ancient varna system, was transformative.[99] As Dirks and Bayly noted, it was when ongoing reform and social movements intersected with colonial projects that colonial governance had its greatest impact on Indian lives. The census reports successively linked correspondence and quotations from European experts alongside commentary from Indian publicists and caste associations. Commissioners began by addressing one public, the official reader, appealing to Indian publics only orally, in meetings intended to ameliorate popular fears about the census operation. However, by the second and third decennial censuses, commissioners were aware of a critical South Asian public, having been inundated with petitions and correspondence challenging colonial classifications. By entextualizing,[100] in a single document, and only partially ever reconciling, reams of contradictory social facts about India, then asserting the universal applicability of its statistics, the census simultaneously produced both new ways of 'seeing' and new ways of 'knowing' India.

References

Ambedkar, B. R. 2014. *Dr. Babasaheb Ambedkar: Writings and Speeches* (Edited by Vasant Moon). (Vol. 1. 17 vols). New Delhi: Dr. Ambedkar Foundation, Ministry of Social Justice & Empowerment, Government of India.

Anderson, Clare. 2004. *Legible Bodies: Race, Criminality, and Colonialism in South Asia*. Oxford and New York: Berg.

---

[99] David Arnold argues that 'colonial governmentality … allows for seeing colonialism as a form of modernity sufficiently powerful and persuasive to impel Indians to rethink themselves. Second, it exemplifies agency in the Indians alone are capable of translating, negotiating, and reconstituting that modernity as their own'. Arnold, 'In Search of the Colonial Subject'.

[100] Entextualization is 'the process of rendering a given instance of discourse a text, detachable from its local context'. Silverstein and Urban (1996, p. 21, quoted in Barber, p. 22).

Appadurai, Arjun. 1993. 'Number in the Colonial Imagination'. In Carol Appadurai Breckenridge and Peter van der Veer (Eds.), *Orientalism and the Postcolonial Predicament: Perspectives on South Asia* (Vol. South Asia Seminar Series). Philadelphia: University of Pennsylvania Press.

Arnold, David. 2009. 'In Search of the Colonial Subject'. In Andrew C. Willford and Eric Tagliacozzo (Eds.), *Clio/Anthropos: Exploring the Boundaries between History and Anthropology*. Stanford: Stanford University Press.

Asad, Talal. 1973. *Anthropology & the Colonial Encounter*. Ithaca Press.

Baines, J. A. 1924. 'The Census of India, 1921'. *Journal of the Royal Statistical Society*, 87(4): 595–598.

Baines, J. A. 1893. *Census of India, 1891: General Report*. London: Printed for the Indian government, by Eyre and Spottiswoode. http://archive.org/details/cu31924023177268.

Baker, Christopher John, and D. A. Washbrook. 1975. *South India: Political Institutions and Political Change, 1880–1940*. Macmillan Company of India.

Bandyopadhyay, Sekhar. 1992. 'Construction of Social Categories: The Role of the Colonial Census'. In K. S. Singh (Ed.), *Ethnicity, Caste and People* (pp. 26–36). Delhi: Manohar.

Barber, Karin. 2007. *The Anthropology of Texts, Persons and Publics*. Cambridge: Cambridge University Press.

Barrier, N. Gerald. 1981. *The Census in British India: New Perspectives*. New Delhi: Manohar.

Bayly, C. A. 1996. *Empire and Information: Intelligence Gathering and Social Communication in India, c. 1780–1870*. Cambridge: Cambridge University Press.

Bayly, Susan. 1999. *Caste, Society and Politics in India from the Eighteenth Century to the Modern Age*. Cambridge: Cambridge University Press.

Beverley, H. 1872. *Report of the Census of Bengal 1872*. Calcutta: Bengal Secretariat Press.

Carroll, Lucy. 1978, February. 'Colonial Perceptions of Indian Society and the Emergence of Caste(s) Associations'. *The Journal of Asian Studies*, 37(2): 233–250.

Cohn, Bernard S. 1987. *An Anthropologist among the Historians and Other Essays*. Delhi; Oxford: Oxford University Press.

Cohn, Bernard S. 1996. *Colonialism and Its Forms of Knowledge: The British in India*. Princeton, NJ; Chichester: Princeton University Press.

Conlon, Frank F. 2008. 'Speaking of Caste? Colonial and Indigenous Interpretations of Caste and Community in Nineteenth Century Bombay'. In Ishita Banerjee-Dube and Saurabh Dube (Eds.), *From Ancient to Modern: Religion, Power, and Community in India*. Oxford, New York: Oxford University Press.

Curtis, Bruce. 2009. 'On the Local Construction of Statistical Knowledge: Making Up the 1861 Census of the Canadas'. In *Twenty Years of the Journal of Historical Sociology* (pp. 253–272). John Wiley & Sons, Ltd.

Dirks, Nicholas B. 2001. *Castes of Mind: Colonialism and the Making of Modern India*. Princeton, NJ, Oxford: Princeton University Press.

Dirks, Nicholas B. 1989. 'The Invention of Caste: Civil Society in Colonial India'. *Social Analysis: The International Journal of Social and Cultural Practice*, 25: 42–52.

Fuller, C. J. 2016, July. 'Colonial Anthropology and the Decline of the Raj: Caste, Religion and Political Change in India in the Early Twentieth Century'. *Journal of the Royal Asiatic Society*, 26(3): 463–486.

Gait, Edward Albert. 1902. *Census of India, 1901*. Bombay: Printed at the Government central press, 1902. https://catalog.hathitrust.org/Record/100188376.

Gottschalk, Peter. *Religion, Science, and Empire: Classifying Hinduism and Islam in British India*. Oxford, New York: Oxford University Press, 2012.

Guha, Sumit. 2003. 'The Politics of Identity and Enumeration in India c. 1600–1990'. *Comparative Studies in Society and History*, 45(1): 148–167.

Hutton, J. H. 1933. *Census of India 1931 Vol. 1 (Report)*. http://archive.org/details/in.ernet.dli.2015.56018. Government of India Publications Department, Delhi, 1933.

Ibbetson, Denzil Charles. 1883. *Report on the Census of the Panjáb Taken on the 17th of February 1881*. India. Census, 1881. [Imperial Census of 1881. Reports, Vols. 26–28]. Lahore: Central Gaol Press (pr.).

Lelyveld, David. 2003. *Aligarh's First Generation: Muslim Solidarity in British India*. Oxford, New York: Oxford University Press, 2003.

Maheshwari, Shriram. 1996. *The Census Administration under the Raj and After*. Concept Publishing Company. New Delhi.

Mantena, Karuna. 2010. *Alibis of Empire: Henry Maine and the Ends of Liberal Imperialism*. Princeton, NJ, Woodstock: Princeton University Press, 2010.

Marten, J. T. 1924. *Census of India 1921 Vol. 1 India Pt. 1 (Report)*.

Natarajan, Swaminath. 1962. *A Century of Social Reform in India*. Asia Publishing House. London

O'Hanlon, Rosalind, and Christopher Minkowski. 2008, 1 September. 'What Makes People Who They Are? Pandit Networks and the Problem of Livelihoods in Early Modern Western India'. *The Indian Economic & Social History Review*, 45(3): 381–416.

Owens, Trevor. 2012, 16 March. 'Defining Data for Humanists: Text, Artifact, Information or Evidence?' *Journal of Digital Humanities*. http://journalofdigitalhumanities.org/1-1/defining-data-for-humanists-by-trevor-owens/.

Peabody, Norbert. 2001. 'Cents, Sense, Census: Human Inventories in Late Precolonial and Early Colonial India'. *Comparative Studies in Society and History*, 43(4): 819–50.

Pennington, Brian K. 2005. *Was Hinduism Invented?: Britons, Indians, and the Colonial Construction of Religion*. Oxford: Oxford University Press.

Pinch, William. 1996. *Peasants and Monks in British India*. Berkeley: University of California Press.

Plowden, William Chichele. 1883. *Report on the Census of British India, Taken on the 17th February 1881*. London: Printed by Eyre and Spottiswoode for H. M. Stationery Office.

Rawat, Ramnarayan S. 2011. *Reconsidering Untouchability: Chamars and Dalit History in North India*. Indiana University Press.

Risley, Herbert Hope, and William Crooke. 1915. *The People of India*. Calcutta & Simla; London: Thacker, Spink & Co., W. Thacker & Co., 1915.

Rocher, Rosane. 'British Orientalism in the Eighteenth Century: The Dialectics of Knowledge and Government'. In Carol Appadurai Breckenridge, Peter van der Veer, and South Asia Seminar (Eds.), *Orientalism and the Postcolonial Predicament: Perspectives on South Asia* (Vol. South Asia Seminar Series). Philadelphia: University of Pennsylvania Press.

Samarendra, Padmanabh. 2008. 'Between Number and Knowledge: Career of Caste in Colonial Census'. In Ishita Banerjee Dube (Ed.), *Caste in History* (pp. 46–66). New Delhi: Oxford University Press.

Seth, Moti Lal. 1905. *A Brief Ethnological Survey of the Khattris*. Agra: Khattri Hitkari Association.

Singh Varma, Kumar Cheda. 1904. *Kshatriyas and Would-Be Kshatriyas: A Consideration of the Claims of Certain Hindu Castes to Rank with the Rajputs, the Descendants of the Ancient Kshatriyas*. Allahabad: Pioneer Press.

Smith, Richard Saumarez. 2000. 'Between Local Tax and Global Statistic: The Census as Local Record'. *Contributions to Indian Sociology*, 34(1): 1–35.

Smith, Richard Saumarez. 1996. *Rule by Records: Land Registration and Village Custom in Early British Panjab*. Delhi: Oxford University Press.

Srinivas, M. N. 'A Note on Sanskritization and Westernization'. *The Far Eastern Quarterly*, 15(4): 481–496. DOI: 10.2307/2941919.

Thapar, Romila. 1989. 'Imagined Religious Communities? Ancient History and the Modern Search for a Hindu Identity'. *Modern Asian Studies*, 23(2): 209–231.

Wagoner, Phillip B. 2003. 'Precolonial Intellectuals and the Production of Colonial Knowledge'. *Comparative Studies in Society and History*, 45(4): 783–814.

Waterfield, Henry. 1875. *Memorandum on the Census of British India of 1871-72*. London: Eyre and Spottiswoode for H. M. Stationery Office.

Yeatts, M. W. M. 1943. *Census of India 1941, Part I Tables*.

CHAPTER 10

CASTE DISPUTES IN COLONIAL INDIA
Conflicts and the Legal Shaping of Caste

JULIE MARQUET

Introduction

On 24 December 1816, members of a weavers' caste in Pondicherry, a small town in the southeast of the peninsula controlled by the French, lodged a complaint with Governor Dupuy. They accused the members of the Pallis caste, most of whom were farm-workers, of wearing the effigy of the tiger, and the five-coloured pavilion in their funeral ceremonies. The weavers claimed the exclusive use of these insignia. The French government did not render judgement, and a few months later, the two castes again came into conflict, on the occasion of the celebration of a temple festival. The Pallis opposed the weavers' request to 'pull the chariot' of the divinity during a procession. Despite the complaints it received, the French administration granted the weavers permission to pull the chariot. In reaction, on 16 September 1817, the Pallis, armed with sticks, daggers, and pistols, attacked the weavers' procession, and burned their chariot. The confrontation ended only with the intervention of two corps of cipayes [soldiers], and the arrest and imprisonment of several notables, and leaders of the Pallis caste.

This is not an isolated case. Caste conflicts, sometimes violent, shook the towns of India from the end of the 17th century to the end of the 19th century, especially port towns where European companies had set up trading posts. These conflicts occurred within a single caste or amongst several castes, in particular between castes belonging respectively to the Left Hand and Right Hand. The two Hands were the division into which castes were distributed in South India; the Left Hand was constituted mostly of craftsmen and merchants, while the Right Hand was the hand of landowners and their tenants and dependants, as well as traders. Caste conflicts concerned the distribution and usage of social and ritual honours in the context of private ceremonies or activities, or of festivals in honour of the deity. Conflicts thus related to passing through specific streets of an area, using palanquins [*tandu*], umbrellas or canes, building a *pandal* in front of one's house, being the first to distribute betel during ceremonies, blowing the conch [*sangu*] for ritual events, sporting a standard, or flag of a particular colour or with particular motifs, such as the tiger of the weavers, in processions, dressing the deity, receiving or distributing *prasadam* in the temple, performing vedic rituals, or causing them to be performed.

This chapter examines how caste identities were shaped by disputes over these honours. It looks at caste conflicts starting in the 17th century, since conflicts developed at that time and therefore most academic work on these conflicts begins with this period. However, conflicts did not suddenly appear in these years. During the preceding centuries, they had shaken the Maratha courts and the expanding towns of the south of the peninsula, where they are seen in watermarks in temple inscriptions recording honours acquired by a caste (O'Hanlon, 2017; Ramaswamy, 1995). Nevertheless, caste conflicts gained visibility from the 17th century onwards by entering the circuits of colonial administration or justice and, possibly, in frequency and intensity, due to the new competition for economic opportunities opened up by the commercial, and then colonial settlement of Europeans, and the changes caused by this settlement. The chapter covers the first centuries of colonial presence, up to the 1880s, when caste identities were crystallized through the census and the creation of caste associations, and when the possibilities of civic or political participation shifted the forms of mobilization of the castes, often in connection with anti-brahmin movements (Washbrook, 1975; Bandyopadhyay, 1997). This chapter thus shows that conflicts between caste-groups were not only elicited by the colonial governments' classificatory practices but were anterior to them. It shows that categorization was the result of long processes of self-presentation and of multiple attempts at social ascendance using open conflict or legal language. This reveals a crucial moment in the shaping of caste identities.

The Changing Patterns of Caste Conflicts

Castes competed for honours throughout the period under consideration, but the objects and forms of conflict evolved over time. In the 17th and 18th centuries, and in a more or less advanced fashion in the 19th century according to locality, the prerogatives which were the centre of the conflicts were the ones bestowed by the sovereigns, and, in the colonial situation, by the European governments, and the executives of commercial companies (Mukund, 1995). The use of palanquins, of horses and vehicles, of weapons, and musical instruments, which were symbols of royal authority in ceremonies marking the cycles of life, was fiercely disputed by the castes. The Left Hand castes, artisans useful to, and favoured by the rulers since the Vijayanagar period, especially sought to appropriate or obtain such prerogatives from the authorities (Ramaswamy,

1985; Stein, 1980). In return, they were violently attacked by the Right Hand castes, who were accused of using the Pariahs as their armed faction. The Right Hand members destroyed the disputed honorary objects, beat their adversaries, and sometimes went so far as to loot and burn their houses. For instance the higher castes Vellajas and their dependants regularly attacked the processions of the castes of artisans of the hammer (blacksmiths, goldsmiths, workers in brass, carpenters, and masons), called Panchalar in Andhra Pradesh, Kamalar, or Kammālan in the Tamil country, and Camalère in the French Settlements of India, as well as the castes of oil pressers and merchants (Vāniyan, Sénécodéar, or Vanouva for the French).

The types of conflicts evolved from the middle of the 19th century onwards. The ancient objects never disappeared, but rivalries were partly reoriented towards the use of urban space and processions' routes, while at the same period the colonial authorities tended to open as public thoroughfares all the main streets and the areas controlled by the higher castes (Bayly, 1989; Frykenberg, 1981; Viguier, 2012). A well-documented case came from Tinnevelly in the Madras Presidency. In December 1858, several violent episodes occurred after the Christian weavers of the Kaikallar caste tried to pass through the main road with a dead body to get to the burying field. This main road, named New Street, had been built in 1847 to give access to funerary sites without crossing the paddy fields and wading through mud and water. It was maintained by the British government and considered as a matter of 'public utility'. However, the use of the road was forbidden to Kaikallars by the local magistrate at the behest of the higher castes, mainly the Vellajas employed by the government. The Kaikallars, supported by the missionaries in Tinnevelly, turned unsuccessfully to the British authorities. While they were waiting for a judgement in their favour, on 21 December, another Christian, belonging to the Pallan caste, died in the hospital. A crowd opposed the transportation of the body though New Street, and the magistrates used military force to open the passage. The soldiers found themselves caught in a riot and shot at the participants, killing ten people. After this episode, widely discussed by British officials throughout the Empire, various social, or religious groups of Tinnevelly guaranteed their respect for everyone's uses of the roads. From that point, it seems that Kaikallars or Pallan processions were no longer contested. The historian Robert Frykenberg placed these events in the broader South Indian context where officials in the different districts of the Madras presidency were calling for the opening of the streets. Frykenberg argues that the middle of the 19th century was marked by an ideological change in the way public space was conceived and in the possible social control of space (Frykenberg, 1981).

As in this case of funerals, processions concerned the ritual times of individuals' lives (weddings, funerals), but they concerned also the festivities in honour of a deity. Circulations on the occasion of temple festivals remained points of conflict after the opening of the main streets of South Indian towns in the 1850s. Similarly, the organization of festivals, the control of the administration of temples, or the attempt by certain castes to enter their precincts were the main motives for disputes in the second half of the 19th century. The transfer of conflicts from honorary objects to temples around the middle of the 19th century, coincided with the passage, identified by Susan Bayly in Indian society, from the model of the man of prowess, and royal and warrior power distributing royal insignias to a model that valued devotion and ritual purity (Bayly, 1993). Bayly notes that in the context of the reorganization of the post-Mughal states, from the late 18th century onwards, the values of the brahminical model had been enhanced by sovereigns, minor warlords, and agrarian elites imitating them. What mattered for status, then, was no longer so much the handling of royal insignias than the display of brahminical devotional practices. In particular, both long-standing and new economic elites invested in the patronage and the construction or restoration of temples. This investment had been a mark of status since the medieval period, but it gained in force by the 19th century. This movement, generally analysed in terms of the development of Hinduism as a religion, also has to be understood in the framework of intense rivalries between caste-groups, or between divisions of the same caste seeking to acquire ritual honours (Bayly, 1989). For instance, the Nadars, an enriched caste of toddy-tapers of Tamil Nadu, sought to gain access to the sanctuaries they sponsored, but the other castes opposed these attempts, sometimes very violently, such as at Sivakasi, in the south of Madurai, in 1899 (Hardgrave, 1981). Although physical attacks always remained a component of caste disputes, there was an evolution in the modalities of these disputes and in the forms of collective action—just as there was an evolution in the objects of the disputes. From the 1860s onwards, complaints and legal actions tended, progressively, to replace street action, and violent conflict (Frykenberg, 1981).

Studying Caste Conflicts

Throughout the 18th and 19th centuries, conflicts were either regulated and arbitrated by caste assemblies or heads of castes, or presented to colonial justice in the form of individual complaints or collective petitions. When they threatened public order, these conflicts also might have been taken on directly by the colonial administration. Addresses to the British or French judicial or administrative system left archival traces that provide precious elements for the study of caste conflict for anthropologists, historians, political scientists, and sociologists. Yet, the study remained peripheral in the existing work on caste, which focused mainly on the formation of caste-groups (Hardgrave, 1969; Roberts, 1982). Researchers who did make caste conflicts the main thrust of their work did not focus on the question of caste identity, but were concerned with specific aspects or types of conflict: of Hands (Appadurai, 1974; Brimnes, 1999; Zimmernan, 1974), those connected with the carrying out of particular private ceremonies (Price, 1991), with the use of public space (Frykenberg, 1981; Viguier, 2012), or with temples (Appadurai and Breckenridge, 1976; Appadurai, 1981). Yet, this chapter build on these two lines of scholarship but replace the conflicts at the centre of the attention. It argues that caste conflicts are a crucial spot to examine the formation and the structuring of caste, considered altogether as a social, religious, ritual, cultural, and legal phenomenon (Jodkha, 2012). Indeed, caste conflicts existed at the intersection of two logics of power—ritual and economic—what makes them a privileged position to examine the underlying logics of the shaping of caste-groups. Thereby, studying caste disputes contributes to the understanding of caste as a phenomenon and as an institution, because they are moments that reveal the structuring of caste-groups and the affirmation of their identities.

This chapter reflects on the shaping of caste through conflict, first by examining the demands and expectations of the litigants, and second by studying the effects of colonial courts' engagement in the regulation of these conflicts.

The Social Definition of Hierarchical Status

Interaction, Sanskritization, and the Regulation of Social Status

Caste conflicts were set off by the specific usage or definitive appropriation of honours conferring social and ritual status by some castes, whose right to do so was not recognized by other castes that considered them as lower. Attempts, called 'encroachments' by their enemies, occurred when the caste or some of its members became rich, producing a discrepancy between the ritual status assigned to the caste, and the economic position it had attained. This meant that a caste regarded as low did not, when it gained power due to economic success, try to oppose the codified system of hierarchical ranks but rather to raise itself within that system. Most of the conflicts were thus between established elites and new ones, whose usefulness in the development of towns and commerce guaranteed them government support since the medieval period (Ramaswamy, 1995). This is the case of the Shanars of Tamil Nadu, named Souraires by the French, and calling themselves Nadars. They were a disadvantaged caste of toddy-tappers, who climbed palm or coconut trees to extract their juice (Hardgrave, 1969; Marquet, 2018). The Nadars, regarded as low caste, were under a series of prohibitions, often physical in nature since they were described as impure in religious prescription texts like the *Manava Dharmasastras*. They were not allowed to wear a stitched or knee length garment and women could not cover their breasts with a wide shawl seen as an attribute of the Nairs, a caste of farm owners, recognized as higher in the Tamil society, and by the British government. They were also supposed to stay away from public wells or from the entrance of temples because of their perceived pollution. From the beginning of the 19th century, the Nadars began to get rich thanks to their traditional activities as sugar or alcohol obtained from the fermentation of palm or coconut juice became important sources of income. Colonial governments derived significant revenues from taxes on these products, and were favourable to Nadar undertakings. The latter, through their enrichment, gradually engaged in transporting goods on the roads newly built by the British, as well as the cloth, cotton seeds, cattle, or tobacco trade. In addition to these activities, many members of the caste migrated to coffee plantations in Ceylon or Malaysia, and bought land in their home region when they returned. With the increase of their wealth, the Nadars changed their way of life, and sought to acquire attributes or rights that their said impure status did not allow them. Their first move in their strategy of social advancement was to adopt the wearing of the shawl of the Nairs to cover the women's breasts.

To designate the appropriation of prerogatives and of attributes recognized as belonging to the higher castes as a means of improving status, most researchers use the term sanskritization coined by M. N. Srinivas. This term, which has been highly debated, identifies the process by which castes attempt to rise by adopting a set of behaviours, practices, deities, and symbols belonging to the 'high' forms of Hinduism (Srinivas, 1989). In this way, the Tamil Nadu Nadars, throughout the 19th century, sought to narrow the existing gap between their economic position and their position in the hierarchy of ritual purity. Since the 1850s, in addition to the shawl, they generally adopted high caste practices: they borrowed their hairstyles and their jewellery models, prohibited widows from remarrying, and dressing in a colour other than white, ordered women to wear water jugs on their hips rather than on their heads, replaced burial practice with cremation, adopted a strictly vegetarian diet, built temples dedicated to Siva, made generous donations to religious institutions, and used palanquins for their movements and ceremonies (Hardgrave, 1969, pp. 107–109).

When a caste decided to raise itself by adopting new practices, its status was not necessarily improved. Its position had to be recognized by the other castes and this has to be apparent in social interactions. Lower castes' attempts to ascend faced vigorous opposition. In the case of the Nadars, women wearing the shawl of the upper castes were attacked. Entrance to some temples remained forbidden to members of the caste and there were riots when they tried to break that ban. Protests arose to forbid their use of palanquins or wearing of sandals. Often as a reprisal for their encroachments, their schools were set on fire. Conflict was the moment when the lower castes who had appropriated honours were attacked, whether physically or through legal processes (these generally going together) by the castes who were the recognized holders of these honours and who considered them their own. It was an affirmation of prerogatives common to the caste-group distinct from other social groups. Conflict thus fixed the boundaries between social groups. At the same time, it strengthened the caste-group cohesion and gave rise to a feeling of identity (defined by honours possessed) and of belonging to a community, structured by mobilization against the appropriation of honours by other castes: gatherings, complaints, and petitions, desertions [*hartal*], or attacks resulted in cohesion, especially because they allowed for appeals to patronage and clientele connections.

The permanent competition for honours and the structural nature of caste disputes in South Indian society demonstrated the interactional dimension of caste identities and the rank of each caste in a given space. The prerogatives and attributes claimed by the castes had a meaning only if they were recognized by other castes, either because those castes accepted their usages, or because they forbade them. They did not function as honorific signs unless identified and mobilized as such by a group of actors. For example, the shawl covering the breast of a woman appeared as the sign of superior status because it was so considered by the Nairs who used it, the Nadars who claimed it and the local or colonial authorities that recognized it as the prerogative of the Nairs. The recognition or opposition of other castes as well as of the higher authority, represented by the colonial government in the majority of the cases studied by academics, determined the status of each one. In the first colonial period, from the 17th to the end of the 19th century, there was no essentially predetermined characterization of caste corresponding to a fixed and immutable ritual status. Caste underwent processes of reconfiguration according to local contexts and levels of wealth. The statuses, excluding those of the lowest castes of agricultural dependants, were therefore flexible and negotiable. The dynamics at work within the caste-groups and between different caste-groups demonstrate, on the one hand, that Indian society was not static, fixed in a traditional system inherited from a pre-colonial past (Washbrook, 1975) and, on the other, that Indians have been active in the shaping of the identities and boundaries of caste, which are not therefore a straightforward effect of colonial domination.

Goals of Self-Presentation: Collective Identities and Personal Means

Studying processes of sanskritization reveals objectives common to a caste-group and enables assessments of the social rise of that group. The collective nature of the claim for honours, or of the opposition to their use, corresponded to modes of self-presentation chosen by the actors in conflicts. Caste identity was thus mobilized to present professional specialization and used to gauge expertise to accede to coveted occupations. In Pune, for example, in the 18th and 19th centuries, the Brahmins and the Kayastha, as caste of the varna of the Sudra, vied with each other for positions as scribes and counsellors of the sovereigns or of their Peshwa ministers. The Kayasthas sought to collectively construct a twice-born identity and claimed the right to perform rituals reserved for such castes. The Brahmins dissented to these claims; they had recourse to the texts of the *Dharmasastras* with the advice of the assembly of pandits to make these honours forbidden and confined the Kayasthas to the varna of the Sudras. In this way, they made them appear to be illegitimate counsellors to the kings, strengthening their own role on the political chess board (O'Hanlon, 2017). Here, litigation allowed for the delimitation of the status of the caste-group in its entirety so as to guarantee or ban its access to strategic resources.

Conflicts over honours did not simply defend a pre-existing essence of caste but, on the contrary, mobilized the argument of caste identity because it was of use to certain actors. Caste identity, therefore, appeared to be instrumental in many cases. This is an important dimension which demonstrates the agency of individuals or social groups: they were not locked into a system that went beyond them but participated in shaping that system. In particular, they used the language of the 'community' and the rights of the caste as a social entity because that language was acceptable to the authorities and it had a mobilizing effect on the members of the caste-group. Thus, while conflicts were always presented in terms of the collective identity of the caste, they may have been motivated by personal or familial interests. Such an example is reported by the well-known broker of the French governor Dupleix, Ananda Ranga Pillai, in the middle of the 18th century. In 1750, the merchant Arunâchala Chetti, himself belonging to the Right Hand, complained to the police that the *bayadères* [dancing girls] of the Left Hand had not stood up to salute him during the wedding of the son of the merchant Muttu Alagappa Chetti, who belonged, as the dancers, to the Left Hand. He was able to procure their arrest and imprisonment. To Ranga Pillai, it seemed that Arunâchala Chetti had used a litigation of honour between the right Hand and left Hand to disgrace a rival merchant. Beyond this example, it is evident that causing a conflict between Hands, between castes or between divisions of the same caste, was a way to build up one's status as a big man (Marquet, 2018; Mines and Gourishankar, 1990). Kanakalatha Mukund, in her study of merchant capitalism on the Coromandel coast in the 17th and 18th centuries, argues that the chiefs of the castes of the right Hand launched attacks against honours obtained by chiefs of the left Hand in order to secure for themselves possession of those honours and, thereby, personal prestige. In presenting the attacks as defences of their entire caste's prerogatives, they called on what she terms populist sentiment, thereby mobilizing the whole caste-group. They thus successfully assimilated their own prestige into that of the whole caste, which allowed them to increase their personal power and demonstrate their strength to the British authorities. Thus, powerful men orchestrated Hands conflicts to secure their control of the cloth business in the 18th century and of the Company's farms in the last years of the century, as well as their access to coveted honours distributed by the British government (Brimnes, 1999; Mukund, 1995). These honours, beyond their social and ritual meaning, were 'the currency of trust' for merchants (Rudner, 1994), guaranteeing their dominant economic position and legitimizing the patron-client relationship they had with lower classes of the urban population. In this way, caste identity has been claimed and thereby reinforced by individuals defending personal interests.

The Legal Shaping of Caste

On the Coromandel Coast, merchant elites actively sought the intervention of the colonial administration or courts in conflicts between the Hands. They expected from the colonial courts an immediate response, a definitive verdict, and the carrying out of their decision. The appeal to the colonial courts and entry into judicial procedure had effects on the constitution of caste identity.

The Legal Sanction of Caste Rights

Judgements provided legal sanction to the prerogatives of each caste. Since demands were presented to the colonial jurisdiction in terms of caste identity rather than for personal reasons, the judgements concerned the specific right of a caste to particular honours. For example, when the high castes filed a complaint against Annassamycramany, from Souraire (Nadar) caste, the rich leaseholder of calou, and arrack alcohols in Pondicherry in the late 1840s, because he had roamed the streets of the city on horseback, the question of the right of the entire caste to use this privilege was raised. The court decision, in the form of an order of the governor, confirmed in 1849 the ban on the whole caste. The decisions obtained, whether in the form of authorizations or interdictions, were treasured by the litigants, and used later on to prove their rights. Obtaining and keeping these legal decisions establishing rights was all the more imperative since there was no code or corpus of customs which would have determined the prerogatives of each. Yet, in all colonial territories, the European authorities were committed to following the cultural and religious traditions and to respecting the manners and customs of Indians. So that, when they had to rule on conflicts between castes, the administrators, or the colonial courts made a point of referring to local usage as it had been under the previous government and of banning all 'innovation'. Preserved judgements thus provided evidence of precedents and allowed the usages to become established. The argument about the antiquity of practices and the rejection of innovations was not the strategy of the colonial government alone; it was used by the caste-groups themselves who fruitfully mobilized the importance of ancestrality and respect for long-standing order. This dynamic dialogue, very clear in the domain of land ownership (Irschick, 1989) and in the organization of religious ceremonies (Prior, 1993), contributed to the production of narratives about the history of the caste and the traditional nature of its prerogatives, well before stories, or mythologies of caste proliferated in vernacular languages at the end of the 19th century.

Besides the specific decisions on which they capitalized, litigants strove to obtain definitive judgements from the colonial courts that would irrevocably fix their rights, even though the allocation of honours had always depended on local equilibriums that were always changing and never frozen. The colonial courts were cautious on determining rights, but the governments sometimes took a stand in favour of castes considered as low but useful to them economically. They then supported their efforts to rise in the name of progress or of Christian morality. For example, in 1813, the British Resident and chief minister of Travancore, John Munro, gave permission for Christian Nadar women to 'cover their breasts as obtains among Christians in other countries', and, in 1859, after decades of conflict, the government of Madras pressured the Maharaja of Tanjore to proclaim the right of all Nadar women to wear a jacket. In Pondicherry, the oil manufacturers and merchants of this caste, whose commercial activity was crucial to the economic success of the town, were, on 17 October 1854, granted the right to travel by vehicle through the main streets of the town, to which the higher Vellaja and Cavaré [Karavai] castes had refused them access.

Colonial Law and the Definition of Caste Conflicts

The very act of bringing the conflicts to colonial courts had the effect of legally fixing prerogatives. It also led the colonial jurists to establish the legal framework for caste conflicts themselves. In so doing, they recognized castes as institutions with legal existence, taking decisions, and organizing the lives of their members autonomously. Colonial law in the British Empire and in the French settlements was very clear: conflicts were to be regulated internally by the castes themselves through inter—or intra-caste policy-making assemblies. Most importantly, colonial jurists defined the social realities that were the subject of the conflicts. They established what came under the jurisdiction of caste as an institution and, still without giving a legal definition of the caste as such, they set its prerogatives as a ritual and religious social unit. Conflicts between castes or within a single caste were considered by the colonial government as related to Hindu law or customary law. It took charge of these through legal exceptionalism outside the usual circuits of the civil and penal courts. In the French Settlements of India, the conflicts were called 'caste affairs' from 1827. The expression designated 'contestations other than those of interest and contentiousness, which are related to the code of religious laws, or to the usage of the caste, that is, to religious ceremonies, private or public, to weddings and burials, to rights and prerogatives of pagodas [temples], to habits and usages, to obligations between members of the same caste, to rights and precedence of castes between themselves, to their administration, to their hierarchy and to their jurisdiction' (Marquet, 2018). Caste affairs were settled directly by the principal administrators. In the course of the 19th century, they progressively restricted the scope of caste affairs and brought some of their subjects before civil courts. They aimed at removing all the political, economic, and social dimensions while retaining only the ritual and cultural dimension of caste affairs. They then proceeded to a form of folklorization of the caste and the litigants turned away from their jurisdiction (Marquet, 2018).

In the British territories, conflicts between castes or within a single caste were designated as 'caste questions', defined as the 'claims of rival factions of the same caste to common caste property, caste leadership, the requiring of voluntary offerings, honours and presents to specific caste members, officiate as a priest, compulsory invitation to dinners' (Kikani, 1912). Caste questions, considered as related to the autonomy of castes, were not dealt with by British courts but left to their own evaluation. All the same, when a civil case was presented as primarily in relation to a question of caste, civil courts might judge the matter. The litigants, seeking the sanction of the colonial courts, were thus able to skew the internal situations of castes in the domain of civil law. Colonial judicial organization, whether British or French, thus had an impact on the delimitation of the borders of caste as an institution and as an experience.

Conclusion

Caste was shaped through conflict and its legal regulations. Caste-groups or powerful individuals sought to appropriate honours in order to enhance their social and ritual status. For this, they were attacked by the castes who considered themselves superior and who refused them the coveted honours. Attempts of appropriation like episodes of confrontation contributed to forging caste-like identities. They had an impact on the way individuals and social groups thought of themselves or were thought of as a caste-group. In confrontation, litigants actively pursued the intervention of colonial authorities into their conflicts. As a result, colonial courts further participated to the fixing of caste prerogatives and caste jurisdiction. The study of caste conflicts, located at the intersection of different logics of power, thus furthers understandings of how caste-like identities have been shaped in the modern period, in particular by taking into account the legal processes for resolving conflicts, which has become a fruitful way to understand caste formation. An integrated long-term approach, incorporating the decisions of Panchayats before or after the independence of India, may allow for clarification of the self-fashioning of caste-groups.

Julie Marquet, Centre d'Etudes de l'Inde et de l'Asie du Sud, and Centre d'histoire de l'Asie contemporaine, Paris Sorbonne University.

References

Appadurai, Arjun 1974. 'Right and Left Hand Castes in South India'. *Indian Economic and Social History Review*, 11(2–3): 216–259.

Appadurai, Arjun, and Breckenridge, Carol. 1976. 'The South Indian Temple: Authority, Honour and Redistribution'. *Contributions to Indian Sociology*, 10(2): 187–209.

Appadurai, Arjun. 1981. *Worship and Conflict under Colonial Rule. A South Indian Case.* Cambridge: Cambridge University Press.

Bandyopadhyay, Sekhar. 1997. *Caste, Protest and Identity in Colonial India: The Namasudras of Bengal, 1872–1947.* Surrey: Curzon.

Bayly, Susan. 1993. *Caste, Society and Politics in India from the Eighteenth Century to the Modern Age.* Cambridge: Cambridge University Press.

Bayly, Susan. 1989. *Saints, Goddesses and Kings: Muslims and Christians in South Indian Society 1700–1900.* Cambridge: Cambridge University Press.

Brimnes, Niels. 1999. *Constructing the Colonial Encounter. Right and Left Hand Castes in Early Colonial South India.* Richmond: Curzon.

Cohn, Bernard S. 1996. *Colonialism and Its Forms of Knowledge. The British in India.* Princeton: Princeton University Press.

Frykenberg, Robert. 1981. 'On Roads and Riots in Tinnevelly: Radical Change and Ideology in Madras Presidency during the 19th Century'. *Journal of South Asian Studies*, 4(2): 34–52.

Hardgrave, Robert L. 1969. *The Nadars of Tamilnadu: The Political Culture of a Community in Change.* Berkeley: University of California Press.

Irschick, Eugene. 1989. 'Order and Disorder in Colonial South India'. *Modern Asian Studies*, 23 (3): 459–492.

Jodkha, Surinder S. 2012. *Caste, Oxford India Short Introductions.* Delhi: Oxford University Press.

Kikani, L. T. 1912. *Castes in Courts. Rights and Powers of Castes in Social and Religious Matters as Recognized by Indian Courts.* Rajkot: Ganatra Printing Works.

Marquet, Julie. 2018. *Droit, coutumes et justice colonial. Les affaires de caste dans les Etablissements français de l'Inde, 1816–1870.* PhD Dissertation supervised by Marie-Noëlle Bourguet et Pierre Singaravelou, Université Paris 7 Paris Diderot.

Mines, Mattison, and Vijayalaskshmi, Gourishankar. 1990. 'Leadership and Individuality in South Asia: The Case of the South Indian Big-man'. *Journal of Asian Studies*, 49(4): 761–786.

Mukund, Kanakalatha. 2005. *The View from Below. Indigenous society, Temples and the Early Colonial State in Tamilnadu, 1700–1835*. New Delhi: Orient Longman.

Mukund, Kanakalatha. 1995. 'Caste Conflict in South India in Early Colonial Port Cities, 1650–1800'. *Studies in History*, 11(1): 1–27.

O'Hanlon, Rosalind. 2017. 'Caste and Its Histories in Colonial India: A Reappraisal'. *Modern Asian Studies*, 51(2): 432–461.

Piror, Katherine. 1993. 'Making History: The State's Intervention in Urban Religious Disputes in the North-Western Provinces in the Early Nineteenth Century'. *Modern Asian Studies*, 27(1): 179–203.

Price, Pamela. 1991. 'Acting in Public versus Forming a Public: Conflict Processing and Political Mobilisation in Nineteenth Century South India'. *South Asia*, 14(1): 91-121.

Ramaswamy, Vijaya. 1995. 'Artisans in Vijayanagar Society'. *The Indian Economic and Social History* Review, 22(4): 417–444.

Rudner, David. 1994. *Caste and Capitalism in Colonial India: the Nattukottai Chettiars*. Berkeley: University of California Press.

Srinivas, M. N. 1989. *The Cohesive Role of Sanskritisation and Other Essays*. Delhi: Oxford University Press.

Stein, Burton. 1980. *Peasant State and Society in Medieval South India*. Delhi: Oxford University Press.

Viguier, Anne. 2012. 'S'approprier le territoire. Les circulations collectives dans les villes d'Inde du Sud au XIXe siècle'. *Liame*, 24.

Washbrook, David. 1975. 'The Development of Caste Organisation in South India 1880 to 1925'. In C. J. Baker and D. Washbrook (Eds.), *South India: Political Institutions and Political Change 1880–1940* (pp. 150–203). Delhi: Macmillan.

Zimmermann, Francis. 1974. 'Géométrie sociale traditionnelle. Castes de main droite et castes de main gauche en Inde du Sud'. *Annales. Economies, sociétés, civilisations*, 29(6): 1381–1401.

CHAPTER 11

CASTE AND THE LAW

GAUTAM BHATIA[*]

As one of the organizing principles of Indian society, it is scarcely surprising that caste has many interfaces with the legal system. The relationship between caste and the law is a complex one: if the law claims to govern a society that is, at least in principle, broadly committed to egalitarianism in the public sphere, it must necessarily take account of—and intervene into—caste structures that are driven by the contrary logic of hierarchy. But the very act of doing so—as we shall see—becomes constitutive of changes in the concept of caste itself, under pressure from the force of law. Law and caste, therefore, are in constant tension with one another, and their relationship remains a fluid and dynamic one.

A complete analysis of the numerous interfaces between caste and the Indian legal system would require many volumes. Here, I shall limit myself to flagging four main themes: *first*, the ways in which caste appears in the Indian Constitution (I); *second*, the role of caste in the Indian Supreme Court's engagement with reservations (II); *third*, the jurisprudential link that has been drawn between caste, territory, and religion (III); and *four*, legislative attempts to prevent and redress caste-based domination and subordination (IV). I have chosen these four themes because, while the first structures any enquiry into the relationship between caste and law, the rest are salient and live issues today; moreover, they are specifically relevant for interdisciplinary studies. Each of these issues has seen the courts drawing upon insights from sociology, anthropology, and history (among other disciplines), to arrive at their conclusions. While the form of reasoning—and the outcome—is, of course legal in character, the important judgements rely upon—and have an impact upon—aspects that go much beyond the field of law, and will probably be of interest and concern to a wide range of scholars.

---

[*] As an upper-caste individual, I acknowledge the biases that stem from my caste location/privileges, in the course of writing about this subject.

Caste in the Constitution

Caste occurs in the Indian Constitution in three interlinked forms: as a ground for the prohibition of discrimination (A); as a ground for enabling affirmative action (B); and as an organizing principle for erecting an institutional apparatus to implement the first two mandates (C).

Discrimination

Liberal Constitutions all over the world possess some form of an equality-and-non-discrimination clause, which guarantees the equal protection of law, and the prohibition of discrimination on the basis of certain defined personal characteristics. Most Constitutions make provisions, for example, for prohibiting discrimination on grounds of race, sex, and religion (at least). Unsurprisingly, the Indian Constitution adds 'caste' to this list, in Article 15(1) (which is a part of the fundamental rights chapter). 'Caste' as a ground—accompanying more generic grounds such as race, sex, and religion—is also found in provisions prohibiting discrimination in public employment (Article 16(2)), in the imposition of compulsory public service (Article 23(2)), and in access to publicly-funded educational institutions (Article 29(2)).

Interestingly, however, the Constitution goes one step further: it not only prohibits the *State* from discriminating on grounds (*inter alia*) of caste, but also—in some domains—prohibits *private parties* from doing so. Article 17, for example, abolishes 'untouchability'—the entire social system of hierarchy and subordination, which has always been enforced primarily by *social sanctions*. More interestingly, Article 15(2) guarantees non-discriminatory access to 'shops, public restaurants, hotels, and places of public entertainment'[1]. This kind of a provision is familiar from civil rights legislation passed by various countries—often after long struggles—but it rarely appears in *Constitutions*, where it can be directly enforced without going through the legislative route. This suggests that the framers of the Indian Constitution were keenly aware of how relationships of power, domination, and subordination, organized around 'grounds' such as religion, caste, or sex, operated within the *private sphere*, and understood that freedom and equality would remain incomplete without at least an effort to address this (Ambedkar 1969).

Constitutional history, indeed, indicates that the final wording of the clauses was, actually, watered down. In an initial draft on fundamental rights, B. R. Ambedkar included a detailed anti-boycott provision, targeted at addressing the debilitating practice of

---

[1] Article 15(2), Constitution of India, 1949. For an explanation of how, in this understanding, the framers of the Indian Constitution departed from the traditional 'liberal' assumptions underlying constitutionalism, see (Bhatia 2019).

caste-based social and economic boycotts.² This provision—which resembled to a greater extent the detailed civil rights laws passed in other countries—was ultimately whittled down into the thinner wording of Article 15(2), which limited protection to only a few spaces, such as shops and schools.³ Even this, however, was radical in recognizing that the rights to equality and non-discrimination could not be enjoyed in any realistic form unless they were also made applicable to social institutions, such as that of caste. Indeed, a perusal of the Constituent Assembly Debates reveals that the framers intended to it to be applied to a broader and more expansive range of private discriminatory acts, than judicial interpretation has allowed it to be.⁴

Affirmative Action

Reservations—often taking the specific form of *quotas*—had a long, pre-constitutional history in India. At the turn of the 20th century, Indian princely states began to establish caste-based quotas in government employment, with a view to ensuring genuine equality in representation.⁵ When representative institutions were first created by the British regime, they came virtually born with quotas, which took the form of separate electorates. These quotas were primarily along the lines of religion, but in the incremental march towards full independence, legislators experimented with quota-based representation on the lines of gender, specific economic interests, and so on. Most famously, of course, under pressure from Ambedkar, the British regime agreed to institute separate electorates along caste lines as well—until Gandhi's notorious fast-unto-death and the Poona Pact put paid to that.⁶

At the moment of the framing, the Indian Constitution drew upon the existing systems of quotas—in public employment and in representative institutions—and constitutionalized them. Interestingly, however, in the case of public employment, it did not use the word 'caste'—preferring, instead, to go with the more neutral 'backward classes'.⁷ 'Castes' would be specifically introduced into these constitutional provisions *via* subsequent amendments, that drew a tripartite distinction between 'Scheduled Castes', 'Scheduled Tribes', and the 'Backward Classes' (it is beyond the scope of this chapter to deal with the distinction in detail⁸).

---

[2] See (Ambedkar, 1969).

[3] But see Indian Medical Association v Union of India, (2011) 7 SCC 179, where the Supreme Court relied upon Ambedkar's comments in the Constituent Assembly to accord a broad meaning to the word 'shops'.

[4] See, for example, the discussion between B. R. Ambedkar and Sardar Nagappa, on 29 November 1948, and the comments of Ajit Prasad Jain on 22 November 1949 (Parliament of India, 1949a and 1949c).

[5] For a comprehensive historical account, see (Galanter, 1984).

[6] For an account, see (Ambedkar, 1946).

[7] See Ambedkar's comments in the Constituent Assembly on 30 November 1948 (Parliament of India. 1949b).

[8] But see (Galanter, 1978) for more details.

It was in parliamentary quotas that castes found specific mention: Article 330 of the Constitution guarantees reservation of seats in the Lok Sabha for members of the 'Scheduled Castes',[9] in proportion to their population (through subsequent amendments, this would be extended to local government, as well as to special jurisdictions, such as Delhi). There are similar provisions for the state legislative assemblies.[10]

Institutions

Creating a class of beneficiaries under the Constitution—or a constituency that was to be afforded special solicitude by the Constitution and the State—would necessarily require the creation of corresponding institutional mechanisms. For the Scheduled Castes, this took the specific institutional form of a National Commission for the Scheduled Castes, constituted under Article 338 of the Constitution, and which has a wide-ranging mandate to look into the welfare of the Scheduled Castes by investigating complaints, looking into grievances, participating in developmental and planning work, and writing reports.[11]

At a more primary level, of course, there was the basic question of taxonomy: how was Scheduled Caste identity to be determined, for the purposes of the Constitution? This necessitated the second institutional mechanism: the Presidential List. Under Article 341 of the Constitution, the President is empowered to specify 'which castes, races, and tribes' are deemed be 'Scheduled Castes', for the purposes of the Constitution. The list can subsequently be modified by Parliament, acting in its legislative capacity.[12]

RESERVATIONS

As we have seen above, when drafting a provision to enable the State to make reservations in public sector employment, the Constituent Assembly opted to use the phrase 'backward class of citizens' (in contrast with, e.g., parliamentary quotas, where 'Scheduled Castes' was used). There was a significant amount of debate in the Assembly over the precise wording to be used, and the final formulation was something of a compromise, that brought together the twin factors of inadequate representation in public services, and 'backwardness'. While the Assembly did not, finally, define 'backwardness', the term 'backward class' had been in vogue through the colonial era,

---

[9]
[10] Article 332, Constitution of India, 1949.
[11] Article 338, Constitution of India, 1949.
[12] Article 341, Constitution of India, 1949.

and had come to acquire a meaning that broadly corresponded to social exclusion and subordination.[13]

After the entry into force of the Constitution, governments nonetheless used caste as the unit for determining the beneficiaries of reservation. In 1962, this was finally challenged, in *M. R. Balaji v State of Mysore*.[14] In *M. R. Balaji*, the Court was faced with a difficult situation: Articles 16(1) and (2) of the Constitution specifically prohibited discrimination in public employment on grounds of caste. Article 16(4) specifically enabled reservations for 'backward classes'. The use of the words 'caste' *and* 'class' in the same constitutional provision suggested that there was at least some measure of distinction between them, because otherwise, the framers could have simply used the same word throughout. But if there was a distinction between the two terms, then all caste quotas would, by definition, be struck down as unconstitutional, since they violated Article 16(1), and fell outside the protective umbrella of 16(4).

The Court's response to this situation was to hedge its bets. While maintaining that there *was* a distinction between 'caste' and 'class', the Court nonetheless held that the legislature could take caste as a 'starting point' in determining class backwardness—because caste was, after all, a form of class, and could often stand in as a useful *proxy* for determining which classes were backward.[15] So while Parliament could not *simply* identify a set of castes and provide them with reservations, what it could do was to *begin* by identifying a set of castes, and then check if social backwardness was mapped onto these castes—or, in other words, if these castes could fairly be classified as socially backward classes. The practical effect of this, of course, was to subsume class into caste, and render the former term analytically empty.

This approach towards the caste/class question under Article 16 of the Constitution has been a consistent feature of the Court's jurisprudence throughout. Its effect has been to conceptualize constitutional social justice or ameliorative measures in terms of caste, and not any other social, cultural, or economic (or a combination of the three) formation. This has been manifested in how the controversies surrounding the identification of the 'Other Backward Classes'—that culminated in the famous *Indra Sawhney* judgement of 1992, which upheld the Mandal Commission Recommendations—have also been contested on the terrain of caste. Consequently—as observed at the beginning of the essay—caste becomes effectively constituted, in the eyes of law, as the *sole* locus around which the constitutionally guaranteed promise of social justice is to be achieved.

There is one other feature of the Supreme Court's reservations jurisprudence that is worth examining. In *Balaji*, the State of Mysore had reserved 68 per cent of available positions. The Supreme Court struck this down on the basis that Article 16(4)—that enabled reservations—was an *exception* to the rule of formal equality of opportunity.

---

[13] See, for example, the census report of J. H. Hutton (Hutton, 1933). See also Ambedkar's testimony to the Committee in (Government of India, 1932). See further the discussion in (Rao, 2009) as well as in (Zelliott, 2012).

[14] *M. R. Balaji vs State of Mysore*, AIR 1963 SC 649.

[15] Ibid.

An exception could never cross 50 per cent, otherwise it would displace the rule itself.[16] This was the origin of the 50 per cent cap on reservations, which—as a judicial rule—continues to this day. While some states have exceeded the cap, the laws enabling that have been placed in the Ninth Schedule of the Constitution, which immunizes them from any challenge.

The 50 per cent cap—which was debated extensively in the Constituent Assembly as well, and seemed to have Ambedkar's implicit support[17]—raises some interesting issues about how the law treats the idea of constitutional equality in relation to the historical fact of caste subordination. Labelling formal equality of opportunity as 'the rule' and reservations as an 'exception' suggests that while the former is the *normal* baseline, the latter is a departure that stands in need of a justification. At a deeper level, it suggests that, when it comes to equality of opportunity, the default assumption is that of a level playing field, which may be slightly tweaked in order to correct some particularly glaring distortions.

This approach, however, seems to run contrary to the entire history of caste-based oppression and subordination in India, which has always been structural and institutional in character (Ambedkar 1936). From time to time, the Supreme Court has been alive to this point, and has advocated different interpretations of Article 16. In *State of Kerala v N. M. Thomas*,[18] for example, a majority of the Court held that Article 16(4) was not an exception to Article 16(1), but a *facet* of it; that is, 16(1) (equality of opportunity) and 16(4) (reservations) embodied the same vision of substantive equality, and 16(4) was only an emphatic restatement of the principle of 16(1). Logically, this would get rid of the 50 per cent cap; later judgements, however, have gone back to thinking about equality and caste-based reservations as embodying conflicting principles that must be 'balanced'; consequently, the 50 per cent cap remains part of Indian constitutional jurisprudence.[19]

Territory and Religion

Although it has been sociologically demonstrated that caste hierarchy and caste subordination exist in other religious communities in India, for the purposes of law, the caste system exists exclusively within Hinduism: the Presidential List under Article 341 contains only defined castes within Hinduism (and Buddhists and Sikhs, who, for various *legal* purposes under the Constitution, are deemed to fall under the same umbrella group as Hindus). A second feature of the constitutional understanding of

---

[16] Ibid.
[17] Ambedkar took the example of 70 per cent reservation, and suggested that it may be constitutionally problematic.
[18] *State of Kerala vs N. M. Thomas* (1976) 2 SCC 310.
[19] For a chronology, see (Sitapati, 2016).

Scheduled Castes is that they exist *state-wise*: that is, the SCs are defined as such within their specific states.

It would be beyond the scope of this chapter to discuss the reasons why the Indian legal system only recognizes the caste system as a function of Hinduism, and bounded by territory. What I want to discuss, however, is how—in circumstances flowing from these constitutional realities—the courts have come to understand caste oppression and disadvantage.

The first set of examples concerns situations involving conversions and *re-conversions*. In 1976, the Supreme Court held that on conversion from Hinduism, in circumstances where the internal rules of the caste decreed that the convert lost her caste status, 'the social and economic disabilities arising because of Hindu religion cease and hence, it is no longer necessary to give [an individual] protection'.[20] The Court then went on to hold that if, after that, a person *re*-converted, then 'the social and economic disabilities once again revive and become attached to him, because there are disabilities inflicted by Hinduism'.[21] Consequently, as long as the reconversion was in accordance with, and permitted by, the rules of the caste, on reconversion, it was assumed that in the intervening period, the individual's caste status (and its attendant entitlements) had only been 'eclipsed', and was now revived.

The underlying assumption, of course, is that through a formal act of conversion, an individual can simply 'step out' of all the social, economic, and cultural subordination that was entailed in her (erstwhile) caste location. In other words, oppression—according to the Court—is simply attached to formal status, and can be shed as easily as a conversion ceremony. In the eyes of the law, therefore, caste is only a *legal* category with purely *legal* consequences flowing from caste status; it does not go any deeper than that.

The conversion/reconversion double-movement by the Court, unsurprisingly, triggered another set of claims that began to push on the boundaries of its logic: conversions and *inter-generational* reconversions. First, the Court held that the logic would continue to apply if the son of a convert (and who, therefore, was not *born* a Hindu) reconverted, and was accepted back into the original caste.[22] But how far could this go? Interestingly, when a case came before the Court involving *two* generations—that is, a reconverted grandson—the Court not only backtracked on its earlier logic, but seemed to subscribe to the opposite view: in *K. P. Manu v Chairman*,[23] the Court went out of its way to argue that caste disabilities were persistent and subsisting, and therefore, *could not* be wiped away in the span of a generation or two. Quoting a wide range of sources—B. R. Ambedkar, James Massey, Archbishop George Zur, the Mandal Commission, a Church of the South India Commission, the Chinnappa Commission Report, and a political scientist, it noted that 'there has been detailed study to indicate the

---

[20] *G. M. Arumugam vs S. Rajgopal* (1976) 1 SCC 863.
[21] Ibid.
[22] *Guntur Medical College vs. Y. Mohan Rao* (1976) 3 SCC 411.
[23] *K. P. Manu, Malabar Cements Ltd vs. The Chairman* (2015) 4 SCC 1.

Scheduled Castes persons belonging to Hindu religion, who had embraced Christianity with some kind of hope or aspiration, have remained socially, educationally and economically backward'.[24]

The Court used this argument to reject the State's contention that a two-generation gap was sufficient for an individual to lose reservation benefits on reconversion, and to reaffirm the doctrine of eclipse. As this was in line with precedent, it would be easy to miss the underlying shift: in previous cases, the Court had held that because disadvantaged was associated with formal caste status, one liberated oneself on converting, and then fell *back* into disadvantage by rejoining. In *K. P. Manu*, on the other hand, the Court reasoned that disabilities were so deeply entrenched, that *one never lost them in the first place*. The two views, thus, are in tension, and it remains to be seen whether, in a future case, the Court will be called upon to resolve them.

The former line of precedent is also *a courant* with another set of cases, involving migration between states. In *Marri Chandra Shekhar Rao vs Dean, Seth G. S. Medical College*,[25] the Supreme Court held that 'extreme social and economic backwardness arising out of traditional practices of untouchability is normally considered as criterion for including a community in the list of Scheduled Castes and Scheduled Tribes. The social conditions of a caste, however, varies from state to state and it will not be proper to generalize any caste or any tribe as a Scheduled Tribe or Scheduled Caste for the whole country'.[26] The Court then went on to note that 'a man does not cease to belong to his caste by migration to a better or more socially free and liberal atmosphere. But if sufficiently long time is spent in socially advanced area then the inhibitions and handicaps suffered by belonging to a socially disadvantageous community do not continue and the natural talent of a man or a woman or a boy or girl gets full scope to flourish'.[27] Consequently, the Court held that a Scheduled Caste individual who had migrated to another state was no longer entitled to avail of reservation. This has been a consistent jurisprudential position.

The similarities between the first line of precedent in the conversion cases, and the migration cases, should be evident. Both sets of cases view caste disabilities and disadvantages as burdens that can be easily shaken off—by migration or by conversion. On the basis that, as a formal matter of law, caste status is a function of religion and of state territory, they hold that once that formal status has been shed, an individual enters the proverbial level playing field, and is responsible for his or her success or failure in open competition. What this view ignores, of course, is the lasting, persisting, and deep-rooted character of caste-based disadvantage. The judgement in *K. P. Manu* provides a hint of an alternative view, but it is a view that requires significant fleshing out before it can displace the dominant approach of the courts.

---

[24] Ibid.
[25] *Marri Chandra Shekhar Rao vs. Dean, Seth G. S. Medical College* (1990) 3 SCC 130.
[26] Ibid.
[27] Ibid.

Civil Rights

From the time that the Constitution was drafted, it was understood that the Scheduled Castes would require special, protective legislation, which would implement the promises made by Articles 15(2) and 17 of the Constitution. Parliament acted upon this by passing the Civil Rights Act of 1955; this was, however, something of a bare-bones legislation, and did not go much beyond the proto-drafts that Ambedkar and his colleagues had prepared in the years before independence.[28]

A far more detailed legislation—the Prevention of Atrocities Act—was passed in 1989 (and recently updated). The Prevention of Atrocities Act prohibits and criminalizes a range of caste-based discriminatory activities, and was in the news last year, when a bench of the Supreme Court diluted some of its more stringent provisions regarding arrest and custody (after significant political pressure, the government re-enacted them into the law).[29] What I want to focus on here, however, is the *asymmetric* character of social power organized around caste, which is recognized by the Prevention of Atrocities Act.

This asymmetry is evident most clearly when we consider Section 3(i)(x) of the Act, which prohibits 'intentionally insult[ing] or intimidat[ing] with intent to humiliate a member of a Scheduled Caste or a Scheduled Tribe in any place within public view'.[30] Unlike other provisions of the Act, which list out specific, prohibited *acts* that are part of a set of practices of caste discrimination, such as forced manual scavenging or disposal of excreta, Section 3(i)(x) is a pure *speech* offence. Under the scheme of the Act, like every other offence, it too is asymmetrical: by definition, *only* a non-SC/ST individual can commit this crime *against* an SC/ST individual. The Act will not apply for anything that occurs *inter se* between SC/ST individuals or non-SC/ST individuals, and it will not apply if an SC/ST individual violates its provisions with respect to a non-SC/ST individual.

The asymmetrical character of the provisions has been something that the Courts have been forced to grapple with. In two judgements examining the scope of Section 3(i)(x),[31] the Supreme Court provided something of an explanation: insulting or humiliating speech, it noted, was not to be construed as simply a set of words, but as an integral element of a set of *practices* that enforced caste hierarchy and subordination. Comparing the use of the word 'chamaar' with the use of the word 'nigger' in the United States, the Supreme Court noted that what made the speech wrongful was not that it caused offence or insult, but that it contributed to maintaining and upholding a system, and a set of institutions, that were responsible for the oppression and subordination of a group

---

[28] Protection of Civil Rights Act, 1955.
[29] Scheduled Castes and Scheduled Tribes (Prevention of Atrocities Act), 1989.
[30] Section 3(i)(x), Prevention of Atrocities Act, 1989.
[31] *Swaran Singh vs State* (2008) 8 SCC 435 and *Arumugam Servai vs. State of Tamil Nadu* (2011) 6 SCC 405. For an extended discussion, see (Bhatia, 2015).

of people. This was why the scheme of the Act was asymmetrical: while anyone could (in theory) verbally insult, humiliate, or hurt another person, it was only in the context of the different sites of power occupied by non-SC/ST individuals in relation to SC/ST individuals, did that insult, humiliation, or hurt, become *legally salient*. In this way, therefore, the Supreme Court laid down an important principle about how—despite its bluntness—the law could address caste inequities by being sensitive to, and aware of, the relationship between caste, social power, and institutional subordination.

Conclusion

As I began this chapter by noting, caste and the law are inextricable. The importance of caste as an organizing principle of Indian society makes legal interference inevitable. The relationship between caste and the law is symbiotic: law's legitimacy in society is (at least in some part) contingent upon how it handles the social phenomenon that is caste, while what *is* caste itself comes under pressure and alters in the shadow of the law.

In this chapter, I have discussed three points of interface between caste and the law. Each of these interfaces present issues that are relevant in the contemporary age, and each of them address, in different ways, the relationship between caste and social power; or, to put it more specifically, they address law's response to how caste organizes society, and social power, in its specific and particular ways. The first interface—reservations, or affirmative action—centres around the State's remedial efforts, to make up for generations of denied social opportunity and mobility, in the teeth of caste-based proscriptions. Ironically, to address this, the State has had to use caste *as* a marker of identification—the very system worse ill-effects it is ostensibly trying to reverse. And even in doing so, we have seen, the Courts are often hesitant to admit the full extent to which caste has acted as a barrier to equality, and how radical a true solution may need to be. Similarly, in cases involving loss of constitutional entitlements on conversion or migration, the Court seemingly understates the deep-rooting and pervasive character of caste disabilities, appearing to believe, instead, that these disadvantages can be tacked merely by a change in formal status. Both sets of cases, therefore, are premised upon an understanding of caste-based oppression and subordination that denies its deep-rooted and persisting character, and believes that it can be resolved through a surface application of law. Interestingly, the one set of cases that does seem to recognize the imbalances of power within the context of caste, arises in the context of the Prevention of Atrocities Act, where the analysis is carried on in the context of hate speech, and how its asymmetrical character tracks persisting and entrenched inequalities of power.

The jurisprudence on these issues continues to evolve. However, the Section 3(i)(x) cases, and the second line of analysis on the issue of conversion, suggest a contrapuntal approach to the issue of caste and the law, which appears more authentic and faithful to reality than the dominant approach. Whether it will ever become a mainstream view, however, remains to be seen.

References

Ambedkar, B. R. 1969. 'Memorandum'. In B. Shiva Rao (Ed.), *The Framing of India's Constitution: Select Documents, Vol. II*. New Delhi: Universal Law Publishing.

Ambedkar, B. R. 1946. *What Congress and Gandhi Have Done to the Untouchables*. Bombay: Thacker.

Ambedkar, B. R. 1936. *The Annihilation of Caste*. Self-published, available at http://ccnmtl.columbia.edu/projects/mmt/ambedkar/web/readings/aoc_print_2004.pdf.

Bhatia, Gautam. 2019. *The Transformative Constitution*. (New Delhi: Harper.

Bhatia, Gautam. 2015. *Offend, Shock, or Disturb: Freedom of Speech under the Indian Constitution*. New Delhi: OUP.

Galanter, Marc. 1984. *Competing Equalities: Law and the Backward Classes in India*. New Delhi: Oxford University Press.

Galanter, Marc. 1978. 'Who Are the Other Backward Classes? An Introduction to a Constitutional Puzzle'. *Economic and Political Weekly*, 13(43/44): 1818.

Government of India. 1932. *Report of the Franchise Committee*. Delhi: Government of India Central Publication Branch.

Hutton, J. H. 1933. *Census of India, 1931: Vol. 1*. Delhi: Government of India, Manager of Publications, available at https://ia802506.us.archive.org/14/items/CensusOfIndia1931/Census%20of%20India%201931.pdf.

Parliament of India. 1949a. *The Constituent Assembly Debates, Vol. VII*, 29 November 1948, available at http://164.100.47.194/loksabha/writereaddata/cadebatefiles/vol7.html.

Parliament of India. 1949b. *Constituent Assembly Debates, Vol. VII*, 30 November 1948, available at http://164.100.47.194/loksabha/writereaddata/cadebatefiles/vol7.html.

Parliament of India. 1949c, *The Constituent Assembly Debates, Vol. XI*, 22 November 1949, available at http://164.100.47.194/loksabha/writereaddata/cadebatefiles/C22111949.pdf.

Rao, Anupama. 2009. *The Caste Question: Dalits and the Politics of Modern India*. Berkeley: University of California Press.

Sitapati, Vinay. 2016. 'Reservations'. In Sunit Chaudhry et al. (Eds.), *The Oxford Handbook for the Indian Constitution*. New Delhi: OUP.

Zelliott, Eleanor. 2012. *Ambedkar's World*. New Delhi: Navayana.

CHAPTER 12

RESERVATIONS AND AFFIRMATIVE ACTION

ASHWINI DESHPANDE

INDIA'S AFFIRMATIVE ACTION PROGRAMME

India has a long-standing set of policies targeted towards its historically disadvantaged sections. These policies are referred to by the originally American,[1] but now international, term 'affirmative action' (AA), but in the Indian discourse are typically called 'reservations', alluding to the fact that these policies are primarily quota-based.

Until January 2019, the Indian AA programme was primarily caste-based. Here, caste is used more broadly to refer to descent groups which comprise in addition to castes, tribes, and communities that have been historically marginalized and stigmatized on account of their low position in the socio-economic hierarchy. In January 2019, via the 124th Constitutional Amendment, the *raison d'etre* of AA was changed by including 'economically weaker sections' (EWS) from the entire population, including from caste groups that are at the top of the caste system in terms of social and ritual status. Since this change is very recent, and has not yet taken effect, the bulk of this chapter will deal with the AA policy before this change.

The reservation policy, as mandated by the Indian constitution after Indian independence in 1947, identified two descent groups: one, the formerly untouchable castes that bore deep stigma, in addition to economic and social handicaps—the Scheduled Castes (SCs), and two, tribal groups that were relatively isolated and marginalized from the mainstream of the population—the Scheduled Tribes (STs). In addition to reservations, spending in several government programmes has been earmarked for SC–STs as a part of the AA programme.

---

[1] This term was first used in 1961 in the United States by John F. Kennedy in the context of policies designed to promote equal opportunity or non-discrimination.

Additionally, at the Central government level, 27 per cent seats are reserved for an intermediate group of castes and communities called 'Other Backward Classes' (OBCs), since 1991 in government jobs, and since 2006 in higher educational institutions. At the level of state governments, such programmes were adopted at different times since independence.

These reservations can be seen as 'vertical' reservations, in the sense that membership of one group does not overlap with the membership of the other group. While the boundaries of these groups are often disputed and changed through legal cases and appeals to government commissions, the boundaries do not overlap. Over time, the use of the reservation instrument has proliferated to include other groups. Thus, in addition to caste-based reservations, there are quotas along other group dimensions: women, disabled, ex-servicemen, on grounds of domicile. These can be viewed as 'horizontal' reservations, as these categories are not mutually exclusive, and they intersect the vertical caste categories.

Pre-Independence

In the 19th century, after the British consolidated their hold on substantial parts of the subcontinent, their policy was one of 'non-interference', which meant recognition of the established social order, but no conscious attempt to change it. Galanter (1984) discusses how the policy of non-interference was not neutral in consequence, in that the conscious actions as well as aloofness of the British, both had an impact on Indian society. The establishment of a nationwide legal system was one such example, as the principle of equality before the law which was implicit in this legal system generated a dynamic of its own, and the various Hindu reform movements, which were already underway, as well as caste organizations, used the concept of formal equality to gradually articulate demands which often amounted to questioning caste hierarchy and inequality. The preferential policies of the British state towards untouchables were followed by several progressive rulers of princely states, for example, in Baroda, Kolhapur, and Travancore, who introduced reservations in administrative positions for backward classes in the first quarter of 20th century.

Post-Independence

The new Indian constitution and the legal system guarantees equal treatment to all citizens, irrespective of their social group identity. The question is whether in fact, individuals are treated as equals under the prevailing social norms and institutions, most notably the caste system. It was clear to Dr B. R. Ambedkar that merely the formal espousal of the principle of 'equality in law' would not actually overcome generations of cumulative disadvantage. Thus, to promote the advancement of untouchables and other 'socially and economically backward classes', in his role as the principle architect of the constitution, he ensured that constitutional provisions safeguard the rights of the untouchables and protect their interests through preferential policies.

There is a tension between the two principles of 'equality in law' and 'equality in fact', and the provisions of the Indian constitution reflect this tension. To ensure the former, the constitution ensures fundamental rights such as the guarantee to all citizens of equality before the law (Article 14); the prohibition of discrimination on grounds of religion, race, sex, caste, or place of birth (Article 15); and the assurance of equality of opportunity in matters of public employment (Article 16). To ensure the provision of 'equality in fact', the constitution needed to depart from the principle of formal equality and institute the principle of *compensatory discrimination* for groups who are otherwise subjected to social and economic discrimination. Thus, Article 46, a 'Directive Principle of State Policy', states[2]:

> The State shall promote with special care the educational and economic interests of the weaker sections of the people, and, in particular, or the SCs and the STs, and shall protect them from social injustice and all forms of exploitation.

The implementation of this article has mainly been in the form of preferences in public sector jobs, educational institutions, in the electoral sphere as well as in special provisions in various development expenditures. The specific clauses of the constitution which outline these special policies are listed as follows.

Reservations in Employment

The constitution bans discrimination in government employment through Article 16(4) and allows the state to make:

> ... any provision for the reservation of appointments or posts in favour of any backward class of citizens which, in the opinion of the State, is not adequately represented in the services under the State.

Clause 4A of the same Article enables the state to provide to reservation to SC–ST in matters of promotion. Moreover, Article 335 asserts that the 'claims of the SCs and STs shall be taken into consideration, consistent with the maintenance of efficiency of administration, in the making of appointments to services and posts in connection with the affairs of the Union or of the State.'

---

[2] The Constitution prescribes it as the duty of the state to apply these principles in making laws.

The concrete implementation of these articles has been through reservation of seats, or quotas, in government employment for SCs and STs. Between 1947 and 1970, of the posts recruited directly on an all-India basis by open competitive examination, 12.5 per cent were reserved for SC and 5 per cent for ST. These were raised to 15 per cent and 7.5 per cent in 1970 (a total of 22.5 per cent), which is the level of current reservation for these groups.

All states, except Orissa, Madhya Pradesh, and Jammu & Kashmir had reservations in effect since 1951. In several states, these reservations were part of a wider reservations for OBCs (the present-day SC–ST–OBC together were the erstwhile 'Depressed Classes'), but after 1951, states were asked to separate the two categories (SC–ST and OBC). Even though the reservation at the central level, which was 17.5 per cent to begin with, later raised to 22.5, reflected the share of the combined SC–ST population at the national level, several states have had varying (typically higher) levels of quotas than what was mandated by the Centre. At the state level, the variation in the proportion of reserved seats is not necessarily in proportion to the population shares. For instance, Tamil Nadu has close to 70 per cent quotas, with 18 per cent for SCs, and 1 per cent for STs; Rajasthan has 68 per cent, including 14 per cent for 'forward' castes.

Reservations in Education

The Constitution also prohibits discrimination (Article 15), and discrimination in government aided educational institutions (Article 29[2]). However, there were two Supreme Court judgements rejecting discrimination in educational institutions, where the court ruled that while the government was empowered to ensure for backward classes, it could not do so on grounds of caste. In the 1951 *State of Madras v. Champakam Dorairajan* case, a Brahmin student who did not get admission into a medical college because of caste quotas, but would have been admitted otherwise, sued on the grounds that the quota policy violated Article 29[2] of the constitution which stipulated that no student shall be denied admission into any educational institution on grounds of caste. The court ruled in favour of the student. Within two months of the decision, the parliament amended article 15 in 1951 to include a new section to Article 15. This introduction of this amendment is one example of the role of the judiciary in continuously shaping the nature of the AA policy.

Thus, the new section 4 of Article 15 explicitly stated that,

> Nothing in Article 15 or Article 29(2) ... shall prevent the State from making any special provision for the advancement of any socially and educationally backward classes of citizens or for the Scheduled Castes and the Scheduled Tribes.

Under Article 15(4), reservations have been provided in higher educational institutions for SC–ST, mirroring the quotas in employment. Other than quotas, there is a whole range of special provisions, designed to enable members of the target groups to take advantage of the quotas. These include age concessions (i.e. relaxation of the minimum age for entry into the service); fee concessions (either in the form of waiver or reduction); reduction in the minimum qualifying marks for admission; and so on. The idea behind these provisions is to reduce or remove some of the barriers which might hinder the ability of the target groups to take advantage of the quotas and to make a greater proportion of the target group eligible for quotas. In addition to the quotas in employment and education, Article 275 requires the central government to provide separate allocations in national development plans for the improvement of SC and ST communities.

Identification of the SCs

The category of the exterior castes (now SCs) originated to serve the needs of preferential policies started by the British. At the conceptual level, it was supposed to capture the 'untouchables', groups who on account of their low ritual status were subject to a range of disabilities. However, the exact identification of these groups has gone through several iterations, starting from the beginning of the 20th century, resulting in a variety of estimates (reported in Galanter, 1984). The most elaborate effort to identify the untouchables was made by J. H. Hutton, the 1931 Census Commissioner. He proposed a series of tests, to identify the untouchable communities, which were designed around the incidence of disabilities:

1. Whether the caste or class in question can be served by Brahmans or not.
2. Whether the caste or class in question can be served by the barbers, water carriers, or tailors, etc., who serve caste Hindus.
3. Whether the caste in question pollutes a high-caste Hindu by contact or proximity.
4. Whether the caste or class in question is one from whose hands a caste Hindu can take water.
5. Whether the caste or class in question is debarred from using public conveniences, such as roads, ferries, wells, or schools.
6. Whether the caste or class in question is debarred from the use of Hindu temples.
7. Whether in ordinary social intercourse a well-educated member of the caste or class in question will be treated as an equal by the high caste men of the same educational qualifications.
8. Whether the caste or class in question is merely depressed on account of its own ignorance, illiteracy, or poverty and but for that, would be subject to no social disability.
9. Whether it is depressed on account of the occupation followed, and whether but for that occupation it would be subject to no social disability.

As can be appreciated, several of these criteria are not easy to observe (e.g. 7), or framed in a way such that the answer might not reveal the extent of disability: for example, 5: roads or schools are typically free for anyone to *use*, but for untouchables, the usage might be restricted in some form, and there might be some wells from which the untouchables are barred, but not from certain other wells. A question like 9 is problematic too, given that often times, the specific occupation is what make the caste group untouchable or low ritual status.

The lack of any single test to determine untouchability led to huge debates. However, Ambedkar pointed out that the aim was to identify groups which suffer the contempt and aversion of high caste Hindus and he warned that 'it is a fatal mistake to suppose that differences in tests of untouchability indicate differences in the conditions of untouchables' (quoted in Galanter, 1984, p. 129). After considerable debate, denial of access to temples and causing pollution by touch or approach were taken as the generally accepted tests of untouchability and groups in this category were listed in a government schedule in 1936. This list reflected a combination of economic and educational criteria to determine untouchability. In the 1941 census, these groups were 19 per cent of the Hindu population and 12.6 per cent of the total population of undivided India.

After independence, the same approach to identify untouchables was carried forward. A SCs Order was promulgated by the President in 1950 which was a restatement of the 1936 list. The major additions were four Sikh castes and the extension of the list to areas which previously had not compiled a list. There were other changes made to the list between 1951 and 1970, and according to the 1971 census, the SCs were 14.6 per cent of the population. As Galanter (1984) elaborates in detail, the changes to the list have been in the form of additions or corrections of groups, rather than any further attempt to reformulate criteria to determine which groups should be in the schedule. It is important to note that other than caste, two other factors determine which groups should be a part of the SC list—territory and religion. SCs are listed by state, and other than Sikh untouchables and Neo-Buddhists since 1990, only Hindu castes are included. There has been a forceful demand for the inclusion of neo-Buddhists (untouchables who converted to Buddhism) and Dalit Christians, which has not been accepted. Before the 1936 order, the recognition existed that Muslims and Christians, within their religions, contained depressed classes which should be considered for inclusion into the SC list. However, in the disputes leading to the formation of the 1936 list, the castes/communities from other religions were not included in the SC list and that situation has prevailed since then, despite periodic demands to the contrary.

IDENTIFICATION OF THE STs

Designation of groups as STs has been much less controversial than the designation of OBCs (discussed later) or SCs. Again, conceptually, this category is supposed to include all those with 'tribal characteristics' (social, religious, linguistic, and cultural distinctiveness), which are spatially and culturally isolated from the mainstream. However, the demarcation between 'tribals' and non-tribals is not unambiguous. Indeed, during the 1950s, some groups which were earlier classified as SCs got reclassified as STs.

The formal mechanism of being listed as a ST is the same as that for SCs. The President consults with the governors of states to designate particular communities SCs or STs. Once the list is promulgated, it can be changed only by an Act of Parliament. In addition to listing tribal groups in the schedule, there are other specific provisions for tribals which are absent in the case of OBCs or SCs. The British started the policy of insulating certain areas (called Excluded Areas or Partially Excluded Areas in the Government of India Act of 1935) to protect the aboriginal people from 'exploitative or demoralizing contact with more sophisticated outsiders' (Galanter, 1984, p. 147). This has continued after independence in a policy to designate certain areas as Scheduled Areas, under the Fifth and Sixth Schedules of the constitution, respectively. The designation of Scheduled Areas is also done by the President, who retains the power to alter or de-schedule them.

The idea behind these supplementary provisions for tribals is to enable them to maintain their distinctiveness, rather than encourage their assimilation with the rest of society. Article 339 (2) provides for direct central control over administration; Article 275 (1) provides for direct central financial responsibility; Fifth Schedule #3 asks for annual reports from the Governors to the President; Fifth Schedule #4 provides extensive executive power over Scheduled Areas in order to protect them from illegal transfer of their land and to insulate them from private moneylenders; finally, Fifth Schedule #5 asks for the formation of Tribal Advisory Councils to participate in the formulation of policy. The Sixth Schedule contains wide ranging recommendations, as mentioned in the previous chapter, relating to the ability of the autonomous regions and autonomous districts to frame land use policies, policies related to reserved forests, related to inheritance and marriage rules, and other important determinants of social and economic life in the areas under the Sixth Schedule.

OBC Reservation

Preferential policies for the 'Depressed Classes' in parts of British India were targeted towards communities which were classified as 'backward', as well as the untouchables, tribals, and some non-Hindu communities. Even though there were preferential policies for the 'Backward Classes', their exact definition had not been clearly articulated and details of the various definitions during the British period are spelt out in Galanter (1984). The constitution of independent India did not define 'OBCs' in a specific way either. However, after the SCs were listed as a separate category, the term Backward Classes started to be used in two senses: as the group of all communities which needed preferential treatment, and as castes low in the socio-economic hierarchy, but not as low as the untouchables. As should be clear, the two usages overlap considerably. However, given the ambiguity surrounding the varna-jati linkage, the exact identification of groups and communities which should be counted as OBCs has been fraught with a great deal of controversy.

As the constituent assembly debated the use of the term 'backward', the final agreement was that the backward classes other than the SCs and STs would be designated at the local level. Galanter (1984, p. 161) suggests that part of the reason for not bringing out a central list of OBCs then could have been the belief that the OBCs were a sufficiently potent political force at the local level 'to look out for their own interests', and unlike the untouchables, 'central control of their designation was not required to ensure the inclusion of the deserving'.

Even before the constitution came into effect, several states formed the category for the first time (e.g. Bihar in 1947; Uttar Pradesh in 1948) and conferred benefits on them, while those states which already had benefits for the backward castes, expanded the existing range of benefits. Thus we see that in 1978, without any central reservations for OBCs, at least 13 states reserved seats for Backward Classes, other than SCs and STs. These reservations were found throughout southern India, in Maharashtra and Gujarat, and in parts of north India, with the heaviest representation in the south (Galanter, 1984, p. 87).

The first Backward Classes Commission, under the chairmanship of Kaka Kalelkar, was established in 1953, which was directed to first determine the criteria to be adopted to determine whether any section of the population could be considered backward (over and above SC and ST), then, according to these criteria, prepare a list of such classes. The Commission prepared a list of 2399 groups, which were roughly 32 per cent of the population. It was generally understood that the classes identified by the commission would be castes or communities. This meant that backwardness was defined or understood in terms of the 'social hierarchy based on caste'. Thus, the commission listed as criteria of backwardness trade and occupation, security of employment, educational attainment, and representation in government service and position in social hierarchy.

There was a rush among communities wanting to be classified as backward due to the potential benefits that this status would confer upon them. However, in deciding on the validity of these multiple claims, the commission was stymied by the lack of data. On the one hand, embracing the ideal of a casteless society had led to the conclusion that caste had to be de-emphasized in various spheres, including in the census; on the other hand, combating backwardness or marginalization based on low-caste origins required a clear identification of the marginalized, whether individuals or groups, and for that, more data were needed, not less. This dilemma between the urge to de-emphasize caste, but the need to collect more caste-based data to assess what had changed and to what extent, resonates very strongly with the debate that arose when the proposal to count caste was mooted for the 2011 census.

Despite the lack of data, the commission made wide-ranging recommendations for benefits to be conferred to backward classes, often relying on just the names of the caste to make its case. However, at the last minute, the chairman repudiated the report of the commission by stating that he found the use of caste as antithetical to democracy and to the eventual creation of a casteless and classless society. Due to several factors (the rush of communities wanting to be classified as backward, the unreliability of data, the extensive recommendations of the commission), the work of the commission was widely criticized. The basic point of contention was the use of caste or community as the chief axis which was used to determine backwardness. There was a forceful plea made to use economic criteria alone to determine backwardness, and hence to determine *individuals* who could be considered backward on the basis of objective economic criteria, rather than *groups*, such as castes or communities, and/ or social criteria. In 1965, when the report was finally tabled in parliament, the central government firmly opposed the definition of backwardness on the basis of communal criteria (i.e. communities or castes), arguing that the use of caste was administratively unworkable and were contrary to the 'first principles of social justice' in their exclusion of other poor. The centre decided not to impose a uniform criterion on the states, but persuaded them to use economic criteria, rather than community-based ones, to identify the backward.

Various state governments set up backward classes commissions, and some followed the economic criteria endorsed by the centre. However, most states have placed a greater emphasis on the caste criterion. The socialist parties in north India, under the ideological leadership of Ram Manohar Lohia, consistently championed quotas for backward castes to the tune of 60 per cent. His famous slogan '*sansopa ne bandhi gaath, pichhda pave sau mein satth*': Sansopa (the Samyukta Socialist Party) is determined, the Backward should get 60 out of 100: became a major rallying point for mobilizing the Backward Castes. Accordingly, the Janata Party government, which was a coalition dominated by various hues of socialists and Lohiaites, set up a commission under the chairmanship of B. P. Mandal in 1978 to examine the entire issue of backwardness, starting with determining the criteria which should be used to identify the backward.

The Mandal Commission used 11 indicators of social and economic criteria, which were grouped under three heads: social, educational, and economic. These were combined using weights (social criteria were given a weight of three, educational got two and economic criteria were given a weight of one). This was done for all the Hindu communities. For non-Hindus, the commission used another set of criteria: all untouchables who converted to other religions and all communities which were identified by their traditional occupations, for which the Hindu counterparts were included in the list of backward classes.

Based on this, the commission identified 3743 caste groups as backward, which were 52 per cent of the population (as against 32 per cent identified by the Kalelkar commission and roughly 44 per cent from NSS data). The 52 per cent figure was arrived at after subtracting from 100 per cent the share of the SC–ST population, the non-Hindu population based on the 1971 census, and the share of the Hindu upper castes extrapolated from the 1931 census. The residual was actually 43.7, to which was added half of the non-Hindu population share.

The announcement of the implementation of the Mandal Commission Report (MCR) was made in 1990 by the then Prime Minister, V. P. Singh. Under the recommendation of the MCR, based on its list as well as the various states lists to identify the OBCs, reservations were extended to include an OBC quota of 27 per cent with effect from August 1990, taking the total quota (SC/ST/OBC) to 49.5 per cent. Based upon a Supreme Court verdict in the 1963 Balaji case, there is a limit on reservations that prohibits reserving a majority of the seats, thus limiting quotas to less than 50 per cent. The figure of 27 per cent for OBCs, therefore, is not in accordance with its share in the population, but is the residual, after accounting for the 22.5 SC–ST quota. Subsequently, the Government of India enacted the National Commission for Backward Classes Act (Act No. 27 of 1993) that set up a National Commission for Backward Classes (NCBC) as a permanent body.[3]

The OBC quota is perhaps the only instance of AA in the world where the designated beneficiary category is not counted in the national census. Given that there is no jati-based census since independence, most of the commissions set up to examine the conditions of the backward classes since then have had to rely on extrapolations from the 1931 census or conduct their own surveys to identify who the backward classes are. The NCBC (as did the MCR) set out guidelines for inclusion into the central list of OBCs. These guidelines are listed in Deshpande (2013). The NCBC uses a composite set of social, educational, and economic criteria to identify backwardness, with four criteria being considered decisive to the identification of backwardness:

(1) Castes and communities, which in terms of caste system, are identified with traditional crafts or traditional or hereditary occupations considered to be lowly or undignified.
(2) Castes and communities, which in terms of the caste system, are identified with traditional or hereditary occupations considered to be 'unclean' or stigmatized.
(3) Nomadic and semi-nomadic castes and communities.
(4) Denotified or Vimukta Jati castes and communities.[4]

The NCBC re-created the central OBC list afresh, irrespective of whether castes and communities that it designated as backward were included in the MCR list or not. The NCBC functions like a tribunal that decides the validity of the claims made by caste groups for inclusion in the OBC list.

---

[3] Article 340 of the Constitution provides for the appointment of a commission that investigates the conditions of and the difficulties faced by socially and educationally backward classes and to make appropriate recommendations.

[4] The term refers to castes/communities which had been categorized as Criminal Tribes under the Criminal Tribes Act, 1924, Act No. VI of 1924, passed by the Indian Legislature and repealed by the Criminal Tribes (Repeal) Act, 1952, Act No. XXIV of 1952 and subsequently referred to as Denotified or Vimukta Jatis.

THE CASE FOR CASTE-BASED AFFIRMATIVE ACTION IN CONTEMPORARY INDIA

The case for a continuation of the caste-based reservation policy rests on several pillars: one, on the evidence on inter-caste disparities in material or standard of living indicators, such as income, expenditure, land ownership, wealth holding, occupation, education, and wages. Deshpande and Ramachandran (2019) provide evidence on the evolution of caste disparities over time on a range of these indicators. Based both on absolute gaps and the specific level of relative gaps, except for the lowest categories of educational attainment, upper castes Hindus have further reinforced their educational advantage in the last five to six decades. The evolution of inter-caste differences in occupational distribution for the most prestigious category of white-collar jobs shows that traditional hierarchies have remained largely static over the past five decades. The findings on the evolution of wages mirror the findings of the education and occupational analysis. As caste gaps have closed in lower categories of education, wage gaps have been closing for workers earning below the median wage. As caste gaps in higher categories of education have increased or remained the same, wage gaps in the upper half of the wage distribution and in access to white-collar jobs have increased. Decomposing the wage gap, they find an increase in the unexplained part of the wage gap between upper castes on the one hand, and SC–STs and OBCs on the other. This suggests an increase in labour market discrimination against lower ranked castes.

The second rationale for continued caste-based reservation is the continuing discrimination against Dalits and Adivasis. Dalits continue to suffer from a 'stigmatized ethnic identity' due to their untouchable past and remained mired in corresponding social backwardness. There is sufficient evidence that amply demonstrates the various aspects of stigmatization, exclusion, rejection, and violence that Dalits continue to face in contemporary India. In rural India, despite the breakdown of the traditional subsistence economy, caste continues to make its strong presence felt in many different dimensions.

The designation of tribals or Adivasis as 'primitive' is a hang-over from colonial practice and while the original intention was to demarcate aboriginal groups, the term is used in a sense antithetical to the idea of modernity and is stigmatizing. In independent India, of the 500 groups which are designated as STs, 75 are designated as 'primitive tribal groups' (PTGs) based on their racial characteristics, spatial location, and habitat. The issue of defining appropriate Adivasi rights is complicated and it is important to recognize the nuances in order to comprehend the multiple ways in which Adivasi rights are violated. For nomadic, semi-nomadic, pastoralist tribes, and tribes engaged in shifting cultivation, preservation of their distinct lifestyles would mean guaranteeing them freedom to be on the move. Other tribes notified under Schedule V and Schedule VI areas need the guarantee that they would not be evicted from these areas and would be able to pursue traditional livelihoods if they wanted to.

The stigmatization of tribes began in the early decades of the 20th century through a process of which the 'primitive' designation was the only one aspect. The Criminal Tribes Act of 1911 enabled local governments to declare any tribe or a class of people a 'criminal tribe' and the government could authorize close surveillance and preventive arrests of people from that community.[5] The criminal designation was deeply stigmatizing, and even though these tribes have been de-notified, the stigma remains.

RESERVATIONS AS AN ALTERNATIVE TO JOB CREATION?

As stated earlier, AA in India is applicable only to government jobs. Over the last two decades and more, due to extensive privatization of the economy, the absolute number of government jobs has declined, leading to a *de facto* shrinkage in the scope of AA. However, the last two decades in India have also seen a jobs crisis, believed to have accelerated between 2014 and 2019.[6] There is, thus, an acute competition for coveted government jobs.

This has prompted further proliferation of the demand for additional vertical reservations. Dominant groups in their respective states, who have traditionally opposed reservations for SC–ST, are now demanding to be classified as OBCs, for example, Jats in Haryana, Patels in Gujarat, and Marathas in Maharashtra. Deshpande and Ramachandran (2017) demonstrate that in terms of a range of material indicators, these groups are, even without reservations, better-off than the existing SC–STs and OBCs. Analysing changes between 2005 and 2012, in key indicators such as educational attainment, per capita consumption expenditure, probability of being classified as poor, these groups have further consolidated their relative advantage. While anxieties due to widespread agrarian changes and lack of livelihood opportunities fuel their demands, their self-perception of insecurity is not backed by the empirical evidence. In the context of caste gaps widening or staying the same between upper castes and the historically marginalized and stigmatized groups (Deshpande and Ramachandran, 2019), extending reservations to richer and socially dominant groups dilutes the already small and shrinking entitlement for those who are genuinely marginalized.

---

[5] Several nomadic tribes got designated as such, as well as those tribes whose traditional occupations got disrupted with the spread of capitalism (e.g. Koravas, an itinerant trading community, which traded in grain, salt, cattle, bamboo, etc. between interior districts and coastal areas in the mid-19th century, became redundant with the spread of the railways and roads).

[6] https://www.business-standard.com/article/economy-policy/unemployment-rate-at-five-decade-high-of-6-1-in-2017-18-nsso-survey-119013100053_1.html, accessed 10 March 2019.

The 10 per cent EWS quota needs to be viewed in this context. It should be noted that the income limit for defining EWS is not the usual poverty line, but a household income threshold of INR 800,000 per annum, which is so high that over 97 per cent of the population falls under it. Thus, the EWS quota is effectively a quota for upper castes, not the poor, and in this sense, it overturns the logic of 'compensatory discrimination' that characterized India's AA policy.

THE PURPOSE AND SCOPE OF AA

Finally, in conclusion, in the context of various debates over the nature and scope of AA internationally, it is worth reiterating what AA is meant to do. Broadly speaking, AA consists of a set of anti-discrimination measures intended to provide access to preferred positions in a society for members of groups that would otherwise be excluded or under-represented. It provides a mechanism to address contemporary exclusion, particularly a mechanism to de-segregate elites. AA can be, and has been, utilized in different parts of the world to change the social composition of elite position holders, making those positions more representative of the caste/ethnic/gender composition of the society as a whole. AA is not a conventional redistributive measure, in the sense that it does not lead to a redistribution of wealth or assets in the same way that, say a policy of land reforms, would achieve. It simply alters the composition of elite positions in society.

It is not meant to be an anti-poverty measure, nor an employment *generation* measure. It should be noted that class-based government programmes, such as anti-poverty or employment generation programmes, designed to ameliorate poverty, or provide livelihood support, could also reflect underlying social biases, in that deserving members of stigmatized groups could get disproportionately excluded from such programmes. The rationale for AA is that given systematic and multi-faceted discrimination against certain groups, the normal process of development might not automatically close the gaps between the marginalized and the dominant groups, because dominant groups will disproportionately corner the fruits of development. While it is true that the lives of large sections of the marginalized groups might not be touched by AA given its targeting of elite positions, AA nevertheless fulfils an important function by providing some members of disadvantaged communities a voice in decision-making; by placing them in prestigious jobs and elite educational institutions, it provides the community with say.

REFERENCES

Deshpande, Ashwini. 2013. *Affirmative Action in India*. Oxford India Short Introductions, New Delhi: Oxford University Press.

Deshpande, Ashwini, and Rajesh Ramachandran. 2017. 'Dominant or Backward? Political Economy of Demand for Quotas by Jats, Patels and Marathas'. *Economic and Political Weekly*, May 13, LII(9): 81–92.

Deshpande, Ashwini, and Rajesh Ramachandran. 2019. 'Traditional Hierarchies and Affirmative Action in a Globalising Economy: Evidence from India'. *World Development*, (118): 63–78.

Galanter, Marc. 1984. *Competing Equalities: Law and the Backward Classes in India*. New Delhi: Oxford University Press.

CHAPTER 13

'BACKWARDNESS'

Reviewing the Emergence of a Concept

S. ANANDHI AND KALPANA KANNABIRAN

Introduction

The concept of backwardness underwrites affirmative action, reservations, and social welfare policy in India. Mobilizations and movements for equality and dignity since the turn of the 20th century have focused on dignity and on questions of recognition of social disabilities and redistribution of power and resources as ways of combatting backwardness—social, economic, political, and cultural. The articulation of backwardness however is far from linear and encompasses several layers of loss and disentitlement in a hierarchical caste society. The concept itself has a long political and intellectual history that must be traced in order for us to open its multiple meanings out to view.

Especially important is the relationship between backwardness and caste—through the medium of class/untouchability/tribe/socio-religious group/categorization as criminal, nomadic, or semi nomadic. However, these are the visible signifiers of backwardness historically. There are other fields that may be opened out from the standpoint of the contemporary, like disability, gender (not limited to the male–female binary), and region. How may we account for the diversity of 'backwardness' even while signposting its historical trajectories? What is the relationship between 'Minority' (as defined by Ambedkar) and 'Backwardness'? How do the other fields of backwardness relate to caste? How exactly does backwardness fold into inequality and into discrimination? What are its markers? And what are the interconnections between political mobilization, the identification/claim to backwardness, and the concepts of recognition and redistribution?

This essay will attempt to engage with the above questions through a review of writing in the social sciences and law with a view to map the concept of backwardness in India, mainly, the context-specific delineations of the idea of backwardness and its reverberations in legislative, executive, and judicial action, as also in policy research. We will explore the genealogy of linking caste and backwardness in order to understand the limits and possibilities these debates offer in addressing multiple, layered, and interconnected inequalities that require state attention. We examine the missionary and colonial legacy of understanding backwardness and anti-caste philosophy in colonial India. In the post-independence period we look at the official discourse on 'backwardness', the judicial discourse on 'backwardness' and caste, the articulation of women's status and position in the debates on backwardness, the minority question, and the relationship between religion, caste, and backwardness in the deliberations around affirmative action.

Caste, Untouchability, and Backwardness

From the early 19th century, caste was a predominant concern for missionaries. That caste was a major impediment for the progress of converts convinced the missionaries that renouncing caste was possible only by denouncing Hinduism. Rev. Philips for instance wrote 'whatever weakens caste weakens Hinduism' (Phillips, 1912, p. 18; also Dirks, 2001, p. 27). They attributed the backwardness of the lower castes, mainly the untouchables, to their caste-based agrestic servitude and associated socio-cultural disabilities. Missionary conferences and educational efforts concerned themselves in addressing the problem of caste as cause for backwardness.[1] It is in the context of converting the untouchables to Christianity that the missionaries articulated their views on caste as an irrational ideology which bestowed special privileges on dominant caste Hindus while it dehumanized the existence of the 'untouchables' or depressed classes (Phillips, 1912, p. 53). A report in the *Missionary Review of the World* sums up this perspective quite well:

> One of the greatest problems in the Indian empire is that of the depressed classes. There are 50 million of them—men, women and children, ignorant and poor, illiterate and despised, treated like slaves, considered unworthy to be touched and living in an awful state of moral decay. The condition of these masses is especially bad in south India, where it is continually imprest upon them that they belong to a lower order of beings than the members of the castes...[2]

---

[1] See for instance a detailed report on identifying problems of lower castes and their backwardness in the 4th Decennial Indian Missionary Conference held in Madras, 1902 (report published by Christian Literature Society, 1902). Similarly, the missionary magazine *The Harvest Field* carried several reports on missionary approaches to caste and backwardness and the actions to be taken by the church missionaries to address this problem. See, *The Harvest Field*, XXXIX(7), July 1919.

[2] *The Missionary Review of the World*, 1911, 887. For a similar account see also, Phillips (1912).

Missionary records were replete with vivid descriptions of degradations, poverty, and illiteracy of the depressed classes as signs of backwardness, which they sought to remedy by creating alternate livelihoods through industrial and medical missions. In these reflections on backwardness and caste the missionaries used the term depressed classes, untouchables, outcastes, and backward classes interchangeably.[3]

The colonial government in India, like the missionaries, recognized caste as an essential part of Hinduism and Indian society and in 1871, brought caste categories into the census enumeration. H. H. Risley's ethnographic survey of India and the census produced empirical information on caste, based primarily on missionary accounts and orientalist writings (Dirks, 2001, pp. 41–49). These colonial efforts led to systematic formulations of affirmative policy for the backward classes. However, while the colonial government through various commissions recognized the backwardness of women and Muslims in education and employment and accorded special privileges to them, the term 'backward classes' was not applied to them. For instance, the Hartog committee defined backward classes as 'castes or classes which are educationally backward.[4] They include the depressed classes, aboriginals, hill tribes and criminal tribes' (Indian Statutory Commission, 1929, p. 399).

The Madras government was a forerunner which, like the missionaries, attributed 'backward class' status, mainly to the untouchables for their 'impure conditions' imposed by caste system that led to the denial of access to education and public services.[5] Much of their policy recommendations for the backward classes concerned themselves with reservations in public service employment and special incentives such as scholarship and free meals for the backward classes ('illiterate' and 'indigent castes') in the field of public education (Saraswathi, 1974, pp. 108, 110). The colonial government, during this period, used educational backwardness as the main criteria to include certain castes in the list of 'backward', which over the years expanded from 39 in 1895 to 131 in 1920 (Radhakrishnan, 1990, p. 515). Around this time, as a response to colonial state measures, several castes sent in their memorials requesting their inclusion in the government list of backward classes in order to avail special facilities provided to the 'panchamas' or the untouchables.[6] Later on as part of their demands to be included

---

[3] See, London Missionary Society's Records of activities in which mention is made of the society's work among the 'backward classes' mainly the Shanars and Tiyas in Quillon district of the 'Malayalam Country' in Hacker and London Missionary Society (1908, 106).

[4] Hunter Commission in 1882 and the Indian Statutory Commission in 1929 (Hartog Committee) recorded the causes for the backwardness among women and Muslims and suggested legislative measures to overcome the same. See, Report of the Indian Education Commission, 485, 505, and 521.

[5] The Hunter Commission categorically stated that there should be special schools and classes for the children of low-caste communities established from public funds and where there is no such alternative their rights to entry into the cess-school 'must be firmly maintained especially in the secondary institutions...'. For a detailed report on Government efforts to address the backwardness of the 'low caste communities' through educational measures, see, Report of the Indian Education Commission (Hunter Commission) 1882, Calcutta: Government of India, 1883, Chapter IX, 517, 520.

[6] These were mainly the artisanal groups who also demanded through their memorial to the government in 1897 that their skills as artisans should be recognized; that they should be offered specialized

in the backward list, many of these 'low castes' such as the Vanniakula Kshatriyas,[7] Vishwakarma Brahmins, and others contended that they should be recognized as 'politically backward' in order to be nominated to the Legislative Council.[8]

The demand for recognition as 'backward' by various caste groups led to the formation of the Backward Class League mainly among the low-caste Shudras. This was also an attempt to assert their unified identity of backward classes as opposed to the depressed classes and the upper caste non-brahmins.[9] Equally important was the assertion of untouchable castes which demanded that they should be treated as a separate category of 'depressed classes' and not to be confused with the 'backward classes' which were only educationally backward and not disadvantaged by the social, economic, and religious system. Writing in 1925, M. C. Rajah a well-known Dalit intellectual and a former member of the Madras Legislative Council observed:

> The term 'Depressed Classes' should not be confused with the term 'Backward Classes'. Backward Classes are those communities that are only educationally backward but are really high up in the social, economic and religious scale. On the other hand, communities that are called 'Untouchable Classes' are educationally, economically and socially backward and come under the term 'Depressed Classes'. These people have been kept down by the Caste Hindus, through the ages, by systematic tyranny and social oppression. (Rajah, (1925) 2005, p. 4)[10]

Echoing the sentiments of M. C. Rajah and several other members of the depressed classes association, the colonial government in 1925, separated the Depressed Classes (comprising 'untouchables' and 'tribals') and the Backward Classes (comprising 'castes other than Depressed Classes') as two distinct categories.

---

technical education and reservations atleast of one seat in the legislative council for a representative of their caste. There were also few other castes who made their representations for inclusion in the list of Backward. See, Saraswathi (1974, pp. 110, 131, fn 84).

[7] Vanniakula Kshatriyas are the numerically largest OBC caste groups in Tamil Nadu that continues to exert caste power over the Dalits. In the 1920s they frequently asserted that they were backward class and not 'non-brahmins' and that they should not to be equated with the depressed classes. They were the first ones to demand proportionate allocation of government jobs based on numerical strength of their caste in the total population, in addition to their demand for backward status which later became an accepted conception of social Justice in Tamil Nadu. See, Saraswathi (1974, p. 116).

[8] At least until 1919 the British government did not extend the backward class category beyond the depressed classes who were considered as 'poor' and under 'special disabilities'.

[9] The Backward Class League was formed in 1933 in Madras Presidency which unified several 'backward' non-Brahmin Hindus other than the 'depressed classes' and other than the few non-brahmin upper castes such as the Vellalars, Reddis, Nairs, and Mudaliars. This league demanded a special reservation by the revision of the communal order of 1922 which provided for distribution of appointments to public services to various caste groups.

[10] From 1917 onwards, The Depressed Classes Association passed resolutions in their conferences to be treated as separate class from the 'backward classes' and to be provided with special privileges in education. See, Radhakrishnan (1990, p. 517); Rajah ((1925) 2005, pp. 33–37).

Addressing Backwardness: Phule, Periyar, Ambedkar

While colonial policies to address backwardness led to proliferation of caste associations demanding greater concessions from the colonial state without a critique of caste system, anti-caste movements led by Jotirao Phule and Babasaheb Ambedkar in Maharashtra, and Periyar E. V. Ramasamy in Tamil Nadu, on the other hand, engaged in a sustained critique of caste and reconceptualized backwardness with the view to emancipate lower castes, women, tribes, and religious minorities who had been denied equality on several grounds.

Phule and Periyar interpreted the backwardness as something assigned to the lower castes by brahminism and by the dominant castes to erase and make invisible the productive contributions of the cultivator-rural-shudra-atishudras. While positively revalorizing and re-centering the economic and socio-moral contributions of the cultivator-labour images of the Shudras, both these reformers identified the problems of backwardness of these communities or lower castes as lack of modern education, hardship of labour with no adequate recognition, or value attached to their contribution, lack of special knowledge of their interests and demands, and the lack of their capacity to turn this into a claim that may be bargained with the government (O'Hanlon, 1985, p. 258; Pandian, 2007, pp. 204, 207). They underscored the relative nature of backwardness which was based on caste identity of the labourers: for instance, Phule's vivid juxtapositions of the hardships of the toiling masses and the selfishness of the Brahmin castes, as also his comparisons between the lives of toil of the shudra women and the comforts enjoyed by the Brahman women (O'Hanlon, 1985, p. 259).

In trying to understand the demeaning and inhuman existence of the low-caste Shudras and their backwardness, Ambedkar underscored the need to recognize how Brahmins by deliberately introducing the legal system of 'pains and penalties', subjugated the Shudras and erased their original identity, absorbing them as low-class Hindus 'without civilization, without culture, without respect and without position' (cited in Rodrigues, 2002, p. 387).

What is to be noted here is that the leaders of the anti-caste movements like Phule or Periyar did not approve certain non-brahmin caste groups' claim to upper caste status and a share in the backward status for their own narrow benefits of education and employment. Phule, for instance, disapproved the claims to Maratha status by the Kunbis and pointed to their folly of keeping to the caste divisions that led to social oppression (O'Hanlon, 1985, pp. 260–262). Similarly, Periyar was concerned that the socially and economically backward Shudras, being co-opted by the Brahminic Hinduism, deployed their caste prowess by claiming Kshatriya status and thus in his view, they perpetuated caste violence on others.[11] Ambedkar too was critical of the Shudra's interest in

---

[11] Periyar's Speech at the Salem Vanniakula Kshatriya Conference reported in *Kudi Arasu*, 1 June 1930.

sustaining the Brahmanic four varna system which led to their social and economic backwardness (Rodrigues, 2002, p. 395).

Another significant aspect of the anti-caste movements was the expansive conceptions of social and economic backwardness to address the problems of the low social status of women, tribes, and certain Muslims. Ambedkar held caste and Hinduism as primarily responsible for the backwardness of the aboriginal tribes and blamed the upper caste hindus for keeping the former as savages without reforming them (Rodrigues, 2002, p. 270). The anti-caste intellectuals recognized the simultaneous and intersecting aspects of caste, gender, class, and religion in social injustice and therefore demanded recognition of these and claimed an inclusive social justice for these different socially and economically backward groups.

OFFICIAL DISCOURSE ON BACKWARDNESS IN INDEPENDENT INDIA

In the 1950s, the fledgling national government recognized that special redistributive measures were required to address caste inequalities in addition to the development programmes meant to redress other forms of inequalities. Jawaharlal Nehru, for instance, moved a resolution in the Constituent Assembly for providing adequate safeguards to the 'minorities, backward and tribal areas and depressed and other backward classes'. Following this, within the Constituent Assembly, the advisory committee on rights of citizens, minorities and tribal and excluded area, of which Ambedkar was part, extended the definition of 'backward class' to include minorities.

The reservation of certain proportion of posts of public services to be prescribed for these 'backward citizens' then became a clause within the Article 16 of the Indian Constitution. These 'backward class of citizens' were more clearly marked as those that are 'socially and educationally backward' in the Article 15(4) of the Constitution. However, the ambiguity that surrounded the interpretation of who the backward classes were and Ambedkar's own explanation that a 'backward community is a community which is backward in the opinion of the state Government' posed challenges for defining the Backward Classes category at the all-India level and also for the lower castes who had organized themselves as a backward class league to demand special privileges. Mainly, the ambivalence of the category OBCs and the unevenness in providing special concessions in education and employment were quite evident in the manner in which two and a half million tribes, left out of the list of Scheduled Tribes were later added to this category. A disparate OBC list was prepared by various state governments, depending upon the state's history of affirmative actions for the backward communities. Christophe Jaffrelot argues that although Ambedkar was clear that caste determined backwardness he was unwilling to come up with definite criteria for defining the category 'backward classes' (unlike in the case of SCs and STs), for he was 'apprehensive that a clear-cut definition of the OBCs would transform them into an all-powerful social coalition involving the bulk of the society' (Jaffrelot, 2008, p. 217).

The result was an unevenness in the redistributive politics of various state governments with states like Madras and Bombay offering various special welfare measures to the OBCs for which the state expenditures in the 1950s went up significantly. In accordance with the constitutional provisions, the Madras state reserved 25 per cent of seats in public services separately for the backward classes including the reservations for the SCs and STs. The intervention of the Supreme Court to strike down the Madras government's Communal Order that provided reservations for backward classes in educational and government employment paved the way for the First Amendment in the Indian Constitution empowering the states to make special provisions for the socially and educationally backward classes.

Undoubtedly, the framing of the Indian constitution provided an important occasion to define the category 'backward classes'. Ambedkar, while introducing the first amendment bill to the Constitution in 1951, was categorical in stating that 'Backward Classes ... are nothing else but a collection of certain castes' (in Thorat and Kumar, 2008, p. 352). Taking cue from this, various national and state commissions for backward classes as well as the Indian constitution linked backwardness to caste, thus recognizing the formidable role of caste in backwardness of several marginalized communities, including some non-Hindus (Galanter, 1991, p. 281). Notwithstanding this, caste as criteria for assessing backwardness had come under severe criticism.

Kaka Kalelkar, who led the First Backward Classes Commission constituted by the government under Article 340 of the Constitution on 29 January 1953, hints at the complexity underlying the concept of backwardness:

> The problem of backwardness is not one of serving a few minorities here and there, but it is a problem of the reconstruction of society itself. It is a changeover from the medieval feudal society to the modern democratic society based on the equal respect for the personality of every individual ... If our recommendation in this regard is accepted, the Government will have to find for this ministry a statesman of the first rank, having the widest sympathy, tact, courage and vision. (Kalelkar Commission, 1955, xxv–xxvi)

In an attempt to open the complexity out in order to eliminate backwardness, the Kalelkar Commission delineated the criteria for backwardness: women, rural peoples, manual workers in unsheltered worksites, landless labourers, unskilled labour, clerical workers, menial servants, unlettered parents, lack of resources, illiterate, lacking in capacity for self-improvement, and religious obscurantism. Social backwardness was based on assessing the low social positions, and educational and economic disadvantages caused by caste-based hierarchies. Importantly, the discussion on backwardness in the Commission report encompassed both social disabilities and regional disparities—notably the entrenchment of backwardness in rural areas in the context of widespread rural dispossession and feudal exploitation, reflected in livelihoods, housing, landownership patterns, access to public goods, especially education—rooted in an extremely inegalitarian social order.

Arguably one of the most nuanced reports on the conditions of backward classes in India, the Kalelkar Commission's recommendations provided for an inclusive and expansive definition of backwardness but was rejected by the parliament. This is because the Commission used the caste criteria to assess backwardness, that is, assessing the social and economic status as an effect of caste-based discrimination. Critics of the report included eminent sociologist M. N. Srinivas, who in his presidential address to the Indian Science Congress (1957) noted that, 'it is time to give serious thought to evolving "neutral" indices of backwardness... The criteria of literacy, landownership and income in cash or gain should be able to subsume all cases of backwardness' (cited in Galanter, 1991, 175, fn 109).

Echoing these sentiments, the first five-year plan document in the chapter on 'Welfare of Backward Classes' noted that, '[t]he term "backward class" is difficult to define. Backwardness is expressed in lack of adequate opportunity for group and individual self-development, especially in economic life and in matters of health, housing, and education. It is measured in terms of low levels of income, the extent of illiteracy, and the low standard of life demonstrated by living conditions' (Planning Commission, 1951, chap. 37, para 2). The states were advised to enumerate only economic backwardness without using caste or community as criteria for providing special privileges (Galanter, 1991, p. 176).

However, the state appointed commissions followed their own tradition of defining backwardness. For example, the Sattanathan Commission (1971), appointed by the Tamil Nadu Government, suggested that the social backwardness should be linked to caste standing, mainly of the low caste Shudras. It also held that poverty was not the sole criteria for defining social backwardness. Working under the constraints of court orders, the commission came up with the concept of 'upper crust' and suggested a revision to the existing reservation for backward classes in Tamil Nadu. It noted with concern that 'the benefit of reservation has gone mostly to the few top castes among the backward and to an increasing layer of upper crust in each caste' (Sattanathan, 2007, p. 188). The Andhra Pradesh and Kerala Backward Classes Commissions too emphasized the caste-based occupation associated stigma, the heritage of purdah and the lack of English education as indicators of backwardness among the low castes to be considered for reservation (Galanter, 1991, pp. 236–237). In contrast, North India and Central India witnessed a strong resistance to affirmative action programmes for the backward classes at least until the arrival of the Backward Class movement which was fostered by the first backward class commission's report (Jaffrelot, 2008, p. 253). From the early 1980s, OBC politics across various states and the recommendations of the Second Backward Classes Commission (Mandal Commission) significantly connected caste with backward class identity.

The Mandal Commission's identification of the backward classes was based primarily on the list of backward classes provided by various state governments which were mostly various low caste groups in addition to the converts to other religion who had their traditional occupations as the Hindu Backward Classes. The commission recommended 27 per cent reservations and financial assistance for the identified backward classes in central government services, autonomous bodies, public sector undertakings including nationalized banks, universities, and colleges and those private undertakings that received financial assistance from the state. As many as 3743 caste groups in India benefitted from this policy of reservation. As historian Susan Bayly has argued, the recognition of backward class for state benefits had led to an increase in caste groups' claims to backwardness:

> India's non-untouchable 'Backward' populations [the 'Other Backwards'] claimed that social and material 'backwardness' was not just an affliction of untouchables and so-called tribals. On the contrary as bearers of titles denoting 'clean' non-proprietary caste origin [it was] argued that these 'communities' too had been collectively demeaned over the centuries by the pretensions of the pure Brahman and the 'lordly' Rajput. They too were educationally and materially deprived; they too should be entitled to state aid to compensate for these historic 'disabilities'. (Bayly, (1999) 2002, p. 288)

In the recent past, well-off caste groups with numerical majority like the Patels and Marathas have pressed for inclusion in the OBC list, under threat of conversion, and leveraging their numerical strength. This led to the introduction by the government of the controversial bill amending Articles 15 and 16 of the Indian Constitution (124th amendment of the Constitution) passed after Presidential assent on 12 January 2019, providing for reservation in public employment and education for 'economically weaker sections' (EWS). Widely known as 'upper caste quota', this amendment brought in a new category of 'economically backward', delinking caste-based social backwardness as the core of reservation policy of the state. As Zoya Hasan observes, 'the definition of backwardness remains contested despite attempts to list groups in schedules invoking a set of normative concepts of social justice, equality, and secularism' (Hasan, 2009, p. 197).

JUDICIAL INTERPRETATION OF BACKWARDNESS

Discussions in court and the cross-talk with sociologists and socio-legal scholars illuminate our understanding of the trajectories of public discourse on the question of backwardness (see Kannabiran, 2012, pp. 163–205). The *Vasanth Kumar* judgement set out the guidelines for states to frame reservation policy.[12] One of the four concerns

---

[12] Justice Y. V. Chandrachud in his opening statement makes this clear: 'We were invited by the counsel not so much as to deliver judgements but to express our opinion on the issue of reservations; which may serve as a guideline to the Commission which the Government of Karnataka proposes to

stated by Justice Y. V. Chandrachud, relevant to this discussion was that for backward classes to come within the purview of reservation, their situation must be comparable to the scheduled castes and scheduled tribes *and* they should satisfy the means test.[13]

Justice D. A. Desai even while recognizing that India was a 'stratified and hierarchical society' described the claim to reservation as a movement downwards '(Anulom)' by those who set out to move upwards '(Pratilom)'. What preoccupied him however was the contradiction between sociological and jurisprudential methods of interpretation. In order to resolve this, he invoked the debate between IP Desai (1984), Ghanshyam Shah (1985), and Upendra Baxi (1985) on the subject that took place in the early 1980s. Because of its significance to the interpretation of backwardness by courts, it is useful to recall the salient points of this triangular debate. IP Desai argues that the identification of socially and educationally backward classes must take note of the following:

> (1) The unit must be completely secular, (2) It must be in consonance with the new society that has emerged and is developing, (3) The new society is based on recognition of the individual as a citizen, and his rights and obligations are defined by secular political authority. (4) The class to which an individual belongs can be identified by the activity he engages in for earning livelihood, and the social relations in which he enters in the course of his activity are governed by contract into which he enters of his free-will and which can also be annulled by the will of either party. (5) The backwardness of the class is to be judged by the existence or non-existence of various impediments in exercising the choice in selecting the activity for earning the livelihood and in entering into the contract. The impediments collectively characterize the backwardness of class. (Desai, 1984, p. 1113)

Since the Constitution, in Parts III and IV, envisages the abolition of caste, not its legitimization, Desai argued,

> [I]t needs to be stressed that the directive principles of the Constitution of India envisages a society in which there will be no discrimination on the basis of religion and caste. The Constitution (Parts III and IV) . . . definitely enshrines the element of egalitarianism in it unlike any other state of political authority in the past in India...If those unfavourably placed in respect [of economic and political power] are supported with a view to enabling them to compete with those favourably placed . . . it is in consonance with the principle and spirit of the Constitution. (Desai, 1984, p. 1110)

---

appoint, for examining the question of affording better employment, and educational opportunities to Scheduled Castes, Scheduled Tribes, and other Backward Classes. A somewhat unusual exercise is being undertaken by the Court in giving expression to its views without reference to specific facts. But, institutions profit by well-meaning innovations. The facts will appear before the Commission and it will evolve suitable tests in the matter of reservations.' *K. C. Vasanth Kumar and Another vs State of Karnataka*, 1985 AIR (SC) 1495.

[13] *K. C. Vasanth Kumar and Another vs State of Karnataka*, 1985 AIR (SC) 1495.

Desai's framing of the question of caste within constitutionalism, as Baxi observed, was rare among sociologists (Baxi, 1985, p. 426). Extending Desai's articulation, Baxi points out that in recognition of the subjective and objective bases of antagonistic class interests, Desai's suggestion of 'a secular criterion for the identification of backwardness' positions the Constitution 'as the means or the agenda for the transformation of the class in itself into the class for itself' (Kannabiran, 2012, p. 204). The problem of the class/caste contradiction remained unresolved theoretically. While it is true, as Baxi argues, that 'class' and not 'caste' found place in Article 15(4) (Baxi, 1985, p. 427), the fact that the principle of reservation in the constitution is based on caste as the unit and on the recognition of the fact that caste is a source of discrimination, it can perhaps be argued that class in this instance is co-terminus with caste in a secular, that is non-religious sense. Also, if class is 'a division based on status, rank or caste' as Justice Venkataramaiah points out in *Vasanth Kumar*, the reading of backward classes as castes for the purpose of reservation can scarcely be faulted, since there is widespread agreement among jurists, sociologists, and vedic scholars [the third scholastic category invoked in this judgement] that caste is about status and rank or hierarchy. This is the point Justice Chinnappa Reddy makes as well:

> Despite individual exceptions, it may be possible and easy to identify socially backwardness with reference to caste, with reference to residence, with reference to occupation or some other dominant feature... If they reflect poverty which is the primary source of social and educational backwardness, they must be recognised for what they are along with other less primary sources.[14]

Justice Chinnappa Reddy echoes IP Desai's concern on the diversity of caste locations across a state or the country creating a problem for identification of rights bearers from among the backward classes, and recognizes that courts are ill-equipped to embark on this exercise:

> The question really is how to identify these backward classes to entitle them to entry through the doors of Arts. 15(4) and 16(4). And, the further question, naturally, is about the limits of reservation... We are afraid the courts are not necessarily the most competent to identify the backward classes or to lay down guidelines for their identification except in broad and very general way. We are not equipped for that; we have no legal barometers to measure social backwardness... A test to identify backward classes which may appear appropriate when applied to one group of people may be wholly inappropriate and unreasonable if applied to another group

---

[14] *K. C. Vasanth Kumar and Another vs. State of Karnataka*, 1985 AIR (SC) 1495. When the Constitution (First Amendment) Bill was introduced to include Article 15(4), Dr Ambedkar referred to Article 16(4) and said that backward classes are 'nothing else but a collection of certain castes' (Parliamentary Debates 1951, Third Session, Part II Vol. XII at p. 9007 cited in *Vasanth Kumar*).

of people. There can be no universal test; there can be no exclusive test; there can be no conclusive test.[15]

The discussion by the early 1990s shifted from the need to eliminate discrimination based on caste to identifying who the legitimate claimants for reservation are, apart from the scheduled castes and scheduled tribes. Did class in its plain sense mean caste? How was the identification of backward classes to be carried out?

> [C]aste neither can be the sole criterion nor can it be equated with 'class' for the purpose of Article 16(4) for ascertaining the social and educational backwardness of any section or group of people so as to bring them within the wider connotation of 'backward class'. Nevertheless 'caste' in Hindu society becomes a dominant factor or primary criterion in determining the backwardness of a class of citizens.[16]

In the definitions of 'class' and 'caste' that were cited from various lexical and anthropological sources by the court however, caste and class co-constituted each other. To cite Justice Pandian in the *Indra Sawhney vs Union of India*, '[a] group of persons having common traits or attributes coupled with *retarded* social, material (economic) and *intellectual (educational)* development in the sense *not having so much of intellect and ability* will fall within the ambit of 'any backward class of citizens' under Article 16(4) of the Constitution'.[17]

In the context of reservation, therefore, this definitional overlap between caste and class described the condition of 'backwardness':

> Unless 'caste' satisfies the primary test of social backwardness as well as the educational and economic backwardness which are the established accepted criteria to identify the 'backward class', a class per se without satisfying the agreed formulae generally cannot fall within the meaning of 'backward class of citizens' under Article 16(4), save in given exceptional circumstances such as the caste itself being identifiable with the traditional occupation of the lower strata—indicating the social backwardness.[18]

In the final analysis, the courts settled uneasily on the view that a caste, when it satisfies the test of backwardness may be denoted as a backward class. This could be either through the demonstration of social, educational, and economic backwardness, or through the performance of traditional occupations by the lower strata in the caste order.

---

[15] *K. C. Vasanth Kumar and Another vs State of Karnataka*, 1985 AIR (SC) 1495.
[16] Justice Pandian in *Indra Sawhney vs Union of India*.
[17] Ibid., para 58.
[18] Ibid., para 82.

Gender and Backwardness

The recognition of caste and gender as intersecting regimes that produced backwardness of women and gender inequality led feminists in India to demand gender justice through special privileges for women in education, employment, and nomination to public bodies. As early as 1929, Muthulakshmi Reddi, an eminent activist from Madras, while representing women's interest in accessing education and employment at the Indian Statutory Commission and demanding special incentives and professional training, held illiteracy and caste control over women through early marriage, and purdah system as reasons for their backwardness.[19]

The Kaka Kalelkar Commission report, which stated that *all women as a class should be treated as backward*, in fact highlighted the gender dimensions of backwardness. The Mandal Commission (1980) took this further in its delineation of eleven indicators of backwardness, in which two out of four social indicators pointed to women's status—percentage of women married as minors and female work participation.

The National Commission for Religious and Linguistics Minorities, also known as Ranganath Mishra Commission (2007), according to Lata PM (2018), adopted the most forward-looking approach to the gendered inflections of backwardness: that India lags behind in the matter of women's status because of 'disparities on the level of caste, religion, class, linguistic, sects, tribes, ethnicity etc.'; that although there has been some relief from complete subordination, 'the promise of equality and dignity remains an unfinished agenda', the gender gap in educational attainment is significant, and 'tremendously high MMR [Maternal Mortality Rate] and higher female infant and child mortality persists in most parts of the country. Millions of girls and women are missing between each census;' that status of women is dependent on the developmental status of the areas they come from and the socio-economic strata they belong to; that marked son-preference ('apartheid of gender') gravely truncates women's life choices and well-being in several arenas; that organized religion plays a major role in the subjugation of women; and that there are intra-religious disparities in status that must be taken into account in a discussion on backwardness and disentitlement (cited in Lata, 2018, chap. 3).

In their national survey of the status of Muslim women in India, Zoya Hasan and Ritu Menon draw attention to the fact that disadvantage—backwardness—is compounded by Muslim women's minority status, and underscore the fact that class, gender, community, and state intersect and produce mutually reinforcing forms of deprivation and disadvantage (Hasan and Menon, 2005, p. 241).[20]

---

[19] See, Muthulakshmi Reddi's Notes of Dissent at the Indian Statutory Commission (Hartog Committee) in the *Report of the Review of the Growth of Education in British India* (Delhi: Government of India Press, 1929), pp. 378–375.

[20] The All-India Muslim Women's Survey was the first national survey of its kind and covered 9541 women, 80 per cent of them Muslim, 60 per cent urban, spread over 40 districts in 12 states, and focused on 10 parameters: socio-economic status, education, work, marriage, mobility, decision-making,

Minorities, Caste, Backwardness

The discussion on minorities in the Constituent Assembly was not limited to religious minorities, but encompassed racial, religious, and caste minorities across which there were common axes of disentitlement and 'backwardness' (see Kannabiran, 2012, pp. 272–303). Within the minority Sikhs, for instance, sects like Mazhabis, Ramdasias, and Kabirpanthis were on par with the Scheduled Castes—and required commensurate protections (Rao, 1968, pp. 770–772). The discussions on these intersections in the process of constitution-making are immediately relevant to discussions on whether religious minorities come within the meaning of backward classes—especially given the complex interweaving of class and caste in the entire debate on identification. That the Constituent Assembly did not mark borders between minorities of different kinds, even while it acknowledged the specificities is important. Are there castes among Muslims? And from this question, we approach the next one, namely, are there backward castes/classes among Muslims?

The 1911 census showed that out of 12 million followers of Islam in Punjab, 10 million reported caste names like Rajput, Jat, Arain, Gujar, Muchi, Tarkhan, and Teli, while only 2 million were of 'foreign origin' like Ashraf, Pathan, Baluch, etc. (Krishnan, 2007, p. 50). A study of Muslims in Bihar points to the fact that while status ascriptions among Muslims do not intersect with the Hindu caste order, there is a long history of parallel realities of caste among them (Ahmed, 2003; Alam, 2003). There are approximately 170 backward Muslim communities in India—with ajlaf [commoner] communities stratified by caste (Mondal, 2003, p. 4893). The Sachar Committee in its 2006 report on the Status of Muslims in India adopted the three-fold categorization of Muslim castes into Ashraf, Ajlaf, and Arzal (Sachar Committee, 2006). The P.S. Krishnan Committee on *Identification of Socially and Educationally Backward Classes in the Muslim Community of Andhra Pradesh and Recommendations* constituted by the Government of Andhra Pradesh applies indices of backwardness to different classes of Muslims. Arzal consists of castes analogous to the 'untouchable castes' among Hindus whose primary occupation is civic sanitation (Krishnan, 2007, pp. 62–63).

While conversion to Christianity is well documented, in the case of Islam there are few accounts. The Manual of the Kistna District 1883 records how the outcastes' conversion to Islam enabled them to access village commons. The accounts from Bengal spoke of conversions to Islam from Namasudras and Rajbansis among the Scheduled Castes and 'the poor aborigines of eastern and deltaic Bengal . . . fishermen, hunters, pirates and peasants . . . the impure or unclean out-castes, popularly called the untouchables, spurned and neglected by the caste-proud Brahmanical Hindu-Society [who] adopted Islam to escape from social injustice or secure social status' (Krishnan, 2007, p. 33).

violence, access to social welfare and media, and political participation. See also Zoya Hasan and Ritu Menon (2005).

These conversions were sometimes triggered by violence against Dalit communities, like in the Meenakshipuram conversions in 1981, which spread to the neighbouring districts and saw a total of 1713 conversions of Dalits to Islam (Krishnan, 2007, p. 20).

While it is far from settled whether Muslims as a whole constitute a backward class, official positions (starting with the Kalelkar Commission) acknowledge stratification and recommend identifying backward sections for special treatment, including all untouchable communities, and all occupational groups that are known by their occupational name and whose Hindu counterparts have been identified as backward.[21]

The question of 'backwardness' then lies at the core of the lived experience of religious minorities in India—both because of an inbuilt stratification system based on status ascription within the religious community, and because conversions saw the movement of the most oppressed and deprived castes from Hindu caste orders to other religions, carrying the material markers of backwardness with them even while they asserted dignity and self-respect through the act of conversion. Yet, the reluctance to recognize social backwardness among sections of Muslims and Christians, comparable to the extreme social disabilities and discrimination suffered by 'Hindu' Dalits results in the proliferation of new forms of discrimination against minorities.

As Hasan observes pertinently,

> as long as the religion bar remains in place, [the SC] category would only include Dalits of religions considered indigenous and exclude others regardless of their social disabilities and status ... The framework of justice must ensure that similarly placed groups are treated equally and evenly without religion being brought into play to deny some equal treatment under the law. (Hasan, 2009, p. 223)

Conclusion

Affirmative action policies carried out by both the colonial and postcolonial state to redress backwardness, as we have seen, offered a new recognition and a social status for the 'backward classes' and opened different possibilities in negotiating caste and backwardness. As we have noted, state recognition of 'backward classes' as eligible for reservation in the government sector and in state representative bodies have led to an expansive mobilization of several caste groups under this category (as Ambedkar anticipated) to claim backward class status. This process has led to a convergence of caste and class interests of the lower castes whose numerical strength as a backward class is the concern for the elected governments. Against this background backwardness continues to be a contested category.

---

[21] For example, Dhobi, Teli, Dheemar, Nai, Gujar, Kumhar, Lohar, Darji, Badhai, etc., as in Mandal Commission Report. See Krishnan (2007, p. 212).

References

Ahmed, Irfan. 2003, 15 November. 'A Different Jihad: Dalit Muslims' Challenge to Ashraf Hegemony'. *Economic and Political Weekly*, 38(46): 4886–4891.

Alam, Anwar. 2003, 15 November. 'Democratisation of Indian Muslims: Some Reflections'. *Economic and Political Weekly*, 38(46): 4881–4885.

Baxi, Upendra. 1985, 9 March. 'Caste, Class and Reservations: In Memoriam: I. P. Desai'. *Economic and Political Weekly*, 20(10): 426–428.

Bayly, Susan. (1999) 2002. *Caste, Society and Politics in India: From the Eighteenth Century to the Modern Age*. Cambridge: Cambridge University Press.

Desai, I. P. 1984, 14 July. 'Should "Caste" Be the Basis for Recognising Backwardness?' *Economic and Political Weekly*, 19(28): 1106–1116.

Dirks, Nicholas B. 2001. *Castes of Mind: Colonialism and the Making of Modern India*. Princeton and Oxford: Princeton University Press.

Galanter, Marc. 1991. *Competing Equalities: Law and the Backward Classes in India*. Delhi: Oxford University Press.

Hacker, Isaac Henry, London Missionary Society. 1908. *A Hundred Years in Travancore, 1806–1906: A History and Description of the Work Done by the London Missionary Society in Travancore, South India during the Past Century*. London: H.R. Allenson.

Hasan, Zoya. 2009. *Politics of Inclusion: Castes, Minorities, and Affirmative Action*. New Delhi: Oxford University Press.

Hasan, Zoya, and Ritu Menon. 2004. *Unequal Citizens: A Study of Muslim Women in India*. New Delhi: Oxford University Press.

Indian Statutory Commission. 1929. September. *Interim Report of the Indian Statutory Commission: Review of Growth of Education in British India* by the Auxiliary Committee appointed by the Commission. Calcutta: Government of India. (Hartog Committee).

Jaffrelot, Christophe. 2008. *India's Silent Revolution: The Rise of the Low Castes in North Indian Politics*. Delhi: Permanent Black.

Kannabiran, Kalpana. 2012. *Tools of Justice: Non-Discrimination and the Indian Constitution*. New Delhi: Routledge.

Lata, Pratibha Madhukar. 2018. 'OBC Political Formations in Maharashtra: A Bahujan Feminist Perspective of Politics of Inclusion and Bahujan Sangharsh Samiti'. Unpublished PhD Thesis, Hyderabad: Council for Social Development and Tata Institute of Social Sciences.

Mondal, Seik Rahim. 2003, 15 November. 'Social Structure, OBCs and Muslims'. *Economic and Political Weekly*, 38(46): 4892–4897.

O'Hanlon, Rosalind. 1985. *Caste, Conflict and Ideology: Mahatma Jotirao Phule and Low Caste Protest in Nineteenth-Century Western India*. London and Bombay: Cambridge University Press and Orient Longman.

Pandian, M. S. S. 2007. *Brahmin and Non-Brahmin: Genealogies of the Tamil Political Present*. Delhi: Permanent Black.

Phillips, G. E. Rev. 1912. *The Outcastes' Hope or Work among the Depressed Classes in India*. London: Church Missionary Society.

Planning Commission. 1951. Chapter 37: 'Welfare of Backward Classes', *First Five-Year Plan*. Delhi: Government of India. https://niti.gov.in/planningcommission.gov.in/docs/plans/planrel/fiveyr/welcome.html Accessed on 27 October 2021.

Radhakrishnan, P. 1990, 10 March. 'Backward Classes in Tamil Nadu, 1872–1988'. *Economic and Political Weekly*, 25(10): 509–517.

Rajah, M. C. (1925) 2005. *The Oppressed Hindus*. New Delhi: Critical Quest.
Rao, B. Shiva. 1968. *Framing of India's Constitution: A Study*. New Delhi: Indian Institute of Public Administration.
Report of the Backward Classes Commission. New Delhi: Government of India, 1980 ('Mandal Commission').
Report of the First Backward Classes Commission. New Delhi: Government of India, 1955 ('Kalelkar Commission').
Report of the Indian Education Commission (Hunter Commission). Calcutta: Government of India, 1883.
Report of the National Commission for Religious Minorities. New Delhi: Government of India. 2007. ('Ranganath Mishra Commission').
Report on Identification of Socially and Educationally Backward Classes in the Muslim Community of Andhra Pradesh and Recommendations, Hyderabad: Government of Andhra Pradesh, 2007 ('Krishnan').
Rodrigues, Valerian (Ed.). 2002. *The Essential Writings of B.R. Ambedkar*. New Delhi: Oxford University Press.
Saraswathi, S. 1974. *Minorities in Madras State: Group Interests in Modern Politics*. Delhi: Impex India.
Sattanathan, A. N. 2007. *Plain Speaking: A Sudra's Story*. Delhi: Permanent Black.
Shah, Ghanshyam. 1985, 19 January. 'Caste, Class and Reservation'. *Economic and Political Weekly*, 20(3): 132–136.
Social, Economic and Educational Status of the Muslim Community of India: A Report. New Delhi: Government of India, Prime Minister's High-Level Committee, 2006 ('Sachar Committee').
Thorat, Sukhadeo, and Narender Kumar (Eds.). 2008. *B.R. Ambedkar: Perspectives on Social Exclusion and Inclusive Policies*. New Delhi: Oxford University Press.

Cases Cited

Indra Sawhney vs Union of India, 1993 AIR (SC) 477.
K. C. Vasanth Kumar and Another vs State of Karnataka, 1985 AIR (SC) 1495.
State of Madras vs Champakam Dorairajan, AIR 1951 SC 226.
Venkataramana vs State of Madras AIR 1951 SC 229.

Abbreviations

AIR: ALL INDIA REPORTER
SC: SUPREME COURT

SECTION III

CASTE AND THE RELIGIOUS REALM

Editors' Introduction

THE popular view of caste has tended to see it as an aspect of Hindu religious belief. Given that it is often equated with *varna*, which finds reference in ancient Hindus scriptures, its identification with Hinduism is taken for granted. How has this relationship evolved over time among sects and sections of the Hindus? What are its dynamics in the modern times? How do we make sense of its practice among the non-Hindus? Chapters in this section deal with all these questions.

In the opening chapter, Mathieu Claveyrolas foregrounds the point that 'Hinduism' and 'caste' are 'both paradigmatic examples of one major paradox haunting social sciences concerned with ... India's social and cultural realities', which is that 'neither of these words ... can be translated accurately into an Indian language'. Underlying such a statement is the obvious recognition of how the western academy and colonial powers have shaped what we see as the obvious core of India. However, the two categories are no longer alien to India or the Indians. They have come to acquire vernacular lives as Claveyrolas shows through his extensive overview of empirical and historical researches on the subject. Meanings and practices of Hinduism and caste continue to vary, across regions of the subcontinent as well as across different caste groups. Such an empirical approach enables him to see the adaptive and enduring nature of caste and, more importantly, its irreducibility to a textual view of Hindu religion. Even though the two tend to be 'consubstantial' as caste draws its ideological matrix from Hinduism, caste still has a life of its own, both 'beyond the limits of Hinduism ... and beyond the limits of religious matters'.

Continuing in a similar mode, Raphaël Voix in his chapter provides an overview of how notions and practices of caste vary across the diversity of Hindu sects. He thus questions the singular view of Hinduism. On ground, not only has the Hindu religiosity been theologically plural but it has also been marked by sociological diversity and has been often contested, from within and from outside. There are sects within Hinduism who have theologically rejected the ideas of hierarchy and varna. Institutionally, they tend to revolve around a charismatic Guru, thereby displacing the pre-eminence of the Brahmin. These differences also have relational implications. 'Sects provide lower castes a psychological and social space where they can defy the pre-eminence of the Brahmins by becoming teachers/masters of religious knowledge and they therefore represent a means of upward social mobility.' However, there are limits. While sects tend to be inclusive, they rarely offer a radical critique of the social order of caste. The alternative values they promote 'mainly relate to the external world', mostly confined to the value of equality in terms of 'equal access to the divine', which does 'not discard hierarchy *per se*'. In some cases, sects get accommodated over time into the social order of Hindu society as a caste group with reworked status; the rise of dissenting sects often coinciding with a kind of Sanskritization of an upwardly mobile section of the 'lower' castes. Viewing it from a longer-term political and sociological perspectives, the sects have also helped in the process of expanding the boundaries of Hinduism, vertically, with growing numbers of those located lower down in the hierarchy identifying with it, religiously and politically.

In the following chapter, George Kunnath takes this discussion forward by focusing on the concept of Sanskritization. The concept emerged during the 1950s, out of field-based studies of the Indian society. These field-based studies of the Hindu and Indian social life claimed to provide a counter view to the colonial and orientalist 'book-view'. M. N. Srinivas, who popularized the term argued that contrary to the then dominant view, caste had always been in a 'dynamic flux'. Sanskritization was one of the mediums through which those occupying lower ranks in the social hierarchy could move upward by 'emulating the beliefs and practices of upper castes, particularly those of the Brahmins'. However, as Kunnath shows in his chapter, its critics questioned the underlying assumptions of such a claim, which represented lower castes as eager imitators of the socio-religious practices of the upper castes, and thereby 'negating their agency and consciousness'. Brahmanical view of hierarchy has never been as hegemonic as the categories like Sanskritization tend to suggest. Its operation in the present time also has political implications, of producing a political Hinduism, vertically united, and socially harmonious.

Joel Lee takes the discussion on caste and Hinduism further in his chapter. He explores this historically, by looking at the 19th century reformers, who invented the idea of Hindu nationalism. At the beginning of the 20th century, Hindutva (a neologism with Sanskrit etymology referring to the idea of hindu-ness), 'crystallized as an ideology and its advocates developed enduring institutions'. The idea of Hindu nationalism required a reimagination of caste and the exclusions that its practice implied. The building of a political community required turning the vertical divisions into horizontal differences so as to make Hinduism comparable with Semitic religions, such as Christianity and Islam. Such a process was to also help in its numerical consolidation, required for the emerging politics during the colonial period. Their biggest challenge for them was 'attracting and incorporating communities previously held in contempt by Hindus into the Hindu fold, while simultaneously alienating these same communities from their Muslim neighbours, with whom they often shared cultural traditions more extensively than with Hindus'. Led almost entirely by the upper castes, the newly emergent Hindu organization popularized a range of myths that attributed the lowly status of untouchables to the Muslim rulers of India. Given that caste was recognized by the British rulers as a Hindu institution, their official inclusion into Hinduism did not create much problem. This remained the norm even after Independence and influenced the framing of public policies such as reservations. Lee also argues that while the success of Hindutva in consolidating a political community seems evident, it should not be taken for granted. Caste divisions continue to mark the ground realities of the Indian social life, often giving rise to inter-caste conflict, sometimes even leading to brutal violence.

Caste also exists among the non-Hindu religious groups in the subcontinent. The Muslims, the Christians, and the Sikhs all practice caste. This is often attributed to their Hindu ancestry. Focussing on 'Caste among the Muslim Communities of India and Pakistan' Julien Levesque in the following chapter questions such an assumption and shows how the real story is far more complex.

The colonial and orientalist theories on the religious life of the Hindus and Muslims saw them as being fundamentally different in terms of their social organization, presence, and absence of caste being a core aspect of this difference. By implication, rarely did they comment on caste among the Muslims. Much of the existing historical scholarship on the region also goes along with such a framework. It was only during the 1950s and 1960s, when the social anthropologists and sociologists started undertaking field-studies of rural social life across regions of the subcontinent that they began to report the presence of caste among the Muslim communities. Their initial explanation of castes among the Muslim communities was in terms of their acculturation, the influence of the local practices on their life, while asserting that Islam *per se* was an egalitarian religion and free of caste. However, the writings of Sylvia Vatuk and Talal Asad helped the academic narratives on the question of caste among the Muslim communities of South Asia move forward, abandoning the orientalist presumptions.

The evolving literature on the religious realm of caste helps us transcend the simplistic and static view of the subject. Religious realm of caste continues to be very critical, but in ways very different from its classical orientalist constructs.

CHAPTER 14

HINDUISM AND CASTE SYSTEM

MATHIEU CLAVEYROLAS

ARE HINDUISM AND CASTE CONSUBSTANTIAL?

'Hinduism' and 'caste' are both paradigmatic examples of one major paradox haunting social sciences concerned with the Indian field. However, crucial to our understanding of India's social and cultural realities, neither of these words—that we can fairly supposed to be among the most widely used through academic literature—can be translated accurately into an Indian language. What is at stake, then, is both defining precisely what we mean when using 'Hinduism' and 'caste', and how these two notions are connected to one-another. Is the caste system Hindu? Is Hinduism necessary for the caste system to exist? Is Hinduism chiefly dependent upon this one-and-only organization (Srivivas, 1956, p. 495)? And would Hinduism inevitably disappear 'if and when caste disappears' as Srinivas also argued (Srivivas, 1956)? Is there such thing as a casteless Hinduism? In other words: to what extent are Hinduism and caste consubstantial?

Behind the misleading conceptions of Hinduism as a homogeneous category, a 'religion' shared by some 80 per cent of the Indian population, one must keep in mind the variety of Hindu practices and representations. Together with other criteria such as sectarian or regional traditions, caste affiliations are crucial to the structural diversity within Hinduism. The need to bring together such heterogeneity under a unique term and category has only grown relatively recently, boosted by colonization, and independence/nationalist fights (Sontheimer and Kulke, 1989; Lorenzen, 1999), without radically undermining neither the diversity between castes, nor the utmost importance of the caste system in Indian social structures, daily life, and religious practices.

Caste, Hinduism, and Society

Most studies of Hindu castes rightfully start with the distinction between *varnas* and *jatis*. On the one hand, castes as *varnas* divide society into four orders: the Brahmins (religious specialists), the Kshatriyas (rulers and warriors), the Vaishyas (farmers and merchants), and the Shudras (servants). Such a conception of caste as *varna* is inherited from Brahminical ideology. On the other hand, castes as *jatis* divide society into thousands of inherited, endogamous social groups—a conception close to the naturalist notion of species.

Castes as *varnas* illustrate the intrinsically socio-religious dimension of Hinduism. Not only does the ability to perform certain rituals and to be initiated depend on one's *varna*, but such religious hierarchy matches a social role embedded in a truly organicist vision of society. The founding myth of *varnas* has them originate from the dismembering of the primordial being (*Purusha*)—Rig Veda hymn X/90: Brahmins are the mouth, Kshatriyas the arms, Vaishyas the thighs, and Shudras the feet.

Together with such social structuring supported by the caste system, another dimension of *varnas* stands for a Hindu model of the interaction between individual life and society. Best formalized in the *Bhagavad Gita* teaching of Krishna to Arjuna, the Hindu ideology demands individuals to support the cosmic order through sticking to their own, individual *dharma*, varying according to *varnas*. Kshatriyas should eat meat and make war whereas Brahmins should be non-violent vegetarians dedicated to the ritual maintenance of the cosmic order. In sharp contrast with any universal morality, the *varna* system founds Hinduism as a structuring model commanding each individual his distinct place and duty within cosmos and society.

Such holism might allow to argue in favour of a supposedly non-segregationist Hindu society, where each *varna* is necessary and complements the others, just as a human body needs all its members. In this perspective, stressing how Hinduism inevitably goes with casteism is often assimilated to a disguised strategy to divide the so-called Hindu community, to weaken its solidarity reflexes in communalist contexts. But the 'naive' apprehension of castes as harmoniously complementary is obviously missing the hierarchy guiding the system—and the shared representations considering the head (Brahmins) as the noblest part of the body and the feet (Shudras) as highly impure.

Relative Purity or the Caste System as Founded on Hindu Ritual Ideology

Indeed, if *varnas* are structured by their relative access to sacrifice, the hierarchy also relates to the Hindu notions of ritual purity and pollution: a Shudra is not pure enough to go through the *upanayanam* (sacred thread) initiation ceremony and become a twice-born *dvija* (a category reserved to the three upper *varnas*). But the relative purity structuring the Hindu caste system is best exemplified by everyday life as governed by the subtle hierarchy of *jatis*. Not only is each individual born within a specific *jati*, not only does he marry and die within it, but *jati* comes to govern his daily interactions. The ancient regulation of the necessary distance (number of steps—Herrenschmidt, 1978) to be respected between a Brahmin and a low-caste individual has been replaced by prohibition of physical contact, commensality, and exogamy. Consequently, the higher one stands in the caste hierarchy, the higher is the risk of pollution, and the subsequent precautions and taboos.

Castes as *jatis* are a relational system. The intrinsic quality (*guna*) of each *jati* is a highly transferable one, primarily through cooking (and serving) food, water, and body fluids (semen, saliva, sweat, faeces). Thus centered on purity, the *jati* identity is also linked to professional activities which, though not necessarily respected today, still retain their value as purity markers: *jatis* whose traditional occupation was dealing with leather (tanner *jati*) or hair (barber *jati*) still suffer from the polluting stigma. Focusing on individual relations and quality transfers, Hindu sacrifice has been studied through a transactional approach of castes. The payment to the ritual specialist (*dakshina*—Malamoud, 1976) can be apprehended as a transfer of inauspiciousness from the patron individual (who benefits from the ritual and pays for it) to the ritual specialist, who needs constant precautions and purification (Parry, 1986; Raheja, 1988).

Accordingly, one must not be misled by the Brahminical understanding of caste as *varna* that puts the Brahmin's archetypical occupation as ritual specialists on top of the social hierarchy. Brahmins are far from being a uniform *varna*-community, and the main criterion ruling hierarchy among them is precisely the public ritual service. For a Brahmin, working in a public temple indeed means enjoying the closest access to the divine, but it also means officiating for clients of various statuses, resulting in lower prestige than other Brahmins without ritual duties (Fuller, 1984). And when in charge of highly impure ritual activities, the Brahmin specialist can even be 'treated like an Untouchable' such as with funeral priests officiating in Banaras (Parry, 1994, p. 3).

Such relational dimension of the caste system goes hand in hand with a certain flexibility, depending on individual, or collective strategies. The system's flexibility builds on a long history of *jati* merging or dividing dynamics accompanied by adjustments at the level of the ritual traditions each new *jati* chooses to follow. Again, the key-issues are relational: more than 'what can I eat?', the question raised is 'who can I eat with?', and 'who cooks what I eat?' While most daily prohibitions are unescapable in public, many are relieved in private settings—a point that counts for the global easing of caste rules in urban contexts. Moreover, even the most polluting activities can be justified for the sake of the whole system. According to this *apad-dharma*, the caste-bound rule one has to follow in times of crises, even the Brahmin individual is allowed (even asked) to eat dog flesh in case of extreme starvation in order to avoid the greatest of loss: the death of Brahmins and the subsequent impossibility to perpetuate the holist caste-system. Other solutions to failure to respect caste prohibitions are rooted in the Hindu logics of ritual purification. Specific rituals (*dana*-gift, purifying bath, head shave, or *mantra japa*-recitation, for instance) and engaging in pilgrimage (*tirthayatra*) are expiation rites (*prayacita*) allowing correction of most caste-wise issues.

Castes in Hindu Temples and Villages

Ritual practices link castes with Hinduism through the complex relational ideology of purity. The *varna* logics misleadingly posits that Brahmins have the monopoly of priestly functions—notwithstanding the many lower caste ritual specialists officiating all over India's Hindu homes, shrines, and ceremonies. As a matter of fact, Hindu ritual traditions widely differ according to castes, and Hindu mythology and pantheon are pervaded by caste considerations (Bouillier and Toffin, 1993). A kind of ritual labour division links Hindu deities and castes: a Brahmin individual can be made to turn towards a low-caste ritual specialist, for instance when facing a danger identified with a spirit only an exorcist is able to deal with. If ritual activities are distinct between higher and lower castes, they can also be complementary, when Dalits are traditionally required to beat the drums during funeral processions, for instance. But then again, the complementarity reading is contested by those who live it as segregation and choose to protest through renouncing their traditional caste ritual attributions (Clark-Décès, 2008).

Within Hindu temples, the social hierarchy along criteria of contact, distance, and ingestion governs both the spatial organization and the ritual pre-eminence rules. Besides the ban for Untouchables to enter high-caste premises, Hindu temples replicate the caste hierarchy and pollution rules through concentric circles (from *garbhagriha* to *mandapa* and surrounding spaces) restricting the approach of the divine according to castes. Enjoying the *prasad* (gods' leftovers of the offerings) can also be reserved to higher castes, or handed out in a specific order.

Beyond temples, Hindu castes and religious practices are jointly rooted in the village territory. The spatial organization according to castes in village India is still widely ordered by the local religious topography. Most village Hindu temples follow caste lines (or groups of assimilated castes): they are situated in a caste-specific neighbourhood, whose caste members generally provide for the devotees, the local priest, and the foremost patrons (Reiniche, 1979; Trouillet, 2008). But the village caste system should also be studied through the relational network linking each individual god, temple, and community with those of other (caste-specific) neighbourhoods. Religious circulations such as processions typically reinstate socio-spatial dynamics, sacralizing caste neigbourhoods as divine jurisdictions—*kshetra* (Berti and Tarabout, 2009). The various village rituals express the sociological unity of the village, and ritual changes typically accompany new adjustments in the village inter-caste relations (Herrenschmidt, 2016).

True enough, with economic changes since several decades and Brahmins widely leaving the villages, some Shudras have become locally dominant castes. But one should not conclude that Hindu ritual hierarchy has totally disappeared. The influence of Hindu ideology in daily caste matters is still pervasive in the village spatial segregation of former Untouchables ('those who cannot be *touched*') neighbourhoods. Most other enduring prohibitions (the right to use the village cremation ground, or the village well), and the most common humiliating punishments for lower caste individuals who fail to comply (having someone wear his shoes on his head) reinstate ritual criteria (Herrenschmidt, 2014).

How Caste Issues Interact with the Definition of Hinduism

As a historically contingent category, Hinduism has been constantly redefined according to its relations with castes, moving from a synonym of Brahminism (when the orientalist perspective excludes lower caste practices, and representations from the realm of 'Hinduism') to an inclusive continuum of heterogeneous traditions.

Strictly speaking, besides being segregated as polluting individuals, Dalits are deprived of castes as *varnas* (they are *a-varna*), a conception which has long kept them outside Hinduism. Still today, Dalit activists regularly use the phrase 'caste Hindus' to refer to those with varnas (*sa-varna*). The 'world of caste' also builds on the opposition with non-Hindu tribal groups, a dichotomy again reified by British administrators and their Brahmin sources (Bayly, 1999). But the political stakes behind the definition of the frontiers of Hinduism have also contributed to strategically *include* groups formerly considered to be non-Hindus. During the 19th-century mobilization for Independence, the need for a unifying category against the British, and the positioning against other religions for census and electoral purposes, gradually led to the inclusion of lower castes into the Hindu community (Roberts, 2016). But the outcome of a Hindu consciousness among Dalits remains debatable (Ilaiah, 1996). Viramma, the Pariah woman whose life story vividly acknowledges the subjective experience of lower castes, hesitates when articulating Untouchability and Hinduness: 'Who are the Hindus, the Muslims, the Christians, that, I don't know for sure ... Hindus must be the name of a caste. Wait, I think I heard it once: the Hindu people, it is us, the Poor, who are called like that in the speeches' (Viramma and Racine, 1994, p. 203).

Indeed, if politically- motivated inclusion processes favoured an understanding of Hinduism as shared by *sa-varnas* and *a-varnas*, they also reinstated caste hierarchy, and segregation as central to Hinduism. The national debate over the ban for Untouchables to enter government-led Hindu temples (first lifted in 1936) has long aroused sometimes violent opposition from higher castes. When the police forced Varanasi Brahmins to let Untouchables enter the Vishwanath temple in 1956, local orthodox Hindus considered that such an issue rendered the Shiva *linga* impure, and decided to build another, private, 'New Vishwanath temple' (Eck, 1998, p. 135). And when, in 1936, Gandhi inaugurated the Banaras Bharat Mata (Mother India) *mandir*, a temple/museum with a marble map of India standing in place of the main *murti*— divine image (Claveyrolas, 2008), he tried to articulate national unity, and an egalitarian Hinduism beyond caste divisions: 'In this temple, there is no statue of gods or goddesses. I hope this temple will play the role of a universal platform for all religions, as well as for *harijan* [untouchables] and for all castes and creeds, and that it will contribute to the sentiments of religious unity, peace and love in this country' (quoted in Gupta, 2001, p. 4292). But the Gandhian ecumenism does not contest caste hierarchy and its Hindu ritual purity criteria: during the Bharat Mata temple's inauguration, so-called 'sons of god' (*harijans*) were handed out pieces of soap in order to 'wash' before being allowed to share the common meal with other participants (Gupta, 2001) . . . The anecdote reveals the deep discomfort of Westernized Indian nationalist elites regarding the ritually sanctioned hierarchy of castes.

Moreover, such focus on castes as an all-inclusive system, ambiguously associated with tolerance as a supposedly Hindu virtue (Halbfass, 1988), often comes back to strengthening the equation between Hinduism and Brahmanism. Hence *sanskritization* strategies (Srinivas, 1956) implemented by those who fight caste segregation within Hinduism: they typically comply with the Brahminical hierarchy, giving up low-caste 'impure' practices (blood sacrifice, meat, and alcohol offerings, trance) to adopt higher caste 'pure' traditions (vegetarianism)—thus hoping to be granted a higher status.

Castes, Domination, and Conversion

Focusing on the Hindu ritual ideology of purity and pollution as the major dimension of the caste system and Indian society, such as in Dumont's (1966) influential theory, has been criticized as a Brahminical bias. Following McKim Marriott's first counter-model (1959) stressing rank rather than purity issues, most recent studies have looked at caste in terms of power and domination (Guha, 2013; Mosse, 2012; Roberts, 2016; Viswanath, 2014). They argue in favour of a more horizontal reading of castes, insisting on non-religious dimensions such as socio-political subordination or empowerment, and electoral lobbies (Jaffrelot, 2005). Such analyses favour castes as bounded communities, with relations and hierarchies focused on the access to resources and power—untied by either ritual ideology or Hinduism *per se*.

Again contrasting with the argument of an intrinsically Hindu-bound ideology, subaltern studies also argued in favour of an initially far more flexible system, only solidified in colonial times by the British taxonomic obsession and 'divide-and-rule' strategies (Cohn, 1996; Dirks, 2001). The representations of the caste system, and of its relations with Hinduism, have indeed greatly evolved during this period, including through the manipulations of Independent leaders eager to put forward a Hindu majority by including Dalits in this category. Following Independence, the Hindu socio-ritual caste system was once thought to be bound to disappear with the advent of modernity, globalization, and urbanization. Though caste rules are more constraining in villages (still the vast majority of Indian population), such hypothesis has long been abandoned. Castes have shown perfectly compatible with social classes: the two different logics somehow join, with social handicaps (poverty, poor access to health, or education) more often than not coupled with ritual lower statuses (Roberts, 2016). Meant to fight such segregation, the quota reservation system has also been decisive in the resilience of caste consciousness and in the legal definition of caste restricted to Hindus (quotas exclude Christian *Other Backward Classes*, for instance).

One of the strongest illustrations of the Indian assimilation of the complex relations of castes to Hinduism lies in the fact that many castes fighting against their segregation finally chose to convert to Islam, Buddhism, or Christianity. Escaping castes through leaving Hinduism seems to confirm that there cannot be a casteless Hinduism. Such perception of how the caste system directly stems from Hinduism—and of the Hindu nature of low-caste oppression—eventually led the 'Father of the Indian Constitution' Ambedkar to convert to Buddhism, thirty years after having publicy burnt (in 1927) the *Laws of Manu*, the *Dharmashastra* text in which the Sage Manu exposes caste rules.

The existence of castes outside Hindu communities is supposed to uphold the so-called Hindu-bias reading of India through the Dumontian theory. Yet, one must keep in mind that such (individual or, rather, collective) conversions rarely put an end to segregation. In fact, if the *jati* hierarchy is flexible and has never been written down for eternity, it remains a relational matter, depending on how others evaluate your relative purity, and consequently engage with you on a daily basis. Indeed, neither Indian Christianism nor Indian Islam can be understood without a close look at their internal caste relations and hierarchy, and at their relations with Hindu castes (Clémentin-Ojha, 2008). Barely changing such relational prospects, conversion cases stress how non-Hindu religions have never been able to go beyond caste domination. Indian Catholicism, for instance, replicated caste hierarchies, even if it fought the religious sanction structuring the caste system, and also contributed in developing a language for social contestation (Mosse, 2012). Moreover, when part of a caste converts to Catholicism for instance, inter-religious marriages do happen, but only as long as caste endogamy prevails.

Beyond the (ritual-religious or political) focus chosen to tackle caste issues, caste stands at the crossroads of various classification systems (referring to religious or kinship terminologies and structures), and various domination systems (whether be it class or gender, for instance—Ghosh & Banerjee, 2018). Hence sometimes confusing identities. If *hijra* individuals are first defined by their gender (transsexual) identity, they are also Hindus or Muslims, and can be from upper or lower castes (Boisvert, 2018). Adding a high-caste patronym to one's name is a common strategy to support upward pretentions of one's family or community, without contesting the caste system. And, an individual from the Jat caste can be a Hindu, a Sikh, or a Muslim; a member of lower castes and a member of the locally dominant class and caste.

A Casteless Hinduism? Challenges to Caste Within Hinduism

Besides lower castes fighting the system's hierarchy, the caste logics is first challenged within Hinduism itself through ascetic individuals and institutions. The caste system has been studied as grounded in the dialectical relation between the world of castes—those householders engaging in actions according to their relative *dharma* (*varnashramadharma*)—and renunciation—those ascetic individuals renouncing not only worldly possessions but the whole world of caste. Though in a sense paradigmatic Hindus, renouncers are dead to their caste: they performed their own death ritual, they are freed from its rules and duties, away from the otherwise unescapable fruits of actions and rituals (Dumont, 1966; Madan, 1988).

With renunciation also comes a challenge to the very necessity of castes for Hinduism to exist. Even if only temporarily and as a theoretical model, the ever-growing numbers of Hindu pilgrims replicate the quest for salvation apart from the world of caste, engaging in a caste-free devotional experience. Matching Turner's *communitas* model, the ideal Hindu pilgrim experience is indeed egalitarian, setting pilgrims free from sociological categories, and constraints (Claveyrolas, 2016). But ethnographical data on actual pilgrim experiences show how this ideal, indeed crucial to the pilgrims' own representations, is hardly consistent with the daily organization of pilgrimage. Pilgrims generally travel with their kins or fellow villagers, making it uneasy to go beyond caste matters (Gold, 1988; Karve, 1988; Lochtefeld, 2010). Furthermore, they are usually housed and ritually guided by pilgrim priests (*panda*) who have been maintaining hereditary patronage (*jajmani*) relations with their fellow-caste members for generations—guaranteeing that basic interaction and commensality rules are still respected during the time of pilgrimage. Even if the kind of priest the pilgrim chooses has come to depend more and more on market rules, pilgrim groups remain rather homogeneous in terms of caste status (Van der Veer, 1988).

Bhakti, a strong contestation of castes in itself, is another reference fuelling Hindu pilgrimage. Devotional (*bhakti*) traditions, starting around the 5th century AD, have regularly put forward anti-Brahmanical ideologies. Targeting the Brahmins' monopoly of ritual, technical mediation, *bhakti* movements have argued in favour of an un-mediated, emotional relation to divinity (Bennett, 1993; Lynch, 1990). In sharp contrast with the *varna* theory, Hindu *bhakti* introduces a 'universal' possibility to reach god and salvation whatever the caste you belong to. Such a move towards universality can also be witnessed in most modern sectarian traditions based on individual gurus and lineages, often replacing, in theory if not in practice, caste-bound ritualism by a caste-free individual devotion. From the 19th-century Arya Samaj to contemporary *guru*-led sectarian movements, caste-free Hinduism is often linked with the promotion of the Indian unity around Hindutva nationalistic ideology, thus bringing back the potential contestation of castes within Hinduism, again understood as all-inclusive and relevant to both social and religious matters.

THE RESILIENCE OF CASTE IN OVERSEAS HINDU COMMUNITIES

One of the most crucial challenges to both the caste system and the apprehension of its link to Hinduism has lied in its outcome in Indian overseas communities—an issue that crystallized the academic interest soon after the Indian diaspora studies first developed (Schwartz, 1967). The issues raised were three-fold: first, that of the possibility/transformation of Hinduism when it leaves its Indian mother-land; second, that of the resilience of the holistic caste system when only some of the individual castes are exported; third, that of the possible emergence of a casteless Hinduism.

As soon as the late 19th century, Bengal witnessed a crucial debate over the consequences faced by high-caste Hindus leaving the Indian sacred territory (*dharmabhumi*) and crossing the ocean's dark waters (*kalapani*) to study, work, or fight in far-away lands (Clémentin-Ojha, 2016). Risking exclusion from their caste, such individuals concretely experimented the possibility of being Hindu in a context where India's caste system and regulations could no longer be respected. For (mainly low-castes) Hindu indentured labourers contracted to work in the Caribbean, Indian Ocean, or Pacific sugar-colonies in the second part of the 19th century, two major challenges to caste persistence are generally stressed: the un-controlled commensality and promiscuity beyond caste barriers during the boat passage, and the disruption of purity regulations ruling endogamy, residence, and work specialization once installed in the colony.

Most studies conclude that while castes still exist in today's communities installed in diaspora or descending from the indentured labourers, the caste *system*, structured by the ideology of purity has waned, or even disintegrated (Hollup, 1994) in favour of a joint brahminization and ethnicization of the system (Van der Veer & Vertovec, 1991). Interestingly, together with stressing the disappearance of purity matters guiding most daily interactions, few of these studies would contest the resilience of caste rules when it comes to marriage and, sometimes, commensality, and ritual matters (Claveyrolas, 2015). Diaspora studies hence open the door to the possible compatibility of castes with overseas Hinduism.

The Dumontian reading of the caste system as founded by the Hindu ritual ideology has been the target of most alternative studies of castes insisting on non-religious (non-Hindu) dimensions in a sometimes too radical swing of the pendulum. It may well be fair to argue that, half a century after Dumont's *Homo Hierarchicus*, castes as a Hindu system initially born out of a Brahminical socio-ritual ideology but pervading the Indian society well beyond upper castes, still stand as a major, if not exclusive, entry-point into Indian society.

As a concluding attempt, let us answer our original interrogation, and argue that castes and Hinduism are indeed, to a great extent, consubstantial. On the one hand, except for marginal or dialectical contexts (renouncement), castelessness in mainstream Hinduism is limited to ideological theories (*bhakti*), and attempts (sects)—more often than not contradicted by actual practices (sects, pilgrimage). On the other hand, castes in India cannot be considered without Hinduism because caste hierarchy, daily practices, and social rules are all directly rooted in an overarching, inextricably social, and ritual, Hindu ideology.

Certainly not the only category relevant to the anthropology of Hinduism and the sociology of India, caste remains a crucial issue because the system is as pervasive as it is flexible, able to transform, and adapt to new contexts. No wonder, then, that castes have been able to prevail at the very core of the Indian society, but also to grow both beyond the limits of Hinduism (see castes in Indian Islam or Christianity), beyond the limits of religious matters (see social contestation movements and political lobbying based on caste affiliations), and beyond the Indian territory and society (see diasporic contexts). Rather than negating the fact that caste is consubstantial to Hinduism, such extensions of the realm of caste actually confirm the enduring relevance of the religious dimension of caste, as all the new avatars of caste have indeed perpetuated the core principle of Hindu ritual ideology: the distinction between the pure and the impure.

References

Bayly, S. 1999. *Caste, Society and Politics in India from the Eighteenth Century to the Modern Age*. Cambridge: Cambridge University Press.

Bennett, P. 1993. *The Path of Grace. Social Organization and Temple Worship in a Vaishnava Sect*. Delhi: Hindustan publishing company.

Berti, D., and G. Tarabout (Eds.). 2009. *Soil, Territory and Society in South Asia*. Delhi: Manohar.

Boisvert, M. 2018. *Les hijras; portrait socioreligieux d'une communauté 'transgenre' sud-asiatique*. Montréal: Presses de l'Université de Montréal.

Bouillier, V., and G. Toffin (Eds.). 1993. *Classer les dieux? Des panthéons en Asie du Sud*. Paris: EHESS (collection Puruṣārtha n°15).

Clark-Décès, I. 2008. 'The Re-Invention of Tamil Funeral Processions'. In K. Jacobsen (Ed.), *South Asian Diasporas on Display: Religious Processions in South Asia and in the Diaspora* (pp. 15–28). London: Routledge.

Claveyrolas, M. 2008. 'Les temples de Mère Inde, musées de la nation'. *Gradhiva*, 7: 84–99.

Claveyrolas, M. 2015. 'The "Land of the Vaish"? Caste, Structure and Ideology in Mauritius'. *Samaj*.
Claveyrolas, M. 2016. 'The Amazement of the Ethnographer: Hindu Pilgrimage beyond Sacred and Profane'. In D. Albera and J. Eade (Eds.), *New Pathways in Pilgrimage Studies. Global Perspectives* (pp. 36–52). New York: Routledge.
Clémentin-Ojha, C. 2008. *Les Chrétiens de l'Inde. Entre castes et églises*. Paris: Albin Michel.
Clémentin-Ojha, C. 2016. 'Kālāpānī ou les limites à ne pas franchir. Le voyage en Angleterre du maharaja de Jaipur (1902)'. In M. Claveyrolas and R. Delage (Eds.), *Purushartha 34, Territoires du Religieux dans les mondes indiens. Parcourir, mettre en scène, franchir* (pp. 251–274). Paris: éditions de l'EHESS.
Cohn, B. 1996. *Colonialism and Its Forms of Knowledge. The British in India*. Princeton: Princeton University Press.
Dirks, N. 2001. *Castes of Mind. Colonialism and the Making of Modern India*. Princeton: Princeton University Press.
Dumont, L. 1966. *Homo hierarchicus. Le système des castes et ses implications*. Paris: NRF/Gallimard.
Eck, D. 1983. *Banaras: City of Light*. Princeton: Princeton University Press.
Eck, D. 1998. 'The Imagined Landscape: Patterns in the Construction of Hindu Sacred Geography'. *Contributions to Indian Sociology*, 32(2): 165–188.
Fuller, C. J. 1984. *Servants of the Goddess. The Priests of a South Indian Temple*. Cambridge: Cambridge University Press.
Ghosh, N., and S. Banerjee (Eds.). 2018. 'Caste-Gender Intersections in Contemporary India'. *Samaj*, 19.
Gold, A. 1988. *Fruitful Journeys: The Ways of Rajasthani Pilgrims*. Berkeley: University of California Press.
Guha, S. 2013. *Beyond Caste: Identity and Power in South Asia, Past and Present*. Leiden: Brill.
Gupta, C. 2001. 'The Icon of Mother in Late Colonial North India'. *Economic and Political Weekly*, 36(45): 4291–4299.
Halbfass, W. 1988. *India and Europe. An Essay in Understanding*. New York: SUNY Press.
Herrenschmidt, O. 1978. 'L'Inde et le sous-continent indien'. In J. Poirier (Ed.), *Ethnologie régionale* (pp. 86–292). Paris: Gallimard.
Herrenschmidt, O. 2014. 'Violences d'un autre âge dans les villages indiens. Actualités d'Ambedkar'. *European Journal of Sociology*, 55(1): 59–81.
Herrenschmidt, O. 2016. 'Le destin humain d'une déesse villageoise en Andhra côtier. Une histoire d'avatars'. In M. Claveyrolas and R. Delage (Eds.), *Purushartha 34, Territoires du Religieux dans les mondes indiens. Parcourir, mettre en scène, franchir* (pp. 303–333). Paris: éditions de l'EHESS.
Hollup, O. 1994. 'The Disintegration of Caste and Changing Concepts of Indian Ethnic Identity in Mauritius'. *Ethnology*, 33(4): 297–316.
Ilaiah, K. 1996. *Why I Am Not a Hindu. A Sudra Critique of Hindutva Philosophy, Culture and Political Economy*. Kolkata: Popular Prakashan Pvt.
Jaffrelot, C. 2005. *Inde: la démocratie par la caste. Histoire d'une mobilisation socio-politique. 1885–2005*. Paris: Fayard.
Karve, I. 1988 [1951]. '"On the Road": A Maharashtrian Pilgrimage'. In E. Zelliot and M. Bernsten (Eds.), *The Experience of Hinduism. Essays on Religion in Maharashtra*. Albany: State University of New York Press.

Lochtefeld, J. 2010. *God's Gateway: Identity and Meaning in a Hindu Pilgrimage Place*. Oxford: Oxford University Press.

Lorenzen, D. 1999. *Who Invented Hinduism? Essays on Religion in History*. Cambridge: Cambridge University Press.

Lynch, O. 1990. *Divine Passions: The Social Construction of Emotion in India*. Berkeley: University of California Press.

Malamoud, C. 1976. 'Terminer le sacrifice. Remarques sur les honoraires rituels dans le brahmanisme'. In M. Biardeau and C. Malamoud (Eds.), *Le sacrifice dans l'Inde ancienne* (pp. 155–204). Paris, Presses Universitaires de France.

Madan, T. N. 1988. *Non-Renunciation: Themes and Interpretations of Hindu Culture*. Oxford: Osford University Press.

Marriott, M. 1959. 'Interactional and Attributional Theories of Caste Ranking'. *Man in India*, 39: 92–107.

Mosse, D. 2012. *The Saint in the Banyan Tree. Christianity and Caste Society in India*. Berkeley: University of California Press.

Parry, J. 1986. 'The Gift, the Indian Gift and the "Indian Gift"'. *Man (n.s.)*, 21–23: 453–473.

Parry, J. 1994. *Death in Banaras*. Cambridge: Cambridge University Press.

Raheja, G. G. 1988. *The Poison in the Gift, Ritual, Prestation, and the Dominant Caste in a North Indian Village*. Chicago: Chicago University Press.

Reiniche, M.-L. 1979. *Les Dieux et les hommes. Etude des cultes d'un village du Tirunelveli. Inde du Sud*. Paris: Mouton.

Roberts, N. 2016. *To Be Cared For. The Power of Conversion and Foreignness of Belonging in an Indian Slum*. Oakland: University of California Press.

Schwartz, B. (Ed.). 1967. *Caste in Overseas Indian Communities*. San Francisco: Chandler.

Sontheimer, G.-D., and H. Kulke (Eds.). 1989. *Hinduism Reconsidered*. New Delhi: Manohar.

Srinivas, M. N. 1956. 'A Note on Sanskritization and Westernization'. *The Far Eastern Quarterly*, 15(4): 481–496.

Trouillet, P.-Y. 2008. 'Mapping the Management of Threatening Gods and Social Conflict: A Territorial Approach to Processions in a South Indian Village'. In K. Jacobsen (Ed.), *South Asian Religions on Display. Religious Processions in South Asia and in the Diaspora* (pp. 45–62). London: Routledge.

Van der Veer, P. 1988. *Gods on Earth. The Management of Religious Experience and Identity in a North Indian Pilgrimage Centre*. London: The Athlone Press.

Van der Veer, P., and S. Vertovec. 1991. 'Brahmanism Abroad: On Caribbean Hinduism as an Ethnic Religion'. *Ethnology*, 30: 149–166.

Viramma, Racine J., & J.-L. Racine. 1994. *Une vie paria. Le rire des asservis. Inde du Sud*. Paris: Plon/Terre Humaine.

Viswanath, R. 2014. *The Pariah Problem: Caste, Religion and the Social in Modern India*. New York: Columbia University Press.

CHAPTER 15

HINDU SECTS AND CASTE

RAPHAËL VOIX

WHILE it has been said that Hinduism is coextensive with the 'caste' (*jāti*) system (Dumont, 1970), it has also been said that Hinduism is made up of a 'mosaic of sects' (*sampradāya*) (Renou, 1953, p. 89). Although they differ, both statements amount to affirming that the primary principle of the religion of the Hindus must be sought not in their beliefs or in their rites, but in the indigenous institutions around which Hindus organize their social and religious identities. Yet, knowing that the caste system is the characteristic mark of the Hindu social organization, how can we understand the sectarian phenomenon that this society is experiencing? To answer the question, this chapter starts by examining the way sects have been defined by indigenous authors as well as by sociologists, before analysing their interactions with the caste system.[1] Although over the course of history, Buddhists and Jains have long interacted with Hindu sects, this chapter will limit itself to the last.[2]

---

[1] This chapter both in its structure and content owes a lot to extensive personal notes taken from C. Clémentin-Ojha's research seminar held at the École des Hautes Études en Sciences Sociales between 2000 and 2017, notably the years 2007–2009 on which two short abstracts have been published (2009–2010) as well as an analytical bibliography (2013). It also draws from classic works on these questions, such as Wilson (1958), Babb (2003), and Lorenzen (2004) and has benefited from the insightful remarks of Véronique Bouillier, C. Clémentin-Ojha, and Brian Hatcher who should all be thanked for this.

[2] While for a long time the term Hinduism was used indiscriminately and carelessly we must bear in mind that it has no obvious meaning. Hindus started to call themselves 'Hindus' and thus acknowledged that they belong a common socio-religious group around the 16th century, but the term 'Hinduism' is of recent (18th century) and foreign origin. In this chapter, following Stietencron, 'Hinduism' is used to designate 'a geographically defined group of distinct but related religions that originated in the same region, developed under similar socio-economic and political conditions, incorporated largely the same traditions, influenced each other continuously, and jointly contributed to the Hindu culture' (1991, p. 20). Far from being monolithic, Hinduism is thus radically 'polythetic' (King, 1999, p. 182) and is crossed by important dividing lines, 'caste' and 'sect' being only one of these.

The Theological, Institutional, and Sociological Logics of Hindu Sects

There is no a singular term in any Indian language to designate the type of organization that, following the first authors who wrote on the phenomenon, we call 'sect'. Indian literature employs numerous terms to designate a specific religious tradition: *sampradāya* (transmission); *mata* (doctrine); *pantha, mārga,* or *prasthāna* (path); *siddhānta* (doctrine); *paramparā* (lineage); or more recently *samāja* (society). While each term has a specific connotation, it is customary for both Indologists and social scientists to designate the groups or schools they refer to by the term 'sect'. The origin of this usage can be traced to the work of Horace Hayman Wilson (1786–1860), considered the precursor of historical studies on India's religious systems (Bhattacharyya, 1996, p. 241). Published posthumously in 1861, his book *The Religious Sects of the Hindus* is the first presentation in a Western language of the history and classification of the different 'religious sects' of the Hindus (Wilson, 1958).[3] It relies on pre-modern descriptions as well as on observations he conducted, which allowed him to describe the then current condition of these sects in British India. While Wilson used the expression 'Hindu Sect', without justifying or explaining it, it was later adopted by other Orientalists such as R. G. Bhandarkar (1913) or J. N. Farquhar (1913, 1920).

The word 'sect' has a long history within European languages where it has borne both a neutral and a pejorative meaning. Derived from the Latin verb *sequi* (to follow), the word 'sect' long referred to 'a line of intellectual or moral conduct, particularly in philosophy'. According to this usage the existence of a variety of 'sects' was 'a sign of 'intellectual health'. The adoption of Christianity as a State religion formalized a 'semantic shift' which gave the term a 'religious overtone' as it became a synonym for the Greek *hairèsis* used to designate 'dissenting or heterodox groups' that place themselves outside the Catholic Church, the 'exclusive religion' that imposed an 'indisputable dogma' (Boulhol, 2002 pp. 391–392). This double meaning was also conveyed in early Indologist works where it could be used to mean both a group of Hindus (such as the Śaiva or Vaiṣṇava) and groups of dissenters such as the Buddhist or Jaïn who broke away from Hinduism (see Hatcher, 2018, p. 19). However, nowadays Indologists and social scientists use it mainly in its non-pejorative sense, closer to its initial meaning. In this sense the term carries some similar connotations as those associated with the traditional occurrence of the Sanskrit term *sampradāya*, which designates an initiated group of people who follow the teaching or discipline given by a guru.[4] Although there

---

[3] It consists of the revised version of two earlier articles that Wilson published in Asiatic researches, 1828, vol. XVI and 1832, vol. II. Let us note that when Aksay Datta recreated Wilson's work in Bengali, he translated 'sect' with the word '*sampradāya*' (Datta, 1888).

[4] As the authoritative thesaurus of Sanskrit, *Amarakośa*, defines *sampradāya* as *guruparaṃparāgatasa dupadeśa* (see Shodhan, 2001, p. 31, quoted in Hatcher, 2020, p. 278, fn. 17).

have been attempts to de-westernize social science on India,[5] this usage has been widely accepted and contemporary Indologists continue to use the term or other synonymous expressions, such as 'Hindu sectarian traditions', to refer to religious groups of different antiquity founded in the Indian subcontinent, which are neither Buddhist, Jain, nor Sikh.[6]

Hindu sects are very diverse. They emerged in most parts of the Indian subcontinent over a very long period. While the first groups, that were considered retrospectively in the historiography of Hinduism as sects, such as the Bhāgavatas,[7] were founded a few centuries before the Common Era, they developed exponentially in medieval times 'fostered' partly by the 'political, social, economic, and demographic changes' prevalent at the time (Lorenzen, 2011, p. 271). In addition to differing in terms of their antiquity, Hindu sects also differ in terms of size: some consist of relatively small groups of followers—sometimes pejoratively called 'minor' or 'obscure'—while others have had a tremendous influence on South Asian history and have millions of followers some of whom are non-Indians. Sociologically, sect membership—which is based on a voluntarily choice, a crucial characteristic, to which we will come back later—is often disparate as not all sectarians originate from the same social *(class/varṇa/jāti)* or cultural (regional) background. Theologically, sects do not share a uniform conception of the divine. Each one has its own set of canonical texts and while some envisage and adore a deity endowed with attributes *(saguṇa)*—sometimes in the form of an anthropomorphic image *(mūrti)*—others reject this approach and revere a supreme being devoid of any attributes *(nirguṇa)*. Sects are often linked to a specific teacher and/or a unique revelation/teaching *(sadupadeśa)*. Lastly, Hindu sects are often regional in origin and extent and even when expanding, may retain strong regional roots (e.g. Swaminarayan and Gujarat).[8] Yet, with a few exceptions, they share a universal soteriology according to which salvation is open to all the 'chosen'. In this respect, they constitute proselytizing movements and have often been disseminated in other parts of India. A sect may even have a wider following in a region other than the one where its revelation/teaching took place.[9] In view of the above facts, and taking into account their strong fissiparous

---

[5] McLeod, has suggested replacing the word 'sect' that he believed to be 'too deeply tainted with Western connotations' with the word 'panth' (Mcleod, 1978, p. 287). This proposition, which reflects the 'Sikh tropism of the author' (Clementin-Ojha, 2013), has however never been followed and since the usage of the term sect has 'been established in Indian Studies for over 200 years' most authors, like Shah himself, have 'no problem in using [it]' (Shah, 2006, p. 2010).

[6] These emic categories were used to classify Hindu sects in the earliest work on Hinduism (Monier-Williams, 1877, p. 135) as well as in the main reference works on Hindu sects (Wilson, 1958; Babb, 2003; Lorenzen, 2004, for example). Certain authors sometimes use the expression 'Indian sect' as including all religious traditions born in South Asia including Buddhists, Jains, or Sikhs (Renou, 1953, p. 90; Dumont, 1999, p. 187).

[7] Early pre-mediaeval groups such as the Ājīvikas, the Jainas, and the Buddhists are more ancient by a few centuries, yet they were not considered retrospectively as 'Hindu sects' but rather as 'new religions'.

[8] For a survey of sects by region, see Lutgendorf (2003).

[9] The case of the Śaiva Siddhānta, which originated in Kashmir but continued to flourish particularly in South India, is a good illustration of this (Brunner-Lachaux, 1963–1998). Contrarily, although it is found predominantly in Tamil Nadu the land of its founder, Rāmānuja (11th century), the Śrīvaiṣṇava

tendencies, Hindu sects do not—by any means—represent either a unified or a homogeneous religious movement. In fact, as brilliantly shown by Hawley (2015), although there were attempts to organize the traditions of North Indian bhakti movements at the turn of the 17th century, the idea of a 'Bhakti movement' only really emerged and spread in the 1930s in the context of the nationalist movement. The modern idea is thus a recent intellectual construct that conveys a politically motivated 'ideal' rather than reflecting any kind of 'social or historical fact'.

Not only do Hindu sects vary immensely they can also be viewed through different disciplines—such as literary studies, history, philosophy, theology, sociology, or anthropology—each approach and even each author giving 'his own slant to the nature of a sect and the way its relation to the larger traditions should be conceptualized' (Lorenzen, 2011, p. 253). Whereas pre-modern Indian scholars have mainly viewed sects through the prism/study of their literature, and thus described them principally according to their own metaphysical background, 19th-century Orientalists, in collaboration with Indian scholars, developed a more 'empirical, historical, and ethnographic epistemology' (Lorenzen, 2011). In the 20th century, Hindu sects became a legitimate object of study for the social sciences. Although not deprived of the peculiar 'lens' of nation, which created the idea of *bhakti* as a movement (Hawley, 2015), a more complete view of the religious, political, cultural, and social phenomenon they represent emerged. Yet, sects share, beyond their diversity, a number of common features that allow for some generalizations. As proposed by Clémentin-Ojha (2009–2010), they are constructed around different logics that work together: (1) theological; (2) institutional; (3) sociological.

A Theological Logic

The first characteristic of a Hindu sect is its organization around the quasi-exclusive cult to one particular deity. This theological characteristic was identified by ancient authors such as Wilson or Farquhar as being a form of 'monotheism' (Bhattacharyya, 1996, p. 246). It is, however, more appropriate to designate this theological specificity as a form of 'theism' as sects do not deny the existence of a multiplicity of gods as strict monotheism does, their teachings stating that only one specific deity has the power to grant liberation *(mokṣa)*.[10] In other words, 'each sect acknowledges the existence of gods other

---

sect spread to other parts of India notably to Gujarat (Rangajan, 1996). Some sects have developed significant followings overseas thanks to the conversion of non-Indians—for example the International Society for Krishna Consciousness, an off-shoot of the Gauḍīya Vaiṣṇava (Vaiṣṇavas of Bengal)—or exclusively among the Hindu diaspora, as in the case of the Puṣṭimārga (The way of grace) another Vaiṣṇava sect (Richardson, 2014).

[10] In its strict sense, monotheism is 'not only the belief in one unique God, but the explicit negation of all other gods' (Geffré, 2019, my translation). Theism finds its full literally expression in the post-classical *Purāṇas* and notably in sects such as the Bhāgavatas or the Liṅgāyats.

than their own god(s), suitable for others to worship, though they might not care to worship them themselves' (Doniger, 2009, p. 42). It is therefore only in terms of salvation that sects are exclusivist: in the more devotional sects, to deserve the saving grace, the devotee has to totally surrender his/her Self to the deity through intense devotion *(bhakti)*, or in less devotional contexts to engage himself in an active spiritual discipline *(sādhana)*—yogic practices or physical austerities—through which one interacts with the divinity and acquires his/her power. Although not all sects manifest this exclusivism to the same degree, the theism of a sect must be differentiated from the 'preference' for one or another of the deities of the Hindu pantheon that many Hindus demonstrate as the result of a personal religious sensibility or a preference transmitted within the family or the caste (Clémentin-Ojha, 2013).

The importance of this theological conception in a sect's self-definition is reflected in one of their common endogenous classification as two groups—Śaiva and Vaiṣṇava—depending on the main deity worshipped.[11] Śaiva sects consist of devotees (Śaivas) who '*follow the teachings* (my emphasis) of Śiva *(śivaśāsana)*' (Flood, 2003, p. 119; Sanderson, 1988, p. 664). Vaiṣṇava sects consist of devotees 'who *worship* (my italics) Viṣṇu and his different aspects as well as the traditions they follow' (Colas, 2003, p. 229). Both groups have a long and complex history and great internal diversity. However, Śaiva and Vaiṣṇava remain important emic sectarian categories as reflected, for example, in the logic of the sectarian mark drawn on the forehead *(tilak)*: while all Śaiva sectarian markings have horizontal stripes, the Vaiṣṇava sectarian marks consist of vertical lines. Thus, if few Indians are able to identify a specific Hindu sect by looking at the *tilak*, everyone is able to distinguish between a Vaiṣṇava and a Śaiva. In times of conflict this mark may even become an important trait of self-identification (Clémentin-Ojha, 1999).

While Brahmanic orthopraxis is pan-Indian and refers to the Vedas as the ultimate authority, the sects, without denying the Vedas, also have their roots in the Tantras, a set of scriptures considered as revealed by Śiva (or the Goddess) and Viṣṇu. These Tantras often prescribe the worship of deities according to rites that do not use Vedic mantras, but do not, however, reject or replace the Veda. They rather supplant it on an esoteric plane and consider themselves as belonging to a parallel system. For instance, they respect the orthodox norms of behaviour *(vaidika)* from the social point of view but consider these as inferior from the metaphysical point of view. In other words, they see the Veda and its Brahmanic social order as the 'common religion' while they dispense esoteric teaching that is available only to those who through an initiation (or a series of initiations) become members of lineages of masters and are able to perform these cults.

As attested by abundant primary sources, especially in Sanskrit and vernacular languages, the sects attached to these two dominant Indian religious traditions—Śaiva

---

[11] While early emic sources can distinguish between *Saura* (worshippers of the sun god Sūrya), Gaṇapatyas (worshippers of the elephant headed god Gaṇeśa/Gaṇapati), *Pāśupatas* (worshippers of Rudra), *Śāktas* (worshippers of the Goddess), etc.; later sources would distinguish between Vaiṣṇava, Śaiva, and *Śāktas*, the last being considered as belonging to Śaiva as the Goddess is considered as Śiva's partner (Padoux, 2000b).

and Vaiṣṇava— have engaged in constant exchanges and interactions. These include religious and economic tensions and sometimes intense rivalry—notably between Śaiva *(saṃnyāsin)* and Vaiṣṇava *(bairāgi) a*scetics during the Mughal era (Lochtefeld, 1994)— which sometimes contributed to weakening their authority. In fact, already in King Asoka's time (ca. 269–232 BC), sects did not always 'behave [...] in a courteous manner', to say the least (Lorenzen, 2011, p. 256). However, relations between sects also included mutual influences and exchanges, such as reciprocal patronage and absorption of another sect's figures. These influences emerged both from within the Hindu fold, between sects of different obedience, and from outside it. In medieval Bengal, for example, some minor Hindu religious groups such as the medieval Sahajiyās cult inherited traits from Buddhist Tantric lineages and from local islamic traditions.

An Institutional Logic

For their revelation and/or teaching to be transmitted over generations, Hindu sects have developed specific institutions within which religious authority is legitimized in a specific fashion. This constitutes its second characteristic. In fact, quite significantly, the Sanskrit term *sampradāya* (What is handed over) refers not only, as its early usage attests, to a 'formalized transmission of knowledge' but also, in its later use, to, 'a distinct form of social organization and institutionalization' (Malinar, 2013, p. 157). In other words, the term *sampradāya*, which was first used to designate a particular teaching, went on to signify the community or institution within which this teaching is transmitted.

This transmission takes place over generations by means of a spiritual lineage called *guru-paramparā* (from one guru to the next). Whereas, in theory, these spiritual genealogies are uninterrupted and go back to the guru who received, through a dream or an experience, the revelation/teaching, and founded the sect, historians have shown that they are often marked by processes of inclusion and exclusion. Nevertheless, they are most often constituted by historical characters who ensure the transmission of the doctrine and the reproduction of the social group from generation to generation. Because it is precisely the historical inscription of these spiritual genealogies that establishes the doctrine's legitimacy, practices of remembering the lineages of gurus play an important role in the disciple's socialization within the sect. This has led sects to develop a sense of history that is less prevalent in the rest of Hinduism.

Theoretically, one joins a sect as the result of a voluntary and individual choice, and this point is of crucial importance: in order to become a member of a sect one must make a request—hence the voluntary choice. But this choice must also be accepted by the master, this approval constituting another important dimension of the sectarian entry process. Entry into the sect is than ritually marked by an initiation *(dīkṣā)*. Like the Brahmanic initiation *(upanayana),* this sectarian initiation is a rite of consecration *(saṃskāra)*: it confers a specific ritual qualification upon the person who receives it; in this case, the *dīkṣā* introduces the sectarian to the cult of a particular divinity through the transmission of a specific, and sometimes secret, *mantra*. The initiation also seals a personal relationship with a *guru*; one usually chooses to be initiated into a particular Hindu sect not because of a specific theological predilection but as the result of an encounter—physical or magical—with a specific master.[12] The importance of the guru-disciple relationship in the sectarian context lies in the fact that the *guru* acts as an intermediary between the disciple and the divinity. In the Tantric context, he is even considered as *the* divinity (Padoux, 2000a). Sectarian initiation makes it possible to clearly distinguish members from non-members and confers upon the sectarian a social identity that differs from that of their caste. While only sons of twice-born *(dvija)* are qualified to receive the *upanayana* and become twice-born in turn, sectarian initiation does not make birth a criterion: sectarian initiation is granted not according to social criteria (status) but to spiritual criteria (religious qualification).

The importance of transmission (*parampara*) and initiation *(dīkṣā)* has led sects to develop a particular method of legitimizing religious authority. Founders of sects are often deified and, when they are, they themselves become objects of worship. This is because, contrary to Brahmanism, 'where the only role of the religious authorities is to transmit the revealed texts and comment on them', within a sect the founders are 'themselves the origin of the truth they teach': they are often presented as individuals having received a revelation, having been in direct contact with the divinity (Clémentin-Ojha, 2013). This characteristic is reflected in the sect's literature and centres. Without rejecting the Veda per se—which would have excluded them from the Hindu fold and made them *nāstikas*—Hindu sects have developed their own literature. We find theological exposés, ritual treatises, discipline and organization rules or aesthetic scriptures. This feature is so important that 'fundamentally religious books can be defined as *books written for the use of a sect* (Renou, 1953, p. 50, my emphasis). However, some scriptures—that is several *Upaniṣads*, the *Bhagavadgītā,* or the *Bhāgavatapurāṇa*—can be common to many sects, and indeed, may also be appreciated by non-sectarian Hindus (Renou, 1953, p. 92). Among the vast body of literature produced by sects, hagiography constitutes a genre in its own right. There are edifying life histories that record the master's actions and contribute to deifying him. They present many similarities, often reduplicating each other: the person who is the subject of a hagiography often appears to be a superhuman being, an ascetic with extraordinary powers, or a divine incarnation. His life becomes a model recognized by the community of disciples that often seeks to imitate him or her (Mallison, 2001). His story is transmitted and repeated among members who identify and remember him as the founder of their community. Not only do hagiographies play a role in developing the legitimacy of the cult by preserving and transmitting the founder's charismatic authority

---

[12] The importance of the *guru* is related to the fact that 'Indian traditions always gave precedence to the oral/aural/verbal, rather than to the written form of religious teaching' (Padoux, 2000a, p. 41). This means that lay-members usually remain little aware of the sect's theology and not 'much concerned with philosophical issues' (Shah, 2006, p. 216): ritual behaviour is learnt first and initiation is primarily an agreement to adhere to certain tenets of the sect and its rules of conducts.

through what Weber identified as the 'routinization of charisma', they are also propaganda tools designed to spread the cult while contributing to the construction of the sectarian identity itself.[13]

Besides these common features, sects experience diverse modalities of religious organization. They are often, but not necessarily, based on a nucleus made up of celibate ascetics[14] surrounded by lay disciples (Renou, 1947, p. 622; Dumont, [1970] 1999, p. 187). This configuration is sometimes loosely recognizable and includes variations, as in the case of the Rāmānandīs (Van Der Veer, 1988). Whatever their organizations, sects usually maintain temples, monasteries, and sacred pilgrimage centres that contribute to anchoring the distinctiveness of the community in the religious landscape.

A Sociological Logic

In addition to its theological and institutional characteristics, the sect is a type of social formation that structures religious activity within a distinct community that consciously cultivates its cultural heritage. It is this sociological dimension—a specific form of religious communalization—that sociologists noticed early on and examined.

The first sociological approach to the sectarian phenomenon was that of the German sociologist Max Weber. Developing his arguments on the basis of the religious history of the Christian West, but seeking sociological concepts and analytical tools that could be used in other contexts, Weber opposed two contrasting modes of social existence of religion: the Sect and the Church.[15] For him the Sect differs from the Church in that it is a voluntary, elitist, and autonomous association that has at its core a charismatic authority (Weber, 1958, pp. 291–329).[16] Adapting this model for interpreting Hindu Society, he contrasted the Sect with Caste. Whereas, in the case of Caste, the individual is subordinate to his or her birth group, the Sect provides a possible means of individual

---

[13] On the analysis of the relationship between hagiographic construction and the construction of sectarian identity, see the remarkable work of Stewart (2010) on Caitanya (1486–1533) and the Gaudīya-Vaiṣṇava.

[14] Following Clémentin-Ojha (2006, p. 536), I use the term 'ascetic' as a 'generic term' and the term 'renouncer' as a translation of *saṃnyāsī*. This Sanskrit term can refer either to the 'twice-born' who has entered the fourth Brahmanical stage of life (*āśrama*) or to a 'member of an ascetic lineage whose rules of conduct, though modeled on the former's pattern, have integrated later sectarian developments'. This distinction is important since 'not all Hindu ascetics are strictly speaking renouncers'. Some sects can be highly structured with different autonomous lineages that are loosely coordinated and work together, for example, in the case of the Daṇḍī ascetics of Benares who belong to the wider Daśanāmī *sampradāya* (Sawyer, 1993). There are also some exceptions: the hard core of the Vallabhis, for example, is formed by lay disciples whereas the *daśanāmī* have only an order of celibate ascetics with no lay disciples.

[15] In this article, Sect—with a capital S—denotes the ideal-type of the sect. It is used as a 'pole of reference for the study of empirical reality' (Hervieu-Léger and Willaime, p. 73).

[16] We should note that Weber does not specify the religious dimension of Hindu sects: he does not explicitly mention the fact that this type of communitarian formation is based on the exclusive cult to a specific god considered as the only one who can bring salvation.

emancipation.[17] Beyond identifying the dyadic opposition between Caste and Sect, Weber introduced useful distinctions between different types of membership of the Hindu Sect by recognizing that the 'the typical dualistic organization of Hindu sects' is: a 'nucleus' consisting of celibate ascetics and a community of lay devotees under their authority (Weber, 1958, p. 196).

Weber's Caste/Sect ideal-type represented a milestone in the sociology of Hinduism. With a structuralist approach that sought to order the 'proliferation' of Hinduism (Dumont, 1970, p. 185) by providing a 'unitary vision' (Dumont, 1970, p. xix), Dumont took this ideal-typical opposition between Caste/Sect further by adding a theological level and associating each group with a specific religious pursuit, respectively that of Householder and Renouncer. Therefore, for Dumont, Sect and Caste are opposed at different levels: Caste is the product of the man-in-the-world (Householder). It is theologically inclusive—it accepts a plurality of cults—but it is sociologically exclusive—as it only accepts members of a similar birth group. On the other hand, a Sect is the product of the man-out-of-the-world (Renouncer); it is 'theologically exclusive'—the revealed teachings and the grace of a single God are the direct means of salvation—but sociologically 'inclusive'—it accepts members of all castes (Dumont, 1970, pp. 284–285). He thus opposes the 'religion of the group' which is common to the 'religion of the individual', which is superior because it rests on a choice.

Shah (2006) provides a recent and interesting sociological approach to sects as a sociological phenomenon, acknowledging that sects are a structural principle of Hindu society as a whole, and he makes them the focus of his analysis: rather than the Caste/Sect distinction, it is the Sect/Non-Sect distinction that needs to be considered and, more than the behaviour of celibate ascetics, it is that of the lay sectarians that is central to his analysis. For Shah, a non-sectarian configuration is characterized by an 'inclusive attitude' towards the pantheon. Non-members of sects keep pictures of different Hindu gods and saints, sometimes even the Buddha or Guru Nanak, in their homes, prayer rooms, or on their car dashboards. They can indifferently offer worship *(pūjā)* to the major gods of Hinduism but also to local deities, by visiting their temples, accepting their consecrated leftovers *(prasād)*, participating in their festivals, singing devotional hymns to them, or visiting different pilgrimages sites (Shah, 2006, pp. 211–212).

In contrast, the sectarian attitude is 'exclusive'. In his prayer room or on his car dashboard, a member of a sect only displays pictures of the main deity, and possibly minor deities associated with him. He will only visit temples, go on pilgrimages, and participate in festivals dedicated to his deity. A sectarian attitude towards other deities would be that of 'respect'—in this sense, he is not, as we saw, a 'strict monotheist'—but he will refuse to eat the *prasād* of other deities. Members of specific sects not only avoid the cult of other deities, they also assert their exclusive faith in their deity and adopt a common behaviour clearly displaying their sectarian affiliations to outsiders, through sectarian

---

[17] Weber not only underlines the sociological importance of the sectarian community but other dimensions, too, including the economic and psychological repercussions of belonging to a sect (Weber, 1921).

markings mentioned above. This takes place notably through the daily/constant reiteration of a sectarian 'sacred phrase' glorifying the sect's deity: when greeting one another, while exchanging e-mails, etc. (Shah, 2006, p. 214). Moreover, each sect uses specific 'diacritical marks' (Shah, 2006, p. 215). One is the sectarian mark drawn on the forehead *(tilak)* whose form, material, and colour are unique to each sect (even though, as we have seen, the horizontal and vertical logic of the *tilak* has some pan-Indian significance). Another is the ornamentation that each sectarian has to wear, be it a necklace (varying in material, form, number of beads, etc.), staff, trident, particular way of wearing hair, turbans, etc. which is also specific to each sect. More important is the fact that each sect has its own literature. This not only consists in the sacred texts containing the sect's revelation/teaching, but also includes certain 'selected passages' from ancient texts as well as some specific 'periodicals', 'scholarly journals', or sect review's (Shah, 2006, p. 215). But more importantly, sects have developed their own 'music, dance, painting, sculpture, and temple architecture' (Shah, 2006, p. 216).

Hindu Sects Within a Caste Society

The Hindu social order *(varṇāśramadharma)* is based on the acknowledgement of the Veda as the Revelation *(Śruti)*, Sanskrit as the unique sacred language, and Brahmins as exclusive figures of religious authority. By affirming that they follow a revelation/teaching of their own and that a Supreme Being grants his saving grace to all those who surrender themselves to him, Hindu sects contest these Brahmanical values. Although these affirmations are theological in nature, they have certain sociological implications that explain why sects have often been seen as protest movements.[18] Hindu sects are thus perceived as contributing to the development of a 'counter-culture' in South Asia because they present an alternative to the social and ritual duties based on the hierarchical order of caste, which became the dominant form of social organization in about the same period (Thapar, 1979, 2000).

Sects as Subversive Social Groups

The potential of sects for social subversion is partly predicated on *bhakti*, a religious attitude they all share to some extent (Renou, 1953, p. 93). While, over the course of history—from its first occurrence in the 4th century BCE in the late Vedic Upaniṣads to the Bhagavadgītā and the Purāṇas as well as to its contemporary usage—the word *bhakti* has referred to various religious experiences and practices, it nevertheless

---

[18] On this topic, see notably Reiniche and Stern (1995). Let us also note that this perception might have originated with the European-Christian understanding of the church-sect relationship whereby 'sect' appears as being 'schismatic' from an original 'church' (Hatcher, 2020, p. 88, 259 fn. 44).

conveys a particular conception of relationship with the divine. Derived from the root verb BHAJ—to 'share with or in', to 'partake of'—the term *bhakti* is polysemic but often refers to an 'affective participation' on the part of the devotee in the divine's own nature (Renou, 1953, p. 70). It is also rendered as an 'intense devotion'—that can take the form of wonder, fear, love, affection, or even passion (Francis and Vaudeville, 2014)—towards a deity with whom the devotee (*bhakta*) has a personal relationship. Whereas *bhakti* is prevalent all over India (Renou, 1953, p. 72) and nowadays constitutes the 'dominant form' of Hinduism (Johnson, 2010, p. 93)—with practices such as the offering of flowers, perfumes, food, music, singing, dancing, and the veneration of particularly sanctified places—it is in the sectarian context that it emerged, developed, and expressed itself to the greatest extent, and where it constitutes a direct challenge to the basis of caste hierarchy (ibid).

By promoting *bhakti* as a means of liberation, sects presume the possibility of a direct relationship between the devotee and his or her divinity, and hold that anyone with the ad hoc spiritual requirement can qualify for liberation. This principle has deep social outcomes. First, if all devotees are deemed equal before the divine, regardless of their social status, Brahmans are no longer required to serve as religious intermediaries. Their domination over religious life can hence be rejected, leaving room for *Śūdras* to acquire positions of power within the sect, which has happened within many sects, notably tantric ones. Thus sect literature abounds with edifying stories in which low-caste men and women, through their pure love of God, have attained spiritual superiority. Second, given their universalistic view of liberation, sects tend to be socially open, and to make their message accessible to the masses by preaching in vernacular languages (Tamil, Braj, Kannada, Telugu, Bengali, Marathi, Oriya, etc.).[19] They thus challenge the pre-eminence of Sanskrit as the unique religious language in India and have contributed to the emergence of an important body of vernacular literature (poetry, etc.). Third, through their shared values and practices, sectarians form a brotherhood, which represents a social alternative to the caste group. Therefore, within the sectarian context—in monasteries, ashrams, etc.—devotees from different social backgrounds can eat together irrespective of the usual rules of ritual pollution. In some cases, sects challenge caste rules of endogamy by promoting marriage between their members and/or inter-caste marriage.

The Ambivalence of Sects towards the Caste System

While sects have often contested the values upon which the Hindu social order is based, they have not always done so with the same radicalism nor has this always involved conflict.

---

[19] This does not exclude the fact that some sects may also favour a greater degree of esotericism by adopting 'secret writings' (Renou, 1953, p. 95).

First, all sects have not challenged or resisted the Brahmanic tradition and its social order to the same extent. According to Lorenzen (1995), those that developed a view of the Supreme without attributes *(nirguṇa)* and for whom the Supreme principle is impersonal and cannot be represented, were far more challenging. On the other hand, sects that envisaged the Supreme Being as endowed with attributes *(saguṇa)*—that is to say as a personal god incarnated in a divine image *(mūrti)* that can be worshipped—were more likely to endorse the dominant (hierarchical) ideology and serve the interests of the Brahmins. This can be easily understood, as it is the *saguṇa bhakti* currents that have built temples and statues throughout India.

Second, because religion cannot be separated from social forces, most of the dissenting Hindu sects have been confined to social categories of inferior ritual status. Sects have provided lower castes with a psychological and social space where they can defy the pre-eminence of the Brahmins by becoming teachers/masters of religious knowledge and they therefore represent a means of upward social mobility. In fact, the rise of dissenting sects has usually coincided with the economic and political affirmation of lower castes (Juergensmeyer, 1982). This clearly shows the extent to which 'theological differences are [...] symptomatic and expressive of differences in social identities' (Lorenzen, 1995 p. 2).

Third, the alternative values promoted by sects mainly relate to the external world. The foundation of a sect usually aims to transform one's relation to the divine but not to transform the world Their teaching of devotional egalitarianism is often paired with respect for caste hierarchy and gender difference. In fact, many sects disseminate the conviction of 'the unchangeable nature of the order of the world' (Weber, 1958, p. 313).[20] Their principles of equality exclusively target salvific ends: ideally all men, on an equal footing, have direct access to the divine, and therefore a man cannot be ranked according to his birth—or caste. However sects have not discarded hierarchy *per se*. They have merely displaced its basis by invoking other criteria such as personal ability, talent, or merit, which are different from birth criteria. In fact, because they are founded by renouncers (Dumont, 1960), sects have, for example, often shaped a new hierarchical order with renouncers at the top. Going beyond this, a few sects have developed a complete alternative to the Hindu social order, while continuing to participate in it. Through a complex socioreligious process, by which they gradually lose their radicalism, sects have often been co-opted into the caste system following at least three different schemas.

Reintroducing caste values within the sect. Thus, although they are ideologically dissenting, equality within sects is often only acknowledged on the metaphysical level and not on the social level of everyday life. Most strikingly, over time, sects tend to readopt the values of mainstream society and reintroduce caste hierarchies within their fold. In the case of the *Gauḍiya Vaiṣṇavas* (Vaiṣṇavas of Bengal), founded by the Bengali mystic Caitanya, although this sect helped people of 'lower caste to construct

---

[20] There are a few exceptions of sects that tried, without much success, to produce a real alternative social order. On this subject, see Voix (2011).

a new sense of self-respect and assert it in a wider social sphere', over the course of time, it promoted the image of a 'neo-Brahman order', supporting the teleology of the establishment, rather than 'social revolution' (Chakravarti, 1985, pp. 90, 332; quoted in Bandyopadhyay, 2004, p. 62). Sects that claim the equality of all their members can in some cases restrict non-Brahmans from accessing the status of spiritual master, as in some Śaivasiddhanta monasteries (Koppedrayer, 1991). By comparing the procedures of selection and installation of abbots belonging to two different Hindu sects—the Daśanāmī and the Nimbārkī *sampradāyas*—Clémentin-Ojha (2006) has shown that spiritual lineage follows caste and sometimes even kinship rules. In Madras, devotional singing *(bhājana)* groups dedicated to the love of Rādhā and Kṛṣṇa defend an ideal of complete equality, while recruiting disciples within the middle class and among Brahmans (Singer, 1966).

Reinforcing caste solidarity. Whereas in theory, Hindu sects include members of different castes, it can happen that they indeed restrict themselves to proselytizing within a specific social stratum, rendering the link between caste and sect inextricable. In these cases, the sectarian affiliation contributes to reinforcing the cohesion and social unity of a caste. By acting as arbitrators of social behaviour, sectarian authorities can 'enforce social norms among members of the same caste', something we find among the Gauda Sarasvata Brahmanas (Conlon, 1977). In other cases, interacting with caste councils *(pañcayat)* or sectarian institutions *(maṭha)* contributes to unifying caste, as shown in monasteries belonging to different sectarian traditions in Karnataka (Gnanambal, 1973).

Becoming a caste. Lastly, this represents the ultimate moment off the co-optation of a sect into mainstream society. This occurs when a sect reproduces itself along caste lines or according to birth and, paradoxically, the condition of being a member is to be born within the sect. The sect hence gradually begins to function as a caste and becomes considered as such. The process is gradual, as the Satnami sect in Madhya Pradesh consisting mainly of members originating from the Cāmar caste (Babb, 2003, p. 235) or as Ravidāsī who are mainly of either Cāmar or Yādava castes. 'Sectarian caste'—an expression due to Blunt (1931, pp. 132–134)—can also be made of fallen ascetics, such as the Sannyāsis of Nepal, a caste made up of the offspring of Daśnāmī saṃnyāsīs who have taken wives (Bouillier, 1979).

Sect and Caste: Imbrication and Tension

It is 'indisputable' that 'considered over the long historical period, sects fail to overturn the hierarchical order of society despite their egalitarian ideal and their clear subversive potential. They do not become religions in their own right; they operate *within* the framework of the Hindu order' (Clémentin-Ojha, 2013, 'my italics'). Different causes can be invoked to explain this situation.

First, sects have never been able to unite because of their incessant rivalries and their internal divisions, themselves the product of dissent. Their resistance to the established order has been deprived of effectiveness, because it has been played out solely on the basis of rivalry. Second, sects have been constantly torn between their stated principles of equality and their respect for the hierarchy of the caste system. All sects, in fact, are usually marked by what Parry called an 'ambivalence' towards caste society: 'On the one hand, the inequality of man is explicitly denied, while on the other hand, cult members are urged to adopt a lifestyle and a set of customs calculated to enhance their standing in the eyes of orthodox society' (1974, p. 177). It is, for example, very common that in terms of pollution rules, sectarians follow their caste affiliation, particularly when these are still prevalent as they are for the lay members. In the Kabīrpānth, while the followers have their own rituals and norms that replace those of caste Hinduism, the lay members obey the pollution rules applicable to their caste (Lorenzen, 1987, pp. 267–268). Among the Rāmānandīs, unfailing devotion theoretically prevails over caste affiliation and other markers of social identity. But when it comes to commensality or matrimonial exchanges, Rāmānandīs adopt the same avoidance behaviour that marks the social relations between high and low castes. Moreover, their temples are served by Brahmin priests (Van der Veer, 1988, p. 88) and for large community meals the cook is a Brahmin (Gross, 1992, p. 145).

The extent to which this ambivalence is central to a sect's doctrine, or reflects a systemic difficulty in overthrowing the hierarchy of a caste-based society, is a matter of debate. Discussing Śaiva sects and drawing from O'Flaherty's work on the ambiguous nature of Śiva (1981), both 'erotic' and 'ascetic', 'family man', and 'vagabond', Flood argues that indeed Śaiva traditions characteristically contain this ambivalence: 'on the one hand, the Saiva imagination has been in line with the instituting power of particular regions, on the other, it has brought to life a world that undermines that power through its promotion of a vision of the self that transcends social institutions and political stability' and it is precisely in this ambiguity that Flood sees the 'genius' of these traditions (2003, p. 200).

It is perhaps Louis Dumont who most clearly articulates the connection between caste and sect: 'In theory, for the man-in-the-world, adherence to a sect is an individual matter, *superimposed* on caste observances, though *not obliterating them*, and the sect respects these observances even though it relativizes them and criticizes worldly religion from the point of view of individualist religion' (1999, pp. 187–188, 'my italics'). Although he had not done any fieldwork on Hindu sects, Dumont had rightly noted that sect and caste operate on 'different' levels: most Hindu sects are 'otherworldly'. They contest the caste system only in the name of the supramundane purpose of liberation, but on all other levels, operate within the caste system, and its specific system of organizing social relations. They find their source and justification in the sectarian doctrines themselves which, partly based on the Veda, perpetuate its hierarchical ideology. If sects do not offer any alternative to the specific organization of social relations with which they interact closely (not without tension), nor therefore to *dharma* understood as a sociocosmic order, this is because to a certain extent they constitute individual religions which are superimposed on the group religion according to the dictates of caste, in a logic of aggregation of optional practices with mandatory practices. To put it differently, we can rephrase Weber's famous sentence, 'The truly devout Hindu is not merely a Hindu but a member of a Hindu sect as well'. (Weber, 1958, pp. 24–25).

Conclusion

Hinduism is characterized by diversity that defies any attempt to organize it because it has never ceased to be 'constructed, deconstructed, and reconstructed' (Lorenzen, 2011, p. 271). Although they have always involved only a minority of Hindus, sects have undoubtedly played a crucial role in historical change. They have been both a source of resistance and a source of innovation. Because, in Hinduism, 'The notion of orthodoxy lacks stability' (Renou and Filliozat, 1947, p. 621), sectarian literature as well as practices have often been integrated into the main Hindu fold. The way the Hindu tradition has assimilated these currents is one of the most striking manifestations of its flexibility and of the fact that it has never been fixed or monolithic. Sects have not only 'infused new life' but might even be responsible for the 'very survival of Hinduism' (Renou, 1953, p. 89). Therefore addressed from a historical perspective that takes into account the social construction of its boundaries, the sectarian phenomenon is a privileged means of studying the dynamics of the internal divisions of Hinduism as well as their resorption.

Similarly, the distinction between caste and sect has been a fecund one through which to apprehend the diversity of Hinduism as these categories represent two antagonistic, yet compatible, types of religious communalization. While sects assert the fundamental irrelevance of caste in obtaining salvation and thus challenge the social hierarchy, they are not isolated from the surrounding society, but operate within the framework of its social stratification. However, one should bear in mind that used as sociological concepts these two terms do not cover all scales of Hindu religious groups: while some groups are difficult to classify in one or another category,[21] under the ideal-type of the Sect co-exist a great variety of social groups that can differ in their theological or institutional characteristics (i.e. *sampradāya*, reform movements or contemporary guru based religious movements, etc.). Moreover the 'limit' cases where a group at a particular time of its history is identified as a Hindu sect while being later identified as a new religion also reminds us that these categories do not represent fixed natural entities but rather some social realities as viewed at a particular time.[22] Therefore, the recent attempt by some sociologists of religion in India to overtake the caste-sect dyad that has often been denounced as embedded in a Europocentric view of religion must be welcome. Following Inden (1990)—who was inspired by

---

[21] For example, on the case of the Bāuls of Bengal being categorized both as a sect and as a caste, see Openshaw (2002, p. 20).

[22] As the famous case of Gurū Nānak (1469–1539) who was at his times considered a Bhakti guru and latter the founder of Sikhism (Oberoi, 1994).

Collingwood (1942)—Shodhan (2001) and most notably Hatcher (2020) develop the concept of 'religious polities' to designate communities of choice that maintain their distinctiveness through the establishment of a self-ruling power. What makes the usage of 'religious polity' interesting for the social scientist is that it reminds us that these types of communities are not self-existent, radically bounded, and settled forever but constantly altered and renewed through interactions with their environment and, notably, with the competing authorities of their time (be these local landlords and rulers, legal procedure, bureaucracy, State apparatus, etc.). Not only are religious polities thus 'historically conditioned' and exist 'along a scale of forms' (Hatcher, 2020: 82) but they build themselves up through interactions that exceed their sole opposition to/interactions with caste.

References

Assayag, J. 1995. 'Semence de sang ou de son? Une caste de prêtrise sectaire dans le sud de, l'Inde (Karnataka)'. In M.-L. Reiniche and H. Stern (Eds.), *Les ruses du salut: Religion et politiques dans le monde indien* (pp. 55–85). Paris: Éditions de l'École des Hautes Études en Sciences Sociales, *Puruṣārtha* 17.

Babb, Lawrence A. 2003. 'Sects and Indian Religions'. In Veena Das (Ed.), *The Oxford Companion to Sociology and Social Anthropology* (Vol. 1, pp. 802–826). New Delhi: Oxford University Press.

Bandyopadhyay, S. 2004. *Caste, Culture and Hegemony. Social Domination in Colonial Bengal*. New Delhi: SAGE.

Bhandarkar, R. G. 1913. *Vaisnavism, Saivism and Minor Religious Systems*. Strassburg: Karl J. Trübner.

Bhattacharyya, N. N. 1996. *Indian Religious Historiography*. Delhi: Munshiram Manoharlal.

Blunt, E. A. H. 1931. *The Caste System of Nothern India*. London: Oxford University Press.

Bouillier, V. 1979. *Naître renonçant, une caste de Sannyāsi Villageois au Népal Central*. Nanterre: Société d'ethnologie.

Bouillier, V. 1995. 'Une secte en forme de caste? Documents judiciaires du monastère Kānphaṭā jogī de Caughera (Dang, Nepal)'. In M.-L. Reiniche and H. Stern (Eds.), *Les ruses du salut: Religion et politiques dans le monde indien* (pp. 43–54). Paris: Éditions de l'École des Hautes Études en Sciences Sociales, *Puruṣārtha* 17.

Boulhol, P. 2002. '*Secta*: de la ligne de conduite au groupe hétérodoxe. Evolution sémantique jusqu'au début du Moyen-Âge'. *Revue de l'histoire des religions*, 219(1): 5–33.

Brunner-Lachaux, H. 1963–1988. *Somaśambhupaddhati. Rituels dans la tradition Śivaite selon Somaśambhu*, 4 vols. Pondicherry: French Institute of Pondicherry.

Chakravarti, R. 1985. *Vaiṣṇavism in Bengal, 1486–1900*. Calcutta: Sanskrit Pustak Bhandar.

Clémentin-Ojha, C. 1999. *Le Trident sur le Palais. Une cabale anti-vishnouite dans un royaume hindou à l'époque coloniale*. Paris: École française d'Extrême-Orient.

Clémentin-Ojha, C. 2006. 'Replacing the Abbot: Rituals of Monastic Ordination and Investiture in Modern Hinduism'. *Asiatische Studien/Etudes Asiatiques*, 40(3): 535–573.

Clémentin-Ojha, C. 2009–2010. 'Dynamique des mouvements religieux dans le monde indien. De l'anthropologie à l'histoire'. *Annuaire de l'École des Hautes Études en Sciences Sociales*. Paris: EHESS. http://journals.openedition.org/annuaire-ehess/19314 and /20008.

Clémentin-Ojha, C. 2013. 'Sociological Approaches to Hinduism'. *Oxford Bibliographies Online*. DOI : 10.1093/OBO/9780195399318-0129. https://www.oxfordbibliographies.com/view/document/obo-9780195399318/obo-9780195399318-0129.xml.

Colas, G. 2003. 'History of Vaiṣṇava Traditions: An Esquisse'. In Flood Galvin (Ed.), *The Blackwell Companion to Hinduism* (pp. 229–270). Oxford: Blackwell Publishing.

Collingwood, R. G. 1942. *The New Leviathan, or Man, Society, Civilization and Barbarism*. New York: Oxford University Press.

Conlon, F. F. 1977. *A Caste in a Changing World: The Chitrapur Saraswat Brahmans, 1700–1935*. Berkeley: University of California Press.

Datta, A. 1888. *Bharatvarshiya Upasaka Sampraday*. Calcutta: Notun Sangha.

Doniger, W. 2009. *The Hindus: An Alternative History*. New York: The Penguin Press.

Dumont, L. 1960. 'World Renunciation in Indian Religions'. *Contributions to Indian Sociology*, 4: 33–62.

Dumont, L. 1999 [1970]. *Homo Hierarchicus. The Caste System and Its Implications*. New Delhi: Oxford University Press.

Eisenstadt, S. N., Reuven Kahane, and David Shulman (Eds.). 1984. *Orthodoxy, Heterodoxy and Dissent in India*. Berlin: Mouton.

Farquhar, J. N. 1913. *The Crown of Hinduism*. London: Oxford University Press.

Farquhar, J. N. 1920. *An Outline of the Religious Literature of India*. London: Oxford University Press.

Flood, G. 2003. 'The Śaiva Traditions'. In Flood Galvin (Ed.), *The Blackwell Companion to Hinduism* (pp. 200–228). Oxford: Blackwell Publishing.

Francis, E. and C. Shmidt. 2014. 'Introduction: Towards and Archaeology of Bhakti'. In E. Francis and C. Shmidt (Eds.), *The Archaeology of Bhakti I: Mathurā and Maturai, Back and Forth* (pp. 1–29). Pondicherry: Institut Français de Pondichery & École Française d'Extrême Orient.

Geffré, Claude. 2019, 6 August. 'Monothéisme'. In *Encyclopædia Universalis* [online], viewed 6th August 2019. https://universalis.aria.ehess.fr/encyclopedie/monotheisme/.

Gnanambal, K. 1973. *Religious Institutions and Caste Panchayats in South India. Memoir, Anthropological Survey of India 18*. Calcutta: Anthropological Survey of India, Government of India.

Gross, R. 1992. *The Sadhus of India: A Study of Hindu Asceticism*. Jaipur: Rawat.

Hardy, F. 1983. *Viraha-bhakti. The Early History of Kṛṣṇa Devotion of South India*. Delhi: Oxford University Press.

Hawley, J. S. 2015. *A Storm of Songs. India and the Idea of the Bhakti* Movement. Cambridge, London: Harvard University Press.

Hatcher, B. 2018. 'Situating the Swaminarayan Tradition in the Historiography of Modern Hindu Reform'. In R. B. Williams and Y. Trivedi (Eds.), *Swaminarayan Hinduism. Tradition, Adaptation and Identity*. London: Oxford University Press.

Hatcher, B. 2020. *Hinduism before Reform*. Cambridge: Harvard University Press.

Hiden, R. 1990. *Imagining India*. New York: Basil Blackwell.

Juergensmeyer, M. 1982. *Religion as Social Vision: The Movement against Untouchability in 20th Century Punjab*. Berkeley: University of California Press.

Johnson, W. J. 2010. *Oxford Dictionary of Hinduism*. Oxford: Oxford University Press.

King, R. 1999. 'Orientalism and the Modern Myth of "Hinduism"'. *Numen*, 45(2): 146–185.

Koppedrayer, K. I. 1991. 'The Varṇāśramacandrika and Śūdra's Right to Preceptorhood: The Social Background of a Philosophical Debate in Late Medieval South India'. *Journal of Indian Philosophy*, 19: 297–314.

Lochtefeld, J. G. 1994. 'The Vishva Hindu Parishad and the Roots of Hindu Militancy'. *Journal of the American Academy of Religion*, 62(2): 587–602.

Lorenzen, D. N. (Ed.). 1995. *Bhakti Religion in North India: Community Identity and Political Action*. Albany: State University of New York Press.

Lorenzen, D. N. 2011. 'Hindu Sects and Hindu Religion Precolonial and Colonial Concepts'. In Talbot, C. (Ed.), *Knowing India—Colonial and Modern Constructions of the Past* (pp. 251–278). New Delhi: Yoda Press.

Lorenzen, D. N. 2004. 'Introduction'. In David N. Lorenzen (Ed.), *Religious Movements in South Asia, 600–1800* (pp. 16–44). New Delhi: Oxford University Press.

Lorenzen, D. N., et al. 1984/1987. 'Śaivism: An Overview'. In Mircea Eliade (Ed.), *The Encyclopedia of Religion* (Vol. 13, pp. 6–20). New York: Collier Macmillan.

Lorenzen, D. N. 1987. 'Tradition of "Non-Cast" Hinduism: The Kabir Panth'. *Contributions to Indian Sociology*, 21(2): 263–283.

Lutgendorf, P. 2003. 'Medieval Devotional Traditions: An Annotated Survey of Recent Scholarship'. In A. Sharma (Ed.), *The Study of Hinduism* (pp. 200–260). Columbia: University of South Carolina Press.

Malinar, A. 2013. 'Sampradāya'. In K. Jacobsen et al. (Eds.), *Brill's Encyclopedia of Hinduism* (pp. 156–164). Leiden: Brill.

Mallison, F. (Ed.). 2001. *Constructions hagiographiques dans le monde indien. Entre mythe et histoire*. Paris: Librairie Honoré Champion.

McLeod, W. H. 1978. 'On the Word *Pānth*: A Problem of Terminology and Definition'. *Contribution to Indian Sociology*, 12(2): 287–295.

Monier-Williams, M. 1877. *Non-Christian Religious System: Hinduism*. London: Society for Promoting Christian Knowledge.

Monier-Williams, M. 1899. *A Sanskrit-English Dictionary: Etymologically and Philologically Arranged with Special Reference to Cognate Indo-European languages*. Oxford: Clarendon Press. https://sanskrit.inria.fr/MW/284.html#sampradaaya, accessed 13 July 2019.

Oberoi, H. 1994. *The Construction of Religious Boundaries: Culture, Identity, and Diversity in the Sikh Tradition*. New Delhi: Oxford University Press.

Openshaw, J. 2002. *Seeking Bāuls of Bengal*. London: Oxford University Press.

Padoux, A. 2000a. 'The Tantric Guru'. In D. G. White (Ed.), *Tantra in Practice* (pp. 41–51). Princeton: Princeton Readings in Religion.

Padoux, A. 2000b. 'Introduction'. In H. Brunner, G. Oberhammer, and A. Padoux (Eds.), *Tāntrikābhidhānakośa* (Vol. 1, pp. 11–36). Vienne: Verlag Der Osterreichischen Akademie der Wissenschaften.

Parry, J. 1974. 'Egalitarian Values in a Hierarchical Society'. *South Asian Review*, 7(2): 95–121.

Rangarajan, H. 1996. *Rāmānuja Sampradāya in Gujarat: A Historical Perspective*. Bombay: Somaiya.

Reiniche, M.-L., and H. Stern (Eds.). 1995. 'Les ruses du salut. Religion et politiques dans le monde indien'. *Puruṣārtha* (Vol. 17). Paris: Éditions de l'École des Hautes Études en Sciences Sociales.

Renou, L. 1953. *Religions of Ancient India*. London: The Athlone Press.

Renou, L., and J. Filliozat. 1947. *L'Inde Classique. Manuel des études indiennes*. Paris: Payot.

Richardson, A. E. 2014. *Seeing Krishna in America. The Hindu Bhakti Tradition of Vallabhacharya in India and Its Movement to the West*. Jefferson: McFarland & Company.

Sanderson, A. 1988. 'Śaivism and the Tantric Traditions'. In S. R. Sutherland, P. Clarke, F. Hardy, and L. Houlden (Eds.), *The World's Religions* (pp. 660–704). London: Routledge.

Sawyer, D. W. 1993. 'The Monastic Structure of Banarsi Dandi Sadhus'. In B. R. Hertel and C. A. Humes (Eds.), *Living Banaras: Hindu Religion in Cultural Context* (pp. 159–180). Albany: State University of New York Press.

Shah, A. M. 2006. 'Sects and Hindu Social Structure'. *Contributions to Indian Sociology*, 40(2): 209–248.

Singer, M. 1966. 'The Radha-Krishna Bhajanas of Madras City'. In M. Singer (Ed.), *Krishna: Myths, Rites and Attitudes* (pp. 139–172). Honolulu: East-West Center Press.

Shodhan, A. 2001. *A Question of Community: Religious Groups and Colonial Law*. Delhi: Samya.

Stietencron, H. von. 1991 [1989]. 'Hinduism: On the Proper Use of a Deceptive Term'. In G. D. Sontheimer and Hermann H. Kulke (Eds.), *Hinduism Reconsidered* (pp. 11–20). Delhi: Manohar.

Stewart, Tony K. 2010. *The Final Word. The Caitanya Caritâmrita and the Grammar of Religious Tradition*. New York: Oxford University Press.

Thapar, R. 1979. 'Dissent and Protest in the Early Indian Tradition'. *Studies in History*, 1(2): 177–195.

Thapar, R. 2000. 'Renunciation: The Making of a Counter-Culture?' In R. Thapar (Ed.), *Cultural Pasts: Essays Indian History* (pp. 876–913). Oxford: Oxford University Press.

Van Der Veer, P. 1988. *Gods on Earth. The Management of Religious Experience and Identity in a North Indian Pilgrimage Centre*. London: The Athlone Press.

Voix, R. 2011. 'Une utopie en pays bengali: De l'idéologie sectaire hindoue à l'édification d'une alternative communautaire'. In C. Clémentin-Ojha (Ed.), *Convictions religieuses et engagement en Asie du Sud depuis 1850* (pp. 165–188). Paris: Ecole Française d'Extrême-Orient.

Weber, M. 1958 [1921]. *The Religion of India. The Sociology of Hinduism and Buddhism*. Glencoe: The Free Press.

Wilson, H. H. 1958 (edited by Ernst R. Rost) [1861]. *Religious Sects of the Hindus*. Calcutta: Susil Gupta.

CHAPTER 16

SANSKRITIZATION

The Inheritance of an Ideational Category

GEORGE KUNNATH

Introduction

The concept of Sanskritization should be understood in the context of the wider study of the caste system in India. Its various conceptualizations reflect the changing emphases in scholarship on Indian society and culture during the colonial and postcolonial periods. Colonial scholarship portrayed caste hierarchy as a rigid and static system of social stratification; this view being primarily derived from interpretation of the Hindu religious texts. However, in the 1950s, a field-based analysis supporting social mobility began to emerge. This new approach was primarily reflected in the work of Indian anthropologist Mysore Narasimhachar Srinivas (1916–1999), or simply known as M. N. Srinivas. Srinivas argued that the caste system was in dynamic flux, with the castes in the lower ranks of the hierarchy constantly striving for upward mobility. Central to his argument was the concept of Sanskritization, which he defined as a process that entailed lower castes emulating the beliefs and practices of upper castes, particularly those of Brahmins, in order to raise their status in the caste hierarchy. Srinivas and several others provided ethnographic evidence that linked emulation of upper caste norms with social mobility. In contrast, other studies pointed out that Sanskritization falsely represented lower castes as eager imitators of the socio-religious practices of upper castes because it negated their agency and consciousness. These studies emphasized that lower caste participation in politics, and new economic and educational opportunities have enabled their upward mobility, and not Sanskritization. They also maintained that, in some instances where Sanskritization did occur, it was a manifestation of resistance to caste domination rather than compliance to upper caste norms, and that emulation did not result in mobility in the hierarchical structure of caste.

Examination of these contrasting perspectives on Sanskritization is the focus of this chapter. The chapter is divided into three sections. The first section, drawing on Srinivas' definition, provides a comprehensive overview of Sanskritization. The second section identifies and probes the ambiguities of this concept by examining its two primary assertions regarding social mobility and emulation. The final section, while demonstrating the problematics inherent in this category, points out that the concept tends to be ideational in its conceptualization of the caste system, especially regarding its integrative functions, while the empirical evidence suggests otherwise. In this sense the use of the term 'ideational' denotes imagined, ideological, ideal, and aspirational. I conclude the chapter with three observations, which further clarify the ideational underpinnings of Sanskritization. The first two observations relate to Srinivas' emphasis on harmony, consensus, and unity in his presentation of Sanskritization. In his vision of a unified India, the Hindu religion and the caste system were central, and Sanskritization functioned as the connecting link between them. Following on from this, the third observation relates to Sanskritization in relation to the contemporary ideology of Hindutva. Although they might differ in their approaches, both Sanskritization and Hindutva seem to share common ideological ground regarding Indian civilization as Hindu, and Sanskritic culture as its unifying force.

SANSKRITIZATION: THE CONCEPT

Srinivas first defined Sanskritization in his book *Religion and Society among the Coorgs of South India*. He says:

> The caste system is far from a rigid system in which the position of each component caste is fixed for all time. Movement has always been possible, and especially so in the middle regions of the hierarchy. A low caste was able, in a generation or two, to rise to a higher position in the hierarchy by adopting vegetarianism and teetotalism, and by Sanskritizing its ritual and pantheon. In short, it took over, as far as possible, the customs, rites, and beliefs of the Brahmins, and the adoption of the Brahminic way of life by a low caste seems to have been frequent, though theoretically forbidden. This process has been called 'Sanskritization' in this book, in preference to 'Brahminization,' as certain Vedic rites are confined to the Brahmins and the two other 'twice born' castes. (1952, p. 30)

Although the centrality of the Brahmin underpins his ideology of emulation, Srinivas (1956) prefers the term Sanskritization over Brahminization because according to him some Brahmin sects did not adhere to vegetarianism or teetotalism, two significant features of Sanskritization. Further, drawing on the writings of anthropologists studying other regions of India (Panikkar, 1955; Pocock, 1957), Srinivas points out that it was not just the Brahmins who were emulated, but also other locally dominant castes, and these were often Kshatriyas or Vaishyas. Thus, he spoke of three models of Sanskritization— Brahmin, Kshatriya, and Vaishiya (Srinivas, 1989, p. 18). Castes in these three *varnas* were called 'twice-born' or *dwija* castes because only they were 'entitled' to don the sacred thread at an initiation ceremony which symbolized a 'second birth' (Srinivas, 1966, p. 8). The term Sanskritization became an appropriate category as only upper castes were considered the custodians of Vedic knowledge and Sanskritic culture (Srinivas, 1966). Moreover, Srinivas noticed that this process was not limited to low castes, but extended to tribal groups who were outside the Hindu caste order. These communities too imitated upper caste and Brahminical values and practices. In his later work, therefore, Srinivas broadened the definition of Sanskritization to include the above factors. Accordingly, he defined Sanskritization as 'the process by which a low caste or tribe or other group takes over the customs, rituals, beliefs, ideology and style of life of a high and in particular "twice born" (*dwija*) caste' (Srinivas, 1989, p. 56).

However, the emulation of the Kshatriya or Vaishya did not take away the centrality of the Brahmin in Srinivas' scheme of Sanskritization. He commented that the locally dominant caste was emulated in the short term but, over a long period of time, Brahminical practices spread among the lower castes 'in a chain reaction ... each group took from the one higher to it, and in turn gave to the group below' (Srinivas, 1956, p. 483). Srinivas thought that the Brahminical model became the most sought after because it was considered more 'puritanical' than all other models due to its emphasis on vegetarianism and teetotalism, which were recognized as superior practices in the Hindu religious context. Further, 'ambitious castes' that aspired to higher status 'were aware of the legitimizing role of the Brahmin' (Srinivas, 1966, p. 27).

Further, Srinivas claimed that Sanskritization was not limited to the adoption of Brahminic customs and rituals, but also included adoption of a host of ideas and values, both sacred and secular, which have their origins in Sanskrit literature. Theological ideas like *karma* (destiny), *dharma* (duty), *papa* (sin), *punya* (good deed), *maya* (illusion), and *moksa* (liberation from the cycle of birth and death) reached the common people through myths and stories. These ideas then frequently occurred in the conversations of ordinary people, including members of the lower castes (Srinivas, 1956, pp. 485–486). Along with theological ideas, he asserted that the lower castes also emulated some of the practices prevalent among the Brahmins, such as early marriage for girls before puberty, prohibition of widow remarriage, and increased restrictions on women in general, which included seclusion, and veiling among others (Srinivas, 1956, p. 484).

Srinivas claimed that Sanskritization could lead to social mobility when it successfully met certain conditions. First, the emulation became effective when it was a group process. It required that an entire caste or tribe, or the majority of its members in a region collectively took various steps to raise its position. It was important that the group was large enough to maintain itself as an endogamous entity. Second, Sanskritization was likely to succeed when it was accompanied by economic and/or political power. According to Srinivas, these two forms of power, alongside the ritual, functioned as 'the three axes of power in the caste system' (1956, p. 483). Third, it was a long-drawn-out process. It usually took one or more generations before a caste's claim to be of a higher position came to be recognized by other castes. Meanwhile, the caste in question had to continuously put forward its claims through appropriate myths, rituals, and practices before other castes accepted these claims. There was also a strong likelihood that the claims would never get recognized, or perhaps they would become accepted in one region, but not in another (Srinivas, 1956, pp. 492–493). Fourth, there was more mobility in the middle rungs of the caste hierarchy than at the top or bottom. Unlike the 'extremities of the system which were relatively fixed' (Srinivas, 1956, p. 491), among the middle castes there was a certain vagueness regarding the rank of each caste. With new opportunities for improving their economic status during the colonial period, the middle castes often successfully staked their claim to higher status. This was not the case, however, in relation to the 'untouchable' castes which, in spite of their many efforts (Srinivas, 1956, p. 493), rarely succeeded in raising their status. Their only chance to raise their caste status depended on moving to a new place where their caste background remained unknown.

Srinivas' conceptualization of Sanskritization raises two main concerns that can be expressed through a number of interrelated questions:

1) Sanskritization and Mobility: What is the type of change triggered by Sanskritization? Does it lead to cultural or structural change? Can 'untouchable' communities achieve social mobility through Sanskritization? What are the implications of Sanskritization for women?
2) Nature of Emulation: Is the desire to emulate Brahmins/upper castes inherent among lower castes? Does emulation depend on the time and context? Does emulation suggest consensus on the caste system? Is emulation a form of resistance? How do upper castes respond to emulation?

These questions will be examined in the following section, based on a number of studies that engaged with Srinivas' concept in field situations, including my own work among Dalit communities in Bihar.

Sanskritization: A Critical Appraisal

Srinivas' primary thesis of social mobility through Sanskritization remains contentious, as do many other aspects of this concept, such as emulation as an inherent and historical process in the caste system. In one of his later writings, *The Cohesive Role of Sanskritization and Other Essays* (1989, p. 17), he reiterated the claim made earlier regarding the two dimensions of mobility associated with Sanskritization—cultural and structural. The changes in customs, ritual, ideology, and life-style indicated cultural change. The gradual entry of outside or marginal groups into the Hindu fold, and the upward mobility of the lower castes in the local caste hierarchy demonstrated evidence of structural change. Singer (1992, p. 145), in his review of the above book, endorses Srinivas' 'belief' that this concept continues to remain a 'valid description' of 'cultural and structural changes' all over India.

The concept of Sanskritization has been applied in several ethnographic studies explaining social mobility, especially in the 1960s and 1970s (Bailey, 1957; Rowe, 1968a, 1968b; Singer and Cohn, 1968; Lynch, 1969; Berreman, 1993;). Rowe, for instance, mentions the significant role of Sanskritization in the changes in the 19th-century caste system, especially among the Nonyas and Kayasthas. Kayasthas used various platforms—pamphlets, caste histories, petitions to the colonial courts—to advance their claim as Kshatriyas during the colonial period (1968a). The Nonya, an 'untouchable' caste, tried to establish their identity as Chauhan, a Rajput community, through Sanskritization and appropriate myths (1968b). Rowe pointed out that in the post-Independence period, new avenues for social change opened up in urban areas, especially for the wealthy Nonyas, but in rural India Sanskritization remained the primary mode of social mobility. The scholarship on mobility was not limited only to lower castes' imitation of the higher castes, but also extended to tribals who were normally considered outside the Hindu fold, and its caste hierarchy (Bailey, 1960; Majumdar, 1972). Majumdar's work (1972) described the adoption of Sanskritic Hindu practices by the Garo tribe. Sanskritization facilitated the transformation of this tribe into a caste. Further, the implications of Sanskritization for the position of women also came under the purview of the research on caste mobility. When a caste adopted the practices of the 'twice-born' castes, increasing restrictions were placed on women. These included prohibition of widow and divorcee remarriage, and introduction of dowry, patrilineal inheritance, seclusion, and veiling (Srinivas, 1989; Berreman, 1993; Mosse, 1994).

It is likely that Sanskritization led to changes among certain lower castes and tribal groups in the sphere of culture, especially in dietary habits, ritual practices, status of women, and withdrawal from 'polluting' occupations. But, there is no evidence to suggest that it contributed to a change in the structural location of these castes in the caste hierarchy. Lynch's (1969) seminal work among the Jatavs in Agra, for example, demonstrated that their efforts to claim Kshatriya identity through emulation did not raise their position in the caste hierarchy. Instead, political participation, and new education and employment opportunities opened up by the reservation policy and the leather industry in Agra, contributed to their upward mobility. A similar finding from my ongoing research among Dalit communities in Bihar's Jehanabad district indicates that impetus for change in their social status in the 1970s came not from emulation of upper castes, but from their collective assertion against caste-based exploitation spearheaded by the Maoist movement. Dalit mobilization and armed resistance ended upper caste dominance in Jehanabad villages, especially with the defeat of the Bhumi Sena, caste militia of the Kurmi landowners (Kunnath, 2017). The nature of resistance to caste oppression itself changed from covert and individual actions, which James Scott (1985) termed as everyday forms of resistance, to overt, and collective protest. The structures of local power relations were reconstituted with the formation of village committees primarily under the leadership of Dalit men and women. These committees replaced dominant caste *panchayats*, and managed village affairs, including settling local disputes, fixing daily wages, and regulating labour relations. The changing power relations enabled Dalit communities to make their caste identities visible in the villages by initiating Dalit festivities and installing statues of Dalit heroes. Ravidasis (Chamars) organized the Sant Ravidas Jayanti (birth anniversary of Sant Ravidas) every year with great pomp and ceremony. Dusadhs installed statues of Chuharmal to commemorate the myth of a legendary Dusadh warrior. As local narratives go, Chuharmal is said to have killed 700 Bhumihar landlords on the battle field (Narayan, 2001; Kunnath, 2020). These actions made Dalit identity visible rather than obliterating it through imitation of upper castes.

However, while there are several examples of counter-culture among lower caste communities, they do not negate the widespread practice of emulation in the caste system across India. An appraisal of Sanskritization, therefore, calls for closer scrutiny of the nature of this emulation itself. Srinivas viewed the caste system as the central ordering feature of Hindu society. Since the Brahmins remained at the apex of the system, Brahminic culture became esteemed and desired by everyone. Consequently, Srinivas (1952, p. 31) maintained, 'Every caste tended to imitate the customs and rituals of the top most caste, and this was responsible for the spread of Sanskritization.' He asserted that this process has been in operation 'over a period of at least 2500 years' and has penetrated the culture and beliefs of even the most remote hill tribes (Srinivas, 1952).

At the centre of the concept of Sanskritization, in Srinivas' view, was the perception that there is a general consensus in India regarding the hierarchical ordering of castes with Brahmins at the top, and 'untouchables' at the bottom. Dumont in his influential book *Homo Hierarchicus* (1980) shares this perception. Caste, according to him, is fundamentally based on the principle of hierarchy, which is constituted by the Hindu religious ideas of purity and pollution. The opposition between ritual purity and pollution defines the hierarchical position and relationship of the castes, with the Brahmins and 'untouchables' at extreme opposite ends of the pole, the former being the 'most pure' and the latter the 'least pure' (Dumont, 1980, pp. 43–44). According to him, in a traditional society like India, hierarchy is viewed through the prism of holism, and not in terms of social stratification or inequality. Each caste accepts its place in the hierarchical system, and helps to maintain the system by following the *dharma* assigned to it. Moffatt (1979) reiterated the same idea by pointing out that the lower castes are in consensus with the values of the system. According to him 'The view from the bottom is based on the same principles and evaluations as the view from the middle or the view from the top' (Moffatt, 1979, p. 3). The lower castes replicated among themselves 'the entire set of institutions and of ranked relations from which they have been excluded by the higher castes by reason of their extreme lowness' (Moffatt, 1979, p. 5). In Moffatt's view, there was cultural consensus at work among all caste groups regardless of their position in the hierarchy, which manifested in principles of inclusion and exclusion, complementarity and replication.

However, emulation did not always stem from consensus on the caste system as Srinivas and others asserted, but also from dissent and resistance. Jha (1977), for instance, using government records of conflicts between lower caste peasants, particularly Yadavs, and upper caste landlords in Bihar from 1921 to 1925, demonstrated that the former turned to Sanskritization because of social and economic exploitation by the latter, and not rising economic prosperity, as Srinivas claimed. Adoption of various practices, especially donning the sacred thread, and prioritizing education, '... *was to bring themselves on a level with the higher castes*' (Jha, 1977, p. 550; emphasis in the original). Lower castes used Sanskritization as a mechanism to end economic and social oppression by claiming their equality with upper castes. Similar alternative explanations characterized the adoption of certain Sanskritic practices in my fieldwork area. Some Dalit men and women who were members of the Kabirpanth, a devotional sect that preached equality, advocated strict adherence to teetotalism and vegetarianism. When quizzed as to whether or not this amounted to following Brahminical norms, some of them retorted that their emphasis on vegetarianism had nothing to do with Brahminism, but respect for all living beings (Kunnath, 2017).

Many recent writings representing a Dalit perspective have critiqued Sanskritization as an elite model that denies agency and autonomous consciousness to Dalits. They have claimed that within this model, which 'valorises consensus over conflict', Dalit protests are viewed 'as mere aspirational imitations' of upper caste practices (Rawat and Satyanarayana, 2016, pp. 10–11). Instead they have presented alternative Dalit articulations that are in conflict with the Brahminical model. Ilaiah (2002), for instance, argued that there is nothing in common between the socio-cultural worlds of the Dalitbahujan—the oppressed majority comprising lower castes—and upper caste Hindus. In fact, they are opposed to each other. He advocated that the only way to establish an egalitarian India is the *Dalitization* of the entire society, where Dalit values of humanism, equality, and tolerance will replace the repressive and hierarchical character of Hindu society. Iliah's conceptualization had antecedents in the powerful anti-Brahmin movements advocated by Phule, Periyar, and Ambedkar in western and southern India (Omvedt, 1976; O'Hanlon, 1985; Jaffrelot, 2003), and the *Ad Dharam* movement in the north, especially Punjab (Ram, 2012). These movements called for the rediscovery of the culture and identity of the lower castes, where there was no place for the emulation of upper castes.

Another aspect questioned was Srinivas' claim that Sanskritization has been in operation for 2500 years (1952), and that the change in the colonial period was 'only a quantitative one' (1956, p. 492). Critics pointed out that this assertion appears ahistorical (Carroll, 1977; Lee, 2019). The emulation of upper castes does not seem to have been an inherent tendency among lower caste populations since ancient times, but the product of certain policies and programmes of the colonial regime (Cohn, 1996; Dirks, 2001). Movements for caste mobility became widespread in the 19th and 20th centuries when British officials used Brahminical norms to rank the social and ritual status of various caste groups for the census enumeration in 1891 and 1901. Caste became politicized, and caste *sabhas* or associations sprung up to contest the officially assigned position if it was perceived as 'low' in the caste hierarchy (Dirks, 2001). Kayasth, Yadav, Kurmi, Koeri, all formed their caste *sabhas*, and campaigned to raise their status in various ways—through organizing protest meetings, petitioning the government, writing caste histories, and encouraging their respective caste communities to adopt Sanskritic practices to claim higher status (Rudolph and Rudolph, 1967; Rowe, 1968a;

Frankel, 1989). One of the first Dalit castes to form a caste association was the Dusadh in Bihar, who formed the *Dusadh Sabha* in 1911, and took forward its claim for Kshatriya status (Pinch, 1996). Undoubtedly, the colonial preoccupation with caste in the census, especially the gradation of castes along the Brahminical scale of purity and pollution, led caste associations to initiate Sanskritization for social mobility (Carroll, 1977). Therefore, the surge in Sanskritization was ignited by an external impetuous rather than an inherent desire to emulate upper castes as Srinivas has claimed.

There is substantial evidence to argue that emulation, whether we call it Sanskritization or use other terms for it, was a widespread phenomenon, especially in the wake of colonial policies of caste enumeration, and that still continues today, at least in some form. However, to deduce from the spread of this phenomenon that there is an inherent desire to emulate upper castes is problematic because it falsely represents lower caste communities as being in consensus with the caste system. Equally problematic is the claim that all acts of Sanskritization represent collective resistance against caste hierarchy and exploitation. For instance, acts like donning the 'scared thread' or inventing myths to claim Kshatriya identity might offer an immediate challenge to upper caste dominance in a locality, but in the long run, they reinforce the caste system. Ironically these acts of both compliance and resistance emphasize the significance of caste (Kunnath, 2020). As Srinivas said, 'Caste is so tacitly and completely accepted by all including those who are most vocal in condemning it that it is everywhere the unit of social action' (Srinivas, 1962, p. 41). The framework of analysis, therefore, has to go beyond the consensus and conflict models. A possible explanation could be based on the contribution of Pierre Bourdieu. Bourdieu (1977) pointed out that experience of the enduring effects of dominant structures could lead to their internalization and subsequent reproduction. Bourdieu (Bourdieu, 1977, p. 86) used the term *habitus* to refer to such internalized dominant structures. They give rise to certain perceptions and actions which operate 'below the level' of conscious decision making and the 'controls of the will' (Bourdieu 2001, p. 37). At the same time, Bourdieu also argues that the *habitus* generates practices which, while reproducing the relations of domination, also change these relations. Emulation of upper caste norms is the product of the enduring effects of power relations centred on caste; it is not a conscious or consensual adoption of upper caste practices. And, in their everyday practices, lower castes might reproduce some of these norms, but they do so in their own terms, often modifying them to their advantage. Bourdieu's concept of *habitus* thus offers a useful framework for understanding complicity and resistance in the act of Sanskritization, which takes place in the context of the enduring effects of power and domination.

Sanskritization: An Ideational Category

In this section, I make three concluding observations on Srinivas' model of Sanskritization, which I argue presents a specific view of Indian society that is ideational in character and guided by the integrative role of the caste system. First, the concept of Sanskritization provided the connecting link between the colonial model of Indian society drawn from the Hindu religious texts, and the idea of India constructed through field studies. The common thread that runs through both perspectives was an idealized and harmonized view of the caste structure, ensuring cooperation, and stability. Second, Srinivas conceived Sanskritization as an ideational principle that would ensure the integration of diverse castes and communities under Hindu civilization, built on Brahminical culture. Third, although different in their approaches, the concepts of Sanskritization and Hindutva seem to share a common ideology that views Indian civilization as Hindu, and Sanskritic culture as its unifying force. In the discussion below, I shall examine each feature separately.

My first observation relates to Sanskritization as a 'harmony ideology (cf. Nader, 2002)'. Knowledge of Indian society during the colonial period was primarily constructed from the interpretation of the Hindu scriptures. In this 'book view' of Indian society, as Jodhka (1998) calls it, the caste system became the central ordering principle, ensuring harmony, and cooperation between different caste groups. This idealized view of society was then transported to village India, which became 'the signifier of "authentic native life", a place where one could observe the "real" India …' (Jodhka, 1998, p. 311). With the rise of village studies in the last decades of colonial rule, and with its growth in the post-Independence era, the idealized Indian village became the mainstay of the anthropological imagination. In this 'field view' of Indian society, just as in the 'book view', caste continued as the ordering principle. The ideology of Sanskritization functioned as a mechanism to further reinforce the idea of harmony with the emphasis on willing emulation of upper caste cultural and religious beliefs and practices among lower castes, thus bridging the textual and field studies. The empirical evidence, however, suggested that the village hierarchy was riddled with conflict. The concept of Sanskritization served an ideological purpose and could effectively mask conflict and inequality among caste groups. In this sense, Sanskritization functioned as 'harmony ideology'. This concept refers to a set of beliefs that 'conflict resolution is inherently good and that its opposite, continued conflict or controversy, is bad or dysfunctional' (Nader, 2002, p. 32).

Further, Sanskritization as harmony ideology effectively managed conflict by allowing some room for mobility within the system. But this mobility was limited only to the 'positional changes in the system'. Through Sanskritization a caste might move up within the *varna* system, but the caste system 'itself does not change' (Srinivas, 1966, p. 7). In this sense, Sanskritization functions as a 'self-sealing mechanism' for negotiating conflicts arising out of low status within the hierarchy (Lynch, 1969, p. 80).

The theoretical rationale of Sanskritization is located in the structural-functional approach, which held that specific functions are indispensable for the continuance of any social structure, for coordinated patterns of human relations, and for the maintenance of equilibrium within society. Srinivas followed Radcliffe-Brown's holistic structural functionalism, which considered that every part of society is functionally integrated in order to maintain the solidarity of the society (Radcliffe-Brown, 1952). The caste system provided for various functions necessary to social life, ranging from education to scavenging, from village governance to domestic service, and from agricultural production to marketing. Thus, the theory provided a justification for caste stratification as a functional necessity.

The second observation relates to Sanskritization as a unifying principle in Indian society. In an essay originally published in 1969 (and republished in 1980), Srinivas talked about the diversity of India, manifested in many caste, ethnic, and religious groups. He also identified unifying factors, including the constitution of India, and importantly, Hinduism. With its sacred places, salient features of Sankritic culture, and castes found throughout the country, he claimed, 'the concept of the unity of India is inherent in Hinduism' (Srinivas, 1980, p. 2). He further noted, 'Hinduism is best described as a loose confederation of innumerable cults, the connecting threads of which are found in Sanskritization, and, in the last resort, Brahmins' (Srinivas, 1989, p. 58). Srinivas viewed Sanskritization as the unifying principle, which enabled the Hindu Sanskritic culture to permeate different regions of the country. From an ideational perspective, he saw the importance of this process in the newly emerged independent India, in bringing together 'all sections of India's heterogeneous population into the national mainstream' (Srinivas, 1989, p. 71). Sanskritization thus became a useful conceptual tool to assert the 'cultural continuity of India's past' and the 'political unity of its future' (Carroll, 1977, p. 368; Charsley, 1998).

As mentioned earlier, Srinivas claimed that the process of Sanskritization has been at work for over 2500 years. Sanskritic values of Hinduism and Indian civilization, the repository of which is Brahminic culture, gradually spread among different castes and tribes through a process of emulation. Although the immediate target of emulation often involved locally dominant 'twice-born' castes, Brahminical customs and ways of life gradually spread among all castes, and also among groups outside the Hindu caste order, including some tribal communities. Even 'untouchables', Srinivas (1956) claimed, who achieved little mobility through Sanskritization, eagerly adopted Sanskritic rituals and ways of life. He argued that there was a widespread movement among 'untouchables' to give up eating 'carcass beef, domestic pork and toddy, and to adopt Sanskritic customs, beliefs and deities' (Srinivas, 1956, p. 494). He asserted that some of them have become even more Sanskritized than the Shudra castes (Srinivas, 1956, p. 494). Just as harmony ideology played a role in reinforcing Brahmin and upper caste dominance, Sanskritization, as the unifying force, further cemented the hegemony of Hinduism and Sanskritic culture across India.

My third observation concerns the ideological link Sanskritization seems to share with Hindutva in contemporary India. Both concepts are located in the idea of Indian civilization as Hindu, and they visualize the unity of India based on Sanskritic values and practices. Both processes reinforce Brahminical hegemony. While Sanskritization has to some extent succeeded in doing so through a process of generating consensus, Hindutva employs the methods of violence and coercion. Both concepts, linked to upper caste dominance, call for a closer examination.

In elaborating the concept of hegemony, Antonio Gramsci says that 'the supremacy of a social group manifests itself in two ways, as "domination" and as "intellectual and moral leadership"' (Gramsci, 2014, p. 57). Domination is characterized by physical force and violence. Hegemony, in contrast to domination, is located in 'intellectual and moral leadership'. Dominant classes, according to Gramsci, seek to generate the willing support of the masses in order to legitimize their dominance. It is when a crisis in hegemony occurs due to the non-compliance of the dominated classes that force and violence become tools for maintaining supremacy.

Sanskritization in general functioned as an ideological apparatus for building and reinforcing the hegemony of upper castes. As mentioned earlier, the process of emulation facilitated the spread of hegemonic Brahminic values, ensuring the entrenchment of the caste system and its ritual hierarchy. As a harmony ideology, it generated consensus and compliance among lower castes. It succeeded in creating illusions of mobility, and even provided space for conflict. In situations where lower castes resisted the caste hierarchy, by donning the sacred thread or claiming Kshatriya identity, their actions amounted to a self-sealing mechanism rather than a fight against the caste system itself. However, since the 1980s, the rise of Dalit consciousness and collective mobilization has threatened Brahminic hegemony and, as a result, upper castes have taken to the aggressive ideology of Hindutva to reinforce their dominance. Consumption of beef, for instance, has become not just a 'polluting' act, but an antinational transgression punishable by mob lynching. Although their approaches might differ, Sanskritization and Hindutva represent a continuum—an ideology that reinforces the mutuality of Hinduism, the caste system, and upper caste dominance.

References

Bailey, F. G. 1957. *Caste and the Economic Frontier*. Manchester: Manchester University Press.
Bailey, F. G. 1960. *Tribe, Caste, and Nation: A Study of Political Activity and Political Change in Highland Orissa*. Bombay: Oxford University Press.
Berreman, Jerald. 1993. 'Sanskritization as Female Oppression in India'. In B. Miller, D. Fessler, and N. Quinn (Eds.), *Sex and Gender Hierarchies* (pp. 366–391). New York: Cambridge University Press.
Bourdieu, Pierre. 1977. *Outline of a Theory of Practice*. London: Oxford University Press.
Bourdieu, Pierre. 2001. *Masculine Domination*. Cambridge: Polity Press.
Carroll, Lucy. 1977. '"Sanskritization," "Westernization," and "Social Mobility": A Reappraisal of the Relevance of Anthropological Concepts to the Social Historian of Modern India'. *Journal of Anthropological Research*, 33(4): 355–371.

Charsley, Simon. 1998. 'Sanskritization: The Career of an Anthropological Theory'. *Contributions to Indian Sociology*, 32(2): 527–549.
Cohn, Bernard. 1996. *Colonialism and Its Forms of Knowledge: The British in India*. Princeton: Princeton University Press.
Dirks, Nicholas. 2001. *Castes of Mind: Colonialism and the Making of Modern India*. Princeton: Princeton University Press.
Dumont, Louis. 1980. *Homo Hierarchicus: The Caste System and Its Implications*. Delhi: Oxford University Press.
Frankel, Francine. 1989. 'Caste, Land and Dominance in Bihar: Breakdown of the Brahmanical Social Order'. In F. Frankel and M. Rao (Eds.), *Dominance and State Power in Modern India: Decline of Social Order* (Vol. I, pp. 46–131). New Delhi: Oxford University Press.
Gramsci, Antonio. 2014. *Selections from the Prison Notebooks*. Chennai: Orient Longman Limited.
Ilaiah, Kancha. 2002. *Why I Am Not a Hindu: A Sudra Critique of Hindutva Philosophy, Culture and Political Economy*. Calcutta: Samya.
Jaffrelot, Christophe. 2003. *India's Silent Revolution: The Rise of the Lower Castes in North India*. New York: Columbia University Press.
Jha, Hetukar. 1977. 'Lower Caste Peasants and Upper Caste Zamindars in Bihar (1921–1925): An Analysis of Sanskritization and Contradiction between the Two Groups'. *The Indian Economic and Social History Review*, 15(4): 549–559.
Jodhka, Surinder. 1998. 'From "Book View" to "Field View": Social Anthropological Constructions of the Indian Village'. *Oxford Development Studies*, 26(3): 311–331.
Kunnath, George. 2017. *Rebels from the Mud Houses: Dalits and the Making of the Maoist Revolution in Bihar*. London: Routledge.
Kunnath, George. 2020. 'Dalit Responses to the Caste System: Rethinking Resistance'. In S. Murru and A. Polese (Eds.), *Resistances: Between Theories and the Field* (pp. 189–205). London: Rowman & Littlefield.
Lee, Alexander. 2019. 'The Origins of Ethnic Activism: Caste Politics in Colonial India'. *The Journal of Race, Ethnicity, and Politics*, 4(0): 148–179.
Lynch, Owen. 1969. *The Politics of Untouchability: Social Mobility and Social Change in a City of India*. New York and London: Columbia University Press.
Majumdar, D. N. 1972. 'A Study of Tribe/Caste Continuum and the Process of Sanskritization among the Bodo-speaking Tribes of the Garo Hills'. In K. S. Singh (Ed.), *Tribal Situation in India* (pp. 263–270). Shimla: Indian Institute of Advanced Study.
Moffatt, Michael. 1979. *An Untouchable Community in South India: Structure and Consensus*. Princeton: Princeton University Press.
Mosse, David. 1994. 'Idioms of Subordination and Styles of Protest among Christian and Hindu Harijan Castes in Tamil Nadu'. *Contributions to Indian Sociology*, 28(1): 67–106.
Nader, Laura. 2002. *Life of the Law: Anthropological Projects*. Berkeley: University of California Press.
Narayan, Badri. 2001. *Documenting Dissent: Contesting Fables, Contested Memories and Dalit Political Discourse*. Shimla: Indian Institute of Advanced Study.
O'Hanlon, Rosalind. 1985. *Caste, Conflict and Ideology: Mahatma Jotirao Phule and Low Caste Protest in Nineteenth-Century Western India*. Cambridge: Cambridge University Press.
Omvedt, Gail. 1976. *Cultural Revolt in a Colonial Society: The Non-Brahman Movement in Western India: 1873 to 1930*. Bombay: Scientific Socialist Education Trust.
Panikkar, K. M. 1955. *Hindu Society at the Crossroads*. Bombay: Asia Publishing House.

Pocock, David. 1957. 'Inclusion and Exclusion: A Process in the Caste System of Gujarat'. *South Western Journal of Anthropology*, 13(1): 19–31.

Pinch, William. 1996. *Peasants and Monks in British India*. Berkeley: University of California Press.

Radcliffe-Brown, A. R. 1952. *Structure and Function in Primitive Society*. London: Cohen and West.

Ram, Ronki. 2012. 'Beyond Conversion and Sanskritisation: Articulating an Alternative Dalit Agenda in East Punjab'. *Modern Asian Studies*, 46(3): 639–702.

Rawat, Ramnarayan, and K. Satyanarayana. 2016. 'Introduction'. In R. Rawat and K. Satyanarayana (Eds.), *Dalit Studies: New Perspectives on Indian History and Society* (pp. 1–30). Durham: Duke University Press.

Rowe, W. L. 1968a. 'The New Cauhans: A Caste Mobility Movement in North India'. In J. Silverberg (Ed.), *Social Mobility in the Caste System in India* (pp. 66–77). The Hague: Mouton.

Rowe, W. L. 1968b. 'Mobility in the Nineteenth-Century Caste System'. In M. Singer and B. Cohn (Eds.), *Structure and Change in Indian Society* (pp. 201–208). Chicago: Aldine Publishing Company.

Rudolph, Lloyd, and S. Rudolph. 1967. *The Modernity of Tradition: Political Development in India*. Chicago: University of Chicago Press.

Scott, James. 1985. *Weapons of the Weak: Everyday Forms of Peasant Resistance*. New Haven: Yale University Press.

Singer, Milton, and B. Cohen (Eds.) 1968. *Structure and Change in Indian Society*. Chicago: Aldine Publishing Company.

Singer, Milton. 1992. 'The Cohesive Role of Sanskritization and Other Essays by M. N. Srinivas Review'. *Journal of the American Oriental Society*, 112(1): 149–150.

Srinivas, M. N. 1952. *Religion and Society among the Coorgs of South India*. Oxford: Clarendon.

Srinivas, M. N. 1956. 'A Note on Sanskritization and Westernization'. *Far Eastern Quarterly*, 15(4): 481–496.

Srinivas, M. N. 1962. *Caste in Modern India and Other Essays*. Bombay: Asia Publishing House.

Srinivas, M. N. 1966. *Social Change in Modern India*. Berkeley: University of California Press.

Srinivas, M. N. 1980 [1969]. *India: Social Structure*. Delhi: Hindustan Publishing Corporation.

Srinivas, M. N. 1989. *The Cohesive Role of Sanskritization and Other Essays*. Delhi: Oxford University Press.

CHAPTER 17

CASTE AND HINDUTVA

JOEL LEE

AT first glance, caste and Hindutva may appear to have little to do with one another. While caste is often represented as an internal, vertical stratification of Hindu society with roots in antiquity, Hindutva—the ideology of Hindu nationalism—is known for the horizontal divisions it promotes between the Hindu 'race' and Muslim and Christian others, and for the inspiration it draws from 19th-and early 20th-century European nationalism. Given only this inherited view of things, one might expect caste to be, at most, an embarrassment for Hindutva, an irritant to its efforts to project a united Hindu front against its putative Muslim antagonists. In fact, caste has played a far more integral role in the genesis of Hindutva in the late colonial period, and in its spectacular resurgence since the 1980s, than is generally recognized. Reciprocally, moreover, Hindutva has influenced in no small degree Indian and global representations of caste—the fact that untouchability, and thus 'untouchables', are so widely imagined to be internal to the Hindu body politic in a transhistorical sense is one of Hindutva's more astonishing successes. Indeed a number of ideas about caste that enjoy mainstream credibility in India today—that the caste-based occupation of manual scavenging was introduced to India by Muslims, for example, or that Dalit conversions to Hinduism in the present can plausibly be understood as a 'homecoming' or 'ghar wapsi'—can be traced to the first generation of Hindutva ideologues, who put them into circulation a mere century ago.

The first three decades of the 20th century, when Hindutva crystallized as an ideology and its advocates developed enduring institutions, were a period of sharply intensified awareness of and mobilization around numbers. This was a consequence of policies, techniques, and representational strategies of colonial governance. Though the first all-India census took place in 1871–1872, initiating the gradual conceptual transformation of groups like sects, castes, and language speakers into 'enumerated communities' whose relative 'strength' could be measured against one another statistically (Kaviraj, 1992), it was not until the Partition of Bengal along religious lines in 1905 that the stakes of enumeration became abruptly apparent. The Indian Councils Act of 1909 and the Montagu-Chelmsford Reforms of 1918–1919 further underscored the political significance of numbers; as institutions of limited self-governance by elected bodies expanded, it became increasingly evident that governance in the emerging nation would be a matter of mobilizing numerical majorities. In large swaths of British India the question of which group constituted a majority was unsettled; this was particularly the case in regions like Punjab and Bengal, where both Muslims and Hindus (and Sikhs, in Punjab) could make persuasive claims, depending on how populous but socially marginalized groups were counted.

It was in this context that a section of educated Hindus began to turn their attention to the subordinated castes—'Shudras' as well as, especially, 'untouchables'—and to regard their religious affiliation as a matter of concern. The colonial state had been classifying 'untouchables' as Hindus by default in the decennial censuses, but this policy had met resistance: from Hindu census enumerators, who objected to being clubbed in the same category as sweepers; from some 'untouchable' communities, such as the Satnamis, who defined themselves in opposition to Hindus; and from a number of British officials, who described the policy as 'absurd' on account of its variance from the self-understanding of those thus classified. With the arrival of enumerative politics, this heretofore quiet debate among census administrators erupted into a highly charged public struggle over the religious classification of a fifth of the population of the subcontinent, and thus of the very conditions of possibility of a Hindu—or Muslim—majority India. The newly formed Muslim League petitioned Lord Minto in 1906 that 'untouchables' should not be counted as Hindus. While the government did not ultimately change its policy, the spectre raised by this potential 'loss' to Hindu numbers—periodically revivified by events such as the Gait Circular (1911), Mohammad Ali's Kakinada Speech (1926), the Ad Dharm's assertion of Dalit religious autonomy in the census (1931), Ambedkar's declaration of intent to convert (1936), and others—impressed themselves permanently on the character of Hindu nationalism, making control over subordinate castes, and over the representation of their religious life an imperative at the very heart of Hindutva. The solution that Hindutva's originators devised to the perennial threat of numerical loss was a set of discourses and practices aimed at attracting and incorporating communities previously held in contempt by Hindus into the Hindu fold, while simultaneously alienating these same communities from their Muslim neighbours, with whom they often shared cultural traditions more extensively than with Hindus. Hindutva's answer, that is, was a project of majoritarian inclusion: the forging and sustaining of a majority status vis-à-vis a perceived rival by the induction of a heretofore despised outgroup.

The study of Hindutva has often been bifurcated along disciplinary lines, with historians providing accounts of its first wave, from the early 1920s to the assassination of Gandhi by a Hindu nationalist in 1948, and social and political scientists examining its recrudescence from the 1980s to the present. Yet despite profound differences in the political context of the two periods, Hindutva anxieties and strategies with respect to caste show remarkable continuity. The spectre of loss of numerical strength—what Arjun Appadurai (2006) calls 'the fear of small numbers'—is common to both phases, with the Meenakshipuram conversions of Tamil Dalits to Islam in 1981 and the implementation of the recommendations of the Mandal Commission in 1990 triggering, in the current wave, what colonial policy decisions, and early assertions of Dalit autonomy provoked in the first. In what follows, we will briefly consider key texts and practices in Hindutva's century-long grappling with caste.

TEXTS

While there is no official Hindutva canon, the institutional fortunes of the Rashtriya Swayamsevak Sangh (RSS) since the post-1980s rise of its affiliate, the Bharatiya Janta Party (BJP), to political power have encouraged a foregrounding of literature written by RSS leaders and their inspiration, V. D. Savarkar. Here, we will take note of three texts that decisively shaped Hindu nationalist ideology and practice and that illuminate the role played by caste in both.

A Dying Race, a pamphlet composed by the retired military officer (Lieutenant Colonel) and Bengali brahmin U. N. Mukerji in 1909, is arguably the first systematic Hindu majoritarian formulation of the caste problem. It begins with an uncritical reading of the decennial censuses of 1872, 1881, 1891, and 1901, with attention to reported Muslim and Hindu population growth in Bengal. In 'the space of 30 years', Mukerji (1929, p. 1) concludes from a brief survey of the numbers, 'the Mahomedans who were at the start in a minority of 4 lakhs had not only made up the deficiency, but were nearly *25 lakhs more numerous* than the Hindus'. Having mentioned aboriginal Americans, the Irish, and the Maoris of New Zealand as examples of 'peoples [who] have dwindled and finally disappeared from their own country', Mukerji contends that,

> We are also a decaying race. Every Census reveals the same fact. We are getting proportionately fewer and fewer. There is no actual decrease; but the rate of increase compared with that of the Mahomedans is *extremely small* . . . Why should it be so? (Mukerji, 1929, pp. 4–5)

Mukerji postulates several reasons, among them the superior physique, diet, and work ethic he ascribes to 'the Mahomedans,' as well as the 'love or lust' behind intermarriage between Muslim men and Hindu women (Mukerji, 1929, pp. 6–8). The bulk of the essay, though, is devoted to what Mukerji diagnoses as the ultimate cause of Hindu diminution: 'our caste system'. Caste, it turns out, 'is an insuperable bar' to the attainment of the kind of unity and solidarity, the sense of being 'fellow countrymen' that Mukerji (1929, p. 33) believes to be exemplified by Muslims and the English. Caste contempt prevents brahmins and 'so-called high castes'—13 per cent of the Hindu population, by Mukerji's reckoning—from having anything to do with the 'contaminating' castes—57 per cent of the Hindus—other than extracting their labour. Deprived of contact with their cultured social betters, the 'low castes' either lead lives of 'hopeless degradation' characterized by drunkenness and disease, or they are attracted to Christianity or Islam, and thus deplete Hinduism's numbers while swelling the ranks of its rivals (1929, p. 46). Mukerji's conclusion is stark:

> The wages of sin is death. We Hindus have sinned deeply, damnably, against the laws of God and nature, and we are paying the penalty. In our treatment of our co-religionists lies the germ of our self-destruction. (1929, p. 97)

In conjoining an argument animated by the enumerative logic of the modern state, a narrative of Hindus threatened by Muslim growth, and a naming of caste division as an existential threat to the Hindu 'race,' Mukerji articulated a discourse from which Hindu nationalism has continued to draw ever since. By linking these concerns to the moral language of sin and guilt, Mukerji also prepared the ground for Gandhi's expiatory approach to the untouchability question.

Impressed with Colonel Mukerji's ideas after meeting him in 1912, the Arya Samaj and Congress leader Swami Shraddhanand (1856–1926) popularized the dying race thesis on an all-India level. In a host of pamphlets published in the 1910s and 1920s, and in his 1926 manifesto, *Hindu Sangathan: Saviour of the Dying Race*, Shraddhanand further developed Mukerji's diagnosis of the caste problem and also formulated a solution. Beginning, like Mukerji, with appeals to colonial demography, Shraddhanand (1926, p. 14) declared that 'within the next 420 years the Indo-Aryan race would be wiped off the face of the earth unless steps were taken to save it'. But whereas Mukerji's concerns were confined to the Hindu 'race,' Shraddhanand augmented the racial with the political community, infusing the same fear of small numbers into a clear nationalist vision of a post-British state in which the religion of the subordinated castes would determine the configuration of power. 'If all untouchables became Muslims then these will become equal to the Hindus,' he wrote in *Vartamān Mukhya Samasyā* ('Today's Foremost Problem'), 'and at the time of independence they will not depend on the Hindus, but will be able to stand on their own legs' (quoted in Jordens, 1981, p. 144). In this way, Shraddhanand fused the prospect of Dalit autonomy with the fear of Hindus becoming a political minority, and this in turn to the existential danger of Hindus being 'wiped off the face of the earth'.

To combat these threats, Shraddhanand proposed a program of Hindu *sangathan*—organization or consolidation—that included as one of its central planks the 'resuscitation' or 'revival' of the four-tiered Varna system of ancient Vedic social theory.

> Down with the caste system! that is the dictum of every true son of Mother India. The present day unnatural, immovable division into a hundred castes and thousands of sub-castes must go, if the Hindu Community is to be rescued from total extinction.
>
> In the first place all distinctions of sub-castes must cease [. . .] I realize the difficulty in remodeling the Hindu Samaj according to the ancient Varnadharma at once. But there should be no difficulty in all the sub-castes, and even non-castes consisting of the socalled untouchables, being absorbed in the four principal castes. [. . .]

[C]haracter and conduct should become the determining factors in fixing the Varna of a Hindu. (Shraddhanand, 1926, pp. 135–136)

How these exhortations were to be put into practice was another matter, one we will address when we turn from texts to practices. What is notable here is the resolution of the problem of hierarchy in the present by simplification (from 'hundreds' and 'thousands' of divisions to four), a 'return' to an idealized Vedic past, and a switch from birth to 'character and conduct' as criteria for caste. In a more radical vein, Shraddhanand (1926) also advocated the introduction, albeit 'gradually,' of intercaste marriage—including the forbidden 'Pratiloma' variety of 'higher' women with 'lower' men—without attempting to justify it on Vedic grounds.

As a concept in which Hindu nationalist praxis in this period was crystallized, *sangathan*, indefatigably promoted by Shraddhanand and his many admirers, dominated highly charged public debates over caste and communalism in the 1920s and into the 1930s. Sangathan was joined and eventually eclipsed by the concept of Hindutva ('Hindu-ness'). This term was first popularized in 1923 with the publication of *Hindutva: Who Is a Hindu?*, written in prison by the anti-colonial nationalist and Maharashtrian brahmin Vinayak Damodar Savarkar (1883–1966). Much has been written about Savarkar's romance with European nationalist ideas of blood, soil, and patriotism, manifested in his triadic definition Hindutva—'a common nation (Rashtra) a common race (Jati) and a common civilization (Sanskriti)'—and about his portrayal of Indian Muslims and Indian Christians as fifth columnists whose 'holyland is far off in Arabia or Palestine,' whose 'ideas and heroes are not the children of this soil' and whose 'names and ... outlook smack of a foreign origin' (Savarkar, 1969 [1923], pp. 113, 116). Less acknowledged is Savarkar's attempt, in *Hindutva*, to address the caste problem.

Savarkar, like Shraddhanand, prized the four-tiered varna system of the Vedic period as a distinctively Hindu contribution to global social theory worth preserving. Celebrating varna, however, presented a problem for the contention that Hindus constitute a single race. Savarkar did not adopt Shraddhanand's fantasy that varna in the Vedic golden age was determined by action rather than descent. But if varna kept society divided into separate hereditary classes, what basis could there be for the 'common flow of blood from a Brahman to a Chandal [the paradigmatic untouchable]' on whose existence Savarkar (1969 [1923], p. 85) insisted—and without which, indeed, the entire racial dimension of his argument would collapse? Here Savarkar's marriage of brahminical sociology and European race theory reveals its complexity: miscegenation, perforce, would supply the explanatory link, but only upon making distinctions between good and bad miscegenation. On the one hand, 'on the north-western side of our nation the commingling of races was growing rather too unceremonious to be healthy'; that is, at the territorial 'border' that Savarkar projects into the subcontinent's past (the Indus river), the mixing of 'Hindus' and others was a danger to be thwarted by boundary regulation (1969 [1923], p. 28). On the other hand, *within* the fatherland, miscegenation was healthy, insofar as it was regulated by brahminical principles. Savarkar accomplishes this counterintuitive claim by treating the abhorrence of inter-varna and especially pratiloma unions in normative literature as evidence of a kind of benevolent eugenics.

> All that the caste system has done is to regulate its noble blood on lines believed—and on the whole rightly believed—by our saintly and patriotic law-givers and kings to contribute most to fertilize and enrich all that was barren and poor, without famishing and debasing all that was flourishing and nobly endowed. (1969 [1923], p. 86)

Noble blood, that is, is a gift of the higher varnas to the lower, retained and distributed according to judicious principles favouring the overall health of the race.

Having provided a novel interpretation of the Hindu past, Savarkar advocates its continuation in the present: '[Let] intermarriages between provinces and provinces, castes and castes, be encouraged where they do not exist' (1969 [1923], p. 138). In this prescription, as in his attention to numbers—'The numerical strength of our race is an asset that cannot be too highly prized' (1969 [1923], p. 134)—Savarkar hewed close to the path carved by Shraddhanand.

Practices

How, in the face of early 20th-century social realities—deep divisions between castes, longstanding local traditions of Dalit religious autonomy, and widespread disaffection from dominant caste politics of many subordinated caste communities—were the dreams of the architects of Hindutva to be realized? Much of the work of putting into practice the ideas formulated in texts like *Hindutva* and *Hindu Sangathan* fell to volunteers in Hindu nationalist organizations, especially the Arya Samaj, the Hindu Mahasabha (of which Savarkar assumed leadership in 1937), and the RSS and its many offshoots. But as is often and rightly noted, the leadership of these organizations and much of their rank and file membership have been, from their inception, dominated by men of the 'twice-born' and especially brahmin and baniya castes. For the first seven decades of its existence, the RSS was led by brahmins of Maharashtra, as indeed it is today. Of the six men to hold the Sangh's highest position of *sarsanghchalak*, five have been brahmins (K. B. Hegdewar, M. S. Golwalkar, M. D. Deoras, K. S. Sudarshan, and Mohan Bhagwat), and one (Rajendra Singh) a kshatriya. The Hindu Mahasabha's early leaders—Madan Mohan Malaviya, B. S. Moonje, and Savarkar—were also brahmins. The Arya Samaj's leadership featured brahmins (Dayanand Saraswati) alongside Punjabi mercantile castes (Lala Lajpat Rai, Swami Shraddhanand). Given the relatively narrow caste composition of organized Hindu nationalism, especially in its early decades, how was 'consolidation' and 'unity' to be brought about?

The discourses and practices by which proponents of Hindutva sought to expand their base—and thereby secure what they saw as the greatest vulnerability of the Hindu body politic—involved a fundamental reworking of the everyday categories of sociality, of the texture of quotidian social relations, and of ways of inhabiting public space. Let us take each of these interrelated transformations in turn.

Since fear regarding the unsettledness of the question of the religious affiliation of 'untouchables' was chief among the factors that gave rise to Hindutva, one of the primary tasks of Hindu nationalists was to persuade Hindus and 'untouchables' that they were, in fact, co-religionists. This often meant changing the terms by which people referred to themselves and others, introducing the language of 'co-religionist' (*sahdharmi* in north Indian languages), and inventing historical explanations for the *de facto* remoteness of most Dalit communities from the Hindus with whom they were now to be identified. This work was carried out almost entirely in the vernacular: in pamphlets, speeches, articles in the vernacular press, quips, slogans, *bhajan*s, and other musical and performance genres. Through these media myths were introduced that 'untouchables' and other subordinated castes were the descendants of Hindu Kshatriyas whose fierce defense of Hinduism and refusal to convert to Islam provoked Muslim invaders to force these communities into degrading occupations centuries ago. Having 'forgotten' their former kinship, Hindus and Dalits were invited now to rediscover one another as brothers estranged only by misfortune, and united against a common foe. Dalits were urged to identify themselves as Hindu during the census, to adopt Hindu rather than Muslim names, to take up cremation instead of burying their dead, to cease eating beef, and to sever ties with Muslim employers and neighbours. Hindus were exhorted to curtail practices of untouchability, to cease addressing 'untouchables' with contemptuous names, to educate their rediscovered co-religionists in the ways of Hinduism, and to cultivate towards them feelings of solidarity rather than disgust (Gould, 2005; Gupta, 2016; Prashad, 2000; Lee, 2021; Shyamlal, 1984).

While the transformation of everyday categories of sociality proceeded at varying paces and unevenly across regions through the first half of the 20th century, the changes were ratified and given uniformity by a legislative act rarely considered in the literature on Hindu nationalism. This was the Constitution (Scheduled Castes) Order of 1950, a presidential order enacted by the first Congress government of independent India, which specified that 'no person who professes a religion different from the Hindu religion shall be deemed to be a member of a Scheduled Caste'. This linking of compensatory discrimination (or affirmative action) to the profession of Hinduism—later amended to include Buddhism and Sikhism, but not Christianity or Islam—has arguably done as much to secure the 'numerical strength' of the Hindus, to undermine Dalit religious autonomy, and to legitimate Savarkar's xenophobic taxonomy of religion, as have decades of grassroots labours by Arya Samaj and RSS volunteers. Scholars of law have noted that it represents a kind of 'legal Hindutva' (Conrad, 2007, p. 216) and that in upholding it the courts are 'endorsing a form of "gharwapasi"' (Fazal, 2017, p. 23).

Mention of 'ghar wapsi' brings us to our second set of key Hindu nationalist practices: those oriented to the transformation of the texture of everyday social relations between castes. As Mukerji and Shraddhanand both observed, assertions of Hindu unity lacked credibility when privileged castes abhorred contact with 'low' castes and observed a host of practices that reinscribed the degradation of the latter daily. The Arya Samaj under Shraddhanand tackled this problem by means of a ritual practice called shuddhi or 'purification'. Developed in the late 19th century to re-admit to their Hindu communities 'high caste' Hindus who had converted to Islam and Christianity, shuddhi was then repurposed as a means for inducting 'untouchables' into the Hindu fold—a few dozen in 1900, tens of thousands by the 1920s and 1930s. That these 'untouchables,' who were not Muslim or Christian, were nonetheless initially seen as exterior to the Hindu community is revealed in early remarks by Samaj leaders such as Lala Lajpat Rai's explaining two means of joining the Samaj in 1908: 'With Hindus merely signing the declaration of faith is sufficient. In the case of non-Hindus a *shuddhi* ceremony of a simple kind is obligatory' (quoted in Graham, 1943, p. 465). By the 1920s the Samaj was committed to the narrative of untouchables as fallen Kshatriyas; bringing practice into alignment with the new discourse, shuddhi was again recast, less as an elevation of the impure, and more as a 'return' of primordial Hindus to their forgotten home.

Crucially, the shuddhi that Shraddhanand advocated involved not merely the ceremony but was to be accompanied by concrete changes in social relations that would secure the initiates' 'full rights and privileges' as Hindus. This began with interdining, or different castes eating together. Shuddhi rites were concluded with feasts in which the largely brahmin and baniya Arya Samajists sat down to eat with their new compatriots. Though opposition to intercaste meals eventually yielded to the logic of majoritarian inclusion, in shuddhi's initial years Hindu traditionalists (sanatanists) objected strenuously, often excommunicating and boycotting Arya Samajists for, as one critic put it, 'defiling Hinduism and destroying its purity' (quoted in Adcock, 2014, pp. 123–124, cf. Graham, 1943; Jordens, 1977, 1981). Equally controversial were the opening of wells and school admissions to 'untouchables' that Arya Samajists, heeding the demands of groups that expressed interest in shuddhi, sometimes brought about. For Hindus and Dalits to eat together, draw water from the same wells, and study in the same schools was unprecedented. These were substantive transformations with considerable social and economic ramifications that undoubtedly lent shuddhi what appeal it held for sections of the Depressed Classes (Adcock, 2014).

Strategies for reconfiguring social relations pioneered by the Arya Samaj in the first half of the 20th century have been redeployed, with variations, by the RSS and its affiliates in the Hindutva resurgence of the 1980s to the present. In their overtures to subordinated castes during the mobilization to destroy the Babri Masjid (mosque) in Ayodhya and build a Ram Mandir (temple) in its place, the RSS and the Vishwa Hindu Parishad (VHP) asked Dalit residents of UP to host *kar sevak*s (militant Hindu volunteers) travelling to Ayodhya and in particular to cook food for them, drawing attention to the willingness of Hindu nationalists to eat food prepared by Dalits. More generally, the RSS makes interdining a key feature of its outreach programs to Dalits (Narayan, 2009). At pains to demonstrate an inclusive attitude, the RSS leadership also seeks out individual Dalits to perform symbolic roles in public displays of Hindu unity; a Dalit, for example, was selected to lay the foundation stone for the proposed

Ram Mandir in Ayodhya in 1989 (Andersen and Damle, 2018, p. 170; Hansen, 1999; Narayan, 2009).

Emboldened by the electoral victory of the BJP and the installation of an RSS member (Narendra Modi) to the position of Prime Minister, VHP and RSS activists in 2014 launched a campaign of 'ghar wapsi' in which Christians and Muslims of Dalit, Tribal, and otherwise 'low caste' background were encouraged to 'return home' to Hinduism. In its narrative of 'reclamation' and in its organizers' explicit concern with Christian and Muslim 'threats' to Hindu numerical strength, ghar wapsi is a renewal of shuddhi under a different name. In the place of access to wells and school admissions a century ago, potential participants in ghar wapsi are now promised assistance in obtaining biometric Aadhaar cards (Katju, 2015).

Changes in modes of sociality are closely tied to transformations in ways of inhabiting public space. One Hindu nationalist strategy, repeated across cities in north and west India over the last century, is to support the construction of Hindu shrines and temples on or adjacent to Muslim graveyards or mosques in low-income urban neighbourhoods where Dalits and Muslims live side by side, provoking communally polarized property disputes gauged both to instil in Dalits—who often had no previous tradition of temple-going—a sense of identification with Hinduism, while simultaneously undercutting existing or potential Dalit–Muslim solidarity (Hansen, 1999, pp. 124–126; Prashad, 2000, pp. 109–110). Another tactic for reconfiguring public space along majoritarian lines has been to invite both Dalits and 'the shudra labouring poor' to participate in militant Hindu religious processions, as Hindu nationalists began to do in the 1920s and 1930s (Freitag, 1989; Gooptu; 2001). Nandini Gooptu (2001, pp. 191–241) describes how subordinated castes in urban UP, attracted to the 'fallen Kshatriya' trope of Arya Samaj propaganda, came to enact the role of defenders of the Hindu faith—often armed and costumed as the 'monkey army' of the Ramayana legend—in Holi and Ram Lila processions newly orchestrated by baniya sponsors as displays of Hindu virility. Similar efforts characterize the current phase of Hindutva pre-eminence. Badri Narayan (2009) documents a host of ongoing projects in which RSS, VHP, and BJP activists have, since the 1990s, sought to refashion the local gods and heroes of particular Dalit castes of north India into avatars of Ram and Hindu warriors by sponsoring plays, songs, temples, statuary, and other cultural forms. In Bahraich, for example, where Hindus, Muslims, Dalits, and others have long participated together in the centuries-old annual festival of the eleventh century Muslim prince Ghazi Miyan, Hindutva activists now sponsor a counter-festival to celebrate the local king Suhaldev who killed Ghazi Miyan, depicting Suhaldev as a Dalit (Pasi) leader whose goals were the defense of Hinduism and the protection of cows (2009, pp. 80–100).

The most extreme outcome of the transformations wrought by Hindu majoritarian inclusion is the involvement of subordinated castes in organized anti-Muslim violence or 'riots,' as, for example, in Noakhali in Bengal in 1946, in western UP townships in 1990–1991, or in Gujarat in 2002. The irony of Dalits, in particular, becoming 'footsoldiers of Hindutva' has attracted considerable interest, given the structural, and at times spectacular violence to which Dalits themselves continue to be subjected by

Hindu dominant castes (Basu, 1996; Menon, 2010; Narayan, 2009; Teltumbde, 2005; Shani, 2007; Prashad, 2000). At the same time it is important to invert the question and consider the equally remarkable fact of Hindutva's failures, in most of India, to enlist Dalits in acts of majoritarian violence, despite a century of assiduous efforts. Recent analyses of how Ambedkarite Dalits thwarted an incipient communal riot (Jaoul, 2012) and how enduring traditions of subterfuge enable Dalits to appear to acquiesce to Hindu nationalist demands while quietly undermining them (Lee, 2021) suggest lines of enquiry into subaltern tactics that act to contain Hindutva.

The limits of Hindutva's inroads among Dalits and other subordinated castes point to the contradiction at the heart of the project of majoritarian inclusion: the 'high caste' men who have always constituted Hindu nationalism's base simultaneously need 'low castes' Tribals and Dalits, and hold them in contempt. Arya Samajists acknowledged this in their own writings in the early 20th century, describing the *ghrna*, or disgust, that they struggled to overcome as they sought to reimagine Dalits as their co-religionists (e.g. Sharma, n.d.). That a discourse of contempt towards both 'shudras' and Dalits, along with a lively sense of superiority on caste grounds, continues to prevail among organizers of Hindu nationalist violence is revealed in ethnographic studies of the RSS and its affiliates (Hansen, 1999; Shani, 2007), as well as in first-hand autobiographical accounts (Meghvanshi, 2020). One effect of this contradiction is the subordinate role that subaltern communities are usually assigned when incorporated in Hindu nationalist narratives and mobilizations—from being cast as the 'monkey army' in Ram Lila processions in the 1920s to being told that Hanuman was a Tribal Dalit by the BJP chief minister of UP in 2018. Another effect is the limited degree to which Hindutva has managed to win over the bulk of those whose numbers it so insistently claims.

References

Adcock, C. S. 2014. *The Limits of Tolerance: Indian Secularism and the Politics of Religious Freedom*. New York: Oxford University Press.

Andersen, Walter K., and Shridhar D. Damle. 2018. *The Rss: A View to the Inside*. Gurgaon: Penguin Viking.

Appadurai, Arjun. 2006. *Fear of Small Numbers: An Essay on the Geography of Anger*. Durham: Duke University Press.

Basu, Amrita. 1996. 'Mass Movement or Elite Conspiracy? The Puzzle of Hindu Nationalism'. In D. Ludden (Ed.), *Making India Hindu: Religion, Community, and the Politics of Democracy in India* (pp. 55–80). Delhi: Oxford University Press.

Conrad, Dieter. 2007. 'The Personal Law Question and Hindu Nationalism'. In V. Dalmia and H. v. Stietencron (Eds.), *The Oxford India Hinduism Reader* (pp. 187–230). New Delhi: Oxford University Press.

Fazal, Tanweer. 2017. 'Scheduled Castes, Reservations and Religion: Revisiting a Juridical Debate'. *Contributions to Indian Sociology*, 51(1): 1–24.

Freitag, Sandria B. 1989. *Collective Action and Community: Public Arenas and the Emergence of Communalism in North India*. Berkeley: University of California Press.

Gooptu, Nandini. 2001. *The Politics of the Urban Poor in Early Twentieth-Century India*. Cambridge: Cambridge University Press.

Gould, William. 2005. *Hindu Nationalism and the Language of Politics in Late Colonial India*. Cambridge: Cambridge University Press.

Graham, James Reid. 1943. 'The Arya Samaj as a Reformation in Hinduism with Special Reference to Caste'. PhD Dissertation, Religion, Yale University.

Gupta, Charu. 2016. *The Gender of Caste: Representing Dalits in Print*. Seattle: University of Washington Press.

Hansen, Thomas Blom. 1999. *The Saffron Wave: Democracy and Hindu Nationalism in Modern India*. New Delhi: Oxford University Press.

Jaoul, Nicolas. 2012. 'The Making of a Political Stronghold: A Dalit Neighbourhood's Exit from the Hindu Nationalist Riot System'. *Ethnography*, 13(1): 102–116.

Jordens, J. T. F. 1977. 'Reconversion to Hinduism, the Shuddhi of the Arya Samaj'. In G. A. Oddie (Ed.), *Religion in South Asia: Religious Conversion and Revival Movements in South Asia in Medieval and Modern Times* (pp. 140–159). Columbia, MO: South Asia Books.

Jordens, J. T. F. 1981. *Swami Shraddhananda: His Life and Causes*. Delhi: Oxford University Press.

Katju, Manjari. 2015. 'The Politics of Ghar Wapsi'. *Economic and Political Weekly*, 50(1): 21–24.

Kaviraj, Sudipta. 1992. 'The Imaginary Institution of India'. In P. Chatterjee and G. Pandey (Eds.), *Subaltern Studies Vi: Writings on South Asian History and Society* (pp. 1–39). Delhi: Oxford University Press.

Lee, Joel. 2021. *Deceptive Majority: Dalits, Hinduism, and Underground Religion*. Cambridge: Cambridge University Press.

Meghvanshi, Bhanwar. 2020. *I Could Not Be Hindu: The Story of a Dalit in the Rss*. (Trans. by N. Menon). New Delhi: Navayana.

Menon, Dilip M. 2010. 'The Blindness of Insight: Why Communalism in India Is about Caste'. In A. Singh and S. Mohapatra (Eds.), *Indian Political Thought: A Reader* (pp. 123–135). London: Routledge.

Mukerji, U. N. 1929. *A Dying Race*. Calcutta: Bhaskar Mukerji.

Narayan, Badri. 2009. *Fascinating Hindutva: Saffron Politics and Dalit Mobilisation*. New Delhi: SAGE.

Prashad, Vijay. 2000. *Untouchable Freedom: A Social History of a Dalit Community*. Delhi: Oxford University Press.

Savarkar, Vinayak Damodar. 1969 [1923]. *Hindutva: Who Is a Hindu?* Bombay: Veer Savarkar Prakashan.

Shani, Ornit. 2007. *Communalism, Caste and Hindu Nationalism: The Violence in Gujarat*. New Delhi: Cambridge University Press.

Sharma, Shriram. n.d. *Patitoddhār*.

Shraddhanand, Sanyasi. 1926. *Hindu Sangathan: Saviour of the Dying Race*. Delhi: Arjun Press.

Shyamlal. 1984. *The Bhangis in Transition*. New Delhi: Inter-India Publications.

Teltumbde, Anand. (Ed.). 2005. *Hindutva and Dalits: Perspectives for Understanding Communal Praxis*. Kolkata: Samya.

CHAPTER 18

CASTE AMONG MUSLIMS IN NORTH INDIA AND PAKISTAN

JULIEN LEVESQUE

From a textualist point of view, Muslims, in the South Asian subcontinent or elsewhere, can hardly be said to have castes. Islam as a set of beliefs and religious practices based on the foundational Quranic text and the subsequent Islamic tradition (*hadith, sunna, fiqh*) excludes the possibility of a caste-based social order, which can then only appear as an unorthodox deviation from the Islamic ideal of equality among believers. Proponents of this view thus describe caste among Muslims as the result of an 'acculturation' through which a supposedly pure Islam—champion of an egalitarian ideal—adapted to local cultural contexts as it spread across the world (G. Ansari, 1960). However, social scientists have criticized such a dichotomous view that pins a pure Islam against multiple local deviations. Relying on empirical observation, they have argued against making hierarchical judgements between the many ways of being Muslim, differentiated by language, cultural habits, sects, beliefs, religious practices, and social stratification. To reconcile the contradiction stemming from the identification of multiple practices as Islam by the practitioners themselves, one position has been to 'adapt the Orientalist distinction between orthodox and nonorthodox Islam to the categories of Great and Little Traditions' (Asad, 1996, p. 6). This implied that social scientists should refrain from judging what is Islamic from what is not. In other words, 'anyone who tried to look for any hierarchy or truth-value in various Islams was trading in theology' (Anjum, 2007, p. 657). In order to reject both 'the idea of an integrated social totality in which social structure and religious ideology interact [as well as the idea that] anything Muslims believe or do can be regarded by the anthropologist as part of Islam', Talal Asad proposes to conceptualize Islam as a 'discursive tradition' (Asad, 1996, p. 14). According to Ovamir Anjum, 'Paying attention to a discursive tradition is not to essentialize certain practices or symbols as being more authentic but to recognize that the authenticity or orthodoxy of these has to be argued for from within the tradition and embraced or rejected according to its own criteria' (Anjum, 2007, p. 662).

The question for scholars becomes, then, not whether caste exists in South Asian Muslim societies, but how Muslims in the subcontinent engage with caste practices and discourses. To use Talal Asad's formulation, how are Muslims inducted into caste practices and discourses *as* Muslims? Can caste practices be argued from within the discursive tradition of Islam?

Caste is also the object of conflicting definitions. The term encompasses two indigenous notions: *varna*, that designates the four broad Hindu caste-families (Brahmin, Kshatriya, Vaishya, Shudra), and *jati*, or the caste that is part of one's lived experience and to which are attached a number of prescriptions and prohibitions regarding social behaviour and intercourse (endogamy, commensality, occupation). Muslims themselves generally use the terms *baradari* and *zat* in the northern parts of the subcontinent (Alavi, 1972), which are somewhat comparable with the notion of *jati*. Moreover, as we will see in greater detail below, scholars have identified three broad categories—*ashraf*, *ajlaf*, *arzal*—that are evocative of *varna*. Other terms may be employed by Muslims across the subcontinent, such as *qaum, samaj, sampraday, samuday*, or the English word 'community'.

From colonial census administrators to social scientists, scholars have debated whether Muslims in the subcontinent can be said to have castes. In the last decades, the discussion also entered the political arena over the issue of reservations in India. In order to offer an overview of the debates concerning caste among Muslims, mainly in North India and Pakistan, this chapter first shows that colonial scholars and administrators tended to understand the phenomenon as the product of a history of conquest and miscegenation. I then turn to socio-anthropological debates of the second half of the 20th century that opposed scholars on whether a caste *system* existed among Muslims. Finally, I explore how new legal conceptions of caste among Indian Muslims became a stepping stone for political mobilization from the 1990s.

Conquest and Miscegenation: Muslim Caste in Colonial Knowledge Production

Among historians, much of the debate on caste has centred on the extent to which colonialism shaped what we now know as caste. Contrary to some colonial writings that lauded the British presence in India for curtailing the oppressive role of caste, recent historiography has highlighted the deep impact of colonization in the transformation of social categories. Scholars of the postcolonial and the Subaltern schools consider the colonial enterprise of Orientalist knowledge production and the subsequent use of caste as an official administrative category responsible for what we now know of as caste (Dirks, 2001). Other accounts—historians of the 'Cambridge school' in particular—see the advent of colonialism not so much as a sharp rupture than as a process, and consequently throw light on developments at work before the colonial period (Bayly, 2001). However, as noted by Margrit Pernau, historians have not specifically examined the ways in which colonialism transformed social stratification among non-Hindus (Pernau, 2013, p. 62).

In the first half of the 19th century, British knowledge of social distinctions among Indian Muslims relied on the 'uncoordinated efforts of [. . .] regional datagatherers' (Bayly, 2001, p. 103). Locally prominent figures composed reports or volumes, often on the request of colonial administrators. Consequently, such accounts of South Asian Muslim life shared the perspective of dominant groups. In 1832, two such books targeting a British audience described the ways of life of Indian Muslims (Shurreef, 1832; Hassan Ali, 1832). They offered much details about the higher social groups among Muslims: the four categories that claim foreign descent—Sayyid, Shaikh, Mughal, Pathan—and form the *ashraf* or *tabqa-i ashrafiyya*. However, they almost totally disregarded artisan or service castes. In his *Qanoon-e-Islam, the Customs of the Moosulmans of India*, the Hyderabadi notable Jafar Sharif explained in a footnote running several pages that 'Mohummudans are divided into four great classes, distinguished by the appellations *Syed*, *Sheikh*, *Mogol*, and *Putt'hans*' (Shurreef, 1832, p. 8).

Mrs. Meer Hassan Ali, the English wife of a Lucknowi Shi'a aristocrat of *sayyid* lineage, was mainly interested in religious practices, but acknowledged in her *Observations on the Mussulmauns of India* the existence of social ranking among Muslims, including 'poorer classes of the people' (Hassan Ali, 1832, p. 21). She only rarely used the term 'caste', and then only for Hindus. Mrs Meer Hassan Ali conceived of Muslims and Hindus in dichotomous terms, distinguishing the 'aborigines' from the 'invaders'. Yet she observed instances of 'borrowings' or acculturation: commenting on the reaction to lunar eclipses, she noted that 'Many of the notions entertained by the lower classes of Mussulmauns upon the nature of an eclipse are borrowed from the Hindoos' (Hassan Ali, 1832, pp. 158–159).

In spite of the differences in their regional (Lucknow, Hyderabad) and sectarian (Shi'a, Sunni) contexts, these two accounts of South Asian Muslim life share commonalities that set the tone for later colonial scholarship. They adopted the perspective of dominant groups, in which 'true Muslims' were those whose ancestors supposedly came from outside as 'invaders', while other Muslims were examined in a way that sought to gauge the extent to which Islam transformed itself through extended contact with Hinduism. In this narrative of 'pure origins' and subsequent mixing, Muslim caste, described in a variety of terms that included tribe, class, and race, appeared as the typical product of the civilizational encounter between Islam and Hinduism, each assumed to possess their own social structures.

From the second half of the 19th century, colonial scholarship aspired to greater representativeness. It began relying on large-scale surveys put in place by the 'ethnographic state' (Dirks, 2001, pp. 43–60). From 1844 to 1941, the nearly fifteen 'castes and tribes' surveys all included Muslim groups in their listings, while the Census, starting in 1871, allowed for the quantification of these group populations (G. Ansari, 1960,

p. 2). Regarding Muslims, such surveys helped abandon the *ashraf*-centred perspective by including other groups and complexified the simple Hindu-Muslim dichotomy. Thus in 1869, the *Report of the Census of Oudh* by J. Charles Williams, in a section dedicated to detailing the different 'classes of Muhammadans', identified three broad categories: the 'higher castes of Muhammadans' (the four *ashraf* groups), the 'Muhammadans descended from high caste Hindu converts' (mostly Rajput), and the 'lower classes of Muhammadans', the latter 'split up into thirty-five different castes' (Williams, 1869, Vol. 1, pp. 74–82). In the revision of Henry Miers Elliot's *Glossary* by John Beames, the author noted that in the variety of artisan and service castes such as Julahas, Nais, Bihistis, and Dhobis, each 'had Hindu counterparts—or Hindu members' (Lelyveld, 2003, p. 13). Hence, not only did such surveys point to the divisions within Muslims, they also indicated overlaps between Hindu and Muslim social groups and provided an explanation for the origin of castes among Muslims. In his report, J. Charles Williams felt the need to justify the use of the term 'caste' for these groups, unlike in the case of 'higher castes': 'I use this word advisedly and in opposition to mere professions', for 'the converts to Muhammadanism (of Northern India at any rate) did not, when adopting a new religion entirely abandon the habits and prejudices of their forefathers—on the contrary they remained in many respects observers of caste customs' (Williams, 1869, Vol. 1, p. 79).

William Crooke, one of the major voices among British administrators-ethnographers, extended the use of the term 'caste' to all Muslims. In his four-volume study on the religious and social customs of caste groups, Crooke adopted an inclusive, non-cultural definition of caste. He did not see it as 'confined to the votaries of the Hindu faith'. According to him, 'Islam has boldly solved the difficulty by recognising and adopting caste in its entirety. Not only does the converted Râjput, Gùjar, or Jât remain a member of his original sept or section; but he preserves most of those restrictions on social intercourse, intermarriage and the like, which make up the peasant's conception of caste' (W. Crooke, 1896, Vol. 1, p. xvii).

Crooke thus acknowledged the scale of conversion to Islam but retained the narrative of conquest and intermixing. Almost a hundred years after their original publication, he reedited Mrs Meer Hassan Ali's and Jafar Sharif's books. He presented the latter as an authoritative description of 'Islam in India', the new title for the book. One of Crooke's numerous edits was the addition of an initial chapter entitled 'Ethnography', which once more described the 'four [*ashraf*] classes'. But the 'ethnography' was actually preceded by an historical account of the spread of Islam in India in the form of a listing of the various Muslim conquests and kingdoms. For Crooke, South Asian Islam seemed best understood as the result of the encounter between Hinduism and a foreign religion along a linear north-west to east axis: 'Thus the present distribution of Islam has followed the course of the Muhammadan conquests from the north and west, and they are strongest in proportion to their vicinity to the head-quarters of the Faith in western Asia' (Sharif, 1921, p. 1).

The underlying racial assumption that associated physical with cultural traits appeared even more clearly in the first full chapter dedicated to analysing 'Caste and

Islam' in Edward A. H. Blunt's volume *The Caste System of Northern India*. Although Blunt counted as an opponent to the racial and anthropometric theory, his deterministic vision combined cultural, religious, behavioural, and physical traits, and was expressed in terms of pure origins, conquest, and miscegenation. He narrated the spread of 'the new 'militant religion of Muhammad' in India through a 'fresh series of invasions' (Blunt, 1931, p. 161), and its subsequent decay to the point when the 'Muhammadan domination, in short, had become the rule of the half-caste; and Muslim, like Saka, Kushan, and Hun before him, was in danger of being absorbed into Hinduism' (Blunt, 1931, p. 173).

With Blunt, the conception of caste among Muslims as the result of a civilizational encounter came to full fruition. Colonial writings saw Hinduism and Islam as two fundamentally antagonistic religions, rooted in different scriptures and civilizations. Caste among Muslims could only appear as an anomaly due to Hindu influence, conceived by its degree of resemblance, or difference, with the Hindu standard. The various colonial understandings of caste among Muslims tended to be influenced by racial conceptions and sought evolutionary explanations based on notions of purity and intermixing. What emerged was the '*ashraf-ajlaf* dichotomy', that is, the distinction between the four 'higher classes', or those who claimed foreign descent, and the descendants of converts, the latter being more likely to follow caste practices retained from Hinduism (I. Ahmad, 1966). These conceptions informed the anthropological debate on Muslim caste after India and Pakistan's independence.

Muslim Caste as a System and the Socio-Anthropological Debate

After independence, social scientists studying Muslim social stratification followed the changes of Indian anthropology and sociology, which experienced 'a transition from a descriptive to an analytical period' (Keda and Gupta, 2004, p. 231). In 1960, the first monograph on caste among Muslims focused on Uttar Pradesh and reignited the debate on the applicability of the term 'caste' for South Asian Muslims. Its author, Ghaus Ansari, adopted a structuralist and holistic approach, insisting that caste worked *as a system* among Muslims:

> Caste attitude and behaviour among the Ashraf castes can only be analysed in relation to the Muslim community as a whole. [. . .] If we once accept the fact that the Indian Muslims in general have a caste system, however modified, we must come to the conclusion that the Ashraf constitute the highest stratum within this structure. [. . .] Thus both the Sayyid and Shaikh, as competent religious pedagogues and priests, are almost identical with the Brahman; whereas both the Mughal and Pathan, being famous for their chivalry, appear to be equal to the Kshatriya. (G. Ansari, 1960, pp. 39–40)

Building on colonial sources, Ansari proposed a general picture of a South Asian 'Muslim caste system' composed of four broad categories: the *ashraf*, supposed to be the descendants of Muslim immigrants and divided into the four categories Sayyid, Shaikh, Mughal, and Pathan; the *ajlaf*, descendants of converts from service or 'clean occupational castes' (such as Qasab or butcher, Hajjam or barber, Darzi or tailor, etc.), sorted according to their level of proximity with their Hindu counterparts (by the degree of conversion of their members, understood as more or less correlated with the degree of Islamization of their customs); and the *arzal*, or untouchable castes (notably the tanners or Chamars and the sweepers or Bhangi or Lalbegi). The fourth category stands somewhat separately from the others, as the Muslim Rajputs, who retain many Hindu practices, do not wish to be associated with lower castes, yet are not considered suitable marriage partners by the *ashraf* (G. Ansari, 1960, pp. 40–41). Thus, Ansari depicted the 'Muslim caste system' as an inter-connected hierarchical chain that runs from the *Sayyid* on top to the untouchable castes at the bottom. If Ghaus Ansari's study had the merit of seriously raising the question of Muslim caste, it may be criticized for its lack of attention to contemporary developments (such as Partition-induced migration or the effects of the Zamindari Abolition Act) and its rather uncritical use of colonial sources. Thus, Ansari's work can be approached as a final synthesis concluding a long line of British surveys.

Starting in the 1960s, however, several scholars broke from the survey tradition and conducted empirically grounded ethnographic research in South Asian Muslim contexts. While earlier scholarship on social stratification among Muslims tended to adopt a static, atemporal vision, most of these case studies sought to grasp observable transformations rather than unchanging patterns. They included village ethnographies (Eglar, 1960), regional studies (Misra, 1964), or monographs on marriage customs, and gender-relations (Vreede-de Stuers, 1968). From the 1970s, the discussion took the form of a four-volume series edited by sociologist Imtiaz Ahmad (1973, 1976, 1981, 1983), as well as articles in *Contributions to Indian Sociology* (Gaborieau, 1972; Madan, 1972; Lindholm, 1986), later compiled as a book (Madan, 1976, 2001). These authors were divided on whether Muslims could be said to have castes. The central premise of Imtiaz Ahmad's work was that Muslims and Hindus, being part of the same society, shared the structural features of their social organization. By arguing that caste existed among Indian Muslims, Imtiaz Ahmad's endeavour stressed their 'Indian-ness', challenging both the position of the Hindu Right (who saw Muslims either as foreign invaders or as converts bound to revert back to Hinduism), and the religious scholars among Muslims (who tended to highlight the egalitarian norm in Islam and downplay inegalitarian practices or discourses).

Imtiaz Ahmad's research also contradicted Hindu-centric visions of caste among scholars, not least French anthropologist Louis Dumont's then recently published systemic theory that defined caste as the concrete transformation of the ideological principle of purity and impurity, embodied in the figure of the Brahmin at the top of the hierarchy (Dumont, 1966). Authors adopting a holistic approach, such as Dumont or Célestin Bouglé, used the terms 'caste system' to insist on the idea that castes only make sense in hierarchical relation to each other. Therefore, one particular occurrence of caste cannot be conceptually detached from the working of the integrated whole that the 'caste system' forms. For Dumont, caste only exists in Hinduism and in the Hindu cultural sphere, or what Edmund Leach called the 'Pan-Indian Civilization' (E. R. Leach, 1960, p. 5). Caste, then, is an Indian or South Asian specificity. Others have argued, to the contrary, that caste should be conceived of as a social structure rather than as a culturally embedded system (Berreman, 1979). Therefore, one could well apply the word caste to various forms of social stratification, for instance in Africa (Todd, 1977), in the Americas (McCaa, Schwartz, and Grubessich, 1979), or in other parts of Asia (Barth, 1960; Potter and Potter, 1990, pp. 296–312). South Asia would be only one among many 'caste societies', and 'the similarities between South Asian Muslims and Hindus [could thus be argued to be] not a result of assimilation, but rather of structural correspondence' (Lindholm, 1986, p. 67).

For many scholars, the absence of strict notions of ritual purity and untouchability seems to be a distinguishing feature of caste among Muslims (Barth, 1959, pp. 16–22). Noting divisions between scholars on this point, Imtiaz Ahmad concluded that 'the notion of ritual purity and pollution is not as elaborate among the Muslims as it is among the Hindus. As a matter of fact, it is considerably weak, so weak that it is not immediately obvious and must be inferred from indirect evidence' (I. Ahmad, 1973, p. 9). For Dumont, the principle of purity and pollution gives ideological cohesion to the caste system. To him, because of the absence of the Brahmanic figure, caste among Muslims appears as 'truncated', and therefore 'not caste at all', as in the case of the Swat Pathans (Lindholm, 1986, p. 68). Instead of apprehending the system from the top, French anthropologist Marc Gaborieau pointed to documented cases of untouchability among Muslims. He argued that Muslims 'retain certain elements of caste hierarchy to the extent that these elements allow for the exclusion of lower impure service castes' (Gaborieau, 1993, p. 292). Some recent scholarship has attempted to provide broader evidence of the practice of untouchability among Muslims (Trivedi, Srinivas, and Kumar, 2016).

Some empirical studies focused on the local level to see how caste functions as a system among Muslims. Zekiye Eglar's village ethnography of a Punjabi village in Pakistan described in a static way the system of exchange based on contractual functions similar to the complementary relations described as the *jajmani* system in North India or *bara balutedar* in Maharashtra (Eglar, 1960). Unlike previous scholars, Eglar did not delve into the historicity of Muslim caste, made no attempt to explain its origins, or to compare it with Hindu caste, and did not even discuss the pertinence of the term 'caste' in a Muslim context. In the contractual relationships (*seyp*) between a landholding or *zamindar* family and a number of artisan castes or *kammi* families (Eglar, 1960, pp. 28–41), the latter provide goods and services to the *zamindars* in exchange for grain, and perform a number of other customary and ritual roles (for instance, the barber cooks in the house of the *zamindar* on special occasions, acts as messenger and matchmaker, and performs circumcision). By shifting the focus away from identifying the elements of a graded hierarchy, Eglar showed that the Muslim context did not fundamentally change inter-caste relations. This conclusion was later criticized by sociologist Hamza Alavi, who rejected the 'assumption that these [South Asian rural] societies are structurally similar, if not identical in every detail, and that the distinguishing feature of the structure of social institutions in those societies is their focus on caste and the related *jajmani* system as bases of social organization' (Alavi, 1972, p. 1). He argued that in West Punjab, 'it is the kinship system rather than caste which embodies the primordial loyalties which structure its social organization' (Alavi, 1972, p. 1). According to Alavi, the crucial social unit is the *baradari* (brotherhood or patrilineage), a term which describes various circles of kinship relations. However, Alavi's description of *baradari* relationships does not depart greatly from descriptions of caste relationships elsewhere in South Asia, especially if combined with contractual relations.

Scholars also paid attention to dynamic transformations among South Asian Muslims, such as social mobility. To describe such changes, Cora Vreede-de Stuers drew on M. N. Srinivas' analysis of 'sanskritization' to introduce the distinction between 'Islamization' and 'ashrafization'. She calls '"ashrafization" [the] attempts at social climbing by groups or individuals through hypergamy and adopting the way of life of higher classes', to be contrasted from Islamization, that is, when 'groups or individuals [...] wish to distinguish themselves clearly from non-Muslims by purifying themselves of so-called un-Islamic customs and "practices"' (Vreede-de Stuers, 1968, p. 6). Several subsequent studies have examined the upward social trajectories of Muslim caste groups, such as the Shaikh Siddiquis (I. Ahmad, 2018), the Julaha/Ansari (Mehta, 1997), or the Qasab/Qureshi (Z. Ahmad, 2018).

Among the wide range of case studies, several scholars also highlighted regional variation to argue that caste was not an accurate paradigm to describe social stratification among Muslims in South Asia (Wakil, 1972). Scholars of South India, in particular, questioned the dominant, North-India centric trope. Mattison Mines wondered why Tamil Muslims, unlike Hyderabadi and North Indian Muslims, do not seem to fit in any definition of caste (Mines, 2018). Also in the Tamil context, Frank Fanselow invited scholars to examine how Muslim converts have 'disinvented' caste (Fanselow, 1996). Observations of Muslim social stratification in the Konkan, the Malabar coast, or the Maldives also challenge the tripartite framework—*ashraf, ajlaf, arzal*—drawn from the North Indian situation. For this reason, some have suggested alternative terms to describe Muslims' caste-like practices. Pervaiz Nazir, for instance, spoke of 'caste labels' (Nazir, 1993), while Leela Dube preferred 'caste analogues' (Dube, 1973).

The socio-anthropological debate on whether caste exists among Muslims has not led to the emergence of a clear consensus. Driven by the intention to construct 'a comprehensive and systematic coverage of all the facets of Islam in India' (I. Ahmad, 1981, p. 3), the debate on Muslim caste has been useful in fostering a wide range of empirical research highlighting regional variations and examining contemporary observable dynamics. Such a project, however, seems to have stopped inspiring new empirical studies since the 1990s. As a result, some, like Syed Ali, argued that 'the question of the existence of caste among Muslims in India is no longer fruitful' (Ali, 2002, p. 602). Ali further stated: 'How much Muslim caste is similar to, or different from, Hindu caste gives us no better understanding of how caste functions for Muslims, or of how and why it is or is not important in different contexts' (Ali, 2002, p. 603). Syed Ali's statement echoes an earlier suggestion by Sylvia Vatuk (1996, p. 229). Vatuk invited scholars to explore research questions that allow them to address Muslim social stratification in South Asia 'in its own terms'—for instance by focusing on the notion of *khandan*—and to look at the justifications offered by Muslims themselves for social distinctions. In recent decades, social scientists focusing on South Asian Muslims have avoided overarching or systemic representations—abandoning any project of a 'systematic coverage'. Instead, the interest for social structures among Muslims has been included in broader ethnographic studies of 'lived Islam', 'Muslim lives', or 'Muslim belonging', without necessarily attempting to synthetize distinct situations.

CASTE AS LEGAL CATEGORY AND POLITICAL PLATFORM AMONG MUSLIMS

According to Joel Lee, 'the prominence of caste in South Asian Islamic life has been almost entirely obscured in global representations of the region [by, among several factors, the] non-recognition of Muslim caste by the postcolonial states of India, Pakistan, and their neighbors; to be ignored by the census and related technologies of modern governance is in significant ways to be rendered invisible to the world' (Lee, 2018a, p. 168). The question of caste remains largely taboo in Pakistan, whether among Muslims or between Muslims and low-caste non-Muslims, in which case caste hierarchy reinforces the exclusion of minority religious groups (Gazdar, 2007; Hussain, 2019). In India, the political environment of the 1980s and 1990s sparked new conceptualizations of Muslim caste that served an agenda of collective mobilization and made Muslim caste visible. In particular, in the wake of the 1980 Mandal Commission report (B. P. Mandal Commission, 1980), marginalized castes (especially, in India's administrative categorization, OBCs or Other Backward Classes) became powerful political forces (Jaffrelot, 2003).

The main problem for marginalized Muslim castes was their exclusion from caste-based government benefits, in particular quotas (reservations) in public service and universities. The Presidential Order of August 1950 stated that 'no person who professes a religion different from Hinduism shall be deemed to be a member of a Scheduled Caste'. However, later official reports noted that some Muslims were also victims of caste discrimination, despite their exclusion from the Scheduled Caste and OBC categories. The Mandal Commission report, which recommended a quota for OBCs, stated that 'Though caste system is peculiar to Hindu society yet, in actual practice, it also pervades the non-Hindu communities in India in varying degrees' (B. P. Mandal Commission, 1980, p. 55). Referring to sociological literature, the 2006 Sachar report concurred, noting 'the presence of descent based social stratification among [Muslims]. Features of the Hindu caste system, such as hierarchical ordering of social groups, endogamy, and hereditary occupation have been found to be amply present among the Indian Muslims as well' (Sachar Committee, 2006, p. 192). Finally, the 2009 Ranganath Mishra Commission report recommended a 10 per cent quota for Muslim OBCs, as well as the abrogation of the 1950 Presidential order.

This indicated a shift in the official understanding of caste by the Indian state, from a religiously sanctioned to a socio-economic definition not specific to Hindus. In line with this change, the central government and several states introduced affirmative action for certain Muslim castes as part of the OBC category in the 1990s. The legal translation of the official recognition of Muslim caste has, however, been ambiguous: in the 1992 *Indra Sawhney* case, the Supreme Court 'recommended the inclusion of only those Muslim castes whose analogous Hindu castes had been included in the backward class category' (Bhat, 2018, p. 184). The public debate on whether Muslims should benefit from reservations still opposes proponents of religious-specific quotas to those who argue that some Muslims should be included in SC and OBC categories if they fit certain socio-economic criteria but more importantly if they are victims of particular exclusionary practices.

Since the 1980s, a new voice emerged in this debate when several groups were established to represent marginalized Muslim castes (OBC) and Dalit Muslims (SC)—often denoted by the general term *pasmanda* (roughly translated as 'marginalized'). Caste-based organizations among Muslims—such as the Momin Conference or the Jamiat-ul Quresh, representing respectively the weavers (Julaha) and the butchers (Qasab)—had since the early decades of the 20th century acted as platforms of solidarity and catalysts of social mobility for specific '*jati*-clusters' (Manor, 2010, p. xix). However, some now argued in the pages of the magazines *Dalit Voice* and *Muslim India* that Dalits and Muslims shared common interests—countering Hindu high-caste domination—and should therefore unite (Marková, 1990; Sikand, 2001, 2004). Others stressed the need for *pasmanda* Muslims to break the monopoly of the *ashraf* over the representation of Muslims as a single community (Anwar, 2001). This was the line of the Pasmanda Muslim Mahaz (PMM), founded by Ali Anwar in October 1998 in Patna. When several Muslim organizations demanded reservations for Muslims as a whole in the Muslim Agenda 1999, the PMM released its own Pasmanda Agenda 1999 and lobbied for caste-based reservations applicable to Muslims (Alam, 2007, 2009; K. A. Ansari, 2009; Waheed and Mujtaba, 2017, pp. 121–22). Similar demands were put forward by the All-India Muslim OBC Sangathan in Maharashtra and by the All-India Backward Muslim Morcha, set up by Aijaz Ali in Patna in 1994 (Khanam, 2013, p. 136). Such groups helped making Dalit Muslim voices heard and led to a few electoral victories, notably in Bihar, but have not profoundly changed the composition of the leadership of the Muslim organizations.

Yet such movements renewed the historical and socio-anthropological debates on caste among Muslims. The dispute among social scientists became irrelevant as a section of Muslims themselves started denouncing the domination of higher castes in the name of representing the 'Muslim community', without focusing on matters of definition. By stepping into the political and scholarly debate, *pasmanda* Muslim organizations defended the idea that caste exists as a tool of oppression among Muslims and should therefore be combatted. They targeted the religious and political leadership, mainly of *ashraf* extraction, accusing it of perpetuating inequality among Muslims by denying caste-based exclusion. Their argument in favour of equality drew on the normative principle often put forward by *ulama* as one of the core tenets of Islam—that of equality, or *masavat*, among believers. At the same time, *pasmanda* intellectuals investigated the justifications provided for caste practices within South Asian Muslim thought, such as the concept of *kafa'a/kufu* invoked by *ulama* in support of endogamy (Sikand, 2004, pp. 27–43). Interestingly, the most comprehensive argument denouncing caste practices among Muslims came from an *alim* associated with the Jama'at-i Islami Hind, Masud Alam Falahi, who nonetheless rejected sectional interest groups like the various *pasmanda* organizations (Falahi, 2009). Falahi notably brought to light the writings of medieval *ulama*, hence showing that caste practices and discourses among Muslims could be traced to precolonial times. The critique addressed by *pasmanda* scholars like Falahi and Ali Anwar to the Muslim leadership is also indicative of the failure of Islamic reform movements to tackle the *de facto* inequality within Muslims and its perpetuation through hierarchical social practices. Overall, the emergence of *pasmanda* demands has thus contributed to fostering new research on Muslim social stratification. Its political relevance brought activists on the academic stage (Quadri and Kumar, 2003), while new investigations by anthropologists provided historical depth as well as ethnographic thickness to our understanding of Muslim caste (Lee, 2018b).

Concluding Remarks

Muslim caste can no more be a fruitful object of scholarly enquiry if it consists of assuming an underlying social structure that researchers should unearth. The debate on the applicability of the term 'caste' to Muslims or on whether castes existed among Muslims largely relied on just such an assumption. Scholarly exchanges on the question became an exceedingly redundant discussion over the years. This does not mean, however, that scholars should shun from examining caste practices and discourses among Muslims. First, we may heed Sylvia Vatuk's call for appraising social stratification among South Asian Muslims not only insofar as it relates to Hindu caste but in Muslims' own terms (Vatuk, 1996). Second, following Talal Asad, caste should be seen as 'an instituted practice (set in a particular context, and having a particular history) into which Muslims are inducted *as* Muslims' (Asad, 1996, p. 15). This implies that caste among Muslims should be seen as a dynamic process that needs to be studied in its relation to Islam as a discursive tradition, rather than as a static core structuring principle that would impose itself on people in the subcontinent, Hindu or not. This forces us to consider seriously the dynamics of social distinction in which Muslims actively participate: at the discursive level (discourses, texts, visuals that construct representations about caste practices), in daily practices (the maintenance of occupational specialization, endogamy, or caste-based exclusionary practices; or, conversely, the active engagement in egalitarian endeavours), and in collective and political mobilization, where the goal of dismantling caste privilege becomes a way of engaging with the state.

New scholarship could bring forth fresh empirical material and thus further our understanding of Muslim social stratification in the subcontinent. Using the wide literature produced by individuals and organizations, historians could throw light on the evolution of caste categories over time, the position of religious and political authorities with regard to Muslim caste, and the trajectories of 'Muslim communities of descent' (Pernau, 2013, p. 62). Social scientists with their range of methods—ethnography, life-stories, mixed methods, experiments, or surveys—could provide insights into contemporary usages of caste among Muslims as a marker of social distinction, a political platform of mobilization, or a legal category, as well as into the intersection of caste with other social identities—gender or sect (*maslak*). I would suggest three possible avenues for further study on Muslim social stratification in the South Asian subcontinent: first, the study of formal caste associations or organizations; second, the exploration of the intersection of caste and sect, to question varying attitude towards caste hierarchy; third, comparative studies across religious groups and across regions of the subcontinent. This list, of course, is not exhaustive, but scholarship on these questions would no doubt enhance our comprehension of the way South Asian Muslims produce and reproduce their categories of social distinction, including caste.

References

Ahmad, Imtiaz. 1966. 'The Ashraf-Ajlaf Dichotomy in Muslim Social Structure in India'. *Indian Economic & Social History Review*, 3(3): 268–278. DOI: https://doi.org/10.1177/001946466600300303.

Ahmad, Imtiaz (Ed.). 1973. *Caste and Social Stratification among Muslims in India*. Delhi: Manohar.

Ahmad, Imtiaz (Ed.). 1976. *Family, Kinship, and Marriage among Muslims in India*. New Delhi: Manohar.

Ahmad, Imtiaz (Ed.). 1981. *Ritual and Religion among Muslims in India*. New Delhi: Manohar.

Ahmad, Imtiaz (Ed.). 1983. *Modernization and Social Change among Muslims in India*. New Delhi: Manohar.

Ahmad, Imtiaz. (Ed.) 2018. 'Endogamy and Status Mobility among the Siddiqui Sheikhs of Allahabad, Uttar Pradesh'. In Imtiaz Ahmad (Ed.), *Caste and Social Stratification among the Muslims in India* (3rd ed., pp. 171–206). Delhi: Aakar Books.

Ahmad, Zarin. 2018. *Delhi's Meatscapes: Muslim Butchers in a Transforming Mega City*. New Delhi: OUP India.

Alam, Arshad. 2007. 'New Directions in Indian Muslim Politics the Agenda of All India Pasmanda Muslim Mahaz'. *History and Sociology of South Asia*, 1(2): 130–143. DOI: https://doi.org/10.1177/223080750700100206.

Alam, Arshad. 2009. 'Challenging the Ashrafs: The Politics of Pasmanda Muslim Mahaz'. *Journal of Muslim Minority Affairs*, 29(2): 171–181.

Alavi, Hamza A. 1972. 'Kinship in West Punjab Villages'. *Contributions to Indian Sociology*, 6(1): 1–27.

Ali, Syed. 2002. 'Collective and Elective Ethnicity: Caste among Urban Muslims in India'. *Sociological Forum*, 17(4): 593–620. DOI: https://doi.org/10.1023/A:1021077323866.

Anjum, Ovamir. 2007. 'Islam as a Discursive Tradition: Talal Asad and His Interlocutors'. *Comparative Studies of South Asia, Africa and the Middle East*, 27(3): 656–672.

Ansari, Ghaus. 1960. *Muslim Caste in Uttar Pradesh: A Study of Culture Contact.* Lucknow: Ethnographic and Folk Culture Society.

Ansari, Khalid Anis. 2009. 'Rethinking the Pasmanda Movement'. *Economic and Political Weekly*, 44(13): 8–10.

Anwar, Ali. 2001. *Masavat ki jang.* New Delhi: Vani Prakashan Publisher.

Asad, Talal. 1996. 'The Idea of an Anthropology of Islam'. In John A. Hall and Ian Jarvie (Eds.), *The Social Philosophy of Ernest Gellner* (pp. 381–403). Amsterdam, Atlanta: Rodopi B.V.

B. P. Mandal Commission. 1980. 'Report of the Backward Classes Commission'. New Delhi: Backward Classes Commission.

Barth, Fredrik. 1959. *Political Leadership among Swat Pathans.* London: University of London, Athlone Press.

Barth, Fredrik. 1960. 'The System of Social Stratification in Swat, North Pakistan'. In Edmund Leach (Ed.), *Aspects of Caste in South India, Ceylon & North-West Pakistan* (pp. 113–146). Cambridge: University Press.

Bayly, Susan. 2001. *Caste, Society and Politics in India from the Eighteenth Century to the Modern Age.* Cambridge: University Press.

Berreman, Gerald Duane. 1979. *Caste and Other Inequities: Essays on Inequality* (Vol. 2). Meerut: Folklore Institute.

Bhat, M. Mohsin Alam Bhat. 2018, February. 'Muslim Caste under Indian Law: Between Uniformity, Autonomy and Equality'. http://dspace.jgu.edu.in:8080/jspui/handle/10739/1383.

Blunt, Edward Arthur Henry. 1931. *The Caste System of Northern India with Special Reference to the United Provinces of Agra and Oudh.* London: Oxford University Press.

Crooke, W. 1896. *The Tribes And Castes of the North Western India* (Vol. 1. 4 vols). Calcutta. http://archive.org/details/in.ernet.dli.2015.149957.

Dirks, Nicholas B. 2001. *Castes of Mind: Colonialism and the Making of Modern India.* Princeton: Princeton University Press.

Dube, Leela. 1973. 'Caste Analogues among the Laccadive Muslims'. In Imtiaz Ahmad (Ed.), Caste and Social Stratification among the Muslims in India. New Delhi: Manohar.

Dumont, Louis. 1966. *Homo hierarchicus: le système des castes et ses implications.* Paris: Gallimard.

Eglar, Zekiye. 1960. *A Punjabi Village in Pakistan.* New York: Columbia University Press.

Falahi, Masʿud ʿAlam. 2009. *Hindūstān menzāt pāt aur Musalmān.* Mumbaʾī: Āʾiḍiyal Fāʾūndaishan.

Fanselow, Frank S. 1996. 'The Disinvention of Caste among Tamil Muslims'. In C. J. Fuller (Ed.), *Caste Today* (p. 295). Delhi: Oxford University Press.

Gaborieau, Marc. 1972. 'Muslims in the Hindu Kingdom of Nepal'. *Contributions to Indian Sociology*, 6(1): 84–105. DOI: https://doi.org/10.1177/006996677200600105.

Gaborieau, Marc. 1993. *Ni brahmanes ni ancêtres: colporteurs musulmans du Népal.* Nanterre, France: Société d'ethnologie.

Gayer, Laurent, and Christophe Jaffrelot (Eds.). 2011. *Muslims in Indian Cities: Trajectories of Marginalisation.* London: Hurst & Co.

Gazdar, Haris. 2007. 'Class, Caste or Race: Veils over Social Oppression in Pakistan'. *Economic and Political Weekly*, 42(02): 86–88.

Hassan Ali, Mrs. Meer. 1832. *Observations on the Mussulmauns of India: Descriptive of their Manners, Customs, Habits and Religious Opinions, Made during a Twelve Years' Residence in Their Immediate Society*. London: Parbury, Allen, and Co. http://archive.org/details/in.ernet.dli.2015.217679.

Hussain, Ghulam. 2019. 'Understanding Hegemony of Caste in Political Islam and Sufism in Sindh, Pakistan'. *Journal of Asian and African Studies*, 54(5): 716–745. DOI: https://doi.org/10.1177/0021909619839430.

Jaffrelot, Christophe. 2003. *India's Silent Revolution: The Rise of the Lower Castes in North India*. London: C. Hurst & Co. Publishers.

Keda, Satish, and Giri Raj Gupta. 2004. 'Theoretical Trends in Post-Independence Ethnographies of India'. In Surendra K. Gupta (Ed.), *Emerging Social Science Concerns: Festschrift in Honour of Professor Yogesh Atal* (pp. 231–243). New Delhi: Concept Publishing Co.

Khanam, Azra. 2013. *Muslim Backward Classes: A Sociological Perspective*. New Delhi: SAGE Publications India.

Leach, Edmund Ronald. 1960. *Aspects of Caste in South India, Ceylon and North-West Pakistan* (Vol. 2). Cambridge: Cambridge University Press.

Lee, Joel. 2018a. 'Caste'. In Zayn R. Kassam, Yudit Kornberg Greenberg, and Jehan Bagli (Eds.), *Islam, Judaism, and Zoroastrianism* (pp. 167–176). Encyclopedia of Indian Religions. Dordrecht: Springer.

Lee, Joel. 2018b. 'Who Is the True Halalkhor? Genealogy and Ethics in Dalit Muslim Oral Traditions'. *Contributions to Indian Sociology*, 52(1): 1–27.

Lelyveld, David. 2003. *Aligarh's First Generation: Muslim Solidarity in British India* (2nd ed.). New Delhi: Oxford University Press.

Lindholm, Charles. 1986. 'Caste in Islam and the Problem of Deviant Systems: A Critique of Recent Theory'. *Contributions to Indian Sociology*, 20(1): 61–73.

Madan, T. N. 1976. *Muslim Communities of South Asia: Culture and Society*. New Delhi, Inde: Vikas Publishing House.

Madan, T. N. (Ed.). 2001. *Muslim Communities of South Asia: Culture, Society and Power* (3rd ed.). New Delhi: Manohar.

Madan, T. N. 1972. 'Religious Ideology in a Plural Society: The Muslims and Hindus of Kashmir'. *Contributions to Indian Sociology*, 6(1): 106–141. DOI: https://doi.org/10.1177/006996677200600106.

Manor, James. 2010. 'Prologue: Caste and Politics in Recent Times'. In Rajni Kothari (Ed.), *Caste in Indian Politics* (2nd ed., pp. xi–lxi). Hyderabad: Orient Blackswan.

Marková, Dagmar. 1990. 'Efforts at Uniting Indian Muslims and Dalits in the 1980s'. *Archiv Orientální*, 58: 33–42.

McCaa, Robert, Stuart B. Schwartz, and Arturo Grubessich. 1979. 'Race and Class in Colonial Latin America: A Critique'. *Comparative Studies in Society and History*, 21(3): 421–433.

Mehta, Deepak. 1997. *Work, Ritual, Biography: A Muslim Community in North India*. Delhi: Oxford University Press.

Mines, Mattison. 2018. 'Social Stratification among Muslim Tamils in Tamilnadu, South India'. In Imtiaz Ahmad (Ed.), *Caste and Social Stratification among Muslims in India* (pp. 159–169). Delhi: Aakar Books.

Misra, Satish Chandra. 1964. *Muslim Communities in Gujarat: Preliminary Studies in Their History and Social Organization*. Asia Publishing House.

Nazir, Pervaiz. 1993. 'Social Structure, Ideology and Language: Caste among Muslims'. *Economic and Political Weekly*, 28(52): 2897–2900.

Pernau, Margrit. 2013. *Ashraf into Middle Classes: Muslims in Nineteenth-Century Delhi*. India: OUP.

Potter, Sulamith Heins, and Jack M. Potter. 1990. *China's Peasants: The Anthropology of a Revolution*. Cambridge: Cambridge University Press.

Quadri, Safdar Imam, and Sanjay Kumar (Eds.). 2003. *Marginalisation of Dalit Muslims in Indian Democracy*. Delhi: Deshkal Publication.

Roy, Asim, and Mushirul Hasan (Eds.). 2005. *Living Together Seperately: Cultural India in History and Politics*. New Delhi: Oxford University Press.

Sachar Committee. 2006. 'Social, Economic and Educational Status of the Muslim Community of India'. New Delhi: Prime Minister's High Level Committee, Cabinet Secretariat, Government of India.

Sharif, Jafar. 1921. *Islam in India, or, The Qanun-i-Islam; the Customs of the Musalmans of India; Comprising a Full and Exact Account of Their Various Rites and Ceremonies from the Moment of Birth to the Hour of Death*. [Edited by William Crooke. Translated by Gerhard Andreas Herklots]. London, New York [etc.] H. Milford: Oxford University Press. http://archive.org/details/islaminindiaorqnoojafa.

Shurreef, Jaffur. 1832. *Qanoon-e-Islam, or the Customs of the Moosulmans of India*. [Edited by Gerhard Andreas Herklots] (1st ed.). London: Parbury, Allen, and Co. https://archive.org/details/in.gov.ignca.13877.

Sikand, Yoginder. 2001. 'A New Indian Muslim Agenda: The Dalit Muslims and the All-India Backward Muslim Morcha'. *Journal of Muslim Minority Affairs*, 21(2): 287–296. DOI: https://doi.org/10.1080/1360200120092860.

Sikand, Yoginder. 2004. *Islam, Caste and Dalit Muslim Relations in India*. New Delhi: Global Media Publications.

Todd, D. M. 1977. 'Caste in Africa?' *Africa*, 47(4): 398–412. DOI: https://doi.org/10.2307/1158345.

Trivedi, Prashant K., Fahimuddin G. Srinivas, and S. Kumar. 2016. 'Does Untouchability Exist among Muslims: Evidence from Uttar Pradesh'. *Economic and Political Weekly*, 51(15): 32–36.

Vatuk, Sylvia. 1996. 'Identity and Difference or Equality and Inequality in South Asian Muslim Society'. In C. J. Fuller (Ed.), *Caste Today* (pp. 227–262). Delhi: Oxford University Press.

Vreede-de Stuers, Cora. 1968. *Parda: A Study of Muslim Women's Life in Northern India*. Assen: Van Gorcum.

Waheed, Abdul, and Sheikh Idrees Mujtaba. 2017. 'Aspiring to Rise: Agitation of Muslim "Other Backward Classes" in Uttar Pradesh'. *Islam and Muslim Societies: A Social Science Journal*, 10(1): 105–126.

Wakil, Parvez A. 1972. '"Zat" and "Qoum" in Punjabi Society: A Contribution to the Problem of Caste'. *Sociologus*, 22(1/2): 38–48.

Williams, John Charles. 1869. *The Report on the Census of Oudh* (Vol. 1). Lucknow: Oudh Government Press.

SECTION IV

LOCAL POWER AND THE POLITICAL PROCESS

Editors' Introduction

THEORETICALLY, the institutionalization of a liberal democracy was to outdo the institution of caste from Indian political life. The voting power was vested with the individual, with no formal recognition of caste. However, the history of democratic politics in the region has turned out to be very different. Caste quickly adapted itself to the new political realities. In the process, it also underwent changes. Chapters in this section discuss various aspects of the unfolding of this process.

In the opening chapter, Nicholas Martin explores the changing dynamics of caste and power at the local level, in rural India, by focusing on the category of 'dominant caste', popularized by M. N. Srinivas. Based on his fieldwork in a south Indian village, Srinivas had argued in 1955 that dominance in the Indian rural context was generally enjoyed by the landowning middling castes, who also tended to be larger in numbers and were ritually never too low in the local caste hierarchy. Their ability to educate their children in urban institutions and have members of their community employed in white-collar jobs added to their advantage. As Martin shows, his formulation was widely contested by scholars working on rural India around that time. While some pointed to the critical role played by individual leaders and patrons, some others pointed to the hurdles faced by those wanting to mobilize their peers along caste lines to capture power. Local dominance was not simply an ascribed attribute. Still others argued that power in rural India was acquired through vertical alliances of different caste groups around 'factions', often led by a rich landowning individual farmer. Power was thus held by individual leaders and not by the entire caste group.

These debates around the notion of 'dominant caste' were mostly carried-out during the 1960s. The sources of dominance in rural India have since undergone many changes. With the introduction of democratic process, growing migrations, and extensive mechanization of farm production, the older structures of hierarchy have largely disintegrated. However, the democratizing impact of these changes over the rural social life has been limited and the traditionally dominant castes continue to wield power, but this time through their hold over the bureaucratic and political networks outside the village, which enables them to operate the clientage and patronage politics at the village level.

Another important category through which caste and power have been discussed in the social science writings is that of 'caste association', subject of the following chapter by Rajeshwari Deshpande. On the face of it, caste association is a contradictory term. Castes are traditional, ascription-based communities. Associations are modern, formed by the voluntary coming together of individuals around a commonly held interest. Thus, their emergence during the early decades the 20th century reflected a kind of churning in the social and political life of caste. These early caste associations were mostly formed by the mobile upper castes to help members of their communities negotiate the emerging modern spaces, like providing hostels to children going to cities for studies. Some were more political and lobbied with the colonial government for status recognition and other interests of their caste groups. In the second phase of their life, during the early decades after Independence, they acted as mediators between local communities and emerging democratic political processes. As was famously argued by Susanne and Llyod Rudolph and Rajni Kothari, they functioned as adaptive institutions, helping caste-based communities to transition from 'sacred' to 'secular' domains of the Indian social life. The third moment of caste association arrives during the 1990s, after the introduction of the Mandal Commission Report. Even though caste emerges as a legitimate political actor during this period, it is also a time when they are undergoing internal differentiation and experiencing a process of fragmentation. This period also sees growing awareness among smaller and peripheral caste groups. They too begin to form associations making claims over political resources.

Echoing an overlapping point, Christophe Jaffrelot revisits the popular assumption that the Indian electorates 'vote their caste while casting their vote'. Using data from the 2014 and 2019 national elections, he argues that the relationship of caste to the electoral behaviour of Indian voters is far more nuanced than what is popularly believed. While caste does matter during elections, it does not matter in the same form or format everywhere, and all the time. For example, during the 2014 elections, class too had been a significant factor. However, it appears to have changed a bit during the 2019 elections, when the persona of Narendra Modi seems to have played a role of its own, independently of caste or class. He also shows how the localized caste communities, such as the *jatis,* appeared to matter more at the local levels of electoral politics. Value of caste in electoral politics further differs vertically. Questions of identity and honour seem to matter more for those at the extreme ends of the traditional hierarchy, the upper and the lower caste communities. Those in the middling positions, do not seem to be too anxious about their status positions while engaging with electoral political processes.

In the last chapter of this section, Lucia Michelutti explores a rather difficult and less researched subject, though much talked about in the popular media. Her chapter focusses on the criminalization of Indian politics in relation with the changing nature of patronage and caste. The chapter provides a broad overview of different formulations around the questions of patronage and criminal activity. It shows how in the 'goonda raj' caste continues to matter in electoral politics and thereby influences the nature of Indian democracy. However, she also underlines that quite like the institution of caste and the dynamics of Indian democracy, the nature of criminal activity and its involvement with the political domain has been changing over time. Her ethnographic fieldwork shows that the institutions of caste and kinship are important in structuring the 'criminal economies in many ways but they *are not totally indispensable*'. Individual personality of the 'boss' is an equally important variable, she observes.

Chapters in this section reinforce the point that while caste continues to matter in the Indian political and social life, it matters in diverse and complicated ways, constantly changing with time, and intersecting with other variables.

CHAPTER 19

THE DOMINANT CASTE

NICOLAS MARTIN

'The Dominant Caste' in Context

M. N. Srinivas (1955) used the concept of 'dominant caste' to explain the relationships between caste, authority, and power, and today both scholars and journalists continue invoke it to analyse rural power configurations and election results in India. In this chapter, I seek to unpack the term, and to shed light on the factors that today determine power and authority in rural India.

Srinivas wanted to explain hierarchical caste relations in terms of observable power relations on the ground, rather than with reference to religious ideas and ritual considerations. He dubbed his approach, and that of other sociologists doing empirical research in villages, the 'field view of caste'. His account emphasizes power relations above religious ideas and ritual practices, and seeks to explain the fact that 'middling' castes that do not rank particularly high in Hindu ritual hierarchy often command the most power and authority at village level.

In advocating the 'field view of caste' Srinivas was reacting against the Indological representation of caste as Varna, a view of caste derived from classical Indian texts and that Srinivas in turn dubbed 'the book view' of caste. The 'book view' is essentially one according to which the vast number of endogamous castes (or Jatis) that exist on the ground can be fitted into a fourfold hierarchical classification known as 'Varna'. This scheme—mentioned in the Rig Veda dating back to 1000 BC—divides and ranks society into Brahmins (priests), Kshatriyas (warriors), Vaishyas (farmers and traders), and Shudras (artisans and menials). The Code of Manu (c. 200 BC–AD 200) stipulates that to sustain social harmony and cosmic stability, each of these separate groups needs to perform a specific function. Thus the Brahmin's duty is to study, teach, sacrifice, and receive gifts; the Kshatriya must protect the people, sacrifice, and study; the Vaishya is to sacrifice and study, but his chief function is to breed cattle, till the earth, pursue trade, and lend money; the Shudra's duty is to serve the three higher classes. European scholars had usually taken it as axiomatic that these groups were organized hierarchically with Brahmins at the top, followed by the Kshatriyas and then the Vaishyas and with the Shudras at the bottom.

In his essay on Varna and Caste Srinivas (1962) argued that to understand caste it was essential to free oneself of the Varna model. What mattered on the ground was power rather than the ritual hierarchy of Varna. Srinivas observed that even Brahmins sometimes needed to pay their respects to people lower down the Varna hierarchy, but who happened to be wealthier and more politically influential. In Rampura, for example—Srinivas' field site village in South India—Brahmins often had to pay respect to members of the Okkaliga caste: a caste that ranked as Shudra on the Varna scale.

For Srinivas the relevant social unit on the ground was connected to *Jati* rather than Varna. The term *Jat* (*zaat* in Urdu) refers to the units that make up the so-called caste system rather than to the system itself. It can be used to refer to 'birth' or 'genus' and is used for 'any set of beings supposed to cohere as a biological and or social community (*samaja*)—a race, clan, region, occupation, religion, language, nation, gender or varna' (Kane, 1958, pp. 1632–1633). Jatis remain separate from each other primarily, but not solely, through marriage endogamy. Thus, even today in India it is often taken for granted—particularly in rural areas—that people will marry within their own Jati, albeit often in a different sub-Jati (or sub-caste). Finally, Jatis are segmentary; they are frequently subdivided into several sub-Jatis (see Béteille, 1964).

Researchers who approach caste through the 'field view' are more likely to encounter Jati than they are to encounter Varna. When asked about their Caste, Indians tend to first refer to their Jati. Furthermore, in parts of South Asia where Sanskritic Hinduism was never particularly influential, and where caste nevertheless clearly exists, people may not even know where their caste fits into the Varna scale. This is the case, for example, in much of the Punjab where the dominant religions have been Islam and Sikhism. In his work on Sanskritization, Srinivas (1956) argues that even in Hindu dominated regions particular Jatis only begin to claim their slot the Varna hierarchy when they are seeking upward mobility by adopting elite Sanskritic values and behavioural norms.

The Criteria for Dominance

So what is, according to Srinivas, 'a dominant caste'? In his own words:

> A caste may be said to be 'dominant' when it preponderates numerically over the other castes, and when it also wields preponderant economic and political power. A large and powerful caste group can be more easily dominant if its position in the local caste hierarchy is not too low. (Srinivas, 1955)

Srinivas adds that since at least independence another increasingly important ingredient for caste dominance is the number of educated persons and white-collar workers. Castes possessing large numbers of educated people working in government are more likely to be dominant. He argues that castes possessing all of the above attributes—numerical preponderance, economic power, political power, and graduates with government jobs—are 'decisively dominant' (Srinivas, 1959, p. 2) but that 'decisive dominance' is uncommon. However, Srinivas argues that former untouchables cannot achieve dominance even when they are numerous because they are generally too poor to do so, and because they face social discrimination on account of their polluted ritual status. I will return briefly to the issue of former untouchables later.

Take the *Okkaliga*, or as Srinivas calls it the, the 'Peasant' caste in Rampura. They are Shudras in terms of Varna, but nevertheless dominate all the other village castes—including the ritually higher-ranking Brahmins and Lingayats—because they are numerically preponderant, own the most land, and possess the most graduates.

Numerical strength matters because 'the capacity to 'field' a number of able-bodied men for a fight and a reputation for aggressiveness are relevant factors in determining the position of a caste vis-à-vis other castes' (Srinivas, 1959, p. 5). Thus, where a particular caste is numerically strong and where its members are willing to use force, it can impose its will on other castes. Srinivas gave the example of a South Indian regional caste of ritually impure 'fishermen' who could impose their will when they were in the majority, but who had to bow down to the dictates of other castes when in the minority. When in the majority, they could take their wedding processions through Brahmin and Peasant neighbourhoods without fear of retaliation. When in a minority, such as in the village of Kere, both the Brahmins and Peasants could easily prevent them taking their processions through their neighbourhoods.

In fact, Srinivas goes on, members of minority castes often feel that they are at the mercy of numerous castes, and that they may be 'abused, beaten, grossly underpaid for work done, or their women required to gratify the sexual desires of the powerful men in the dominant caste' (Srinivas, 1959). Thus, Srinivas suggests that members of the same caste tend to live together in separate village neighbourhoods to get a sense of security in numbers, rather than merely to maintain their ritual purity. Thus while Brahmins may agglomerate in separate neighbourhoods for purity related reasons, they also do so for the sake of physical safety.

In contexts where agriculture is the principal source of employment landownership is also crucial for the achievement of dominance. Historically in India, agricultural land was not only a source of income but also a source of political power (Neale, 1969). Landownership was coupled with political power because it implied dependents in the form of sharecroppers, farm servants, and casual labourers. Moreover, as Jan Breman (1974) once illustrated, the relationship between landlords and their dependents was not of the limited contractual variety characteristic of capitalist relations of production. In addition to remunerating them for their services, landlords were expected to provide their tenants, farm servants, and labourers with patronage and protection. They were, for example, expected to lend them money, to intervene with the authorities on their behalf, and to mediate their disputes. In exchange, dependents were expected to render a variety of services that could include performing corvée labour and providing their patrons with muscle power during factional disputes, or with votes during elections.

Finally, Srinivas argues that with the rise of the modern administrative state, education became a key criterion for dominance. It allowed members of dominant castes to gain employment within the state administration, and thereby to influence the course of village affairs, and also to act as gatekeepers between villagers and the state.

Srinivas argues that Dominance—resulting from the combination of the above factors—is most visible in the context of dispute resolution. Thus, it is members of the dominant caste who settle most village disputes, including disputes internal to other castes. Srinivas reports that in Kere, Peasant elders could even threaten to outcaste members of castes other than their own. He reports that the Peasants threatened to expel a fisherman from his caste based on accusations that he had committed incest. Crucially, as Oliver Mendelsohn (1993) argues, their ability to do so was premised on the fact that subordinate castes accepted their authority.

Critiques

Srinivas' concept has been highly influential, and both scholars and journalists continue to use it to refer to certain castes that appear to dominate particular villages or even entire regions. Thus, Jats in western Uttar Pradesh, Haryana, and Punjab have been described as a dominant caste, and so have the Bhumiars (Chakravarti, 2001) in north Bihar, the Anavils in Gujarat (Breman, 2007), the 'Marathas' in Maharashtra (Hansen, 2001), and the Kammas in coastal Andhra (Benbabaali, 2018).

While the term dominant caste is widely used to refer to a salient feature of rural power relations, some scholars have questioned Srinivas' framework. Others, such as Mendelsohn (1993), recognize that it may have helped describe village-level power relations in the past, but that it is no longer relevant because economic transformations and democratization have fatally eroded the power of once-dominant castes.

Some scholars have questioned Srinivas' tendency to assume that dominant castes constituted cohesive social and political units. Oommen points out that 'In order that the possession of resources [namely land, numbers, graduates, and ritual status] should result in the act of power being exercised, the group concerned should be highly articulate and politicised' (1970, p. 75). Dube's work (1968, pp. 58–81) suggests that so-called dominant castes were perhaps never highly articulate and politicized. Instead of dominant castes, she argues that Indian villages possessed 'dominant individuals'. Power in rural India, in other words, was not exerted by cohesive and politicized dominant castes, but rather by influential individuals within them.

Along parallel lines, Hamza Alavi's work on the Pakistani Punjab (Alavi, 1971) and Joyce Pettigrew's work on the Indian Punjab Pettigrew (1975) both emphasize the fact that Jats—often described as a dominant caste—were only rarely united as a caste at the village level, and they both also emphasize the role of individual village patrons above that of dominant castes as corporate entities. For Pettigrew, as for Alavi, influential village-level patrons—who also tended to be rich landlords—commanded the political allegiances of both fellow Jats and that of a dependent clientele comprises tenants, labourers, and artisans. Pettigrew emphasizes the fact that the building block of Punjabi politics was the faction—which Paul Brass in his work on Uttar Pradesh defined as 'a vertical structure of power which cross cuts caste and class divisions' (1965, p. 236). For Pettigrew therefore, caste did not play a significant role in structuring Jat politics, and nor did class or even political party allegiances.

Louis Dumont, on similar grounds, found Srinivas' numerical preponderance criterion 'somewhat surprising' (1980, p. 161). He argued that numbers did indeed facilitate the exercise of power, but that leaders frequently gained strength in numbers by drawing on a pool of dependent clients rather than upon members of their own caste. Drawing on the same insight, Hamza Alavi's work on the Pakistani Punjab (Alavi 1971) illustrates how the existence of a dependent clientele, in fact, obviates the need for caste-based political unity. He demonstrated how patrilineal clans (*biraderis*) with big landowners tended not to be particularly cohesive, and to be frequently riven by factional disputes over land and political power. He likewise showed how economically dependent biraderis were not particularly cohesive either. Members of landless service castes—such as potters, cobblers, carpenters, barbers, and sweepers—rarely acted as cohesive political blocks because they tended to be compelled to take sides with their employers/patrons, and were therefore divided in ways that mirrored divisions among the latter.

On the other hand, biraderis made up of economically independent peasant farmers tended to be the most cohesive. These did not possess a clientele because they had to cultivate their own land and employed few if any labourers. Because they could not draw on a dependent clientele, they needed to unite if they wanted to assert themselves politically. Thus, unlike members of wealthy landlord biraderis, and also unlike members of poor service caste biraderis, independent peasant farmers tended to vote as a block. What Alavi thereby demonstrated was that a biraderi's numerical strength mattered more for some communities than it did for others.

So where does this leave Srinivas' numerical criterion? In a later essay, Srinivas suggests that,

> The numerical strength of caste groups has become critical in a political democracy based on universal adult suffrage, and dominance based on economic power and education alone was not enough. Dominant castes tried everywhere to increase their strength by ignoring subdivision among them previously regarded as important. (Srinivas, 1996, p. 153)

What this would suggest is that strength in numbers became more important with the onset of electoral democracy in independent India. Indeed, the political rise of the numerous Other Backward Castes in states such as Bihar and Uttar Pradesh would seem to confirm this. In these states, deepening democracy in the decades after independence eventually allowed members of larger castes, such as the Yadavs (Michelutti, 2007) to displace traditional political elites whose power was based more on landownership than on their numbers. It is even the case, as Jaffrelot (2003) has most famously documented, that numerically strong Dalit castes have used their numbers to gain political power.

However, the fact that numerous castes have used their numbers to gain power at state level still doesn't mean that they have shed all their village-level divisions, nor that their members have all equally benefitted from their newfound political power and influence either at village or state level. It may indicate that an electorally significant proportion within their ranks united for electoral purposes, but not that the entire caste has now become dominant. Moreover, the fact that either Yadav's or even Dalits might be in power at state level does not necessarily mean that they are always in control in the villages. This is particularly true in the case of Dalits. As Jeffrey and Lerche (2001) have illustrated, Dalits did not necessarily always gain influence at village level when the Bahujan Samaj Party—a Dalit political party—was in power at state level in Uttar Pradesh. To claim, as dominant caste farmers often do (see Martin, 2015), that Dalits have become the new dominant caste just because they play a growing role in politics is therefore misleading. Thus, while the position of some Dalits may have improved thanks to reservations, and that some may have gained political power (Jaffrelot, 2003), the majority of Dalits still suffer poverty and social discrimination and wield little if any genuine political power (Javid and Martin, 2020).

This leaves us with the two other factors singled out by Srinivas as necessary for dominance: landownership and education. Landownership was the critical asset that allowed people to mobilize a clientele and to wield power in the village. In the Pakistani village where this author carried his doctoral fieldwork, the Gondal subcaste of Jats constituted only 10.5 per cent of the village population, but they had always controlled village politics because they owned 74 per cent of the land around the village (Martin, 2015). Traditionally, land ownership had given the Gondals the monopoly over people's livelihoods because there was little work to be found outside agriculture. Depending on the extent of their landholdings, landlords employed either tenants or labourers to cultivate their lands.

From around the 1960s however, the mechanization of agriculture reduced farmers' need for both tenants and labourers. Here it is important to remember that before tractors had become widespread, farming was a labour-intensive activity because it was carried out with teams of bullocks and labourers (see Chakravarti, 2001). 'Tractorization' allowed landlords and farmers to replace tenants and their bullock teams with tractors. According to one estimate from Pakistan, each tractor introduced in the 1960s displaced between nine and twelve labourers (Sayeed, 1996). In some areas, the introduction of citrus orchards (see Martin, 2015) or of mango orchards (see Breman, 1974) likewise contributed to the displacement of both tenant cultivators and labourers.

In comparatively developed areas of both India and Pakistan, improved transportation links allowed displaced labourers and tenants to find mostly informal sector work in nearby urban centres. In these areas, land is no longer always a critical source of power.

Mendelsohn (1993) reported that in a village in the area of North Eastern Rajasthan, near Haryana and Delhi, predominantly lower caste agricultural wage labourers managed to find work as rickshaw pullers, in brick kilns, and in construction. This allowed them to escape the grip of the Ahir landowning caste. Moreover, the spread of democratic and egalitarian values meant that they no longer readily submitted to Ahir authority. Dalits in particular, as Jaffrelot (2003) has argued, no longer accepted their subordination to the upper castes from around the 1990s onwards. Mendelsohn, furthermore, reported that the Ahirs of Rajasthan themselves, thanks to their higher levels of formal education, were increasingly employed outside the village in—among other things—clerical, accountancy, and teaching positions and that they were increasingly uninterested in village affairs. Mendelsohn reported that they no longer even held caste panchayats and thus lacked the solidarity necessary to resolve disputes at the village level.

Crucially, however, Mendelsohn nevertheless reported that the Ahirs tended to still dominate in village level elected bodies, although his article did not explore in detail what this meant for Ahir power. This, however, does not necessarily contradict his argument regarding the decoupling of land and power; it merely suggests that power may have become more closely linked to access to the state than to land ownership— as Breman (2007) suggests with reference to the powerful Anavil Brahmins of Gujarat. Other more recent work (Benbabaali, 2018; Martin, 2015; Jeffrey, 2001) indicates that power has likewise become more closely linked to political and business clout as after the green revolution farmers diversified into sectors such as agro-industry and transport.

Craig Jeffrey (2001) illustrates how in the prosperous region of Western Uttar Pradesh, some Jats continued being able to get away with many exploitative practices—including paying labourers below the minimum wage. They could do so because they invested in education and obtained government jobs and therefore controlled state institutions in charge of implementing minimum wage laws. Their dominance in electoral politics also gave them discretion over the police and over the allocation of government resources.

Like Craig Jeffrey's work on Western Uttar Pradesh, this author's more recent work on the Indian Punjab (Martin, 2015) illustrates how prosperous Jat farmer/businessmen use their control over panchayats—and state-level politics more broadly—in ways that frequently deprive Dalits of their entitlements. Because of their control over panchayats, prosperous Jats can, for example, deprive Dalits of their reserved share of village common lands. Jat village councillors also frequently divert and use panchayat funds in ways that benefit them and their close allies at Dalits' expense. In some cases, Jat councillors either implicitly or explicitly threaten to withhold state benefits—such as access to the NREGA scheme, or to housing plots—from Dalits, and others, if they vote in the wrong way during elections. Thus, even if Jats no longer entirely control Dalit livelihoods as they once did (see Jodhka and Louis, 2003), and that Dalits have been able to distance themselves from Jats by seeking employment elsewhere, Jats involved in politics are still able to exert various forms of pressure on them.

None of this is to say that it is necessarily the case that land and power have decoupled everywhere. Chakravarti's work (2001) on an underdeveloped region of Bihar, for example, demonstrates how landless labourers were until comparatively recently—when the OBCs came to power (see Witsoe, 2013)—still very much at the mercy of powerful landlords. In the 1990s, this was a region in which 87 per cent of the population was rural—compared with 74 per cent for India as a whole—and that was marked by the lack of both infrastructure and industry. Moreover this was a region in which rural literacy was around 33 per cent, and only about 17 per cent for Dalits. The literacy rate among Dalit males was 28.3 per cent whereas it was just 5.54 per cent for Dalit females. The lack of non-farm work opportunities coupled with low levels of literacy meant that Dalits had little choice but to continue working for local Bhumiar and Rajput landlords. Due to the lack of agricultural work throughout the year, many Dalits resorted to seasonal migration to states such as Punjab, Haryana, West Bengal, Assam, and Karnataka. However, seasonal migrants didn't entirely escape the grip of landed power because their families stayed behind, and their women often continued working for local landlords.

However, in addition to lacking bargaining power vis-à-vis the landlords because of the absence of non-agricultural labour, they also lacked bargaining power because landlords used the state to crush any signs of labour unrest or resistance. Because they possessed many graduates within their ranks, landlords occupied most positions within the state administration, including the police. Thus, any labourer seeking, for example, to enforce his or her right to the minimum wage was unlikely to be successful. In fact, Chakravarti reports that when landlords deployed armed goons to quash labour unrest they did so with tacit and sometimes explicit consent from the police.

To sum up then: the links between landownership, power, and authority have partially unravelled in more developed regions but may remain somewhat in place in less developed ones. Nevertheless, in both types of region members of the 'dominant castes' buttress their power by obtaining government jobs as well as elected positions at local and state levels. Srinivas' claim that in modern India the number of graduates would become more important in determining dominance, therefore, appears to stand. However, one factor that Srinivas did not fully explore relates to the importance of business clout subsequent to the green revolution. Several of the works cited above indicate that wealthy farmers who benefitted from the green revolution invested their surpluses into urban businesses, and that it is such farmers who increasingly control politics.

Conclusions

The concept of the Dominant Caste as formulated by Srinivas was invaluable to the extent that it drew researchers' attention away from textual sources and towards the observable, empirical, reality of caste on the ground. It drew scholars' attention to the fact that there was regional variation in the castes that happened to be at the top of the village pecking order, and also that those in such positions could be low ranking on the Varna ritual hierarchy. Crucially, Srinivas drew scholars' attention to power relations, and to the realities of violence and exploitation that British colonial officers and then

Indian nationalists had overlooked in their romanticized accounts of village life (see Jodhka, 2002).

What is not entirely clear is whether all the criteria identified by Srinivas to explain inter-caste power relations at village level were relevant at the time, and whether any of them remain relevant today. The idea, for example, that dominant castes drew strength from their own numbers is questionable based on the widely reported fact that individuals from dominant castes often drew strength in numbers from a dependent and frequently mixed-caste clientele. The existence of a dependent clientele, as Hamza Alavi argued, precluded the need for caste unity as reflected in the fact that dominant castes were often split into rival factions. Nor is it entirely clear that democracy provided caste dominance with a new lease of life through the principle of numbers. While it is undeniable that numerous OBC castes, and even Dalits, have obtained political power, the use and benefits of such power remained unevenly distributed within these communities and did not necessarily produce corporate caste blocs.

While, on the other hand, we can safely agree that land ownership was once a crucial determinant of village level power, it is not so clear that this remains universally true today. Landownership may remain a source of power in less developed regions of South Asia—perhaps in parts of Bihar and of the Pakistani Punjab—but it appears to play less of a role in certain more prosperous regions of North Western India where landless labourers have been able to find work outside agriculture and partially beyond the influence of landlords. Moreover, as this author (Martin, 2015) and also Benbabaali (2018) have argued, it is often farmers who have diversified into business who today are most likely to wield political power. In other words, in addition to landownership, business clout has become essential.

The one criterion for dominance that still seems to play an important role is the one relating to the number of graduates. The literature indicates that members of erstwhile dominant castes have used their educational credentials to colonize the state administration and have used the positions obtained to further their interests. Moreover, such people have also frequently managed to control the political sphere, at both village and higher levels, and to thereby bolster their interests at the expense of lower castes.

It is nevertheless important to emphasize that the political and business clout of particular castes in contemporary India does not necessarily signal anything like the caste dominance Srinivas described. Thus it would be mistaken to see caste-based and communal political parties (Chandra, 2007) as straightforward extensions of caste dominance. This is because caste-based parties often fail to create united caste blocs due to factionalism (see Martin, 2018) and also because they often serve the interests of privileged segments of their communities rather than their communities as a whole (see Hassan and Martin, 2020). Furthermore, as Jonathan Parry (2007) has argued, there is evidence to suggest that while politics may have given caste a new lease of life in certain respects, socio-economic differentiation within castes has further undermined caste unity. Punjabi Jats or Dalits in white-collar jobs may, for example, have more political, economic, and even social interests in common with others in similar class positions than they might have with impoverished community members in their home villages.

All of this suggests a need for restraint in the application of the term 'dominant caste' in sociological and political analysis, and also suggests the importance of class as a lens through which to analyse power in contemporary India.

Acknowledgements

Nicolas Martin would like to thank the Swiss National Science Foundation (SNF) for contributing to this paper by funding the project entitled 'The Reproduction of Caste? Economic, Political and Kinship Strategies among Jats in Punjab' [Grant no. 10001A_185411/1]. He would also like to thank Surinder Jodhka, Jules Naudet, the anonymous reviewers, and Clemence Jullien for their helpful comments.

References

Alavi, H. 1971. 'The Politics of Dependence: A Village in West Punjab'. *South Asian Review*, 4(2): 111–128,

Alavi, H. A. 1972. 'Kinship in West Punjab Villages'. *Contributions to Indian Sociology*, 6(1): 1–27.

Benbabaali, D. 2018. 'Caste Dominance and Territory in South India: Understanding Kammas' Socio-Spatial Mobility'. *Modern Asian Studies*, 52(6): 1938-1976.

Béteille, A. 1964. 'A Note on the Referents of Caste'. *European Journal of Sociology/Archives Européennes de Sociologie*, 5(1): 130–134.

Brass, P. R. 1965. *Factional Politics in an Indian State: The Congress Party in Uttar Pradesh*. Berkeley and Los Angeles: University of California Press.

Breman, J. 1974. *Patronage Exploitation*. Berkeley and Los Angeles: University of California Press.

Breman, J. 2007. *The Poverty Regime in Village India*. New Delhi: Oxford University Press.

Chakravarti, A. 2001. 'Caste and Agrarian Class: A View from Bihar'. *Economic and political weekly*, 1449–1462.

Chandra, K. 2007. *Why Ethnic Parties Succeed: Patronage and Ethnic Head Counts in India*. New York: Cambridge University Press.

Dube, S. C. 1968. 'Caste Dominance and Factionalism'. *Contributions to Indian Sociology*, 2(1): 58–81.

Dumont, L. 1980. *Homo Hierarchicus: The Caste System and Its Implications*. Chicago and London: University of Chicago Press.

Fuller, C. J. 1996. *Caste Today*. Oxford: Oxford University Press.

Hansen, T. B. 2001. *Wages of Violence: Naming and Identity in Postcolonial Bombay*. Princeton: Princeton University Press.

Javid, H., and N. Martin. 2020. 'Democracy and Discrimination: Comparing Caste-Based Politics in Indian and Pakistani Punjab'. *South Asia: Journal of South Asian Studies*, 43(1): 136–151.

Jaffrelot, C. 2003. *India's Silent Revolution: The Rise of the Lower Castes in North India*. London: C. Hurst.

Jeffrey, C. 2001. 'A Fist Is Stronger than Five Fingers': Caste and Dominance in Rural North India'. *Transactions of the Institute of British Geographers*, 26(2): 217–236.

Jeffrey, C and Lerche, J. 2001. 'Dimensions of Dominance: Class and State in Uttar Pradesh', in C. J. Fuller and Véronique Bénéï (Eds.) *The Everyday State & Society in Modern India* (pp. 91–114). London: Hurst & Company.

Jodhka, S. S. 2002. 'Nation and Village: Images of Rural India in Gandhi, Nehru and Ambedkar'. *Economic and Political Weekly*, 3343–3353.

Jodhka, S. S., and P. Louis. 2003. 'Caste Tensions in Punjab: Talhan and Beyond'. *Economic and Political Weekly*, 2923–2926.

Jodhka, S. S. 2014. 'Emergent Ruralities: Revisiting Village Life and Agrarian Change in Haryana'. *Economic and Political Weekly*, 49(26): 5–17.

Kane, P. V. 1958. *History of Dharmasastra*. Bhandarkar Oriental Research Institute, Poona.

Martin, N. 2015. *Politics, Landlords and Islam in Pakistan*. India: Routledge.

Martin, N. 2015. 'Rural Elites and Limits to SC Assertiveness in Rural Malwa, Punjab'. *Economic and Political Weekly*, 50(52): 37–44.

Martin, N. 2018. 'Corruption and Factionalism in Contemporary Punjab: An Ethnographic Account from Rural Malwa'. *Modern Asian Studies*, 52(3): 942–970.

Mendelsohn, O. 1993. 'The Transformation of Authority in Rural India'. *Modern Asian Studies*, 27(4): 805–842.

Michelutti, L. 2007. 'The Vernacularization of Democracy: Political Participation and Popular Politics in North India'. *Journal of the Royal Anthropological Institute*, 13(3): 639–656.

Neale, W. C. 1969. 'Land Is to Rule'. *Land Control and Social Structure in Indian History*, 3–15.

Oommen, T. K. 1970. 'The Concept of Dominant Caste: Some Queries'. *Contributions to Indian Sociology*, 4(1): 73–83.

Parry, J., 2007. A Note on the 'Substantialization'of Caste and Its 'Hegemony'. *Political and Social Transformation in North India and Nepal*, 479–495.

Pettigrew, J. 1975. *Robber Noblemen: A Study of the Political System of the Sikh Jats*. London: Routledge/Thoemms Press.

Sayeed, A. 1996. 'Growth and Mobilisation of the Middle Classes in West Punjab: 1960–1970', In Singh P. and Thandi S. S., eds., 1996. *Globalisation and the Region: Explorations in Punjabi Identity*, 259–286. Coventry: APS Publications.

Srinivas, M. N. 1955. 'The Social System of a Mysore Village'. *Village India*, 1–36.

Srinivas, M. N. 1956. 'A Note on Sanskritization and Westernization'. *The Journal of Asian Studies*, 15(4): 481–496.

Srinivas, M. N. 1959. 'The Dominant Caste in Rampura'. *American Anthropologist*, 61(1): 1–16.

Srinivas, M. N. 1962. 'Varna and Caste'. *Caste in Modern India and Other Essays*, 63–69. New York: Asia Publishing House.

Srinivas, M. N. 1966. *Social Change in Modern India*. Berkeley and Los Angeles: University of California Press.

Witsoe, J. 2013. *Democracy against Development: Lower-Caste Politics and Political Modernity in Postcolonial India*. Chicago and London: University of Chicago Press.

CHAPTER 20

CASTE ASSOCIATIONS AND THE POST-MANDAL POLITICS OF CASTE

RAJESHWARI DESHPANDE[1]

The life and politics of caste in India during the past few decades inevitably took shape in conversation with 'Mandal'.[2] The 'Mandal' project was not only about the policy of affirmative action of the state to extend benefits of reservations to the OBCs (Other Backward Classes). It unfolded a twin institutional and political logic around caste in the 1990s. This logic reinforced the status of caste as a legitimate political and social category. It also put in place an overarching caste framework of Indian politics that competed with the other dominant ideological frameworks of the time. At both these levels the Mandal project marked a new phase of politicization of caste, with important implications for its life and politics. The post-Mandal moment of caste essentially internalized and thrived on the (gradually defunct) logic of Mandal. At the same time, it complicated and defied that logic in several ways. The present chapter looks back at the politics of caste associations from the vantage point of the post-Mandal moment.

The arrival of the post-Mandal phase of caste was a convergence of three interrelated processes. The first was the unfolding of a much contextualized democratic politics in post-independence period. It has been amply noted how the practices of Indian democracy transformed caste and how caste in turn 'vernacularized' the democratic idiom in a variety of ways (Michelutti, 2008; Yadav, 2010). Much has also been written about the politicization of caste and its implications for the early phase of democracy (Rudolph

---

[1] The chapter draws on my earlier work on caste associations in Maharashtra that was published as an occasional paper by the Department of Politics and Public Administration, SPPU (Deshpande, 2010). The argument on post-Mandal moment of caste was also developed in a piece in Seminar magazine (Deshpande, 2009).

[2] The reference here is to the second backward classes commission appointed by the government of India in 1978, popularly known as Mandal commission after its chairman Mr B. P. Mandal.

and Rudolph, 1967; Kothari, 1970; Frankel and Rao, 1990). However, the consequences of the post-Mandal phase of politicization of caste since the nineties are still unfolding in a messy way. On the one hand, the Mandal politics encouraged construction of caste blocs and the subsequent redefinitions of boundaries of caste. On the other hand, the rediscovery of caste as a resource also led to fragmentation of caste blocs and to the assertions of single caste identity. Caste associations of the post-Mandal phase had to simultaneously negotiate with both these processes.

The second factor that helped shape the caste-politics interaction, more specifically after the implementation of Mandal, was the distinctive institutional logic around caste put forward by the post-independence state. State discourses on caste recognized it as a legitimate criterion for identifying backwardness. At the same time, the state successfully managed to manipulate caste rights by confining them to reservations (Deshpande, 2005). The reservation policy ensured only a thin dispersal of resources controlled by the state and thus encouraged contestations among castes over their share in the meagre resources made available to them.

These contestations escalated in the context of changes induced in the material realm of caste. On the one hand, the routine processes of modernization like urbanization, spread of education, and spatial reconfiguration of communities led to gradual secularization of caste and waning of caste hierarchies (Sheth, 1999; Jodhka and Manor, 2018). On the other hand, the post-independence skewed model of capitalist development also had a deep impact on the life of caste that resulted in a complicated economic existence for the present-day caste communities. Studies on economic conditions of caste groups have indicated a continued reinforcement of caste and class relations at the macro level. At the same time, the traditional links between caste and occupation are breaking (although slowly) and complex patterns of intra- and inter-caste economic stratification have emerged (Heath and Kumar, 2002; Deshpande-Palshikar, 2008; Deshpande Ashwini, 2011). The post-liberalization turn of the early 1990s intensified these economic divisions within castes and aggravated the material crisis faced by the small and marginal castes, forcing them to fall back on their caste identity for material, and symbolic survival. These identities acquired a more complex form when, along with the poor, the emerging middle classes from each caste also invoked their caste identity in a more emphatic manner, mainly as a weapon for consolidating their social and political power.

The contemporary politics of caste associations emerged at the cusp of these processes and signified the contradictory existence of caste in its post-Mandal avatar. Unlike the traditional caste *panchayats*, the caste associations always operated in a more modern setting and mainly served mobilizational/political rather than regulative/sanctimonious functions. The arrival of these associations symbolized an important adaptive moment in the journey of caste, as caste prepared to operate in the modern democratic context. The more recent phase of the journey began when caste became the dominant idiom of politics but the caste communities began to disintegrate.

Earlier studies of caste associations (Kothari, 1970; Rudolph and Rudolph, 1967; Shah, 2002; Hardgrave, 1969) discussed their role in the process of secularization, politicization, and democratization of caste. For Kothari, the emerging democratic framework in India had two implications for the working of the caste system. One is that the caste system provided structural ideological bases for political mobilization. On the other hand, in its efforts to appropriate the power structure of the caste system, modern politics had to make consultations with the local bases of power. These two processes led to emergence of a more complex power structure of the caste system and the newly emerging caste associations became an important aspect of this power structure (Kothari, 1970, pp. 9–10). The complex power structures also led to formation of new caste identities on the basis of more secular—political/material interests.

In their foundational study of the sociology of caste associations, Rudolph and Rudolph (1967) described them as 'para communities'. For them the characteristics of the caste para communities resembled in many ways those of the voluntary associations or interest groups. At the same time these communities could be distinguished in a number of ways, not only from the voluntary associations but also from the natural association of caste out of which they had developed. This was because the membership of caste associations was no longer purely ascriptive and birth in a caste was necessary but not a sufficient condition for it. Second, the caste associations had acquired a political agency to them as they spoke for a much wider group than their active followers and nurtured a potential constituency. Third, Rudolphs noted how caste associations became increasingly specialized in terms of their functions and interests as against those of caste which were wide-ranging and diffused. In their early interactions with modernity and democracy, the caste associations aspired to control and influence the centres of political power and demanded favourable allocations of resources, opportunities, and honour. At the organizational level, these associations abandoned the latent structure of caste and opted for internal beauracratization. Caste associations worked parallel to administrative/political units and the more influential among them even aspired for a pan Indian status. And yet, for Rudolphs, these associations could retain distinctive linkages with caste in their shared sense of culture, character, and status. As a result, they could maintain higher levels of solidarity among the members than are usually found among modern/strictly voluntary associations. The caste paracommunities thus became an adaptive institution and contributed to a fundamental structural and cultural change in the post-independence Indian society (Rudolph and Rudolph, 1967, pp. 29–34).

The multiple histories of these changes are invariably linked to three distinctive historical moments of Indian democracy when caste was exposed to democratic power play. The first one came in the early 1920s when the idea of democracy was introduced to the Indians as a part of the official colonial discourse. This moment, in the form of constitutional reform packages of the colonial state, initiated a wide debate on issues related to democratic rights and representation, and caste rights were articulated for the first time as part of these debates. The early efforts to mobilize caste in the secular democratic context led to establishment of caste associations in many parts of the country. The history of most of the present-day caste associations therefore typically goes back to the late 19th/early 20th century when they prepared ground for caste to operate in the changing social and political context. Carroll argues that the arrival of caste organizations in particular and caste polemics in general in the late 19th and early 20th centuries was an unintended but direct consequence of the foreign definitions of Indian society (Carroll, 1978, p. 233). The colonial classifications and categories of division had important political and economic repercussions in the changing social context. In order to manage these repercussions, the early caste associations put forward twin demands of material and cultural—ritual up gradation of the community to the colonial power (Carroll, 1978; Templeman, 1996; Khare, 1970).

The practices of democracy in the post-independence context altered the role of caste associations in a significant way. There was a clear shift from sacred to secular in the work of these organizations and that undermined the hold of traditional culture and society. The organizations acquired a secular form as they made demands on the state for upgradation of the position of their caste in social hierarchy, for extension of privileges, and rights for the community and generally worked towards upward mobility of the group. These claims were essentially political in nature. The leadership of the caste organizations depended on the capacity to articulate and represent these claims in the political sphere. These associations also created conditions under which local sub castes could be linked together in geographically extended associations.

Caste associations of the early post-independence period acquired the form of an adaptive institution where traditional and modern social features can meet and fuse. They contributed a great deal in gradually levelling the sacred, hierarchical caste order, and replacing it under the new political circumstances. Formation of caste associations led to homogenizing of the caste identities on the one hand and also to the democratization of caste in the long run. Although the democratic politics introduced several profound changes in the working of the traditional caste system, caste did not completely disappear as a result of these. Instead, from a static system of stratification caste changed its form to a more dynamic base of competition and integration, and accommodated itself with politics. The dynamic interactions of caste and democratic politics in the sixties traditionalized Indian politics and caste became a legitimate platform for political mobilization. Politics, on the other hand, secularized and politicized caste leading to complex versions of identity politics in the later period.

The post-Mandal phase marks the third distinctive moment of caste politics interaction that provided a new visibility to the associations of castes. The politics of Mandal contributed to the process of regionalization of politics and to the already emerging multipolar competitions in the electoral arena (Palshikar, 2006; Palshikar and Yadav, 2009). At the same time processes of regionalization and the subsequent rise of a competitive party system in the 1990s provided a possibility for many marginal, localized castes to take an active part in politics, and to assert their bargaining powers. Their mobilizations challenged the dominance of the regionally dominant castes, upset the earlier tone of regional politics and encouraged a further dispersal of political competition—not only at the regional, but at the local sub regional level.

The arrival of the Bahujan idiom in politics had brought in new mechanisms of political bargaining at the regional and sub regional level. The Mandal project of creation of Dalit Bahujan majority required some kind of federative processes in which castes and communities could come together to form loose alliances. At the same time, this politics, as it shaped in the context of competing multi polarities, also encouraged constant fragmentation and realignments of social blocs due to its extremely competitive, tentative character. Political (re) alignments and social churning during the last three decades thus unleashed a variety of patterns of identity politics. The peculiar nature of political competition of this phase, the advent of caste framework, and the weaving of complex patterns of identity politics led to revival of the role of caste associations in the electoral and mobilizational arenas. The associations contributed to the redefinition of caste consciousness, to the rise of caste-based mobilizations including formation of single caste-based parties, and most importantly to the process of regionalization and further dispersal of party/electoral politics.

The process of Mandalization was not limited to those castes which were officially included in the State list of OBCs. It engulfed many other smaller castes that were confined to certain sub regions, had a marginal yet significant presence in the earlier electoral politics and were desperate to consolidate their claims of representation. Both at the national and at the State level the logic of Mandal inaugurated a new phase of caste politics—mainly a politics of presence—in which each small caste wanted to participate and be visible.

Manor (2012) revisited Rudolphs' analysis of caste associations to understand their changing role and importance in more recent times. He argues how economic differentiation and emergence of alternative channels to gain foothold within the political system have affected the fate of caste associations and how their influence is waning at the national and regional level of politics. At the same time, we see proliferation of a large number of caste associations at the local level, especially in the urban and semi-urban areas in different parts of the country. Our studies[3] in four states listed a large number of caste associations claiming to represent a range of individual castes placed at different levels of traditional social hierarchy. Internal differentiation in each caste and the changing political context in the post-Mandal period have led to formation of many caste associations from within the same caste. Rudolphs' reading of the caste associations happened at a time when mainly the traditionally influential and resourceful caste communities were active in politics and sought social mobility, representation, and share in power through caste-based platforms. The new caste associations operated with a rather different mandate as they mainly represented the hitherto discrete, marginal castes in politics; negotiated with the almost vacuous affirmative action policy, and asserted downward rather than upward mobility in the traditional caste hierarchy. The erstwhile 'dominant' castes like Jats, Marathas, and Lingayats have also used caste

---

[3] I refer here to studies that I conducted with the help of three of my research students in the states of Maharashtra, Karnataka, Madhya Pradesh, and Uttar Pradesh during the past ten years. We studied politics of an erstwhile 'dominant' caste of Lingayats in the adjoining regions of Maharashtra and Karnataka (Deshmukh, 2006); of the OBC community of shepherds in the states of Maharashtra and Madhya Pradesh (Gholwe, 2013); and that of a Dalit caste of Charmakars in Uttar Pradesh and Maharashtra (Agwane, 2019).

association platforms for their politics during the post-Mandal phase. However, this version of politics, despite the subtexts of power engulfed within it, strangely resorted to assertions of 'backwardness' of these castes (Deshpande, 2004, 2014; Jenkins, 2004) and turned them into vulnerable communities in the wake of political and material crisis.

The 'new age' caste associations retain some (especially the organizational) features of the past that Rudolphs had noted. At the same time, the changing democratic political context and the state actions in the realm of caste compel them to adopt new ways of doing politics. The simultaneous processes of mandalization and regionalization of Indian politics ushered in complete interpenetration of caste and politics in the nineties. On the other hand, castes were 'ethnicized' and were rapidly losing their integrative potentials. Both these aspects had important consequences for the work of the caste associations. Rather than operating at the national/regional level most of the organizations became localized in nature during this period. They revolved around a single leader who used the organization mainly to build up his (always men as women play a very marginal role in the organizational ranks) political constituency at the local/sub-regional level. In the 1960s, the political role of these associations was federative as they tried to build up horizontal and vertical caste alliances. Since the 1990s though, they have been part of the process of splintering of caste alliances. The project of Mandal had expected them to further its ideological agenda of Dalit Bahujan unity. However, in practice, the project led to formation single caste parties and encouraged political bargaining on behalf of each small caste. The 'democratic upsurge' of the nineties also contributed to this process when the political participation of the hitherto marginal sections of Indian society significantly increased (Yadav, 2000). The work of caste associations in this period contributed to the political fragmentation of caste blocks and defied the ideological logic of Mandal. Instead, the idea of politics was reduced to bargaining in elections and representation was reduced to politics of presence. The competitive nature of the party system, its organizational weakening, and the resultant dispersal of political contestations further encouraged internal fragmentation of the caste communities in political sphere. Caste associations acquired a completely instrumental role in the process and could not even effectively serve as interest groups on behalf of the community. Their work constituted one important aspect of the constant configuration and fragmentation of caste blocs at the time. These associations worked to create social alliances that shaped coalitional politics at a more formal level. However, since both social and political alliances were essentially weak, incoherent in nature, the work of the caste associations became a difficult task for them in the post-Mandal phase. Thus, in spite of their proliferation in large numbers and in spite of celebrations of caste as a dominant idiom of Indian politics, this phase of the work of caste associations in a way marked an end of the caste logic as caste only symbolically and clumsily survived in their politics.

Typically, these organizations put forward three sets of demands to the state that brought out the contradictory nature of politics of caste. In their efforts to rewrite the past, each caste invented their own community heroes and their first set of demands involved a request to the state to name some institution after that person or to erect his statue at some place. Secondly, they demanded that the state should protect their traditional community based economic rights so that they could survive amidst the economic hardships induced by the skewed capitalist developmental model. This has been a prominent concern for many artisan castes in recent years. But as their material anxieties amplified even the established agrarian castes like Marathas and Jats also joined them in seeking community based economic concessions from the state (Deshpande and Palshikar, 2017; Jaffrelot and Kalaiyarasan, 2019). They used caste associations as one of many mobilizational channels to articulate these demands. The third kind of demands were obviously about the reservation policy. These ranged from state recognition to 'backward' status of a community (Jenkins, 2004; Shatrugna, 1994) to demands for a separate quota within quota or demands to shift a particular community from this to that group of beneficiaries of reservation policy (Gholwe, 2013; Roy, 2018). At this level, the caste communities and their associations tried to appropriate the discursive space of Mandal to keep alive and assert the caste logic. At the same time, the common economic hardships experienced by different caste communities compelled these organizations to extend their membership beyond the members of a caste when they doubled up as trade unions/professional organizations. As Rudolphs discussed, though necessary, the membership of caste was never a sufficient requirement to be a member of a caste association in the 1960s. The increasing intra-caste economic differentiation of the 1990s made it even more difficult for the caste associations to create and nurture their clientele from within the caste. As a result, these associations lost their distinctive linkages with caste and were unable to maintain solidarity among the members. Instead, these organizations acquired the form of routine interest groups which moved in and out of weakening caste logic. At all these levels, the contradictions surrounding caste politics of the post-Mandal phase mirrored in the work of caste associations as they struggled to construct a coherent identity of the community for purposes of political mobilization.

In his early studies of changing identities in south Asia, Barnett (1977) argued how community discourses become meaningful in the presence of particular institutional possibilities and socio-economic conditions. In order to operate in the post-Mandal context, the caste associations had to construct the caste identity in a skilful manner. In this process, the caste communities remained porous, were fractured, and were constantly reshaped in the multiple grids of identity politics. They remained open to competing identity claims and had to constantly negotiate with these claims in order to keep their political presence alive. At this level, duality, incoherence, and implicit contradictions defined the politics of caste associations in more recent period. In the context of overall political instability and disintegration of communities, caste associations had to traverse a difficult path in shaping identity politics around caste ideology.

They had to cope with simultaneous processes of state identifications and categorizations of castes as backward and forward, the political processes shaping around caste that demanded both shaping of caste blocs and assertions of individual caste, the politics of Hindutva that provided a new framework of identity politics and also with the material anxieties of caste(s). Caste associations resorted to many symbolic acts as they tried to negotiate with the democratic politics as it unfolded since the

1990s. At the same time, they tried to navigate a variety of identity politics that sometimes colluded with the state, sometimes tried to evade its logic, and sometimes tried to subvert it. The organizations had to keep testing all the ideological choices that were contextually available to them for the construction of caste identity.

The politics of Lingayat organizations in the bordering regions of Maharashtra and Karnataka (Deshpande, 2010; Deshmukh, 2006) presents an interesting case. As is well known, the elite Lingayat organizations of the 1960s could successfully manipulate its religious—sectarian identity for internal consolidation of the caste community and for facilitating its secular material interests (Bairy, 2009; Khare, 1970; Manor, 2012). In the decade of 1990s though, each sub caste within the Lingayat fold tried to assert itself. When the competition for backward status became extreme in the post Mandal phase, many small castes from the Lingayat fold in Karnataka suggested that the suffix 'Lingayat' should be dropped from the caste names so that they would be treated on par with their Hindu counterpart backward castes. One organization of the Lingayats claimed that for purposes of affirmative action, all Lingayats be considered as 'Lingders'[4] and be included in the category of Scheduled Castes! The same organization, however, also came up with the slogan '*Garv se Kaho Hum Lingayat Hain!*'[5] when it joined hands with the BJP in municipal elections. The recent politics of caste associations was thus a curious mix of desperations and assertions, of frustrations and material anxieties, and mostly of political bargaining on behalf of communities that were fast disintegrating.

And yet these associations survive and multiply in the 'contextual Indian democracy' (Frankel, 2000) where the crisis of representation deepens despite democratic expansions. As Yadav (2010) suggests, viewed in a more comparative light, the connection between caste and politics becomes the Indian version of operations of social cleavages in politics. However, the specificity of democratic encounter complicates these operations at multiple levels. The failure of the Mandal project points to one such complication. The project was about democratization of caste and contained possibilities of mobilizations in the form of collective resistance to caste-based discriminations. However, the project was ripped off its democratic content when the 'contest' notion of social justice in it was replaced by the 'sponsored' one (Guru, 2010). Caste associations of the 1990s remained trapped in the vacant rhetoric of Mandal and despite their growing numbers could not contribute much to the processes of democratization of caste.

The changing nature of political competition and the structuring of party system in Indian democracy introduced another angle to the complications surrounding caste and politics. The rise of a competitive party system in the 1990s contained rich possibilities of democratic expansion and empowerment. However, these possibilities were lost when meaningful choices available to the voters shrunk significantly. Caste associations acted like a crucial local level hinge in this large scale social and political churning taking

---

[4] Lingders are one of the lowly communities within the Lingayat fold who have been included among the scheduled castes.

[5] Literally, say proudly that we are Lingayats as a follow-up slogan of Garv Se Kaho Hum Hindu Hein! (say proudly that we are Hindus) popularized by the militant Hindu organizations of the 1990s.

place in Indian democracy over the past few decades. However, as the substantive ideological contestations receded, caste associations too were forced to resort to 'politics of presence' through symbolic, token gestures. More importantly, as the communities they tried to represent began to disintegrate, the associations were forced to cling to the vacant and (therefore) shrill rhetoric of caste in even more aggressive ways.

The shrill noises of caste associations are often seen as instances of 'casteism' in Indian politics that undermine the agency of politics and instead reduce it to the social power play. In reality though the functioning of caste associations in the post Mandal phase not only signifies a complete interpenetration of caste and politics but also reveals how democratic politics has changed caste in a profound way. It also reveals the contradictions in the contemporary life of caste where caste survives clumsily in a democracy that lacks pure interest-based agencies of mobilization and substantial representation.

REFERENCES

Agwane, Rajendra. 2019. *Maharashtra ani Uttar Pradeshatil Charmakar Sanghatananche Rajkaran* (Marathi- Politics of Charmakar Associations in Maharashtra and Uttar Pradesh) unpublished PhD dissertation, Department of Politics and Public Administration, Pune, S P Pune University.

Barnett, Steve. 1977. 'Identity Choice and Caste Ideology in Contemporary South India'. In David Kenneth (Ed.), *The New Wind: Changing Identities in South Asia* (pp. 393–414). The Hague: Muton Publishers.

Bairy Ramesh, T. S. 2009. 'Brahmins in the Modern World: Association as Enunciation'. *Contributions to Indian Sociology*, 43(1): 89–120.

Carroll, Lucy. 1978. 'Colonial Perceptions of Indian Society and the Emergence of Caste(s) Associations'. *Journal of Asian Studies*, 37(2): 233–250.

Deshmukh, Appasaheb. 2006. *Solapur Jillhyatil Lingayat Samajyachya Sanghatana* (Marathi-Associations of Lingayat Community in Solapur District), unpublished M.Phil. Dissertation, Pune, University of Pune.

Deshpande, Aswini. 2011. *The Grammar of Caste: Economic Discrimination in Contemporary India*. New Delhi: Oxford University Press.

Deshpande, Rajeshwari. 2004. 'Inevitability and Inadequacy of Caste: Some Dilemmas for Mobilisation of Backward Classes'. In B. V. Bhosale (Ed.), *Mobilisation of Backward Communities in India* (pp. 200–216). New Delhi: Deep and Deep Publications.

Deshpande, Rajeshwari. 2005. *State and Democracy in India: Strategies of Accommodation and Manipulation*, occasional paper series III no.4, Special Assistance Programme, Department of Politics and Public Administration, Pune, University of Pune.

Deshpande, Rajeshwari. 2006, 8–14 April. 'Maharashtra: Politics of Anxieties, Frustrations and Outrage'. *Economic and Political Weekly*, 146–175.

Deshpande, Rajeshwari. 2009, September. 'Breaking Free of the Post Mandal Deadlock'. *Seminar*, 76–80.

Deshpande, Rajeshwari. 2010. 'Caste Associations in the Post-Mandal Era: Notes from Maharashtra'. CAS occasional paper series no.2, Centre for Advanced Studies, Department of Politics and Public Administration, Pune, University of Pune.

Deshpande, Rajeshwari. 2014, June–December. 'Seeking OBC Status: Political Strategies of Two Dominant Castes'. *Studies in Indian Politics*, 2: 169–183.

Deshpande, Rajeshwari, and Suhas Palshikar. 2008, 23–29 August. 'Patterns of Occupational Mobility: How Much Does Caste Matter?' *Economic and Political Weekly*, 43: 61–70.

Deshpande, Rajeshwari, and Suhas Palshikar. 2017. 'Political Economy of a Dominant Caste'. In R. Nagaraj and S. Motiram (Eds.), *Political Economy of Contemporary India* (pp. 77–97). Cambridge: Cambridge University Press.

Frankel, Francine R. 2000. 'Introduction/Contextual Democracy: Intersections of Society, Culture and Politics of India'. In Francine Ruth Frankel, Rajeev Bhargava, Balveer Arora and Zoya Hasan (Eds.), *Transforming India: Social and Political Dynamics of Democracy* (pp. 1–25). New York: Oxford University Press.

Frankel Francine, and M. S. A. Rao (Eds.). 1990. *Dominance and State Power in Modern India*. (Vols. I and II). Delhi: Oxford University Press.

Gholwe, Sominath. 2013. *Maharashtra ani Madhya Pradeshatil Dhangar Samajache Rajkaran: Ek Toulanik Abhyas* (Marathi—Politics of Dhangar Community in Maharashtra and Madhya Pradesh: A Comparative Study), unpublished PhD dissertation submitted to the Department of Politics and Public Administration, SP Pune University.

Guru, Gopal. 2010. 'Social Justice'. In Niraja Gopal Jayal and Pratap Bahnu Mehta (Eds.), *The Oxford Companion to Politics in India* (pp. 361–380). New Delhi: Oxford University Press.

Hardgrave, R. L. 1969. *The Nadars of Tamil Nadu: The Political Culture of Community in Change*. Berkeley: University of California Press.

Heath, Anthony, Oliver Heath, and Sanjay Kumar. 2002, October 5. 'Changing Patterns of Social Mobility'. *Economic and Political Weekly*, 37(40): 4091–4096.

Jaffrelot, Christophe, and A. Kalaiyarasan. 2019, 16 February. 'The Political Economy of the Jat Agitation for Other Backward Class Status'. *Economic and Political Weekly*, 54(7): 29–37.

Jenkins, Rob. 2004. 'Reservation Politics in Rajasthan'. Working Paper. Crisis States Programme. London: London School of Economics.

Jodhka, Surinder S., and James Manor (Eds.). 2018. *Contested Hierarchies Persisting Influence: Caste and Power in Twenty First Century in India*. Hyderabad: Orient Blackswan.

Khare. Ravindra. 1970. *Changing Brahmans: Associations and Elites among the Kanya-Kubjas of North India*. Chicago: University of Chicago Press.

Kothari, Rajni (Ed.). 1970. *Caste in Indian Politics*. New Delhi: Orient Longman.

Manor, James. 2012, June. 'After Fifty Years of Political and Social Change: Caste Associations and Politics in India'. *Pacific Affairs*, 85(2): 355–361.

Michelutti, Lucia. 2008. *The Vernacularisation of Democracy: Politics, Caste and the Religion in India*. New Delhi: Routledge.

Palshikar, Suhas. 2006. 'Caste Politics through the Prism of Region'. In Rajendra Vora and Anne Feldhaus (Eds.), *Region, Culture and Politics in India*. New Delhi: Manohar Publishers.

Roy Kapil, Chandra. 2018, 3 November. 'Demand for Scheduled Tribe Status by Koch-Rajbangshis'. *Economic and Political Weekly*, 53(44): 19–21.

Rudolph, L., and Susanne H. Rudolph. 1967. *Modernity of Tradition: Political Development in India*. New Delhi: Orient Longman.

Shah, Ghanshyam (Ed.). 2002. *Caste and Democratic Politics in India*. New Delhi: Permanent Black.

Shatrugna, M. 1994, 10 September. 'Andhra Pradesh-All Kapus as BCs: Reducing Reservation to a Farce'. *Economic and Political Weekly*, 29(37): 2397–2400.

Sheth, D. L. 1999, August. 'Secularization of Caste and Rise of New Middle Class'. *Economic and Political Weekly.*

Templeman, Dennis. 1996. *The Northern Nadars of Tamil Nadu: An Indian Caste in the Process of Change.* New Delhi: Oxford University Press.

Yadav, Yogendra. 2000. 'Understanding the Second Democratic Upsurge: Trends of Bahujan Participation in Electoral Politics in the 1990s'. In Francine Frankel et al. (Eds.), *Transforming India.* New Delhi: (pp. 146–175). Oxford University Press.

Yadav, Yogendra. 2010. 'Representation'. In Niraja Gopal Jayal and Pratap Bahnu Mehta (Eds.), *The Oxford Companion to Politics in India* (pp. 347–360). New Delhi: Oxford University Press.

Yadav, Yogendra, and Suhas Palshikar. 2009. 'Ten Thesis on State Politics in India'. In Sandeep Shastri, K. C. Suri, and Yogendra Yadav (Eds.), *Electoral Politics in Indian States: Lok Sabha Elections in 2004 and Beyond* (pp. 46–63). New Delhi: Oxford University Press.

CHAPTER 21

DO INDIANS VOTE THEIR CASTE—OR THEIR *JATI*, OR THEIR CLASS, OR . . .?

CHRISTOPHE JAFFRELOT

ACCORDING to common parlance, analysts of India's politics assume that 'Indians vote their caste while casting their vote'.[1] The 2014 general elections have reflected a certain erosion of the influence of caste compared to the growing importance of class elements.[2] In the first part of this chapter, we will focus on this evolution that is partly due to the socio-economic differentiation of caste groups that has resulted, in particular, in the formation of a 'neo-middle class'.

However, caste continues to play a significant role at the *jati* level, a more relevant unit of analysis than the large categories of 'upper castes', 'Other Backward Classes', and 'Scheduled Classes' which need to be disaggregated. We will make this point in the second part of this chapter by using data of the 2014 and the 2019 elections and by focusing on the state level. We will then highlight the fact that socio-economic differentiation is also taking place within *jati*, a process that is bound to affect the voting pattern at that level too. Finally, we will scrutinize the impact of urbanization over the act of voting in relation to caste, as this variable also plays an important role at the *jati* level.

---

[1]

[2] C. Jaffrelot, 2013, Juin. 'Gujarat Elections: The Sub-text of Modi's "Hattrick"—High Tech Populism and the "Neo-middle Class"', *Studies in Indian Politics*, 1(1): 79–96; and C. Jaffrelot, 2015, June. '"The Class Element in the 2014 Indian Election and the BJP's Success with Special Reference to the Hindi Belt", in "Understanding India's 2014 Elections"', *Studies in Indian Politics*, 3(1): 19–38.

Caste or Class? The Social Determinants of Electoral Behaviour in 2014 and 2019—A Tale of Two Elections

Voters decide to support a certain political party at the time of election for many different reasons, including the ideology reflected in its programme, the records of its leader(s), the profile of its local candidate(s), etc. But their decision also partly results from their social profile in terms of religion, caste, and class. Traditionally, caste has been considered as the most important factor and political parties have carefully analysed the caste composition of every constituency at the time of candidates' selection. Lately, however, two other variables—religion and class—have gained momentum. The former because the rise of Hindu nationalism has blurred other social markers, the BJP's propaganda inviting all members of the majority community to look at themselves as Hindu first (see the chapter by Joel Lee in this volume), and the latter because of the socio-economic differentiation of Indian society. In the context of the post-1991 liberalization, this process has been fostered by a very high growth rate that has helped some poor people to become part of what Narendra Modi has called 'the neo-middle class'.

2014: The Emergence of Class in Electoral Politics

This very amorphous social category known as 'the neo-middle class' is made of aspiring people who have initiated some upward mobility—and sometimes some geographical mobility too, as they have shifted from rural to urban or semi-urban localities in order to get a non-agricultural job (as we will see in the last section). Most of the members of this 'neo-middle class' come from the OBCs—the largest caste-based grouping of India— and have supported BJP to a large extent in 2014. According to the Lokniti-CSDS post-election survey, the proportion of the BJP voters among the OBCs belonging to the lower category in terms of class jumped by 14 percentage points to reach 37 per cent, whereas 'only' 28 per cent of the poor OBCs supported BJP.

In 2014, the impact of class differentiation within caste aggregates was also significant among the upper castes. While 'only' 37 per cent of the poor upper castes supported BJP in 2014 (+12 percentage points compared to 2009), 55 per cent of the rich of this grouping did the same (+ 22).

The support of the OBC 'neo-middle class' in favour of the BJP was particularly obvious in the largest Hindi belt states, UP and Bihar where we even observe a bell curve

Table 21.1 The 2009, 2014, and 2019 LS Elections: The OBC Vote by Class in India

	INC			BJP			BSP		
Class	2019	2014	2009	2019	2014	2009	2019	2014	2009
Poor	14	15	24	39	28	19	7	2	3
Lower	21	14.8	24	35.5	37	23	7	3	4
Middle	18	15.8	26	37	33	23	7.5	2	4
Rich	19	13.7	23	44	37	27	4	1	3

Source: Nation Election Studies (NES) 2019, 2014, and 2009 conducted by CSDS. All the tables of this chapter are based on the 2019, 2014, and the 2009 NES, except when mentioned otherwise.

Nota bene: Row percentages. All Figures are in per cent. Row figures do not add up to 100 since 'Others' are not included.

Table 21.2 The 2009 and 2014 Lok Sabha Elections: The Upper Caste Vote by Class

	INC			BJP			BSP		
Class	2019	2014	2009	2019	2014	2009	2019	2014	2009
Poor	19.5	12.7	23	31.5	37	25	5	1	3
Lower	20	10.8	26	37.5	48	29	4	1	3
Middle	20	14.8	27	43	46	30	3	2	1
Rich	27	13	29	40	55	34	4	1	2

Source: Same as for Table 21.1.

Note 1: Row percentages. All Figures are in per cent. Row figures do not add up to 100 since 'Others' are not included.

as the poor and the 'upper' class OBCs did not support the BJP as much as the 'lower' and 'middle' categories.[3]

The 2019 Elections and the Erosion of Class Explanatory Power

While class played a major role in the 2014 elections for explaining the success of BJP, in 2019, the gap between the 'poor' and the 'rich' has dropped from 14 percentage points to

---

[3] For more detail, see Ibid.

Table 21.3 The 2009, 2014, and 2019 Lok Sabha Elections: Class-wise Support for Main Parties—All-India

	2019	2014	2009	2019	2014	2009	2019	2014	2009	2019	2014	2009
Poor	17	20	27	36	24	16	7	5	8	6,908	3,901	11,791
Lower	21	19	29	36	31	19	7	5	6	7,566	6,686	9,894
Middle	21	20	29	38	32	22	6	3	4	4,975	7,298	5,964
Rich	20	17	29	44	38	25	4	4	4	2,932	2,322	1,814
All	19.5	19	29	37.5	31	19	6.5	4	6	22,381	20,207	29,463

Source: Same as for table 1.

4, and to 2 only if we compare the 'poor' with the 'middle' stratum. While the 'poor' used to lag behind the average performance of BJP—31 per cent of the valid votes—by 5 percentage points in 2014, it was only 1.5 percentage point below the average performance of BJP—37.7 per cent—in 2019.

The erosion of the class factor did not necessarily reinforced the relevance of caste considered at the level of national aggregates. Certainly upper castes voted more for the BJP than the OBCs (52 per cent against 44 per cent), but the increase of the OBC vote for BJP was such (+ 10 percentage points compared to 2014), that even the OBC vote was well above the average score of the BJP (37.5 per cent). In fact, to make sense of the role of caste in the 2019 election—and in the 2014 election as well—one needs to study the political behaviour of the *jatis* at the state level—the only relevant one for these social categories.

The large aggregates we have considered so far—'upper castes', 'OBCs', and 'SCs'—have always been very heterogeneous and their voting patterns rather diverse, except, for a brief moment of unity, in the wake of the Mandal affair of the early 1990s. Already in the 2000s, *jatis* were the relevant units of analysis, at least in the Hindi belt where Yadavs would support SP and RJD, the Kurmis would vote for the JD(U), the Jatavs for the BSP, etc. Simultaneously, upper castes aligned themselves more and more on the BJP.

THE RESILIENCE OF *JATI* POLITICS

The voting pattern of both extremes of the caste system—the *savarna* and the Dalits—is not very much class sensitive. In fact, the correlation observed above about the 2014 election—the richer, the more BJP-oriented—did not apply even then (and even less in 2019). Brahmins and Rajputs are a case in point, as these two *jatis* do not vote more for BJP (and its allies) the richer they are. On the contrary: poor Rajputs and pour brahmins tend to vote more for the BJP (and its allies) than the others—including the 'middle' and,

Table 21.4 The 2009, 2014, and 2019 LS Elections: The Brahmin Vote by Class

Class	Congress+ 2019	Congress+ 2014	Congress+ 2009	BJP+ 2019	BJP+ 2014	BJP+ 2009	BSP 2019	BSP 2014	BSP 2009
Poor	9	13	31	67	48	48	2	2	6
Lower	13	12	33	62	65	44	1	1	3
Middle	12	15	30	66	59	51	1.5	3	1
Rich	10	14	32	66.5	59	49	1	0	3

Source: Same as for Table 21.1.
NB: Row percentages. All Figures are in per cent. Row figures do not add up to 100 since 'Others' are not included.

Table 21.5 The 2009, 2014, and 2019 LS Elections: The Rajput Vote by Class

Class	Congress+ 2019	Congress+ 2014	Congress+ 2009	BJP+ 2019	BJP+ 2014	BJP+ 2009	BSP 2019	BSP 2014	BSP 2009
Poor	14.5	11	23	71	78	56	2	0	0
Lower	15	1	29	72	73	59	2	1	3
Middle	18	17	38	68	64	51	1	0	2
Rich	18	15	30	68	70	50	2	2	2

Source: Same as for Table 21.1.
Note: Row percentages. All Figures are in per cent. Row figures do not add up to 100 since 'Others' are not included.

in the case of the brahmins, the 'upper' classes. This atypical phenomenon has probably something to do with the 'neo-middle class' effect, but it probably also reflects the will of these poor *savarna* to demonstrate (and assert) their status by supporting a party associated with the Hindu great tradition and not in favour of caste-based reservations.

At the other end of the caste system, Dalit voters are not following the standard pattern either. In 2014, class made little difference till the higher social echelon so far as the BJP vote was concerned. And in 2019, the Dalit voters almost inverted the standard correlation according to which, the richer the voter, the more BJP-oriented too. In 2019, a counter intuitive correlation has taken shape: the poorer the Dalit voters, the more BJP-oriented too (with one exception, the 'rich' category).

One can make sense of this surprising correlation only by factoring *jatis* as an explanatory variable, preferably at the state level where these social units are more relevant. In Uttar Pradesh, the BJP has attracted poor Dalits more because it has become the rallying point of

Table 21.6 The 2009, 2014, and 2019 LS Elections: The Dalit Vote by Class

Class	Cong. 2019	Cong. 2014	Cong. 2009	BJP 2019	BJP 2014	BJP 2009	BSP 2019	BSP 2014	BSP 2009
Poor	14	17	24	34	22	10	13	13	23
Lower	22	17	31	32	22	13	10	13	20
Middle	26	18	34	27	22	16	8	14	14
Rich	24	20	35	30.5	27	19	4	13	14

Source: Same as for Table 21.1.

Note: Row percentages. All Figures are in per cent. Row figures do not add up to 100 since 'Others' are not included.

the non Jatav voters by cashing in on the resentment of these small and poorer Dalit groups vis-à-vis Jatavs—who are indeed better off than other Dalits (see below) and who are often accused by other Dalits of monopolizing access to reservations. The BJP wooed the non-Jatavs because the Jatavs are closely connected to the BSP—especially in Uttar Pradesh. In this state, in 2019, the BSP has given more than 20 per cent of its tickets to Jatavs, whereas BJP has nominated only 5 per cent of Jatavs, 7.7 per cent of Pasis, and 9 per cent of 'Other SCs'.[4] Certainly, the BSP-SP got 75 per cent of the Jatav vote, but it received only 42 per cent of the 'Other SCs' vote, against 48 per cent which went to the BJP. Interestingly, at an all India level, the BSP can only get more supporters than the BJP among the 'poor' Jatavs—all the other Jatavs prefer the BJP over the BJP, which suggests that class considerations are gaining momentum (see Table 21.7), even if jati identity continues to prevail in UP.

However, some *jatis* are more sensitive to class than other. The Jatavs are a case in point, as their voting pattern reveals a reverse correlation, compared to what we have observed so far. Till now, the impact of the class element meant that the richer they were, the more BJP-oriented the voters tended to be, irrespective of their caste. In the case of the Jatavs, this correlation works, not vis-à-vis the BJP, but vis-à-vis the BSP. This is probably due to ideological reasons and to the fact that Mayawati's rule has benefited the most to this group when she was in office. The Jatavs have become an interest group with a political instrument too.

While the OBC voters tended to be directly influenced by class considerations in 2014, the voting patterns of brahmins, Rajputs, and Jatavs/Chamars show that at both extremities of the caste system, *jati*-based identities matter more and class matter less—in 2014 as well as in 2019. This is probably due, in part, to the fact that upper castes and Dalits are more sensitive to status (positively or negatively) and to reservation-related

---

[4] G. Verniers, 2019, 28 May. 'Breaking Down the Uttar Pradesh Verdict: In Biggest Bout, Knockout', *The Indian Express*. https://indianexpress.com/article/explained/lok-sabha-elections-uttar-pradesh-bjp-modi-amit-shah-yogi-5751375/.

Table 21.7 The 2009, 2014, and 2019 LS Elections: The Jatav/Chamar Vote by Class

Class	Congress+ 2019	Congress+ 2014	Congress+ 2009	BJP+ 2019	BJP+ 2014	BJP+ 2009	BSP 2019	BSP 2014	BSP 2009
Poor	16	17	26	21	29	10	35.5	28	41
Lower	23	14	367	26	26	11	21	31	32
Middle	25	16	35	28	34	12	19	32	25
Rich	21.5	14	33	26	23	21	25	44	29

Source: Lokniti-CSDS, National Election Survey (NES), 2009, 2014, and 2019.

Note: Row percentages. All Figures are in per cent. Row figures do not add up to 100 since 'Others' are not included.

issues. To test this hypothesis, we need to look at the way OBC *jatis* vote. And, we need to do it at the state level again as, in fact, most of the OBC *jatis* are not politically meaningful beyond the limits of one state.

JATIS' VOTING PATTERN CLASS AT THE STATE LEVEL: THE CASE OF THE YADAVS

Jati remains one of the most relevant units of analysis for understanding electoral behaviour of OBCs at the state level because a relative majority of each *jati* aligns itself with one party. This is true, at least, in the case of the demographically numerous *jatis* for which data are available (samples are too small for the others). For instance, Yadavs tend to support the Samajwadi Party in UP and the Rashtriya Janata Dal in Bihar.[5] Jatavs support the Bahujan Samaj Party in UP and Rajputs as well as Brahmins support BJP.[6] This state of things may result from emotional attachment to the leader of these parties which belong precisely to the same *jati*. But it can also be explained by clientelistic practices. In that case, the members of a *jati* will vote for a certain party, not only because its leader is from the same caste group, but also (and possibly, more importantly) because if elected this leader will acknowledge this support by giving government jobs to members of his caste, will redistribute state resources, etc.[7]

---

[5] This is a legacy of the 'yadavisation' of the states of UP and Bihar that Mulayam Singh Yadav and Laloo Prasad Yadav initiated in the 1990s (Jaffrelot, 2003, pp. 366–386).

[6] See C. Jaffrelot, 'The Class Element in the 2014 Indian Election'.

[7] This is the main argument of Kanchan Chandra, 2004. *Why Ethnic Parties Succeed: Patronage and Ethnic Headcounts in India* (Cambridge: Cambridge University Press).

Table 21.8 The 2009, 2014, and 2019 LS Elections: The OBC Vote by Class in UP

Class	Congress+ 2019	2014	2009	BJP+ 2019	2014	2009	BSP+SP 2019	BSP 2014	2009	SP 2014	2009
Poor	4	4	17	59	44	15	33.5	10	15	37	41
Lower	7	8.4	15	46.5	53	25	41	8	11	23	44
Middle	8	11.6	20	42	47	18	47	7	19	24	32
Rich	7	14	21	46.5	46	15	40.5	2	8	26	45

Source: Same as for Table 21.1.

Note: Row percentages. All Figures are in per cent. Row figures do not add up to 100 since 'Others' are not included.

However, this logic did not fully neutralize the class element in 2014, as evident from the voting pattern of the Yadavs in UP. While 82 per cent of the poor Yadavs voted for the SP in 2014 in UP, less than 50 per cent of those who were better off (but sometimes marginally so) did the same because of the new popularity of BJP among them. In 2019, the situation changed completely. Then, two things were noticeable: certainly *jatis* continued to matter, but class *within* the Yadav *jati* played also a major role. *Jatis* continued to matter among OBCs like among Scheduled Castes: in UP like the Jatavs, the Yadavs tend to dominate their category[8]—the OBCs in their case—and are, therefore resented by smaller, subaltern OBC *jatis* which accuse them of cornering all the reservations and of benefitting from the SP's clientelistic practices when this party is in office. The BJP has successfully targeted these caste-groups by nominating many candidates from this milieu. Whereas 27 per cent of the SP candidates were Yadavs in 2019, Yadavs represented only 1.3 per cent of the candidates of the BJP which, on the contrary, gave tickets to 7.7 per cent Kurmis and 16.7 per cent 'Other OBCs', who often came from small caste groups.[9] This strategy translated into votes: while 60 per cent of the Yadavs voted for the SP–BSP alliance, 72 per cent of the 'Other OBCs' supported the BJP.[10]

However, class played a role *within* the Yadavs in 2019. Certainly, 'poor' Yadavs and 'rich' Yadavs voted for the SP–BSP alliance in the same proportions, but the 'poor' Yadavs have been more attracted by BJP this time, in contrast to the situation that had prevailed five years later, when the richer the Yadav, the more BJP-oriented too. In

---

[8] C. Jaffrelot and A. Kalaiyasaran, 2019, 14 January. 'Quota and Bad Faith'. *The Indian Express*.
[9] Verniers. 'Breaking Down the Uttar Pradesh Verdict'.
[10] M. A. Beg, S. Pandey, and S. Kare, 2019, 26 mai. 'Post-Poll Survey: Why Uttar Pradesh's Mahagathbandhan Failed', *The Hindu*. https://www.thehindu.com/elections/lok-sabha-2019/post-poll-survey-why-uttar-pradeshs-mahagathbandhan-failed/article27249310.ece.

Table 21.9 The 2009, 2014, and 2019 LS Elections: The Yadav Vote by Class in UP

Class	Congress 2019	Congress 2014	Congress 2009	BJP 2019	BJP 2014	BJP 2009	BSP+SP 2019	BSP 2014	BSP 2009	SP 2014	SP 2009
Poor	1.5	4	12	27.5	11	7.6	68	0	3	82	76
Lower	4	6	19	24	32	6.3	58	6	3	49	70
Middle	15	10	8	22	29	5.6	59	3	8	49	78
Upper	7	11	5	18	26	5.4	66	2	5	47	77

Source: Same as for Table 21.1.

Note: Row percentages. All Figures are in per cent. Row figures do not add up to 100 since 'Others' are not included.

2019, the correlation is exactly the reverse. This transformation may be explained by the alliance that the BSP and SP made in 2019: first, the 'poor' Yadavs[11] were probably not willing to join hands with Dalits—with whom they are often locked in conflict and competition at the grassroots level; second, the same 'poor' Yadavs possibly identified the SP as the party of the 'rich' Yadavs—those who benefitted from its policies when it governed UP.

To conclude: class-related variations of *jatis*' voting pattern are more pronounced for the Yadavs than for the brahmins and the Rajputs. This state of things may be due to the intermediary position of OBCs in the caste system that makes them less status sensitive, but it may also reflect the 'neo-middle class' effect. This effect can also be measured beyond class indicators by studying the urbanization pattern of *jatis*.

Conclusion

While class played an important role in the 2014 election—and contributed to the success of Narendra Modi, the situation has been very different in 2019, when the Prime minister appeared to be equally popular among all the strata of society, including the poor.

---

[11] According to the India Human Development Surveys conducted in 2004–2005 and 2011–2012 show increasing inequalities within the rich and the poor Yadavs. This gap partly comes from the fact that 17 per cent of the Yadavs of UP are agricultural labourers (in other words, landless peasants). (C. Jaffrelot and A. Kalaiyasaran, 2019, 14 January. 'Quota and Bad Faith', *The Indian Express*. https://indianexpress.com/article/opinion/columns/yogi-adityanath-quota-reservation-bjp-uttar-pradesh-5536651/.

If class has lost some of its relevance for explaining the results of the 2019 elections, caste is showing some unexpected relevance. In spite of the BJP's claim that the party's ideology was allergic to any consideration which may divide the nation, its strategists have meticulously studied the caste equation at the local level in order to select the right candidates. They have, in particular, nominated representatives of small OBC and Dalit *jatis* which resented the domination of other caste groups of their categories—whose quotas they cornered. Yadavs and Jatavs of UP are two cases in point: in this state, the BJP could consolidate the anti-SP and anti-BSP voters among OBCs and Dalits. This tactic reconfirms that the role of caste in politics must be analysed at the state level and at the *jati* level.

While we can still partly explain Indians' electoral behaviour on the basis of their caste background, caste does not make the same impact in any uniform manner: if OBCs are more influenced by class-related considerations, *savarna* and Dalits, because they occupy both ends of the caste system, are more status-sensitive—even though, in the case of the latter, the class element started to play a bigger role in 2019. As a result, their voting pattern continues to be more overdetermined by caste. Second, caste matters more significantly at the *jati* level, as large aggregates like 'OBCs' or even 'Dalits' have only been politically relevant in the context of crisis like the 'Mandal affair' of the 1990s. Correlatively, as *jatis* are mostly meaningful at the state level, it is also at the state level that one must study the politics of caste. The cases of the Jatavs and the Yadavs of UP show some variations as class *within* these *jatis* played a more important role among the latter that the former.

Two caveats must be added to these conclusions. First, caste may play an even more complicated role at the local level, according to the arithmetic of caste groups at the constituency level and the parties' strategies of ticket distribution. Second, in some cases, the relevant unit of analysis may not be the *jati*, but its subdivisions. Patels are a case in point in Gujarat, as evident from the following table showing the voting preference of the Karwa Patels and the Leuva Patels. These figures reconfirm the importance of the caste of the parties' leaders: the fact that the founder of the GPP, Keshubhai Patel, was a Leuva larley explain why almost one-third of the Leuva Patels supported this party.

In addition to the above conclusions, this chapter suggests that political scientists now have to examine the role of caste in terms of voting behaviour in a more sophisticated manner, but the paucity of data, remains a huge challenge in this regard.

Table 21.10 Voting Preference of Karwa and Leuva Patels

Sub Patel Caste Groups	BJP	Congress	GPP	Others
Karwa	80 (−5)	6 (−2)	6 (+6)	8 (+1)
Leuva	52 (−3)	12 (−22)	32 (+32)	4 (−7)

Source: same as for Table 21.16.

Appendix The Growing Impact of Urbanization on Castes' Electoral Behaviour

Electoral behaviour is increasingly over determined by the urban/rural divide, to such an extent that we need to factor in this variable too, in addition to class, if we want to measure the resilient influence of caste over voting patterns. Certainly, class and urbanization overlap in the sense that villagers are generally not as affluent as those living in towns and cities. But the rural/urban divide implies two other dimensions. First, the decline of agriculture in relative terms vis-à-vis other sectors of the economy, affects all groups, including the most affluent farmers.[12] Second, urban dwellers are exposed to a different kind of politics: they are immersed in a universe where propaganda is much more intense and where ghettoization along communal lines also tends to be more pronounced.[13]

In 2014, the impact of urbanization on caste groups was minimal on the *savarna*, whereas OBCs, and to a lesser extent to Dalits, rallied more around the BJP when they got urbanized. However, the correlation was far from linear, as OBCs and the Dalits tended to support the BJP more in towns and cities than in the large metropolises. This invert U curve was partly due to the competition of the AAP which gets 14–15 per cent of the OBC and Dalit votes in the metropolises.

Interestingly, there were major variations state-wise. The invert U curve mentioned above simply did not exist in the case of the OBCs of Gujarat, a very urbanized state where the 'neo-middle class' effect played a big part: the larger their locality, the more supportive of the BJP Gujarati OBCs appear to be. This linear relation is also observed in Karnataka in the case of the Dalits.

Table 21.11 The Upper Caste Vote Layered by Locality

Locality	Congress	BJP	Left	BSP	SP	AAP	Total
Village	14.7	46.5	4.4	1.3	1.5	.8	100 N = 2533
Towns and cities	11.3	47	4.9	1.5	.5	2.2	100 N = 1418
Metro	9.8	50.9	.7	.2	0	9.0	100 N = 458

---

[12] For more details see C. Jaffrelot, 2017, 8 December. 'Fields of Despair', *The Indian Express*. https://indianexpress.com/article/opinion/columns/indian-farmers-rural-economy-bjp-fields-of-despair-4973039/.

[13] For more details, see C. Jaffrelot and Sanjay Kumar.

Table 21.12 The OBC Vote Layered by Locality

Locality	Congress	BJP	Left	BSP	SP	AAP	Total
Village	15.4	32.3	3.7	2.3	5	.7	100 N = 5046
Towns and cities	14.5	37.5	2.7	1.2	2.7	1.7	100 N = 1742
Metro	13.9	33.3	1.9	1.9	0	13.9	100 N = 366

Table 21.13 The Dalit Vote Layered by Locality

Locality	Congress	BJP	Left	BSP	SP	AAP	Total
Village	18.9	22.4	7.9	14.6	1.3	.5	100 N = 2373
Towns and cities	19.3	29.5	5	13.8	.6	2.1	100 N = 860
Metro	9.1	18.9	1.1	4.6	0	14.9	100 N = 366

Table 21.14 The OBC Vote by Locality in Gujarat

Locality	Congress	BJP	Total
Villages	31.2	63.8	100 N = 224
Towns and cities	15.5	77.5	100 N = 71
Metros	9.5	90.5	100 N = 21

Table 21.15 The OBC Vote Layered by Locality in Karnataka

Locality	Congress	BJP	JD(S)	Total
Villages	36.6	41.3	16.1	100 N = 317
Towns and cities	26.5	51.2	17.6	100 N = 170
Metros	28.6	50	0	100 N = 14

Table 21.16 The OBC Vote Layered by Locality in Maharashtra

Locality	Congress	NCP	BJP	Shiv Sena	Total
Villages	13.2	13.9	27.4	33.6	100 N = 453
Towns and cities	9.3	0	38.9	25.9	100 N = 54
Metros	7.9	2.6	31.6	23.7	100 N = 38

Table 21.17 The Dalit Vote Layered by Locality in Karnataka

Locality	Congress	BJP	JD(S)	Total
Villages	51.3	29.1	7.7	100 N = 117
Towns and cities	26.3	47.4	24.6	100 N = 57
Metros	0	100	0	100 N = 1

The case of BJP where the OBC BJP voters jumped from 63.8 per cent to 90.5 per cent needs to be scrutinized. The sample of the NES 2014 being too small for conducting a serious analysis, we need to use the data that the CSDS had collected in 2012 at the time of the state elections. It showed that the impact of urbanization was indeed very significant, especially in the case of the Kolis, the largest OBC caste of their state. Indeed, if a linear relation is at work for all the OBC groups, it is especially dramatic in the case of the Kolis: while 53.2 per cent of the rural Kolis voted for the Congress, only 18.5 per cent of the semi-urban members of the caste did the same. Symmetrically (almost), only 44 per cent of the rural Koli voted for the BJP but 65.2 per cent of the semi-urban ones did the same. More generally speaking, all the castes and communities tend to be more Congress oriented when we consider their village dwellers—except the Patels.

Table 21.18 The Impact of Urbanization on the Voting Pattern of Castes and Communities

Castes and Communities	Congress			BJP			GPP		
Categories	rural*	semi urban°	urban#	Rural	semi urban	urban	rural	semi urban	urban
Upper caste		16.1	22.5		64.5	60.5	16.1		
Patel	12.4	16.1	10.7	62.8	71	72.9	24.8	6.5	6.4
Kshatriya	45	41.1	36.2	51.2	51.8	53.2	0.7	-	2.1
Koli	53.2	18.5	-	44	65.2	0.8	-	3.3	-
Other OBC	40.7	26.6	17.9	50.9	51.6	65.5	3.1	3.5	5.5
Dalit	81.3	45	59.7	18.8	36.3	16.9	-	1.3	-
Adivasi	47.3	41.1	20	29.6	35.6	66.7	0.8	10	-
Muslim	70.2	81.4	68.5	20.7	7	29.6	0.8	2.3	1.9
Total	45.7	32.2	27.5	43.3	50.8	57.7	3.3	4.6	3.2

Source: Post poll survey conducted by the CSDS for CNN-IBN.[14]

* Rural constituencies have 75 per cent or more village-based voters.
° Semi urban constituencies have between 25–75 per cent urban voters.
Urban constituencies have 75 per cent to more urban voters.

[14] This poll was conducted across 60 assembly constituencies between 13 and 18 December. A total of 3,755 respondents participated in it.

CHAPTER 22

CASTE, PATRONAGE AND CRIMINALIZATION OF POLITICS

LUCIA MICHELUTTI

Introduction

This chapter discusses what is the role of caste in current muscular political-economic systems of governance, popularly known in the region as 'Mafia Raj' or 'Goonda Raj' (rule by mafia/gangsters). It mainly draws on ethnographic material collected in Uttar Pradesh over the past decade. During this period, concerns about the 'criminalization of politics' in this part of the world have surpassed worries about endemic nepotism or the mismanagement of public funds and patronage practices. 'Criminal politicians' are accused not simply of embezzlement or vote buying but more so of kidnapping, murder, and rape. Thus the political landscape is not only corrupt and 'clientalistic' but also highly violent. The Association for Democratic Reform (ADR) and National Election Watch have created a unique database of affidavits submitted by candidates contesting state and national elections since 2002, illustrating the presence of politicians with criminal records in Indian politics. From this data we know that 43 per cent of current elected Members of Parliament (MPs) have criminal histories, but what do these statistics actually mean? Crime mostly remains a matter of 'background' or quantifiable 'cases' (Michelutti and Harriss-White, 2019). Although 'crime' is said to pay off (Vaishnav, 2017; Kapur and Vaishnav, 2018) what goondagardi (criminal work) is and how it gets politicized and what is the role of caste in these systems of power remains quite nebulous. By contrast research tends to focus on patronage (rather than racketeering): on the corrupted clientalistic exchanges (or lack of them) between politicians, party workers, and voters at election time. Thus, on the one hand, we have scholars who argue that patronage is still central to Indian politics and informs electoral choices (Chandra, 2004; Kitschelt and Wilkinson, 2007; Vaishnav, 2017). Many in this camp view patronage as a statecraft tool *deeply intertwined with caste and kinship, local moral economies and old kingly/religious practices* (Berenshot, 2010; Gilmartin, 2012; Singh, 2012; Michelutti, 2014). Some go as a far as proposing a theory that conceptualizes patronage as what determines Indian politics (Piliavsky, 2014). On the other hand, there is an opposing strand of research that argues that patronage (*and by extension hierarchy and caste*) are not central key elements of contemporary Indian social-political life. According to this view the 'common man' no longer simply appeals to the idioms of traditional patron—client relations, but engages in 'politics' (Khilnani, 1997; Chatterjee, 2004; Banerjee, 2008). Issues like 'ideology' have also been identified as more important than clientalistic (caste) exchanges and ultimately as informing political choices (Chibber and Verma, 2018). We are often told that money do not buy votes (Björkman, 2014). We are also told that cash flows should viewed as rhetorical tools—as part of campaign spectacle and pomp (Chibber and Verma, 2018, chap. 6).

In this chapter, I argue that both the 'clientalistic thesis' and the 'anti-clientalistic' one fail to ask a simple question: *where do the money that is displayed and distributed at elections times come from? What is the relation with caste, if any?* Answering these key questions bring us back to the need of understanding the nature of 'criminal work' not merely as a background to the criminalization of politics but as the engine of it. Failing to engage with 'criminal work' and how it entangles with caste and kinship may preclude a full understanding of everyday Mafia Raj social-political and economic exchanges and to appreciate how they constantly blur 'patronage into racketeering; protection into extortion; informal economic practices into organized crime; systems of patronage democracy into 'mafia owned democracies' (Armao, 2000, 2015); and 'caste/clans' into Mafia Companies and 'Mafia families'. It should be noted that Mafia Raj, are original systems of political and economic governance where not only criminals, businessmen, and politicians meet but also where the 'public becomes implicated as clients, customers, and voters' (Micheutti et al., 2018, p. 14). Most importantly, Mafia Raj are also environments that are inherently 'fraught with uncertainty, distrust, suspicion, paranoid anxiety, and misunderstanding' (Von Lampe and Johansen, 2003; see Michelutti, 2018a) and this is because illegality and competition are pervasive. In this context, caste heritage, mythological origins, and kinship strategies that aim at the long-term perpetuation of forms of protection/racketeering and domination become important but as I will argue in the following sections, *not essential.*

Patronage or Racketeering?

We are commonly told that '. . . the display of money during elections is socially approved . . . is a political necessity, and is born of cultural expectations' (Chibber and Verma, 2018, p. 22). Following this assumption Indian political leaders have often been described as having the duty 'to care for the material interests of [their] followers' (e.g. Brass, 1990, p. 96). Pamela Price has described this idea as heir to the persistent, historically embedded models of lordship, pointing out the long assumed duty of the king to provide (1989, p. 47, 1999, 2010). The raja's 'beauty and dazzle', she wrote, 'symbolised the potentialities of wealth for the community as a whole'. The relation between king and subject is then refracted to local big men down to village/lineages heads and from dominant castes leaders to clan/lineage ones. Against this socio-cultural matrix after India's independence the Congress Party is said to have appealed to 'traditional' political systems like *jajmani* village patronage and caste-based village factions to mobilize its electorate and transform relations between the village dominant castes and their clienteles into relations between Congress politicians and their vote banks (Brass, 1965; Rudolph and Rudolph, 1967, pp. 36–64).[1] Soon after the independence, however, the cumulative effect of rising electoral competition, spreading education, the policies of affirmative action, and land reforms prompted transformations in the local structures of dominance and authority, opening political spaces for formerly marginalized groups. Marguerite Robinson, who conducted 25 years of field research in the villages and district centres of Andhra Pradesh, showed that by the early 1970s people substantially stopped voting for traditional elites (1988). She concluded that this change reflected *the broader delegitimation of caste hierarchies* and the political rise of the landless (Robinson, 1988, p. 248). Similarly, Jan Breman argued on the basis of extensive research in Gujarat that in post-independence India *inequality lost its social legitimacy, precipitating a shift from 'vertical' (inter-caste) to increasingly 'horizontal' (intra-caste) patterns of political mobilisation* (1993, p. 262). Policies that reserved places of education, civil service, and politics for historically downtrodden communities (SC, ST, and OBC) further reshaped how people related to old-time patrons and prompted the rise of *'new' patronly classes*.

In democratic India castes begun to claim an equal share, proportionate not to their status but to the size of their population. As political scientist Kanchan Chandra (2004) argues, Indian citizens make electoral choices on the basis of 'ethnic head counts': they vote for parties that contain most members of their own community instead of comparing their policy platforms. Because parties also count their voters' 'heads', it follows that the main demand of caste-based political parties is distributive 'social justice' related to the narrowly defined social upliftment (jobs, access to government pro-poor or pro-rural programmes, and a sense of empowerment/dignity) of their voter communities. This is what Chandra (2004) famously characterized as a 'patronage democracy'. This is a democracy in which political leaders have the power to distribute the vast resources controlled by the state to voters on an individual basis. *Redistributions is here key and caste matters*. It matters because to vote for a caste fellow is considered an efficient way to assure some sort of political power, which is because politicians first help their caste (*samaj/parivar*) members is an accepted political fact. In reality, however, this might not happen, indeed, many times it does not happen (see

---

[1] I have explored in detail these trends in Michelutti (2018) and Michelutti (2014).

Chandra, 2004, p. 136). However, people continue to think that by supporting a caste fellow they maximize their chances of getting a share of the state resources. It is in the mid-nineties, that Hansen marvellously captured the ways in which old forms of patronage—the donor-servant ideal—and the values attached to it had been adapted to and transformed by democracy and vice versa and in the process have been shaping popular politics. He argues that by the 1980s 'India's democratic revolution gradually undermined the idiom and practices of *ma-baap'ism* [paternalism/patronage]' and explained how it was 'the performance of a certain style of public authority—generous but also with a capacity for ruthless violence—that determines who can defend and represent "the community", defend neighbourhoods, punish and discipline' (2005, p. 136). Politicians are said to be known to be corrupt and to resort to violence, but if seen as 'our men' loyal to 'our community', they may often command wide support in majoritarian electoral politics. In this environment politicians choose to project an image of men of action: men who can 'get things done for their people' (see Michelutti, 2010; Berenschot, 2012).

In the late 90s and the first decade of the 21st century Indian economic liberalization has prompted a scramble for resources and a further demand for muscular politics. Across India we witnessed an increasing number of violent entrepreneurs entering into politics (Jaffrelot, 2002). In this environment, 'democratic rajas' had to be not only generous benefactors (Piliavsky, 2014; Price, 1996) but also crucially violent protectors. It is at this time that the ideal of kingly protection begun to mix with forms of protections which are at the heart of 'mafia capitalism' (Schneider and Schneider, 2011). Long back scholars of mafia expressed the salience of these intimate entanglements, complicities, and opportunistic partnerships with the Italian concept of 'intreccio', meaning an intertwining like a tightly woven braid. Historically, such 'intrecci' are said to occur under conditions of abrupt and rapid capitalist development for which violent entrepreneurs are useful aides. Building on this literature, Michelutti et al. (2018) and Harriss-White and Michelutti (2019) argued that India is yet another established democracy in which intense electoral competition combined with predatory forms of capitalism is producing particular forms of criminal (political) governance. This work shows how 'mafias' and many captains of industry are at the apex of much more extensive criminal economic systems embedded in formal, registered, and regulated institutions and, crucially, the political sphere and its bureaucracy. As of today, the workings and the social consequences of this *intreccio* have hardly been taken into dialog with classical South Asian understandings of 'the donor-servant ideal', with the concept of *sewa* and the role of caste sovereignties in Indian democracy.

My work on *dabangs* (bosses/enforcers) has provided (Michelutti, 2014, 2019) some insights into how lordly ideals have been refashioned vis-à-vis the emergence of mafia's styles of protection in Western Uttar Pradesh. I showed how the dabangs I met over the course of my fieldwork represent a qualitative shift from the traditional figures of the *bhai* or *dada* (strongman) in any North Indian provincial town until about two decades ago. The traditional town and neighbourhood bosses used to establish their sovereignty through protection rackets, moneylending, and adjudicating disputes. These old style protectors-cum-social bandits boasted an exceptional muscular physique and reputed fighting techniques—usually acquired through wrestling. They employed their force to establish domination in the *mohalla* (neighbourhood) and to acquire 'violent' credibility with their patrons (who were often the local politicians). They also tend to come from 'martial castes' or local dominant castes like Rajputs, Jats, Gujars, or Ahirs. However, today in the words of an aspiring *dabang*, 'You just need a pistol, courage, and to get involved in the *bhumi* [land] mafia' (Michelutti et al., 2018, p. 154). Small-town bosses (often independently from their caste background) become involved in the booming construction industry and use the new capital to build up their political strongholds. '... In short, traditional specialists of violence stopped supplying their services to the big (upper caste/dominant caste) leaders: they stopped acting as mercenaries for their landlords and patrons and instead began to use their muscular skills to stage a better life for themselves and their families and create their political mafiaesque clans' (Michelutti et al., 2018 p. 154).

'THE ART OF BOSSING': FROM 'PATRONAGE DEMOCRACY' TO 'MAFIA-OWNED DEMOCRACY'

Despite this economic and cultural shifts a great deal of work on clientalism and patronage in South Asia tends still to focus on how leaders mediate or distribute resources as 'generous benefactors' rather than their role as violent protectors and enforcers. For example, Berenschot (2010) emphasizes that the state's limited capacity to implement access has fuelled both the demand for and the supply of fixers. Because the state is too understaffed and under resourced to implement these schemes, fixers take up the job. The dark side of 'patronage' is however left underexplored and with it the shift from a 'patronage democracy' to a 'mafia-owned democracy' (Armao, 2015). Let me explain. As explored in the previous section 'patronage democracies' have been conceived as democracies in which elected political leaders have the power to distribute the vast resources controlled by the state to vote on an individual basis. In a mafia-owned democracy, however, what is crucial is not redistribution but *criminal partnerships between the state and private capitalism based on the power of enforcement by force and intimidation*. To run and protect their economic activities (legal and illegal), violent entrepreneurs tend to develop symbiotic relations with the state—and in the process they sometimes become 'criminal-politicians'.

In a co-author volume 'Mafia Raj: The Rule of Bosses in South Asia' (2018) Michelutti, Hoque, Martin, Picherit, Rollier, Ruud, and Still explore the everyday life of racketeering and protection/extortion as statecraft tools and instruments of accumulation by ambitious violent political business entrepreneurs. This collaborative ethnography reminds us that that 'protection' is a shadowy contract in which violence, personal interests, and fantasies of power intersect (Strathern, 2012, p. 401). Its exploration contributed to the conceptualization of 'the art of bossing' as the performance of personal sovereignty. 'This art form refers to the violent, criminal, business, and "democratic" tactics and strategies that some men (seldom women) deploy to *control* people and resources to pursue a better life for themselves, their families, and, at times, their communities. Enacting personal sovereignty requires a capacity for violence and for making money, repeated acts of give and take, figurations and mythologies' (Michelutti et al., 2018, p. 8). Michelutti et al. illustrate how these ingredients are put together, joined, mixed, and packaged and how such an art brings political-economic authority into existence. Importantly, what is documented is *the uncontrollable nature of such processes* and the perpetual instability of bosses' power.

Mafia Raj exchanges are certainly more complex than simple and 'straightforward' acts of redistribution and vote buying practices and/or acts of coercion and intimidation at election times. For a start, the unstable and evanescent relations between bosses and their citizen-subjects distinguish this relationship from idealized patron-client or king-servant relations and their spectacular acts of generosity (Price, 1996). What ethnographies of bossism question empirically *is the idea that patrons automatically command respect from the people.* This does not mean that violent self-interest and profit-driven individual actions are not embedded in the local social fabric, on the contrary. However, the relationality of bossism should be not viewed as embedded in pregiven mythical bonds between the individual patron and his or her adoring followers but rather as the product of hard quotidian work. This is work that is shaped (yet not determined) by specific sociocultural and economic situations and institutional milieus.

What Is the Role of Caste, Kinship, and Family in Mafia Raj?

The fusion of muscle power with capitalism and democracy represents certainly a break with the past. Today's violent protectors are nurtured in different spaces and have diverse sociological backgrounds as mentioned above. The personality of the boss becomes particularly important precisely because the power of the boss is often detached from hereditary status and caste/community sovereignties (Hoque and Michelutti, 2018). Thus, what becomes a source of conversation and admiration is not always heritage: instead, what is of celebrated are *personal individual achievements*. A number of bosses I have encountered have checkered histories and come from a life of hardship; some are from lower castes and others come from more privileged backgrounds and the traditional martial dominant caste and communities. Mostly, bosses origins are not so predictable: some are literally fighting their way to the top. Importantly, their stories suggest that in present conditions even people from a privileged background need to assert themselves by force, at least in the early stages of their career (Michelutti et al., 2018,

p. 239). This is not to say that caste, ethnic identity, and class are not important. Caste and kinship structure criminal economies in many ways but they *are not totally indispensable*. Take for example the case of a woman boss in Western UP whose caste origins were dubious but claimed Brahmin status. The lady in question built up her career as a fearless and violence entrepreneur. Enacting her personal sovereignty required a capacity for violence and for making money and—crucially—the cultivation of a personal mythology and charisma. Locally, her sovereign power is deeply shaped by the figurative power of Phulan Devi, aka the Bandit Queen—one of the icons of North Indian low-caste politics and Indian feminism. Somewhere else I described how the lives (and afterlife/myth) of these two women interact, and how such interactions are helping the production of the lady' authority, the awe she inspires and her capacity to 'boss' and win elections in this corner of the world. The fact that she was a Brahmin was not crucial in shaping her career but it certainly helped her to get tickets from regional parties like the Bahujan Samaj Party—a party whose strategy has been to combine the vote of Dalits and Brahmins. However, she was not successful in mobilizing the Brahman and/or the Dalit vote and won elections only when she run as an independent.

Kinship and family (rather than caste) are however very important. Kinship bonds should be treated as an essential coping mechanism to control risk in the making of 'Mafia families'.[2] As a local boss well exemplifies it: 'I can't further enlarge our firm [he runs a very successful construction company] because expansion means the involvement of workers from outside the family and one can't trust outsiders in our business.' This comment well exemplifies the fragility and potential volatility of political-criminal configurations (Gayer, 2014, p. 134). It should also be noted that while bosses try to minimize risks by employing family members, they also thrive on instability and often make a virtue out of it. Uncertainty, if well-staged, has the capacity to spread paranoia and enhance the magnitude of bosses. Thus, the cultivation of insecurity becomes an integral part of the charismatic power of the boss. It is in these unstable but opportunity-rich arenas that bosses' dynasties are performed. *Dabangs* certainly command respect and they are valued for what they have achieved, not for what they are (Michelutti, 2010, p. 46).

Force and instability also help lower castes and Dalits to establish themselves as muscular leaders and to challenge local hierarchies and power structures, but with some limitations. Take for example, the henchman, Kondappa, who David Picherit (Michelutti et al., 2018, chap. 4) shadowed in Andhra Pradesh. He is a Dalit and a boss in his own right. He rules over his jurisdiction but his power is linked to the one of his higher caste Reddy's boss. Far from being fixed, relations between him and his boss are however uncertain, fluid, and temporary, with ever-growing uncertainty. This impacts the ways bosses watch over their henchman: 'Money has become important; it doesn't guarantee loyalty, but it does help keeping people around. I still

---

[2] See, for example, the literature on organized crime where trust is treated as a feature of mafia-like enterprises (Paoli, 2002, p. 84).

have people following me whatever I do; I'm like a part of their family. But now people also want money' (Michelutti et al., 2018, p. 110) explains Kondappa's higher caste boss. Traditional hierarchies and relations of domination are thus not straightforward and money are needed to consolidate them. It follows that bosses are in a constant state of competition and fear losing power.

This is not to say that kinship bonds and marriage alliances are not important conditions to becoming a boss; intergeneration and inherited feuds are often key circumstance in some instances (Rollier, 2016). In addition, local structures of caste dominance have often important electoral affinities with bosses' electoral successes but not in as straightforward a manner as might be first thought (Martin and Michelutti, 2017). Control over territories by bosses who belong to the so-called dominant caste is strategically used to run markets, extract resources, and win elections. 'Territorial' forms of democracy, as Witsoe conceptualized them, go hand to hand with bossism. 'In such systems electoral outcomes are influenced by relations of dominance and subordination within specific territorial spaces, and conversely, the ways in which electoral practice reinforces, and can even produce, territorial [mafia-like] dominance' (2009, pp. 65–66). It follows that in some areas elected politicians become guarantors of provision and protection who often share imagined kin relations with the people they represent. People see kin who can protect them as the best form of guarantee in a world where authorities and the legal system are trusted less and less every day (Michelutti, 2014).

It is against this background, in the case of Uttar Pradesh, for example, criminal economic sectors—from 'sand mafia' to 'oil mafia' or 'coal mafia' are often run by dominant castes that claim Kshatriya origins such as Thakur, Yadavs, Jats, and Gujars (Michelutti, 2019a). These are castes that have a reputation for being capable of using violence (*dandaniti*) and more importantly they are thought as 'entitled' to use it. These are castes that still often describe themselves as natural protectors and as the 'ones' who can legitimately administer justice ('We have justice in the blood', they often say). 'Yadavs used to be the muscle power of Brahmins and Thakurs [Rajputs]'. A powerful Yadav government administrator reminded me: 'We (Yadavs) were always active in the industry of violence—but now rather than doing it for the Brahmins and Rajputs—we do it for ourselves ... we became self-employed—it is for this reason we did much better than the Kurmis.' Danda (*force*) is indeed still one of the constitutive elements used to define the identity of many social groups in North India and this is strategically and indirectly used in today's Mafia Raj political and economic systems. This model of boss-king entrenched in traditional warrior-rules ethos has been recently emblematically embodied by the figure of the current Chief Minister of the state a Thakur. Yogi Adityanath, a controversial spiritual figure with a respectable criminal record himself, made his reputation by transforming a gangster-dominated constituency, Gorakhpur, into a 'safe' Hindu territory. The charismatic Kshatriya Yogi fuses in his persona divine kingship, 'danda' and democratic popular sovereignty (Chaturvedi, 2017). Ultimately, he is also a 'king-boss' (Michelutti, 2019) and his election has visibly embolden the Rajput community. Since Adityanath's appointment caste riots rather than communal riots have been rampant in Western Uttar Pradesh. The Thakurs are taking revenge against the Dalits and backward castes that have been in power for the previous 15 years. Multiple revenge wars are unfolding. These 'battles' spread further insecurity and with it a need for protection that provides a fertile ground for Mafia Raj/Hindu sovereignty to grow and prosper, and reinvent itself this time in the name of Hindu Rashtra (polity) and its dharma. Many years ago, Gambetta (1993) argued that lack of trust in a context where the state is unable to provide basic security generates the popular demand for Mafia-like protection. In the case of western Uttar Pradesh, it is not only a lack of confidence in the government (although it undeniably exists) that provides a 'robust pillar for mafia business' but also local animosities and conflicts between and within castes and communities provide fertile ground for bossism to prosper (Martin and Michelutti, 2017). More research is urgently needed to map out the politics of caste and kinship complicities, the balance between the roles of culture, political power, and the logic of profit-making in criminal accumulation.

References

Armao, F. 2000. *Il sistema Mafia: Dall'economia-mondo al dominio locale*. Torino: Bollati Boringhieri.
Armao, F. 2015. 'Mafia-Owned Democracies: Italy and Mexico as Patterns of Criminal Neoliberalism'. *Revista de Historia Actual*, 1: 4–21.
Banerjee, Mukulika. 2008. 'Democracy, Sacred and Everyday: An Ethnographic Case from India'. In Julia Paley (Ed.), *Democracy: Anthropological Perspectives* (pp. 63–95). Santa Fe: Advanced Research Press.
Berenschot, Ward. 2010. 'Everyday Mediation: The Politics of Public Service Delivery in Gujarat, India'. *Development and Change*, 41(5): 883–905.
Björkman, Lisa. 2014. '"You Can't Buy a Vote": Meanings of Money in a Mumbai Election'. *American Ethnologist*, 41: 4.
Brass, Paul. 1965. *Factional Politics in an Indian State*. Berkeley: University of California Press.
Brass, Paul. 1990. *The Politics of India since Independence*. Cambridge: Cambridge University Press.
Breman, Jan. 1993. *Beyond Patronage and Exploitation: Changing Agrarian Relations in South Gujarat*. New Delhi: Oxford University Press.
Chandra, Kanchan. 2004. *Why Ethnic Parties Succeed*. Cambridge: Cambridge University Press.
Chatterjee, Partha. 2004. *The Politics of the Governed: Reflections on Popular Politics in Most of the World*. New York: Columbia University Press.
Chaturvedi, Shashank. 2017. 'Khichdi Mela in Gorakhnath Math Symbols, Ideas and Motivations'. *Society and Culture in South Asia*, 3(2): 1–22.
Chaturvedi, Shashank, David Gellner, and Sanjay Kumar Pandey. 2019. 'Politics in Gorakhpur since the 1920s: The Making of a Safe "Hindu" Constituency'. *Contemporary South Asia*. DOI: 10.1080/09584935.2018.1521785.
Chibber, Pradeep, and Verma Rahul. 2018. *Ideology and Identity: The Changing Party Systems of India*. Delhi: Oxford University Press.
Gambetta, Diego. 1993. *The Sicilian Mafia: The Business of Private Protection*. Cambridge,
Gilmartin, D. 2012. 'Introduction to Election Law in India'. *Election Law Journal*, 11, 2 (June 2012) [Guest edited issue with Robert Moog]. MA: Harvard University Press.

Gayer, L. 2014. *Karachi. Ordered Disorder and the Struggle for the City*. London, Delhi, New York, Karachi: Hurst, HarperCollins, Oxford University Press.

Hansen, Thomas B. 2005. 'Sovereigns beyond the State: On Legality and Public Authority in India'. In Ravinder Kaur (Ed.), *Religion, Violence and Political Mobilisation in South Asia* (pp. 109–144). New Delhi: SAGE.

Harriss-White, B., and L. Michelutti (Eds.) 2019. *The Wild East. Criminal Political Economics in South Asia*. London: UCL Press.

Hoque Ashraf, and Lucia Michelutti. 2018, November. 'Brushing with Organized Crime and Democracy: The Art of Making Do in South Asia'. *The Journal of Asian Studies*, 77(4): 991–1011.

Jaffrelot, C. 2002. 'Indian Democracy: The Rule of Law on Trial', India Review, 1(1): 77–121.

Kapur, D., and M. Vaishnav (Eds.). 2018. *Costs of Democracy: Political Finance in India*. New Delhi: OUP.

Kitschelt, Herbert, and Steven I. Wilkinson (Eds.). 2007. *Patrons, Clients, and Policies: Patterns of Democratic Accountability and Political Competition*. Cambridge: Cambridge University Press.

Khilnani, Sunil. 1997. *The Idea of India*. London: Hamish Hamilton.

Martin, N., and L. Michelutti. 2017. 'Protection Rackets and Party Machines. Comparative Ethnographies of "Mafia Raj" in North India'. *Asian Journal of Social Science* 45 (6) pp. 693–723.

Michelutti, L., A. Hoque, N. Martin, D. Picherit, P. Rollier, A. Ruud, and C. Still. 2018. *Mafia Raj: The Rule of Bosses in South Asia*. Stanford: Stanford University Press.

Michelutti, L. 2010. 'Wrestling with (Body) Politics: Understanding "Goonda" Political Styles in North India'. In P. Price and A. E. Ruud (Eds.), *Power and Influence in South Asia: Bosses, Lords, and Captains*. Delhi, London: Routledge.

Michelutti, Lucia. 2014. 'Kinship without Kings in Northern India'. In A. Piliavsky (Ed.), *Patronage as Politics in South Asia*. Cambridge: Cambridge University Press.

Michelutti, Lucia. 2018. 'Parivar Raj (Rule of Family): The Role of Money and Force in the Making of Dynastic Authority'. *Studies in Indian Politics*, 6(2): 196–208.

Michelutti, Lucia. 2019. 'Circuits of Protection and Extortion: Sovereignty in a Provincial North Indian Town'. In D. Gilmartin, P. Price, and A. E. Ruud (Eds.), *South Asian Sovereignty: The Conundrum of Worldly Power*. Delhi, London: Routledge.

Piliavsky, Anastasia (Ed.). 2014. *Patronage as Politics in South Asia*. Cambridge: Cambridge University Press.

Price, Pamela. 1989. 'Kingly Models in Indian Political Behaviour'. *Asian Survey*, 29(6): 559–572.

Price, Pamela. 1996. *Kingship and Political Practice in Colonial India*. Cambridge: Cambridge University Press.

Robinson, Marguerite. 1988. *Local Politics: The Law of the Fishes: Development through Political Change in Medak District, Andhra Pradesh (South India)*. Delhi: Oxford University Press.

Rollier, Paul. 2016. 'Vies de caïds et justice informelle à Lahore (Pakistan)'. *L'Homme*. Nr 3: 219–220.

Ruud, Arild Engelsen. 2014. 'The Political Bully in Bangladesh'. In Anastasia Piliavsky (Ed.), *Patronage as Politics in South Asia*. Cambridge: Cambridge University Press.

Rudolph, Lloyd I., and Susanne H. Rudolph. 1967. *The Modernity of Tradition: Political Development in India*. Chicago: University of Chicago Press.

Schneider, Jane, and Peter Schneider. 2011. 'The Mafia and Capitalism. An Emerging Paradigm'. *Sociologica*, 2: 1–22.

Singh, B. 2012. 'The Headless Horseman of Central India: Sovereignty at Varying Thresholds of Life'. *Cultural Anthropology*, 27(2): 383–407.

Strathern, M. 2012. 'Gifts Money Cannot Buy'. *Social Anthropology*, 20(4): 397–410.

Vaishnav, M. 2017. *When Crime Pays: Money and Muscle in Indian Politics*. New Haven, CT: Yale University Press.

Von Lampe, K., and P. O. Johansen. 2003, 29 August. 'Criminal Networks and Trust. Paper Presented at the 3rd Annual Meeting of the European Society of Criminology (ESC) Helsinki, Finland'. Retrieved from http://www.organized-crime.de/criminalnetworkstrust.htm.

Witsoe, Jeffrey. 2011. 'Corruption as Power: Caste and the Political Imagination of the Postcolonial State'. *American Ethnologist*, 38(1): 73–85.

Witsoe, J. 2009. 'Territorial Democracy: Caste, Dominance and Electoral Practice in Postcolonial India'. *Political and Legal Anthropology Review*, 32(1): 64–83.

SECTION V

COMMUNITY PROFILES AND REGIONAL TRAJECTORIES

Editors' Introduction

SCHOLARSHIP on caste has steadily moved away from the conventional view that looked at it as a single pan-Indian system. The emerging empirical and historical research has shown how caste-based hierarchies have evolved differently across regions of India. It has further shown that caste is not an internally integrated system as it has been believed to be. Over the past century, different caste communities or *jatis*, and sections within them, have marked out their own trajectories of change and mobility. These processes have also transformed their self-images and identities in diverse ways. This section has chapters on profiles of a selection of caste communities as well as on caste formations in select regions of the subcontinent.

Occupational specialization is commonly viewed as a defining feature of caste. Such a view is not only present in the textbook entries on the Indian caste system but has also influenced a wide range of political agendas, including state policy. However, such a view is largely drawn from the classical orientalist writings on India. Exploring the history of the Chamars of Uttar Pradesh, Ramnarayan Rawat shows how their lived reality radically differs from their popular image. While they are imagined as a community occupied exclusively with leather related activities, in fact a very small proportion of them, only around 4 per cent according to the 1881 Census, engaged in leather work. Rest of them were engaged in diverse forms of occupations, agricultural work being the most common. Such a discrepancy between popular notions and ground realities remains true even today, across caste communities, and region of the subcontinent.

In the following chapter, Haripriya Narasimhan provides an overview of the Brahmins of urban India. Brahmins are perhaps the only caste group that is spoken of as a pan-Indian category. However, they too are characterized by significant diversities among them. They are divided regionally along specific identities, besides their internal hierarchies. The Brahmins of Tamil Nadu, for example, are very different from the neighbouring Namboodiris of Kerala. Not only would they not marry each other, but their material conditions, and their trajectories of economic mobility have also varied significantly. These regional boundaries of Brahmin-ness are carefully protected and reproduced even when they move to a metropolitan city, or even to a foreign country in the global North.

The following chapter by Ujithra Ponniah provides a historical account of the changing trajectory of a business caste, the Aggarwal Banias in Delhi. Her focus is mainly on their mobility trajectories, spatial as well as social. Her chapter shows how while moving from rural hinterlands and small towns of northern India to the city of Delhi, they also moved up, from a middling status group to becoming an 'upper caste' in the urban setting of the capital city. They were able to do so by consolidating networks through setting-up associations and community structures. They also reworked gender relations by actively involving their women in building, what she calls, a 'moral economic universe', in which women acquire agency but only by showing allegiance to the community. Such a 'modern' organization of 'caste as networks in business' enables them to 'inhabit class through caste', without belonging to one or the other completely. Caste and class are thus co-constituted and visibilized through the crafting of subjectivities.

The remaining four chapters focus on regional trajectories of caste. First of these is Zoe E. Headley's chapter on the South Indian state of Tamil Nadu. Her historical anthropology shows how the specificity of caste in the region came to be carved out during the latter half of the medieval period (11th and 13th century), as the influence of merchants and artisans was growing and that new castes (jatis) emerged. These castes got organized around supra-local organizations (the 'nadu' assemblies) and were characterized by 'a horizontal supra-community ordering'. The region has also had the practice of dividing groups into 'left' handed and 'right' handed caste groups, a division that was unique to the Tamil region and remained popular until the early 20th century. Tamil Nadu was also a region that saw the early rise of a counter-vailing religious movement against the authority of the Brahmin, the Bhakti, sometime in the 6th century CE. It was from here that the movement gradually spread to other parts of the subcontinent and emerged as 'an incredible force', which challenged both the authority of the Brahmin as well as 'the hegemony of Sanskrit by expressing itself in the vernacular languages'. The social and political trajectories of caste have also followed a distinctive path during the colonial and post-colonial period, a path structured by the anti-brahmin Dravidian movement.

The next two chapters focus on two 'peripheral' regions of India, Bengal, and Punjab. Having large Muslim population, they were both partitioned at the time of India's independence and ended up becoming border states. While the Indian state of West Bengal continues to have a significant proportion of its population still following Islam, the Indian Punjab saw a near complete exodus of the Muslims and the arrival of Sikh–Hindu population from across the border. Even though both states are seen as regions where caste has been less significant, they have a large proportion of their population listed as Scheduled Caste, Bengal around 24 per cent, and Punjab around 32 per cent. Finally, they both provide enlightening narratives of the subterranean trajectories of caste and of the complex ways in which caste manages to survive, even when it is not so visible, or politically active.

In her chapter on Bengal, Sarbani Bandyopadhyay shows how caste has persisted in the region through its complex intersections with the communal (Muslim–Hindu) and the class questions. In the pre-Partition Bengal, the Hindu communal organizations were successful in turning the 'low' caste mobilizations against the Muslim landlords into a communal question. With the Muslim landlords gone after Partition, the middle-class and upper-caste Bengalis, the Bhadraloks, on the Indian side, were able to marginalize the lower-caste social movements. Near absence of caste-centric violence further gave the impression that caste had been forgotten in Bengal. However, it suddenly re-surfaced during the first decade of the current century when a section of the urban middle-class Dalits began to demand implementation of SC quotas in the government jobs. As she concluded, far from being casteless, West Bengal remains a caste-society, 'inflicting invisible wounds' on those who have historically been on its margins, the Dalits.

The Punjab story is a bit different. Even though here too caste actively intersected with religious identities and communal politics, it has remained visible, politically and socially. The region has also witnessed powerful mobilization of Dalits since the early decades of the 20th century. Even though Sikhism theologically and politically decries caste, it does not deny its existence. Its elite lobbied with the national leadership for the inclusion of their Dalit castes into state list of Scheduled Castes. As Surinder S. Jodhka shows in his chapter, the caste question has remained alive in the state through the past century, even though its dynamics saw significant changes with the success of

Green Revolution technology, which brought about far-reaching changes in the social organization of its rural life. While Punjab has not witnessed a significant political churning, despite the large numbers of SC population, Dalit identities remain active and creatively engaged with questions of dignity and rights. If the grammar of caste relations got transformed along with the growing assertion of Dalit politics and the deep transformations of the agrarian structure, caste nonetheless remains at the heart of Punjabi regimes of inequality.

The final chapter of this section by David Gellner provides an overview of caste in Nepal, another country with a majority Hindu population but that did not experience colonial rule. As he shows in his chapter, 'caste as a fundamental principle of social organization' has been as important in Nepal as in India and it continues to be 'a fact of everyday life' though 'much less constraining than in the past'. However, the nation has a different mode of classifying caste groups, with Khas Aryas at the top, followed by the Madheshis, the Dalits, and the Janajatis. Janajatis are closer to the Scheduled Tribes of India. Sociologically, they are more like ethnic groups, than castes. Unlike India, Nepal also enumerates all the groupings of caste even though it does not have a reservation system for historically marginalized groups. Gellner further argues that it may be theoretically useful to take the Nepal case seriously for a comparison with the Indian situation as 'the Nepali case shows clearly that British colonialism and the schemes of British Orientalists cannot be blamed' for the invention of caste.

Chapters in this section provide clear evidence about the diversities of caste relations and its trajectories on ground, across regions of the subcontinent. In the process, they also question many popular assumptions about caste and its functioning, in the past as well as in the present.

CHAPTER 23

HOW TO WRITE NEW HISTORIES OF CASTE

A Dalit History of Chamars

RAMNARAYAN S. RAWAT

The two largest castes in the most populous state of India, Uttar Pradesh, are Chamars and Brahmans—in that order. According to the 1881 census, Chamars constituted 14.09 per cent (5.3 million), and Brahmans constituted 12.23 per cent (4.6 million) of the total population of the Uttar Pradesh—together forming nearly a quarter of population in the largest province of India. Even today, they comprise two of the largest caste groups in the state. Both of these groups have deeply influenced politics, both in the region and in the national arena. We have rich ethnographies of the Chamars of Uttar Pradesh (UP) but we have no comparable studies of Brahmans in the province. There exists a number of ethnographies of other castes in the region, such as the Yadavs, Jats, and Rajputs. We can note this uncanny absence of the Brahmans in the bibliographical pages of prominent recent studies of caste, which contain long lists of monographs on Chamars but very few, if any, on Brahmans.[1] Given the population of Brahmans in Uttar Pradesh, who occupy a spectrum of occupations within the agrarian regime in northern India well beyond stereotypical priestly occupations, the comparative absence of studies on the Brahmans needs urgent attention. In addition, sections of Brahmans are invested in maintaining hierarchies which have historically offered members of their caste inherited advantage. The burgeoning field of Dalit Studies have documented the critical

---

[1] See the bibliographies, Sumit Guha, 2013. *Beyond Caste: Identity and Power in South Asia, Past and Present* (Leiden: Brill); Surinder Jodhka, 2012. *Caste: Oxford India Short Introductions* (Delhi: Oxford University Press); and Susan Bayly, 1999. *Caste, Society and Politics in India from the Eighteenth Century to the Modern Age* (Cambridge: Cambridge University Press).

role of anti-caste ideology in constituting the Dalit political. In the absence of studies on Brahmans, the theorization of caste has relied on Brahmanical/Hindu sources and analyses of anti-caste Dalit writings and practices, but not on the lived conditions and experiences of Brahmans. Indeed, the study of untouchability has received substantial scholarly attention, emerging as a significant field in the study of caste.[2]

Three main frameworks have dominated the study of caste to explain ideological motivations and practices that have contributed to its persistence.[3] The most familiar model highlights the 'purity and pollution' framework to explain the workings of caste, the dominance of Brahman and Kshatriyas, the subordinate status of Shudra (low-caste), and the stigmatized and excluded status of Untouchable groups in India. The study of South Asian society through this dyadic framework acquired a new sociological and historical depth with the rise of the Indological view of caste, informed by the Hindu theological texts and associated with the colonial knowledge production. In the caste and tribe surveys and in the census, the study of Indian society was organized around the five-fold varna model with Brahmans at the top and 'untouchable' groups at the bottom.

The second framework have challenged the 'purity-pollution' model by bringing perspectives of the 'untouchable' castes. A number of ethnographic studies, beginning in the 1950s and associated with the rise of empirical village studies, sought to challenge this Brahman-centred view by studying Dalit groups such as Chamars in the north to Paraiyars in the south. Scholars such as Kathleen Gough, Gerald Berreman, Joan Mencher, and Robert Deliege, among a large number of scholars, have argued that the 'untouchable' groups have rarely accepted the dominant explanation about their status or the dominant position of Brahmans.[4] The third framework have emphasized the power/kingship model to highlight the non-Kshatriya status of caste groups who had occupied a dominant position within a local caste society. Several historical-anthropological studies, especially by Susan Bayly and Nicholas Dirks, have documented the leading role of the kingship and the political power of rulers over the primary role assigned to Brahmans.[5] These ethnographic studies in the 1970s and 1980s had challenged the structuralist view of caste embodied in Louis Dumont's work.

The 'purity-pollution' framework had the greatest impact in the study of modern South Asia. Building on this viewpoint, the nationalist assumption of the caste underlined the principles of reciprocity and interdependence among various caste groups. M. N. Srinivas's notion of Sanskritization prized elements of consensus and willfully ignored elements of conflicts involving lower castes and Dalit groups, interpreting

---

[2] This is evident in the discussion more centrally in Jodhka, but also in Bayly.

[3] These themes are discussed in Guha, *Beyond Caste*, Jodhka, *Caste*, and Bayly, 2001. *Caste, Society and Politics in India. Castes of Mind: Colonialism and the Making of Modern India* (Princeton, NJ: Princeton University Press). And of course, Susan Bayly, *Caste, Society and Politics*.

[4] Kathleen Gough, 1996. 'Brahman Kinship in a Tamil Village', *American Anthropologist*, New series, vol. 58, no. 5. Gerald Berreman, 1963. *Hindus of the Himalayas* (Berkley: University of California Press). Joan Mencher, 1974. 'The Caste System Upside Down, or The Not-So-Mysterious East', in *Current Anthropology*, vol. 15, no. 4. Robert Deliége, 1997. *The World of the Untouchables: Paraiyars of Tamil Nadu*. Translated by David Phillips. (Delhi: Oxford University Press).

[5] Nicholas Dirks, 2001. *Caste, Society and Politics in India. Castes of Mind: Colonialism and the Making of Modern India* (Princeton, NJ: Princeton University Press); and Susan Bayly, *Caste, Society and Politics*.

them as aspirational imitations of caste Hindu practices.[6] Such a model was coeval with the nationalist civilizational understanding of India because of its inherent cultural unity sustained by the caste system. By highlighting features of consensus and mobility within the caste system, by ignoring the role of caste as a mode of power and marker of domination, the nationalist discourse was able to postulate India as a secular and casteless space. Indeed, the thesis of modernization of caste argued that, 'caste is a traditional system, its central principle is ritual hierarchy and its known structure is vertical'.[7] The nationalist standpoint, reaffirmed by sociological research in independent India, insisted that caste is an anachronism in modern India and the affirmative action a legacy of colonial policy of divide and rule.

In post-colonial India caste entered the public domain in a new, and violent fashion in the 1990 over the Indian government's decision to implement the Mandal Commission report.[8] Caste became extremely conspicuous in urban India during the student protests in the cities and towns, such as Delhi, Mumbai, Kolkata, Hyderabad, and Bengaluru. Several student groups had organized demonstrations, at times violent, in the urban centres in India in the autumn of 1990 against the government.[9] Even sections of the middle-class caste Hindu women protested against the report to express their concern at finding good, well employed, partners.[10] The post-Mandal context created an extraordinary new debate in the public sphere over the political and personal role of caste in modern India. A large section of Indian intelligentsia, including leading sociologists, opposed the use of caste as a category of governmentality because such a policy would further solidify caste divisions in newly independent nation.[11] Emboldened by growing opposition, the progressive mainstream media favoured those who opposed the implementation of the Mandal Commission Report in 1990. Yet, the denial of caste contributed to the emergence of Dalit student organizations in university campuses all over India. This active discussion over caste also challenged the general perception that caste is relic of rural India.

The caste-Hindu student organizations defence of their caste entitlements in the post-Mandal context of 1990s exceeded the frameworks of studying caste. The power/kingship framework, for instance, prioritized the practices of governmentality in colonial and postcolonial India to explain the emergence of caste political activity. Crucial to the model of governmentality was the assumption that colonial state, 'developed [its] understanding of Indian society and the caste system from [the Hindu] scriptural sources'.[12] Bernard Cohn's foundational work have documented the critical role of

[6] Chapter 2 in M. N. Srinivas, 1962. *Caste in Modern India and Other Essays* (Bombay: Media Promoter and Publishers).
[7] K. Satyanarayana, 2014. 'Dalit Reconfiguration of Caste: Representation, Identity and Politics', *Critical Quarterly*, 56(3): 51.
[8] The Report is available at the National Commission on Backward Classes website. http://www.ncbc.nic.in/.
[9] *India Today*, 15 October 1990.
[10] Uma Chakravarti, 2003. *Gendering Caste: Through a Feminist Lens* (Calcutta: Stree), chapter 1.
[11] K. Balagopal, 1990. 'This Anti-Mandal Mania', *Economic and Political Weekly*, 25(40); Gail Omvedt, 1990. '"Twice-Born" Riot against Democracy', *Economic and Political Weekly*, 25(39).
[12] Jodhka, *Caste*, p. 72. For additional discussion, see the Introduction in Susan Bayly, *Caste, Society and Politics in India*, and 'The Birth of Caste' (especially pp. 30–43), in Guha, *Beyond Caste*. Bernard Cohn,

the census in 'classifying and making objective to the Indians themselves their culture and society', and the role of 'caste in terms of social precedence'.[13] Indeed, 'the ethnographic state' emerged in the 1870s when caste became the primary category to classify South Asian society, which created caste and tribe volumes, district gazetteers, and the census.[14] Emphasis on the critical role of the colonial state emerged because of its focus on elite all-India set of sources consisting of census, caste, and tribe survey volumes, and the gazetteers. This elite all-India body of material became a major source of writing a revisionist history by highlighting the role of colonial construction of caste.[15] This revisionist history of caste could not explain caste-Hindu anti-Mandal agitators' motivations to use untouchable occupational stereotypes to humiliate the community. In these demonstrations' the middle class student had set up mock-stalls of shoemakers or pretended to be city-municipal sweepers. More recently, the right-wing Hindu vigilantes are using these stereotypes to launch violent attacks on Dalit.[16]

A new history of caste must recognize its entanglement with modes of power that has ensured caste Hindu privilege and sustained the Brahmanical framework. K. Satyanarayana has described the post-Mandal era of Indian politics in the 1990s as one marked by the 'Dalit politics of caste'.[17] The caste identities played a critical and visible role for the first time in public domain, especially in the towns and cities of India and they were no longer a feature of rural India. Dalit writers and activists sensed the new political in modern India by highlighting the role of social origins of identities in shaping Indian politics. The stereotypical representations of Dalit occupations during these protests, and the subsequent increased violence on Dalits have fundamentally shaped Indian politics, especially the rise of right-wing Hindu nationalist groups. Therefore, it is incumbent on us to rethink existing histories of caste and write new histories of caste by highlighting themes of humiliation, hierarchy, and domination, which were brought to the fore by caste Hindu student opposition to Mandal recommendations.

Writing new histories of caste must entail addressing two critical elements central to its religious and economic role in maintaining hierarchy. Caste had a strong role in the organization of land tenure relations in rural India and studies of caste can profit

1994. 'The Census, Social Structure and Objectification', and 'Notes on the Study of Indian Society and Culture', in *An Anthropologist among the Historians and Other Essays* (Delhi: Oxford University Press).

[13] Cohn, "The Census, Social Structure and Objectification," *Anthropologists among the Historians*, p. 230.

[14] Nicholas Dirks, *Castes of Mind*, pp. 44–45.

[15] Rashmi Pant, 'The Cognitive Status of caste in colonial ethnography: A review of some literature on the North West Provinces and Oudh', *Indian Economic and Social History Review*, 24(2); Sanjay Nigam, 'Disciplining and Policing the "Criminals by Birth": The Making of Colonial Stereotype; The Criminal Tribes and Castes of North India'. Parts 1 and 2. *Indian Economic and Social History Review*; Ronald Inden, 1986. 'Orientalist Constructions of India', *Modern Asian Studies*, 20(3).

[16] *The Hindustan Times*, 27 August 1990. *The Times of India*, 28 August 1990, *The Times of India*, 2 September 1990.

[17] K. Satyanarayana, 2016. 'The Dalit Reconfiguration of Modernity: Citizens and Castes in the Telugu Public Sphere', in Rawat and Satyanarayana (Eds.), *Dalit Studies* (Durham, NC: Duke University Press), p. 166.

by investigating relationship between caste and the organization of land tenures.[18] Caste hierarchy have shaped the structure of rent rates on occupancy and non-occupancy peasants favouring the upper-castes. It has ensured distribution of best quality of landholdings to the privileged caste groups. The very first set of detailed land settlement reports between the 1870s and 1880s in northern India have systematically documented the extensive role of caste in determining revenue and rent rates for land. The settlement officers recognized the powerful role of caste in structuring the mechanics of land control and the appropriation of agrarian surplus which was most detrimental to the 'untouchable' castes. They highlighted castes' critical role in shaping the organization of villages, detailing the organization of jati mohallas in a village and the segregated untouchable villages, replicating the ideals of Manusmriti in the local society.[19] Shahid Amin has argued that John Reid's 1881 Azamgarh settlement report, particularly the agrarian glossary, 'opens a window on to north Indian peasant society and not simply on peasant agriculture'.[20] As I will show in this chapter, an investigation of the settlement reports offers dramatic possibilities for writing a new history of caste, providing material to offer an innovative understanding of Chamars relationship with agrarian life, especially the land tenure regime.[21]

Caste hierarchy, including practices of untouchability, had determined the spatial organization of villages, with dominant castes occupying the main streets, low-castes occupying the periphery, and a segregated Dalit village far removed from the main village. Dalit autobiographies have particularly underlined spatial character of caste in promoting stigma, exclusion as means of domination.[22] A prominent Hindi writer and activist, Mohan Das Namishray has highlighted features of spatial exclusion in his 1995

---

[18] Several studies on agrarian relationships documented the role of caste in land tenure rights, see Vol. 2 of *Cambridge Economic History of India*. Edited by Dharma Kumar. Cambridge: Cambridge University Press, 1982.

[19] Reports by Settlement Officers: Crosthwaite and Neale, *Report of the Settlement of the Etawah District* (Allahabad: North-Western Provinces and Oudh Government Press, 1875), p. 20; E. G. Clark, 1873. *Report on the Revision of Settlement of the Bharaich District, Oudh* (Allahabad: North-Western Provinces and Oudh Government Press), p. 66; Robert G. Currie, 1874. *Report on the Settlement of the Shahjehanpore District* (Allahabad: North-Western Provinces and Oudh Government Press, 1874), p. 61; J. R. Reid, 1881. *Report on the Settlement Operations in the District of Azamgarh* (Allahabad: North-Western Provinces and Oudh Government Press), p. 31; T. E. Smith, 1882. *Report on the Revision of Settlement in the District of Aligarh* (Allahabad: North-Western Provinces and Oudh Government Press), p. 130; F. N. Wright, 1878. *Report of the Settlement of the Cawnpore District* (Allahabad: North-Western Provinces and Oudh Government Press), p. 46.

[20] Shahid Amin ed., 2005. *A Concise Encyclopedia of North Indian Peasant Life. Being a Compilation from the Writings of William Crooke, J.R. Reid, G.A. Grierson* (New Delhi: Manohar), p. 45.

[21] It would an important new dimension to Jodhka and Guha's calls to examine the relationship between caste with political economy. 'Introduction,' in Jodhka (Ed.), *Caste* (2012) 'Introduction,' in Guha, *Beyond Caste* (2013).

[22] Mohan Dass Namishray, 2006. *Apne-Apne Pinjare: Ek Dalit ke Atmakatha* (New Delhi: Vani Prakashan); Omprakas Valmiki, 2003. *Jhutan* (Delhi: Radhakrishna Prakashan); Vasant Moon, 2000. *Growing up Untouchable in India: A Dalit Biography*. (Trans. by Gail Omvedt) (Lanham, MD: Rowman and Littlefield).

autobiography *Apne-Apne Pinjare* (Prisons of Oneself) and the title captures the theme of separate caste *mohallas* (quarters). He narrates the lived experience of Jati *mohallas* (caste quarters) and the stigmatized Dalit *mohallas* in imprisoning people into caste consciousness. Elsewhere I have argued that we need to bring this spatial element more centrally into the discussion of Dalit and Caste studies.[23] Attention to caste-spatial feature of village life is a critical feature of Dalit historiography. B. R. Ambedkar's 1948 study, *The Untouchables*, historicized the powerful presence of separate untouchable villages in India in order to explain the historical origins of Dalit as a segregated community.

New History of Caste: The Chamars, Occupational Stereotype, and the Hindu Imagination

The Hindu ideology of caste was built on associating Dalit groups with polluting occupations to exercise domination and exclusion. The new histories of caste entails unravelling the occupational stereotypes that are critical to the caste-Hindu imagination which draws ideological sustenance from the Varna model in the Hindu scriptures and evident in the organization of neighbourhoods in rural areas, including the location of Hindu temples with its insistence on purity and humiliation. The period between the 1920s and the 1930s in Maharashtra, Kerala, and Uttar Pradesh witnessed several conflicts between caste Hindus and Dalit groups over latter's right to enter Hindu temples. Further, it requires investigating the relationship between Dalits and the land tenure regime, examining the role of caste in shaping new economic opportunities in modern India, and recovering political activism by Dalit groups. The historical and anthropological accounts have provided valuable information on the religious and ritual aspects of caste and untouchability. However, the study of Dalit identities and of activism might benefit from examining the occupational stereotypes associated with 'untouchable' castes.[24] An investigation into the history the occupational stereotypes of Chamars offers us a compelling caste study into the role of dominant narratives. The occupational stereotype has equated leather work with all Chamars, portraying it as a historical fact, which have hindered investigation into new histories of untouchability (and caste). Hence, writing new histories of caste requires examining the historiographical assumptions behind the caste analytical frameworks.

---

[23] Ramnarayan S Rawat, 2013. 'Occupation, Dignity, and Space: The Rise of Dalit Studies', *History Compass*, 11(12). See also Sharika Thiranagama, 2019. 'Respect Your Neighbor as Yourself: Neighborliness, Caste, and Community in South India', *Comparative Studies in Society and History*, 16(2).

[24] I have discussed this point in detail in the 'Introduction', in Rawat, 2011. *Reconsidering Untouchability: Chamars and Dalit History in North India* (Bloomington, IN: Indiana University Press), pp. 6–18.

The occupational stereotype of Dalit castes has provided justification for the continued exploitation, and abuse of Chamars and other untouchable castes. Aspects of humiliation and discrimination were evident during the 1990 autumn of caste Hindu student agitation against the implementation of the Mandal commission report. Student demonstrations in Delhi included burning copies of University degrees and performing caste stereotypical occupations such as shoe repair (associated with Chamars) and street sweeping (associated with Balmikis). Such performances embodied students' sense of caste privilege and entitlement to secular occupations against those that belonged to untouchable groups.[25] The student protestors during their demonstrations imagined 'untouchable' futures for all Hindus in contemporary India. Oppression has also taken the form of falsely accusing Chamars of cattle poisoning for hides and skin and launching violent attacks with complete disregard for evidence. During my doctoral research in Delhi, in 2002, brutal murder of five men from Chamar community in Jhajjar in the nearby state of Haryana made national headlines. The men were dragged from their houses into the street, beaten, and stoned to death.[26] In the last decade cow vigilantes have openly attacked Chamars and brazenly streamed their violence in online media. The public floggings of four Dalit men in the town of Una in south-west Gujarat in July 2016 over suspicions of poisoning and killing cows received national and international news coverage.[27] In both these episodes Chamars were falsely accused of poisoning the cows even though they had purchased old, sick, dying cows sold by Hindu farmers because it was no longer feasible to keep them alive. These types of segregation and occupational stereotyping have provided contexts for humiliating and marginalizing Dalit groups in India.

Allegations of cattle poisoning against Chamars dates back to the nineteenth century and even then occupational stereotype had played a critical role. Yet, these claims were critical to the caste-Hindu mobilization for an assertive Hindu identity formation, and to its agendas of reform. Several studies have documented critical role of the cow protection movement (1892–1893) in the north Indian states of Uttar Pradesh and Bihar and contributed to a violent struggle which successfully promoted a new, aggressive, Hindu identity. Led by the *Gau-rakshini sabhas* (cow-protection associations), the movement directed its ire not only against the Muslims, protesting the sacrifice of cows (*qurbani*) during the Eid festival but also targeted the Chamars and other 'untouchable' communities. The *Gau-rakshini sabhas* portrayed Chamars as criminal using caste occupational stereotype that explained Chamar participation in the leather trade. The *Gau-rakshini sabhas*' sources and associated police reports provided extensive material

---

[25] *The Hindustan Times*, 27 August 1990. *The Times of India*, 28 August 1990, *The Times of India*, 2 September 1990. *The Wire*, 7 July 2017. Damayantee Dhar, 'One Year on, "There Is No Justice" for Una Flogging'.

[26] *Frontline*, 19, no. 23 (9–22 November 2002).

[27] *The Hindustan Times*, 12 July 2016. *The Indian Express*, 20 July 2016.

indicting Chamars of cattle poisoning solely because of their caste background. The cow-protection movement threatened Chamar lives and livelihood. The Hindu middle class in northern India readily shared such views. The Hindi and English language newspapers circulated the popular discourse on Chamars caste-based criminality in the 1890s and these charges continued to appear in the media throughout the early-twentieth century, offering a much longer genealogy for today's cow protection activism against Dalits and Muslims.[28]

Accusations against Chamars first appeared in the 1850s as part of the massive police campaign to contain cattle poisoning. The police actively pursued the crime of cattle poisoning in UP between 1860s and 1880s because of concerns about the local peace and stability and to protect the vibrant leather trade. However, police investigations into the crime of cattle poisoning petered out by the 1890s because the police reports along with those by the judicial department increasingly recognized that in most cases the convictions of Chamars were based primarily on the caste occupational stereotypes of the police constables less on evidence. The police and judicial inquiries provide fascinating information about the critical role of fictitious evidence in criminal convictions of Chamars. Such investigations relied, for example, on Chamar neighbourhoods (Chamrauti or Chamrauli) as the source of crime. The 1855 'Memorandum by Judge M. Smith', explained that village level constables would regularly seize 'the inhabitants of the Chamars quarter, searching their houses', with the objective of extracting a confession.[29] The police investigations, at times, would result in violent infringements against Chamars. The 'report on cattle poisoning', mentions number of such cases between 1850 and 1890.[30] A key body of evidence in police investigations was the use arsenic by Chamars and their confession of the crime. However, as the official police inquiries noted with alarm, the amount of arsenic submitted as evidence would not even kill a mouse. Using arsenic as evidence was convenient because it was easy to find in Chamar households because those involved in the leather trade would typically have a portion in the house to clean freshly flayed skin.[31] The indictment by the local police, who belonged to caste Hindu communities, relied on the association of Chamars with leatherwork. Chamars became easy scapegoats for a crime they rarely committed.

The last four decades of the nineteenth century had witnessed a robust export trade in hides and skins from the northern Indian state of Uttar Pradesh, constituting a quarter of its total export trade to the port of Calcutta. The annual reports of the inland trade of Uttar Pradesh suggests that the export of hides and skins increased from

---

[28] For a detailed discussion, Rawat, *Reconsidering Untouchability*, pp. 48–53.
[29] "Memorandum by M. Smith," p. 694, Cattle Plague Commission, Report of the Commissioners, appendix 4, 'Report on Cattle Poisoning', pp. 690–702.
[30] Ibid.
[31] Extract from the Report of W. Walkers, M. D., Chemical Examiner to Government, North-Western Provinces, 1869, in Cattle Plague Commission, *Report of the Commissioners* (Calcutta: Superintendent of Printing, Government of India, 1871), pp. 726–727. 'Note on Cattle Poisoning by Dodd', Judicial Progs (Home Dept.), no. 34, August 1870, NAI, pp. 3–5. Also, the annual police proceedings of UP government, 1870s–1890s.

20 per cent of annual trade in the 1880s to nearly 30 per cent in the 1890s.[32] Hides and skins was a prominent Indian export commodity from the port of Calcutta. Thus, old and sick cattle had become a valuable commodity and peasant communities had begun to sell cattle to Chamars who were increasingly purchasing cattle to fulfil the great export demand. As the district magistrate of Ghazipur noted, cattle sold at state pounds were 'bought by Chamars' because they were 'animals of small value, barren cows or worthless bullocks abandoned by their owners'.[33] Leather workers and traders became very involved in figuring out ways to procure cattle from the countryside, including in times of calamities arising from foot and mouth diseases, cattle plague, and monsoon floods. The leather trade had become so lucrative that zamindars began to sell Chamar contractors the 'rights' to purchase cattle for a large annual sum.[34] This trade was particularly robust in the Bhojpuri speaking areas of eastern Uttar Pradesh and parts of western districts of Bihar. One of the sharpest observers of rural India and the author of numerous settlement reports, D. M. Stewart in his 1922 'Cesses in Oudh' (Awadh) enquiry reported the emergence of a new *thekadari* (contractorship) system in the 1890s in response to leather trade. The landlords had begun to auction off to Chamar *thekadars* (contractors) the right to collect hides and skins in their respective areas (zamindari).[35]

The dominant Hindu assumption about the status and position of Chamars relationship to leatherwork shaped the colonial policies in creating modern leather industries in Uttar Pradesh. Provincial government monographs published between 1903 and 1904 claimed that leather industries provided Chamars a new opportunity.[36] The 1918 Indian Industrial Commission report summed up the dominant perception about the benefits of leather industries for Chamars, 'who were originally village tanners', and deemed as a ready work force for the leather industry. These considerations played an important role in the selection of Kanpur as the site of the first modern industrial leather factory in northern India. The British government established the first leather factory at the abandoned military harness depot in Kanpur, known locally as the Kila (fort) factory. The factory location was very close to the Chamar neighbourhoods.[37] By the early-twentieth century, Kanpur had emerged as a major leather industry centre in South Asia.

---

[32] *Annual Report of the Inland Trade of North-Western Provinces and Oudh (1880–1901)* (Allahabad: North-Western Provinces and Oudh Government Press, 1890). *Annual Statement of the Sea-Borne Trade and Navigation of the Bengal Presidency (1880–1901)*. (Calcutta: Superintendent of Government Printing, 1880–1900).

[33] The annual police proceedings UP government, Vol. 91, 1889, p. 30, and Vol. 93, 1890, p. 68.

[34] Ibid., annual volumes, 1885–1897.

[35] D. M. Stewart, 'Cesses in Oudh, 1922', Revenue (A) Progs., May 1925, UPSA, pp. 38–39.

[36] Rowland N. L. Chandra, 1904. *Monograph on Tanning and Working in Leather in the Province of Bengal* (Calcutta: Secretariat Press), p. 17; C. G. Chenvix-Trench, 1904. *Monograph on Tanning and Working in Leather in the Madras Province* (Madras: Government Central Press), p. 13; H. G. A. Walton, 1903. *Monography on Tanning and Working in Leather in the United Provinces of Agra and Oudh* (Allahabad: Government Press, United Provinces), pp. 1–2.

[37] File no. 434, 7 December 1866, L/MIL/7/13506, Harness and Saddlery Factories, Cawnpore, Military Department, OIOC, British Library, London.

Yet, the presence of Chamar workers in leather industries had less to do with their association with leatherwork and more with the opportunities available to them. Most Chamar workers in leather industry typically came from agrarian backgrounds, hoping to augment their earnings. A British leather manufacturer from Kanpur in his presentation to the Indian Industrial Commission in 1916 observed that 'Chamars as a rule do not take up leather working as their life-work. Most of them are cultivators and only leave their villages for the leather factories when they wish to earn a little money.'[38] Indeed, in the context of another enquiry on the question of the primary producers of leather in India, J. C. Donaldson, director of industries in Uttar Pradesh in 1930, argued that in India the primary producer of leather, 'is a butcher or a hide merchant or both'. He insisted that a Chamar did 'not necessarily become a primary producer of hides' merely because of his caste, insisting that 'the Chamar is largely an agriculturist like others holding land ranging between 2 and 5 bighas paying Rs 9–51 rental, and having as assets the grain he raises and proceeds he obtains from sale thereof'.[39] Chamars were the largest group of workers in the leather industry in Kanpur but they also occupied a similar position in the textile industry in Kanpur, and the Jute industry in Bengal, and were also the largest group of emigrants from India to plantation colonies of the Empire.[40]

Chamars' relationships with leatherwork and leather trade were far more complicated than the occupational stereotype that reduced all of them as leather workers. The 1923 district industrial survey reports of Uttar Pradesh governments, comprising forty district volumes, have underlined the role of *qasbas,* market towns as centres of leather production and trade in North India, where leather-workers and shoemakers were important fixtures of these towns. The Rae Bareli district report identified the unique feature of the leather trade: 'Specialisation and large scale production at central places and not the principle of self-sufficient economy for every village is the order of the day.'[41] The forty districts surveys in Uttar Pradesh identified two kinds of leather production centres based in the *qasbas*. The first kind were those associated with the finished leather products and especially in the districts of Jhansi, Saharanpur, Lucknow, Jaunpur, Ghazipur, and Rae Bareli.[42] The second kind were those associated with the export

---

[38]

[39] Letter from J. C. Donaldson, Director of Industries, 18 February 1931, Files and Proceedings of the Government, Industries Department, UPSA.

[40] Ranjit Das Gupta, 2001. 'Factory Labour in Eastern India: Sources of Supply, 1855–1946 Some Preliminary Findings', *Indian Economic and Social History Review*, 38(1): 316–317; Brij V. Lal, 2001. *Chalo Jhajji: A Journey through Indenture in Fiji* (Canberra: The Australian National University Press), pp. 106–107.

[41] *Report on the Industrial Survey of the Rae Bareli District, 1923* (Allahabad: Superintendent of Government Press, United Provinces, 1923); B. K. Ghoshal, p. 29.

[42] *Report on the Industrial Survey of the Ghazipur District of the United Provinces* (Allahabad: Superintendent of Government Press, United Provinces, 1923); B. R. Bhatta, *Report on the Industrial Survey of the Jhansi District of the United Provinces*; G. N. Bhargava, *Report on the Industrial Survey of the Lucknow District of the United Provinces*; B. K. Ghoshal, *Report on the Industrial Survey of the Jaunpur District of the United Provinces*; B. R. Bhatta, *Report on the Industrial Survey of the Rae Bareli District*

of raw hides and skins particularly in the districts of Azamgarh, Agra, Kanpur, and Hamirpur. The workforce in these qasbas consisted primarily of workers belonging to Muslim, Chamar, Pasi, Bhangi, and Khatik untouchable communities.[43]

Given the *qasba* character of leather trade, the Muslim merchants, and artisans dominated the industry, especially in the shoe and boot business because they produced all varieties of products. By the 1920s, the Agra shoe industry had emerged as a major retail business in northern India and it employed nearly 25,000 persons out of which 95 per cent were Muslims.[44] The Uttar Pradesh government had sponsored leather training schools in qasbas to better train Chamar workers. Yet, as the government enquiry revealed, the Muslim students comprised more than 90 per cent of pupils in such schools. Out of 45 pupils in Kanpur leather training school, 38 were Muslims in 1919, echoing their pronounced role in leather industry.[45]

The occupational stereotypes relating to the position and status of Chamars have actively prevented the exploration of their relationships with agrarian life. The theory of occupational stereotype has continued to inform the dominant sociological understandings of caste. *The People of India* national series volumes on the Caste, published in 1993, perpetuated the occupational stereotype, arguing that leather work was the age-old work of Chamars, and therefore their name and identity is drawn from the Sanskrit word *Charmakara*.[46] Indeed, very few postcolonial studies have challenged these occupational stereotypes. An exception is *Untouchable Pasts* by Saurabh Dube, which documents Satnami's relationship with land and struggles around it.[47]

The settlement officers, some of whom have written innovative ethnographies of the district's economic and social life, were the first to question occupational stereotype in their writings in 1870s. C. Crosthwaite and W. Neale, authors of the 1875 Etawah settlement report challenged the classification of Chamars as a non-agricultural caste because a 'great many [of them], however, live, entirely by farming, while numbers of those who habitually labour for hire have a few bighas of land as well'.[48] Indeed, the settlement officers of Aligarh, Shahjahanpur, Kanpur, Bahraich, Azamgarh, and Basti found the assumption about caste and occupation unsustainable. J. Hooper wrote in the 1891 Basti settlement report that, 'many Chamars are genuine cultivators, that is to say, they earn their subsistence entirely by farming on their own account, but a great many are ploughmen or labourers depending chiefly for their living on wages'.[49] The settlement

of the United Provinces; B. K. Ghoshal, *Report on the Industrial Survey of the Saharanpur District of the United Provinces*; Mohammed Zia-Ur-Rub.

[43] *Report on the Industrial Survey of the Moradabad District, 1923*, R. Saran, p. 22.
[44] *Report on the Industrial Survey of the Agra District, 1924*, M. Zia-Ur-Rubb, pp. 61–65.
[45] Industries Proceedings, Vol. 23, January–June, 1920, UPSA, p. 43.
[46] Kumar Suresh Singh, 1993. *The Scheduled Castes* (National Series 2: People of India (Delhi: Oxford University Press), p. 301. See also Robert Deliege, 1999. *The Untouchables of India* (New York: Berg), pp. 27–50.
[47] Saurabh Dube, 1998. *Untouchable Pasts: Religion, Identity, and Power among a Central Indian Community, 1780–1950* (Albany: State University of New York Press).
[48] *Report of the Settlement of the Etawah District, 1875*, C. Crosthwait and W. Neale, p. 20.
[49] *Final Report of the Settlement of the Basti District* (Allahabad: North-Western Provinces and Oudh Government Press, 1891); J. Hooper, pp. 28 & 212.

reports capture Chamars' active engagement with agricultural production at various levels, including vigorous social and cultural relationship with the agrarian rhythm. In the 1911 census Chamars emerge primarily as cultivators, with 40 per cent possessing occupancy tenants and non-occupancy tenants, 40 per cent identified as agricultural labourers, 9 per cent as labourers, 4 per cent as industrial workers, 3 per cent as livestock owners and milkmen, and 4 per cent leatherworkers.[50]

The settlement reports highlight the presence of Chamars as one of the more prominent rent-paying caste in the western districts of Uttar Pradesh. Their visible role in this part of the region had to do with the *bhaiyachara* tenure regime because the revenue paying Jat proprietors were actively involved in the cultivation of land and had no qualms in recognizing the tenancy of Chamar cultivators to fulfil stiff revenue obligations. The tenure regimes of the *zamindari* (landed magnates) in the eastern parts and the *taluqdari* (landed aristocracy) in the central parts (or Awadh region) of the state conditioned Chamars ability to acquire occupancy tenancy rights. The *talqudari* tenure regime discriminated against all low-caste tenants by denying them security of tenure provided to them in the bhaiyachara and, to some extent in, zamindari tenures. This unique condition of tenants under the *taluqdari* regime may also account for the only *Kisan Sabha* peasant movement in the state of Uttar Pradesh, in Awadh region, in which the Chamar and the Pasi tenants actively participated. Majority of peasant demonstrators killed in the movement belonged to these two castes.[51] Yet, the untouchable status of Chamars, marked most visibly and notably by their segregated villages, ensured their discrimination at various levels of the agrarian life. For instance, Chamars paid higher rents compared to caste Hindus, they were denied access to the best land for cultivation, and they were required to provide services to elite castes, consisting of *hari* (ploughing, harvesting, and so on) or tributes at various occasions and contexts.[52]

A history of caste that challenges and moves beyond the frameworks of 'purity and pollution', and 'occupational stereotypes', must also question assumptions of 'Sanskritization', or 'social mobility' to explain Dalit activism. These two frameworks posited the goal of attaining the status of caste Hindus for Dalits and other subordinated castes. Gopal Guru has argued that Indian historiography in the last two decades has

---

[50] *Census of India, 1911*, Vol. 15, pt. 2 (Allahabad: Superintendent of Government Press, United Provinces, 1912), pp. 756–762.

[51] For a Dalit point of view see, 'Introduction', in Rawat (Ed.), *Reconsidering Untouchability*, pp. 12–15. For a low-caste peasant point of view see, Gyan Pandey, 1982. 'Peasant Revolt and Indian Nationalism: The Peasant Movement in Awadh, 1919–1921', in Ranajit Guha (Ed.), *Subaltern Studies* (Vol. 1) (Delhi: Oxford University Press); Majid H. Siddiqi, 1978. *Agrarian Unrest in Northern India: The United Provinces, 1918–1922* (Delhi: Vikas Publishers).

[52] D. M. Stewart, 'Cesses in Oudh, 1922', Revenue (A) Progs., May 1925, UPSA, pp. 20–24. 'Rasad Begari Agitation in UP, 1920', File no. 694, box no. 153/1920, GAD, UPSA, pp. 1–3. 'William Crooke's Report on Etah District', in *A Collection of Papers Connected with an Inquiry into the Conditions of Lower Classes of the Population* (Allahabad: North-Western Provinces and Oudh Government Press, 1888), pp. 62–63.

begun to pay critical attention to the question of caste inequality and cultural and political initiatives by Dalits in modern India.[53] Chamar groups addressed questions of caste hierarchy, dignity, and equality from two vantage points. Chamar writers and activists claimed Kshatirya status as 'equal' to that of the dominant Hindu castes in the early-twentieth century. Several books, such as *Shree Chanvar Purana* (1916), *Suryvansh Kshatriya Jaiswar Sabha* (1926), *Jatav Jivan* (1929), and *Yaduvansh ka Aitihas* (1942), claimed equal status similar to other peasant communities such as Yadavs and Kurmis based on Chamars' position in agrarian society.[54] The methodological claims in these histories to a 'clean or pure' historical past was modelled on the mainstream Hindu 'itihasa-purana' practice of history writing. Such widely recognized practices allowed non-Kshatriya and low-caste groups to claim equal status. Chamar groups in western region of Uttar Pradesh established associations and organized meetings to assert a noble or Kshatriya status, adopting vegetarian diet, restricting women from agrarian work, and advocating non-leatherwork.

The Adi-Hindu Mahasabha movement founded primarily by Chamar leaders who articulated an anti-caste inclusive *achut* identity in the 1920s. In public speeches, petitions, and in chapbooks, the Mahasabha activists claimed that all untouchables were *achuts*, untouched and pure, because they were the original inhabitants of India before the arrival of Aryans, progenitors of Hindu religion. The Mahasabha activists highlighted the questions of equality and dignity as critical elements of their struggle, which the Hindu groups were unwilling to acknowledge. In concrete terms, they demanded adequate safeguards for *achuts* in the legislative institutions through separate electorates, proportional representation, and reservations of places in educational institutions and in government service. The Adi-Hindu Mahasabha organized a series of meetings and demonstrations between 1923 and 1940 to mobilize Dalits in northern India. It mobilized Dalit groups in the towns of Uttar Pradesh to welcome the Simon Commission visit in March–April 1928 to discuss questions of caste inequality and affirmative action, at the same time that the Congress had organized a boycott of the delegation. The Mahasabha also played an important role in organizing meetings to send petitions and telegrams to the Round Table Conference in 1931 and 1932. It orchestrated a series of processions in Lucknow, in April 1937, to demand that the newly elected Congress government of Uttar Pradesh provide greater representation for Dalits in the legislative assembly and institute tenancy reforms. In the 1940s, the leaders and activists of the Adi-Hindu Mahasabha founded the Scheduled Castes Federation at the regional and district levels. The remarkable electoral success of the Republican Party in Uttar Pradesh, and more recently of the Bahujan Samaj Party, draws from this earlier half-century of Chamar activism.[55]

---

[53] 'Introduction: Theorizing Humiliation'. In Gopal Guru (Ed.), *Humiliation: Claims and Context* (pp. 1–22). (New Delhi: Oxford University Press, 2009).
[54] This paragraph is based on Chapter four Rawat, *Reconsidering Untouchability*.
[55] Chapter 5, Id.

Conclusion: Towards New Histories of Caste

A new history of caste, with a Dalit perspective, can intervene in the study of caste in two critical fields. First, it must address the persistence of caste as an institution that emphasizes hierarchy, stigma, and exclusion.— The anti-Mandal agitation led by urban caste Hindu groups in the autumn of 1990 have starkly illuminated the entailment of caste with power, privilege, and hierarchy. Dalit student associations emerged in the 1990s to defend the principles of equality and dignity guaranteed in the Indian constitution and support policies of affirmative action, advanced by the Mandal Commission report. Further, it must clarify the intricate role of caste in shaping ethical motivations that have informed the actions of caste Hindu actors, in this case the students. It is for these reasons, we need new caste histories of Brahmans in north India. Indeed, the new histories caste focusing on the 'untouchable' castes have illuminated the engaged relationship between Dalit political activism and caste in late colonial India, transforming our understanding of the nationalist project. In the last decade, the emerging field of Dalit Studies have invigorated the study of caste by disentangling it from earlier focus on 'purity and pollution' and recovering a history of Dalit activism.

Second, writing a new history of caste require that we prioritize the land tenure regimes and the spatial organization of villages because caste hierarchy had deeply implicated the workings of these two institutions. This must include attention to the institutions of land tenure rights, the caste-spatial organization of village life, and the organization of religious and devotional practices. Instead of relying on traditional sources of caste history such as, the census and provincial level caste and tribe volumes, the new histories of caste must engage with other types of sources. These may include the settlement reports, the rent and revenue reports, and the tenancy rights reports which contain valuable information on the institution of caste. An emphasis on these body of sources takes us beyond 'occupational stereotype' and 'purity and pollution' frameworks and provide a 'bottom up' view of caste by offering its intrinsic role in shaping the political economy of rural life. If caste determines land tenure rights, revenue and rent rates, privileges and entitlements of the dominant castes, and even the spatial organization of villages, then we must surely recognize it an as an administrative category because of its central role in the built environment of rural village life. Redefining our relationship with sources by drawing from more local documents like district settlement reports, land tenure enquiries, and reports on local trade and economic conditions—can provide materials to understand the regime of caste hierarchy. A new history of caste must highlight the critical role of spatial organization of rural, and even urban, lived conditions, identifying ways that caste geography engages with the varna model/ideal. The commitment to the working of this model is independent of the presence of Brahmans in positions of power, yet equally embraced by locally dominant castes and lower caste groups with stakes in maintaining their local authority.

CHAPTER 24

THE BRAHMINS OF URBAN INDIA

HARIPRIYA NARASIMHAN

Dharwad doesn't agree with Vasudevachaar these days. The pace and the way of life that is fast moving away from traditional customs confuses him.
—Shrinivas Vaidya, *A Handful of Sesame* (2018, p. 200)

INTRODUCTION

Sometime in 1942, Vasudevachaar, the protagonist of the Kannada novel 'A Handful of Sesame', comes to his nephew Keshav's house in Dharwad, and misses the slow and steady pace of life in Navalgund, where he knew himself and his position in the village life. Dharwad was too fast for his taste. He even bemoans that the 'new waters' of Dharwad does not suit him (p. 220). The Kannada novel translated in English chronicles the life of the ayurvedic physician Vasudevachaar and his extended family, from the late 19th century till Independence. From the village of Navalgund, the family slowly move to Dharwad and further to Bombay. For a deeply religious and orthodox man, managing a large family with just his medical practice, the intercaste marriage of his descendants, granddaughters riding a bicycle, children donning Gandhi caps, was tumultuous to say the least. He wished he could pass his life in his native village, rather than stay in a city that he simply did not understand. In some ways, Vasudevachaar voices the bewilderment of the urban for the Brahmin in India, which continues well into the 21st century.

This chapter highlights some facets of this 'bewilderment', for want of a better word, as seen through the eyes of ethnographers who studied Brahmin communities in urban India. But before doing that, there is a need to clarify why the focus is on the 'urban' Brahmin. What has the 'urban' got to do with the 'Brahmin'? What has the urban got to do with caste in general? Isn't the popular assumption the one where the 'urban' collapses inequalities such as caste and renders them unnecessary for a city living? We know from numerous scholarly works on contemporary India, and indeed on urban areas outside that inequalities and differences do not just vanish into the abyss because the city demands them to be. Rather, in a strange way, the city might exacerbate these differences even more. City living is fraught with various tensions amongst which caste is a prescient one in the Indian scenario. Setha Low (1996) writing on the city points out how 'everyday practice' might reveal 'the linkages of macroprocesses with the texture and fabric of human experience' (Low, 1996, p. 384). Taking this forward, I look at how one might conjure up the image of an urban Brahmin in 21st century, by looking at some recent ethnographic works exploring issues of caste and class. Four major themes crop up—a yearning sense of nostalgia for the bygone days by the young, gendering of space and movement, aspiration for education and jobs tempered by a feeling of 'castelessness', and creative approaches to continuity with respect to religion.

It's difficult to write about Brahmins in urban India as a homogeneous community. Most of the recent works are from southern India, where Brahmins faced antagonism through various reform movements and anti-brahmanical sentiment, which was less pronounced in the rest of the country. Even so, urban way of living renders a number of challenges common to Brahmins everywhere, and that will be the focus of this chapter.

The story of Brahmins in India has been reasonably well documented in anthropology and hence this paper will not go into detail in that direction. Instead, it will look at the more recent works on Brahmins in India, and highlight how the 'urban' intervenes as a significant marker in the story of the Brahmins in the contemporary. Studies by Bairy (2009), Béteille (1996), Fuller (1984, 2003), Gough (1981), Hancock (1999), Khare (1971), Madan (1989), Parry (1994), and Ulrich (1987) have richly documented the varied trajectories of Brahmin lives in India. Many of them have located their work in rural India. In this chapter, I will revisit the works pertinent to the discussion on urban Brahmins. More recently, scholars like Srinivas (2018) and Gallo (2018) have brought into focus the urban as well as the Brahmin, and the negotiations with modernity and globalization. Fuller and Narasimhan (2014) in their study of Tamil Brahmans reinforce the point about the caste group strongly emphasizing middle class identity so much so that it's become a 'middle class caste' (2014, p. 17). A review of research on Brahmins (2014, pp. 212–237) shows that education, migration to urban areas and employment in government jobs were the enablers in becoming middle class.

'Balance' between modernity and 'tradition' has been a key theme for Brahmins as is evidenced by Bengali and Maharastrian Brahmin public discourse during the colonial times debating the difficulty in achieving it. This debate played out in the public domain through reform movements as well as through popular culture (Fuller and Narasimhan, 2014, pp. 212–216). This was not common amongst all Brahman communities, like Tamils and Telugus, who were not so preoccupied with these questions. A new middle class did arise, mainly due to occupations in the colonial administration. In responding to the debate on modernity, education (and its connection to employment), and marriage reforms were central. There was not so much anxiety in the southern states, unlike the Bengali Bhadralok or the Maharastrian Brahmins.[1] Even within southern India, while Tamil and Telugu Brahmins moved to urban areas and got their sons educated in English, and jobs in the British administration, the Namboodri Brahmins rejected such opportunities, being seen as 'backward' in contrast (Gallo, 2017). Brahmin communities have therefore responded to changes in different ways. My aim here is to seek the connecting thread between the classical works mentioned earlier, and the more current sociological work coming out, and what that might tell us about what urban does to Brahmins, and vice-versa.

Gender

We will start with gendering the Brahmin movements in the urban sphere. Norms of purity and pollution are an inflection point in urban living. In the 1980s Hancock (1999) documented Smarta women of Chennai (then Madras) trying to organize festivals like Navaratri Golu, and at the same time confirm 'transmission of modernity by rationalized home management and by undergoing (and enacting) educational and social reform' (Hancock, 1999, p. 244). She profiled many women who ensured functioning of temples, organizing of chanting in those spaces, and even becoming gurus, following the orthodox guru Shankaracharya.

Her epilogue marks the 'commercialization' of Golu by local newspapers. Prizes are awarded for the best display, and photos are featured in the papers along with that of the lady organizing them. The nine-day Navratri is no small affair. It involves planning and coordination between relatives, friends, and neighbours, to ensure every 'eligible' woman (*sumangali*, the auspiciously married one) receives '*thamboolam*' (betel leaves and nut) from every other woman of similar stature. The dolls have to be placed in the proper order, guests have to be received, and boiled lentils (*sundal*), and other gifts handed over, while at the same time, ordering girl children of the house to invite other women in the neighbourhood. Mornings are kept aside to visit close relatives. Office going women, from the 1990s onwards, would send postcards to their kins mentioning a specific date to collect thamboolam, so as to not miss work. Now, it is all done on WhatsApp. The Tamil Brahmin diaspora, especially in the US, has taken this festival to another level, causing their relatives back in Chennai to complain about how one has to go to New York to see what a Golu display should actually look like.

'Achara', the cornerstone of Brahman observance of rules and regulations is no longer possible to be observed in cities, especially in smaller apartments (Srinivas, 2018, p. 94). Menstruation is a major problem for achara. As I have noted elsewhere about the problems in observing menstrual pollution amongst Tamil Brahmins in Chennai

---

[1] Also see Sathaye (2015) on Maharashtrian Brahmins and reform (2015, pp. 214–216).

(Narasimhan, 2011), modern times force several twists and turns around menstruation. A menstruating woman has to remain in seclusion for the first three days, and can enter the household (i.e. the kitchen) only after a ritual bath on the fourth day. At least the village homes have multiple sections for segregation. What are women supposed to do in small flats in Chennai, or in Mumbai, where flats are even smaller? There is a lot of 'adjustment' that happens, as in the segregated space being reinterpreted to mean anything from a whole room to a corner of a hall, to all of the house excluding kitchen. Where the woman has to enter the kitchen to take charge of cooking, then the door of the 'god's room' (or shelf) is closed. In the age of Zomato and Swiggy, it is quite possible that a woman can observe segregation, or not, without worrying about cooking for her family. Nonetheless, a Brahmin woman would still be hard pressed to manage the ritual space of her home during menstruation, particularly during festivals and life cycle ceremonies. Srimathy, a yoga teacher profiled by journalist Biswanath Ghosh (2012) finds living in Chennai with her sister's family more traditional (observing menstrual pollution) than in small town Kumbakonam where the liberal father gave her more freedom (Ghosh, 2012, p. 71). Urban need not always mean liberal.

The constraints on movement are also about disciplining the female body. Tulasi Srinivas (2018) sees the space of the temple as a landscape where her own gender and caste identities create tensions, for herself, and for regular temple goers. By wearing a kurta and not a sari, and in not always standing in the women's queue at the temple, she was challenging unspoken, but well established norms. The temple space eventually taught her 'what it means to be a Brahmin middle-class woman' (Srinivas, 2018, p. 19). Her attire invited criticism and comments, which would be familiar to many female ethnographers who have worked in India. Not wearing jewellery, hair untied, not being adorned with *mangalsutra* (the sign of marriage), all of these marked Srinivas not just as inappropriately dressed for the setting, but as she remarks, 'un-Brahmin-Brahmin and unwomanly-woman' (2018, p. 21). She lacked *najuka* (2018, p. 47) or 'finesse'. Brahmin women (and men) brought up in households less observant about orthodoxy and rituals, living abroad were in some sense estranged from their native 'trifold' (2018, p. 21). Such chastening has its effect as seen in subsequent visits to the temple where Srinivas is dressed in a sari, and wearing the right amount of jewellery needed to mark a woman as married.

Another area where gendering of caste ideas amongst Brahmins has been studied is on the topic of marriage. While 'companionate marriage' has emerged as a neat arrangement linking individual desires and family priorities (see Fuller and Narasimhan, 2014, pp. 138–143), it is not without critique, especially from parents of the 'boys'. An interesting scene Ghosh (2012) depicts in his book on Chennai is of a 'swayamvaram' or a matrimonial meeting. Families of prospective grooms and brides gather to exchange 'biodata' and horoscopes and find the best possible partners. Ghosh follows two families as they negotiate this exercise and finds out that the bride earning more than the groom is a downer. The prospective groom's cousin tells Ghosh that now girls' families have started placing more demands (Ghosh, 2012, p. 67).

Religion

How has the urban Brahmin fared when it comes to religion and ritual? Krishna Bhattar, one of the main characters in the eloquent ethnography by Srinivas on Bengaluru voices both 'bewilderment' and 'wounded sadness' at the present (Srinivas, 2018, p. 11). The author also feels a sense of nostalgia for the city where 'fracture' is a dominant sense. This sense of fracture is strongly tied to the neoliberal times that India has gone through since 1991, where people feel 'being on the edge' (2018, p. 11).

The Brahmin is defined in classical ethnographies as one who is very religious and observant. Fuller's work on the Adisaiva priests of Madurai and Parry's discussion of the Mahabrahmans of Varanasi are, just to mention two, well known in the sociological literature of India. A more recent addition is that of Datta (2016), on Kashmiri Pandits. The Kashmiri Pandits have had to endure violence and what they see as erasure of memory and experience, after their exodus in 1990. As the only Hindu caste present in a place where the majority is Muslim, Kashmiri Pandits have been seen for a long time as 'elites' (Datta, 2016, p. 133). With a strong presence in the administration of the state, both pre-colonial and after Independence, the Pandits were seen as having usurped the powers of the majority community, and being cunning in their ways. The largest exodus of the Kashmiri Pandits out of the valley to Jammu in 1990 has led to them being refuges inside the country, a rather unique situation. Therefore, a lot of their outpourings are about fracture or 'loss'—of heritage, in this case, such as rituals and temples.

For instance, major shrines for the Pandit community have been recreated in Jammu. But people still feel that it does not have the same resonance as the original ones which are in Kashmir. Pandits did eventually become 'attuned' to the new shrine in Jammu, as years went by. Initially dismissed as a 'Xerox copy' (Datta, 2019, p. 282), the temple has slowly begun to seep into the consciousness of the Pandits. Ethnographic attention also brings out the fact that even if people complain that the replica of the temple does not contain the 'spiritual' strength of the former, it still allows for them to be used as a place for recreation (2019, p. 283).

The lamenting of 'loss of culture' (Datta, 2016, p. 140) is materialized in change of offerings to temple deities, for instance. Instead of meat offerings that were mandatory in the original shrine of Sharika Mata at Hari Parbat, in the replica, devotees only offer vegetarian items so as to not offend the locals. Such changes deeply mark not only the migration of Kashmiri Pandits from the valley, but also larger transformations. Change in marriage practices is another such issue. Marrying people outside the community also marks a 'loss' of some sort (2018, p. 141), as does change in marriage rituals and practices.

Saavala (2010) narrates a similar incident in Hyderabad, far away from Jammu, where the real temple, and replica of an idol have similar resonance. A group of young people, men, and women, go to Ramoji film city, on the outskirts of Hyderabad. Built in 1999 on a massive space, the film city is equipped to handle all requirements of a film or television shoot, including different kinds of 'settings', be it a bus top, a restaurant, a village, or a temple. People come from Hyderabad and outside to see this representation of the global in Hyderabad city. Saavala documents the layout of the place, and consumption practices of the middle class, or wannabe classes. Her friends, however, were disenchanted. They then went to another temple close by, not run by Brahmins, with another young Brahmin man Arun. There too, Mohan expressed his displeasure by not really worshipping the deities but instead doing meditation. For Arun, it didn't matter though. The girls had observed all the rules about visiting temple—had a bath, wore clean, washed clothes, and yet Mohan decided not to worship along with them. This former IT employee who had lived abroad just didn't feel the temple holy enough.

In later chapters, Saavala documents religious practices of young people in Hyderabad. Ayyappan, a Hindu deity whose main temple is located in Sabarimala in Kerala is extremely popular in the Telugu states, particularly amongst the youth. Men take a vow of celibacy for about forty-one days, before visiting the temple by foot. Called 'swami', they can be seen in blue, black, or orange dhotis, with upper chest uncovered, unshaven, and eating sparse meals after bath twice a day, and going to temples. Men are supposed to immerse themselves in religious thoughts and practices. Movies, and non-devotional gatherings are prohibited during this time. One Brahmin man who undertook pilgrimage to Sabarimala recounted his fascination with the rigor of the whole exercise and looks forward to keeping the *vratam*. He also mentioned that his father did not maintain Ayyapa vratam. A number of people pointed to the scholar that their religious beliefs were different from that of their parents (2010, pp. 160–161). Young people preferred more community-based, devotional movements rather than orthodox, Sanskrit rituals that required 'purity' of their homes. It is also for this reason that urban Brahmins, as well as people from other caste groups increasingly follow devotional movements as has been charted by Warrier (2005). One can also see this religiosity played out increasingly in the social media and on television, in the following visible amongst self-claimed gurus like Sadhguru and Sri Sri Ravishankar. Suave, speaking in English, comfortable with using analogies understood by today's youth, these men attract the youth especially from urban areas, many of whom are upper caste as well, though not just Brahmin.[2]

'Religion' has moved from rituals conducted in the privacy of the home to the public space of a temple or a bhajan group or a satsang congregation.[3] In apartments that have come up along the IT corridor in the southern cities of Hyderabad, Chennai, and Bengaluru, one can often see public gatherings for festivals which not so long ago were entirely observed at home, amongst very close family members. However, bringing devotees into the temple and obtaining their support is no easy task, as the priests Dandu Sastri and Krishna Bhattar know very well (Srinivas, 2018). They come up with many 'cutting edge' innovations (2018, p. 142) to keep devotees interested. In the techno

---

[2] Note the absence of similar, female global gurus except for Mata Amritanandamayi, documented by Warrier.

[3] Members of bhajan groups and satsangs gather to sing songs and chant names of Hindu deities. These are not exclusively urban, but more common and popular in urban areas, particularly among women. For more, see Nicole Wilson (2015)

age, that meant taking help from technology to give some kind of 'shock and awe' to the followers. Dandu Sastri for instance, came up with the idea of hiring a helicopter to shower petals from the sky on a newly consecrated Devi shrine in his temple (2018, pp. 143–144), or to take help from IT engineer devotees to light up a mechanical Devi idol during Navratri to give viewers an almost graphic experience of *Mahisashura Vadam* (the killing of Mahisasura) (2018, p. 139).[4] In that sense, priests have not 'failed to come to terms with the modern world' (Fuller, 1984, p. 165).

Fuller (1984) does point out the demoralization that had set in amongst priests in Tamil Nadu back in the 1970s, who did not see any prospects for upward mobility for their sons in that occupation. Belonging to groups considered lower in Brahmin hierarchy, such as Mahabrahman (Parry, 1994), or Adisaiva (Fuller, 1984), priests did not necessarily enjoy status of the wealthier, urban, educated, middle class, salaried brahmins. However, things are certainly changing for priests in urban areas, but whether this is pan-Indian remains to be seen. In Bengaluru, Srinivas documents the ways in which the urban middle-class, largely Brahmanical neighbourhood of Malleswaram learns 'to act, look and sound middle class through status-based practices' (2018, p. 14), part of which is about performing temple rituals. Through the eyes of priests of two temples in the area, who she has been in touch with for nearly two decades, Srinivas traces their move from being small neighbourhood temples to those with 'computer lamps' and the like (2018, p. 17). These priests are an exception. Generally, priests are seen as 'morally corrupt', embodied in their 'fat' bodies (2018, pp. 133–136), too greedy, and trying to juggle too many commitments while actually knowing little and less interested in pursuing knowledge. The priest riding fast on a two wheeler with a mobile clipped to his ear is an often-derided figure in the public discourse. But Srinivas also shows what priests and temples have come to mean for urban religiosities to exist.

The Hindu diaspora is instrumental in keeping these religiosities going as sites of consumption. Temples are present online, in Facebook, and perhaps even Instagram. Devotees, both local and long distance, express their attachment through 'like's on the pages when photos of the latest events in the temple are uploaded (Srinivas, 2018, pp. 162–163). There are 'virtual seva' of the rituals performed, available on videos to be seen at times convenient for the worshippers, and to imbibe the 'blessings' virtually. In fact, the author describes a ritual done on her own family's behalf in the temple in Bengaluru and watched by her and her family members in USA, live, through facetime on Ipad (2018, pp. 164–167). Savvy priests have creatively utilized technological developments to keep their demanding clientele engaged with the goings-on in the temples. Srinivas and her family in USA saw the priests performing various rituals in the Bengaluru temple for their welfare. It is also a sociological fact that religiosity has increased in the post-liberalization India. Temples in urban areas are doing bigger and costlier rituals. The situation might not be the same in rural areas. However, discerning priests like Dandu

---

[4] Mahisasura is the buffalo faced demon whose slaughter is symbolic of the ego of the human overcome by the power of the divine.

Sastry are not impressed. He feels that all this interest in pujas and rituals are only as 'insurance' to protect the middle-class urban residents from adverse consequences (2018, p. 187). Inauspicious times like Rahukala have the same value as the auspicious times in the world run by neoliberal logic. It's only 'insurance' like temple rituals that can safeguard one in such times, so goes the argument.

Education and Employment

Brahmin communities would rather talk about 'class' than 'caste'. In particular, they identify themselves as 'middle class'. Employment and education are key in this role-playing. Many Kashmiri Pandits today run businesses in Delhi and elsewhere but still prefer jobs in state administration. This feeling is exemplified in the words of one migrant thus—'we have lost everything. And now our children will have to do *mazdoori*' (Datta, 2016, p. 145). This is very telling in the story Datta mentions, of a girl from a poorer Pandit family who was learning tailoring. Such jobs were seen as demeaning, manual labour (mazdoori) in earlier times. But this kind of nostalgia can be a 'burden' as well for poorer families, as in the case of two young men who would rather be unemployed than work as labourers repairing buses (Datta, 2016, p. 151). While not all Pandits belonged to the same class background, their past elite status in Kashmir meant that even adversity would not force a woman to go for occupation such as tailoring. But times have changed, with the loss of what the community held close in the past.

Employment in administration meant moving to urban areas. While Tamil Brahmins capitalized on this move, educating themselves in the city colleges and then working in colonial administration, Namboodri Brahmins in neighbouring Kerala did not, and were seen as 'backward'. In order to overcome this image, which was also because of strict rules of marriage,[5] lack of literacy, lack of participation in the colonial government, restrictions on women, middle classness was seen as essential (Gallo, 2017, p. 248). This middleclassness was achieved by a long fight by the younger generation of the Namboodris for marriages with Nair women, and in other castes to be recognized, by migrating to cities like Bombay and Madras (as they were called then) for jobs, and in building houses which incorporate both the Tharavad style and modern amenities. It was a long road to shed the tag of backwardness, and extremely painful for many Namboodri men and women whose relationships with other caste members were rejected, and families ostracized. Class markers do not mean though that caste has receded as a signifier. As one Pandit man remarked to Datta, 'Brahmins have become Sudras' by migrating from Kashmir to Jammu, and becoming just one amongst many castes in the predominantly Hindu region (Datta, 2016, p. 147). Younger Namboodri

---

[5] See Gallo (2017, pp. 30–31) for details on Namboodri forms of marriage and close relations with Nairs.

men active in organizations like the Yoga Kshema Sabha see the struggles of their ancestors as a loss of 'old customs' (Gallo, 2017, p. 247).

Another key issue for Brahmins is education. Recent work on caste and its connections to education foreground the sense of 'castelessness' that envelops discussions of caste in urban spheres, the kind of 'we don't talk about caste' disclaimer that Gilbertson (2017) points out in Hyderabad. Talking to parents, teachers, and students in two schools of Hyderabad, and in two neighbourhoods, Gilbertson found that 'cosmopolitan castelessness', a denial of 'intimate connections between caste and class' (Gilbertson, 2017, p. 100) was pervasive. Her informants talked about 'persistent denial of caste's relevance in contemporary public life' (2018, p. 100). Conversations about caste in urban India, in professional settings, and in private discussions, are almost filled with a sort of disdain for even thinking about caste. It is as if someone has committed an inexcusable faux pas in asking about or talking about caste.

This denial often expresses itself in subtle forms. Brahmin teachers in one elite school felt that they were 'natural teachers' because of their caste (Gilbertson, 2018, p. 101). 'Regardless of the actual significance of caste in daily life, it was important in positioning oneself as middle class to declare that caste is irrelevant' (Gilbertson, 2018, p. 104). Reservations of jobs in government and colleges were a particularly vexing topic where parents and teachers argued that 'merit' should be given more importance. With a well-developed IT industry, the 'software' culture in Hyderabad is projected as evidence for the non-utility of caste and focus on merit (2018, p. 105).

Subramaniam (2015) demystifies this myth of 'merit' in her detailed study of the 'social life of caste' in elite higher education institutions like the IITs. In pitting the debate about castelessness and merit, she insists that we see this as 'responses to subaltern assertion' (Subramaniam, 2015, p. 293). Since 'reservation' as affirmative action is known in India is a volatile topic in relation to education, the notion of 'merit' is tied into the notion of being without caste, and only with talent, which those coming under 'general' category presumably possess. Graduates in premier institutions like IITs seem to have a particular disdain for jobs in government and set their sights on going abroad (Subramaniam, 2015, p. 301).

Urban Spaces

Ghosh (2012) sees the city of Chennai as 'worship(ing) tradition' (Ghosh, 2012, p. 61). For an outsider like Ghosh, Chennai is a 'brahmin motif'. A (Tamil) Brahmin today may be similar to the British monarch in that it's all 'regalia, no power' (Ghosh, 2012, p. 65) but Brahmanical ideologies have not given way in the globalized world, as can be seen in the gated communities. These secluded housing colonies by another name have become a symbol of the post-liberalization, IT industry-driven visions of the contemporary. They are the evidence of 'development' currently sweeping urban India. Does caste exist in these supposedly modern, or post-modern constructions?

In Gurugram (known more commonly as Gurgaon), the landscape is littered with high rise exclusive enclaves. Quoting Upadhya's work on similar housing areas in Bengaluru (Upadhya, 2008), Srivastava mentions the largely upper-caste profile of the inhabitants in such places (Srivastava, 2015, p. 177). There the quandary was, 'how to explicitly broach caste in the condominium, a space putatively aligned to all those processes that speak of lives beyond such affiliations?' (2015, p. 184). Sabitha, a resident, occupied an almost loner lifestyle in the condo. Originally from south India and married to a European, she could not identify herself with largely Hindi-speaking women who were into 'satsangs and karva chauth' (2015, p. 185). Tales of a separate 'servants' lift', of domestic helps being chased through the apartment by their female employers, being asked to sleep in the foyer at night, abounded. Everyone understood and kept their space.

In rapidly globalizing Bengaluru, independent apartments in sleepy suburbs like Malleswaram gave way to massive high rises, with amenities like swimming pool, guarded entry, elevators, etc. Along with obsession for technology, residents engaged with rituals, and traditions that could secure them an obstacle-free future. Vaastu, the supposed science of architecture was important in ensuring this requirement (Srinivas, 2018, p. 52). Many developers mention in their advertisements about apartments being 'vaastu compliant'. Knowledge of the vedic texts allowed these 'vasstu consultants', who may not necessarily be Brahmin, to suggest changes to the homes in order to restore 'premodern harmoniousness' by bringing in good 'vibrations' (2018, p. 52). Just like a human body, the house also has problems that needs cure and the vaastu consultant offers just that, becoming some kind of a 'space doctor' (2018, p. 54). Modernity brings along worries—financial, physical, and emotional—for which some indigenous correction is mandatory. Vaastu fits the bill neatly for the middle class Bangaloreans, who may also be upper caste, since it is seen as 'science' (2018, p. 53).

Nostalgia

Revival of 'native' places, be it towns or villages, is an ongoing task amongst Brahmans settled in urban areas, and in the diaspora. There is a certain nostalgia for the time when Brahmans occupied the top positions in the village hierarchy. Gallo's work on the Namboodris of Kerala illustrates it evocatively. Namboodris were seen as 'deyvam' (gods or deities) till 19th century (Gallo, 2017, p. 38). In the early 20th century, they were also seen as unwilling to participate in building a modern state, refusing education, and clinging on to kinship practices making them almost anthropological specimens.

The Yoga Kshema Sabha (YKS) which played a pivotal role in Namboodri society during the 1920s, led by stalwarts like E. M. S. Namboodripad, has resurrected itself in the areas near Kochi. Mostly followed by young men, the new YKS is aimed at bringing back the glory days of the community. Lamenting on the loss of crucial elements of identity for the Namboodris, one informant said that 'past YKS people were great in destroying our old customs, to challenge the backwardness of our community ... but eventually they were not able to preserve our history ... they were quite heedless of rituals, religion ...' (Gallo, 2017, p. 247). Two aspects of Namboodri transformation come in handy for the new YKS—migration, and increasing middle-class identity. Through the internet, a vast network is created amongst Namboodris who are keen on revival of the past glory. YKS thus successfully makes 'a case for their existence' (Bairy, 2009, p. 92).

Conversation between two Namboodri men with diverse opinions shows how pervasive this sense of nostalgia for the glorious past is, particularly among youth. Krishnan, a young man who sobbed on taking leave from village and family elders, asked for Gallo to be seated away from him so that he is not polluted by touch, and his cousin Sanjay who is very sceptical reveals the fault lines in this desire for resurrection of the past (pp. 258–261). This selective memory obfuscates the huge amount of literature available in the public domain about the hardships faced by Namboodris in the past. Men who wanted to recognize their Nair partners as wives and give legitimate recognition to children were ostracized. Women married as children to old men and widowed young were condemned to a life inside the *illam*, till they fought back for rights to education, remarriage. These facts are in dire need of forgetting for the younger generation to form networks across cities and countries.

This 'going back to the roots' endeavour uses genealogy as a participatory tool. Smart digital technologies only exacerbate this attempt, as will be obvious to anyone who has recently been made part of any number of WhatsApp groups. But this is emotionally tense for those who have memories of past relationships that ended up being treated badly (excommunicated, ostracized, denied inheritance). The family trees of the present are expected to have neat arranged marriages and not the complicated relationships Namboodris had in the past. Gallo calls this 'virgin cosmopolitanism' (2017, p. 267).

Similar attempts in connecting to lineage members across the world and bringing the 'native village' into limelight is seen among Tamil Brahmans as well. New digital technologies are very crucial in enabling this process.

Conclusion

The urban Brahmin's sense of the world might be summed up in 'bewilderment and wounded sadness of the contemporary everyday' (Srinivas, 2018, p. 11). Loss of prestige, status, heritage, memory, time, space, ritual ... the Brahmans see as a huge sense of loss with a way of life that they feel they had for a long time. The 20th-century and early 21st-century Brahmin of urban India is therefore living in the 'loss' era. The sense of loss is not just directed to those 'others' who challenged Brahmanical hegemony, but also within, at the youth, at women, and at attempts to question past norms.

The four major issues highlighted here suggest that Brahmins are also creatively reinventing traditions, rituals, and religion itself, using technology to keep the spectacular intact. Technology also comes in handy to keep in touch, be it with families back home, or with villages inhabited long back. Marriage is still largely arranged though women have more say. Women are still in charge of performing rituals at home, though there is gap in the literature about what men think about doing (or not doing) life cycle rituals. The urban does complicate the picture for Brahmins heavily, making it difficult to talk about caste outside, or in maintaining lines of purity and pollution inside the home. However, a belief in living in a 'casteless' world makes it possible to gloss over the existence of inequality. Castelessness is most visible in talking about class and particularly the middle class. It's here that Brahmins, those living in urban areas especially, have arrived at to talk about caste ideologies in subtle ways. 'Middle class' is like a pseudonym, subsumed under which are notions of purity and pollution. One has to only scratch the surface about 'vegetarian food' in urban residential enclaves to understand this point. The most recent work on urban Brahmins suggests that a yearning for the past is a strong undercurrent in the urban brahmin's outlook in 21st century India.

References

Bairy, Ramesh, T. S. 2009. 'Brahmins in the Modern World: Association as Enunciation'. *Contributions to Indian Sociology (n.s.)*, 43(1): 89–120.

Béteille, Andre. 1996. *Caste, Class and Power: Changing Patterns of Stratification in a Tanjore Village*. New Delhi: Oxford University Press.

Datta, Ankur. 2016. *On Uncertain Ground: Displaced Kashmiri Pandits in Jammu and Kashmir*. New Delhi: Oxford University Press.

Datta, Ankur. 2019. '"That Was *Natural*. This Is Just *Artificial*"!: Displacement, Memory, Worship, and Connection at a Kashmiri Hindu Shrine Replica'. *History and Anthropology*, 30(3): 276–292.

Fuller, C. J. 1984. *Servants of the Goddess: The Priests of a South Indian Temple*. Cambridge: Cambridge University Press.

Fuller, C. J. 2003. *The Renewal of Priesthood*. Princeton: Princeton University Press.

Fuller, C. J., and Haripriya Narasimhan. 2014. *Tamil Brahmins: The Making of a Middle Class Caste*. Chicago: The University of Chicago Press.

Gallo, Ester. 2018. *The Fall of Gods: Memory, Kinship and Middle Classes in South India*. New Delhi: Oxford University Press.

Ghosh. Biswanath. 2012 *Tamarind City*. Chennai: Tranquebar Press.

Gilbertson, Amanda. 2017. *Within the Limits: Moral Boundaries of Class and Gender in Urban India*. New Delhi: Oxford University Press.

Gough, Kathleen. 1981. *Rural Society in South East India*. Cambridge: Cambridge University Press.

Hancock, Mary. 1999. *Womanhood in the Making: Domestic Ritual and Public Culture in Urban South India*. Boulder, Colorado: Westview Press.

Khare, R. S. 1971. 'Home and Office: Some Trends of Modernization among the Kanya-Kubja Brahmans'. *Comparative Studies in Society and History*, 13(2) 196–216 .

Low, Setha M. 1996. 'The Anthropology of Cities: Imagining and Theorizing the City'. *Annual Review of Anthropology*, 25: 383–409.

Madan, T. N. 1989. *Family and Kinship: A Study of the Pandits of Rural Kashmir*. New Delhi: Oxford University Press.
Narasimhan, Haripriya. 2011. 'Adjusting Distances: Menstrual Pollution among Tamil Brahmins'. *Contributions to Indian Sociology*, 45: 243.
Parry, Jonathan. 1994. *Death in Banaras*. New Delhi: Cambridge University Press.
Saavala, Minna. 2010. *Middle Class Moralities: Everyday Struggle Over Belonging and Prestige in India*. Hyderabad: Orient Blackswan.
Sathaye, Adheesh. 2015. *Crossing the Lines of Caste: Visvamitra and the Construction of Brahmin Power in Hindu Mythology*. New Delhi: Oxford University Press.
Srinivas, Tulasi. *The Cow in the Elevator: An Anthropology of Wonder*. New Delhi: Oxford University Press.
Srivastava, Sanjay. 2015. *Entangled Urbanism: Slum, Gated Community and Shopping Mall in Delhi and Gurgaon*. New Delhi: Oxford University Press.
Subramanian, Ajantha. 2015. 'Making Merit: The Indian Institutes of Technology and the Social Life of Caste'. *Comparative Studies in Society and History*, 57(2): 291–322.
Ulrich, Helen. 1987. 'Marriage Patterns among Havik Brahmins: A 20 Year Study of Change'. *Sex Roles*, l.16(11/12).
Upadhya, Carol. 2008. 'Rewriting the Code; Software Professionals and the Reconstitution of Indian Middle Class Identity'. In C. Jaffrelot and P. van der Veer (Eds.), *Patterns of Middle Class Consumption in India and China* (pp. 55–87). New Delhi: Sage Publications.

A 20-Year Study of Change 1

Vaidya, Shrinivas. 2018. *A Handful of Sesame*. Translated by Maitreyi Karnoor. Manipal: Manipal University Press.
Warrier, Maya. 2005. *Hindu Selves in a Modern World: Guru Faith in the Mata Amritanandamayi Mission*. New York: Routledge.
Wilson, Nicole Allyse. 2015 'Middle-class identity and Hindu women's ritual practice in South India'. Unpublished PhD dissertation, Syracuse University.

CHAPTER 25

AGARWAL BANIAS OF DELHI

UJITHRA PONNIAH

INTRODUCTION

Businesses in India have been structured by caste and family ties (Tripathi, 1984; Markovits, 2008; Damodaran, 2008). Studies empirically documenting the workings of caste and family ties in business are emergent (Naudet and Dubost, 2016; Daljit et al., 2012; Munshi, 2019; Mosse, 2018; Harris-White, 2002; Prakash, 2015). Scholars have observed the continuing importance of family and caste networks, trust, reputation, and loyalty to structure Indian businesses in neoliberal India (Khanna and Palepu, 2000; Chen et al., 2014; Naudet and Dubost, 2016; Schoettli and Pohlmann, 2017). The primacy given to the institution of the family and a treatment of the family as a black box without its share of internal power contestations, however, has resulted in the invisibilization of women in family businesses. Policy interest focusing on upper-class women has been around their right to inherit property and be business successors. Women were denied the right to inherit property under the Hindu Undivided Family (HUF), a legal entity till 2005 (Das Gupta, 2013). Also as per the Companies Act, 2013 it is mandatory to now appoint at least one-woman director as a board member in listed companies. Despite these promising legal developments, in popular imagination women in family businesses appear as consumers of luxurious lifestyles alone, and remain missing in academic writings

Scholars working on caste observe that a decline in caste hierarchy has been accompanied by a persistence in the reproduction of caste-based inequalities and privileges (Srinivas, 1995; Fuller, 1996; Béteille, 1997; Jodhka, 2015; Jodhka and Manor, 2017). An increase in violence against Dalits has been observed even when untouchability is on a decline (Gorringe, 2012; Teltumbde, 2010). Vertical mobility in India is blocked by caste, even as caste loses its ideological hold (Thorat and Attewell, 2007; Vaid and Heath, 2010).While those at the lower end of caste hierarchy find their lives marked by stigma, discrimination, and a lack of opportunities; those at the higher end of the spectrum are seen to dominate wealth accumulation, institutions, and corner opportunities. Caste-based inequalities are captured by studies on wealth inequality in India which show that 10 per cent of the 'upper' castes in India owning 60 per cent of the total wealth (Bharti, 2018; Zacharias and Bakulabharanam, 2011). As caste is an ever-adapting institution, scholars have identified the organization of caste as networks as one of the ways in which the newer caste hierarchies have been organized in the urban. (Jodhka, 2015; Mosse, 2018). Caste as a network process, Mosse (2018) observes has mostly been undertaken by economists and shows the adaptive and flexibility of the institution. A sociological investigation is required to understand the processual formation of these networks and the changing ways in which individuals inhabit them.

This chapter, using the case study of a North Indian business caste, Agarwals will contribute towards the understanding of one of the social outcomes of the 'modern' organization of caste as networks in business, that is—the reproduction of gender inequalities. The Agarwals are a business caste that have a visible presence across the country, although academic literature has focused on their more popular cousins, the Marwari. I argue that the movement of Agarwals from a middle caste to an urban 'upper' caste is in the ways in which they engage with the woman's question. This transformation leads to a gendered inhabitation of class through caste, This chapter has been structured in the following manner: Section 'Caste as Social Capital in Business', will engage with the debates on caste as social capital in business; Section 'Women in Family Businesses' will show the ways in which the women's question in Indian businesses has been engaged; Section 'Agarwal Banias of Delhi' will present the Agarwal Bania caste study with a sociological focus on how they build caste networks in Delhi and the reproduction of gendered inequalities; and Section 'Conclusion' will conclude.

CASTE AS SOCIAL CAPITAL IN BUSINESS

Caste as social capital occupies an important role in business. The continual importance of caste networks in business can be seen in globalized India, through an increase in the density of interlocking directorates, despite a global trend towards 'fracturing' and 'disintegrating' (Naudet and Dubost, 2016). Scholars note that caste networks allow better access to credit, capital, and information, it encourages people to take risks, navigate cumbersome regulations, provide cheap local labour, and mitigates failure (Tripathi, 1984; Markovits, 2008; Damodaran, 2008; Vaidyanathan, 2019).

The continual dependence on caste has made scholars argue that it is an important cultural institution that gives India a global edge in business (Das, 2002; Vaidyanathan, 2019). Vaidyanathan (2019) argues there has been a 'vaishyavization' of large parts of the civil society. Drawing on the Economic Census of 2005, he shows that 43.29 per cent of social groups (SC – 6.97 per cent, ST – 2.13 per cent, and OBC – 34.19 per cent) are owners of enterprises. This leads him to argue that all case groups have networks for social capital for business. He proposes that ownership of business, as opposed to reservations, is the route to upward mobility of caste groups. There are two problems with Vaidyanathan's (2019) argument: first, he does not account for the hierarchy of networks shared by different caste groups. Damodaran (2008) shows the difference in caste networks regionally. He argues that while in southern and western India, features of 'inclusive capitalism' can be seen through the incorporation of non-mercantile castes in business, North India continues to be dominated by Banias, Marwaris, or Khatris. The Jats (Both Hindus and Sikh) Yadvas, Gujjars, and other intermediates caste in the North, Damodaran (2008) observes are at the production level of sugarcane, paddy, wheat, cotton, etc. They are however not visible at the level of textile tycoons, sugar millers, and grain exporters. Second, Vaidyanathan (2019) does not unpack the category of the entrepreneur. A business which has one hired help and hundreds of hired help is clubbed together in the caste—class neutral category of the entrepreneur.

Scholars have shown the hierarchy, strength, and quality of caste networks in business through a focus on Dalit entrepreneurs. Prakash (2015) through his study of Dalit entrepreneurs argues that market outcomes are governed by formal economic institutions present in the market and state but also by social institutions, collective behaviour, and social values shaped by caste. He argues that the Dalits are faced with an 'adverse inclusion' in market processes for they lack the network resources of the upper caste entrepreneurs. Vijayabaskar and Kalaiyarsan (2014) through their study of the garment industry in Tiruppur show how the Dalit entrepreneurs lack caste-based kinship networks shared by the Gounders. Hence, despite the initial push provided by the state, their growth is limited. The functioning of caste in business has led Basile and Harriss-White (2000) to argue that caste functions as a civil society, that helps regulate the conflicts within a capitalist society, and makes it compatible to the needs of accumulation. They argue that caste functions as an 'ideological backcloth' on which modern institutions of business associations, labour unions, and political parties can function following capitalist norms but structured by primordial caste hierarchies. These studies show how caste as social capital excludes by including only one's own through a focus on subaltern business enterprises. However, a sociological investigation is required to know the institutions and processes that helps the dominant business groups organize their caste networks especially in the urban contexts in globalized times.

Women in Family Businesses

Kinship studies have contributed to the study of women in family businesses both sociologically and historically. These studies show how women are essential for the social reproduction of family businesses.

Historians in India have engaged with the women's question in family businesses through an engagement with questions of reform (child marriage, sati, and women's education) in the late 19th century (Hardgrove, 2004; Birla, 2011). Caste associations of business caste groups had sent numerous petitions to the British and to each other to resolve the women's question in ways that did not go contradictory to their mercantile interests linked world views. Birla (2011) goes on to show how the regulation of the women's question had direct implications on how the British perceived the Marwaris as legitimate business partners. Other historians have tangentially engaged with the women in the family business, however keeping the focus on the role of the family vis-à-vis the business (Fox, 1969; Hardiman, 1996; Bayly, 1983). Hardiman (1996) writing about 19th-century Western India says that there were two markers of wealth for a Bania—size of his house and the jewellery that hung around his wife's neck. Bayly (1993) writing about the North Indian Merchant in 18th century shows that the firm was linked with the family through conceptions of 'right marriage', piety, and credit. Business practices and unorthodox behaviour reflected both on the social and economic status of the group since merchant families had to have respectable marriage partners as well as trustworthy traders. While revealing, the family as opposed to women in the families is the primary concern of historians.

Ethnographic studies using the elite studies framework have engaged with women in family businesses through the following approaches: a focus on social reproductive roles undertaken by women in families (Ostrander, 1984; Ponniah, 2017; Glucksberg, 2018); consumptive practices mediated through the social relations of money (Osburg, 2013); and intertwined cultural practices of capital with kinship and gender (Yangaisako, 2002; Chari, 2004). Glucksberg (2018) shows how the social reproductive labour of business elite women in London is sustained by an industry of other women workers. Hambata (1991) reveals the hidden role of women, children, and ancestors in the power play in the board room, as brokers between families that are linked by marriage. Laidlaw (1995, p. 358) in his study of Jain family businesses in Jaipur, says that women keep long fasts while their wealthy merchant husbands make donations recognizing them. The man's generosity while helping him display his wealth comes across as an 'expression of piety' facilitated by their pious wives. Yanagaisako (2002) shows how capitalists in Italy are made not through struggles with other classes or fractions of bourgeoisie but through their struggles in their own families. This struggle she shows constitutes not just the family and firm relationships but also class-making and self-making. Contributing to the existing literature, the Agarwal Bania case study in Delhi shows the sustenance of caste networks through an engagement with the woman's question within their families.

Agarwal Banias of Delhi

Agarwals are part of a large community of Banias. The term 'bania' is a reference to anyone who is involved in business, usually the owner of a small neighbourhood store. It has also become a generic term used when someone is being stingy and calculative with money. The business community in North India primarily consists of four *jatis*—Agarwals, Marwaris, Oswals, and Maheshwaris. There are also Marwari Agarwals. The difference between Marwari and Agarwals is their region of origin and who they trace their descent from. Agarwals trace their descent from Maharaja Agrasen, which Marwaris don't. Agarwals hail from parts of Haryana and Uttar Pradesh while Marwaris hail from two regions in Rajasthan-Mewar and Marwar. Those Agarwals who hail from Rajasthan call themselves Marwari Agarwals. The Agarwal *jati* from Haryana is further divided into eighteen gotras that are used as surnames—Bansal, Bindal, Goel, Garg, Jindal, Kansal, Kanchal, Mittal, Singhal, Mangal, Nagal, Tayal, Teran, Tungal, Eran, Makukal, Dhalan, or Dheran, and Rashtogi. In the last two decades, there have been attempts to change one's surname to Agarwal, to increase community solidarity and visibility. The spelling of Agarwal has been standardized with a single 'g', although many continue to use 'gg'. The caste associations in Delhi put their population at 20 per cent, however, there is no way of confirming this in the absence of a caste census. In Delhi, I focussed on Agarwals who had migrated from parts of Haryana and were involved in business. Three intergenerational routes of mobility were found amongst Agarwal families in Delhi—bazaar to factory; agriculture to bazaar; education to factory. The time of a family's migration and geographical area of settlement in Delhi from Haryana depended on their route of mobility.

Building Caste Networks in Delhi

The building of caste as networks required the formation of caste identity that gave its members a common ground. Many of the Agarwal families migrated to Delhi post-independence. By the 1970s, as some of them had begun to find their economic foothold they found the need to script an identity to unite the Agarwals in Delhi. This was both for electoral gains and to have a sense of belonging in the urban. Scripting an identity led to a re-energization and re-scripting of roles of Agarwal caste associations that had been dormant since the 1920s–1930s. Three Agarwal caste associations were formed in Delhi: Akhila Bhartiya Agarwal Sammelan (ABAS); Delhi Parishad Agarwal Sammelan (DPAS); and All India Vaish Federation (AIVF). While the first two focused on the Agarwal *jati* the third was a corporate caste association. In the 1970s, a temple trust called Agroha Vikas Trust was set up in Agroha, Haryana. The person at the helm of these organizations was Banarsi Das Gupta, two-time Chief Minister of Haryana, and Member of the Parliament, freedom fighter, and social reformer. He was supported by known businessmen like Nand Kishore Goenka (the father of Subhash Chandra Goenka of the Essel group) and O. P. Jindal of the Jindal group.

The caste associations have a central committee and function by connecting to associations at the neighbourhood level. ABAS works at an all India level while DPAS functions in Delhi in consultation with ABAS. Both these associations have an apex body which has a central working group along with a separate youth and women's wing. The heads of the central working group, youth, and women's wing are elected for a fixed term. The apex body is in touch with the neighbourhood Agarwal caste association, which in many places in Delhi again has a separate working group for men and women. The women's wing in the affluent neighbourhood where I had conducted my field work had won many awards from ABAS and was the oldest functioning women's caste association.

To answer who one is, it becomes important to think about what one was. Accounts of what one was in the past reflects how one wishes to be perceived in the present. One of the stated aims of ABAS was to script an 'authentic' history of Maharaja Agrasen, Agroha, and Agarwals. From the 1970s to the late 1980s, ABAS wrote origin accounts by using 'mytho-historical' knowledge. The usage of the term 'mytho', does not mean that it is untrue, but that its authority does not come from the systematic testing using evidence the way the historical accounts function. Myth is a lens into the organizing themes, ideas, and perceptions of a social group.

The defining theme emergent from the descent myth of Maharaja Agrasen is legitimization of wealth making through business. The myth highlights the non-violent and sacrificial self of Agarwal men by virtue of being Maharaha Agrasen's descendants. by highlighting their *non-violent* and *sacrificial* self through Maharaja Agrasen. Maharaja Agrasen was portrayed not as a god himself, however worthy enough to be seated next to them. Maharaja Agrasen was a Kshatriya who embraced Vaishnavism by denouncing animal sacrifice. This is not to say that the Agarwals were necessarily non-violent, however, it shows the way in which they wanted to be perceived. The story of descent from Maharaja Agrasen was written by drawing on a version written by the celebrated Hindi poet Bhartendu Harishcandra in late 19th century.

Once the story of origin had been standardized and the link between Agarwal and Agrasen had been established. The Agroha Vikas Trust and Agarwal caste associations worked towards visibilizing the caste identity by constructing sites and naming places after Maharaja Agrasen. Agroha in Haryana was identified as the kingdom for the king. Foundation stone was laid in Agroha and it was blessed by the Chief Minister of Haryana. An excavation of Agroha was undertaken for the first time in 1888 by C. T. Rogers. The second round of excavation was undertaken by H. L. Srivastava under the Archaeological Survey of India in 1938–1939. The third and last excavation was undertaken by the Haryana government in 1979–1980. Writers and historians from the Agarwal community like Champalal Gupt, Dr Parmeshwari Lal Gupta, and Dr Satyaketu Vidyalandkar have made special effort to associate the archaeological remains of Agroha with Maharaja Agrasen and Agarwal. Hence by the late 1980s, the Agarwal identity was established by linking Agrasen-Agroha-Agarwal.

This stable identity allowed the elites from the community to then undertake philanthropic efforts through registered societies in the name of Maharaja Agrasen. Participation in philanthropic efforts helped increase caste networks amongst the community's elites in Delhi, Haryana, Calcutta, and Mumbai, These caste networks strengthened credit, capital, and information for business while regulating competition for business. Schools, hospitals, and colleges were also built through registered societies, allowing the Agarwals to gain proximity to the nation-state, by subsidizing its development initiatives. The role of the associations is central in making the caste identity that grounds networks. The reproduction of these networks however happens within the family through a negotiation of the women's question.

Negotiating with the Women's Question: Reproducing Gendered Inequalities

As caste is an ascriptive category, the reproduction of a caste group even in its modern form as network happens through a control of women's sexuality (Ambedkar, 1979). The preoccupation with women's sexuality, however, is not for the purity of women or the caste group as discussed by Chakravathy (1993). In the contemporary it is for the sustenance of durable caste networks through endogamous marriages. The changing motivations associated with the social reproductive strategies employed by the caste group comes from processes of secularization that might play out from inhabiting the urban. The individualizing potential embodied by education, socialization in diverse groups, financial mobility, travel, and consumption practices needs to be in sync with maintaining the caste group as a resource. The way in which a balance is struck between processes of individualization and capital's reliance on caste as networks determines how a caste group embodies the 'modern'. One needs to inhabit class and caste identities similarly, simultaneously without belonging to either completely. This process can be understood through a sociological focus on micro processes of gendered power within caste communities and families.

Women are invisibilized in writings by community intellectuals in newspapers and journals produced by caste associations funded by wealthy businessmen till the 1990s. Associational writings in Delhi before the 1990s among other things focused on commemorations to noted businessmen and politicians, lessons learnt from the community's role in nationalist struggle, contribution to the Hindu language and various philanthropic efforts undertaken in Delhi. Kumar (1994) notes a similar invisibilization of women in the writings produced by the Agarwal caste association in Banaras. She argues that a reference to women as mothers and housewives does not find a mention in Agarwal records. In Delhi, post the 1990s, women find a mention in associational writings and events through an engagement with the institution of marriage. Inter-related issues of how weddings should be organized, marital choices made, what qualifies as marital compatibility and what is the ideal way for daughters-in-law to behave in their marital homes are discussed in the writings. What emerges in these writings is the fear and anxieties that animate the community in Delhi post the 1990s and the ways they deem fit to resolve frictions. In these writings' women are asked to undertake 'right' decisions, not through an appeal to wifely duty instituted in Hinduism (although it hangs in the background) but for their own welfare. Women are prodded in a liberal language of 'choice' to think of the individual as being squarely located within the community. This tone marks a departure from earlier didactic accounts on 'how women should behave?', written about by historians of late 19th century.

Moving from the space of the caste associations to the families, in my study I found older elite women in Agarwal families as mothers, wives, and mothers-in-law help actualize the ideological message of the caste association at the level of the family. Through their actions they help create the moral-economic universe of caste by *first*, forging fictive kinship ties across the caste group through 'social work'. This 'social work' involves the organization of Hindu religious festivals like Teej, exhibitions, and fairs. Elite women through the organization of morally sanctioned cultural spaces of socialization, consumption, and self-expression for the less fortunate Agarwal women, whose mobility is curtailed by their families feel that they are contributing to their upliftment. In the process, elite women create aspirational standards for other Agarwal women in Delhi on how to inhabit their class-caste identity in morally permissible and desirable ways while actively enjoying what might be construed as the 'corrupting' influence of consumption font for this sentence appears different. and South Delhi culture. Investing in these events, helps elite women differentiate themselves and their families amongst their own peer group. *Second*, elite women help forge fictive kinship ties amongst class peers through sustained socialization. For example, in DPAS organizes trips on an annual basis. There are some trips where the cost per person is low enough for all Agarwals in Delhi to participate. There are also exclusive trips with a higher cost per person in which community elites participate. The last such trip was to temples in Nepal. A special train with security guards and cook was organized from Safdarjung station in Delhi. This train did not stop to pick others and was exclusive for the DPAS members. The head of a business group famous for well-known chain of restaurants in India helped organize the rail requirements showing the political and economic clout of the community. In these informal spaces of socialization as families, women help strengthen the affective with the economic aiding business interests. *Third*, women in families help steer individualising desires of marriage and work. Mothers as friends and confidants of their children ensure children undertake caste-status appropriate marriages and educated daughters-in-law not allowed to work after marriage stay happy by indulging in part time hobbies and consumptive lifestyles. Marriage is seen as a route for attaining social adulthood, responsibility, and prioritizing the needs of the family while also finding happiness (Ponniah, 2017). Older women in families then help in processes of individualization by making the individual realize the importance of the collective.

The economics of newer hierarchies of caste as networks is realized through the socio-cultural negotiations within families. By making women internalize their domestication through endogamous marriages and their desires mediated through their mothers and mothers-in-law, the family ensures the continued reproduction of gendered subjects in the family. The transformation of a middle caste to an urban upper caste group is anchored through the historical accruement of capital, and capacity to undertake capital conversions. This process of transformation is morally grounded through a negotiation of women's question in ways that class is inhabited through caste. This process which is spread over time is self-contradictory, dynamic, and carries with it the threat of failing through the secularization in the urban context. Hence, to be an urban upper caste group with durable networks, it is essential to find a tandem between processes of capital conversion and the processes of secularization as negotiated by 'caste-d' actors.

Conclusion

The emergent studies on business in India have been concerned about the ways in which caste facilitates the formation of social capital. While the exclusionary nature of these networks has been established through a focus on the struggles of Dalit entrepreneurs in the market, the making of these networks in upper caste contexts has been seldom investigated. The case study of Agarwal Banias in Delhi using a lens of caste and kinship shows how caste as a networks process is forged through identity making and a negotiation of the women's question at the caste association level and an interlinked process of gender making within families. In the process, the case study shows how the Agarwal Banias inhabit class through caste, without belonging to either completely. Sociological studies on business, while embedding economic processes within social structures, need to show how both are co-constituted, and visibilized through changing processes of self-making of its actors.

References

Ambedkar, B. R. 1979. 'Castes in India: Their Mechansim, Genesis and Development'. In Frances Pritchett (Ed.), *Dr Babasaheb Ambedkar: Writings and Speeches* (Vol. 1, pp. 3–22). Bombay: Education Department, Government of Maharashtra.

Basile, E., and Harris-White Barbara. 2000. *Corporative Capitalism, Civil Society and the Politics of Accumulation in Small Town India*. Working Paper no 38, Oxford University: Queen Elizabeth House.

Bayly, Christopher A. 1983. *Rulers, Townsmen and Bazaars: North Indian Society in the Age of British Expansion*. Cambridge: Cambridge University Press.

Béteille, A. 1997. 'Caste in Contemporary India'. In C. J. Fuller (Ed.), *Caste Today* (pp. 150–179). Delhi: Oxford India Paperback.

Bharti, Nitin Kumar. 2018. 'Wealth Inequality, Class and Caste in India'. World Inequality database, World Inequality Lab.

Birla, Ritu. 2011. *Stages of Capital: Law, Culture and Market Governance in Late Colonial India*. Durham: Duke University Press.

Chakravarthy, Uma. 1993. 'Conceptualising Brahmanical Patriarchy in Early India: Gender, Class and State'. *Economic and Political Weekly*, 579–585. Volume 28.

Chari, Sharad. 2004. *Fraternal Capital: Peasant-Workers, Self-Made Men and Globalisation in Provincial India*. Standford: Standford University Press.

Chen, G., R. Chitoor, and B. Vissa. 2014. 'Modernizing without Westernizing: Social Stucture and Economic Action in the Indian Financial Sector'. Volume 58. *The Academy of Management Journal*, 511–537.

Daljit, Han Donker, and Ravi Saxena. 2012. 'Corporate Boards in India: Blocked by Caste'. *Economic and Political Weekly*, 39–43. Volume 47.

Damodaran, Harish. 2008. *India's New Capitalists: Caste, Business and Industry in a Modern Nation*. UK: Palgrave Macmillan.

Das Gupta, Chirashree. 2013. 'The Tenacity of the Hindu Undivided Family: Gender, Religion and Tax Concessions'. *Economic and Political Weekly*, 73–75.

Das, Gurcharan. 2002. *The Elephant Paradigm: India Wrestles with Change*. Delhi: Penquin Books.

Douglas, Lisa. 1992. *The Power of Sentiment: Love, Hierarchy and the Jamaican Elite*. Boulder: Westview Press.

Fox, Richard G. 1969. *From Zamindar to Ballot Box: Community Change in a North Indian Market Town*. Ithaca: Cornel University Press.

Fuller, Chris (Ed.). 1996. *Caste Today*. Delhi: Oxford University Press.

Glucksberg, Luna. 2018. 'A Gendered Ethnography of Elites: Women, Inequality and Social Reproduction'. In Paul Gilbert and Jessica Sklair (Eds.), *Focaal: Journal of Global and Historical Anthropology*, 81: 16–28.

Gorringe, Hugo. 2012. 'Caste and Politics in Tamil Nadu'. *Seminar*, 633: 38–42.

Hambata, Mattews Masayuki. 1991. *Crested Kimono: Power and Love in the Japanese Business Family*. New York: Cornell University Press.

Hardgrove, Anne. 2004. *Community and Public Culture: The Marwaris in Calcutta*. Delhi: Oxford.

Hardiman, David. 1996. *Feeding the Baniya*. Delhi: Oxford University Press.

Harris-White, Barbara. 2002. *India Working: Essays on Society and Economy*. Delhi: Cambridge University Press.

Jodhka, Surinder, and James Manor. 2017. 'Introduction'. In Jodhka and Manor (Eds.), *Contested Hierarchies, Persisting Influence: Caste and Power in Twenty-First Century India* (pp. 1–38). Hyderabad: Orient Black Swan.

Jodhka, Surinder. 2015. *Caste in Contemporary India*. Delhi: Routledge.

Khanna, Tarun, and Kishna Palepu. 2000. 'Is Group Affiliation Profitable in Emerging Markets? Analysis of Diversified Indian Business Groups'. *The Journal of Finance*, 55: 867–891.

Kondo, Dorinne. 1990. *Crafting Selves: Power, Gender and Discourse of Identity in a Japanese Workplace*. Chicago: University of Chicago Press.

Kumar, Nitya (Ed.). 1994. *Women as Subjects: South Asian Histories*. US: University of Virginia Press.

Laidlaw, James. 1995. *Riches and Renunciation: Religion, Economy and Society among the Jains*. Oxford: Clarendon Press.

Markovits, Claude. 2008. *Merchants, Traders, Entrepreneurs: Indian Business in the Colonial Period*. UK: Palgrave Macmillan.

Mosse, David. 2018. 'Caste and Development: Contemporary Perspectives on a Structure of Discrimination and Advantage'. *World Development*, 110: 422–436.

Munshi. 2019. *Caste and the Indian Economy. Journal of Economic Literature*, 57(4): 781–834. Retrieved from http://www.histecon.magd.cam.ac.uk/km/Munshi_JEL1.pdf.

Naudet, Jules, and Claire-Lise Dubost. 2016. 'The Indian Exception: The Densification of the Network of Corporate Interlocks and the Specificities of the Indian Business System (2000–2012)'. *Socio-Economic Review*, 15(2): 405–434.

Osburg, John. 2013. *Anxious Wealth: Money and Morality among China's New Rich*. Standford: Standford University Press.

Ostrander, Susan. 2017 [1984]. *Women of the Upper Class*. Temple University Press: Philadelphia.

Ponniah, Ujithra. 'Reproducing Elite Lives: Women in Aggarwal Family Businesses'. In Surinder Jodhka and Jules Naudet (Eds.), *SAMAJ* (p. 15). South Asia Multidisciplinary Academic Journal, https://journals.openedition.org/samaj/.

Prakash, Assem. 2015. *Dalit Capital: State, Markets and Civil Society in Urban India*. India: Routledge.

Schoettli, Jivanta, and Markus Pohlmann. 2017. 'A "New" Economic Elite in India: Transnational and Neoliberal'. In Surinder Jodhka and Kules Naudet (Eds.), *SAMAJ* (p. 15). South Asia Multidisciplinary Academic Journal, https://journals.openedition.org/samaj/.

Srinivas, M. N. 1995. *Social Change in Modern India*. Delhi: Orient Longman.

Teltumbde, Anand. 2010. *The Persistence of Caste*. New Delhi: Navyana.

Tripathi, Dwijendra. 1984. *Business Communities of India: A Historical Perspective*. New Delhi: Oxford University Press.

Thorat, Sukhdeo, and P. Attewell. 2007. 'The Legacy of Social Exclusion: A Correspondence Study of Job Discrimination in India'. *Economic and Political Weekly*, 31: 4141–4145.

Vaidyanathan, R. 2019. *Caste as Social Capital*. New Delhi: Thomson Press.

Vaid, Divya, and Anthony Heath. 2010. 'Unequal Opportunities: Class, Caste and Social Mobility'. In Anthony Heath and Roger Jeffery (Eds.), *Diversity and Change in Contemporary India* (pp. 129–164). Oxford: Oxford University Press.

Vijaybaskar, M., and A. Kalaiyarsan. 2014. 'Caste as Social Capital'. *Economic and Political Weekly*, 49(10): 35–39.

Yanagisako, Junko Sylvia. 2002. *Producing Culture and Capital: Family Firms in Italy*. Princeton: Princeton University Press.

Zacharias, Ajit, and Vamsi Vakulabharanam. 2011. 'Caste Stratification and Wealth Inequality in India'. *World Development*, 10: 1820–1833.

CHAPTER 26

CASTE LOGOS
A View from Tamil Nadu

ZOE E. HEADLEY

DESPITE the uneven distribution of anthropological attention in India (Berger, 2012), the Tamil speaking region[1] has widely captured the attention of scholars over the last century. A recent comprehensive article on the anthropology of Tamil Nadu illustrates the conspicuousness of caste in the scholarship produced since the 1950s in this region (Alex and Heidemann, 2013) and some of the most heated debates on caste originate from scholars, such as Louis Dumont and Nicholas Dirks, who cut their (field working) teeth in Tamil Nadu before earning their (academic) stripes. Addressing the incredible complexity of caste in Tamil Nadu and reviewing its rich and diverse literature in so few pages is a thankless task and it will largely be circumvented by addressing the issue of 'caste' only through its most elementary definition, that of a birth group through which an ascribed social identity is inherited. Hence 'caste' is not taken here to signify a 'system' or an 'idea', therefore paramount issues such hierarchy, purity, and pollution are not addressed. The scope of this short investigation is further narrowed down by examining solely elements of language through which caste, as an inherited social identity, is enunciated. The focus will be on specific sets of words, the *logos* of caste in Tamil, thereby setting aside the daily practice(s) of caste, ignoring its *grammar* of inequality and discrimination (Deshpande, 2013), overlooking its *idioms* of honour (Guha, 2013) and subordination (Mosse, 1994). I address here three broad fields which can yield some understanding of the logos of caste in its regional setting. Firstly, 'Inscribing caste', takes stock of the epigraphic exception that is the Tamil region in a bid to challenge the notion of caste immobility during the pre-colonial period. Secondly, 'Naming caste', examines the staggering complexity and transformation of modern Tamil caste society

---

[1] The state of 'Tamil Nadu' was created on the 14th of January 1969, following the reorganization of states according to linguistic boundaries.

through the politics of castes titles. Thirdly, 'Speaking caste', addresses the language of belonging to the birth group where one hears little about 'identity' and a lot about 'relationship'. Finally, the annex, 'Reading Caste' proposes an indicative table of publications according to the castes and sub-castes.

Inscribing Caste

The exceptionally rich inscriptional corpus which archaeologists and historians have been collecting and studying for over a century now is yielding substantial information on local pre-colonial structures of social stratification in the Tamil region. In this regard, the Tamil situation resembles no other in the Indian subcontinent with 28,000 inscriptions in Tamil and 16,000 inscriptions in other Dravidian languages against 'only' 7,800 inscriptions in Sanskrit and 5,000 inscriptions in other Aryan languages (Subbarayalu, 2011). These stones and copperplates are whispering[2] a rather different story of Tamil society which strikes down paradigmatic representations of society in South Asia such as Metcalf's 'village republic' (1830) and Marx's 'stagnant Orient' (1867). The study of Tamil inscriptions remains vitally important for contemporary research as it challenges an enduring paradigm of postcolonial studies, that of the relative immobility of caste formations prior to the colonial period. Though a systematic investigation of social morphology in Tamil inscriptions and textual traditions has yet to be carried out, several features of jati formations and caste ideology in pre-modern Tamil society warrant the attention of the scholars of the modern period to weed out the idea, however eloquently spelt out by Dirks (2001), that caste is a British artifact.

Though a handful of inscriptions date as far back as the 3rd century BCE and the number increases steadily from the 6th and 9th century BC, the real momentum occurs from the 10th to the 16th century under the reign of the Chola, Pandya, and Vijayanagara states (Karashima, 2009).[3] In the earliest inscriptions (Tamil-Brahmi) available, individuals' identities are enshrined according to occupation, sect, and sometimes lineage, but 'caste', whether varna or jati, is yet to be seen (Mahadevan, 2003). As the noted historian Champakalakshmi describes, 'in the Sangam classics there is clearly no assertion of caste as an organizing principle of society, and there is often an ambivalence, suggestive of the absence of stratification based on varna, although *Brahmana* households existed [...] and Vedic sacrifice was performed' (2008, p. 151). In the early medieval period (AD 700–1300), mention of the *caturvarṇa* (the four varnas) as qualifiers of social identity is also absent from Saiva and Vaishnava temple inscriptions,

---

[2] Karashima, 2014

[3] The history of Tamil society is conventionally chapterized into four periods: the early historical period (Sangam, 300 BC–300 AD), followed by the early medieval (Pallava and Chola dynasties, AD 700–1300), the medieval period (Vijayanagara AD 1450–1650), and the colonial period.

and the 'only means of determining identities is through suffixes like *bhatta* (brahmana) *velan* (agriculturalist), *kon* (cowherd), and so on' (2008, p. 150).

In the midst of a society structured largely around the temple, with organized sectarian groups who managed and protected land grants and other gifts made by royal patrons (Stein, 1980; Hall, 2001; Karashima 2009), a theistic devotional trend, Bhakti, emerged in the Tamil region in the 6th century, and gradually spread through to other Indian regions, languages, and religions (Islam, Jainism and Sikhism). A number of poet-saints, the Saiva Nayanars and Vaishanava Alvars, produced a vast corpus of hymns in Tamil describing an individual's personal emotion in his direct encounter with 'god'. This direct access to divine grace circumvented the Brahmins' hegemony in the religious sphere, and thereby opened salvation to all, regardless of social and ritual status. Despite the debates that have stormed around the correct interpretation of the social impact of this cult of devotion (Hawley, 2015), '[…] no one disputes that, between the 6th and 16th centuries, Bhakti was an incredible force that everywhere challenged the established religion built on the ideas, practices and institutions of the Brahmins […], swept away the hegemony of Sanskrit by expressing itself in the vernacular languages, and established itself as a model of holiness for men and women whose lives were hardly in conformity with the conventions established by the Brahmin texts' (Clementin-Ojha, 2016).

During the latter half of the medieval period, (11th and 13th century), in the context of an increase in the power of merchants and artisans (partly due to the development of maritime trade in the Indian ocean), the rising conflicts between the Brahmanas and peasants (Subbarayalu, 2011) inscriptions testify to important transformations within Tamil society: the proliferation of new castes (jatis), the emergence of supra-local organizations (the 'nadu' assemblies) as well as the advent of a horizontal supra-community ordering (Karashima, 2009, 2014). This horizontal ordering of a large number of castes is a distinctive feature of the pre-modern caste organization in South India (excluding the Malayali region). Originally denoting regiments in the Chola army, the terms *iṭaṅkai* ('left hand') and *valaṅkai* ('right hand') came to designate a set of two distinct aggregations of professional groups (Subbarayalu, 2011, pp. 167–174). There is some disagreement among scholars over the composition of these groups. One view holds that the *valaṅkai* comprised agriculturalists and *iṭaṅkai* was composed of artisans. However, what is striking is that the groups are mainly, but not exclusively, composed of the lower sections of Tamil society (Karashima, 2014, p. 177). This division into moieties, which was unknown in North India, led to intense and sometimes violent competition between the right and left hand castes over economic concerns and visible ritual status (such as the use of insignias and routes of processions) and by the early 18th century carved out an active role of caste leadership as the preoccupations and conflicts over honour were increasingly brought to the attention of the British (Brimnes, 1999). Described by Arjun Appadurai as 'source of bewilderment to scholars' (1974, p. 216) and Pamela Price as a 'long-term mystery of South Indian history' (1996, p. 10), the causes of the disappearance of the right and left hand caste division by the turn of the 20th century has yet to reach a consensus among scholars, though Pamela Price's argument that the 'traditionalizing forces' of Anglo-Indian law and the introduction of 'social totality of stable, fixed identities and relationships, the now famous caste system' is quite convincing.

Naming Caste. A Performative Utterance?

A straightforward approach to the topic of 'caste in Tamil Nadu' would be: 'which castes are present in Tamil Nadu'? However, to know a caste by its name is a byzantine terrain. If you were to ask today a member of the Pramalai Kallar sub-caste (Madurai district) to name his or her 'caste', you will be given 8 different answers: Tevar, Kallar, Mukkulathor, B. C., Indrakula, D. N. C, Pramalai Kallar, Muvendar. All these answers are 'correct' and contribute to the definition of his social identity. However, they are not all synonymous and their morpho-sociological, administrative, and political significance is heterogeneous. The number and diversity of caste names that a single Pramalai Kallar individual may choose to name his or her birth-group allows us to appreciate the complexity of the Tamil sociological landscape (Headley, 2013). These fieldwork observations among the Pramalai Kallar echo numerous instances recorded in the ethnographic literature throughout Tamil Nadu. For instance, among the Valaiyars in Ramnad district there is a measure of uncertainty and even confusion as to which caste title to use: 'Like many of those castes, however, the Valaiyars' social position displays some important regional variations, which are expressed in their very caste names since they are also known as Mooppanars, Muthurajas, Muthuraiyars, and Ambalakkarrars. The Valaiyars of Alamgkulam are not sure what to call themselves. They all agree that the name Valaiyar is demeaning, and they tend to reject it accordingly; they have started using the word Mooppanar but it is not very widespread [. . .]'. (Deliège, 1996, p. 72). The complexity of identifying a sub-caste or caste by its name, which can take on other twists,[4] is partially reflected in the official list of Backward Classes approved by Government of Tamil Nadu, which enumerates 252 'classes and communities', subdivided into three categories (BC, MBC, and DNC), presently entitled to benefits and reservations.[5] A thorough search through the BC and DNC list for the six names and titles (Tevar, Kallar, Mukkulathor, Indrakula, Pramalai Kallar, Muvendar) enumerated by the Pramalai Kallar subcaste offers the following information:

---

[4] For instance, a sub-caste in one district will be using caste name A and the very same sub-caste caste name B in another district, whereas these two names (A & B) correspond to very distinct sub-castes in a third district

[5] On the creation of the administrative categories of the different castes by the British, and subsequent evolution (until the 1970s), see: Galanter (1984).

Table 26.1 Classification of the 'Kallars' in the Official BC List*

1. Backward Classes		
43	Kallar, Easanattu Kallar, Gandharva Kottai Kallars (*except* Thanjavur, Nagappattinam, Tiruvarur, and pudukottai Districts), Kootappal Kallars (*except* Pudukottai, Tiruchirapalli, Karur, and Perambalur Districts), Piramalai Kallars (*except* Sivaganga, Virudhunagar, Ramanathapuram, Madurai, Theni, Dindigul, Pudukottai, Thanjavur, Nagappattinam, and Tiruvarur Districts), Periyasooriyur Kallars (*except* Tiruchirapalli, Karur, Perambalur, and Pudukottai Districts)	59
44	Kallar Kula Thondaman	
3. Denotified Communities		
208	Gandarvakottai Kallars (Thanjavur, Nagappattinam, Tiruvarur, and Pudukottai Districts)	59
216	Kootappal Kallars (Tiruchirappalli, Karur, Perambalur, and Pudukottai Districts)	59
229	Piramalai Kallars (Sivaganga, Virudhunagar, Ramanathapuram, Madurai, Theni, Dindigul, Pudukkottai, Thanjavur, Nagappattinam, and Tiruvarur Districts)	59
230	Peria Suriyur Kallars (Tiruchirapalli, Karur, Perambalur, and Pudukkottai Districts)	59

*The left-hand column indicates the slot number in the state-wide list of Tamil Nadu and the right-hand column indicates the slot number in the Central OBC list for Tamil Nadu.

Despite its frugal appearance, this table yields significant information about the complexity of the socio-morphology of caste in Tamil Nadu today, albeit without any explanation. First, we may note an abundance of caste names appended to the title 'Kallar' (Easanattu, Gandharva Kottai, Kootappal, etc.), second, we may wonder over the conspicuous absence of four out of six titles (Tevar, Mukkulathor, Indrakula, Muvendar) and, third, we may question the district-wise criterion of distinction among two groups (the Pramalai Kallars and the Periya Suriyur Kallars). Making sense of this table lies in the history of colonial and postcolonial administration of the population and the vigorous responses and collective mobilizations the successive policies elicited. Since Bernard Cohn's landmark essay (1987), there has been much scholarly production on the shapes taken on by caste once it became a privileged entry point into Indian society to identify, classify, and control the Indian population. The first censuses in the Madras Presidency,[6] introduced in 1822, recorded information about caste 'in open-ended questions, that is without forcing them to fit into a pre-established category' (Guilmotto, 1998, p. 51). This method proved too confusing and burdensome for British administrators, who then set out to identify the correct denomination of the different castes and tribes composing

---

[6] The Madras Presidency was the southernmost province of the British Empire, bordered on the east, west and south by the sea, and on the north by the Bombay Presidency, the states of Mysore and Hyderabad, the central provinces and Bihar and Orissa. Among its members were independent states (Tranvancore, Cochin, Pudukkottai, Banganapalle, and Sandhuur).

South India and to order them into comprehensible groupings. In 1901, assisted by their Brahmins informants,[7] they resorted to the varnas as a classifying principal of local society. However, the central distinction was not between the twice born varnas (brahmin/kshatriya/vaisya) and the others (sudra and out-caste) but between Brahmins and the vast heterogeneous mass of 'non-Brahmins', contributing to fuel the (anti-brahmin) Dravidian movement, whose profound political, social, and cultural effects on Tamil society have been multifarious (Irschick, 1969; Barnett, 1976; Baker, 1976; Pandian, 1987; Ramaswamy, 1997; Ryerson, 1988). Previously inexistent material and symbolic interests of being administratively recognized as belonging to a varna category paved the way to new forms of inter-caste competition have been well accounted for in the literature. Indeed, the colonial administration, and subsequently the Indian government, progressively introduced an increasing number of benefits for a growing number of castes and communities.[8]

As early as the 1870s, the Tamils vigorously responded to this vertical objectification of South Indian society through a novel form of horizontal mobilization, caste-clusters (or meta-castes) which were largely formulated and promoted by a new socio-political institution, the caste association (Washbrook, 1975; Hardgrave, 1969; Verma, 1979). Indeed, a number of sub-castes, that were socially, ritually, geographically, and economically disparate, grouped together behind a single caste title, thereby garnering numerical strength, whilst formulating greater internal social homogeneity (modifying practices of diet, worship, commensality, connubiality, etc.) to advance and defend the status and rank of their 'caste'(-cluster) in the colonial administration. Such is the case of the titles 'Mukkulathor', 'Muvender' as well as 'Tevar' aimed at unifying three distinct castes: the Kallar, the Maravars, and the Agamudayars. While the title 'Tevar' was in use, both the titles "Muvender" and Mukkulathor' (*mu* denoting the number 'three') were re-created to add antiquity to this new horizontal caste formation. To gain historical legitimacy, caste leaders sought to spell out, in writing, a common history, resting largely on a mythological, or historical justification of the caste name.[9] These strategies

---

[7] The privileged relationship established by the administrators with the various Brahmin castes is a now well-known chapter of Indian colonial history: it is through them that they are introduced to Indian languages, and that they recruit the majority of the employees of their huge imperial machinery. The inequality of access to the world of education and work, intensified by the low proportion of Brahmins among the population of the Madras Presidency—just over 3 per cent at the turn of the 19th century—precipitates a lasting antagonism in Tamil society between Brahmins and 'non-Brahmans' which took an important political turn that we will not develop here (Irschick, 1969).

[8] For instance: 'Study and housing allowances, places in medical colleges and engineering schools, jobs allocated in the public service, reserved seats in the legislative assemblies of the Indian Union and each state, etc.' (Lardinois, 1985, p. 78). On the creation of the administrative categories of the different castes by the British, and subsequent evolution (until the 1970s), see M. Galanter (1984).

[9] These strategies were implemented through the creation of newspapers of community interest, the drafting of petitions and memoirs that engorged the Madras High Court, and the publication of historical works legitimizing their desire to be (re)classified in the hierarchy.

contributed to an extraordinary social, economic, and political ascent of certain groups in Tamil Nadu, such as the Nadars (formerly known as Shanars) and the Vanniyars (formerly known as Pallis).[10]

The colonial administration was overwhelmed by what they considered 'false caste name's. T. C. Boag, in charge of the 1921 census for the Madras Presidency, reported the increasing 'number of errors due to intentional false statements by members of certain castes who cherish the repeated claims made in each census, when they present petitions requesting that they be described in a certain way in the census tables […]' (Boag, 1922, p. 152). At least four strategies were deployed in the manipulation caste names, of which Rowe (1968) identified three: 'Some castes [. . .] choose the name of a known higher caste. Others choose to add the name of a varna higher than their own after the usual names of the castes. [. . .]. Another type of petition calls for the change of a functional Sudra caste name such as Teli (oil manufacturers and sellers) in Vaishya, the varna of traders, which is not at all a caste name' (Rowe, 1968, p. 87 cited by Pandian, 1983, p. 191). The fourth strategy is to 'maintain' the caste name but to justify, through publications and petitions, an etymology different from that commonly attributed to demonstrate the belonging of the said caste to a particular varna.

Over the course of the 20th century (administratively recognized) caste names came to function as performative utterances (Austin, 1962): they were aimed not only at identifying a specific social group but at changing its social inscription within official (colonial and postcolonial) classifications and the State. Though their 'truth-value' was frequently challenged by the colonial administration, in numerous instances, re-modeled caste names became performative utterances of an adaptive collective identity. Though the stakes attached to caste names changed significantly after Independence, with the introduction of reservations and affirmative action programs, their performative charge, so to speak, remains considerable, and very poorly documented. Indeed, if the successive central and state policies have been studied, their economic and political impact scrutinized, the issue of false caste certificates, whereby an individual 'proves' to be of a lower caste than that of his or her birth group (in order to benefit from reservation policies, Gatade, 2005), or the opposite phenomenon, found in some sections of the informal sector, of pretending to be from a higher caste (namely to access employment in upper caste households) has failed to gather proper attention.

---

[10] The Nadars are mainly present in the regions of Madurai, Kanyakumari, Tirunelveli, and Ramanathapuram. Hardgrave, 1969. Vanniyars are mainly found in the regions of Chingleput, North Arcot, South Arcot, and Salem. K. K. Verma, 1979. *Changing Role of Caste Associations* (New Delhi: National Publishing House).

'Speaking Caste'

An individual's belonging to caste, her/his caste identity, is sustained by a number of collective resources that are summoned, in certain circumstances, to inform and orient discourse as well as shape and anchor social practices.[11] These collective resources, such as I have observed them among the Pramalai Kallar, include: sub-caste name (Pramalai Kallar), caste name (Kallar), caste-cluster title (Tevar, Muvender, Mukkulathor), dialect, collective memory, lineage cult, ideal of preferential marriage (maternal uncle), and practice of endogamy, traditional territory (Kallar Nadu), martial ideology (conveyed by their caste associations and cinema), administrative classification ('Criminal Tribe' under the British and DNC/BC after Independence), values attached to the former traditional occupation (*kāval* guardian), economic situation, representation in popular culture (folklore, proverbs, urban legends, cinema, and the press, i.e. caste stereotypes), and political affiliation. It is more or less possible to distinguish these resources according to their emic or etic perspectives as well as their subjective and objective characteristic. However, it is significant here to borrow Brubaker's distinction (2001) between 'communality' (the simple sharing of a common attribute), 'connectedness' (the sharing of relational attachments), and 'groupality' (the combination of these two modes of identification). If caste names and titles evidently denote the sharing of a common attribute, they serve to distinguish one caste (sub-caste, caste, caste-cluster) from another.

It is a striking fact that given the centrality 'caste' still holds today in Tamil society that, at first ear-shot, the anthropologist hears 'it' so little during fieldwork. The very utterance of the term, whether 'caste' or 'jāti', is in many conversational circumstances avoided. Indeed, the term jāti is frequently replaced by a set of other terms suggesting the (similar) idea of a set of people sharing common attributes and/or relational attachments: 'vakuppu' (class, section), 'vakai' (division, branch, gender), *kuṭṭam* (crowd, meeting), *makkaḷ* (human being, people), 'camutāyam' (society). Similarly, in English conversations, or in the use of English in Tamil conversations the word 'caste' is replaced very frequently by 'community'. This socio-linguistic practice produces confusions in many conversational situations on 'caste': 'who' exactly is being talked about? The complexity of grasping the precise social morphology of a specific caste or sub-caste is further thickened in the most elementary forms of Tamil grammar. Indeed, while talking about social, political, and religious practices of their locality with a high priest of a local temple, a mother working in the fields, or a village tailor, the informants systematically explain, describe, and answer, not by using the first person singular ('I do this and that'), but with the first-person plural: 'we do like this' and 'we

---

[11] Some of these resources can be openly mobilized by 'neighboring' groups (structurally close castes) to justify various forms of rapprochement (such as the 'creation' of caste-cluster as we have seen, justifying the expansion of the endogamy, ad hoc or sustainable political coalitions) but also by antagonistic groups to stigmatize, resist, or challenge statements and actions of members of this group.

don't do that'. So far, so good. However, in Tamil, there are two forms of 'we': nāma and naṅka. The first one (nāma) is inclusive: it specifically includes the addressee, that is 'you and I (and possibly others)'. The second one (naṅka) is exclusive: 'myself and others but not you'. This grammatical distinction, coined 'clusivity', is found in all Dravidian languages, as well as a handful of Indo-Aryan languages (Gujurati, Marathi, Punjabi, Marwari).[12]

How then does one 'speak' overtly of caste belonging in contemporary Tamil Nadu? What features of speech can be heard to comprehend an individual's belonging to the birth group? Despite the rich and varied scholarship on caste in Tamil Nadu, sociolinguistic studies of caste have been few and far between. The very first study on caste dialects in India and, for many decades, the only one (Shapiro and Schiffman, 1981), concerned precisely the Tamil speaking region. Jules Bloch's 1910 study (*Castes et Dialectes en Tamoul*),[13] the result of linguistic surveys between 1906 and 1907 in five localities,[14] established clear distinctions in caste dialects between the brahmin castes, non-brahmin castes, and the so-called untouchable castes. The variations in Tamil dialects follow a number of social parameters besides those of caste belonging, and include urban/rural, educated/uneducated, formal/informal, Hindu/Muslim, etc. Nearly 60 years after, the issue of Tamil caste dialects resurfaced in Milton Singer and Bernard Cohn's landmark volume on caste, *Structure and Change in Indian Society* (1968). Here, A. K. Ramanujan records the endurance of caste dialect through a comparison between Mudaliar (non-brahmin) and Iyengar (Brahmin) dialects. Though other in-depth studies were conducted, notably by the department of Linguistics of Annamalai University in the 1970s and early 1980s, since then research on the manifestation of caste in language and verbal interactions has been largely discarded. Though many anthropologists, such as myself, are poorly equipped to embark on the study of variations of isoglosses (which mark the linguistic boundary between dialects), studies on the role of language and speech acts in the performance of clusivity and caste ascription would certainly shed very significant information on the day-to-day currency of caste in Tamil society.

Such research being far beyond the ambit of my academic training, I will endeavour here to point the reader towards a set of words with which Pramalai Kallars express the sharing of relational attachment within their birth group which is constitutive both of caste belonging and of the notion of personhood. The Tamil language offers a wide range of terms to express both the notion of 'relationship' and the people included in it. Three terms are most commonly used: *uṟavu, contam, campatam*. The term *uṟavu* can

---

[12] Clusivity is also present in all Austronesian languages and several Sino-Tibetan languages. See E. Filimonova (Ed.) 2005. *Clusivity: Typology and Case-studies of Inclusive-exclusive Distinction*. John Benjamin: Philadelphia-Amsterdam

[13] Though it was never translated into English, this foundational contribution to the study of the manifestations of caste in language and verbal interactions was picked up and transmitted by the different generations of linguists working on South Asia The (French) text was reprinted by Colette Caillat in 1985 in *Recueil d'articles de Jules Bloch 1906–1955*. Publications de l'ICI, Fascicule 52, pp. 8–37.

[14] Madras, Chengalpattu, Chidambaram, Kumbakonam, and Tirumangalam (near Madurai).

be described as 'generic' in the sense that it has the capacity to cover the distinction between two categories of relationship within the kinship and by extension the sub-caste: prescribed relationships and non-prescribed relationships. On the other hand, two terms derived from *uṟavu* refer to a third category of relationships, that of the relationship generated by the common membership of the sub-caste: *uṟaviṉar* and *uṟavumuṟai*. All relationships governed by kinship are included in the term *contam*, which can be translated as 'bond' to differentiate it from the term *uṟavu*. The term *contam* is characterized by its inalienable nature and is underpinned by particular representations of the individual's physical constitution (Headley, 2021). Commonly in Tamil, the term '*campantam*' refers to the relationship(s) created by marriage. Many castes use the term '*campati*' to refer to 'the parents of the son-in-law or daughter-in-law'. However, on my field of study (the Pramalai Kallars of Madurai district) it means on the contrary the linking of two people or two groups of people who do not have a previous 'bond' and 'relationship'. In the context studied, this term has a completely neutral value and does not imply a friendly, affectionate relationship, or their opposites. The ramifications of the articulation and expression of relationship within the birth group are of course not bounded solely by the differentiated use of the terms discussed here. The articulation of caste belonging is based, reiterated, modified, and contested on the basis of very heterogeneous representations and practices of daily life. Two fundamental notions largely escaped the historical re-inscriptions and political manipulations of 'caste' and contribute significantly to 'belonging to caste the Tamil way'[15] are the notion of *murai* (rules, norms) and that of *kuṇam* (intrinsic character of animate and inanimate groups).

Afterword

This brief overview of caste in Tamil Nadu attempted to address, through the narrow lens of its logos, the scope, diversity, and complexity of caste—understood as an ascribed identity inherited by birth—has displayed over time. We have seen that diverse forms of vertical stratifications and horizontal categorizations have alternated over the centuries and that different types of binary and ternary oppositions have conditioned intra-caste competitions and inter-caste solidarities. Though the literature on caste in Tamil Nadu is rich and fairly textured, it had been until recently relegated to the dustbin of anthropology along other maligned colonial concepts, notably since the demise of village studies. The content, articulations endurance, and transformations of Tamil categories of personhood and belonging which contribute significantly to understand the daily lived experience of caste as an ascribed collective identity deserve more attention. A further terrain of exploration is to examine situations where the inherited caste identity of

---

[15] I borrow here directly the title of Valentine Daniels inspirational work among the Aru Nattu Vellalars: 'Fluid Sign. Being a Person the Tamil Way' (1984).

an individual is challenged. Indeed, since belonging to a specific caste is determined by birth, a natural presupposition is that belonging to that caste is immutable. However, there exist at least six different situations or predicaments where one ascribed social identity is contested, lost, removed, or disguised. These are conversion, renunciation, or repudiation of the birth group, children from inter-caste marriages, children from inter-confessional marriages, caste 'passing' (namely in the field of formal and informal employment) and caste exclusions (or 'excommunication'). These situations, which reflect in one way or another, transgressions and violations of enduring kin-caste rules, local legal culture and modern Indian law, are in need of renewed investigations to better understand the contemporary articulations of belonging to the birth group.

Annexe: 'Reading Caste'

The following table offers an indicative caste-focused bibliography of books, chapters, articles. A number of publications cited are centered on topics other than social morphology and stratification (such as land tenure, kinship, devotion, etc.), but offer useful specific ethnographic data on specific Tamil castes and sub-castes.

Caste	Location(s)	Date–Author
Kongu Vellalar (Goundar)	Coimbatore	1972–B. Beck
Kongu Vellalar (Goundar)		2018–S. Ponnarasu
Pramalai Kallar (Tevar)	Madurai	1957(1986) –L. Dumont
Pramalai Kallar (Tevar)	Madurai	2009–A. Pandian
Pramalai Kallar (Tevar)	Madurai	2014–I. Nabokov
Thondaiman Kallar (Tevar)	Pudukottai	1987–N. Dirks
Kallar (Tevar)	Madurai	2009–A. Pandian
Paraiyar (and Reddyar)	Chingleput	1979–M. Moffat
Paraiyar (Reddiar, Vanniyar)	Pondichery	1997–J. & J.L. Racine
Pallar	Ramnad	1980–R. Deliege
Pallar (and 20 castes)	Madurai	2012–D. Mosse
Aru Nattu Vellalar (Vellalar)		1984–V. Daniels
Konttaikatti Vellallar (Vellalar)		1976–S. Barnett
Nadukottai Chettiyars (Chetiyar)	Chettinad	1994–D. Rudner

Caste	Location(s)	Date–Author
Kaikkoolar or Sengunthar Mudaliar (Mudaliar)	Kongu Nadu and Madras	1984–M. Mines
Nadar		1969–R. Hardgrave
Nadar	Madurai	1996–D. Templeman
Brahmin	Madurai	2003–C. Fuller
Brahmin		2014–C. Fuller and N. Haripriya
Vagri, Muttaraja, Kallar	Tanjore	2009–G. Alex
Brahmin, Kallar, Padayachi, Vellalar, Pallar	Tanjore	1965–A. Béteille
Pallar, Christian Paraiyar, Muthurajah, Vellan Chettiar, Telugu Brahmins	Tiruchirapalli	1998–K. Kapadia
Maravar, Vellalar (Mudaliar, Pillai), Brahmin, Konar, Muppanar, Pallar, Paraiayar	Tirunelvelli	1978–M. L. Reiniche
Pallar, Valaiyar	Ramnad	1996–R. Deliège
Kaikkolar or Sengunthar Mudaliar, Nagarattu Chettiyar, Vellan Chettiyar, Kongu Vellalar	Salem (Tiruchengodu)	1996–M. L. Reiniche
Agambadiyar, Padayachi, Konar, Muppanar, Vanniyar, Pallar/Adi-dravidar, Brahmin, Kallar, etc. (20 castes)	Tanjore	1969–K. Gough
Tevar, Pallar, Pillaimar, Mippanar, Paraiyar, Illuttuppillai, Aiyars, etc. (14 castes)	Tirunelvelli	2005–Mines
Vanniyar, Paraiyar Reddiar, Acari, Vannan, Ambattan	Villupuram (Irulvelpattu)	1918–Slater 1940–Thomas and Ramakrishnan 1967–Haswell 1983–Guhan and Mencher 2012–Harriss, Jeyaranjan, and Nagaraj

References

Alex, G., and F. Heidemann. 2013. 'Tamil Nadu: Inequality and Status'. In P. Berger and F. Heidemann (Eds.), *The Modern Anthropology of India* (pp. 260-275). London and New York: Routledge.

Appadurai, A. 1974. 'Right and Left Hand Castes in South India'. *The Indian Economic and Social History Review*, 11(2-3): 216-259.

Austin, J. L. 1962. *How to Do Things with Words: The Williams James Lectures Delivered at Harvard University in 1955, 1962*. Oxford: Clarendon Press.

Baker, C. J. 1976. *The Politics of South India: 1920-1937*. Vikas Publishing House, New Delhi.

Barnett, M. R. 1976. *The Politics of Cultural Nationalism in South India*. Princeton: University Press, Princeton.

Bean, Susan. 1974. *Linguistic Variations and the Caste System in South Asia.* in *Indian Linguistics*, 35(4): 77-277-294

Berger, Peter. 2012. 'Theory and Ethnography in the Modern Anthropology of India'. *HAU: Journal of Ethnographic Theory*, 2(2): 325-357.

Boag, T. C. 1922. Census of India. 1921. Madras, 13, Part I; Madras. Printed by the Superintendent, Government Press

Brimnes, N. 1999. *Constructing the Colonial Encounter. Right and Left Hand Castes in Early Colonial South India*. Richmond: RoutledgeCurzon.

Caroll, L. 1978. 'Colonial Perceptions of Indian Society and the Emergence of Caste(s) Associations'. *Journal of Asian Studies*, XXXVII(2): 233-250.

Clémentin-Ojha, C. 2016. 'Compte-rendu de "John Stratton Hawley, A Storm of Songs. India and the Idea of the Bhakti Movement"'. *Archives de sciences sociales des religions*, 176-390.

Champakalaskshmi, R. 2008. 'Caste and Community: Oscillating Identities in Pre-modern Tamil Society'. In R. Cheran, Darshan Ambalavanar, and Chelva Kanaganayakam (Eds.), *New Demarcations. Essays in Tamil Studies* (pp. 149-171). Toronto: Canadian Scholars Press Inc.

Deliège, R. 1996. 'At the Threshold of Untouchability. Pallars and Valaiyars in a Tamil Village'. In Fuller, J. C. (ed.), *Caste Today* (pp.65-92). New Delhi: OUP.

Deshpande, Satish. 2013, 13 April. 'Caste and Castelessness: Towards a Biography of the "General Category"'. *Economic and Political Weekly*, 48(15): 32-39.

Dirks, N. 2001. *Caste of Mind. Colonialism and the Making of Modern India*. Princeton & Oxford: Princeton University Press.

Gatade, S. 2005. 'Phenomenon of False Caste Certificates'. *Economic and Political Weekly*, 40. 4587-4588. 10.2307/4417318.

Guha, S. 2013. *Beyond Caste. Identity and Power in South Asia, Past and Present*. Leiden: Brill.

Guilmoto, C. Z. 1998. 'Le texte statistique colonial: à propos des classifications sociales dans l'Inde britannique'. *Histoire et Mesure*, XIII(1/2): 39-57.

Hall, K. (Ed.). 2001. *Structure and Society in Early South India: Essays in Honour of Noboru Karashima*. Oxford: Oxford University Press.

Hardgrave, R. L. 1965. 'The Dravidian Movement'. *Bombay*, Popular Prakashan, 8-11.

Hardgrave, R. L. 1969. *The Nadars of Tamil Nadu: The Political Culture of a Community in Change*. University of California Press, Berkeley.

Hawley, J. S. 2015. *A Storm of Songs. India and the Idea of the Bhakti Movement*. Cambridge, London: Harvard University Press.

Harriss, J. 2010. 'Land, Labour and Caste Politics in Rural Tamil Nadu in the Twentieth Century: Iruvelpattu 1916–2008'. *Economic and Political Weekly*, 45(31): 47–61 (with J. Jeyaranjan and K. Nagaraj).

Headley, E. Z. 2013 'Nommer la Caste : Ordre Social et Catégorie Identitaire en Inde Contemporaine.' In Naudet, J., (ED.), *Justifier l'Ordre Social: Caste, Race, Genre et Classe*. PUF/La Vie des Idées, Paris.

Headley, E. Z. 2021. 'A Sociological Grammar of Belonging. Relation and Substance in a South Indian Subcaste'. In M. Claveyrolas and P. Y Trouillet (Eds.), *Les Hindous, les Autres et l'Ailleurs Frontières et relations* (pp. 41–67). Purusharta n°38, Editions de l'EHESS.

Irschick, E. F. 1969. *Politics and Social Conflict in South India: The Non-Brahman Movement and Tamil Separatism, 1916-1929*. University of California Press, Berkeley.

Jeffrey, R. (1974). 'The Social Origins of Caste Association 1875–1905: The Founding of SNDP Yogam'. *South Asia*, IV: 39–59.

Karashima, Noboru. 2009. *Ancient to Medieval, South Indian Society in Transition*. New Delhi: Oxford University Press.

Karashima, N. 2014. 'Emergence of New Jatis and Supra-Local/Community Organizations'. In N. Karashima (Ed.), *A Concise History of South India. Issues and Interpretations* (pp. 175–182). New Delhi: OUP.

Mahadevan, I. 2003. *Early Tamil Epigraphy: From the Earliest Times to the Sixth Century A.D.* Harvard Oriental Series 62. Harvard: Harvard University Press.

Mosse, D. 1994. 'Idioms of Subordination and Styles of Protest among Christian and Hindu Harijan Castes in Tamil Nadu'. *Contributions to Indian Sociology*, 28(1): 67–106.

Pandian, J. 1983. 'Political Emblems of Caste Identity. An Interpretation of Tamil Caste Titles'. *Anthropological Quartely*, 56(N°4): 190–197.

Pandian, J. 1987. *Caste, Nationalism and Ethnicity: An Interpretation of Tamil Cultural History and Social Order*. Popular Prakashan, Bombay.

Price, P. 1996. *Kingship and Political Practice in Colonial India*. Cambridge: Cambridge University Press.

Ramanujan, A. 1968 K. (Ed.). 'The Structure of Variation: A Study in Caste Dialects'. In Singer, M. and Cohn B.S. (Eds.), *Structure and Change in Indian Society* (pp. 461–474). Chicago: Aldine Transaction.

Ramaswamy, S. 1997. *Passions of the Tongue: Language Devotion in Tamil India, 1891–1970*. Berkeley University Press, Berkeley.

Rowe, W. L. 1968. 'The New Cauhans'. In J. Silverberg (Ed.), *Social Modernity in the Caste System*. The Hague: Mouton.

Ryerson, C. 1988. *Regionalism and Religion: The Tamil Renaissance and Popular Hinduism*. Christian Literature Society, Madras.

Shapiro, M. C., and H. F. Schiffman. 1981. *Language and Society in South Asia*. Delhi, Varanassi and Patna: Motilal Barnasidas.

Stein, B. 1980. *Peasant State and Society in Medieval South India*. Oxford: Oxford University Press.

Subbarayalu, Y. 2011. *South India under the Cholas*. New Delhi: Oxford University Press.

Verma, K. K. 1979. *Changing Role of Caste Associations*. New Delhi: National Publishing House.

Washbrook, D. 1975. 'The Development of Caste Organizations in South India 1880-1925'. In C. J. Baker and D. Washbrook (Eds.), *South India: Political Institutions and Political Change, 1880–1940*. Delhi: Macmillan Co. of India.

CHAPTER 27

THE INVISIBILITY OF CASTE IN BENGAL

SARBANI BANDYOPADHYAY

CASTE has long been considered to hold little significance in structuring lives in Bengal while class, religion, and gender were placed at the centre of debates. Studies on Bengal have by and large underplayed caste by accentuating focus on the emergence of the bhadralok, colonial modernity, class, class mobilization, and the communal question (Bhattacharya, 2005; Chatterjee, 1997, 1999, 2016; Ghosh, 2002; McGuire, 1983; Mukherjee, 1970, 1975). This sense of a Bengali exceptionalism continued well into the 1990s. The absence of stark and widespread caste-based physical violence in Bengal helps account for the lack of significance of caste there (Ghosh, 2001). In both private and public conversations on the nature of caste in Bengal, the reference point is a focus on the few occurrences of caste-based outrageous physical violence and comparisons are often drawn with Bihar, Uttar Pradesh, or southern Indian states. This understanding has effectively been questioned by Sekhar Bandyopadhyay, in particular through his research on the Namasudras (Bandyopadhyay, 1990, 2004, 2011; Bandyopadhyay & Basu Ray Chaudhury, 2016). Recently, there has been a renewed interest in caste in Bengal (Bandyopadhyay, 2012, 2016; Sen D., 2012, 2014, 2016; Sen U., 2014) and, despite assertions to the contrary by some social scientists (Chatterjee, 2016, for instance), one can assume to a fair extent that while there still is scepticism around the degree of significance of caste, Bengal can no longer be considered casteless.

THE BHADRALOK QUESTION, *DALADALI*, AND CASTE

Drawing from Sanskritic texts and historical sources, Hitesranjan Sanyal (1981) gives us an analysis of caste structure and social mobility in Bengal. Among the most effective strategies for upward social mobility available to so called 'lower' castes, one can mention the attempt of moving from a traditional occupation to one that requires the use of modern technologies; going where one's caste is not known and claiming high ritual status; rewriting the origin myths of one's community; breaking away from one's original caste group; enforcing new norms of endogamy; building temples; making actions of charity towards Brahmins, etc. These modes are also fairly common to other regions beyond Bengal. Sanyal underscores that although the Brahmin was at the top of the varna hierarchy it was not the only upper 'caste' (*uchha jati*) in Bengal. In the 14th century the two powerful castes of Kayastha (scribes) and Baidya (practitioners of traditional medicine) were elevated by the Bengali lawgiver Raghunandan to the status of *uchha jati* though they remained Shudra in terms of varna. Thus, in Bengal, the upper castes comprised of the Brahmins, the Kayasthas, and the Baidyas. 'Lower' caste writings of the 19th century such as those of the Sadgop and Mahishya communities (two dominant agricultural castes) highlight such methods of claiming high status and also illustrate the disdain they had for those considered to be at the bottom of the hierarchy who were making competing claims to higher caste status (Ghosh, 1938, 1939). From the 19th century till the Partition of the Province in 1947, Bengal witnessed vibrant caste movements, yet caste suddenly seems to have 'disappeared' post-1947. Bengal came to be characterized by an absent-presence of caste.

Many caste studies in India focus on the legitimation-contestation and domination-resistance axes (Bairy, 2010). While such understandings and explanations are important, they tend to invisibilize the ways in which caste truly plays out in Bengal. The absence of strong assertive movements, particularly 'Ambedkarite' ones in post-Partition West Bengal has been taken as an indicator of an absence of a significant caste question in West Bengal. This chapter intends to depict the lives of caste in Bengal in some of its variety.

Hitesranjan Sanyal's book Social Mobility in Bengal (1981) has been one of the earliest comprehensive studies on caste in Bengal. But until then, Bengal's intellectual history had mostly been consumed by a fascination for the bhadralok and the caste question became in some ways reduced to simple binaries: bhadralok/chhotolok, high culture/low culture, Hindu/Muslim, conservative/reformer, peasant/zamindar, middle class/working class, inside/outside.

Around the 17th-century European trade expanded its investments in the silk and weaving industries and people from the cultivating, trading, and service castes and the higher castes of Brahmans and Kayasthas found new opportunities in the field of trade and commerce (Sanyal, 1981, p. 56). Jyotirmoyee Sarma (1980) pointed out some distinctive features of the 'bhadralok' and its other, the '*chhotolok*': only a small number of the higher castes were involved in their traditional occupations as most took advantage of the opportunities offered by colonial rule and shifted to more lucrative occupations.

In contrast, the vast majority of marginalized castes confined themselves to the practice of their traditional occupations. Sarma argues that while the bhadralok was an open group, caste status continued to be significant (Sarma, 1980). *Chhotolok* originally was 'meant to include those who were found to be wanting in money and position, were lacking in education, and were of low caste ranks' (Sarma, 1980, p. 102). These elements continued to remain integral in 19th- and 20th-century understandings[1] of bhadralok and *chhotolok*.

In the 18th century, these upper castes along with the prosperous sections of the Weaver, Tili and Subarnabanik castes acted as *dewans*, and *banias* to European trading companies. Due to the nature of their trade/occupation these castes had closer ties with the city and the European traders than many other castes had (Sanyal, 1981, p. 57). While the 1793 Permanent Settlement gave the high castes control over most of the land, in most cases these landlords migrated to Calcutta and the neighbouring towns and functioned as absentee landlords. By the time British rule was being established here the upper castes were the most advantageously placed and could have easy access to English education, the modern professions, and opportunities (Ghosh, 2001, p. 48).

The bhadralok (genteel folk or broadly the middle classes) category that started taking shape towards the beginning of the 19th century were not a homogeneous category: it included the rentier property class, a middle class holding administrative positions, and engaged in higher urban professions, lower-grade clerks (kerani), *tol* teachers, and priests (Bandyopadhyay, 1823; McGuire, 1983; Sarkar, 1997). Links with land ownership in some capacity was a crucial marker of the bhadralok (Bhattacharya, 2005). Along with this what made these varied sections part of the bhadralok were their dis-engagement with manual labour and their high caste status.

Caste was also much more prominent from the mid eighteenth till the middle of the 19th century as was reflected through the importance of the institutions of caste *cutcherries*[2] and caste factions called *dals* (Mukherjee, 1970, 1975).

The *dals* played a major role in the rise of the Kayasthas in the city. Their control over many powerful *dals* helped them in their conflict against the Brahmins following their claims over a higher ritual status. A measure of their challenge could be gauged from the fact that in 1851, the Bengali Brahmin reformer Vidyasagar and then Principal of Sanskrit College, allowed entry to Kayastha boys in this once Brahmins and Baidyas-only College, while denying the same to other Shudra castes on the ground that they were 'at present lacking in respectability' and that their status was 'very low' (Bayly, 2012, pp. 144–145).

---

[1] For instance in Bengali high-caste literature marginalized castes seeking upward mobility and cultural acceptance were often derided.

[2] Caste courts.

Mukherjee points out that the entire bhadralok population of Calcutta came under the control of these *dals* and competition for control over these *dals* was intense (1975, p. 69). The chief function of the leaders of these dals (*dalapatis*) was 'to preserve caste, lives and religion of his *dal*' (Mukherjee, 1975, p. 68) and that they used the 'old caste sanction of excommunication to keep men under control' (Mukherjee, 1975, p. 68). He further states that *'the primary function of a dal was to settle disputes concerning caste, inheritance, marriage, caste rank and intercaste relationships'* (1975, pp. 17–18).

Despite such clear markers of a strong presence of caste, Mukherjee (1970, 1975) believes that caste was of minor significance for the bhadralok. Describing the power of the *dals* controlled by the *abhijat*[3] *bhadralok*, a specifically west Bengali phenomenon, he argues that till about the 1870s the *dals* ruled Bengali society in close association with colonial patronage. But with the introduction of liberal elective principles from the latter half of the 19th century, the migration of East Bengali students and of new bhadralok families into the city, the *dals* began to lose their hold. McGuire (1983) also claimed that the significance of caste began to decline towards the end of the 20th century.

We can read Dwaipayan Sen (2012, 2014) here who contests this dominant view around caste and Bengali exceptionalism. Drawing upon archival evidence, he highlights the patterned ways in which the bhadralok undermined marginalized caste interests. He calls this unrecognized phenomenon of caste-based discrimination as 'absent-minded casteism'. Such absent-minded casteism continued to mark post-Partition West Bengal (Sen, 2016).

Broomfield (1968) is perhaps the one who best described the bhadralok's relation with caste:

> We now have of the Bengali bhadralok at the beginning of the twentieth century: a socially privileged and consciously superior group, economically dependent upon landed rents and professional and clerical employment; keeping its distance from the masses by its acceptance of high-caste proscriptions and its command of education … and maintaining its communal integration through a fairly complex institutional structure that it had proved remarkably ready to adapt and augment to extend its social power and political opportunities …
>
> Membership [to the bhadralok category] was not wholly ascriptive. For a low-caste Hindu or for a Muslim it was difficult to enter the charmed circle of the respectable, but it was not impossible and education was the means … There were however, formidable difficulties to be overcome. To the normal initial handicap of cultural deprivement common to lower-class children in all societies, was added the problem of competing for an English-language education with boys from English-literate upper-caste families, many of whom had received their elementary education from private tutors
>
> … The education system was costly and exclusive. It was controlled by the bhadralok primarily in the interest of the bhadralok. And for those non-bhadralok who did get the necessary education, there was still the formidable task of securing

---

[3] Those who belonged to the upper rungs such as zamindars, banias, the local nobility.

employment and reasonable promotion in offices under the regime of high-caste *bara babus* (chief clerks), for whom the exercise of patronage or outright nepotism was the accepted rule (Broomfield, 1968, pp. 7–10).

CASTE MOVEMENTS AND HINDU REVIVALISM

Sekhar Bandyopadhyay studied a protest movement through which, from 1872 onwards, the Namasudras of Bengal began to develop a community identity and to organize themselves into one of the most powerful castes in Bengal (Bandyopadhyay, 2011). From there, he analyses the eventual disintegration of the movement and its merger with other dominant political streams in colonial India. This work has been the first one to make visible the caste politics of the bhadralok society albeit through the lens of a Dalit community. In a later study, Bandyopadhyay and Basu Ray Chaudhury (2016) also point out the dispersal of the marginalized castes after Partition as a significant reason behind the decline of the caste movements in West Bengal. They also rightly point out the conflict within the marginalized castes in particular among the Namasudras around the alliance with Muslim politics and the Muslim League. This has been significant in weakening the community's challenge to bhadralok aspirations in the 1940s and later in West Bengal.

Referring to Shibnath Shastri's text *Jatibheda* (1963[1884]) Sumit Sarkar (1997) underscores that education and economic wealth were not enough to grant a lower caste high social status. Referring specifically to the caste of Subarnabaniks (a highly prosperous mercantile caste) he shows that despite their wealth and education they remained subjects of contempt for the Brahmins and Kayasthas of Calcutta (1998, p. 366). This fact reaffirms the significance that caste held for the bhadralok. Not only were the Subarnabaniks rich bankers and leaders in the Province's financial enterprises, they also were the caste that accounted for the highest rate of literacy in English. This ability to humiliate through abuse, through caricature, through calling names probably emerges from the symbolic power that upper castes hold. Subarnabaniks thus remained on the margins of bhadralok society although they possessed all of their attributes, other than that of being high caste. Indeed, as historical records and compilations show, Subarnabaniks were engaged in a large number of charitable and philanthropic work that included setting up numerous schools across Bengal (Laha, 1940). Despite all these accomplishments, the Subarnabaniks could not match the symbolic power of higher castes and it resulted in their consequent social marginalization.

It is often argued that the Hindu–Muslim and class questions have been able to dent the challenge of caste (Bandyopadhyay, 2011) or make caste less real (Chatterjee, 1982, 1984). Class mobilizations did break caste solidarities to an extent. Yet, one also needs to compare the differences in agenda when the movements are led by the marginalized castes and when they are led by the bhadralok. The 1940s Tebhaga movement is a case in point. Their demand for two-thirds share of the agricultural produce for the sharecroppers led to fracturing the caste-based solidarities in those regions where dalit castes held substantial amount of land as zamindars or jotedars.

However, one should not forget an earlier and much more radical agrarian movement that was waged around 1928, when dalit and Muslim sharecroppers as well as other marginal producers had gathered against Hindu upper caste and Muslim landholders to demand the abolition of zamindari and the abolition of intermediary interests. Tanika Sarkar (1987) argues that the force of this movement was such that different Hindu religious organizations consequently developed programmes of temple-entry, *shuddhi*, and granting of higher ritual status to these labouring castes. The famous Patuakhali Satyagraha (Bandyopadhyay, 2011) led by the Hindu Mission under the leadership of Swami Satyanand (who hailed from a marginalized caste) took place in this context.

Class, communal and caste politics intersect and these intersections often result into a 'Hindu dividend'[4] that benefits those identifying with the encompassing 'Hindu' dominant identity rather than with a particular caste identity. This is amply demonstrated by the Bharat Sevashram Sangha and its Hindu sangathan (community-building) project (Bandyopadhyay, 2016): the aim was to build among the dalit/marginalized castes the 'consciousness' of belonging to the 'Hindu' community, to uphold and fight for that identity. It was explicitly meant to 'Hinduise' these castes and to place them in direct conflict with the Muslims thereby taking them away from their anti-caste politics.

Partha Chatterjee (2016) has discussed the reasons behind the disappearance of caste in West Bengal and pointed out the crucial role of Partition in this. He explains that the Partition, by weakening the power of the Muslim elite, helped in the re-establishment of upper caste dominance in West Bengal. This dynamic was specific to Bengal. However, despite a growing scholarship on the visibility of caste in pre-Partition Bengal, Chatterjee claims that the challenge to Brahmanism and upper caste dominance in colonial Bengal came from the Muslims and not the marginalized castes. In his oversimplifying view, religion and communalism—rather than caste—were among the main engines of social change in Bengal.

CASTE IN POST-INDEPENDENCE AND MARXIST BENGAL

Ruud (1994, 1999) offers interesting insights into caste and Left political mobilizations in West Bengal through his study of a Burdwan village. He calls for a nuanced approach to *'the totalizing nature of hegemony'* (1999, p. 728). Tracing the alliance between the Marxists and the peasants in cultural hierarchy and role-obligations, he suggests:

---

[4] Drawing from RW Connell's concept (2005) of the patriarchal dividend.

> ... the CPI(M) vis-a-vis the peasantry came to fill a role homologous to that of a patron to his supporters. This implies that the alliance between Marxist and peasants was an exchange of moral and physical support for self-defined interests between unequal but interdependent partners rather than ties based on any expectation of near or future economic return. Though the two partners were not subject to the same moral or ideological code, their goals and interests coincided sufficiently to create this alliance. (Ruud, 1994, pp. 359–360)

He further elaborates:

> A tentative answer to the question of how the Marxists could mobilize peasants in such numbers during the late 1960s, has here been sought in the readily understood moral support the Marxists offered its followers ... But there is another element: this support would not automatically have been forthcoming to any organization or movement in a dominant position. CPI(M) and Kisan Sabha's explicit pro-poor agitation and leadership of high ritual rank, their inclusion of previously (politically) excluded groups, and practical accommodation of most socio-economic groups, and their ready involvement in local political issues ... contributed more towards creating ties between organization and followers than did the often bleak prospects of land redistribution. In addition, the humiliating dependency created by near or complete landlessness-a humiliation the CPI(M)/Kisan Sabha could do little about- was for many softened through participation in and recognition from the Marxist movement. (Ruud, 1994, pp. 378–379)

Studying the changing world of Calcutta's cultures of servitude, Ray and Qayum (2003) analyse the changes and continuities that mark bhadralok forms of distinction among the older and new generations. Through a study of the evolution of domestic servitude in Bhadralok households, they highlight the emergence of new 'notions of privacy and ideologies of the nuclear family' as well as of 'capitalist and corporate discourses about employers and employees'. These new repertoires inform and transform employer-servant relations. It nonetheless remains that benefiting from the help of domestic employees constitutes a distinctive category in terms of lifestyles, desires, and habits. Ray and Qayum argue that distinction between the bhadralok and its other 'is "naturally" reflected in a caste-inflected class distinction within the bhadra home' (2003, p. 541). The contradictory pulls of a modern capitalist ethos and the older hierarchical values of inequality bring out the tensions that mark domestic relations between employers and servants. The complex emergent relations around desires and expectations revolve around the maintenance of distinction in the 'home'. These tensions within the home are also reflective of the tensions that mark the outside: '[Q]uestions about servants' space and subjectivity are questions about a changing social order' (Ray and Qayum, 2003). Unlike in the past, when servants could be from lower or upper caste according to the nature of the task to be performed, the authors found that today's servants were overwhelmingly lower caste and that more than half of the domestic employees belong to scheduled castes. Asserting one's

Bhadralok status is thus closely linked to the capacity—or incapacity—to hire domestic employees: 'Employers and domestics engage in a complex choreography of expectations and disappointments as they negotiate the terrain of a newly emerging culture of servitude. It is clear, however, that the identity of Kolkata's respectable classes continues to rest on the maintenance of clear distinctions from the serving classes. New servant aspirations and servants who are seen to "pass" as non-servants cause anxiety because they threaten erasure of crucial distinction' (Ray and Qayum, 2003, pp. 547–548). Fear of contamination—passed off as a concern for hygiene—structures the relationship between the employer and the servants.

It is this same idea of contamination and of the transgression of boundaries that fuel the taboo of inter-caste marriage, particularly if the hierarchical distance is beyond 'permissible' limits. The concern is around the maintaining of the '*achar-bichar* or rules and customs of the house' (Donner, 2002). Examining Bengali marriage, caste, and kinship, Donner (2002) points out that reproduction is integrally related with '*cultural-differences and socio-biological differences (gun)*'. The primary concern against inter-caste marriage that Fruzzetti points out is '*the worry that the offspring of an inter-caste union will be born of bad moral character*' (Fruzetti, 2013, p. 48). Situating marriages within the wider contexts of caste, class, religious, and regional affiliations, Donner argues that traditional Bengali hierarchical values have been integrated into locally accepted class distinctions and that middle-class women are the custodians of the boundaries between households.

Hindu Reformism and the Countering of Marginalized Castes Mobilizations

Census operations reinforced the importance of caste. However, colonial exercise is not the only reason behind the importance of caste in Bengal. It is in what is seen as constitutive of the middle class (i.e. modern education, professional employment, literature, and 'culture' and politics) that we find the patterns of the predominance of upper-castes, hidden behind the veil of castelessness.

Joya Chatterji (2002) analyses the spectacular rise of the bhadralok till the Swadeshi movement and the beginnings of its meteoric fall from 1911. The Dignity Movement of 1872–1873 led by the Namasudras of the deltaic eastern Bengal made the caste question a thorn in the very existence of the Bengali bhadralok. This assertion of the marginalized caste in colonial Bengal led to a variety of responses from the bhadralok. Sandwiched between an onslaught on their legitimacy from below and the colonial perceptions of the Indian society as caste-ridden, the upper castes felt the necessity to reclaim their legitimacy. This was not sought simply through the re-establishment of their dominance but also through a questioning and reconstituting of upper caste selfhood.

Of these responses two are noteworthy for our analysis: one was the Hindu Mahasabha project of building an organized 'Hindu' society (*sangathan*) and related to this a radical response through the activities of a Vaishnav pandit from eastern Bengal, Digindranarayan Bhattacharya. The Bharat Sevashram Sangha and Hindu Mission for who Digindranarayan worked were among the central organizations that carried out the work of the Hindu sangathan. While Digindranarayan called upon the marginalized castes to unite and to refuse to serve the upper castes till they mended their ways and embraced the marginalized castes as their brethren, the Sangha was clearly opposed to any radical restructuring of the caste system. Indeed, in the literature of the Sangha, Digindranarayan remains conspicuous by his absence. However, Digindranarayan's radical politics was instrumental in bringing a large section of the marginalized castes under the banner of the Hindu Mahasabha. This brings us to an interesting aspect of the Bengali caste question. A large section of western Bengali marginalized castes were quite effectively mobilized under the Hindu Mahasabha while the same Hindu Mahasabha found it a labourious task to expand its influence among the marginalized castes in eastern Bengal. Eastern Bengal (which was primarily agriculture-based) had a Muslim majority population, particularly among the lower rungs of the agrarian hierarchy. This often led to collective struggle gathering Muslims and marginalized castes against the zamindars who were mainly Hindu upper caste but also included Muslims. Breaking these modes of cooperation required communalizing the existing conflicts between marginalized castes and Muslims. It therefore called for greater effort and, in the light of the complex historical relationship between the Muslims and Namasudras, this task proved to be a protracted one.

Despite fundamentalist movements, Eastern Bengal had also been witness to sustained movements against the zamindars waged by marginalized caste and Muslim tillers of agricultural lands. It was in eastern Bengal that the marginalized castes led by the Namasudras in alliance with the Muslims had declared non-cooperation with the Swadeshi movement and indeed gave support to the government's plan of partitioning the province. The Matua sect, founded in the latter half of the 19th century by Harichand Thakur, explicitly stood against the Hindu social order: Harichand Thakur had forbidden Matuas from worshipping Hindu deities and making pilgrimage to Hindu sacred places (Biswas, 2014; Sarkar, 1916). His son Guruchand took the Namasudra movement to new heights by bringing together the need to organize along with the need to educate. Education and organization became the twin pillars of the marginalized caste movements in eastern Bengal right from 1905 and they were often waged in close association with the Muslims of eastern Bengal. In his fight for education for the marginalized, Guruchand Thakur was generously aided by the Australian Baptist Mission (Bandyopadhyay, 2011; Sen, 2012).

It was around this time that we see bhadralok organizations taking up social reform issues on a massive scale. The Hindu Mahasabha and organizations such as the Bharat Sevashram Sangha and Hindu Mission plunged themselves into rebuilding Hindu society. The caste question got tied with the Muslim question and with the idea of the 'nation', and increasingly so following the Swadeshi movement (1905–1911).

The fault-lines between marginalized castes and Muslims were fully exploited by these organizations. The more the demands for increased participation and sharing of societal resources gained momentum among the marginalized castes, the more organized and widespread became the campaign for Hindu *sangathan*. The Patuakhali Satyagraha mentioned earlier is a case in point. The 1937 elections saw the Scheduled Caste MLAs ally with the Muslim-led political parties such as the Krishak Praja Party and the Muslim League. But this was not enough to keep the bhadralok out of the government. Before the 1941 Census, the Hindu Mahasabha and its allied organizations actively campaigned among the marginalized castes so that they would identify as 'Hindu' only and not as Depressed Classes. Along with this, the War forced the government to leave the census field personnel (who were predominantly upper caste) almost unsupervised. This came in handy for the Hindu bhadralok. As a result, the Depressed Classes population came down by 1.8 million for Bengal as compared to the 1931 Census (Sen, 2014).

The historical anti-brahminical and anti-caste joint mobilizations of the Namasudras and the Muslims notwithstanding, it is important to bear in mind that there were powerful Namasudra factions which were aligned with the Hindu Mahasabha or the Congress. Acutely aware of what the caste system holds for the marginalized, their identification of being 'Hindu' stemmed from their understanding that they were among the original inhabitants of Bengal and that the Muslims came from 'outside'. Regardless of the few conversions into Islam of some members of marginalized castes, most non-Muslim marginalized caste members had identified Islam as an 'outsider' religion.[5] This did open up possibilities for the politics of Hindu sangathan (Bandyopadhyay, 2016a).

The Hindu sangathan also rested upon the desire of some powerful (mostly western Bengali)[6] marginalized castes to be recognized as 'Hindu' and to be placed among the three twice-born varnas. Indeed the powerful Paundra caste split over the tag of 'depressed class'. The 'Hindu' identity was seen as more 'universal' and more 'respectable' especially in the context of a rising Muslim community. However, the Hindu bhadralok could never trust the loyalty of marginalized castes to the Hindu sangathan and this resulted in marginalized caste majority districts to be finally left out of the new West Bengal that was being carved out of the Bengal province. Partition somehow solved the twin problem of marginalized caste politics and of Muslim assertion.

---

[5] This was one of the dominant views, I gathered from fieldwork among the Namasudra refugees. Noting my facial expression one of the wittiest and most articulate of participants asked me if I found in his interview anything close to Savarkar's position on who was a Hindu and then dismissed such speculations by asserting that as untouchables they stood outside and against the caste system. Therefore their notions of a 'Hindu' was at odds with that of Hindu Mahasabha.

[6] The Hinduisation of the Matua sect also began taking place almost immediately after the death of Guruchand Thakur when Matua writers began to claim that Harichand and Guruchand were reincarnations of Brahma and Shiva the most important deities in the Hindu pantheon.

Partition and the Invisibilization of Caste in West Bengal

Post-Partition, when marginalized caste refugees started arriving in large numbers from East Pakistan, most of them were forced to live in government camps or move into the interior districts. Bhadralok refugees could stay in Calcutta and the neighbouring areas and could utilize their caste networks to secure their stay (Sen, U., 2014). Lands of absentee landlords, inoperative barracks, idle government land and land belonging to Muslims were primarily occupied by the bhadralok refugees in and around Calcutta. In the interior districts, the marginalized castes were encouraged to occupy the lands of Muslims and settle there, driving away the local Muslim population from their lands. This aspect makes the caste question take an interesting turn here whose relevance can be felt acutely now in the context of the Citizenship Amendment Act, 2019 and the National Register of Citizens. One can witness the 'Hindu dividend' come into play. Initially, marginalized caste members saw their pleas for the inclusion of their districts into West Bengal rejected. But when they later came as refugees and as later entrants, with little or no social networks, they were unlikely to pose any serious challenge to the bhadralok domination. As refugees, they made the best out of their situation: identifying themselves as refugees and as 'Hindu' rather than as marginalized caste. Their claim to belonging to this nation could be measured only against their (antagonistic) distance from the Muslims.[7] This historical burden is still intensely felt today, especially among the descendants of Namasudra refugees.

Post-Partition West Bengal therefore saw almost no upsurge along the lines of caste. Caste had indeed lost its visibility and the discriminatory refugee rehabilitation policy of the government was an important reason for this. The marginalized caste challenge to bhadralok domination came primarily from eastern Bengal through autonomous movements and organizations. The Partition thus successfully suppressed this opposition to the bhadralok hegemony. It is in this sense that one could say following Sen (2012) that the Partition was a 'nationalist resolution of the caste question' in West Bengal. The discriminatory refugee rehabilitation policy of the state help understands the dalit position according to which the refugee question is actually the caste question in post-Partition West Bengal. It is thus clear that the intersection of caste and religious identities complicated the caste question. While Sen (2012) is right in pointing out that 'the analytical tyranny of communalism' has for long overshadowed dalit insights into the communal problem, it still remains crucial to take into account the way the Hindu 'dividend' that refugees benefitted from countered the political influence of the marginalized castes.

---

[7] In his study, Bandyopadhyay (2009) mentions that the refugee dalits, in particular Namasudras had led riots against the Muslims in the border districts of West Bengal and occupied their lands as a form of rehabilitation.

The 'Muslim' remains a significant 'other' for Dalits and this figure shapes their sense of collective identity.

Such a 'caste-free' West Bengal led to severe violations to the rules of reservations.[8] West Bengal introduced the West Bengal Reservations in Vacancies (Recruitment of Scheduled Castes and Scheduled Tribes) Act in 1976 in order to ensure that reservation rules were implemented in the state. Even then, till the 1980s the recruitment roster was not in order. Moreover, most recruitment till about the mid-1980s occurred through personal networks. The absence of any official will to implement reservations in recruitment and the personal nature of such recruitment allowed Dalit candidates to enter the teaching profession as 'uncasted' and therefore as meritorious individuals. This allowed them to become part of the bhadralok society but their narratives reveal that their belongingness was contingent on their caste identity remaining unknown to these circles (Bandyopadhyay, 2016a). The Partition of 1947 had thus swept away the possibility of an educated, articulate, and assertive marginalized caste population from West Bengal. The middle-class spaces continued to remain dominated by upper castes and, in these spaces, raising the issue of caste was viewed with scepticism and even suspicion. By default, the bhadralok universe was an upper caste one, but one never recognized as such. The marginalized castes who entered the middle-class spaces could thus only do so by keeping their caste identity away from scrutiny and by resorting to 'passing' (Goffman, 1963; Renfrow, 2004). When, on occasions, their caste identities got revealed, they were greeted with surprise, shock, and other reactions that often pointed out they had 'tres-passed' into forbidden territory (Bandyopadhyay, 2016a). Their personhood and their right to react back were denied, leading to deeper wounds in their sense of identity.

The 1976 Act was a turning point and led to 'marking' the hitherto 'unmarked' marginalized castes in middle-class spaces. They got stigmatized as 'sarkari pushyiputra' (adopted/domesticated kids of the government). Such labels became important in bhadralok attempts to maintain the boundaries of the middle-class and keep 'intruders' and 'encroachers' away.

Forms of lifestyle and cultural capital that the bhadralok had access to and could appropriate as theirs have not, unlike in Tamil Nadu (Fuller, 1999) been dissociated from caste in West Bengal. Bhadralok lifestyle since its inception has been intimately connected with upper caste lifestyle and value systems. In Tamil Nadu, as Fuller (1999) argues, the decline of Brahmanical superiority in the political domains allowed for the dissociation of brahmanical cultural values from the Brahmin caste and made them available as universal values for all Tamils. This kind of disjunction between caste status, class position, and political power has not happened in West Bengal. The real possibilities of this happening were cut short by the Partition of the Province in 1947. Since then, West Bengal has witnessed a large-scale re-securing of bhadralok domination in all spheres. Consequently, this prevented the possibility of any dis-empowerment of upper-castes,

---

[8] WB Assembly Proceedings 1976.

a process that Fuller (1999) identifies as having contributed to the dissociation of brahminical values from the Brahmins in Tamil Nadu.

The prejudice and everyday discrimination against marginalized castes in the workplace was revived when in 2005 a dalit organization waged an agitation for the filling up of 900 vacancies in reserved category posts (Bandyopadhyay, 2016a). Such an agitation and the resultant recruitment of some 300 reserved category candidates across colleges in West Bengal over four years renewed a sense of siege that had gripped the middle class in 1991 over the Mandal controversy. This entry seemed to have breached an unwritten accord that under the patronage of bhadralok society 'lower castes' could 'progress'. Self-assertions on the part of the latter finally forced some of the caste practices to become visible.

Anjan Ghosh (2001) has rightly pointed out that it is largely the absence of overt physical violence that has fuelled the idea that Bengal is an exceptional case for caste. He further argued that the Partition was responsible for the migration of a substantial rich Muslim peasantry to East Pakistan, thus suppressing the most serious contenders to bhadralok domination in post-Partition West Bengal. However, the Partition simultaneously took away the presence, the visibility, and the challenge from the assertive marginalized castes. That is why despite West Bengal recording 24 per cent Scheduled Caste population (Rana, 2009) this state has also been marked by a near complete absence of caste as part of the social vocabulary and with little challenge to bhadralok domination. In a recent piece, Maroona Murmu (2019) has rightly underscored the symbolic violence that Bengali bhadralok society imposes on marginalized castes.

West Bengal, far from being casteless, is a caste-society inflicting invisible wounds. It is therefore not surprising that Bengali Dalits consider the past to be better than the present. This is in contrast to Dalit positions from other parts of the country that generally approach the past as characterized by more oppression and humiliation than the present. For Bengali Dalits, the temporality is reversed: the past was a time of relatively greater political assertion, dignity, and empowerment. Partition of 1947 opened a new cycle of violence against them, silencing their voices and their political subjectivities.

References

Assembly Proceedings, Official Report, West Bengal Legislative Assembly. West Bengal Government Press, Alipore, 1976.
Bairy, R. 2010. *Being Brahmin, Being Modern: Exploring the Lives of Caste Today*. New Delhi: Routledge.
Bandyopadhyay, B. 1823. *Kalikata Kamalalay*. Calcutta: Bhabanicharan Bandyopadhyay.
Bandyopadhyay, Sarbani. 2008. 'Caste and Bengali Middle Class Self'. *West Bengal Sociological Review*, 1(1): 53–67.
Bandyopadhyay, S. 2011. *Caste, Protest and Identity in Colonial India: The Namasudras of Bengal, 1872–1947*. New Delhi: Oxford University Press.

Bandyopadhyay, S. 2012. 'Caste and Politics in Bengal'. *Economic and Political Weekly*, 47 (50): 71–73.
Bandyopadhyay, S. 2016. 'Another History: Bhadralok Responses to Dalit Political Assertion in Colonial Bengal'. In U. Chandra, G. Heierstad, and K. B. Nielsen (Eds.), *The Politics of Caste in West Bengal*. New Delhi: Routledge.
Bandyopadhyay, S., and A. B. R. Chaudhury. 2016. 'Partition Displacement, and the Decline of the Schedule Caste Movement in West Bengal'. In U. Chandra, G. Heierstad, and K. B. Nielsen (Eds.), *The Politics of Caste in West Bengal*. New Delhi: Routledge.
Bandyopadhyay, S. 2016a, December. 'The Lives of Caste among the Bengali Middle Class: A Study of the Contemporary'. Unpublished PhD thesis submitted to IIT Bombay.
Bayly, C. A. 2012. *Recovering Liberties: Indian Thought in the Age of Liberalism and Empire*. Cambridge, Cambridge University Press.
Bhattacharya, T. 2005. *The Sentinels of Culture: Class, Education, and the Colonial Intellectual in Bengal (1848–1885)*. Delhi: Oxford University Press.
Biswas, D. K. 2014. *Sri Sri Harililamrita: Prasanga Harichand Thakurer Nishedhagwa*. Kolkata: Janamon.
Broomfield, J. H. 1968. *Elite Conflict in a Plural Society: Twentieth-Century Bengal*. Berkeley and Los Angeles, University of California Press.
BSS. 2006. *Sangha Gita*. Kolkata: Sangha.
Chatterjee, P. 1984. *Bengal 1920–1947: The Land Question*. Calcutta: KP Bagchi.
Chatterjee, P. 1982. 'Caste and Politics in West Bengal'. In G. Omvedt (Ed.), *Land, Caste and Politics in Indian States*. Delhi: Authors Guild Publications.
Chatterjee, P., 1997. *The Present History of West Bengal: Essays in Political Criticism*. New Delhi, Oxford University Press.
Chatterjee, P. 1999. *The Partha Chatterjee Omnibus*. New Delhi, Oxford University Press.
Chatterjee, P. 2016. 'Partition and the Mysterious Disappearance of Caste in Bengal'. In U. Chandra, G. Heierstad, and K. B. Nielsen (Eds.), *The Politics of Caste in West Bengal*. New Delhi: Routledge.
Chatterji, J. 2002. *Bengal Divided: Hindu Communalism and Partition, 1932–1947*. Cambridge: Cambridge University Press.
Donner, H. 2002. ' "One's Own Marriage": Love Marriages in a Calcutta Neighbourhood'. *South Asia Research*, 22(1): 79–94.
Fruzzetti, L. 2013. *When Marriages Go Astray: Choices Made, Choices Challenged*. New Delhi: Orient Blackswan Private Limited.
Fuller, C. 1999. 'The Brahmins and Brahminical Values in Modern Tamilnadu'. In R. Guha and J. P. Parry (Eds.), *Institutions and Inequalities: Essays in Honour of Andre Béteille*. New Delhi: Oxford University Press.
Fuller, C. J., and H. Narasimhan. 2015. *Tamil Brahmans: The Making of a Middle-Class Caste*. New Delhi: Social Science Press.
Ghosh, A. 2001. 'Cast(e) Out in West Bengal'. *Seminar-India, New Delhi* (508): 47–49.
Ghosh, A. 2002. 'Revisiting the "Bengal Renaissance": Literary Bengali and Low-Life Print in Colonial Calcutta'. *Economic and Political Weekly*, 37(42): 4329–4338.
Ghosh, S. 1938. *Sadgop Tattwa* (Vol. 1). Sameeksha Trust: Calcutta.
Ghosh, S. 1939. *Sadgop Tattwa* (Vol. 2). Calcutta.
Goffman, E. 1963. *Stigma. Notes on the Management of Spoiled Identity*. New York: Simon and Shuster, Inc.

Jodhka, S. S., and K. Newman. 2007. 'In the Name of Globalisation: Meritocracy, Productivity and the Hidden Language of Caste'. *Economic and Political Weekly*, 42(41): 4125–4132.

Juktananda, 2007. *Hindu Milan Mandir*. Kolkata: Sangha.

Laha, N. 1940. *Subarnabanik – Katha o kirti* (Vol. 1). Calcutta: Oriental Press.

Mandal, M. 1926. *Bange Didindranarayan*. Kanthi.

McGuire, J. 1983. *The Making of a Colonial Mind: A Quantitative Study of the Bhadralok in Calcutta, 1857–1885*. Canberra: Australian National University.

Menon, D. M. 2006. *The Blindness of Insight: Essays on Caste in Modern India*. Chennai: Navayana Publishing.

Mukherjee, S. N. 1975. 'Daladali in Calcutta in the Nineteenth Century'. *Modern Asian Studies*, 9(01): 59–80.

Mukherjee, S. N. 1970. 'Class, Caste and Politics in Politics, 1815–38'. In E. R. Leach and S. N. Mukherjee (Eds.), *Elites in South Asia*. Cambridge: Cambridge University Press.

Murmu, M. 2019. 'Structural Violence of Casteism: A Personal Narrative by an Adivasi University Teacher'. *India Forum*. https://www.theindiaforum.in/article/structural-violence-casteism, accessed 23 September 2019.

Rana, S., and K. Rana. 2009. *Paschim Bange dalit o Adivasi*. Kolkata: Camp.

Renfrow, D. G. 2004. 'A Cartography of Passing in Everyday Life. *Symbolic Interaction*, 27(4): 485–506.

Ray, R, and S. Qayum. 2003. 'Grappling with Modernity: India's Respectable Classes and the Culture of Domestic Servitude'. *Ethnography*, 4(4): 520–555[1466–1381(200312)4:4;520–555;039219] www.sagepublications.com, accessed 7 November 2019.

Ruud, A. E. 1994. 'Land and Power: The Marxist Conquest of Rural Bengal'. *Modern Asian Studies*, 28(02): 357–380.

Ruud, A. E. 1999. 'The Indian Hierarchy: Culture, Ideology and Consciousness in Bengali Village Politics'. *Modern Asian Studies*, 33(03): 689–732.

Sanyal, H. 1981. *Social Mobility in Bengal*. Calcutta: Papyrus.

Sarkar, T. C. 1916. *Sri Narayana Harililamrita*. Faridpur.

Sarkar, T. 1987. *Bengal, 1928–1934, the Politics of Protest*. New Delhi: Oxford University Press.

Sarkar, S. 1997. *Writing Social History*. New Delhi: Oxford University Press.

Sarma, J. 1980. *Caste Dynamics among the Bengali Hindus*. Calcutta: Firma KLM.

Sen, D. 2012. '"No Matter How, Jogendranath Had to Be Defeated": The Scheduled Castes Federation and the Making of Partition in Bengal, 1945–1947'. *Indian Economic & Social History Review*, 49(3): 321–364. SAGE.

Sen, D. 2014. 'An Absent Minded Casteism?' *Seminar*, 645.

Sen, D. 2016. 'An Absent Minded Casteism?' In U. Chandra, G. Heierstad, and K. B. Nielsen (Eds.), *The Politics of Caste in West Bengal*. Routledge: New Delhi.

Sen, U. 2014. 'The Myths Refugees Live By: Memory and History in the Making of Bengali Refugee Identity'. *Modern Asian Studies*, 48(01): 37–76.

CHAPTER 28

CASTE IN PUNJAB

SURINDER S. JODHKA

In the literature and imaginations of caste in India, Punjab has been an interesting kind of outlier, a periphery, where caste matters but its popular theories do not seem to apply so easily. Punjab has not been a land of Brahmanical Hinduism, a religion that supposedly sanctifies the practice of caste, the fountain head of its ideology. However, this did not mean absence of caste from the region. Like most other parts of India, caste remains quite central to the social, spatial, and political life of Punjab. This is true not only about its demographic minority, the Hindu population, but also about the social landscape of other communities of the region. The institution of caste shapes or influences almost everything: kinship and family structures, electoral politics and power relations in the everyday life, designs of rural and urban settlements, the patterns of land ownership and the agrarian economy, as well as social relations across communities, and classes of its populace.

Punjab has also been important in the modern/contemporary history of caste and caste-based identity politics. For example, it was for a lecture to be delivered here, in Lahore, to the members of the *Jat-Pat-Todak Mandal*, a reformist Hindu organization that claimed to be focused on 'dismantling' of caste, that B. R. Ambedkar wrote in 1935 his most celebrated text *Annihilation of Caste*. The region has also been witnessed to some of the most influential Dalit mobilizations, some of which have been important markers in the history of Dalit politics, nationally and globally. The most prominent of these has been the Ad-Dharam movement during the 1920s. Led by California-returned Mangoo Ram, the Chamars of the Doaba region of Punjab were among the first of the Dalit communities in the region to effectively mobilize against the hierarchical culture of caste. They demanded from the colonial rulers that instead of being listed as an untouchable Hindu caste, which placed them among the lowest in the Hindu social hierarchy, they be recognized as a separate religious community, the believers of Ad Dharam. Their listing as a separate religion was to make them a distinct *kaum*, outside the hierarchical frame of caste and thus enlisting them horizontally as one among the religious communities of the region, different but equal, at par with the Hindus, the Sikhs, or the Muslims of Punjab (see Jurgensmeyer, 1988; Jodhka, 2016).

Their mobilizations were spirited and significant enough to make British rulers concede to the demand and during the Census enumerations of 1931 they were listed as a separate religion (see Jurgensmeyer, 1988). Sections of Dalit population have remained politically active and continue to mobilize around a range of issues. Dalit population in Punjab is also very large in numbers, larger than any other state of the country in proportional term. The 39 communities listed as Scheduled Caste in the state list of such communities together made for 32 per cent of the total state population of Punjab in 2011, nearly double the national average of around 16 per cent. Some of the prominent leaders of the national level Dalit politics have been from Punjab. Perhaps the most prominent of them has been Kanshi Ram, the founder of Bahujan Samaj Party (BSP). Even though it has not been able to be of much significance in the state politics of Punjab but at the national level BSP has been electorally the most successful of Dalit led political parties.

The Regional Context: The present-day Indian Punjab, the focus of this chapter, has been a fluid region. Its demographics and administrative boundaries have changed several times over the past two centuries. Until 1947, when it was partitioned at the time the India's independence from the British colonial rule, Punjab was a much larger region, with the Muslims making for the majority of its population. However, the Sikhs and the Hindus were also in substantial numbers. Almost the entire Sikh population lived here but they made for only around 13 or 14 per cent of its total population. Even in the Sikh kingdom of Ranjit Singh during the early half of the 19th century, a majority of the population of his Empire were followers of Islam.

The Partition of Punjab in 1947 was accompanied by large-scale communal violence. Almost the entire Sikh and Hindu population was forced to leave their homes and move to the Indian side of the newly drawn international border. Similarly, Muslims of Punjab were also made to migrate to Pakistan. Besides many other things, Partition changed demographic balance of communities. The Hindus emerged as a majority population in the Indian side of Punjab. However, their demographic dominance was short lived. Following the Punjabi-Suba movement by the Sikh Akalis, the province was once again divided and administratively re-organized in 1966. The Hindi speaking and Hindu majority pockets were separated out of the state; some of these were merged with the hill state of Himachal Pradesh and the others made into the new state of Haryana. Thus, Punjab became a Sikh majority state of the Indian union (see Jodhka, 2006a) and its demographic profile has not seen much change after 1966.

According to the 2011 Census, Sikhs made for nearly 58 per cent and Hindus 38 per cent of the total population of Punjab. The Muslims were nearly 2 per cent and the Christians a little above 1 per cent. The Buddhists, Jains, and those who did not state their religions were all together less than 1 per cent.[1] Size of the Hindu population of

---

[1] https://www.census2011.co.in/data/religion/state/3-punjab.html, accessed 25 June 2019.

Punjab is slightly overstated in the Census because after the introduction of caste-based quotas, the Ad Dahrmi Dalits gave up their insistence on being listed as a separate religion and were clubbed along with the Hindus. However, their sense of distinctive identity has only become stronger over time. The rise of Ravidassia-movement during the first decade of the 21st century has further reinforced this process. Their religious practices continue to differ from the local Hindus and have historically been closer to Sikhism (see Jodhka, 2009; Ram, 2017).

Given its social and political history and religious demographics on the one hand and the reality of persistent hierarchies of caste on the other, the present-day Indian Punjab provides an interesting case that raises several compelling questions, which have important implications for the popular theoretical understanding of caste. The mainstream and textbook literature on caste almost universally locates the source of its origin and persistence in the Hindu faith and its ritual order. The Punjab case also calls for recognition of diverse trajectories of caste as they have evolved in different regional contexts and its intersections with material processes such as the agrarian economy and business cultures. Given that caste in the region has remained a fact of life without the overarching figure of the Brahmin, the Punjab case also raises question about the value of the *varna* model of hierarchy, empirically as well as theretically. How does then caste survive and reproduce itself? This chapter attempts a broad overview of the dynamics of caste in the regional context of Punjab, with a focus on the Indian Punjab.

Religion and Caste[2]: Caste has for long been viewed as a traditional system of hierarchy prevalent among the Hindus of south Asia/India. Though not all Indians are Hindus, this popular view also underlines the claim that foundational values of Indian culture are quintessentially drawn from Hindu religious philosophy. The Muslims, the Christians, the Sikhs, or even the Buddhists, and Jains of the Indian origin have either converted out of Hinduism (such as the Indian Muslims or the Indian Christians), or their faith systems are branches and varieties of Hinduism. Caste in such narratives is almost always presented as a critical element and evidence of the claim of India's Hinduness. In other words, the presence of caste or caste like divisions and hierarchies among the non-Hindu communities of India is thus viewed as a proof of their Hindu ancestry.

Much of this was popularized by indologist and orientalist writings on India. However, this view of India was also enthusiastically endorsed and accepted by colonial rulers, native 'reformers' and the mainstream nationalist leadership. The British colonial rulers also institutionalized some of this when they initiated Census enumerations in 1870s. Similarly, the religion-centric view of caste was also accepted quite uncritically and reinforced by the makers of Indian Constitution when they made religion a fundamental marker for the identification of Scheduled Castes among the socially deprived communities.

This Hindu-centric view of caste frames it as a religiously constructed structure of hierarchy, first codified in an ancient Hindu text, the *Manusmṛti*. The textual model

---

[2] This section partially draws from Jodhka (2017).

of caste ranked the Hindus into four *varṇa*s with Brahmans at the top, followed by Kṣatriyas, Vaiśyas, and Śūdras. Outside the *varṇa* hierarchy and lowest in the rank are the untouchables. Even when the details and names of *jāti*s varied across regions and time, the structure of hierarchy remained intact for centuries. As suggested above, in this framework, conversions to Islam or Christianity made little difference to the hierarchical mind of the Indians. The local movements that articulated critiques of the hierarchal system and offered alternative views on transcendence similarly failed to erase the values of hierarchy from the lay minds of the local communities. It was only during the British colonial rule, when modern ideas were infused into Indian life through the introduction of Western-style secular education, modern technology, and urban life, that the reality of caste began to loosen its grip.

An engagement with the contemporary realities of caste in a region like the Indian Punjab thus must begin with a critique of this view, much of which has already been done by the recent and not so recent historical scholarship on caste and the broader subject of Hinduism, orientalism, and the 'colonial forms of knowledge', to use Bernard Cohn's expression (Cohn, 1996). According to the alternative view presented by this scholarship, the popular and dominant view of caste, and Indian history and culture is founded on several untenable assumptions (Frykenberg, 1989; Smith, 1989; Fuller, 1997; Thapar, 1989; Oberoi, 1994). First of all, it constructs caste as singular pan-Indian reality with no variations across regions (For example, in Dumont, 1998; for its critique, see Dirks, 2001) and Hinduism as a cohesive faith system with a unified theological structure and without any variations in its social organization across geographical regions and vertical hierarchies. By implication, Hinduism is presented as a monotheistic faith system, comparable to other religious systems, such as Christianity and Islam, which are similarly presumed to be monotheistic in their ideological moorings. Second, it views caste purely as a religious value, the structural logic of which lay almost exclusively in Hindu religious philosophy and ritual practice, which alone shapes the Indian mind and everyday social life. While it is true that, quite like many other social institutions, such as marriage and family, caste too has an ideational dimension, and does find its articulation in Hindu religious philosophy, the diverse realities of caste could not be entirely reduced to religion and ritual practice (Jodhka, 2015). Third, such a view of India and Hinduism or caste and village life allows no agency to the Indian people and also negates any possibility of change through internal processes and critiques (see Inden, 1990; Cohn, 1996).

Religion, Caste, and the Punjabi Social: Theologically speaking, Sikhism, and South Asian Islam, actively decry caste. It was in Punjab that the founder of Sikh faith, Guru Nanak, and other Sikh Gurus preached their message of human equality. Though the ten Sikh Gurus were all from upper caste Hindu Khatri families, their crusade against Brahminical hierarchy and ritualism was indisputable. Not only were the Sikh gurus 'beyond all doubt, vigorous and practical denouncers of caste' (McLeod, 1996, p. 87) they advocated equality of human beings, at a social plane as well as in relation to God. The second guru standardized the Gurumukhi script, which eventually became a vehicle for the Punjabi language and identity. Earlier Guru Nanak had consciously rejected Sanskrit in preference of the indigenous spoken language. When the fifth guru, Guru Arjun compiled the canon of the faith, the Adi Granth, he included the writings of some of the contemporary saints from the so-called Shudra and 'untouchable' castes (such as Kabir, a weaver; Ravidas, a cobbler; Sadhan, a butcher; and Sain, a barber). Bhai Budha who was appointed the first reader and custodian (*granthi*) was a Jatt by caste. Of the 'five beloved' who were the first to be baptized as Khalsas on the day of Baisakhi in 1699 by the tenth guru, four reportedly came from castes belonging to 'middle' or 'lower' categories in the given social hierarchy.

The Sikh Gurus also initiated several communitarian institutions that defied the logic of caste, pollution, and hierarchy. The most prominent of these were the *sangat*, congregational worship and the *langar*, practice of sitting together, and eating from the same source irrespective of one's identity. W. H. McLeod describes these as initiatives that promoted 'compulsory commensality' (1996, p. 86). Besides the influence of the Sikh movement, Islamic and Sufi ideas of common humanity would have played a role in shaping the everyday social life in the region.

Given its current demographics, it will perhaps be useful to say a bit more about Sikhism. For the founder Guru, Nanak, the aim of salvation was union with God that transcended the cycle of birth and death. Since the divine presence was everywhere, it was available to everyone. He denounced ritualism, ascetic practices, and idol worship. An important aspect of Guru Nanak's philosophy was his emphasis on the values of everyday life, a 'this worldliness'. In other words, against the choice available within the classical Hinduism of getting out of the caste system through renunciations (see Dumont, 1998, pp. 184–185; Srivastava, 1999), Guru Nanak denounced caste while living within the social world.

Persistent Caste and Dynamics of Change: Despite these radical moves targeting the hierarchical ritual order and the changes it produced in the local culture and normative frames of social life, caste did not go away from the region. As indicated above, its presence and practice is also not denied by anyone. From colonial enumerations and reports, the ethnographic accounts of rural social life and urban settlements produced by social anthropologists and other social scientists to the popular fiction, everyone has reported the significance of caste in everyday life of the Punjabis, in Punjab and those living outside, including in the Punjabi diaspora.

However, the presence of caste does not imply a common structure or framework of social life everywhere. As a dynamic institution, its practice varies with space and time, across communities and settlements. For example, an important aspect of the religious demographics of the state is its important intersection with the rural-urban divisions of the Punjabi population, which has some interesting implications for the diverse ways in which caste is practised in the state. For various historical and sociological reasons, the Sikhs of Punjab are more concentrated in the rural areas while the reverse is true of the Hindus. Almost all the major cities of Punjab have Hindu majority population. Even in district like Amritsar, where Sikh made for more than 90 per cent of the rural population in 1981, the city area had nearly 55 per cent Hindus in the same year (see Jodhka, 2000, p. 384).[3]

Even the upper caste Sikhs in urban Punjab tend to be of different jatis than those who dominate the rural Punjab. It was with this context in mind that W. H. McLeod argued that the Punjabi society had two 'general hierarchies': one urban and the other rural (1996, p. 103). He goes on to elaborate that in urban Punjab, the trading caste of Khatris occupied a superior ranking and Aroras closely followed them. In contrast the rural hierarchy had neither of them in position of dominance or superior status. Instead, the landowning cultivating Jatts occupy the superior-most position in a typical village of Punjab. They are followed by the Ramgarhias in the middle and the Dalit castes Mazhabis and Ramdasias at the bottom (1996, p. 103; also see Judge, 2010).

A large majority of the urban Khatris and Aroras of Punjab would identify themselves as Hindus and their position in the status hierarchies of urban Punjab is very similar, irrespective of religious identification. Perhaps the only difference among them is their relationship with the local Brahmins. While Sikh religion has no priesthood or any specific caste group tied to its ritual life, the Hindus do have their Brahmins. However, their requirement for ritual life did not give them a high status within the Hindu community of the region. In an interesting commentary on social life in colonial Punjab, Prakash Tandon, a Hindu Khatri himself, writes in his autobiographical *Punjabi Century* that it was difficult to find 'an affluent Brahmin' in the region (Tandon, 1988, p. 77). They lived a 'frugal life' and in his native village the Brahmins were generally treated as members of the menial castes. Like other menials, they too depended for their livelihood on their *jajmans*:

> With us brahmins were an underprivileged class and exercised little or no influence on the community ... Our brahmins did not as a rule even have the role of teachers, because until the British opened regular schools, teaching was done by Muslim mullahs in the mosques or by Sikh granthis ... in the Gurudwaras. Our brahmins were rarely erudite; in fact many of them were barely literate, possessing only a perfunctory knowledge of rituals and knowing just the necessary mantras by heart. (Tandon, 1988, p. 76)

Anthropologist Satish Saberwal who studied a small town of Punjab during the 1960s corroborates Tandon's observation: 'In Punjabi the word *pandat* (pandit) denotes a brahmin and may connote some respect for the latter. But the word *bahman* (brahmin) almost always carries a little contempt' (Saberwal, 1976, p. 10).

Perhaps this 'status poverty' of Brahmin in the region also implied that even when divisions and hierarchy of caste existed or even when its normative order persisted, its ideological scaffolding remained weak.

---

[3] Data on religion-wise distribution across rural and urban settlements is not available for later period.

When the British extended their rule to Punjab after defeating Ranjit Singh in 1839, the colonial observers appeared to have been surprised at the absence of rigid caste hierarchy in the region. Some of them went to the extent of saying that Punjab was a 'notable exception' to the caste system in India (O'Malley in Nayar, 1966, p. 20). Commenting on the status of 'low castes' in the province, a colonial government report, for example, observed in the 1920s:

> It would be misleading to attach too great importance to the existence of caste in the Punjab .... Not only is it the case that the Brahman has no practical pre-eminence among Hindus, but as between 'caste' and 'non-caste' Hindus the distinction is not so strongly marked as to create the political problem found elsewhere in India.[4]

Social differentiation in Punjab, some of them felt, resembled Europe more than mainland India. As another observer wrote:

> Nowhere else in Hindu India does caste sit so lightly or approach so nearly to the social classes of Europe.[5]

Ethnographic accounts produced by social anthropologists during the 1960s and 1970 too report on similar lines. Joyce Pettigrew, an anthropologist, who conducted her fieldwork in Punjab during the early 1970s goes to the extent of saying that the rural society of Punjab differs radically from the Hindu India because of the absence of caste among the Sikhs (Pettigrew, 1975, p. 4). However, Paul Hershman, another anthropologist who carried out his fieldwork in a village near Jalandhar contested Pettigrew's claim and accused her of writing 'from the premise of Sikh theology that there is no caste among the Sikhs' (Hershman, 1981, p. 21). He was right. While recognizing that caste divisions existed in the region, the available literature also indicates that the changes experienced in the attitudes towards caste during the last century have been significant. Evidence for this is available from studies of individual villages and towns, as well as from the writing on social reform movements during the early half of the 20th century, particularly those targeting 'low castes'.

Reporting from a village near Amritsar during the late 1950s, anthropologist I. P. Singh (1975, 1977), found the village being divided into two groups, the Sardars (the upper castes), and the Mazhabis (the lower caste scavengers). The first group included the Jatts, Kambohs, Tarkhans, Kumhars, Sunars, and Nais (in the Hindu caste hierarchy, they would all be clubbed as Shudras and with the exception of Jatts, in the official list of the 'Other Backward Classes'). Though the agriculturist Jatts considered themselves higher than the other groups in this category, Singh found no feeling of caste-based avoidance or prejudice among them. They visited each other's house, inter-dined and

---

[4] Great Britain Indian Statutory Commission, *Memorandum Submitted by the Government of Punjab (1930)* as in Nayar (1966, p. 20).

[5] See James Drummond Anderson (1913, p. 26) as in Nayar (1966, p. 20).

attended marriage functions and celebrated most of the festivals together. In terms of the village settlement also, no demarcation existed in the houses of these groups.

However, the Mazhabis, who constituted nearly half of the village population, were treated differently. They lived on one side of the village. They had a separate well for their drinking water needs while all the other castes used a common well. In the village feasts, where everyone was invited, the Mazhabis sat separately. Since many of them worked as labourers in the fields of the Jatt landowners, the latter visited the houses of the Mazhabis but they did so as a patronizing gesture.

There were also occasions where untouchability was either not practiced or its extent had been declining. Many Jatts in the village let the Mazhabis enter their houses and did not consider their touch polluting. One of them had also employed a Mazhabi to clean utensils in his house. Untouchability was practiced minimally among the drinkers in the village. The Mazhabis were the traditional brewers of country liquor in the village.

> Mazhabis and Sardars drink liquor together at the fair and occasionally in the fields. We saw them drinking from the same glass which was passed from one to the other. However, in their homes they usually drink only among their own caste members. On festivals like Lohri and Holi, when villagers indulge in heavy drinking, no caste distinctions are observed. (Singh I. P., 1977, p. 76)

The practice of untouchability was also less in religious affairs. There was only one gurudwara (the Sikh holy place) in the village where everyone was allowed entry. They also sat together while eating food in the gurudwara. The priest, who himself belonged to a low caste (Cheemba, washer-man), served all the castes without any discrimination. He had performed all the marriages in the villages irrespective of any caste distinction. This was quite in contrast to the way a Brahmin priest functioned. The Brahmin priest used to perform rituals for the Sikhs in the village as well until they began appointing their own priest for the gurudwara. But he served only the upper caste Sikhs.

The religious reform movements among the Sikhs during the 1920s launched by the Singh Sabhas and Akalis had a lasting impact on the religious life of the Sikhs in the village. The insistence of Sikh reformers to distance the 'community' from the Hindus and the legal recognition to weddings through the Sikh rituals, the Anand Karaj, made the village Brahmin priest redundant. Unlike the Brahmin, the Sikh priest could be from any caste and, as mentioned above, the priest in this particular village was from a lower caste. He had been trained to be a priest at the Sikh Missionary College, Amritsar. Priesthood among the Sikhs had thus become an achieved, rather than an ascribed status!

Agrarian Change and Caste: Punjab emerged as a frontline state during the early decades after India's independence. Until around early 1990s, it was the richest state of the country in terms of the per capita income. Though the state has several vibrant urban centres where industry and service economy flourished, the locus of its growth story was 'agriculture'. It was in Punjab that the economic outcomes of the Green Revolution technology, introduced during the later part of 1960s, were first realized. Even though the new technology was introduced in many districts across the country, it was Punjab that came to signify its success. The Green Revolution was a critical landmark in the history of modern India and a major achievement of India's developmental state. The surplus food grains produced in Punjab became the primary source of India's food reserves.

Most of the social science research carried out during the 1970s and 1980s remained preoccupied with economic variables exploring patterns of agricultural growth. The Marxist scholars raised questions about the changing nature of class relations in Punjab agriculture and elsewhere in India and debated on characterization of emergent 'mode of production' in Indian agriculture (see Rudra, 1969; Thorner, 1982). These writings remained virtually blind to 'caste'. However, the agrarian change and the new technology had significant implications for prevailing structures of caste relations as well. They transformed the older forms of social arrangements and dependencies in the local agrarian economy. For example, the traditional ties of *jajmānī* relations disintegrated very rapidly. The new technology and increasing productivity of land made farmers prefer formalized relations with labouring classes. The customary system of bigger landowners hiring individuals and families from the landless dependent caste, mostly Dalits and 'backwards' on share-bases soon were abandoned in favour of formalized contracts and daily wage labour (Bhalla, 1976; Jodhka, 2002). The new technology and intensive agriculture also required more labour. Labour coming from outside the state met the increased demand.

The Green Revolution also changed the nature of social and political power. Given that most of the agricultural land in rural Punjab is owned by Jaṭṭs, prosperity brought about by the Green Revolution further strengthened their economic and political position. They consolidated their position in the local and emerging regional power structure. Their influence also grew within the Sikh religious institutions, which changed the earlier caste equations in the power structure of the Shiromani Gurdwara Parbandhak Committee (SGPC), significantly weakening the position of the urban upper castes, the Khatrīs and Aroṛas.

Disintegration of jajmani structure of formalization of labour relations also provided space for the Dalits to re-negotiate their relationship with dominant caste groups at the local levels. Weakening of dependencies produced frictions and political awareness among them leading to many changes in local level caste relations. I have conceptualized these changes through the categories of *dissociation, distancing,* and *autonomy* (Jodhka, 2002).[6] The economic growth with the Green Revolution also induced changes in the larger economy thereby generating opportunities for employment outside agriculture. With growing political awareness, Dalits began consciously *dissociating* themselves from their traditional 'polluting' occupations. The Chamars (including Ad Dharmis and Ramdasis) have almost completely given up their traditional occupation of dealing with dead cattle. Some of these occupations are no longer identified with any specific caste group in rural Punjab. For example, picking up of dead cattle became a completely

---

[6] This discussion draws from my earlier work (Jodhka, 2002).

commercialized enterprise. The village *panchayat* generally gives the work on contract to an individual contractor, who could even be from another village or a nearby town. Most of those involved in this 'business' are quite well off and are often seen with envy even by the upper castes. Similarly, some degree of commercialization has taken place in case of other Dalit or *jajmani* occupations as well. Barbers, carpenters, blacksmiths, all now have shops. Some from the Dalit castes have also taken-up the job of carpenters, particularly in villages where the traditional carpenters have left for the towns.

The only 'unclean' occupation where a degree of continuity exists is that of scavenging. Though a large majority of those involved with scavenging work are the Balmikis and Mazhabis (earlier known as Chuhras), the castes with which it was traditionally identified, only a few families from these castes actually work as scavengers. Even in scavenging, the traditional structure of *jajmani* relations has almost completely changed. The cleaning of drains and toilets or sweeping of the houses is mostly done on commercial basis. In most villages a scavenger is employed for an individual street. Each household in the street pays a fixed sum to the scavenger on a monthly basis. In order avoid any element of familiarity, some of them preferred working in the neighbouring village rather than their own. There has also been a degree of feminization of the occupation. Even among those household involved with the scavenging work, men went out of the village to work and women worked as part-time scavengers. Another survey of 800 Dalit shows that 82 of them reported to be working as sweepers, mostly in urban centre (76),[7] while in case of their previous generation (fathers) the number was 180 (Judge and Bal, 2009, pp. 89–93).

Even though labouring on land for cultivating farmers remains an important source of employment for the landless Dalits, they rarely enter long-term labour-tying arrangements. Given the choice, they also prefer working in the non-farm economy. Such *distancing* from the local farm economy gave them a sense of dignity by not being dependent on the locally dominant for employment. Judge and Bal show that the number of those reporting agricultural labour as their primary occupation came down to nearly half over a generation, from 404 to 225 of the 800 Dalits they surveyed. (Judge and Bal, 2009, pp. 89–92).

Working towards gaining autonomy from the collective or 'community life' of the village is yet another strategy that Dalits deploy to uphold their dignity. In many pockets of the state, Dalits have also been investing in building their autonomous cultural institutions, such as gurudwaras and community centres. Though in principle there are no restrictions on Dalits entering the Sikh gurudwaras, caste prejudice at the local level seems to work quite strong in the religious institutions as well. Dalits often felt that they were not really welcomed by the locally dominant castes in the village gurudwaras. Their children would be asked to come for the *langar* after everyone else had finished eating or they would be asked to sit in separate queues. While the gurudwara management formally invited all the others, Dalits were not even informed about special programmes

---

[7] Urban jobs are all formalized and generally better paid.

and festivities. Rarely were they allowed to participate in the cooking and serving of the *langar* in local gurudwaras.[8]

There were some other significant changes in the caste relations in rural Punjab. We observed an interesting trend of declining significance of segregated settlements. With the growing population and a continual expansion of residential areas, the old settlement structure of the village has, to some extent, been diluted. As the newly prosperous upper castes make newer and bigger houses on the peripheries of the village, Dalit settlements do not remain as isolated as they were before. In fact, all categories of villagers have constructed new houses on the peripheries. There were also some interesting cases where upwardly mobile Dalits had purchased houses in upper caste localities from those who had left the village for towns or had emigrated to the West.

Much has changed with regard to the access to drinking water as well. Wells are no longer the primary source of drinking water anywhere in rural Punjab. While in some villages taps have been installed under government-funded programmes, at others, hand-pumps have replaced wells. Though the sources of drinking water were as such separate for Dalits and the upper castes, there were much lesser restrictions on the access of Dalits to the taps and hand pumps used or owned by upper castes. However, it may be useful to add here that though Dalits could and did access water from the upper caste sources quite regularly, the frequency of upper castes taking water from the sources used by Dalits was much lesser, though not completely absent.

However, these changes did not imply growing equality among caste groups. Inequalities and distinctive identities persist. One way of reproducing them is through education. Even when the older forms of untouchability and caste-based segregation is no longer practiced in the local state-run schools, newer forms of segregations seemed to be emerging. The quality of education being imparted in the state-run village schools is so poor that the locally dominant castes have nearly withdrawn their children from such schools. The number of teachers employed was normally lesser than required. Even those employed did not take their work very seriously. Rarely did rural schools have enough infrastructures in terms of rooms, labs, and furniture required for proper functioning of the school. As a consequence, the more ambitious and well-to-do parents had started sending their children to urban schools. One could also notice mushrooming of private schools, mostly at the nursery and primary level of teaching in some of the villages. The main attraction of these schools was that they claimed to carry out teaching in 'English medium'. However, they charged fees while the government schools were virtually free. Only the landed upper caste and better-off families could afford to send their children to these schools. This withdrawal of upper castes from government-run schools has had a further negative impact on the quality of education in these schools. In some of the villages, the government schools have begun to be called Dalit or 'Harijan' schools. Since the influential upper castes do not send their children to

---

[8] It may be mentioned here that the practice of untouchability in Hindu temples in Punjab villages is much greater even today (see Jodhka, 2002).

the government school, there is little interest among them to demand improvement in standards of teaching in local schools.

Thus, even when traditional hierarchies are contested and the pre-capitalist structures of patron-client ties, the jajmani relations, disintegrate, ascription-based identities persist and they tend to overlap with emergent economic disparities producing a new regime of inequalities, which also remains embedded in caste (see Jodhka and Manor, 2018).

Concluding Comments

While speaking to a social anthropologist sometime in the late 1970s, a Scheduled Caste student from the local Chamar community at the Punjabi University in Patiala summed up his experience of caste in following words:

When someone says, 'I am a Jatt', his chest expands. But when we say 'Chamar', we contract to nothing.[9]

This brief sentence articulates the core of caste, institutionalized culture of humiliation and power. Such a reality of caste has indeed been in place for centuries. Even when it changes, it persists. Some of the changes are quite significant, if not radical. Quite like many other regions of the country, Dalits of Punjab have become assertive and socially organized, even when acutely divided around their specific jati or community identity. Persistence of caste is not simply a fact about the Dalits, it is also true about the larger social formations. However, taking note of Dalit assertion is also important because they are the ones who call-out that caste persists and it does so as a structure of power and hierarchy, and they are the one who bear its outcomes: exclusions, deprivations, and discrimination.

However, this is not to deny the value of some important changes that have taken place in the region. They have also altered the grammar of caste relations. An implication of these changes has been the growing autonomy of Dalit political agency, which has made them assertive about their rights of being citizens. They value their dignity much more than they did or could do and fight for it.

Growing Dalit assertion in the region is manifesting itself in two sets of processes. First, increasing cases of inter-caste conflicts that invariably involve Dalits on one side and the dominant landowning Jatts on the other. These conflicts became particularly prominent in the popular narrative on the state politics following a case of violence across communities reported from a village called Talhan located near the city of Jallandhar in June 2003. Talhan was followed by a large number of cases of Dalit-Jatt conflict reported from different parts of the state. Even though their contexts and storyline varied, they all seemed to present a common thread, that is assertion for equal rights and a share in the resources that belong commonly to the village and had so far been in the exclusive control of the locally dominant caste, the Jatts (Jodhka and Louis, 2003; Jodhka, 2006b; Judge, 2010).

[9] Aggarwal (1983, p. 24).

The second manifestation of this has been the consolidation of community specific identities among individual Dalit communities. The most important case in this context is that of the Ravidasis. Originally, Chamars of doaba region have actively used the persona of the saint guru Ravidas to construct a distinct religious identity of their own. They have built their own Deras (congregation centres), schools and hospitals. They have been among the most mobile of the SC communities in the country. It was from within this community that the Ad Dharam movement emerged during the early 20th century. A good number of them also live in United Kingdom and North America, who have been actively participating in the community building activities (see Jurgensmeyer, 1988; Ram, 2008; Jodhka, 2009; Singh, G., 2012). A similar trend is observable among the caste traditionally identified with scavenging work, the Balmikis and the Mazhabi Sikhs (see Jodhka, 2015).

Does it imply ethnicization of caste or its substantialization? The answer is in the negative. Identity and assertion are clearly pointer to change in relational structures of caste, they do not imply a new form of equality among communities. Persistent inequalities produce regimes of inequality that over-lap and intersect with the preexisting structures of ascription-based hierarchies. In other words, even when caste is contested and undergoes changes it persists and influences the shapes and shades of the emergent orders.

References

Aggarwal, P. C. 1983. *Halfway to Equality*. New Delhi: Manohar Publications.
Ambedkar, B. R. 1936. *Annihilation of Caste*. Available at http://ccnmtl.columbia.edu/projects/mmt/ambedkar/web/readings/aoc_print_2004.pdf, accessed on 14 June 2019.
Bhalla, S. 1976. 'New Relations of Production in Haryana Agriculture'. *Economic and Political Weekly*, 11(13): A23–A30.
Cohn, B. 1996. *Colonialism and Its Forms of Knowledge: The British in India*. Princeton: Princeton University Press.
Dirks, N. B. 2001. *Castes of Mind: Colonialism and the Making of Modern India*. Princeton: Princeton University Press.
Dumont, L. 1998 (1971). *Homo Hierarchicus: The Caste System and Its Implications*. Delhi: Oxford University Press.
Frykenberg, R. 1989. 'The Emergence of Modern "Hinduism" as a Concept and as an Institution: A Reappraisal with Special Reference to South India'. In G. D. Sontheimer and H. Kulke (Eds.), *Hinduism Reconsidered* (pp. 29–49). Delhi: Manohar.
Fuller, C. J. (Ed.). 1997. *Caste Today*. Delhi: Oxford University Press (paperback edition).
Hershman, Paul. 1981. *Punjabi Kinship and Marriage*. Delhi: Hindustan Publishing Corporation.
Inden, R. B. 1990. *Imagining India*. Oxford: basil Blackwell.
Jodhka, S. S. 2000. 'Prejudice without Pollution?: Scheduled Castes in Contemporary Punjab'. *Journal of Indian School of Political Economy* (special issue on Scheduled Castes edited by Andre Béteille). 12(3–4): 381–402.

Jodhka, S. S. 2002. 'Caste and Untouchability in Rural Punjab'. *Economic and Political Weekly*, 37(19): 1813–1823.
Jodhka, S. S. 2006a. 'Regions and Communities: Social Identities in Contemporary Punjab'. In Rajendra Vora and Anne Feldhaus (Eds.), *Region, Culture and Politics in India* (pp. 299–316). Delhi: Manohar.
Jodhka, S. S. 2006b. 'Caste and Democracy: Assertion and Identity among the Dalits of Rural Punjab'. *Sociological Bulletin*, 55(1): 4–23.
Jodhka, S. S. 2009. 'The Ravi Dasis of Punjab: Global Contours of Caste and Religious Strife'. *Economic and Political Weekly*, 44(24): 79–85.
Jodhka, S. S. 2015. *Caste in Contemporary India*. New Delhi.
Jodhka, S. S. 2016. 'From *Zaat* to *Qaum*: Fluid Contours of the Ravi Dasi Indentity in Punjab'. In Ramnarayan S. Rawat and K. Satyanarayana (Eds.), *Dalit Studies* (pp. 248–270). Durham: Duke University Press.
Jodhka, S. S. 2017. 'Caste from a Contemporary Perspective'. In Knut A. Jacobsen Gurinder Singh Mann Kristina Myrvold and Eleanor Nesbitt (Eds.), *Brill's Encyclopedia of Sikhism. History, Literature, Society beyond Punjab.* (pp. 234–42). Leiden: Brill.
Jodhka, S. S. and James Manor (Eds.). 2018. *Contested Hierarchies, Persisting Influence: Caste and Power in 21st Century India*. Hyderabad: Orient Blackswan.
Jodhka, S. S., and Prakash Louis. 2003. 'Caste Tensions in Punjab: Talhan and Beyond (with Prakash Louis)'. *Economic and Political Weekly*, 38(28): 2923–2926.
Judge, P. S., and Gurpreet Bal. 2009. *Mapping Dalits: Contemporary Reality and Future Prospects in Punjab*. Jaipur: Rawat Publications.
Judge, P. S. 2010. *Changing Dalits: Exploration across Time*. Jaipur: Rawat Publications.
Juergensmeyer, M. 1988. *Religious Rebels in the Punjab: The Social Vision of Untouchables*. Delhi: Ajanta Publications.
McLeod, W. H. 1996. *The Evolution of the Sikh Community: Five Essays*. Delhi: Oxford University Press.
Nayar, B. R. 1966. *Minority Politics in the Punjab*. New Jersey: Princeton University Press.
Oberoi, H. 1994. *The Construction of Religious Boundaries: Culture, Identity and Diversity in the Sikh Tradition*. Delhi: Oxford University Press.
Pettigrew, Joyce. 1975. *Robber Nobleman: A Study of the Political System of the Sikh Jats*. London: Routledge and Kegan Paul.
Ram, Ronki. 2008. 'Ravidass Deras and Social Protest: Making Sense of Dalit Consciousness in Punjab (India)'. *The Journal of Asian Studies*, 67(4): 1341–1364.
Ram, Ronki. 2017. 'The Genealogy of a Dalit Faith: The Ravidassia Dharm and Caste Conflicts in Contemporary Punjab'. *Contributions to Indian Sociology*, 51(1): 52–78.
Rudra, Ashok, A. Maiid, and B. Talib. 1969. 'Big Farmers of the Punjab: Some Preliminary Findings of a Sample Survey'. *Economic and Political Weekly*, 5(39), Review, 143–146.
Saberwal, S. 1976. *Mobile Men: Limits to Social Change in Urban India*. New Delhi: Vikas Publishing House.
Singh, Gurharpal. 2012. 'Religious Transnationalism and Development Initiatives: The Dera Sachkhand Ballan'. 52(13): 53–60.
Singh, I. P. 1975. 'A Sikh Village'. In M. Singer (Ed.), *Traditional India: Structure and Change* (pp. 273–297). Jaipur: Rawat (Indian reprint).
Singh, I. P. 1977. 'Caste in a Sikh Village'. In H. Singh (Ed.), *Caste among Non-Hindus in India* (pp. 66–83). New Delhi: National Publishing House.

Smith, B. K. 1989. *Reflections on Resemblance, Ritual and Religion*. New York.

Srivastava, V. K. 1999. 'Renunciation from Below'. In Ramachandra Guha and Jonathan P. Parry (Eds.), *Institutions and Inequalities: Essays in Honour of Andre Béteille* (pp. 170–200). Delhi: Oxford University Press.

Thapar, R. 1989. 'Imagined Religious Communities: Ancient History and the Modern Search for a Hindu Identity'. *Modern Asian Studies*, 23(2): 209–231.

Tandon, P. 1988. '*Punjabi Century* (first published 1961)'. In *Punjabi Saga* (1857–1987). New Delhi: Viking, Penguin Books.

Thorner, A. 1982. 'Semi-Feudalism or Capitalism? Contemporary Debate on Classes and Mode of Production in India'. *Economic and Political Weekly*, 17(49–50): 993–999; 2061–2086.

CHAPTER 29

CASTE, ETHNICITY, AND THE STATE IN NEPAL

DAVID N. GELLNER

INTRODUCTION

Castes, from the point of view of sociological theory, are a special kind of ethnic group.[1] There is an old joke that defines a nation as a group of people with a shared illusion about their common origins and a shared aversion to their neighbours. The joke captures the way in which both national and ethnic identities are forged from a combination of self-identification, on the one hand, and categorical relationships and enmities with nearby outsiders, on the other. Following Smith (1986, pp. 22–31), we may take an ethnic group to be a set of people who share (1) a collective name, (2) a common myth of descent, (3) a shared history, (4) a distinctive shared culture, (5) an association with a specific territory, and (6) a sense of solidarity. If the sense of solidarity is missing, we are dealing with an ethnic *category* as opposed to an ethnic *group*. One or other of these dimensions may well be lacking or differently evaluated in particular cases; in some cases language is also a key criterion. To these dimensions, more contemporary theories of ethnicity, building on the insights of Max Weber and Frederick Barth, add a stress on the centrality of boundary work in creating and maintaining ethnic groups, as well as an insistence that the actual facts of shared culture or history are less important than people's beliefs about them (Wimmer, 2008, 2013).

Castes share ethnic groups' boundary-making, cultural distinctiveness, concern for separation, and presumed recruitment by descent, but they add two crucial elements on top: (1) there are multiple castes in any given territory (one of them,

---

[1] This chapter draws on forty years of research on caste and ethnicity in Nepal. Most recently it has been supported by grants from the ESRC [ES/L0024OX/1] and the British Academy [HDV190020]. Thanks for comments on an earlier version are due to G. Kunnath, D. P. Martinez, S. Thebe Limbu, K. Hachhethu, A. Shah, J. Whelpton, and K. Adhikari. I alone am responsible for any errors that remain.

usually the dominant caste, who usually identify as Kshatriyas, may have a closer symbolic and affective link to that territory than others); and (2) they are arranged hierarchically and in accordance with a division of labour. Dumont famously and controversially argued that all the various principles underlying such local caste hierarchies can be reduced to one: the opposition of the pure to the impure (Dumont, 1980, p. 43). Many today would argue that the key principle is that of graded honour and contempt, with those deemed higher feeling entitled to despise those lower on the scale (Ambedkar, 2014).

Caste as a fundamental principle of social organization is as important in Nepal as it is in India. Thanks to its unique history Nepal should be 'good to think with' for South Asianists, but unfortunately it is often ignored. Culturally, religiously, linguistically, and economically, Nepal is a full part of South Asia. However, unlike India, Nepal effectively avoided the imposition of colonial rule and all the momentous direct and indirect changes, all the reworkings of caste, religion, and other traditions, that colonialism set in train. In Nepal the caste hierarchy was supported by the full force of state law until 1963 and Nepal was still officially a Hindu kingdom until May 2006. For all these reasons, Nepal-India comparisons and contrasts, if we take the trouble to make them, could be particularly fruitful.

In Nepal today, both in Nepali and in English, a distinction and opposition is drawn between caste (*jat*) and ethnic group (*janajati*). This is a modern distinction—*janajati* is a modern neologism—that has emerged in practice and in dialogue with the state.[2] Until the 1950s those who now see themselves as ethnic groups or indigenous nationalities were obliged to present themselves as castes. Today, in the changed political circumstances of 'new Nepal', it is the other way around: castes have to organize as ethnic groups (Adhikari and Gellner, 2016), as described below. From the formal sociological point of view, however, both castes and ethnic groups are equally forms of ethnicity.

Nepal is a sovereign political unit and indeed is proud to be the oldest political unit in the subcontinent. It goes back—more or less within its present boundaries—to the 'unification' or 'conquest' campaign of Prithvi Narayan Shah (1722–1775), which started when he ascended the throne of the small hill principality of Gorkha in 1743 (Whelpton, 2005). The new regime is conventionally dated from Prithvi Narayan's conquest of Kathmandu in 1768. Although Prithvi Narayan referred to Nepal as 'a yam between two boulders', Nepal's relationship to its two neighbours is completely asymmetrical. In line with the Nepal–India Peace and Friendship Treaty of 1950, the border between the two countries is 'open', meaning that the citizens of each country can move freely and work freely in the other (goods are supposed to be controlled). Many Nepalis study, work, and live in India. Nepali politicians have always taken refuge in India. Many Nepali women, especially from the Tarai-Madhesh region, marry in India, and many of their

---

[2] Changing usages of the terms *jat* and *jati* in Nepal, before the acceptance of *janajati*, are traced in Ishii et al. (2007). On the tribe-caste/tribe-Hindu contrast in Nepal, see Gellner (1991).

brothers marry Indian brides. In short, the cultural distance of the hills of Nepal from the states of the Indian Union with which Nepal shares a border is less than the cultural and linguistic distance between north India and south India, and the cultural distance between Nepal and India is miniscule when compared to the distance between Nepal and China.[3]

Caste is a fact of everyday life in contemporary Nepal. It is much less constraining than in the past, but still pervasive. Nepal is, for its geographical and population size, highly diverse. That diversity has often been celebrated. Prithvi Narayan famously called his kingdom a 'flower garden of all castes' (*sabai jatko phulbari*) (Sharma, 1997, p. 479). Whether this made him a multiculturalist in the modern sense, as often claimed, is highly doubtful and he may even have been warning against it, but at any rate it showed a keen awareness of cultural difference. Nowadays Nepal, like many other countries, faces two seemingly contradictory social trends. On the one hand, there are powerful processes of cultural change and adaptation (to Nepali, to Hindi, and to English, to name just the most important). As more and more children attend schools in which they learn the national culture through the national language, Nepali, or increasingly go to English-medium private schools, local languages go into decline. More and more people travel abroad for work and even those who do not go outside the country are exposed to foreign influences through the mass media, especially TV and social media, and through mass tourism. At the same time there is a counter-current, certainly weaker than the homogenizing trend, but present nonetheless, by which old cultural identities are re-evaluated, reformed, revived, and made the basis for political action. There are activists working day and night to preserve disappearing languages, to teach old cultural traditions, and to make use of the most modern technologies to stem the tide of modernity or at least to repackage their cultural traditions in modern forms.

In the new post-1990 world of free elections, following the overthrow of the partyless Panchayat regime (1960–1990), political parties were able to organize, and compete for votes. Starting in 1991 the national census recorded caste/ethnic group, right down to the lowest level of local government. This means that, since the 1990s, the proportions of different groups have been known (unlike in India where only Scheduled Caste and Scheduled Tribe figures are collected and published). The combination of political competition and unequal outcomes, both in politics and in other spheres, has meant that people are increasingly aware of, and see themselves as belonging to, one of four large and newly emerging super ethnic groups, which I call 'macro-categories' (see Table 29.1).[4] The category of 'others', where Muslims are

---

[3] I have argued the point that most of Nepal is almost wholly south-facing in Gellner (2016).

[4] There is a complication here, because of the ambiguity of 'Madheshi' and the fact that Madheshis are divided by caste. Dalits, Janajatis, and Muslims who live in the Tarai plains belt of Nepal can (depending on context) be classified as, and think of themselves as, belonging to two different macro-categories simultaneously: Dalit/Madheshi, Janajati/Madheshi, and Other/Madheshi, respectively. There is also some ambiguity about whether Hill Dalits should be considered to be part of the Khas-Aryas.

Table 29.1 Major Castes, Ethnic Groups, and Macro-Categories of Nepal

Parbatiyas ('hill people'), now 'KHAS-ARYA'	Hill JANAJATIS	Language loss among hill JANAJATIS	Taraians/MADHESHIS ('plains people')	Others
Bahun 12.2%	Magar 7.1%	68%	Tharu 6.6%	Muslim 4.4%
Chhetri 19%	Tamang 5.8%	11%	Yadav 4%	
DALIT (hill) 8.1%	Newar 5%	34%	DALIT (plains) 4.4%	
	Rai 2.3%	16%	(+ many small groups)	
	Gurung 1.9%	50%		
	Limbu 1.4%	14.5%		
Totals 39.3%	+ c.27.2%		+ c. 28%	+ 5% = 100%

Sources: Nepal Census 2011 census (total: 26,494,504) with figures for hill minority language loss calculated from the 1991 census (Whelpton, 1997, p. 59). Otherwise percentages are as analysed in Tamang et al. (2014, pp. 6–9).

Notes:

1. Macro-categories are in small capitals; Janajati groups are underlined; in English 'caste' tends to be used for groups within the Parbatiyas/Khas-Arya and within the Madheshis, 'ethnic group' for groups within the Janajatis; but in Nepali all are equally *jat* ('species', 'kind', 'birth').

2. Dalits = former Untouchables; Janajatis are mainly those who were formerly called hill tribes. All figures and some labels are likely to be disputed. The label 'Madheshi' is particularly disputed (see fn. 4).

placed, may be considered a fifth macro-category. The broad categories themselves are not new, but they have acquired a new salience due to electoral competition and the perceived imbalance in proportionality at every level (of the 13 Prime Ministers since 1990, ten have been Bahuns and three Chhetris, for example). The formal *names* of these macro-categories, however, are entirely new. They were either virtually or completely unknown before 1990.

The first two macro-categories to emerge were (1) the Janajatis, formerly known as 'hill tribes' in English and *matwali* or 'alcohol-drinkers' in Nepali; and (2) the Dalits (former Untouchables). Later came (3) the Madheshis (the most contested category: at its most expansive, it refers to anyone dwelling in the plains; at its most restrictive, it covers only caste Hindus in the eastern Tarai). Finally—and in line with the widespread logic that the dominant group comes to define its identity only when challenged from below, and therefore belatedly—the Bahuns and Chhetris, along with small associated castes such as Thakuris and Sanyasis, have come, since around 2012, to be known by the single catch-all term (4) 'Khas-Arya'. For those familiar with north India, Khas-Aryas correspond to Forward Castes. Janajatis, though technically equivalent to STs, are far more numerous and politically significant in Nepal; they therefore fill the political slot occupied by OBCs in India.

Diversity and the State before 1951

Cultural differentiation was certainly encouraged in the past by the sheer diversity of geographical niches to be found in Nepal's highly vertical topography. It was also encouraged by the internal logic of caste systems, in which the fetishism of small distinctions is given the greatest play; outsiders—even outsiders who speak the same language and live around the corner—are assumed to be ignorant of insiders' conventions and rules. Cultural complexity, expressed in ritual and sub-dialects, was a form of self-protection, a way of preventing rulers from being able to command or see inside the collective units over which they presided. Ambedkar (2014) referred to this endlessly fissiparous tendency in his famous aphorism that 'the Caste System is not just a division of labour. It is also a division of labourers'.

These tendencies towards cultural complexity were perhaps most pronounced in the agro-cities of the Kathmandu Valley, whose ancient royal cores are now UNESCO World Heritage Sites. Robert Levy, in his magisterial survey of all the caste sub-groups and festivals of the city of Bhaktapur (Levy, 1990), calls such cities 'climax communities'. This leads to the paradox that the Newars, the original inhabitants of the Kathmandu Valley and categorized as Janajatis and therefore supposedly tribal, disadvantaged, and with a cultural predilection for egalitarianism, are subdivided into an elaborated and sophisticated caste hierarchy, far more so than the hierarchy of the Khas-Aryas who are classified as Hindu and caste-like (Gellner and Quigley, 1995; Gellner, 2003).

Yet another factor encouraging great diversity is the fact that Nepal is a meeting place of different cultural areas, an idea expressed in the notion of the 'Indo-Tibetan Interface' (Fisher, 1978). Nepal's relationship to the north and south is not, as noted above, symmetrical; for most of the population Nepal's ties to its southern neighbour are far deeper and more important than those to the north. Nonetheless, along the northern fringe of Nepal there are people who speak Tibetan dialects, are culturally Tibetan, and follow Tibetan religious traditions. They are relatively few in number, so their political clout and strategic importance are much less than that of the far more numerous Madheshis, who are Nepali citizens speaking Awadhi, Maithili, and Bhojpuri, and other languages found on both sides of the India-Nepal border. Still, the Tibetan presence and historical link is not insignificant. These Tibetan groups are counted among Nepal's many minorities, known today as Janajatis or Adivasi-Janajatis, for which the formal English translation is now 'indigenous nationality', but who are usually known colloquially as 'ethnic groups' or 'minorities'.

In every part of the country one finds also the dominant group, today formally known as Khas-Aryas, who collectively amount to almost 40 per cent of the population; colloquially other groups refer to them as 'Bahun-Chhetris' or 'Chhetri-Bahuns'. Sometimes they are also labelled as Parbatiyas or Pahadis (literally 'hill people'), but this term is ambiguous, since it can also be used, and generally is so used in the Tarai, to include hill Janajati people. Some authors also refer to the Khas-Aryas as 'Indo-Nepalese', but this is a purely external category which begs several questions about history and identity and so it is best avoided. Khas-Aryas are divided into Bahuns (Brahmins), Chhetris (Kshatriyas), and Dalits, the service castes who were traditionally treated as untouchables. Khas-Aryas form the overwhelming majority in the far western districts (which also make up the poorest part of the country), but are found in considerable numbers everywhere else, except in the heavily Madheshi-dominated parts of the eastern Tarai. There was considerable internal hierarchy both within Bahuns and within Chhetris in the past, though those differences are of little interest to most people today (for the purposes of the present exposition, Thakuris, 1.6 per cent of the total population, and Sanyasis, 0.8 per cent, are grouped together with the Chhetris). In the 19th and early 20th centuries many successful Chhetri and Bahun men had secondary Janajati wives and their offspring all counted as Chhetris, even when the father was a Bahun, which is part of the explanation for the fact that the Chhetris are the largest group in the country.

The Khas-Aryas' language, known in the past as Khas *kura*, 'the speech of the Khas', and later as Gorkhali, and finally, from the early-20th century, as Nepali, was always the lingua franca of the Himalayas. It was the inevitable choice as the national language of the country (Burghart, 1984; Hutt, 1988). The Khas-Arya caste system, simpler and more basic than that of the Newars, is the main framework for caste in the country as a whole. However, the Madheshis have a separate hierarchy, with essentially the same castes as are found on the other side of the border in India.

The Janajati groups, though divided by language, culture, and even religion, amount, collectively, to over one-third of the total population (if one adds the Tharus and similar groups in the plains to the Janajatis of the hills). All Janajati groups either have their own Tibeto-Burman language or had one in the past, with the exception of the c. 40,000 Santals in the far south-east of the country who speak a Munda language. The Tharus now speak dialects of the local plains languages and may have spoken a non-Tibeto-Burman language in the past. The extent of language loss varies enormously, being most advanced (if one puts the Tharus aside) among the Magars, who have the longest history of cultural and religious assimilation to the Khas-Aryas (see Table 26.1). One large and important group, the Tamangs, living around the Kathmandu Valley, is strongly attached to Tibetan Buddhism. Another large group, the Gurungs, is also Buddhist, though less unequivocally so. Two groups, the Magars and the Tharus, have, in an Ambedkarite spirit of opposing Hinduism, embarked on an opening to Buddhism in the modern period (Letizia, 2014). The Kirat groups in the east of the country (Rais, Limbus, and others) are much less influenced by Buddhism. Like all these groups, they have their own shamanic traditions.

The Janajati groups have diverse origins. Some have myths linking them to the north, others to the east, yet others include a southern sojourn. Most have a 'homeland', a set of districts where they are the largest single group. It is in these 'homelands' that the language is likely to be most spoken and where cultural traditions are thought of as most pure. Hill Janajatis and Chhetris were recruited into the British Gurkhas, though the ideology of 'martial tribes' evolved considerably over time (Caplan, 1995). The Janajatis were slotted into the Khas-Arya caste hierarchy between the Bahuns and Chhetris at the apex and the Dalits at the bottom. In fact, Janajatis were often introduced to the ideas of caste first by Dalit artisans who were invited into their villages in order to provide the necessary services as they adapted to rice agriculture (Höfer, 1986; Allen, 1997; Adhikari and Gellner, 2019).

The social order of the Nepali state was systematized by the famous law code (Muluki Ain) of 1854, written by Brahmin legal pundits at the behest of Jang Bahadur Rana, the first hereditary Rana Prime Minister of Nepal, following his visit to England and France. It has been comprehensively studied by Höfer (1979). Based on the Hindu *dharmasastras*, it enacted caste rules into law. Brahmins, as 'gods on earth', were exempted from capital punishment. All the subjects of the state were classified into three broad categories: the unclean (subdivided into those whose touch required purification and those who could be touched but from whom water could not be accepted); the 'alcohol-drinkers' (*matwali*), today's Janajatis, subdivided into the 'enslavable' (*masinya*) and the 'non-enslavable'; and the 'wearers of the sacred thread' (*tagadhari*), who, again, were subdivided into the Chhetris and the Bahuns. Both Chhetris and Bahuns had internal status grades, with the Bahuns ranked into priestly and non-priestly categories.

The social hierarchy was expressed spatially in most places, with Dalits relegated to separate hamlets outside or on the outskirts of the settlements of the 'clean' castes. Dalits could be recruited into the army or into the Indian Gurkhas only as specialists, such as cobblers, tailors, and blacksmiths. Occasionally Dalits might acquire education or wealth, but they were very likely to lose it in subsequent generations. Caplan's (1972) study in west Nepal showed how Bahuns were able, thanks to their better links to the state, to resume, over time, much of the land of the Mijars/Sarkis, in a place where at one time the latter had reasonable landholdings. Dalit specialists existed in patron/client relationships with the other castes; often these were ongoing hereditary relationships similar to the *jajmani* relationships of northern India; in Nepal they are known as *balighare* or (in western Nepal) as *ritibhagya* (Gaborieau, 1977; Cameron, 1998).

The position of women varied quite considerably according to caste, ethnicity, and locality. Dalit women had and still have more autonomy than women of the 'high' Khas-Arya castes (Bennett, 1983; Cameron, 1998; Galvin, 2005). Janajati women likewise had considerably more autonomy (McHugh, 2001; March, 2002, 2018), though it would be a mistake to accept the idea, advanced by some Janajati activists, that they have anything like complete equality with their menfolk (Des Chene, 1997). Crude stereotypes of the supposedly freer tribal woman have been commonplace both among Nepalis and in the writings of foreign observers, but historical and contemporary realities are inevitably a good deal more complex (Gellner, 1991). Today, caste/ethnic differences are overlaid by emerging middle-class norms of femininity, with powerful expectations about fashion and deportment (Liechty, 2003; March, 2018).

Despite all this diversity, and the framework of hierarchy and separation designed to keep everyone in their place, there was, between 1850 and 1950, much migration, considerable social change, and the emergence of a common culture. This national culture, based partly on the Nepali language, as noted above, spread throughout the middle hills. It was also based on religion: common shrines and pilgrimage sites, and common cults, such as Mankamana and the uniquely Nepali goddess, Swasthani (Birkenholtz, 2018). Admittedly, the Tarai was not really included in this process. Large-scale migration to the Tarai from the hills did not begin until the 1950s and 1960s. The Tarai castes, apart from their Brahmins, were not included in the synthetic national caste order outlined in the 1854 law code. By the mid-20th century, historian Kumar Pradhan's claim (1991, p. 201)—'the Gorkhali conquests created a unified kingdom, but not a unified society'— was arguably no longer true in the hills, but it remained true of relations between the hills and the plains of Nepal.

THE POLITICS OF ETHNICITY SINCE 1951

With the fall of the Rana regime in 1951 and the end of legal backing for the caste hierarchy in 1963, Nepal entered a new era. Huge social change has occurred in the decades since then. Before 1951 Dalits who failed to warn other people of their caste, for example causing them to become impure by offering water to them, faced severe punishment. Dalit men who 'seduced' higher caste women likewise were severely punished. Taking up the occupations of others was also hazardous and risked one's caste status.

There was an expectation after 1951 that a new caste-free, egalitarian society would suddenly emerge (Sharma, 2004, Chs. 16–17). This did not happen, mainly because, unlike in India, there were no steps taken to penalize caste discrimination and there were no reservations, that is, no affirmative action. Dalits and Janajatis remained relatively excluded from modern professions. The period of the Panchayat regime, with political parties banned and operating underground and from bases in India, was a time when overt expressions of ethnicity were frowned upon. Schools were established throughout the country for the first time, Radio Nepal had a monopoly of the airwaves, and the idea of Nepal as a nation-state was consolidated. Inevitably perhaps, the image of the nation-state was dominated by the culture, practices, and presuppositions of the dominant castes, the Bahuns and Chhetris.[5] The new middle class that emerged with urbanization and education, expanding rapidly after 1990 (Liechty, 2003), contained members from all backgrounds, but proportionately far more of them were Bahuns, Chhetris, and upper-caste Newars, leading to the acronym 'BCN' as a shorthand for the elite. The kinds of obstacles faced by Dalits in India, as documented by Mosse (2018), are faced equally by Dalits in Nepal, as well as, to a lesser extent, by Janajatis and Madheshis (Bennett, 2006; Bennett et al., 2013).

Politically and culturally there were far-reaching changes after 1990. 'If the period 1960 to 1990 was one of *nation*-building, the [period] since then has been a time of *ethnicity*-building' (Gellner, 2007, p. 1823).[6] It was only with the collection of ethnicity data after

---

[5] There is a considerable literature on this theme. See, i.a., Ragsdale (1989), Pigg (1992), Onta (1996), and Chalmers (2003).

[6] Emphasis added. On the rise of ethnicity in Nepal see Hangen (2010), Fisher (2001), Guneratne (2002), Lawoti (2005), Gellner (2007), Gellner et al. (1997), Lecomte-Tilouine (2009a, 2009b),

1990 that the full extent of the exclusion began to be understood. Statistics were collected which showed that Khas-Aryas were massively over-represented in all leadership positions, whereas Madheshis, Janajatis (with the exception of Newars), and Dalits were hugely under-represented.[7] Furthermore, Janajatis, Madheshis, and Dalits performed worse on all human development indicators. These disparities and inequalities have led to the rise of movements on behalf of all these macro-categories. The Janajatis organized first, from 1991, as the Nepal Federation of Nationalities (NEFEN), with one representative organization for each Janajati group. Following the UN's declaration of a year and then a decade of indigenous people, the equivalence of 'nationality' (*janajati*) and 'indigenous' (*adivasi*) in the Nepalese context was affirmed. The name of the organization was changed to the Nepal Federation of Indigenous Nationalities in 2003.

Just how many Janajati groups there are (or should be) was in flux for some time. When NEFEN was founded in 1991 there were only seven members. Ethnic activists encouraged the smaller groups to form organizations and to become affiliated members of NEFEN/NEFIN. Eventually the number stabilized at 59 Janajati groups of which 56 have member organizations represented within NEFIN.[8] Some of the recognized groups have a population of only a couple of hundred people. The largest (Magars, Tharus, Tamangs, Newars) count over a million members. It was a major success of NEFIN to achieve government recognition and the establishment in 2002 of a permanent National Commission for Janajatis, known as NFDIN, one year after it had established Commissions for Women and Dalits. There is now also a National Commission for Madheshis. However, Nepal lacks the elaborate tribal-oriented bureaucracy of India, whose workings are analysed in Middleton (2015). In August 2007 the Nepal parliament ratified the Indigenous Tribal and Peoples Convention (1989), also known as ILO 169, the only mainland Asian country to do so; in September of the same year it also adopted the less binding but more radical UNDRIP (Jones and Langford, 2011).

Lying behind these successes for the ethnic movement was the fact that the Maoists had made ethnicity a major plank of their revolution (1996–2006).[9] Early in 2004 they divided the country into nine 'autonomous regions' and, in eight of the nine, established 'people's governments' through elaborately choreographed and filmed public ceremonies (Ogura, 2008). Six of these regions were named after the ethnic group whose

---

Hachhethu and Gellner (2010), Lawoti and Hangen (2012), Adhikari and Gellner (2015), and Shneiderman (2015).

[7] These figures were collected first by Neupane (2000) and have been reworked and republished in many other places, for example, Lawoti (2005, pp. 104–106), Maharjan (1999, pp. 63–64), Hachhethu and Gellner (2010, p. 138), Sijapati (2013, pp. 153–154), Bennett et al. (2013), and Gurung et al. (2014).

[8] The government commissioned a report from anthropologist Professor Om Gurung in 2009 to investigate Janajatis. His report recommended expanding the number to 81, but by then the issue of ethnicity had become controversial and the report was shelved and never published (Adhikari and Gellner 2016, p. 2022).

[9] On the Maoist movement, including its relationship to the ethnicity question, see de Sales (2003), Hutt (2004), Tamang (2006), Ogura (2007, 2008), Lecomte-Tilouine (2009a, 2013), Shah and Pettigrew (2012), Pettigrew (2013), Adhikari (2014), Jha (2014), Ismail and Shah (2015), and Zharkevich (2019).

homeland they were supposed to be. The Maoists dissolved their parallel governments in January 2007, because they had come 'above ground' and were about to participate in elections, eventually held in 2008, which they went on to win. In this unprecedented and semi-revolutionary political situation, ethnic issues were pushed high up the agenda. It had already been decided by the interim parliament in 2007 that Nepal would become a federal republic. Ethnic activists hoped that there would be 'prior rights' (*agradhikar*) for the key ethnic groups. This situation provoked a massive backlash among Bahuns and Chhetris who began to organize on the same national basis as the Janajati groups. In other words, under extreme political pressure castes became ethnic groups (Adhikari and Gellner, 2016). This led to the collapse of the first Constituent Assembly and new elections in 2013, in which the Maoists were defeated by the two older parties, the Congress and the UML (Gellner, 2014). This in turn led, following the earthquakes of 2015, to the declaration of a new federal constitution which largely disappointed the hopes of the Janajati activists.[10]

Conclusion

Nepal's position as a formally independent state, not part of the British Raj, meant that changes that began in India in the 19th century did not happen, if at all, till much later in Nepal. Nepal retained a Hindu king until 2006. Until 1951 the Rana regime enforced the caste hierarchy in the name of the king; very limited mobility was possible for some individuals and some caste fragments, but only if legitimated by the palace; the free-for-all of collective upward mobility and Sanskritization unleashed by the British in India, and especially by their decennial censuses, did not happen in Nepal. Right up to the monarchy's demise in 2006 Hinduism was central to its legitimacy to such an extent that, in voting for a republic, MPs felt obliged, in that revolutionary situation, to vote also for secularism, that is, to remove the privileged position of Hinduism from the constitution, even though many of them were not, in their hearts, convinced that this was the right thing to do.[11] Thus, ruling through caste, was, until 1963, a key part of the legitimation of the monarchical state. From that time onwards many aspects of caste continued, under the guise of culture and tradition, and only came to be contested after 1990 and, even more so, after 2006. Change has come so recently that Dalits in Nepal, with their relatively smaller middle class and continued dependence on mainstream

---

[10] On the process leading to the promulgation of the 2015 Constitution, see Hutt (2020).

[11] Letizia (2016, p. 40). The position of Hinduism was surreptitiously protected in the 2015 Constitution by a special 'explanation' that defined secularism as 'protection of religion and culture being practiced since ancient times and religious and cultural freedom', the key word for 'ancient' being *sanatan* (Gellner and Letizia, 2016, pp. 5–7). On the process of removing the king from the polity, see Gellner (2022).

political parties, remain substantially behind Dalits in India in many respects (Gellner, Adhikari, and BK, 2020).

In the modern period, since 1951, the traditionalist framework, consciously erected by the Ranas to buttress their patrimonial regime, has been gradually and systematically destroyed, despite the resistance of those who would like to defend aspects of it as traditional culture. In 2003, at a time when the whole government system was under severe pressure from the Maoist insurgency, Prime Minister Surya Bahadur Thapa accepted the principle of reservations for the civil service. Shortly after the fall of the monarchy, on 16 May 2006, the restored parliament declared Nepal to be 'untouchability-free'. In 2007 the Civil Service Act of 1993 was amended to reserve 45 per cent of places for disadvantaged groups (33% for women, 27% for Janajatis, 22% for Madheshis, 9% for Dalits, 5% for the disabled, and 4% for backward regions) (Sunam and Shrestha, 2019). Similar levels of representation were guaranteed in all elections from 2008 onwards (Khanal et al., 2012). Around the same time social benefit transfers were increased substantially, targeting those over 60, the disabled, those classified as belonging to 'endangered indigenous groups', and Dalit children as well as all children in the Far West of the country (Drucza, 2019). In May 2011 the Caste-Based Discrimination and Untouchability (Offence and Punishment) Act, 2068 (2011) was passed. This gave teeth to laws against untouchability by extending their coverage to the private domain as well. The punishments for offences under this act were increased substantially in 2018. With these measures, Nepal policies in the area of affirmative action began to approach those adopted by India decades earlier.

Whether and how these new laws are being and will be implemented is, needless to say, another matter. Caste is not the same as class but nonetheless there is a considerable correlation in contemporary Nepal. Dalits are far more likely to be poor and they are far less likely to be able to make use of the courts, the police, and other arms of the state in order assert their rights under these new laws. As noted above, Dalits are massively under-represented in all state employment, except as municipal cleaners.

From a comparative point of view, the Nepali case shows clearly that British colonialism and the schemes of British Orientalists cannot be blamed for the existence of the caste system, however tempting such a position might be. British colonialism may certainly have led to greater rigidity between castes and may well have reinforced the power of Brahmins at the system's apex; but it simply flies in the face both of deep historical evidence and of the more recent history of Nepal to pretend that caste as we know it today was somehow invented by colonialism. It is possible, as some historians have claimed, that Jang Bahadur Rana was inspired, following his visit to Paris, by the Code Napoléon to draw up the 1854 law code. But he had no need of Orientalists or colonialism to do so. The content was thoroughly Hindu and the Hindu pundits who wrote it were drawing entirely from their own knowledge of scripture as well as from their practical experience of administering Hindu law.

References

Adhikari, A. 2014. *The Bullet and the Ballot Box: The Story of Nepal's Maoist Revolution.* London: Verso.

Adhikari, K. P., and D. N. Gellner 2016. 'New Identity Politics and the 2012 Collapse of Nepal's Constituent Assembly: When the Dominant becomes "Other"'. *Modern Asian Studies,* 50(6): 2009–2040.

Adhikari, K. P., and D. N. Gellner. 2019. 'International Labour Migration from Nepal and Changing Caste-based Institutions and Inter-caste Relations'. *Contributions to Nepalese Studies,* 46(1): 167–191.

Allen, N. J. 1997. 'Hinduization: The Experience of the Thulung Rai'. In Gellner D. N., J. Pfaff-Czarnecka, and J. Whelpton (Eds.), *Nationalism and Ethnicity in a Hindu Kingdom: The Politics of Culture in Contemporary Nepal* (pp. 303–323). Amsterdam: Harwood Academic Publishers.

Ambedkar, B. 2014 (1936). *Annihilation of Caste.* London: Verso.

Bennett, L. 1983. *Dangerous Wives and Sacred Sisters: The Social and Symbolic Roles of High-Caste Women in Nepal.* Columbia University Press. Reissued Himal Books, Kathmandu, 2004.

Bennett, L. 2006. *Unequal Citizens: Gender, Caste and Ethnic Exclusion in Nepal.* Kathmandu: DFID and World Bank.

Bennett, L., B. Sijapati, and D. Thapa. 2013. *Gender and Social Exclusion in Nepal: Update.* Kathmandu: Himal Books.

Birkenholtz, J. Vantine. 2018. *Reciting the Goddess: Narratives of Place and the Making of Hinduism in Nepal.* New York: OUP.

Burghart, R. 1984. 'The Formation of the Concept of Nation-State in Nepal'. *Journal of Asian Studies,* 44: 101–125. Reprinted 1996 in R. Burghart, *The Conditions of Listening: Essays on Religion, History and Politics in South Asia* (edited by C. J. Fuller and J. Spencer) (pp. 226–260). Delhi: Oxford University Press.

Cameron, M. 1998. *On the Edge of the Auspicious: Gender and Caste in Nepal.* University of Illinois Press.

Caplan, L. 1995. *Warrior Gentlemen: 'Gurkhas' in the Western Imagination.* Oxford: Berghahn.

Caplan, A. P. 1972. *Priests and Cobblers: A Study of Social Change in a Hindu Village in Western Nepal.* San Francisco: Chandler.

Chalmers, R. 2003. '"We Nepalis": Language, Literature and the Formation of a Nepali Public Sphere in India, 1914–1940'. Ph.D, SOAS, University of London.

Des Chene, M. 1997. '"We Women Must Try to Live": The Saga of Bhauju'. *Studies in Nepali History and Society,* 2(1): 125–172.

Drucza, K. 2019. '"At Least the Government Is Watching out for Us Now": Dalit Perceptions and Experiences of Governance and Cash Transfers in Three Villages in Sarlahi, Nepal'. *Modern Asian Studies,* 53(6): 2041–2078.

Dumont, L. 1980. *Homo Hierarchicus: The Caste System and Its Implications* (complete recd English ed.). Chicago: The University of Chicago Press.

Fisher, J. (Ed.). 1978. *Himalayan Anthropology: The Indo-Tibetan Interface.* The Hague: Mouton.

Fisher, W. F. 2001. *Fluid Boundaries: Forming and Transforming Identity in Nepal.* New York: Columbia University Press.

Gaborieau, M. 1977. 'Systèmes traditionelles des échanges de services spécialisés contre remuneration dans une localité du Népal Central'. *Purusartha,* 3: 1–70.

Galvin, K.-L. 2005. *Forbidden Red: Widowhood in Urban Nepal*. Pullman: Washington State University Press.

Gellner, D. N. 1991. 'Hinduism, Tribalism, and the Position of Women: The Problem of Newar Identity'. *Man (n.s.)*, 26(1): 105–125. Reissued 2001 in D. N. Gellner, *The Anthropology of Buddhism and Hinduism: Weberian Themes*, Ch. 11. Delhi: OUP.

Gellner, D. N. 2003. 'From Cultural Hierarchies to a Hierarchy of Multiculturalisms: The Case of the Newars of Nepal'. In M. Lecomte-Tilouine and P. Dolfuss (Eds.), *Ethnic Revival and Religious Turmoil in the Himalayas* (pp. 73–131). Delhi: Oxford University Press.

Gellner, D. N. 2007. 'Caste, Ethnicity and Inequality in Nepal'. *Economic and Political Weekly*, 42(20): 1823–1828.

Gellner, D. N. 2014. 'The 2013 Elections in Nepal'. *Asian Affairs*, 45(2): 243–261. (bit.ly/1pe2hal).

Gellner, D. N. 2016. 'The Idea of Nepal' (M. C. Regmi Lecture 2016) (soscbaha.org/lecture-series/the-idea-of-nepal/).

Gellner, D. N. 2022. 'The Last Hindu King: How Nepal Desanctified Its Monarchy'. In A. Azfar Moin and A. Strathern (Eds.), *Sacred Kingship in World History: Between Immanence and Transcendence* (pp. 271–298). New York: Columbia University Press.

Gellner, D. N., and D. Quigley (Eds.). 1995. *Contested Hierarchies: A Collaborative Ethnography of Caste among the Newars of the Kathmandu Valley*. Oxford: Clarendon.

Gellner, D. N., J. Pfaff-Czarnecka, and J. Whelpton (Eds.). 1997. *Nationalism and Ethnicity in a Hindu Kingdom: The Politics of Culture in Contemporary Nepal*. Amsterdam: Harwood Academic Publishers. Reissued 2008 by Vajra Books, Kathmandu, as *Nationalism and Ethnicity in Nepal*.

Gellner, D. N., and C. Letizia 2016. 'Introduction: Religion and Identities in Post-Panchayat Nepal'. In D. N. Gellner, S. L. Hausner, and C. Letizia (Eds.), *Religion, Secularism, and Ethnicity in Contemporary Nepal* (pp. 1–32). Delhi: Oxford University Press.

Gellner, D. N., K. P. Adhikari, and A. B. BK. 2020. 'Dalits in Search of Inclusion: Comparing Nepal with India'. In A. S. Rathore (Ed.), *B.R. Ambedkar: The Quest for Social Justice, Vol. 2: Social Justice* (pp. 91–115). Delhi: OUP.

Guneratne, A. 2002. *Many Tongues, One People: The Making of Tharu Identity in Nepal*. Ithaca and London: Cornell University Press.

Gurung, Y. B., B. R. Suwal, M. S. Pradhan, and M. S. Tamang. 2014. *Nepal Social Inclusion Survey 2012: Caste, Ethnic and Gender Dimensions of Socio-Economic Development, Governance, and Social Solidarity*. Kathmandu: Central Department of Sociology/Anthropology, Tribhuvan University.

Hachhethu, K., and D. N. Gellner. 2010. 'Nepal: Trajectories of Democracy and Restructuring of the State'. In P. Brass (Ed.), *Routledge Handbook of South Asian Politics* (pp. 131–146). London & New York: Routledge.

Hangen, S. I. (2010). *The Rise of Ethnic Politics in Nepal: Democracy in the Margins*. London: Routledge.

Höfer, A. (1979). *The Caste Hierarchy and the State in Nepal: A Study of the Muluki Ain of 1854*. Innsbruck: Universitätsverlag Wagner. Reissue 2004, Kathmandu: Himal Books.

Höfer, A. 1986. 'Wieso hinduisieren sich die Tamang?' In B. Kölver and S. Lienhard (Eds.), *Formen kulturellen Wandels und andere Beiträge zur Erforschung des Himālaya* (pp. 157–187). Sankt Augustin: VGH Wissenschaftsverlag.

Hutt, M. J. 1988. *Nepali: A National Language and Its Literature*. London/Delhi: SOAS/Sterling.

Hutt, M. J. (Ed.) 2004. *Himalayan 'People's War': Nepal's Maoist Rebellion*. London: Hurst & Co.

Hutt, M. J. 2020. 'Before the Dust Settled: Is Nepal's 2015 Settlement a Seismic Constitution?' *Conflict, Security & Development*, 20(3): 379–400.

Ishii, H., D. N. Gellner, and K. Nawa. 2007. 'Introduction'. In H. Ishii, D. N. Gellner, and K. Nawa (Eds.), *Nepalis Inside and Outside Nepal* (pp. 1–14). Delhi: Manohar.

Ismail, F., and A. Shah. 2015. 'Class Struggle, the Maoists and the Indigenous Question in Nepal and India'. *EPW*, 50(35): 112–123.

Jha, P. 2014. *Battles of the New Republic: A Contemporary History of Nepal*. London: Hurst; Delhi: Aleph.

Jones, P., and M. Langford. 2011. 'Between Demos and Ethnos: The Nepal Constitution and Indigenous Rights'. *International Journal on Minority and Group Rights*, 18: 369–386.

Khanal, K., F. S. Gelpke, and U. P. Pyakurel. 2012. *Dalit Representation in National Politics of Nepal*. Kathmandu: NNDSWO.

Lawoti, M. 2005. *Towards a Democratic Nepal: Inclusive Political Institutions for a Multicultural Society*. Delhi: SAGE.

Lawoti, M., and S. Hangen (Eds.). 2012. *Nationalism and Ethnic Conflict in Nepal: Identities and Mobilization after 1990*. London and New York: Routledge.

Lecomte-Tilouine, M. 2009a. *Hindu Kingship, Ethnic Revival, and Maoist Rebellion in Nepal*. Delhi: OUP.

Lecomte-Tilouine, M. 2009b. 'Ruling Social Groups—From Species to Nations: Reflections on Changing Conceptualizations of Caste and Ethnicity in Nepal'. In D. N. Gellner (Ed.), *Ethnic Activism and Civil Society in South Asia* (pp. 291–336). Delhi: SAGE.

Lecomte-Tilouine, M. (Ed.) 2013. *Revolution in Nepal: An Anthropological and Historical Approach to the People's War*. Delhi: OUP.

Letizia, C. 2014. 'Buddhist Activism, New Sanghas and the Politics of Belonging among Some Tharu and Magar Communities of Southern Nepal'. In G. Toffin and J. Pfaff-Czarnecka (Eds.), *Facing Globalization in the Himalayas: Belonging and the Politics of the Self* (pp. 289–325). Delhi: SAGE.

Letizia, C. 2016. 'Ideas of Secularism in Contemporary Nepal'. In D. N. Gellner, S. L. Hausner, and C. Letizia (Eds.), *Religion, Secularism, and Ethnicity in Contemporary Nepal* (pp. 35–76). Delhi: OUP.

Levy, R. (with K. Rajopadhyaya) 1990. *Mesocosm: Hinduism and the Organization of a Traditional Newar City in Nepal*. Berkeley: University of California Press.

Liechty, M. 2003. *Suitably Modern: Making Middle-Class Culture in a New Consumer Society*. Princeton and Oxford: Princeton University Press.

Maharjan, P. 1999. 'Problems of Democracy in Nepal'. *European Bulletin of Himalayan Research*, 17: 41–68.

March, K. S. 2002. *'If Each Comes Half Way': Meeting Tamang Women in Nepal*. Ithaca: Cornell University Press.

March, K. S. 2018. 'Tamang Gendered Subjectivities in a Migrating World'. In D. N. Gellner and S. L. Hausner (Eds.), *Global Nepalis: Religion, Culture, and Community in a New and Old Diaspora* (pp. 467–506). Delhi: OUP.

McHugh, E. 2001. *Love and Honor in the Himalayas: Coming to Know Another Culture*. Philadelphia: University of Pennsylvania Press.

Middleton, T. 2015. *The Demands of Recognition: State Anthropology and Ethnopolitics in Darjeeling*. Stanford: Stanford University Press.

Mosse, D. 2018. 'Caste and Development: Contemporary Perspectives on a Structure of Discrimination and Advantage'. *World Development*, 110: 422–436.

Neupane, G. 2000. *Nepalko Jatiya Prasna: Samajik Banot ra Sajhedariko Sambhavana* (Nepal's Nationality Question: Social Structure and the Possibilities of Compromise). Kathmandu: Centre for Development Studies.

Ogura, K. 2007. 'Maoists, People, and the State as Seen from Rolpa and Rukum'. In H. Ishii, D. Gellner, and K. Nawa (Eds.), *Political and Social Transformations in North India and Nepal: Social Dynamics in Northern South Asia* (pp. 435–475). New Delhi: Manohar.

Ogura, K. 2008. 'Maoist People's Governments, 2001–05: The Power in Wartime'. In D. N. Gellner and K. Hachhethu (Eds.), *Local Democracy in South Asia: Microprocesses of Democratization in Nepal and Its Neighbours* (pp. 175–231). Delhi: SAGE.

Onta, P. R. 1996. 'Creating a Brave Nation in British India: The Rhetoric of Jati Movement, Rediscovery of Bhanubhakta and the Writing of Bir History'. *Studies in Nepali History and Society*, 1(1): 37–76.

Pettigrew, J. 2013. *Maoists at the Hearth: Everyday Life in Nepal's Civil War*. Philadelphia: Pennsylvania University Press.

Pigg, S. L. 1992. 'Inventing Social Categories through Place: Social Representations and Development in Nepal'. *Comparative Studies in Society and History*, 34(3): 491–513.

Pradhan, K. 1991. *The Gorkha Conquests: The Process and Consequences of the Unification of Nepal with particular Reference to Eastern Nepal*. Calcutta: OUP.

Ragsdale, T. 1989. *Once a Hermit Kingdom: Ethnicity, Education and National Integration in Nepal*. Delhi: Manohar.

Sales, A. de. 2003. 'The Kham Magar Country: Between Ethnic Claims and Maoism'. In D. N. Gellner (Ed.), *Resistance and the State: Nepalese Experiences* (pp. 326–357). Delhi: Social Science Press.

Shah, A., and J. Pettigrew (Eds.). 2012. *Windows into a Revolution: Ethnographies of Maoism in India and Nepal*. Delhi: Orient Blackswan and Social Science Press.

Sharma, P. R. 1997. 'Nation-Building, Multi-Ethnicity, and the Hindu State'. In D. N., J. Pfaff-Czarnecka, and J. Whelpton (Eds.), *Nationalism and Ethnicity in a Hindu Kingdom: The Politics of Culture in Contemporary Nepal* (pp. 471–493). Amsterdam: Harwood Academic Publishers. Republished in Sharma (2004).

Sharma, P. R. 2004. *The State and Society in Nepal: Historical Foundations and Contemporary Trends*. Lalitpur: Himal Books.

Shneiderman, S. 2015. *Rituals of Ethnicity: Thangmi Identities between Nepal and India*. Philadelphia: University of Pennsylvania Press.

Sijapati, B. 2013. 'In Pursuit of Recognition: Regionalism, Madhesi Identity and the Madhes Andolan'. In M. Lawoti and S. Hangen (Eds.), *Nationalism and Ethnic Conflict in Nepal: Identities and Mobilization after 1990* (pp. 145–172). Abingdon: Routledge.

Smith, A. D. 1986. *The Ethnic Origins of Nations*. Oxford: Blackwell.

Sunam, R. and K. Shrestha. 2019. 'Failing the Most Excluded: A Critical Analysis of Nepal's Affirmative Action Policy'. *Contributions to Nepalese Studies*, 46(1): 143–165.

Tamang, M. S. 2006. 'Culture, Caste and Ethnicity in the Maoist Movement'. *Studies in Nepali History and Society*, 11(2): 271–301.

Tamang, M. S., P. S. Chapagain, and P. K. Ghimire. 2014. *Social Inclusion Atlas of Nepal: Ethnic and Caste Groups*, Vol. 1. Kathmandu: Central Department of Sociology/Anthropology, Tribhuvan University.

Whelpton, J. 1997. 'Political Identity in Nepal: State, Nation, and Community'. In Gellner, D. N., J. Pfaff-Czarnecka, and J. Whelpton (Eds.), *Nationalism and Ethnicity in a Hindu*

Kingdom: The Politics of Culture in Contemporary Nepal (pp. 39–78). Amsterdam: Harwood Academic Publishers.

Whelpton, J. 2005. *A History of Nepal*. Cambridge: CUP.

Wimmer, A. 2008. 'Elementary Strategies of Ethnic Boundary Making'. *Ethnic and Racial Studies*, 31(6): 1025–1055.

Wimmer, A. 2013. *Ethnic Boundary Making: Institutions, Power, Networks*. New York: OUP.

Zharkevich, I. 2019. *Maoist People's War and the Revolution of Everyday Life in Nepal*. Cambridge: CUP.

SECTION VI

DALIT LIVES AND PREDICAMENTS OF CHANGE

Editors' Introduction

CHAPTERS in this section focus on the margins of caste, the Dalit experiences of untouchability and violence, their assertions for change, including their political mobilizations. Two chapters in the section also focus on communities that share a similar experience of discrimination and humiliation with Dalits, the Scheduled Tribes, and the De-notified Communities. Almost all the chapters in this section look at caste from below as well as from the perspectives of change in the context of economic growth, social development, and democratization.

The opening chapter by Anand Teltumbde provides a broad introduction to 'the legacy of B.R. Ambedkar', to the life and ideas of a person who has come to be the most influential figure in the writings on caste in India since the late 1980s and early 1990s. A Dalit by caste, Ambedkar went on to become the most educated Indian of his time, with two PhDs, from two of the top academic institutions of the world (Columbia University and the London School of Economics). He not only produced a large volume of writings on the 'oppressive' side of caste but also initiated social and political movements for its 'annihilation'. The legacy he left behind was not merely his persona but also a plethora of institutions and organizations. He also left behind an ideological and symbolic legacy, which has provided a new sense of self and a vision of emancipation to those on the margins of the caste system across the subcontinent, and beyond. Through his own political work, Ambedkar also evolved new modes of fighting caste discrimination. Institutionalization of quotas for the Scheduled Castes, mostly thanks to his effort, enabled the emergence of a Dalit middle class, which has emerged as the key critical agent of caste, which too could be seen as his legacy. At another level the persona of Ambedkar has emerged as a mode of thinking about caste, in the framework of democracy and human rights.

The following chapter by Suryakant Waghmore focuses on the dynamics of untouchability. The practice of untouchability has been at the core of caste. Though the logic of pollution applies to the entire spectrum of the hierarchy, the caste order also identified some groups as being 'permanently impure' who were 'located at the lowest rung' of the social order. His focus is primarily on the strains on the caste system produced by processes such as Dalit migration to urban centres, institutionalization of protective legal measures, reservations, and their political mobilizations. He provides a broad view of the literature that shows how the traditional hierarchies are undergoing some profound changes. These include changing status of the ex-untouchables. Such changes are also often accompanied by 'increased violence against untouchables in rural areas and newer forms of exclusion of untouchables in urban areas'. However, despite many persistent aspects of caste hierarchy, these are indeed positive, and migrations to urban centres does 'promise better possibilities of dignity and equality to ex-untouchables'.

Continuing in a similar vein, Hugo Gorringe and Karthikeyan Damodaran, provide a broad overview of the anti-caste social mobilization in India. They begin their discussion with the word Dalit, its origin, its political value in bringing together diverse communities who have been victims of untouchability across the subcontinent and beyond, and the contestations that such an experience trigger. They go on to discuss the various Dalit movements as they emerged during the colonial period and took shape with the rise of a middle-class from within the ranks of the ex-untouchable communities. They also provide a brief account to the different modes of politics of leaders like Ambedkar and Kanshi Ram, their priorities—culture, political, economic—and their strategies of dealing with the violence of caste. Despite differences and internal disagreements, Dalit movements in India 'remain at the forefront of efforts to highlight persistent inequalities, change social norms and discourses and introduce "new norms of civility" and ways of being', they conclude.

The following chapter by Harish Wankhede provides an account of the Mahar Dalits of Maharashtra and their anti-caste mobilizations over the past century or so. After providing a broad history of the community and its mobilizations, he lists five emerging tendencies within the regional Dalit politics of Mahars. First, as caste persists, atrocities against Dalits also persist. Dalits continue to carry out militant protest against such injustices, whenever required. Second, there is growing tendency towards 'caste-community specific assertions', resulting in the fragmentation of the Dalit identity at large. Third, there is a growing tendency among the members of the rising Dalit middle classes of engaging with the caste question through civil society or NGO-centric activism. This leads to a move away from active and direct politics. Fourth, there is a growing emphasis on marking their symbolic presence through promoting Dalit icons and their memorials. Finally, one can witness an emerging right-wing shift among a section of the Mahar Dalits. Thus, disagreeing with Gorringe and Damodaran, Wankhede feels that the emerging Mahar elite 'utilizes the democratic spaces to raise sectarian concerns and remains distanced from the ground level political processes'.

With growing mobilities across caste communities and changing realities on ground, Dalit social movements are diversifying in many different ways. While a section of them localize and sectarianize their activities, there are others who network with the larger world, with all those who experience discrimination because of their identity. In the following chapter, Eva-Maria Hardtmann provides an overview of the growing transnational mobilization by Dalit activists. Beginning with sometime in the later years 1990s and early 2000s, they actively began to network with a range of global actors in order to enhance the weight and value of their work. She goes on to identify four different spheres of their transnational engagements. First, they began to actively network with the already settled Dalits in the diaspora, such as the Ravidasis of Punjab; second, they began to actively work with their anti-caste agenda in the relevant platforms of the international institutions, such as the United Nations, the World Bank, IMF, and WTO; third, they began to network with the Global Justice Movement and the World Social Forums; and four, they began to actively communicate with 'other activists on Internet and in social media'. She also points to some of the initiatives by Dalit women's movements and their growing engagements with feminists globally.

Taking the discussion on growing global engagements of Dalits forward, Deepa Reddy provides an interesting theoretical twist to the subject, underlining its larger implications. Locating her argument in the context of extensive mobilizations by Dalit groups for a recognition of 'caste' at par with 'race', the practice of which implies discrimination and violation of human rights, she argues that such a move becomes possible only when the underlying grammar of caste has undergone a significant change. By arguing their case in the language of rights, Dalit groups are also transcending the hierarchical view of caste, its cultural localism, which sees it as a unique system of ritual life among the Hindus of India. Invoking the language of exclusion and discrimination enables the ex-untouchables to imagine their position as being globally comparable to racial and ethnic minorities elsewhere. Caste, thus appears as a system of injustice and not as a localized cultural tradition.

The last two chapters in the section focus on neighbouring social categories, the so-called Scheduled Tribes and the De-notified Communities (DNTs), and their relationship with the Dalits.

In the state narratives of communitarian margins, the Scheduled Tribes are often clubbed with the Scheduled Castes, resulting in the common acronym 'SC-STs'. They were also the two categories identified for reservations by the Constituent Assembly and were provided with common provisions for their uplift soon after Independence. However, as Jai Prasad shows in his chapter, the term Scheduled Tribes is deployed to describe a wide range of communities who live away from the so-called mainstream Hindu society. Quite like caste, the term has come to acquire a life of its own and has also been institutionalized in the Indian administrative structure. However, the sociological and anthropological narratives on tribe-caste relationship remained embedded in the colonial and evolutionary frameworks, which saw the so-called tribal groups as 'primitive' and speculated their future in being absorbed into the Hindu society through their Sanskritization. However, this has not been the case. Beginning with the late 1980s there is an increasing tendency towards identity assertion, which also implies claims for their ethnic autonomy, even while many among them continue to encounter growing marginalization.

In her chapter on De-Notified Communities, Kalpana Kannabiran begins with a discussion of the term DNT and its origin in the colonial law, the Criminal Tribes Act, 1871, enacted by the British rulers 'to regulate and control vast and diverse communities'. They were not all similar to those they described as 'tribes' and included a range of groups such as 'acrobats, dancers, singers, jugglers, fortune-tellers and street performers of various kinds' along with some artisans and traditional healers. Many of them are currently listed as SCs. The second category were those who earned their livings by training 'wild' performing animals. They too are now listed as SCs or OBCs. The third category were the nomadic and pastoral communities, including some hunters and gatherers, many of whom are currently listed as STs. Even though the colonial law characterizing them as traditionally criminals has been scrapped, they (a total 312 of them) remain marked by the DNT administrative label, even though expressly for welfare purpose. Their access to public goods and systems of justice remains extremely poor. They continue to experience stigmatization and segregation. Their education levels being among the poorest, their access to decent employment, even within the reservation quotas, remains insignificant. Some still encounter untouchability while others face the stigma and humiliation of being deemed criminals. Their voice is also rarely heard as they remain on the margins of Dalit movements.

The chapters in this section provide a diverse picture on what is happening on ground to those traditionally marginalized, excluded, and humiliated by the caste system.

CHAPTER 30

AMBEDKAR'S LEGACY

ANAND TELTUMBDE

Bhimrao Ramji Ambedkar, Babasaheb (the lord father) as Dalits respectfully refer to him, suffered neglect of the mainstream for most part of his life and almost for a decade thereafter. Today, one of the most memorialized persons in history, he did not have a simple structure in memory until his son Yashwantrao Ambedkar, who built a small stupa as a memorial at Chaityabhumi in 1967, the place where he was cremated in 1956 (Teltumbde, 2018c, p. 34). The most prominent cause for this change was the transformation of political configuration of rural India with the economic policies followed by the postcolonial regime.[1] These changes led to political parties looking for vote blocks in terms of castes and communities. Dalits being, relatively cohesive, politicized, numerically significant but economically vulnerable group became the target for the ruling parties. The strategy for attracting them included destroying their autonomous politics with co-optation of its leadership, supplemented by the promotion of Ambedkar, sans his radicalism, who had emerged as a demigod for Dalit masses having replaced their erstwhile Hindu gods after their conversion to Buddhism under his leadership.

MAKING OF THE LEGACY

The advent of the British in India brought huge opportunities to the Untouchables. Many of them found jobs in British army, in households as domestic help, in their clubs

---

[1] The policies of the postcolonial state, particularly the Land Reforms followed by the Green Revolution resulted in creating a class of rich farmers and flooding capitalist relations into rural India. This class, engineered by the ruling Congress to be its political ally in rural areas, however, slowly developed its own political ambitions, which began to manifest into autonomous political blocks to hard-bargain with the Congress and into regional parties, if the latter. It thus threatened the Congress monopoly in elections, making them increasingly competitive (Anand Teltumbde, 2012; Anand Teltumbde and Yengde, 2018b, p. xv).

as butlers and attendants; in their army as soldiers, and more importantly, got access to education in schools started by Christian missionaries to public, and by military to army men and their families. Centuries of ostracization as the untouchables and ideological indoctrination by the theory of Karma (Jayaram, 2010; Smith, 1994)—whereby one's status was predetermined by one's conduct in the past life and could improve in subsequent lives by one's observance of dharma (assigned caste duties) in the current life—became a rational explanation for the caste system and provided much needed solace for those who were disadvantaged by it. Centuries of indoctrination that they themselves were responsible for their low status had sapped their spirits of self-esteem. For the first time, they woke up to their human identity and potentialities during the colonial rule. While various job opportunities brought them economic benefit, the military service and education had a catalytic impact on their morale. Ambedkar himself was a product of these opportunities, his two generations, from both maternal and paternal sides, having served in the army of the East India Company (Khairmode, 1968, Vol. 1, pp. 9–15).

Ambedkar was born when his father ranked as subhedar and was posted as the headmaster in the military normal school in MHOW cantonment (Khairmode, 1968, Vol. 1, pp. 9–15; Keer, 1974, p. 9). Soon after his retirement, they shifted to Dapoli, close to his native village, a favourite place for Mahar military retirees (Keer, 1990, p. 10). One of such retirees Gopal Baba Walangkar had begun social activism among the Untouchables in Western Maharashtra taking inspiration from Jotiba Phule, himself a beneficiary of Christian Missionary School (Keer, 1974, p. 59), who had pioneered a non-Brahmin or anti-Brahmin movement. Ambedkar would consider him as one of his three gurus, after Buddha and Kabir (Keer, 1990, p. 59; Ninan, 2018, p. 59).

Ambedkar was lucky to get timely financial support from Maharaja of Baroda (Keer, 1990, p. 26; Khairmode, Vol. 1, 1968, p. 66) to go to Columbia University in the United States to do his post-graduation and doctoral degrees. Later, he also obtained D. Sc. from London University and Bar-at-Law from Gray's Inn (Keer, 1990, pp. 48–49). With two doctoral degrees in Economics from the renowned universities in the world, he became one of the most educated persons of his time, an incredible feat for a Dalit when the community did not have even countable matriculates. However, even this educational achievement could not save him from the heat of humiliation on account of his caste. When he had to return to India abruptly due to the expiry of his scholarship and join the service of Baroda Government as per the agreement (Keer, 1990, p. 32), the office staff would throw files at him from distance, no one would rent a house to him, and he would be thrown out of a Parsee Guest House where he had taken shelter incognito, when identified as untouchable. Frustrated, he returned to Mumbai and modestly begun his public life when invited to give a testimony before the Southborough Committee on Franchise. He started a weekly, *Mooknayak* (Leader of the dumbs) with the financial help from Maharaja of Kolhapur, a princely state, and participating in various community conferences. He managed to return to England after three years to complete his studies. Only after his return to India in April 1923, having completed his studies, he plunged into public life by founding the Bahishkrit Hitakarini Sabha (Kadam, 1991, pp. 80–81; Keer, 1974, p. 55) (Association for the well-being of the excluded) at Bombay in July 1924.

In course of his illustrious public life of over four decades, Ambedkar founded many organizations—Bahishkrit Hitkarini Sabha (1924), Samata Samaj Sangh (1927), Bharat Bhushan Printing Press (1927), Samata Sainik Dal, Depressed Classes Education Society' (1928), Mumbai Municipal Kamgar Sangh (1934), 'Independent Labour Party (1936), Municipal Workers Union' (1937), Mahar Dnyati Panchayat Samiti (1941), Scheduled Castes Federation (1942), Peoples Education Society (PES) (1945), 'Scheduled Castes Improvement Trust' (1944), Bhartiya Boudha Jansangh (1951) transformed as 'The Buddhist Society of India (1954), Mumbai Ilakha Kanistha Gaokamgar Sangh' (1955), Buddha Bhushan Printing Press'(1956), and posthumously Republican Party of India (1957). Some of which were superseded by the newer ones but most survived. His ideological vision—Liberty, 'Equality, Fraternity' informed his entire life. He proposed certain programmes—State socialism vide his book States and Minorities (1947), conversion to Buddhism (1956), parliamentary democracy vide drafting the Constitution of India (1950). While they all constitute his legacy, it necessarily manifests in the struggles, euphoria, contradictions, frustrations of Dalits who claim to be following him.

Ambedkar's legacy is significantly shaped by this history as well as contemporary social, economic, and political forces. The spread of education among Dalits and rise of a Dalit middle class that extended to constitute a sizable Dalit diaspora abroad; a section of it becoming entrepreneurs and advocating Dalit capitalism, the reservation policies that played a prominent role in catalysing these changes, and consequent identitarian instincts it induced in the upwardly mobile Dalits are all due to this legacy. The cultural assertion of Dalit masses in terms of Buddha Viharas, Ambedkar statues, and alternate cultural goods, and practices are also pervasively seen as his legacy. Likewise, Ambedkar's legacy could be noted in general constitutional discourse, civil rights activism, women's struggles against gender discrimination, and political activism of vast political class to which numerous Dalit parties, including Bahujan Samaj Party belong. Ambedkar's multi-dimensional legacy encompassing all these multi-layered influences is thus a complex whole, which may not be easy to grasp and still difficult to analyse. In this chapter, I attempt to take stock of some broad aspects of this legacy.

Ambedkar's legacy is conceived in five parts: One, Organizational legacy, which is seen in the state of organizations that he founded; two, Ideological legacy, that refers to his ideals, his vision of human emancipation; three, Programmatic legacy, which is seen in the state of the programmes he proposed to accomplish his ideal; four, the symbolic legacy in terms of representation of himself and his movement and five, the conduct of his legatees, the followers who claim to follow him.

Organizational Legacy

Ambedkar founded many organizations as vehicles for his mission. To start with he had founded Bahishkrit Hitkarini Sabha (1924). It was superseded by organizations for various purposes, which lived longer and existed when he died. The prominent ones are Samata Sainik Dal (Social Equality Corps), Bombay Scheduled Caste Improvement

Trust, People's Education Society, Buddhist Society of India, and Republican Party of India. All of them seem to survive but in such a state that may place his legacy in disrepute.

Samata Sainik Dal

Samata Sainik Dal (SSD) was formed in the wake of the Bahishkrit Conference at Mahad that was organized on 19–20 March 1927 (Teltumbde, 2016, pp. 105–172) as a volunteer force of youth to take care of organizational and security requirements. During its preparatory phase, Dr. Ambedkar Seva Dal was formed with the initiative of a youth Ramchandra Babaji More[2] on the pattern of Dr. Hardikar Seva Dal of the Indian National Congress. According to Ambedkar's instruction, this band of volunteers was renamed as the Samata Sainik Dal (SSD) (Teltumbde, 2016, pp. 273–274). As the concluding act of the conference, the delegates marched to the Chavadar tank and asserted their legal right by drinking its water. This defilement of tank by the untouchables provoked the caste Hindus to attack the delegates after they returned from the march, seriously injuring 60–70 people (Teltumbde, 2016, 127 Mahad). Ambedkar, angered by this development, himself organized the next conference as Satyagraha Conference from 25 December, just nine months later. The SSD performed important role in enlisting support for this conference. For many years, it functioned informally as volunteer corps and was formally inaugurated at a national level on 20 July 1942 at Nagpur (Kshīrasāgara, 1994, p. 102).

The youth were supposed to be trained in physical fitness and military techniques so as to create an effective defence shield for the leadership. They became an integral part of the Ambedkarite movement and were a visible force in the conversion ceremony that took place in Nagpur in 1956 and thereafter in the funeral procession of Ambedkar in Mumbai. Unlike the Rashtriya Swayamsevak Sangh (RSS), the organization of the Hindu-Right, incidentally founded in Nagpur in 1925, SSD was formed as an adjunct outfit to defend various organs of the movement. After the death of Ambedkar, the split in the Republican Party of India impacted the SSD like all other organs. It exists in autonomous fragments in most major centres of Ambedkarite movement such as Mumbai, Nagpur, Jalandhar, Delhi, Agra, and some others in the form of their poorer selves. There have been conscious attempts to revive them by such veteran leaders like the late Bhagwan Das and Lahori Ram Balley of Jalandhar but without much success. It does show up at major congregations like that takes place in Mumbai on 6 December to observe death anniversary of Ambedkar, Deeksha Bhumi in Nagpur on the Dussehra Day and 14 October[3] and newer ones like Bhima-Koregaon, etc. but much in a symbolic manner.

---

[2] R. B. More was a young activist who conceived and organized the Mahad Conference. He would later join the Communist Party and be known as Comrade More (Teltumbde, 2016, p. 105).

[3] Even the anniversary of the conversion also split into two, one faction observing it on the day of a Hindu festival, the Dussera, and the other following the English calendar, and observing it on 14 October, following the English calendar.

The Bombay Scheduled Caste Improvement Trust

In order to establish a social centre for the overall development of the Dalits, Ambedkar had begun to mobilize building fund. He had called upon the people to contribute Rs 2 per male and Re 1 per female. In response, Rs 45,095 was collected under this fund. Ambedkar bought two plots of land admeasuring total 2332 square yards on Gokuldas Pasta Road in Dadar East for Rs 23,535 and built a temporary office on the land with the balance amount. He founded the Bombay Scheduled Caste Improvement Trust on 29 July 1944. Its objects in the trust deed mainly emphasized advancement of general literacy, eradication of social evils, and superstitious practices among Dalits, and safeguarding their civil rights. It included supporting organizations engaged in such works. When Ambedkar's printing press in Naigaon was burnt down in the caste riots, Ambedkar shifted it to this plot of land and began depositing its rent and maintenance charges. The trust was dormant all these years but came into a limelight controversy when the Ambedkar Bhavan standing on the trust land, was demolished with bulldozers at 3 a.m. on 26 June 2016. A huge public uproar ensued and the trust came into disrepute. It was alleged that a retired Dalit IAS Officer, Ratnakar Gaikwad, whose father was one among the 20 students Ambedkar sent abroad in 1943, was instrumental in demolition (Bavadam, 2016).

Peoples Education Society

Right from the Mahad Conference, Ambedkar voiced the need for the Dalits to take higher education. In line with his Fabian proclivities, he imagined that if Dalits occupied important posts in bureaucracy, they could influence the state to be congenial to Dalit interests. In July 1944, when he was a member of the viceroy's executive council, he founded People's Education Society (PE) and two years later in April 1946, opened Siddharth College of Arts and Science in Mumbai. Another college, Milind College was started at Aurangabad in September 1950. These colleges played a yeomen's role in providing poor Dalit students access to higher education and still maintained respectable standards of education. Many of its alumni (like M. L. Shahare, UPSC Chairman; Sukhdeo Thorat, Chairman, UGC, Narendra Chapalgaonkar, Justice, High Court, etc.; and scores of noted litterateurs like Yashwant Manohar, Raosaheb Kasbe, etc.) reached high positions, as envisaged by Ambedkar, but a few, if at all, may be said to have performed the role he expected them to perform. The PE society grew over the years in terms of number of colleges and schools but lost its respectability with its poor standards of both faculty as well as students. In recent years, it is embroiled into the tussle between politicians, viz., Ramdas Athwale, Prakash Ambedkar, and Anandraj Ambedkar, to take its control through court battles as well as physical scuffles. It is engulfed in the cobweb of court cases and a galore of controversies and is reduced to its it's dilapidated self (Sunday Guardian, 2019; Mumbai Mirror, 2019).

The Buddhist Society of India

The Buddhist Society of India or the Bharatiya Bauddha Mahasabha (BMS) (in Marathi) was established by Ambedkar on 4 May 1955 in Mumbai for promotion of Buddhism in

India. Ambedkar reflected strong attraction towards Buddhism although in the context of conversion he never gave any indication that Buddhism was his choice until he decided to do so (Teltumbde, 2018a, pp. 219–242). The mass conversion of estimated half a million Dalits on 14 October 1956 that followed his own was a momentous event. However, soon after his death, it was overtaken by politics and as such the presidentship of the BMS, which was seen politically unimportant, came to his son Yashawantrao Ambedkar almost uncontested (Teltumbde, 2018a, p. 235). The schism in politics spread to other spheres and BMS also did not escape it. After the death of Yashwantrao Ambedkar, by which the BMS became a sizable property, the contest for its control ensued. When the mantle of presidentship was assumed by his wife Meeratai Ambedkar, dispute was raked up, and taken to the courts (Bombay High Court, 2013; Janwalkar, 2014). The BMS fragmented with people forming their own BMSs but without any affiliation to the central body (Teltumbde, 2011).

Republican Party of India

Ambedkar formed two political parties, viz., Independent Labour Party in August 1936, in the wake of the first provincial elections that were to be held in 1937 (Keer, 1974, p. 285; Rao, 2013, pp. 43–58). Ambedkar thought that his own caste following could not help him win elections unless he widened his appeal to broader masses of people. He therefore decided to found a party of the working class, which would naturally subsume all Dalits (Jaffrelot, 2006, p. 74; Rao, 2013, p. 46). He took inspiration from its name sake, a British political party of the left, established in 1893. The declared aims and objectives of ILP were: State Sponsored industrialization to be given high priority, strong labour laws to protect factory workers, legislation to provide remunerative wages, to fix maximum hours of work, leave with pay, and a sanitary dwelling at reasonable amount; the need for abolition of the Jagirdari system; extensive programme for the improvement of educational facility in technical institute; abolition of the exclusion of Dalits from the lucrative jobs in industries (BAWS, 2003b, pp. 413–420). The manifesto of the ILP reeled off mostly the Fabian agenda and had reference to caste only once and that too in a passing manner. ILP secured a total of 14 seats out of 17 in which they contested. This included 11 reserved (out of 13) and 3 general seats (out of 4) (Jaffrelot, 2003, pp. 103–104; Ambedkar, 2003b, p. 296). He sincerely carried out his class-caste struggles until 1942 when he took a decision to dissolve the ILP and form the Scheduled Caste federation (SCF) in response to the Crisp Mission Report that acknowledged claims of communal parties but ignored ILP's (Cháirez-Garza, 2018, pp. 1–28). The foundation of the SCF coincided with his joining the viceroy's executive council. In September 1946, his membership was annulled with the reconstitution of the viceroy's executive council as the interim cabinet of the future government of India with members from Congress and Muslim League. Ambedkar was replaced by Jagjivan Ram by the Congress. Ambedkar remained in political bewilderment during the parleys for transfer of power. When the constituent assembly was formed, Ambedkar did not have numbers in the provincial assemblies to elect him to the constituent assembly. However, he managed to get elected with the help of Jogendranath Mandal from Khulna-Jessore constituency in East Bengal. But it was a short-lived solace as his membership came to an end with the declaration of June 1947 Mountbatten Plan for the partition of India. The Congress decided to get him elected from Bombay, shelving its own plan, and made him even the chairman of the Drafting Committee. He was also inducted into the first all-party cabinet as law minister.

On account of the lack of promised support from Nehru to the Hindu Code Bill, he ambitiously drafted, he resigned from the cabinet (Keer, 1990, pp. 434–435). He tried unsuccessfully two elections to the Lok Sabha. In this spell of dejection, Ambedkar contemplated a non-Communist anti-Congress party and conceived an idea of the Republican Party of India (RPI). He wrote to various socialist leaders inviting them to join it (Jaffrelot, 2006, p. 86). He had also set up a 'training school for entrance to politics' in 1956 (Keer, 1990, p. 496). He even announced his decision to form RPI to his audience in Nagpur during his stay there for conversion ceremony. Unfortunately, he died shortly thereafter. The next layer of leadership had formed a presidium to thwart the internecine rivalry amongst them but it did not help. They fought the 1957-elections under the SCF banner and thereafter announced the formation of the RPI in deference to Ambedkar's wishes but sans its content. It just proved a change in the name. But even then it could not survive. A section of leadership disputed the proposition of the party to take up struggles for the livelihood issues of the Dalits and accused it to be anti-Ambedkarite and inspired by the communists (Teltumbde, 2017). The party split and went on splitting (Teltumbde and Yengde, 2018b, p. xiii). Today, their innumerable factions flaunting 'republican' in their names to claim their 'Ambedkariteness' allude to their lost legacy.

Ideological Legacy

Ambedkar's ideology may be crystallized into his fond phrase, 'Liberty, Equality, Fraternity'. Ambedkar mapped his ideal society, ideal democracy, and almost every ideal with it (Kadam, K. N., 1997, p. 26). This Trinitarian slogan of French Revolution was usurped by bourgeois; its Liberty overwhelming Equality and neglecting Fraternity altogether. The reason that the French Revolution did not produce either liberty or equality is that the major power holders and their heirs have successfully maintained that they were separate objectives. Ambedkar acutely realized it and therefore claimed that he took his slogan from Buddhism (Teltumbde, 2018d). He extended its meaning to raise it to the utopian heights by stressing the coexistence of all its three attributes that he envisioned in his ideal society.

Liberty is liberalism's motto, its flagpost. Ambedkar, a liberal, however, was acutely aware of its historical pitfall. It tended to become its antithesis inasmuch as it became liberty for the capitalist to exploit workers and became a cause for inequality and strife. Liberalism's liberty thus ignored both equality and fraternity. Socialism emphasized equality but ignored other two, liberty and fraternity. And some religious traditions propagated fraternity but ignored liberty and equality. His conception of liberty was 'not merely the negative conception of the absence of restraint' or was 'confined to the mere recognition of the right of the people to vote', it was very positive. It involved the idea of Government by the people (BAWS, 1991a, p. 37). Likewise, his conception of equality meant 'abolition of privileges of every kind in law, in the civil service, in the Army, in taxation, in trade and in industry: in fact the abolition of all processes which lead to inequality'. He defined fraternity as 'an all-pervading sense of human brotherhood, unifying all classes and all nations, with 'peace on earth and goodwill towards man' as its motto' (BAWS, 1991a, p. 37).

When an opportunity arose, he tried to imbue the constitution with these ideals but it proved empty rhetoric in practice. The postcolonial state that he helped construct was actually the continuation of the colonial state—three-fourth of its constitution (the India Act 1935) being adopted nearly verbatim into the new constitution—the entire institutional structure as well processes of the state remaining unchanged, its draconian laws having been stay put, and entire societal ethos remaining feudal. These oddities, instead of being arrested and diminished, have only grown over the years. The caste ridden society symbolized the antithesis of his ideal—Liberty, Equality, Fraternity—was rather reinforced by re-implanting castes from its parched ground of traditions into the modernist constitutional soil with the help of reservations (Teltumbde, 2018c, pp. 46–90). Fraternity was thus sacrificed at the altar of caste and communal divide; liberty was lost to a plethora of draconian laws, and equality proved still born with systematic promotion of capitalism and capitulation to feudalism (Teltumbde, 2018c, pp. 46–90).

Programmatic Legacy

Ambedkar tried out his strategies towards realization of his ideal 'liberty, equality, fraternity'. These are constitutionalism with state socialism embedded into it and Buddhism.

State Socialism

While Ambedkar repeatedly invoked the revolutionary republican principles of liberty, equality, and fraternity, he left no ambiguity about equality's pre-eminence (Maxwell, 2015, p. 75). Ambedkar proposed state socialism to be hardcoded into the constitution (BAWS, 1979b, pp. 381–452). The plan contained provisions like nationalization of land, parcelling it out to village cooperatives for cultivation with state-providing inputs, state-run key, and basic industries, compulsory life insurance, etc. It did not disregard private property and provided for compensation if it was taken over by the state. It's still death only proved impossibility of changing economic structure of the society with any such wishful propositions. When Ambedkar, as the representative of Jessore-Khulna constituency, was invited to speak on Nehru's Objective Resolution, he did touch upon its essence, saying how without the structure of the society being socialist, one could conceive justice social, economic, and political (BAWS, 1994, Vol. 13, p. 9). However, the compulsions of realpolitik made him to hasten that he was prepared to leave it at that (BAWS, 1994, p. 9). While it spelt a kind of patch up with the Congress, which got him elected from Bombay assembly when he lost his membership due to the Partition plan, and subsequently made him a chairman of its most important committee, the drafting committee. He could never make a mention of this plan in the CA and when others spoke of socialism, vehemently countered them. In November 1948, when Prof. K. T. Shah, representing Bihar, proposed the amendment that 'India shall be a Secular, Federal, Socialist Union of States' (BAWS, 1994, p. 326), Ambedkar opposed the amendment, saying that secularism was inherent to the constitution's structure and he felt that mentioning it in the preamble would be redundant. While opposing socialism, he argued that 'how the society should be organized in its social and economic side, are matters which must be decided by the people themselves according to time and circumstances. It cannot be laid down in the Constitution itself, because that is destroying democracy altogether' (BAWS, 1994b, p. 326). Not only that, he also called Shah's amendment 'purely superfluous'. He interestingly observed that the directive principles in the Constitution, which did not have any force and therefore would be ignored by the rulers with impunity, were socialist in their direction: '... apart from the Fundamental Rights, which we have embodied in the Constitution, we have also introduced other sections which deal with Directive Principles of State Policy... What I would like to ask Professor Shah is this: If these directive principles... are not socialistic in their direction and in their content, I fail to understand what more socialism can be' (Teltumbde, 2018d).

It did not take even two years for Ambedkar to get disillusioned with the constitution. On 2 September 1953, during a debate on the role and power of the governor in the Rajya Sabha, he retorted to the charge that he was the architect of the Constitution, saying,

> 'My answer is I was a hack. What I was asked to do, I did much against my will.... Sir, my friends tell me that I have made the Constitution. But I am quite prepared to say that I shall be the first person to burn it out. I do not want it. It does not suit anybody ...' When someone interjected commenting, 'But you defended it,' Ambedkar shot back saying, 'We lawyers defend many things...'[4]

While creating an illusion of 'Nehruvian socialism', India merrily promoted capitalist developments giving fillip to existing inequality. (Yengde and Teltumbde, 2018, pp. xiv–xviii). In July 1991 India adopted neoliberal market reforms that further aggravated inequality (Bhattacharyya, 2013, p. 1; Mooij, 2005). Today, India is one of the most unequal societies in the world (Sinha, 2018). Ambedkar's legacy was not only undermined by the State he helped in constructing but also by his so-called followers, who enthusiastically advocated capitalism and neoliberal economic reforms (Chandrasekaran, 2018; Prasad and Kamble, 2013).

---

[4] Rajya Sabha Debates, 2 September 1953, col. 877 (Teltumbde, 2018d).

Buddhism

Ambedkar had proposed religious conversion as the way of escaping caste. His analysis led him to conclude that annihilation of caste was not possible unless the Hindus came forward to dynamite their dharmashastras, which, according to him, were the source of castes (BAWS, Vol. 1, 75 AoC). Religious conversion, therefore, symbolized a complete break from Hinduism, and 'resistance to the power constituted by Hinduism and the caste system' (Naudet, 2019). In 1935, he had taken a vow to not die as a Hindu. Next year in a special conference organized to explain the rationale behind this declaration, he provided the existential logic. He said that Dalits were treated badly because they lacked in all the three strengths—strength of numbers, strength of finance, and strength of spirit. In order to overcome their plight, the only way was to merge into some existing religious community by converting to its religion. The manner in which he made approving references to Islam, it appeared he favoured Islam for conversion (Ambedkar, 1936). However, when he actually did convert after two decades, it was Buddhism. Leave apart having a community, Buddhism was not even known to common people. The rationale he then proffered was its legacy of anti-Brahmanism and congruence with modern science. He wrote a 'gospel' for the new converts 'The Buddha and His Dhamma' (BAWS, 1992), which provided his own interpretation of Buddhism, away from its prevailing schools. He hoped that all Indians would appreciate this heritage and become Buddhists. But apart from his own castemen who converted at Nagpur after him, not many people, even belonging to the untouchable castes accepted Buddhism. As a matter of fact, until 1990, when the Prime Minister VP Singh extended the SC reservations to the SC-converts to Buddhism, even the people who had embraced Buddhism would not officially register themselves as Buddhists lest they should lose their safeguards and concessions. Spread of Buddhism apart, his followers could not keep up with his radical outlook and deviated in various directions, within the familiar frame of Hindu practices. They have completely failed to preserve the heritage of rationality and scientific outlook Ambedkar's engaged Buddhism, expected of his followers (Yengde and Teltumbde, 2018, pp. 219–242, Strategy).

Symbolic Legacy

Ambedkar in his own life time had become a cult figure for his followers who adored him as Babasaheb (Lord Father), Bhim Raja (lord Bhim), celebrated his birth anniversaries, used a greeting, Jai Bhim (victory to Bhim),[5] and composed songs and waved myths

---

[5] It was coined by Babu L. N. Hardas, a leader of Independent Labour Party, on 16 February 1937. Ramteke (2016).

around him. After his death, the cult only grew, with thousands of statues, and busts spread all over India (Tartakov, 2012); songs and hymns written in praise for him[6]; pictures and posters adorning homes and offices; seminars and conferences to discuss various aspects of his thoughts; celebrations of birth anniversaries; huge congregations in his name being held at various locations connected with him, etc. They served to counter the hegemonic presence of Hindu gods and goddesses in the popular culture create a new culture of resistance with Ambedkar as its central figure. Later, with the spread of education among the Dalits, there emerged the study centres in colleges and universities on him. In its sheer magnitude, there may not be any person in history who could rival him in this symbolic legacy. Originated as a cultural arsenal of struggle, it, however, reduced to an inert articles of obeisance to Ambedkar. Apart from the nostalgic devotion of Dalits in making this phenomenon, the state has played a big role. In order to woo Dalit voters, display of devotion to Ambedkar, who emerged as a pivotal icon for Dalits, became a common theme across all political parties. While Ambedkar's other legacies are doldrums, his symbolic legacy is growing with increasing crisis the Dalits face.

His Legatees

Ambedkar's legacy ultimately reflected in his followers, particularly the educated middle class who have been major beneficiaries of his struggle. He expected them to become protectors of interests of the Dalit masses and catalyse their uplift. However, during his own life time, he lamented that they had betrayed him (Darapuri, 2016). These educated individuals occupied high positions in bureaucracy and in process underwent class transformation that snapped their umbilical cord with the masses, although in caste terms they still belonged to them as their new class would not socially accept them. In reaction, they promoted identitarian trend which especially thwarted possibilities of associating the Dalits with the progressive forces and opened reactionary possibilities of aligning with the ruling classes. The masses merely took Ambedkar as their god replacing their erstwhile Hindu gods and could not create an alternate cultural paradigm. Socially and politically they splintered along various versions of Ambedkar—the one who asked them to follow 'educate, agitate and organize', one who asked them to shun agitation and follow constitutionalism; one who asked them to follow Buddhism, and such like—reducing Ambedkar to an inert and worst a reactionary identity.

[6] For instance, Hema Rairkar and Guy Poitevin, who co-founded the Centre for Cooperative Research in Social Sciences (CCRSS) in Pune, transcribed more than 110,000 folk songs of Maharashtra over a period of 20 years during 1990s (Mohan, 2017).

Conclusion

In the failed legacy of leaders, the blame is always heaped on the followers. The reasons behind the loss of radical legacy of Ambedkar are however complex than indicated by such a dictum. The foremost is the intrinsic difficulty in definition of Ambedkar's legacy. It is because Ambedkar's thoughts and actions actually evolved in their spatial and temporal context. There are many instances wherein he said one thing at one time but quite opposite at other time. For instance, in States and Minorities, he proposed his plan of state socialism, and thought it should be hard coded into the constitution as without it, democracy would remain flawed. However, while dealing with the K. T. Shah's amendment (BAWS, 1994b, p. 326), he took the opposite view. Likewise, in States and Minorities, he proposed compensation in the form of debenture to the owners while taking over their lands, however, while discussing in Parliament whether the government could acquire land by compensating the owners under the then Article 31 of the Constitution, Ambedkar was the only one who opposed it. Ambedkar termed it murderer of land reforms and so ugly that he would not even like to look at it. The same could be said even in relation to the constitution. Initially, he was against the idea of the constituent assembly but later, when it was getting formed, he was desperate to enter it. In the ecstasy of being the chief architect of the constitution, he exhorted his followers to discard all other methods and follow the constitutional ones to redress their grievances. However, within two years, he was so disillusioned with the constitution that he angrily disowned it declaring it useless to anyone. Such contradictions and inconsistencies were indeed numerous and he would just brush them away by invoking Emerson who said: 'consistency is a virtue of an ass. No thinking human being can be tied down to a view once expressed in the name of consistency. More important than consistency is responsibility. A responsible person must learn to unlearn what he has learned. A responsible person must have the courage to rethink and change his thoughts'. It could also be traced to his Pragmatism which relied on choosing best course of action in an unfolding situation.

The other contributing factor, and arguably more significant is the ruling classes realizing the importance of Ambedkar as an icon for Dalit aspirations in the face of elections becoming competitive by the end of 1960s as depicted in the first para of this chapter. It, in turn, led to the conception of vote banks in terms of castes and communities. Dalits, the most populous section of them who considered Ambedkar as their icon, were relatively the most politicized people and hence became prime targets of power seekers. They could be swayed and manipulated by manipulating Ambedkar icon. In order to woo Dalits, the ruling classes began promoting Ambedkar by naming roads, public places after him, putting up his statues, launching schemes, programmes and institutions after him and so on. They systematically destroyed autonomous politics of the Dalits and reduced it to mere symbolism. They induced ideological pollution suppressing radical aspects of Ambedkar and highlighting aspects that were congenial to them. It necessarily blurred his legacy.

Still another reason for damaging Ambedkar legacy was making him a godhead by the Dalits as his devotees. It entwined the process of iconization of Ambedkar. With the promotion from the ruling classes, big congregations began happening in the name of Ambedkar, which in turn led to not only politicians basking in popular appeal to Dalits but even the intellectuals reinforcing the same to gain popularity with the Dalit masses. Ambedkar was greatly simplified in the resultant hagiographic output. It was an irony that a man who so eloquently decried the blind devotion to so-called great people (BAWS, 1991b, p. 240), was himself turned into a godhead by his own followers.

These processes manifested in many things like, seeing communists as enemy number one, suicidal neglect of material aspects just because they were identified with the communists, excessive identitarian orientation that turned them into antithesis of what Ambedkar spoke, creating cult of devotees of Ambedkar, and so on, all contributing to the systematic destruction of Ambedkar's legacy. It paved the way to right wing Hindutva forces saffronizing Ambedkar and pushing Dalits into the dark past from where they were barely extricated during the last century.

References

Abbreviation followed in Bibliography:
BAWS: Babasaheb Ambedkar: Writings and Speeches, Education Department, Govt. of Maharashtra, Mumbai.
B. R. Ambedkar. 1936. What Path to Salvation? http://www.columbia.edu/itc/mealac/pritchett/00ambedkar/txt_ambedkar_salvation.html, accessed 08 October 2019.
BAWS. 1979a. Vol. 1 (Annihilation of Caste).
BAWS. 1979b. Vol. 1 (States and Minorities in).
BAWS. 1991a. Vol. 10 (Why Indian Labour Is Determined to Win The War).
BAWS. 1991b. Vol. 10 (Ranade Gandhi and Jinnah).
BAWS. 1992. Vol. 11 (The Buddha and His Dhamma).
BAWS. 1994. Vol. 13 (Resolution Regarding Aims and Objects).
BAWS. 1994b. Vol. 13 (Section Four, Clausewise Discussion: 15th November 1948 to 8th January 1949).
BAWS. 2003a. Vol. 17 Part 1, 2003 (Struggle For Human Rights).
BAWS. 2003b. Vol. 17 Part 2 (Independent Labour Party: Its formation and Its Aims).
Bavadam, Lyla. 2016, 19 August. 'Rumble in Mumbai'. *Frontier*. https://frontline.thehindu.com/dispatches/article29477909.ece, accessed 07 October 2019.
Bhattacharyya, Sudipta (Ed.) 2013. *Two Decades of Market Reform in India: Some Dissenting Views*. London, Anthem Press, p. 1.
Bombay High Court, Trustee of Buddhist Society vs Meeratai Y. Ambedkar on 21 June 2013. https://indiankanoon.org/doc/31186001/.
Cháirez-Garza, Jesús Francisco. 2018. 'Bound Hand and Foot and Handed over to the Caste Hindus': Ambedkar, Untouchability and the Politics of Partition'. *The Indian Economic and Social History Review*, 55(1): 1–28.
Chandrasekaran, Balakrishnan, and B. R. Ambedkar. 2018. *The Greatest Free Market Economist of India*. http://missionbhim.com/2018/03/03/b-r-ambedkar-the-greatest-free-market-economist-of-india-by-balakrishnan-chandrasekaran/.

Darapuri, S. R. 2016. 'Dr. Ambedkar's Historical Speech At Agra'. https://countercurrents.org/2016/08/dr-ambedkars-historical-speech-at-agra, accessed 13 October 2019.

Deivasigamani, T. 2018. *Subaltern Discourses*. Chennai: MJP Publishers, 59.

Jaffrelot, Christophe. 2006. *Dr Ambedkar and Untouchability: Analysing and Fighting Caste*. Delhi: Permanent Black.

Jaffrelot, Christophe. 2003. *India's Silent Revolution: The Rise of the Lower Castes in North India*. London: C. Hurst & Co. Publishers.

Janwalkar, Mayura. 2014, 16 April. 'Battle to Head Ambedkar's Society Nears End in HC'. *Indian Express*. https://indianexpress.com/article/india/india-others/battle-to-head-ambedkars-society-nears-end-in-hc-2/, accessed 07 October 2019.

Jayarama, V. 2010, November 14. '"Hinduism and Caste System" Hinduism, Buddhism, Jainism, Sikhism, Zoroastrianism and Other Resources'. *Web*.

Kadam, K. N. 1991. *Dr. Babasaheb Ambedkar and the Significance of His Movement: A Chronology*. Bombay: Popular Prakashan.

Kadam, K. N. 1997. *The Meaning of the Ambedkarite Conversion to Buddhism and Other Essays*. Mumbai: Popular Prakashan.

Keer, Dhananjay. 1990. *Dr. Ambedkar: Life and Mission*. Mumbai: Popular Prakashan.

Keer, Dhananjay. 1974. *Mahatma Jotirao Phooley: Father of the Indian Social Revolution*. Mumbai: Popular Prakashan.

Khairmode, C. B. 1968. *Bhimrao Ramji Ambedkar, Charitra Khand Pahila* (Biography, Vol. 1). Mumbai: Ambedkar Education Society.

Kshīrasāgara, Rāmacandra. 1994. *Dalit Movement in India and Its Leaders, 1857–1956*. New Delhi: M D Publications, 1994.

Maxwell, Barry. 2015. *No Goads. No Masters. No Peripheries: Global Anarchisms*. Oakland: PM Press.

Mohan, Shriya. 2017, 30 June. 'Songs of Grit and Grist, Businessline'. https://www.thehindubusinessline.com/blink/watch/songs-of-grit-and-grist/article9741903.ece#, accessed 08 October 2019.

Mooij, Jos (Ed.). 2005. *The Politics of Economic Reforms in India*. New Delhi: SAGE.

Naudet, Jules. 2010, November 5. 'Ambedkar and the Critique of Caste Society'. https://booksandideas.net/Ambedkar-and-the-Critique-of-Caste.html, accessed 08 October 2019.

Ninan, M. M. 2018. 'Ambedkar's Philosophy of Hinduism and Contemporary Critiques'. Lulu.com.

Prasad, Chandra Bhan, and Milind Kamble. 2013, 23 January. 'Manifesto to End Caste: Push Capitalism and Industrialization to Eradicate This Pernicious System'. http://timesofindia.indiatimes.com/articleshow/18136744.cms?utm_source=contentofinterest&utm_medium=text&utm_campaign=cppst, accessed 08 October 2019.

Ramteke, P. T. 2016. 'Jai Bhim che Janak (The Originator of Jai Bhim) Babu Hardas L. N. (in Marathi)'. https://ambedkareksoch.wordpress.com/2016/10/12/jai-bhim-%E0%A4%9C%E0%A4%AF-%E0%A4%AD%E0%A5%80%E0%A4%AE-%E0%A4%9C%E0%A5%88%E0%A4%AD%E0%A5%80%E0%A4%AE-%E0%5%8D/, accessed 08 October 2019.

Rao, Anupama. 2013. *Revisiting Interwar Thought: Stigma, Labour, and the Immanence of Caste-Class*, in Cosimo Zene, *The Political Philosophies of Antonio Gramsci and B. R. Ambedkar: Itineries of Dalits and Subalterns*. New York: Routledge, 2013.

Sinha, Vikram. 2018, 25 August. India Is One of the World's Most Unequal Countries: James Crabtree'. *Live Mint*. https://www.livemint.com/Companies/FeRwRFEQJu8mKx7wcVN5FL/India-is-one-of-the-worlds-most-unequal-countries-James-Cr.html, accessed 08 October 2019.

Sunday Guardian. 2019, 7 October. http://www.sunday-guardian.com/news/grandson-seeks-control-of-ambedkars-legacy. *Mumbai Mirror*, https://mumbaimirror.indiatimes.com/mumbai/other/trust-row-worsens-colleges-staff-shortage/articleshow/62274139.cms, accessed 07 October 2019.

Smith, Brian K. 1994. *Classifying the Universe: The Ancient Indian Varna System and the Origins of Caste*. New York: Oxford University Press [Print].

Tartakov, Gary Michael (Ed.). 2012. *Dalit Art and Visual Imagery*. New Delhi: Oxford University Press.

Teltumbde, Anand. 2011, 22 April. 'Crisis of Ambedkarites and Future Challenges'. Countercurrents.org. https://www.countercurrents.org/teltumbde220411.htm, accessed 07 October 2019.

Teltumbde, Anand. 2012. 'Identity Politics and the Annihilation of Castes'. https://www.india-seminar.com/2012/633/633_anand_teltumbde.htm.

Teltumbde, Anand. 2016. *Mahad, The Making of the First Dalit Revolt*. Delhi: Aakar, 2016.

Teltumbde, Anand. 2017. 'Caste, Gender and Other Such Issues Should Be Dealt with as Class Struggle'. https://countercurrents.org/2017/04/caste-gender-and-other-such-issues-should-be-dealt-with-as-class-struggle-anand-teltumbde, accessed 07 October 2019.

Teltumbde, Anand. 2018a. *Strategy of Conversion to Buddhism: Intent and Aftermath in Suraj Yengde and Anand Teltumbde, The Radical in Ambedkar: Critical Reflections*. New Delhi: Penguin Random House.

Teltumbde, Anand, and Suraj Yengde. 2018b. *Introduction in Suraj Yengde and Anand Teltumbde, The Radical in Ambedkar: Critical Reflections*. New Delhi: Penguin Random House.

Teltumbde, Anand. 2018c. *Republic of Caste*. New Delhi: Navayana.

Teltumbde, Anand. 2018d. *Ambedkar's Socialism: Some Reflections*. http://www.india-seminar.com/2018/701/701_anand_teltumbde.htm, accessed: 08 October.

CHAPTER 31

CHANGING DYNAMICS OF UNTOUCHABILITY

SURYAKANT WAGHMORE

> Caste is a state of mind. It is a disease of the mind. The teachings of the Hindu religion are the root cause of this disease. We practise casteism, we observe untouchability, because we are asked to do it by the Hindu religion in which we live. A bitter thing can be made sweet. The taste of anything can be changed. But poison cannot be made *Amrit*.
>
> B. R. Ambedkar (1936)

THE above epigraph from Ambedkar could help us pose several questions about the past, present, and future 'untouchability'. What is untouchability? Is untouchability a thing of past in rural and urban India? Can caste exist without untouchability? If caste and untouchability persist, what are the newer forms that untouchability takes in contemporary India? How does the changing dynamics of untouchability configure equality and citizenship in rural and urban spaces? This chapter argues that the traditional forms and ideas of untouchability are under severe duress due to migration, urbanization, protective-preventive, and compensatory legal measures and more importantly due to assertion and activism of ex-untouchable castes. Paradoxically withering of caste system and eradication of untouchability is accompanied with increased violence against untouchables in rural areas and newer forms of exclusion of untouchables in urban areas. Despite limitations, urban India promises better possibilities of dignity and equality for ex-untouchables.

UNTOUCHABILITY—FROM NORMAL TO CRIMINAL

What is untouchability? In a conversation on priesthood in Hinduism with some non-Dalits, I asked a Maratha youth in Beed district, if a Mang could become a temple priest?

He replied with clarity and confidence, 'that was impossible' (Fieldnotes: 3 December 2009). He meant no offence to the Mang youth accompanying me. He was simply sure of what was 'impossible' in local rural society. Similar were the views of touchable castes about marrying untouchables, sharing water with them, or living with them in same locality—all of this was impossible. I came across exceptional cases of untouchables crossing these lines but there continued to be some normality in understanding the pollution attached to untouchable castes.

Untouchables thus constitute the permanently impure castes located at the lowest rung. In being so they offer clarity to the ideological whole of caste system, as other castes get stacked above them in terms of purity and status. The practice of 'untouchability' involves maintenance of social, physical, and ritual distance from untouchables and untouchables evoke pollution and disgust. Untouchability is considered both natural and normal by caste subjects—sometimes even by the untouchables. Not surprisingly in February 2017, *Times of India* reported electoral campaign of an untouchable candidate, Rajvir Diler who while visiting upper caste localities would sit on the floor and carried his own glass and termed this practice as *paramparagat adat* (traditional habit).

Those emphasizing caste as a form of consensual system suggest therefore that untouchables agree to their location and function in caste system and are largely in consensus with the ideology of purity and pollution that governs caste (Moffatt, 1979). While others like women face temporal impurities (during menstrual cycles), it is the permanent impurity of the untouchables that helps construct the unity of opposites—the pure and impure (Dumont, 1980). Thus separate settlements for untouchables, assigning of untouchable—occupations that are considered impure and lowly and their simultaneous inclusion in rituals (death, marriage, and so on) only point to the central function untouchables played in the sustaining order, peace, and hierarchy of caste system. Untouchability was thus normal and central part of Hindu ethical life, and it faced very little political opposition till colonial advent. Much opposition to untouchability was voiced in spiritual terms before colonial rule. The normality of untouchability, social condition of untouchables and its ethical basis came to be partially challenged during the colonial rule. Such challenges were a product of economic changes, church sympathy, untouchable protest, and limited *savarna* radicalism. The British policy towards caste and untouchability was largely a policy of non-interference (Galanter, 1963).

Untouchability came to be increasingly considered 'abnormal' in urban public life following the mobilization by non-Brahman reformers and untouchable movements. The legal blow to the normality of untouchability was laid in the Constitution of Independent India as Article 17 of the Constitution banned untouchability. In banning untouchability, the untouchables also came to be recognized as 'equal' citizens in public life. Any form of untouchability in public life was considered a punishable offence and it was recognized that only untouchables faced untouchability. What had largely been a normal and popular understanding of untouchables and untouchability in caste society was now rendered criminal.

While Article 17 laid the broader foundations for criminalizing untouchability, the Untouchability (Offences) Act was enacted only in 1955. UoA also required the courts to presume crimes against untouchables as arising out of caste-untouchability—unless proved otherwise. Galanteer (1963) however notes the limitation of this UoA in defining untouchability and its inevitable failure, as neither the society at large nor the judges remained sympathetic to the cause of untouchables. Due to its limitations the UoA was revised, renamed, and re-enacted with changes as Protection of Civil Rights (1955) in 1977. While PCR was an outcome of progressivism of Congress party by late 1980 untouchables were a political force and the incidence of violence against untouchables kept swelling. To overcome the limitation of previous laws, the Prevention of Atrocities (Scheduled Caste and Scheduled Tribes) Act was introduced in 1989. Besides collective and individual violence, this Act listed several normalized practice of untouchability as cases of 'caste atrocity'. In 2015, Dalit activists further mobilized and expanded the purview of this Act to include newer practices of 'untouchability' as atrocity. Besides legal checks on untouchability, caste too has been undergoing rapid changes in postcolonial times rendering the practice of untouchability difficult in rural areas and void in urban spaces.

Withering Caste Withering Untouchability?

Caste and its socio-cultural and economic forms are fast changing in rural and urban India. These changes are not merely limited to prosperous parts of developed states and can be observed in the underdeveloped regions as well. Such changes of varying scales in the role, form, and practice of caste seem to be a pan-India phenomenon. Sociologists have therefore rightly questioned the tenacity of caste and have announced the collapse of the caste system in the village (Srinivas, 2003) and waning of hierarchies (Gupta, 2005). The collapse of caste (Gupta, 2005) or tentatively at least the processes of such collapse bring under strain the normalized ideas of purity-pollution and touchability—untouchability.

Hierarchical values however continue to inform social relations and interactions in rural areas. This is witnessed in the desire of the middle and lower castes in embodying purity and to be part of the pure Hindu universe. This process of embodying purity and aspiring higher status was also termed as *sanskritization* by Srinivas (1956). Srinivas's (1956) focus on acculturation however undermined complexities involved. Gupta (2005) punctured this universality of acculturation through raking up discrete nature of castes and hierarchies. The discrete nature of castes and hierarchies that Gupta (2005) develops help us better gather the commonalities in these discrete units—all aspire to be *pure* in different ways. No caste is suggesting their dis-allegiance to ideology of purity they are rather insisting upon discrete logics that make them part of the higher universe of purity. Sanskritization held limited promise of accommodation for the untouchables and Srinivas indeed pointed out that an Untouchable group may be unable to cross the barrier of untouchability despite sanskritization (Srinivas, 1956).

We also observe rise of new Hindu religious movements like the Swadhyay that attempt to bring together ideas of caste purity and untouchable-accommodation towards forging larger Hindu spiritual solidarity. The aspiration of embodying and performing purity has multiplied with processes of economic mobility amongst the middle castes and classes. Untouchable castes are not necessarily out of these hyper-circulating visceral desires to embody purity—however the newer logic of purity is not free of hierarchy—particularly ideas of pollution; as middle castes embody purity ex-untouchables are inadvertently pushed into polluted bodies and spaces. Purity thus is increasingly de-brahmanized, simplified, and banalized, and it becomes ever more important to demonstrate one's disgust with and distance from untouchables. Caste thus continues to be an adaptive structure (Lynch, 1969) and untouchability is indeed changing its form and content in keeping with changes in policy, culture, and economy.

Economic Dependence to Labour Mobility

Caste-based occupations and labour practices that stigmatized untouchable bodies socially and politically are increasingly waning. These are also termed as 'slavery' (following Ambedkar's maxim—'tell a slave that he is a slave and he will revolt') by activists and Dalits influenced by Ambedkarite movements. Labour practices linked with traditional *jajmani* relations caused social stigmatization of untouchables while sustaining their economic (inter)dependence on non-Dalits. Dalit activists and labourers increasingly emphasize liberation in not being dependent on dominant castes for their livelihood sources in villages.

The changing labour practices, increased monetization of economy, increase in non-farm activities, and migration for livelihood has led to reconfiguring of caste relations in rural areas. For instance in Marathawada, migration as sugarcane-cutting workers to the sugar belts of northern Karnataka and western Maharashtra has facilitated economic mobility and independence amongst several ex-untouchable families. It is not rare to come across Dalit families who had bought land, built houses, or invested in their children's education based on their earnings as sugarcane-cutting workers. Dalits also try to make the most out of other non-farm employment opportunities in neighbouring towns.

One Dalit activist in his early thirties described to me how the practice of traditional exchange constructed, humiliated, and stigmatized the existence of Dalits in public spaces. He used to go door to door through the village in the evening for *bhakri* (a flattened bread made out of jowar, bajra, or maize flour), as part of village tradition till he was fifteen, 'I used to feel that we are supposed to live like this' (Field notes: 7 June 2009). It is increasingly difficult to find families now who strictly survive on traditional occupations and practices. Other caste-based practices are also being challenged or changed. The traditional *halagi*[1] playing, for instance, is now turned into commercial music playing groups called *banjo* parties who perform during marriages. Traditional labour exchange in caste were non-monetary transactions—as labour was mostly being exchanged for grains. Besides denying Dalits a respectable social status, this practice also sustained extreme poverty and indebtedness amongst them. Such economic changes though substantial are largely precarious for rural Dalits across India. There is also no direct relationship between economic mobility of Dalits and their claims to dignity in rural public spaces. As rural economy changes, it alters traditional ideas of hierarchy and untouchability. However, competition between castes turn prejudice and discrimination into a strategy of the dominants to maintain status distinctions. Jodhka observes;

> The old local-level systems of hierarchy have indeed disintegrated but a new hierarchy of networks based on the institutions of caste and kinship appears to be thriving. These hierarchies work through 'monopolies' over social and cultural capital and enable reproduction of caste [....] Prejudice and discrimination become significant and more active when old hierarchies disintegrate and groups begin to compete for scarce resources in domain of economy, politics, and culture/social-status. (Jodhka, 2015, p. 15)

Untouchability could thus be reproduced in newer forms. In an exhaustive study of untouchability covering eleven states, Shah et al. (2006) suggest untouchability as an extreme vicious aspect of caste system has survived. Three important dimensions of untouchability that the authors mention are exclusion, humiliation-subordination, and exploitation (p. 21). This study had listed 64 practices of untouchability to document untouchability in its varied forms. The study captures untouchability and discrimination against Dalits in state services; secular public sphere; religious, cultural, and personal spheres; economic realm and also discrimination in the *market*. Out of the total survey villages it is found that untouchability is practiced in one form or the other in 80 per cent of the villages.

Not all Dalits who experience (partial) economic independence (i.e. those who were not dependent on dominant castes) turn their opposition to hierarchic practices of caste into practice. Dalits, despite being aware of the discrimination they face, may be neither united nor willing to question their exclusion. A Dalit informant from a village in Beed

---

[1] *Halagi* is a type of drum that Mangs (ex-untouchable caste) traditionally played on occasions such as marriages and religious or ritual processions.

Taluka who was a sugarcane migrant worker, discontent with the Marathas' dominance in his village shared;

> Our village is baara bodyacha[2], they do not let us touch their water pots and pour water from above [a distance] for us to drink. They do not even pay our wages properly; they pay it once in fifteen days rather than weekly.

Despite achieving some economic mobility Dalits may continue to face sociopolitical and economic dominance of upper castes. Further assertive and autonomous actions of Dalits that challenge the authority of powerful castes evoke violent reactions making Dalit assertion a risky proposition, particularly for Dalits dependent on dominant castes. Quantitative studies too have reiterated the fact that lessening income gaps between Dalits and non-Dalits could mean increased chances of violence against Dalits (Sharma, 2015). Upper castes may also consider violence against Dalits as altruistic and necessary to impose caste norms and culture (Hoff, Kshetramade, and Fehr, 2011).

John Harriss suggests that, 'the agrarian production relations, when they have involved dominant caste landholders and untouchable labourers, have a significant religious dimension because of the religious services that untouchables have also supplied historically—and still do, to an extent, in the present'. Dalits thus may continue to face caste exclusion in various forms and their status in villages varies according to the struggle they initiate in their local context against such discrimination (limited or prohibited access to natural or common property resources, public spaces, temples, water, schools, transport, restaurants, etc.).

Rural Untouchability—Violence and Subversive Politeness

Changes in economy and rural polity has brought in the possibility of new status roles beyond traditional authority embedded in caste, thus creating opportunity for Dalits to challenge status-authority based in caste. Robert Deliége (2011) suggests that discrimination based on ritual pollution has perhaps not totally vanished, but is clearly on wane however the separation of untouchables for protective measures and increasing 'Dalitism' has widened socio-political gap between touchable and untouchables (Deliége, 2011). Dalits on the other hand point to continued untouchability (Still, 2013; Waghmore, 2015; Gorringe, 2005), while non-Dalits tend to emphasize erasure of caste and withering untouchability. Dalits are also accused of misusing the protective laws

---

[2] A verbal abuse in Marathi, *baara boda* literally translates into twelve vaginas, a slang generally used to comment on a woman's sexual promiscuity or loose character.

not just by non-Dalits even by the courts (Waghmore and Gorringe, 2018). There is a definite disagreement between untouchables and touchable-s over the practice of untouchability and the nature of untouchable accommodation. In consistently pushing the social norms and boundaries of touchability and untouchability and by evoking protective laws, Dalits push rural sociabilities towards new standards of civility.

This has resulted in broadly two newer forms of response towards ex-untouchables—one violent and other subversive politeness, challenging the latter could also result in the former. Subversive politeness demands docility from Dalits in public spaces and also forgiveness in minor cases of humiliation and injustice facing Dalits. Politeness serves as a repertoire that regulates the carnal desires of disgust towards untouchables in modern caste sociality—For Dalit respondents such disgust and hatred seem hidden in the bodies/minds of dominants, if not overtly performed (Still, 2013, Waghmore, 2013).

Mendelsohn and Vicziany (1998) distinguish traditional forms of violence against Dalits in the past (like unreported rapes) from the present forms, which they suggest are also related to modern forms of Dalit resistance. Violence that Dalits face in the villages are also related to their struggles for democratization of public spaces (Waghmore, 2013). These could be linked to dignified access claims to public spaces and offices or Dalit political assertion. Lynch's (1969) termed separate political organization and political participation of ex-untouchables as functional alternative to *sanskritization* (p. 126), which also evokes violent response from dominant castes in rural areas (Waghmore, 2013). In villages where the dominance and traditional authority of landholding castes is overwhelming Dalits tend to be invariably constructed as lower subjects relegated to margins. Dominant castes do coalesce traditional and modern authority thus bringing in values of hierarchy and caste in rural public spaces (Anderson, Francois, and Kotwal, 2011; Jeffrey, 2000). Rural democracy thus perpetuates dominance of land holding castes and the 'neutral' bureaucratic apparatus of state mostly ceases to be caste-neutral while dealing with untouchables and untouchability.

The NCRB for instance lists 704 and 707 murders of Dalits in the year 2014 and 2015 respectively. Rapes against Dalit women were stable at 2233 and 2326 rapes in the year 2014 and 2015 respectively. Such recurring incidence of violence against Dalits reaffirms the tension between constitutional ideals and societal norms. The ideals of equality for all irrespective of social status is still not in sync with the normalized rituals of inequality as a social practice—that insists on permanent impurity of Dalit bodies. Thus, rural democracy affirms economic and political power of dominant castes.

In March 2018, the Supreme Court of India ruled against immediate arrest (non bailable) in cases filed under Scheduled Castes and Scheduled Tribes (Prevention of Atrocities) Act, 2015. This judgment while diluting the stringent act echoed the popular understanding of 'untouchability' long being over and of ex-untouchables misusing protective legislations. What followed was nation-wide protest by Scheduled Castes across India. The SC–ST Act has been a dividing line between the 'touchables' and 'untouchables' since it is used widely by Dalits to challenge routinized forms of humiliation like caste-based abuses or banal nature of violence and caste discrimination. Use of the laws by Dalits have in turn only disguised (does not eliminate) disgust and violence against Dalits. Absence of violence against Dalits does not mean end of untouchability what we see now is a new form of politeness extended towards Dalits that simultaneously demands Dalit docility in rural areas (Waghmore, 2018). Any transgression either for love beyond caste or genuine equality in public spaces mostly results in violence against Dalits.

Urban spaces as compared to rural areas provide anonymity to Dalits and caste restriction on Dalits tend to be much lesser due to the dynamic density of cities. The intimate nature of caste sociality or regulation in rural spaces is difficult to find in urban areas but urban India is not uncongenial to caste, and caste constitutes a linkage between city and country-side. Caste in its plasticity took the form of guilds and trade unions with urbanization and industrialization. Caste in cities thrived under the British as the colonial government maintained their policy of non-interference in indigenous religion. Cities like Bombay saw reorientation of primordial groups (castes and religious sects) as a response to ideological and political changes and a new form of urban leadership that had primordial linkages (Dobbin, 1972).

Caste interaction in city increasingly emphasizes distinction, and separation over hierarchy (Cort, 2004). Emphasis on separation and difference is not void of violence and exclusion against untouchables. In a recent study, Coffey et al. (2018) speak of 'explicit prejudice' and untouchability though low but still present in metros like Delhi and Mumbai. Mumbai has minimal cases of violence and untouchability against Dalits. On the other hand cities like Bengaluru and Hyderabad have incidents of crimes against Dalits that are comparable with Lucknow and Patna (Deshpande, 2017). Despite limitations, urbanism, and rising individualism in cities offers more chances of undoing untouchability and caste prejudices.

Conclusion

Rajvir Diler the untouchable candidate who attracted attention of media for campaigning with his own tea cup also managed to win the reserved assembly seat in the UP assembly elections of 2017. On the other hand Dalit protestors opposing the regressive Supreme Court verdict on SC–ST Act resulted in death of nine Dalits, some were shot down by police and others allegedly by caste Hindus who joined the police. Paradoxically the dynamics of untouchability in India demands docility of Dalits for peace and their assertion invites violence in rural and semi-urban areas.

The making of the democratic state and modern sociality in postcolonial India has not reduced the salience of caste in public life. Despite its dynamic nature, caste continues to construct moral and political impediments to the possibilities of full citizenship for Dalits and other marginal groups. Caste as an adaptive structure continues to govern and discipline rural populations and the popular practice of democracy is not void of quotidian violence against Dalits. Dalit protest in postcolonial times has, however, considerably altered the social meanings of power and hierarchy in popular culture and politics. Dalit assertion has also transformed the regressive nature or rural and urban publics (Waghmore, 2013) and Dalit separatism paradoxically results in greater integration and articulation with the larger society (Lynch, 1969).

Dalits continue to be placed at the periphery or the outer rungs of the growing universe of pure subjects. Subversive politeness includes processes of working out a consensus with respect to Dalits and of securing their consent over the nature of limited Dalit inclusion. This is in keeping with hierarchy as a civilizational principle of caste, one that is based on consent and not violence (Dumont, 1980). Dalit struggles for citizenship and dignity on the other hand stretches the boundaries of popular democracy in postcolonial India, making genuine equality a substantive possibility.

References

Ambedkar, B. R. 1936. *Annihilation of Caste, Social Justice and Political Safeguards for Depressed Classes*. New Delhi: Shree Publishing House.

Anderson, Siwan, Patrick Francois, and Ashok Kotwal. 2011. 'One Kind of Democracy'. Canadian Institute for Advanced Research. Retrieved from http://ciar.ca/one-kind-of-democracy/$file/onekind.pdf.

Coffey, Diane, Payal Hathi, Nidhi Khurana, and Amit Thorat. 2018. 'Explicit Prejudice'. *Economic & Political Weekly*, 53(1): 46–54.

Cort, John. 2004. 'Jains, Caste and Hierarchy in North Gujarat'. In Dipankar Gupta (Ed.), *Caste in Question: Identity or Hierarchy?* (pp. 73–112). New Delhi: SAGE.

Deliége, Robert. 2011. 'Caste, Class and Untouchability'. In Isabele Clark-Decés (Ed.), *A Companion to Anthropology of India* (pp. 45–61). Oxford: Wiley-Blackwell.

Deshpande, Ashwini. 2017, 11 December. 'The Ugly Reality of Caste Violence and Discrimination in Urban India'. *The Wire*.

Dobbin, C. E. 1972. *Urban Leadership in Western India: Politics and Communities in Bombay City, 1840–1885*. Oxford University Press.

Dumont, Louis. 1980. *Homo Hierarchicus*. Chicago: University of Chicago Press.

Galanter, Marc. 1963. 'Law and Caste in Modern India'. *Asian Survey*, 3(11): 544–559.

Gorringe, Hugo. 2005. Untouchable Citizens: Dalit Movements and Democratisation in Tamil Nadu. Untouchable Citizens: Dalit Movements and Democratisation New Delhi: SAGE.

Gupta, Dipankar. 2005. 'Caste and Politics: Identity over System'. *Annual Review of Anthropology*, 34(1): 409–427. DOI: 10.1146/annurev.anthro.34.081804.120649.

Hoff, Karla, Mayuresh Kshetramade, and Ernst Fehr. 2011. 'Caste and Punishment: The Legacy of Caste Culture in Norm Enforcement'. *The Economic Journal*, 121(556): F449–F475.

Jeffrey, Craig. 2000. 'Democratisation without Representation? The Power and the Political Strategies of a Rural Elite in North India'. *Political Geography*, 19(8): 1013–1036.

Jodhka S, 2015. 'Ascriptive Hierarchies: Caste and Its Reproduction in Contemporary India'. *Current Sociology*. 1–16.

Lynch, Owen. 1969. *The Politics of Untouchability*. New York: Columbia University Press.

Mendelsohn, Oliver, and Marika Vicziani. 1998. The Untouchables: Subordination, Poverty and the State in India. In Jan Breman, C. G. P. Hawthorn, Ayesha Jalal, Patricia Jeffrey, Atul Kohli, and Dharma Kumar (Eds.), *Contemporary South Asia*. Cambridge: Cambridge University Press.

Moffatt, Michael. 1979. 'Harijan Religion: Consensus at the Bottom of Caste'. *American Ethnologist*, 6(2): 244–260. DOI: 10.1525/ae.1979.6.2.02a00020.

Shah, Ghanshyam, Harsh Mander, Sukhdeo Thorat, Satish Deshpande, and Amita Baviskar. 2006. *Untouchability in Rural India*. New Delhi: SAGE.

Sharma, Smriti. 2015. 'Caste-Based Crimes and Economic Status: Evidence from India'. 204–226 *Journal of Comparative Economics*, 43(1).

Srinivas, M. N. 1956 'A Note on Sanskritization and Westernization'. *The Far Eastern Quarterly*, 15(4): 481–496.

Srinivas, M. N. 2003. 'An Obituary on Caste as a System'. *Economic and Political Weekly*, 38(5): 455–459. DOI: 10.2307/4413162.

Still, Clarinda. 2013. 'They Have It in Their Stomachs but They Can't Vomit It Up: Dalits, Reservations, and Caste Feeling in Rural Andhra Pradesh'. *Focaal*, 2013(65): 68–79. DOI: 10.3167/fcl.2013.650107.

Waghmore, Suryakant. 2013. *Civility against Caste: Dalit Politics and Citizenship in Western India*. New Delhi: SAGE.

Waghmore, Suryakant. 2015. 'Challenging Normalised Exclusion: Humour and Hopeful Rationality in Dalit Politics'. In Hugo Gorringe, Roger Jeffery, and Suryakant Waghmore (Eds.), *From Margins to Mainstream: Institutionalising Minorities in South Asia* (pp. 169–193). New Delhi: SAGE.

Waghmore, Suryakant. 2018. 'From Hierarchy to Hindu Politeness?' In Surinder Jodhka and James Manor (Eds.), *Waning Hierarchies, Persisting Inequalities: Caste and Power in 21st Century India*. Delhi: Orient Blackswan.

Waghmore, Suryakant, and Hugo Gorringe. 2018, 2 April. 'By Diluting SC/ST Atrocities Act, Supreme Court Undermines Dalit and Adivasi struggles for dignity'. *Scroll*.

CHAPTER 32

DALIT MOVEMENTS IN INDIA

HUGO GORRINGE AND KARTHIKEYAN DAMODARAN

INTRODUCTION

Dalit movements were barely out of the news in 2018 when we started writing this piece. In January, the 200th anniversary celebrations of a battle between British forces including a Mahar regiment and the local Peshwa army witnessed mass mobilization and caste-based violence. Upper-caste groups reportedly co-ordinated the attacks, yet the police targeted Dalits in their arrests (Thakur and Moharana, 2018; India Today, 2018; Roy, 2018). Not long thereafter, a Supreme Court judgement on an individual case sought to amend the provisions of the Scheduled Caste and Scheduled Tribe Prevention of Atrocities Act (George, 2018). Dalit Government Ministers demanded a judicial review of the order (PTI, 2018) and Dalit groups across the country mobilized in protest for a *Bharat Bandh* (India Blockade) that witnessed marches, rallies, road, and rail blockades across much of the country (Lakhani, 2018). Dalit leaders were ubiquitous in the media, Dalit politics gained centre stage and commentators like Ajay Gudavarthy (2018) suggested that opposition to the BJP Government should coalesce around Mayawati—the female Dalit leader of the Bahujan Samaj Party.

Against this backdrop, in September that year, the Ministry of Information and Broadcasting issued an advisory notice to satellite and television channels calling on them to 'avoid the nomenclature "Dalit" for members belonging to the Scheduled Castes' (Yadav, 2018). Earlier, on the 15 March 2018, a similar circular from the Indian Government's Ministry of Social Justice and Empowerment was sent to chief secretaries of state governments and Union Territories. Scheduled Caste is the official denomination for formerly untouchable castes listed as requiring affirmative action measures in the Constitution. To order Government departments to abide by the language of the state, thus, has a certain logic to it. To advise media outlets to do the same, however, suggests that the term is controversial or contentious. What then is the meaning and history of the term and the mobilizations in its name? In this chapter, we offer an overview of why Dalits are called Dalits, and explore the history of anti-caste protest, before considering more contemporary developments and debates.

What Is in a Name?

The term Dalit, literally meaning 'broken' or 'ground down,' most commonly refers to those at the foot of the caste hierarchy; members of castes previously seen as untouchable. Whilst untouchability was rendered a punishable offence by the Constitution of India in 1950, practices of discrimination and exclusion persist (Shah et al., 2006; Jodhka and Manor, 2018). Faced by continued stigmatization, radical groups inspired by the Black Panthers popularized the word in the 1970s. 'The Marathi word Dalit', as Zelliot (1996, p. 267) argues, 'like the word Black, was chosen by the group itself and is used proudly'. It seeks to invert the stigma attached to those who have been systematically excluded, by infusing the name with pride and rebellion. As opposed to the Scheduled Caste label, it incorporates those who have converted to egalitarian religions like Islam or Christianity and yet continue to experience casteism. Various titles have been foisted on the group, but 'Dalit' Charsley notes, originates from 'a political and cultural movement amongst Buddhists and Scheduled Castes in Maharashtra, [and] is the politically correct term used increasingly by the Indian media' (Charsley, 1996, p. 16).[1]

Charsley (1996) documents the many names and tags applied to the group, and notes how the British term 'Untouchable' fostered a pan-Indian category that had not existed before. As this suggests, the small word 'Dalit' encompasses a huge variety of castes across different regions. Not all individuals or all castes accept the label (Ciotti, 2010; Kapadia, 2017), and some contest their classification as Scheduled Castes and lay claim to higher status (Damodaran, 2018). Indeed, the Government intervention into the politics of naming followed a writ-petition by a Scheduled Caste activist claiming that it was derogatory and ran counter to the community's search for dignity (Shantha, 2018). Insofar as 'Dalit' is now a proxy for formerly Untouchable castes, one could argue that it *has* lost some of its radicalism. The Dalit Panthers in the 1970s envisaged it as a catch-all term incorporating the poor and exploited of all castes. As Ambedkar—first law minister of India, Chairman of the committee that drafted the constitution, and pre-eminent leader of India's Dalits—astutely noted, however; 'the Caste System is not merely a division of labour. *It is also a division of labourers*' (1979, p. 47). Efforts by Communist parties and others to unify the oppressed of all castes have foundered on the divisions

---

[1] Simon Charsley sadly passed away in 2017. His work helped to popularize and establish Dalit studies and his articles, co-edited volume *'Challenging Untouchability'*, and edited series on Cultural Subordination and the Dalit Challenge remain touchstones in the field.

created by caste. 'Dalit', as a result, signifies those ground down by caste and fighting for equality. Even though it is contested, as Kancha Illaiah puts it, 'it has brought the community together across the states, irrespective of language, and cultural differences. It has constructed a national identity for the community' (Quoted in Shantha, 2018). Whilst the term 'Dalit' is relatively recent, decisions about what terminology to use when describing this category of people have long been contested and speak to larger questions of how Dalits perceive themselves and are perceived.

CONFORMITY OR CONFLICT: THE CULTURAL CONSENSUS DEBATES

There are debates surrounding whether slavery in India is comparable with servitude elsewhere, and about the applicability of the term 'slavery' to define the condition of the landless serfs in India (Washbrook, 1993). The caste system may have perpetuated the social and economic deprivation of the lowest castes, but it is said to have accorded them certain 'rights' or obligations, such as working on a particular piece of land. The landowner had an obligation to employ serfs born on the land and, in this sense, according to Kumar (1965), the labourers were arguably not 'landless'. British officials conspired with landlords to present an image of slavery in India as relatively benign and sometimes beneficial (Viswanath, 2014, p. 5). Such arguments, however, are pure casuistry. Karashima (1997) notes that land deeds often recorded the number of slaves that were part of the sale, and Viswanath (2014, p. 3) notes that landless labourers were 'described as slaves (Tamil, *atimaiyatkal*) in native discourse'. Most types of servile status were hereditary, and they were confined to members of the lowest castes (Hjele, 1967; Ludden, 1989).

Slavery was deemed to be an inappropriate concept in the caste context for another reason. Critiquing the propensity for scholars to analyse Indian society through an individualistic, Western lens, Dumont (1980) argued that caste should be viewed holistically as a harmonious and interdependent system. The existence of Dalit movements is an anomaly according to such an approach, because oppression in Hinduism is unlike exploitation or racism due to people's belief in *Karma* (the idea that one's actions are responsible for one's fate) and *Dharma* (moral duty). Indeed, as Gupta (2005, p. 411) notes, 'If traditional scholarship on caste were to be accepted, then even those who were considered low or impure in the ritual order would consider their position to be just and befitting their status'. Moffatt's (1979, p. 98) contested ethnographic work in Tamil Nadu offers the most forceful articulation and defence of this view, and argues that the lowest castes demonstrate a 'deep cultural consensus with', and 'replicate', those structures from which they are excluded. Understood in this light, those at the foot of the caste hierarchy accept their fate and buy into the values that afford them so lowly a position. Others reach a similar conclusion without necessarily endorsing the diagnosis of cultural consensus. B. P. Mandal, author of the Second Backward Classes Commission for example, argued that 'The real triumph of the caste system lies not in upholding the supremacy of the Brahmin, but in conditioning the consciousness of the lower castes in accepting their inferior status in the ritual hierarchy as part of the natural order of things' (Mandal, 1980, p. 14).

If untouchables accept their status, whether they believe in the system or not, then the history of Dalit movements is hard to explain. Indeed, a school of thought inspired by Balagangadhara of Ghent University views those who critique the inequities of caste as informed by 'colonial consciousness' or influenced by Christian missionaries (Sutton, 2018; Mosse, 2020). Similarly, Prakash Shah (2016, p. 57) argues that Indian scholars such as Ambedkar suffer from colonial consciousness and understand caste through a colonial lens. Such accounts not only deny agency to anti-caste activists, but obscure a long history of struggle, flight, and critique including by Buddhist, Sikh, and Bhakti practitioners (Zelliot, 1996; Gorringe, 2005). Viswanath (2014) and Irschick (2015) note how untouchable subjects actively engaged with missionaries and colonial powers to alter their status and position. Moreover, as Deliege (1992) and Mosse (1994) argue, analysis of untouchable 'myths of origin' demonstrate that they interpret their lowly standing as the product of past errors, accidents, or tricks by others. Untouchables, Deliege (1992, p. 166) observes from his research in Tamil Nadu, 'view themselves as *taazhttapattor*, "those who are forced to be low", and they do not agree that it is their caste which possesses inherent impurity'.

A number of other scholars similarly reject the suggestion that untouchables are in complete agreement with their subordination. Berreman (1991) and Mencher (1974) observe that the view from the bottom-up is quite different from that described by Dumont, and emphasizes the compulsion to perform menial and degrading tasks. As Mosse (1994) argues, untouchables describe their situation in terms of servitude and poverty rather than ritual impurity. As Karanth (2004, pp. 159–160) observes, dependence is emphasized in such accounts, meaning that 'what may appear to be replication is not indicative of consensus (as Dumont and Moffatt assume)'. On the contrary, replication may be a claim to higher standing or an assertion of equal status; it is, in this sense, an 'attempt to redefine their identities, and to protest against humiliation'. Such perspectives, we contend, better explain the long history of anti-caste protests and do not conflate statements that show *familiarity* with caste rationalizations with adherence to those norms (Deliege, 1992). Take the example of Viramma, the Dalit agricultural labourer whose life-story Viramma, Racine and Racine (1997) vividly recount. In reflecting on her experiences, Racine and Racine (1998, p. 7) echo Moffatt in opining that she 'shares the consensus that places the Dalits at the bottom of the caste hierarchy and accepts the rationale of a system based on "purity"', including the 'concepts of *Karma* and *dharma*'. Their theoretical model of caste, however, blinds them to the agency that Viramma displays in challenging her fate by educating her son, engaging in small acts of resistance, and envisaging a different future.

What Place for Us in Swaraj?

Zelliot's (1996) pioneering work traces the lineage of contemporary movements back to the socially conservative but spiritually radical *Bhakti* (devotional) Hindu saints. She notes how they articulated searching critiques of inequality that still resonate today and find an echo in a common question posed by Dalits experiencing discrimination: 'if we are cut do we not bleed?' Zelliot (1996, p. 34) argues that what differentiates more recent movements against caste is the emergence of a leadership that was released from dependency and service. Whilst movements often emerge from an upwardly mobile middle-class, our focus on them may also reflect the absence of ordinary voices from the historical record. Viswanath's path-breaking study in Tamil Nadu focuses on the actions of officials that are the only traceable indications of 'the many mostly unnamed Dalit men and women who were often willing to risk everything in an ongoing effort to transform the conditions of their existence' (2014, pp. 9–10). Taken together, these works emphasize the undercurrent of resentment and anger without which we cannot comprehend the uprisings against caste oppression and the alternatives to caste-based society that are articulated following the advent of colonial rule (Omvedt, 1994).

To say that colonialism creates the conditions for Dalit political assertion, however, is not to argue that the British supported such action. Indeed, colonial rule if anything tended to reinforce the position of Brahmins and modernize their domination (Omvedt, 1994, p. 90). Whilst deeply critical of the British on this and of the economic devastation occasioned by their policies, Dalits seized on the separation between 'state and societal power' to demand change (Shah, 2001, p. 30). If Dalits sought to escape caste bonds through flight or conversion in the past, the 19th century is when coherent anti-caste sentiments begin to be articulated as part of a wider socio-political project. A number of prominent individuals stand out at this point. One is Jotiba Phule (1826–1890)—not himself a Dalit—who saw caste as a form of slavery based on both violence and the illusions of religion. Phule took on and reformulated British racial theories to present Brahmins as Aryan invaders who subjugated the original inhabitants of the subcontinent (Omvedt, 1995). He joined hands with Pandita Ramabai—founder of the *Arya Mahila Samaj*—to offer a critique of brahminical patriarchy (Chakravarti, 1993). Both sought to establish schools for the lower castes and girls who were denied access to education in textual formulations of caste.

Dalit mobilization at this point, as Jaffrelot (2003) notes, primarily occurred in western and southern areas where the non-Brahmin movements were strongest. In what was then Madras Presidency, the Paraiyar campaigner Iyothee Thass offered a similar analysis of caste and likewise portrayed Dalits as the original inhabitants of India (Geetha and Rajadurai, 2011). Both Phule and Iyothee Thass also sought to undermine the justifications for caste hierarchy through religious change. Iyothee Thass prefigured Ambedkar, in arguing that Dalits were originally Buddhists and converting to Buddhism, whereas Phule attempted to create 'a new theistic and egalitarian religion'

(Omvedt, 1995, p. 19). Phule was little known outside Maharashtra, according to Omvedt (1995, p. 23), both because he wrote in Marathi, but also because 'the lack of a communication network among low castes and the revulsion for his writings felt by most of the brahman elite'. It would be mistaken, however, to see Dalit assertion in the late 19th century as only localized. Research on Iyothee Thass and others points to a thriving network of communicative practices based around the journals such as *Paraiyan* and *Oru Paisa Tamilan* which circulated as far afield as Myanmar and other countries in South-East Asia where migrant Dalits had settled (Ayyathurai, 2011; Balasubramaniam, 2012). This was a time when Dalits in Madras Presidency ran close to forty different magazines, newspapers, and journals that instilled a sense of Dravidian social consciousness and acted as precursors of the Dravidian movement (Balasubramanian, 2017; Gorringe, 2017).

Dalit networks, in other words, preceded the formation of the Indian Nationalist Congress and were pivotal to making the issue of caste inequality central to debates around Independence. It was not, therefore, that the introduction of limited self-determination fostered political awakening, but that engaged and enraged Dalits sought to make the most of institutions of self-rule by demanding representation. M. C. Rajah—a nominated member of the Madras Legislative Council in the 1920s and 1930s—thus, demanded that seats should be set aside for Untouchables in local bodies, schools and colleges (Shah, 2001, p. 31). Such reservation policies continue today and have been key to the emergence of an educated Dalit middle class. This period also saw the emergence of the pre-eminent leader of Dalits and the first to have a pan-Indian following in Dr Ambedkar (1891–1956). Having received degrees from the US and UK, Ambedkar fast became one of the most articulate representatives of the Untouchables. This led him into conflict with nationalist leaders, most notably Gandhi, in ways that continue to shape Dalit politics.

Ambedkar was a vocal critic of the nationalist movement, but he was in no sense a pawn of the British. He offered a clear-eyed condemnation of the ravages wrought by colonial rule, but argued that just as no country should rule over another, equally no class should dominate. Ambedkar was increasingly disillusioned with an upper-caste and class leadership that expressed concern for the Untouchables but failed to support their Gandhian struggles for temple-entry or access to water sources. Matters came to a head at the Round Table Conference where Ambedkar demanded and gained approval for separate electorates for the Dalits. They would vote in general constituencies, but also in a special constituency for a number of reserved seats (Zelliot, 1996). Gandhi, who was in prison at the time, questioned Ambedkar's right to represent Untouchables rather than his own, and claimed that separate electorates would prevent Dalits from being integrated into the nation. He went on a fast unto death demanding that the decision be over-turned. Faced by immense pressure and hostility, Ambedkar was compelled to accede to a compromise—called the Poona Pact—in which there would be no separate electorates but instead a number of reserved constituencies in which only Dalits could contest (Kumar, 1985). As Dalits do not comprise a majority in most constituencies, the upshot is an emasculation of Dalit institutional politics in which non-Dalits decide which Dalit will win (Gorringe, 2005).

Ambedkar's scepticism about the inclusiveness of Congress is captured in his pithy statement: 'under Swaraj of the Congress variety, the Untouchables will have no way of escape from the destiny of degradation which the Hindus and Hinduism have fixed for them' (1991, p. 494). Ambedkar's disillusionment with caste-based society is seen in his shifting politics. He moves from the Independent Labour Party which tried to unite labourers across all castes, to the Scheduled Caste Federation (SCF) before finally converting out of Hinduism as the only means of escaping the stigma of untouchability. Whilst the electoral strategies of Ambedkar and other Dalits may not have borne fruit at this time, they succeeded in placing debates around caste at the centre of the independence struggle and ensuring that reservation was etched into statute. It is for this reason that, despite the poor electoral showing of the SCF, Ambedkar was invited to become the first Law Minister of India and to Chair the committee drafting the Constitution (Jaffrelot, 2005).

Post-Independence Trajectories: Prioritizing the Political?

The post-Independence period in Dalit politics may be characterized as one of growing disillusionment. It did not take long for Ambedkar's fears about caste dominance to be realized. In 1957, for instance, Immanuel Sekaran an anti-caste campaigner and Congress supporter from Tamil Nadu was violently murdered following an altercation with the locally dominant Muthuramalinga Thevar (Damodaran, 2018). Fear of such incidents led Ambedkar to declare that he would be the first to burn the Constitution if it did not safeguard the rights of minorities. Pankaj and Pandey (2019, p. 9) argue that the Dalit movement in India moves through three phases: '(a) reformative, (b) transformative, and (c) confrontational', but we contend that these three *approaches* are discernible in each phase of the movement. Both Phule and Iyothee Thoss lobbied for reforms which often generated confrontations and led to demands for greater change. Both also sought to transform both themselves and their communities by turning to alternate religions.

Likewise, in the post-Independence era, Dalits sought to work with Congress and realize the gains of citizenship on one hand, whilst pressing for deeper changes on the other. If one characteristic differentiates Dalit movements at this point in time it is, perhaps, an emphasis on the cultural aspects of change. Ambedkar, thus, not only converted to Navayana Buddhism, but led 500,000 of his followers out of Hinduism, exhorting them to reject the religion and its discriminatory practices (Jaoul, 2018). Some followers took up Ambedkar's ideas and launched the Republican Party of India, but this had limited success. In the late 1960s and early 1970s, therefore, young educated

Dalits, disaffected by the slow pace of change and inspired by Civil Rights and Black Power activists in the United States, launched the Dalit Panthers (Joshi, 1986). The Dalit Panthers popularized the term 'Dalit', which means broken or ground down, insisting that they would call themselves what they were and fight against the stigma of caste as well as its structural inequalities. Dalit movements at this point tackled forms of untouchability head on by smashing up tea-stalls that served Dalits with separate glasses and walking down high-caste streets. Alongside political protests, though, there was an outpouring of poetry, literature, and theatre seeking to showcase Dalit lives. The reverberations of this cultural movement continue to be felt,[2] though they have faded into the background since this high-point of Dalit cultural activism.

The Dalit Panthers succumbed to factionalism, personality clashes, and the temptations of institutional politics (Waghmore, 2013).[3] They were also critiqued for failing to develop a coherent socio-economic programme (Omvedt, 1994). Against this backdrop, a political entrepreneur called Kanshiram sought to mobilize a Dalit middle class of professionals and government workers to offer support and guidance to the marginalized. He formed the Backward (SC, ST, OBC) and Minority Communities Employees Federation (BAMCEF) in 1973 as the 'think bank' of the masses, but when affiliates started to be harassed and transferred at work he allowed the organization to fade into the background (Jaffrelot, 2003, pp. 388–396). Given the harassment of a purely social network, Kanshiram declared that political power was the 'master key' to social change and the network of financial contributors and activists became a springboard for the formation of the Bahujan Samaj Party (BSP—Majority People's Party) in 1982 (Waghmore, 2013, p. 45). The BSP was not the only Dalit organization to turn to politics. In the 1980s and 1990s, the decline of Congress dominance paved the way for an era of coalition politics in which smaller parties could make demands and gain power (Corbridge and Harriss, 2000).

In 1990, furthermore, the V. P. Singh Government's announcement that it would implement the recommendations of the Mandal—or Backward Classes Commission Report—ushered in an explosion of OBC politics (Jaffrelot, 2000). Fearing that socially weak, but politically dominant Backward Castes would dominate political institutions and on the back of Kanshiram's critique of Dalit politicians in mainstream parties as *chamchas* (stooges), autonomous Dalit movements began to organize and institutionalize (Gorringe, 2005). The Dalit parties demonstrated an abiding faith in democratic institutions and reliance on the state as a provider of welfare and employment, but also a disillusionment with established parties which continued to use Dalit voters and politicians 'like curry leaves to be thrown away after use' as the Tamil Dalit MP, Thirumavalavan put it (Interview by Gorringe, 2012). Autonomous Dalit parties,

---

[2] See the excellent work of the network co-ordinated by Nicole Thiara and Judith Misrahi-Barak here: https://dalitliterature.wordpress.com/

[3] The Panthers established branches in different states including Tamil Nadu, where the Dalit Panthers of India morphed into the *Viduthalai Chiruthaikal Katchi* (Liberation Panther Party).

however, were hamstrung by the fact that Dalits are widely dispersed and had to reach out to non-Dalits in order to win elections.

The BSP's attempt to unite Scheduled Castes, Dalits, and Backward Castes had mixed success given that those just above Dalits in the caste hierarchy are the ones who most bitterly resent their assertion. The BSP, therefore, developed a political strategy that saw them tie up with Brahmins and upper castes and ally with other parties including the BJP in order to secure power (Pai, 2002). These political strategies enabled the BSP to form the state government in Uttar Pradesh twice with outside support before it gained an unprecedented outright majority in 2007. Commentators are divided on the impact of BSP rule, with some arguing that it has made significant social and political alterations in UP, expanded the public sphere, and underscored the ability of Dalits to wield political power (Pai, 2002; Ciotti, 2010), whilst others contend that there is a 'marked disjuncture between formal political change and ground-level political realities' (Jeffrey, Jeffery, and Jeffery, 2008, p. 1392). As Pai (2002, p. 1) puts it, the BSP—like other Dalit parties elsewhere—needs to decide whether it is a movement for social change or political party focused on gaining electoral victories. This dilemma is inescapable and means that, whilst the BSP's political successes engendered numerous attempts to emulate their formula elsewhere, Dalit politics is said to have reached an 'impasse' (Shah, 2004, p. 131).

Key Questions and New Directions

As Jaoul (2007) and Waghmore (2013) argue, talk of an impasse applies only to institutional Dalit politics. Looking beyond formal politics reveals vibrant networks of socio-political engagement, activism, and debate extending across the country. Thus, even when Dalit political parties fail to win seats or stagnate, processes of social change continue. Given the embodied and material nature of caste identities (Gorringe and Rafanell, 2007), Dalit movements must needs operate on multiple scales. Drawing on Foucault, Irschick (2015, p. 137) notes how Dalit politics involve 'technologies of the self' that reject caste stereotypes and construct new and destigmatized subjectivities. This can, however, be a double-edged sword as when attempts to improve social standing for the community result in the adoption of gender norms that are disadvantageous to Dalit women (Still, 2014; Kapadia, 2017). Dalit politics has tended to operate within an identitarian logic that is insufficiently attuned to the intersecting variables of caste, class, and political engagement (Govinda, 2017). Indeed, to speak of Dalit activists, means to focus on assertive members of the community.

Increasingly such activists are tied into networks that extend not only across each state but across India as a whole and increasingly span the globe. From the late 1990s at least, Dalit campaigners have joined hands with activists across the globe to argue that Dalit rights are human rights and that casteism should be recognized as a form of hereditary or racial discrimination (Bob, 2007; Hardtmann, 2009). Dalits in the diaspora have domesticated their struggles and sought to change legislation in the UK and

USA (Waughray, 2009; Mosse, 2020).[4] Links across countries are long-standing, but the density of such networks has increased with the rise of social media. The spread of mobile phones and internet across India has enabled Dalit networks to reach into rural areas and connect those in villages with activists on the other side of the world (Dhillon, 2016). Such links mean that caste abuses can be called out, challenged, and condemned with greater regularity than in the past. Indeed, some groups placed above Dalits in the social hierarchy have complained of processes of 'reverse-casteism', in which Dalits are said to enjoy and abuse their position to victimize members of the higher castes (Gorringe, 2012). This was the argument at the heart of contentious debates over the SC/ST Prevention of Atrocities Act discussed at the head of this chapter.

Claims of Dalit dominance ring hollow in the face of continued caste violence, poverty, and practices of untouchability (Shah et al., 2006). Indeed, even the commonality of the coronavirus lockdown in 2020 failed to curb casteist sentiments and highlighted the structural inequalities of the system (Ganguly, 2020). Accounts of Dalit privilege, instead, should be read as an indication that Dalits are increasingly challenging the taken-for-granted nature of caste. This is seen in refusals to perform degrading work such as manual scavenging and removing carcasses (Gorringe and Waghmore, 2019), in the emergence of strong Dalit characters and themes in mainstream films (Damodaran and Gorringe, 2017; Yengde, 2018), and in the way that all groups and parties now seek to honour and appropriate Ambedkar. It is, however, perhaps best seen in two ways: Firstly in the increased repression of Dalit activists, and second in the increasing attention paid to caste inequalities. Several years on from the events in Bhima-Koregaon, as we edited the chapter, police were still harassing Dalit academics (several of whom remain in prison, including our colleague and contributor to this volume, Anand Teltumbde) and activists in relation to it (Scroll Staff, 2020). That Dalit activists are now seen as a threat speaks to their prominence, even as it emphasizes their weakness in relation to the State. It also highlights that Dalit movements have revealed the privilege that underpins claims to castelessness and begun to challenge the social processes that lock them within caste identities whilst portraying others as free from caste (Mosse, 2018). This was seen most clearly in the protests following the killing of George Floyd in the United States of America, when Dalit activists called out the hypocrisy of their co-nationals who insisted that Black Lives Matter whilst remaining silent on Dalit deaths (Singh, 2020).[5] Not having the luxury of disregarding caste, Dalit movements remain at the forefront of efforts to highlight persistent inequalities, change social norms and discourses, and introduce 'new norms of civility', and ways of being (Waghmore, 2013, p. 207).

---

[4] In August 2020, California brought a test case against the multinational corporation CISCO on grounds of caste discrimination: Opinion | California's lawsuit against Cisco shines a light on caste discrimination in the U.S. and around the world - The Washington Post https://www.washingtonpost.com/opinions/2020/07/13/new-lawsuit-shines-light-caste-discrimination-us-around-world/

[5] For a sharp critique of the tokenistic embrace of Black Lives Matter by the Indian cricket team, see here: https://thewire.in/sport/when-political-yogis-take-the-knee-they-reveal-the-perverse-politics-of-indian-cricket

References

Ambedkar, Bhimrao. 1991. *Dr. Babasaheb Ambedkar: Writings and Speeches Vol. 10*. Compiled by V. Moon. Mumbai: Education Department, Govt. of Maharashtra. Retrieved from https://www.mea.gov.in/Images/attach/amb/Volume_10.pdf.

Ambedkar, Bhimrao. 1979. *Dr. Babasaheb Ambedkar: Writings and Speeches Vol. 1*. Compiled by V. Moon. Mumbai: Education Department, Govt. of Maharashtra. Retrieved from https://www.mea.gov.in/Images/attach/amb/Volume_01.pdf.

Ayyathurai, Gajendran. 2011. *Foundations of Anti-caste Consciousness: Pandit Iyothee Thass, Tamil Buddhism, and the Marginalized in South India*. PhD, Columbia University. Retrieved from http://academiccommons.columbia.edu/item/ac:163650.

Balasubramaniam, J. 2012. *Dalits and Print Media: A Historical Study*. Unpublished PhD Thesis. Chennai: Madras Institute of Development Studies.

Balasubramaniam, J. 2017. *Suryodhayam Mudhal Udhayasooriyan Varai: Dalit Idhazhgal, 1869–1943* (From Suryodhayam till Udhayasooriyan: Dalit Magazines 1869–1943). Nagercoil: Kaalachuvadu Publications.

Berreman, Gerald. 1991. 'The Brahminical View of Caste'. In D. Gupta (Ed.), *Social Stratification* (pp. 84–92). Delhi: Oxford University Press.

Bob, Clifford. 2007. '"Dalit Rights Are Human Rights": Caste Discrimination, International Activism, and the Construction of a New Human Rights Issue'. *Human Rights Quarterly*, 29(1): 167–193.

Chakravarti, Uma. 1993. 'Conceptualising Brahminical Patriarchy in Early India'. *Economic and Political Weekly*, 27(14): 579–585.

Charsley, Simon. 1996. ' "Untouchable". What Is in a Name?' *Journal of the Royal Anthropological Institute*, 2(1): 1–23.

Ciotti, Manuela. 2010. *Retro-Modern India*. London: Routlegde.

Corbridge, Stuart, and John Harriss. 2000. *Reinventing India*. Cambridge: Polity.

Damodaran, Karthikeyan. 2018. *Contentious Spaces: Caste, Commemorations and Production of Political Community in South India*. University of Edinburgh: Unpublished PhD Thesis.

Damodaran, Karthikeyan, and Hugo Gorringe. 2017. 'Madurai Formula Films: Caste Pride and Politics in Tamil Cinema'. *South Asia Multidisciplinary Academic Journal* [Online]: http://samaj.revues.org/4359.

Deliege, Robert. 1992. 'Replication and Consensus: Untouchability, Caste and Ideology in India'. *Man*, 27(1): 155–173.

Dhillon, Amrit. 2016, 25 July. 'How Social Media Is Empowering India's Dalits'. *The Globe and Mail* 2016. https://www.theglobeandmail.com/opinion/how-social-media-is-empowering-indias-dalits/article31091710/, accessed on 30 March 2018.

Dumont, Louis. 1980. *Homo Hierarchicus: The Caste System and Its Implications*. Chicago: University of Chicago Press.

Ganguly, S. 2020. 'India's Coronavirus Pandemic Shines a Light on the Curse of Caste'. *The Conversation*. https://theconversation.com/indias-coronavirus-pandemic-shines-a-light-on-the-curse-of-caste-139550, accessed on 28 August.

Geetha, V., and S. V. Rajadurai. 2011. *Towards a non-Brahmin Millennium*. Kolkatta: Samya.

George, Anisha. 2018, 3 April. 'Caste-Blind Justice'. *The Indian Express*. http://indianexpress.com/article/opinion/columns/supreme-court-sc-st-atrocities-act-dalit-bharat-bandh-caste-blind-justice-5121060/, accessed on 3 April.

Gorringe, Hugo. 2005. *Untouchable Citizens*. New Delhi: SAGE.

Gorringe, H. 2012. 'Caste and Politics in Tamil Nadu'. *Seminar* 633 (May): 38–42. http://www.india-seminar.com/2012/633/633_hugo_gorringe.htm.
Gorringe, Hugo. 2017. *Panthers in Parliament*. New Delhi: Oxford University Press.
Gorringe, Hugo, and Irene Rafanell. 2007. 'The Embodiment of Caste'. *Sociology*, 41(1): 97–114.
Gorringe, Hugo, and Suryakant Waghmore. 2019. 'Go Write on the Walls that You Are the Rulers of This Nation': Dalit Mobilisation and the BJP'. *Indian Politics & Policy* [Online]: http://www.ipsonet.org/publications/open-access/inpp.
Govinda, Radhika. 2017. 'Different Dalit Women Speak Differently'. In K. Kapadia and S. Anandhi (Eds.), *Dalit Women: Vanguard of an Alternative Politics in India* (pp. 218–245). New Delhi: Routledge.
Gudavarthy, Ajay. 2018. *India after Modi: Populism and the Right*. New Delhi: Bloomsbury.
Gupta, Dipankar. 2005. 'Caste and Politics: Identity over System'. *Annual Review of Anthropology*, 34: 409–427.
Hardtmann, Eva-Maria. 2009. *The Dalit Movement in India: Local Practices, Global Connections*. New Delhi: Oxford.
Hjele, B. 1967. 'Slavery and Agricultural Bondage in S.India in the 19th Century'. *Scandinavian Econ History Review*, 15(1–2): 71–126.
India Today. 2018, 14 March. 'Right-Wing Leader Milind Ekbote Accused of Instigating Bhima-Koregaon Violence Arrested'. *IndiaToday.in*. https://www.indiatoday.in/india/story/bhima-koregaon-violence-right-wing-leader-milind-ekbote-arrested-1189366-2018-03-14, accessed 19 December 2018.
Irschick, Eugene. 2015. *A History of the New India*. London: Routledge.
Jaffrelot, Christophe. 2000. 'The Rise of the Other Backward Classes in the Hindi Belt'. *The Journal of Asian Studies*, 59(1): 86–108.
Jaffrelot, Christophe. 2003. *India's Silent Revolution*. London: Hurst.
Jaffrelot, Christophe. 2005. *Dr Ambedkar and the Caste System: Analysing and Fighting Caste*. New Delhi: Orient Blackswan.
Jeffrey, Craig, Patricia Jeffery, and Roger Jeffery. 2008. 'Dalit Revolution? New Politicians in Uttar Pradesh, India'. *Journal of Asian Studies*, 67(4): 1365–1396.
Jodhka, Surinder, and James Manor. 2018. 'Introduction'. In S. Jodhka and J. Manor (Eds.), *Contested Hierarchies, Persisting Influences: Caste and Power in India Today* (pp. 1–36). New Delhi: Orient BlackSwan.
Jaoul, Nicolas. 2007. 'Political and "Non Political" Means in the Dalit Movement'. In S. Pai (Ed.), *Political Process in Uttar Pradesh: Identity, Economic Reform and Governance* (pp. 142–168). New Delhi: Pearsons.
Jaoul, Nicolas. 2018. 'The Politics of Navayana Buddhism'. In S. Yengde and A. Teltumbde (Eds.), *The Radical in Ambedkar: Critical Reflections* (pp. 281–292). Gurgaon: Penguin Random House.
Joshi, Barbara (Ed.). 1986. *Untouchable! Voice of the Dalit Liberation Movement*. London: Zed.
Kapadia, Karin. 2017. 'We Ask You to Rethink: Different Dalit Women and Their Subaltern Politics'. In K. Kapadia and S. Anandhi (Eds.), *Dalit Women: Vanguard of an Alternative Politics in India* (pp. 1–50). New Delhi: Routledge.
Karanth, Gopal. 2004. 'Replication or Dissent? Culture and Institutions among "Untouchable" Scheduled Castes in Karnataka'. *Contributions to Indian Sociology*, 38 (1–2): 137–163.
Karashima, Noboru. 1997. 'The Untouchable in Tamil Inscriptions & Other Historical Sources'. In H. Kotani (Ed.), *Caste System, Untouchability & the Depressed* (pp. 21–30). New Delhi Manohar.

Kumar, D. 1965. *Land and Caste in South India*. Cambridge: Cambridge University Press.
Kumar, Ravinder. 1985. 'Gandhi, Ambedkar and the Poona pact, 1932'. *South Asia*, 8(1–2): 87–101.
Lakhani, S. 2018, 3 April. 'Mocked for Wearing Slippers, Punished for Winning a Game Why Thousands Marched'. *The Indian Express*. Retrieved from http://indianexpress.com/article/delhi/dalit-protests-mocked-for-wearing-slippers-punished-for-winning-a-game-why-thousands-marched-5121186/.
Ludden, David. 1989. *Peasant History in South India*. Delhi: Oxford University Press.
Mandal, B. P. 1980. *Report of the Backward Classes Commission, First Part*. New Delhi: Backward Classes Commission. Retrieved from http://www.ncbc.nic.in/Writereaddata/Mandal%20Commission%20Report%20of%20the%201st%20Part%20English63522871510 5764974.pdf, accessed 28 September 2018.
Mencher, Joan. 1974. 'The Caste System Upside Down, or the Not-So-Mysterious East'. *Current Anthropology*, 15(4): 469–493.
Moffatt, Michael. 1979. *An Untouchable Community in South India*. Princeton: Princeton University Press
Mosse, David. 1994. 'Idioms of Subordination and Styles of Protest among Christian and Hindu Harijan Castes in Tamil Nadu'. *Contributions to Indian Sociology*, 28(1): 67–104.
Mosse, David. 2018, October. 'Caste and Development: Contemporary Perspectives on a Structure of Discrimination and Advantage'. *World Development*, 110: 422–436.
Mosse, David. 2020. 'Outside Caste? The Enclosure of Caste and Claims to Castelessness in India and the United Kingdom'. *Comparative Studies in Society and History*, 62(1): 4–34.
Omvedt, Gail. 1994. *Dalits & the Democratic Revolution*. New Delhi: SAGE.
Omvedt, Gail. 1995. *Dalit Visions*. Delhi: Orient Longman.
Pai, Sudha. 2002. *Dalit Assertion and the Unfinished Democratic Revolution*. New Delhi: SAGE.
Pankaj, Ashok, and Ajit Pandey. 2019. 'Dalits, Subalterns and Social Change in India'. In A. Pankaj and A. Pandey (Eds.), *Dalits, Subalternity and Social Change in India* (pp. 3–26). New Delhi: Routledge.
PTI 2018, 6 September. 'Union Minister to Challenge HC Directive against the Use of Word Dalit in SC'. *The Wire*. https://thewire.in/law/union-minister-to-challenge-hc-directive-against-the-use-of-word-dalit-in-sc, accessed 20 December 2018.
Racine, Jean-Luc, and Josiane Racine. 1998. 'Dalit Identities and the Dialectics of Oppression and Emancipation'. *Comparative Studies of South Asia, Africa and the Middle East*, 18(1): 5–20.
Roy, Debayan. 2018, 29 August. 'Bhima Koregaon: How and Why the January Violence Snowballed into Arrest of Rights Activists'. *News18.com*. https://www.news18.com/news/india/bhima-koregaon-how-and-why-the-january-violence-snowballed-into-arrest-of-rights-activists-1860141.html.
Scroll Staff. 2020, 29 July. 'Bhima Koregaon: Arundhati Roy Criticises Centre for Arresting DUprofessor Hany Babu'. *The Scroll*. https://scroll.in/latest/968919/bhima-koregaon-arundhati-roy-criticises-centre-for-arresting-du-professor-hany-babu.
Shah, Ghanshyam. 2001. 'Introduction: Dalit Politics'. In G. Shah (Ed.), *Dalit Identity and Politics* (pp. 17–43). New Delhi: SAGE.
Shah, Ghanshyam. 2004. *Social Movements in India*. New Delhi: SAGE.
Shah Ghanshyam, Harsh Mander, Sukhadeo Thorat, Satish Deshpande, and Amita Baviskar. 2006. *Untouchability in Rural India*. New Delhi: SAGE.
Shah, Prakash. 2016. 'A Weak Defence of an Indefensible Caste Law: A Reply to DavidKeane'. *International Journal of Discrimination and the Law*, 16(1): 55–58.

Shantha, Sukanya. 2018, 4 September. 'If Community Recognises Itself as "Dalit", How Can Court, Government Dictate Terms?' *The Wire*. https://thewire.in/caste/dalit-media-bombay-high-court, accessed 19 December 2018.

Singh, Surabhi. 2020, 17 June. 'Black Lives Matter Should Be a Wake-Up Call for India'. *The Diplomat*. https://thediplomat.com/2020/06/black-lives-matter-should-be-a-wake-up-call-for-india/, accessed 10 July 2020.

Still, Clarinda. 2014. *Dalit Women: Honour and Patriarchy in South India*. Delhi: SocialScience Press.

Sutton, Deborah. 2018. ' "So-called Caste": S. N. Balagangadhara, the Ghent School and the Politics of Grievance'. *Contemporary South Asia*, 26(3): 336–349.

Thakur, Sai, and Byasa Moharana. 2018. 'Bhima Koregaon and Politics of the Subaltern'. *Economic and Political Weekly*, 53(7): 12–14.

Viramma, Josiane Racine, and Jean-Luc Racine. 1997. *Viramma: Life on an Untouchable* (Trans. W.Hobson). London: Verso:

Viswanath, R. 2014. *The Pariah Problem: Caste, Religion and the Social in Modern India*. New York: Colombia University Press.

Waghmore, Suryakant. 2013. *Civility against Caste*. New Delhi: SAGE.

Waghmore, Suryakant, and Hugo Gorringe. 2018, 2 April. 'By Diluting SC/ST Atrocities Act, Supreme Court Undermines Dalit and Adivasi Struggles for Dignity'. *Scroll.in*. https://scroll.in/article/873678/by-diluting-sc-st-atrocities-act-supreme-court-harms-dalit-and-adivasi-struggles-for-dignity, accessed 02 April 2018.

Washbrook, David. 1993. 'Land and Labour in Late 18th Century South India: The Golden Ageof the Pariah?' In P. Robb (Ed.), *Dalit Movements & The Meanings of Labour* (pp. 68–86). Delhi: Oxford University Press.

Waughray, A. 2009. 'Caste Discrimination: A Twenty-First Century Challenge for UK Discrimination Law?' *The Modern Law Review*, 72(2): 182–219.

Yadav, Yatish. 2018, 4 September. 'Months before I&B Ministry Advisory, Centre Told States to Avoid Word "Dalit" in Official Docs; Seen as Move to 'Suppress' Unrest'. *Firstpost*. https://www.firstpost.com/india/months-before-ib-ministry-advisory-centre-told-states-to-avoid-word-dalit-in-official-docs-seen-as-move-to-suppress-unrest-4417773.html, accessed 19 December 2018.

Yengde, Suraj. 2018. 'Dalit Cinema'. *South Asia*, 41(3): 503–518.

Zelliot, Eleanor. 1996. *From Untouchable to Dalit*. Bombay: Manohar.

CHAPTER 33

THE MAHARS AND DALIT MOVEMENT OF MAHARASHTRA

HARISH WANKHEDE

Introduction

'Dalit' means broken, oppressed, or mutilated, invoked mainly to describe the pitiful location of the Untouchable castes in the Indian society. Even though leaders like Jyotiba Phule and Babasaheb Ambedkar occasionally used this term in lieu of the conventional caste categories, it was not a popular adjective within the anti-caste movements during the 19th century. It was during the 1970s that the Dalit Panthers proudly defined 'Dalit' as a universal revolutionary identity for all the oppressed and marginalized communities and proclaimed that the ex-untouchables must become the vanguards in the battle against oppressive order of caste and Brahmanism (Teltumbde, 2017, p. 2). Over time the term 'Dalit' has come to be recognized as a 'secular' denominator to address the Untouchable castes and their social and political movements. However, such an attempt at the community making has not been equally successful as the Dalits have continued to claim their individual caste identities and have developed diverse groupings that disallow them to function as an effective political category.

With a focus on Mahar Dalits, this chapter attempts to draw a chronological account of three major phases of Dalit Movement in Maharashtra. The first part narrates the social and political background responsible for the emergence of nascent 'Mahar Movement'. The second phase is crucial as it witnessed the entry of Ambedkar as the most powerful leader of the untouchable castes. He offered Dalits a collective social identity and revolutionary political ideology to enable them effectively intervene in modern democracy. Finally, it maps the contemporary Dalit social and political life to showcase the arrival of newer complexities and divisions that could be described as the emerging Dalit conundrum.

In the post-Ambedkar period. the Mahars of Maharashtra have been actively engaged in campaigns against caste atrocities and in asserting their cultural rights through the use of Buddhist symbols. Alongside, new Dalit groups have also mushroomed, donning visible association with the bourgeois right-wing ideological camps. These segments have pluralized the Dalit public sphere and disturbed the ethical principles of Ambedkarite struggles. Especially during the last three decades, we could observe five major trends that demonstrate the shifts in the Dalit movement in Maharashtra. The last section of the chapter would be discussing the new trend.

THE ORIGIN OF DALIT MOVEMENT IN MAHARASHTRA

There are four major Scheduled Castes (SC) communities in Maharashtra: Mahars, Mangs, Chambhars, and Bhangis. The regional Dalit politics of the state has mostly revolved around the Mahars as they are the largest group, followed by the Matangs and Chambhars.[1] In the traditional village society, these three castes had to perform compulsory services, duties, and menial jobs (Watan) under the Balutedari system.[2] In comparison to other Untouchable caste groups, the Mahars were viewed as the better-off as they were relatively flexible in terms of professional choices and social relationships. Mahars have historically nurtured the cultural and intellectual landscape of the Dalits and provided leadership to the anti-caste struggles. Eleanor Zelliot called the early Dalit activism that emerged during the colonial period as 'Mahar Movement' as it was led by the social and economic mobility seeking Mahars. They were the first to migrate to urban centres (Nagpur and Mumbai) and gained access to modern education. They were also able to find employment in colonial institutions before the others. Ambedkar had initiated his social and political activism as leader of the Mahars. It was only in the later phase that he emerged as the national leader of the Depressed Classes (Zelliot, 2012).

The origin and development of the Dalit movement in Maharashtra have been traced in the Bhakti or the Warkari traditions. Popular saints like Tukaram, Namdeo, and Chokhamela preached equality of all before God, rejecting caste hierarchies, and ritual status. Though the Bhakti saints did not directly confront the powerful authority of the priestly Brahmins or the conservative religious values (O'Hanlon, 1985, p. 14), they did

---

[1] According to the Census of India 2001, out of 59 Scheduled Castes, Mahar, Mang, Bhambi/Chambhar, and Bhangi together constitute 92 per cent of the SC population of the state. Mahar are numerically the largest constituting 57.5 per cent followed by Mang (20.3 per cent), Chambhar (12.5 per cent), and Bhangi (1.9 per cent).

[2] Till the mid-19th century, certain professions, assets, and properties in the agrarian economy were distributed by the dominant elites as 'Balute' between 12 major castes. They have the traditional rights to obtain it as 'Watan'.

invent a critical language to interrogate the religious order. In the agonized words of saint Chokhamela, the Dalits for the first time found a space to claim equality, mainly in the spiritual domain, which later become a rallying point for the *Mahars* to demand improvement of their position in society (Zelliot, 1981, p. 141).

Inspired by ethical modern ideas coming from the West, Maharashtra witnessed sporadic rise of social reform movement under the progressive minded social elites in the mid-18th century. Balshastri Gangadhar Jambhekar (1812–1846), Govind Vitthal Mahajan (1815–1900), and Lokhitvadi Gopal Hari Deshmukh (1823–1892) were the first set of reformers who attacked various forms of social prejudices and advocated abandoning of social evils like the caste system. They published newspapers and journals to educate the masses about modern ideas (Naito, 1993, p. 177). However, it was only with the arrival of Jyotiba Phule (1827–1890) that the reform movement took a radical anti-caste non-Brahamin turn and the texture and tone of the social movement witnessed significant shift. He visualized an alliance between *Shudhras* (the Backwards) and *ati-Shudhras* (Untouchables) as equal partners in the battle against Brahmanical hegemony. He emphasized on education for all. In 1849, along with his wife, Savitri Bai, he established the first ever school for Dalit children, which was also open to girls. His *Satyashodhak Samaj* (Society for Searching the Truth) proclaimed the unity of the oppressed communities, challenged the authority of the Brahamins, and aspired to established a new society based on modern values (Bhadru, 2002).

As the British colonial rule expanded in India, the ideas of religious reform, demand for modern education, and concerns for social justice increasingly became part of early nationalist discourse. Phule inspired the future generation of leaders, initiated political reforms, and substantively influenced the budding Mahar movement. During the First World War period, the Mahars also attempted to improve their social position through economic mobility and by accessing modern education and urban professions, including enrollment in the British Army. Leaders like Gopal Baba Walangkar, G. A. Gawai, and Kisan Fago Bansode emerged as the earliest Dalit leaders. They mobilized the community for greater social reforms within the caste system. Walangkar claimed 'Kshatriya' status for the Mahars and started the first journal 'Vital Vidhvansak' (Destroyer of Brahmanical Pollution) to highlight the deprived conditions of the Untouchables (Kadam, 1993, p. 10). Bansode and Gawai established modern caste forums like the Depressed Castes Association in 1915 and organize national conferences like *Akhil Bhartiya Bahishkrit Parishad* in 1920 to claim participation in the newly available modern institutions (Jaffrelot, 2005, p. 44).

Chatrapati Shahu (1874–1922) of the Princely State of Kolhapur was also influenced by Phule and continued his legacy by arguing for vital social and political reforms to improve the conditions of the Dalit-Bahujan masses. During his realm, he rejected the Brahminic authority as the advisors to the court, annulled the need of the Brahmin priest for religious and social rituals, asked for special quota for the Backward Communities in state's jobs, and universalize primary education. These initiatives offered a limited but bold entry of the socially marginalized communities into the political discourse of Maharashtra, making them an integral part of the non-Brahmin social consciousness

(Naito, 1999, p. 170). Importantly, Shahu was instrumental in starting Ambedkar's weekly newspaper 'Mooknayak' in 1920. He presided over the first Depressed Class Conference during the same year where he announced that Ambedkar would be the new national leader of the oppressed communities.

This period established a nascent but impressive politics of recognition and representation and opened-up a new arena of critical engagement against the power and authority of the social elites. The two separate compartments emerged between the non-Brahmin intellectual tradition and conservative upholders of social privileges and domination. It proved to be a defining road—map for Ambedkar's movement and also provided the much needed intellectual and financial resources. Ambedkar's leadership revitalized the Mahar movement with liberal modernist ideas and he was able to build an impressive national movement of the Untouchables in the following years.

Ambedkar, Democracy, and the Dalit Question

B. R. Ambedkar (1891–1956) believed that democracy as a system of governance was not only about procedural electoral norms or about the accountability of the ruling elites but it must also function as a 'good society' based on equality, liberty, and solidarity (Dreze, 2019, p. 171). Social justice and ideas of representation are integral concepts in Ambedkar's thought on democracy. Modern liberal state must take adequate measures for substantive participation of the minorities and the socially marginalized communities in the decision-making processes (Rodrigues, 2017). Ambedkar maintained that the principle aim of any democratic constitution was to dislodge the governing classes from its position of power in favour of the servile classes (Ambedkar, 2002, p. 64).

Ambedkar was hopeful that the newly Independent India would adopt constitutional morality as a virtue and would generate greater public conscience towards its minorities and the downtrodden people. He visualized that the liberal constitution would also help the ex-untouchables to escape the caste prison and allow them to enter democratic polity as right bearing and dignified citizens. He tried to energize the political space by founding a new political party, the Republican Party of India (RPI). He hoped that the RPI would emerge as an effective political opposition to the Congress Party and would help in making the Indian democracy more accountable.

However, Ambedkar's ambitious political project has only been partially successful. Dalit politics has remained largely insignificant in providing leadership to most of the marginalized and oppressed communities. It ended-up being a narrow movement of the Mahar community or the neo-Buddhists of Maharashtra. It failed to amplify the agenda of social justice and in mobilizing diverse section of the working poor and in building an effective opposition against the hegemonic domination of the Congress Party. The post-Ambedkar Dalit politics under RPI has also remained in perpetual crisis due to the rampant factionalism (Mendelsohn, 2000, pp. 212–213). It has mostly been a passive political entity without any audible or impressive voice. In contrast, its social counterpart, the Dalit Civil Society witnessed vibrant visibility in 1970s and 1980s.

The Dalit 'social' has been largely groomed by autonomous modes of mass protest and innovative strategies. Inspired by the Black Panther Party of the United States, some of the young Dalit leaders of Maharashtra like Namdeo Dhasal, Raja Dhale, J. V. Pawar along with some others formed in 1972 the Dalit Panthers in Mumbai. Dhasal insisted that Panthers should avoid the Mahar community-centric Dalit agency and promote a revolutionary class-like politics so that a wider 'collective struggle of the disposed and marginalized' communities could be formed (Rao, 2010, p. 192). It announced the return of Ambedkarite radical heritage and brought the issues of caste atrocities, victimization, and violence of the Dalits to the centre stage. The Panthers' organized militant street struggles against the domination of the Shiv Sena, which had emerged as a masculine right-wing force. The term 'Dalit' rapidly becomes a popular metaphor to describe emerging revolutionary consciousness of the 'oppressed people' and transformed the passive and compromising political language of the RPI-led Dalit politics.

Alongside, Kanshriam and D. K. Khaparde started the All India Backward and Minority Communities Employees Federation (BAMCEF) in 1978 to organize the government employees. Soon after (1979), a socio-religious organization names Trilokya Baudha Mahasangha Sahayak Gana (TBMSG) was established in Pune. All these organizations kept a critical distance from the electoral politics and focused on social engagements with middle-class communitarian concerns. Further, the rise of Marathi Dalit literature movement introduced a new class of public intellectuals, critical writers, and political commentators. Their writings demonstrated the wretched and brutal social conditions, especially of the rural Dalits. These non-political Dalit organizations, were very different from each other and had no centralized coordination, their rise demonstrated through rich democratic aspirations, and ethical courage. Together with the Dalit political parties, including the Bahujan Samaj Party (BSP), they brought about a visible social vibrancy to the Dalit question and pressurized the state to function under the directives of social justice policies.

However, the Dalit movement dwindled during the post-liberalization period as new Dalit actors began to shift towards a pragmatic rationalism, which emerged alongside the flagbearers of Ambedkarite values. It adopted compromising position towards the traditional social elites, flagged aspirations to work with the neo-liberal economic development, and also found ideological comradery with the right-wing political forces.

The Emergent Dalit

Ambedkar had hoped for Dalits to emerge as an enlightened political community through the RPI. The Panthers' revolutionary rhetoric also ended up being moribund and inconsequential. This is evident from the contemporary Dalit social spectrum, which appears to be moving towards a fluid political condition. In absence of a strong political normative, there is no single privileged moral force or actor that can determine the nature of political voice. The social and political actors operate in plural fashion, challenging the authorities from their segmented location.

The following section discusses five major tendencies that dominate Dalit consciousness in Maharashtra today. Though, each segment has its distinct operative field and their differences are well pronounced, however, these are not sectarian or compartmentalized processes. These emerging Dalit actors recognize the degraded social location of their communities and claim to fight caste-based discrimination and atrocities. In intervals they also work with each other on various social programs and often flag their commitment towards an Ambedkarite moral outlook and a sense of social responsibility. However, the arrival of strong right-wing tendencies has disturbed the equivalence that bonded the earlier Dalit fragments together. The new language of Dalits is context based, rational and directed to achieving immediate targets without contemplating much to build a normative political force.

The first of these tendencies is the persistent Dalit Militancy. Dalits continue to experience caste atrocities, social discrimination, and economic exploitation in their everyday life. Despite changes, the Maharashtrian society remains Brahmanical and resists all initiatives that give dignity and fraternity to Dalits with brutal attacks, humiliation, and discrimination. In given situation, Dalits have no choice but to build resistance though community mobilizations. They have over time acquired ability to counter everyday casteist slurs, discrimination in schools and government institutions, harassment, and rape of Dalit women, social boycott by the upper caste elites, non-payment of wages, social prejudices, and exploitative customs, and not allowing the victims of caste atrocities to lodge FIR against the perpetrators of violence. Dalits are engulfed in such social tragedies persistently and only through numerous small, local, and sporadic struggles, such discriminatory social attitudes are being challenged.

On occasions, Dalits have also organized statewide massive protests. In the post-1990 phase, the major Dalit mobilizations with militant spirits have been on three occasions. First was in 1997 when the Dalits took to the streets to protest against the desecration of Dr Ambedkar's statue in Mumbai. It was a massive protest where they encountered police bullets and 10 Dalit youths were killed in police firing. Second, was on 29th of September 2006 when four members of the Bhotmange family belonging to Mahar caste were murdered in a small village called Khairlanji in Bhandara district. The women of the family were paraded naked before being murdered. Almost two months after the incidence, the news began to circulated on electronic media, and Dalits started protesting against the atrocities in all major cities of Maharashtra. The news became global and pressure was built upon the government for speedy action. Third was a case of vibrant and powerful Dalit protests on the streets of Maharashtra when at Bhima Koregaon, near Pune, some lumpen right-wing groups attacked the Dalits who had gathered to commemorate an annual community event of historic significance. The Dalit response was spontaneous, angry, and the protesters brought the normal functioning of the state to halt.

Such sporadic awakening of Dalit masses is the testimony that Dalit movement has retained its radical uncompromising character and retains the capacity to take militant street action against the Brahmanical forces. These civil society struggles are often delinked from its political counterparts as several local Dalit groups protest as flash mobs, often autonomously organized to raise their grievances. In the recent times, Ambedkarite protesters have faced extreme hostility from the state-society combine and are being projected as militant hate-mongers against the Hindus and the Hindutva-led nationalist-state. In the current context, there is an increasing imposition of tags like miscreants, lawbreakers, Naxals, and even anti-national on the protesters. Arrest of Anand Teltumbde, a known Dalit intellectual, on a false premise of sedition and anti-state activities is a visible example of state's anti-Dalit character (Bajoria, 2019). A nationalist collective-Hindu self is being evoked to target the 'separatist' political voices of the Dalits. Thus, the resisting Ambedkarite Dalits are now projected with unlawful and criminal categories. These strategies on the social fronts have cunningly projected the Ambedkarites as an 'other' social minority. From being revolutionary and radical, like the *Dalit Panthers* of 1980s, the vocal and agitating Dalits in the contemporary statist narrative are framed as Maoists, 'urban-naxals', and anti-nationals.

The second emerging tendency is that of caste-community specific assertions. As discussed above, the Ambedkarite movement in Maharashtra is often associated with the assertion of the Mahar community. However, in the post-1980s, the region has witnessed significant mobilizations of non-Mahar Dalit castes as well, especially amongst the Matang and Charmkar castes. They have been highlighting questions of disparity, inequalities, and exclusion within the Dalits. The mobilization of Matangs over the demand of separate sub-quota within the SC reservation is made in order to overcome their relative deprivation (Hiwrale, 2018). They further advanced their demands for appointment of an autonomous state commission to examine the social, economic, and educational backwardness of the non-Mahar Dalit castes and also to establish welfare institutions for the promotion and safeguards of the poorest Dalits. Such demands became the rallying point for other Dalits communities as well and became a move towards democratizing the Dalit sphere in a substantive manner. The awakening of the poorer and more-marginalized Dalit communities demanding access to middle class positions and participation in institutionalized political process is a progressive churning and has the capacity to build greater solidarities for social justice.

Within the conventional Dalit discourse the independent mobilizations of Mang-Matang and Chamakars are judged as a divisive strategy crafted by the political elites to keep the traditional social ruptures intact. Such claims for nominal benefits by evoking immaterial social difference are treated as anti-Ambedkarite in spirit and are presented as attempt to derail the political project of Dalit unity (Gopani, 2019, p. 181). For example, in conventional social discourse the Charmakar caste is identified as superior over Mahars and therefore its distance from the Ambedkarite movement is justified. It pushes the group to become an alibi of right-wing politics. Such social divisions become useful during the local elections to defeat the dominant Mahar/

neo-Buddhist candidates. Increasingly, the Mang-Matang communities provided an independent Ambedkarite leadership and political objectives. Leaders like Anna Bhau Sathe and Lahuji Salve become the new icons of social dignity alongside Babasaheb Ambedkar and Mahatma Phule. Numerous community-based organizations like *Akhil Bhartiya Matang Sangh, Manviya Hakk Abhiyan, Anna Bhau Sathe Foundation* have influenced the community to raise critical issues of representation. These assertions have been critical of the dominant Mahar leadership for appropriating most of the benefits of state policies, however new claims for Dalit solidarity for political action are also evoked.

There are also those who argue for the need of forming broader solidarities across Dalit communities. This has also been visible on ground. Mang-Matang castes have been joining the Ambedkarite social movement. Their organic demands for separate quota and special packages for community welfare are still intact but it hardly creates visible contestations or divisions. Thus there is also a counter-tendency of Dalit caste community coming together and creating new alliances and solidarities, specifically over the issues of caste atrocities and land question.

Third major emerging trend is the growing visibility and active politics of the Dalit Middle class. The emergence of an active Dalit middle class is an important and visible phenomenon. A significant Dalit section has entered the realm of middle-class comfort by gaining higher education, utilizing the facilities of reservation and other welfare measures of the state. This section had been the backbone of Ambedkarite political parties like the RPI till 1970s. They also promoted the BSP when it emerged in the 1980s. However, during the 1990s, the Dalit middle class shifted its priorities and began to engage in civic society activities by establishing NGOs, running faith-based Buddhist organizations, building community centric welfare associations, starting educational institutions, running cultural collectives, and opening associations for economic advancement of their communities and the Dalits at large. More recently, they have shown interest starting independent print and visual media platforms with a focus on the Dalits. As a result, the state of Maharashtra has a dozen daily newspapers, numerous magazines, and periodicals and three 24X7 television channels that mainly focus and deliberate on aspects of Dalit politics and Buddhist faith.

One of the major initiatives that emerged in Maharashtra was the establishment of Dalit Indian Chamber of Commerce and Industry (DICCI), with an objective to foster entrepreneurial attitude within the Dalits. The organization aims to transform Dalits into 'job givers and not job seekers'. It also argues that state policy of affirmative action should be extended to support Dalits businesses to enable them succeed in the realm of market (DICCI, 2019).

Given that the state has backtracked from its welfare agenda, the focus must shift to democratizing the market economy. In the emerging global order, the DICCI looks at the state as a moral partner that would bring new modes of safeguards, protection, and benefits and would initiate policy framework so that the Dalits could be integrated as equal partners in the neoliberal economic development. It demands that a proactive affirmative action by the state and the market leaders would reduce vulnerability of the Dalits and would help benefit from the opportunities being opened by the globalizing economy.

This is a crucial shift in the post economic reform period. The new middle class is not agitating or forcing the state to return to its socialist promises and provide state support for economic empowerment. This eventually can provide some solace to the marginalized groups. However, such initiatives also attract criticism for they completely neglect the large masses of extreme poor, Dalits and Adivasis, and provide legitimacy to the neo-liberal market reforms. The critics argue that at the end, such manifestations of the new Dalit middle class end up becoming 'low intensity spectacle' that is used to justify the hegemony of market over its people (Guru, 2012).

The fourth is the growing visibility of Dalits symbolism in the public spaces. Social symbolism based on public events, memorials, conferences, rallies has emerged as a major feature of the Dalit movement in Maharashtra. The public spaces are increasingly becoming inclusive and democratic because of the active presence of Dalits. Major cities like Mumbai, Pune, Nagpur, and Aurangabad have periodically witnessed the growing presence of Dalit cultural and Buddhist symbols through public ceremonies, memorials, and monuments. These social symbols and public installations have an emotional appeal among the Dalits as the common Dalits look upon these icons with a poised aspiration and as a mark of social empowerment and dignity. In last three decades, Deekshabhumi in Nagpur, Chaityabhumi in Mumbai, and Bhima-Koregaon memorial near Pune have emerged as robust Dalit heritage sites.

Erecting Ambedkar's statue and mobilizing people around it seems to be the focal point for renewed Dalit aspirations towards democracy and equality. Dalit public symbolism has the capacity to dethrone the hegemony of abstract elitist standards of public and national spaces. It democratizes the secular spaces substantively and provides a new meaning to public life (Wankhede, 2010). These symbols have demonstrated that the Dalits are endowed with reflexive agency having capacity to promote themselves as a group of equal beholders of all the public spaces.

The ionization of the Dalit heroes in public is the most assertive gesture of growing democratic consciousness of the socially deprived sections. The cultural and social symbols have amplified significantly in the last few years with massive public assemblies of the Dalits to celebrate and commemorate the anniversaries of the Dalit-Bahujan icons. The critical conjecture is that the continuous appearances of such Dalit public through celebrations and other symbolic gestures can contribute in projecting them as bourgeois culturists, away from the ethical concerns for substantive social emancipation. These annual functions are massive and occupy public spaces without much conflict or antagonisms towards the dominant castes. The new Dalit middle class has converted the annual Dalit gatherings into popular public rituals mainly to showcase the newly acquired self-confidence of the community and its new economic pride. In the recent times, there is also a growing intervention of the state and the Hindutva parties in these events with the clear objective of appropriating these public ceremonies and emerging autonomous Dalit imagination.

Until the 1990s, these were local and sporadic celebrations and the Dalits were largely organized around local *Viharas*, community centres with Ambedkar's statues. However, since the turn of the century there is an increment in political patronage and middle-class engagements into these events. The Hindu right-wing political parties appear to understand these claims better than the Congress Party and they have tend to address the Dalit anxieties better. For example, the BJP actively invokes Ambedkar's name during its elections campaigns, promises not to disturb the reservation policy, and extend affirmative actions for their economic empowerment. Such associational endeavour by the right-wing party to promote Dalit symbols has helped it to attract a sizeable Dalit mass into its fold.

The fifth tendency is an emerging rightward shift among a section of Dalits. Dalit identity in Maharashtra is a powerful political block. Its legacy of struggles for social justice has gained an iconic presence in contemporary democracy. The Ambedkarite Dalits, especially the neo-Buddhists, have resisted the Brahmanical cultural assimilation by asserting their religious and political autonomy. Dalit identity has remained a bête noire to the Hindutva project and in the past, the right wing has avoided an open engagement with the caste question. The Rastriya Swayamsevak Sangh (RSS) understands the dynamic legacy of the Dalit movement in disturbing the Hindutva's ideological agenda. Hence, to neutralize the impact of Dalit assertion on the political and social fronts, the right-wing forces have improvised their tactics (Wankhede, 2020, p. 165).

Since the inception of BJP government in Delhi in 2014, the popular representations of Ambedkar as a Hindu reformist nationalist icon have taken precedence over his radical anti-caste identity. The BJP wishes to showcase that they are equally sensitive to the ideas of Ambedkar and committed to the values of social justice. On 14 April 2017, the Prime Minister Narendra Modi visited Deekshabhumi at Nagpur and made a loud political statement by announcing various welfare measures for the Dalits. Newer monuments, cultural programs, statues, memorials, and other symbolic events are built, or expanded by the BJP to showcase its sincerity towards Ambedkar and his followers. Further, the BJP in Maharashtra has promoted its pro-Dalit image by building a political alliance with Ramdas Athawale led faction of RPI. It has helped the party in expanding its electoral support base in the regions like Mumbai, Nagpur, and Solapur.

Such strategies have surely helped the BJP in changing its conventional anti-Dalit character. The inter-community factionalism within the Dalits helps the BJP mobilize the more-marginalized Dalits into its fold through various socio-cultural initiatives. The BJP appears to be also gaining support amongst the Dalit middle classes and within a section of the neo-Buddhists. The right-wing Hindu party is also cultivating a new Dalit leadership that often speaks the political language of the RSS without being apologetic to its communal character. A small but influential segment of the Dalits in the right-wing politics regard it as a pragmatic and rational option, especially when the other political forces have failed in bringing any substantive material benefits to the community. It is not a substantive turn towards rightwing, as a large section within the Dalits have remained committed voters of the Congress, BSP, or the RPI factions.

Ambedkar, Ambedkarism, and the emergent Dalit Conundrum: 'Without Equality, liberty would produce the supremacy of few over many. Equality without liberty would kill individual initiative. Without fraternity, liberty, and equality could not become a natural course of things' (Ambedkar, 2014, p. 1216). These are among the most quoted words of B. R. Ambedkar from his speech made to the Constituent Assembly on 25 January 1949. Fraternity is idealized as the necessary attribute to reconcile the classical debate between liberty and equality. Democracy offers this promise of linear progress while acknowledging and arranging a sum of many contradictions. Ambedkar's nuanced ideas on annihilation of castes, Buddhism and constitutional democracy envisage a social-democratic sphere that moves towards substantive transformation of social and economic conditions. As a political ideologue he was closest to the tradition of democratic socialism. In this arrangement, he hoped that the Dalit intellectual class and political leadership would play a crucial role in shaping the agenda of democratic polity. He envisaged a reformed social milieu, effective liberal institutions, representative democracy, and an expansion of welfare state. He thus offered multitudes of social and political solutions for the empowerment of the Dalits. Alongside, Ambedkar also envisaged a dynamic political location for the Dalits in the new democracy hoping that his community would emerge as a vanguard revolutionary class. The RPI was formed mainly for this grand purpose.

In Maharashtra this political project appears to have failed as the political hegemony of the social elites remained unchallenged. Further, the current sociological mapping of the Dalit conditions suggests that it has taken a new turn. It utilizes the democratic spaces to raise sectarian concerns and remains distanced from the ground level political processes. The multitudes of social assertions are not utilized to imagine new political roadmap supplementing to Ambedkar's idea of democratic socialism. Instead, the rising multitudes disturb the normative Ambedkarite agenda of crafting a fraternal social life too. Certain social assertions are further distanced from the agenda of social justice, as they often remain exclusively committed to particularistic caste-class interests. It is increasingly visible that the effects of neo-liberal rightwing ideology has also influenced the contemporary Dalit social condition and its political consciousness. The Dalit middle-class tendencies are increasingly tilted towards bourgeois consumer values, cultural festivities, and appear to be finding comfort in ritualistic social practices. Increasingly, it is only in the non-political locations that the Dalit voices have been loud, visible, and active. The plural Dalit subjectivities thus enrich social democracy and sharpen the struggle for recognition and redistribution at varied levels. However, they do not share any serious commitment which would pose a radical challenge to the conventional political authorities.

REFERENCES

Ambedkar, B. R. 2002. 'Democracy'. In Valerian Rodrigues (Ed.), *The Essential Writings of Ambedkar* (pp. 60–64). New Delhi: Oxford University Press.

Ambedkar, B. R. 2014. 'Government of India Act Amendment Bill'. Complied by Vasant Moon, *Dr. Babasaheb Ambedkar Writings and Speeches* (Vol. 13, pp. 1194–1218). New Delhi: Reprinted by Dr. Ambedkar Foundation.

Bajoria, Jayashree. 2019, 14 February. 'There Is No Democracy without Dissent'. *Outlook*. New Delhi.

Bhadru, G. 2002. 'Contribution of Shatyashodhak Samaj to the Low Caste Protest Movement in 19th Century'. *Proceedings of the Indian History Congress*, 63: 845–854.

DIICI. 2019. 'About Us' on DICCI's Official Website, accessed on 12 June 2019, https://www.dicci.org/about.php.

Dreze, Jean. 2019. 'Dr. Ambedkar and the Future of Indian Democracy'. In Suraj Yengde and Anand Teltumbde (Eds.), *The Radical in Ambedkar*. New Delhi: Penguin Press.

Hiwrale, Anup. 2018, April. 'Mangs in Maharashtra: Politics of Mobility and Change'. *Indian Journal of Dalit and Tribal Studies and Action* 3(1&3): 39–52.

Gopani, Chandraiah. 2019, 'New Dalit Movements: An Ambedkarite Perspective' in Suraj Yengde and Anand Teltumbde (Eds) *The Radical in Ambedkar: Critical Reflections*; New Delhi: Penguin Random Books.

Guru, Gopal. 2012, December. 'Rise of the "Dalit Millionaire": A Low Intensity Spectacle'. *Economic and Political Weekly*, 47(05).

Jaffrelot, Christophe. 2005. *Dr Ambedkar and Untouchability: Analysing and Fighting Caste*. New Delhi: Permanent Black.

Kadam, K. N. 1993. *Dr. Babasaheb Ambedkar and the Significance of His Movement*. Bombay: Popular Prakashan.

Mendelsohn, Oliver, and Marika Vicziany. 2000. *The Untouchables: Subordination, Poverty and the State in Modern India*. New Delhi: Cambridge University Press.

Naito, Masao. 1997. 'Anti-Untouchability Ideologies and Movements in Maharashtra from the Late Nineteenth Century to the 1930s'. In H. Kotani (Ed.), *Caste System, Untouchability and the Depressed*. New Delhi: Manohar Publications.

Rao, Anupama. 2010. *The Caste Question: Dalits and the Politics of Modern India*. Berkeley: University of California Press.

Rodrigues, Valerian. 2017, 15 April. 'Ambedkar as a Political Philosopher'. *Economic and Political Weekly*, LIL(15).

Teltumbde, Anand. 2017. *Dalits: Past, Present and Future*. New York: Routledge.

Wankhede, Harish. 2010, 13 March. 'Dalit Symbolism and the Democratisation of Secular Spaces'. *Mainstream*, XLVIII(12).

Wankhede, Harish. 2020. 'Caste, Dalits and BJP's Social Engineering'. In Zaheer Ali (Ed.), *Communities as Vote Bank: Elections in India*. New Delhi: Aakar Books.

Zelliot, Eleanor. 1981. 'Chokhamela and Eknath: Two Bhakti Modes of Legitimacy for Modern Change' In Jayant Lele (Ed.), *Tradition and Modernity in Bhakti Movements*. Leiden: E.J. Brill.

Zelliot, Eleanor. 2012. *Ambedkar's World: The Making of Babasaheb and the Dalit Movement*. New Delhi: Navayana Publications.

CHAPTER 34

DALIT ACTIVISM AND TRANSNATIONAL MOBILIZATION

EVA-MARIA HARDTMANN

Introduction

Today, Dalit is a familiar concept far beyond India, associated with activism, self-respect, and struggle. People outside of India may now have heard about Dalit feminism. Dalit writers and poets have been translated into a number of foreign languages and participated in international literature festivals. We have seen Dalit artists exhibit their paintings abroad and Dalit hip-hop and rap have more recently received recognition outside of the country, particularly among youth.

The situation with Covid-19 has drastically changed the world. People in India and across the world have been affected in different ways. A crisis like the pandemic situation increases inequalities, gives rise to new vulnerabilities, and hits people at the margins even more than others when they lose income, a place to stay, something to eat, and their health.[1] My focus in this chapter is not on activism in the pandemic situation, but I note that the crisis has opened up new possibilities to the activists, as contradictory as this may seem. Activists seem to create and recreate networks and new social media platforms. In the time of quarantines and social distancing many activists, Dalits included, seem, strangely enough, to have multiplied their connections across the world.

In India, as well as abroad, the concept of Dalit was for a long time understood in its literary meaning of downtrodden or broken.[2] A change took place in the 1970s when it was given a new meaning by the Dalit Panthers[3] and in the 1980s and 1990s it was used

---

[1] See for example discussions in *EPW* (2020).
[2] For a detailed discussion about the history of the concept, see for example, Zelliot (1992).
[3] For an overview and the *Dalit Panther* manifest, see for example, Murugkar (1991).

with its new meaning in a more massive way by small Dalit grassroots organizations in villages and cities across India. During these decades political parties such as BSP and RPI also attracted Dalits and gave them influence as a vote bank. In the 1990s and 2000s, Dalits made their voices heard in new ways and collaborated transnationally using the United Nations as a platform. They later joined forces with activists across the world within the Global Justice Movement.

The new millennium has increasingly seen transnational mobilization by Dalit activists. Internet and social media have played important roles for social movement activists more generally, and as Internet cafés have multiplied and cell phones get cheaper, Dalit activists reach out to others to an even larger extent than before.

The mobilization could be dealt with in three categories: Dalit activists in India mobilizing transnationally in relation to (1) Dalit activists in the diaspora; (2) the international context of United Nations, the World Bank, IMF, and WTO; and (3) the Global Justice Movement and the World Social Forums. Furthermore, Dalit women's movements and Dalit feminists relating to feminists globally have the last decades been in the forefront in the movement, not least in relation to the UN and the Global Justice Movement. It is well worth mentioning that scholars have also come across Dalit activists when studying movements from other perspectives, such as writing about the Burakumin in Japan[4] or feminism more generally in the Global Justice Movement or the World Social Forums.[5]

To be sure, the three categories above are analytical constructs and there are of course overlapping and complex entanglements between these categories, with activists and networks belonging in more than one category. There are also frictions between activists in the diverse groupings, as well as individual moral dilemmas for those taking part in diverse networks with sometimes contradictory messages and strategies. We find complex relations between Dalit activists in networks on an international or global scale, in relation to local and regional Dalit activist networks in India.[6]

In this chapter, I will focus on activists self-identifying as Dalits and mobilizing transnationally. The chapter begins with a brief background to recapitulate how regional Adi movements organized across India in the 1920s and 1930s and how Ambedkarites and Ravidasis inspired by Ad Dharm, began to mobilize transnationally in the 1950s and 1960s.[7] I will further examine what shape the Dalit transnational mobilization took after independence. Next, I will discuss the more recent context of neoliberal economic globalization and describe how Dalit activists became involved in international and global contexts. Finally, I will end by reflecting on the local struggles in India in the context of Dalit transnational mobilization.

---

[4] See, for example, Hankins (2014).
[5] See, for example, Eschle and Maiguashca (2010) and Conway (2013).
[6] Furthermore, Dalit activists stand in a complex relation to 'scheduled castes', who are not activists and not active in any Dalit movement networks.
[7] For a detailed overview of Ad Dharm and Adi movements, see, for example, Juergensmeyer (1982) and Omvedt (1994).

Background

The so-called untouchables began to mobilize regionally and nationally in the 19th and beginning of the 20th century.[8] Even though they were inspired by ideas, visions, and strategies outside of India, they were still not organized in a more practical way in terms of transnational networks. Caste associations and caste federations were local and regional, and it was not until the Adi movements in the 1920s that activists came to be related on an All-India level (Omvedt, 1994).

During the 1930s two kinds of struggle crystallized among the so-called untouchables; one strand was Hindu social reformist; and the other strand was more radical in its approach and the activists were autonomous in relation to Hinduism. These strands were represented in different social organizations at the time, which were not all-Indian in themselves, but they were still *linked* to political parties on an all-India level (Omvedt, 1994). The Depressed Classes Federation was Ambedkarite and connected to Ambedkar's Independent Labour Party. The Depressed Classes League (or the Harijan League), on the other hand, was Gandhian and connected with the Congress Party.[9] When we look at them in terms of the two traditions mentioned; The Depressed Classes Federation associated with Ambedkar's Independent Labour Party belonged in the more radical tradition, which was autonomous in relation to Hinduism. The Depressed Classes League (or the Harijan League), on the other hand, belonged within the Hindu social reform tradition.

The Depressed Classes Federation was similar to the earlier Adi movements mentioned, in terms of emphasizing their autonomous identity in relation to the Hindus, but also when it came to organizational form. This means that the Depressed Classes Federation, in the tradition of the Adi Movements, could be regarded as the forerunner to today's transnational Dalit movement, combining cultural, social-political, and economic struggle in an all-India network.[10]

With independence in 1947 and the new constitution in 1950 there were new rights for 'scheduled castes'. However, social practices and economic circumstances did not change on a grassroots level in the villages and cities and discrimination against 'scheduled castes' continued as before. In the decade to come, there was a growing dissatisfaction when the new laws were not implemented and this resulted in protest writings as well as social and political activities. As early as the 1950s we find the protests in Dalit authors' and Dalit poets' literature, but it was not until the end of the 1960s that Dalit Sahitya got the status of a school of literature.

---

[8] This section is to a large part also found in Hardtmann (2009).
[9] There was also 'The Depressed Classes Association', linked to the Hindu fundamentalists in the Hindu Mahasabha (Omvedt, 1994).
[10] For a more detailed description, see for example Omvedt (1994).

In 1972, the Dalit Panthers were founded. They identified in new ways with struggles among economically exploited and discriminated-against people in other parts of the world. Inspired by Ambedkar they combined social work with writing, Marxism with Buddhism, and they criticized the nation-state for not fulfilling the promises in relation to the Dalits and in accordance with the law. The earlier self-accusations and silence was in the 1970s exchanged for outwardly directed accusations in literature, poetry, and politics, against representatives of an oppressive caste system and an unequal economic system. Dalit activists made it clear that they belonged within a broader struggle against discrimination and exploitation in the world.[11]

The historical processes of knowledge production among Dalit activists are of importance for an in-depth understanding of their more recent transnational mobilization and involvements in the struggle against discrimination and global economic neo-liberalization[12] and their roles in this context, which I will come to.

THE DIASPORA: THE EXAMPLE OF AMBEDKARITES IN GREAT BRITAIN AND PUNJAB

The first more systematic efforts to build transnational networks in this context we find among the 'scheduled castes' who immigrated to Great Britain from Punjab in the 1950s and 1960s as a working force, with dreams about a better future (Juergensmeyer, 1982). Many among the 'scheduled castes' who left Punjab often stayed in New Delhi for some years, before leaving for Great Britain, and their new life. Some of them got in touch with Ambedkarites while in New Delhi, while others were drawn into Ambedkarite networks after their arrival to Great Britain. The volume *Ambedkar; Life and Mission*, by Dhananjay Keer, written in 1954, is described by many senior activists in the diaspora to be an eye-opener and the reading of it as an enlightened moment in their lives. They very suddenly understood their own life and the discrimination they had been subjected to in a new light. The book describes in a colourful and emotional way the life of Ambedkar, his hardship and how he was cruelly discriminated against, just because of the community he had happened to be born into, at the very bottom of the caste hierarchy.

In the 1960s a number of Scheduled Castes organizations, Buddhist organizations, and political organizations were founded among the 'scheduled castes' diaspora in Great

---

[11] This has been dealt with in detail by scholars. For an overview of the history of Dalit Panthers in Maharashtra see, for example, Murugkar (1991).

[12] For a definition and an overview of neoliberalization, see for example, Harvey (2010), Peck and Tickell (2002), and Ortner (2011).

Britain, which were transnationally connected to India. Ambedkarite networks were formed from within the Ravidasi community and blended with already fused networks of Ambedkarite Buddhists and political networks. Over a few years in the mid-1960s the small and informal group of Ambedkarite friends had grown to a few hundred activists, with many more supporters starting to organize in a new way (Hardtmann, 2009, p. 166).

Their relations with their families, but also with Ambedkarite organizations and political parties in Punjab were kept up at a distance and new ones were formed in the new country. From being informal networks between friends, coming together in pubs, keeping in touch over phone to help out with practical matters in the new country, the Ambedkarite and also Ravidasi organizations were gradually organized in more formal ways with membership fees and formal meetings, also economically supporting their counterparts in India. New houses were built, such as Buddha viharas, and houses were also rented by the Ambedkarite organizations so they could come together in a more organized manner when the membership grew.

The Ambedkarite and Ravidasi immigrants, in cities such as London, Birmingham, and Wolverhampton, methodically created networks over the years, between Great Britain and their cities and villages of origin in Punjab. Scholars have in detail discussed their common history, but also the more recent religious and political frictions between Ambedkarites and Ravidasis in Great Britain.[13,14]

This is just one example of how the early relations were created and how Ambedkarites mobilized transnationally between India and Great Britain. Ambedkarites also emigrated to the United States and Canada; to other European countries; and to other continents such as Australia, Africa, and South America.

Dalit activists have not only mobilized in terms of keeping up bonds with emigrated scheduled castes in other parts of the world, but increasingly also related to marginalized people from other parts of the world. From the 1980s and 1990s, disappointed Dalit activists were increasingly bypassing the Indian state, similar to what happened at the same time in other parts of the world. We can distinguish between two broad and diverse approaches to reaching out transnationally among Dalit networks. The first approach was to reach out internationally in relation to the intergovernmental United Nations, international NGOs, and a human rights discourse in the 1990s, and the later approach was to reach out in relation to the Global Justice Movement and the WSF.

---

[13] For related discussions, see Dhanda (2009), Jodhka (2015, p. 161), Ram (2004a, 2004b), and Taylor (2014).

[14] On a local level in Punjab, Ad-Dharmi (Ravidasis) was competing with Ambedkar's movement in Punjab, but on a national level Mangoo Ram, the leader of Ad-Dharmi, showed a united front with Ambedkar in 1932. He was similarly as Ambedkar in favour of separate electorates and in strong opposition to M. K. Gandhi, who started a fast to protest against separate electorates (Juergensmeyer, 1982, p. 128).

International and Global Mobilization

International Mobilization

To discuss how Dalit activists have mobilized in international and global contexts, I will take the transnational collaboration between Dalits in South Asia and the Burkaumin in Japan as an example.[15] The Burakumin in Japan have experienced a similar kind of discrimination as the Dalits in India. Scholars have described how, like the Dalits, Burakumin lived outside the main villages and were discriminated against because of their occupations that were often associated with death, such as preparing the dead for burial or tanning hides. They were seen as the ritually most impure, even as non-human. Like Dalits, Burakumin were not allowed into the houses of other people and not allowed into hot springs or into bath houses in Japan (Pharr, 1990, p. 77; Hankins, 2014). Burakumin is not a fixed category that has existed in constant form throughout Japanese history, but according to Amos (2011, p. 22) it rather refers to people who have experienced similar social marginalization.

Interestingly, the Burakumin mobilized early on, and we find social reform movements as well as more radical movements, which could be compared to the social reform movements and the autonomous movements in India, described earlier (for a detailed comparison see Hardtmann 2017: 73–101). The comparison should however not be taken too far, since we talk about activism in different cultural, political, and socio-economic contexts.

In the 1980s and 1990s there was an NGO-boom in India. The (I)NGOs was an organizational form requested by the UN to be accepted as legitimate discussion partners within the UN framework. The discourses on caste discrimination among the Dalit and Burakumin activists were now framed into a discourse on human rights, and caste was translated into the language of discrimination based on 'work and descent', a language adapted by (I)NGOs, which wanted to get access to and operate within a UN framework (cf. discussions by Bob, 2007; Lerche, 2008).

With the UN as a platform, the Dalit women's movement and Dalit feminism became during the 1990s related to women and feminism in other parts of the world. It happened within the UN framework at the same time as when neoliberalism was on the rise. This was also the time when Dalit feminists began to collaborate within South Asia and the contacts with Japan were more formalized in organizational collaborations and (I)NGOs.[16]

---

[15] A similar and more detailed discussion is found in Hardtmann (2017).
[16] National Federation of Dalit Women (NFDW) in India and the Federation of Dalit Organisations (FEDO) in Nepal began, for example, to collaborate. In this context other networks were later included and formalized in the broader The International Movement against all Forms of Discrimination and Racism (IMADR), with consultative status within the UN.

Dalit feminism in this international context was also gradually tied to the human rights discourse as well as a development discourse. This changed discourse within many Dalit (I)NGOs was in line with a general trend among social movements across the world, drawn into a human rights discourse (cf. Mosse, 2011). The change in discourse was accompanied by a change in focus. The earlier socio-cultural, economic, and political claims on the state, by historically radical social movements, were now gradually turned into a discourse in which focus turned to the individual and the moral issues on a personal level between individuals.[17] Human rights in Japan were now talked about in terms of 'human rights mentality' and 'human rights consciousness' (Amos, 2011, p. 177). In South Asia it was a shift, from a focus on structural inequalities and economic and moral claims on the cultural, economic, and socio-political elite, to a focus on the economic, and moral responsibility of poor individuals on a micro-level, who were requested to enter the market as entrepreneurs by the support of micro-loans.[18]

The Global Justice Movement and World Social Forums

At the end of the 1990s and in the 2000s, there was disappointment among activists globally with international institutions such as the United Nations and severe criticism was directed against the so-called UN family,[19] including specialized agencies such as the World Bank, the IMF, and the WTO.[20] It was to a large extent the so-called structural adjustment programs, enforcing states in a neoliberal direction that was criticized for increasing inequalities rather than being a supportive.[21]

There was a growing resistance against economic globalization and neoliberalism among many groups and activist networks. Marginalized people discriminated-against in different parts of the world began to show their discontent in local protests and newly formed social movements. Inspired by the Zapatistas and others they looked for new platforms outside of the UN in their struggle for economic and social justice.[22] United Nations had begun to collaborate closer with the World Bank and IMF and was thus seen as part and parcel of the problem rather than the solution to the problems of discrimination and economic inequalities.

This is the context during the first decade of the 2000s when Dalit activists created contacts with activists across the world—outside of the UN framework, such as the Landless Workers' Movement (MST) in Brazil, No-Vox the urban homeless in France, and others struggling for recognition. World Social Forum is an annual large conference

---

[17] Amos (2011, p. 177), and Hardtmann (2017, p. 94).
[18] Cf. Elyachar (2005) writing about Cairo in Egypt.
[19] http://www.un.org/en/sections/about-un/funds-programmes-specialized-agencies-and-others/.
[20] The United Nations had announced a closer collaboration with the World Bank.
[21] The severely criticized 'Structural adjustment programs', were in 2005 transformed into and replaced by 'Poverty Reduction Strategy Papers' (PRSP), see Anders (2008) for a related and interesting discussion.
[22] For more about the Mexican revolutionary Zapatista movement see, for example, Olesen (2004).

cum festival. It was first held in Brazil in 2001 and was an initiative to bring activists and social movements together from different parts of the world to protest against discrimination and economic inequalities. The World Social Forum came to overlap with movements such as Occupy, The Arab Spring, and others (Juris, 2008). There are a large number of studies of the Global Justice Movement, also called the movement of movements.[23] These studies have to a large extent focused on activists in Europe, the US, and Latin America. The Dalit activists and more specifically Dalit women and Dalit feminists, however, took a lead in the World Social Forums and in Mumbai in 2004 they became recognized by activists and scholars globally.[24]

Dalit activists participated actively in the formation of the Global Justice Movement. They entered transnational activist networks with their unique historical experiences of activist struggle, combining cultural, socio-political, and economic struggle. They were inspired by Ambedkar's writings, more specifically *Buddha and His Dhamma*, in which Ambedkar combined Buddhism with Marxist ideas in a way that was understandable to people without any scholarly knowledge (Ambedkar, 1991 [1957]). The Dalit activists were influenced by Ambedkar's direct actions outside of party politics, but also, by his socialist party politics, in ILP.

Transnational Mobilization and Local Struggles

Much of the Dalit struggles in India take place on a local grassroots level, engaging people in questions related to their mundane and immediate regional surroundings. The everyday struggles against caste discrimination and economic hardship with all its regional diversity have been ethnographically well described by scholars. There are a large number of contemporary local struggles among Dalits and also Adivasis arising across India, as shown by Shah, Lerche et. al (2018, p. 215) and Kunnath (2012), among others. These local struggles sometimes include transnationally engaged Dalit activists and may be linked to social movements in other parts of the world, but sometimes the struggle is exclusively local or regional.

Looking at India there is still a deep-seated social and economic inequality. Scholars have shown how economic inequalities have increased in India due to economic globalization and neoliberalism. This has worsened the situation economically for 'scheduled castes' in India.[25] This is part of a larger global trend and the wealthiest 0.1 per cent of

---

[23] Eschle and Maiguashca (2010), Della Porta (2007), Conway (2013), Routledge, Nativel and Cumbers (2007), Smith, Karides et al. (2008).

[24] In previous writings (Hardtmann, 2017), I have dealt in detail with the South Asian activists and more specifically the Dalit activists in the Global Justice Movement.

[25] See, for example, Randeria (2007), Thorat and Newman (2007), Kannan (2018), and Banerjee and Piketty (2004).

people on the planet now possesses nearly 20 per cent of total global wealth (Piketty, 2014, p. 438). We have come to a point in history when wealth accumulated in the past grows more rapidly than output and wages. In other words, capital reproduces itself faster than output increases (Piketty, 2014, p. 571).

Coming to the end of this chapter, it is time to briefly reflect on the local Dalit struggles in the context of the transnational mobilization. There are many processes at play at the same time. The radical struggle by activists in one locality may look different in another locality. Doing fieldwork, Taylor (2014) found for example how the two Indian protest traditions discussed above are combined locally in Punjab in complex ways.[26] New forms of status symbols have been locally introduced and the caste structure is often reinforced, also by the transnational diaspora, in spite of having radical ideas in opposition to the caste hierarchy.[27] This is not to say that global transnational mobilization by Dalit activists has been without effects when it comes to opposing caste hierarchies on the local level in India, but rather to highlight that there are many processes at play at the same time; at different levels and in diverse localities.

When we look at the Dalit activists, who were engaged in transnational activities within the UN framework, the fact that Dalit activists bypassed the Indian state to lobby within the UN did not have any actual and lasting impact on the Indian government or on the situation on local levels. The 'boomerang effect'[28] did not happen in any real sense. The Indian government found caste-related issues to be a matter, not for the international community or the UN, but to be dealt with internally.[29] The UN, however, served as an important platform for Dalit activist networks to connect with marginalized and socially discriminated-against and economically exploited people in South Asia and other parts of the world. This platform was also the starting point of transnational collaborations between Dalit feminists in India and feminist networks in South Asia and other parts of the world. Furthermore, it gave international media visibility to Dalit activists and their messages about contemporary and local caste discrimination in India.

Concerning the Global Justice Movement, caste discrimination, and economic exploitation were in the global networks translated by Dalit activists into a language that attracted and was understood by others, who similarly combined struggles in the cultural, socio-political, and economic spheres. Already in the 1920s and 1930s, we could find forerunners to the Dalit movements in India, similar to what scholars have referred to as the 'new social movements' in Europe and the US from the end of the 1960s. Dalit activists were thus well equipped to take an active part in the Global Justice Movement (cf. Escobar 1992).

---

[26] To recall these two traditions were the Hindu caste-reform tradition vs. the autonomous anti-caste tradition (cf. Omvedt, 1994; Hardtmann, 2009, pp. 45–86)
[27] Cf. Dhanda (2009) and Ram (2012).
[28] An expression coined by Keck and Sikkink (1998).
[29] See also, for example, Bob (2007) and Lerche (2008).

Coming into this transnational movement Dalit activists already knew from historical experiences, how to contextualize messages, from local to regional to global levels, and also how to interrelate and form a counterpublic over vast geographical areas.[30] With their unique experiences Dalit activists—in transnational collaboration with Burakumin activists from Japan—were in a strong position within the Global Justice Movement to share experiences with activists from Latin America, Africa, Europe, and the US, among others, during the World Social Forums in the 2000s. The combination of socialism, Ambedkarite Buddhism, and feminism were uniquely put forward by Dalit activists in the Global Justice Movement as ways to challenge global neoliberalism, the caste system, and patriarchal structures.[31] Dalit activists and more specifically Dalit feminists took a lead in the World Social Forum in Mumbai in 2004 and thus found a common language and bridges for communication with activists from other parts of the world.

During the last decade South Asia has partly and gradually been marginalized in the Global Justice Movement. The World Social Forums have been held in other parts of the world, making it difficult for Dalits and other South Asian activists to participate. Looking closer at the discourses among participant in the (I)NGOs and within the UN framework, they came as earlier mentioned to be influenced by neoliberalization at the time. When they later participated in the World Social Forums the discourses were partly and gradually entangled in complex ways with more radical discourses within the Global Justice Movement. Similarly the organizational forms of (I)NGOs and social movements have been drawn closer together. At the same time as a professionalization is taking place among employees in Dalit (I)NGOs, there are temporary, project-funded employees, often in precarious situations, moving flexibly between diverse activist, and organizational network.[32]

A younger generation of activists communicates now in new forms and with the help of more direct channels of communication. Dalit musicians, artists, and authors have a better capability to keep in touch with others across the world, but also to reach out more massively to those who were not reached before (cf. Jeffrey and Doron, 2011 and 2013; Thirumal and Tartakov, 2011).

To say that Dalit activists have become known outside of India in roles such as authors, artists, and musicians or have collaborated internationally or with activists globally is not to say that caste discrimination in India has faded away. It is not something of the past, belonging to an already gone era. Caste discrimination is still very much alive and closely related to poor economic circumstances.[33] It has taken new forms, as has been convincingly shown by scholars and also confirmed in this volume. Similarly, struggles are transformed, change and take new local but also transnational forms; activists find new friends, new strategies, and new channels for communication. Let me

---

[30] For a more detailed review, see Hardtmann (2017).
[31] Patriarchy was not dealt with separately, but seen as essential for global capitalism.
[32] For a more detailed discussion, see Hardtmann (2016).
[33] See, for example, Kannan (2018).

finally summarize. The Dalit activists gained media attention in an international context as they adapted to the UN's vocabulary 'work and descent'. Paradoxically, they got a larger activist support in the Global Justice Movement, when they did not primarily adapt, but rather highlighted the uniqueness of the Dalit experiences. They thus became a driving force in the Global Justice Movement through the contribution of the unique combination of socialism, Ambedkar Buddhism and feminism. An additional factor to the Dalit activists' strong position in the broader Global Justice Movement during a period, was also the unique historical experience of having, early on, in the 1920s and 1930s found strategies for combining cultural, socio-political, and economic struggles over a large geographical area.

Allow me to end with a brief reflection. The uncertainties and tragic effects of the pandemic seem, as strange as it may be, to have spurred creative ideas among activists world-wide and the pandemic situation will certainly also transform the transnational mobilization among Dalit activists. We may see even more numerous and additional forms of communication and alliances, new ways of protesting and also new themes and activities. All this may launch a combination of local, regional, and transnational processes which we are still not even able to imagine.

References

Ambedkar, B. R. 1991 [1957]. *Buddha and His Dhamma*. Bombay: Siddhartha Publications.

Amos, Timothy D. 2011. *Embodying Difference—The Making of Burakumin in Modern Japan*. Honolulu: University of Hawai'i Press.

Anders, Gerhard. 2008, November. 'The Normativity of Numbers: World Bank and IMF Conditionality'. *Political and Legal Anthropological Review*, 13(2): 187–202.

Banerjee, Abhijit, and Thomas Piketty. 2004, September. 'Top Indian Incomes 1922–2000'. Discussion Paper No. 4632. London: Centre for Economic Policy Research. Available at piketty.pse.ens.fr/fichiers/public/BanerjeePiketty2005.pdf, accessed 31 March 2019.

Bob, Clifford. 2007. '"Dalit Rights Are Human Rights": Caste Discrimination, International Activism, and the Construction of a New Human Rights Issues'. *Human Rights Quarterly*, 29: 169–193.

Conway, Janet M. 2013. *Edges of Global Justice: The World Social Forum and Its 'Others'*. London and New York: Routledge.

della Porta, Donatella, ed. 2007. *The Global Justice Movement: Cross-National and Transnational Perspectives*. Boulder and London: Paradigm Publisher.

Dhanda, M. 2009. 'Punjabi Dalit Youth: Social Dynamics of Transitions in Identity'. *Contemporary South Asia*, 17(1): 47–64.

Economic and Political Weekly (Mumbai, India). 2020, 25 July. 'Editorials: "Impacts of Covid19 on Labour" and "Locked Out at the Margins"'. 55(30); 7–8.

Elyachar, Julia. 2005. *Markets of Dispossession: NGOs, Economic Development, and the State in Cairo*. Durham and London: Duke University Press.

Eschle, Catherine, and Bice Maiguashca. 2010. *Making Feminist Sense of the Global Justice Movement*. Lanham: Rowman and Littlefield Publishers.

Escobar, Arturo. 1992. 'Culture, Practice and Politics—Anthropology and the Study of Social Movements'. *Critique of Anthropology*, 12(4): 395-432.
Hankins, Joseph D. 2014. *Working Skin: Making Leather, Making a Multicultural Japan*. Oakland, CA: University of California Press.
Hardtmann, Eva-Maria. 2009. *The Dalit Movement in India: Local Practices, Global Connections*. New Delhi: Oxford University Press.
Hardtmann, Eva-Maria. 2016. 'Transnational Dalit Feminists in between the Indian State, the UN and the Global Justice Movement'. In Kenneth Bo Nielsen and Alf Gunvald Nilsen (Eds.), *Social Movements and the State in India: Deepening Democracy?* London: Palgrave Macmillan.
Hardtmann, Eva-Maria. 2017. *South Asian Activists in the Global Justice Movement*. New Delhi: Oxford University Press.
Harvey, David. 2010 [2005]. *A Brief History of Neoliberalism*. Oxford: Oxford University Press.
Jeffrey, R., and A. Doron. 2011. 'Celling India: Exploring a Society's Embrace of the Mobile Phone'. *South Asian History and Culture*, 2(3): 397-416.
Jeffrey, R., and A. Doron. 2013. *The Great Indian Phone Book: How Cheap Mobile Phones Change Business, Politics and Daily Life*. London: Hurst Publisher.
Jodhka, Surinder S. 2015. *Caste in Contemporary India*. New Delhi: Routledge.
Juergensmeyer, Mark. 1982. *Religion as Social Vision: The Movement against Untouchability in the 20th Century Punjab*. Berkeley/Los Angeles/London: University of California Press.
Juris, S. Jeffrey. 2008. *Networking Futures—The Movements against Corporate Globalization*. Durham: Duke University Press.
Kannan, K. P. 2018. 'Macro-Economic Aspects of Inequality and Poverty in India'. In Shah, Lerche et al. (Eds.), *Ground Down by Growth: Tribe, Caste, Class and Inequality in Twenty-First-Century India*. London: Pluto Press.
Keck, Margaret E. and Kathryn Sikkink. 1998. 'Transnational Advocacy Networks in the Movement Society'. In David S. Meyer and Sidney Tarrow (Eds.), The Social Movement Society: Contentious Politics for a New Century. Lanham, MD; Boulder, CO; New York and Oxford: Rowman and Littlefield Publishers.
Keer, Dhananjay. 1990 [1954]. *Dr. Ambedkar, Life and Mission*. Bombay: Popular Prakashan.
Kunnath, George J. 2012. *Rebels from the Mud Houses: Dalits and the Making of the Maoist Revolution in Bihar*. New Delhi: Social Science Press.
Lerche. Jens. 2008. 'Transnational Advocacy Networks and Affirmative Action for Dalits in India'. *Development and Change*, 39(2), 239-261.
Mosse, David (Ed.). 2011. *Adventures in Aidland: The Anthropology of Professionals in International Development*. New York, Oxford: Berghahn Press.
Murugkar, Lata. 1991. *Dalit Panther Movement in Maharashtra*. London: Sangam Books.
Olesen, Thomas. 2004. 'The Transnational Zapatista Solidarity Networks: An Infrastructure Analysis'. *Global Networks*, 4(1): 89-107.
Omvedt. Gail. 1994. *Dalits and the Democratic Revolution—Dr Ambedkar and the Dalit Movement in Colonial India*. New Delhi, Thousand Oaks, and London: SAGE.
Ortner, Sherry. 2011, May. 'On Neoliberalism'. *Anthropology of This Century (AOTC)*. (1). Available at http://aotcpress.com/articles/neoliberalism/, accessed 31 March 2019.
Peck, Jamie, and Adam Tickell. 2002, July. 'Neoliberalizing Space'. *Antipode*, 34(3): 380-404.
Pharr, Susan J. 1990. *Losing Face: Status Politics in Japan*. Berkley, Los Angeles, and Oxford: University of California Press.

Piketty, Thomas. 2014. *Capital in the Twenty-First Century*. Cambridge and London: The Belknap Press of Harvard University Press.
Ram, Ronki. 2004a, September–December. 'Untouchability, Dalit Consciousness, and the Ad Dharm Movement in Punjab'. *Contributions to Indian Sociology*, 38(3): 323–349.
Ram, Ronki. 2004b, November–December. 'Untouchability in India with a Difference: Ad Dharm, Dalit Assertion, and Caste Conflicts in Punjab'. *Asian Survey*, XLIV(6): 895–912.
Randeria, Shalini. 2007. 'The State of Globalization'. *Theory, Culture and Society*, 24(1): 1–33.
Shah, Alpa, Jens Lerche, Richard Axelby, Dalel Benbabaali, Brendan Donegan, Jayaseelan Raj, and Vikramaditya Thakur. 2018. *Ground Down by Growth: Tribe, Caste, Class and Inequality in Twenty-First-Century India*. London: Pluto Press.
Smith, Jackie, Marina Karides, Marc Becker, Dorval Brunell, Christopher Chase-Dunn, Donatella della Porta, Rosalba Icaza Garza, Jeffrey S. Juris, Lorenzo Mosca, Ellen Reese, Peter (Jay) Smith, and Rolando Vasquez, Eds, 2008. *Global Democracy and the World Social Forums*. Boulder and London: Paradigm Publishers.
Taylor, Steve. 2014, May–August. 'Religious Conversion and Dalit Assertion among Punjabi Dalit Diaspora'. *Sociological Bulletin*, 63(2): 224–246.
Thirumal, P., and G. M. Tartakov. 2011. 'India's Dalits Search for a Democratic Opening in the Digital Divide'. In Patricia Randolph Leigh (Ed.), *International Exploration of Technology Equity and the Digital Divide: Critical, Historical and Social Perspectives*. Hershey and New York: Information Science Reference.
Thorat, S., and K. S. Newman. 2007. 'Caste and Economic Discrimination: Causes, Consequences and Remedies'. *Economic and Political Weekly*, 42(41): 4121–4124.
Zelliot, Eleanor. 1992. *From Untouchable to Dalit—Essays on Ambedkar Movement*. New Delhi: Manohar.

CHAPTER 35

CASTE, RACE AND ETHNICITY

DEEPA S. REDDY

From Caste to Race to Ethnicity

In her 2016 Report to the UN Human Rights Council, Special Rapporteur on minority issues Rita Izsák-Ndiaye makes the following two foundational assertions:

1. 'a minority rights approach can provide a valuable platform for the protection of the rights of caste-affected communities and that minority rights standards, including equality, non-discrimination, consultation, participation, and special measures, should be applied to combat discrimination based on caste and analogous systems'; and
2. 'discrimination based on caste and analogous systems exists in many countries,' resulting in 'extreme exclusion and dehumanization' and the restriction or denial of 'most basic civil, political, economic, social, and cultural rights.'[1]

While the first assertion applies a minority rights framework to caste groups such as Indian Dalits who do not constitute an official minority (Waughray, 2010), the second adapts the idea of caste into such form as can then globally mark out areas of 'extreme exclusion and dehumanization'. In both instances, analogies are implied: castes must be likened to minorities, and presumably Indian caste forms the basis for the identification of 'caste-like' groups elsewhere. Thus, caste both retains its recognizable associations with hierarchy, heredity, occupational segregation, purity/pollution, and endogamy—but it also 'broaden[s] in meaning, transcending religious affiliation,' and

---

[1] Report of the Special Rapporteur on minority issues 2016, UN doc. A/HRC/31/56, III-A-21, 22.

comes to represent a new association of 'work and descent'. Geographically, it is both 'primarily South Asian', and not. As such, the Special Rapporteur's position simultaneously tightens and loosens common understandings of caste to meet one core aim: establishing international frameworks to address caste-based discrimination.

What has brought us to this moment of internationalism—and what can we say about the character of caste within it? Curiously marginal to this report is much mention of race, which has historically been so critical to establishing knowledge about India's 'castes and tribes', and making claims about governance and caste reform. Early colonial ethnographers 'looked to avowedly scientific ideas of race for the means to interpret their material' (Bayly, 1995, p. 168); racial typologies and race science informed H. H. Risley's anthropometric research aimed at categorizing and enumerating the castes of India (Bates, 1995, pp. 20–26); Max Müeller's articulation of the Aryan theory of race has had famously wide-ranging impact on modern Dalit and Dravidian politics (Thapar, 1996). If race science came early on from Europe, global analogies followed later from the United States. Late 19th century reformers would marshal the history of race-relations in the United States to variously denounce caste hierarchy (Slate, 2011); a Maharashtrian group calling itself the Dalit Panthers in the 1970s would inflect 'Black Power' to imagine a 'Third Dalit World' which 'question[ed] the integrity of the Third world itself' (Slate, 2012, p. 128); and the Indian government's refusal to include caste on the agenda of the 2001 UN World Conference Against Racism, Racial Discrimination, Xenophobia and Related Intolerance (WCAR) held in Durban spurred a massive Dalit opposition campaign, and several heated debates about the relationship (or lack thereof) of race to caste.

It is this last controversy about race that leads into ironically to the sidelining of race in the 2016 report and the present constitution of caste as a matter of minority rights, as we shall see. At the heart of this unfolding contest is the question of how caste must be framed to invoke legal and other condemnatory mechanisms at a supra-national level—to become 'globally mobile' (Ilaiah, 2001b). Caste has long suffered from particularism, or its association in academic and popular discourses as a phenomenon peculiar to the Indian subcontinent (Visvanathan, 2001, p. 2513). At the same time, a series of mechanisms have allowed caste to be released from its socio-cultural and geographic particularity into international regulatory frameworks, even to become a reference point for other 'analogous systems' of discrimination. What emergent lexicon makes such translations of 'caste' possible—and with what implications?

This chapter examines a present moment of caste internationalism, beginning with the debates over caste inclusion at the 2001 UN World Conference Against Racism (WCAR or 'Durban I'), and coming to the present sidelining of race in what we might call a 'caste school of minority relations': an oblique nod to the 'caste school of race relations' of 1930s US scholarship, which used caste as a framework to make sense of race hierarchies in the American South (Thomas, 2015; Fuller, 2011; Slate 2011). I make three imbricated arguments. First, race is central to the emergent lexicon that allows Dalit groups to search out wider discursive affinities; it is the tool that folds the multiple, diverse, and subjective experiences of slavery, apartheid, and untouchability into the broader framework of human rights. Lifting away from local turfs to seek out global discursive affinities, however, does not do away with the particularism of caste. Rather, it reifies it. My second argument, therefore, is that the quest for universal, non-specific paradigms ironically re-situates caste as a particularly extreme form of oppression whose prime instance and, indeed, benchmark is Indian caste. Caste continues to mark out a territory of essential difference much as it did in colonial ethnography, except now it is Dalits (and Dalit advocates) appropriating ideas about caste and religion that have long been used to mystify the local, precisely to resist the conditions of their oppression.

In these multiple movements is a further irony which leads me to my third argument: although caste continues to be formally defined as a hereditary, endogamous, and doctrinally-based system of determining relative rank, just these classic identifiers no longer express its total reality. For at least as long as caste has been a category of modern governance, it has transformed into a series of 'political faction[s]' in competition with 'other such factions for some common economic or political goal' (Leach, 1960, p. 6). Such divisions may reach back into pre-colonial contestations (O'Hanlon, 2017) but the modern state has nonetheless played no small role in catalyzing new factionalization. Dumont (drawing on Ghurye) described such transformations as the 'substantialization of caste': bringing about the 'transition from a fluid, structural universe in which the emphasis is on interdependence [. . .] to a universe of impenetrable blocks, self-sufficient, essentially identical, and in competition with one-another,' in which 'structure seems to yield to substance, each caste becoming an individual confronting other individuals' (Dumont [1970] 1998, pp. 222, 227). Several theorists have likened these transformations to *ethnicization* (Barnett, 1975, pp. 158–159; Chakrabarty, 2002; Washbrook, 1989, p. 174; Jaffrelot, 2000; see Reddy, 2005). C. J. Fuller observes that the process Weber described, whereby status groups can develop into ethnic and then caste groups 'is now proceeding in reverse in contemporary India': '[c]astes are ... being historically constructed, or perhaps more aptly being "deconstructed," as a vertically integrated hierarchy decays into a horizontally disconnected ethnic array' (1996, pp. 22, 26). Vertical hierarchy and horizontal arrays need not, however, be mutually exclusive: while ethnicization certainly weakens older caste hierarchies, it can simultaneously strengthen the wider social frameworks that sustain caste in contemporary personal and social life (O'Hanlon, 2017; also Jodhka, 2016). Finally, for Susan Bayly, the ethnic character of caste lies in its becoming an 'urgent moral mandate' in Independent India, 'a bond of collective virtues and obligations' which function as a 'call to arms' (1999, p. 307).

Such arguments tend to see ethnicity as a powerful (if somewhat unstable and volatile) re-organizational force, which it no doubt is. Rarely, however, does the available literature incorporate more subjective Dalit readings into an understanding of caste as a specific refraction of ethnicity itself (Comaroff, 1987, p. 311). My working definition of ethnicity is a simple one. On the one hand ethnicity is 'the reach for groundings' within the 'post-modern flux of diversity' (Hall, 1991, pp. 36, 35); on the other it defines 'distinctive groups ... of solidarity', or strategic alliances demanding recognition, conceptual, and material (Parsons, 1975, p. 53). This essay focuses on the cultural ideologies contained within the ethnic boundary and the impact of these on the changing shape of the boundaries themselves, on tracking how affinities are alternately established, and then undone (cf. Barth, 1969, p. 15). 'Ethnicity' in this context simply highlights two important and intimately related features of caste in contemporary India: its fluidity, in contrast to its presumed doctrinally-given rigidity, and therefore its capacity to strategically deploy established, essentialized notions of itself in a movement that seeks less to undermine caste than to restore dignity to re-claimed caste identities.

CASTE AT DURBAN I

Caste arrives at Durban I as a result of concerted transnational lobbying by Dalit organizations to claim Dalit rights as human rights, via a likening of caste to race (Bob, 2009; Lennox, 2015; Waughray and Keane, 2017). This strategy met with outright opposition from the Government of India. At the Regional Preparatory Meeting held in Tehran earlier in 2001, Attorney General Soli Sorabjee called it 'misconceived' (2001): Dalit issues were best left out of inter-governmental forums since both State and Central governments had taken steps towards the elimination of untouchability and other caste inequities. The Government had an ally in veteran social anthropologist Andre Béteille, who called the race-caste analogy both 'scientifically nonsensical' and 'politically mischievous' (2001). 'Old and discredited idea[s] of race' would get a 'new lease on life,' he argued; '[e]very social group cannot be regarded as a race simply because we want to protect it from discrimination'.

Béteille's article was met with a range of responses, some calling his social scientific approach pedantic, bordering on the offensive, but most clarifying that indeed, castes are not races (biologically defined), but that, as Berreman once said, 'racism and casteism are indistinguishable in the annals of man's inhumanity to man' (1972, p. 410). In other words, the *experiences* associated with race are virtually indistinguishable from those produced by caste, and both constructs are 'work and descent' forms as named by instruments like the Convention on the Elimination of All Forms of Racial Discrimination (ICERD, 1965). The issue, for Dalit activists, was simply one of prejudice: caste discrimination is inherently systemic and institutionalized, comes attached to notions of purity and pollution, results in social segregation, causes violence and untold forms of social suffering, has specific material consequence—and so for all these reasons, is not only comparable but in fact tantamount to racial discrimination.

That Dalit activism should coalesce in this fashion around the WCAR was not a coincidence. By the time of the Conference, the Dalit movement was just over a decade old, but the limitations of articulating Dalit concerns through the established agendas of women's rights and development have spurred Dalit intellectuals to search out independent modes of articulation. Affirmative action or 'reservations' frameworks were in place but had limitations. A UN Working Paper on work and descent-based discrimination prepared at the time noted 'that improvements have taken place cannot be doubted' and the list of actions taken by the Government of India to address caste-based discrimination is long and 'impressive'.[2] Acknowledging these measures, but also recognizing the significant lag in attitudinal change and the attendant problems with law enforcement, the focus of the paper and also of Dalit discourse in the lead-up to Durban I shifted to the 'hidden or invisible discrimination that a Dalit would encounter'.[3]

At this juncture, two key concepts laid ground for the linking of caste to race: human rights and apartheid. The National Campaign on Dalit Human Rights (NCDHR) was established on 10 December 1998 (World Human Rights Day) with support from the Ford Foundation and Human Rights Watch (Bob, 2009, p. 39). Focused on ensuring that 'India and the International Community recognize and uphold that Dalit rights are human rights', the organization sought to lobby the Government of India and 'statutory bodies of the UN and other international organizations to give top priority to Dalit issues'.[4] This human rights emphasis then facilitated the convergence of a range of international 'organizations, institutions and individuals' working on caste discrimination in isolated fashion, so that the International Dalit Solidarity Network (IDSN) was established in 2000 to help expand NCDHR work into more global contexts. By this time, too, the focus of Dalit activism both nationally and internationally was preparation for the WCAR: while Phase I of the NCDHR was to focus on raising awareness and documenting atrocities against Dalits, one of the primary outcomes of Phase II of the Campaign was meant to be strong representation of Dalit issues at the WCAR. Of prime importance was the goal of creating a set of obligations that would be legally binding on the Government of India to ensure Dalit human rights. The Government of India's insistence that it had already taken numerous steps towards this goal needed to be set against the Mandal furor, which Dalit writers and advocates read as a national betrayal (Ilaiah, 1996a, 1998; Tharu and Niranjana, 1996). The only recourse was to obtain and solidify the disapproval and sanction of the International community. For Dalit activists, then, the internationalization of caste was the means of emphasizing the need for accountability, and the WCAR was a key opportunity to create policy ensuring it. Humanitarianism expressed as 'human rights', or human rights as principled stratagem as it were, appeared the fastest, most effective vehicle to move towards that goal.

The WCAR took its focus on human rights from the ICERD's definition of 'racial discrimination' as essentially antithetical to the enjoyment of human rights and fundamental freedoms (Article 1). Both the Programme of Action for the Third Decade to Combat Racism and Racial Discrimination (towards the end of which the WCAR was scheduled), and the WCAR's own final declaration held racism and racial discrimination as 'among the most serious violations of human rights in the contemporary world', which 'deny the self-evident truth that all human beings are born free and equal in dignity and

---

[2] Working paper by Rajendra Kalidas Wimala Goonesekere on Discrimination Based on Work and Descent 2001, UN Doc.E/CN.4/Sub.2/2001/16, p. 8.
[3] Ibid., p. 9.
[4] http://www.dalits.org/, 3 December 2004.

rights'.[5] The WCAR further found, in the 'faithful implementation of all international human rights norms and obligations, including enactment of laws and political, social and economic policies', crucial methods to 'combat racism, racial discrimination, xenophobia and related intolerance'.[6] In other words, not only was racism an explicitly acknowledged human rights concern, but adherence to human rights norms and obligations was proclaimed its most effective antidote. The link to caste came first via the 1996 ICERD clarification 'that the term "descent" mentioned in Article 1 of the Convention does not solely refer to race [. . . and] that the situation of the scheduled castes and scheduled tribes falls within the scope of the Convention'.[7] A 2000 resolution declaring discrimination based on 'work and descent a violation of human rights law' then drove home the claim for caste discrimination as human rights violation.[8] By these connections, both overt and 'hidden or invisible discrimination that a Dalit would encounter'[9] are labeled and given form, the latter especially ironically rendered internationally visible by its transformation into what an IDSN statement to the WCAR Preparatory committee would call a 'hidden apartheid' (2000).

The analogy was a pointed one, for 'apartheid' was by then an incontrovertible signifier of extreme oppression. The ICERD, which became the 'model for devising in 1966 the implementation machinery for the International Covenants on Human Rights',[10] was drafted at a time when colonialism and, even more, apartheid were signifiers of extreme injustice. ICERD broke down the dimensions of race only into 'segregation and apartheid'. The two prior World Conferences to Combat Racism and Racial Discrimination (1978 and 1983, both held in Geneva) and, indeed, the UN's first two decades to combat racism, had been preoccupied with the regime of apartheid in South Africa. As a result, 'apartheid' already provoked 'general condemnation' as a 'criminal policy and practice and as a crime against humanity'[11]; it was poised to define a 'common platform of struggle' against racism and racial discrimination worldwide.[12] The link to caste was then just another analogy away: V. T. Rajshekhar's well-known booklet *Apartheid in India*, written in the wake of India's participation in the International Anti-Apartheid year (1978), had insisted that 'the prejudices in this country *are as terrible*' (emphasis added). Even the Indian journal *Seminar* titled its issue on the WCAR debates 'Exclusion', with the 'X' dramatically enlarged on the cover: a wry comment on

---

[5] Implementation of the Programme of Action for the Third Decade to Combat Racism and Racial Discrimination 1995, UN Doc E/RES/1995/59: bullet 1; Report of the WCAR 2001, UN Doc A/CONF.189/12, p. 7.

[6] Ibid., p. 19.

[7]

[8] Discrimination Based on Work and Descent 2000, UN Doc. E/CN.4/SUB.2/RES/2000/4

[9] UN Doc. E/CN.4/Sub.2/2001/16, p. 9. Working paper by Rajendra Kalidas Wimala Goonesekere on Discrimination Based on Work and Descent 2001, UN Doc.E/CN.4/Sub.2/2001/16: 9, available online https://documents-dds-ny.un.org/doc/UNDOC/GEN/G01/142/20/PDF/G0114220.pdf?OpenElement

[10] Background paper prepared by Theodor van Boven on United Nations strategies to combat racism and racial discrimination 1999, UN Doc. E/CN.4/1999/WG.1/BP.7: 4–d.

[11] Ibid.

[12] Ibid.

the barring of Dalits from a conference that, in effect, celebrated South African victory against apartheid. If 'exclusion' unified all of South Asian lower caste experiences, as Guru (2003) has suggested, then exclusion was also the link that likened caste discrimination to apartheid, and caste to race.

THE ETHNICITY OF CASTE

'The goal is not identity but affinity', writes Visvanathan.

> Race was the most universal language of condemnation. Race moved mountains like the UN, the foundations and the corporations. If caste were defined as 'race in India,' one retained local turfs but could use international forums to embarrass the official Indian image. A moralistic, moralizing state could be caught flatfooted in international forums. (2001, p. 2513)

Visvanathan writes of the politics of international shaming, but more needs to be said about the retention of "local turfs" precisely to acquire global mobility. Two underlying narratives about caste that emerge around the WCAR speak to the simultaneity of its expansion and contraction, the reaching outwards in the search for discursive affinity as well as the retention of 'local turfs'. On the one hand, a UN working paper on work-and-descent-based discrimination[13] and a Human Rights Watch report prepared specifically for the WCAR list affected communities worldwide. Together, these establish 'the prevalence and global dimensions' of '[d]iscriminatory, cruel, inhuman and degrading' practices that are each 'justified on the basis of caste' (HRW, 2001, p. 2). The HRW report notably emphasizes birth over faith, characterizing caste as a fundamentally social institution with necessary no basis in Hinduism. This disassociation of caste from religion allows HRW to then establish its global generalizability under the 'work and descent' rubric.

On the other hand, ideas of caste as rooted in India and Hindu practice remain oddly tenacious. The HRW report de-emphasizes religion, but still introduces Indian caste as 'the world's longest surviving social hierarchy' a rigid, inescapable, hereditary, and doctrinally sanctioned system 'more than 2000-year[s]-old' (2001, p. 2). As such, it is both starting point and benchmark for any conversation on caste. Both HRW's WCAR report and a prior (1999) report on violence against 'India's "untouchables"' identify caste as the 'defining feature of Hinduism'—and 'untouchability' as the essence of caste, tellingly associated only with South Asian communities. That 'untouchability' in India has historically named a set of issues faced by more than one caste group, complicating state

---

[13] UN doc E/CN.4/Sub.2/2001/16. Working paper by Rajendra Kalidas Wimala Goonesekere on Discrimination Based on Work and Descent 2001, UN Doc.E/CN.4/Sub.2/2001/16: 9, available online https://documents-dds-ny.un.org/doc/UNDOC/GEN/G01/142/20/PDF/G0114220.pdf?OpenElement

efforts at formal categorization, is a background either ignored or forgotten. Both literally and symbolically, 'untouchability' now stands proxy for Dalit experience. At the same time, however, ideas of purity/pollution and filth/cleanliness are globally prevalent, so untouchability as a practice must be qualified locally, but also can be generally understood as the 'imposition of *social disabilities* on persons by reason of birth into a particular caste' (emphasis added). In this, the concept also recalls earlier analogies with pre-civil rights black experience on one side of the color line[14]; it thus finds affinity with race expressed as racism by evoking comparable ethical and moral outrage. And as once with South African apartheid, so also now does untouchability signify new extremes: Dalit writers are quick to insist that Indian atrocities 'more horrendous' than any other (Louis, 2001; Ilaiah, 2001a; Rashidi quoted in Slate, 2012, p. 138) and *therefore* 'crime[s] against humanity' (HRW, 2001). Indian caste is the ultimate extreme; other instances are 'analogous'.[15]

'Untouchability' thus tethers caste to its place of origin, while enabling its participation in a global economy of ideas and emotions; indeed, transforming its very specificity into its most fluid global currency. Paradoxically, conceiving of caste (and Hinduism) in India as timeless, unchanging, oppressive, and rigid via tropes like 'untouchability' enables the transformation of caste. Quite simply, 'caste' needs stasis to achieve mobility, the local to reach the global, particularity in order to stake its claims to universal resources.

In the specific details of its movement between local and global, in the simultaneity of its expansion and contraction, caste comes to resemble an entity sociologists have averred caste is *not*, and that is ethnicity. To be sure, caste continues to exist as an endogamous, hereditary, hierarchical social institution, but when that traditional form, unevenly reformed and substantialized over the past hundred years, becomes a vehicle for global mobility caste comes to express more and more its ethnic character. Writings about ethnicity typically drive at either its capacity to foment violence, or celebrate multiculturalist ethnic diversity. Much less gets said about ethnicity as that which enables the cultural flows of people, ideas, and capital—or, to borrow Spivak's words from another context, about ethnicity as a 'provisional field and a provisional traffic of essences' (1993, p. 36). And yet, insofar as caste becomes 'boundary-oriented, holistic, primordialist' (Appadurai, 1990, p. 20), it functions as an effective platform for political claims-making, much in the way that other corporate groups do. The result is not exactly the disappearance of older vertical hierarchies, but perhaps their dis-integration as possibilities for more horizontal configurations open up. The paradox of caste at this moment is that without this dual constitution, it would have continued to remain an institution with only the most intimately local significance.

---

[14] But see Immerwahr's documentation of the disagreements 'over whether being black is like being colonized or like being untouchable' (2007, p. 276).

[15] Thematic Discussion of Discrimination based on Descent 2002, UN Doc. CERD/C/SR.1531.

THE ASCENT OF DESCENT AND MINORITY RIGHTS

Post-Durban discussions skirt any further overt debate on race, though the category remains foundational. Rather, attention turns to 'descent' as a related category named by CERD that 'no doubt' includes caste but is also 'wider and can encompass other situations'.[16] Descent lifts caste from any specific cultural mooring, so the work of establishing and identifying *caste-like* systems continues through thematic discussions of descent-based discrimination,[17] General Recommendations,[18] and subsequent working papers.[19] Emphasis shifts tellingly to 'caste and analogous systems': a vague concession of both caste's Indian particularity and an insistence on its commensurability. The 2016 accretion of 'minority rights'[20] to this international lexicon adds both new dimension and new complexity: while highlighting non-dominance and intersectionality, the report opens the door to the paradox of re-consolidating and valuing caste group identity while also working towards the elimination of its imposed and derogatory effects (cf. Gorringe, 2013; Waughray, 2010, p. 333).

Such malleability is a key mark of the ethnic character of caste. Theorists have long-since characterized ethnicities as interests motivated by 'the pragmatics of calculated choice and opportunism' (Tambiah, 1996, p. 21, also see Barth, 1969), noting their tendency to expand (assimilate) and contract (differentiate) to 'fill the political space available for [their] expression' (Horowitz, 1975, p. 137; see also 1985, pp. 64–74). Ambedkar, too, had long-since recognized the 'spirit of rivalry among the different castes for dignity', underscoring its fissiparous ethnic nature (Moon, 1987, p. 48). The micro-processes of power and domination, replete with variations and contradictions, that have been the real interest of social scientists expounding the value of comparative studies are of less relevance here (see Berreman, 1972; Sharma, 1993; Fuller, 2011). Nor is there much room to consider the changing dynamics of caste in modern India, in response to decades of reservations, urbanization, media, and technology penetration, globalization, and more (Gupta, 2000). International political space as marked out by UN bodies and procedures

---

[16] Expanded working paper submitted by Asbjørn Eide and Yozo Yokota on Discrimination based on work and descent 2003, UN Doc. E/CN.4/Sub.2/2003/24.

[17] CERD/C/SR.1531. Thematic Discussion of Discrimination based on Descent 2002, UN Doc. CERD/C/SR.1531 Available online: https://unispal.un.org/DPA/DPR/unispal.nsf/0/2A4CF1AA901904F985256C3300638F30

[18] General Recommendation XXIX on descent-based discrimination 2002, UN Doc. CERD/C/61/Misc.29/Rev.1.

[19] UN Doc. E/CN.4/Sub.2/2003/24 Expanded working paper submitted by Asbjørn Eide and Yozo Yokota on Discrimination based on work and descent 2003 and Expanded working paper submitted by Asbjørn Eide and Yozo Yokota on Discrimination based on work and descent 2004, UN Doc. E/CN.4/Sub.2/2004/31.

[20] UN Doc. A/HRC/31/56. Report of the Special Rapporteur on minority issues 2016, UN doc. A/HRC/31/56

is one that calls for generalities and commensurabilities as frameworks for national (but not so much local) experiences. Placing caste thus 'squarely within the old framework of international right defined by pacts and treaties' (Hardt and Negri, 2000, p. 5) privileges certain categories and mechanisms and reifies the 'spirit of rivalry' in the quest for dignity in this significantly wider context. The search for discursive affinities anchors caste via such tropes as untouchability and 'hidden apartheid'—also the title of a 2007 Human Rights Watch shadow report presented to CERD—which mark both old essences and new extremes. Such moves accentuate the moral function of comparison, no doubt, but also the ethnic character of caste by drawing on the sort of 'emotively charged ideas of inheritance, ancestry and descent [and] place or territory of origin' (Tambiah, 1996, pp. 20–21) which typically ground ethnic imaginaries. They also rely on a definition of racial discrimination as a 'widespread and enduring phenomenon that exhibits remarkable powers of persistence,' as one-time CERD member Patrick Thornberry has said (2004, p. 130). There is thus a paradox at the heart of this phenomenon called ethnicity which caste in its internationalized turn now mirrors: it is a set of relationships and an accompanying ideology that is always refashioning itself according to historical context and need, but its claims are in the process naturalized, their ultimate authority given not by immediate historical context and need but, by their essential persistence, birth-ascribed permanence, and ahistoricity. It is this tendency of groups to strategically deploy immutable ideas about themselves that enables the transformation of caste into something other than itself—precisely at moments when it insists it has never been transformed.

References

Appadurai, Arjun. 1990. 'Disjuncture and Difference in the Global Cultural Economy'. *Public Culture*, 2(2): 1–24.
Barnett, Stephen A. 1975. 'Approaches to Changes in Caste Ideology in South India'. In Burton Stein (Ed.), *Essays on South Asia*. Hawaii: University Press of Hawaii.
Barth, Frederick. 1969. 'Introduction'. In Frederick Barth (Ed.), *Ethnic Groups and Boundaries: The Social Organization of Culture Difference* (pp. 9–37). Boston: Little Brown.
Bayly, Susan. 1995. 'Caste and Race in the Colonial Ethnography of India'. In Peter Robb (Ed.), *The Concept of Race in South Asia* (pp. 165–218). Delhi: Oxford University Press.
Bayly, Susan. 1999. *Caste, Society and Politics in India from the Eighteenth Century to the Modern Age*. Cambridge: Cambridge University Press.
Berreman, Gerald D. 1972. 'Race, Caste, and Other Invidious Distinctions in Social Stratification'. *Race & Class*, 13(4): 385–414.
Béteille, Andre. 2001, 10 March. 'Race and Caste'. *The Hindu* (March 10).
Bob, Clifford. 2009. '"Dalit Rights Are Human Rights": Untouchables, NGOs, and the Indian State'. In Clifford Bob (Ed.), *The International Struggle for New Human Rights* (pp. 31–51). Philadelphia: University of Pennsylvania Press.
Chakrabarty, Dipesh. 2002. *Habitations of Modernity: Essays in the Wake of Subaltern Studies*. Chicago: University of Chicago Press.

Comaroff, John L. 1987. 'Of Totemism and Ethnicity: Consciousness, Practice and the Signs of Inequality'. *Ethnos*, 52: 301–323.

Dipankar Gupta. 2000. *Interrogating Caste: Understanding Hierarchy and Difference in Indian Society*, Penguin Books, New Delhi.

Dumont, Louis. [1970] 1998. *Homo Hierarchicus: the Caste System and Its Implications* (Trans. Mark Sainsbury, Louis Dumont, and Basia Gulati). New Delhi: Oxford University Press.

Fuller, C. J. 1996. 'Introduction: Caste Today'. In C. J. Fuller (Ed.), *Caste Today* (pp. 1–31). New Delhi: Oxford University Press.

Fuller, C. J. 2011. 'Caste, Race, and Hierarchy in the American South'. *Journal of the Royal Anthropological Institute*, 17: 604–621.

Gorringe, Hugo. 2013. 'Dalit Politics: Untouchability, Identity, and Assertion'. In Atul Kohli and Prerna Singh (Eds.), *Routledge Handbook of Indian Politics*. London: Routledge.

Guru, Gopal. 2003. 'Spectre of Exclusion'. Paper presented at a symposium on 'The Agenda of Transformation: Inclusion in Nepali Democracy,' organized by Social Science Baha. 24–26 April 2003, Birendra International Convention Centre, Kathmandu, Nepal. http://www.himalassociation.org/baha/baha_conf_gopalguru.htm, accessed on 19 December 2003.

Hall, Stuart. 1991. 'The Local and the Global'. In Anthony D. King (Ed.), *Culture, Globalization and the World System: Contemporary Conditions for the Representation of Identity* (pp. 19–40). London: Macmillan.

Hardt, Michael, and Antonio Negri. 2000. *Empire*. Cambridge, MA: Harvard University Press.

Horowitz, Donald. 1975. 'Ethnic Identity'. In Nathan Glazer and Daniel P. Moynihan. (Eds.), *Ethnicity: Theory and Experience*. (pp. 111–40). Cambridge, Mass.: Harvard University Press.

Human Rights Watch. 1999. *Broken People: Caste Violence against India's 'Untouchables'*. New York: HRW.

Human Rights Watch. 2001. *Caste-Based Discrimination: A Global Concern*. New York: Human Rights Watch.

Human Rights Watch, and CHRGJ. 2007. *Hidden Apartheid: Caste Discrimination against India's 'Untouchables'*. New York, NY: Centre for Human Rights and Global Justice, New York University School of Law and Human Rights Watch.

International Dalit Solidarity Network (IDSN). 2000, 1–5 May. Statement to the First Preparatory Committee for the WCAR Durban, Geneva.

Ilaiah, Kancha. 1996a. 'Productive Labour, Consciousness and History'. In Shahid Amin and Dipesh Chakrabarty (Eds.), *Subaltern Studies IX* (pp. 165–200). New Delhi: Oxford University Press.

Ilaiah, Kancha. 1998. 'Towards the Dalitisation of the Nation'. In Partha Chatterjee (Ed.), *Wages of Freedom: Fifty Years of the Indian Nation-State* (pp. 267–291). New Delhi: Oxford University Press.

Ilaiah, Kancha. 2001a, 11 June. 'Durban, Caste, and Indian Democracy'. *The Hindu*.

Ilaiah, Kancha. 2001b. 'Towards a Constructive "Globalization"'. Interview with Uma Maheshwari. *Seminar*, 508. http://www.india-seminar.com/2001/508.htm.

Immerwahr, Daniel. 2007. 'Caste or Colony? Indianizing Race in the United States'. *Modern Intellectual History*, 4(2): 275–301.

Jaffrelot, Christophe. 2000. 'Sanskritization vs. Ethnicization in India: Changing Identities and Caste Politics before Mandal'. *Asian Survey*, 40(5): 756–766.

Jodhka, Surinder. 2016. 'Ascriptive Hierarchies: Caste and Its Reproduction in Contemporary India'. *Current Sociology*, 62(2): 228–243.

Leach, Edmund. 1960. 'Introduction: What Should We Mean by Caste?' In Edmund Leach (Ed.), *Aspects of Caste in South India, Ceylon and North-West Pakistan* (pp. 1–10). Cambridge: Cambridge University Press.

Lennox, Corinne. 2015. 'Norm-Entrepreneurship on Caste-Based Discrimination'. In David Mosse and Luisa Steur (Eds.), *Caste Out of Development? The Cultural Politics of Identity and Economy in India and Beyond*. NJ: Routledge.

Louis, Prakash. 2001. *Casteism Is Horrendous than Racism: Durban and Dalit Discourse*. New Delhi: Indian Social Institute.

Moon, Vasanth (Ed.). 1987. 'Dr. Babasaheb Ambedkar: Writings and Speeches'. Vol. 3. New Delhi: Dr. Ambedkar Foundation, Ministry of Social Justice & Empowerment, Govt. of India. https://mea.gov.in/images/attach/amb/volume_03.pdf.

O'Hanlon, Rosalind. 2017. 'Caste and Its Histories in Colonial India: A Reappraisal'. *Modern Asian Studies*, 51(2): 432–461.

Parsons, Talcott. 1975. 'Some Theoretical Considerations on the Nature and Trends of Change of Ethnicity'. In Nathan Glazer and Daniel P. Moynihan (Eds.), *Ethnicity: Theory and Experience* (pp. 53–83). Cambridge, MA: Harvard University Press.

Reddy, Deepa S. 2005. 'The Ethnicity of Caste'. *Anthropological Quarterly*, 78(3): 543–584.

Sharma, Ursula. 1993. Berreman Revisited; Caste and the Comparative Method. *The Sociological Review*, 41(1_suppl):72–91. doi:10.1111/j.1467-954X.1993.tb03401.x

Slate, Nico. 2011. 'Translating Race and Caste'. *Journal of Historical Sociology*, 24(1): 62–79.

Slate, Nico. 2012. 'The Dalit Panthers: Race, Caste, and Black Power in India'. In Nico Slate (Ed.), *Black Power beyond Borders* (pp. 127–143). New York: Palgrave Macmillan US.

Sorabjee, Soli J. 2001, March 4. 'Racism, Name Changing and Toilets'. *Times of India*.

Spivak, Gayatri Chakravorty. 1993. ' "An Interview with Gayatri Chakravorty Spivak". By Sara Danius and Stefan Jonsson'. *Boundary 2*, 20(2): 24–50.

Tambiah, Stanley. 1996. *Leveling Crowds: Ethnonationalist Conflict and Collective Violence in South Asia*. Berkeley: University of California Press.

Tharu, Susie, and Tejaswini Niranjana. 1996. 'Problems for a Contemporary Theory of Gender'. In Shahid Amin and Dipesh Chakrabarty (Eds.), *Subaltern Studies IX* (pp. 232–260). New Delhi: Oxford University Press.

Thapar, Romila. 1996. 'The Theory of Aryan Race and India: History and Politics'. *Social Scientist*, 24(1–3): 3–29.

Thomas, Deborah A. 2015. 'Cox's America: Caste, Race, and the Problem of Culture'. *Canadian Journal of Latin American and Caribbean Studies*, 39(3): 364–381.

Thornberry, Patrick. 2004. 'Race, Descent and Caste under the CERD'. In Kenji Nakano, Mario Jorge Yutzis, and Ryo Onoyama (Eds.), *Peoples for Human Rights,* Vol 9: Descent-based discrimination (pp. 119–137). Tokyo: IMADR.

United Nations. 1965. International Convention on the Elimination of All Forms of Racial Discrimination. Available online: https://www.ohchr.org/en/professionalinterest/pages/cerd.aspx.

Washbrook, David. 1989. 'Ethnicity in Contemporary Indian politics'. In Hamza Alavi and John Harriss (Eds.), *South Asia* (pp. 174–185). New York: Monthly Review Press.

Waughray, Annapurna. 2010. 'Caste Discrimination and Minority Rights: The Case of India's Dalits'. *International Journal on Minority and Group Rights*, 17: 327–353.

Waughray, Annapurna, and David Keane. 2017. 'CERD and Caste-Based Discrimination'. In David Keane and Annapurna Waughray (Eds.), *Fifty Years of the ICERD* (pp. 121–149). Manchester: Manchester University Press.

Visvanathan, Shiv. 2001, 7 July. 'The Race for Caste: Prolegomena to the Durban Conference'. *Economic and Political Weekly*, 36(27): 2512–2516.

CHAPTER 36

CASTE AND TRIBE

JAI PRASAD

Introduction

From days of early colonial encounter in the Indian subcontinent when modern conceptions of Indian civilization and nationhood took shape, to the present times when India is recognized as a major global power, *caste* has remained a key locus of academic, politico-administrative, and social discourse in and about India.[1] Casteism in Indian politics, affirmative action based on caste status, Dalit resurgence, and socio-economic predominance of upper castes are issues that continue to draw heated debates in contemporary India. The cognitive universe of this discourse is located in contested ideas about the nature and content of 'Indian tradition' that emerged in the last two centuries. It is widely agreed upon in postcolonial scholarship that India's colonial experience consecrated caste as a defining feature of Hinduism, granting the idea of caste a teleological validity across space and time. As Cohn (1997, p. 162) states, '[In] the conceptual scheme, which the British created to understand and to act in India ..., they reduced vastly complex codes and associated meaning to a few metonyms .... Once the British had defined to their own satisfaction what they constructed as Indian rules and customs ... the Indians had to conform to these constructions.' However, it is also understood that caste as a form of social organization, and one of the many social markers, did exist in pre-colonial India, and should not be treated simply as a colonial invention. Attention must be directed to the historical and ideational processes that rendered a caste-centric view of Indian civilization[2] into a key cultural and cognitive component of modern state

---

[1] Marie Sklodowska-Curie European Training Network titled 'Global India' (Grant Agreement 722446) supported this work. The training network is funded by the European Commission's Horizon 2020 programme. I thank Professors Virginius Xaxa, Surinder Jodhka, and Rahul Mukherji for their encouragement and valuable suggestions.

[2] The most powerful exposition of this view remains Louis Dumont's *Homo Hierarchicus* (1970). See, O'Hanlon (2017) for a fine summation of the histories of caste, underlining the importance of understanding the historical roots of concretization of caste identities in organic protests against hierarchies.

making in the Indian subcontinent (Dirks, 2001; Inden, 1990; Metcalf, 1995; Washbrook, 1976). Inextricably linked to the 'caste-view' of Indian society is another colonial construction that has had a long shadow in modern India: the term or category of 'tribe' and 'Scheduled Tribe (ST)'. The former is a much-beleaguered term embedded in the history of anthropology, first used in India by colonial administrator-anthropologists, and the latter an administrative term that emerged with the adoption of the Indian Constitution inheriting a deep colonial legacy. The techniques of state making in British India such as census classification and administrative descriptions, in tandem with colonial anthropology, were central to identification, governance, and development of so-called tribal communities and their perceived sociological characteristics. In colonial discourse, however, the imagination of India as an ancient, predominantly Hindu civilization came to be centred on the recognition of caste as a core structure of Indian society. This epistemological determination of communities that appeared to lay beyond the perceived boundaries of so-called Hindu mainstream as 'tribes' reflects the power of this top-down approach, entrenched in a Brahminical textual view of Indian social organization and predominant race theories. Consequently, the search for what undergirds the institution of 'caste' remains a preoccupation for those studying Indian social life, and the terms of discourse around citizenship claims of India's 'tribal' communities obfuscate both the dynamics of social change as also the extent and depth of structural violence they experience. In this chapter, we will outline the main aspects of this epistemological connection between caste and tribe in Indian society: How have we understood tribes vis-à-vis non-tribes over the last century or so? What has been the basis of this differentiation and its implications? How has the changing scenario of tribal identity engendered their political voice in recent times?

It is to be noted that the term 'tribe' is not being used here as a *sui generis* category reflecting uncomplicated social reality of so-called tribal communities, but as an indicative term illustrating the coaxial historicity of two predominantly, and in many ways contrasting, colonial constructs, i.e., 'caste' and 'tribe'. India's tribal communities, including those enlisted as ST by the Indian state for protective and welfare guarantees, seldom identified with, or created, the variety of labels applied to them during colonial and post-independence periods. A host of *outsiders*—administrators, missionaries, social reformers, politicians, anthropologists, and public intellectuals—reflecting a range of locations and power equations used these labels, many of which survive and pervade public, academic, and policy discourses.[3] In contemporary India, the term 'Adivasi' (original inhabitant, autochthon) is used for collective self-identification by tribal communities (except in the northeast) as a marker of cultural and political assertion,

---

[3] A plethora of terms essentializing tribal backwardness, primitiveness, isolation, or remoteness from civilization, and cultural attributes persist in public, policy, and political discourse. For example, words such as *janjaati* or *adimjaati* (primitive people), *vanyajaati/vanvaasi* (forest people), and *junglee* (a derogatory term meaning wild folk).

reflecting, with its own ambiguities, an emergent Adivasi consciousness deeply rooted in a shared history of dispossession and marginalization (Radhakrishna, 2016). In this context, it is also indispensable to understand the immense diversity of India's tribal communities. The Indian state categorizes about 104 million people, 8.6 per cent of India's population, as ST (GoI, 2013) but the term does not capture the lived experiences of numerous, similarly placed communities, who may or may not identify themselves as tribes. Even if we take the communities enlisted as ST, they vary immensely in every possible way—population size, occupation, educational, and social development, integration in regional socio-cultural lives, language, food habits, cultural moorings, political voice, and religious affiliation (Sundar, 2016). Wide differences exist within regions, tribes, and within tribes. For example, India's northeast, where nearly 12 per cent of India's ST live, is viewed as a single region in popular imagination but it has over 200 tribes and sub-tribes with distinct language, culture, and political systems. In terms of administrative frameworks, tribal communities in India's northeastern states of Assam, Meghalaya, Tripura, and Mizoram, enjoy much greater autonomy under the the Sixth Schedule of the Indian Constitution, compared to communities that are governed by the Fifth Schedule. Many of the larger tribal communities live across states, with populations that run into millions, divided into sub-tribal groups, integrated into their regional political economies following occupations across sectors of the economy. On the other hand, there are many particularly vulnerable tribal groups (PVTGs) with very small populations. For example, as per the Census of 2001, the Birijia and Asur of Bihar were 17 and 181, respectively. Occupations among ST can range from high-powered bureaucrats, politicians, and landless labourers to hunter-gatherers, shifting cultivators, artisans, and pastoralists and nomads. Over 80 per cent work in the primary sector as cultivators, against 53 per cent of the general population. Linguistic diversity among the tribes is equally mindboggling. Of the four major linguistic families in the nation, namely, Indo-European, Dravidian, Austro-Asiatic, and the Tibeto-Burman, the tribes mainly speak the Dravidian, Austro-Asiatic (spoken only by tribes), and Tibeto-Burman families, while over three-fourth of India's population speaks Indo-European languages (about 1 per cent of tribes, mainly the Bhil) (GoI, 2014).

Defining 'Tribal' India

Tribes as distinct communities have always existed in the political and cultural imaginaries of the Indian subcontinent. Ancient Indian myths and legends speak of forest-dwelling tribes and their contestations with intruders.[4] Modern historians of

---

[4] For example, the stories of the burning of the Khandava forest and the destruction of the Naga people in the *Mahabharata* have been read as encounters between Aryans and indigenous populations (Karve, 1999).

ancient India contrasted settled or herding communities with an egalitarian social organization, or *janas*, with *jaatis*, which were hierarchically organized (Ray, 1972). While no one today argues that present day tribes and castes could be equated with these categories (Roy Burman, 1983, 1994), co-existence of regionally interdependent communities that formed a dynamic spectrum of autonomous egalitarian communities at the margins of 'civilization', marked by contrasting hierarchized social forms in pre-colonial India remains an unfolding debate (Kosambi, 1975; Thapar, 1971; Guha, 1998, 2013). According to Béteille, 'Tribes have existed at the margins of Hindu civilization from time immemorial, and these margins have always been vague, uncertain, and fluctuating' (Béteille, 2005 [1975], p. 133). Even today, the popular notion of what constitutes the margins of Hindu society carries a large imprint of race theories predominant during the colonial era. Historians have, however, never found any substantial archaeological backing for the clash of races myth in India, which, as Sumit Guha (1998, p. 438) states, 'took shape when brown sahibs and white sahibs sought to escape their fears about the instability of social hierarchy by giving it a biological basis and projecting it into the past—thus covering extant hierarchies with the mantle of the natural and the primordial'. The predominant conception of tribes as different from the 'civilized', mainstream in their essential and/or necessary characteristics—isolated, uncorrupted, or pristine, primitive, self-sufficient, timeless—emerged as a complex process in which colonial masters and their collaborators went about creating the colonial state. Close collaboration of the Brahmanical order with the Raj (and the pervasive use of racial theories) must be located in the material and ideational contestations over British interventions, such as in land and forest rights, taxation, policing, and judiciary. The shifts in life-chances that these changes brought for vulnerable communities, and their struggles and strategies to adapt, resist, and survive, form the contours of the historic processes of dispossession and marginalization that continues till date (see Pati, 2011; Sivaramakrishnan, 1997; Gadgil and Guha, 1993). Unlike mainstream India, they had none of the sophisticated literature, spokespeople, or common knowledge about their struggles, which makes the discourse around 'tribes' more of a colonial construct than that of 'caste' (Béteille, 1986).

Attempts at describing groups and communities of India began with European travellers, administrators, and missionaries from 18th century onwards and intensified as the Raj expanded. The period between establishment of The Asiatic Society in Calcutta in 1784 to the early 1920s saw gradual consolidation of efforts to map Indian society. The connotations of the term 'tribe', however, stood contested since the middle of the 19th century when anthropologists first began describing social formations encountered by European explorations and colonial agendas across the world.[5] Following a broadly evolutionist scheme, European anthropologists until the early 1930s concentrated

---

[5] Lewis Henry Morgan (1818–1881) was the key proponent of evolutionary stages of societies from simple, primitive hunter-gatherers, to settled agricultural communities to the highest and most complex, urban civilization. The image of a tribe as unique type of society, corresponding to a specific stage of evolution, may be traced to his influence on modern anthropology.

on 'simple, pre-literate, small-scale, and isolated societies in Australia, Melanesia, the Pacific Islands, North and South America, and sub-Saharan Africa', and defined tribes as self-contained, primitive, segmentary units (Béteille, 1986, p. 297). As anthropology progressed to a study of 'larger wholes', such as India, Japan, the Arab world, or 'civilizations', a historical framework that delved into the co-existence of groups and communities constituting these societies started emerging. However, there were clear inconsistencies between European ethnographic models that dealt with the so-called 'new world' and the realities of the 'old world' civilizations like India. Unlike the former where culturally, politically, and territorially a clear-cut distinction between the indigenous and the intruder could easily be made, tribal communities in India had been living in close interdependence with the non-tribal for millennia, with several examples of encompassing tribal kingdoms. It is not surprising that the first ethnographic descriptions of tribes and castes of different parts of India exhibited ambiguities about definitions, identification, and characteristics of tribes vis-à-vis the larger society. Throughout the late-19th century up to the 1901 census the terms 'tribes' and 'caste' were used more in an ethnic-descriptive sense, often interchangeably (Xaxa, 2008). Terms like 'aborigines', 'semi-Hinduized aborigines', or 'hill tribes', were in use since the middle of the 19th century that later became incorporated in census and anthropological definitions. In the 1881 census, the term 'forest tribes' was used as a sub-classification within the category agricultural and pastoral castes. Areas inhabited by them were classified as 'backward regions', to be governed directly by the governor-generals. In the 1901 and 1911 censuses, however, religion became the prime criteria for differentiation. Tribes were classified as 'animists' within the list of castes and others, which was changed to 'tribal religion' in the 1921 census. Gradually, the lack of utility of such a generic category from an administrative point of view made it important to capture other traits, such as geographical location/isolation; state of backwardness, or primitiveness[6] vis-à-vis other segments of the population (Xaxa, 2008). The association of tribal identity with isolated territories and the imperative to protect them from destructive influences of the mainstream took shape in British administrative reforms such as the Scheduled Districts Act 1874, and Government of India Acts of 1919 and 1935. The GoI Act 1935 classified backward regions inhabited by tribal communities into 'partial' or 'fully excluded areas', creating a road map for notification of Scheduled Areas in Independent India. On Independence, the state was empowered vide Article 342 to notify tribal communities living in erstwhile 'fully and partially excluded areas' as ST, and vide Article 244 to create the administrative mechanisms for so-called Scheduled Areas. To date, there exists no consensus on how to define a tribe in India. As the Dhebar Commission (GoI, 1961, p.1) noted,

> No standard term has been accepted to denominate the people who are classified as of tribal origin. Even the Constitution has not defined them clearly except by

---

[6] Large populations were also notified as so-called criminal tribes since 1871, turning all members of that group into potential outlaws. These tribes were 'de-notified' only after Independence.

declaring that the Scheduled Tribes are 'the tribes or tribal communities or parts of or groups within tribal communities' which the President may specify by public notification (Article 342).... In classifying them, different and sometimes contradictory criteria tend to be used by administrators, anthropologists or social workers, who may take as a basis of their designation the colour of the skin, language, customs, or living conditions or other considerations that they consider necessary.

Enlisting of tribes, thus, emerged as an administrative exercise and as it involved governmental safeguards and benefits, a deeply political exercise.

LOCATING THE TRIBE-CASTE CONTINUUM: THE HINDUIZATION MODEL

Numerous ethnographic accounts of tribes[7] since the late 19th century note the rapidity with which tribal culture was vanishing under a host of economic, political, and social changes brought about by colonial rule. While British forestry, land revenue, agrarian, and irrigation policies irreversibly altered tribal lives from late 18th century onwards, mostly for the worse, the political and administrative debate over appropriate governmental policy towards protection or accelerated assimilation of tribes started in the 1920s. From the early 1920s onwards, Indian nationalist opinion and academic literature on Indian society imbued with the nationalist sentiment, viewed India's tribal communities in relation to Hindu society, setting the terms of discourse about their identity and social transformation. Tribal communities were considered a primitive part of the Hindu cultural whole, and their isolation from the mainstream the most important reason for their backwardness. Socio-economic integration and cultural improvements that would remove their propensity for drunkenness, superstition/witchcraft, promiscuity, propensity to violence, and so on, were part of the early Gandhian-nationalist reformist agenda for India's tribes that continued for several decades into independent India (Hardiman, 1987, 2003).

Among others, the most prominent social scientists that shaped our understanding of tribes through the lens of Hindu civilization were G. S. Ghurye (1893–1983) and N. K. Bose (1901–1972), both of whom relentlessly advocated a historically situated, dynamic, and civilizational, albeit predominantly Hindu, view of Indian society. In Ghurye's legacy, 'sociology came to be defined as the study of Indian (i.e. Hindu) civilization and of the history and structure of its basic social institutions—family, kinship, caste, and religion—through textual and empirical fieldwork methods' (Upadhya, 2007, p. 243). In two of his most discussed books, *Caste and Race in India* (1932) and

---

[7] For example, Bradley-Birt (1910), S. C. Roy (1928), D. N. Majumdar (1937), Verrier Elwin (1944), and Furer-Haimendorf (1982).

The Aborigines-so-called and Their Future (1943, enlarged and published in 1959 and 1963 as *The Scheduled Tribes*), the idea of a caste-tribe continuum takes shape. In the first work concerning the caste system, its characteristics, origins, functions, and future, Ghurye draws upon the *varna* system of ritual status. He embeds his analysis in racial theorizing on Aryan expansion and racial admixture as the basis of the caste system. Here, the caste Hindu society emerges as the main body of the nation into which all other social formations naturally flow over time, if left undisturbed. In his view, the spread of Brahmanical Hinduism produced what we know as Indian society held together by its unique cultural traditions and social institutions (Upadhya, 2007). Ghurye's second book was directed at debunking Verrier Elwin's forceful advocacy of protection of tribal identity, habitat, livelihood, and culture from their interaction with caste Hindu outsiders and exposure to 'civilization' (Elwin, 1944).[8] He underplays the differences between tribal and Hindu society, and goes on to describe them as 'backward Hindus', based largely on ethnographic-administrator and Indological accounts, parallels between tribal religions and lower caste Hindu rituals as well as similarities between Dravidian and tribal language families. Assimilation of tribes into Hindu society, to him, has occurred historically and naturally, though with inevitable 'strains and stresses' in regions where tribes existed in contact with Hindu society, such as the Khonds and Kharias of Orissa, Raj-Gonds of the Central Provinces, Santhals and Mundas in Chota Nagpur, and Bhils of western India. Adaptation of 'tribal traits' to a process of voluntary or natural Hinduization would then seem to be the best scenario for solving the problem of the tribes in modern India, which were, according to him, essentially the creation of colonial rule (Dirks, 2013). Ghurye's preoccupation with textual and scriptural sources led him to adopt the 'Brahmanical model of Indian society, which is too idealistic and over-arching' (Momin, 1996, p. vi). Despite the immense value of Ghurye's scholarship in bringing out the shortcomings of romanticizing tribes and protectionist policies, his foregrounding of continuities between Hindus and tribes was based on thin empirical data. An overemphasis on harmony as an inherent feature of Indian society nurtured a long-lasting legacy in Indian sociology that was by design less attentive to tribals' lived experience and contestations—what Oommen (2011) calls a kind of 'cognitive dissonance'.

From the time of Ghurye, it has been an abiding preoccupation among social anthropologists and historians alike to define tribal societies in religio-cultural terms—in how they fit in the larger Hindu map. An Indologist and indefatigable ethnographer, N. K. Bose (1941, 1971), following the 'cultural zone' and 'diffusionist' model of ethnography promoted by Franz Boas, Alfred Kroeber, and his followers, focused on cultural similarities and cultural diffusion across regions, including castes and tribes inhabiting

---

[8] For a forceful critique of assumptions about tribal societies underlying Elwin's advocacy of tribal protection, see Archana Prasad (2003); see Ramachandra Guha (1996) for a detailed discussion on Elwin's contestations with both the assimilationist and integrationist views.

that area in a sort of zonal unity.[9] To him, as also to many of those times, national reconstruction and integration was a looming problem, and anthropology had a critical 'application' in (a) unravelling the cultural unity of India in historical terms, and (b) providing a 'scientific' basis for social reconstruction. This view, which later pervaded the idea of applied or constructive anthropology, is based on a relentless search for civilizational unity and harmonious history, obscuring 'the fact that it is often structures of social and politico-economic dominance which create developmental problems' (Bose, 2007, p. 300). Bose presents a five-fold classification of tribal communities based on their livelihood or mode of production with which they are associated: (a) hunters and gatherers; (b) shifting cultivators; (c) settled agriculturists with ploughs and cattle; (d) nomads; and (e) plantation and factory workers. The 'Hindu method of tribal absorption', according to Bose, is a process of diffusion of the Hindu social organization due to its technological and cultural superiority. In his view, caste organization based on division of labour at the local and regional levels offers economic security to people in its fold. This presents incentives for tribal communities to become a part of caste-based social order. Tribes who were Hinduized in their customs and/or had ties of interdependence with non-tribal peasantry are in the process of becoming a part of the caste order. This is akin to the formulation by D. D. Kosambi (1975), who considers adoption of productive technologies of the Hindu castes by tribal communities as the driving force behind their absorption into Hindu society.

Ghurye and Bose's work may be seen as precursors to the Sanskritization model of status mobility within Hindu caste society formulated by M. N. Srinivas (1966). Sanskritization presents the cultural emulation of upper castes by lower castes in a regional setting as a historically ongoing mode of upward social mobility within caste hierarchy, thereby absorbing tribal communities into the Hindu fold. Terms akin to the concept are 'Khsatriyisation' and 'Rajputisation' (Xaxa, 1999).

Hindu absorption models are criticized on several counts. For example, Hinduization, or give and take of material or cultural practices should not be equated with social absorption through Sanskritization. In cases where 'peasantization' has happened, it fails to recognize the resilience of tribal ethnic identities that survive Hinduization—and that stays true even if Kshatriya status is sought. K. S. Singh (1985) mentions a reverse process 'tribalization', among non-tribal outsiders living in tribal villages. A member of the Chotanagpur Oraon tribe, for example, remains Oraon even when parts of the tribe follow settled agriculture, some parts have converted to Christianity, and the tribe, over generations, has become significantly differentiated. Moreover, despite Hinduization, tribes may or may not aspire to become a part of the caste structure, which would inevitably accommodate them at the lower levels. The groups of Hindu society that might appear as their aspirational reference would necessarily remain arbitrary. Again, tribes may or may not sanskritize as a whole, with some parts getting integrated into a caste order while others live along more customary ethnic lines. This remains true of tribal languages as well, as less-isolated segments of tribes adopt regional mainstream languages, but overall tribal languages stay as a key marker of identity (Xaxa, 2008).

---

[9] His study of the spread of the spring festivals in the eastern and central parts of the Indian subcontinent (among the Nagas, Oraons, Kandh, and Gond tribes) and the festival spreading from this region to north and northwestern India and beyond is a classic example of this view. Bose (1927).

The Hindu model of tribal studies tends to strengthen orthodox ethno-administrative representations of what a tribal society means. David Mandelbaum (1970), for example, comparing tribe and *jati*, maintains that tribes in India live mostly in isolated tribal villages in hilly or forested terrain, with sparse population and difficult communication, and a strong sense of distinctive identity vis-à-vis *jati* villages. These tropes form a cosmological categorization wherein tribes appear as *essentially different* from the mainstream Hindu society, which in turn, is essentialized as a caste society. These essentializing tropes have taken myriad forms—of isolated people with a non-willingness to mix with outsiders; mired in myths and folklore without a sense of history; backwardness due to inherent 'wild' propensities for drinking, eating of forbidden meats; love for dancing, idling, promiscuity, and prone to violent outbursts. Ideal-typical images of tribal person's closeness with nature, a romantic infantile, lacking shrewdness, and so on and so forth, lurk widely in public, artistic, and cultural domains. This inability to look at Indian society beyond caste and tribe, but as a plural, disaggregated conglomerate of autonomous communities of citizens undergirds that long-lasting administrative preoccupation with idea of a tribal economy and society—defined as a self-sufficient, territorially identifiable mode of production maintained by a distinct tribal type that is historically undifferentiated (Corbridge, 1988).

Beyond Tribal Absorption

The models of so-called tribal absorption into the Hindu fold continued to hold sway until at least the late 1970s and have not lost their appeal till date. As Xaxa (1999, p. 1519) pointed out,

> The conventional wisdom among anthropologists has been that when a tribe undergoes change through a loss of isolation and through close integration with the wider society, sooner or later, and with unfailing regularity, it becomes a caste. While this may have been true to a greater or lesser extent till the forties, the argument is no longer valid. Yet anthropologists have gone on making such a generalisation—and despite inadequacy of data, concept and argument to support it. Now, while tribes continue to undergo changes of many kinds, these no longer transform them into castes. ... This argument has implications not only for the understanding of tribes but also for the understanding of Indian society as a whole.

Comparison between castes and tribes took myriad forms. Similarities and distinctions were drawn with the Hindu mainstream as a reference point for tribal transformation, development, and integration. Surajit Sinha (1958, 1962, 1965, 1987), for example, in his studies on the Bhumijs, Rajputs, and other tribes of central and eastern India, viewed tribal (folk) cultures as 'little traditions' that intricately get articulated into regional caste configuration (represented by peasantry), and thereby in the Great tradition of Hinduism (reflected in indigenous urban centres). The neat division of Indian society into tribal, peasantry, and urban (see, e.g., Vidyarthi and Rai, 1985), however, was marred with conceptual inconsistencies. Tribal and caste groups interpenetrated the class portrayed as the peasantry (Béteille, 2005[1975]), and the term peasantry, much like the term tribe was widely contested. Most accounts of tribal transformation and development in this period were obsessed with incorporation into the Hindu mainstream, either as peasantry or castes, through a variety of means (see, for example, Roy-Burman, 1972). Issues of ethnic identity, language, and embedded structures of local and regional power were effectively sidelined. Gradually, however, a disaggregation of the 'unity in diversity' view occurred, in which the move from 'book view' to the 'field view' of Indian society played a significant role (Jodhka 2015). It could also be seen as a move from the predominant structural-functionalist view to a more pragmatic approach, which took the conceptual and methodological inadequacy of the term 'tribe' in India and its administrative categorization, the ST into account (Radhakrishna, 2016). Weaknesses of neat distinctions between tribes vis-à-vis castes or peasantry (Bailey, 1961; Béteille, 2005[1975]; Pathy, 1984; Roy-Burman, 1983, 1994 Singh, 1985) became evident by the early 1980s. Caste-society came to be interrogated from below without the baggage of finding a unifying theme in the otherwise fault-line-ridden Indian society. Dimensions of coercion in maintenance and change of social order was highlighted in this process of revisiting sociological categories categories of Hinduisation or peasantisation. Rise of ethno-regionalism occasioned studies of tribal autonomy movements that challenged the extant notions of tribes (Devalle, 1992; Corbridge, 1988). Critical works on the politics of natural resources and environment, land alienation, displacement, dispossession, and forced migration, sharpened the focus on linkages between nationalistic agendas and ethnic politics (Gadgil and Guha, 1994; Baviskar, 1995). Expanding agendas of historical-anthropological enquiries started discrediting modes of tribal representation firmly held by conventional tribal studies (see for example, Guha, 1997; Skaria, 1997; Sundar, 1997; Sivaramakrishnan, 1997 Nilsen, 2019; Bhukya, 2017). As Dube (2007, p. 763) states, 'anthropologists and historians have rethought theory, method and perspective, archival materials have been read through anthropological filters and field work has been harnessed to the historical imagination ... . Historical sensibilities have informed ethnographic explorations of the interplay between culture and power within elaborations of colonialism and empire, nation and nationalism, domination and resistance, and environment and ethnicity'. It became critical to interrogate how identity, group solidarity, and ongoing economic and political processes at the regional level interacted and shaped each other in multiple material and ideological ways, and continued to perpetuate themselves. The importance of interpreting and analysing organic voice of tribal collectives became apparent.

Towards Adivasi Identity and Politics

The term Adivasi (of Sanskrit origin, meaning primal inhabitant) has emerged as a collective identity marker among a host of tribal communities across northern, eastern, and central India with diverse languages, sizes, and regional identities. Beyond the ST status, this term forms a potent rubric that can bring together multiple meanings, forces, and causes. Historically, it has been traced to the mobilization of Chotanagpur tribes in the 1920s (Hardiman, 1987), much before the terms 'indigenous' became an international rallying point for protection of indigenous peoples' rights through the ILO (1957, 1989) conventions and the UN Declaration on the Rights of Indigenous Peoples (2007). As Xaxa (2016) points out, Adivasi identity transcends multiple tribes and dialects. Joined by little but their shared historical experience of exploitation by the nontribal outsiders, individuals belonging to multiple dialects, lineages, and tribal names, came together in religious congregations afforded by Christian gatherings. This created associational opportunities beyond religious practice among the educated tribal 'elites', and made the beginning of a political voice possible.

In contemporary India, this voice is slowly galvanizing against the ills of a development framework that excludes and marginalizes Dalits and Adivasis (Xaxa and Ambagudia, 2021). The tribes in India, however, continue to remain at the bottom of socio-economic ladder, far behind the mainstream on most social, educational, economic, indicators (GoI, 2013). It is noteworthy that over 60 per cent of India's forests are found in tribal areas, and these areas are among the richest in terms of mineral deposits, water sources, and divertible land for infrastructural and industrial development.[10] Hence, tribal concentration districts are under severe strain for their forest and mineral resources, and a disproportionate burden of India's extractive economy and growth falls on them. Tribal citizens constitute nearly 40 per cent of all the citizens displaced due to developmental activities between 1951 and 1990, nearly 8.5 million people, of whom a mere 24 per cent have been rehabilitated till date (Wahi and Bhatia, 2018, p. 11). A large section of the tribal population depend upon forests for their livelihood and cultural survival. Creation of reserved and protected forests and wildlife sanctuaries and national parks through a historical process before and after independence have extinguished their customary rights in the forests. Even after the passing of the Scheduled Tribes and Other Traditional Forest Dwellers (Recognition of Forest Rights) Act (FRA) 2006, which aims to reverse this historical injustice, their struggle to reclaim these rights has been anything but easy. (Lele, Sharachchandra and Ajit Menon, 2014).

Adivasi politics rooted in struggles of tribal peasant, worker, and forest-dwellers against dispossession, forced dislocation, and exploitation, have helped advance their claims of substantive citizenship. India's environment politics since the 1970s, for example, has foregrounded issues of forest rights, development induced displacement, and protection of natural resources critical to survival of Adivasi communities (Gadgil and Guha, 1994). Important milestones in terms of powerful legislations protecting Adivasi interests, such as the Panchayati Raj (Extension to Scheduled Areas) Act 1996 and FRA

---

[10] Odisha, Chhattisgarh, and Jharkhand, for example, have considerable mineral reserves. These three States alone account for 70 per cent of India's coal reserves, 80 per cent of its high-grade iron ore, 60 per cent of its bauxite, and almost 100 per cent of its chromite reserves (MoTA, 2014).

2006 have been accomplished in the last two decades. In a cultural as well as political sense, assertion of indigeneity and redefinition, or re-assertion of Adivasi, tribal, or indigenous identity is now becoming an integral part of collective responses by a large group of communities that have hitherto remained marginal to India's development story (Karlsson, and Subba, 2013). It has also brought Adivasi identity in a dialectical relation with anthropological and historical knowledge, resistance to structural violence, and socio-political aspirations. Knowledge created by administrator-ethnographers that lay not only the very framework for tribal governance in colonial India, but also the representations of tribes as backward, wild, isolated, and timeless, is, interestingly, now being reconstructed in parts to strengthen claims on the state (Upadhya, 2011; Karlsson, 1997, 2011; Middleton, 2013).

While on one hand, caste and tribe, both colonial constructions and 'sticky' identities, continue to deeply impact life chances of the marginalized, the road to political assertion is especially arduous for Adivasis. While Dalit assertion entails a fight for dignity within a loosely defined boundary of religious identity conflated with linguistic and caste alliances, the axes of tribal exclusivity are fundamentally ingrained in the idea of nationhood and national identity in contemporary India. Adivasis are not only pitched against material dispossession, they are also compelled to fight the ever-persistent 'otherness' that pervades the mainstream, popular consciousness. Their internal divergences in terms of affiliation and participation in regional caste, language, religious, or gendered structures, weakens their political voice in the implicit, or explicit boundaries of nationhood in India. As Xaxa (2016, p. 225) argues, Indian national identity has been defined in a way that excludes existing tribal cultural forms, and the only 'commonality shared by tribes is exclusion from many social groupings [language, religion, caste, region] that have historically, socially, and culturally been associated with India'. While both Dalit and Adivasi assertion are weakened by internal differentiation and elite hijack, the latter is frequently termed anti-development, Maoism-inspired, misguided politics. Compulsions to connect with nation-level political parties, and failures to bring together scattered movements across the nation, often mar their capacity towards realizing inclusive citizenship.

As the force and scope of Adivasi identity grows in today's India, the enterprise of defining and differentiating caste and tribe at the margins of Hinduism by tracing similarities and differences, in history and in space, seems more and more pointless. Not unlike caste, the ideology, usage, and materiality of tribal communities has changed radically. However, shared experiences of oppression and marginalization are very real for both Dalits and Adivasis. Entrenched power structures within policy, law, and governance structures in India demand political projects that can bring different interests and identities together, and Adivasis and Dalits have to learn to walk together. Material aspirations, protection of identity and culture, and a growing hunger for dignity joins Dalits and Adivasis movements today. Fortunately, Adivasi resurgence has seen a growth of strongly motivated, widely networked, organic leadership from among the tribes who can be at the forefront of programmatic alliances with other marginalized communities. The importance of civil-society networks and grassroots movements, and their numerous alliances and federations that have emerged since the 1980s cannot be overestimated. The rise of the rights-based regime of social welfare since the early 2000s, the growing importance of subnational governments and politics, continues to give hope for Adivasi resurgence in India. However, the rise and consolidation of Hindu majoritarianism and shrinking space for democratic deliberations has thrown fresh challenges of populist redefinitions of cultural citizenship alongside neo-liberal onslaught on Adivasi rights. As Hindu-nationalist organizations attempt to force distinct cultural identities into an overarching straitjacket, the coming together of India's indigenous communities to fight for a socially just and environmentally sustainable developmental agenda has acquired immense importance.

References

Ambagudia, Jagannath and Virginius Xaxa (Eds.). 2021. Handbook of Tribal Politics in India. Delhi: Sage India.

Bailey, F. G. 1961. *Tribe, Caste, and Nation: A Study of Political Activity and Political Change in Highland Orissa*. Manchester: Manchester University Press.

Baviskar, Amita. 1995. *In the Belly of the River: Tribal Conflicts over Development in the Narmada Valle*. Delhi: Oxford University Press

Béteille, Andre. 1986. 'The Concept of Tribe with Special Reference to India'. *European Journal of Sociology*, 27(2): 297–318.

Béteille, Andre. 2005 [1976]. 'Tribe and Peasants'. In Dipankar Gupta (Ed.), *Anti-Utopia: Essential Writings of Andre Béteille*. New Delhi: Oxford University Press.

Bhukya, Bhangya. 2017. *The Roots of the Periphery: A History of the Gonds of Deccan India*. New Delhi: Oxford University Press.

Birt-Bradley, F. 1910. *Chota Nagpore: A Little-Known Province of the Empire*. London: Smith, Elder and Co.

Bose, Pradip Kumar. 2007. 'The Anthropologist as "Scientist": Nirmal Kumar Bose'. In Patricia Uberoi, Satish Deshpande, and Nandini Sundar (Eds.), *Anthropology in the East: Founders of Indian Sociology and Anthropology*. New Delhi: Permanent Black.

Bose, Nirmal Kumar, 1927. 'The Spring Festival in India', In *Man in India*, Vol. 7.

Cohn, Bernard. 1997. *Colonialism and Its Forms of Knowledge*. New Delhi: Oxford University Press.

Corbridge, Stuart. 1988. 'The Ideology of Tribal Economy and Society: Politics in the Jharkhand, 1950–1980'. *Modern Asian Studies*, 22(1): 1–42.

Devalle, Susana, B. C. 1992. *Discourses of Ethnicity: Culture and Protest in Jharkhand*. Delhi: Sage India.

Dirks, Nicholas. 2001. *Castes of Mind: Colonialism and the Making of Modern India*. New Delhi: Permanent Black.

Dirks, Nicholas. 2013. 'G.S. Ghurye and the Politics of Sociological Knowledge'. *Sociological Bulletin*, 62(2): 239–253.

Dube, Saurabh. 2007. 'Historical Anthropology of Modern India'. In *History Compass 5/3*: 763–779.

Dumont, Louis. 1970. *Homo Hierarchicus: The Caste System and Its Implications*. London: Weidenfeld and Nicolson.

Elwin, Verrier. 1944. *The Aboriginals*. Bombay: Oxford University Press.

Fürer-Haimendorf, C. von. 1982. *The Tribes of India: The Struggle for Survival*. Berkley: University of California Press.

Government of India, 1961, Report of the Scheduled Areas and Scheduled Tribes Commission, vol. 1. New Delhi: Ministry of Home Affairs, GoI.

Government of India. 2013. *Statistical Profile of Scheduled Tribes in India*. New Delhi: Ministry of Tribal Affairs.

Government of India. 2014. *Report of the High Level Committee on Socio-economic, Health and Educational Status of Tribal Communities of India*. New Delhi: Ministry of Tribal Affairs.

Gadgil, Madhav, and Ramachandra Guha. 1993. *This Fissured Land: An Ecological History of India*. Delhi: Oxford University Press.

Gadgil Madhav and Ramachandra Guha. 1994. 'Ecological Conflicts and Environmental Movements in India'. Development and Change, Vol.25 (1994), pp. 101–136.

Guha, Ramachandra. 1996, September. 'Savaging the Civilized: Verrier Elwin and the Tribal Question in Late Colonial India'. *Economic and Political Weekly*, 31(35/37): 2375–2389.

Guha, Ranajit (Ed.), 1997. A Subaltern Studies Reader, 1986-1995. Minnesota: University of Minnesota Press.

Guha, Sumit. 1998. 'Lower Strata, Older Races, and Aboriginal Peoples: Racial Anthropology and Mythical History Past and Present'. *The Journal of Asian Studies*, 57(2): 423–441.

Guha, Sumit. 2013. *Beyond Caste: Identity and Power in South Asia, Past and Present*. Leiden: Brill

Ghurye, G. S. 1943. *The Aborigines-So-Called and Their Future*. Bombay: Popular Prakashan.

Hardiman, David. 1987. *The Coming of the Devi: Adivasi Assertion in Western India*. New Delhi: Oxford University Press.

Hardiman, David. 2003. *Gandhi in His Time and Ours*. Delhi: Orient Blackswan.

Inden, R. B. 1990. *Imagining India*. Oxford: Blackwell.

Jodhka, Surinder S. 2015. *Caste in Contemporary India*. Delhi: Routledge

Karlsson, B. G. 1997. *Contested Belonging: An Indigenous Peoples' Struggle for Forest and Identity in Sub-Himalayan Bengal*. Monographs in Social Anthropology 4, Lund: Department of Sociology, Lund University.

Karlsson, B. G. 2011. 'Sovereignty through Indigenous Governance: Reviving Traditional Political Institutions in Northeast India'. In Daniel J. Rycroft and Sangeeta Dasgupta (Eds.), *The Politics of Belonging in India: Becoming Adivasi*. New York: Routledge.

Karlsson, B.T. and Subba, T.B. eds., 2013. Indigeneity in India. Routledge.

Karve, Irawati. 1999. *Yuganta: The End of an Epic*. Hyderabad: Disha Books.

Kosambi, D.D. 1975. The Culture and Civilisation of Ancient India in Historical Outline. Delhi: Vikas Publishing House.

Lele, Sharachchandra and Ajit Menon, eds., 2014. Democratizing forest governance in India (p. 432). New Delhi: Oxford University Press.

Mandelbaum, David G. 1970. *Society in India: Continuity and Change*. California: University Press.

Metcalf, T. R. 1995. *Ideologies of the Raj*. Cambridge: Cambridge University Press.

Middleton, Townsend. 2013. 'Scheduling Tribes: A View from inside India's Ethnographic State'. *Focaal—Journal of Global and Historical Anthropology*, 65(1): 13–22.

Momin, A. R. 1996. *The Legacy of G.S. Ghurye: A Centennial Festschrift*. Bombay: Popular Prakashan.

Nilsen, A. G., 2019. Adivasis and the State: Subalternity and Citizenship in India's Bhil Heartland (Vol. 7). Cambridge University Press.

Sundar, N., 1997. Subalterns and Sovereigns: An Anthropological. History of Bastar 1854–1996. Oxford: OUP.

Oommen, T. K. 2011. 'Scheduled Castes, Scheduled Tribes, and the Nation: Situating G. S. Ghurye'. *Sociological Bulletin*, 60(2): 228–244.

O'Hanlon, Rosalind. 2017. 'Caste and Its Histories in Colonial India: A Reappraisal'. *Modern Asian Studies*, 51(2): 432–461.
Pathy, J. 1984. *Tribal Peasantry*. New Delhi: Inter-India Publications.
Pati, Biswamoy (Ed.). 2011. *Adivasis in Colonial India: Survival, Resistance, and Negotiation*, New Delhi: Orient Blackswan.
Prasad, Archana. 2003. *Against Ecological Romanticism: Verrier Elwin and the Making of an Anti-Modern Tribal Identity*. Delhi: Three Essays Collective.
Radhakrishna, Meena (Ed.). 2016. *First Citizens: Studies on Adivasis, Tribals, and Indigenous Peoples in India*. New Delhi: Oxford University Press.
Ray, Niharranjan. 1972. *Nationalism in India*. Aligarh: Aligarh Muslim University.
Roy Burman, B. K. 1983. 'Transformation of Tribes and Analogous Social Formations'. *Economic and Political Weekly*, 18(27): 1172–1174.
Roy Burman, B. K. 1994. *Tribes in Perspective, Vol. 1*. Delhi: Mittal Publications.
Singh, K. S. 1985. *Tribal Society in India*. New Delhi: Manohar.
Sinha, Surajit. 1958. 'Tribal Culture of Peninsular India as a Dimension of Little Tradition in the Study of Indian Civilization: A Preliminary Statement'. *The Journal of American Folklore*, 71(281): 504–518.
Sinha, Surajit. 1962. 'State Formation and Rajput Myth in Tribal Central India'. *Man in India*, 42(1): 35–80.
Sinha, Surajit. 1965. 'Tribe—Caste and Tribe—Peasant Continua'. *Man in India*, 45(1): 57–83.
Sinha, Surajit. 1987. *Tribal Polities and State Systems in Pre-Colonial Eastern and North-Eastern India*. Calcutta: KP Bagchi and Company.
Sivaramakrishnan, K. 1997. *Modern Forests: Statemaking and Environmental Change in Colonial Eastern India*. New Delhi: Oxford University Press.
Skaria, Ajay. 1997. 'Shades of Wildness: Tribe, Caste, and Gender in Western India'. *The Journal of Asian Studies*, 56(3): 726–745.
Srinivas, M. N. 1966. *Social Change in Modern India*. California: University of California Press.
Sundar, Nandini (Ed.). 2016. *The Scheduled Tribes and Their India: Politics, Identities, Policies, and Work*. New Delhi: Oxford University Press.
Thapar, Romila. 1971. 'The Image of Barbarian in Early India'. *Comparative Studies in Society and History*, 13(4): 408–436.
Upadhya, Carol. 2007. 'The Idea of Indian Society: G.S. Ghurye and the Making of Indian Sociology'. In Patricia Uberoi, Satish Deshpande, and Nandini Sundar (Eds.), *Anthropology in the East: Founders of Indian Sociology and Anthropology*. New Delhi: Permanent Black.
Upadhya, Carol. 2011. 'Colonial Anthropology, Law, and Adivasi Struggles: The Case of Jharkhand'. In Sujata Patel (Ed.), *Doing Sociology in India: Genealogies, Locations, and Practices*. New Delhi: Oxford University Press.
Vidyarthi, L. P., and B. K. Rai. 1985. *Tribal Culture in India*. Delhi: Concept Publishing.
Wahi, Namita, and A. Bhatia. 2018. *The Legal Regime and Political Economy of Land Rights of Scheduled Tribes in the Scheduled Areas of India*. New Delhi: Centre for Policy Research.
Washbrook, David. 1976. *The Emergence of Provincial Politics: The Madras Presidency 1870–1920*. Cambridge: Cambridge University Press.
Xaxa, Virginius. 1999, 12–18 June. 'Transformation of Tribes in India: Terms of Discourse'. *Economic and Political Weekly*, 34(24): 1519–1524.
Xaxa, Virginius. 2008. *State, Society, and Tribes: Issues in Post-Colonial India*. New Delhi: Pearson Longman.
Xaxa, Virginius. 2016. 'Tribes and Indian National Identity: Location of Exclusion and Marginality'. *Brown Journal of World Affairs*, 23(1): 223–237.

CHAPTER 37

DENOTIFIED COMMUNITIES

KALPANA KANNABIRAN

The land was ours
Even the rivers were ours
Our elders wandered the jungles and the plains
When we were hungry we would beg
If we couldn't beg we would steal
The British came
They made laws
They made us 'born criminals'.

The British came and oppressed us
They beat us till our skin was flayed
The British left and the police came
Freed from the camps we were put in jails
The jungle disappeared
The land disappeared
The rivers disappeared
The rivers disappeared
The rivers disappeared.

—Chhara children's song (2006) (cited in Schwarz, 2010, p. ix)

INTRODUCTION

Denotified tribes draw their name from a colonial law, the Criminal Tribes Act, 1871, that was enacted by the colonial British government to regulate and control vast and diverse communities of mostly itinerant traders and migrant communities—'coin-makers, entertainers, migratory peasants, stray wandering groups, nomadic communities, long-distance traders' (Devy, 2012, p. 29)—forcing them into 'settled' residence and wage labour. Meena Radhakrishna identifies four categories of communities classified as criminal tribes: the first are 'acrobats, dancers, singers, jugglers, fortune-tellers and street performers of various kinds; artisans/craftspeople; and traditional healers/medicine men and women—largely classified as Scheduled Castes and targeted by anti-beggary legislations;' the second category consists communities 'dependent on wild performing animals for livelihood and which train bears, monkeys, owls/other birds, snakes'— classified as Scheduled Castes or Other Backward Classes trapped by wildlife conservation laws; the third set consists of nomadic pastoral communities classified as Other Backward Classes or Scheduled Tribes; the fourth are nomadic forest dwelling communities that practice shifting cultivation, hunting, and gathering classified as Scheduled Tribes (Radhakrishna, 2008, pp. 202–203).

As is evident from this distribution, the use of the term 'tribe' to describe these communities does not in fact restrict the communities so identified to tribes alone. As Tolen points out colonial gazetteers used 'criminal caste', 'criminal class', and 'criminal tribe' interchangeably (Tolen, 1991, p. 108). At the time of its enactment, the Criminal Tribes Act was an 'Act for the Registration of Criminal Tribes and Eunuchs', brought into force because the colonial government felt it was 'expedient to provide for the registration, surveillance and control of certain criminal tribes and eunuchs'. The interchangeability of caste and tribe in the case of criminal tribes is an important one because the specific use of the terms 'caste' and 'tribe' performed specific functions, as Tolen points out:

> ['Tribe'] evoked both an evolutionary stage and certain values and images ... 'Tribe' was situated on a lower rung than 'caste' on an evolutionary scale. But the peculiar use of the term 'tribe' to evoke a set of images is clear from the logic used to explain the causes of crime: criminal tribes committed crime because it was dictated by their caste to do so. 'Caste,' rather than 'tribalism,' was the distinctive causal feature of this breed of criminality. But the term 'tribe' could evoke qualities of savagery, wildness, and otherness in a way that 'caste' could not. The term 'criminal tribe' was often favored because of the signs it was able to produce in British consciousness. (Tolen, 1991, p. 109)

Henry Schwarz presents the intertwining of criminal tribe and caste in the British imaginary somewhat differently:

> Hereditary criminal tribes became the ultimate guarantor of the theory of rigid caste identity ... The antithesis of individuals who committed crimes, and so could be controlled by liberal, rational law, these groups were bound by a strictly determinist notion of caste in a timeless and ahistorical parallel universe to what the British envisioned as their ideal of a stable, settled agrarian India rooted in village community. (Schwarz, 2010, p. 69)

This ambiguity was carried into postcolonial categorizations of the 'denotified tribes'/ 'vimukta jati' where a cursory glance shows that 60 per cent of communities listed belong to the Other Backward Classes and only 20 per cent fall under the Scheduled Tribes. Complicating this further is the fact that the same communities are listed under different categories in different states, the only commonality being that they are 'denotified tribes' DNT being the official acronym. The suggestion for this nomenclature came from the Kaka Kalelkar Committee, in 1955: 'They should not be called Tribes. Nor should the names "Criminal" or "Ex-criminal" be attached to them. They could be simply called denotified communities' (Kalelkar, 1956, p. 36). Although the Kalelkar Commission takes a sympathetic view of Denotified Communities, it reproduces the stigmatizing stereotypes in its description of these communities and their livelihood practices (Kalelkar, 1956, pp. 34–37).

This chapter will look at the specific ways in which the four criminal tribes enactments (of 1871, 1897, 1911, and 1924) marked this community for posterity. The discussions around criminality, nomadism, surveillance, and stigmatization need to be understood in the historical context of these colonial enactments, and their afterlives in independent India. Although the first of these enactments, the 1871 Act continued to define 'criminal tribe' ambiguously, important for our present purposes is the fact that the identification and labelling of 'denotified tribes' originates through their description, definition, and treatment prescribed by a penal law. Section two, 'Legislating Criminality' that follows this introduction will look at these enactments, with a brief account of their legislative history. Section three, 'Colonizing Itinerant, Disaffected Lives', critically examines ethnographic and historiographical accounts of the colonial period that speak of criminal tribes and their 'regulation' and 'reform'. Section four, 'Fragmentation of Family, Kinship, Neighbourhood', focuses on the practices of segregation and fragmentation of families and communities through the legally mandated policy of settlements and reformatory schooling. Section five, 'Discontents and Paradoxes of Inclusion', discusses briefly the problem of inclusion, categorization, and barriers against the backdrop of access to education, employment, and affirmative action through the findings of a study that examined the socio-economic and educational status of denotified communities in nine states in India. Section six is the 'Conclusion.'

LEGISLATING CRIMINALITY

A large, amorphous cluster of communities—'Denotified Tribes'—is constituted by *The Criminal Tribes Act*, 1871 (Act XXVII of 1871) (CTA 1) in Punjab, Oudh, and the North-West Frontier Provinces in British India, and was at this constitutive moment 'An Act for the Registration of Criminal Tribes and Eunuchs', which provided 'for the registration, surveillance and control of certain criminal tribes and eunuchs'.[1] The identification of a 'criminal tribe' was simple—and since the identification in the first instance was to a

---

[1] Part 1 of the Act pertains to Criminal Tribes, Part 2 pertains to Eunuchs. For the purposes of this essay, we will only look at the provisions relevant to Part 1. For the legislative debates around this early enactment see Radhakrishna (2001, pp. 27–44).

governmental notification of a 'tribe' with 'criminal' attributes, this stands in for the definition. Section 2 of the Act answers the question, 'Who are Criminal Tribes?':

> If the Local Government has reason to believe that any *tribe, gang* or *class* of persons *is addicted* to the systematic commission of nonbailable offences, it may report the case to the Governor General in Council, and may request his permission to declare such tribe, gang or class to be a criminal tribe. (emphasis added)

The *Criminal Tribes Act, 1871,* required the local authority to provide reasons for requesting such permission, details of the kinds of offences such tribe, gang, or class is supposed to be addicted to, and alternative livelihoods they will be provided with after the application of the provisions of this act. Where residence is not settled, details are sought, and where the local authority observes the engagement in 'lawful occupation' besides commission of/addiction to crime, the authority must determine whether this is 'the real occupation of such tribe, gang, or class, or a pretense for the purpose of facilitating the commission of crimes, and shall set forth the grounds on which such opinion is based'. Of particular concern to the British government were 'wandering tribes' with 'no fixed place of residence'. This legislation provides for the compulsory registration of all persons designated to be 'criminal tribes' in this manner and provides for the removal of children from their parents and their confinement to reformatories under the guardianship of a superintendent, a colonial officer. The act placed the villages and settlements where such tribes resided under inspection and surveillance, provided a schedule of punishments which ranged from whipping to transportation for life—for child 'offenders' in the reformatories as well, whipping was a prescribed punishment.

The subjugation of these communities through confinement, surveillance, and corporal punishment—whipping 'to be inflicted in the manner prescribed by any law in force for the time being in relation to whipping'—rendered them vulnerable *as a class* to violent subjugation both by the colonial state and by agencies like the Salvation Army that worked in the service of the colonial state. Radhakrishna quotes from the Salvation Army newspaper in 1909: 'One man in our settlement (in Gorakhpur) had been flogged 15 times, another 6 times. They are now happily at work in our Salvation Army factory' (cited in Radhakrishna, 2001, p. 72).

The *Criminal Tribes (Amendment) Act, 1897* introduced two major amendments to the 1871 Act. The first was the amendment to Section 17A, which authorized the local government to '*establish and maintain* reformatory settlements for children' (emphasis added) who could be removed from their parents who were 'registered members of any tribe, gang, or class which has been declared to be criminal' and placed in these settlements under the guardianship of the superintendent. A child was 'a person under the age of eighteen and above the age of four years'. The guardian was authorized to apprentice the children in the settlement in accordance with the rules set out in the *Apprentices Act, 1850* (Act XIX of 1850). The second amendment to Section 19 introduced more stringent punishments in section 19A—whipping, rigorous imprisonment, transportation, and life imprisonment for repeat offenders. Section 19B prescribed rigorous imprisonment up to three years for 'registered members' 'found in any place under such circumstances as to satisfy the Court that he was about to commit, or aid in the commission of, theft or robbery, or that he was waiting for an opportunity to commit theft or robbery'.

The *Criminal Tribes Act, 1911* (Act III of 1911) was a new enactment that dropped eunuchs from its purview, and was applicable only to 'criminal tribes'. It consolidated the 1871 and 1897 enactments, by providing for the registration, control of surveillance of tribes and any parts of such tribes; the establishment and maintenance of settlements and schools; and a schedule of punishments. It introduced finger-printing as part of the registration of members—sections 5 to 9 speak of the need to record 'finger impressions' of registered members, if necessary, by an order of the magistrate. Refusal to record finger impressions invited penalties under section 21 of the act. A child under the 1911 act was a person between the ages of six and eighteen years (the minimum age increased from four to six). Village headmen, village watchmen, owners of land where members resided were all drawn into the regime of surveillance by the colonial authority and invited penalties for not providing information on the activities of members residing in territories under their charge/in their possession.[2]

This law—the Criminal Tribes Acts—was the medium through which the colonial government rendered the intractable (to colonial comprehension), mobile, fluid, lives of a large, and amorphous cluster of communities that were constituted in and through cultures of nomadism and migration, visible, and legible. These acts were part of a long process that began with thugs and culminated in the 'enshrinement of the principle of hereditary criminality' (Schwarz, 2010, p. 64). Anderson details the invention of 'thuggee' and the development of regimes of control around it in the mid-19th century connecting the first 1871 Act to earlier colonial discourses on this subject—a quintessentially Indian crime, marked by its 'secretive, timeless nature' (Anderson, 2004, p. 6). The introduction of protocols of naming ('criminal tribes'), categorization, surveillance, finger-printing, and forced fragmentation of community (especially through the removal of children) served to subjugate and mark bodies, holding them in captivity to be deployed in ways that served colonial interests. In South Asia, as in other parts of the empire, as Clare Anderson notes, 'new modes of identification were invoked to record and describe similarly anomic criminal bodies, particularly unknown persons picked up in the growing cities on the suspicion of being habitual offenders, and itinerant social groups who could not be anchored to particular localities' (Anderson, 2004, p. 2). Most importantly however, 'criminality' became an ascriptive trait of entire communities, transmitted by birth—mirroring the technologies of caste—with the violation of protocols of surveillance set down by the law constituting proof of criminality and inviting incarceration and punishment of varying degrees. The actual commission of crime by a person or group of persons and investigation of such crime in accordance with a code of criminal procedure was no longer the condition for the operation of this

---

[2] The *Criminal Tribes Act, 1924* re-enacted the provisions of the CTA 1911.

law in respect of the tribes listed under it. And yet as Tolen argues, the constitution of the notion of the 'criminal castes' was a gradual process that drew on the growing British 'knowledge' of Indian society and on the ideas of crime, criminality, and social order in Britain during colonialism (Tolen, 1991, pp. 107–108).

Colonizing Itinerant, Disaffected Lives

By the time of the 1897 Amendment to the Criminal Tribes Act, the colonization of the body (to echo David Arnold) had taken a different turn. Criminal tribes were by this time marked as 'hereditary criminals' belonging to particular castes and tribes. It is however, important to note that at the time of the first enactment in 1871, while we do see the developments around thuggee and its insertion into the ordering of castes and tribes, the definition of a 'criminal tribe' in the law did not speak of particular castes and tribes—it was a category left open that could suck into its vortex, the widest aggregation of 'deviant' bodies ranging from gangs and classes to eunuchs. The law therefore provided the apparatus for colonizing 'criminals' who were identified through the production of colonial knowledge in various genres ranging from travellers' accounts to colonial ethnography and orientalist fiction. How might colonial government deal with the constant 'anarchic' blurring of boundaries and the impossibility of confining or controlling peripatetic communities that proliferated outside a sedentary context that yielded revenue and recognizable labour that could be appropriated:

> mendicant and pilgrim throngs, pastoralist and hunting bands, and other itinerant communities ... [traveling] in and out without sufficient scrutiny. Pack-traders moving along hazardous routes and between famine and plenty, provisioning warring camps, [keeping] themselves independent of political authority. A buoyant military market [that] encouraged armed cavalry men from Central Asia and mercenaries from Arabia to filter into Hindustan and the peninsula by land and sea ... At the local level, 'hereditary predatory communities' [that] seemed to get away with forms of blackmail—cattle theft or poisoning, vengeful arson, or crop pilfering—to enforce their employment as herdsmen, village watchmen, ferrymen or messengers. (Singha, 2000, pp. 151–152)

Ranajit Guha maps the trajectory of agrarian disturbances over 117 years, from 1783 to 1900 that ruptured the emergent colonial state again and again right till the end of the 19th century (Guha 1983). The disturbances, Guha argues drew their logic from a negative class consciousness that identified the enemy—the nobility, the landed aristocracy, and moneylenders, whose interests converged with the interests of the state. The disturbances were upheavals in that they attempted an inversion of all dominant codes in waves of insurgent acts/actions—speech, dress, religion, and assets. In these upheavals, insurgency in colonial terms was reduced to dacoity and crime, although the two derive from two very different codes of violence.

Dacoities were only one of the manifestations of rural violence—the others were brought under the offences of murder, theft, robbery, arson, hurt. On closer examination, Guha finds that the focus on class enemies—local elite, moneylender, colonial authority—and the concerted use of several forms of violence against one target, forces us to reckon with these as forms of militant collective action supported by the local population, rather than as isolated crimes. The object of the action was to overturn authority, not just to loot.

Colonial criminal law takes shape through the translation of claims for equitable distribution of food and resources into crime; the interpretation of resistance to gross inequality and dispossession as dacoity in a period of ascendant colonial capitalism; the forging of networks of solidarity and kinship across the immediate boundaries of tribe, caste, and gender in order to make this resistance more focused, better equipped, and more concerted, were read as the submissiveness of Indians before the depredations of thugs and dacoits.

After the rebellions of 1857–1858, the British convicted a range of 'ordinary criminals'—those sentenced for murder or armed gang robbery—to imprisonment in the penal settlement at Port Blair. By the end of the 19th century, about twelve thousand convicts lived on the island. The object of the penal settlement, Satadru Sen argues, was to create a 'social, political and physical order that conformed to the normative order of colonialism' (Sen, 2000, p. 248). It was imperative for the state to fashion a system which was conducive to policing—the policing of the recalcitrant subject by the colonial state and over time, through systems of rewards and punishments, the policing of subjects by subjects on behalf of the colonial authority—creating the limited identification that would strengthen the modern regime (Sen, 2000, pp. 67–69). Rural migrants, casual poor, the marginally employed sub-proletariat, factory hands, goondas, badmashes, the unorganized labour sector all faded into each other as did the distinctions between drug peddling, wage work, and working in organized crime in the service of wealthy men and politicians (Chandavarkar, 1998, pp. 145–146). In general, the writing on crime, criminality, surveillance, and its relationship to subalternity under colonialism underscored the greater propensity for spontaneous violence by subaltern mobilization.

Colonial law was alive to the fact that disaffection towards the government—its personnel, installations, and all things European—was a logical consequence of colonial rule. Criminal law addressed this prospect directly, with the focused object of disciplining the working classes and itinerant communities (who were always in very immediate ways in confrontation with the government), breaking resistance, forcing sedentarization, and repressing political movements. This volatility and violent resistance of the poor to colonial rule was by Guha's account something that began in the middle of the 19th century—in fact before the enactment of the Penal Code—and the Criminal Tribes Acts. Were the surveillance regimes under these acts then structured to deal with disaffection and with mobile, peripatetic lives that were a threat because of their itinerant intractability?

Towards the end of British colonialism, the criminal tribes act was increasingly seen by Indian nationalists as a 'negation of civil liberty' (Nehru, cited in Gandhi, 2008, p. 11) with Pattabhi Seetharamayya declaring that criminal tribes are treated worse than cattle bought and sold in the market, wild animals hunted out of villages and worms trodden under the feet (cited in Gandhi, 2008, p. 11). However, the discomfort with uprooting the idea of inherent criminality was evident in the virtual replacement of the Criminal Tribes Act with the Habitual Offenders' Act, in Madras in 1948 and in Andhra Pradesh in 1962, the provisions of which mirrored those of the criminal tribes acts—registration, maintenance of settlements, surveillance, fingerprinting, provisions of arbitrary arrests, and incarceration. Not surprisingly, of the 5268 persons registered under the Madras Restriction of Habitual Offenders' Act of 1948, 4097 were from 'ex-Notified tribes' (Gandhi, 2008, p. 20, fn 45). The Rajasthan Habitual Criminals (Registration and Regulation) Act 1950, under section 4(1) defines a 'habitual criminal' as 'a person who, being a member of a notified tribe, has not ... been declared by an order ... of the District Magistrate as no longer a habitual criminal ...'; it defines a 'notified tribe' as 'any tribe, community, gang, group, or class of persons which had, previous to ... this Act been declared to be a criminal tribe ...' (Krishnan, 2014, p. xxviii).

FRAGMENTATION OF FAMILY, KINSHIP, NEIGHBOURHOOD

No discussion of criminal tribes under colonialism is complete without a discussion of the incarceration of entire families and the subjugation of wives and children of male suspects to intense surveillance and confinement in settlements.

The formation of settlements of different kinds—penal, reformatory, voluntary, agricultural, and industrial (Gandhi, 2017, p. 59)—and the confinement of registered members of criminal tribes to 'settlements' as prescribed by the Criminal Tribes Acts,[3] coincided with the handing over of the management of settlements to Christian missionary agencies like the Salvation Army, American Baptist Mission, London Mission, and similar such agencies (Gandhi, 2008, p. 162), which were entrusted with the task of extracting labour under conditions of incarceration. This was variously described at the time as similar to slavery or the conversion of free labour

---

[3] *Criminal Tribes Act, 1924*: Section 16. The [Provincial Government] may establish industrial, agricultural, or reformatory settlements and may order to be placed in any such settlement any criminal tribe, or any part or member of a criminal tribe, in respect of which or of whom a notification has been issued ... 17. (1) The [Provincial Government] may establish industrial, agricultural or reformatory schools for children, and may order to be separated and removed from their parents or guardians and to be placed in any such school or schools the children of members of any criminal tribe or part of a criminal tribe, in respect of which a notification has been issued ...

into indentured labour (Radhakrishna, 2001, p. 87); educating children who had been removed from parental custody in reformatories with the specific aim of teaching them skills that could then rein them into the emergent industrial workforce; and proselytizing this amorphous cluster of communities that had little in common except the label they shared. Meena Radhakrishna observes that confinement in settlements was a practice that was 'in absolute violation of the principle laid down by the CTA that settlements were to be formed for 'extreme cases' among those notified and registered, and were for those found to be 'incorrigible"—that is those who were believed by the administration to be beyond deterrence (Radhakrishna, 2001, p. 71). Importantly, she points out that the idea of settlements and its inclusion into the Criminal Tribes Acts was the result of the Salvation Army's correspondence in 1910 with the Governor-General-in-Council, that is before the act was formulated, urging the government to address the problem through reformation and employment and not only through repression and punishment (Radhakrishna, 2001, pp. 72–73). And yet both reformation and employment were repressive and punitive:

> The whole of the settlement was fenced in with a stout barbed wire fence on steel rail posts and reinforced with a thorn hedge, the exit being under control… day and night. Besides this, the lines where settlers lived were illuminated by electricity… This arrangement has… been a great factor in counteracting many a vicious tendency… (cited in Radhakrishna, 2001, p. 84).

Alongside this confinement of families in settlements, the colonial government in Madras established 'reformatory schools' that segregated children from criminal tribes, removed them on the one hand from proximity to their families and familiar neighbourhood, and on the other hand kept them apart from the regular schooling system. Reformatory education, industrial training, night schools, and particular forms of missionary education served to deprive children of a basic education and reproduced extreme forms of vulnerability and stigma. The first reformatory schools were established in 1880, starting in north India for Dom children and in Chingleput in Madras for children of 'criminal gangs'. These schools were affiliated to and located in close proximity to prisons, often functioning as sub-jails. Gandhi cites correspondence from HB Grigg, the jail superintendent, advising the government to set up reformatory schools as a way of reducing the convict population in jail (Gandhi, 2017, p. 61). Supervision in reformatory schools was modelled on prison surveillance regimes, and the former very soon functioned like open jails:

> Children were isolated from their parents, community and village at a tender age. Parents were never allowed to meet their children [who] were trained to cope with arduous work… The Missionary schools alienated children from proper education. As the community and parents were always under strict supervision of the CTA provisions, they could not seriously resist reformatory schooling system… Parents who resisted the kind of treatment received in these schools were strictly penalized. (Gandhi, 2017, p. 60)

The forced removal of children and the reverberations of child-reform projects especially among the criminal tribes continue to be relevant in postcolonial India. Importantly for our present purposes, the segregation, confinement, and strict policing through violent means by the state and local dominant communities (torture in illegal custody and lynch mobs respectively), as also the perpetuation of stigma intergenerationally echoes in distinct ways the prescriptive ascription of 'untouchability' in caste society, and its morphing of form in contemporary Indian society.

Discontents and Paradoxes of Inclusion

Although Nehru described this legislation as 'a blot on the law book of independent India', these communities re-christened the 'denotified' tribes continued to be the target of criminal law in the newly independent Indian State (Radhakrishna, 2009).

Results from a 2015 survey by CSD highlighted yet again the specific and continuing vulnerabilities of 'denotified', nomadic, and semi-nomadic tribes—especially in relation to the persistent disparities in access to education and employment and the ever-looming fear of stigma and criminalization faced by these communities.[4] In the past, these issues were already highlighted by the National Commission for Denotified, Nomadic, and Semi-Nomadic Tribes (NCDNT, 2008), and in the Report of the National Advisory Council Working Group on Denotified and Nomadic Tribes (2011), and the Report of the High Level Committee on Socio-economic, Health, and Educational Status of Tribal Communities of India (Xaxa Committee, 2014), among others.

Of the 306 communities listed by the NCDNT, this study covered 76 (66 per cent Other Backward Classes, 16 per cent Scheduled Caste, and 18 per cent Scheduled Tribe) and included communities that were victims of labelling as well as those that did not face criminal targeting. A separate segment of the questionnaire explored the specific impacts of criminal labelling. Overall, the study reiterated the close relationship between poor socio-economic conditions, stigmatization, residential segregation, and low educational attainment of the 'denotified' and nomadic tribes.

The communities surveyed were predominantly rural, reporting a long duration of stay (around 30 years) in their present location indicating a shift from nomadism to settled residence. The proportion of households still engaged in traditional work as the

---

[4] Given the paucity of reliable data on socio-economic and educational status of these communities, the Indian Council of Social Science Research (ICSSR) sponsored a study covering nine states to examine the socio-economic status and educational attainment of these communities. The Council for Social Development, Hyderabad (CSD), carried out the study between 2012 and 2015 and covered 13,000 households in Madhya Pradesh, Chhattisgarh, Gujarat, Goa, Maharashtra, Karnataka, Tamil Nadu, Andhra Pradesh, and Telangana. This section is a revised version of Kannabiran (2017). For a detailed account, see Kannabiran et al. (2018).

primary occupation was marginal across the states except Gujarat (25 per cent of the households) and Madhya Pradesh (22 per cent). The study showed that many of these families were moving to the lowest levels of other livelihoods like non-agricultural labour. Forced migration has a direct bearing on family stability and educational access. A distinction must be made between cultures of nomadism (where the community negotiates mobility, settlement, and residence in familiar ways that are culturally rooted), and forced/distress migration, which throws communities into precarity at every level. Migration was high in Tamil Nadu and Chhattisgarh at 40 per cent, and 59 per cent in Telangana. In Telangana, 54 per cent of migrant households reported migration once a year with around 80 per cent reporting one— to three-month duration. Wage labour accounted for 31 per cent of total households. In Tamil Nadu, 53 per cent of households reported non-agricultural labour as their primary occupation. The educational status of 'denotified' communities across states reveals that the 'never-enrolled' were high across states, more than a quarter, except in Maharashtra (5.5 per cent), Tamil Nadu (18 per cent), and Andhra Pradesh (21 per cent). However, the 'completion' reported by respondents indicates discontinuation of education after primary or at best secondary school in a majority of cases. Migration was cited as a major reason for dropping out of school or not enrolling children across states. Interviews with teachers in Madhya Pradesh, for instance, revealed the pervasiveness of negative stereotypes that inhibit teacher–pupil relations, aggravate absenteeism, and retard retention at the school level. Hostels and ashram schools have been part of efforts to universalize education among vulnerable Adivasi communities.

The first NCDNT report (2008) revealed a sharp gender disparity in accessing hostels at primary and upper primary levels, but also a virtual disappearance of boys at the secondary and higher secondary levels. The CSD study did not show that provision of residential schools for children from denotified communities had significantly enhanced educational attainment.

Across the states, the involvement of parents in decision-making with respect to education and schooling of children was found to be lacking. While this might be in part due to the lack of education and awareness among parents, a deeper reason lies in the physical, and social distance of the school from their habitations. Notwithstanding this trend, parents wanted both their sons and daughters to study well and secure government jobs. Given that distance to the school was a major factor in obstructing uninterrupted schooling, our findings suggested that reduction in dropouts, and increase in retention by schools might be possible by locating schools in the proximity of neighbourhoods and habitations. This could also ensure more active participation of parents and community in the school lives of their children—a concern that connects back to the forced removal of children from parents and community in the era of colonial settlements discussed earlier.

A majority of the students across the nine states that participated in this study attended government schools—between 88 per cent and 90 per cent in Madhya Pradesh, Gujarat, Maharashtra, Chhattisgarh, Karnataka, Tamil Nadu, and Andhra Pradesh, and 75 per cent in Telangana and Goa. Despite the proliferation of private schools across the country, this study demonstrated yet again that children from the most marginalized communities continue to attend government schools, leading to the inference that strengthening government schooling is an immediate need—in terms of infrastructure, teacher capabilities, and curricular reform. More generally, the study findings pointed to the inadequacy of existing institutional arrangements which are minimal and poor in quality, and ridden with in-built forms of exclusion that obstruct schooling. The findings also highlighted how specific local factors influenced the access communities had to these arrangements. Evidence suggests that many existing measures do not recognize the specificities of aspirations and needs of these vulnerable communities, and more seriously there is a continuing reproduction of vulnerability which is reflected directly in the arenas of education and livelihood choices available.

Conclusion

A recent report of the National Commission for Denotified, Nomadic, and Semi Nomadic Tribes lists a total of 1100 communities, of which 312 are denotified tribes. Their poor access to public goods, systems of justice and reparations, and their continuing stigmatization despite the formal dismantling of segregation practices continue to subjugate and repress the largest section of these communities. Education and stable, decent employment are aspirations largely unrealized with affirmative action being fragmented across categories in which these communities are arbitrarily distributed. Some of them suffer the humiliation of untouchability practices, others the stigma, and humiliation of criminalization, yet others slide off the radar of affirmative action policy and social protection completely, forced to remain servile, and invisible. Existing policy regimes have not improved the status of denotified and nomadic communities. They continue to be denied effective voice, and suffer from an inter-generational neglect that deprives them of real, and viable opportunities for social and economic mobility.

Regimes of dispossession in India are marked by histories of occupation and surveillance under different state regimes and by dominant social groups on the sub-continent. As Levien observes (2015, p. 147), 'the concept of regimes of dispossession encourages us to see dispossession as a form of coercive redistribution that states use to facilitate different forms of accumulation and class interests in different periods'. While Levien applies this concept to land under capitalism, I suggest that it is useful to understand the experience of 'denotified communities' through the concept of regimes of dispossession, where territoriality (as distinct from land) is at the core and geographies of experience become intelligible through the prism of territory (Delaney, 2005). For these more than any other group, the life experience of entire communities is intimately connected to their spatial organization—whether these are homelands or the mobile territory of peripatetic communities or indeed incarceration in settlements under surveillance or custodial facilities, as the case may be. The criminalization of nomadic, peripatetic, and foraging and petty trading communities under the Criminal Tribes Acts of the British government importantly brought into play notions of proprietorial control by the state of commodities, trading, access to lands, and forests, the freedom of movement and autonomy of livelihoods (Radhakrishna, 2008).

Dispossession itself has been complex and layered, homogenizing livelihoods, and lifeworlds while delegitimizing them. The most common description of foragers and hunters-gatherers for instance, has been that they have lived in isolation. Yet, there is ample evidence that for centuries, foraging communities have lived in contact with rural and urban agglomerations (Rao and Casimir, 2003, p. 13); studies have shown that very few nomadic communities subsist solely on foraging—a significantly larger number sustain themselves in a mixed economy of foraging and trading in wild produce (Rao and Casimir, 2003, pp. 23–24). Importantly for our purposes, there is evidence of shifts that communities have made from cultivation to foraging and peripatetic livelihoods consequent on displacement, thus challenging the linear narratives of tribal development and progress from nomadism to sedentarism (Rao and Casimir, 2003, pp. 22–25). Social relations and hierarchical socialities have been at the centre of the stigmatization of denotified and nomadic tribes. In the case of the foragers for instance, forager/non-forager relations are characterized by a 'suspicious subservience met by contemptuous paternalism' (Rao and Casimir, 2003, p. 23)—with foragers forced to reckon with a society that treats them as almost subhuman. Social humiliation is enmeshed in dispossession.

The violence of the colonial state transmitted through the CTA that overlaid the penal code rendered aggravated surveillance, carcerality and degrading punishment like whipping legitimate and lawful in the matter of 'hereditary criminals,' and conflated intersecting vulnerabilities. This vulnerability is carried forward on 'denotification' into the constitutional democracy in the form of fatal stigmatization, custodial violence, and death as evident in the narratives of Laxman Gaikwad and the case of Budhan Sabar.[5] The reverberations of colonial punitive regimes interlocked with and often indistinct from violent caste practices are felt in the successive decades after 1950. The prison and police lock-up—custodial institutions of the state—are the frames through which we first begin to 'see' the denotified tribes—Laxman Gaikwad and Budhan Sabar's case present us with two narratives that fold together notwithstanding the physical distance between them or the fact that they belong to different tribes from different regions that are widely different from each other.

The arrest of Budhan Sabar in February 1998, on charges of theft, his torture in police custody, his judicial remand and eyewitness accounts of his torture in jail and death in judicial custody became a milestone in resistance against social and state oppression by members of denotified communities. In his entry in the General Diary pertaining to the arrest of Budhan Sabar, police officer Asoke Roy wrote:

> I interrogated accused Budhan Sabar thoroughly when he voluntarily disclosed that he along with Jagan Sabar, Kalipada Sabar, Paru Kirtan Sabar and others of one Akarbaid and neighbouring villages had committed dacoity at Balaji Bus about five

---

[5] Also Renke, Balkrishna, Lakshmibhai Patni, Meena Radhakrishna. 'The Myth of Vigilante Justice', NCDNT press statement, 21 September 2007 (on file with author).

months ago and sold the stolen articles [to] Kalipada Pramanick, Kartick Pramanick and others of Akarbaid.

The Paschim Banga Kheria Sabar Kalyan Samity under the leadership of Mahasweta Devi took Budhan's case to Calcutta High Court and secured compensation for his custodial murder for his wife—a breakthrough in the law that has historically only been pitted against these communities, undermining basic constitutional claims to freedom and justice.

Laxman Gaikwad's poignant account in a sense sums up the current predicament of the denotified communities:

> If a bird is confined to life in a house by clipping its wings lest it flies away, it is forced to remain in the same house all its life. Even if it wishes to fly, it cannot. Absolutely in the same way once a person from these tribes is shoved into jail right at his birth, he gets inextricably bonded to it. Even if … the person himself tries to escape from it he cannot come out of that hell … He bears the indelible brand of a criminal on his forehead for all to see. (Gaikwad, 1998, p. 200)

References

Anderson, Clare. 2004. *Legible Bodies: Race, Criminality and Colonialism in South Asia*. Oxford & NY: Berg.

Chandavarkar, Raj. 1998. *Imperial Power and Popular Politics: Class, Resistance and the State in India, c. 1850–1950*. Cambridge: Cambridge University Press.

Delaney, David. 2005. *Territory: A Short Introduction*. Oxford: Blackwell Publishing. Ebook.

Devy, Ganesh N. 2012. 'The Tejgadh Experiment: Culture and Development'. *India International Centre Quarterly*, 39(2) (Autumn): 27–40.

Gaikwad, Laxman. 1998. *The Branded* (Trans. P. A. Kolharkar). New Delhi: Sahitya Akademi, 1998. (Trans. of *Uchalya*).

Gandhi, Malli. 2008. *Denotified Tribes: Dimensions of Change*. New Delhi: Kanishka Publishers.

Gandhi, Malli. 2017. *Educating Ex-Criminal Tribes: Issues and Concerns*. New Delhi: Rawat Publications.

Guha, Ranajit. 1983. *Elementary Aspects of Peasant Insurgency in Colonial India*. Delhi: Oxford University Press, 1983.

Kannabiran, Kalpana. 2017, 28 October. 'Vulnerable Communities'. Editorial, *Economic and Political Weekly*, 52(42–43): 9.

Kannabiran, Kalpana, Sujit Kumar Mishra, Soumya Vinayan, and K. Jafar. 2018. 'Education and Its Discontents: Investigating Barriers to Schooling among De-Notified and Nomadic Communities'. *Journal of Social Inclusion Studies*, 4(1): 80–103.

Krishnan, P. S. 2014. 'Introduction'. In Malli Gandhi (Ed.), *Denotified Tribes: Retrospect and Prospect* (pp. xxi–lviii). New Delhi: Manak Publications.

Radhakrishna, Meena. (2001) 2008. *Dishonoured by History: Criminal Tribes and British Colonial Policy*. Hyderabad: Orient Longman.

Radhakrishna, Meena. 2008, October. 'Stratification among the Disadvantaged: Identifying the Rock-bottom Layers'. *Indian Journal of Industrial Relations*, 44(2): 201–208.

Radhakrishna, Meena. 2009. 'The Hunter and the Hunted: Nomadic Communities and Indian Conservation Strategies'. Paper presented at the international conference on 'Terrestrial environments and Their histories in modern India'. 1–2 May 2009, organized by South Asian Studies Council and the MacMillan Center, Anthropology Department, Yale University.

National Advisory Council (2011). Working Group on Denotified and Nomadic Tribes. Available at http://www.nirmanindia.org/Report/dnt_draft.pdf, accessed on 6 July 2017.

Rao, Aparna, and Michael J. Casimir. 2003. 'Nomadism in South Asia: An Introduction In Aparna Rao and Michael J. Casimir (Eds.), *Nomadism in South Asia*, New Delhi: Oxford University Press.

Report of the Backward Classes Commission. New Delhi: Government of India, 1956 (Kalelkar Commission).

Report of the High Level Committee on Socio-Economic, Health and Educational Status of Tribal Communities in India. Government of India, 2014 (Xaxa Report 2014).

Report of the National Commission for Denotified, Nomadic and Semi-Nomadic Tribes. Government of India, 2008 (NCDNT).

Schwarz, Henry. 2010. *Constructing the Criminal Tribe in Colonial India: Acting like a Thief*. West Sussex: Wiley Blackwell.

Sen, Satadru. 2000. *Disciplining Punishment: Colonialism and Convict Society in the Andamans*, New Delhi: Oxford University Press.

Singha, Radhika. 2000. *A Despotism of Law: Crime and Justice in Early Colonial India*. Delhi: Oxford University Press.

Tolen, Rachel. 1991, February. 'Colonizing and Transforming the Criminal Tribesman: The Salvation Army in British India'. *American Ethnologist*, 18(1): 106–125.

SECTION VII

EMERGING ENTANGLEMENTS OF CASTE

Editors' Introduction

THIS section has chapters on entanglements of caste with spheres of social life where it is least expected to matter. These chapters further show its plasticity and unpredictability. They allow us to shift our perspective on the subject, in a manner that enables us to re-emphasize that caste needs to be studied on ground, as a lived reality, and without a prejudged path of its inevitable evolution.

Of all the social scientists, economists have been among the last to recognize caste as a reality that needed to be taken into account for analysing structures and processes of economic life. It is perhaps hard for the mainstream economics to deal with a subject like caste, given that caste continues to be popularly seen as a collective identity belonging to the religious and cultural realms, unique to traditional India. As such a culture-centric understanding implied its inevitable disappearance with the process of economic growth and the rise of modern institutions, its investigation by economists did not appear as a priority. However, this has changed. A good number of economists have come to recognize that collective processes like ethnicity and caste or jati have relevance for economic analysis and it is now clear to them that these cultural and relational identities structure networks and markets. Such processes also become important in the policy domain, where economists are often called-upon to provide suggestions and models. Guilhem Cassan maps this journey in is chapter. As he stresses, what is perhaps the most decisive reason behind the economists' growing involvement with the subject of caste is on the growing availability of hard data, that helps take the study of caste beyond speculation and domains of rituals and past traditions. It has also enabled them to engage with subjects like discriminations and inequalities more concretely and to understand the role of caste in the shaping of labour markets.

In the following chapter, Ajantha Subramanian spells out how the idea of merit has come to be deployed to conceal and legitimize the privileges of caste in contemporary India. Those occupying positions of privilege invoke the classical liberal binary between ascription and merit where the latter is invoked and understood as 'a democratizing force favoring individual achievement over inherited privilege'. However, the reality on ground is very different. Invoking her own work on engineering education, she argues that 'the institutional spaces most identified as meritocratic continue to be overwhelmingly upper caste in composition'. Attempts at opening up these spaces to lower castes through affirmative action and other democratizing measures are consistently met with fervent opposition, not in the name of caste, but in the name of preserving merit'. She goes on to argue that a way out of the prevailing scenario does not lie in erasing caste from the public sphere by going back to either 'liberal individualism or class politics' but in confronting the reality of persistent ascription-based hierarchies.

Continuing this discussion from another and more quantitative angle, Divya Vaid, in the following chapter, provides an overview of the patterns of social mobility in relation to caste. As is also discussed in several other chapters, despite the popular view of caste being a stable structure, it did not induce complete immobility. There were possibilities of social mobility even within the hierarchical logic of caste. Vaid's focus is on contemporary times, when individual social mobility becomes the dominant norm across caste communities, through education and/or migration. However, caste continues to matter even in processes of individual mobility and it does so in different ways. Those from the upper castes invariably find their caste fellows helping them in the process of going-up in the modern economy, both in class and status, and those lower down in the traditional hierarchy find caste working as an inhibiting factor. Besides caste, gender also matters, though it intersects with caste and class mobilities in complicated ways. Class mobility, for example, could be detrimental for work participation for a woman from a traditionally lower caste background.

The question of the intersection of gender with caste has indeed been critical, both in writings on caste as well as in the politics of Dalit groups. Given that caste continues to shape kinship and marriage practices, it also structures gender relations. In his chapter on caste and gender, Pushpesh Kumar shows how the question of the intersection between the two began to be discussed in India much before the gender-race intersection became a central issue among western feminist academics. It was during the second half of the 19th century and the early 20th century that caste-reformers like Jyotirao Phule, Periyar E. V. Ramasamy, and B. R. Ambedkar took it up. Not only did they politicize the question but they also provided us with important theoretical leads. The feminist scholarship in India also engaged with it while looking at subjects like kinship and marriage. However, the question acquired major visibility only when it was taken-up by Dalit feminists in the 1990s. Kumar also points the limitations of identity-centric articulations of gender and caste by bringing-in a brief discussion of the questions of sexual citizenship in relation to queer individuals and their sense of marginality, even within the Dalit feminist movements.

Finally, in the age of globalization, one necessarily wonders what happens to caste when Indians go out of India. Radha Modi begins her chapter on 'caste and diaspora' with a clear assertion that they take their caste along. However, as she shows through an extensive review of writings on the subject, the trajectories of such a process are very diverse. Indian migrations abroad have been happening for a long time, starting with colonial rulers taking them to other colonies as indentured labour to the migrations of well-qualifies professionals to North America occupying high-end jobs in the service sector. Caste and kinship networks help them stabilize in foreign land. Though a large majority of the Indians in diaspora are from privileged upper castes, Dalits too have been part of these migrations. Her chapter provides an extensive account of the nature of the relationship between the upper caste Indians and Dalits in diasporic settings. While there is evidence of the persistence of caste prejudice and discriminatory practices, replicating the 'homeland', it is relatively easier for Dalit groups to contest such practices when abroad. As also discussed by Eva-Maria Hardtmann in her chapter, Dalits in diaspora are rather well networked. Generational changes further have implications for caste relations. Second and third generations of diaspora appear less attached to their caste identities as the first generation is. However, this is not a simple process of moving out of caste over time. Successive generations tend to stay embedded in the kinship and caste networks they inherit.

Though seemingly different in focus, these chapters open-up important questions, which are not only empirically exciting to explore but they also have major theoretical implications.

CHAPTER 38

THE ECONOMICS OF CASTE

GUILHEM CASSAN

CASTE plays a central role in the daily life of more than a billion Indians. Indeed, it affects their most private choices, such as marriage (Banerjee et al., 2009): in 2011–2012, 95 per cent of married women declared that they had married within caste,[1] with very little change in this pattern over time, as illustrated in Figure 38.1. It also affects important economic decisions such as employment: in 2011–2012, 17.3 per cent of working age males were working in their jati's traditional occupation (Cassan et al., 2022).[2] The participation in collective action is also affected by caste as is exemplified by the importance of caste in political mobilization.

In fact, caste is an important determinant of most economic decisions in India. However, despite this role of caste in economic behaviour, it is only recently that economics has begun studying caste in depth.

The growing availability of micro datasets since the late 1970's combined with a growing willingness to study the role of each country's specific institutional and cultural arrangement in economic behaviour have enabled economists, and development economists in particular, to delve into what they often loosely called 'informal institutions' or 'culture'. In the case of India, this has meant, among other things, a growing attention to the caste system.

The first focus of economists has been to study caste as an object of public policies: economists have very fruitfully contributed to the debate about the effect of the various dimensions of reservations for low castes (Cassan, 2019), as is detailed in Ashwini Deshpande's chapter in that handbook. In that literature, however, by construction, the definition of caste tends to be restrained to official categories: Other Backward Classes, Scheduled Castes, and Scheduled Tribes. Economists are now broadening their scope to other dimensions of the role of castes, in particular at the jati level.

---

[1] *Source*: IHDS, 2011–2012, computations of the author.
[2] If individuals were allocated randomly across occupations, only 12 per cent of the population should be working on its traditional occupation.

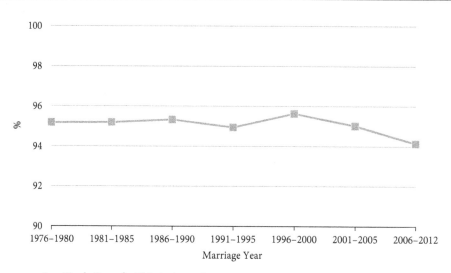

FIGURE 38.1 Evolution of within jati marriage.
Source: IHDS 2011-12, author's computation
Key: in 1976-1980, roughly 95% of marriages took place within jati.

To understand the approach taken by economists, it is may be useful to rely on the often used dichotomy of ethnicitization versus sanskritization of caste (Jaffrelot, 2000), since it reflects quite well the way economists have approached the caste system. Indeed, a first approach taken by economists to analyse the role of jatis has been to consider it as a network of mutual help, very similar to any other ethnic group. According to this view, jatis offers many services to its members, which may come at the cost of a lack of mobility, as network effects tend to lead to a lower socio-economic mobility, which may be hurtful in the long run.

A second approach, influenced by the contributions of other social sciences, considers jatis as part of a system: a single jati cannot be studied independently from the others, since one key feature of the caste system is that it determines inter-caste relationship.

Finally, a new promising field of research begins to look into the interaction between jati and gender, showing how the variations in gender norms across castes may lead to unexpected responses to a changing political or economic environment.

Caste as an Ethnic Group

The dominant economic approach to the caste system is that of a network which provides services to its members, very similar to the role offered by the membership in an ethnic group: access to information, access to insurance, access to employment, etc...

In that view, there is nothing specific to the caste system that would distinguish it from an ethnic group. Indeed, each jati is seen as a network, providing services to its members, while the system as a whole is ignored.

In the economists' perspective, one key role of the state is to help resolving 'market imperfections', the frequent situations in which the market left alone is dysfunctional. Take the case of the insurance market, for example. In most OECD countries, there exists a state organized compulsory social insurance scheme that will protect everyone against risks such as diseases or accidents. The state will also organize the protection against risks such as the loss of employment. As a matter of fact, it has long been documented that market forces by themselves will not be able to provide such highly needed services, justifying the intervention of the state in these sectors.

However, the state itself may not be able to correct these market imperfections: it may suffer from imperfections of its own. The 'public choice' school of thought has for example long documented that the state itself is not a benevolent actor whose sole objective is to maximize the welfare of its citizens. The state faces its own constraints and own objectives, which may different from the interest of the citizens. What is more, even if the state was indeed benevolent, if may not always have the means of its benevolence. Lant Pritchett (2009) has for example famously called the Indian state a 'flailing state', a state with a well-functioning head, with willing, and competent public servants, but a dysfunctionning body, not able to implement the decisions taken at the head.

Therefore, in a context in which both market and state fail to provide such vital services as access to finance and insurance, other alternatives are necessary.

Economists, and in particular, development economists and economic historians, have studied extensively such alternatives, often labelled 'informal institutions', and which rely on some form of mutual help network (Greif, 1993; Fafchamps and Lund, 2003; La Ferrara, 2003), typically relying on an ethnic, religious, or caste network. One key aspect of these networks of mutual help is that they rely on informal sanction mechanisms, typically based on reputation, trust, and threat of ostracism. One may rely on the help of the members of the network only provided that the other members think that their help may be rewarded in the future, very much in the spirit of the gift-counter gift approach emphasized by Mauss (1925).

The caste system provides a way for economists to test this theory of ethnic networks as mutual help groups. Indeed, the diversity of jatis, even at the local level, is unique, and allows economists to look at these network effects within fairly small geographical areas, such as cities or villages. However, collecting large quantitative data at the jati level—a requirement for mainstream economics analysis, which relies on statistical approaches—is notoriously complex, due to the numerous synonyms that a same jati can have, as well as to the polysemy of the word caste itself. One only needs to look into the first attempts of the British census colonial administration in the late 12th century, to convince oneself of the difficulty of the task (Conlon, 1981). It is therefore only relatively recently that economists have managed to apply their tools to jatis, either by collecting their own data, or by exploiting systematically the colonial census data, which contains a wealth of jati level statistics (Banerjee and Somanathan, 2007; Cassan, 2015).

This availability of data has enabled economists to deepen their analysis of the role of jatis. Munshi and Rosenzweig (2009) for example used the REDS data, representative of rural India in 1999, to show that 20 per cent of the households they surveyed participated in some form of jati based insurance in the previous year. Households sending either loans or gifts to fellow jati members would send an amount close to 9 per cent of their income, while those loans and gifts would represent more than 40 per cent of the income of those that benefited from them. It is therefore true that the jati network represents a quantitatively important resource of mutual help.

To understand the way in which jati network and insurance motives interact, Rosenzweig and Stark (1989) propose an interpretation of the organization of the rural Indian marriage practices as a way to provide insurance. Indeed, in a rural setting, in which agriculture is the main source of income, income tend to be volatile: it will rely extensively on variable climatic conditions, which have strong consequences on the harvest. In such a risky context, access to insurance is paramount. Marriages in rural India tend to be organized across villages but within jati. For Rosenzweig and Stark (1989), the reason why this is the case is that the local weather may vary across villages, and therefore, the weather induced fluctuations in income will not be exactly similar across villages. As a consequence, by having married a daughter in another village, households may ask for help in bad years. The fact that the marriages are organized within jati helps building a reputation which may be tarnished if the family proves not to be reliable.

Jatis have also been shown to help providing information, in particular for accessing employment. Munshi (2011) for example studies the market of diamond in Mumbai. In this specific market, most transactions do not rely on explicitly written contract, but rather on the trust between the buyer and the seller, when the seller typically accepts to sell the diamond at credit. In the absence of written contract, trust is paramount: the seller needs to know that the buyer is worthy enough to be trusted with an important credit with no formal contract written, and therefore, no possibility to turn to the court in the eventuality of a default. In such a context, the reputation of buyers is crucial. To enter in such a market, one needs to be introduced by an insider, and to benefit from his recommendation. Historically, this market has been dominated by two jatis, the Marwaris and the Palanpuris, whose traditional occupation is linked to trade. However, a third jati, the Kathiawari, has managed to enter this sector, despite being a relatively lower caste, whose traditional occupation is linked to agriculture. Following a sudden increase in the supply of diamonds, some Kathiawari managed to move from the low skilled occupation of diamond cutting to diamond selling in the 1970's. These new entrants managed to help fellow jati members set up their own business in the sector, leading to a large increase in the share of diamond firms owned by Kathiawaris from the 1980's onwards. That is, in this specific setting, the sharing of information and the density of the caste network[3] allowed members of a relatively low caste to successfully enter a new, more skilled occupation, despite its original disadvantage.

In the political world as well, jatis have been shown to offer several services to its members. Munshi and Ronsenzweig (2010), using the REDS data, for example argue that jati network at the ward level in a panchayat allow for a better control of the actions of local politicians. Elected personnel coming from a jati with a large population in the ward will tend to see their behaviour monitored, and will face social sanctions in case of misbehaviour. In the context of these very local elections, thus, the existence of jati network may increase the quality of political action.

Therefore, jatis do appear to indeed offer services to its member akin to those offered by other informal network such as ethnic groups. And these services are quantitatively important.

Caste and Inefficiency

However, those network-based services typically come at a cost. Greif (1993), in his study of the community of Maghribi traders in 11th-century Mediterranean, famously underlined how the establishment of such networks can be extremely beneficiary in the short run, but may lead to long run costs, if the economic environment changes and individuals are caught in a network that doesn't allow them to benefit from these new economic opportunities.

These insights have been applied to the caste system (Munshi, 2019). Munshi and Rosenzweig (2009) for example explored whether attachment to the jati network, may not be a reason why the level of rural to urban migration is so low in India. Indeed, India's urbanization rate stands out compared to countries comparable in terms of economic development. As a matter of fact, compared to China, Indonesia or Nigeria, India's urbanization rate was quite similar until the late 1970's, when it started to diverge drastically, with a level of urbanization remaining remarkably low. Could it be that the importance of the services offered to its members by the jati network is in fact so high that in spite of the development of new economic opportunities in urban areas, people tend to prefer to remain in rural areas, with their fellow jati members? Using the REDS data, a very detailed data on migration, marriage, and caste-based insurance arrangement, Munshi and Rosenzweig show strong supportive evidence that the characteristic of the insurance services offered by a jati strongly affects the probability to both marry outside the jati and migrate. They show that jatis do offer a

---

[3] The author notably underlines the role of within jati and within industry marriages in strengthening the network.

strong level of insurance to their members, as measured by tests of risk sharing,[4] and that individuals associated to the benefits of these insurance tend indeed to migrate less, and to out marry less than individuals that benefit only marginally from these services.

However, this result is only suggesting that there may be dynamic inefficiencies: we do not know if indeed, in the long run, it would have been better for individuals to migrate or no, even if this evidence is quite suggestive.

Munshi and Rosenzweig (2006) go further in developing evidence of these dynamic inefficiencies. Looking into the schooling choices in Mumbai, they show that the returns to being educated in an English-speaking school increases with the economic liberalization of the early 1990's. However, the jatis who tend to rely heavily on jati network to gain access to employment (typically low castes in blue-collar type of jobs) will tend to maintain their children in Marathi speaking schools despite the constraint that this represents for the professional career of their children. Indeed, their children will be less able to speak English, and therefore, to benefit from the newly developing economic activities of the city. Obviously, one may think that the reason why these children are not scholarized in English-speaking schools may be linked to discrimination against lower castes. That is indeed possible. However, Munshi and Rosenzweig show that this pattern is only true for male and not female children: female children are increasingly scholarized in English-speaking schools, while male children are not, which is at odds with a simple discrimination explanation. The explanation of the authors is that the jati networks enabling the access to these blue-collar jobs were typically useful only for males (since females would not work in these occupations). Therefore, the social identity of the male members of these jati revolved around working in a blue collar occupation. Putting one's male child in an English-speaking school would be an indication of a betrayal of that identity, which may come at a cost (either an individual cost, the feeling of betraying one's identity, or a social cost, with some form of social sanction against the parents putting their male children in an English-speaking school), while no such cost would exist for girls. Therefore, while their parents have benefited from the jati network, which has allowed them to enter blue-collar occupations, male children may suffer from the very existence of these networks, which forces them into a career path which may not be relevant anymore, given the changes in economic conditions.

Do these rigidities matter at the level of the entire Indian economy? Cassan et al. (2022) combined jati level information from the 1911 census, the Indian Human

---

[4] Which measures the extent to which an income shock faced by a member in a given year affects the consumption of that member during that year, if other members of the network do not face that shock. If risk sharing is high, then facing an income shock at the individual level should not affect individual consumption, since network level insurance mechanism would allow that individual to spend more than her income: consumption in a given year should only depend on the total income of the network. In the absence of risk sharing mechanism, then consumption in a given year should be highly correlated to income in that same year, at the individual level, but not at the network level.

Development Survey (2011–2012), the Demographic and Health Survey (2005–2006) as well as the People of India Project (Singh, 1996) to compute a large-scale database on occupation choices, wages, and jati traditional occupation. They use this dataset to estimate the cost that the rigidities linked to the caste system may impose on the economy. By preventing individuals from freely choosing their occupation, the caste system may slow down economic activities, as already alluded to by Ambedkar.[5] Indeed, the caste system, which imposes an occupation on individuals may lead to 'misallocation of talent': individuals end up working in an occupation not best suited for them, which comes at a cost for the economy as a whole. Indeed, these authors find that individuals tend to be twice as likely to work in the traditional occupation of their jati than in any other occupation. On top of that, they find evidence that within a given jati, individuals working in the traditional occupation appear less productive than individuals working in another occupation. That is, there is evidence that members of jatis working in their traditional occupation may very well have been more productive in another occupation.

Therefore, even when controlling for network and human capital transmission effects, jati is a strong determinant of occupational choice, which prevents individuals to work in the occupation in which they would be more productive, leading, in general equilibrium, to worst economic performances. The authors however show that this effect is largely attenuated by the positive effect on productivity of having both a strong caste network and strong intergenerational human capital transmission in traditional occupations.

In the political sphere, also, there are drawbacks related to the reliance on jati networks. While at the very local level, as already discussed, there may be evidence of benefits of an increased control of a jati on its representative, at other levels of representation, these benefits may disappear. Banerjee and Pande (2007) have for example shown that for legislative elections, the tendency to vote for ones' caste leads to a lower quality of elected personnel. Indeed, if electors vote for candidates based on their caste identity, and, because the elections are at the state level and not at the panchayat level, they cannot exert any direct control on their action, then the caste identity of the candidates may compensate for the lack of skill.

Along the same lines, Lehne et al. (2018) have shown that the delivery of contracts for road construction in the PMGSY program may be diverted due to jati based linked between the members of the legislative assembly in whose constituency a road is being built and contractors. Indeed, they show that when members of the legislative assembly and contractors share the same last name (a proxy for sharing the same jati), the probability for the contractor to win the road construction contract increases by 83 per cent.

---

[5] '[Industry] undergoes rapid and abrupt changes. [. . .] an individual must be free to change his occupation. [. . .] Now the Caste System will not allow Hindus to take to occupations where they are wanted, if they do not belong to them by heredity. [. . .] By not permitting readjustment of occupations, Caste becomes a direct cause of much of the unemployment we see in the country' (Ambedkar, 1936).

Hence, caste networks appear to impose significant costs on the economy: by restraining socio-economic mobility and by affecting the functioning of the state, it affects the performance of the economy as the whole.

Caste as a System: Homo Economicus Meets Homo Hierarchicus

Studying jatis as a network has yielded very useful results, and has deepened our knowledge of its role in the Indian economy. However, this approach also neglects many of its important aspects. In particular, it puts aside that castes are part of a system, and that studying each jati independently from the other does not allow a full understanding of the role of jatis in economic decisions.

A new strand of studies, often drawing from contributions of other social sciences, is embracing the specificities of castes. Indeed, castes are part of a system which codifies relationship across castes, often in a hierarchical manner.

A novel strand of research is specifically focusing on these aspects of the caste system, often by collecting specifically tailored dataset, or by offering a new take on already existing datasets.[6]

Anderson (2011) has for example studied the trade of water across jatis in rural Uttar Pradesh and Bihar. Embracing the concept of caste dominance (Srinivas, 1955, 1987), she studies how the constraint put on the sharing of water across castes affects agricultural productivity. In particular, she shows that in villages in which low castes are the dominant castes, then access to water for members of these castes is not an issue, while the opposite is true when high castes are dominant. This results in dramatic differences in agricultural productivity for low castes in villages not dominated by them, despite the fact that there are no differences across those two types of villages in terms of the quantity and quality of land these castes own. Her main finding is that the agricultural yields of low castes relying on water buying and residing in villages in which high castes are dominating (and controlling water access) is 45 per cent lower than those of low castes relying on water buying but residing in villages in which water sellers are of the same caste.

Anderson et al. (2015), despite not explicitly referring to it, analyse the political consequences of the jajmani system (Wiser, 1936). Collecting a novel dataset on political and socio-economic relationships in rural Maharashtra, they offer an explanation to the puzzle of how, in a democracy such as India, in which the large majority of the population lives in poverty, the policies implemented often are not to the benefits of the poor. In the specific context that they study, they analyse how, at the panchayat level,

---

[6] Note that I do not to present here the large body of work pertaining to caste-based discrimination, as this is covered in Ashwini Deshpande's chapter.

the Maratha jati came to maintain its political dominance in a democratic context, and to implement policies going against the interests of the poor majority.[7] Their argument is that Maratha landlords, in the villages that they dominate, will buy the votes of agricultural labourers by offering them insurance. This will allow the local dominant Maratha to get the upper hand on policy delivery at the local level and therefore a better control of the local labour force. Thanks to the depth of their data collection, Anderson et al. (2015) can show that indeed, in Maratha dominated villages, landless household tend to report that they have more often access to informal insurance than in non-Maratha dominated villages, but that in those same villages, those same household have a lower access to pro-poor policies, while Maratha landlords obtain higher profit from their land.

Therefore, by considering castes as embedded within a system, economists have been able to uncover and measure how important this system of relations affect economic decisions, as exemplified by the economic costs due to the absence of trade of water across castes, as well as the capture of local electoral offices by dominant castes.

Caste and Gender

A burgeoning field in the economics literature delves into the interaction between caste and gender. One main focus of attention of this literature is the fact that gender norms, and in particular, women mobility and labour force participation, widely differ across jatis. Indeed, it has long been documented that women of lower castes background tend to be facing less constraints in that dimension than women from high caste background (Mencher, 1988; Chakravarti, 1993; Kapadia, 1997; Drèze & Sen, 2002; Joshi et al., 2017).

Therefore, differences in jati level reaction to changes in the economic or political environment may be linked to these differences in gender norms.

Luke and Munshi (2011) show that in the context of the tea estates of the High Range in Kerala and Tamil Nadu, low caste households who have migrated to work on these tea estates seem to give a higher education to their children than high caste household working in the same estates, despite having similar income. In particular, they show that when the relative income of the mother in the household is high, the education of children increases, but only for low caste household. Their interpretation is that while women may want to educate their children more than men do, and that women with a relatively high income within their household may have a higher bargaining power, it is only women of low caste that succeed in rising the education of their children when

---

[7] As measured by the non implementation of pro-poor policies such as the distribution of Below Poverty Line cards or access to Employment Guarantee Scheme programs.

Table 38.1 Reservations and Panchayat President's characteristics

	No Reservations	Reserved for Women	Reserved for LC
HC men	50.9%	0%	3.1%
LC Men	42.6%	4.6%	87.6%
HC Women	3.7%	30.8%	0%
LC Women	2.8%	64.6%	9.3%
Number of Elections	108	65	97

Source: The REDS 2006 data. Elections reserved for both women and LC are excluded.

their relative income is high. That is, it is likely that the social norms against women participation in household decision among high castes may be too high for them to be able to influence the education of their children, compared to low castes.[8] In their view, this is indicative that novel economic opportunities may be seized more easily by women of low castes, one of the group the most disadvantaged in India, due to the fact that they are less constrained by social norms.

In the same line of thought, Cassan and Vandewalle (2021) look into how the relatively high physical mobility of low caste women may interact with gender specific policies. Analysing the implementation of quotas for women in panchayat's presidents elections, using data representative of rural India, they show that in elections reserved for women, the representation of low castes increases drastically. Table 38.1 shows that when an election is not reserved, 50.9 per cent of the elections are won by high caste males.[9] However, when the election is reserved for women, the candidate that wins that election is a low caste woman in 64.6 per cent of the cases. That is, the gender quota not only changes the gender of the president but also, often, its caste. Taking advantage of the wealth of information available in the dataset, they can then show that the women elected under this quota do not only implement policies closer to the preferences of women (as documented in Chattopadhyay and Duflo, 2004) but also closer to the preferences of low castes.

The research on the interaction between gender and caste therefore appears to be a promising field, providing novel and thought provoking findings. It shows in particular that the dynamic inefficiencies and the caste hierarchy discussed above may become questioned as women of low castes managed to benefit from novel political and

---

[8] Note that the authors also find evidence of backlash, as marital violence also seem to be higher against women of low castes whose relative income is high.

[9] They define high caste as non OBC, non-SC, and non-ST, while low castes are defined as OBC, SC, or ST. Muslims are almost not represented in their sample. In that definition, high castes represent around 20 per cent of the population, and high caste males 10 per cent of the population. They are therefore over represented.

economic opportunities better than their high castes counterpart, which may prove to have far reaching consequences for the caste system as a whole in the long run.

Discussion

In the last decades, economists have entered the debate on the role of jatis in the Indian economy. Using both tools that were developed for different contexts, and developing specific ones for the study of the caste system, the contribution of economists has allowed to greatly broaden our knowledge of the role of caste in the Indian economy. In particular, we now have a better grasp of the quantitative extent of this importance.

However, there are only few datasets available to scholars. Indeed, scholars have either relied on datasets that they had collected by themselves, which may not be an option for many, or on one specific dataset, the REDS data, the access to which implies high administrative costs. Until recently, economists had remained shy of systematically analysing the jati data available in public datasets such as the Indian Human Development Survey or the Demographic and Health Survey. With the decrease in data treatment cost, this has become possible (Cassan, 2019; Cassan et al., 2022): the quantitative analysis of jati data is 'democratizing' and economists are now more and more able to study the role of jati with such publicly available data or via clever ways of treating administrative data (Lehne et al., 2018). We can therefore hope for an important increase in the study of jatis in the forthcoming years.

References

Ambedkar, Babasaheb. 1936. *The Annihilation of Caste*.
Anderson, Siwan. 2011. 'Caste as an Impediment to Trade'. *American Economic Journal: Applied Economics*, 3(1).
Anderson, Siwan, Patrick François, and Ashok Kotwal. 2015. 'Clientelism in Indian Villages'. *American Economic Review*, 105 (6).
Banerjee, Abhijit, and Rohini Somanathan. 2007. 'The Political Economy of Public Goods: Some Evidence from India'. *Journal of Development Economics*, 82.
Banerjee, Abhijit, and Rohini Pande. 2007. 'Parochial Politics: Ethnic Preferences and Politician Corruption'. Working Paper.
Banerjee, Abhijit, Esther Duflo, Maitreesh Ghatak, and Jeanne Lafortune. 2009. 'Marry for What? Caste and Mate Selection in Modern India'. *American Economic Journal: Microeconomics*, 5(2).
Cassan, Guilhem. 2015. 'Identity Based Policies and Identity Manipulation: Evidence from Colonial Punjab'. *American Economic Journal: Economic Policy*, 7(4).
Cassan, Guilhem. 2019. 'Affirmative Action, Education and Gender: Evidence from India'. *Journal of Development Economics*, 136.
Cassan, Guilhem, Dan Keniston, and Tatjana Kleineberg. 2022. 'A Division of Laborers Identity and Efficiency in India'. NBER Working Paper 28462

Cassan, Guilhem, and Lore Vandewalle. 2021. 'Identities and Public Policies: Unexpected Effects of Political Reservations for Women in India'. *World Development*.

Chakravarti, U. 1993. 'Conceptualising Brahmanical Patriarchy in Early India: Gender, Caste, Class and State'. *Economic and Political Weekly*, 28(14): 579–585.

Chattopadhyay, R., and E. Duflo. (2004). 'Women as Policy Makers: Evidence from a Randomized Policy Experiment in India'. *Econometrica*, 72 (5).

Conlon, Frank F. 1981. 'The Census of India as a Source for Historical Study of Religion and Caste'. In N. Gerald Barrier (Ed.), *The Census in British India: New Perspectives* (pp. 103–118). New Delhi: Manohar Publications.

Drèze, Jean, and Amartya Sen. 2002. *India: Development and Participation* (2nd edition). Oxford University Press.

Dumont, Louis. 1966. *Homo Hierarchicus: essai sur le système des castes*. Paris: Gallimard.

Fafchamps, Marcel et Lund, Susan. 2003. 'Risk Sharing Networks in Rural Philippines'. *Journal of Development Economics*, 72(2).

Greif, Avner. 1993. 'Contract Enforceability and Economic Institutions in Early Trade: The Maghribi Trader's Coalition'. *American Economic Review*, 83(3).

Jaffrelot, Christophe. 2000. 'Sanskritization vs. Ethnicization in India: Changing Identities and Caste Politics before Mandal'. *Asian Survey*, 40(5).

Joshi, S., N. Kochhar, and V. Rao. 2017. 'Are Caste Categories Misleading? The Relationship between Gender and Jati in Three Indian States'. WIDER Working Paper 2017/132.

Kapadia, K. 1997. 'Mediating the Meaning of Market Opportunities: Gender, Caste and Class in Rural South India'. *Economic and Political Weekly*, 32(52): 3329–3335.

La Ferrara, Eliana. 2003. 'Kin Group and Reciprocity: A Model of Credit Transactions in Ghana'. *American Economic Review*, 5(93).

Lehne, Johnathan, Jacob Shapiro, and Oliver Vanden Eynde. 2018. 'Building Connections: Political Corruption and Road Construction in India'. *Journal of Development Economics*, 131.

Luke, Nancy, and Kaivan Munshi. 2011. 'Women as Agents of Change: Female Income and Mobility in India'. *Journal of Development Economics*, 94(1): 1–17.

Mauss, Marcel. 1925. 'Essai sur le don. Forme et raison de l'échange dans les sociétés archaïques'. *L'Année sociologique*; rééd. F. Weber (éd.) 2012. *Essai sur le don. Forme et raison de l'échange dans les sociétés archaïques*. Paris: PUF.

Mencher, J. P. 1988. 'Women's Work and Poverty: Women's Contribution to Household Maintenance in South India'. In D. Dwyer and J. Bruce (Eds.), *A Home Divided: Women and Income in the Third World*. Stanford University Press.

Munshi, Kaivan. 2011. 'Strength in Numbers: Networks as a Solution to Occupational Traps'. *Review of Economic Studies*, 78.

Munshi, Kaivan. 2019. 'Caste and the Indian Economy'. *Journal of Economic Literature*, 57(4).

Munshi, Kaivan et Rosenzweig, Mark. 2006. 'Traditional Institutions Meet the Modern World: Caste, Gender, and Schooling Choice in a Globalizing Economy'. *American Economic Review*, 96(4).

Munshi, Kaivan et Rosenzweig, Mark. 2009. 'Why Is Mobility in India So Low? Social Insurance, Inequality and Growth'. Working Paper.

Munshi, Kaivan et Rosenzweig, Mark. 2010. 'Networks, Commitment, and Competence: Caste in Indian Local Politics'. Working Paper.

Murdock, George Peter. 1959. *Africa: Its Peoples and Their Cultural History*. New York: McGraw-Hill Book Company.

Murdock, George Peter. 1967. *Ethnographic Atlas*. Pittsburgh: University of Pittsburgh Press.

Pritchett, Lant. 2009. 'Is India a Flailing State? Detours on the Four Lane Highway of Modernization'. Working Paper.

Rosenzweig, Mark et Stark, Oded. 1989. 'Consumption Smoothing, Migration, and Marriage: Evidence from Rural India'. *Journal of Political Economy*, 97(4).

Singh, K. S. 1996. *Communities, Segments, Synonyms, Surnames and Titles*. People of India National Series Volume VIII.

Srinivas, M. N. 1955. 'The Social System of a Mysore Village'. In M. Marriott (Ed.), *Village India*. Chicago: University of Chicago Press.

Srinivas, M. N. 1987. *The Dominant Caste and Other Essays*. New Delhi: Oxford University Press.

Wiser, William. 1936. *The Hindu Jajmani System: A Socio-Economic System Interrelating Members of a Hindu Village Community in Services*. Lucknow Publishing House.

CHAPTER 39

CASTE AND MERIT

AJANTHA SUBRAMANIAN

It may seem paradoxical to propose a relationship between caste and merit. After all, caste is the social institution most emblematic of ascriptive hierarchy while meritocracy is typically understood as a democratizing force favouring individual achievement over inherited privilege. However, even a cursory look at the uppermost echelons of Indian higher education reveals a far more entangled history. Decades after independence, the institutional spaces most identified as meritocratic continue to be overwhelmingly upper caste in composition. Moreover, attempts at opening up these spaces to lower castes through affirmative action and other democratizing measures are consistently met with fervent opposition, not in the name of caste, but in the name of preserving 'merit'.

Historicizing Merit

Merit is a loaded term that does similar political work as an earlier discourse of republican 'virtues and talents'. In this sense, Indian meritocracy is part of a much longer history of modern political thought within which universal equality has been reconciled with naturalized social hierarchy. As historians of the Enlightenment have shown, virtues and talents became the focus of philosophers and political writers concerned with engendering a new society based on principles of nature and reason. They argued that a sociopolitical order founded on these principles would best ground the emergent notions of the republican citizen and the enlightened society. Most presumed that hierarchies would necessarily remain within a democracy; now, however, they would be rooted in legitimate differences and not the legacy of family or rank. Despite the widely circulating language of equality and universal rights, they argued that the 'natural superiority' of some over others—men over women, adults over children, or Europeans over other people—made them best suited to govern. Even for those, like John Adams, who fretted about the substitution of an aristocracy of birth with an 'aristocracy of talent', there was little question that stratification would persist as an integral part of the social order, in large part because of differences in peoples' 'natural' endowments. For 18th-century ideologues, naturalized difference became a key alibi for the perpetuation of social hierarchy after the advent of republican democracy.[1]

As with 18th-century republicanism, post-independence India witnessed heated debates over how to reconcile the formal ideal of equal citizenship in the new republic with persistent social hierarchies. At the same time, Indian republicanism was far more radical than its 18th century predecessor. Universal adult franchise symbolized a radical break with colonial subjecthood. Departing from the explicit colonial invocation of caste as the organizational basis of society and economy, postcolonial statesmen, and planners sought to overcome colonial 'underdevelopment' and the purported social barriers to Indian modernity.

Caste was one of these social barriers. Unlike the colonial treatment of caste as a foundational category of Indian society, postcolonial statesmen viewed caste as inimical to modern social life with no place in a democratic polity. Caste thinking with its basis in hierarchy, stigma, and segregation was to be rooted out in favour of civic principles of equality and fraternity. But much like the hierarchies embedded within 18th century Enlightenment thought, some Indians were thought to have achieved this enlightened consciousness of castelessness sooner than others, and were thus suited to lead. Although the material legacies of caste continued to profoundly structure post-independence life, those upper castes who were its greatest beneficiaries were the first to proclaim their own transcendence of caste and their right to rule on the basis of merit.

The intimacy between caste and merit seen in upper caste claims to meritocracy throws into question the widespread assumption that the political leveraging of caste is limited to the socially marginalized. In the Indian context, this assumption is reflected in arguments about caste as a more salient basis of social distinction and self-definition for lower than for upper castes. From the 1970s, media and scholarly attention has been far more focused on the impact of lower caste mobilization on Indian society and politics. Attention to lower caste politics has illuminated the transformative potential of subaltern agency; on the other hand, it has also produced an equation between caste politics and subaltern identitarianism. As a result, the proliferation of writing on lower castes that points to caste as a sociopolitical category operating through various registers and at different scales has not led to similarly robust engagement with upper caste self-definition and maneuver.[2]

---

[1] James Kloppenberg. 1987. 'The Virtues of Liberalism: Christianity, Republicanism, and Ethics in Early American Political Discourse', *Journal of American History*, 44(1): 1–33; John Carson. 2006. *The Measure of Merit: Talents, Intelligence, and Inequality in the French and American Republics, 1750–1940* (Princeton: Princeton University Press).

[2] But see Sara Dickey. 2016. *Living Class in Urban India* (New Brunswick: Rutgers University Press; Delhi: Permanent Black); Raka Ray and Seemin Qayum. 2009. *Cultures of Servitude: Modernity, Domesticity, and Class in India* (Stanford: Stanford University Press); C. J. Fuller and Haripriya Narasimhan. 2014. *Tamil Brahmans: The Making of a Middle Class Caste* (Chicago: University of Chicago Press); Ramesh Bairy. 2010. *Being Brahmin, Being Modern: Exploring the Lives of Caste Today* (New Delhi: Routledge).

It is undoubtedly true that non-elites have embraced caste as a vehicle of empowerment, and that collective mobilization for lower caste rights in both formal and informal political arenas has changed the contours of Indian society and politics. However, this only underscores the need for work on how caste operates at the other end of the spectrum. Many upper caste individuals think of themselves as modern, meritocratic subjects with sincere commitments to universalistic ideals of equality, democracy, and rationality. At the same time, they are able to inhabit this worldview precisely because a history of accumulated advantages allows them a unique claim to certain forms of self-fashioning. Whereas at an earlier moment, status might have been more explicitly tied to caste, the social bases of merit continue to be constituted in ways that allow the same social groups to inhabit merit as an embodied ideal. This begs the question of how castelessness as a subjectivity is produced, and what its relationship is to caste belonging in the postcolonial, democratic present. When do upper castes mark their own caste identities and when do they not?[3]

Higher Education and the Production of Castelessness

Higher education is an ideal site for thinking through the interplay between caste marking and un-marking that is evident in upper caste claims to merit. Within Indian higher education, engineering, arguably the most coveted field of study in the country, is a particularly generative focus. My own work looks at the role of engineering education in transforming caste privilege into merit. More specifically, I focus on how caste histories of technical training have given rise to the current stratification of engineering institutions, with the Indian Institutes of Technology (IITs) occupying the uppermost echelon. To understand the ubiquitous perception of upper caste IIT graduates as emblems of Indian meritocracy, I look at how three technologies of caste production—testing, affirmative action, and diasporic mobility—have allowed for the remaking of upper caste engineers as meritocratic moderns. While I look specifically at engineering and the IITs, this account has broader relevance for understanding the importance of merit as a caste claim. Let me take up each technology briefly.

---

[3] For other work on the reconstitution of upper castes as casteless, meritocratic individuals, see Satish Deshpande. 2013. 'Caste and Castelessness: Towards a Biography of the "General Category"', *Economic and Political Weekly*, 48(15): 32–39; Ashwini Deshpande and Katherine Newman. 2007. 'Where the Path Leads: The Role of Caste in Post-University Employment Expectations', *Economic and Political Weekly*, 42(41): 4133–4140; Surinder Jodhka and Katherine Newman. 2007. 'In the Name of Globalization: Meritocracy, Productivity, and the Hidden Language of Caste', *Economic and Political Weekly*, 42(41): 4125–4132; Carol Upadhya. 2007. 'Employment, Exclusion and "Merit" in the Indian IT Industry', *Economic and Political Weekly*, 42(20): 1863–1868.

Mass Examination

The reconstitution of upper castes as casteless, meritocratic moderns was facilitated by the modern mass examination. Unlike earlier processes of selection that explicitly favoured a high-born elite, the mass examination was underwritten by an ideology of middle class achievement where labour would find its just rewards. Its presumed apolitical character, its scale, and its finely calibrated system of ranked outcomes constituted merit as an index of individual achievement within an egalitarian system.[4] However, the promise of open access and equal opportunity is belied by the structuring force of economic and social relations and the ideological power of cultural assumptions. Historical and contemporary work on the mass examination clearly shows that success is made possible by the accumulated advantages of unequal opportunity. Moreover, threats to expected outcomes posed by phenomena such as the contemporary coaching industry or the colonial 'crammer' are met by efforts to restructure exams to once again produce the desired results. These results in turn reinforce assumptions about who is or is not innately talented. In other words, the examination is profoundly social and cultural in both its structure and its effects.

A case in point is the Joint Entrance Exam (JEE) to gain admission to the IITs, which arguably represents the fullest realization of the country's examination fetish. The expanding scope of the exam has had a significant effect on the perception of its outcomes. As an all-India exam, it has come to be seen as a national arbiter of merit. Over the 1970s and 1980s, engineering education was a growth industry, particularly in southern India. Through this period, the JEE sealed its reputation as the ultimate test of conceptual prowess and stepping stone to economic mobility, attracting increasing numbers of students who wanted to try their hand in a national competition. Through this process, the JEE All-India Rank has become an index of innate abilities.

Significantly, the JEE as a mass examination did not have the anticipated democratizing effect. Through the 1970s, 1980s, and 1990s, the IIT student body was heavily weighted towards upper caste, middle-class urbanites. Most were children of central government service employees, graduates of the prestigious Union Public Service Commission exam who made a point of training their children to succeed in the intense competitiveness of examination culture. In addition to these structural continuities that made caste and class history so key to exam success, the perceptions of the UPSC and

---

[4] For social scientific and historical work on the mass examination, see Pierre Bourdieu and Claude Passeron. 1977. *Reproduction in Education, Society, and Culture* (London: Sage); Satish Deshpande. 2010, 3 March. "Pass, Fail, Distinction: The Examination as a Social Institution," Third Marjorie Sykes Memorial Lecture, Regional Institute of Education, Ajmer; Bernard Cohn. 1966. 'Recruitment and Training of British Civil Servants in India, 1600–1860', in Ralph Braibanti (Ed.), *Asian Bureaucratic Systems Emergent from the British Imperial Tradition* (Durham: Duke University Commonwealth Studies Center, 1966); Krishna Kumar. 1985, 27 July. 'Reproduction or Change? Education and Elites in India'. *Economic and Political Weekly*, 1280–1284; Clive Dewey. 1973. 'The Education of a Ruling Caste: The Indian Civil Service in the Era of Competitive Examination'. *The English Historical Review*, 88(347): 262–285.

JEE as objective filters of individual ability disassociated from other structural factors have reinforced an ideology of meritocratic achievement. Assumptions about the mass examination as a social leveler have allowed those who succeed to disavow ascriptive inheritances and foreground middle-class achievement. In this way, a claim to middle classness has become a crucial alibi for caste ascription.

Affirmative Action

A second technology for transforming caste into merit is affirmative action. In the immediate postcolonial period, official opinion was divided between a recognition of enduring caste inequalities and the perception of caste as an outmoded category of social belonging with no place in a modern polity. Redress for caste 'disabilities' found expression in a system of affirmative action where reserved seats, or quotas, were set aside for the 'socially and educationally backward'.[5] Over the past 70 years, the Indian legislature and courts have moved more definitively towards an embrace of quotas as a necessary mechanism of recompense and redistribution. Supreme Court judgements from the 1950s through the 2000s illuminate shifts from a more categorical stand in favour of formal equality towards an embrace of measures to bridge the gap between formal and substantive equality.

But even as more and more ink was spilt in debating the appropriate limits to quotas and the caste versus class contours of social disadvantage, the inheritances that underwrote achievement slipped out of view. For the judiciary, the high caste subject remained the ideal citizen defined by individual merit. By contrast, the reserved were marked by history and identity. The invisibility of caste privilege was especially pronounced in the educational domain. Those who qualified for educational quotas on the basis of social disadvantages were identified within the 'reserved category' through their caste affiliation whereas those who did not qualify were simply classed under the 'general category' of 'merit-based' admissions. The absenting of caste from the postcolonial administrative classification of upper caste students marked a key transition in official parlance that came to intersect in critical ways with their self-fashioning as modern meritocratic subjects. This categorical distinction between the meritorious/ casteless and the reserved/caste-based has profoundly shaped the debate around educational equality in India. It has allowed those who fall within the general category to argue that it is the system of reservations, and not the inheritances of caste that undermines the democratic ideal of equal citizenship. Moreover, the admissions categories of 'general' and 'reserved' have generated their own caste effects within and beyond higher education by producing caste distinction and discrimination at a different scale. As a result, the antagonists of the debate over educational equality are now these consolidated

---

[5] For an exhaustive account of India's approach to affirmative action, see Marc Galanter. 1984. *Competing Equalities: Law and the Backward Classes in India* (New Delhi: Oxford University Press).

caste groupings of the 'general' and 'reserved'. Even when the finer gradations of caste give way, stigma persists through these consolidated forms.[6]

Claiming merit in opposition to the 'reserved' is a pervasive trend in elite higher educational institutions. This pattern has been exacerbated after 2006 when new quotas for intermediate castes were extended to the most elite, centrally funded institutions, like the IITs. The expansion of quotas has set in motion an incessant diagnostics of caste on college campuses through which everything from clothing to accents become indices of caste belonging. It has also more sharply polarized the 'general' and 'reserved' as consolidated caste categories. The distinction between the 'general' and 'reserved' has also had ramifications beyond campus life in shaping career trajectories. Now, job recruiters routinely use these admissions categories as a basis of evaluation, in the process reproducing caste stigma in hiring.[7] In the Indian private sector, which is beyond the purview of reservations, the absence of quotas, discriminatory hiring practices, and the systematic disavowal of caste all combine to shore up a claim to being a caste-free space that is the inverse of the supposedly caste-ridden public sector.[8]

Diasporic Mobility

Finally, the transnational mobility of upper castes to the United States has been a third technology for the remaking of caste privilege as merit. Caste inheritances have long been key to diasporic migration. The late 19th-century wave of Indian migration to Burma, Ceylon, Malaya, Africa, the Caribbean, and the Pacific mostly consisted of lower caste, indentured labourers. A second wave of traders, clerks, and bureaucrats followed indentured labourers to East and South Africa and other British colonies. A third wave of headed for the United States from the 1880s. With changes in immigration policy in the 1960s, upper caste professionals became the largest contingent of Indians in the

---

[6] For an in-depth analysis of economic discrimination on the basis of caste, see Ashwini Deshpande. 2011. *The Grammar of Caste: Economic Discrimination in Contemporary India* (Oxford University Press, 2011). For an ethnographic account of the Dalit experience of stigma as a result of reservations, see Clarinda Still. 2013. '"They Have It in Their Stomachs but They Can't Vomit It Up": Dalits, Reservations, and "Caste Feeling" in Rural Andhra Pradesh', *FOCAAL*, 65: 68–79. My analysis of the political work of the 'general category' builds on Satish Deshpande. 2013. 'Caste and Castelessness: Towards a Biography of the "General Category"', *Economic and Political Weekly*, 48(15): 32–39.

[7] Odile Henry and Mathieu Ferry. 2017. 'When Cracking the JEE Is Not Enough: Processes of Elimination and Differentiation, From Entry to Placement, in the Indian Institutes of Technology'. *South Asia Multidisciplinary Academic Journal*, 15.

[8] For work on private sector claims to merit as an expression of caste sentiment and belonging, see Carol Upadhya. 2007. 'Employment, Exclusion and "Merit" in the Indian IT Industry', *Economic and Political Weekly*, 42(20): 1863–1868; C. J. Fuller and Haripriya Narasimhan. 2007. 'Information Technology Professionals and the New-Rich Middle Class in Chennai (Madras)', *Modern Asian Studies*, 41: 121–150, Surinder Jodhka. 2015. '"Caste Blinding" and Corporate Hiring', in *Caste in Contemporary India* (New Delhi: Routledge); Marilyn Fernandez. 2018. *The New Frontier: Merit vs. Caste in the Indian IT Sector* (New Delhi: Oxford University Press).

U.S.[9] Their professional successes have been hugely significant for reinforcing the link between meritocracy and caste. With geographical distance from India and from rising challenges to caste entitlement, upper caste achievement abroad appears to be a form of self-made success that has nothing to do with caste. It helps that in the United States, caste privilege is consistently misrecognized as middle class labour and racial talent. This has been all the more so after the Information Technology boom of the 1990s. The sizable presence of Indian engineers in the Silicon Valley boom of the 1980s and 1990s has endowed them with a mystique as the most risk-free sites of capital investment. The fetishizing of Indian technical talent has to be situated in the context of a late 20th and early 21st century politics of ascription. Whereas the explicit invocation of particularistic genealogies as a basis for social worth or market value was once parochialized as non-modern, we are now witnessing the resurgence of claims on these grounds. The return to genealogy has been accorded new legitimacy by the neoliberal marketplace for identities and entrepreneurial ideologies of self-made success. In this context, elite engineering graduates in the United States are seen, not as beneficiaries of caste or the developmental state, but simply as naturally gifted 'technological Indians'.[10]

Among diasporic engineers, IIT alumni are the most visible successes of the global knowledge economy. Moreover, IITian networks have been very active in protecting their brand value to ensure its exceptional standing. Some alumni have done this by using media coverage while others use their influence to induct younger IIT graduates into university campuses and entrepreneurial ventures. Although caste distinction is at the heart of these forms of transnational institutional kinship, IITians represent themselves merely as uniquely talented, middle class Indians whose success was only possible outside a homeland doomed to mediocrity by measures such as affirmative action.

These three technologies—mass examinations, affirmative action, and global market success—have all mediated the transformation of caste inheritances into merit. At the same time, other trends have complicated the reconstitution of upper castes as casteless, meritocratic moderns. The naturalization of upper caste merit has not gone unchallenged. The proliferation of rights discourses and politics, the extension of universal franchise, and the entry of new social groups into spaces previously monopolized by upper castes have posed real challenges to caste hierarchies. Through the 20th century, constitutional amendments, policy initiatives, and regional politics have variously illuminated the persistence of caste as a structural determinant of opportunity and success. These interventions have advanced competing notions of equality that presume, not the level playing field of formal democracy, but the historical accumulation of advantages and disadvantages.

---

[9] Vivek Bald, *Bengali Harlem and the Lost Histories of South Asian America* (Cambridge, MA: Harvard University Press, 2015); Devesh Kapur. 2010. *Diaspora, Development, and Democracy: The Domestic Impact of International Migration from India* (Princeton: Princeton University Press, 2010); Vijay Prashad, *The Karma of Brown Folk* (Minneapolis: University of Minnesota Press, 2000).

[10] Ross Bassett. 2016. *The Technological Indian* (Cambridge: Harvard University Press).

The Dialectic of Achievement and Ascription

Attention to caste histories of accumulation has been particularly pointed in regions where a politics of lower caste assertion has interrupted the transformation of privilege into merit. In my work, I look in particular at the role of Tamil Nadu as an important precedent for the re-marking of upper castes *as castes* and how this has shaped a proliferating politics of meritocracy. As the discursive target of the Non-Brahmin and Dravidian movements that swept the southeastern region from the early 20th century, Tamil Brahmins in particular came to be hyper-visible and their claims to knowledge inextricably linked to caste privilege. Their explicit marking as caste subjects has in turn produced a heightened consciousness among Tamil Brahmins of their own caste belonging. For them, however, being Brahmin is an expression of both modernity and merit. Tamil Brahmin claims to educational rights as modern, meritocratic subjects arose as early as 1951 with the first post-independence court case against reserved quotas in higher education.[11] What is evident in the framing of the case and the judgement is that, for both the Tamil Brahmin claimants and the judges, to be Tamil Brahmin was an expression of both caste culture and modern merit.

The Tamil Brahmin example illuminates the importance of lower caste challenges in illuminating the dialectic of achievement and ascription that is at the heart of upper caste claims to merit. Such challenges have elicited strident reactions from upper castes which reveal, not the wholesale disavowal of caste, but the back-and-forth movement between self-marking through expressions of caste sentiment and affiliation and unmarking through claims to modernity and democracy. Situating upper caste claims to merit in relation to lower caste politics thus allows us to see how meritocracy encodes forms of ascription. It is only as a response to lower caste claims that the identitarian underpinnings of meritocracy are laid bare.

With the spread of Backward Caste politics to the 'Hindi belt' in the 1990s and 2000s, what was once a southeastern regional dialectic of lower caste claims to rights and upper caste claims to merit has assumed national proportions. Now, it is not only Tamil Brahmins who claim merit as both a caste characteristic and an expression of individual achievement. The expansion of lower caste rights politics to national scale—particularly, the rise of Dalit and Other Backward Class (OBC) political parties in the 1990s and the expansion of reserved quotas in 1990 and 2006—has witnessed a similar expansion of an identitarian politics of meritocracy. As a result, upper castes across India have embraced merit as a collective caste trait that distinguishes them from lower castes.[12]

---

[11] The Supreme Court of India. 1951, 9 April. *The State of Madras vs. Srimathi Champakam Dorairajan*.

[12] For more on the upper caste claim to ascriptive caste traits as the basis of business acumen, see Surinder S. Jodhka and Jules Naudet. 2017. 'Towards a Sociology of India's Economic Elite: Beyond the Neo-Orientalist and Managerialist Perspectives', *South Asia Multidisciplinary Academic Journal*, 15.

As noted above, the return to ascription as the explicit basis of achievement is an instance of the neoliberal commodification of identity.[13] Culturalist, genealogical, even genetic claims to merit have become an increasingly common feature of the 21st century. In naturalizing achievement as the expression of innate qualities, such claims illuminate the ascriptive bases of meritocracy that belie its democratizing promise.

Conclusion

In India, consolidated categories of upper and lower caste have acquired outsized importance in political life. In many contexts, these identitarian categories overshadow the salience of caste at a smaller scale. Understanding a proliferating upper caste politics of meritocracy also sheds light on the complex relationship between caste and class in contemporary India. On the one hand, upper castes routinely use middle classness as an alibi for disavowing caste inheritances. On the other, the leveraging of merit has allowed for a process of upper caste retrenchment in both domestic and diasporic private sectors and sharply exacerbated wealth disparities. Class is thus both a discursive trope and a structural effect of an upper caste politics of meritocracy. Finally, the focus on higher education and the private sector as battlegrounds of caste politics has produced its own exclusions by foregrounding middle class aspirations to social mobility at the expense of more far-reaching measures of distributive justice.

We may be tempted to conclude that the only answer to these forms of polarization is a return to either liberal individualism or a class politics cleansed of caste considerations. To my mind, these would be grave mistakes. Instead, we need to recognize the importance of reclaiming a social democratic politics that acknowledges the inheritances of caste and the work of ascription within putatively universal frameworks. Only then can we build democratic societies that work with and through the legacies of history and not by attempting to transcend them.

---

[13] For work on the relationship between ascription and democracy, see S. Jodhka, 'Ascriptive Hierarchies: Caste and Its Reproduction in Contemporary India,' *Current Sociology*, 64(2): 228–243; Charles Tilly. 1998. *Durable Inequality* (Berkeley: University of California Press). For work on the return to ascription under neoliberal conditions, see John and Jean Comaroff. 2009. *Ethnicity, Inc.* (Chicago: University of Chicago Press), George Paul Meiu, 2017. *Ethno-Erotic Economies: Sexuality, Money, and Belonging in Kenya* (Chicago: University of Chicago Press).

CHAPTER 40

CASTE AND MOBILITY

DIVYA VAID

INTRODUCTION

Social mobility, closely tied to notions of (in)equality, is the intra-generational (over a person's life-time), or inter-generational (from one generation to another), movement between different strata.[1] This mobility can include either upward, downward, or horizontal movement between strata such as caste, or between classes which has been indexed by either occupation, income, wealth, or education.[2] Beyond this movement, social mobility research looks at the articulation, aspiration, and strategies of achieving upward mobility, and the anxieties, and barriers faced in this process.

Intra-generational or career mobility often involves studying the movement and changes over ones working life especially looking at what helps or hinders occupational access and income at different stages of one's career (Kalleberg and Mouw, 2018). This intra-generational mobility is tied to patterns and experiences that might reproduce across generations. However, since there is less work in this area in India and more engagement with the reproduction of advantages and disadvantages across generations,

---

[1] There are multiple approaches to capture social mobility as discussed briefly in the next section. For more on definitions of mobility, contrasting approaches to mobility and concepts, see Heath (2003), Fields (2019), and Iversen et al. (2021).

[2] I use the term class to imply social class and do not engage at this point with the definitions of class and how to measure it specifically in the context of a social mobility study (see Vaid, 2018 for a discussion on this). With regard to the term caste, rather than using *varna* or *jati*, around which there have been long stranding debates covered by other chapters in this volume, I use the broader term caste to mean either *jati*, or groups of *jatis*, or at times Constitutional categories as used in the research reviewed here. In this chapter, I also limit myself to the broader work on Hindu castes in India—this doesn't preclude caste in other religions or in the diaspora where use of networks for social mobility is of interest (see other contributions to this volume for a discussion on these themes; see also Vaid and Datta, 2019).

in this review I focus on inter-generational social mobility.[3] This inter-generational mobility has been viewed in two ways: either as movement of entire groups, or as movements of individuals. An example of the former could be a caste claiming a particular position, or moving up or down a local hierarchy; and, an example of the latter could be an individual's occupational or income mobility as compared to their parents (Heath, 2003; see Vaid 2014 for a review). This chapter begins by discussing the various approaches and methods used for the study of mobility; it then explores both forms of inter-generational movement mentioned above: first, by covering studies that have discussed the social mobility of entire castes or the possibility of such movement; and second, by summarizing work on the patterns of mobility of individuals from different castes. It then briefly discusses the significance of space and spatial mobility that either constrains or encourages social mobility. The chapter ends by looking at the experiences, aspirations, and anxieties tied to mobility.

Mobility Approaches and Methods

Mobility to some extent assumes a language of hierarchy, though movement need not only be vertical (i.e. mobility between classes or castes placed in a more or less accepted hierarchy), but could also be seen as horizontal (i.e. movement between classes or castes placed at the same or similar levels of the social strata). Further, spatial mobility makes this picture more complex. For example, migration from one location to another could entail social mobility in terms of a better, or worse, occupational position, but this could be complicated by status dissonance.[4]

The study of social mobility in India, especially in the context of caste, has entailed the use of a variety of methodological approaches. Sociologists and economists who study individual level mobility through occupations or incomes tend to use macro datasets and quantitative approaches. Within sociologists, there have been divisions between those who use the class mobility approach using parent to child mobility tables, where often class is indexed by occupation (Kumar et al., 2002; Vaid, 2018; see Goldthorpe, 2003 for a discussion on this approach); and, those that have used a multi-dimensional approach with some similarities to the status attainment approach (Ram, 1988; see Blau et al., 1967 for more on the status attainment approach; see Vaid, 2018 for a broader discussion of mobility approaches). To study socio-economic mobility, economists have used either measures of income, wealth, education or occupation,

---

[3] While there are fewer studies on career mobility in India, the literature on labour market inequalities and the hurdles faced by groups to enter, remain, and progress in valued positions such as the professions, points to the barriers that exist due to caste or class location (see Vaid, 2014 for an overview; also see Deshpande 2011).

[4] For instance, an Indian immigrant to the US may feel socially mobile, however, their occupation in the host country may be lower in an occupational hierarchy than the one in their home country.

and a range of techniques from mobility matrices, to regression models (Emran and Shilpi, 2019).[5]

These macro studies have also relied on the use of both absolute and relative rates of mobility to capture patterns and trends. Absolute mobility is the raw numbers who move either up, down, or horizontally. This figure captures the extent of parent to child inheritance, or the lack of it, in class terms. In contrast relative mobility captures the mobility net of structural change. For instance, we expect to find some absolute mobility simply due to changes in the occupational structure; for example, a decline in agriculture, or an increase in the services is likely to either push people out of agriculture, or pull them into the services. Relative mobility, also referred to as social fluidity, captures mobility net of this structural change. In other words, it is the mobility of individuals from a certain group in relation to others when structural change is kept constant (Heath, 2003; Vaid, 2018).[6]

Social-anthropologists who have looked at experiences of mobility or stagnation, or at aspirations, or at the burgeoning size of the middle class, and how that relates to caste, have more often used in-depth interviews, or the ethnographic approach (Osella and Osella, 2000; Dickey, 2012, see Vaid, 2021 for a review of ethnographic research on social mobility), including life histories (Benei, 2010). Some anthropologists, such as Benei (2010), are critical of the quantitative approach for the study of social mobility, since they believe it privileges the individual over the family. 'Thus many quantitative studies tend to disregard the fact that mobility is not only a matter of individual agency but also of family praxis, and that individuals are embedded within family, occupational and local contexts' (Benei, 2010, p. 199). While quantitative work has had a rather different aim, usually to establish trends and patterns, it has also in different ways looked at social networks, location, strategies such as education, and so on, as factors that constrain or encourage mobility (Iversen et al., 2021).

While different methods have been used for the study of caste and social mobility, this chapter attempts a brief overview of the research in this area (see also Vaid, 2014; Vaid, 2018). Before we move on to the next section, a brief word on gender and mobility. A majority of work on social mobility in India that looks at broader patterns and trends, either by economists or sociologists, has tended to focus on the mobility patterns for men, usually by looking at father-to-son mobility (Luke, 2019). The reasons for this have ranged from the absence of sufficient data on women in many national surveys that use household level sampling, to the absence of women from the active labour market

---

[5] Data, variables, concepts, and measures all influence patterns of mobility. Studies that consistently use similar measures and the same datasets over time allow one to capture change and persistence. Datasets that collect household level information, such as the National Sample Survey for instance, underrepresent women who may have left their parental home, and are less useful for the study of women's social mobility. Individual level datasets, such as the National Election Studies, allow for an inclusion of women and men irrespective of who they live with, either alone or with their parents. Results from studies using different datasets are covered in the section on mobility patterns.

[6] There are a few different ways to capture absolute mobility from a mobility table, or mobility matrix, such as inflow, outflow, and total mobility (see Heath, 2003 for definitions).

especially in the generation of 'mothers'. Some exceptions to these studies are discussed later in this chapter (see also Vaid, 2018). However, this is an area that requires more research especially given the role gender plays in caste and occupational practices and their reproduction (Dube, 1996).

Caste Mobility

The association of caste with hereditary occupation (Bougle, 1971; Gupta, 1991) can be seen as limiting the possibilities of social mobility. Dumont's (1970) structuralist view of India as 'homo hierarchicus' or a society characterized by hierarchy, contrasted with the 'homo equalis' of the West, along with his emphasis on the binary oppositions of 'pure' and 'impure' may seem to imply an absence of, or limited, mobility. However, others have argued that castes were never entirely closed (Fuller, 1996), though the amount of movement away from 'traditional occupation' may have been constrained. Caste and class (especially with regard to occupation) were seen as closely related, if not synonymous, particularly at the two extremes—the lower classes with the so-called lower castes; and, the higher classes with so-called higher castes (see Naudet in this volume for a discussion, see also Vaid, 2018).[7]

In this context the discussion on the 'book' versus 'field' view of caste (Jodhka, 1998) throws light on the empirical evidence in support of mobility opportunities. Srinivas in his work on the Coorgs (1952, see Charsley, 1998) captures mobility of castes through the concept of Sanskritization: essentially mobility through emulation. This emulation of rituals, lifestyle practices such as food and dress, of the 'upper', and in his later work 'dominant' castes, of the region, were mirrored by those lower down the local hierarchy to lay claims to higher status and upward mobility. The practice of emulating a reference group (as discussed in contributions in Silverberg (1968) especially in the context of Merton's reference group theory, and earlier by Ambedkar (1916) with reference to Tarde's work) were group endeavours which were slow to bring about change, and were often contested by those in more privileged locations. In this regard, claims to social mobility went hand in hand with claims for political mobility (see discussions in Still, 2015, and see the work on the Izhavas by Osella and Osella, 2000).

Further to group endeavours, reservation policies were meant to provide opportunities for disadvantaged castes and tribes to overcome historical inequalities in

---

[7] In the literature on mobility, the terms 'higher', 'upper', and 'lower' are used in the sense of hierarchy as discussed in the next section. This can be contentious in terms of using and applying a specific hierarchy of castes (or classes). Also, using terms such as lower and higher does not imply that individuals or castes do not have any agency or that they simply accept their position as given, but it is used to enable a tracing of movement from a less advantaged or deeply marginalized location to one of greater advantage.

education and occupation and to encourage social mobility. There is evidence of the positive outcomes of these reservations (as discussed in the next section of this chapter). However, persistence of inequalities, of an underrepresentation of Scheduled Castes, Scheduled Tribes and Other Backward Classes in government, including academic jobs, tells us another story. Hence, regardless of state policy, certain castes have experienced disproportionately more discrimination and inequality in attempting to gain access to secure and privileged occupations and in attaining social mobility (see Still, 2015 for a collection of research on marginalization of Dalits and their social mobility). The barriers faced by these castes to gain access to education, to convert education to reasonable jobs in the labour market, and to avoid precarity are steep. Some of these barriers including, for instance, the constraints due to residential segregation, are discussed later in this chapter.

Studies on specific castes have observed the ways in which caste barriers are overcome, or strategies of adapting to structural changes are followed. An example of a specific caste and their experiences of mobility is the work on the Izhavas, a former 'untouchable' caste of Kerala, by Osella and Osella (2000). The strategies comprising familial and individual, as well as group based religious and political movements, migration, and remittances, provide an overall picture of one castes' experiences. In contrast to the Izhavas, is the work of Fuller and Narasimhan (2015) on the Vattima Brahmins of Tamil Nadu who by virtue of their caste status, and their ties to land, were able to transition earlier to urban areas, and from there to take up newer jobs, such as those in the IT sector. This prior advantage, coupled with English language proficiency, and local and global networks provided upward mobility opportunities to some members of this caste.

Castes, however, are not homogeneous and experiences of mobility vary not only between, but also within castes or *jatis*. Harriss (2016), for instance, finds some evidence of the upward mobility of Dalits, and the 'decline' of 'landed caste power' with an 'increasing assertion of Dalits'; however, not all Dalits have been equally successful across the 'Slater' villages of Tamil Nadu that he had re-studied (p. 30). This differentiation within a caste has also been highlighted by Parry (1980) in his work on the funeral priests of Banaras (Varanasi), whose occupation, and in turn their status position, is lower in the caste hierarchy according to other Brahmins. Ethnographic studies of caste group mobility capture these differentiations, and the strategies used by different castes. To see whether individuals from certain castes have been mobile or not, especially with reference to individuals from other castes, we turn to the next section.

Mobility Patterns

Economists have studied intergenerational mobility between a range of categories including income, occupation, and education which have often been seen as markers of 'class'.[8] Sociologists have predominantly used occupation as a marker of class, followed by education.

With regard to results from studies by economists, Iversen et al. (2016) find evidence of more downward occupational mobility for SCs and STs as compared to those from other backgrounds in their men-only study using the second round of the Indian Human Development Survey (IHDS). However, Asher et al. (2020), also using the IHDS, focusing more on educational mobility (from fathers to sons and daughters), find support for the benefits of reservations for SCs. They find a large geographic difference in their patterns; however, their disaggregation shows that SCs/STs have had major gains which they find has been offset by major losses for Muslims. They expect that this could be due to reservation benefits for SCs/STs. They find 'constant and high upward mobility over time' for men from the higher castes (p. 4) and state that men from the 'Scheduled Castes and Scheduled Tribes, have crossed respectively 50 per cent and 30 per cent of the mobility gap to Forwards/Others'. However, SC/ST girls have not closed the gap as effectively. Interestingly they conclude:

> Upward mobility is highest in urban areas, and in places with high consumption, education, school supply, and manufacturing employment, which are broad correlates of development. High mobility is negatively correlated with caste segregation and land inequality. Geography-subgroup interactions are important; for instance, girls have higher mobility than boys in urban areas, but lower in rural areas. (Asher et al., 2020, p. 4)

Azam and Bhatt (2015) in their men-only study using the IHDS also find support for an increase in educational mobility over time and a decline in 'educational persistence'. However, they find that the impact of father's education on son's education has declined for father's with lower education; while it has increased for father's with higher education.

Majumder (2010) looks at both educational and occupational mobility using the National Sample Survey Organization data from 1993 and 2004 and finds some support for social mobility; however, general castes experience more upward mobility than the 'excluded' castes. He also finds that education mobility is greater than occupational mobility which he interprets as highlighting labour market discrimination where education progress is not necessarily translating into occupational advantage. This finding may help explain some of the variation in the other studies discussed above that have looked either at occupational mobility or education mobility and not at the two together.

Fewer sociologists studying mobility in India have used a quantitative or macro approach. This could in part be due to the evolution of the discipline of sociology in India which more closely resembles social anthropology. Of the few studies on mobility patterns, occupational mobility, similar to the class mobility approach (Treiman and

---

[8] For more on the definitions and concepts used by economists see Fields (2019), and on different measures and methods see Emran and Shilpi (2019).

Ganzeboom, 2014; Goldthorpe, 2003; Heath, 2003), has been studied by Kumar et al. (2002), McMillan (2005), Vaid and Heath (2010), and Vaid (2018) to establish broader patterns of mobility and comment on the disadvantages faced by certain castes. Fewer studies have focused on women as previously mentioned (Vaid and Heath, 2010 and Vaid, 2018 are some exceptions to this), and mobility has mostly been seen in terms of the father-son transfer of resources.

The general conclusion from these studies is that in absolute terms while all groups, including the SCs and STs, have been socially mobile and have experienced some amount of 'upward' mobility, when it comes to mobility in relative terms these groups continue to experience some 'relative disadvantage' (McMillan, 2005, p. 149). While the so-called upper castes are not protected directly from possibilities of downward mobility, barriers to mobility still persist which make it harder for the so-called lower castes to be relatively socially mobile, or to cross 'lower-middle level positions in the class schema' (Vaid, 2014, p. 399; see also Deshpande, 2011).

Kumar et al.'s (2002) study using the male-only data from the individual-level National Election Study from 1971 and 1996 reports on the absence of the weakening of caste and class; and, also finds evidence of persisting stability in terms of father to son mobility. McMillan (2005) uses the same datasets but combines the data for women with that for men and reports that absolute mobility may have increased for SCs and STs, but in relative terms, there is actually evidence of an increase in disadvantage when compared to the non-SCs and non-STs. Findings from Vaid (2018), who uses the series of NES datasets from 1996 to 2014 comparing patterns for women and men separately, shows some weakening of the association between class destination (respondent's class) and their caste and community. For access to professional class destination, both caste and father's class (class origins) have an impact. However, while the importance of class seems to be stronger and more persistent over birth cohort, the significance of caste does not disappear. SCs do face more barriers to upward class mobility, though non-SC castes are not entirely protected from downward mobility. Women in general, and those from reserved castes in particular, have a tougher time in being upwardly mobile. Interestingly, the urban also comes across as a site of both opportunity and precariousness (especially for women) with heightened chances of downward as well as upward mobility.

Beyond the work on occupational mobility using mobility tables, and predating much of the recent work on the rise of the middle classes in India, Nandu Ram (1988) in one of the first volumes on social mobility among the Scheduled Castes and the 'rise of a middle class' uses a multi-dimensional approach for the study of father-son social mobility. In this approach, while including occupation, he also includes education, income, consumption, and power as dimensions (p. 18). He draws the theoretical framework from a range of work including Lipset and Zetterberg on multidimensional social mobility, Homans on 'status congruence', and Merton and Rossi on 'reference group behaviour' (Ram, 1988, p. 16). The empirical work included interviews with 240 public sector employees from the Scheduled Castes in Kanpur city in Uttar Pradesh. He found that SCs with relatively better socio-economic origins experienced upward mobility more easily than other SCs did. He also reported an absence of 'complete social mobility' and a disjuncture between what he terms 'composite' (made up of occupation, education, and income) and 'corporate' (caste) status as perceived by the respondents thus leading to some dissonance (Ram, 1995, p. 453).

In his discussion, for Ram (1988) mobility can occur 'both in caste and class hierarchies' (p. 3). Hence, for him, 'middle and lower level castes' could improve their position in the existing caste hierarchy through 'the adoption of reference group behaviour' (p. 3), while 'mobility in the class hierarchy occurred in the form of improving one's socio-economic position' (p. 4). However, it has been seen that no claims to mobility or aspirations of mobility are without some sort of resistance. Violence or resentment against the actual or imagined mobility of the Dalits, for instance, has been a part of the experience of social mobility (Ram, 1988; Jodhka, 2012).

In addition to this work on occupational mobility and on the congruence of caste and class, there is much research on the persistence of the 'language of caste' in the labour market which has important repercussions on how mobility may be experienced by people from different castes. Jodhka and Newman (2007) in interviews with Human Resource managers in private sector firms in the Delhi National Capital Region bring out the various ways in which caste pervades recruitment. Interestingly, while the recruitment managers they interview do not feel that caste is a significant factor anymore, they persist in using 'family background', a catch-all term that captures what remains significant in recruitment. 'Family background' when analysed is seen to be composed of caste, class and regional location among other things. Deshpande and Newman's interviews (2007) with students about to enter the labour market also underline the expectations of persisting caste stereotypes and how these expectations constrain the aspirations that students have and in turn their mobility chances.

Clearly then, in studies on the broader or macro patterns of individual level class mobility by caste there are some consistent and some contrasting findings. However, there is an overall sense of low levels of mobility generally, especially for SCs, STs, and OBCs, along with the persisting though weakening association between class and caste.

Space and Spatial Mobility

The possibility of being spatially mobile as well as space itself, are both clearly tied to how social mobility is experienced and understood. Spatial mobility, as seen through migration, is of interest to understand experiences of social mobility. In some cases, geographic movement is a pathway to social mobility, either upward or downward. We see in the ethnography of Osella and Osella (2000) the ways in which Izhava migrants' employment in various Gulf states enabled their personal and familial economic advancement due not only to remittances, but also to status enhancement accrued by working 'abroad'.

In contrast to studies on blue-collar labour migrants, as discussed previously Fuller and Narasimhan (2015) throw light on the more educated white-collar migrants in their work on the Tamil Brahmins. Prior advantage (due to land ownership) and an earlier stage of migrating to urban areas enabled them to enter professions, including IT work, when the country liberalized. Further, this migration did not remain regional, and some Tamil Brahmins moved abroad to take up professional positions. These connections to both regional and international migration chains enabled this group to experience mobility.

On the flip side, we find that forced migration, due to a host of reasons ranging from climatic change to violence or strife, while leading to precarity for many may also lead some people belonging to the upper strata to experience downward mobility. One example of this can be seen through Datta's (2017) work on the Kashmiri Pandits. This research captures the sense of decline and stagnation, and the absence of opportunities for social mobility for the Kashmiri Pandits living in migrant camps in Jammu city. Both the sense of a camp, and spatial dislocation, heighten the experience of stagnation.

Beyond the intertwining of spatial mobility with social mobility, space by itself as seen through residence can limit or encourage social mobility. Inglis (2019) in his work on golf caddies in Bangalore (Bengaluru) shows how certain castes (and minorities such as the Muslims) are constrained by their neighbourhoods. While the caddies who live in these segregated neighbourhoods may interact and work with others on the golf courses by day, and some claim that caste is not salient, the possibility of 'performing middleclassness' is restricted for them, as are the possibilities of mobility for their children due to the barriers of access to good schooling. Further, when it comes to visiting other caddies' homes, or temples, and the opportunities to leave behind their 'origins', caste is clearly 'there' and visible. In this way space and the ability to transcend space impacts on social mobility opportunities.

Experiences, Aspirations, and Anxieties

Beyond establishing patterns and trends of social mobility, the way people experience mobility or its absence, the familial, and individual strategies they use (including networks, see Munshi, 2011; or educational strategies, see Donner, 2008) have been explored extensively. Tied to the aspiration of social mobility are the anxieties of attaining, maintaining, and transmitting their position and opportunities to the next generation. Hence, this section will address the role of experiences, aspirations, and anxieties in mediating social mobility.

We have already seen how certain castes, due to their earlier position (such as land ownership) have been able to take advantage of opportunities of mobility both locally and globally. For others, their caste has in effect been a barrier to opportunities

(Jeffrey et al., 2008). However, some studies have dwelt on the long-range mobility of castes that were previously disadvantaged. For instance, Naudet (2018) explores how Dalits who have been successful in entering elite positions make sense of their mobility while also feeling the pressures and anxieties of 'giving back' to their community. Further to this, are the frustrations and pressures certain castes may experience in not only being able to enter, but also to remain, in the middle class. Dickey's (2012, 2013) work on Madurai captures some of the excitements and possibilities that newer employment opportunities engender, while also capturing the anxieties of maintaining middle-classness and ensuring status stability, or upward mobility, for the next generation. This research highlights the familial and individual strategies people follow to overcome unexpected road bumps, as seen in long-term ethnographies such as by Dickey and by Inglis. Familial strategies of thrift and using social capital, coupled with individual strategies of gaining forms of cultural capital such as English language education, are important to analyse.

An important familial strategy for social mobility is to keep others out, since recourses such as good schools and good jobs are scarce (Béteille, 1993). In this context we see how those who are on the precipice of the middle class looking in, feel the additional pressure to provide similar benefits to their own children, while those who are privileged have much to gain by maintaining social distance. This is captured by Inglis' work (2019). The caddies he observes are essentially informal workers, and are privy to the lives, decisions, and luxuries of the elites who they work with. Some are, through luck, effort, benevolence of the members, and familial support, able to provide a better life for their children and position themselves more firmly on the social mobility ladder. However, some have only a tentative hold on the bottom rungs of this ladder and others are not able to get anywhere near it. For these individuals this precarious hold rarely translates into improved opportunities for their children leading to heightened anxieties. Inglis shows how caste is intertwined with these frustrations and precarity. We also observe the strategies members in these clubs use to maintain the status quo and keep a distance between themselves and the caddies, for instance by not regularizing the caddies' work.

And, while residence matters as discussed in the previous section, and we see that landowners are in relatively securer positions, we also find that not all landowning castes are protected from the anxieties of downward mobility. Inglis (2019) shows that when his research began in 2007, landowning caddies from the Vokkaligga caste seemed to be protected from some of the precarity and anxieties that other caddies faced; however, over his decade of research during which land was sub-divided or sold-off due to broader economic changes, caddies from this caste were exposed to more precarity, and had few other resources to prevent their downward mobility.

These anxieties around precarity and the frustrations of stagnation are also captured by Datta (2017) in his study of Kashmiri Pandit migrants to Jammu who were displaced due to the violence in the region in the early 1990s. Frustrations around the absence of opportunities of social mobility and the limits to aspirations among the younger generations, some of whom were too young to remember the migration and displacement, are seen. He also discusses how the experience of dispossession and loss relates to the anxieties around the loss of status and the fear of not being able to recover this loss for a group that is in caste terms *Brahmin,* and of whom some sections had enjoyed opportunities for upward mobility or had seemed protected from downward mobility in the past. These migrants also see themselves in reference to others in the region who did not face displacement. The disjuncture between caste and loss of status is apparent.

Interestingly, in the context of a gendered experience of mobility, there is evidence of the familial strategies of withdrawal of women from the labour market to indicate a higher status. Heyer (2015) in her work on Dalit women of Tiruppur, Tamil Nadu, had observed that these women who worked in garment factories would withdraw from the workforce if the income earning capacities of their husbands improved significantly (see also De Neve 2011). By withdrawing from the labour force and becoming homemakers they could claim to be middle class. While this is contrary to modernist theory which argues for increased participation of women in the work force, this withdrawal indicates the importance of the intersection of the logics of caste and the aspirations of class in situations of social mobility. This also further emphasizes the need for more work on gender, aspirations, and anxieties around mobility (Luke, 2019).

Discussion

This chapter has provided a brief overview of the literature around social mobility of castes as well as patterns of occupational mobility by caste. While there is a persistence of the association of caste with class, especially at the extremes of the caste system, there is some evidence of group level mobility which is a slow, long-term, and much contested process, as well as mobility at the individual occupational and educational level. However, the burden of caste remains.

Through looking at results of both macro studies and in-depth field-based research we find that not all members of a caste are mobile even if a few have been. This is what Osella and Osella (2000) show with their study of the Izhavas who had followed a group mobility project of rejecting their 'stigmatized caste identity' (p. 16) in the early 20th century by embracing 'education, respectable employment, thrift and accumulation of wealth, abolition of untouchability, entry into the mainstream Hindu fold' (p. 16). However, not all Izhavas have been successful in this project though major advances have been made. It is in effect the differentiation between and within castes that leads to possibilities of mobility for certain members of a caste, but that may also prevent the mobility of an entire caste. This example underlines the need to marry studies on both broader patterns of social mobility to capture how castes may have broadly moved up or down, to studies that explore in more detail the specific experiences, aspirations, and frustrations that mobility or its absence entails.

Finally, the absence of a gender dimension to much of this research, especially that at the macro level, is glaring. Through a few studies that exist, it is clear that women experience mobility differently and experience distinct barriers which also vary by caste. Further research would do well to look at the interaction of caste, class, and gender in the context of social mobility.

References

Ambedkar, B. R. 1916. 'Castes in India: Their Mechanism, Genesis and Development, Anthropology Seminar of Dr. A.A. Goldenweizer at The Columbia University, New York, U.S.A. on 9th May 1916'. *Source*: Indian Antiquary, May 1917, XLI. Available online at http://www.ambedkar.org/ambcd/01.Caste%20in%20India.htm, accessed September 2019.

Asher, Sam, Paul Novosad, and Charlie Rafkin. 2020. 'Intergenerational Mobility in India: New Methods and Estimates across Time, Space, and Communities'. *Compare: A Journal of Comparative International Education*, 40(2): 199–212. A version available at: http://www.dartmouth.edu/~novosad/anr-india-mobility.pdf, accessed September 2020.

Azam, Mehtabul, and Vipul Bhatt. 2015. 'Like Father, Like Son? Intergenerational Educational Mobility in India'. *Demography*, 52(6): 1929–1959.

Benei, Veronique. 2010. 'To Fairly Tell: Social Mobility, Life Histories, and the Anthropologist'. *Compare: A Journal of Comparative and International Education*, 40(2): 199–212.

Béteille, Andre. 1993. 'The Family and the Reproduction of Inequality'. In Patricia Uberoi (Ed.), *Family, Kinship and Marriage in India* (pp. 435–451). Delhi: Oxford University Press.

Blau, Peter M., Otis D. Duncan, and Andrea Tyree. 1967. *The American Occupational Structure*. New York, London: Free Press; Collier Macmillan.

Bougle, Celestin. 1971. *Essays on the Caste System* (Trans. with an Intro. by D. F. Pocock). Cambridge: Cambridge University Press.

Charsley, Simon. 1998. 'Sanskritisation: The Career of an Anthropological Theory'. *Contributions to Indian Sociology*, 32(2): 527–549.

Datta, Ankur. 2017. *On Uncertain Ground: Displaced Kashmiri Pandits in Jammu and Kashmir*. New Delhi: Oxford University Press.

De Neve, Geert. 2011. '"Keeping It in the Family": Work, Education and Gender Hierarchies among Tiruppur's Industrial Capitalists'. In H. Donner (Ed.), *Being Middle-class in India: A Way of Life* (pp. 73–99). London: Routledge.

Deshpande, Ashwini. 2011. *The Grammar of Caste: Economic Discrimination in Contemporary India*. New Delhi: Oxford University Press.

Deshpande, Ashwini, and Katherine Newman. 2007. 'Where the Path Leads: The Role of Caste in Post-University Employment Expectations'. *Economic and Political Weekly*, 42(41): 4133–4140.

Dickey, Sara. 2012. 'The Pleasures and Anxieties of Being in the Middle: Emerging Middle Class Identities in Urban South India'. *Modern Asian Studies*, 46(3): 559–599.

Dickey, Sara. 2013. 'Apprehensions: On Gaining Recognition as Middle Class in Madurai'. *Contributions to Indian Sociology*, 47(2): 217–243.

Donner, Henrike. 2008. *Domestic Goddesses: Maternity, Globalization and Middle-class Identity in Contemporary India*. Hampshire: Ashgate Urban Anthropology Series.

Dube, Leela. 1996. 'Caste and Women'. In M. N. Srinivas (Ed.), *Caste: Its 20th Century Avatar*. Delhi: Viking Penguin.

Dumont, Louis. 1970. *Homo Hierarchicus: The Caste System and Its Implications*. London: Weidenfeld & Nicolson.

Emran, M. Shahe, and Forhad Shilpi. 2019. 'Economic Approach to Intergenerational Mobility: Measures, Methods, and Challenges in Developing Countries', WIDER Working Paper 2019/98. Helsinki: UNU-WIDER.

Fields, Gary S. 2019. 'Concepts of Social Mobility'. WIDER Working Paper 2019/106. Helsinki: UNU-WIDER.

Fuller, C. J. 1996. *Caste Today*. Delhi: Oxford University Press.

Fuller, Chris J., and Haripriya Narasimhan. 2015. *Tamil Brahmans: The Making of a Middle-Class Caste*. New Delhi: Social Science Press.

Goldthorpe, John H. 2003. 'Progress in Sociology: The Case of Social Mobility'. Sociology Working Papers, Paper No. 2003-08, Department of Sociology, University of Oxford.

Gupta, Dipankar. 1991. *Social Stratification*. Delhi: Oxford University Press.

Harriss, J. 2016. 'The Story of the "Slater Village": Studies of Agrarian Change in Tamil Nadu, and Methodological Reflections upon Them'. In Himanshu, P. Jha, and G. Rodgers (Eds.), *The Changing Village in India: Insights from Longitudinal Research* (pp. 20–34). New Delhi: Oxford University Press.

Heath, Anthony F. 2003. 'Social Mobility'. In J. Mokyr (Ed.), *Oxford Encyclopaedia of Economic History* (pp. 521–524). Oxford: Oxford University Press.

Heyer, Judith. 2015. 'Dalit Women Becoming "Housewives": Lessons from the Tiruppur Region 1981/2 to 2008/9'. In Clarinda Still (Ed.), *Mobility or Marginalisation: Dalits in Neo-Liberal India*. New Delhi: Routledge.

Inglis, P. 2019. *Narrow Fairways: Getting by and Falling behind in the New India*. New York: Oxford University Press.

Iversen, Vegard, Anirudh Krishna, and Kunal Sen. 2016. 'Rags to Riches? Intergenerational Occupational Mobility in India'. GDI Working Paper 2016-004. Manchester: The University of Manchester.

Iversen, Vegard, Anirudh Krishna, and Kunal Sen. 2021. *Social Mobility in Developing Countries: Concepts, Methods, and Determinants*. Oxford: University Press.

Jeffrey, Craig, Patricia Jeffery, and Roger Jeffery. 2008. *Degrees without Freedom? Education, Masculinities and Unemployment in North India*. Stanford, CA: Stanford University Press.

Jodhka, Surinder S. 1998. 'From "Book View" to "Field View": Social Anthropological Constructions of the Indian Village'. *Oxford Development Studies*, 26(3): 311–331.

Jodhka, Surinder S. 2012. *Caste: Oxford India Short Introductions*. Oxford: Oxford University Press

Jodhka, Surinder S., and Katherine Newman. 2007. 'In the Name of Globalisation: Meritocracy, Productivity and the Hidden Language of Caste'. *Economic and Political Weekly*, 42(41): 4125–4132.

Kalleberg, Arne L., and Ted Mouw. 2018. 'Occupations, Organizations, and Intragenerational Career Mobility'. *Annual Review of Sociology*, 44(1): 283–303.

Kumar, Sanjay, Anthony Heath, and Oliver Heath. 2002. 'Changing Patterns of Social Mobility'. *Economic and Political Weekly*, 37(40): 4091–4096.

Luke, Nancy. 2019. 'Gender and Social Mobility: Exploring Gender Attitudes and Women's Labour Force Participation'. WIDER Working Paper 2019/108. Helsinki: UNU-WIDER.

Majumder, Rajarshi. 2010. 'Intergenerational Mobility in Educational and Occupational Attainment: A Comparative Study of Social Classes in India'. *Margin: The Journal of Applied Economic Research*, 4(4): 463–494.

McMillan, Alistair. 2005. *Standing at the Margins: Representation and Electoral Reservation in India*. Oxford: Oxford University Press.

Munshi, Kaivan. 2011. 'Strength in Numbers: Networks as a Solution to Occupational Traps'. *The Review of Economic Studies*, 78(3): 1069–1101.

Naudet, Jules. 2018. *Stepping into the Elite: Trajectories of Social Achievement in India, France and the United States*. New Delhi: Oxford University Press.

Osella, Filippo, and Caroline Osella. 2000. *Social Mobility in Kerala: Modernity and Identity in Conflict*. London: Pluto Press.

Parry, Jonathan. 1980. 'Ghosts, Greed and Sin: The Occupational Identity of the Benares Funeral Priests'. *Man*, 15(1): 88–111.

Parry, Jonathan. 1999. 'Lords of Labour: Working and Shirking in Bhilai'. *Contributions to Indian Sociology*, 33(1–2): 107–140.

Ram, Nandu. 1988. *The Mobile Scheduled Castes: Rise of a New Middle Class*. Delhi: Hindustan Publishing Corporation.

Ram, Nandu. 1995. 'Social Mobility and Status Identification among Scheduled Castes: A Synoptic View'. In K. L. Sharma (Ed.), *Social Inequality in India: Profiles of Caste, Class, Power and Social Mobility* (pp. 440–58). Jaipur, India: Rawat.

Silverberg, James. 1968. *Social Mobility in the Caste System in India: An Interdisciplinary Symposium*. Comparative Studies in Society and History (Suppl. III). The Hauge: Mouton.

Srinivas, M. N. 1952. *Religion and Society among the Coorgs of South India*. Oxford: Oxford University Press.

Srinivas, M. N. 2003. 'An Obituary on Caste as a System'. *Economic and Political Weekly*, 38(5): 455–459.

Still, Clarinda. 2015. *Dalits in Neoliberal India: Mobility or Marginalisation?* New Delhi: Routledge.

Treiman, Donald J., and Harry B. G. Ganzeboom. 2014. 'The Fourth Generation of Comparative Stratification Research'. In Stella R. Quah and Arnaud Sales (Eds.), *The International Handbook of Sociology* (pp. 123–150). London: SAGE.

Vaid, Divya. 2014. 'Caste in Contemporary India: Flexibility and Persistence'. *Annual Review of Sociology*, 40: 391–410.

Vaid, Divya. 2018. *Uneven Odds: Social Mobility in Contemporary India*. New Delhi: Oxford University Press.

Vaid, Divya. 2021. "Ethnography and Social Mobility: A Review". In Vegard Iversen, Anirudh Krishna and Kunal Sen (Eds.), *Social Mobility in Developing Countries: Concepts, Methods, and Determinants (247-270)*. Oxford: Oxford University Press.

Vaid, Divya, and Ankur Datta. 2019. 'Caste and Contemporary Hindu Society: Community, Politics and Work'. In Torkel Brekke (Ed.), *The Oxford History of Hinduism: Modern Hinduism* (pp. 216–243). Oxford: Oxford University Press.

Vaid, Divya, and Anthony F. Heath. 2010. 'Unequal Opportunities: Class, Caste and Social Mobility.' In Anthony F. Heath and Roger Jeffrey (Eds.), *Diversity and Change in Modern India: Economic, Social and Political Approaches* (pp. 129–164). Oxford: Oxford University Press.

CHAPTER 41

CASTE AND GENDER

PUSHPESH KUMAR

THIS chapter dwells upon the feminist concerns on the caste in relation to gender. The chapter begins by briefly sketching the anti-caste movements in the western and southern India to demonstrate the latter's specific focus on the role of caste in sustaining gender oppression and goes on to discuss kinship literature in explicating the linkage between caste and gender. The sections following this draw on the existing scholarship emerging through the Dalit women's assertion against the *savarnization* of the 'mainstream' women's movements and 'masculinization' of Dalit movements. It also focuses on the writings of Dalit women that began to be published during the 1990s, bringing forth the multifaceted nature of oppression and exploitation experienced by Dalit women. The final section of the chapter throws light on to the question of sexual citizenship and its relation to caste, focusing on the issues of LGBTQI movement in India, and its relation with anti-caste movements. The chapter concludes by putting forth narratives of two Dalit non-heterosexual subjects and their intertwined experiences of caste and sexuality.

GENDER AND CASTE: THE ANTI-CASTE MOVEMENTS

Much before academic concerns, the issue of caste and women's position in it emerged in India in the second half of the 19th century in anti-caste struggles. Phule, Periyar, Iyothee Thass, and Ambedkar, in their scathing attack on the privileged social order, imagined caste, and gender discriminations as closely related phenomena. Women's liberation was integral to their anti-caste articulations. Jotirao Phule, the ideological-political founder of the anti-caste movement in Maharashtra established the Satyasodhak Samaj (Society for Seekers of Truth) in 1873 with the vision of bringing fundamental change in society (Mani, 2005). Phule included women of all castes and communities in his notion of the oppressed and contended that the subordination of women and toiling castes, by denying them the right to education, was the main cause behind the appalling backwardness of Indian society (Mani, 2005, p. 275). He negated Brahmanical Hinduism and its caste system and thereby negated the in-built structures of gender relations in caste which instituted repressive sexual codes for women (Chakravarti, 2003). Phule opened his first school in Poona, the seat of Brahmanical conservatism, in 1848 for lower caste, untouchable girls, challenging the Brahmanical order by making knowledge an instrument of power, and creating the ability to develop critical faculty for both low caste and women (Chakravarti, 2003). Phule and his wife Savitribai launched their vehement campaign against enforced widowhood on upper caste women and opened orphanages for children born to Brahmin widows. Phule spearheaded the barbers' strike to motivate them to refuse to perform enforced tonsure on widows (Chakravarti, 2003).

Phule supported both Pandita Ramabai and Tararbai Sindhe for their courage in contesting both Brahmanical and non-Brahmanical patriarchies. Ramabai refused Brahmanical Hinduism by adopting Christianity and set up a widow home at a bigger scale, while Tarabai Sindhe, one of the active members of the Satyasodhak Samaj developed a fierce critique of patriarchy through her revolutionary pamphlet *Stree-Purush Tulana* (A Comparison between Women and Men) in 1882, wherein she questioned the hypocrisies of men and dominant patriarchal norms (see Chakravarti, 2003a). Inviting hostile reactions from the mainstream conservative patriarchs and the male dominated press of the time, Tarabai's essay is considered as the first modern feminist text in India (Chaudhuri, 2004).

E. V. Ramaswamy Naicker, better known as Periyar, founded the anti-caste organization Self Respect League in Tamil Nadu in 1926 bearing striking similarity to Phule's Satyasodhak Samaj (Mani, 2005). He called for the annihilation of caste, opposed Brahmanical hegemony, and championed the liberation of subjugated classes (*adidravida*) and women (Mani, 2005). Many adidravida women were active participants in the Self-Respect Movement [SRM] (Geetha, 1998) which developed a critique of upper caste nationalist women for participating in Brahmanical ideals like pativrata (worshipping husband) and celibacy. They campaigned for equal wages for women and advocated for household work to be recognized as (paid) work (Geetha, 1998). Voicing against the devdasi system, they denounced degrading religious practices for low caste men and women (Geetha, 1998). Periyar exposed the asymmetrical gender relation within marriage by questioning the differential sexual ethics for men and women, as V. Geetha (1998, pp. 13–14) writes,

> Marriage seemed to Periyar . . . sexual unfreedom thrust on women . . . and in order to counter this . . . Periyar exhorted women to . . . claim a free, self-validating desire . . . choose a life of economic self sufficiency and abjure the responsibility of motherhood . . . The freedom also implied that women could look on their bodies as their own, as part of their being . . . They could resist reification either into chaste wives and devoted mothers and could think of themselves as sports women, adventurous workers and thinkers.

Dr Ambedkar also saw a correlation between caste and gender oppressions. In Ambedkar's view, caste emerged through the regulation of women and hence, the annihilation of caste is a prerequisite to dismantle patriarchy (Pardeshi, 2003, p. 358). Ambedkar's idea of how upper caste patriarchy dealt with a 'surplus woman', a woman whose husband is dead, reflects his deeper understanding of the gendered codes of Brahmanical patriarchy. To him, the surplus woman is 'disposed of' in one of the two ways viz sati—burning a woman on her husband's pyre and if that is not possible, subjecting her to forced and degraded widowhood (Rege, 2013, p. 61). A surplus man (a widower) was, however, allowed to remarry even beyond the circle of endogamy if required. In Ambedkar's formulations, three operations central to the origin and development of caste come to light: the intra-group organization of reproduction, violent control of surplus women's sexuality, and legitimizing this control through ideology (Rege, 2013).

Ambedkar, in his essay 'Rise and Fall of the Hindu Women' published in his journal *Maha Bodhi* in 1951, dispelled the myth of the 'Vedic Golden Age' articulated by nationalists to show the high status of Hindu women, and held Manu responsible for the downfall of women (Rege, 2013). He publicly burnt Manusmriti, as this text ideologically justified the enslavement of shudras and women (Pardeshi, 2003). The participation of Dalit women in the various struggles launched by Ambedkar for dalit and women's liberation is well documented (Moon and Pawar, 2014; Zelliot, 2003). As the Labour Member in the Viceroy's Executive Council (1942–1946), Ambedkar drafted the Mines Maternity Benefit Act (Rege, 2013). His most important contribution towards gender equality was the promulgation of his Hindu Code Bill as the Law Minister in Nehru's first Cabinet (Zelliot, 2003). Through the Bill, Ambedkar sought to abolish compulsory endogamy, the indissolubility of marriage for Hindu women (read upper caste), to ensure women's rights to property, and questioned polygamy which subordinates the interests of individual woman (Rege, 2013). The Hindu Code Bill is seen as a manifesto of women's liberation (Rege, 2013).

Feminist Movements and Caste

Feminist movements, both in pre - and in post-Independent India, have worked on issues of domestic and public violence and legal reforms to empower women. They have mobilized women around land struggle, work and wage discriminations, reproductive health and care, etc. Issues of bodily autonomy and sexual control, dowry, sati, and poverty have informed feminist concerns (see Sen, 2004). While feminist movements talked about caste and class, it could not develop a thorough critique of the caste system from the perspective of dalit women, foregrounding the latter's experiences in the discourse and struggle for women's liberation. Gail Omvedt (1975) held economic inequalities as the prime factor responsible for the plight of lower caste-class women rather than 'traditional' cultural patriarchy. To Omvedt (1975), economic necessity forces these women into the lowest paid occupations for survival, but such work makes these women independent, vigourous, and extremely militant. Similarly, Chhaya Datar (1999) finds ecofeminist movements focus on caste-class oppression primarily in terms of environmental destruction, displacement and unjust distribution of natural resources, with poor women losing livelihood. Of course, these poor women belonged mostly to dalit and adivasi communities. Datar (1999) highlights that, during 1975–80, the focus of the left-oriented women's movement was mainly on the issue of discrimination in wage rates and legal rights at the work place. It does not mean that there was a complete absence of caste in feminist mobilizations, as feminists in Maharashtra did show solidarity with the protest around renaming of Marathwada University at Aurangabad after Dr Ambedkar. Another landmark feminist mobilization took place around the custodial rape of the Adivasi woman Mathura, affirming the commitment of feminist mobilization around marginal women. However, feminist mobilizations could not insert caste as a major concern in historically instituting what Anupama Rao (2003) calls the 'extraction of labour and surplus', material dispossession, and sexual appropriation of lower caste women which continue to exist in subtle and not so subtle ways in contemporary India amidst formal equality and legal empowerment. The essay by Kannabiran and Kannabiran (1991) reflecting the incidents of upper caste violence in Tsunder, Chilakurti, and Gokakarajapalli villages of Andhra Pradesh in South India can be considered as the first of its kind in developing a nuanced understanding of caste and gender as intermeshed social phenomena, and how each of these can only be understood with reference to the other. Writing about the differences between upper caste women's protest against alleged molestation of Reddi girls on the one and dalit women's protest on the other, the authors (Kannabiran and Kannabiran, 1991) point out the differential treatment meted out by the police and the state. While upper caste women's protest in the public sphere is legitimized, dalit women's protests are seen as transgressive.

Kinship, Gender, and Caste

The question of caste and gender primarily emerged through feminist investigations of family and kinship, after the institutionalization of women's studies. It is kinship as a structural principle and ideological norm that (re)produces caste simultaneously bear specific implications for women. Dube (2000) demonstrates in her essay on 'caste and gender' how a distinctive culture of caste, reflected in the modes of worship, fasts and festivals, purity and pollution, food practices, and the organization of space, is reproduced through the active participation of women in everyday life within the domestic sphere. She writes (Dube, 2000, p. 159), 'Women's practices in relation to food play a critical role in the hierarchical ordering of caste.' Maria Mies's study (2012) *Lace makers of Narsapur* reveals the entrapment of Kapu caste women in the purdah and housewife ideology, disabling them from taking up work outside, whereas the low caste Mala and Madiga women are able to earn more money through wage work outside, precisely because they were not 'respectable housewives'. Karin Kapadia's (1997) study of a rural Tamil Nadu region demonstrates the primacy of the matrilateral principle among Non-Brahmin castes, while patrilineal norms controlled upper caste Brahmin women. Kapadia's comparative perspective to analyse women located in different castes by using kinship, religion, and sexuality discourses of various castes, explain the degree of control each caste exercises on their own women. She also provides account of the lowest caste Pallar women of her fictive village Aruloor who are juxtaposed between the freedom and mobility they enjoy by virtue of being providers of their families, and the exploitation and discrimination they suffer as female members of an 'untouchable' caste (Kumar, 1998). Gloria Goodwin Raheja (1996) describes gendered norms of the dominant Gujar caste in rural north India through the term *besharam* indicating a woman without modesty, used for those women who would to go about with uncovered head, or loosely flowing hair.

Prem Chowdhry's (2004) research shows the policing of marriages by caste panchayats in Haryana, subsuming the individual will to village/collective will. Shalini Grover (2011), in her ethnographic study of marriage and cohabitation of low-income Scheduled Caste women in Delhi, talks about conjugal stability within love and arranged marriages respectively, secondary or consensual unions following widowhood or breakdown of marriages, and the role of informal women's courts in settling marital disputes. Puberty rituals and menstrual practices have been studied by feminist anthropologists, showing how caste purity, and gendered identities are symbolically produced through such practices (Kapadia, 1997; Narshimhan, 2011). Despite such richness and vigour of feminist reflections on kinship, gender, and caste, *dalit woman's standpoint* in problematizing caste remained absent till the 90s. Though kinship and gender studies made significant contributions in understanding caste dynamics and gendered realities, they remained silent on certain symbolic and material privileges which upper caste women might enjoy vis-à-vis dalit men and women despite the former being oppressed and subordinate within the caste order. As discussed in the subsequent section, the participation of upper caste women in Anti-Mandal Commission protests, and their defence of endogamous marriages reveal that 'women's solidarity' around the 'common oppressive' is illusive and untenable.

SAVARNIZATION AND MASCULINIZATION: DALIT WOMEN SPEAK OUT

Dalit women's perspective emerges through their assertion against what Sharmila Rege (2004, p. 216) calls the Masculinization of dalithood and Savarnization of womanhood. The Dalit Panther movement in 1970s Maharashtra was radical and counter-cultural. Rooted in Ambedkar's thought, dalit literary movements reflected an uncompromising critique of caste and Savarna literary sensibilities. However, both the Dalit Panthers and its literary arm remained unable to engage with the complex multiple marginalities of dalit women through the latter's subordination within Brahminical and dalit patriarchies. Encapsulated firmly in the role of 'mother' and 'victimized sexual beings' (Rege, 2004), women's productive and reproductive labour in sustaining upper caste patriarchies and reproducing dalit households on an everyday basis was simply ignored. The historically institutionalized appropriation of 'sexual labour', the stigmatization and marginalization of dalit women belonging to certain communities and their continuing plight within these multiple discriminations in their 'modern avatar'[1] did not inform male dalit writings.

The left party-based women's organizations and 'autonomous women's groups', emerging in the 1970s failed to engage with caste and untouchability as gendered experiences. While for the former, 'caste' was contained in class, for the latter, 'sisterhood' became 'pivotal' (Rege, 2004). Feminist organizations were formed and run by upper-caste/middle-class women with many dalit and tribal women as (only) members having no decision-making powers (Sowjanya, 2014). Feminist interventions into dalit and tribal women, especially in cases of rape and molestation, have been criticized as 'occasional interventions' (Sowjanya, 2014).

It is against this backdrop that National Federation of Dalit Women (NFDW) was founded in 1993 by Ruth Manorma, and the 'Dalit Mahila Snagthan' by Maharashtra Dalit Women in 1995 (Guru, 2003). Participation of many upper caste women in the anti-Mandal protests in early 1990s jumping on the 'meritocratic' bandwagon against caste reservation (Tharu and Niranjana, 1994) and the absence of dalit women leadership and decision-making within mainstream feminism (Sowjanya, 2014) formed the basis for the instating of these organizations. The formation of separate groups of dalit women is not simply a politics of *difference* or *mere inclusion*; it would constitute: (i) revisiting the issue of labour and surplus from the perspective of caste and its sexual economies,[2] and (ii) examining caste enforced dispossession either as the perpetuation of poverty or the lack of access to various forms of social capital (Rao, 2003). Rao (2003) argues that the symbolic economy of gender and sexuality and the material reality of the economic dispossession of dalit women need to be viewed together. Here, I draw upon Sharmila Rege's (1995) scholarly work on low caste 'entertainer' Kolhati women, the Lavani[3] performers in Maharashtra, demonstrating the appropriation and extraction of sexual and erotic labour, their marginalization and dispossession, and their simultaneous entanglement in upper caste and dalit patriarchies. Apart from Kolhati women,

---

[1] Rege talks about sexual slavery during the Peshwa period which transformed into a different kind of bondage through colonial interventions and the postcolonial modern state decried slavery without preparing the material conditions for the slaves to abandon and transform into 'free citizens'.

[2] The phrase 'sexual economies' here indicates the appropriation of sexual and physical labour of lower caste women in a system of upper caste domination with simultaneous regulation and control of upper caste women's sexuality.

[3] Lavani is an erotic dance performed traditionally by lower caste women for upper-caste men. In postcolonial India, the Marathi cinema appropriated this erotic form to give it a cinematic twist by projecting the lavani performers as hot chilli (*mirchi*). See Rege (1995).

many lower caste women have had been associated with this folk art and subjected to similar marginality and appropriation.

The Kolhatis in Maharashtra, a nomadic community in postcolonial India, were assimilated within the caste system in Maharashtra as part of *balutedari* (patron-client) relations, with women of the community traditionally being the entertainers of elite castes (read male). Rege describes these performing women as travelling or nomadic *balutedars,* who travel from village to village performing lavani. For learning the skills of erotic (*shringarik)* lavani, these women had to remain unmarried. In popular imagination, the shringarik or erotic became one of the modes of constructing the bodies of these lower caste women as either constantly arousing or satiating male desire (1995, p. 25). Troupes of Kolhati women performers are called sangeet bares,[4] often labelled as obscene and immoral. Many of the Kolhati women were part of slavery, instituted during pre-colonial Peshwa times; the mode of recruitment into the slavery system was through the accusation of lower caste women as adulterous, and then incorporating them into royal slavery to appropriate their productive and sexual labour.[5] Rege (1995) argues that Marathi cinematic representation has over-sexualized these women's bodies by coining the word 'mirchi' (hot chilli), who would be tamed and reformed by the hetero-hero [invariably a Patil's son or school master, always from an upper caste] (Rege, 1995). Hot chilli indicates an uncontrolled female; her taming by the upper caste hetero-man highlights not only the dichotomy of passive and pure wives against the wild and impure *nacchis,* but also reiterates the inability of lower caste men to control the sexuality of their women, thereby legitimizing the hegemony of dominant caste men whose women are emblems of 'controlled sexuality' (Rege, 1995). Apart from providing erotic and sexual labour to the upper caste,[6] Kolhati women and their decision-making are controlled by their own family, kin networks, and caste Panchayat who sustain from their earnings. Once she is put out for business (by her kin) in sangeet barees, she cannot marry and any transgression of this norm is punishable by the caste Panchayat (Rege, 1995). Through the Kolhati performer's sexuality, Rege demonstrates how women of low caste perform 'impure' and 'degraded' sexual labour, historically instituted through the mechanism of procuring female slaves. Even in the absence of slavery system, Kolhati women, along with other low caste female performers, are subordinated through both upper caste and dalit patriarchies, and their labour is not

---

[4] Rege (1995, p. 29) mentions that the Sangeet Baree troupes were formed by Kolhati women around 1900s. In precolonial India, the ruling elite, Peshwas were the patrons of these folk artists. But with the end of Peshwa rule around 1818, the *lavani tamasha* troupes had to shift to rural areas patronized by the feudal lords and Zamindars of the village. Further, with the emergence of the Marathi theatre and its association with the emerging middle-class, lavani performing women and their art were viewed as licentious and immoral. Rege (1995) speculated the emergence of sangeet barees through the initiatives of these low caste women in which Kolhati women took the lead.

[5] These Kolhati performers have definite linkages with their predecessor slave sisters (Rege, 1995).

[6] The highest bidders are invariably the upper-caste and middle-caste men despite the mixed male audience who watch these performances.

rewarded through proper remuneration, unlike the many non-dalit heroines who perform lavani onscreen in Marathi cinema.

The assertions of dalit women during the 1990s surfaced through their writings including autobiographies, fictions, historical accounts (Moon and Pawar, 2014) and poetry. Filled with memorialization of the 'untouchable' past, stigma, dispossession, back-breaking work, and violence, these literary sensibilities expose, satirize, and critically reflect on upper caste customs as well as domination by their own (dalit) men. The dialectics of belonging to dalit communities while also being aware of dalit patriarchies inform their articulations. It is not possible to list out all the names and the entire spectrum of dalit feminist writings in this chapter, but it is worthwhile to provide a brief account of some of the most circulated texts from Maharashtra and a few southern states. Meenakshi Moon and Urmila Pawar's collection (trans. Sonalkar) *We Made History Too,* comprise accounts of dalit women's participation in Ambedkar's struggle against untouchability. These women participated in the Mahad Satyagraha (1927), the conferences of Scheduled caste Federation in the 1940s, the Satyagraha against the Pune Pact (1946), Buddhist Mahila Mandals in the 1950s and in the conversion to Buddhism (Rege, 2005, p. 53). Emerging as leaders, some of them established schools, hostels, and orphanages for girls while others shouldered leadership in the labour movement, land struggles, and movements to extend reservation to dalits (Moon and Pawar, 2003, p. 55).

Sharmila Rege's book, *Writing Caste, Writing Gender* (2004), contains an elaborate introduction to the inseparability of gender and caste in dalit women's perspective as well as testimonies of eight dalit women translated to English from Marathi. In her testimony, Babytai Kamble (in this volume) argues that the memories of humiliation of enslaved lives need to be reiterated because future generations must know about the fiery ordeal that the earlier generations have gone through (2006, p. 194). Detailing her life in the *marahwada*, the residential quarters of Mahars on the outskirts of the village in the 1920s, Babytai describes how most houses were 'plastered with mud' and 'decorated with eternal poverty'. Describing the reproductive labour of women in her community, Babytai writes (Rege, 2004, p. 206),

> Mothers who give birth ... have to tie up their stomach just after child birth ... in the pregnant woman's hut, there is no grain even to make simple gruel. After the woman delivers the baby, her stomach becomes empty, and it needs to be layered with soft food. ... The woman ... just delivered the baby ... asks repeatedly for food, laying on torn rags, crying in pain ...

Kumud Pawade, another dalit feminist in her account titled *Antasphot* (Outbursts), *inter alia* narrates her journey of becoming a Sanskrit Professor as a dalit woman; she remembers the laughter and ridicule among interviewers after she left them, 'Now they want to teach Sanskrit eh?' (2004, p. 245). Pawade mentions how her marriage to a Savarna person and the subsequent change in her surname—from Somkuvar to Pawade (a Kunbi Maratha surname)—projected her identity as a Savarna and fetched her a lecturer's job in Sanskrit (2004, p. 246). Urmila Pawar derives the title of her autobiography *Aiadan*[7] (bamboo baskets) from her mother's work of bamboo weaving as she narrates her humiliation of delivering baskets, which her mother would weave, to the customers. She hated that people would sprinkle water to 'purify' the baskets which she delivered. At school too, her teacher, Harkekar Guruji, often picked on her to clean the dung in the school grounds when it was the turn of her class to do so (2004, p. 284). As an activist in dalit movement also, she experienced the secondary treatment given to women (2004, p. 292). She writes about the casteism in urban metropolitan spaces. On the occasion of her little daughter Manini's birthday, the latter's friends were invited. When these children went home and described the figurines of Buddha and Ambedkar that they had seen in their house, one of the friends' mother informed how Maratha castes were not to eat food at her house (2004). Pawar, mentioning the tensions of her marital life and her husband's patriarchal attitude, reflects on dalit women's lives and labour, and dalit men's patriarchal control. She further cites instances of dalit men's hegemony in dalit movement and the simultaneous absence of a foregrounding of Ambedkar's perspective in the women's movement leading to the formations of dalit women's collectives.

Dalit Feminism: Southern India

The 1990s also witnessed dalit activism and writings throughout South India and parts of Northern India. The literary works of Telugu, Tamil, and Malayalam dalit feminists are included in exclusive Oxford anthologies of dalit writings from each of these three regions. Such scholarship published in regional languages with powerful articulations of anger and protest against caste and patriarchy are being translated to English. It is difficult to capture voices from all regions and of all dalit feminist writings here. Apart from Marathi dalit feminists,[8] names of prominent Tamil dalit feminists include Bama Faustina with her two famous writings—*Karukku* and *Sangati*; Meena Kandasamy's poetry collection *Touch and Militancy* has won accolades for its unapologetic critique of caste in its traditional and modern avatars through a dalit feminist lens. Telugu dalit feminist Gogu Shyamala's work '*Father May Be an Elephant and Mother only a Small Basket But . . .*' depicts the lives of the most marginal Madiga community bringing out many facets of the exploitation of women of lower castes, including the forced *Jogini* system instituting the sexual exploitation of dalit women by the privileged caste under a religious garb. Here, I limit myself to a couple of dalit feminist writings which portray the different material and symbolic worlds of dalit

---

[7] Urmila Pawar's autobiography has been translated by Maya Pandit (2009) titled *The Weave of My Life: A Dalit Women's Memoir*.

[8] Maya Pandit (2019) lists out three generations of dalit feminists in Maharashtra with shifting focus in their literary work.

women, enabling, and disabling their agency.[9] Jupuka Subhadra, a Telugu dalit feminist in her poem, *My Kongu Is Not a Sooty Rag*, delineates the function of the drape of the saree which for upper caste women implies covering the bosom for modesty and respectability (see Rani, 2012). For Subhadra, her drape (*Kongu*) becomes the cushion for pots which bring head-loads of water from a distance. It becomes a wrap around her waist during agricultural activities like sowing, weeding, reaping, and harvesting. Vijila, a Malayali dalit poet, in her poem *I can't grow my Nails*, contrasts the privileged caste women whose long painted nails move around the computer and phone keypads with that of a poor dalit woman's nails which are stunted with wounds and calluses, as her nail polish begins to flake along the blackened vessels she washes everyday (see Dasanet et al., 2012). These caste-based material conditions of life surround dalit women's everyday life and writings.

Though many members of dalit communities have experienced upward mobility with modernity touching their lives, the upper-caste, middle-class discriminatory attitude persists, and orchestrates in visible and invisible forms. Rekha Raj (2013) discusses about dalit women and their protests gaining media attention in Kerala post-1990s and the controversy in Kerala's public sphere about C. K. Janu, a dalit woman activist. When Janu appeared on TV channels in a silk saree and with 'full make-up', she was accused of being 'funded'. Dalit woman activists are reprimanded by the police as Saleena Prakkanam, a woman dalit activist, asks—'Would anybody have sufficient courage to scold Sreemathi or Ayisha Potti,[10] as the policemen do to me'? (Raj, 2013, p. 61).

Dalit women are subjected to structural violence on account of their poverty, resourcelessness, poor nutrition, and overwork, besides caste-based violence in the form of sexual assault particularly in the rural context. Under the Jogini system, girls between the ages of 5–13 years are dedicated to temple deities. They are not allowed to marry and are forced into prostitution, eventually auctioned into urban brothels (Aloysius et al., 2011, p. 12). Aloysius et al. (2011) list out and empirically demonstrate verbal abuse, physical assault, sexual violence, kidnapping, abduction, and forced incarceration, medical negligence, child abuse, and domestic violence as the several forms of violence against dalit women. One of the most humiliating methods of caste-based violence is the stripping off women naked and parading them in public (Rao, 2009). This brings us to the question of sexual assault of dalit women as a mechanism to reinforce upper caste male domination by demonstrating the helplessness of dalit men to protect their women. The dalit men then are considerably emasculated, and are not only taught a lesson through their women's sexual assault, but are rendered marginalized and subordinate in the masculinist economy of the village (see Kannabiran and Kannabiran, 2003).

---

[9] My choice of these writings is to reiterate certain points and not based on any other consideration.
[10] These two are privileged and well-known female political figures in Kerala.

Caste and Sexual Citizenship

The hitherto illegal subjects in India, the LGBTQIA+, have been extended citizenship through two Supreme Court Verdicts viz. the NALSA Verdict of 2014 recognizing Transgender communities as legal subjects, and the Navtej Singh Johar vs Union of India verdict, 2018 which legalized gay sex in private. The politicization of 'sexual and gender minorities' began in the early 1990s when International NGOs took up intervention programmes to prevent the growing incidence of HIV/AIDS in India. Sex workers, working-class male homosexuals, and transfeminine persons were identified as target groups practicing 'unsafe sex' by international donor agencies. The international HIV/AIDS interventions simultaneously imported the language of rights for the sexually subjugated, resulting in the mobilization of these minorities since 1990s. Their mobilization centred around legal reforms, particularly the reading down of Section 377 of the Indian Penal Code introduced by the colonial administration which made gay sex punishable by law and rendered non-heterosexual publics illegal. So, the recent legal reforms following the long struggles of the sexual and gender minorities were followed by celebratory moments and assertions of queer subjects in contemporary India. Legal reforms being the major focus of the LGBTQI+ movement, the question of caste and class remained untouched and under-theorized even here.

It is, however, important to highlight that a fair chunk of transgenders, particularly Hijras and Kothis, belong to dalit-bahujan castes. For many privileged gay and lesbian persons in India, the strategy has been to downplay their sexual orientation viz-a-viz family and kin, and 'come out' only when the prospect of financial independence becomes a possibility. Poor effeminate men from lower caste-class backgrounds only find support and succour in the hijra culture and take on the hijra-kothi identity. In my own study of Kothi in western India, I mostly came across men from dalit-bahujan backgrounds, while the more privileged persons with non-heterosexual erotic preferences never identified with the hijra-kothi culture.

The hijras and other transgender communities mobilized in solidarity following the suicide of dalit scholar Rohit Vemula at the University of Hyderabad, and forged alliances with dalit groups, and dalit feminists in the city. Placards of Ambedkar and Phule in the LGBT pride marches in Hyderabad city have become common. The community had called the Bahujan scholar, Kancha Ilaiah, to flag off the Pride March. A dalit activist from Hyderabad, Sharath Naliganti, composed a song glorifying the sphere of hijras following which 'glory to hijras' (Jai hijra!) became the key slogan in the pride marches in Hyderabad. However, the experiences of dalit-trans solidarity in Hyderabad are limited, and do not constitute an ideal model either for transgender communities or dalit groups as issues of non-heterosexual subjects within the context are not easily welcomed.

Here, I offer two narratives of dalit, non-heterosexual subjects articulating their dilemma as both 'dalit' and 'queer'. V. Angayarkanni (2017) from rural Tamil Nadu depicts her dilemma of being a queer woman which is not understood by her dalit family, kin, and community, while her dalit identity and poverty limits her possibilities of participating in queer life which exists outside her family and kin contexts. Angayarkanni (2017) writes,

> I have spent much of my life trying to forget the woman I loved and abandoned in fear of myself. I spent much time sitting by the riverbed wishing we would hold hands again and wishing she would tell me one more time how she loved me. She took her own life. She did not want to be married to the man her family forced her to. She left me with one more person to see hung to death in my lifetime ... I am also Dalit. Unlike my queerness, I do not know well enough what this means. I know that I have seen my brothers fight the Vellalar boys and not come home, at least not with breath. I know that my ancestors were slaves, bought and sold between landlords. I know my grandmother couldn't look herself in the face on even the good days. I know that my parents, my cousins, my sisters and brothers, they all show me their scars. I show them mine... I also know I am not wanted as a queer in my Dalit family. I am not held, I am not heard in political spaces. I am told Ambedkar did not speak of queerness. But, I told myself, Ambedkar likely didn't speak about coconut trees, or the platypus, or cancer, or predict global warming. I don't know. Maybe he did ... So whoever I am, I am not proud. Not yet. I also will wait for the queer community to unfurl and recognize that it was the work of oppressed caste people and oppressed caste transwomen who have given them whatever pride they have today.

The second narrative is taken from OUTCASTE, a project initiated by Sangama, a Bangalore based NGO working with the LGBT community (see Kumar 2018). Here 'A' from rural India narrates 'his' story as a 'low caste' and a 'non-heterosexual' youth (2018). He discusses the spatial segregation of caste settlements in his village and how he is addressed by his caste name—'Chambhar' by an upper caste landlord and by his own principal in the school, who himself is a Dalit (2018). 'A' also has experiences of sexual violence which he finds difficult to articulate; he is raped and sexually assaulted for possession of a sexually non-coherent self, his male anatomical sex, and his masculine gender mismatch with his same-sex erotic desire (2018). His gesticulation does not correspond to his masculine gender and he fails to conform to local homosocial norms. He cannot look for community support when his body is violated unlike that of women of his (dalit) community (2018). He fears of being branded as *gandu* (bugger) and prefers silence to retain his existence within his family and community. From this narrative, it appears that the dalit as a group can organize against caste dominance and state power; dalit women mobilize against dalit patriarchy, and Brahminical feminism (see Rage, 2004), but it is not easy for a 'dalit faggot' to mobilize his (dalit) community for justice (Kumar 2018).

Conclusion

The linkage between caste and gender oppression was first addressed by anti-caste movements in mid- and late 19th century and continued in Ambedkar's writings and his activism till 1950s. The assertion of radical dalit movements post- Ambedkar in 1970s and parallel growth of women's movements in India at this time ignored the question of dalit women allowing the latter to form their own separate groups and articulate and foreground their marginality while highlighting the inadequacies of the former movements. Dalit women's voices add radical and fierce critique of masculinization of anti-caste movements and savarnization of mainstream feminist concerns while reflecting on multiple and intersectional marginalities and oppressions. This radicalism of dalit women, however, could not connect to non-conforming genders and sexualities even when the latter belonged to dalit caste groups. The chapter includes two narratives of such dalit gender non-conforming persons whose vantage points, if included, will certainly democratize anti-caste transformatory politics.

References

Angayarkanni, V. 2017. 'Queer, Dalit, and Not Yet Proud: This Is My Story'. Retrieved from, Queer, Dalit And Not Yet Proud: This Is My Story (youthkiawaaz.com).
Cahudhuri, Maitrayee (Ed.) 2004. *Feminism in India*. London: Zed Books.
Cahudhuri, Maitrayee (Ed.) 2005. *Feminism in India*. London: Zed Books.
Chakravarti, Uma. 2003. *Gendering Caste* through *Feminist Lens*. UK: Bhatkal and Sen.
Chakravarti, Uma. 2003a. 'Reconceptualizing Gender: Phule Brahmanism and Brahmanical Patriarchy'. In Anupama Rao (Ed.), *Gender and Caste* (pp. 164–79). London: Zed Books.
Chowdhry, Prem. 2004. 'Caste Panchayat and Policing of Marriage in Haryana'. In Dipankar Gupta (Ed.), *Caste in Question: Identity or Hierarchy?* (pp. 1–42). Delhi: SAGE.
Datar, Chhaya. 1999. 'Non-Brahmin Rendering of Feminism in Maharashtra: Is It a More Emancipatory Force?' *Economic and Political Weekly*, 34(41): 2964–2968.
Dasan, M. et al. (Ed.) 2012. *The Oxford India Anthology of Malayalam Dalit Writing*. Delhi: OUP.
Dube. Leela. 2000. 'On the Construction of Gender: Socialization of Hindu Girls in Patrilineal India'. In Leel Dube (Ed.), *Anthropological Explorations in Gender* (pp. 87–118). Delhi: SAGE.
Geetha, V. 1998. 'Periyar, Women and Ethics of Citizenship'. *Economic and Political Weekly*, 13(17): WS-9–15.
Grover, Shalini. 2011. *Marriage, Love, Caste and Kinship Support*. Delhi: Social Science Press.
Guru. Gopal. 2003. 'Dalit Women Talk Differently'. In Anupama Rao (Ed.), *Gender and Caste* (pp. 80–85). London: Zed Books.
Irudayam S. J., Aloysius et al. 2011. *Dalit Women Speak Out: Caste, Class and Gender Violence in India*. Delhi: Zubaan.
Kannabiran, Vasanth, and Kalpana Kannabiran. 1991. 'Caste and Gender: Understanding Dynamics of Violence and Power'. *Economic and Political Weekly*, 26(37): 2130–2133.
Kannabiran, Vasanth, and Kalpana Kannabiran. 2003. 'Caste and Gender: Understanding Dynamics of Violence and Power'. In Anupama Rao (Ed.), *Gender and Caste* (pp. 249–260). London: Zed Books.
Kapadia, Karin. 1997. *Siva and Her Sisters: Gender, Caste and Class in Rural South India*. Delhi: OUP.
Kumar, Pushpesh. 1998. 'Book Review, Shiva and Her Sisters: Gender, Caste and Class in Rural South India'. *Sociological Bulletin*, 47(1): 108–111.
Kumar, Pushpesh. 2018. 'Queering Indian Sociology: A Critical Engagement'. *Explorations, E-journal of Indian Sociological Society*, 2(1): 60–85.

Mani, Braj Ranjan. 2005. *Debrahmanising History: Dominance and Resistance in Indian Society.* Delhi: Manohar Publishers.

Meis, Maria. 2012. *The Lace Makers of Narsapur.* London: Zed Books.

Moon, Meenakshi, and Urmila Pawar. 2003. 'We Made History, Too: Women in Early Untouchable Liberation Movement'. In Anupama Rao (Ed.), *Gender and Caste* (pp. 48–56). Delhi: Zubaan.

Nrashimhan, Hripriya. 2011. 'Adjusting Distances: Menstrual Pollution among Tamil Brahmins'. *Contributions to Indian Sociology*, 45(2): 245–268.

Pandit, Maya. 2019, 10 October. 'How Three Generations of Dalit Women Writers Saw Their Identities and Struggle?' Retrieved from https://indianexpress.com/article/gender/how-three-generations-of-dalit-women-writers-saw-their-identities-and-struggle-4984202/.

Pardeshi, Pratima. 2003. 'The Hindu Code Bill for Liberation of Women'. In Anupama Rao (Ed.), *Gender and Caste* (pp. 346–362). London: Zed Books.

Pawar, Urmila (trans. Maya Pandit). 2009. *The Weave of My Life: A Dalit Women's Memoir.* New York: Columbia University Press.

Pawar, Urmila, and Meenakshi Moon (Trans. Bandana Sonalkar). 2014. *We Also Made History: Women in Ambedkarite Movement.* Delhi: Zubaan.

Raheja, Gloria Goodwin. 2016. 'The Limits of Patriliny: Kinship, Gender and Women's Speech Practices in Rural North India'. In Mary Jo Maynes, Ann Waltner, Birgitte Soland and Ulrike Strasser (eds) Gender, Kinship and Power: A Comparative and Interdisciplinary History (pp 149-174). New York: Routledge.

Raj, Rekha. 2013. 'Dalit Women as Political Agents: Kerala Experience'. Economic and Political Weekly, Engage, 48 (18) Dalit Women as Political Agents: A Kerala Experience | Economic and Political Weekly (epw.in)

Rani, Suneetha K. 2012. *Flowering from the Soil: Dalit Women's Writings.* Delhi: Prestige Publishers.

Rao, Anupama. 2009. *The Caste Question: Dalits and Politics of Modern India.* California: university of California Press.

Rege, Sharmila. 1995. 'The Hegemonic Appropriation of Sexuality: The Case of *Lavani* Performers in Maharashtra'. *Contributions to Indian Sociology (n.s.)*, 29: 23–38.

Rege, Sharmila. 2004. Writing Caste, Writing Gender: Narrating Dalit Women's Testimonios. Delhi: Zubaan.

Rege, Sharmila. 2005. Writing Caste, Writing Gender. Delhi: Zubaan.

Rege, Sharmila. 2013. *Against the Madness of Manu: B.R. Ambedkar's Writings on Brahmanical Patriarchy.* Delhi: Navayana.

Rao, Anupama. 2003. 'Introduction'. In Anupama Rao (Ed.), *Gender and Caste* (pp. 1–47). Delhi: Kali For Women.

Sen, Ilina. 2004. 'Women's Politics in India'. In Maitrayee Chaudhuri (Ed.), *Feminism in India* (pp. 187–210). Delhi: Women Unlimited.

Sen, Ilina. 2013. *Against the Madness of Manu: B.R. Ambedkar's Writings on Brahmanical Patriarchy.* Delhi: Navayana.

Sowjanya. T. 2014, April–June. 'Forever Other: Understanding Dalit Feminism'. *The Philosopher*, 145–157.

Tharu, Susie, and Tejaswini Niranjana. 1994. 'Problems for a Contemporary Theory of Gender'. *Social Scientist*, 3(4): 93–117.

Zelliot, Eleanor. 2003. 'Dr Ambedkar and Empowerment of Women'. In Anupama Rao (Ed.), *Gender and Caste* (pp. 204–217). London: Zed Books.

CHAPTER 42

CASTE AND THE DIASPORA

RADHA MODI

[Caste] has been carried far beyond the border of the subcontinent with the spread of the Indian diaspora. Wherever Indians have gone, it has followed them; wherever they have settled, caste has also established itself.

Anand Teltumbde (2010, p. 11)

INTRODUCTION

The above quote by Anand Teltumbde, a prominent Dalit scholar, aptly captures the enduring reality of caste in the diaspora. The South Asian diaspora is the largest, with a long history of out-migration from the subcontinent, and as such the patterns of caste reproduction vary. The goal of this chapter is to examine those patterns of caste migration, reproduction, and transformation in the diaspora, highlight the deleterious impact of caste discrimination on lower caste communities, recommend new enquiries, and methodologies for the study of caste in the diaspora, and call for a rigorous scholarly commitment to Dalit-centred research.

The South Asian caste system, historically rooted in Hinduism, is a deeply entrenched form of division that stratifies based on fixed occupational status and duties and is passed down from one generation to the next. As Dr Ambedkar states, 'the Caste System is not merely a division of labourers which is quite different from division of labour—it is a hierarchy in which the divisions of labourers are graded one above the other' (1936, p. 14). The hierarchical system is bolstered by cultural, legal, and political traditions and structures that foster exclusion and inequality. *Brahmins* are at the top of the caste hierarchy, while *Sudras* (farmer workers) are at the bottom. Along this hierarchy, various other middle castes exist such as the *Kshatriyas* (warriors) and *Vaishyas* (merchants). *Dalits* (formerly known as 'Untouchables') and *Adivasi* (indigenous South Asians), cast even lower than *Sudras*, are completely excluded from society. This hierarchy, while less prevalent, also manifests in Pakistan, Bangladesh, Sri Lanka, Nepal, Maldives, and Bhutan.

The significance of caste in the South Asian subcontinent as well as in the diaspora continues to be a contested issue. Central to this debate is the question of mobility along the caste hierarchy. Current Indian scholarship argues that a 'closed' characterization of the caste system is an orientalist understanding of caste, and the system is more dynamic than previously understood (Srinivas, 1994; Vaid, 2014; Jodhka, 2015). At the same time, violence against Dalit communities by upper caste members continues and has increased over the last decade (Jodhka, 2015). Within India, there is a continued pattern of caste discrimination with systemic disparities along educational, income, and social network lines (Thorat and Newman, 2007; Desai and Dubey, 2012; Jodhka, 2015).

The ongoing debate also points to a fundamental enquiry in caste scholarship. Can the *system of caste* endure outside of the South Asian subcontinent? Grieco (1998) argues that the system of caste cannot be viable beyond its symbolic form abroad because the same structures that uphold caste socially, economically, politically, and culturally in India do not exist in those new destinations. Lal (2005) and Kumar (2012) indeed find migration and settlement on plantations interrupted caste practices and identities among some indentured migrant communities. However, even among those with lineage to indentured communities, caste has not been fully disrupted as it plays a subtle role in social relations today (Claveyrolas, 2015). Further, those who migrated voluntarily and under more humane conditions have reproduced caste hierarchical relations abroad. Other scholars, as a result, assert that while migration and settlement contexts may weaken or transform the system of caste among diasporic communities, potent caste practices beyond the symbolic form do persist and are impactful for important life outcomes (Waughray, 2009; Kumar, 2009; Teltumbde, 2010; Herzig, 2010; Harilal, 2015; Modi, 2016; Pariyar, 2019). If caste ideologies and practices do endure, what are the mechanisms of that reproduction? Does reproduction persist across generations as diasporic communities create long-term settlements abroad? Further, what criteria do scholars utilize to evaluate the development or erosion of the caste system? The answers to these questions depend on multiple factors such as the type of migration (indentured or free), caste status at the time of migration, quality, and continuity of family structure and networks in both sending and receiving countries, immigration policies in host countries, institutionalization of religious practices, transnational political influence, intercaste relations, and caste discrimination.

CASTE SELECTION IN MIGRATORY PATHWAYS

One critical element of caste persistence is the selection process of migration with two primary pathways: the coerced, and at times involuntary, migration under the colonial indentured labour system and the voluntary migration for economic, educational, and occupational opportunities abroad. The impact of migration and the context of resettlement on the reproduction of caste is varied. Those that were part of the earlier indentured labour had weak or symbolic connections to the caste system in daily life with some exceptions. Conversely, those who engaged in voluntary migration decades later have maintained a stronger alliance with the caste system.

The inhumane colonial indentured labour system disproportionately contracted lower caste South Asians. Their lower caste status made them vulnerable to various push and pull factors: harsh living conditions due to widespread famine, revolts, and persecution by the British rule, and the tyranny of the caste system in South Asia as well as targeting by recruiters for indenture work abroad. Recruiters relied on coercion and false promises to contract labourers into indentured servitude to meet labour demands with the abolition of slavery (Eriksen, 1992). A total of five million South Asians from the subcontinent were contracted for indentured labour (Kumar, 2009) from Calcutta, Madras, Bombay, and United Provinces of Bihar (Kale, 1998). Nearly a million were indentured to work on sugar and tea plantations on British colonial locales such as Mauritius, Fiji, British Guyana, Trinidad, Malaysia, and South Africa (Bhat and Narayan, 2010). The French and Dutch also recruited and contracted South Asians to work in locales such as Reunion, Martinique, Guadeloupe, and Suriname (Kumar, 2009). While lower caste members were overrepresented in indentured migration, the scholarship reveals a more complex picture of caste diversity among migrants. Lal (2012) finds indentured labourers in Fiji originated from varying caste communities including Brahmins. Communities living in Mauritius, Guyana, Trinidad, and Suriname originated from the very lowest of caste communities, as well as from upper caste groups, such as Brahmins and Rajputs (Schwartz, 1967).

The coerced migration and the colonial indentured system shattered networks, family systems, and communal religious practices weakening the caste system. The migration story of indentured labourers reveals a weakly held connection to caste (Lal, 2005; Grieco, 1998) that continues today in subtle and symbolic form (Claveyrolas, 2015). The lack of continuity of networks with the homeland and loose networks among the indentured consequently allowed for anonymity. Many lower caste South Indians traveling to South Africa changed names to shed the stigma of lower caste status, as documented by ship log discrepancies (Kumar, 2012). The structural limitations of plantation life also made it difficult for migrants to maintain the caste system. As Lal (2005) writes, 'People lived and worked together, slept under the same roof in the lines, shared the same well and toilet facilities. Even if they wanted to, they did not have the cultural resources to sustain the caste system. Most immigrants were young and illiterate and ignorant of the rituals and ceremonies associated with the caste system. The disproportionate sex ratio on the plantations produced cross-caste marriages. Breaches of caste rules could not be punished' (p. 12). The indentured community in South Africa, a majority Tamil- and Telugu-speaking lower caste community that came between 1860 and 1910, also did not reproduce a durable caste system under the harsh realities of plantation life. Kumar (2012) suggests that caste now may be more symbolic among South African South Indians who are descendants of indentured migrants, as they weakly maintain marital endogamy, do not practice vegetarian dietary restrictions, and have access to class mobility. South Asians in the Caribbean also symbolically maintain caste through porous marital endogamy. Despite diluted caste practices, communities in Mauritius subtly hold on to ancestral caste identities while also engaging in caste deniability (Claveyrolas, 2015). Teltumbde (2010) argues the lack of dominant caste identities in these regions is the result of majority lower caste positions among migrants. These communities had minimal incentive to sustain a system that had oppressed them. The contemporary example of the Gulf region's labour camps may mirror the experiences of indentured migrants on plantations. Migrant labour that travels to Gulf countries for semi-skilled and unskilled work face harsh conditions in labour camps. A Brookings Institute report suggests that caste boundaries are hardly observed in labour camps due to overcrowded housing, precarious and difficult work, and a lack of belonging (Pethiyagoda, 2017). In this case, the caste system is temporarily suspended and may resume when workers return home.

In contrast to the indentured migration, those that travelled and settled abroad voluntarily were more likely to maintain casteist ideologies and reproduce the caste system in these new locales. Voluntary migration is strongly associated with selective characteristics such as possessing resources to travel and settle abroad, continuing transnational social and political networks, migrating with intact family structures, overrepresenting middle and upper caste backgrounds and engaging in caste-based religious practices. Upper caste South Asians did not migrate in larger numbers until the liberalization of immigration policies in many Western countries in the 1950s and 1960s. The Immigration and Naturalization Act of 1965, in particular, attracted upper class and upper caste professionals to the U.S. As of 2003, the vast majority of immigrants from India were from upper caste communities, making up 90 per cent of Indians in the U.S. (Kapur, 2010). The over selection of middle and upper caste South Asians in voluntary migration is further fuelled by family unification policies in places such as the U.S., Australia, and New Zealand. Families sponsor relatives to migrate to the same destination with the aid of their upper caste and upper class resources and networks (Leckie, 1998). This form of chain migration consolidates dominant caste access to spatial mobility allowing their networks to stay intact with successive waves of emigration.

Voluntary Dalit migration post-independence also occurred but at a smaller scale. The highly selective immigration process, coded for upper class and caste migrants, prioritized professionals with human and social capital and consequently limited higher rates of Dalit migration to the West. Only Dalits, who came from urban middle-class families, had access to competitive educational training that would eventually open up doors for migration. Dalits, currently, make up a smaller share of the South Asian diaspora population in countries such as the U.S., U.K., Australia, Kenya, and New Zealand, but comprise a larger share of migrant labour in the Gulf regions. In Britain, Dalits from the *Chamar* (leather-working) caste came as part of the large Punjabi waves of emigration to Britain, with hopes of improving their social positionality on the heels of newly acquired resources from the increased value of leather in India post-independence (Judge, 2002; Bahadur, 2017). These hopes were quickly dashed, as many Dalits came to learn that caste had followed them to these new locales where upper caste compatriots reproduced their exclusive networks and organizations.

CLOSED NETWORKS AND ENDOGAMY IN CASTE REPRODUCTION

Within the literature on caste and diaspora, continuity and maintenance of closed networks and relations are critical for the persistence of caste. For example, the Gujrati South African population that originally came as merchants, did utilize caste ideologies, and practices to ostracize lower caste communities from their networks. They maintained 'caste consciousness' throughout the migration process by sustaining transnational family relationships, establishing caste-based organizations, and practicing marital endogamy (Greico, 1998).

The high concentration and saturation of upper caste South Asian immigrants in Western countries has resulted in a dynamic of unchecked casteist practices and shoring up of resources within upper caste-based closed networks. Within the U.S., Roohi (2017) argues that high-skilled workers rely on 'caste capital' to access upper caste formal and informal networks for educational and occupational opportunities. Tech recruitment agencies are often headed by upper caste members increasing chances of mobility for these high-skilled workers. Britain, an older immigrant gateway, seems to have the strictest and most solidified caste system due to the large networks of South Asians that arrived at the same time, especially as large family units (Kumar, 2012). This has allowed for subcaste formation and flourishing caste associations (Pariyar, 2019). Dalits have not been able to escape casteist violence in the U.K. by changing their name because of the strong presence of close-knit networks that make anonymity impossible. There have been numerous accounts of Punjabi Jatt upper caste violence against Punjabi Dalits (Human Rights Watch, 2001).

The use of caste-based networks has successfully aided Patels in the U.S. in creating a niche of hotel and store owning communities. Literature paints a picture of Patels, belonging to the *Paridar* (originally *Kanabi*) caste, as adept in their use of caste to access mobility (Chandra, 1997). The community is adherent to caste-based practices such as endogamy, vegetarianism, and engagement in caste-based associations resulting in exclusive, tight-knit networks. Dhingra (2012) demonstrates, through his ethnographic document of Indian motel owners, their extensive reliance on networks to generate capital for motel investments, recruit extended family members in hotel management, and dominate the U.S. motel industry.

Endogamic marriages, in particular, are opportunities to reinforce caste divisions and the status of upper castes. In Kenya, where occupational boundaries of caste have withered among its long-standing South Asians communities of Brahmins, Patels, Oshwals, Sikhs, Muslims, Ismailis, and Jains, endogamous marriages along class, caste, linguistic, and religious lines continues to be a driving force in perpetuating allegiance to caste and consequently reinforcing the reliance on communal closed networks to aid in partner selection (Herzig, 2010). Partner selection often involves input from multiple generations, and caste backgrounds are explicitly matched before further involvement. High-skilled workers in the U.S. utilize 'caste capital' to secure high class, high caste partners (Roohi, 2017). The resulting marriage alliances boost the socio-economic status and social capital for both parties and allow upper caste Indians to strategically negotiate social mobility within the transnational marriage market. Among the U.K. Sikh diaspora, where there is laxity around intercaste marriage, Dalit Sikhs are largely excluded from the social structure (Kumar, 2012). Taylor (2014) reveals that the U.K. Punjabi Dalits in his sample all engage in intra-caste marriages. As one participant explained, intercaste marriage ' "causes too many tensions" and he does not "encourage [his] children do it for these reasons" ' (Taylor, 2014, p. 242).

Transnational networks perpetuate closed networks as overseas Indians of professional and skilled background maintain strong ties with global networks that are linguistically, regionally, religiously, and caste specific. The Gujarati diaspora, for example, has various networks that connect Gujaratis globally such as the Shree Swaminarayan Gadi Sansthan or Vishwa Gujarati Samaj. Similar transitional alliances are utilized by the Tamil, Telugu, Bhojpuri-speaking Diaspora (Bhat and Narayan, 2010). According to Pande (2013), caste has become an important avenue to retain a connection to the nation-state. For example, the government of specific states in India has sponsored world conferences for non-resident Indians. These meetings include the World Gujarati Conference or the World Tamil Conference (Bhat and Narayan, 2010). Transnational conferences allow the nation-state of India to strengthen connections with the diaspora and promote Hindu-Indian nationalism abroad.

However, as online communities become prominent, traditional networks, and endogamous relations may not be as critical for caste reproduction as previously thought. Pariyar (2019) finds that in emerging gateway countries such as Australia, closed networks, endogamous relationships, and caste associations have less of a presence in daily life. She suggests that social media instead plays a key part in reproducing the caste system as these applications employ algorithms that promote network clusters based on location, similar backgrounds, common surnames, and congruous viewpoints. Social applications, such as *WhatsApp*, allow for diasporic connection with transnational familial networks particularly ones based in the South Asian subcontinent. Political and cultural hot button issues are transmitted, shared, and discussed on these platforms often reinforcing caste cleavages. The upper caste Australian-based Nepalese community, that is younger and more liberal, for instance, practices Brahminical Hinduism and engages in anti-Dalit joking online.

The exclusion from dominant diaspora social structures has pushed Dalits to create their own organizations, places of worship, and networks. Dalit diaspora communities have established Buddhist Vihars, Gurudwaras, and Hindu temples in Britain (Dalit Solidarity Network U.K., 2011). Kumar (2009) identifies multiple regional and international organizations developed on improving the lives of Dalits such as FABO

(Federation of Ambedkarite and Buddhist Organizations in the U.K.) and IDSN (International Dalit Solidarity Network). Diasporic Dalit activists have also developed social justice initiatives with oppressed communities globally, including Adivasi in India, Burakumin in Japan, and Blacks in America. The historically oppressed roots of both Black and lower caste South Asian communities provide an opportunity for solidarity and critical engagement. The partnerships with Black leaders have a long history in the U.S. Specifically, transnational efforts to accomplish this have been present since the late 19th century and brought to light by Ambedkar's letter to W. E. B. Dubois. Dalit organizers also partnered with the Black Panthers in a worldwide effort for the liberation of all oppressed people (Kumar, 2009). The relationship continues with a new generation of Dalit and Black collaborators in the U.S. (Ray, 2019).

CASTE REPRODUCTION THROUGH RELIGIOUS INSTITUTIONALIZATION

Castes hierarchies exists not only in Hindu communities but also in other South Asian religious communities (Ambedkar, 1936; Vaid, 2014). In his 1937 essay, *Annihilation of Caste*, Dr Ambedkar states that while caste is a Hindu construction, 'the Hindus have fouled the air all over, and everybody is infected—Sikh, Muslim, and Christian'. The institutionalization of South Asian Hinduism, Sikhism, and Christianity is key to how religion perpetuates caste in the diaspora.

The Hindu diaspora has been fervently institutionalizing Hinduism since the 1970s as a way to preserve ethnic identity in the U.S. (Kurien, 2007). Institutionalization here refers to the construction of temples by monied Hindu sects, formalization of Hindu education for youth, and the development of Hindu associations. Brahmanical Hindu ideologies of 'purity' and preserving purity through diet, hygiene, prayer, and appointing Brahmin priests are embedded within the ritualized practices and the standardized education. The focus on Brahmanical purity fortifies caste cleavages as Dalits are commonly perceived as 'impure' and ostracized from dominant temples, rituals, and worships (Equality Labs, 2016). Upper caste Hindus have also formed associations to promote pro-Hindu cultural and political projects (Kurien, 2017). The institutionalization of these Brahmanic ideologies and practices coupled with the construction of Hindu temples and associations reproduce aspects of the caste system in host countries. Hindu communities in Kenya, for instance, continue to identify along caste lines (Herzig, 2010).

Sikhs and Christians have also institutionalized caste divisions in their places of worships. Despite renunciation of caste by all major Sikh Gurus, upper caste Sikhs (*Jats-Sikhs*) actively segregate from lower caste Sikhs (*Ad-Dharmis* and *Ravidasis*). This segregation has been maintained through the exclusion of lower caste Sikhs from dominant caste Gurudwaras (Sato, 2012). While there is no religious scripture that encourages divisions between Christians, South Asian Christians accomplish caste segregation through the institutionalization of denominations. Originally only upper caste Hindus could convert to Christianity with the eventual mass conversion of Dalits later on (Fuller, 1976). Conversions did not change the social status of converts. Upper caste Hindus who converted became upper caste Christians: *Syrian Christians, Bamonns,* or *Chardos*. Lower caste Hindus who converted became lower caste Christians: *Sudirs* or Dalits. Upper caste Christian diaspora communities maintain their separation through denominational places of worship such as the Syrian Christian Church (Kurien, 2017).

A part of the institutionalization process has required collaboration with co-religious groups in South Asia through transnational religious networks. This collaboration authenticates diasporic claims to an ethno-religious identity in the host country (Kurien, 2007). Through this connection, the value of caste is continuously transmitted from the homeland to the diaspora. One Christian priest divulges that his efforts to attract lower caste members into his church are counteracted by caste prejudices prevalent among his parishioners (Kurien, 2017). For diaspora Hindus, global Hindutva is driving their local agenda of promoting a unified image of Hinduism, sweeping caste into the shadows, and consolidating Hindu-based political power (Bhatt and Mukta, 2000; Kurien, 2007).

In contrast, counterexamples demonstrate that institutionalization of caste is weakened by certain migratory pathways, competing forms of division, and Dalit assertion. For instance, even Hindu Brahmanical practices lost their significance among indentured communities as non-Brahmins took over ritual responsibilities in South Africa (Kumar, 2012) and the Caribbeans (Kannabiran, 1998). Further, since Muslim diasporas officially segregate by sect (i.e. Sunni or Shia), caste segregation is secondary. Muslims from various castes will worship alongside each while maintaining social distance (Herzig, 2010). Caste in Muslim communities includes Ashrafs or Syeds (higher status as related to ancestry to Prophet Muhammed), Ajlaf (considered lower born or non-Arab Muslims), or Arzal (Dalits who converted to Islam) (Shaban, 2018). Dalit conversion away from Hinduism is another way the caste system is destabilized. Many Dalits convert to Buddhism and to a lesser degree Christianity and Islam to escape Brahminical casteist practices. According to Taylor (2014), conversions are an act of Dalit assertion and resistance. Those in the diaspora that convert to Buddhism identify as Buddhist Ambedkarites to remember Dr Ambedkar's resistance against caste tyranny in Hinduism.

Caste Reproduction Across Generations

As South Asian diasporas establish permanent settlements abroad, the question of caste reproduction across successive generations becomes vital to diaspora scholarship. Caste reproduction is most likely to occur among upper caste communities who have a stake in maintaining caste hierarchies. Upper caste South Asians have settled in plural societies where competing forms of stratification exist such as class and racial hierarchies. Within the context of plurality, caste plays a dynamic albeit implicit role in the everyday lives of later generation South Asians.

U.S.-born upper caste South Asians passively learn caste ideologies and practices through socialization from first generation family members, engagement in caste segregated religious and organizational spaces, transnational family systems, and consumption of Bollywood (Modi, 2016). Inherent in these multiple socializing pathways is the prominence of colourism. Lighter skin colour often becomes a proxy for upper caste status, utilized by the first generation, co-ethnic communities, and popular culture. Family members will police their children's appearance to reproduce caste status in future generations. As the second generation comes of age, many deny the significance of caste in their lives, while continuing to engage in colourism and marital endogamy bolstered by U.S. racial logics (Modi, 2016).

In post-apartheid South Africa, where there has been a longer presence of South Asians, later generation of Gujaratis have secularized, and disengaged from caste-based events. Caste-based Gujarati organizations are losing membership with subsequent generations. Unlike their parents, newer generations do not view caste as a reliable form of mobility, and instead, utilize educational opportunities. A similar dynamic may occur in other regions as second and third generation South Asians come of age.

As such, reproduction of caste through endogamy has become complex in places such as Australia, the U.S., and South Africa, where the practice is declining or becoming more implicit with subsequent generations. Both native-born South African Gujaratis (Harilal, 2015) and U.S. South Asians (Modi, 2016) are less likely to favour caste endogamous marriages. However, matrimonial discussions among second generation South Asians in the U.S. convey implicit casteist motives such as preferences for light skin, certain occupations, diets, religious, and geographical background (Modi, 2016). Ramachandran (2019) suggests caste blindness might be an outcome of upper caste privilege. Deniability of caste may also be occurring alongside the prominence of colour-blind and multicultural ideologies in host countries. I find second generation South Asians living in the New York metro area engaged in both colour—and caste—blind values (Modi, 2016). As such, even implicit caste-based partner preferences manifest caste endogamy among second generation South Asians.

Among youth in Australia, caste hierarchies are maintained through 'assertions of diasporic "Indianness"' (Ramachandran, 2019) and for youth in the U.S., through assertions of 'model minority' (Modi 2016). Wanting to present an authentic Indian identity, participants knowingly and unknowingly engage in upper caste Indian cultural practices. For these communities, caste ideology, and caste behaviour not only assist in maintaining status but also preserve ethnic identity in plural societies. Preserving symbolic ethnic identities become paramount among later generation South Asian in the

U.S., as they simultaneously resist racialization post-9/11 and make efforts to integrate into American society (Modi, 2016).

Caste Discrimination

Caste discrimination remains hidden in various South Asian diasporic communities, allowing upper caste members to have unimpeded dominance in certain regions. Awareness raising and fighting discrimination have disproportionately fallen on the shoulders of Dalits. Dalit-led organizations collect data and disseminate information on trends of upper caste abuse, discrimination, and violence against Dalits within the diaspora. Push from organizers has brought the issue of caste discrimination to the mainstream, propelling policy organizations to collect state-wide evidence of casteist practices. Considering both Dalit and non-Dalit scholarship, caste discrimination manifests in overt and covert ways in interpersonal interactions, exclusive networks, and community level organizations.

A 2010 report by the National Institute of Economic and Social Research on caste discrimination in Britain, based on 32 semi-structured interviews with lower caste Britains, reveals self-reported accounts of discrimination in every major aspect of daily life: bullying at school, harassment at work, unfair treatment for services, exclusion from upper caste spaces and associations, and physical assaults for caste transgressions (Metcalfe and Rolfe, 2010). Caste-based discrimination is not limited to the Hindu diaspora and occurs across all South Asian communities in the U.K. (Waughray, 2009). British Punjabi Dalit youth, often bullied by upper caste peers, refrain from crossing caste boundaries, and developing inter-caste relations for the fear of reprisal (Dhanda, 2006). Sato (2012) describes the ongoing caste segregation within four British Gurdwaras. Caste divisions are also a common cause of fragmentation in a Pakistani Muslim community in Bradford (Alam and Husband, 2006). Metcalfe and Rolfe (2010) stress the potential for mental health issues among lower caste individuals from long-term exposure to caste-based harassment in Britain. These outcomes are also bolstered by reports from the Dalit Solidarity Network U.K.

Consistent with the findings in Britain, caste discrimination also impacts major aspects of daily life for Dalits and other lower caste subgroups in the U.S. Self-reported experiences of discrimination are documented in a 2016 report by the Dalit-led organization, Equality Labs. A majority of surveyed Dalit South Asians disclosed occurrences of prejudice in the workplace and one in three indicate facing harassment in school. The report also finds that 25 per cent of Dalit respondents have been verbally and physically assaulted, 39 per cent have been excluded from places of worship, and 40 per cent have been rejected in a romantic relationship because of their caste. Exploratory vignettes by the Pulitzer Center reveal that Dalit women, in particular, face harassment and sexual assault by upper caste men but do not report it for the fear of backlash (Ray, 2019).

Conclusion: A Way Forward

Evident in the patterns from the literature, while caste may decline or transform due to migration and settlement, caste is both a persisting, and dynamic force in South Asian diasporic communities. In particular, for those engaged in voluntary migrations post-independence, caste is a significant social organizing tool that has a meaningful impact on important life outcomes. Social exclusion and discrimination of lower caste communities are the most prominent caste-based practice within the diaspora. Dalits are excluded from upper caste associations and religious spaces in the U.K., U.S., and Australia. The institutionalization of Hinduism overseas adds to the further entrenching of caste divisions. Closed-networks, reinforced by martial endogamy, allow upper caste members to maintain status and privilege, preserve ethnic identity, and potentially reduce competition in access to mobility abroad. Even among the descendants of indentured migrants where the prevalence of the caste system has been weak, certain levels of marital caste endogamy and the reliance on caste narratives prevail to maintain distance from other minority populations. An important transformation of caste abroad is the use of caste logics alongside racial logics in multicultural societies across South Asian generations. As such, scholars on caste should move beyond the question 'does caste persist' to questions of how, when, and where does caste endure. The answers to these questions will offer more clarity on the divergent mechanisms of caste reproduction in the diaspora.

Academic scholarship on caste and diaspora must also centre the experiences and goals of lower caste communities. There is a dearth of systematic research on the material and psychological costs of caste discrimination for lower caste and Dalit diaspora. This is partly due to institutional and methodological limitations. The underrepresentation of Dalits in academic institutions and the limited knowledge of caste outside of South Asia often lead to an underwhelming interest in Dalit-centred research projects. If broad interest is there, securing funding and formulating a sampling methodology that will garner a representative sample of lower caste and Dalit participants are additional concerns. To counteract these barriers, one promising model utilizes partnerships between academics and Dalit-let organizations. Community-based surveys that are Dalit-led are one of the most valuable sources on the experiences of Dalits. Much of the existing work has relied on a snowball methodology and small sample sizes to document anti-Dalit discrimination. With the leadership of Dalits, South Asian community members and academics can conduct multiple community-level projects to capture both quantitative and qualitative data on caste discrimination. An example of a successful partnership is a comprehensive 2010 report on 'untouchability' based on 1589 randomly selected villages in Gujarat by the Navsarjan Trust and the RFK Center for Human Rights that outlines both vertical and horizontal discrimination. A similar systematic investigation will deepen understanding of caste discrimination and will also support policy initiatives on casteism within the diaspora.

Further, ongoing and changing contexts of diaspora demographics, globalization, and technology will continue to play a role in the dynamism of caste in the coming years. The most promising research on caste and diaspora will focus on these shifts. Aligned with these themes, I offer potential avenues for future scholarship.

Implicit caste-based bias is understudied in diaspora scholarship. As second and third generation South Asians, the descendants of voluntary migrants post-independence, come of age outside of the subcontinent, the role of caste is less clear-cut. Later generation upper caste South Asians are less likely to see caste as a factor in their upward mobility and offer other reasons such as hard work and education. They use implicit markers of caste in partner selection such as skin colour, diet, language, and educational background (Modi, 2016). In what ways do these micro implicit practices relate to aggregate patterns of caste inequality and segregation within the diaspora? Audit studies offer an inexpensive method of studying implicit caste-based bias present in the diaspora. They can be utilized to investigate bias in partner selection on dating sites, apartment rentals in South Asian ethnic enclaves, access to South Asian professional networks, or job callbacks from South Asian employers.

New scholarship should also make further inroads in studying the Hindutva movement, and its clout within the diaspora. For example, how has Hindutva's growing influence transformed caste among Indo-Caribbeans, where historically caste has been weak? The movement's goals are to consolidate Hindu political power by reframing the caste hierarchy as benign. The aim is not to destroy caste and systematic caste oppression but instead to convey an illusory image of caste diversity. Those firmly engaged in the Hindutva neoliberal project use caste blindness as a tactic to delegitimize Dalit assertions. A study of Hindutva will illustrate the macro, transnational processes involved in caste consciousness.

The third avenue of research should focus on the role of technology in both disrupting and reinforcing the caste system within the diaspora. An example of research along these lines is the work of Pariyar (2019). Pariyar's research alludes to the eclipsing of traditional networks by online communities in caste reproduction. The study of online networks will require creative methodologies and tackling new ethical concerns from scholars. Additionally, advancements in artificial intelligence, machine learning, and robotics make surveillance and censorship a growing concern for Dalit resistance globally. Scholarship on caste will need to centre a critical treatment of technology in caste replication.

It is clear that caste endures in the diaspora, as it endures in the subcontinent. The future of caste will not be its passive disappearance but an active confrontation by South Asians globally to its systematic dehumanization. Along with Dalit assertion, scholarship on the diaspora will be instrumental in illuminating the workings of the caste system and bringing caste biases to the surface.

References

Alam, Mohammad Yunis, and Charles Husband. 2006. 'British-Pakistani Men from Bradford'. York: *Joseph Rowntree Foundation*: https://www.jrf.org.uk/report/reflections-young-british-pakistani-men-bradford, accessed October 2021.
Ambedkar, Bhimrao Ramji. 1990 (1936). *Annihilation of Caste: An Undelivered Speech*. New Delhi: Arnold Publishers.

Bahadur, Bali. 2017. 'Tracing the Roots of Dalit Diaspora'. *International Journal of Applied Social Science*, 4(9&10): 383–392.

Bhatt, Chetan, and Parita Mukta. 2000. 'Hindutva in the West: Mapping the Antinomies of Diaspora Nationalism'. *Ethnic and Racial Studies*, 23(3): 407–441.

Bhat, Chandrashekhar, and K. Laxmi Narayan. 2010. 'Indian Diaspora, Globalization and Transnational Networks: The South African context'. *Journal of Social Sciences*, 25(1–3): 13–23.

Bose, Purnima. 2008. 'Hindutva Abroad: The California Textbook Controversy'. *The Global South*, 2(1): 11–34.

Chandra, Vibha Puri. 1997. 'Remigration: Return of the Prodigals—An Analysis of the Impact of the Cycles of Migration and Remigration on Caste Mobility'. *International Migration Review*, 31(1): 162–170.

Claveyrolas, Mathieu. 2015. 'The "Land of the Vaish"? Caste Structure and Ideology in Mauritius'. *South Asia Multidisciplinary Academic Journal*, 6.

Dalit Solidarity Network U.K. Caste-based Discrimination in the United Kingdom, 2011, https://www2.ohchr.org/english/bodies/cerd/docs/ngos/IDSN_UK79.pdf, accessed March 2019.

Desai, Sonalde, and Amaresh Dubey. 2012. 'Caste in 21st Century India: Competing Narratives'. *Economic and Political Weekly*, 46(11): 40.

Dhanda, Meena. 2009. 'Punjabi Dalit Youth: Social Dynamics of Transitions in Identity'. *Contemporary South Asia*, 17(1): 47–64.

Dhingra, Pawan. 2012. *Life behind the Lobby: Indian American Motel Owners and the American Dream*. Stanford, California: Stanford University Press.

Equality Labs. 2016. 'Caste in the United States'. https://www.equalitylabs.org/caste-survey-read, accessed March 2019.

Eriksen, Thomas Hylland. 1992. 'Indians in New Worlds: Mauritius and Trinidad'. *Social and Economic Studies*, 41(1):157–187.

Fuller, C. J. 1976. 'Kerala Christians and the Caste System'. *Man*, 11(1): 53–70.

Grieco, Elizabeth M. 1998. 'The Effects of Migration on the Establishment of Networks: Caste Disintegration and Reformation among the Indians of Fiji'. *International Migration Review*, 32(3): 704–736.

Harilal, Kalpana. 2015. 'Changing Caste Identities in the Indian Diaspora'. In *Indian Diaspora: Socio-cultural and Religious Worlds*, edited by Pratap Kumar (pp. 158–176). Brill.

Herzig, Pascale. 2010. 'Communal Networks and Gender: Placing Identities among South Asians in Kenya'. *South Asian Diaspora*, 2(2): 165–184.

Judge, P. S. 2002. 'Punjabis in England: the Ad-dharmi Experience'. *Economic and Political Weekly*, 37(31): 3244–3250.

Jodhka, Surinder S. 2015. *Caste in Contemporary India*. India: Routledge.

Kale, Madhavi. 2010. *Fragments of Empire: Capital, Slavery, and Indian Indentured Labor in the British Caribbean*. Philadelphia, PA: University of Pennsylvania Press.

Kannabiran, Kalpana. 1998. 'Mapping Migration, Gender, Culture and Politics in the Indian Diaspora: Commemorating Indian Arrival in Trinidad'. *Economic and Political Weekly*, WS53– WS57.

Kapur, Devesh. 2010. *Diaspora, Development, and Democracy: The Domestic Impact of International Migration from India*. Princeton, NJ: Princeton University Press.

Kumar, Vivek. 2009. 'Dalit Diaspora: Invisible Existence'. *Diaspora Studies*, 2(1): 53–74.

Kumar, P. Pratap. 2012. 'Place of Subcaste (jati) Identity in the Discourse on Caste: Examination of Caste in the Diaspora'. *South Asian Diaspora*, 4(2): 215–228.

Kurien, Prema. 2007. *A Place at the Multicultural Table: The Development of an American Hinduism*. New Brunswick, NJ: Rutgers University Press.

Kurien, Prema. 2017. *Ethnic Church Meets Megachurch: Indian American Christianity in Motion.* New York, NY: NYU Press.
Lal, Brij V. (Ed.) 2005. *Bittersweet: The Indo-Fijian Experience.* Canberra: Pandanus Books.
Lal, Brij V. 2012. *Chalo Jahaji: On a Journey through Indenture in Fiji.* Canberra: Research School of Pacific and Asian Studies, Australian National University and Suva: Fiji Museum.
Leckie, Jacqueline. 1998. 'The Southernmost Indian Diaspora: From Gujarat to Aotearoa'. *South Asia: Journal of South Asian Studies,* 21(s1): 161–180.
Metcalf, Hilary, and Health Rolfe. 2010. 'Caste Discrimination and Harassment in Britain'. *National Institute of Economic and Social Research.* https://www.niesr.ac.uk/sites/default/files/publications/caste-discrimination.pdf, accessed March 2019.
Modi, Radha. 2016. 'Brown: The Asianization of the US Racial Divide'. http://repository.upenn.edu, accessed on 2016.
Navsarjan Trust and RFK Center. 2010. 'Understanding Untouchability'. http://www.indianet.nl/pdf/UnderstandingUntouchability.pdf, accessed March 2019.
Pariyar, Mitra. 2019. 'Travelling Castes: Nepalese Immigrants in Australia'. *South Asian Diaspora,* 11(1): 89–103.
Pande, Amba. 2013. 'Conceptualising Indian Diaspora: Diversities within a Common Identity'. *Economic and Political Weekly,* 59–65.
Pethiyagoda, Kadira. 2017. 'Supporting Indian Workers in the Gulf: What Delhi Can Do'. *Brookings Institute.* https://www.brookings.edu/research/supporting-indian-workers-in-the-gulf-what-delhi-can-do/, accessed March 2019.
Ramachandran, Vidya. 2019. 'But He's Not Desi: Articulating 'Indianness' through Partnership Preference in the Indian-Australian Diaspora'. *South Asian Diaspora,* 1–17.
Ray, Tinku. 2019. 'The US Isn't Safe from the Trauma of Caste Bias'. *Pulitzer Center.* https://pulitzercenter.org/reporting/us-isnt-safe-trauma-caste-bias, accessed March 2019.
Roohi, Sanam. 2017. 'Caste, Kinship and the Realisation of "American Dream": High-skilled Telugu Migrants in the USA'. *Journal of Ethnic and Migration Studies,* 43(16): 2756–2770.
Sato, Kiyotaka. 2012. 'Divisions among Sikh Communities in Britain and the Role of Caste System: A Case Study of Four Gurdwaras in Multi-Ethnic Leicester'. *Journal of Punjab Studies,* 19(1).
Schwartz, Barton M. (Ed.) 1967. *Caste in Overseas Indian Communities.* Chandler Publishing Company.
Shaban, Abdul. (Ed.) 2018. *Lives of Muslims in India: Politics, Exclusion and Violence.* Taylor & Francis.
Srinivas, M. N. 1994. *The Dominant Caste and Other Essays.* Revised and Expanded edition. Delhi: Oxford University Press.
Taylor, Steve. 2014. 'Religious Conversion and Dalit Assertion among a Punjabi Dalit Diaspora'. *Sociological Bulletin,* 63(2): 224–246.
Teltumbde, Anand. 2010. *The Persistence of Caste: The Khairlanji Murders and India's Hidden Apartheid.* Zed.
Thorat, Sukhadeo, and Katherine S. Newman. 2007. 'Caste and Economic Discrimination: Causes, Consequences and Remedies'. *Economic and Political Weekly,* 4121–4124.
Vaid, Divya. 2014. 'Caste in Contemporary India: Flexibility and Persistence'. *Annual Review of Sociology,* 40: 391–410.
Waughray, Annapurna. 2009. 'Caste Discrimination: A Twenty-First Century Challenge for UK Discrimination Law?' *The Modern Law Review,* 72(2): 182–219.

Name Index

A

Adityanath, Yogi, 352
Ahmad, Imtiaz, 295–296
Alavi, Hamza, 297, 313
Alha, Akhil, 81
Ali, Aijaz, 299
Ali, Meer Hassan, 292
Ali, Syed, 297–298
Aloysius, G. R., 618
Anderson, Clare, 558
Anderson, Siwan, 580–581
Angayarkanni, V., 619–620
Ansari, Ghaus, 294–295
Anwar, Ali, 299
Appadurai, Arjun, 162, 280, 401
Asad, Talal, 155, 290–291, 300
Asher, Sam, 600
Azam, Mehtabul, 600

B

Bailey, F. G., 94
Baines, J. A., 164, 169
Bandyopadhyay, Ritajyoti, 82
Bandyopadhyay, Sekhar, 413, 417
Banerjee, Abhijit, 579
Bansode, Kisan Fago, 504
Barbosa, Duarte, 32
Barnett, Steve, 326
Barth, M., 164
Baxi, Upendra, 222–223
Bayly, Christopher, 76–77, 155, 156, 159, 172, 391
Bayly, Susan, 156, 178–179, 221, 362, 529
Beames, John, 293
Benveniste, Émile, 32
Berenschot, Ward, 349
Berreman, Gerald, 68, 362, 491, 530

Beteille, Andre, 530, 542
Béteille, André, 94
Bhagwat, Mohan, 284
Bhandari, Parul, 113
Bhandarkar, R. G., 248
Bhatt, Vipul, 600
Bhattacharya, Digindranarayan, 421
Biedelman, 64, 65
Birla, Ritu, 77, 80, 85, 391
Bloch, Jules, 407
Blunt, Edward A. H., 294
Boag, T. C., 405
Boas, Franz, 545
Bois, WEB du, 149
Bose, N. K., 544, 545–546
Bouglé, Célestin, 55–56
Bourdieu, Pierre, 18, 272
Breman, Jan, 311, 315, 347
Bronger, Dirk, 66
Broomfield, J. H., 416

C

Caldwell, Bruce, 70
Caplan, A. P., 449
Carroll, Lucy, 145, 169, 322
Cassan, Guilhem, 579, 582
Chakravarthy, Uma, 394
Chakravarti, A., 315–316
Chandra, Kanchan, 347
Chari, Sharad, 85
Charsley, Simon, 489
Chatterjee, Partha, 418
Chatterji, Joya, 420
Chaudhury, Basu Ray, 417
Chowdhry, Prem, 116, 613
Clémentin-Ojha, Catherine, 250, 254n14 259
Coffey, Diane, 485

NAME INDEX

Cohn, Bernard, 11, 121, 155, 157, 168, 363, 403, 407, 431, 539
Collingwood, R. G., 262
Commander, Simon, 62, 65, 69
Comte, Auguste, 48
Cornish, W. R., 163
Crooke, William, 164–165, 293
Crosthwaite, C., 371
Curtis, Bruce, 158

D

Damodaran, Harish, 81, 390
Datar, Chhaya, 612
Datta, Ankur, 379, 382, 603, 604
Deliége, Robert, 362, 483, 491
Deoras, M. D., 284
Desai, I. P., 222–223
Deshmukh, Lokhitvadi Gopal Hari, 504
Deshpande, Ashwini, 208, 209–210, 602
Dharmakirti, 33
Dhingra, Pawan, 627
Dickey, Sara, 604
Dirks, Nicholas, 155, 157, 163, 168, 172, 362, 399–400
Donaldson, J. C., 370
Donner, H., 420
Dube, Leela, 297, 312, 612
Dube, Saurabh, 548
Durkheim, Emile, 4

E

Eglar, Zekiye, 296
Elder, Joseph, 71, 72
Elwin, Verrier, 545

F

Falahi, Masud Alam, 300
Fanselow, Frank, 297
Farquhar, J. N., 248
Ferry, Mathieu, 97
Flood, G., 260
Freed, Stanley, 109
Frykenberg, Robert, 178
Fukazawa, Hiroshi, 65–66
Fuller, Chris, 63, 67, 113, 164, 171, 376, 381, 424–425, 529, 599, 603

G

Gaborieau, Marc, 296
Gaikwad, Laxman, 566
Gait, E. A., 164, 165
Galanter, Marc, 200, 204–206, 480
Gallo, Ester, 376, 384–385
Gambetta, Diego, 353
Gandhi, Malli, 562
Gawai, G. A., 504
Geetha, V., 149, 610
Ghosh, Anjan, 425
Ghosh, Biswanath, 378, 383
Ghurye, G. S., 11, 544, 545, 546
Gidwani, Vinay, 85
Gilbertson, Amanda, 383
Glucksberg, Luna, 391
Godelier, Maurice, 93
Golwalkar, M. S., 284
Gooptu, Nandini, 287
Gottschalk, 157, 158, 159
Gottschalk, Peter, 156
Gough, Kathleen, 67, 362
Gould, Harold, 68, 69
Gramsci, Antonio, 276
Greif, Avner, 577
Grieco, Elizabeth M., 624
Grover, Shalini, 613
Gudavarthy, Ajay, 488
Guha, Ranajit, 559–560
Guha, Sumit, 63, 64, 68, 128, 156, 542
Gupta, Akhil, 84
Gupta, Dipankar, 55–56, 92, 480, 490
Guru, Gopal, 83, 148, 372, 533

H

Hambata, Mattews Masayuki, 391
Hancock, Mary, 377
Hardgrove, Anne, 80
Hardiman, David, 391
Hariss-White, Barbara, 93
Harper, Edward, 66
Harriss, John, 79, 483, 599
Harriss-White, Barbara, 83, 348, 390
Hasan, Zoya, 221, 225, 227
Hatcher, B., 262
Hawley, J. S., 250
Headley, Zoe, 99

Heath, Anthony F., 601
Hegdewar, K. B., 284
Hegel, Georg Wilhelm Friedrich, 48
Hershman, Paul, 434
Heyer, Judith, 605
Hocart, A. M., 127
Höfer, A., 449
Hooper, J., 371
Hutton, J. H., 166, 203

I

Illaiah, Kancha, 272, 490
Inden, 261
Inglis, P., 603–604
Irschick, Eugene, 156, 491, 496
Iversen, Vegard, 600
Izsák-Ndiaye, Rita, 527

J

Jaaware, Aniket, 140, 148
Jaffrelot, Christophe, 11, 95, 99, 314, 315, 492
Jambhekar, Balshastri Gangadhar, 504
Jaoul, Nicolas, 496
Jeffrey, Craig, 315
Jha, Hetukar, 271
Jodhka, Surinder S., 82, 97, 98, 274, 602
Jones, William, 148

K

Kalaiyarasan, A., 99
Kalaiyarsan, A., 390
Kalelkar, Kaka, 219–220, 227, 556
Kannabiran and Kannabiran, 612
Kapadia, Karin, 613
Karanth, Gopal, 491
Karashima, Noboru, 490
Kaushal, M. P., 72
Kessinger, Tom, 72–73
Khare, Ravindra, 148
Kolenda, Pauline, 55, 61
Kosambi, 128
Kroeber, Alfred, 545
Kumar, Adarsh, 97
Kumar, D., 490
Kumar, Nitya, 394
Kumar, P. Pratap, 624, 625
Kumar, Sanjay, 601

Kumar, Vivek, 628
Kunnath, George J., 521

L

Laidlaw, James, 391
Lal, Brij V., 624, 625
Lambert, Helen, 104, 109
Lata, P. M., 225
Lehne, Johnathan, 579
Leonard, Karen, 112
Lerche, Jens, 93, 314, 521
Levien 2015, 565
Levy, Robert, 447
Lewis, Oscar, 70
Lorenzen, D. N., 258
Lorenzen, David, 34, 36
Low, Setha, 376
Luke, Nancy, 581
Lynch, Owen, 270, 484

M

Mahajan, Govind Vitthal, 504
Majumdar, D. N., 270
Majumder, Rajarshi, 600
Malamoud, Charles, 41
Malaviya, Madan Mohan, 284
Mandal, B. P., 491
Mandelbaum, David G., 109, 546
Manor, James, 82, 324
Mantena, 157
Mantena, Karuna, 157
Marriott, McKim, 240
Marten, J. T., 165, 166
Mauss, Marcel, 576
Mayer, Peter, 60, 67–68, 70, 104
McGuire, J., 416
McLeod, W. H., 432
McMillan, Alistair, 601
Mencher, Joan, 71, 362, 491
Mendelsohn, Oliver, 312, 315, 484
Menon, Ritu, 225
Metcalf, Hilary, 632
Metcalf, Thomas R., 400
Michelutti, Lucia, 19, 99, 348–350
Mies, Maria, 612
Miller, 63
Mines, Mattison, 79, 297

Moffatt, Michael, 271, 490, 491
Moon, Meenakshi, 616
Moonje, B. S., 284
Mosse, David, 3, 84, 96, 389, 450, 491
Müeller, Max, 528
Mukerji, U. N., 281–282, 285
Mukherjee, S. N., 416
Mukund, Kanakalatha, 183
Munshi, Kaivan, 576, 577, 581
Murmu, Maroona, 425

N
Namishray, Mohan Das, 365
Nandy, Ashish, 82
Narasimhan, Haripriya, 113, 376, 599, 603
Narayan, Badri, 287
Naudet, Jules, 97, 99, 604
Nazir, Pervaiz, 297
Neale, W., 371
Neve, Geert de, 109
Newman, Katherine, 602
Nobili, Roberto de, 31

O
O'Flaherty, 260
O'Hanlon, Rosalind, 12, 156, 529
Omvedt, Gail, 93, 493, 611
Oommen, T. K., 545
Orenstein, Henry, 65
Osella, Caroline, 599, 602, 605
Osella, Filippo, 599, 602, 605
Owens, Raymond, 82

P
Pai, Sudha, 496
Pande, Amba, 628
Pande, Rohini, 579
Pandey, Ajit, 494
Pandey, Gyanendra, 172
Pankaj, Ashok, 494
Pariyar, Mitra, 628, 634
Parry, Jonathan, 114, 317, 599
Pawar, Urmila, 616
Peabody, Norbert, 156
Pernau, Margrit, 292
Pettigrew, Joyce, 434
Philips, Rev., 214

Phule, Jyotiba, 56
Pinch, William, 170
Plowden, W. C., 162
Pocock, David, 62–63, 68, 74, 111
Polanyi, Karl, 128
Ponniah, Ujithra, 80, 99
Pradhan, Kumar, 450
Prakash, Aseem, 83
Prakash, Assem, 390
Price, Pamela, 347, 401
Pritchett, Lant, 575

Q
Qayum, S., 419
Quigley, D., 127
Quigley, Declan, 112

R
Racine, Jean-Luc, 491
Radcliffe, Cyril, 172
Radcliffe-Brown, A. R., 275
Radhakrishna, Meena, 554, 557, 562
Raheja, Gloria Goodwin, 613
Rai, Lala Lajpat Rai, 284, 286
Raj, Rekha, 618
Rajah, M. C., 216
Rajshekhar, V. T., 532
Ram, Nandu, 601, 602
Ramachandran, Rajesh, 209–210
Ramachandran, Vidya, 631
Ramanujan, A. K., 407
Rao, Anupama, 612, 614
Rawat, Ramnarayan S., 170
Ray, R., 419
Reddi, Muthulakshmi, 225
Rege, Sharmila, 613, 614, 616
Reid, John, 365
Risley, H. H., 163, 164, 165, 172, 215, 528
Robinson, Marguerite, 347
Rolfe, Health, 632
Roohi, Sanam, 100, 627
Rosenzweig, Mark, 576, 577, 578
Roueff, Olivier, 97
Rowe, W. L., 270, 405
Roy, Tirthankar, 76
Rudner, David, 79
Rudolph, L., 322, 324–326

NAME INDEX

Rudolph, Lloyd, 10
Rudolph, Susanne, 10
Rudolph, Susanne H., 322, 324–326
Ruud, A. E., 418–419

S

Saavala, Minna, 379–380
Sabar, Budhan, 566
Saberwal, Satish, 433
Samaddar, Ranabir, 82
Samarendra, Padmanabh, 168
Sanyal, Hitesranjan, 414
Sapre, S. G., 72
Sarkar, Sumit, 417
Sarkar, Tanika, 418
Sarma, Jyotirmoyee, 414–415
Sarukkai, Sundar, 148
Sato, Kiyotaka, 632
Satyanarayana, K., 364
Savarkar, Vinayak Damodar, 283–284
Schneider, David, 106
Schwarz, Henry, 555
Scott, James, 270
Seetharamayya, Pattabhi, 561
Sen, D., 423
Sen, Dwaipayan, 416
Sen, Satadru, 560
Shah, A. M., 111, 255
Shah, Alpa, 93, 100, 521
Shah, Ghanshyam, 222, 482
Shah, K. T., 471, 474
Shah, Prakash, 491
Shahu, Chatrapati, 504–505
Sharif, Jafar, 293
Sharma, R. S., 130
Shastri, Shibnath, 417
Sheikh, S., 132
Shodhan, A., 262
Shraddhanand, Swami, 282–283, 284, 285–286
Silverberg, James, 598
Simon, Henri de Saint, 48
Singer, Milton, 269
Singh, I. P., 434
Singh, K. S., 546
Sinha, Surajit, 547
Smith, A. D., 443
Smith, Richard, 157

Srinivas, M. N., 11, 93, 480, 546
Srinivas, Tulasi, 376, 378–379
Stark, Oded, 576
Stein, 128
Stein, B., 132–134
Stewart, D. M., 369
Still, Clarinda, 113
Subrahmanyam, Sanjay, 77
Subramanian, Ajantha, 383
Sudarshan, K. S., 284

T

Tandon, Prakash, 60, 433
Taylor, Steve, 522, 628, 630
Teltumbde, Anand, 626
Thakur, Guruchand, 421
Thakur, Harichand, 421
Thass, Iyothee, 56
Thornberry, Patrick, 536
Tilly, Charles, 19
Timberg, Thomas A., 78
Tolen, Rachel, 555, 559

U

Upadhya, Carol, 384

V

Vaid, Divya, 97, 601
Vaidyanathan, R., 389–390
Vandewalle, Lore, 582
Varma, Kumar Cheda Singh, 169–170
Vatuk, Sylvia, 298
Vicziani, Marika, 484
Vijaybaskar, M., 390
Vikas, Ram Manohar, 65, 73
Viramma, Josiane Racine, 491
Visvanathan, Shiv, 533
Viswanath, R., 490, 491
Vreede-de Stuers, Cora, 297

W

Wadley, Susan, 64, 73
Waghmore, Suryakant, 496
Wagoner, Philip, 156
Walangkar, Gopal Baba, 504
Warrier, Maya, 380
Waterfield, Henry M., 160–162

Weber, Max, 15
Williams, J. Charles, 293
Wilson, Horace Hayman, 248
Wimmer, Andreas, 20
Wiser, William, 60, 61–62, 64, 67, 68, 70
Witsoe, Jeffrey, 84

X
Xaxa, Virginius, 547, 549–550

Y
Yadav, Yogendra, 327
Yalman, N., 115
Yalman, Nur, 110
Yanagisako, Junko Sylvia, 391
Yeatts, M. W. M., 167

Z
Zelliot, Eleanor, 489, 492, 503

Subject Index

A

Ad Dahrmi Dalits, 430
addressivity, 154
Adi Movements, 516
Adivasi identity and politics, 548–51, 623
Adivasis, 9, 510
  rights of, 209
advaita, 148
Afghans, 35
Agarwal Banias of Delhi, 80, 358, 388–89, 391–95
  caste associations, 392
  elite women of, 394–95
  identity, 393
Agrasen, Maharaja, 393
Agroha Vikas Trust, 392–93
Ahirs, 35
Akhila Bhartiya Agarwal Sammelan (ABAS), 392–93
Akhil Bhartiya Matang Sangh, 509
Al- Biruni, 35
All India Backward and Minority Communities Employees Federation (BAMCEF), 506
All-India Backward Muslim Morcha, 299
All-India Muslim OBC Sangathan, 299
All India Vaish Federation (AIVF), 392
Ambedkar, B. R., 2–3, 14, 16, 26, 39, 105, 110, 140, 144, 147, 171, 193–94, 200, 459, 474, 489, 493–94, 505, 535, 571, 609, 617, 623
  anti-caste movements, 217–18
  basis of caste hierarchy, 56–57
  celebrations of birth anniversaries, 473
  conception of liberty and fraternity, 470–71, 512
  conversion, 40
  correlation between caste and gender oppressions, 611
  declaration of intent to convert, 280
  defining Hindu identity, 40
  educational achievement, 464–65
  as a Hindu reformist nationalist icon, 511
  idea of democratic socialism, 512
  ideological legacy, 470–71
  Independent Labour Party, 516
  Mooknayak, 465
  organizational legacy, 466–70
  organizations founded by, 465–70
  political solution to caste, 147
  programmatic legacy, 471–73
  relationship between religions, 40
  on *sampradaya*, 40
  sociological criticism of caste system, 39–40
  spread of education among Dalits, 465
  state socialism, 471–72
  symbolic legacy, 473
  thought on democracy, 505–6
Ambedkar, Yashwantrao, 463
Ambedkarite movement, 508, 512
  in Great Britain and Punjab, 517–18
Anavils, 312
Anglo- Indian law, 142
Anna Bhau Sathe Foundation, 509
anti-caste movements, 14, 105, 146, 217–18, 460, 489, 491, 502, 609. *See also* Dalit movements
  Ad-Dharam movement, 146, 428
  Adi-Hindu Mahasabha movement, 373
  bhakti and, 34
  women's position, 609–11
apad-dharma, 238
apartheid, 528, 531–34, 536
Apprentices Act, 1850, 557

SUBJECT INDEX

Arab Spring, 521
aristocracy, 586
Aroras, 433, 436
Arthashastra (Kautilya), 128
Article 330 of the Constitution, 191
Arya Mahila Samaj, 492
Arya Samaj, 40, 170, 282, 286
asceticism and *samnyas*, 53, 254
ascription-based hierarchies, 12, 15–16, 19
Asiatic Society of Bengal, 542
Association for Democratic Reform (ADR), 345
Athawale, Ramdas, 511
a-varna, 239–40
Azamgarh settlement report, 365

B

Babri Masjid demolition, 286
Backward Class League, 216n9
backwardness, 11, 124–25, 191–92, 325, 610
  borders between minorities and, 226–27
  condition of, 224
  definition of, 218–21
  demand for recognition, 216
  gender and, 225
  identification of, 208, 222–23
  judicial interpretation of, 221–24
  Kalelkar Commission's recommendations, 219–20
  Mandal Commission's identification of, 220–21
  Muslim communities, 225–26
  policy recommendations for, 215
  relationship between caste and, 213–14
  reservations for, 218–19
  of women and Muslims in education and employment, 215
Backward (SC, ST, OBC) and Minority Communities Employees Federation (BAMCEF), 495
Bahujan Samaj Party (BSP), 333–39, 341–42, 429, 495–96, 506, 509, 511, 515
  political strategy, 496
Bahun-Chhetris, 447–48, 450
Bahuns, 446
baluta system, 66, 68
balutedari (patron-client) relations, 615

Banias, 18, 55
banjo parties, 482
Bansode, Kisan Fago, 504
Barbosa, Duarte, 31–32
Bedias, 107
bhadralok, 376–77
  distinctive features of, 414–15
  education system and, 416–17
  evolution of domestic servitude, 419
  land ownership, 415
  lifestyle, 424
  nature of trade/ occupation, 415
  relation with caste, 416
Bhagavadgītā, 253
Bhāgavatapurāṇa, 253
Bhagwat, Mohan, 284
bhaiyachara tenure, 372
bhakti, 34, 54, 148, 242–44, 250, 256–57, 359, 401, 492
Bhangis, 503
Bharatiya Janta Party (BJP), 281, 332–34, 511
Bharat Sevashram Sangha, 418, 421
Bhattacharya, Digindranarayan, 421
bhayats, 131
Bhumiars, 312, 316
Bhumijs, 547
Bihistis, 293
Black Lives Matter, 497
Black Panther Party, 506
blood purity, 33
Bombay Census Bill, 1863, 160
Bombay Scheduled Caste Improvement Trust, 467
Boston Brahmins, 7
brahmadeya settlements, 134, 136
Brahmanical Hinduism, 16, 428, 545, 610
Brahmanical Hindu-Society, 226
Brahmanical model of Indian society, 545
Brahmanical patriarchy, 394, 611
Brahmanical textual tradition, 105, 107–8
Brahmanism, 33, 253
Brahman-*jajman* relationship, 63
Brahmans, 35, 431
  dominance of, 362
  population in UP, 361
Brahminical hierarchy and ritualism, 240, 431
Brahminical Hinduism, 164

Brahminical model of Sanskritization, 267–68
brahminical patriarchy, 492
Brahminical practices, 268
Brahminical understanding
    of caste, 9, 237
    of Indian social organization, 540
Brahminization, 267
Brahmins, 18, 31, 33, 41, 55, 140, 142, 144, 236–39, 267, 309, 417, 623, 627
    Bengali, 376–77
    communities in urban India, 375–76, 383–84
    employment and education, 382–83
    gendering of caste ideas, 377–78
    Kashmiri Pandits, 379
    of Kerala, 358
    Mahabrahmans of Varanasi, 379
    Maharastrian, 376–77
    Namboodris of Kerala, 384–85
    of Nepal, 449
    religious thoughts and practices, 379–82
    Tamil, 376–77, 425, 603
    of Tamil Nadu, 358
    Telugu, 376–77
    of urban India, 358
    as vasstu consultants, 384
    woman, observance of caste rules and regulations, 377–78
Brahmo Samaj, 40
Buddhism, 6, 17, 144, 241, 285, 472–73, 512, 517
    criticism of caste, 33–34
    ideals of kingship, 128–29
Buddhist Society of India/Bharatiya Bauddha Mahasabha (BMS), 468
Bunt chiefdoms, 134
business communities, 358
    Aggarwals, 80, 358, 392. See also Agarwal Banias of Delhi
    Bohras, 79
    Gounders, 81–82, 85, 390
    Jats, 390
    Kammas, 81
    'Kathiawari' Kanbi Patels, 80
    Khatris, 390
    Maheshwaris, 391
    Marathas, 81
    Marwaris, 78, 80, 85, 390–91

Muslim mercantile groups, 79, 81
Nadars, 81
Naidus, 81
Nakarattar community, 79
Nattukottai Chettiars, 79
Oswals, 391
ownership of business, 389
Palanpur Jains, 80
Parsis, 79
Patels/Patidars, 80–81
Reddys, 81
Syrian Christians of Kerala, 81

C

candalas, 35
caste, 93–94. *See also* economics of caste
    as an endogamous group, 29
    as an ethnic group, 575–77
    associations, 10, 169–70, 306, 327–28, 392, 516
    based community networks, 9
    based discrimination and violence, 114
    based inequality and discrimination, 3
    based political parties, 347
    based politics, 13
    brahminical view on, 9, 33
    Brahmin- nonbrahmin divide, 142
    colonial invention of, 141–43
    communities in past, 28
    conceptual trajectory of, 2
    culture-centric view of, 5, 17–18
    Dalit perspectives on, 9–10
    in Deccan (15th-18th centuries), 34
    dialects, 407
    at Durban I, 530–33
    essentialist view of, 20
    etymology, 31–32
    European point of view, 32–33
    field view of, 38–39, 309–10, 548, 598
    'fissiparous' dimension of, 12
    as a form of racism, 3
    as graded system of sovereignties, 147
    groupings, 28
    Hindu religion- centric view of, 6
    identities, 10, 15, 83, 99–100, 123–24, 182, 364
    in Indian Constitution, 189–91
    Indo-Persian view of, 35
    inequalities, 83

caste (*cont.*)
   inheritances, 591
   inter-disciplinary understanding of, 12
   as *jatis*, 237
   and kinship dynamics, 29
   legal definition of, 185
   link between meritocracy and, 586–94
   as marker of identification, 123–24
   material side of, 13
   middle-class elite view of, 2, 8
   Orientalist/colonial view of, 5–8, 11
   patriotism, 11
   as a phenomenon, 140, 146
   political scientists' view on, 10
   polythetic definition of, 16
   as power, 98
   re-framing of, 20
   related violence, 3
   relationship with landlessness, 12
   relationship with state system, 17
   in relation to class, 28
   religious historians on, 34
   role in electoral processes, 10–11
   in rural setting, 8
   segmentation of class, 100
   as social capital in business, 389–90
   social distinctions of, 34
   social science engagements with, 7–10
   social science research on, 12
   as a special spatial identity, 7
   unity of, 9
caste conflicts
   basis of ritual status and, 180
   as caste affairs, 185
   colonial law on, 183–85
   of hands, 177–79
   on occasion of temple festivals, 178–79
   over honours, 181–83
   patterns of, 177–79
   resolution method, 179
   shaping of caste identities, 177
   in social interactions, 181
   for use of palanquins or wearing of sandals, 177, 181
   for use of urban space and processions' routes, 178–79
   weavers' caste *vs* Pallis, 176

caste hierarchy, 139, 144, 364–65, 388–89, 395, 480, 587, 629
   Ambedkar's view, 56–57
   mobility and, 269
   pre-modern caste organization in South India, 401
   religious communities and, 193–95
   spatial exclusion, 365–66
   violence and, 145–46
caste-Hindu student politics, 363
caste mobility, 276, 297, 299, 310, 323–24, 332, 358, 363, 372, 388, 587–88. *See also* Sanskritization
   case of Izhavas and Vaatima Brahmins, 599
   of Dalits, 599
   diasporic migration, 591–92
   downward occupational mobility for SCs and STs, 600–601
   educational and occupational mobility, 600–602
   gendered experience, 605
   inter-generational mobility, 595–96
   intra-generational or career mobility, 595
   methodological approaches, 596–98
   patterns, 599–602
   role of experiences, aspirations, and anxieties, 603–5
   social and spatial mobility, 602–3
caste networks, 12, 81–84, 390, 571
   benefits of, 81–82
   business transactions and capital accumulation, 78, 81–82, 84–86
   in capital-labour relations and sourcing finance, 82
   dominance and exclusion of others, 84
   effect on business, 84
   in informal economy, 83
   production and distribution, 83
caste or class debate, 91–92
caste questions, 185
   within constitutionalism, 223
caste societies, 92
caste system model, 38–39
caste-tribe continuum, 544–47
caste uplift movements, 169–70
census categories, 36–37, 122–23, 143, 154, 159–68, 364

basis of social standing, 162
Calcutta's 1866 census, 160
1871-1872 census, 160–61
colonial categories, 37
Hindu and Muslim categories, 161–62
new caste identities, 166
racial distinctions, 164–65
racialized distinctions, 161
religion basis, 166–67
scientific form, 160
self-consciously enumerated communities, 167
untouchables, 161
use of varna, 163
census commissioners, 168–69, 172
census ethnography, 155–58, 171–72
advantages of, 160
decennial censuses from 1871 to 1941, 158
precolonial precursors, 156
publication of, 159
as public property, 168–71
stages, 159
use of legal and surveillance systems, 157
Chamars, 358, 361, 428, 436, 626
allegations of cattle poisoning against, 367–68
claim of Kshatriya status, 373
ethnographies of, 371–72
humiliation and discrimination against, 367–68
'Kshatriya' status for, 373
in leather industries, 369–70
as a non-agricultural caste, 371–72
population in UP, 361
relationship with agrarian life, 365
as rent-paying caste, 372
thekadars (contractors), 369
violent infringements against, 368
Chambhars, 503
Charmkar, 508
chaturvarna frame of social organization, 26
Chauhans, 35
Chaulukya kingdom, 132
Chhetris, 446, 452
child marriage abolition, 146
Cholas, 134
Christianity, 6, 17, 184, 233, 241, 244, 248, 283, 285–87, 429–31, 489, 546, 610, 629–30

clerical hierarchies, 26, 48
conversion to, 144, 164, 195, 214, 226, 281, 286
Dalit Christians, 204
nobility of 'old Christians,' 31–32
Syrian Christians, 81
Christian missionaries, 124, 464, 491
Christians, 6, 31
citizenship, 3
Citizenship Amendment Act, 2019, 423
civil rights, 196–97
Civil Rights Act of 1955, 196
civil society, 3
classes, 8
Brahmanic theory of, 33
congruence between caste and, 96–97
disparities within caste group, 99
dissociation from caste, 94–96
in electoral politics, 332–34
hierarchy, 145, 602
inequalities within caste group, 99–100
intersections of caste with, 28
mobility, 93–94, 570
mobilizations, 417
overlap between caste and, 192, 224
segmentation of caste, 100
State, 41–43
struggles, 92–93, 98
Code of Manu, 309
colonial categorization of caste, 6, 121–22
colonial criminal law, 560
colonial India, 6
colonial invention of caste, 141–43
Anglo-Hindu law, 142
education and caste mobility, 143–45
emergence of caste associations, 142–43
transformation of matrilineal systems in Kerala, 143
colonialism, 139
commensality, 19
The Committee on the Customary Rights to Scavenging, 64
communal solidarity, 19
communitarian political structure, 128
community, 8
centric social exclusion, 12
community identities, 124
Companies Act, 2013, 388

Comte, Auguste, 48
Congress Party, 347
Constitution (103rd Amendment) Act of January 2019, 42
Constitution (Scheduled Castes) Order of 1950, 285
conversion/ reconversion, 144, 164, 194–95, 226–27, 281, 286
　of Tamil Dalits to Islam, 280
criminalization of politics, 345–46
criminal tribes, 554–56
　access to education and employment, 563–65
　Budhan Sabar, case of, 566–67
　colonization of body, 559–61
　Criminal Tribes enactments, 556–59
　family and kinship, 561–63
　forced/distress migration, 564
　formation of settlements, 561–62
　identification of, 556–57
　proof of criminality, 558–59
　reformation and employment, 562
　stigmatization, 556, 562–63, 566
　subjugation of, 557, 561–63, 566
Criminal Tribes Acts, 565
　1871, 554–55, 557
　1911, 210, 558
Criminal Tribes (Amendment) Act, 1897, 557
culturalization of caste, 77
cultures of caste, 5, 17–18

D

dakshina, 237
Dalit feminism, 514–15, 519–22, 571, 617–18
　feminist writings, 617–18
Dalit Indian Chamber of Commerce and Industry (DICCI), 83, 509
Dalit Mahila Snagthan, 614
Dalit mobilization, 270–71, 461, 507, 515
　in international and global contexts, 519–24
　structural adjustment programs, 520
　transnational mobilization, 515–24
Dalit movements, 309, 460, 488–96, 502, 530–31
　Bharat Bandh, 488
　in India, 521–24
　in Maharashtra, 503–5
　post-Independence period, 494–96
Dalit-Muslim solidarity, 287

Dalit Panthers, 9, 489, 495, 502, 506, 514, 517, 528, 613–14
Dalits, 9, 13, 18, 82, 99, 149, 209, 315, 362, 436, 446, 459, 529, 623
　atrocities on, 14
　Bengali, 425
　capitalism, 83, 465
　celebrations and commemoration of icons, 510
　civil society organizations, 10, 506
　consciousness, 507
　de facto remoteness of, 285
　diaspora communities, 628–29
　in diasporic settings, 571
　economic mobility of, 481–83
　emerging rightward shift among, 511
　entrepreneurs, 83, 390
　feminism., 514
　Hindu consciousness among, 239
　human rights, 531
　literacy rate among, 316
　literature, 10
　middle classes, 460–61, 463, 465, 493, 509–10, 512
　migration, 626–27
　migration to urban centres, 460
　mobility, 599
　movements, 461, 488–97, 503–6, 508
　as muscular leaders, 351–52
　names and tags applied to, 489–90
　networks, 493, 497
　political activism, 314, 364, 374, 494–96, 505
　public symbolism, 510–11
　of Punjab, 429
　rights of, 496
　Sikhs, 628
　solidarity, 509
　student associations, 374
　villages, 365
　violence against, 227, 367, 388, 484–85, 507, 617–18
　women's perspective, 613–17
Dalit Sahitya, 516
dals, 415–16
Delhi Parishad Agarwal Sammelan (DPAS), 392, 395
democracy, 2, 586

democratic politics, caste in, 10–11, 17
democratic rajas, 348
denotified communities, 554–56, 563–64, 566
   current predicament of, 567
   educational status of, 563–64
   Kalelkar Committee on, 556
   provision of residential schools for children, 564
   regimes of dispossession, 565
   stigmatization of, 566
De-notified Communities (DNTs), 462
Deoras, M. D., 284
Depressed Classes Association, 216n10
Depressed Classes Federation, 516
deprivations, 7
Deshmukh, Lokhitvadi Gopal Hari, 504
dharma, 36, 131, 236
Dharmasastras, 34, 182
dharm relationships, 109
Dhobis, 293
diasporic migration, 591–92
Dignity Movement of 1872-1873, 420
discrimination, 3, 416, 528
   caste, 95, 108, 139, 196, 298, 450, 460, 463, 484, 519, 521–23, 530–33, 571, 632
   compensatory, 211
   in government employment, 201
   against marginalized castes, 420–25
   prohibition of, 202
   racial, 531–32
division of labourers, 39, 56
dominant castes, 276, 306, 309, 580, 626
   Ahirs, 315
   criterion for dominance, 310–15
   critique of, 312–16
   Gondals, 314
   as guarantors of provision and protection, 352
   Jats, 312–13, 315
   links between landownership, power, and authority, 315–16
   Okkaliga, 311
Dumont, Louis, 5, 15, 17, 26, 38, 77, 92, 105, 399, 444, 529
   caste hierarchy, 49–54, 134, 141, 244
   distinction between caste and sect, 255
   forms of asceticism and *samnyas*, 53
   hierarchical relation between king and Brahmin, 122, 127
   holism- hierarchy relationship, 50
   Homo Hierarchicus, 38–39, 49, 244, 271
   notions of individualism and equality, 50–51
   power, 53–54
   on practice of untouchability, 56
   segregation between castes, 55–56
   social order, 52
   status hierarchy, 52
   substantialization of caste, 94
Dusadhs, 271, 273
   'Kshatriya' status for, 273
Dusadh Sabha, 273
A Dying Race (Mukerji), 281

E
East India Company (EIC), 141–42
economically weaker sections (EWS), 42, 199, 211, 221
economics of caste, 12, 17, 77, 573–74
   role of jatis in economic decisions, 573, 576, 583
   in terms of inefficiencies, 577–80
   trade of water, 580
economic well-being, 3
education
   and caste mobility, 143–45, 591–92
   higher, 588–92
ekavarna, 33
electoral democracy, 2
electoral politics, 2014–2019
   Brahmin votes, 335
   BSP-SP vote share, 336–39
   class-wise support for main parties, 332–34
   Dalit votes, 335–36, 342–43
   impact of urbanization, 341, 344
   Jatav/Chamar vote, 337
   jatis' voting pattern, 337–40
   Karwa Patels votes, 340
   Kolis votes, 343
   Kurmis votes, 334, 338
   Leuva Patels votes, 340
   OBC votes, 332–34, 337–38, 342–43
   Rajput votes, 335, 337
   support for BJP, 332–36
   upper caste vote, 333, 341
   Yadavs votes, 334
   Yadav votes, 338–39
entanglements of caste, 569

Equality Act, 3
equality of status and
    opportunity, 43–44
ethnic boundary-making, 20
ethnic communities, 15
ethnic group, 443
ethnicity, 529–30
    of caste, 533–34
ethnicization, 11
Ezhavas, 144

F
Fazal, Shaikh Abu'l, 35–36
    A'in- i Akbari, 35
feminist movements, 611–12
flailing state, 575
fraternal capital, 85

G
Gama, Vasco da, 31–32
Gandhi, Mahatma, 40, 146, 166
    issue of separate electorates for
        untouchables, 147
Garo tribe, 270
Gau-rakshini sabhas (cow- protection
    associations), 367
Gawai, G. A., 504
gender and caste, 581–83, 609–11
    gendered norms of Gujars, 613
    marriage and cohabitation of low-income
        SC women, 613
    matrilateral principle among
        Non- Brahmin castes, 613
    participation of women in everyday
        life, 612
    puberty rituals and menstrual practices, 613
General Category (GC), 41–42, 44
genti, 32
Global Justice Movement, 515, 520–24
Golwalkar, M. S., 284
Government of India Act 1935, 543
graded inequality, 16, 39–40, 56, 110
Green Revolution technology, 360
Gudavarthy, Ajay, 488
Gujarat riots, 2002, 287
Gupta, Dipankar, 55–56
guru- paramparā, 252

H
Habitual Offenders' Act, 561
harijans, 240
Hartog committee, 215
Hegdewar, K. B., 284
Hegel, Georg Wilhelm Friedrich, 48
hierarchical structuralism, 50
hierarchy/hierarchies
    Brahmanical view of, 52, 232
    of caste, 1, 13, 19, 26–27
    of castes, 13, 19, 26–27, 43
    defined, 48
    Dumont's view, 49–53
    duplication of, 52
    in Hindu temples, 238–39
    holism relationship, 50
    ritual, 52
    social, 52
    in terms of purity, 51
    ways of approaching, 49
hijras, 242, 619
Hindu-bias, 241
Hindu Code Bill (HCB), 40, 611
Hindu diaspora, 629
Hinduism, 5–6, 16, 35, 39, 148, 162, 164, 179, 193,
    214–15, 231–33, 235–36, 247n2, 294, 516,
    550, 623. *See also* varnas
    castes in Hindu temples and villages,
        238–39
    challenges to caste within, 242–43
    devotional (*bhakti*) traditions, 242–43
    Hindu ritual purity criteria, 240
    ideal Hindu pilgrim experience, 242
    inclusion processes, 239–40
    in Indian overseas communities, 243–44
    notions of ritual purity and pollution,
        237–38
    Orientalist view of, 5
    power and domination, 240–42
    relations with castes, 239–40
    ritual ideology of purity and
        pollution, 237–38, 240–42
Hindu Mahasabha, 284, 421
Hindu mind, 5
Hindu nationalism, 233, 282–85
Hindu population diminution, 281–82
Hindu reform movements, 200

Hindu religious worldview, 4
Hindu right-wing organizations, 14
Hindus, 2, 20, 35, 233
   way of doing business, 85
Hindu Sangathan, 282–84, 421
Hindu Sects, 248–50
   within caste society, 256–61
   importance of transmission (*parampara*) and initiation (*dīkṣā*), 251–52
   institutional characteristics, 252–54
   literature and centres, 253
   nature of, 249
   personal relationship with a *guru*, 253
   Śaiva sects, 251–52
   sectarian mark on forehead (*tilak*), 251
   sect membership, 249
   sociological approach, 254–56
   as subversive social groups, 256–57
   in terms of salvation, 251
   theological characteristics, 250–52
   use of Tantras, 251
   Vaiṣṇava sects, 251–52
   view of Supreme, 258
Hindu Sena dynasty, 130
Hindu social order, 34, 39, 256–58, 421
Hindu society, composition of, 35
Hindu temples
   religious thoughts and practices, 379–82
   and villages, caste in, 203, 238–40, 366
Hindutva, 233, 275–76, 279
   changes in modes of sociality, 287
   discourses and practices, 284–88
   failures of inclusion, 287–88
   legal, 285
   reconfiguring public space along majoritarian lines, 287
   texts, 281–84
Hindu Undivided Family (HUF), 85, 388
Hindu worldview, 6
historical research on caste, 11–12, 123
holism, 50
homecoming or ghar wapsi, 279, 285, 287
Homo Hierarchicus, 5
human well-being, 12
hypergamy, 110
hypogamous relationships, 110

I

Iberian populations, 31
identity politics, 11
Immigration and Naturalization Act of 1965, 626
India
   democratic politics, 10–11
   development planning, 8
   exceptionalism, 11
   HIV/AIDS in, 619
   Indian democracy, 148–49
   modernization, 29
   Mughal power, 35
   past tradition, 1–2
   'progress deficit', 15
   religious systems, 248
   rural life, 8–9
   sex ratio, 116
   social and political life, 3
   urbanization rate, 577
Indian Act 1935, 41
Indian businesses, 78, 388. *See also* business communities
   business networks, 19
Indian Constitution, 3
   creation of institutional mechanism, 191
   ground for affirmative action, 190–91
   principle of compensatory discrimination for groups, 201
   principles of 'equality in law' and 'equality in fact', 201
   prohibition of discrimination, 189–90, 202
Indian Councils Act of 1909, 279
Indian Institutes of Technology (IITs), 588–89
Indian National Congress, 146
Indian national identity, 550
Indian republicanism, 587
Indian society, 100, 123, 157, 159, 200, 540, 548
   categorization, 41–43
   field view of, 8, 274, 548
   'neo-orientalist' vision of, 92
Indian state's role, economists' perspective, 575
Indian villages, 104, 109, 134–35, 141. See also *jajmani* system
   marriages in, 113–16
   power structure, 85–86
   rituals, 134

Indian villages (*cont.*)
  spatial organization in, 283
  types of, 136
  zamindari villages, 132–34
India's affirmative action programme, 190–91, 199–200, 209–10
  post-independence, 200–201
  pre-independence, 200
  purpose and scope, 211
India's Silent Revolution: The Rise of the Lower Castes (Jaffrelot), 11
individualism, 50–51
  of capitalist market, 69
individualization, 54
Indological view of caste, 362
Indo-Tibetan Interface, 447
Indra Sawhney vs Union of India, 224
industrial capitalism, 76
inequalities, 4, 13–14, 20, 28
  durable, 19
inscribing caste, 399–402
  Saiva and Vaishnava temple inscriptions, 400
  in Tamil inscriptions, 400–401
institutional dimensions of Hindu Sects, 252–54. See also Hindu Sects
  entry by initiation (*dīkṣā*), 251–52
institutionalized caste divisions, 629–30
inter-caste marriages, 14
International Convention on the Elimination of Racial Discrimination (ICERD), 530–32
International Dalit Solidarity Network (IDSN), 531, 629
intra-caste inequalities, 99–100
Islam, 17, 35, 241, 244, 285

J

Jagannath temple, 129
Jainism in South India, 129
Jains, 6
jajmani relations, 8–9
jajmani system, 13, 18, 26–28, 94, 141, 242, 481
  argument against, 63–64
  debt bondage, 66
  definition, 60–62
  dissolution of, 70–74
  Dumont's argument, 62–63
  economic rationality, 69–70
  exploitative relations, 64–65
  market nature of relations, 70
  origins of, 66–68
  payments, 68–69
  political consequences of, 580
  relations, 62–64
  village patronage, 347
Jama'at- i Islami Hind, 300
Jambhekar, Balshastri Gangadhar, 504
Janajatis, 446–47, 451–52
jataka, 35, 128
Jatavs, 270
jati
  intra-jati inequalities, 99
jatis, 4, 25, 32–34, 38–39, 55, 139, 291, 307, 310, 331, 392, 406, 546, 574–75
  based identities, 336
  to gain access to employment, 576–78
  hierarchy, 241
  identity, 237
  information on, 579
  intrinsic quality (*guna*) of, 237
  jati mohallas (caste quarters), 366
  Jativiveka (Discernment of jati), 142
  naturalization of, 33
  networks, 576–80
  politics, 334–37
  purity markers, 237
  role in economic decisions, 573, 576, 580
Jat-Pat-Todak Mandal, 428
Jats, 35, 312, 390, 434, 436
Jews, 31–32
jholi relationships, 109
Jnandev, 34
Joint Entrance Exam (JEE), 589–90
Julahas, 293

K

K. C. Vasanth Kumar and Another vs. State of Karnataka, 221–23
K. P. Manu, Malabar Cements Ltd vs. The Chairman, 194–95
Kabir and Kabir Panth, 34
kafa'a/ kufu, 300
Kaikallars, 178

Kallars, 402–6
Kamalar, 178
Kammas, 312
Kanshiram, 495
karma, 13
Kashmiri Pandits, 603
  businesses, 382
  migration of, 379
Kathiawaris, 577
Kayasthas, 35, 182, 270, 417
Keralamahatmyan, 108
Keralolpatti, 108
Khaparde, D. K., 506
Khas-Aryas, 446–48, 451
Khatris, 433, 436
Khattri Hitkari Association, 170
Khedawal Brahmins, 111
kingship
  brahmadeya settlements, 134, 136
  Buddhist and Jain ideals of, 128–29, 134
  Bunt chiefdoms, 134
  centralized political order, 132–33
  communitarian structure, 128
  Dumont's proposition, 122, 127
  in early medieval Saurashtra and Rajasthan, 131, 133
  Guptas era, 129
  heroic, 134–35
  in Kali age, 130–31
  king-Brahmin nexus, 136
  king- tribe alliance, 131
  king-tribe alliance, 135
  as microcosm of Cosmic Man, 129
  moral, 128–30, 133
  in Muslim states, 132
  in Nepal, 135
  paternal role of, 127
  Rajput caste and political system, 131, 133
  ritual, 134, 136
  ruler-merchant nexus, 130
  specific to South India, 133–34
  Tamil kingdoms, 129, 133–34
  tentative typology of, 135–36
  tribal chiefdoms, 131, 133–35
  in zamindari village, 132
kinship, 28, 104–7, 612
  bonding, 14
  boundaries, 29
  of caste, 107–10
  fictive, 108–9
  networks, 82, 571
  relationships, 109
  theories of, 107–8
Kolhati women, 614–16
Krishnavanshi Yadav, 19
Kshatriyas, 33, 41, 53, 55, 107, 236, 267, 270, 285, 309, 623
Kunhambu, Potheri, 144
Kushanas, 130

L

labour markets, 12, 17
  discrimination, 600
  indentured labour system, 145–46, 243, 561–62, 571, 591, 624–26, 630, 633
  occupational mobility, 599–602
  withdrawal of women from, 605
labour movement, 145–46
  diasporic migration, 591–92
  economic dependence to, 481–83
Landless Workers' Movement (MST), 520
landownership, 314–16
law-caste relationship, 188
Laws of Manu, 107
leather trade, 368–69
  Chamars' relationships with, 369–70
  export of hides and skins, 368–69
  kinds of leather production, 370
  qasba character of, 370–71
legal sanction of caste rights, 183–84
LGBTQI movement, 609, 619
liberal capitalism, 77
liberal democracy, 2
Lingayats, 70
lower castes, 13, 217, 257, 298, 351, 362, 365, 373, 416, 425, 480, 491, 570, 587–88. *See also* backwardness; Dalits; Sanskritization; untouchability/untouchables
  claim to Kshatriya status, 107, 169, 217, 273, 373, 504, 546
  dialectic of achievement and ascription, 593–94 (*see also* meritocracy)
  discrimination against, 578
  women of, 581

M

M. R. Balaji v State of Mysore, 192
ma-baap'ism, 348
Madheshis, 446, 448, 451
Madras Restriction of Habitual Offenders' Act of 1948, 561
mafia-owned democracy
    acts of redistribution and vote buying practices, 350
    control of people and resources, 350
    criminal partnerships, 349
'Mafia Raj' or 'Goonda Raj,' 345–46, 348
    mafia capitalism, 348
    mafia's styles of protection, 348–49
    role of caste, kinship, and family in, 350–53
Mahajan, Govind Vitthal, 504
Mahars, 460–61, 502–3
    atrocities against, 507
    'Kshatriya' status for, 504
    movement, 503–5
Malamoud, Charles, 41
Malaviya, Madan Mohan, 284
Malla dynasty, 131
Malnad system, 66
Mandal Commission, 281, 298, 374, 495
    report, implementation of, 207–8, 281, 306, 363, 367
Mang-Matang castes, 508–9
Mangs, 503
Manusmriti, 121, 130, 142, 148, 365
Manviya Hakk Abhiyan, 509
Maratha jati, 581
Marathas, 312
marginalities, 7
marginalized castes, 417
marriage practices, 29
    among Tamil Brahmans, 112
    arranged, 112n25, 113
    caste positioning of couple in self-chosen relationship, 116
    consanguineal, 110
    endogamy, 19, 110, 114–17, 627
    hypergamous relationships, 110–11, 117
    hypogamous relationships, 110
    idea of *kanyadaan,* 110
    inter-caste, 113
    inter-caste or inter-religious, 113
    intra-subcaste rules of prohibited degrees of relationships, 112
    isogamy, 112
    of Kayasths, 112
    non-endogamous, 110, 113, 115
    policing of marriages, 613
    polygynous, 111
    primary and secondary, 114
    rules of, 111
    in rural India, 576
    sambandham, 111–12
    self-arranged, 113, 116
    widow remarriage, 111
    'wife-givers' and 'wife takers,' 110
Marri Chandra Shekhar Rao vs Dean, Seth G. S. Medical College, 195
Marwaris, 577
Marx, Karl, 6, 27
Marxism, 92–93
Marxist understanding of caste, 92–93
Matangs, 508
materiality of caste, 84
Mauryan empire
    under Ashoka, 128
    commerce and political control during, 128
    end of, 130
Mayawati, 488
Mayer, Peter, 26–27
Mazhabis, 433–35
mercantile castes. *See* business communities
mercantile groups, 146
meritocracy, 586–88
    affirmative action, 590–91
    and diasporic migration, 591–92
    meritorious/casteless *vs* reserved/caste-based, 590
    modern mass examination, 589–90
    of Tamil Brahmins, 593–94
middle classes, 1–2
migration
    caste selection in, 624–27
    continuity and maintenance of closed networks and relations, 627–29
    indentured labourers, 145–46, 243, 561–62, 571, 591, 624–26, 630, 633
    voluntary, 626
Mines Maternity Benefit Act, 611

minorities, 226–27
minority rights, 527, 535–36
Miyan, Ghazi, 287
mleccha, 35
modernity, 1, 43, 93
modernization, 14, 28
Modi, Narendra, 332, 339, 511
monism, 148
monotheism, 250
Montagu-Chelmsford Reforms of 1918- 1919, 279
Moonje, B. S., 284
Moors, 31
Mosse, David, 3
Mukerji, U. N., 281–82, 285
Muslim League, 280, 417
Muslims, 6, 233
   ajlaf, 291, 294
   artisan and service castes, 293
   arzal, 291
   ashraf, 291–94
   caste among, 290–91
   Crooke's study, 293
   Dalits, 299
   high caste Hindu converts, 293
   higher castes, 293
   Mughal, 292
   pasmanda, 299–300
   Pathan, 292
   Sayyid, 292
   SC and OBC categories, 298–99
   Shaikh, 292
   social distinctions among, 292
   socio-anthropological debate, 294–99

N
Nadars, 107, 144, 179–81, 405
Nairs, 180–81
Nais, 293
Namasudra movement, 144
Namasudras, 417, 420
Namboodripad, E. M. S., 384
Namboodris of Kerala, 384–85
Nambudiris of Kerala, 111–12
naming caste, 399, 402–5
National Campaign on Dalit Human Rights (NCDHR), 531
National Commission for Backward Classes (NCBC), 208
National Commission for Denotified, Nomadic, and Semi- Nomadic Tribes (NCDNT), 563–64
National Commission for Religious and Linguistics Minorities (Ranganath Mishra Commission), 225
National Commission for the Scheduled Castes, 191
National Election Watch, 345
National Federation of Dalit Women (NFDW), 614
National Register of Citizens, 423
naturalism, 33
Naudet, Jules, 28
Navayana Buddhism, 494
Nayars, 111
Nehru, Jawaharlal, 2
Nepal, 55
   Brahmins of, 449
   caste hierarchy in, 444
   castes, ethnic groups, and macro-categories of, 446–49
   cultural differentiation in, 447
   cultural distance between India and, 444–45
   Dalits of, 446, 449–51
   ethnic group (*janajati*), 444
   ethnicity, 450–52
   hereditary relationships, 449
   languages in, 447–49
   national culture, 449–50
   position of women, 449
   Prithvi Narayan Shah era, 444–45
   Radio Nepal, 450
   social order in, 449
   Tibetan religious traditions in, 447
   ties to southern neighbour, 447
Nepal, caste in, 360
Nepal Federation of Nationalities (NEFEN)/ Nepal Federation of Indigenous Nationalities (NEFIN), 451
Nepal-India Peace and Friendship Treaty of 1950, 444
Newars, 112, 450
new nation, 7
nominalism, 33

non-Brahmin castes, 3, 216–17, 404, 407, 464, 505
non-brahmin movements, 112–13, 142, 164, 492, 613, 630
Nonyas, 270

O

occupational specialization, 357
occupational stereotype, 161, 364, 374
  of Dalit castes, 366–73
  theory of, 371
Occupy Movement, 521
Okkaliga caste, 310
opportunity hoarding, 19
orientalism, 36
'other,' 4, 19
Other Backward Classes (OBCs), 9, 17–18, 41–42, 98, 108, 124, 192, 200, 205–8, 218–19, 316, 347, 389, 446, 462, 555, 573, 593, 602
  electoral behaviour of, 332–34, 337–38, 342–43
  of Gujarat, 341
  Muslim, 299
  reservation, 205–8
  reservations, 202, 205–8, 210, 218–19, 221, 298, 320, 324
  voting pattern, 332–34, 338, 343
  wealth and economic power, 82
out-caste, 36, 226, 404

P

Palanpuris, 577
Pallavas, 134, 136
Pallis, 176
Panchalar, 178
Panchayati Raj (Extension to Scheduled Areas) Act, 1996, 549
Pandyas, 134
Paraiyars, 362
Parbatiyas/Pahadis, 447
Paschim Banga Kheria Sabar Kalyan Samity, 567
Pasmanda Agenda 1999, 299
Pasmanda Muslim Mahaz (PMM), 299
Patidars, 111
patronage democracy, 346–49
Pawade, Kumud, 616

Pawar, Urmila, 616–17
People of India Project, 579
People's Education Society (PE), 468
Phule, Jotirao, 464, 492–93, 504, 571, 609–10
  anti-caste movements, 217
  campaign against enforced widowhood, 610
Poona Pact, 147, 190, 493
Portuguese, 31–32, 34
post-Mandal phase of caste, 320–28, 363
  caste associations, changing role and importance, 322–28
  caste para communities, 322
  creation of Dalit Bahujan unity, 323–25
  democratic rights and representation, 322
  identifications and categorizations of castes, 326
  identity politics, changing nature of, 324, 326
  intra-caste economic differentiation, 326
  politics of Lingayat organizations, 327
  process of regionalization of politics, 323
  process of secularization, politicization, and democratization of caste, 321–22
poverty, 7–8, 12–13, 96, 106, 211, 215, 220, 241, 314, 433, 482, 491, 497, 581, 611, 614, 618, 620
power, 17, 53, 362–63
Pramalai Kallars, 402–3, 406–8
Presidential List, 191
Presidential Order of August 1950, 298
Prevention of Atrocities Act, 1989, 196
Prevention of Atrocities (Scheduled Caste and Scheduled Tribes) Act, 1989, 480
primitive tribal groups (PTGs), 209
Protection of Civil Rights, 1955, 480
"proto- industrial" economies' of India, 27
Punjab, 359–60, 428
  access to drinking water, 438
  caste divisions, 434–35
  community life, 437
  Dalit population in, 429
  disintegration of jajmani structure, 436–37
  Green Revolution and agrarian change, 435–36
  influence of Sikh Gurus, 431–32
  Muslims of, 429
  Punjabi language and identity, 431–32

Punjabi society, hierarchies, 433
religion and castes, 430–31
religious reform movements, 435
ritual order and changes, 432–35
rural society of, 434
settlement structure of villages, 438
as a Sikh majority state, 429
purity and impurity, idea of, 51, 55–56, 70, 273, 362, 479–80, 527, 629

R
racial segregation, 38
Rai, Lala Lajpat, 284, 286
Rajasthan Habitual Criminals (Registration and Regulation) Act 1950, 561
Rajputs, 35, 547
Ram, Kanshi, 460
Ram, Mangoo, 146
Ramabai, Pandita, 492, 610
Ramachandra, Baba, 146
Ramasamy, Periyar E. V., 217, 571, 609–10
Rama temples, 133
Ramdasias, 433
Ranganath Mishra Commission report, 2009, 299
Rashtriya Swayamsevak Sangh (RSS), 281, 284
Ravidasis (Chamars), 271
Ravidassia-movement, 430
reading caste, 409–10
rebellions of 1857-1858, 560
Reddi, Muthulakshmi, 225
reformatory schools, 562
regional trajectories of caste, 358–59
religious domain of caste, 122
religious institutionalization, 629–30
religious sects, 248
Report of the National Advisory Council Working Group on Denotified and Nomadic Tribes, 563
Republican Party of India (RPI), 468–70, 494, 505, 512, 515
reservations, 191–93, 200, 209–10, 493, 598–99
demand for additional vertical reservations, 210
distinction between general vs, 590–91
in education, 202–3
in employment, 201–2

as employment generation measure, 210–11
levels of quotas, 202–3
OBCs, 205–8
policy, 41, 218
quota, 241, 460
Vasanth Kumar judgement, 221
for women, 582
ritual labour division, 238
rural economy, 12

S
Sadhguru, 380
salvation, 34
Salvation Army, 557
Samata Sainik Dal (SSD), 466–67
sampradaya/ sampradāya, 34, 248, 252
Sanskritic values of Hinduism and Indian civilization, 275
Sanskritization, 39, 93, 105, 123, 144, 164, 181–82, 232, 240, 266–67, 310, 362, 372, 462, 480–81, 484, 574, 598
adoption of Sanskritic Hindu practices, 270, 272–73, 275
among Dalit communities, 270–71
as an ideational principle, 274–76
appraisal of, 269–73
changes in social status, 270
conditions for social moblity, 268
critique of, 272
ethnographic studies, 270
as harmony ideology, 274, 276
models, 267–68
Moffatt's view, 271
in rural India, 270
as a 'self- sealing mechanism,' 274
Srinivas' conceptualization of, 267–69
theoretical rationale of, 275
through emulation, 269–73, 598
Santals, 131
Sanyasis, 446
Saraswati, Dayanand, 284
Saraswativijayam, 144
Sardars, 434–35
sati abolition, 146
Satnamis, 280
Satyashodhak Samaj (Society for Searching the Truth), 504

Savarkar, V. D., 281, 283
sa-varna, 239–40, 341
savarnization, 609
 of womanhood, 613–17
Scheduled Areas, 543
Scheduled Caste Federation (SCF), 494
Scheduled Castes and Scheduled Tribes (Prevention of Atrocities) Act, 2015, 484, 488, 497
Scheduled Castes (SCs), 17, 41–43, 124, 191, 196–97, 218–19, 359, 462, 488, 540, 543, 555, 573
 downward occupational mobility, 600–602
 employment reservation, 201–2
 government AA programmes for, 199–200
 identification of, 191, 203–4
Scheduled Tribes and Other Traditional Forest Dwellers (Recognition of Forest Rights) Act (FRA) 2006, 549
Scheduled Tribes (ST), 41–43, 124, 196–97, 218, 462, 540, 543, 548, 555, 573
 downward occupational mobility, 600–602
 employment reservation, 201–2
 government AA programmes for, 199–200
 identification of, 191, 204–5
schooling choices in Mumbai, 578
segregated settlements, 19
Self Respect League, 610
Self-Respect Movement (SRM), 610
sexual citizenship, 619–20
Shahu, Chatrapati, 504
Shanars, 180
Shiromani Gurdwara Parbandhak Committee (SGPC), 436
Shivaji, 34
Shraddhanand, Swami, 282, 284–86
Shree Swaminarayan Gadi Sansthan, 628
shuddhi ceremony, 286
Shudra/Sudras/ *Śūdras*, 33, 35, 39, 41, 147, 182, 216, 236, 239, 257, 275, 280, 288, 309–10, 415, 504, 623
Sikh-Hindu population, 359
Sikhism, 17, 285
Sikhs, 6, 40, 429, 628
Simon, Henri de Saint, 48
Sindhe, Tararbai, 610
slavery, 145, 490, 615, 625

social capital, 14, 27, 77–78, 81, 389–90, 604, 614, 626, 628
social division of labor, 27
social justice, 34, 192, 207, 218, 221, 327, 347, 504–6, 508, 511–12, 520, 629
social mobility, 143–45, 570
social reform movement, 114
social stratification and exploitation, 38
sociological criticism of caste system, 39–40
sociological dimensions of Hindu Sects, 254–56. *See also* Hindu Sects
 display of sectarian affiliations, 255–56
 distinctions between caste and sect, 255
solidarities, 12, 19, 72, 236, 259, 275, 281, 285, 287, 299, 315, 322, 326, 392, 408, 417–18, 443, 481, 505, 508–9, 529
South Asian caste system, 623–24
South Asian diasporas
 caste discrimination in, 632
 caste reproduction across successive generations, 630–32
 closed networks and relations, 627–29
 countries, 626
 edogamic marriages, 627–28
 institutionalized caste divisions, 629–30
 transnational networks, 628
South Asian society, 171, 362, 364
 Muslim societies, 291–92, 298
speaking caste, 400, 406–8
Sreni, 129
Sri Narayana Dharma Paripalana Yogam (SNDP) movement, 144
Srinivas, M. N., 38–39, 93–94, 105, 181, 266–67, 305, 316. *See also* Sanskritization
 acculturation, 480
 The Cohesive Role of Sanskritization and Other Essays, 269
 diversity of India, 275
 dominant caste, 309–10
 numerical strength of caste groups, 313–14
 Religion and Society among the Coorgs of South India, 267
Sri Sri Ravishankar, 380
State of Kerala v N. M. Thomas, 193
State of Madras v. Champakam Dorairajan, 202
State taxation, 36

status group, 15
stigmatization
　of criminal tribes, 556, 562–63, 566
　of denotified communities, 566
　stigmatized ethnic identity, 209–10
Subarnabaniks, 417
substantialization of caste, 11–12, 49, 94, 440, 529
Sudarshan, K. S., 284
symbolic boundaries, 18

T
taluqdari (landed aristocracy), 372
Tamil Nadu, 358–59
Tarai castes, 450
Tebhaga movement, 418
Thakuris, 446
Thass, Iyothee, 492, 609
Thevar, Muthuramalinga, 494
Thiyyas, 107–8, 114
tradition-governed hierarchies, 9
transgender communities, 619–20
　dilemma of being queer, 619–20
transnational caste networks, 80
tribes, 540
　as 'animists,' 543
　assimilation with Hindu society, 545
　Bhils, 545
　closeness with nature, 547
　comparison between castes, 547–48
　criminal (*see* criminal tribes)
　definition, 541–44
　'denotified tribes'/ 'vimukta jati,' 555–56
　differences between Hindu society and, 545
　forest, 543
　Ghurye and Bose's work on, 544–46
　Hindu model of tribal studies, 546
　Kharias, 545
　Khonds, 545
　linguistic diversity among, 541
　livelihood, 549
　Mundas, 545
　particularly vulnerable tribal groups (PVTGs), 541
　protection of tribal identity, 545
　Raj-Gonds, 545
　Santhals, 545

through Hindu civilization, 544–45
traits, 545
tribal absorption, 547–48
Trilokya Baudha Mahasangha Sahayak Gana (TBMSG), 506
twice-born (*dvija*), 34, 41, 44, 182, 237, 268, 284

U
UN Declaration on the Rights of Indigenous Peoples, 549
Union Public Service Commission exam, 589
Untouchability (Offences) Act, 1955, 479–80
untouchability/untouchables, 5, 18, 43, 56, 85, 114, 140, 199, 201, 203–4, 226, 280, 285, 365, 407, 460, 533–34
　ban of, 479
　criminalization of, 479–80
　definition, 478–79
　discrimination and exclusion, 479, 482, 489
　freedom and, 148–49
　legislations against practice of, 479–80, 484
　names and tags applied to, 489–90
　occupational stereotypes, 366
　practices of, 479, 482
　prohibitions, 238–39
　rural, 483–85
　social norms and boundaries of touchability and, 483–84
　in terms of servitude and poverty, 491
　waning of, 480–81
UN World Conference Against Racism (WCAR), 528, 531–32
Upadhya, Carol, 27
upanayanam (sacred thread) initiation ceremony, 237, 252–53
Upaniṣads, 253, 256
uravu, 407–8

V
Vaishyas, 33, 41, 78, 236, 267, 309, 623. *See also* business communities
vaishyavization, 389
Valaiyars, 402
Vanniakula Kshatriyas, 216
Vanniyars, 405

varnas, 4, 6, 25, 31–35, 39, 41, 121, 139, 231, 236, 267–68, 291, 544
    Brahmanic view of, 33
    classification, 140
    colonial classifications, 37
    distinction between *jatis* and, 236
    founding myth of, 236
    Indo-Persian view of, 35
    interaction between individual life and society, 236
    racialized understanding of, 163
    religious historians' view of, 34
varnasrama, 147
Vedic myth of origin, 35
Vedic ritualism, 34
Vellajas, 178
Vellalars, 136
Vijayanagara Empire, 132
village life, 8–9, 141, 317, 366, 374–75, 431
violence, caste-based, 13–14, 413
Vishnudharmottarapurana, 129, 133
Vishwa Gujarati Samaj, 628
Vishwanath temple, 240
Vokkaligga, 604

W

Walangkar, Gopal Baba, 504
wealth inequality in India, 389
Weber, Max, 27, 40, 54
    analysis of capitalism, 76
    caste/sect ideal- type, 39, 49, 255

West Bengal, 359. *See also* bhadralok
    Bengali marriage, caste, and kinship, 420
    Calcutta's cultures of servitude, 419
    caste-free, 424
    caste in Post-Independence and Marxist Bengal, 418–20
    cultural hierarchy and role- obligations, 418–19
    invisibilization of caste post-partition, 423–25
    marginalized castes mobilizations, 420–22
    migration of Muslim peasantry, 425
West Bengal Reservations in Vacancies (Recruitment of Scheduled Castes and Scheduled Tribes) Act, 1976, 424
westernization, 145
widow remarriage, 40, 105, 111, 146, 268
women
    Brahmin woman, observance of caste rules and regulations, 377–78
    in family businesses, 390–91
    invisibilization in writings, 394
World Gujarati Conference, 628
World Social Forum, 520–21
World Tamil Conference, 628

Y

Yoga Kshema Sabha (YKS), 384–85

Z

zamindars, 131–32, 136, 372, 418

The manufacturer's authorised representative in the EU for product safety is
Oxford University Press España S.A. of el Parque Empresarial San Fernando de
Henares, Avenida de Castilla, 2 – 28830 Madrid (www.oup.es/en or product.
safety@oup.com). OUP España S.A. also acts as importer into Spain of products
made by the manufacturer.

www.ingramcontent.com/pod-product-compliance
Lightning Source LLC
Chambersburg PA
CBHW081812290825
31867CB00005B/432